MW01012713

but let her know, yt this week & next I
have thoughts of going both for Rochester, & for Reading; both on [illegible] acct.
soone, & on our acct. to the other; & by
that time I may write more positively to thy Mother as to wt I have already
writt to her about. The Great God &
Lord of & over us all, keep ~~[illegible]~~ thee &
us in his fear & love, & then it shall be
well wth us. I hear, all our frds are well
but the Cos: [illegible], in this town. And tell
Mother, I know not any one here
yt can tell me the Lady Pools age, but
I beleive she was abt. 13 years older
than I am: Married in 1654, & 20
when married. I sent by the Horse Carrier
yesterday, yt comes from ye 3 Cups
in Bread street, his name Samll
Whippin, a Box, directed for Bri-
~~[illegible]~~ Draper in ~~[illegible]~~ Wine Street;
Webb, [illegible] I desire my
tell mother also that I [illegible] desire
love to [illegible] Osborn; Pray order
also to know how he does. [illegible] leave
the poor little Horse, & ask Mother leave
wch you desire to ride him. So with
my dearest love to her & most to you
and [illegible] Johnne, Tommy, Peggy, Richard &
all [illegible] to hers & yrs. WPenn

THE PAPERS OF WILLIAM PENN

Volume Four · 1701–1718

GRAVE OF WILLIAM PENN IN THE FRIENDS BURI AL GROUND AT JORDANS IN BUCKINGHAMSHIRE EL.

THE PAPERS OF WILLIAM PENN

Volume Four · 1701–1718

EDITORS

Craig W. Horle · Alison Duncan Hirsch
Marianne S. Wokeck · Joy Wiltenburg

GENERAL EDITORS

Richard S. Dunn · Mary Maples Dunn

UNIVERSITY OF PENNSYLVANIA PRESS 1987

Library of Congress Cataloging-in-Publication Data
(Revised for vol. 4)

Penn, William, 1644–1718
The Papers of William Penn.

Includes bibliographical references and indexes.
CONTENTS: *v. 1. 1644–1679.—v. 2. 1680–1684.—v. 3. 1685–1700.—v. 4. 1701–1718.—v. 5. William Penn's published writings 1660–1726*
1. Penn, William, 1644–1718. 2. Pennsylvania—History—Colonial period, ca. 1600–1775—Sources. 3. Society of Friends—History—17th century—Sources. 4. Society of Friends—History—18th century—Sources. 5. Society of Friends—Biography. 6. Pioneers—Pennsylvania—Correspondence. I. Dunn, Mary Maples. II. Dunn, Richard S. III. Title.
F152.2.P3956 1986 974.8'02'0924[B] 80–54052
ISBN 0-8122-7800-3 (v. 1)
ISBN 0-8122-7852-6 (v. 2)
ISBN 0-8122-8029-6 (v. 3)
ISBN 0-8122-8050-4 (v. 4)
ISBN 0-8122-8019-9 (v. 5)

Designed by Adrianne Onderdonk Dudden
Maps by Quentin Fiore and Bernard Gollotti

To
CAROLINE ROBBINS
and
to the
memory of
ALBERT COOK MYERS
HANNAH BENNER ROACH
and
FREDERICK B. TOLLES

Preparation and publication of this volume
was made possible by a major grant from
the Program for Editions
The National Endowment for the Humanities
an independent federal agency

•

and by generous supporting grants from

The American Philosophical Society
The Atlantic Richfield Foundation
The Barra Foundation
Bryn Mawr College
Haverford College
The Historical Foundation of Pennsylvania
The Historical Society of Pennsylvania
The McLean Contributionship
The National Historical Publications and Records Commission
The J. Howard Pew Freedom Trust
The Philadelphia Center for Early American Studies
The Philadelphia Yearly Meeting of the Religious Society of Friends
Adolph G. Rosengarten, Jr.
Smith College
The University of Pennsylvania
Stephanie G. Wolf
The Yarway Foundation

ADVISORY BOARD

ACKNOWLEDGMENTS

The editors are deeply grateful to the following for permitting us to publish documents from their collections: the American Philosophical Society, Philadelphia; the Berkshire Record Office, Reading, England; the Trustees of the Boston Public Library; the British Library, London; the Chester County Historical Society, West Chester, Pennsylvania; Friends Historical Library, Swarthmore College, Swarthmore, Pennsylvania; Lady Ravensdale and the Hertfordshire Record Office, Hertford, England; the Historical Society of Pennsylvania, Philadelphia; The Huntington Library, San Marino, California; Kent County Archives, Maidstone, England; the Library Company of Philadelphia; the Library of the Religious Society of Friends in Ireland, Dublin; the Library of the Religious Society of Friends, London; Weyerhauser Library, Macalester College, St. Paul, Minnesota; the New York Public Library; Penn Mutual Life Insurance Company, Philadelphia; the Division of Archives and Manuscripts, Pennsylvania Historical and Museum Commission, Harrisburg; Princeton University Library; the Public Record Office, London; the Royal Commission on Historical Manuscripts, London; and Van Pelt Library, the University of Pennsylvania, Philadelphia.

Four institutions, Bryn Mawr College, Haverford College, the Historical Society of Pennsylvania, and the University of Pennsylvania—all participants in the Philadelphia Center for Early American Studies — are the sponsors of this edition. The editors are deeply appreciative of this cooperative institutional support. We are also very grateful to the National Endowment for the Humanities and the National Historical Publications and Records Commission for their continuing support, and to the American Philosophical Society, the Atlantic Richfield Foundation, the Barra Foundation, the Historical Foundation of Pennsylvania, the McLean Contributionship, the J. Howard Pew Freedom Trust, the Philadelphia Yearly Meeting of the Religious Society of Friends, Adolph G. Rosengarten, Jr., Smith College, Stephanie G. Wolf, and the Yarway Foundation for their generous grants.

The editors wish to thank Peter J. Parker, director of the Historical Society of Pennsylvania; Linda Stanley, manuscripts and archives curator; David Fraser, librarian; and the other members of the Society staff, for providing the editors with attractive working space and congenial company, free access to the Society's manuscript and book collections, and expert help whenever needed. The editors have also received indispensable assistance from John Van Horne and his staff at the Library Company of Philadelphia; J. William Frost and the staff of the Friends Historical Library at Swarthmore College; Edwin B. Bronner and the staff of the Quaker Collection at Haverford College; James Tanis at the Canaday Library of Bryn Mawr College; and the staff of the Van Pelt Library at the University of Pennsylvania. Farther afield we have been courteously received by Roland M. Baumann and Harry Parker at the Pennsylvania State Archives. In London, we were helped by the staffs of the Public Record Office, the British Library, and the Library of the Religious Society of Friends.

A special word of thanks is due to Scott M. Wilds and Jean R. Soderlund, formerly associate editors of the Papers of William Penn, for their contribution in initiating work on Volume Four. They selected most of the documents and began the annotation for this volume. We also wish to thank William Offutt and Lisa W. Waciega, fellows of the Philadelphia Center for Early American Studies, for their work on a number of documents in this volume. Jerisse Fogel of Smith College and Alan L. Karras of the University of Pennsylvania worked as research assistants during the summer of 1986. Sister Irma Corcoran's index to the microfilm edition of The Papers of William Penn continues to be very useful to us. Members of our Advisory Board have been extremely helpful whenever called upon. Margaret Yasuda and June Peggs assisted with word processing. Patricia Wells did the index, and Deborah Stuart did the copyediting. Adrianne Onderdonk Dudden designed the book, and Bernard Golotti did the maps. Barton L. Craig at the Winchell Company and Arthur Evans, Alison Anderson, and Carl Gross at the University of Pennsylvania Press have worked closely with us to produce this complex volume. Finally, we wish in particular to thank Kathy Fuller of the National Endowment for the Humanities for her advice and help. Without the active and continuing support of the federal agency she represents, this volume could never have been produced.

CONTENTS

ILLUSTRATIONS AND MAPS

THE PAPERS OF WILLIAM PENN

Volume Four · 1701–1718

INTRODUCTION

This is the fourth volume in a select edition of *The Papers of William Penn,* designed to present the most interesting and representative correspondence, religious and political papers, journals, and business records of WP—as he will be referred to henceforth. In a companion fifth volume, Edwin Bronner and David Fraser present an interpretive bibliography of WP's published writings. The overall plan of the work is described in the introduction to our first volume. Volume One, spanning the years 1644 to 1679, documents WP's proceedings as a young Quaker activist. Volume Two, spanning the years 1680 to 1684, documents the founding of Pennsylvania. Volume Three, spanning the years 1685 to 1700, documents WP's controversial career in England before and after the Glorious Revolution, his efforts to govern Pennsylvania in absentia, and his return to America in 1699. Volume Four documents the final eighteen years of WP's life, from 1701 to 1718. It opens with his last months as resident proprietor of Pennsylvania—a moment of great importance in the political history of the colony, since WP on the eve of his departure in 1701 agreed to a constitutional reorganization that shaped the character of Pennsylvania politics until the American Revolution. After returning to England, WP spent a busy decade defending his proprietorship from a series of crippling attacks by opponents on both sides of the Atlantic, a situation further complicated by a protracted legal struggle with the heirs of Philip Ford, his former steward. In 1708, with the fate of his proprietorship in the hands of Lord Chancellor Cowper, and after a lengthy stay in debtor's prison, WP paid £7600 to the Fords. But his continuing financial pressures in England, and his political reverses in Pennsylvania, persuaded WP as early as 1703 to seek the surrender of his colony's government to the crown, and he was on the point of completing this surrender in 1712 when he suffered a series of disabling strokes. After lingering for nearly six more years as an incapacitated invalid, he died on 30 July 1718.

For a chronology of WP's actions and related events from 1701 to 1718, see pp. 20–22. The documents in this fourth volume are arranged in thirteen sections designed to articulate the principal phases of WP's career from his last months in Pennsylvania to his death. Within each section, headnotes introduce groups of documents or individual documents and supply a running commentary on WP's activities. The many hundreds of persons and places mentioned in these documents are identified (whenever possible) in the footnotes; these identifications may be located easily by the **boldface** page references in the index. The maps illustrating this volume are likewise designed to aid the reader in locating many places mentioned in the text. The appendix summarizes WP's most important surviving business records for the period, including family settlements with his son William Penn, Jr., and his son-in-law William Aubrey; the sale of his principal English property at Warminghurst; and the financial resolution of the Ford case.

A very high proportion of WP's surviving manuscripts dates from the eighteen years chronicled in Volume Four. The microfilm edition of The Papers of William Penn, issued by the Historical Society of Pennsylvania in 1975, contains 311 documents for the years 1644–79 covered in Volume One, 512 documents for the years 1680–84 covered in Volume Two, 794 documents for the years 1685–1700 covered in Volume Three, and 939 documents—37 percent of the total—for the years 1701–18 covered in this volume (see the list on pp. 774–94, below). We have added to our master file another 57 documents dating from these eighteen years (see the list on pp. 795–97, below). In preparing Volume Four, we have selected 208 documents for publication and have abstracted another 26 in the appendix. Only 115 of these have previously been published, and they are scattered in dozens of books and journals, most of them printed long ago, often in extracts, with inaccurate texts and lacking annotation.

Two-thirds of the documents printed in Volume Four are held by the Historical Society of Pennsylvania. The others come from the nineteen additional repositories listed in the Acknowledgments. Most of WP's family correspondence for the final years of his life, as for the earlier years, has been lost or destroyed. The chief exception is a group of fourteen letters to his wife, Hannah, and his young sons, John and Thomas, in 1709–10, of which we print seven (see docs. 167–69, 171, and 173–75). No travel journals equivalent to docs. 35, 70, and 119 in Volume One, or autobiographical writings equivalent to docs. 93–94 in Volume Three, survive for this period. There is, however, a very large corpus of legal records: nearly one hundred documents concerning the Penn-Ford case, of which twenty-five are printed or abstracted in this volume (see docs. 108–21 and 211); and another forty documents concerning WP's family settlements, of which twenty-one are printed or abstracted in this volume (see docs. 30, 107, 145, 193, and 209–10). Most of the documents printed in Volume Four are political in character, and they focus more on events in Pennsylvania than in England. A central feature of this volume is WP's extensive correspondence with James Logan, his secretary in Pennsylvania. This correspondence has been unusually well preserved because Logan was a meticulous record keeper who preserved the letters he received as well as copies of the letters he sent; in this volume we print thirty-one of WP's letters to Logan and eighteen of Logan's letters to WP. Crucial as this correspondence is to an understanding of political developments in Pennsylvania, it must always be remembered that Logan was a strongly opinionated writer who gave his master a highly partisan running account of events in the colony. And though WP trusted his secretary completely, he rarely expressed his innermost thoughts to him — or to anyone else in the Penn papers that have survived. As in the earlier volumes, the interior life of this complicated and contradictory man remains a mystery.

Volume Four deals with WP's declining years, when he was often in poor health, and never as creative, vigorous, or idealistic as in the 1670s and 1680s. Nevertheless, the story told here is a dramatic and absorbing one: through these documents we can see WP struggling against a formidable circle of adversaries as he tried to preserve his Quaker commonwealth and his proprietary estate in a rapidly changing world. The volume begins on a promising note: in 1701 WP was still robust and high-spirited, holding court in his colony. But problems that he had never resolved in the 1680s and 1690s were resurfacing with a new urgency. In many respects he was the victim of circumstances beyond his control: the efforts of the English government in the early 1700s to establish mastery over the proprietary colonies (see, in particular, docs. 17–20); the inevitable thrust of colonial representative assemblies to challenge and restrict executive authority (docs. 22, 24, 27–28, and 83); the resentment of Anglicans and other non-Quakers in Pennsylvania against Quaker dominance in government (docs. 66, 69, and 142); and the impact of the War of the Spanish Succession on a colony with a tradition of pacifism and a dependence on international trade (docs. 74, 123, and 129–31). Yet WP exacerbated these trends by his own inadequacies: his tendency to treat the colonists as disobedient children; his cavalier attitude toward those who served him, especially his deputy governors, whom he consistently underpaid (docs. 127, 129–30, and 157); his careless and extravagant way of life, harshly exposed by the Ford case; and his inability to recognize the dangers inherent in absentee landlordship. On the other hand, the Quakers in Pennsylvania seemed to feel more at home in opposition than in control of government, chronically carping at WP and his officers, and refusing to appreciate WP's need to spend much of his time in England warding off new threats to the colony, whether from Lord Baltimore, the Board of Trade and its agents, or Parliament. Only when WP began negotiating a surrender of his rights to govern Pennsylvania did the colonists understand his importance in shielding their political, religious, and economic freedom. The on-again, off-again attempts by WP to sell these rights to the English government are thoroughly documented in this volume (docs. 62, 87–90, 96, 140, 180, and 198).

Out of this welter of conflicting forces emerged a new constitution for Pennsylvania, which shifted the focal point of legislative power away from the Provincial Council to the Assembly (doc. 28); a corporate charter for Philadelphia; and a political division between Pennsylvania and the Lower Counties (now Delaware). Property rights, quitrents, and rents, however, remained very much in limbo, complicated by the Ford case and the surrender negotiations. During this period the colony was managed by a succession of four deputy governors — Andrew Hamilton, John Evans, Charles Gookin, and William Keith — all of whom, except Hamilton (whose service was cut short by death), were poor choices. Evans, in particular, was an unfortunate appointment, for his inappropriate and childish antics furthered the opposition to both WP and Quaker control of government (docs. 129 and 138).

In 1701 WP returned to England to defend his proprietorship against the formidable efforts by the Board of Trade to reshape English colonial administration through the resumption of royal control over the proprietary colonies. To WP's credit, he effectively defended the chartered colonies, despite repeated negative reports sent to the Board of Trade by Robert Quary, judge of the vice-admiralty court (docs. 40, 42–44, 50, and 77). By 1703 WP's proprietorship of Pennsylvania was no longer threatened from that source. But another implacable and able foe emerged: David Lloyd, a Pennsylvania Quaker lawyer, who often served as speaker of the Assembly. Lloyd's opposition was especially damaging, for he had an agenda of considerable validity, which he combined with a cutting ability to expose the hollowness of WP's paternalistic pretensions (see docs. 83 and 102). Nor did he hesitate to call on prominent members of the London Meeting for Sufferings to pressure the proprietor on a variety of issues, including the dismissal of Deputy Governor Evans (docs. 84, 133, and 143). Lloyd's ability to enlist the aid of powerful English Friends must have been particularly galling, since it challenged WP's credibility and status within the Quaker community in England.

In purely personal terms, the closing years of WP's career yielded mixed results. The long and bitter lawsuit with the Ford family, which is fully chronicled for the first time in this volume (docs. 108–21), exposed his financial incompetence, short-sightedness, and poor character judgment, and led to his embarrassing imprisonment. Historians have generally and correctly faulted Philip Ford for overcharging his former employer, but they have also exonerated WP from wrongdoing. In fact, WP was by no means blameless. Despite his delaying tactics and his belief in his innocence, it was obvious to his lawyers and supporters that his own actions had precluded any effective defense (docs. 130–31), and that an accommodation with the Fords was imperative if he wished to retain his proprietorship. His crushing debts also forced him in 1707 to sell Warminghurst, which he had owned for more than thirty years (docs. 145 and 210). He had to provide for a large family: two surviving children from his first marriage and five from his second. He had loving relations with his second wife, Hannah, and their young children, as his letters to them indicate (docs. 167–69 and 173–75), but stressful relations with his two grown children. He was deeply hurt by the behavior of William Penn, Jr., whose renunciation of Quakerism and adoption of a scandalous way of life were tragic indications of a rebelliousness toward WP far more violent and negative than his own rebellion against Admiral Penn (docs. 73, 82, and 86). Nor was WP happy with his son's choice of spouse, Mary Jones, whom he regarded with some disdain, especially when she objected to the sale of Warminghurst (doc. 139). Yet his contempt for her paled in comparison with his antagonism toward Laetitia's husband, William Aubrey (docs. 139 and 199), whom even Hannah Penn characterized as "that muck worm" (doc. 70). Aubrey, however, may have been unfairly maligned, for like many others harshly criticized by WP, he was a creditor of the proprietor. But despite these personal frictions and fiscal problems, WP did manage to make beneficial financial arrangements for all of his children and their heirs.

In the years 1709–12, when the Ford case was resolved and his allies in Pennsylvania were rallying to his support, WP enjoyed a final period of renewed activity. He secured a boundary victory over the Calvert family of Maryland, he tried to influence the peace terms for the War of the Spanish Succession, he encouraged further immigration to Pennsylvania, he continued to fight for the right of Quakers in his colony to affirm for all offices and legal proceedings, and he published several short pieces (docs. 151, 154, 159, 161–63, and 165). His preface to John Banks's *Journal* (1712) was his last publication.

But despite these efforts, WP had become a marginal figure, a fact he himself recognized when he wrote to the earl of Oxford in 1711: "I am heartily Sorry I am now Good for nothing. twas otherways in former days" (doc. 189). One measure of his declining vitality was that his last major publication had been *More Fruits of Solitude,* in 1702. Yet in 1712 he nearly accomplished one final dramatic action — the surrender to the English crown of the government of Pennsylvania. Having agreed upon a price of £12,000 for the surrender, WP received a down payment of £1000 in September 1712 (doc. 198). In October and December, however, he suffered major strokes, which finished his active career. Although Hannah Penn continued to press for completing the surrender, these efforts never succeeded — a fact of immense significance for the future of Pennsylvania and the Penn family. Hannah carried on with great competence in managing, with others, WP's business and political affairs (docs. 201–2 and 204). In the final section of the volume, we have a few intimate glimpses of the last years of WP as his health steadily deteriorated (docs. 201 and 203). The impact on Hannah of his death in July 1718 (doc. 205) and the moving tributes to him from Friends at home and abroad (docs. 206 and 208) bear testimony to the love and respect many felt toward this complex, flawed, but remarkable individual, whose contributions to Quakerism, religious toleration, and the development of political institutions in America are only now becoming fully understood.

EDITORIAL METHOD

In this edition we pursue a literal, rather than a modernized, method of textual reproduction. Our reasons for doing so are discussed in *PWP,* 1:15–16. We aim to print a completely faithful transcript of each original text, including blemishes and errors. When the original text has been lost, we aim to print a completely faithful transcript of the best surviving copy. In this way we try to preserve the form and style of WP's eighteenth-century papers and to introduce no further changes into his modernized papers. In general, our editorial interpolations [enclosed in square brackets] within the text are minimal. On the other hand, we provide considerable annotation. In the footnotes we clarify textual passages and identify persons and places. In both headnotes and footnotes we comment on the chief substantive issues raised in the documents. In this way we try to make each text fully intelligible to the reader. Some editors prefer to let the texts speak for themselves, but we believe that many of WP's documents are difficult to understand or appreciate without considerable editorial assistance.

Our editorial rules may be summarized as follows:

1. Each document selected for publication in *The Papers of William Penn* is printed in full. The only exception to this rule occurs in the appendix, where we have abstracted 26 documents relating to WP's business affairs (docs. 209–11).

2. Each document is numbered, for convenient cross-reference, and is supplied with a short title.

3. The format of each document (including the salutation and complimentary closure in letters) is rendered as in the original or copy, with the following exceptions: Endorsements are treated like dockets and entered into the provenance note (see below). If a document is undated, an initial date line is supplied [within square brack-

ets]. If a document is dated at the close but not at the top, an initial date line is supplied [within square brackets], and the closing date line is retained.

4. The dating of documents poses a further editorial problem. In WP's lifetime, the English employed the Julian, or Old Style, calendar, which by 1700 was eleven days behind the Gregorian, or New Style, calendar used by most continental Europeans—and adopted in England and the English colonies in 1752. The English in the early eighteenth century began the new year officially on 25 March, but since 1 January also had currency as New Year's Day, some writers double-dated for the period 1 January to 24 March. In addition, the Quakers employed their own nomenclature. They numbered the months, counting March the first month and February the twelfth. They also numbered the days of the week, with Sunday the first day and Saturday the seventh.

In this edition, when a document is dated in Quaker form, a "heathen" translation of the month is supplied [within square brackets]. When a document written between 1 January and 24 March is dated according to the previous year, a "modern" translation of the year is supplied [within square brackets]. Otherwise, the Old Style calendar is retained. For example, the date of WP's letter to Friends in Pennsylvania (doc. 181), stated in the document as "10. 12mo 1710/1," is rendered as [10 February 1711] and is not changed to 21 February, the Gregorian, or New Style, date for this letter.

5. The text of each document is rendered as follows:

a. Spelling is retained as written. Misspelled words are not marked with an editorial [*sic*]. If the sense of a word is obscured through misspelling, its meaning is clarified in a footnote.

b. Capitalization is retained as written. In eighteenth-century manuscripts, the capitalization of such letters as "c," "k," "p," "s," and "w" is often a matter of judgment, and we cannot claim that our reading is definitive. Whenever it is clear to us that the initial letter in a sentence has not been capitalized, it is left lowercase.

c. Punctuations and paragraphing are retained as written. When a sentence is not closed with a period, we have inserted an extra space.

d. Words or phrases inserted into the text are placed {within braces}.

e. Words or phrases deleted from the text are ~~crossed through~~.

f. Slips of the pen are retained as written and are not marked by [*sic*].

g. Contractions, abbreviations, superscript letters, and ampersands are retained as written, except raised brevigraphs for "-or,"

"-ur," "-our," "-er," or "-re," which have been lowered and written out. When a contraction is marked by a tilde, it is also expanded.

h. The thorn is rendered as "th," and superscript contractions attached to the thorn are brought down to the line and expanded, as in "the," "them," or "that." Our justification for this procedure is that we no longer have a thorn, and modern readers mistake it for "y." Likewise, since modern readers do not recognize that "u" and "v" as well as "i" and "j" were used interchangeably in the eighteenth century, we have rendered "u" as "v" or "v" as "u," and "i" as "j" or "j" as "i," whenever appropriate.

i. The £ sign in superscript is rendered as "l."

j. The tailed "p" is expanded into "per," "pro," or "pre," as indicated by the rest of the word.

k. The long "s" is presented as a short "s." The double "ff" is presented as a capital "F."

l. Words underlined in manuscript are italicized.

m. Blanks in a manuscript, torn sections, missing words, and illegible words are rendered as [blank], [torn], [missing word], [illegible word], or [illegible deletion]. If a missing word can be supplied, it is inserted [within square brackets]. If the supplied word is conjectural, it is followed by a question mark.

6. Immediately following each document, a provenance note supplies the following information:

a. An indication of the nature of the document, such as ALS or Copy. See the list of Abbreviations and Short Titles, pp. 13–17, for the explanation of these abbreviations.

b. A reference to the source of the document, such as the manuscript collection where the original is located or the book where the best surviving transcript is located. See the list of Abbreviations and Short Titles, pp. 13–17, for the symbols used to identify the chief depositories and printed sources.

c. A reference to the HSP microfilm edition of The Papers of William Penn (1975), indicating on which reel and frame the document in question can be found. For example, *Micro.* 9:521 means that the document begins on the 521st frame of the 9th microfilm reel. See the Calendar of Microfilmed WP Documents, 1701–1718, on pp. 774–94. Documents not included in the microfilm edition are listed on pp. 795–97.

d. The docket and address, if any. Comments on the physical condition of the document are added here, whenever appropriate.

In preparing the text and editorial apparatus for the printer, we have used a Wang Office Information System 115–2. Each document selected for the volume was keyed onto a magnetic disk, compared twice with the original manuscript (or best surviving transcript), and corrected as necessary. Footnote numbers, editorial interpolations, provenance notes, headnotes, document titles, and footnotes were also entered into the word processor. We also used the word processor to index the volume. When the text was in finished form, we inserted a series of codes designed to command a computer-driven typesetter to produce different sizes and fonts of type for headings, text, and notes; to lead the lines of type; and to position the text on each page. From our encoded diskettes, the Winchell Company of Philadelphia then processed the text through its Penta computer and produced galleys and page proofs in Baskerville type on its Linotron 202 typesetter. Thanks to these technical procedures, we have been able to produce this complex volume with relative speed.

ABBREVIATIONS AND SHORT TITLES

ACM
: Albert Cook Myers Historical Collection, Chester County Historical Society, West Chester, Pa.

Acts of Privy Council
: W. L. Grant and James Munro, eds., *Acts of the Privy Council of England: Colonial Series*, 6 vols. (1908–12; reprint, Nendeln, Liechtenstein, 1966).

AD
: Autograph document, not signed.

ADf
: Autograph draft.

ADfS
: Autograph draft, signed.

ADS
: Autograph document, signed.

AL
: Autograph letter, not signed.

ALS
: Autograph letter, signed.

Alumni Cantabrigienses
: John Venn and J. A. Venn, *Alumni Cantabrigienses*, pt. 1, *From the Earliest Times to 1751*, 4 vols. (Cambridge, 1922–27).

Alumni Oxonienses
: Joseph Foster, *Alumni Oxonienses: The Members of the University of Oxford, 1500–1714*, vol. 1, *Early Series* (Oxford, 1891).

Andrews, *Colonial Period*
: Charles M. Andrews, *The Colonial Period of American History*, 4 vols. (New Haven, 1934–38).

APS
: American Philosophical Society.

Baronetage
: G. E. C. [George Edward Cokayne], *Complete Baronetage*, 5 vols. (Exeter, 1900–1909).

Baxter, *William III*

Stephen B. Baxter, *William III and the Defense of European Liberty, 1650–1702* (New York, 1966).

Besse

Joseph Besse, *A Collection of the Sufferings of the People Called Quakers* (London, 1753).

BFHA

Bulletin of Friends' Historical Association.

BL

British Library, London.

Black's Law Dictionary

Henry Campbell Black et al., eds., *Black's Law Dictionary* (St. Paul, 1979).

Blackstone

William Blackstone, *Commentaries on the Laws of England,* 4 vols., 8th ed. (Oxford, 1778).

Braithwaite, *Second Period*

William C. Braithwaite, *The Second Period of Quakerism,* 2d ed., ed. Henry J. Cadbury (Cambridge, 1961).

Burke's *Landed Gentry*

Bernard Burke, ed., *A Genealogical and Heraldic Dictionary of the Landed Gentry of Great Britain and Ireland for 1852* (London, 1852).

Burke's *Peerage*

Bernard Burke, *Burke's Peerage, Baronetage, and Knightage,* 96th ed., 2 vols. (London, 1938).

Burnet

[Gilbert Burnet], *Bishop Burnet's History of His Own Time* (London, 1857).

Charter and Laws

Staughton George et al., eds., *Charter to William Penn and Laws of the Province of Pennsylvania* (Harrisburg, 1879).

Copy

Contemporary copy.

CSPC

W. Noel Sainsbury et al., eds., *Calendar of State Papers, Colonial Series, America and West Indies,* multivolume series in progress (London, 1860–).

CSPD

Mary Anne Everett Green et al., eds., *Calendar of State Papers, Domestic Series, 1603–1704,* 85 vols. (London, 1857–1972).

CTB

William A. Shaw et al., *Calendar of Treasury Books, 1660–1718,* 32 vols. (London, 1904–1962).

D

Document in the hand of a clerk, not signed by the author.

DAB

Allen Johnson and Dumas Malone, eds., *Dictionary of American Biography,* 20 vols. with index and supplements (New York, 1928–38).

Df

Draft in the hand of a clerk, not signed by the author.

DfS

Draft in the hand of a clerk, signed by the author.

DNB

Leslie Stephen and Sidney Lee, eds., *Dictionary of National Biography,* 63 vols. with supplements (New York and London, 1885–1900).

DQB

Dictionary of Quaker Biography, typescript, Quaker Collection, Haverford College, Haverford, Pennsylvania.

Drinker, *Hannah Penn*

Sophie Hutchinson Drinker, *Hannah Penn and the Proprietorship of Pennsylvania* (Philadelphia, 1958).

DS

Document in the hand of a clerk, signed by the author.

Early American Indian Documents

Donald H. Kent, ed., *Early American Indian Documents: Treaties and Laws, 1607–1789* (Washington, D.C., 1979).

FLL

Library of the Religious Society of Friends, London.

Fox

Norman Penney, ed., *The Journal of George Fox,* 2 vols. (Cambridge, 1911).

Fox, *Short Journal*

Norman Penney, ed., *The Short Journal and Itinerary Journals of George Fox* (Cambridge, 1925).

Futhey and Cope

J. Smith Futhey and Gilbert Cope, *History of Chester County, Pennsylvania* (Philadelphia, 1881).

GSP

Genealogical Society of Pennsylvania Collections, housed at HSP.

Hazard, *Annals*

Samuel Hazard, *Annals of Pennsylvania, from the Discovery of the Delaware* (Philadelphia, 1850).

Hinshaw

William Wade Hinshaw, *Encyclopedia of American Quaker Genealogy,* 6 vols. (Ann Arbor, 1936–50).

HMC

Historical Manuscripts Commission.

HSP

Historical Society of Pennsylvania, Philadelphia.

Janney

Samuel M. Janney, *The Life of William Penn* (Philadelphia, 1852).

Jenkins

Howard M. Jenkins, *The Family of William Penn, Founder of Pennsylvania, Ancestry and Descendants* (Philadelphia, 1899).

JFHS

The Journal of the Friends' Historical Society.

Laymon, *Commentary on the Bible*

Charles M. Laymon, *The Interpreter's One-Volume Commentary on the Bible* (Nashville, 1971).

LBC

Letterbook copy.

Lewis, "Courts of Pennsylvania"

Lawrence Lewis, Jr., "The Courts of Pennsylvania in the Seventeenth Century," *PMHB*, 5:141–90.

LS

Letter in the hand of a clerk, signed by the author.

Luttrell

Narcissus Luttrell, *A Brief Historical Relation of State Affairs*, 6 vols. (1857; reprint, Wilmington, Del., 1974).

MBE

Minute book entry.

McCusker, *Money and Exchange*

John J. McCusker, *Money and Exchange in Europe and America, 1600–1775: A Handbook* (Chapel Hill, N. C., 1978).

Md. Archives

William Hand Browne et al., eds., *Archives of Maryland*, multivolume series in progress (Baltimore, 1883–).

Micro.

The Papers of William Penn, HSP, 14 reels and guide (microfilm, 1975). References are to reel and frame.

Minutes of the Provincial Council

Minutes of the Provincial Council of Pennsylvania (Philadelphia, 1852).

Mortimer, 1

Russell Mortimer, ed., *Minute Book of the Men's Meeting of the Society of Friends in Bristol, 1667–1686* (Bristol, 1971).

Mortimer, 2

Russell Mortimer, ed., *Minute Book of the Men's Meeting of the Society of Friends in Bristol, 1686–1704* (Bristol, 1977).

Myers, *Immigration*

Albert Cook Myers, *Immigration of the Irish Quakers into Pennsylvania* (1902; reprint, Baltimore, 1969).

Nash, *Quakers and Politics*

Gary B. Nash, *Quakers and Politics: Pennsylvania, 1681–1726* (Princeton, 1968).

New York Col. Docs.

E. B. O'Callaghan and Berthold Fernow, eds., *Documents Relative to the Colonial History of the State of New York*,. 15 vols. (Albany, 1856–87).

NJA
William A. Whitehead et al., eds., *Archives of the State of New Jersey*, 1st ser., 42 vols. (Newark, 1880–1949).

OED
The Oxford English Dictionary, 2 vols. (Oxford, 1971).

Oxford Classical Dictionary
N. G. L. Hammond and H. H. Scullard, *The Oxford Classical Dictionary*, 2d ed. (Oxford, 1970)

Oxford Companion to Law
David M. Walker, *The Oxford Companion to Law* (Oxford, 1980).

PA
Pennsylvania Archives (Philadelphia and Harrisburg, 1852–).

Peare
Catherine Owens Peare, *William Penn* (Philadelphia, 1956).

Peerage
G. E. C. [George Edward Cokayne], ed., *The Complete Peerage*, 13 vols., 2d ed., ed. Vicary Gibbs et al. (London, 1910–59).

Perry, *Historical Collections*
William S. Perry, *Historical Collections Relating to the American Colonial Church* (1871; reprint, New York, 1969).

PGM
Pennsylvania Genealogical Magazine.

PMHB
Pennsylvania Magazine of History and Biography.

Pomfret, *East New Jersey*
John E. Pomfret, *The Province of East New Jersey, 1609–1702* (Princeton, 1962).

Pomfret, *West New Jersey*
John E. Pomfret, *The Province of West New Jersey, 1609–1702* (Princeton, 1956).

PRO
Public Record Office, London.

Proceedings and Debates
Leo F. Stock, ed., *Proceedings and Debates of the British Parliament Respecting North America* (Washington, D.C., 1924–30), vols. 1–3.

PWP, 1
Mary Maples Dunn and Richard S. Dunn, eds., *The Papers of William Penn*, vol. 1 (Philadelphia, 1981).

PWP, 2
Richard S. Dunn and Mary Maples Dunn, eds., *The Papers of William Penn*, vol. 2 (Philadelphia, 1982).

PWP, 3
Marianne S. Wokeck, Joy Wiltenburg, Alison Duncan Hirsch, and Craig W. Horle, eds., *The Papers of William Penn*, vol. 3 (Philadelphia, 1986).

PWP, 5

Edwin B. Bronner and David Fraser, *The Papers of William Penn*, vol. 5, *William Penn's Published Writings, 1660–1726: An Interpretive Bibliography* (Philadelphia, 1986).

Raimo, *Governors*

John W. Raimo, *Biographical Directory of American Colonial and Revolutionary Governors, 1607–1789* (Westport, Conn., 1980).

Root, *Relations of Pennsylvania*

Winfred T. Root, *The Relations of Pennsylvania with the British Government, 1696–1765* (New York, 1912).

Scharf, *Delaware*

J. Thomas Scharf, *History of Delaware, 1609–1888*, 2 vols. (Philadelphia, 1888).

Scharf and Westcott

J. Thomas Scharf and Thompson Westcott, *History of Philadelphia, 1609–1884*, 3 vols.(Philadelphia, 1884).

Shepherd

William Robert Shepherd, *History of Proprietary Government in Pennsylvania* (New York, 1896).

Smith

Joseph Smith, *A Descriptive Catalogue of Friends' Books*, 2 vols. and supplement (London, 1867 and 1893).

Soderlund, *William Penn*

Jean R. Soderlund, ed., *William Penn and the Founding of Pennsylvania: A Documentary History* (Philadelphia, 1983).

Statutes

James T. Mitchell and Henry Flanders, comps., *The Statutes at Large of Pennsylvania, 1682–1701*, 2 vols. (Harrisburg, 1896–1915).

Statutes at Large

The Statutes at Large from Magna Carta to 1806, 46 vols. (Cambridge, 1762–1807).

Steele, *Colonial Policy*

I. K. Steele, *Politics of Colonial Policy: The Board of Trade in Colonial Administration, 1696–1720* (Oxford, 1968).

Transcript

Modern (post–1718) copy.

Trigger, *North American Indians*

Handbook of North American Indians, ed. William C. Sturtevant, vol. 15: *Northeast*, ed. Bruce G. Trigger (Washington, D.C., 1978).

VCH

W. Page et al., *The Victoria History of the Counties of England*. (London, 1900–).

Votes and Proceedings

Votes and Proceedings of the House of Representatives of the Province of Pennsylvania (Philadelphia, 1752), vol. 1.

Watson, *Annals*

John F. Watson, *Annals of Philadelphia, and Pennsylvania, in the Olden Time,* 3 vols., rev. ed., ed. Willis P. Hazard (Philadelphia, 1905).

Wing

Donald Wing, ed., *Short-Title Catalogue of Books Printed in England, Scotland, Ireland, Wales, and British America and of English Books Printed in Other Countries, 1641–1700,* 3 vols. (New York, 1951).

WMQ

The William and Mary Quarterly.

Works

[Joseph Besse, ed.], *A Collection of the Works of William Penn,* 2 vols. (London, 1726)

A WILLIAM PENN CHRONOLOGY, 1701–1718

1701 *January.* Living in Pennsylvania, sends instructions to William Penn, Jr., as his agent in London.

23 April. Signs treaty with Indians settled on the Susquehanna.

September. Decides to return to England, to defend his proprietorship.

October. Signs Charter of Philadelphia; provisionally approves Charter of Property; permits the Lower Counties to have a separate assembly.

November. Leaves Pennsylvania, naming Andrew Hamilton as deputy governor of Pennsylvania and the Lower Counties.

December. Arrives in England and takes up temporary lodgings in London, while his family goes to Bristol.

1702 *January.* Following the death of Philip Ford, signs an agreement with Bridget Ford to pay back rent on Pennsylvania.

8 March. William III dies; bill to reunite proprietary colonies to the crown is dropped by Parliament.

9 March. Birth of son Thomas Penn.

April–May. Defends his proprietorship against the charges of Robert Quary before the Board of Trade.

May. Presents Quaker address of gratitude to Queen Anne.

19 August. Daughter Laetitia Penn marries William Aubrey.

October. Has an audience with Queen Anne at Bath.

Publication of *More Fruits of Solitude,* his last major work.

1703 *21 January.* Andrew Hamilton approved as lieutenant governor of Pennsylvania.

26 April. Death of Gov. Andrew Hamilton.

May–June. Begins negotiations for surrendering Pennsylvania government to the crown.

May. Leases Pennsylvania lands to provide for Laetitia's marriage settlement; borrows £2500 from son-in-law William Aubrey.

July–August. John Evans approved as deputy governor of Pennsylvania.

30 August. Birth of daughter Hannah Margarita Penn.

1704 *2 February.* Gov. John Evans and William Penn, Jr., arrive in Pennsylvania.

25 August. Assembly sends remonstrance written by David Lloyd.

November. William Penn, Jr., leaves Pennsylvania for England.

7 November. Birth of daughter Margaret Penn.

1705 *29 March.* Philip Ford, Jr., writes to Pennsylvania, claiming to be the proprietor.

5 April. Drafts new proposal to surrender Pennsylvania government to the crown.

4 October. Bridget Ford probates Philip Ford's will; the Fords' claim becomes public.

20 October. Writes a new will, ignoring the Fords' claim.

31 October. The Fords file suit in Chancery.

1706 *17 January.* Birth of son Richard Penn.

23 February. Files cross Bill of Complaint against the Fords.

March. The Ford case is heard in Chancery.

5 June. The Fords respond to Bill of Complaint.

November. Assembly initiates impeachment of James Logan.

December. Drops initial Bill of Complaint against the Fords and files a new bill.

1707 *26 February.* Birth of son Dennis Penn.

21 April. The Fords respond to second Bill of Complaint.

14 May. Replies to the Fords' answer.

28 June. Prosecuted in Common Pleas for payment of back rent on Pennsylvania.

14 August. Defends before the Board of Trade the right of Pennsylvania Quakers to affirm.

22 November. Sells Warminghurst, Sus., his principal property in England.

23 November. Lord Chief Justice Trevor sanctions jury verdict that WP owes the Fords £2908 in back rent.

1708 *7 January.* Refuses to pay the Fords and enters Fleet Prison in London.

February. death of daughter Hannah Margarita.

9 March. Lord Chancellor Cowper rebuffs the Fords' petition for proprietorship of Pennsylvania.

18 July. Charles Gookin approved as deputy governor of Pennsylvania and the Lower Counties, replacing John Evans.

5 September. Birth of daughter Hannah Penn.

September or October. Released from debtors' prison.

5–7 October. Settles with the Fords on payment of £7600, all but £1000 of it loaned by a group of English Quakers, to whom Pennsylvania is mortgaged.

1709 *24 January.* Death of daughter Hannah Penn.

May. Sends peace proposals to the duke of Marlborough.

23 June. Lord Baltimore's claim to the Lower Counties dismissed.

December. James Logan leaves Pennsylvania for England after being impeached by the Assembly.

1710 *Spring.* Settles at Ruscombe, Berks., with his wife Hannah and their children.

29 June Chides the Assembly for its disregard of his proprietorship.

31 July. Resumes negotiations for surrender of Pennsylvania.

October. Pennsylvania election results in first Assembly favorable to WP in five years.

1711 *15 February.* Has an audience with Queen Anne about the surrender of Pennsylvania.

1712 *January.* Logan leaves England to return to Pennsylvania.

January–February. Lobbies for revision of the English Affirmation Act.

23 February. Writes preface to John Banks's *Journal,* his final published work.

April. Suffers his first apoplectic stroke and writes his last will.

July. The Treasury approves payment of £12,000 in four years for surrender of the Pennsylvania government.

28 September. Receives initial payment of £1000 from the Treasury.

October. Suffers second stroke in Bristol.

November. Travels to London to meet with the Board of Trade.

December. Suffers third, debilitating stroke at Ruscombe.

1713 Now an incapacitated invalid; Hannah Penn takes charge of proprietary affairs.

1714 *March 20.* Privy Council recommends that surrender agreement be perfected by act of Parliament, which is prevented by death of Queen Anne.

1715 *June.* Is taken to Bath for treatment but does not improve.

1716 Condition worsens; no longer can attend Quaker meetings at Reading.

November. William Keith is commissioned as deputy governor, replacing Gookin.

1717 Worsens further; can barely walk or speak.

1718 *30 July.* Dies at Ruscombe.

5 August. Buried at Jordans, Bucks.

THE PROPRIETOR IN RESIDENCE

January–September, 1701

By January 1701 WP had been living in Pennsylvania for thirteen months. It had taken the fifty-six-year-old Quaker proprietor fifteen years to return to his colony, and, though he had initially been reluctant to undertake the journey, he seems to have enjoyed being back in charge of his most successful enterprise. He had brought with him his second wife, Hannah, and his only surviving daughter, Laetitia, and had seen the birth of Hannah's first child, John, in Philadelphia. His grown son, William, Jr., was acting as one of his agents in London. Except for a bad leg which troubled him for much of his stay, WP was in robust health and extremely active. He had seemingly accomplished in Pennsylvania all that the English government had demanded from him. He had convinced the Assembly to enact legislation against piracy and illegal trade; dismissed Attorney General David Lloyd, Deputy Governor William Markham, and Justice Anthony Morris; encouraged vigorous assessment of the penny-per-pound tax on tobacco; and supported the royal customs officials and vice-admiralty court. On a personal level, he had obtained from the Assembly an excise tax and a supply bill that would be helpful in ameliorating his substantial debts.

Nonetheless, despite these achievements, WP had incurred the enmity of many Pennsylvania and Lower County colonists, already severely factionalized before his visit and highly resistant to proprietary and royal claims. Anglicans were alarmed at the dominance of Quakers in government. Merchants were upset with enforcement of the English Navigation Acts and the Pennsylvania laws against piracy and illegal trade, and with the growing interference of royal customs officials and the vice-admiralty court. Many colonists complained that their land titles were insecure. The Lower Counties were anxious to disengage from Pennsylvania and to establish their own legislative assembly. Since June 1700 Pennsylvania had been without a constitution. Royal officials were continuing to attack WP's management of his colony, particularly what they viewed as his infringements on the jurisdiction of the vice-admiralty court. In December 1700 a concerned WP twice wrote to Charlwood Lawton, his agent in London, providing detailed arguments for Lawton to use in lobbying members of Parliament. As 1701 began, WP's status as proprietor was in severe jeopardy (see *PWP*, 3:565–67).

During the first nine months of 1701 WP traveled often from his manor of Pennsbury in Bucks County to Philadelphia, where he had to deal with such problems as the repair of Front Street (doc. 2) and the tax status of the inhabitants of Germantown (doc. 3). In the summer of 1701 he visited Sussex County, where the border dispute with Maryland was still continuing (doc. 12), and he traveled to the Susquehanna Valley in order to make peace with the local Indians and prepare for a new settlement (doc. 11). He also addressed the perennial problem of nonpayment of quitrents, particularly in the Lower Counties. WP appointed James Logan to settle titles of lands, to order resurveys where appropriate, and to rationalize the quitrent system (see *Micro.* 9:243, 268; doc. 16). Unfortunately, this caused Logan to travel away from Philadelphia on numerous occasions; in mid-July (doc. 14) WP angrily chastised him for remaining absent for so long when decisions needed to be made on such issues as nonpayment of taxes; William III's request for £350 from Pennsylvania to assist the New York militia; the Maryland border dispute; and the prorogued Assembly.

The most serious issue for WP, of course, was the threat from the English government to the proprietary colonies. Having already appointed Charlwood Lawton as his agent, WP decided also to enlist the support of his son, William, Jr., to whom he wrote in early January (doc. 1). In the spring of 1701 WP wrote to the commissioners of the customs (doc. 4), the Board of Trade (*Micro.* 9:096), and Robert Harley (doc. 9), reiterating the great strides he had made against piracy and illegal trade and asserting the value of proprietary Pennsylvania to the crown. WP was alarmed at the rumored decision of the New Jersey proprietors in England to surrender their charter to the crown. He wrote in March 1701 to the proprietors (doc. 8), calling upon them not to surrender their charter, while in April he wrote angrily to Governor Andrew Hamilton (doc. 10) denouncing both the anti-proprietary riots in that colony and the defeatist attitude of the proprietors in England.

Unfortunately, WP in America was far less informed than were the New Jersey proprietors in England. There was certainly cause for concern. The Board of Trade was mounting a major campaign against the proprietary governments in 1701. A Reunification Bill aimed at voiding all proprietary governing rights had been introduced in the House of Lords on 24 April 1701, but it fell with Parliament's dissolution that summer. As late as 16 August WP had not yet heard of the bill (doc. 17), but by 27 August he knew that it had fallen and that another would be introduced during the next session (doc. 18). On 6 September (doc. 20) he protested that he did not want to undertake a long and dangerous voyage to England, but two days later (doc. 21) he was preparing to return. For further discussion of WP's response to the Board of Trade's challenge in August-September 1701, see the headnote to doc. 17.

1
TO WILLIAM PENN, JR.

[2 January 1701]

Remember these points.[1] 1. that it was the Govermt wch engaged me & those that adventur'd wth me, for as to Land it is the Natives, & I could have bought that of them on my one[2] account, but that would not have engaged us to have gone above 3000 miles of to convirt a meer Desert into an improved & fruitfull Country. In Eng. all is ready to our hands, but here was nothing but meer Creation, & that there is a vast difference between improveing it from that condition, & a place improved to ones hand. The Govermt was our greatest inducement, & upon that public[k] faith, wee have buried our blood & bones as well as ~~C~~estates to make it wht it is, for being Dissenters, we therefore came that we might enjoye that so farr of wch would not be allowed us any share of att home, & wch we so much needed to our security and happiness abroad.

2. Whereas they tell us they will not med{d}le wth our P~~o~~roperty, only the Govermt, I say that is the Property the Crown granted. In all Mannours, Courts Leets or Barron~~s~~ in Eng. especially in Courts Paramount, the powers are as much the Lords Property as the Land Rents or Royaltys thereof; but more especially in Palatines, or Seignorys like unto the title of Propri~~a~~etary govermts[3] this was our encouragement & the only reward we have from the Crown for addi[ng] another Cololony to it, & so considerable a one too. The Land was but as the shell, or ring & Govermt the kernell or Stone, the ring may be worth 20 ss, & the stone 100 pounds there can [be] no proportion, yet t'is called a ring as tother is Prop~~r~~erty, but still this without powers, is as that wthout the Diamond a Name and no more.

3 but next there can be wisdome[4] as well as no Justice in such a proceeding since, the Condition of Colonys young ones especially, calls for Encouragement and where Improvements ar che{c}kt the Crown looses. The more improvement, the more trade, & so the more Revenue to the Crown, directly, or by Circulation as Barbadous &c: & so for Eng.[5] now is it reasonable to think that tempor{ar}y & mer-

cinary Govermts will feel the same obligations to to improvement as one whose Estate it is, & that for this age does litle that can turn to account & so sowes in hope mostly; Certainly the Comparison gives it on our side They come to squeez, but propri~~a~~etarys to Improve.

4 Nor is the king so well secur'd, for where there is most to Lose there must be the best security to the Crown, for a Just Conduct, since Proprietarys have not onely Heireditary Govermts but Countrys to make the ~~P~~King satisfaction, & the Govermts in those places, equall care & paines wth Ks. Govermts without Salerys from the King & at their one[6] Charges being bound to observe the same laws of Trade & Navigation as his more Imediat Govermts ~~without~~

5 Besides the Law of the 7th & 8th of this king, gives Him the approbation of the Deputy Governours of Proprietarys, wch is all but mame{i}ng[7] them, & if Proprietarys are answerable for them, I think the king safe, & the Proprietarys are therein under hardships enough.[8] It seemed to me an Expedient to preserve the Proprietarys Govermts & secure the kings business together, wch is the most that could in any pretence be amed at, whn that Law was made why more?

6 If they say but you will not fight, I answer king Charles King James & ki[ng] William[9] knew that: we are a Quaker Colony, it was so intended: howbeit rather than Loose our Govermt for that let the Governour of new York be Colonell of the forces here;[10] but let but lett not us be persecuted in our Co~~n~~untry whe[11] our Co~~n~~nsciences are tender, that came so farr & have endured and spent so much that we might enjoye them with more ease than at home: In short, if it should press, get time that we may be sent to, & our resolutions known, or I may have liberty to go home & answer for myself.

7 who will pay me for Settling maintaning the Govermt for 20 years, I have not got 500 pounds of the people yet & at this rate must not expect it has cost me so much.

8 the very Name of a kings Governour will immediatly Sinck the intrincick value of Property, as they call it, wch will be more than Cent perct.[12] pray how shall this be repared. I was tould by an understanding person, and no friend to the sentiments of the New England people that the king had spent 40000 pounds to make that Colony 100000 pounds worse then it was. So false are those notions that it is the kings interest to suppress or change Proprietory Govermts Had the kings Govermts improved in proportion to us, they had been as well improved as Irland by this time or little short of it; ours is but 20 years old & the kings 100. I may add new england & Rood Island, the last still a propriety and as finely improved as any part of Sussex or Hamshire downs[13] Sprinkled wth houses & cloathed wth sheep. But no more of this ~~if~~only if should be sayd they too[14] great friends to Pyrats, I offer to joyn Issue wth them, & give 5 to 3, & be in no Danger of the success of that inquiry. so unjust is that Imputation Compare this[15] wt I have write C Lawton[16] & the best of both will make a

memorial for the Parl: or Lords of Trade, or the king himself. The heads I wish in the hands of Ld Sunderland Ld Godalphin, Ld Rochester, L^{d} Mo~~u~~nmoth, Marqu~~a~~es of Normanby, Ld Carbery, Lord Cholmly, D. of Devonshire, L^{d} Ma{c}klesfeild; S^{r} ~~C~~Ch: Mussg Sr Ed. ~~seinor~~ Seimor Sq^{r} Harley[17] Coll: Grim~~e~~ill[18] &c: Not forgetting ~~the~~to move the Earl of Shas{t}bury, & Bath & one Amy of the City a sencible man (& often at the Carolina Coffee house) to int~~re~~erest themselves warmly in this affaire being Lords of Carolina,[19] also L^{d} ~~Berly~~ Berley whose wives Sister, & widdow to his Brother is maried to the Earle of Portland[20] If they had each of them a memorial att larg, it would do well.

Copy. Records of the Proprietary Government, Miscellaneous Papers, Division of Archives and Manuscripts, Pennsylvania Historical and Museum Commission, Harrisburg. (*Micro.* 9:007.) Endorsed in WP's hand: A Copy of my leter to my | Son. | 2. 11^{m} 1700 | by way of new | york: | to write againe. The edges of this letter have been repaired with archival tape which obscures numerous words and letters. The editors have consulted a printed version in *PA*, 2d ser., 7:11-13, and, where applicable, have inserted conjectural words and letters within square brackets.

1. WP is instructing his son, William Penn, Jr. (1681-1720), on how to act as his agent in England. The arguments pursued here closely resemble those in WP's letter to Charlwood Lawton of 21 Dec. 1700 (*PWP*, 3:629). William Penn, Jr., was the oldest surviving son of WP and his first wife, Gulielma, and had married in 1699 Mary Jones (1677-1733), daughter of Charles Jones, Jr., a Bristol Quaker merchant. They had three known children: Gulielma Maria (1699-1740), Springett (1701-1731), and William III (1703-1747). *PWP*, 2:281n; Jenkins, pp. 127-29, 204-12, 245.

2. WP means "own."

3. WP is arguing that his powers as proprietor were equivalent to those of an English feudal lord or head of a county palatine, with jurisdiction within his territory which elsewhere belonged to the sovereign alone.

4. WP or the copyist omitted the word "no."

5. WP is arguing that Pennsylvania benefits England indirectly by circulating its exports to colonies such as Barbados.

6. See n. 2, above.

7. Probably the copyist's mistake for "naming."

8. Although the Navigation Act of 1696 had given the crown the right to approve deputy governors, WP and other colonial governors had successfully resisted royal demands for bond to be posted by governors for the behavior of their deputies. See *PWP*, 3:538.

9. Charles II (1660-1685); his brother James II (1685-1688); and William III (1689-1702), who took the throne jointly with his wife, Mary, James's daughter.

10. In 1692-94 Gov. Benjamin Fletcher of New York had been granted both military and civil management of Pennsylvania, to WP's great distress. But WP was now willing to turn military responsibility over to a friendlier New York governor, Richard Coote (1636-1701), earl of Bellomont, who at this date was also governor of Massachusetts and New Hampshire and commander-in-chief of the militia of Connecticut, Rhode Island, and East and West New Jersey. Appointed with specific instructions to suppress piracy, Bellomont had arrested Capt. William Kidd in Boston in 1699. *DNB;* Andrews, *Colonial Period,* 4:377-78; Stephen Saunders Webb, *The Governors-General: The English Army and the Definition of the Empire, 1569-1681* (Chapel Hill, 1979), pp. 492, 499.

11. Probably "when."

12. Cent per cent, or hundred for every hundred (*OED*). WP means that his property will lose more than half its value.

13. The chalk uplands of southern England, used primarily for pasturage.

14. WP or the copyist probably omitted the word "are."

15. WP or the copyist omitted the word "with."

16. On 21 Dec. 1700 (*PWP*, 3:629). Charlwood Lawton (1660-1721), educated at Oxford and called to the bar from the Middle Temple though he did not practice law, had been WP's friend since 1686. He was acting as WP's agent at court at this time. Ibid., 3:546n.

17. WP was attempting to recruit as large and varied a group of influential supporters at court as possible. Seven of the men listed in this paragraph were prominent Whigs: Robert Spencer (1641-1702), second earl of Sunderland; Charles Mordaunt (1658-1735), earl of Monmouth and third earl of Peterborough; Hugh Cholmondeley (c. 1662-1725), Baron Cholmondeley of Namptwich; William Cavendish (1640-1707), first duke of Devonshire; Charles Gerard (1659?-1701), second earl of Macclesfield; Anthony Ashley Cooper (1671-1713), third earl of Shaftesbury; and William Berkeley (d. 1741), Baron Berkeley of Stratton. Another eight were prominent Tories: Sidney Godolphin (1645-1712), first baron later earl of Godolphin; Laurence Hyde (1641-1711), first earl of Rochester; John Sheffield (1648-1721), marquis of Normanby; John Vaughan (1640-1713), third earl of Carbery; Sir Christopher Musgrave (1632?-1704); Sir Edward Seymour (1633-1708); Robert Harley (1661-1724), later earl of Oxford and earl Mortimer; and John Granville (1628-1701), first earl of Bath. *DNB; Peerage*, 2:20-21, 149; 3:201-2; Steele, *Colonial Policy*, p. 72.

18. Probably a copyist's error for Sir Bevil Granville (d. 1706), nephew to the earl of Bath (see n. 17) and a favorite of William III. *DNB*.

19. Shaftesbury, Bath, and Thomas Amy, a London grocer, were among the proprietors of Carolina in 1701. M. Eugene Sirmans, *Colonial South Carolina: A Political History, 1663-1763* (Chapel Hill, 1966), p. 72; Michael G. Hall, *Edward Randolph and the American Colonies, 1676-1703* (Chapel Hill, 1960), p. 192.

20. William Lord Berkeley's wife, Frances (d. 1707), daughter of Sir John Temple, was sister of Jane Martha (1672-1751), whose first husband was Berkeley's older brother John (c. 1660-1697), and whose second husband was William Bentinck (1649-1709), earl of Portland, holder of numerous offices and chief confidant of William III. Berkeley (see n. 17, above) had been appointed master of the rolls for life in 1696 (*DNB; Peerage*, 2:148-49; 10:589-91).

2
PETITION FROM PHILADELPHIA CITIZENS

[February 1701]

To the Honourable William Penn Proprietarie & Governour of the Province of Pennsilvania & Counties Annexed Sitting in Counsell at Philadelphia the [blank] day of February anno Domini 1700/1 The Petition of severall of the Inhabitants[1] of s[d] Town Humbly Sheweth.

That by the Running and Wash of the Water at the End of the High Street,[2] the Ground is so worn off that the Front Street is allmost impassible by Cart or Wheel Carriage, and becom Dangerous to Horse-men, Very much to the Disadvantage of the Neighbourhood: and the Detriment & reproach of the Town in Generall; As likewise to the Great discouragem[t] of Severall persons Designing to Build under the Bank; Whose Lotts are at present inaccessible by Cart or Other Carriage, By reason of the Breach at the High Street End; and the want of Making a Cartable Road under the Bank in Kings Street,[3] Much to the incommoditie of the Proprietor's Lotts and Intrest, as well as the loss of his Tenants. We the Subscribers do therefore Crave, on behalfe of our Selves & the Town in Generall, That you would be Courteously pleased speedily to Consider of the redress of this Grievance, According to the Power Given You with Such others of the Freeholders of this Town, as You shall please to Call to your Assistance, To Prescribe Such Methods for the Regulation, & Repair of those streets as to Your Wisdom shall seem Meete;[4] And thereby Promote the Common Good both of Town & Countrey Which is the Glory of all Great & Pious Men who takes the weight of Governmt upon their Shoulders And we as in Duty Bound shall Ever Pray &ct.

James Atkinson	Robt Quary	Samuell Marmion
Joseph Knighte	John Davis	John parker
Richard Love	John Jones	John Mills
John: McComb	Mathias bellis	Joshua Johnson
William Waite	Harbert Corrie	William Kelly
Daniel Ridg	Rob Assheton	Nathaniel Edgcome
Thomas Tresse	Tho: Farmar	Ralph Jackson
Ralph: Ward	Nicholas Pearse	Thomas Coates
Thomas Peart	Randall Spakeman	John Kinsy
Timothy Stephenson		James portrues
Robert Reading		William Snead
pentecoast Teage		William Snowdon

DS. Logan Papers, HSP. (*Micro.* 9:039.) Docketed: A Petition | To | Governour & Councill | for mending the High Street | end— ~~May~~. 1701.

1. A number of the 33 signers of this petition occupied land along the riverfront. See Miscellaneous Papers of Phila. Co., 1:25, 27, HSP; Roach, "Directory," pp. 99, 111, 113, 119-20.

2. Now Market St.

3. King St. (later Water St.) ran parallel to the Delaware River on the beach below the riverbank.

4. This petition was discussed in the Provincial Council on 2 June 1701, at which time WP authorized a commission to oversee the maintenance of streets, landing places, and bridges, as well as the clearing of docks. This was in accordance with an act passed by the Assembly in Nov. 1700 for regulating streets and water courses, which permitted the governor and four members of the Provincial Council to appoint such a commission. On 27 June 1701, having recommended to the Council that £500 was needed for repairs, including Front St., the commission was empowered to levy the rate, appoint collectors, and employ the necessary workmen. *Votes and Proceedings,* 1:136-37; *Statutes,* 2:65-67; *Minutes of the Provincial Council,* 2:23-25; Logan Papers, 3:15, HSP; *Micro.* 9:259.

3
FROM FRANCIS DANIEL PASTORIUS

[17 February 1701]

To William Penn,

Absolute Proprietary and Governr in Chief over Pennsilvania & Territories thereunto belonging, A short Demonstration of the present Case of the German-Town Corporation, Together with an humble Request for his sustaining hand and Authority.

Honourable Governour.

May it please Thee to remember, that these 17 years ago this Township by thy good Advice & Convincing Reasons towards the first Beginners thereof was commenced to be laid out not in Plantations as the most part of this Province is, but in Lots and more compacted Settlements;[1] which method being after followed by our Countrymen who from time to time arrived here, It fell so out that there are now upon the 5700 acres of land, this our said Township consists in, three Score families, besides several single persons: and some dwelling so close and near one to the other, that they have not half as much timber as to fence their small Spots of ground; and by reason of this want we were constrained to fence all our Lots in Germantown in four Quarters, & consequentially must needs take singular Care, lest by one or other mans Carelessness the rest would suffer harm and Injury.

Next to this, Dear Govr Be pleased to call to mind, that in the year 1689 thou wart as favourable to the aforesaid German township as to grant unto the same by Charter[2] some considerable Priviledges, which not only then with due thankfulness have been received by the persons therein Incorporated, but likewise are at this very Moment of time enjoyed by us their Successors with all Imaginable Gratitude; At the other hand a few of our Neighbours (according to the old Poets saying Vicinumque pecus grandius uber habet)[3] did, & may be still do think our German Nation to be smiled on beyond desert or mesure; especially because we hitherto construed the said Charter after the plain words and true meaning thereof most beneficially for us the Grantees, refusing to pay those Taxes, Levies & Impositions, the County Courts do lay, as Necessity requires, on those under their Jurisdiction. For being by the s^{d} Charter exempted from the Jurisdiction of the County Court of Philadelphia, having our own Court of Record as well as our General Court, we cannot but believe that we are freed from all Charges towards the said County, seeing It would rather be a Burthen than a Priviledge to pay both the County-Taxes & also the Taxes of our Corporation;[4]

As for the Provincial Taxes we never made any Exception, but were allways, and still are willing to Contribute thereunto according to our habilities, as good and loyal Subjects.

Now dearly Esteemed Govr, After these two Premises we first Conclude, that whereas our Township is so extraordinarily settled, as above mentioned, the same can not be ruled or Ordered Conveniently by the General good Laws of this Province, unless the greatest Number of our Inhabitants should be forced to leave their first fields & Orchards tilled & toiled on with a great deal of labour; which Parting or Veteres migrate Coloni[5] would be not only tedious to many, who thus should be necessitated to withdraw, but likewise an hard matter for their old friends & acquaintance to be deprived of their Company.

Secondly we humbly Implore thy Benevolence towards those of our

German Nation, that came allready, or are hereafter to come into this thy Province, To defend and support our said Township by the Charter formerly granted, and further by way of Explanation to annex, that our Corporation being at their own Charges within themselves is exempted from all and every County-Taxes, or words to that purpose, as we are really apt to think It was thy good will & mind in granting us the said Charter.

What the general Court of this our Township some time ago represented unto Thee, concerning the difficulty of Upholding our Corporation for want of persons that will serve (the most pretending Conscience for to refuse the same) we hope It may be remedied by People that are expected in, as it is partly since the last arrival of some. So right honourable Govr In expectation of thy kind acceptance of this our humble Petition, we pray to God Allmighty to preserve Thee and all Thine both for your own Satisfaction & the Common good of this new Colony.

Germantown the 17th of XIIth mo: 1701.

By Order of a general Court held at the
said Place and Time.
Fr: Daniel Pastorius, Cler.[6]

ADS. Logan Papers, HSP. (*Micro.* 9:052.) Endorsed: Danl Pastorius | ~~for th~~ In behalf of the German | Corporation | To the Governour and Council | 5—1mo 1700/1.

1. See *PWP,* 2:490.

2. WP granted Germantown's charter on 12 Aug. 1689, although it did not receive the great seal of Pennsylvania until 30 May 1691. *Micro.* 6:327.

3. "In fields not ours the crops are ever more bounteous and the neighboring herd has richer udders." Ovid, *Ars Amatoria,* bk. 1, line 350. The translation is from J. H. Mozley, trans., *The Art of Love and Other Poems* (Cambridge, 1957).

4. Germantown's independent borough government, established under the charter of 1689, is described by Stephanie G. Wolf, *Urban Village: Population, Community, and Family Structure in Germantown, Pennsylvania, 1683-1800* (Princeton, 1976), pp. 165-76.

5. "Old settlers, migrate." Vergil, *Eclogue,* IX, line 4. The editors are grateful to Professor Robert E. A. Palmer of the University of Pennsylvania for providing the source and translation of this passage and the source of the passage in n. 3, above.

6. Francis Daniel Pastorius (1651-c. 1720) was the founder of Germantown and in 1701 clerk of its General Court. On 5 Mar. 1701 the Provincial Council considered this petition but deferred action on it. In 1707, however, Pastorius's position was rejected; Germantown lost its chartered privileges and was reconstituted as a township of Phila. Co., liable to county taxes and court jurisdiction. *PWP,* 2:490; *Minutes of the Provincial Council,* 2:13-14; Wolf, *Urban Village,* pp. 176-77.

4
TO THE COMMISSIONERS OF THE CUSTOMS

Philadelphia 6 1mo [March] 1701

Honoured friends

Last night late your obliging Letter of the 25th of 7^br [1] came to my hand by Captain Hill[2] of Maryland whose return so soon as to morrow morning, his ship waiting on him there ready loaden for England forbids me to be so full or particular as I could wish. I cannot but be pleased that I find you are so with what I have done, I am not so assured as to value my self upon my skill or Ability, but I have some Confidence of my good Intentions and Integrity, & as you help me to employ it I have reason to believe my future Services will meet with a suitable acceptance Your Allowance for Boats is very Seasonable & will ~~allow~~ {leave} your officers without excuse:[3] Lowman[4] residing 150 miles off I seldom see him but suddenly intend to visit that place, poor Birch[5] is dead and one Wood[6] in his place till your Orders determine that Affair He has the Character of an honest Gentleman & man of Substance But to deal freely with you, there comes not the 20th part of the Trade of this Governm^{t} to Lewis or Newcastle and if I displease no body I think the Charge you are at for those parts would be better employed ~~for~~ in double the number of Waiters[7] in the most likely places in this Bay and river, Which with one Collector here will far more effectually answer the end than the present establishment Since 19 parts of 20 of our commerce belongs to this town & consequently the trouble & care must be proportionable to a Collector here You are pleased to establish one at Burlington 20 miles above us, wch has not had three vessels there to or from it I think since I came into the River but a Waiter under the Collector here, at Salem 50 miles below near the Bay will be in the opinion of the most knowing a Sutable place to observe the Motions of Traders Not that there is a vessel of any Burthen fitt for the Sea that belongs to that Province but those that are bound to this place or province who will run goods often land them on that side and take their opportunities of crossing the water wth them as the market presents, the River below not being above 6 miles over & here but about a mile & ½, if so much. But I must beg your pardon for these thoughts at least for my free way of expressing my self upon the subject. I have done w^{n} I have told you that a Waiter at Cape May w^{r} many tricks are or may be play'd being the beginning of W Jersey to the Southward & from the sea will be very necessary for the Ks service and the Salary for the Collector at Burlington will defray the Charge that is 40^{l} Sterl wch is 60^{l} here for Salem & the like for Cape May make up the 80^{l} wch I presume that useless officer costs you all wch I submitt to your more correct Judgement[8] What I have said of Lewis Newcastle Salem & Cape May I must say for Kent County I mean that 2 waiters instead of a Collector at 80^{l} will be a surer Method there being many Creeks and not many Inhabitants I shall discourse your Coll^{r} here wth some of ~~the~~ {our} ablest men that have been traders & given off & by the next opportunity present you wth the Result of these Conferences. I hope before I end you'll lett me acknowledge your obliging Assurances that you will assist any Motion in parliament favouring our people about the Registring[9] & to remind you of the Necessity of it if you will encourage shipping & Trade divers having withdrawn from those Concerns because they cannot employ such as they have long known & that they can be answerable for to you I wish you the truest happiness & am wth Truth & respect

Yo[r] very faithful fr[d] to serve you WP

My last was of the 9th 10[br] [10] w[ch] I hope is come to hand wth an Account of the Naval office

LBC. William Penn Letterbook, 1699-1703, HSP. (*Micro.* 9:091.) Endorsed: Commissioners of the Customs. Also endorsed: per Captain Hill.

1. Not found.

2. Richard Hill (1673-1729), a Maryland Quaker ship captain and merchant, moved to Philadelphia in 1700 after his marriage to Hannah Delavall, widowed daughter of Thomas Lloyd. *PWP,* 3:489.

3. In May 1700 WP had written to the commissioners of the customs supporting the request of Matthew Birch and Samuel Lowman, collectors at New Castle and Lewes, respectively, for money to purchase boats to assist them in their duties. As a result their salaries were raised from £80 to £90 per annum. Root, *Relations of Pennsylvania,* p. 70n.

4. Samuel Lowman, an Anglican, was the collector of customs at Lewes, Del. In 1702 WP transferred Lowman to New Castle. *Micro.* 8:585; 10:360.

5. Matthew Birch (d. 1700), collector, surveyor, and searcher of customs for New Castle, died about the end of Oct. 1700. WP had severely chastised Birch several months before his death for criticizing WP's administration. *PWP,* 3:602; Scharf, *Delaware,* 1:534-36; *Micro.* 8:648.

6. Joseph Wood (1666-1721), an Anglican, was at this time sheriff of New Castle Co., having formerly been sheriff of Chester Co. He later served as a supreme court justice for the Lower Counties. *PWP,* 3:162; Scharf, *Delaware,* 1:536, 562, 622; 2:875; Chester County Miscellaneous Papers, pp. 19, 35, HSP; Miscellaneous Papers, Three Lower Counties, Delaware, 1655-1805, p. 65, HSP; *Micro.* 8:648.

7. Tide-waiters, who awaited the arrival of ships and boarded them to prevent the evasion of custom house regulations. *OED.*

8. In Apr. 1701 the commissioners of the customs, having been advised previously by Robert Quary that a collector at Burlington was unnecessary, ordered that post transferred to Cohansey Creek below Salem, West N.J. They also advised the treasury to station a small vessel in Delaware Bay. *CTB, 1697-1702,* p. 480.

9. WP is reiterating a request he had made to the Board of Trade and commissioners of the customs early in 1700, asking that the next statute dealing with trade include a clause permitting Quakers in the colonies to register and clear their ships by affirmation rather than the prescribed oath (see *PWP,* 3:589, 597; *Micro.* 8:305; 9:096). In July 1700 a copy of the initial request had been sent by the commissioners to WP's London agent, Charlwood Lawton, "that he may take advice thereupon" (*CSPC, 1700,* p. 430).

10. *Micro.* 8:648.

5

HANNAH PENN TO ELIZABETH TAYLOR

Philadelphia 6th 1st month [March] *1700*[/1]

Dear Friend[1]

the love which has long lived in my heart to thee, has very often (even in this desolate land,) brought thee into my remembrance; wth true desires to the God of all our mercys, that he would be pleasd to

Continue his blessings to thee, and give thee an increass of spirituall & tomperoll Comforts, in the room of those wch he in his wisdom has thought fit to deprive thee of (as to the outward: I mean thy dear & honourable father,[2] whose Memory is sweet, & pleasant to us, and I doubt not, but Your, & our, Loss is his eternall gain. I often think on thy Dear Mother[3] under her divers afflictions, espesially that of Loosing so tender & affectionate a husband, as he was to her; & a most carefull as well as Affectionate father, to you his children; may they all walk worthy of such a mercy, & follow his example, is what I greatly desire: and shall be glad to hear that thy brother Robert[4] Lives in a sence thereof. And now my dear friend tho, I have been backward in writing, I do assure thee I have not in wishing, thy happyness & wellfare in this thy Married estate, which ~~th~~as it is the greatest comfort in this world, so is it mixt with greatest exercises, a proof of which I hear thou hast already experienc'd, in the Loss of thy dear little daughter,[5] which I was truly sorry for, but hope it will please the lord to give thee more,[6] wch may be a comfort & pleasure to thee in days to come; but as in this, so in all other things, our Comforts are in his hand, who can withhold, or distribute, as he pleases; & we must not say unto him what does'd thou; I have been a witness of his {great power &} deliveran{ce} t{h}rough many exercises, & have cause to bless his name, who in his own due time, was pleasd to turn his hand, & make me partaker of his mercys, beyond what I could even have expected. which I desire I may always remember wth a thankfull heart while I have a being in this world; now dear betty, as ~~as~~ to perticulars know, that I have had my health much better than in england, my dear Husband is pretty well also, but exceedingly prest in buisness partly by his too long stay in england, which will I fear occasian his stay here to be too long also; I know his dear love is to thee & thine, and to the faithfull every where. the Country has Injoyd health in a great degree since we came hither, and my dear little boy[7] grows bravely, he's very pleasant & lively, much like his father, in whom he takes great delight, is well belov'd of his sister,[8] and indeed proves a great comfort & divertion to us all, I have Suckled him my selfe hitherto but think of Weaning him in a little time he has five teeth, and can go alone very well if he pleases Our friend Sarah Climent[9] is here & well, she has had good service in new england, Rhoad, & long Island, &c and intends for Maryland about 2 months hence she desires her dear love to thee & thy relations as oppertunity offers. pray give mine also, and to thy husband in perticular. I wish you comfort & happyness in each other, for I am as I have always been

Thy reall & Affectionate
Friend Han^{h} Penn[10]

since I wrote the above my poor boy has been taken very ill, is somwhat better, but not yet recovered. I expect by next to hear thy Sister Mary[11] is married to S Turners brother,[12] and wish her well every way. Lætitia gives her dr love to you all. vale

ALS. Friends Historical Library, Swarthmore, Pa. (*Micro.* 9:110.) Addressed: To James Taylor at | the Bear in Cheapside | for Eliz^h | Taylor. these | London. Further addressed: Att John Flyes | on Cock-hill next | dore {but one ~~but one~~} to the Signe | of the Cock. Docketed: Hannah Penn (the second | Wife of William Penn) | to Elizabeth Taylor, one | of the Daughters of | Richard Vickris. | Philadelphia 6th of 1st Mo. | 1700.

1. Elizabeth Taylor (b. 1673), daughter of Richard and Elizabeth Bishop Vickris, was the wife of James Taylor, a Cheapside linendraper. Digests of Quaker Records, London and Middx.; Bristol and Som., GSP.

2. Richard Vickris (d. 1700) of Chew Magna and Bristol, a prominent Quaker merchant. *PWP,* 1:373n; 2:122n.

3. Elizabeth Bishop Vickris (1655-1724), daughter of George Bishop (d. 1668), an early Bristol Friend, married Richard Vickris in 1672. Mortimer, 1:194-95, 218-19; *PWP,* 1:54-55.

4. Robert Vickris (b. 1681) was the eldest of four sons born to Richard and Elizabeth Bishop Vickris. Digests of Quaker Records, Bristol and Som.

5. Elizabeth Taylor, born on 22 Aug. 1700, had died on 7 Jan. 1701. Digests of Quaker Records, London and Middx., erroneously lists the child's age at death as "11 days."

6. In fact, Elizabeth and James Taylor would have at least eight more children, although a second daughter named Elizabeth, born on 15 Sept. 1701, died on 29 Nov. 1701. Digests of Quaker Records, London and Middx.

7. John Penn (1700-1746) was thirteen months old at this date. The only one of WP's children born in Pennsylvania (and hence known as "John the American"), he inherited half of WP's proprietary but returned to America only once, in 1734-35. He never married and his share of Pennsylvania went to his brother Thomas Penn. Jenkins, pp. 71-74.

8. Laetitia Penn (1678-1746), Hannah's stepdaughter, had come with her father and stepmother to Pennsylvania in 1699. She married William Aubrey of London in 1702. Ibid., pp. 67, 71.

9. Sarah Clements, a traveling Quaker minister, received a certificate from Devonshire House Monthly Meeting, London, to journey to Pennsylvania on 9 Aug. 1699. She was present at John Penn's birth and signed his birth certificate. Phila. Monthly Meeting, Abstracts of Minutes, Certificates of Removal, GSP; *PWP,* 3:584n.

10. Hannah Penn (1671-1726) was the only surviving child of Thomas and Hannah Callowhill, leading Quakers of Bristol. She married WP on 5 Mar. 1696 and had seven children, four of whom survived her: John, Thomas, Margaret, and Richard. Drinker, *Hannah Penn; PWP,* 3:394, 411-13, 435-37; *PMHB,* 81:78-79.

11. Mary Vickris (b. 1679). No record of her marriage has been found. Digests of Quaker Records, Bristol and Som.

12. Unidentified.

6
TO THE COUNTESS OF BELLOMONT

[c. 17 March 1701][1]

Noble Friend

My Grief exceeds my Surprize and as I condole so great a Loss to the Lady Bellomont[2] I must not leave my self out that measure my Share in it by the real Honour and Affection I had for him my Noble Friend.[3] I pray God soften this (otherwise) hard Stroke to his Family great Losers not otherwise to be repaired, and resignation is the only way to it. A Friend as well as a husband or a Wife is a double enjoyment wch renders the Loss double also But we are born to dy and Death is the way to the longest as well as the best life He has had many fitts that have alarum'd thee for this great Change, So that the latter part of his Life has been a preparatif for your parting. The way to have so great a Disappointment Sanctified to our Comfort is by this sorrowful Occasion to learn how to wean our Affections from those things that are wont to move us most with pleasure and Satisfaction in this low world I wish my noble Friend, any thing in my power could serve thee, I would religiously employ it for the Wife and Frd of the Earle of Bellomont shall alwayes claim the {right of} Survivorship in the Esteem and Service of her dear Lords and her most faithful frd

WP

Mine[4] send wth me our Salutes in true Mourning

LBC. William Penn Letterbook, 1699-1703, HSP. (*Micro.* 9:179.)

1. This undated letter is copied into WP's letterbook directly after his letter of 17 Mar. 1701 to the New York Council consoling them for the loss of their governor, and before a letter dated 26 Mar. 1701.

2. Catherine Nanfan (c. 1665-1738), countess of Bellomont, daughter of Brydges Nanfan, of Birtsmorton, Worcs., had married Richard Coote, later earl of Bellomont, about 1676 and had her first child at the age of 12. After her husband's death, she returned to England and married thrice more. She succeeded to her father's estate in 1704 and died on 12 Mar. 1738. *Peerage,* 1:313-14.

3. Richard Coote, Baron Coote of Coloony and first earl of Bellomont, had been commissioned royal governor of Massachusetts Bay, New Hampshire, and New York in June 1697. He had been in failing health for some time before his death from a severe attack of gout on 5 Mar. 1701. See *PWP,* 3:481.

4. Hannah and Laetitia Penn.

7
FROM THE COMMISSIONERS OF THE TREASURY

[27 March 1701]

After Our hearty Comendations, Whereas By One Indenture bearing date the 24th day of August 1682,[1] The late King James, then Duke of York, for the Consideracion therein mention'd, did Bargain, Sell, Enfeof and Confirm unto You, Your Heirs and Assignes for Ever all the Lands lying upon Delaware River in America, beg[inning] Twelve miles South from the Town of Newcastle, otherwise called Delaware, and Extending Southward to the WhoreKills, otherwise called Cape Hinlopen,[2] with all Priviledges and Immunities whatsoever of the said then Duke of York therein or to any part thereof, to be held as of the Castle of New-York in America,[3] in free and common Soccage,[4] Under the Yearly Rent of a Rose at the Feast of St Michael,[5] if demanded; By which Indenture It is among other things Covenanted and Agreed, that You, Your Heires or Assignes, should, within one Year Ensuing the date of the said Indenture, Erect or Cause to be Erected and sett up One or more Publick Office or Offices of Registry upon the said Bargained Premises, Wherein You, Your Heires and Assignes should and would among other things truely and faithfully Accompt, set down and Register all Rents and other Profitts, which You and they should make, Raise or Procure in, or out of the said Premises or any Part thereof, and should and would at the Feast of St Michael Yearly Pay to the said Duke of York, his Heires and Assignes One full Moiety[6] of all Rents, Issues and Profitts, as well Extraordinary as Ordinary as should be made or raised by reason of the Premises or any Part thereof. And that if it should appear that the same should be behind and unpaid, in part, or in all, by the Space of Twenty days after the same ought to be Paid or delivered, that then it should be Lawfull for the said Duke of York to Enter into the Premises, or any Part thereof, and to Distrain for the said Moiety and Arrears; And Whereas it does not appear unto Us that, Pursuant to the said Covenant, any Accompt has been made to His present Majesty for the said Moiety of the Rents, Issues or Profitts that have been made by You by reason of the said Lands, Wee do hereby strictly Charge and Require You, forthwith to return an Accompt to Us of the Moiety of all the Rents, Issues and Profitts, Received or made by You by reason of the said Lands, or any Part thereof, since the date of the said Indenture to the End, that His Maty's Dues may be thereupon Satisfied.[7] Wherein your speedy compliance is expected. And so Wee bid You farewell. From the Treasury Chambers in Whitehall the 27th day of March 1701.

Your very Loving Friends.
Godolphin
Ste: Fox
Richard Hill[8]

To Our very loving Friend William Penn Esqr Proprietor of the Province of Pensilvania in America.

LS. Penn Papers, Three Lower Counties, HSP. (*Micro.* 9:137.) Docketed by WP: Comrs of the Treasury | Ld. Godolphin Ste | St. Fox Ric. Hill. Docketed in another hand: Mr Pen | Demand for Moiety of Quittrents | 27th March 1701.

1. *Micro.* 3:576. The indenture was one of two of that date from James, duke of York, to WP. The other gave him the town of New Castle and a circle of land twelve miles in diameter around it. *PWP,* 2:281-84.

2. In this context Cape Henlopen denotes the present southeastern boundary of Delaware. See *PWP,* 2:308n.

3. A variant of the "Castle of Windsor" clause in the royal charter granted to WP, which insured that the grantee owed no quasi-feudal obligations to the grantor beyond the quitrent mentioned in the document. See *PWP,* 2:65, 570-71, 576n.

4. Land held free from feudal incidents, like marriage, wardship, and livery, normally attached to socage *in capite* or to knight-service. *PWP,* 2:74n.

5. Michaelmas, the feast day of St. Michael the Archangel, 29 Sept. by the English calendar. *OED.*

6. Half. *OED.*

7. From the beginning, WP had considerable difficulty in collecting quitrents from the Lower Counties. His tenuous claim to the area, combined with the long-standing boundary dispute with Lord Baltimore, had enabled the inhabitants to resist efforts to enforce payment. WP had failed, therefore, to pay any quitrents owed to the English government. Nonetheless, despite this letter, the English government did not press the matter, and by 1711 the arrears amounted to £8700. Beverley W. Bond, Jr., *The Quit-Rent System in the American Colonies* (New Haven, 1919), pp. 161-73.

8. Sidney Godolphin, first Baron Godolphin; Sir Stephen Fox (1627-1716); and Richard Hill (1655-1727) were commissioners of the treasury. *DNB*.

8
TO THE PROPRIETORS OF EAST NEW JERSEY

[c. March 1701][1]

Esteem'd Friends

I cannot but Think that my Interest in the provinces of East and West Jersey both in Respect of my property there and my past Services Sufficient to Intitle mee to a Right ~~to~~ Of be{ing} Consultd with, Equally wth the first in the Disposall of their Government. So I hope you will Excuse mee if I Shew a Concern at the strang Accot wee have of your proceedings You Expect E Jerseans should Raise mony to Reimburse you for the Charge you have been at in Asserting the Port of Amboy in the business of the Shipp Esther[2] when they are made to believe by J B.[3] that the whole matter of that Tryall was carried on by his Interest and at his Charge as in a Lr to John Royse,[4] he Affirms that buisness Cost him above four hundred pounds, wch if Otherwise Seeing by it he has magnified his own Merit and Lessened the Proprietors in the Eyes of the People, you ought at least to do yourselves the Justice of writing over the true State of that Affair that it may be known who has Right to the Praise to have mony Raised you Should keep your Letter directed to mee, by you, 3 months after its date[5] till by the Same Shipp Jer: B. tells his friends wee had Concerted a Surrender, and that he Staid to Come over the Kings Governor[6] that Severall of the Proprietors had Offerd their Service in Recommending him to that Post but that he rejected it believing it to be rather a Disservice and Vallues himself upon his Own Interest with the Ministry I confess had I not Seen it under A Better hand I could not have ~~believed~~ {Given Credit to} what he writes of a Surrender believing you of better Judgmts that[7] to Offer it now having otherwais obtained what it was only Intended to be Exchanged for,[8] in matters of this Concern I {must} think nothing ought to be Concluded without advising With the Proprietors on this Side also, who as they are to fare well or ill as the thing is Laid So they are the best Judges of what is fitt to be done But I am Really troubled to think that as the Offer made of the Government was an Effect of Necessity that by it a Port might be Obtained, Now that necessity being over Your being Supported by the Opinion of Eminent Councill of {the} Assignabilly[9] of Government and being Also Singularly Affronted by E. Jerseans who Send Agents to force the Government from you, make at this Juncture the Resolves of a Surrender altogether inexcusable.

One thing more that Concerns mee is that by Such proceedings any man of honour would be Discouraged from Serving you by the making the Bows to persons your Governour[10] has been Obliged to Quarrell wth in Defence of your honour & whom he is forced to Correct for Contempt of the Government and as open Disturbers of the Publick Peace who I Assure you Acted a part ~~of~~ Both of Judgment & Spiritt for he bravely bowed their Rage and number to his Authority wth a very Considerable one when they Seemd Determined to Rout both him and it out of E Jersey[11] So that the Provinces Seemd a Clean Sheet of Paper but hereby these men are Justified and the Governour Condemnd and Exposed nor will it be Ever otherwise while American Affairs are weighed with an European Scale for Matters of fact and the Circumstances of persons and things must be known before a Right Judgmt Can be made nor will this Ever attain the Ends proposed Either of Smoothing that people or of getting mony it will only make them more Insolent & the Proprietors Litle and Give a new Life to Faction that the Governor had Subdued and forcd to Capitulation

My Friends I have a hearty Respect and Esteem for those that signd that Letter to mee and hope they will have the Same Regard to mee and my ꝑInterests But Cannot but be Concernd when I see you make Such Steps and that you will be tender in making any Steps that tend not Only to Subvert your Own but that of other proprietary Governmts of America that have been Settled and Supported with Such incredible Charge & difficulties this having been the prevailing motive to us all to seek our Satisfaction and Repose in a Desart So Remote from our Native Country I am

in Ancient love and Esteem your Cordial frd
W: P.

P S

Pray lett your Secretary William Duvra[12] know I have Endeavd to Come to the true state of the Case about his land and find his Informer as full of truth on that Side of the water as his famous Actions shew him to have been here, I am Sorry to find so much of his Injustice Vanity & Ingratitude[13]

LBC. William Penn Letterbook, 1699-1703, HSP. (*Micro.* 9:189.)

1. This letter is difficult to date. On 14 Nov. 1700 Gov. Andrew Hamilton of East and West New Jersey had asked WP to write to his fellow proprietors in England, urging them to stand up against Hamilton's adversary Jeremiah Basse (see n. 3, below) and also protesting their plan to surrender the colony to the crown (*Micro.* 8:640). In doc. 8 WP not only adopted Hamilton's advice but copied his language almost word for word, which suggests that he sent this letter in Nov. or Dec. 1700. On the other hand, doc. 8 appears in WP's letterbook between letters dated 26 Mar. 1701 and 31 Mar. 1701, and since most of the letterbook copies are arranged chronologically, the editors believe the letter was more likely written about Mar. 1701.

2. For years the government of East New Jersey had been trying to establish a free port at Perth Amboy, which would enable ships to pay customs to East New Jersey and not be required to call at New York. To force the issue, Gov. Jeremiah Basse of East New Jersey in Nov. 1698 loaded his ship, the *Hester,* at Perth Amboy, whereupon Gov. Bellomont of New York had the ship seized and taken to New York. Basse took

his case to England and filed suit in the court of King's Bench, where in May 1700 a jury found for the plaintiff, who recovered sizable damages and costs. Basse was now trying to make the people of East New Jersey pay for his charges in bringing the case. Pomfret, *East New Jersey*, pp. 311-24.

3. Jeremiah Basse (d. 1725), staunch Anglican and former agent for WP in West New Jersey, had served a controversial term as governor of East and West New Jersey in 1697-99, and was now back in England trying to obtain appointment as the first royal governor of New Jersey. See *PWP*, 3:489n.

4. John Royce (d. 1709), formerly of New York, was a councilman in East New Jersey who led the anti-proprietary faction that opposed Gov. Hamilton. After the surrender of the Jersey proprietorship in 1702, Royce served in several assemblies (see Pomfret, *East New Jersey*, pp. 279-80, 341-42, 352; *NJA*, 23:396). Basse's letter to Royce, mentioned by WP, has not been found.

5. The East New Jersey proprietors had apparently written a letter (now lost) to WP, announcing the victory over New York in the *Hester* case, but had delayed sending it to America.

6. The proprietors of East New Jersey had been negotiating possible terms of surrender to the crown since July 1699. Many were now ready to surrender, but WP was not one of them. Nor were the proprietors ready to recommend Basse as the first royal governor; they preferred Andrew Hamilton. When the surrender finally occurred in 1702, the crown selected Lord Cornbury instead. See Pomfret, *East New Jersey*, chap. 15.

7. Logan's error for "than."

8. WP, adopting Hamilton's argument, is stating that the *Hester* case had secured the right of Perth Amboy as an independent free port, the major concession previously demanded by the proprietors from the crown in return for their surrendering the charter. WP saw no reason to pursue such a surrender now.

9. Logan's error for "Assignability." It is unclear to which "Eminent Councill" Hamilton and WP are referring. In fact, they seem to be unaware that the attorney and solicitor generals had ruled against East New Jersey's claim to nominate free ports, and by implication had brought into question the right of the proprietors to govern the Jerseys. See Pomfret, *East New Jersey*, chap. 15.

10. Andrew Hamilton, who had been appointed governor of the Jerseys in Mar. 1699. See doc. 10, n. 1.

11. For the violent resistance in East New Jersey against continuation of proprietary rule, see doc. 10, n. 2.

12. William Dockwra (d. 1716), an ambitious non-Quaker London merchant, was a leading proprietor of East New Jersey, the absentee secretary and register of the province, and the executive secretary of the proprietors. By 1690 he had amassed over 20,000 acres. He was removed from office for malfeasance in 1702. He is remembered chiefly for his contributions in initiating the postal service both in London and in the American colonies. See John E. Pomfret, "The Proprietors of the Province of East New Jersey, 1682-1702," *PMHB*, 76:256, 260, 266-67; Pomfret, *East New Jersey*, pp. 225, 231.

13. The "informer" against Dockwra was probably his deputy and receiver general in East New Jersey, George Willocks, who in Dec. 1700 had formally accused him of corruption. Willocks charged him with receiving more choice land than he was entitled to, and also making inequitable dividends of land to other settlers. See Pomfret, "The Proprietors of East New Jersey," p. 267; idem, *East New Jersey*, pp. 349-53.

9
TO ROBERT HARLEY

[c. April 1701][1]

Honored Friend,[2]

I have often blamed my selfe I had not left a memoriall of those things that neerly affect this american empire, since we see so little of an american understanding among those, whose business it is to superintend it. All places as well as people & languages have their peculiaritys, & a just consideration therof Contributes much to proper methods for their respective benefitt. But by w^{t} reaches these quieter parts of the world you are so full of more domestick subjects, that I know not whether this will not come too soon, & call for an Apology. However, this I am well assured of, the Crown of England is deeply interrested in our Prosperity; tho I must easily graunt, there may be affaires neerer home of a more immediate import, & upon which may depend the very being of these Colonys in Consequence.

It were to be wisht, in the first place, that there were added to those ingenious Persons that superintend the Colonys, some of their former Governours that served well: For besides that they deserve notice, they must needs supply the rest with that knowledge their experience has given them; that they who have never been in those parts of the world, cannot, tho otherwise oracles, comparably understand.

Next, that both Gover^{rs} & inferior officers, were men of estates, good morrals & Character at home, or they are a punishm^{t} in lieu of a Benefit. and to encourage persons under those Circumstances to goe so farr, let them have double pay, & make all Gratuitys & Perquisits Punishable; and other oppressive gaines a forfieture of their places.

The People are extreamly ill used on one hand, & the King on the other: For one way the officers are officiously & unnecessarily busy for the King, takeing his name {in vaine} to serve every turn of advantage or revenge, to his dishonour & disprofit too. for instance, Trade is the benefitt england Chiefly has ~~in~~ by these Colonys; now where it is very young & small, the people, [illegible deletion] ignorant in the exactness of the laws, ~~taking~~ fall sometimes under their pow[er], the rich finde ways of comeing off easily, the poor they practice their duty upon to the life, that by overacting their parts, unseasonably as well as unjustly, they may recommend their zeal as merritorious to the Com^{rs} of the Customs, or L^{ds} of Trade & Plant. whereby Trade is Crusht in the Budd, & we only turn planters, or farmers, endeavouring a selfe-subsistance & there's an end of a Colony to the Crown; ~~&~~ for where Trade Ceases the revenue cannot encrease, nor england get by the forraign labour of her inhabitants: settled places & Traffick will not easily be Checkt; they will bear Stricktness that know the laws, & have often been informed; but in New Colonys, all ways possible should be used to excite & encourage Trade, for that is serveing Eng^{d} & the king. Since a pineing one will neither enrich him nor them.

The Trade of {Tobacco,} Furs & Skins for Europe, some fish & whale oyle, & provisions for the west india Islands, are the produce of the Northern Countrys or Colonys; Tobacco comeing only from two of them, Virginia & Maryland, except a little made in our Bay of Delawarr. Now if the Crown would encourage every Clymat; in those things it is proper for, we could produce Silk, oranges, & lemons, fruit, & wine, as well as others of us, Hemp, flax, Tarr, masts &

abundance of Crooks, knees,[3] & Stately planck for shiping. The mines of Eng. have distroyd much of the Timber of Eng. & here is enough of both, if great undertakers there, would fall upon it here we might supply Eng. & give her woods time to recover, & Convert these Countrys to arrable & Pasture, into the bargain.

But there is an other unhappiness that attends us, that must undo us if not cured, and that is ~~the~~ the powr of the Admiralty in the extent practised in this province. our settlements are upon the freshes[4] of navigable Rivers, & creeks, where the River may be {from} two or three miles over, to a stones cast over, & 100 miles from the ocean, & the Court of admiralty by virtue of the 7 & 8th of the King, page 502,[5] pretends not only to try Causes that relate to the Kings revenue, as to unlawfull trade, or Pyracy, but whatever is done in the River {or Creeks,} other ways, as debts for victuals, Bear,[6] Sailes, or any thing relateing to the building of any small Craft; so that they have swallowed up a great part of the Govermt here, because our commerce, by reason of the nature of our settlemts, is so much upon the River & small Creeks of it; and determining these causes without a jury, gives our people the greatest discontent, looking upon themselves as less free here than at home, insteed of greater priviledges, wch were promessed. This law Is weakly penned, & could not be be otherwise, when only Comr Chaddock[7] & Ed. Randol[8] were the framers of it. for p. 497, 502, 505, being compared, show its obscurity, if not inconsistancy, and if it means any thing, it must be this, {either} that in the Court of Admiralty where there is no jury, there the Jury shall be natives of Eng. Irland or the plantations. or that all causes to be tryed in the Plantations by the Court of Admiralty shall be by a jury so qualifyed; and truly ~~this,~~ if that Court must be so powrfull here, it had need do so, or the subjects of Eng. will, at all hazords, disobey that Authority. They expect common law here, & that the laws wch limit the Admiralty powrs there, should here, & not that the Admiral should be above the King, the Civil above the common law, or the Doctors Commons preferr'd to Westminster hall.[9] Counselr Mompessin,[10] thy neighbour, at lincolns Inn,[11] has made himselfe master of this business; and I hope the Parl: will not lett us fall under so despotick a powr as that of the admiralty; Since the Colonys of America were begun upon the publick faith by privat purses; and I am sure 30000 pounds will not pay me, tho people have got (by mistake) an other notion of me, nor 500000 pounds the people.

we have past two laws, one agst unlawfull trade,[12] wherein ed. Randal was the greatest transgressor, who ordered the Collectors to ship tobacco by Content at 350l & 400 pounds per Hogshead, while they weighed 6, 7, 8, & 900 pounds Defrauding the king of one half of the ~~kings~~Risen[?] dues of 1d per pound, for severall years. we have also past an other agst Pyrats & Pyracy,[13] both as well guarded & as Comprehensive as we have been able. I have angerd our Tobacconists, for wch cause they were very barren towards me in the Generall Assembly;[14] but time will ware that off, I hope.

I have had all the Care, vexation, & Charge of a Ks. goverr to do the Kings business, without a farthing Consideration, & I hope none has acquitted with more exactness, whatever malice or envy may insinuate agst us. which leads me to a late suffering that makes us very uneasy, & might be remedied there, viz, the Heat of a few Church men, headed by a flanders Camp Parson,[15] under the Protection of the Bp. of London,[16] who haveing got a few together, make it their business to enveigh agst us, & our Govermt. they came heither poor, & some of them {are} so Still, ~~I~~yet here get their bread, & some of them estates, & cannot be satisfyed to do so, & enjoy more than their proportion to the whole, of the Govermt too; but must in the Pulpit inveigh agst our principles & those that regard the State, as Oaths, ~~Tythes~~[?] &c: as if they would Stir up their people agst those, whose tenderness admits them into shares in the Administration, to turn them out. This is very impertent[17] & provoaking. They will now have no Office in the Govermt unless they swear, & have powr to swear others, ~~though~~ {because} they know our Govermt is under attests only, as may be easily thought, & then complain they cannot be admitted into the Govermt because they are Church men: a most abusive treatment of us. methinks some of thy Church acquaintance might moderate these follys a little. The spring of this in good measure has been from Colonel Nicolson of Virginia,[18] a line from any body to him, & from the Bp.[19] to Doctor Brady, his Suffregan in Maryland,[20] might quench this we cannot yet be so selfdenying as to lett those that had no part of the heat of the day, not 1/3 of the number & not 1/4 of the estate, & not 1/10 of the trouble & labour should give laws to us, & make us dissenters, & worse than that in our own Country. I must begg thy favour in mittegateing these indiscretions, &, in Govermt, insupportable treatmt. This Country encreases in Improvements above some of its Neighbours, ~~tho~~ but not in people; for tho' we have the name of people runing over heither, there came not even this yeare above 1500 souls, & into Maryland & Virginia, each 5000, as is generally Computed. tho I think our people of the better sort, theirs servts & ours, for the most part, free passengers.

I am carefull to preserve a good understanding with the natives, many hundreds of whome I expect in 3 days, above one is come.[21] I hope to settle a lasting friendship with them. The northern & western were never here before.[22] They are in nature a brave people, but much the worse for the vices they have learnt of Europeans, that should have taught them better things. I wish we may be able to retrieve them.

I have Sent thee one of their Otters Skins, wch {one of} the~~y~~m presented me wth some time since, & have orderd it to be made up into a muff, if better lik'd in that form. excuse, worthy Friend, this long letter, & the freedoms in it, wch if more than become me, not more than will be forgiven me, I dare assure myselfe, and lett {tell} me,[23] thee, also, that of all thy Pretenders, none has a more fixt vallue for thee than

Thy very faithfull & affect[t] Friend
Wm Penn

pray let S[r] Ed.,[24] if yet alive, have my respectfull salutes, & all my Frds, as thou pleasest, my good wishes. Thy Bro. Cosin, S[r] C. M. J.H. S[r] F.W. & his son S.[25] this is also great freedom, vale.

ALS. Loan 29/190, fols. 132-41, BL. (*Micro.* 9:153.) Addressed: For my honored | Friend Robert[t] | Harley esq[r]. Notation on bottom of first page: esq[r] Harley.

1. Although this letter is not dated, internal evidence suggests that it was written in Apr. 1701. WP mentions his forthcoming meeting with "hundreds" of Indians, and on 23 Apr. 1701 he signed a treaty of "friendship & Amity" at Philadelphia with numerous Indian kings and chiefs. See doc. 11.

2. Robert Harley, former Whig supporter of dissenters and, with WP, an advocate of liberty of conscience, had shifted into the moderate Tory camp. He was a powerful voice in the House of Commons until elevated to the peerage in 1711. In Feb. 1701 he had been elected speaker, and he was later to serve as secretary of state (1704-8), chancellor of the exchequer (1710-11), and lord high treasurer (1711-14). *PWP,* 3:568; Alison Gilbert Olson, "William Penn, Parliament, and Proprietary Government," *WMQ,* 3d ser., 18:189-90.

3. Crooks are bent pieces of timber, and knees are angled pieces of timber; both are used in building. *OED.*

4. Freshes are lands adjoining a tidal river next above the salt water. *OED.*

5. WP is discussing the part of the Navigation Act of 1696 that established colonial admiralty courts, which heard cases without juries and were not subject to common law. The edition of parliamentary statutes cited by WP is *Anno Regni Gulielmi III Regis . . . Septimo & Octavo: At the Parliament begun at Westminster the Two and twentieth Day of November, Anno Dom. 1695* (London, 1696).

6. Beer.

7. James Chadwick, a commissioner of the customs in 1696. Michael G. Hall, *Edward Randolph and the American Colonies, 1676-1703* (Chapel Hill, 1960), p. 161.

8. Edward Randolph (1632-1703), surveyor of the customs since 1691, strongly opposed proprietary government because of what he perceived as colonial willingness to countenance piracy and illegal trade. He advocated royal takeover of the proprietary and chartered colonies through the Reunification Bill introduced in the House of Lords on 24 Apr. 1701. See *PWP,* 3:512, 513n; *The Manuscripts of the House of Lords, 1699-1702* (London, 1908), pp. 314-55.

9. Doctors' Commons in London housed five civil law courts, including Admiralty; Westminster Hall contained the three superior common law courts— Common Pleas, Exchequer, and King's (or Queen's) Bench. Peter Cunningham, *A Handbook for London, Past and Present* (London, 1849), 1:263-65; 2:897-98.

10. Roger Mompesson (c. 1662-1715), parliamentarian, recorder of Southampton, and barrister, had acted as counsel for WP in England, writing in Aug. 1699 a treatise that called for the use of common law juries in admiralty cases in the colonies. Ironically he later became judge of the admiralty courts with jurisdiction from Pennsylvania to Nova Scotia. See *PWP,* 3:629n; Paul M. Hamlin and Charles E. Baker, *Supreme Court of Judicature of the Province of New York, 1691-1704: Biographical Dictionary* (New York, 1959), pp. 130-42.

11. Lincoln's Inn was one of the four principal Inns of Court in London, which alone could call men to the bar, that is, confer the rank or degree of a barrister. *Black's Law Dictionary.*

12. "An act for the ascertaining the dimensions of cask, and for the true packing of meat for transportation," passed on 27 Nov. 1700, set dimensions and weights for tobacco hogsheads. *Statutes,* 2:95-98.

13. "An act against pirates and sea-robbers," passed 27 Nov. 1700. Ibid., 2:100-104.

14. At the Nov. 1700 Pennsylvania Assembly session, the representatives from the tobacco-growing Lower Counties opposed WP's plea for an increase in the provincial tax. It was finally agreed that the Lower Counties would levy £425 and Pennsylvania £1575. *Votes and Proceedings*, 1:138-39; *Statutes*, 2:114-18.

15. Edward Portlock (d. c. 1718), an Anglican minister in East New Jersey 1698-99 and at Christ Church in Philadelphia 1699-1700, had apparently acted as chaplain to the English forces in Flanders. He left Philadelphia under suspicious circumstances, moving to Virginia where he became rector of Stratton Major parish. *PWP*, 3:635n; Pomfret, *East New Jersey*, p. 388.

16. Henry Compton (1632-1713), bishop of London, had supported toleration of dissenters earlier in his career, but by 1701 he had become a Tory and a stout defender of the Anglican church. Alison Gilbert Olson ("William Penn and Proprietary Government," p. 184n) believes that Compton and WP "disliked each other intensely." *PWP*, 2:35n; *DNB*.

17. Impertinent.

18. Francis Nicholson (1655-1728), a devoted high church Anglican and former governor of Maryland, had been governor of Virginia since 1698. For his earlier dealings with WP, see *PWP*, vol. 3.

19. Bishop Compton.

20. Dr. Thomas Bray (1656-1730), rector of Sheldon, Salop., had arrived in Maryland in Mar. 1700 as the first Anglican commissary. He would return to England in Aug. 1701. Contrary to WP's assumption, Bray was never consecrated a suffragan bishop. Nelson W. Rightmayer, *Maryland's Established Church* (Baltimore, 1956), pp. 37-47, 165.

21. See doc. 11.

22. The northern Indians referred to by WP were the Iroquois; the western Indians were the Conestoga, which comprised the Susquehannocks and the Shawnees.

23. WP means "me tell."

24. Sir Edward Harley (1624-1700), father of Robert, had died on 8 Dec. 1700. *DNB*.

25. Among the six persons listed here are Edward Harley (1664-1735), Robert's brother, who was a Tory M.P. for Leominster and later auditor of the imprest; Sir Christopher Musgrave, a Tory and M.P. since 1661; John Howe, or How (1657-1722), a staunch Tory M.P.; Sir Francis Winnington (1634-1700), a lawyer, former solicitor general, and M.P., who had died on 1 May 1700; and his son Salwey Winnington (d. 1736), another parliamentarian. *DNB; Burke's Peerage*, p. 2609.

10
TO ANDREW HAMILTON

Philadelphia 3. 2m [April] 1701

Honored Friend[1]

I have had the surprizeing news of the Practices of some east Jersians;[2] as unexpected by me as dishonorable & Licentious in them. It will be hard to finde temper enough to ballance extreams; for I know not wt punishmt those Rioters do not deserve; & I had rather live alone than not have such people Corrigaible.[3] Their heads should be eyed, & some forcd to declare them by the rigour of the Law, & those that are found to be such, should bear the burden of such sedition, wch were the best way to be-head the Body without danger. if Lenitives[4] wont do, Corrcives[5] should, but tho naturally we would begin there, yet it is the end of wise men, & a remidy with regrett too.

I was Just comeing as P. R.[6] knows with a dozen of our most reputable people (tho Colonel Q.[7] J.M.[8] & J. Gu.[9] seemed too much ~~too much~~

(the first especially) to take part with the mobs argum^{ts} tho not with their practice) till thyn ~~by~~ to S. Jenings[10] gave me the satisfaction of knowing thy more easy & honorable ~~practices~~ Circumstances, & prospect of Loading them wth their own Confusions. pray make not too much hast from them, but Clench the nale:[11] for examples must be made by thee, of them that acted so unex~~a~~emplarily. I assure thee It was my own thought, that new york would be obliged to take Cognisance of it It was at least an extraordinary Ryote if not [illegible deletion] Rebellion, in armes, to Imprison a Gover^{r}, because one of his Justices refused to stand mute at his ~~being~~ being insolently paraded by a Criminal, & in the solemnity of a Court.[12] But the Gentlemen aforesayd, tax L. M.[13] with haveing used Bass[14] just so, to extenuate this, or recriminate. If by being an ould & not the least Pretender to east Jersy, & a Neighbour, in my station, I can yet be serviceable, to compose or Countenance a just prosecution of Rebellious practices, let an express reach me before I leave these parts, & I shall Immediately take horse, God permitting. Time & a Crowd forbids to be more pe~~a~~rticuler, but with hearty regards I am

Thy Faithfull and affect. Friend
Wm Penn

my salutes to Colonel Morris R. Burnet[15] J. B.[16] &c:

ALS. FLL. (*Micro.* 9:184.) The editors have compared this text with the LBC in the William Penn Letterbook, 1699-1701, HSP.

1. Andrew Hamilton (d. 1703), a Scottish merchant, immigrated to East New Jersey in 1686, where he became governor from 1687 to 1688, later holding the same office for East and West Jersey (1692-97, 1699-1703). Shortly before the 1702 surrender of New Jersey to the crown, when WP was about to return to England, he appointed Hamilton deputy governor of Pennsylvania, a post he held until his death in 1703. *DAB;* Pomfret, *East New Jersey,* chaps. 12, 13, 15; Paul A. Stellhorn and Michael J. Birkner, eds., *The Governors of New Jersey, 1664-1974* (Trenton, 1982), pp. 30-33.

2. In late 1700 and early 1701 a series of popular uprisings in East New Jersey, primarily in Essex and Monmouth Cos., challenged the authority of the unpopular proprietary government. Here WP refers to an incident of 25-26 Mar. 1701 in which a mob, supported by the local militia, disrupted the Monmouth court sessions where Gov. Hamilton presided. Pomfret, *East New Jersey,* chap. 15, esp. pp. 336-41, 346-47. See also n. 12, below.

3. Liable to punishment. *OED.*

4. Lenient or soothing measures. *OED.*

5. The LBC reads "Corrosives." WP meant "coercives."

6. Probably Patrick Robinson (c. 1653-1701), a Pennsylvania merchant and lawyer, at this time secretary to WP's Provincial Council. See *PWP,* 3:36n, 488n.

7. Robert Quary (c. 1645-1714)—as judge of the vice-admiralty court of Pennsylvania, the Lower Counties, and West New Jersey—was the chief representative of royal authority in the Delaware Valley. He was an ardent Anglican and a sharp critic of WP's proprietary government. In 1702 he was named to the first royal council of New Jersey, and two years later he succeeded Edward Randolph as surveyor general of customs in America. See *PWP,* 3:506n; *PMHB,* 24:61-62; Raimo, *Governors,* p. 417; *CSPC, 1704-1705,* p. 50.

8. John Moore (c. 1659-1732) was advocate of the vice-admiralty court of Pennsylvania, the Lower Counties, and West New Jersey from 1698 to 1704, and from 1700 to 1704, register general and attorney general for Pennsylvania. In 1704 he became collector of the port of Philadelphia and deputy judge of the vice-admiralty court.

Moore was an aggressive Anglican, a protégé of Robert Quary, and a proponent of centralized royal control of the colonies. See *PWP*, 3:512n; *DAB*.

9. John Guest (c. 1650-1707), an English lawyer, briefly served on the supreme court of New York in 1699 and was appointed by WP in 1701 as chief justice of the Pennsylvania Supreme Court and a member of the Provincial Council. He was also presiding judge of the Philadelphia Orphans court and the courts of Common Pleas and Quarter Sessions. Paul M. Hamlin and Charles E. Baker, *Supreme Court of Judicature of the Province of New York, 1691-1704: Biographical Dictionary* (New York, 1959), pp. 99-103; James G. Wilson and John Fiske, eds., *Appleton's Cyclopaedia of American Biography*, 3:11.

10. Samuel Jennings (d. 1708), a Quaker yeoman and merchant, came from Buckinghamshire to West New Jersey in 1680 and held office there during the 1680s and 1690s as assemblyman, councilor, deputy governor, and governor. In 1701 he was an ally of Gov. Hamilton's against Jeremiah Basse (see doc. 8). In 1702 he was named to the first royal council of New Jersey and in 1707 was elected to the Assembly and became its speaker. The letter has not been found. *PWP*, 2:481n; 3:41n; Pomfret, *West New Jersey*, esp. pp. 195-202, 212, 214-15; *Appleton's Cyclopaedia*, 3:429; William H. Jennings, *A Genealogical History of the Jennings Families* (Columbus, 1899), 2:338-41.

11. Fix matters securely. *OED*.

12. WP is here referring to the Monmouth riot of 25-26 Mar. 1701, when Justice Lewis Morris (see n. 13, below) drew his sword to resist mob efforts to release a prisoner, a member of Capt. Kidd's crew. The mob then temporarily imprisoned Gov. Andrew Hamilton. See *NJA*, 2:362-64.

13. Lewis Morris (1671-1746), an Anglican member of Gov. Hamilton's Council, had disrupted a court session at Perth Amboy in 1698, when Gov. Jeremiah Basse was presiding. Basse twice imprisoned Morris for his seditious behavior, but both times he escaped from jail. In 1701 Morris went to England as Hamilton's ally and played a primary role in the negotiations with the crown that resulted in the surrender of the propriety. Appointed to the royal council, he soon became an opponent of the new governor, Lord Cornbury. He eventually himself became governor of New Jersey 1738-46. *DAB;* Pomfret, *East New Jersey*, pp. 330-32, 353, 356-61, 364; Eugene R. Sheridan, *Lewis Morris, 1671-1746* (Syracuse, 1981), pp. 5, 22-25, 40-43, 46-50.

14. Jeremiah Basse. See doc. 8.

15. Robert Burnet (d. 1714), a Scottish Quaker and zealous promoter of Scottish settlement in East New Jersey, had emigrated from Aberdeen in 1700; he sat on the Board of Property in 1700 and 1701. Pomfret, *East New Jersey*, pp. 236-37; idem, "The Proprietors of the Province of East New Jersey, 1682-1702," *PMHB*, 77:281-82.

16. Probably John Barclay (d. 1731), brother of the Quaker preacher Robert Barclay. He had immigrated with his family to East New Jersey in 1684, where he became a member of the assembly, held numerous offices, and sat on the Board of Propriety until the crown assumed control of the colony. Pomfret, *East New Jersey*, pp. 240-41.

11
ARTICLES OF AGREEMENT WITH THE SUSQUEHANNA INDIANS

WP took great pride in the fact that his colony had maintained peaceful relations with the various local Indian tribes by treating them fairly in land purchases, in trading, and in the courts. The document printed below, WP's only political treaty with the Indians that appears to have survived, epitomizes his optimism that the colonists and Indians could live together "in true Frienship and Amity as one people," without resorting to arms. On his first visit to Pennsylvania in the 1680s, WP had concluded a treaty with the Delaware Indians; that agreement survives only in tradition and in the famous paintings by Benjamin West and Edward Hicks. By the early 1700s, Pennsylvania's expansion and economic growth required that WP negotiate with the Indians who had recently settled on the Susquehanna River, the Susquehannocks and the Shawnee. In April 1701 the chiefs of these tribes traveled to Philadelphia with about forty of their people. With them were several chiefs of the Conoy, or Piscataway, Indians then living on the Potomac River in Maryland who were considering seeking refuge with the Susquehannocks. In addition, the Iroquois were represented by an Onondaga chief, Ahookasoongh, the brother of the "emperor" of the Five Nations. Although still the most powerful Indian group in the Northeast, the Iroquois were caught in the middle of conflict between English New York and French Canada. WP had sought to negotiate with the confederacy since the 1680s, but his efforts had continually been blocked by New York, which claimed a monopoly on trade and diplomacy with the Iroquois. In 1700 and 1701, however, with the French and English poised for war again, the Iroquois were desperate enough to negotiate with both the French and Pennsylvania without New York's knowledge.

WP had three major objectives in meeting with the Indians. First, he sought to preserve peace between the Indians and the colonists, which meant keeping the Indians allied with the English and protecting them from the French and their Indian allies. Second, he sought to secure the Susquehanna Valley, and particularly its mouth at the head of the Chesapeake Bay, as part of his colony. This property had been claimed by both New York and Maryland, and WP had long been amassing documents to buttress his own claim. Finally, he hoped to secure for Pennsylvania a monopoly of the Indian trade on the lower Susquehanna, trade that would compete with New York's monopoly on the Hudson River. With this treaty, WP achieved all three goals, to the extent that these Indians could grant them; however, he continued to face opposition from neighboring New York and Maryland. At the same time, the several delegations of Indians who met with WP obtained the most they could have expected. The Susquehannocks and Shawnees received the promise that they could continue to live in peace at Conestoga, with the same rights as Pennsylvania's "Christian" inhabitants as long as they acknowledged the authority of WP's government. The Conoy received assurances that they could settle within Pennsylvania's boundaries if and when they were forced to leave Maryland. The Iroquois succeeded in initiating an alliance with Pennsylvania at a time when their own position had been substantially weakened and their relationship with New York, strained.

Two months after this visit from the Indians, WP visited Conestoga, probably to inspect lands there for his proposed settlement as well as to cement his relationship with the various chiefs. *PWP*, 3:477–79, 671–78; *Micro.* 9:234, 268, 294, 306, 672; 10:360; H. Frank Eshleman, *Lancaster County Indians* (Lancaster, Pa., 1908), pp. 159–65; Francis Jennings, *The Ambiguous Iroquois Empire* (New York, 1984), pp. 208–45; Allen W. Trelease, *Indian Affairs in Colonial New York: The Seventeenth Century* (Ithaca, N.Y., 1960), pp. 332–63.

[23 April 1701]

ARTICLES of Agreement Indented Made Concluded & Agreed upon at Philadelphia the Twenty third day of the Second Month called Aprill in the year One thousand Seven hundred and one between WILLIAM PENN, Proprietary and Governour of the Province of Pensilvania and Territories thereunto Belonging on the one part And CONNOODAGHTOH[1] King of the Indians inhabiting upon and about the River Susquehannah in the said Province AND Widaagh (alias Orettyagh) Koqueeash and Andaggy Junkquagh[2] Chiefs of the said Nations of Indians and WOPATHTHA King & Lemoytungh & Pemoyajooagh[3] Chiefs of the Nations of the Shawonnah Indians AND AHOOKASSOONGH Brother to the Emperor[4] for and in Behalf of the Emperor (& Weewhinjough, Cheequittagh, Takyewsan & Woapatkoa chiefs) of the nations of the Indians inhabiting in and about the Northern part of the River Potomock[5] in the said Province for and in Behalf of themselves and Successors and their severall Nations and people on the other part, As followeth—

THAT as hitherto there hath always been a Good Understanding & Neighbourhood between the said WILLIAM PENN and his Lieutenants Since his first Arrivall in the said province and the severall Nations of Indians inhabiting in & about the same so there shall be forever hereafter a firm & lasting peace continued between the said William Penn his heirs & Successors & all the English & other Christian Inhabitants of the said province & the s[d] Kings & Chiefs & their successors & all the severall people of the Nations of Indians aforesaid and that they shall forever hereafter be as one head & one heart & live in true Frienship & Amity as one people.

ITEM[6] that the s[d] Kings & Chiefs (each for himself & his people engageing) shall at no time hurt Injure or defraud or suffer to be hurt Injured or defrauded by any of their Indians any Inhabitant or Inhabitants of the said Province either in their persons or Estates AND that the s[d] William Penn his heirs & successors shall not suffer to be done or Committed by any of the Subjects of England within the said Province any Act of Hostility or Violence Wrong or Injury to or ag[st] any of the s[d] Indians but shall on both sides at all times readily do Justice & perform all acts & Offices of Friendshipp & goodwill to Obliedge Each other to a lasting peace as aforesaid

ITEM That all & every[7] the s[d] Kings & Chiefs & all & every particular of the Nations under them shall at all times behave themselves Regularly & Soberly according to the Laws of this Government while they live near or amongst the Christian Inhabitants thereof AND that the said Indians shall have the full & free priviledges & Immunities of all the said Laws as any other Inhabitant[8] they duely Owning & Acknowledg[g] the Authority of the Crown of England and Government of this Province

ITEM that none of the said Indians shall at any time be Aiding Assisting or Abetting to any other Nation whether of Indians or Others that shall not at such time be in Amity with the Crown of England & with this Government

ITEM that if at any time any of the said Indians by means of Evill minded persons & sowers of sedition should hear any unkind or disadvantageous Reports of the English as if they had Evill Designs ag[st] any of the s[d] Indians in such case such Indians shall Send notice thereof to the s[d] William Penn his heirs & successors or their Lieutenants and shall not give Credence to the said Reports till by that means they shall be fully Sattisfied concerning the Truth thereof and that the said William Penn his heirs or Successors or their Lieutenants shall at all times in such cases do the Like by them

ITEM that the said kings & Chiefs & their successors & people shall not suffer any strange Nation of Indians to Settle or plant on the further side of Susquehannah or about Potomack River but such as are there already seated nor bring any other Indians into any part of his province without the Speciall Approbation & Permission of the said William Penn his heirs & successors

ITEM That for the Prevention of Abuses that are too frequently putt upon the said Indians in trade that the said William Penn his heirs & successors shall not suffer or permitt any person to trade or commerce with any of the said Indians but such as shall be first allowed or approved of by an Instrument under the hand & Seal of him the said William Penn or his heirs or successors {or their Lieut[s]} and that the said Indians shall suffer no person whatsoever to buy or sell or have commerce wth any of them the said Indians but such as shall first be approved as aforesaid.[9]

ITEM that the said Indians shall not sell or dispose of any of their Skinns Peltry or Furrs or any other Effects of their hunting to any person or persons whatsoever out of the said province nor to any other person but such as shall be authorised to trade with them as aforesaid and that for their Encouragement the said William Penn his heirs & successors shall take care to have them the said Indians duely furnished with all sorts of necessary goods for their use at Reasonable Rates

ITEM that the Potomock Indians aforesaid with their Colony shall have Free leave of the said William Penn to settle upon any part of

Potomock River within the Bounds of this province they strictly observing & practiseing all & singular the Articles aforesaid to them relateing[10]

ITEM the Indians of Connostogoe[11] and upon and about the River Susquehannah and more Especially the said Connoodaghtah their King doth fully agree to, And by these presents absolutely Ratifie the Bargain and Sale of Lands lying near and about the said River formerly made to the said William Penn his heirs & Successors and since by Orettyagh & Addaggy junkquagh parties to these presents confirmed to the s^d William Penn his heirs & successors by a deed bearing date the Thirteenth day of September last under their hands & seals duely Executed[12] and the said Connoodaghtoh doth for himself and his nation covenant and Agree that he will at all times be ready further to confirm and make good the said Sale according to the Tenour of the Same, and that the said Indians of Susquehannah shall answer to the said William Penn his heirs and successors for the good Behaviour and Conduct of the said Potomock Indians and for their performance of the Severall articles herein Expressed.

ITEM the said William Penn doth hereby promise for himself his heirs & successors that he and they will at all times shew themselves True Friends and Brothers to all and every of the said Indians by assisting them with the best of their Advices Directions & Councils and will in all things just and Resonable Befriend them they behaving themselves as aforesaid and submitting to the Laws of this Province in all things as the English and other Christians therein Doe to which they the said Indians hereby agree and Obliedge themselves and their Posterity forever

IN WITNESSE whereof the said Parties have as a Confirmacion made Mutuall Presents to Each other the Indians in five parcells of Skinns and the said William Penn in severall English Goods and Merchandises as a binding pledge of the promises never to be Broken or Violated and as a further Testimony thereof have also to these presents Interchangeably Sett their hands and Seals the Day and year above written

Connoodaghtoh[13] ⊗
Widaagh alias Orettyagh
Koqueeash
Andaggyjunquagh
Wopaththa
Lemoytungh
Pemoyajooagh ⊗
Ahookassoongh ⊗
Weewhinjough ⊗
Cheequittagh
Takyewsan ⊗
Woapatkoa ⊗

DS. Indian Deeds and Documents (RG 26), Division of Archives and Manuscripts, Pennsylvania Historical and Museum Commission, Harrisburg. (Not filmed.) This treaty is printed in *Minutes of the Provincial Council,* 3:601-4. The editors have compared this text with a copy that lacks the Indian signatures (*Micro.* 9:211), which is in the Logan Papers, HSP, and is printed in *Minutes of the Provincial Council,* 2:15-18. That copy is docketed in James Logan's hand: Signed Sealed and Deliverd in the presence of Edward Shippen[14] | Nathan Stanbury | Alex^r^ Paxton | Caleb Pusey | James Streater | J Le Tort | John Hans Steelman | James Logan | John Sanders | Indian Harry alias H I Showydoohungh his mark | Pemoqueriuhchan his [⊗] mark | Passaqussay his [⊗] mark. Further docketed: Copy of Govr Penn's Agreem^t^ | wth the Indians the {23^d^ Ap^ll^} 1701. | Thus endorsed in James Logan's writing | Articles of Agreem^t^ between the Prop^y^ | & the Susquehannah Indians | Copy | The Prop^ry^ has the Originall | Parchment. Additional copies (not filmed) are found in CO 5/1261, PRO (printed in *CSPC, 1702,* pp. 283-85), and Penn Manuscripts, Indian Affairs, 1:45, HSP.

1. Connoodaghtoh (d. by 1704?) was chief of the Susquehannock Indians who had reclaimed their homeland along the Susquehanna River in about 1690. He also served as the leader of the other Indian groups that had settled nearby. *PWP,* 3:454n, 602n; *Early American Indian Documents,* pp. 175, 477n, 481n.

2. Widaagh (also known as Orettyagh or Oriteo) and Andaggy Junkquagh (also known as Ojunco) were Susquehannock chiefs who negotiated with the Pennsylvania government in the 1690s and early 1700s. Koqueeash has not been identified. *Early American Indian Documents,* pp. 89-90, 477n, 479n; *Minutes of the Provincial Council,* 1:447-49; 2:45-46, 386-90, 469-72, 516; Charles A. Hanna, *The Wilderness Trail* (New York, 1911), 1:78.

3. Wopaththa, or Opessah, was "king" of the Shawnee who had migrated from Maryland in the 1690s and settled on the east bank of the Susquehanna, near Pequea Creek in present-day Lancaster Co. In 1711 Opessah left the Shawnee and went to live with the Delaware at Paxtang. The other Shawnee chiefs, Lemoytungh and Pemoyajooagh, have not been identified. *Early American Indian Documents,* pp. 477n, 479n; *Minutes of the Provincial Council,* 2:15; Hanna, *Wilderness Trail,* 1:136-43.

4. Ahookassoongh has not been identified; his brother, the "emperor of the Iroquois," was probably Decanisova, or Teganissorens, the chief Sachem of the Onodaga. *New York Col. Docs,* 4:890-91; Jennings, *Ambiguous Iroquois Empire,* p. 251.

5. Weewhinjough was chief of the Conoy, or Ganawese, who were then living on Conoy (now Heater's) Island in the Potomac. By 1719, the Conoy had settled on the Susquehanna, first at Conejoholo (now Washington Borough) and later further upriver at Conoy Town. The other Conoy chiefs— Cheequittagh, Takyewsan, and Woapatkoa — have not been identified. Hanna, *Wilderness Trail,* 1:135n, 151; Paul A. Wallace, *Indians in Pennsylvania* (Harrisburg, 1961), p. 107.

6. The original copy of the treaty in Harrisburg is not paragraphed, although decorative calligraphy precedes each "Item" in the text. The editors have followed the Logan copy and supplied new paragraphs for each "Item."

7. The clerk omitted the word "of," which is supplied in the Logan copy.

8. The Indians evidently understood this language to mean that lands would be reserved for their towns. Jennings, *Ambiguous Iroquois Empire,* pp. 236-37.

9. In 1693 the Assembly had passed a law prohibiting nonresidents of Pennsylvania from trading with the Indians on the grounds that they treated the Indians unfairly and provoked them. In 1705, a new law specified that no natural-born subject of the crown could be denied a license. *Charter and Laws,* pp. 240-41; *PWP,* 3:401n; *Statutes,* 2:230. In early Apr. 1701 WP had seized the goods of John Hans Steelman (n. 14, below), one of the Indian traders who witnessed this treaty, for failing to obtain the required Indian trading license. Steelman had recently come from Maryland to open a trading post at Lechay (Lehigh); the Provincial Council restored his goods but ordered him to pay a bond of £1000 and to apply for a license. *Micro.* 9:194; *Minutes of the Provincial Council,* 2:21-22.

10. WP's invitation to the Conoy shows that he was continuing to claim jurisdiction over Maryland territory well south of the 40th degree of latitude. No part of the Potomac River lies within the borders of Pennsylvania as eventually defined by the Mason-Dixon line in the 1760s.

11. Conestoga was the main settlement of the Susquehannocks.

12. In this deed of 13 Sept. 1700 (*Micro.* 8:557), Widaagh and Andaggy Junkquagh confirmed the sale of the Susquehanna lands to WP by former Gov. Dongan of New York. See *PWP*, 3:477, 671.

13. The Indians endorsed this treaty by signing their marks on the tabs of the 12 seals, half of which are missing.

14. Most of these witnesses are identified elsewhere in this volume. Edward Shippen and Caleb Pusey were provincial councilors; WP appointed Shippen mayor of Philadelphia and Nathan Stanbury (d. 1721) as alderman on his departure for England in the fall of 1701. James Streater, a grocer from New Alsford, Hants., came to Pennsylvania in 1701, probably to work for WP at Pennsbury. He had attended WP's marriage to Hannah Callowhill in 1696. All these men were Quakers; the other witnesses probably were not. Alexander Paxton, probably an Anglican, was one of the wealthier residents of Philadelphia. James Le Tort, the son of French Huguenot refugees and Indian traders (see doc. 41), was an Indian trader at Conestoga and Allegheny from about 1697 to 1742. John Hans Steelman (or Tillman, Tilghman) was a Dutch or Swedish trader of Cecil Co., Maryland, who operated a trading post at Lehigh; he had been one of the first whites to trade with the Shawnee. John Saunders (d. by 1706?) was the nephew of Charles Saunders, a merchant active in the Indian trade (see doc. 41). Indian Harry, or Shouwydaghow, was an Onondaga by birth or adoption who frequently served as interpreter for the Conestoga Indians and Pennsylvania officials. Passakassay was a Delaware sachem who settled at Paxtang sometime before 1709, when he represented the Delaware in a meeting with Gov. Charles Gookin. Pemoqueriuhchan has not been identified. *PMHB*, 9:340; 99:16; Hinshaw, 2:423, 661, 1030; 1715 Chester Co. Tax List, GSP; Digests of Quaker Records, Dorset and Hants., GSP; *PA*, 2d ser., 1:321, 394; *PWP*, 3:436; Hanna, *Wilderness Trail*, 1:100, 129, 143-44, 166-68; 2:315, 335; Phila. Will Bk. A, #230; C, #11, 24; *Early American Indian Documents*, p. 478n; C. A. Weslager, *The Delaware Indians: A History* (New Brunswick, N. J., 1972), p. 181; Logan Papers, 2:84-85, 11:4, HSP.

12
TO NATHANIEL BLAKISTON

Philad[a] the 23[d] 3[mo] [May] 1701

My Honoured Friend[1]
I could not have been so prodigall of my Opertunities had I had no buisness to write as to Lett this Slipp by my good friend Samuel Chews[2] Since I assure my Self it will Come Quickly and Surely to hand:

In my Journey in Sussex County Some weeks past I found three or four[3] my Tenants and Inhabitants of this Government from before my going last for England had been forced off from us by some in Authority in Somerset County in Maryland as the Affidavits which Accompany this Express[4] and in a manner too that was an Aggrevation of the breach of Good Neighbourhood and no Line Runn[5] or order from home to Back it & till the Line was Runn all Was to Stand in Statu quo. I am Sure none of my Officers ever Attempted the least Incroachment in that County or at the head of the Bay,[6] thô I am not Unsencible what hast some made (& their Court to Ld Baltimore[7] thereby) to Anticipate mee by begging Rights and takeing up Vast Quantities of Land since matters Lay disputeable but all this was Long before Governour Blackiston had the Command of that province Except the Action of the Sheriff of Somersett County which I presume was not above 3 or 4 years before Maryland was so happy as to have Colonel Blackiston for their Governour[8] I begg therefore that since the delay of Running of the Line lyes not at my door I may not Suffer by it[9] but what need I Labour a matter so plaine with So good a friend as well as Neighbour & whom in all Occurrances I shall Indeavour to preserve such being with all Sincerity and Esteem

Thy very Affectionate frd

WP

I send none of the Kings speeches tho Sencible thou hast a Swifter Intelligence

LBC. William Penn Letterbook, 1699-1703, HSP. (*Micro.* 9:241.) Endorsed: Governour Blackiston.

1. Nathaniel Blakiston (c. 1663-1722) was governor of Maryland 1698-1702 and later became London agent for Maryland and Virginia. See *PWP,* 3:579-80n.

2. Samuel Chew (c. 1660-1718), of Herring Bay, Maryland, was a Quaker merchant and commissioner of trade for Anne Arundel Co. J. Reaney Kelly, *Quakers in the Founding of Anne Arundel County, Maryland* (Baltimore, 1963), pp. 20, 44, 64-67, 70, 124; *Maryland Calendar of Wills,* 4:177; *Md. Archives,* 7:609-11.

3. WP or the copyist omitted "of."

4. Not found.

5. In Nov. 1685 the English government had ruled in WP's favor in his boundary dispute with Lord Baltimore (see *PWP,* 3:68), but since then no formal agreement for surveying boundary lines had been reached. The critical issue in establishing a boundary between Somerset Co. in Maryland and Sussex Co. in Delaware was the perceived location of Cape Henlopen, which WP construed as a point on the Atlantic coast 25 miles south of the entrance to Delaware Bay (the present Cape Henlopen). Late in 1701 WP employed Isaac Taylor and Thomas Pierson (see *Micro. 9:742)* to survey the Pennsylvania-Delaware boundary, but agreement with Maryland was not reached until much later. The present north-south line between Maryland and Delaware was finally settled in 1732; the present east-west line between Maryland and Delaware was confirmed, as WP had wanted it, in 1760; and the east-west line between Maryland and Pennsylvania, surveyed by Charles Mason and Jeremiah Dixon, was finally ratified in 1769. See Dudley Lunt, "The Bounds of Delaware," *Delaware History,* 2:1-40; Walter B. Scaife, "The Boundary Dispute Between Maryland and Pennsylvania," *PMHB,* 9:241-71; *PWP,* vol. 2.

6. Chesapeake Bay.

7. Charles Calvert (1637-1715), Lord Baltimore, had lost political control of Maryland to the crown in 1691, but still retained his proprietary lands and rents. Baltimore bitterly opposed WP's claim to the Lower Counties and to lands which he believed were included within northern Maryland. See *PWP,* 2:36n and passim.

8. Blakiston was appointed governor of Maryland in Oct. 1698 and took the oath of office in Jan. 1699 (Raimo, *Governors,* p. 97). This would place the dispute mentioned by WP in about 1695, when William Whittington (c. 1650-1720) was sheriff (1695-1698) of Somerset Co. (see Clayton Terrance, *Old Somerset on the Eastern Shore of Maryland* [Richmond, 1935], pp. 379-81). In Mar. 1695 the justices of the Sussex Co. court wrote to the authorities in Somerset Co. protesting that John Barker and Charles Tindall, who lived south of Indian River but probably within the present boundary of Delaware, had been forced to recognize the governance of Somerset Co. over their properties. The Sussex justices insisted that "most of the land on ye said south side of the Indian River, and particularly the land that they live upon" was under WP's jurisdiction (Scharf, *Delaware,* 2:1204). If WP's complaint is correct, this matter had not been resolved by 1701.

9. Lord Baltimore had shown little inclination to accept the 1685 boundary decision, and before his death in 1715 he twice attempted unsuccessfully to have the decision reviewed. See Lunt, "Bounds of Delaware," p. 26; doc. 166.

13
TO CHARLWOOD LAWTON

Pensilvania 2: 5 mo [July] *1701*

Dr Friend.

This I hope will Come Safe to hand & find thee & thyne and all my Friends well I heard but last night of this Oppertunity by N York so must be Short the post Staying and Puckle[1] Going in thirty days by whome I Purpose to be Larger I had 3. from thee[2] by him & am Easy in my affairs because I know I have a friend as well as an Agent and a man of Interest as well as Ability thô wee hear of Terrible things against the poor Proprietary Governments by Basse's[3] L^rs to his fr^ds hereaway but Especially ag^st mee[4] I have better thoughts than that Sr Edwd Seymour Can head Such a Breach of Right & property that has Shown So much Zeal for it[5] an American Understand^g is Necessary to Judge well of what is best here a mighty unhappyness to these poor Collonies that those who Superintend and wee would believe mean well to the Publick should Miss it So very widely as Generally they do. proprietary Governments Improve 5 to 1 it is their buisness their Interest and has been the Advantage they have upon other Governments and their prosperity is their Crime in Reality they are more Cautious also because they have more to loose and are Sure to be watcht and perhaps to find no mercy if Caught which I Largely Insisted upon before the Lords in 94,[6] I think to their great Sattisfaction if any Should move of that kind in Parliament Damp, Clogg, & Delay, if Cannot throw of[7] keep it out Insist upon the Topicks or heads I Sent thee before and to my Sister and Son[8] Power is Property without it wee had never Come hither and the Rest of Prop^ty is our Industry the Countrie's being a wilderness and not Improvd as those of Europe the Diff: of the One from the Other being a Hundred to One, the One Oare and the Other Pure Mettle and that wee Should Injoy that is a Mighty Priviledge indeed if nothing Elce will Serve Lett proprietaries be bound for themselves or Deputies for their Administracion the King has his Own Vice Admiralls his Collectors and Lett him name if he will his own Naval Officers: nay lett him Appoint the Military Officers if he pleases Rather than take the Civill Administracion from those that had that Priviledge granted for their first Incouragement Shall wee after all our Troubles Hazards Charges and many Disappointments in our Essays and after makeing Collonies for the Crown at our Own Cost be made and Treated as Less Creatures than the Mayors of the Meanest Corporation of England or Ireland nay as Criminals and

Publick Enemies & Every Little Mercinary Toole Countenanced agst our Merritt upon the Crown for our Industrious and Successfull Adventures, If it must be thus Commend to the Eng: men a Satyr[9] & would wee had nothing to do with the Character have wee not done Kings Governours Tasks for nothing Conformd to the Regulations of his Ministers, as if his Immediate Governours without his pay & been as Answerable for our Conduct as if wee had had his Salary So Barbarous thing was never Dreamt of in former ages when that which was made the Argument of our Crime was the Reason of their Glory & Reward of the Antient Leaders of Colony's My Case Differs from all others the Crown is my D^{r} above 3000 pounds[10] I came in person and it Cost mee 10500 in the First 2: y^{rs} I have Effected the Undertaking to the Unpresidented and Unparaleld Instance and Sunk and Undone if the Government be wholly taken for I have no pretence or power to Reprize my Self & Indebted fortune if it be in Other hands the Governor of Maryland is Vice Admirall Lett him be Collonell but lett the Civill Government Rest as it is.[11] Elce Lett mee Reimburse what I am out for Government & Sing: Interest (with my Plantations that have Cost 5000 pound) and I Shall Submit. I Rely upon thy Care and Zeale Bl.[12] as S^{r} Th: O.[13] Sent mee word is the man and Poor Basse the Greatest of Villains one of his Tools. I hope my Letter about him Came Safely to hand[14] I can Add now no more but best wishes from all myne and that I am

Truely thy Affectionate and Faithfull Friend
W: P

P: Ford[15] can Inform thee of my Graunts:

LBC. William Penn Letterbook, 1699-1703, HSP. (*Micro.* 9:309.) Endorsed: Ch: Lawton.

1. Nathaniel Puckle (d. 1706), a Quaker merchant and ship captain, sailed regularly between Philadelphia and England as master of the ships *Bristol Trader* and *Philadelphia*. *PWP*, 3:618n.

2. Not found.

3. Jeremiah Basse. His letters have not been found.

4. See headnote to doc. 17.

5. Sir Edward Seymour, former speaker of the House of Commons and a distinguished parliamentarian, was a steadfast Tory. But despite WP's fears that Seymour supported the Reunification Bill (see headnote to doc. 17), he proved to be, along with other Tories, a resolute defender of the proprietary colonies, including Pennsylvania. See Basil D. Henning, ed., *The House of Commons, 1660-1690* (London, 1983), 3:411-20; Alison G. Olson, "William Penn, Parliament, and Proprietary Government," *WMQ*, 3d ser., 18:188-95.

6. See *PWP*, 3:395-96.

7. Off.

8. For WP's earlier letters to Charlwood Lawton and William Penn, Jr., see *PWP*, 3:624, 629; doc. 1, above. WP's letter to his sister, Margaret Lowther, has not been found.

9. A reference to Daniel Defoe's poem, *The True-born Englishman, a Satyr.* See doc. 18.

10. WP probably meant to write £30,000, the figure he often quoted as the crown's debt to him; see, for example, doc. 62.

11. Nathaniel Blakiston was commissioned as vice admiral as well as governor of

Maryland (*CSPC, 1699*, p. 239). WP seems here willing to have Blakiston also commissioned military commander over Pennsylvania.

12. William Blathwayt (c. 1649-1717), the leading member of the Board of Trade, 1696-1706, was, as WP here recognizes, a strong exponent of centralized royal control over the colonies, and an advocate of the Reunification Bill. As manager of the colonial office in 1681, Blathwayt had attempted to limit WP's proprietary rights under the charter of Pennsylvania. *PWP*, 2:37.

13. Possibly Sir Theophilus Oglethorpe (1650-1702), M.P. for Haselmere, Sur., in 1700-1701. *Proceedings and Debates*, 2:413.

14. Not found.

15. Philip Ford (c. 1631-1702), WP's steward, operated a shop in Bow Lane, London. In the 1680s he managed the sale of WP's Pennsylvania lands, and in the 1690s he became WP's major creditor, holding a mortgage on Pennsylvania. After his death his widow, Bridget, and their children sued WP in the courts of Chancery, Exchequer, and Common Pleas to recover the debts they claimed were due Ford's estate, sending WP to debtor's prison before the case was settled. See *PWP*, 1:131-32n; headnote to doc. 108.

14
TO JAMES LOGAN

Philad. first day [13 July 1701]

James[1]

I am sorry the time of my comeing to town is that of thy goeing & absence,[2] w^n^ it is of such moment that thou hadst been here w^n^ I came to town, both with respect to york & maryland affaires as they regard us,[3] the Ks letters,[4] the assembly if Sitt or not,[5] a Lt Govr [6] as well as the excise & tax, wch this one County pays ½ of:[7] Of more moment to me than thy presence yonder by farr. I know not w^t^ service thy stay here was of, where, agst promess to them below,[8] thou hast thought fitt to remain 10 to 12 days if not more beyond myn as well as their expectation, I cannot easily comprehend it, Since nothing was actually done either about excise or rents here, and nobody yet come from maryland that required shipping any flowr. nay T. Masters[9] was let loose by thee from w^t^ he offerd me in case the sloop comes, which the frds there promest before now to be here, so that I was forc'd to re-engage him for 7 tun if not ten. This is the face things have to me. For the nonpayers of the excise I think I have overcome it,[10] but will not say I have done as much as thou promest to do to Perry.[11]

14. 5^m^ [July]

I have wanted thee for a Proclamation for the setting of the assembly at the time, to consider of the kgs ~~let~~ letters &c: that we may not prorogue again, when we should call or hasten the setting of an assembly.[12] as well as divers other things of moment, N. Puckle goeing so soon, with {whom} I would have sent something, tobacco, 20 hhd[13] or 40 if could have cull'd out so many good ones of bright tobacco.[14] In short pray dispatch & be here by this day or tomorrow week. for the Banck there, get it as here, if can, or leave it to the assembly time for me to talk wth them.[15] Judge Guest[16] is this day admitted of the Council. Govr Ham:[17] in town, nothing yet done conclusive, nor shall, till the assembly is over, I think. remember to get wt thou canst in wheat & flowr to comply with the frds of M—land for bills, this to thy selfe. also the mony of the tax lyes at chester with andrew Job,[18] these 2 or 3 months wch wants to be received. I admire how thou Couldst stay so long here, wn nothing required it, & nothing is done. take this repetition well, for I am heartily toucht we thus take our turns to be absent. I am

thy loveing Frd
Wm Penn

for the rent thou writt of, I think 2 Bush per 100 Ac. is reasonable.[19] my mannors to submit to mannor Royal.[20]
P. Rob.[21] will deliver thee the records, pray hear his caution, & D. Lloyds,[22] & see if a medium can be found.
For T. Pearson[23] engage him per day, or a Certain sallery take the best way, & do wt is most beneficiall. wt if I had [illegible deletion] {12d} per foot front to low water mark forever, ~~rent for the Banck~~ So every hundred foot front will make 5 pounds per annum more if thou canst. ~~vale.~~ T.F.[24] comes wth this to clear himselfe & do wt he can in reason for my service. vale.

ALS. Logan Papers, HSP. (*Micro.* 9:314.) Addressed: For James | Logan wth | speed & care. Endorsed: Govr Penn to JL | 14. 5mo 1701.

1. James Logan (1674-1751), an Irish-born Quaker, had accompanied WP to Pennsylvania in 1699 as his secretary. When WP left for England in 1701, he appointed Logan clerk of the Council, secretary of the province, commissioner of property, and receiver general; he also left him in charge of Indian relations. In effect, Logan became WP's chief American representative. *PWP,* 3:609.

2. Logan seems to have left Philadelphia for New Castle in order to secure WP's quitrents there, shortly before WP came to Philadelphia from Pennsbury.

3. See docs. 12, 15.

4. See headnote to doc. 15.

5. The Assembly had been prorogued since 6 Mar. 1701. See *Micro.* 9:105.

6. WP had not yet named a lieutenant governor; on 27 Oct. 1701 he appointed Andrew Hamilton. See *Micro.* 9:716.

7. Here WP is probably referring to two measures passed by the Assembly in Nov. 1700, each calculated to raise money for his own use. One was a two year impost or excise on wines, rum, beer, ale, cider, and other specified goods imported, retailed, and sold in Pennsylvania and the Lower Counties; the other was a tax on the clear value of all real and personal estates and on the polls of all freemen. This last tax was calculated to raise £2000, of which Phila. Co. was called upon to raise £1023. See *Statutes,* 2:105-9, 114-18.

8. The Lower Counties.

9. Thomas Masters (d. 1723), a carpenter from Bermuda, came in 1687 to Philadelphia, where he amassed substantial wealth and property. He was appointed in 1701 as an alderman and a water and street commissioner, and later served as mayor, provincial councilor, and assemblyman. *PWP,* 2:661; *PMHB,* 5:4; 8:284-92; 9:340.

10. WP had gained the right to distrain goods for nonpayment.

11. Samuel Peres (see doc. 38, n. 33). Logan's plan of action against Peres for nonpayment of the excise is not known.

12. WP issued a writ on 14 July 1701 calling for the Assembly to meet on 1 Aug. 1701. See *Micro.* 9:324.

13. Hogsheads.

14. See doc. 38, n. 11.

15. WP wanted Logan to secure rent for Delaware River bank lots in New Castle on the same terms as those in Philadelphia. When the Assembly met, it demanded that

the bank lots at New Castle be granted to those who had the front lots to the low water mark, "or so far as they may improve" at a quitrent of one bushel of wheat per lot. WP agreed to this, but only if the lots reverted to him if they were not improved. *Votes and Proceedings*, 1:146, 149.

16. John Guest.

17. Gov. Andrew Hamilton of West New Jersey.

18. Andrew Job (d. 1722) was a Quaker farmer, sheriff of Chester Co., and member of the Assembly. *PWP*, 3:617n; *Votes and Proceedings*, 1:142.

19. WP is probably referring to a Lower Counties quitrent. "New rents" were normally two bushels per hundred acres. Logan's letter to WP has not been found.

20. Probably a reference to the crown's "Castle of New York" prerogatives in the Lower Counties; see doc. 7.

21. Patrick Robinson.

22. David Lloyd (1656-1731), a Quaker lawyer from Wales, had served as Pennsylvania's attorney general, clerk of the Philadelphia and provincial courts, and deputy master of the rolls, in addition to frequent membership in the Provincial Council and Assembly. In 1700, on order from the Board of Trade, WP removed him as attorney general and councilor, whereupon Lloyd became a lifelong enemy of WP and of James Logan, leading the colony's anti-proprietary faction. Roy N. Lokken, *David Lloyd: Colonial Lawmaker* (Seattle, 1959); Nash, *Quakers and Politics; DAB; PWP*, 3:89n.

23. Thomas Pierson, a Quaker surveyor from Bristol, had come to Pennsylvania in 1683, and was appointed in 1684 as deputy surveyor of New Castle Co. On 28 Oct. 1701 WP named Pierson and Isaac Taylor to survey the Delaware-Pennsylvania boundary. See *PMHB*, 21:506-7; 30:130; 47:244-45; doc. 12, n. 5.

24. Thomas Fairman (d. 1714), a Quaker from Hertfordshire who served as deputy surveyor of Phila. Co., had surveyed the site of Philadelphia as well as WP's manors. At this time, WP was unhappy with Fairman's questionable land transactions, his failure to include some choice Indian land within the manor of Highlands, and his cutting and selling reeds from Petty's Island in the Delaware River which WP claimed for himself. See *PWP*, 2:336-37n; 3:611-15; *Micro.* 9:339; doc. 56.

15
FROM THE PENNSYLVANIA ASSEMBLY

One of the recurring themes in English governmental policy from 1689 to 1713, resulting from almost continual war between England and France, was the need to protect New York from French invasion launched from Canada. Because the English government believed that Quaker Pennsylvania should assist the other American colonies in this effort, it directed WP in 1694 to provide eighty men for the defense and security of New York when demanded by Governor Fletcher. The Pennsylvania Assembly initially responded negatively but finally agreed in November 1696 to send Fletcher £300 to be raised by a one-year tax. Again on 19 January 1701 William III, in a series of circular letters to colonial governors from Rhode Island to Virginia, imposed a special levy totaling £3000, of which Pennsylvania was to contribute £350, "towards . . . Fortifications on the Frontiers of New Yorke." WP read the letter to the Assembly and Council on 2 August 1701, without endorsing or opposing the royal command. The following document is the Pennsylvania Assembly's response. Michael Kammen, *Colonial New York: A History* (New York, 1975), pp. 143-45; *PWP*, 3:506n; *Micro.* 9:024; *CSPC, 1701*, pp. 19-26; *Minutes of the Provincial Council*, 2:28-31.

[6 August 1701]

To William Penn Esquire Propr and Governr of Pennsilvania &c
The Humble Addresse of the Assembly

May it Please our Propr and Governor

We the Freemen of this Province and Territories in Assembly mett having perused the Kings Letter requiring a contribution of £350 ster. towards erecting of Forts on the Frontiers of N: Yorke &c. And having duely weigh'd and consider'd our duty and Loyalty to our Sovereign Doe humbly Addresse and represent.

That by reason of the infancie of this Colony and the great charge and cost the inhabitants have hitherto been at in the Setlement ther'of ~~a~~And because that of late great Summs of money have been ~~imposed~~ {Assessed} on this Province and Territories by way of impost and Taxes Besid's the Arrears of Quitrent owing by the People Our present capacity will hardly admit of Levying money at this time And further taking into our consideration that the adjacent Provinces {have} hitherto (as farr as we can uderstand) done nothing in this matter, We are therfore humbl'y of Oppinon And accordingly move that the further consideracion of the Kings Letter may be refferrd to another Meeting of Assembly. or untill more emergent occasions shall require our proseedings ther'in In the mean time We earnestly Desire the Proprietor would candidly represent our condicions to the King And assure him of our readynesse (according to our abillities) to acquiesce wth and answer his commands so farr as our religeous perswasions shall permitt. As becomes Loyall and Faithfull Subjects {so} to Doe.

Signed on behalf of the Assembly[1]
Jos: Growdon[2]
Speaker

ADS. Logan Papers, HSP. (*Micro.* 9:356.) Docketed: Assembly's Answer | to the Governors Proposals for | the Quotas &c 6th 6 month 1701.

1. Assembly members from the Lower Counties wrote a separate, similar letter to WP. See *Micro.* 9:361.

2. Joseph Growden (d. 1730), a Quaker First Purchaser and one of the largest landowners in Bucks Co., served as a member of the Assembly and the Provincial Council frequently from 1684 to 1722 and was speaker of the Assembly eight times between 1690 and 1722. In 1706 he became a judge of the Provincial Court and in 1715 judge of the Supreme Court. Julianna R. Wood, *Family Sketches* (Philadelphia, 1870); *PWP*, 2:644; 3:111-12n.

16
TO JAMES LOGAN

[12 August 1701][1]

James,

Send us up for Cyder wt *such* barrels thou canst get in town by the very first opertunity; I mean, such as are sweet & have had Cyder in them, they will be Cheapest. Also an empty pipe or two to put the mash of the apples in, being sawd a sunder.

I hear inclose this honest weak mans paper.[2] I think I have convinced him that I am one of the poorest men in the Goverm[t] & that my sin has been neglect of my selfe & not selfishness, & therefore ough[3] & must make the best of every thing. It seems he has much stony & poor mountanous land, & he thinks 2 Bushels a 100 A. an oppression.[4] I tould him I must have but one weight & scale; he says but there are 2, & some pay but one by patents from the Com[rs] under me.[5] I referd it to thee I tould him & did beleive thou wouldst be just & reasonable. quiet him all thou canst, & hasten down again. ask him w[t] Jos. Growden told him, & w[t] the people below[6] say tho of little moment. I think we will send in a day or 2 for the Cask. S. Holt[7] may help us to them cheaply. vale.

WP

ALS. Logan Papers, HSP. (*Micro.* 9:365.) Addressed: For James Lo | gan Secre[r] at | Philadelphia | by Oliver | Matthews. Endorsed by WP: He tels me of the hard | Circumstances of one | James Davis,[8] hear it. Docketed: Gov[r] Penn to JL | 6[mo] 1701.

1. This letter can be dated by month and year from the docket, and by day and place from *Micro.* 9:376, a letter from WP to Logan, written from Pennsbury on 13 Aug. 1701, in which WP notes, "I writt {yesterday} per oliver matthe{ws} of N. Castle county, but this comes first, I suppose."

2. Presumably from Oliver Matthews. See n. 4, below.

3. Ought.

4. Here WP refers to the quitrent chargeable on the 350 acres of land owned by Oliver Matthews (d. 1708) in Christiana Hundred, New Castle Co. It had originally been laid out by James Claypoole on 14 July 1686 by warrant from James Bradshaw to Oliver's father, Thomas Matthews, who was obligated to pay a "new rent" of two bushels of wheat per hundred acres. In 1701 James Logan recorded that only three bushels had ever been paid, all by Oliver, who believed that the quitrent was exorbitant, and that he ought to be credited with payment of "4 bushels more." Logan Papers, Quit Rents, Three Lower Counties, 1701-1713, pp. 26, 31, HSP; New Castle Co. Will Bk. B, p. 161.

5. In the Lower Counties, "old renters" were obligated to pay one bushel of wheat per 100 acres compared with twice that amount for "new renters." The rent depended on whether the date of original ownership was before or after WP assumed control of the Lower Counties. However, James Logan's quitrent accounts imply that WP's commissioners of property may have used other criteria in determining the quitrent to be paid, thus prompting Matthew's objection. See Logan Papers, Quit Rents, Three Lower Counties, 1701-1713.

6. In the Lower Counties.

7. Samuel Hold (d. 1734), of Burlington and Philadelphia, was a cooper and one of the founders of Christ Church. Perry, *Historical Collections,* 2:7; Phila. Will Bk. E, #360; *PGM,* 23:111.

8. James Davis, of Christiana Hundred, New Castle Co., had been settled since 1698 on 100 acres of land, part of a tract formerly taken up by Robert Robinson "but quitt[d]." Although the land was held at "new rent" (see n. 5, above), Davis had never paid anything. In Mar. 1701 he promised James Logan that he would pay 40s and three years' rent at 12s 6d per annum by Mar. 1702, but he was probably unable to meet his obligation. See Logan Papers, Quit Rents, Lower Counties, 1701-1713, p. 26.

The next four documents (17-20) can be viewed as a barometer of WP's emotions as he became aware of the magnitude of the threat posed to his colony by developments in England and realized that he must leave Pennsylvania. In a letter to Sir John Lowther on 16 August (doc. 17), WP insisted that, while he was aware of attacks against his colony, he was intent on remaining in Pennsylvania for at least another year. Two days later he blamed Charlwood Lawton for not keeping him properly informed of developments (doc. 18); it seems that WP had just received news of the Reunification Bill. In fact, for some time he had been concerned over possible parliamentary moves against the chartered colonies and had called upon his son, William, Jr., and Lawton to lobby with influential politicians (see doc. 1). However, not until the summer of 1701 did he learn of related developments that had occurred in England since the beginning of the year. The Board of Trade had been under intense pressure from Robert Quary, Edward Randolph, Jeremiah Basse, William Blathwayt, Francis Nicholson, and others to deal firmly with the chartered colonies. The board showed increasing irritation at proprietary opposition to royal efforts to improve imperial defense and customs collection and to eliminate illegal trade and piracy, and in the spring of 1701 it undertook a parliamentary campaign to resume royal control over the proprietaries. On 24 April it enumerated for the House of Commons the many complaints it had received about judicial and trading abuses and emphasized that the proprietary colonies had been dilatory in taking action. On that same day, the Reunification Bill, strongly supported by the board, was introduced in the House of Lords. This bill was intended not to void the charters but to eliminate all proprietary governing rights. The bill moved very slowly in the Lords and had not yet gone to committee by the time Parliament was prorogued on 23 June 1701 (see Steele, *Colonial Policy,* pp. 62-73). This did not deter the Board of Trade, which sent letters to the governors of Virginia and Maryland and directed Lord Cornbury, Colonel Dudley, and Edward Randolph—all of whom were embarking for America—to collect further proofs of proprietary wrongdoing (see Louis Phelps Kellogg, *The American Colonial Charter* [1904; reprint, New York, 1971], p. 102; *CSPC, 1701,* p. 353).

Almost immediately from the time the bill was introduced in Lords, the Quaker Meeting for Sufferings had lobbied against it and had ordered letters to be written to WP on 20 June and 27 June discussing the bill's progress (*Micro.* 9:272, 274). The second letter mentioned the prorogation of Parliament and apparently included extracts of the Board of Trade's reports to both Lords and Commons, as well as the preamble to the bill. WP probably received the first letter on 15 August and the second, a week later. On 22 August he informed the Council that he had received news from England yesterday of "great and Strenuous endeavours" to annex the proprietary colonies to the crown. The closing section of his letter to Lawton, written on 27 August (doc. 18), presents a detailed defense against each of the charges raised by the reports and the bill. Between 25 August and 27 August, WP wrote separate letters of thanks to eleven members of Parliament who had opposed the Reunification Bill (see doc. 18, nn. 43–53). He also wrote to the Board of Trade defending proprietary government and denouncing the board's role in promoting the bill (doc. 19). By the time he wrote to Lord Romney on 6 September 1701 (doc. 20), asking him to lobby with the king on behalf of the proprietors, WP realized that further efforts to pass a Reunification Bill would be attempted once Parliament resumed. If he was to defend his proprietorship, he must sail for England as soon as possible (see doc. 21).

17
TO SIR JOHN LOWTHER

1701 16 6m [August] Pennsberry

Honored Friend[1]

I would not but have thought my selfe lost in thy country entertainments but I finde that Whitehaven is much kinder than Whitehall to Pennsylvania, for the one sends it good wishes and the other suffers itselfe to be mislead to crush such prosperous beginings — I return my most hearty acknowledgements for thy obligeing remembrance and beg the continuance of thy good word and wishes for our prosperity; for whatever interested men suggest, we are an approved experiment what sobriety and industry can do in a wilderness against heats, colds, wants, and dangers. The Crown gets best by us, but its officers less than by other Governments, and that's our crime; but time will sett truth in a better light, to which I adjourn my resentments. We thrive, our town, I think, too much for the country, not keeping a ballance in all things in Government is (perhaps) the hidden but sure cause of visible obstructions and entanglements in administration. I finde the Country, 70 miles back, the best land, Susquehanah a glorious river, boatable upon freshes.[2] We are planted 170 miles upon Delaware and in some places 16 miles back into the woods. Our staple corn and tobacco, we are trying for rice, converted timber for shipping, and hemp. Returns for England is what we want, and either we must have less from thence or better ways of making them. Barbados and those Islands are our market and we are too hard for our neighbours in our flour and bread being the whitest and preferr'd; we spare much of both to our neighbour Colonys also, as New England, Maryland, Virginia, and Carolina where wheat will hardly grow, but rice to perfection, and silk is got to a good pitch and will certainly be a commodity. We have had a good share of health since our arrival and my family increast by a little son;[3] and, if ill treatment call us not home, are like, if God please to prolong life to pass away a year or two at least. Only my privat affairs could make me leave it any more, but they will compel it once again, and then it would not displease me to lay my bones where I have layd my labour, mony, and solicitation in Pennsylvania.

I shall close with this assurance that I am with great esteem and affection.

Thy very faithfull friend
Wm Penn.

Transcript. ACM. (*Micro.* 9:381.)

1. Sir John Lowther (1643-1706) of Whitehaven, Cumb., was M.P. for Cumberland 1665-1700 and a commissioner of the Admiralty 1689-96. Anthony Lowther, WP's brother-in-law, was his cousin. *DNB; Peerage.*

2. The part of a tidal river next above the salt water. *OED.*

3. John Penn.

18
TO CHARLWOOD LAWTON

Philada 18th 6 mo [August] 1701[1]

Dear Friend.

I hope myne[2] in answer to thy Severall Letters by Puckle &cetera is Long since arrived, and that the Arguments I Offered in Defence of Propry Governments have been well Urged and Improved in their Favour and Mine in particular For which I perceive by a Letter from Captain Hill[3] by Way of Boston there has been an Occation more than Common,[4] I wish I had been favourd with the Notice of it from thy hand the same way for next to those comeing Directly to our own River there is no Conveyance Safer than by Vessels to N York and Boston & from thence by post hither.

My time is Very Short Puckle Sailing (as he says) to morrow or next Day I must only therfore Transcrible what I wrote to my Sister[5] the Day after the Receipt of the News three days agoe which being my First thoughts may perhaps need thy Second ones if there be any time or Room left to say any thing on that subject after such Vigorous Attacks made agst Proprietary Governments at large and mine in particular.[6] But if those Little Tools Can find Credit there that have none here to ruine the Meritorious, The Author of the True born Eng: man a Satyr[7] is not Abundly [8] out of the Way, To Condemn the Absent is to Frustrate the benefitt of Innocency and Justifie Assassinations that are without Notice, & for the most part in the Dark for the Security of the Actors

Beggars Fools and Knaves, are in Good Governments markt not to be Trusted must they be here Rewarded as well as Imployed meerly for the sake of Mischief? But if the parliament can be so Imposed upon as to think it is not best for the Crown to Settle Collonies at the Cost of others, and Direct the Governors of them as Materially as if it paid them I have Done. Or that tis as safe and Beneficiall for the Crown to have Mercenary (and for the Most part hungry) Governors that have no Interest to Improve the Colonies or in them to Secure the Crown against their Abuse of Trust as prop^{ry} ones have that are so much Concernd in their Improvements (wch Augments the Revenue of the Crown by Increase of Trade) and whose Interest in their Colonies is a perpetuall Security and Caution to the Crown for their Conduct I Submitt: But in other Ill things the pretence is Usually Grounded on Some Truth of Fact abused to Serve Ill Turns, while in this Affair the Fact Alledged for the reason of this Vehement Assault is Notoriously false both the Invention and Aggravation of the Tools Imployd to Ruine us

But I hope however if the Parliament will shake our Grants they will pay those Debts of the Crown for which they were given and the Charge of their Government to those that have Supported them and which such a Law of Annexing them to the Crown will Deprive them of paying themselves by the peoples Grants upon that Account.

Can it Enter the head of any man of Common Sence knowing any thing of America that wee came hither to be under a Kings Governour that is Mercenary and that has no Interest in the Country but is changeable every Three years perhaps, at least as often as they are thought to have suckt their Vacancies full out of the people? Pray allow mee to go on are wee come 3000 Miles into a Desart of ony[9] wild people as well as wild Beasts (Surrendring our Lives as well as Bellies to Providence) to have only the same priviledges wee had at home, We I say that were neither Criminals nor Necessitous? But further, must wee make property by our Labour, the Desart being meer Creation, and hardly Deserving the name of any? and Shall {it} be a Favour to have a Speciall Gracious provisoe to preserve that to us? It Seems to me Preposterous that in the age that Kidd[10] is so Solemnly hangd for Piracy, any should be Committed on the highest property, with any Publick Sanction, Since publick faith is Violated not only to prop^{ry} undertakers but whole provinces?

Wee will Enter the Lists[11] with our Adversaries & offer to prove Kings Governments (as they are Distinguished thô not by us for wee as well as the King Ever account and often call proprietary ones such) more Tardy then ours, and shall those that are Three to One greater Sinners than wee are be Motives or Examples for our Conformity in Government believe mee the Argument smells Rankly of a Broag[12] or a Bogg, because Kings Governments have been more Guilty of Countenancing Pirates & Forbidden Trade than those under proprietary Ones Therefore those under proprietaries ought to be taken from them & made Kings Governments I convinced the Lords that Maryland under the care of Governour Nicholson himself, and they Vigilancy & Inspection of that single Eyd Gentleman Edward Randolph was 27 Times a greater Offender then wee were, and Since that hearing[13] I find of the 9 Sail of Sloops and Brigantines that he affirmed went from us to Scotland or Holl^{d} there was but one, and the Master according to Law gave Bond to the Government to Goe for England, all that was Required of us to Expect or Command from him by the Law.

It would become the Wisdom as well as Justice of the Parliament to Inquire. 1st may not Such a Design of planting Collonies at private mens Cost and by their Interest Deserve Such Royalties & Jurisdictions as those Grants Contain when they are to be practised 3000 miles of in a Desart & where all the property is to be made by the Labour and charge of the undertakers thô as Subject to the Laws of Trade as any of the Kings more Immediate Colonies? 2dly if such powers are but a Reasonable Incouragement should they be Forfeitable upon any pretence under the peoples Violateing their Allegiance? 3dly Should not the Accused be fairly Summond & Tryed before Condemned? this is of the Nature of a Bill of Attainder[14] & thus much worse that in Some Cases time is given for the Surrender of the person in order to a Tryall, or Elce attainted for not doing it 4^{thly} But it will be said this touches none of our property, I thank them for nothing in their Sence of the Word, Lands they mean, but I Say the power of making our own Concessions Laws & Constitutions & Executing them for our Security (Keeping Faith and Allegiance) is the best part of our property, & next to all that the Crown gave us in those Grants, and if this be taken from us our Encouragement is with it, and wee are frustrated of o^{r} Greatest End in the Undertak^{g} wee being able to Live at home, & did in Equall Reputation with the best of our own Rank, but Could not think ourselves so Easy and Safe as abroad on those terms.

By no Argum^{t} but that a parliam^{t} can doe any thing can our Grants be vacated Indeed wee may Forfeit them but thats our Own Act & Fault none Elce can doe it but upon a parliamentary Omnipotency as I said before, and what ground there is for such a Measure in Government I Leave to better Judgment.

I think Susannah[15] was heard thô perjury cast her, Lies do us but with Difference wee are unheard too, in short this Jesting or Trifling with publick Faith where men are unavoidably Anchor'd & Fixed at this Vast Distance from their Mother Country & Dearest Relations & their Posterity thereby tyed to a Wilderness is and Ever will be Unaccountable with all Reasonable men and I believe that God will in his Time and Way Publickly Rebuke so great Injustice

What Could the Crown Desire more then the Approbation of the Deputy Governours of Prop^{ries}? If any thing it must be that such Lieutenant Governours should give Security by Bond for the Just Discharge of their Duty in Respect to the Laws of Trade, where the Crown is Chiefly Concernd & that I believe was never Refused,[16]

Besides the King has his Commrs of the Customs, Collectors, Auditors, & Surveyors Generall in all Propry Governments also his Peculiar Vice-Admirall & Judges of the Admiralty, I am amazed what pretence can find weight Enough after all this, to Encline Either house of Parliament to throw away their Time upon takeing from the poor proprietaries the Little which is Left them.

I only wish my Self Twenty years younger & no Englishman & I would hope to Enjoy the Fruit of my Labour and Receive the Returne of my Deep and Sinking Expences: For Instead of Inriching mee it pays not the Debt that the Crown ow'd my Father but Involves mee in 20000l Sterl to bring it to the pass 'tis in, which the Loss of the Government Defeats mee of the Meanes and hopes of being Reimburst. I have Spent I am sure more money on the Country Government and the Defence of it since I had it agst such knaves as now attempt its Ruine and mine to be Sure, this is that which makes my Case Singular & Deserving of a Singular Notice and Distinction from Common proprietaries or Incorporated Bodies thô the Attempt is unjust upon them all

27: 6 month 1701.

Since writeing the above our New Shipp the Messenger[17] Designd as a Packet boat between this and England is arrived 5 days agoe having Left London 5 days after Street[18] of whom wee have yet heard nothing and where I suppose your Packets are for there are none in this However I have Employed my time as well as I could to answer the Intelligence given mee by my other Friends and Send thee a Small Cargoe of Letters to be Delivered to those Lords who I am Informd have been very kind in my affair and if not now by a ship that goes from hence or one from York in a very few dayes I Intend to Some Gentlemen of the house of Commons[19] I am in the Dark as to the Affidavits produced agst us[20] but shall take all the precautions that time will let mee that may be Serviceable to us, If I am Destroyd it is by Villany and not by Truth to say nothing of what has been before my time, the worst of wch was in the Administracion of a Kings Govr here[21] and all of it a Trifle in Comparison of our Neighbours Immediately under the King I challenge the World to Blame my Conduct since my arrivall and that my Confidence is not Ill Grounded I pray that my Letters to the Secry of State[22] the Lds of Trade[23] & Commrs of the Customs[24] may be Called for & Read by the Lords if I should not be Able to gett thither before the next Session in wch it will appear my Solicitousness for the Service of the Crown hath Exceeded my Regard to my private Interest. The Charge agst us by the Extract wee have of the Report of the Lords of Trade to the Lds in Parliamt [25] together with the preamble to the Bill[26] Consists of 4 heads the 1st is Genl, the other 3 particular, the Genl one is a meer Insinuation as it Regards us Vizt that wee are Independant Govmts, Can it be so while wee have a Sovereign & never Refused appeals to him

& Submitt all our Laws to his approbation? and wch is more ourselves to his Discretion from time to time and that of his Ministers by his orders what greater Respect can be Ever p^{d} by any Recond the K^{s} more Immediate Gov^{rs} Independancy is a word I grant that ought to Distast a parl^{mt} of Engl^{d} but when used only to Serve a turn I would hope their greater wisdom & Justice will never make it a measure to break in upon our priviledges & Comforts. Wee Renounce all Independancy both as our Duty & Security, & care not how much the parl^{t} will Fence gst [27] it

For piracy the Second branch of our Charge I know my self to be so Innocent that I think my Self Meritorious in stead of Culpable & the worst of my Enemies here will readily allow 't & have only Censurd mee for overdoing the point some of them no longer agoe then this day nearly Concernd in the Admiralty having said in the presence of Severall of Repute in this towne that he knew no false Steps I had made but the Sending the pirates money out of the province that is Straitnd for want of Coin to carry on trade which Captain Puckle can Attest he being present. I did not take 200 Dollars out of Bradinhams money[28] as a K^{s} Governour in N York did[29] but made him live a prisoner here above 4 months upon his Conceald treasure, That I might send what wee had gott without Defalcations as the Account I sent to the Sec^{ry} of State & Council of Trade will Shew[30] I pray also it may be Observd how faintly to[31] Lords of Trade Express my Care in the buisness of some Old pirates Inhabiting near the Capes and Trafiking on board of Kidd wch was long before my arrivall in this province, & tho that Intercourse was known to the Adm^{ty} Officers yet no means were used by any of them to make Seizure either of their goods or persons ab^{t} which I also Referr to my aforesaid Letter

Somuch for piracy our second particular Offence is my Commission of Water Bailief[32] the Extract says to the sheriffs of all the Counties whereas they were but to two Viz: Philadelphia & Newcastle and those in the Absence of Coll Quarry who was Coasting wth his Merchez[33] to Sev^{ll} provinces above Six months & never Intended but to answer such Extraord^{ry} Ends as fall familiary under the Notice of the Common Law & the Civill Courts of Justice And as one of them never used his, so the other did not his thrice and then in cases not Thwarting the Admiralty Jurisdiction and as Soon as Colonel Quarry made known his Dissatisfaction about it I command^{d} the Sheriff to Act no further till he received Special Directions nor has any thing been done in it to this day but that Gentleman promised to Represent with mee those cases that Seemd Dubious to us to the L^{ds} of the Adm^{ty} & Councill of Trade that their Direccions by Advice of the K^{s} Councill in both Cases might be the Rule of our future Conduct where wee thought ourselves Borderers but that has never been done by him.—The last Branch of our Charge is a secret Trade carried on between

The Delaware Valley
1701–1718
0 5 10 20 30
MILES
NEW YORK
Hudson River
EAST
NEW
JERSEY
WEST
NEW
JERSEY
PENNSYLVANIA
New York
Long Island
Perth Amboy
Sandy Hook
Raritan River
Lehigh
PHILADELPHIA
BUCKS
Perkiomen Ck.
Delaware River
Schuylkill River
Neshaminy Ck.
CHESTER
THE FALLS
Fallsington
Pennsbury
Sepassinck Island
Pennypack Ck.
Conestoga
Brandywine Ck.
Pequea Ck.
Germantown
Manayunk
Burlington
East Caln
Chester Ck.
Merion
Susquehanna
Octoraro Ck.
Darby
Philadelphia
Moyamensing
Passyunk
Rancocas Ck.
Chester
Naaman's Ck.
Lancaster
Marcus Hook
Christiana Ck.
(Mason-Dixon Line)
New Castle
CECIL
Elk River
River
NEW
CASTLE
Salem
Bohemia River
Appoquinimink Ck.
Duck Ck.
KENT
Blackbird's Ck.
St. Jones's River
DELAWARE
BAY
KENT
MARYLAND
TALBOT
CHESAPEAKE BAY
Mispillion Ck.
CAPE MAY
CAPE
HENLOPEN
Lewes
Cedar Ck.
Indian River
ATLANTIC
OCEAN
SUSSEX
DORCHESTER
SOMERSET

this place and Curracao (a Dutch plantacon) Chiefly by some scotch men to a Degree that Wine Iron Linnen &c[t] are Sold as cheap here as in Engl[d]. This Looks as if it were Customary & a Formed Traffick But when the Fact is fairly told this mighty Mountain will be found Less then a Molehill for the story is beaten so very thin that a Child of ten year Old may see through it. all this comes from one poor pitifull Instance w[ch] was thus: In October last when I went down to Newcastle to hold an Assembly there & my people that Used to Inspect such things with mee a small sloop about 20 Tunns belongg Chiefly to Some of N York whose M[r] & Merchant were both Strangers[34] arrived at our Capes from Curracao where meeting with a small Shallop Comeing about from Jarsey Cape to this port she put on board her all her prohibited goods Viz[t] 4 hogsheads Claret 1½ Tun Iron & some peices Linen Cloth and came up herself Empty saving a Few baggs of Cacao Nutts w[ch] are allowed The Shallop Comeing but from Jarsey was not searched at night about 12 she Deld[35] the Goods at a private wharf w[ch] being seen by one of Colonel Quarrys fr[ds] he was forthwith Informd of it, but did not think fitt to take any notice of it till 6 weeks after when the Goods were Secured & Disposed of & chiefly by the Marshal of the Admiralty[36] it was then he Informd the Coll[r] [37] and afterw[ds] mee upon w[ch] the sloop was seized & Condemned when Sold to some honest men of the towne wholly Innocent and Ignorant of the matter the Offenders themselves being first out of the province & all our Reaches The wine either belongd to or was bought by a Tavern keeper here but never one hogshead of it drawn being prickt & Distilld for brandy The Iron Sold at 35/ per ct the Common price of other Iron here whereas 'tis sold in Engl[d] under or about 15 This shred of Fact is what he has Extended to so Generall and high a Charge for who that reads that Report would not believe it to be the Customary trade of this place & that wee are Generally Supplyd wth those goods from thence Besides this Sloop there is but one more come in here since my arrivall ag[st] wch nothing Could be found thô she was Condemnd for being Indirectly ownd in part by Forreigner.—And that I do not mince this matter (herein I am wholly unconcernd) they that have any knowledge of the Chicane & Voracious temper of the Adm[ty] Officers here will Easily believe they would have been Silent in their Informations upon a better bargain, but the Cargoe was not worth their while to loose the Oppertunity of such a charge ag[st] us w[ch] they were sure would take at home with our Sup[rs] And from this may the measure be taken of all their m{i}ghty Outcries, the Least Grain of truth once Given them for a Bottom Serving for a foundation to build the Most Extended General & blackest Accusations on. But after all that Letter[38] sett so heavy on his Stomach that he Could not forbear Revealing it to mee & upon a Conscientiousness of the Gross abuse used his Endeavour to Recover the Letter in the Bay of N York but by Contrary Winds &

weather was Frustrated: He was also so free with mee as to Declare his Motive to this Letter was that he had Advices from Engld & Virga that I had sent over Divers Affidavits agst him wch shews it was rather to meet and Ballance the Informations he Suspected in my Affidavits, than from any Conviction of his Duty or just Occation given for so high a Charge & I would not willingly believe the man means it in the Extent, that the Lds have unkindly Representd it Thou mayst Expect within a very few weeks after this all Requisite Testimonies to Confront our Enemies

I Inclose a bill payble to thy self or order for thy own use and a bill for the Govmt at home to think on[39] that if they will take they must also pay which I desire thee to Show to the best hands in both houses Whatever thou dost Insist upon time my case Differing from all others & to the End I may come safely home to Negociate my affairs of so great Importance to mee and my poor family press the Approveing of a Deputy[40] dureing that Interval or Elce I must Either Abdicate my Goverment or loose it for not appearing pray press Ld Romney to Urge the King that his Influence upon the house may not goe against mee to whom Deliver my Letter Directed for him[41] (I mean the Ld R) at the Same time giving him a Copy of my bill of charges.—I have wrote to the Lds of Trade & Commrs of the Customs not for any favour I Expect but to those great men (as I said before) that have been kind for the Continuance of their favour and Justice[42] Vizt the D of Somerset,[43] D: Devonshire,[44] Marq. Normanby,[45] Earl of Dorset,[46] Ld Jefferis[47] & Ld pawlett,[48] & of the Commons to the Speaker[49] Sr Chr M.[50] or Sr Edwd Sey[51]—wch thou pleases to superscribe it for, to Sr Hennage Finch[52] & J How[53] and all this in the Compass of a few days that this Ship gave mee after the Arrival of the Messenger with the many others of Importance that comeing by her I was obliged to answer So that I have almost Jaded myself with the toil: when thyne by C street Comes to hand I shall be better able to take final measures But one thought that has some days possest my mind I cannot forbear dropping because I think true and may be managd to good Advantage if thou art of the Same Sentiment That next the Rapaciousness of Officers to have more Govmts to Excise and Govnrs to Goe Snacks with[54] the Design Seems to Lye against Proprietary Govmts upon the foot of Dissent in Religion For Except Carolina they were all granted to Non Conformists and then the meaning is that no Dissenters Even in a Wilderness at 3000 Miles Distance & at the other End of the world shall Enjoy the powers first granted them for their Incouragment & Security in their Hasardous & most Expensive Enterprises And if this were well Insinuated ~~with~~ Among the Chief of the Presbyterians Independants & Babtist methinks they would See the Common cause of Dissent at Stake and Consequently make a bold Appearance & stand both within doors & without agst the progress of such a Bill wch I Submitt to thy best

Intelligence & Judgment I shall say no more but Commit my Cause and Friends to the Good Providence of God who first gave mee this Country to prosper all your Indeavours in the protection & preservacion of it I am with Due Regards their & Thy most Assured Faithfull Friend

W P

All myne Salute thee & thyne. Communicate what parts of this thou thinkest fitt to those that are my friends—

LBC. William Penn Letterbook, 1699-1703, HSP. (*Micro.* 9:385.) Endorsed: Cha: Lawton.

1. This letter was written over a period of several weeks; WP dates a later segment "27: 6 month 1701," and he mentions a letter to Lord Romney which appears to be that of 6 Sept. (see n. 41, below; doc. 20). If so, WP did not complete this letter to Lawton until after 6 Sept. 1701.

2. Doc. 13.

3. Capt. Richard Hill. This letter has not been found. WP outlined his defense in a letter to Lawton, 21 Dec. 1700 (*PWP,* 3:629). See also doc. 13.

4. It is likely that WP had learned of efforts by the Board of Trade to encourage passage by parliament of a Reunification Bill. See headnote to doc. 17.

5. Margaret Penn Lowther (1647-1718), sister of WP and wife of Anthony Lowther, resided at Marske, Cleveland, Yorks. (*PWP,* 3:135, 139n). The letter has not been found.

6. See headnote to doc. 17.

7. Daniel Defoe (1661?-1731)—dissenter, Whig journalist, and writer—published in Jan. 1701 *The True-born Englishman, a Satyr,* a satiric attack on the English as a race of mongrels. The long poem, intended to defend William III against the charge of being a Dutchman, proved to be enormously popular (*DNB*). The "Little Tools" mentioned by WP were undoubtedly men like Edward Randolph, Jeremiah Basse, and Robert Quary, whom WP viewed with hostility because of their efforts against his proprietorship.

8. Abundantly?

9. The copyist's error for "only."

10. William Kidd (1654?-1701), a Boston privateer commissioned by Lord Bellomont in 1696 to hunt pirates, turned pirate instead. He was arrested by Bellomont in July 1699 and was executed in London on 23 May 1701. *PWP,* 3:580n; *DNB.*

11. The place of combat. *OED.*

12. A brogue was a cheat, fraud, or trick. *OED.*

13. Here WP is referring to his defense before the House of Lords in 1697 (see *PWP,* 3:485-90), in which he asserted that Randolph had reported 27 Maryland ships engaged in illegal trade with Scotland compared with only 9 from the Lower Counties.

14. A parliamentary measure which convicted an individual of treason or felony without a judicial trial. *OED.*

15. Susanna, wife of Joakim of Babylon, had been falsely accused of adultery by two elders and condemned to death; she appealed to God, who sent Daniel to expose the elders. See the Book of Susanna, in the Apocrypha.

16. Here WP conveniently ignores the fact that the English government in 1697-98 had attempted to force the proprietary governors to give security for the actions of their deputy governors, but that the attempt was stymied by WP and the other proprietors. See *PWP,* 3:538.

17. The *Messenger,* captained by John Guy, was a brigantine that carried mail between Philadelphia and England. ACM, vol. 120.

18. Capt. John Street, who was one of the witnesses in the parliamentary hearings on the Reunification Bill, commanded the *Abraham.* See *Proceedings and Debates,* 2:403-4; Logan Papers, 8:9, HSP.

19. These letters were similar to WP's letter to Lord Romney (doc. 20); see nn. 43-53, below.

20. WP is probably referring to the affidavits that the Board of Trade on 11 June

1701 asked Edward Randolph to obtain from several of his anti-proprietary witnesses, who would be unable to attend the next sessions of Parliament. See Robert N. Toppan, ed., *Edward Randolph: His Letters and Official Papers* (1899; reprint, New York, 1967), 5:174.

21. WP is here referring to the administration of Gov. Benjamin Fletcher, 1692-94.

22. James Vernon (1646-1727) had held the post of secretary of state for the southern department since Dec. 1697 (see *PWP*, 3:544n). For WP's letters to Vernon from Pennsylvania, see *Micro.* 8:277, 691, 738.

23. See *PWP*, 3:587, 592; *Micro.* 8:372, 647a, 755; 9:096, 294.

24. See doc. 4; *Micro.* 8:305, 444, 648; 9:288.

25. Evidently the report of the Board of Trade submitted to the House of Lords on 8 May 1701, the text of which was probably similar to that submitted to the House of Commons on 24 Apr. 1701. See *Proceedings and Debates*, 2:392-401, 406.

26. The Reunification Bill. See *The Manuscripts of the House of Lords, 1699-1702* (London, 1908), pp. 314-15.

27. Against.

28. Robert Bradenham, former physician to Capt. William Kidd, turned king's evidence against him. When captured shortly before WP's arrival in Pennsylvania in 1699, Bradenham had more than 2000 pieces of eight in his possession, and was known to have a concealed cache of gold. See *PWP*, 3:580, 593, 598n, 631, 635n.

29. WP is probably referring to Benjamin Fletcher, governor of New York, 1692-98.

30. Probably WP's letter to Secretary of State Vernon of 30 Dec. 1700, and to the Board of Trade of 31 Dec. 1700 (*Micro.* 8:738, 755).

31. The copyist's error for "the."

32. On 20 June 1700 WP had commissioned Thomas Farmer, sheriff of Philadelphia, to act as a water bailiff with the power to execute all legal process against any person, ship, or goods upon the Delaware River (see *Micro.* 8:493). Believing that the commission infringed upon his authority, Robert Quary complained on 14 Nov. 1700 to the Lords of the Admiralty (*CSPC, 1700*, pp. 651-52). The Reunification Bill echoed Quary's sentiments. See also *PWP*, 3:624.

33. Merchandise?

34. Capt. Gous Bonin and Samuel Peres. See doc. 38, n. 33.

35. Delivered.

36. Robert Webb (c. 1659-1701), Maryland merchant and owner of 2500 acres in Pennsylvania, had served as marshal of the vice-admiralty court. *PWP*, 3:574n.

37. Collector.

38. Robert Quary to the Lords of the Admiralty, 14 Nov. 1700. *CSPC, 1700*, pp. 650-53.

39. These bills have not been found.

40. Although WP commissioned Andrew Hamilton as deputy governor of Pennsylvania on 27 Oct. 1701 (see *Micro.* 9:716), final approval by the crown for this appointment was not received until early in 1703. See doc. 55, n. 4.

41. WP probably means doc. 20, which, however, is dated 6 Sept.

42. See n. 19, above. WP also wrote a general letter to the Board of Trade on 26 Aug. 1701 (doc. 19).

43. Charles Seymour (1662-1748), duke of Somerset, was one of the regents during William III's absence in Holland, July-Nov. 1701. He became particularly influential with Anne, who made him master of the horse and one of the commissioners for the union with Scotland. *DNB*. WP's letter to him is *Micro.* 9:431.

44. William Cavendish, first duke of Devonshire, former parliamentarian, strongly supported the cause of religious toleration. He was one of the most powerful Whig peers in the kingdom. *DNB*. WP's letter to him is *Micro.* 9:418.

45. John Sheffield, marquis of Normanby, former soldier, was leader of the Tory party in the House of Lords, often bitterly opposing the court. His firm Toryism earned him numerous honors during the reign of Anne. *DNB*. WP's letter to him is *Micro.* 9:424.

46. Charles Sackville (1638-1706), earl of Dorset and Middlesex, was a friend of WP's since 1674. He served William III as lord chamberlain of the household, 1689-97, and on three occasions was one of the regents in William's absence from England. *DNB; PWP*, 1:292-93n, 516n. WP's letter to him is *Micro.* 9:448.

47. John Jeffreys (1673-1702), second Baron Jeffreys of Wem, was a Tory who took his seat in the House of Lords in 1694; in 1696 he refused to sign the association recognizing William III as lawful king. *DNB; Peerage,* 7:84. WP's letter to him is *Micro.* 9:434.

48. John Lord Poulett (1663-1743), fourth Baron Poulett, who took his seat in Lords in 1696, was a moderate Tory ally of Robert Harley. He was elevated to Earl Poulett in 1706. *DNB;* Steele, *Colonial Policy,* pp. 74-75. WP's letter to him is *Micro.* 9:427.

49. Robert Harley, earl of Oxford, became speaker of the House of Commons on 10 Feb. 1701. *DNB.* WP's letter to him is *Micro.* 9:468.

50. Sir Christopher Musgrave. WP's letter to him has not been found.

51. Sir Edward Seymour. WP's letter to him as not been found.

52. Heneage Finch (c. 1649-1719), M.P. nearly continuously from 1685 to 1703, was a firm Tory. He was elevated to Baron Guernsey in 1703 and earl of Aylesford at the accession of George I. WP knew him from the 1670s. *DNB; PWP,* 1:542-43; 2:78; 3:636n; Henning, *House of Commons,* 3:323. WP's letter to him is *Micro.* 9:477.

53. John How. WP's letter to him is *Micro.* 9:420.

54. To have a share in the profits. *OED.*

19
TO THE BOARD OF TRADE

Philadia 26th 6mo (Augst) 1701

Honourable Friends

Having received none[1] from You since my last of the 6th of Mar.[2] I send this according to promise to accompany such of our Laws as being past or reviewed by our last Assembly are thought fitt to be presented for the Kings Approbation. And naturally first offer themselves to your Board from whence I request you to favour them with what Dispatch your other affairs will suffer you to allow them. There are some others that yet want a Second hand,[3] which when past upon them, Shall wait on you with all Expedition.

And now I know not how to avoid observing to you That by a Ship last week arrived here from London, I have received the Extracts of two Reports made from your Board the one to the house of Commons, the other to the Lords relating to our Proprietary Governments in which if the Extractors have done you Justice you must excuse me if I complain of the want of it to me.[4]

Some faults doubtless must have been committed in an Infant Colony in the Space of eighteen Years, but this is my Comfort the greatest of them are owing to the Administration of a Kings Government[5] when mine was superseded.[6] yet even those were but Moats in comparison to the beams in some others that you seem to prefer, as I could largely prove,[7] and have been expiated I hope (as you are pleased to acknowledge) upon my Arrival: The Representation of what particulars have been Since, and follows in your Report to the Lords Seems wholly unaccountable.

As to the Commission of Water Bailif to the Sherif of Philadelphia[8] who never served three warrants by it, and that to him of Newcastle[9] (which is all I granted) who never served one ~~by it~~ that I know of, I shall Say litle here, having wrote largely to the Lords of the Admiralty on that head[10] a Copy of my Letter to whom I send inclosed[11] & request your Notice of it, Only this, Had that active Officer[12] of the Kings been in his Post or in the Province at any time for Seven Months together those Commissions had never been granted, and upon his remonstrance at his return they were forthwith vacated. And have I by this made Infractions on the Admiralty or any thing else? No, on the contrary I have been so supine and easy to that Court in all respects, That I have been highly upbraided by Ingenious Lawyers of our neighbouring Colonies for exposing Property for a Prey to those who thinking themselves Secure under the awful Language of Serving the Kings Interest, have stopt at no piece of Rigour that would turn a penny their own way, of which Instances may be given that would be tolerated I must believe by no Kings Governour in America.

The next Charge is a secret Trade between this place and Curacao: Through my care that nothing should pass unobserved, I mentioned this to you in my last,[13] and express'd a concern at[14] it, being Jealous that what had been once done, might again But since it is made a general Imputation and Crime in the Publick, I shall give an account of all I could on the Strictest Inquiry ever hear of on that head. Since my Arrival there have but two Vessels come in here from that Island of which the Collectors and Naval Officers Lists can be sufficient Evidence, the first a Sloop of twenty Tuns in October last, when I was with our Assembly at Newcastle 40 miles from Philadelphia, She brought (as I heard two months after and wch was the ground of my Complaint to you) 4 hogsheads of Claret one Tun & a half of Iron, Some pieces of Linnen besides Cacao Nuts, w^ch^, we have alwayes reckoned, are allowed. of this Colonel Quary was forthwith Informed by a friend of his who saw them landed at midnight out of a Shallop that had taken the S^d^ Goods on board at our Capes from the Sloop that brought them, but thought fitt to take no other notice of it, till above 6 weeks after when the Goods were all Secured and disposed of, than to dress up his Information to you on wch your Report I suppose is grounded. In other cases the Officers of that Court are not wanting where the least dawn of Interest appears, but here the Profit was like to be small, and there was a higher end to be served viz by blackning of us to lay a foundation for greater Advantages to themselves as appears by Colonel Quary being now made Surveyor of this River on both sides with power to putt in and turn out all Officers concerned in the Customs — himself being all the while one of the greatest Traders in these parts, two things that in all other places have been hitherto judged[15] inconsistent, and that must needs redound highly to the prejudice of his Fellow Traders, as well as the Kings Insecurity in his Customs. But no sooner was the Account of the aboves^d^ Traffick brought me, than we used all possible application to discover the Goods, but in vain, it was near two months after the Bird was flown, and their own immediate Officer the Marshal of the Admiralty[16] had no small hand in their Disposal. The Vessel however was Seized and condemned after she had been sold to persons wholly innocent, and the guilty escaped clear.

The other Vessel from Curacao has been guilty of nothing of that kind that we can hear of having brought her Returns in Money,[17] yet was condemned for being indirectly owned in part by a Foreigner. The last Vessel from thence before my Arrival was Seized and condemned also.

What is Said of the Pirates at the Capes[18] I should think bears rather a Merit than any Crime in me, they had been Settled there (as others of that old Crew have in the neighbouring Colonies) for Several years[19] under the Admiralty Officers and upon my Arrival I proceeded against them with the utmost Rigour

Upon all which Give me leave to say that when I see my Diligence in those very things that might have slept had I been Negligent in the Kings Affairs to be turned against me, and made a Crime in my Government, I cannot but think it cruel to the last degree. That one fault committed chiefly[20] by Strangers in which no Officer concerned in the Government Save the Marshal of the Admiralty had a hand, should be made a general Imputation and Crime ~~against~~ {in} the Publick is rigorous beyond example.

That my bleeding expences for 20 years past in raising a flourishing Colony profitable to England by the Consumption of her Commodities as well as other wayes and that only by my private Interest ~~are~~ in which my whole Estate that I could have lived much more comfortably on at home is irrecoverably plunged should be rewarded with the Infamous Brands of illegal Practices in the highest and when I might reasonably expect to be reimbursed, must be cutt out of the means, Seems to carry an Injustice with it, that in smaller matters would be otherwise treated

~~While~~ {That} persons gaping for Preferments under the Specious pretence of Serving the Kings Interest, while all the Kings Thirds in Seizures and Condemnations appropriated to themselves are not thought Sufficient to atone for the want of a Settled Salary, should be countenanced and encouraged, and all their Representations without further Inquiry Credited, and made a bottom for the Ruine of the rather meritorious than culpable, while my Endeavours equal in Sincerity and application, I dare be bold to say, to those of any of the Kings more immediate Governours and this without one farthing allowed by the Crown, are made[21] my Guilt and Crime, looks as if all the old known Rules of Justice were to be read backward.

Excuse me pray, If I thus express the just resentments of my Sufferings, My case is singular Since all meets on my Family and Fortune and if fully stated might justly engage the thoughts of all Englishmen to whom Property is sacred Nor is it the Powers of Government alone that is here to be contended for, our Liberties and the first Inducements to undertake So hazardous and difficult an

Enterprize are Struck at by that Bill,[22] and must inevitably fall, if carried on upon the bottom it now Stands:[23] Of the Preamble to which I cannot but observe that it seems to recommend and Strengthen it self by the word Independant Governments: I know that term cannot relish well with an Engl. Parliament but as it refers to me You also know it is not true, my very Grant making Dependencies in several respects, and if you cannot believe me, the Countrey is a Witness I have been a constant Drudge to all your~~r~~ Directions and a Kings Governour in all things but a Salary. And by nothing but a downright Parliamentary Omnipotency can my pretensions be overruled, but I hope by the Lights they may receive before the next Sessions are over, those that are the Conservators of our Liberties and the last resort of Englishmen for Right will not lightly suffer other mens mistakes or ill designs to prevail with them to ruine Me and my Family.

But I will no longer now take up your time, considering the cause, you will excuse (I hope) this Freedom, with which I shall conclude ~~in~~ wth all due respects

Your Assured Faithful friend
Wm Penn

LS. CO 5/1261/18, PRO. (*Micro.* 9:437.) Docketed: Pensylvania | Letter from Mr Penn to | the Board; Dated at | Philadelphia the 26th | August 1701. | Rec^{d} | Read 15th Octr 1701. This letter has been collated with a copy in William Penn Letterbook, 1699-1701, HSP; significant differences between the two are noted below.

1. The LBC reads "one." In fact, WP received a letter from the Board of Trade on 15 Apr. 1701. *Micro.* 9:201.
2. *Micro.* 9:096. WP here forgets that he wrote to the Board of Trade on 2 July 1701. See *Micro.* 9:294.
3. The Provincial Council on 23 Aug. 1701 perused the laws passed by the previous Assembly held at New Castle and ordered them "to be fairly transcribed & sent over, under the great Seal, to England." It appears from WP's remarks that the transcription had not yet been completed. See *Minutes of the Provincial Council,* 2:32.
4. On 24 Apr. and 8 May 1701, the Board of Trade submitted reports to the House of Commons and House of Lords, respectively, which lent credence to Robert Quary's complaints against WP and his colony. See doc. 18, n. 25.
5. LBC reads "Governor." WP is referring to the administration of Pennsylvania by Gov. Benjamin Fletcher, 1692-94.
6. LBC reads "suppressed."
7. LBC omits this phrase and continues: "and those have been Expiated."
8. See doc. 18, n. 32.
9. Joseph Wood. His commission as water bailiff has not been found.
10. See *Micro.* 8:672, written on 10 Dec. 1700.
11. No longer with this letter.
12. Robert Quary.
13. Here WP is referring to his letter of 6 Mar. 1701. *Micro.* 9:096.
14. LBC reads "for."
15. LBC adds "wholly."
16. Robert Webb.
17. LBC omits this phrase.
18. The Board of Trade reported to the House of Commons that former pirates were settled near the capes of the Delaware River and had assisted Capt. Kidd when he arrived there by removing from his ships quantities of stolen East Indian goods. However, the board also reported that WP had imprisoned the suspects and seized some of the goods. See *Proceedings and Debates,* 2:400.
19. LBC adds "even."
20. LBC omits "chiefly."

21. LBC adds "by a Stranger."

22. The Reunification Bill.

23. LBC now concludes: "But I will not now Take up your time for I must make a more Effectual then this Distant plea; If tis thought absolutely necessary the King should have the Government let our Charges & our Circumstances be Duely Considered. But I confess nothing more afflicts mee than that men of your Abilities should be Imposed upon by Little tools and False Facts to believe prop^{ry} Governm^{ts} Inconsistent with the Benefitt of the Crown that are made at other mens Costs, yet are Equally Directed by the King and his Ministers as those that are accounted his more Immediate Collonies and are so much better a Security to the Cr: for their Behaviour then any Temporary Gov^{rs} can give for their Conduct."

20
TO THE EARL OF ROMNEY

Pennsylvania[1] 6th 7^{br} [September] 1701.

I have heard of the very unfaire treatment some have given me in my absence,[2] which I am apt to think one word from the king, (If I could deserve it) would alter. I was thus attackt in Kg. James's time, & when he came to know the ruine it would prove to me and my family, he Cryed out, God forbid, he would {never} be the author of such a Cruelty.

I received it[3] in Consideration of a debt of 16000^{l} oweing to my Father in 80, and that I have expended above twenty thousand pounds upon it, to begin & carry it on to the condition it is now in, I can prove, as well as solemnly attest; whose interest doubles the Sume.

It was Sett at 1200^{l} to such as would have bought it of York; I took it upon the Encouragem^{t} of my interest to render it Considerable, & not upon its own vallue; & dropt the prosecution of my debt: a Case very well known to the Duke of Leeds,[4] Earl of Dorset,[5] Charles Bertie,[6] Lounds,[7] &c: The Encouragem^{t} was powrs to rule our selves, for our own security (saveing our allegeance to the Crown, & other reservations In the Graunt from it) for we were to make the property when we came theither. Had the land been Cultivated as in Eng. we had fallen into immediate profits for our mony; but after all our hazards in geting theither, as well as Charges, to find only Creation, a rough wilderness, that would cost us 3, 4, & 5^{l} an acre to clear for use, and then tell us they will only take the Goverm^{t} from us, but leave us our Property, might deserve a very hard name. It is to Strip us of our defence both in our Civil & religious capacity, & to introduce that powr & Spirit over us we came heither to avoyd; as indeed all the people that began Proprietary Goverm^{ts} did; those of Carolina excepted: And that after the Goverm^{t} at home was glad to be rid of us, at so cheap a rate as a little parchm^{t}, to be practis'd in a desart 3000 Miles off, our honest Labour, blest by heaven, Should raise envy and tempt any to plot our ruine, & that those who ~~should~~ {ought to} be our last resort for redress, should be imposed upon to attempt ~~our ruine~~ It, is very unaccountable.

But I never knew an ill thing want a good pretence, & such an one this has, viz, the service of the Crown, which, they say, will not allow of such independant Govermts and that they are for that reason, as well as foule trade, to be taken out of the hands that hold them, and reunited (as it is very improperly phraised)[8] to the Crown. But if Govermts that by their Graunts are obliged to allow of Appeals to the king, and whose laws are to have his approbation, & where those of Trade and Navigation are {to be} observed, can properly be termed Independant, myn must be such; Else the pretence is vain, as indeed it is, to take away my limitted one as one Independent.

Besides, I can honestly say that no Kings Goverr has more readily obey'd[9] the kings directions, [illegible deletion] or with more intention applyed himselfe to assure him of their complyance with his Commands; and after haveing this testimony Sent home by our old accusers,[10] to be treated alike, as if a transgressor, is to observe no measure to merrit, or Innocence at least. Here I am come to rectify things, I have at an expensive & hazardous voyage, done it, and now I must be turn'd out, as a delinquent. God help us!

My ould friend, possess the king of this usage. I cannot suffer myselfe to think he will be brought to ruine famelys, to break publick faith, to treat merrit in Gult[11] ~~and undoe fammilys~~ for reason of state. wch yet is no reason, unless it were ~~better~~ {worse} for the king to make Colonys at other folks charge than at his own; and to pay salerys to Goverrs than command Governours at their own Cost, as in the Case of Proprietary ones he has done, & may still do.

When Kings Governours have the same interest to improve the Colonys (so necessary for the Kings service) as Proprietary ones have, and as good a security for their Conduct (who come there only to get mony) as Proprietarys, that have their Provinces at stake for their good behavour; and lastly, when Kings Goverments prove antidotes agst Pyracy & foule Tradeing (that I proved before the lords, 94,[12] were greater sinners than we are) It will be time to urge reason of State to deprive us of our Govermts Else I must take liberty to say, that knaves & beggers {(as Randal[13] Bass[14] &c:)} are employd to ruine us, that some people may have more Goverments to excise, & Governours to goe halves with. A Corruption that has been thought to raigne too long already.

pardon, my ould good Friend, this Freedom, for it is a last point I must either Enjoy my Govermt to live, that laying up my own estate, I may pay the great debts I have contracted for it, or the Crown must pay me; or a Prison insteed of a Govermt must determin my fate;[15] which god almighty prevent for my poor familys Sake. I will depend upon the Kings Justice & goodness, and therefore pray read it to him; tho it seems long, it is soon read, I writeing much paper with but a little matter. At least, I pray for time, Since it is too long & dangerous a Journey to remove presently, as well as that it hath all the dishonorable appearance here, to be tost thus about, ~~as well the~~ b~~y~~oth {to}

Indians a*s*nd Europeans. whos friendship and regaurds, I have notoriously purchass'd at a great, and (if I were a kings Gover[r] (as some will distinguish) for I take every one to be such) at a Generous expence, that must be a debt also upon the Crown, if this work proceed, of reuniteing our Goverm[ts] to It; Inasmuch as it has been a Goverm[t] Charge, and I only have defray[d] it, as well as the Governours for 20 years, without a farthing Consideration till this year, & that not the 7th part of the Sume it has cost me, & ⅔ of that, as yet, unreceived. I have exceeded a letter of respect but not[16] of Friendshipp I hope; a word I have been long allowd to use and hardly Ever needed the Tone of it more than now which as I do most heartily begg So the Good Effects of it will Consequently Obliedge in the Deepest Regards

Thy most Affectionate Respectfull
Faithfull Friend.
W: P.

AL. Penn Papers, Granville Penn Book, HSP. (*Micro.* 9:497.) Endorsed: Lord Romny.[17] The final page of this letter is missing; the editors have supplied the lost text from a copy in WP's letterbook (*Micro.* 9:513).

1. LBC begins "Pensbury in."
2 See headnote to doc. 17.
3. Pennsylvania.
4. Sir Thomas Osborne (1631-1712), duke of Leeds and earl of Danby, an avid Tory, had been Charles II's chief minister 1673-79 but was impeached by Parliament and lay a prisoner in the Tower when WP received his charter for Pennsylvania. William and Mary made him lord president of the Privy Council, but he was out of office in 1701. *DNB.*
5. Charles Sackville, earl of Dorset and Middlesex.
6. Charles Bertie (d. 1711), M.P. for Stamford, Lincs., and brother-in-law of the duke of Leeds, was treasurer of the ordnance in 1681, when WP received his charter for Pennsylvania. *Alumni Oxonienses,* 1:117.
7. William Lowndes (1652-1724), M.P. for Seaford 1695-1714, had been from 1679 to 1695 a clerk in the Treasury who processed petitions. From 1695 to 1724 he was secretary of the Treasury and is said to have coined the phrase "ways and means." *DNB.*
8. Here WP is referring to the Reunification Bill. See headnote to doc. 17.
9. Here WP inadvertently skipped a page, then filled it in and wrote a marginal note: "pleas to read t'other side first."
10. Edward Randolph, Jeremiah Basse, and Robert Quary.
11. WP meant "Guilt."
12. Here WP erroneously gives 1694 as the date of his defense before the House of Lords; this actually took place in 1697. See doc. 18, n. 13.
13. Edward Randolph.
14. Jeremiah Basse.
15. Ironically, WP's prophecy was realized in 1708 when he was imprisoned in the Fleet for refusing to pay debts owed to the widow and children of his former steward, Philip Ford. See headnote to doc. 108.
16. AL copy ends here. The conclusion is from the LBC.
17. Henry Sidney (1641-1704), earl of Romney, had known WP since the 1660s. He played a significant role in bringing about William III's accession to power. At this time, although only groom of the stole, he retained the king's favor, thus prompting WP's letter. See *PWP,* 3:99n; Basil D. Henning, ed., *The House of Commons, 1660-1690* (London, 1983), 3:433-34.

LAST MONTHS IN AMERICA

September–December, 1701

WP's sudden decision to leave Pennsylvania made a rapid settlement of the colony's affairs imperative. On 22 August 1701 WP had explained to the Provincial Council the parliamentary threat that required his presence in England, and an Assembly was called for 15 September to consult on how to meet this crisis (*Minutes of the Provincial Council,* 2:32). Not only would the proprietor once again become an absentee, but the colony might soon find itself under direct royal control. A new constitution was needed to replace the discarded frame of 1683; disputed claims, shoddy record keeping, and proprietary exactions caused widespread dissatisfaction in matters of property; and the Lower Counties were increasingly restive in their alliance with Pennsylvania. With little more than two months between his decision to leave and his departure at the beginning of November, WP sought quick resolutions to these problems. Under pressure of time and in need of money, the proprietor was driven to accept unsatisfactory solutions: a constitution that shifted legislative power into the hands of the Assembly, a charter of property rights that he rescinded immediately on his arrival in England, and a dissolution of the union between the Lower Counties and Pennsylvania. Yet the settlement conceived in such haste was to establish Pennsylvania's basic political structure for the rest of its colonial life.

In September 1701 the most pressing concern, to WP's mind, was the need for a new frame of government to secure the colonists' political privileges — a concern that to the Assembly seemed less urgent than redress of property grievances. On 15 September WP addressed the specially convened Assembly, urging the members to devise "some suitable expedient and Provision for your safety, as well in your Privileges as Property, and you will find me ready to Comply with whatsoever may render us happy, by a nearer Union of our Interest" (*Minutes of the Provincial Council,* 2:35). The Assembly's first action was to draw up a series of demands about property rights (doc. 22), based on a petition from inhabitants of Philadelphia written up by

David Lloyd (*Micro.* 9:536). Nettled at the Assembly's priorities, WP replied point by point in doc. 24: some of the claims he considered reasonable, but a number of them would have cut severely into his proprietary revenues. In particular, WP rejected demands for elimination of rents in Philadelphia, for a 10 percent bonus on all land, for treatment of unsold Philadelphia land as common, and for adherence to old rents despite the rise in land values. Worse was to come in October, when the representatives of the Lower Counties objected violently to a bill for confirmation of the laws passed at New Castle in 1700 (see doc. 27). Without this bill, WP's officials were unable to collect the taxes passed at New Castle, including a £2000 levy for the proprietor's use, since Pennsylvanians claimed that the laws had been made outside the province. The Delaware assemblymen saw the bill as an insult to their equal status and a disincentive to the holding of future sessions at New Castle; twice they walked out of the Assembly, and, though WP's mediation achieved a temporary truce, the Lower Counties were far from mollified — especially since the obnoxious confirmation bill was passed despite their objections. WP reluctantly gave them permission to form a separate government, a promise embodied in the final clause of the Charter of Privileges signed on 28 October (doc. 28). See *Minutes of the Provincial Council,* 2:49-52.

By the fall of 1701 it was clear even to WP that his dream of a unified, godly, and contented colony could not be realized. The forces of discontent among various overlapping groups — Anglicans, landholders, taxpayers, Lower Counties settlers, royal officials, and Pennsylvania assemblymen — were too great for him to overcome. But he could still hope to piece together a settlement that would both preserve some colonial privileges and secure the proprietor an income sufficient to stave off bankruptcy. The results of his intense efforts were dual charters of privileges and property, the first arrived at through negotiation with the Assembly, the second drawn up by David Lloyd and only presented to WP shortly before he was to leave (see the headnotes to docs. 28 and 31). Despite his reservations about some of their provisions, especially the new system for property administration, WP agreed to these charters as the only way to achieve a settlement before his departure. As he later explained, he was eager to preserve the colonists' privileges against the possibility of a royal takeover (see doc. 93). He was probably also unwilling to seem recalcitrant, since he was dependent on taxes that were already proving difficult to collect; he needed the colonists' goodwill, but here again his hopes were unrealized (see doc. 35). It was a disheartening farewell from the once-beloved colony that he would never see again.

In addition to negotiating this major settlement of governmental and proprietary affairs, WP had to tie up political loose ends and set his own house in order. He reserved land for ex-servants in fulfillment of a promise made in 1681 (doc. 23), and he received a testimonial from the Indian leaders who had joined in the treaty of 23 April 1701 (docs. 11 and 25). Taking their leave of the Quakers in Falls Meeting, WP and Hannah were issued a glowing certificate of removal (doc. 26). The extraordinarily busy week from 25 October to 1 November 1701 has left thirty-four extant documents, a greater density of documentation than for any other period of WP's life. The survival of these documents is partly due to James Logan's efficient record keeping, but their number testifies to WP's feverish activity on the eve of his departure. The proprietor was issuing last-minute commissions, instructions, and warrants, authorizing land sales, and receiving petitions, in addition to negotiating with the Assembly on the new constitution and property settlement. At the same time, he chartered a Quaker public school and corporate governments for the city of Philadelphia and the borough of Chester (*Micro.* 9:703, 682, 852). In an attempt to raise much-needed cash, WP also revived the Susquehanna land sale scheme of 1696 (see *PWP,* 3:671-78), collecting new subscriptions and issuing a set of concessions to purchasers (*Micro.* 9:672); this plan was ultimately dropped in 1707 (see doc. 35, n. 22). Just before sailing WP executed a new will (doc. 30) and drew up final instructions for Logan and the commissioners of property, urging them to be zealous in collecting and remitting all possible profits (docs. 32 and 33). Expedients that he would have avoided in better times, such as the selling off of rents and the reversions of bank lots, now seemed urgent. Logan and the commissioners drafted projections of WP's expected revenues (doc. 36), while Logan continued his work on collection of quitrents, and an inventory was drawn up of the goods WP had left behind (doc. 37). In December Logan had fairly high hopes for collection of proprietary income, but the taxes had still not materialized and interest in Susquehanna land was flagging — a foretaste of disappointments to come.

21
TO JAMES LOGAN

Pennsbr 8. 7br [September] 1701

James
The necessity of my goeing, makes it absolutely necessary for me to have a supply, & tho I think 1000l should be forth with raised by frds in a private way, at the least, to help me,[1] yet while land is high & valluable, I am willing to dispose of many good patches that else I should have Chosen to have kept, as every bodys mony. To sett abt

this I desire T. F & D. P.[2] to come to me come heither. I have opened my minde therein to them, and they have assured me that they will forthwith (a week now being more time to me than 6 ms an other Season) they will communicate to thee all they know & can remember, & endeavour to finde out wt Customers they can, & acquaint thee of the vallue, to sett the prises, in order to immediate Supplys. the present welch {from Eng.} are divers of them rich, & will want quantetys, & T. F. undertakes to accommodate them handsomly. loos not the opertunity. D. P. can goe among them to prevent others, & direct them ~~this way~~ {to thee}, for quantetys none else can {s}pa~~y~~{re} them. unless S. Carpenter[3] should sell his, (or part of his 5000 Ac[res)] wch I am apt to thin~~g~~k he will not do. This highly concerns me, wherefore loose no time. They tell me wt D. L.[4] has declared as to my powrs in proprietary matters, by wch I perceive tis publick. let him know my minde (occasionally) in company of S. C. &c: Now or never, & while he is {on the} draught of that ~~pl~~ scheam, follow thou my perticular affaires wth all possible Vigilancy, & expedition; tho how to return it {I know not,} unless in Bills upon Dollars sent to Maryland,[5] & that way I hope I may be helpt. If thou takest in Bror P-ton,[6] it may do well; but all under present secrecy, not to be known, least it stop others from a full & due provision. The Iron is now hot, therefore Strike. I fear as per myn by T. Eberden[7] {today,} too many or more than 2, goeing wth me, will augmt the Charge & so lessen my proportion of {Supply.} who can I take, that would goe, that may be ministerial[8] to me, Caleb,[9] if he could {write} ~~right~~, has the best drudgeing Sence, & would be observant. If some goe, they may, if not Governable by me, act secreetly to my Cloging, & in a way of distrust, wch would obstruct my treaty & negociation. This is a conjecture at large, I'le say no more {of this} now, only th~~i~~us, that those who would stay me for th~~y~~eir own ends may goe for them {too;} tho I have enough to[10] shame them there, and every where else. think of it sedately.

Thy amendments of the Bill of Property deliberate upon,[11] for that is a Cardinal point with me to be sure, and Nicholas Waln[12] and Anthony Morris[13] should be treated with upon that Head. Jos Growdon and J. Swift[14] who had the first choice and would not serve without J. Growdon but against them all, of 100 freeholders there was but 31 present, an ill precident for elections,[15] and which I could reject, for many here are troubled at it, and so declared themselves to me. I think to stay over their Court which will be next fourth day.[16] Poor Phineas[17] ~~was~~ {is} a dying man and was not there,[18] tho he crept, as I may say, to meeting yesterday, I am grieved at it, for he has not his fellow, and without him this is a poor County indeed.

I cannot prevail with my wife to stay, and less with Tishe;[19] I know not what to do; Samuel Carpenter seems to excuse her in it, whatever others do,[20] but to all that speak of it, say, I shall have no need to stay,[21] and a great Interest to return, all that I have to dispose of in this world is here for daughter and son, and all the issue which this wife is like to bring me, and that having no more gains by Government to trust to for Bread, I must come to sell, pay debts and live and lay up for this posterity: as well as that they may see, that my inclinations run strongly to a Country and Proprietary life, which then, I shall have time[22] to follow; together with her promise to return, whenever I am ready to return. I confess this is one of the greatest arguments for some Friends of note going with us: to bring us back again; else they can do but little there, and their expence may better help me.

We want a little good Madeira wine, and some of the last white wine, if thou canst hit upon it. I am troubled at Judge Guests heat, to S: C:,[23] in a Judge it is scandalous, try to Cool him. his being so indiscreet is his great fault. 5th or 6th day expect me. Methinks Capt Finney[24] might help us with english pay, and Thomas Fairman and Cousin Ashton[25] should try to get him to buy off some tracts or patches, and indeed it is his own Interest as well as my conveniency. I shall say no more only let it be a measure fixed that Proprietor and Freeholders can have but one Interest, and that Jealousies as in England, is injurious and not sense.[26] the Ass in the Fable, and the Dog likewise.[27] Vale

Wm Penn

my Leather Stockings are at Christophers,[28] or at T E.[29] or in the House. send them pray.

AL and transcript. Penn Papers, Letters of the Penn Family to James Logan. (*Micro.* 9:521.) The second half of this letter has been lost; the editors have supplied this part of the text from a manuscript copy by Deborah Norris Logan in Logan Papers, Selections from the Correspondence of the Honourable James Logan, HSP. Deborah Logan produced two variant transcripts; the editors have used her earlier version, which seems to contain fewer editorial emendations. Significant differences between the two are noted below.

1. Local Friends' meetings did subscribe to aid WP; see doc. 33, n. 5.

2. Thomas Fairman and David Powell (d. 1734), an immigrant from Wales, who was deputy surveyor of the province and had surveyed the Welsh Tract. Thomas Allen Glenn, *Welsh Founders of Pennsylvania* (Oxford, 1911), 1:202; *PMHB,* 26:42; Phila. Admins. Bk. B, p. 67.

3. Samuel Carpenter (1649-1714), a Quaker from Barbados, was the richest merchant and one of the largest landowners in Pennsylvania, as well as one of WP's most trusted associates and advisors. WP stayed at his "Slate Roof House" on Second St. in Philadelphia in 1699-1701. On WP's departure from Pennsylvania in 1701, he named Carpenter as one of the council of state to govern in the proprietor's absence. *PWP,* 2:542n.

4. David Lloyd was engaged in drawing up a statement of the colonists' claims on land matters, which was adopted by the Assembly and presented to WP on 20 Sept. See *Micro.* 9:536; docs. 22, 24; Edwin B. Bronner, "Penn's Charter of Property of 1701," *Pennsylvania History,* 24:267-92.

5. To avoid shipping proprietary revenues in specie or produce back to England, WP proposed to use bills of exchange based on the piece of eight, or dollar, which served as the commonest colonial currency. Maryland's regular tobacco trade with England gave it a well-established mercantile network for such transactions.

6. Edward Penington (1667-1702), WP's brother-in-law, served as surveyor general of Pennsylvania from 1698 to his death in 1702. *PWP,* 3:543n.

7. This letter has not been found. Thomas Everden, or Evernden (d. 1710), a Quaker shoemaker of Canterbury, had settled in Maryland by 1681 and there became a prominent Friend. He also held property in Philadelphia. Henry J. Cadbury, ed., "John Farmer's First American Journey, 1711-1714," *Proceedings of the American Antiquarian Society*, 53:84-85n.

8. Who would attend and act for. *OED*.

9. Caleb Pusey (1651-1726), a Quaker lastmaker and leading politician of Chester, had emigrated from Berkshire, Eng., as a First Purchaser in 1682. He managed WP's mills on Chester Creek. *PWP*, 3:325n.

10. From here the editors follow the transcript by Deborah Norris Logan.

11. In Nov. 1700 the Assembly had passed and WP approved a Bill of Property to regularize land titles in the colony. WP is now trying to line up support for revisions in this law. When the new Assembly met, it demanded that the Bill of Property of 1700 be inserted in the charter (doc. 22). *Votes and Proceedings*, 1:137-40; *Minutes of the Provincial Council*, 1:600, 623-24; *Statutes*, 2:118-23.

12. Nicholas Waln (c. 1650-1722), a Yorkshire Quaker, immigrated to Bucks Co. in 1682 and moved in 1696 to the Northern Liberties in Phila. Co., where he became a large landowner and frequent member of the Assembly. George E. McCracken, *The Welcome Claimants Proved, Disproved and Doubtful* (Baltimore, 1970), pp. 517-19; John W. Jordan, ed., *Colonial and Revolutionary Families of Pennsylvania* (New York, 1911), pp. 203-8; *PWP*, 2:532n.

13. Anthony Morris (1654-1721), a Philadelphia brewer and property owner, was active in Pennsylvania politics and served in the Assembly from 1698 to 1704. In 1703 he became mayor of Philadelphia and in later years traveled as a Quaker preacher. *PWP*, 3:506n.

14. John Swift (d. 1733), a First Purchaser from Southampton, Hants., was elected regularly to the Assembly for Bucks Co. 1689-1718 and for Philadelphia 1721-29, in addition to frequent service as a J.P. *PWP*, 2:654; *PA*, 2d ser., 9:720-23, 737-38, 762, 770-74; *PMHB*, 2:447n; Abstracts of Bucks Co. Wills, GSP.

15. In Bucks Co., the election return for members of the Assembly was dated 4 Sept. 1701 and named Joseph Growdon, John Swift, Joshua Hoopes, and William Paxson as members. *PMHB*, 18:27-28n.

16. Wednesday.

17. Phineas Pemberton (c. 1659-1702), a leading Quaker of Bucks Co. and a close associate of WP, served frequently in the Provincial Council and Assembly and was a member of the Council in 1701. *PA*, 2d ser., 9:643, 770-71; *PWP*, 3:40n; 247.

18. Deborah Logan's second transcript reads "at the Election" rather than "there."

19. Laetitia Penn, WP's daughter.

20. The second transcript omits the phrase, "whatever others do."

21. In England. WP wants Logan to spread the word that he is coming back to Pennsylvania, despite the fact that his wife and daughter are accompanying him to England.

22. The second transcript reads "be at liberty" rather than "have time."

23. The nature of Chief Justice Guest's dispute with Samuel Carpenter is unknown.

24. Capt. Samuel Finney (d. 1712), a wealthy Anglican merchant from Lancashire who held land in Phila. Co., was named to the council of state on WP's departure in 1701. He served regularly as a J.P. and was appointed a provincial justice in 1706. Phila. Will Bk. C, #239; *PA*, 2d ser., 9:719; 19:343; *Minutes of the Provincial Council*, 2:37, 159, 239.

25. Robert Assheton (1669-1727), a cousin of WP, was appointed as clerk of Philadelphia and prothonotary of Pennsylvania's Supreme Court in 1701; in 1711 he became a member of the Provincial Council. *PWP*, 3:624n.

26. The second transcript reads, "are injurious and unreasonable."

27. WP probably refers to two of Aesop's fables that rebuked envy. In the first an ass coveted the comforts of a petted dog and gained himself a beating by jumping into his master's lap. In the second a dog prevented cattle from eating the oats in their manger, not because he was able to eat the food himself, but only because he envied their enjoyment of it. R. T. Lenaghan, ed., *Caxton's Aesop* (Cambridge, Mass., 1967), pp. 85-86, 153-54.

28. Probably Christopher Blackburn (d. 1722), a Quaker tailor of Philadelphia with whom WP dealt. Phila. Will Bk. D, #256; Hinshaw, 2:338, 466; *Micro.* 9:870.

29. See n. 7, above.

22
FROM THE PENNSYLVANIA ASSEMBLY

[20 September 1701]

May it Please the Governour

Wee the Representatives of the Free Men of the Province & Territories, in Assembly mett having taken into Serious Consideracion some Articles concerning our Priviledges ~~In~~ and Property incited by an Address to this House from the Inhabitants of this place[1] and Encouraged by thy self, in Setting forth thy care of us, & promises of Complyence therewith[2] do humbly offer the Following heads for Confirmation, Requesting they may be Granted the People of the Province & Territories, & Ascertain'd to them in a Cha{r}ter

Imprimis[3] That in Case the Proprietor go for England, due care be Taken that he be represented here by persons of Integrity & Considerable known Estates, who may have full power and Authority not only to grant & Confirm Lands &c as Effectualy as if he were personaly present, but also to make Sattisfaction to those who have short; as well as receive what may be due from those who have too much over Measure according to former Agreemt

2dly That before the Proprietary go for England he grant us such an Instrument as may absolutely Secure & defend us in our Estates and properties from himself his Heirs and Assigns for Ever, or any Claiming under him, them or Any of them, as a~~s~~lso to clear all Indian Purchases, and others

3dly That whereas there hath been great delays in the Confirmacion of Land and Granting of Patents, due care may be taken {By} ~~with~~[?] the Proprietor that no such delays may be for the future, and that the Ten acres in the hundred may be allowed according to the Proprietors Engagements.[4]

4thly. That no Surveyor, Secratary, or any other officer under the Proprietary Presume to Exact or take any Fees but what was, is, or Shall be allowed by the Laws of this Province, under Severe Penalties[5]

5thly. That no person or persons shall or may at any time hereafter be Lyable to Answer any Complaint matter or thing whatsoever relating to Property before the Governour or his Councill, or in any other place but in the ordinary Courts of Justice[6]

6thly. {that} The Antient Records made before the Proprieto~~ry~~'s first arrival here be Lodged in such hands as the Assembly Shall judge to be most Safe

7thly That a Pattent Office and all actual Surveyors thereby Imployed may be moddeled according to the Law of Jamaica,[7] and Such Security taken as may render the Peoples Interest Safe

8thly That Whereas the Proprietor formerly gave the Purchasors an Expectacion of a certain Tract of Land which is since laid out, about two Miles long and a Mile broad, wher{e}on to build the Town of

Philadelphia, and that the same should be a Free ~~f~~ gift, which since has been Clogg'd with divers Rents and reservacions contrary to the first design and grant and to the disatisfaction of the Inhabitants, wee desire the Governour to take it into Consideracion, & make them easie therein[8]

9thly That the Land lying back of that part of the Town already built remain for Common & that no Leases be Granted for the future, to make Inclosures to the damage of the Publick, untill such time as the respective Owners shall be ready to build or Improve thereon; and that the Islands and Flatts nere the Town be left to {the} Inhabitants of this Town to gett their Winter Fodder

10thly That the Streets of the Town be Regulated & bounded: and that the Ends of the Streets on Dellaware and ~~Shy~~ Schuylkill be unLimitted & left free to be Extended on the River as the Inhabitants Shall see Meet, and that Publick Landing places at the Blue Anchor, and peny-Pott-house[9] be confirmed free to the Inhabitants of this Town, not infringing any Mans Property

11th. That the Justices may have the Licensing and Regulating Ordinarys, or Drinking Houses, as in England, And as by thy Letter dated the 5th 9ber 97 did order.[10]

12th That the Letters of Feoffment for the Soyl of the Three Lower Countys from the Duke of York be Recorded in the Territories[11]

13th That all the Lands in the said Countys that are not yet taken up may be disposed of at the old-Rent of a bushell of wheat a hundred[12]

14th That the thousand Acres of Land formerly promis'd by the Governour to the Town of New-Castle for Common be laid out and Pattented for that use[13]

15th That the Bank~~s~~-Lotts at New Castle be granted to those that have the Front-Lotts, to Low-water mark, or so far as they may Improve at a Bushell of Wheat a Lott

16th That all the Bay-Marshes be laid out for Common (Except Such as {are} already Granted)

17th That all Patents hereafter to be Granted to the Territories, be on the same Condicions as the Warrants or Grants were obtained[14]

18th That the Division Lines between the Countys of New-Castle and Chester, be ascertained allowing the bounds according to the Proprietors Letters-Pattent from the King[15]

19th That the ~~See~~ Twenty Second Article in the old Charter Concerning Fishing and Fowling be Confirm'd[16]

20th That the Inhabitants or Possesors of Land may have Liberty to purchase off their Quit-Rents as formerly promis'd[17]

21th That the Bill of Property pass'd at new Castle 1700.[18] Be inserted in the Charter with such Amendmts as shall be agreed on

Signed by order of the Assembly
Jos: Growdon Speaker

DS. Logan Papers, HSP. (*Micro.* 9:547.) Docketed: 2d F | The Assemblys Adress to the | proprietarie 1701 | presented 20 Sept 1701 | Saml Carpenters hand.

1. On 17 Sept. the Assembly had received a petition from the inhabitants of Philadelphia, drafted by David Lloyd, which set forth the articles adopted by the Assembly in doc. 22. *Micro.* 9:536.

2. WP had professed his readiness to comply with the Assembly's judgments on colonial privileges and property in his speech to the Assembly of 15 Sept. *Micro.* 9:527; *Minutes of the Provincial Council,* 2:35.

3. This and the succeeding numerical notations appear in the left-hand margin. The editors have moved them into the text.

4. In an attempt to correct accumulated errors in surveying, the Assembly in 1700 had passed a Bill of Property that empowered WP to order resurveys within two years. Landholders were to be allowed a surplus of 10 acres per 100: 4 percent for differences between surveys and 6 percent to compensate for roads and barrens. The Assembly wanted the extra 10 percent applied to all lands, whether or not a surplus appeared on resurvey, a demand WP rejected as unreasonable; see doc. 24. WP later offered 6 percent, but the Assembly deemed this insufficient, and the issue was left unresolved until 1712. Shepherd, p. 57; Thomas Sergeant, *View of the Land Laws of Pennsylvania* (Philadelphia, 1838), pp. 185-86; *Minutes of the Provincial Council,* 2:55-56.

5. For laws setting fees for provincial officers, see *Charter and Laws,* pp. 147-50, 188, 220.

6. Until 1701 the Provincial Council exercised extensive judicial powers, reviewing the actions of lower courts and reversing judgments it considered inequitable or improper. This article is designed to prevent such procedures; it became the sixth clause of the 1701 Charter of Privileges (doc. 28). WP accepted these restrictions unwillingly, as he believed himself entitled to settle proprietary land disputes himself or through prerogative courts—a claim which the colonial landowners would not accept. See doc. 24; Nash, *Quakers and Politics,* pp. 94-96, 216-17; Lawrence Lewis, Jr., "The Courts of Pennsylvania in the Seventeenth Century," *PMHB,* 5:141-90.

7. Jamaican land law assigned sworn surveyors for each area of the island, prescribed set fees, and provided for a centralized registry of titles and surveys. Colonists had long complained about the disarray of Pennsylvania's land administration, but no effective reforms were adopted until after 1732. C. A. Lindley, "Jamaica, 1660-1678" (Ph.D. diss., University of Pennsylvania, 1932), pp. 81, 221-22; *CSPC, 1669-1674,* pp. 266-68; Shepherd, pp. 27-30.

8. Inhabitants of Philadelphia had made a similar complaint in July 1684. See *PWP,* 2:569, 572, 574, 577n; Hannah Benner Roach, "The Planting of Philadelphia: A Seventeenth-Century Real Estate Development," *PMHB,* 92:188-89.

9. The Penny Pot House, at present Vine St., and Blue Anchor Tavern, at present Dock St., were Philadelphia's earliest public landing sites on the Delaware. WP agreed to allow public landings at the ends of streets in his reply, doc. 24. Watson, *Annals,* 1:153-55; Thomas A. Glenn, "The Blue Anchor Tavern," *PMHB,* 20:427-34.

10. This is an error for 5 Sept. 1697. WP's letter of that date, in response to reports of drunkenness and vice in Philadelphia, urged the Provincial Council to license tavern keepers more carefully. The Council in response decreed that only those recommended by the courts would be licensed, but reserved to the governor the actual issuing of licenses, a resolution to which WP held in his reply (doc. 24). *PWP,* 3:517-18; *Minutes of the Provincial Council,* 1:527.

11. For WP's deeds from the Duke of York for the Lower Counties, see *PWP,* 2:281-84; *Micro.* 3:571, 575, 576.

12. A bushel of wheat per 100 acres had been the standard quitrent under the duke of York's government in the Lower Counties. "Old renters," who had held their land before WP's grant, continued to pay this amount, but WP demanded 2 bushels per 100 acres from new renters. See *PWP,* 3:680; John A. Munroe, *Colonial Delaware: A History* (Millwood, N.Y., 1978), pp. 75, 93.

13. WP issued a warrant for the survey of this land on 31 Oct. 1701; see *New Castle Common* (Wilmington, Del., 1944).

14. Standard procedure for the conveyance of proprietary land to purchasers began with the issuance by WP or his officers of a warrant, an order authorizing the

grant of a certain amount of land and directing the surveyor general to establish its bounds. Upon completion of the survey and payment of the purchase price, a patent, which formalized the transfer of title, could be issued. The particular conditions referred to here are unclear, as WP noted in his reply; see doc. 24. Sergeant, *Land Laws of Pennsylvania,* pp. 36-37.

15. On 28 Oct. 1701 WP signed a warrant for the survey of this boundary line, which according to WP's charter was to lie on a 12-mile circle around the town of New Castle. *Micro.* 9:742; *PWP,* 2:64; Dudley Lunt, "The Bounds of Delaware," *Delaware History,* 2:23.

16. The 1683 Frame of Government allowed fishing and hunting on all unenclosed lands. Soderlund, *William Penn,* p. 271.

17. In 1681 WP had offered to accept a lump sum from purchasers in lieu of quitrents. In the changed conditions of 1701 he was unwilling to part with them. See *A Brief Account of the Province of Pennsylvania in America* (London, 1681); doc. 24.

18. This bill, passed 27 Nov. 1700 and intended to confirm and regularize property rights, is printed in *Statutes,* 2:118-123. For a summary of its provisions see Edwin B. Bronner, "Penn's Charter of Property of 1701," *Pennsylvania History* 24:270-71.

23
WARRANT TO SURVEY A TRACT FOR SERVANTS

[27 September 1701]

William Penn Absolute Proprietary & Governour in Chief of the Province of Pensilvania and Counties Annexed

These are to require thee forthwith to Survey or cause to be survey'd for head land[1] to be divided among such as came servants into this Province at the first Settlement thereof a Tract of Land of about ~~five~~ {Six} thousand Acres to be called Free Town[2] in any County of this Province where it has not been already Survey'd nor taken up nor is concealed nor seated by the Indians and make Returns thereof into my Secretaries Office. Given under my Hand and Seal at Philadelphia the 27th of the 7th Month 1701

Wm Penn

DS. Old Rights D-85/68. Division of Archives and Manuscripts, Pennsylvania Historical and Museum Commission, Harrisburg. (*Micro.* 9:558.) Addressed: To Edward Penington Surveyor General | of the Province of Pensilvania & Territories. Endorsed: Six thousand Acres | J Logan. Docketed: Warrant | For Head Land 6000 A | In this Province | Entered page 40 | 17th 7mo 1701.

1. WP had promised in *Some Account of the Province of Pennsylvania* (1681) that each indentured servant would be granted 50 acres of land (a "headright" or "headland") after his period of servitude was complete. This grant applied only to servants of First Purchasers.

2. This allotment of a separate township for servants seems not to have been pursued, though headland was frequently issued to individual former servants. Edmund Physick in the 1780s estimated that a total of 4571¾ acres had been granted to ex-servants of First Purchasers. Futhey and Cope, pp. 150, 154.

24
TO THE PENNSYLVANIA ASSEMBLY

[29 September 1701][1]

The Answer of the Proprietor & Govr to the addresse of the Assembly head by head

To yr first Proposall
I Shall appoint ~~Such~~[?] {those} In whom I can Confide whose powers Shall {be} Sufficient & publicke for the Security of all Concerned and I hope {they shall be} of honest Caracter {wth out Just Exception} to doe that which is Right betweene you & me

To yr Second head
much of It Is Included In my answer to the first however I am willing to Execute a publicke Instrumt or Charter to Secure you In yr Propertyes according to {~~yr~~ Purchase and} the Law of {Property made lately at ~~Ne~~} New Castle, excepting some Corrections or amendments therof absolutely Necessary[2] ~~according to purchase~~

To yr Third head
I know of no willfull delayes and Shall {use my Endeavors} [illegible deletion] prevent~~ion~~[?] {any} for {the} future and am very willing to allow the Ten acres {per Cent} for the Ends proposed by Law and not otherwise[3]

To yr 4th
I am willing that reasonable Fees {to Officers} shall be ascertained by Law or their Services left to {a} quantum meruit[4] For I hope you doe not thinke they should be maintained at my Charge

To the 5th
I know {of no} person {that} has been obliged to answer before the Govr & Counsill {In Such Cases} but I Conceive that {disputes about} unconfirmed Propertyes must lye before the Proprietary ~~but~~ {tho} not before his Councill as Judges

To the 6th
The records Concerne me as well as the people and are and Shall be In hands of {men of} good fame & to keepe them only dureing good behaviour but those of the County of Philadelphia that Chiefly Concerne the People are in Soe great dissorder by Rasures ~~and~~ blotts and Interlineations that you would doe well to use some method In time for their Rectification

To the 7th
If the Jamaica Law will Improve our Regulacion {as It does augment the Fees} I am Content that wee Coppy after It[5]

To the 8th
You are under a mistake In fact. I have tyed you to nothing ~~which you did Comply wth~~ {in ~~regulateing~~ the alotment of the Citty which the first purchasers then present} ~~& the greatest part therof In time of my absence~~ did not readily Seeme to Comply with and I am Sorry

to find their Names to Such an addresse as that presented to you, who have got Double Lotts by my {Re~~a~~plotment} ~~Reallotm^t^~~ of the Citty from 50 to 102 foot front lotts,[6] and If they ~~will refund~~ {are willing} to Refund the 52 foot, I shall as you desire be Easy ~~to you~~ In the quit Rents although this {matter} ~~onely &~~ Solely Referrs to the first Purchasers & to me as Proprietary.

To the 9th

You are under a great mistake to thinke that a fourth part of the Land laid out for a Citty belongs to any {body} ~~perticule~~ ~~persons whatsoever~~ {but my selfe, It} being reserved for Such as were not First purchasers who might want to build In future time, & when I reflect upon the great abuse done me In my absence by destroying of my Timber and wood and {how the Land is} ~~left to be~~ over Run wth brush ~~&~~ to the Injury & discredit of the Towne It is Small Encouragemt to grant yr Request ~~for Commonage~~, however, I am Content {that some land be layd out for the accommodation of the town, till inhabitants present to settle it,} ~~that a Common Shall be laid out for the Conveniency of the Towne~~ under the Regulations that Shall be thought most Conduceing to the End desired, about which I Shall Consult wth ~~the Chiefe~~ {those} persons ~~of the Towne~~ {cheifly} Concerned {therein}; & for the rest {of the 9th article about} ~~Concerning~~ the Islands I know not which you meane, nor one what Terms {desired} ~~when that Is distinguished I can give you a fuller answer although It looks very odd to make such free demands of that wh my property~~ {~~that is~~} ~~Independent~~ {~~of~~} ~~from~~ {~~from~~} ~~the Towne~~ It being an Independant property from the Towne & province

To the 10th about the Ends of Streets & other publick Landings of this Towne,—

I am willing to Grant the~~m~~ ~~when~~ {Ends of Streets where & when} Improved and the other according to yr Request

To the 11th

I am Content that no lycenses Shall be granted to any ordinary keepers but Such as the Justices Shall recommend nor Suffer them longer then the ma~~g~~jestrates find they behave well

~~As~~ To the 12th

~~I presume they were Recorded by~~

~~I have no Lettrs of Feofment~~

I doe not understand It. for I have no Letters of Feofment, but Deeds, ~~I Cannot but take notice~~ which were Recorded by Ephraim {harman}[7] at New Castle & by Jno West[8] to the best of {my} memory at New Yorke & Since Confirmed by the order of Councill for the line as well as otherwise[9]

To the 13th

I thinke this an unreasonable article, Either to Limit me In that which {is} my owne or to deprive me of the Beneffit of Raiseing In proportion to the advantage which time gives to other Mens Propertyes, &

the rather because ~~I am yet In disbursments of that In~~ {~~So much is d~~ [illegible deletion]} I am yet In Disburse for that long and Expensive Controversy with the Lord Baltamore {promised to be defrayd {~~by the publick~~} as appeares by the minutes of Coun^{ll} [10] by the publick as appears by the minutes of Councill} ~~yet that the Inhabitants thereof may see how willing I am to Improve those parts I am Contented, If they will Engauge to seat~~ {~~the same~~} [illegible deletion] ~~every 500 acres they have taken Up according to~~ [illegible deletion] ~~according to the Condicon there Land was taken Up~~ [illegible deletion]

To the 14th

I allow It, according to what I {lately} Exprest at New Castle, and It is not my Fault It has not been done Sooner

~~As~~ to the 15th

according to their owne proposalls at New Castle I Shall gratify their desire; {vizt that} the Same Revert~~ing~~ to me after a Certaine ~~number of years~~ {time} If not Improved

To the 16th

This I take for a high Imposition, however I am willing that they all lye In Common {and Free} untill {otherwise} disposed off, and shall grant the Same from time to time In reasonable Portions & upon Reasonable terms, {Especially to such as shall Engage to dreigne & Improve the same, always} haveing a Regard to back Inhabitants for their accommodacions ~~Excepting all Marshes~~ [illegible deletion] ~~or to be Surveyed for my owne~~ {~~owne~~} ~~use~~

To the 17th

I Cannot {well} understand It therfore ~~to~~ {it must} be Explained

To the 18th

It is my owne Inclination, & I ~~Should be glad if the~~ {desire} the Representatives of New Castle & Chester {forthwith or} before they leave the Towne ~~would advise wth~~ {to attend} me about the time and Method of Doeing it.

To the 19th

They Shall have Liberty to Fish Fowle & hunt upon their owne Land and on all other Lands {that are myn,} untaken up.

To the 20th

If it Should be my lott to loose a publick Support I must [illegible deletion] depend upon my Rents for a Supply. [illegible deletion] & therfore must not {easily} part wth them {[illegible deletion]} & many years are Elapsed since I made that offer, that was not accepted.

To the 21st

I agree that the Law of Property {made at New Castle} Shall be Inserted In the Charter [illegible deletion] {wth Requisite} amendments.

Df, with some of the corrections in WP's hand. Logan Papers, HSP. (*Micro.* 9:560.) Docketed: Prop^{rs}[?] Answers to the Assembly's | Address 8^{br} 1701 in S Carpenters hand.

1. Having received the Assembly's address (doc. 22) on 20 Sept., WP drafted his reply. The finished document, incorporating the corrections shown on this draft, was presented to the Assembly on 29 Sept. *Minutes of the Provincial Council,* 2:40-43. The Assembly's rejoinder of 30 Sept., with WP's further comments, appears in ibid., pp. 44-45.

2. On the Charter of Property, signed 31 Oct. 1701 but never sealed, see the headnote to doc. 31; for the property law passed at New Castle in 1700, see *Statutes,* 2:118-23. WP in doc. 24 agrees to incorporate the law of 1700 into the Charter of Property, but the incomplete surviving text of the charter does not reveal what amendments it made to the 1700 law. See Edwin B. Bronner, "Penn's Charter of Property of 1701," *Pennsylvania History,* 24:267-92.

3. See doc. 22, n. 4.

4. In law, the amount reasonably deserved by a person hired without a formal contract. *Black's's Law Dictionary.*

5. See doc. 22, n. 7.

6. On arriving in Pennsylvania in 1682, WP had revised the distribution of Philadelphia lots, placing non-immigrant purchasers on land along the Schuylkill to promote prompt development of the city along the Delaware. This enlarged the lots on the Delaware side, so that those on Front Street measured 102 feet. Few signers of the 17 Sept. petition from Philadelphians held such choice parcels, which were allotted only to large purchasers; most of the signers were not among the First Purchasers of Pennsylvania land, to whom WP originally granted city lots. Hannah Benner Roach, "The Planting of Philadelphia: A Seventeenth-Century Real Estate Development," *PMHB* 92:29-38; Gary B. Nash, "City Planning and Political Tensions in the Seventeenth Century: The Case of Philadelphia," *Proceedings of the American Philosophical Society,* 112:54-73; *Micro.* 9:536.

7. In 1682 Ephraim Herrman or Harman (1652-1689), attorney, was clerk of the courts of New Castle and Upland, and held several other offices in the Lower Counties as well. The duke of York's deeds appointed Herrman and John Moll as his agents in effecting the transfer of the Lower Counties to WP. See *PWP,* 2:281-84, 305-8.

8. John West (d. c. 1693), a merchant who had accompanied Sir Edmund Andros to New York in 1678, served as secretary of the province 1680-83, in addition to his offices as clerk of the Court of Assizes (1680-83) and the City of New York (1680-87). *New York Col. Docs.,* 3:657n; *Collections of the New-York Historical Society* (New York, 1892), 1:235.

9. See *PWP,* 3:68-70.

10. The Provincial Council had resolved on 28 July 1684 that WP's expenses in connection with this dispute should be borne by the public. A portion of the £500 "freewill offering" that the colonists promised WP in lieu of customs was designated for the purpose, but this sum proved uncollectable. *Minutes of the Provincial Council,* 1:117-18; Nash, *Quakers and Politics,* pp. 83, 99-100; *PWP,* 3:171n.

25
FROM THE SUSQUEHANNOCK AND SHAWNEE INDIANS

[c. 7 October 1701][1]

We the Kings and Sachems of the Ancient Nations of the Sasquehannah and Shavanah[2] Indians; understanding that our Loving and good Friend and Brother William Penn is to our great Grief and the trouble of all the Indians of these parts obliged to goe back for England to speak with the great King and his Sachems about his Government can doe no less than acknowledge that he has been not only alwayes just but very kind to us as well as our ancient Kings and Sachems deceased, & careful to keep a good Correspondence with us, not suffering us to receive any Wrong from any of the People under his Government

Giving, us as is well known, his House for our Home at all times and freely entertaining us at his own Cost and often filling us with many presents of necessary Goods for our Cloathing, & other Accommodations, besides what he has paid us for our Lands, which no Governour ever did before him, and we hope and desire that the great King of the English will be good and kind to him and his Children, and grant that they may alwayes Govern these parts,[3] and then we shall have Confidence, That we and our Children and People will be well used and be encouraged to continue to live among the Christians according to the Agreement that he and We have solemnly made[4] for us and our Posterity as long as the Sun and the Moon shall endure, One head, One Mouth, and one Heart. We could say much more of his good Council and Instructions, which he has often given us and our People to live a Sober and Virtuous Life as the best Way to please the great God and be happy here and for ever But lett this Suffice to the great King and his wise Sachems in love to our good Friend and Brother William Penn.

Connodaghtoh ⊗ his Mark
Wopechthah ⊗
Orettyagh ⊗ their Marks
Tegoamaghsaw ⊗
Shouwydaghow ⊗ Harry
Moyonthguagh ⊗[5]

DS in the hand of James Logan. Penn-Forbes Collection, HSP. (*Micro.* 9:587.) Endorsed: Deliverd to the Governer in | Presence of us Witneses | Edwd: Shippen | Caleb pusey | Antho: Morris | Joseph Kirkbride[6] | Samuel Darke.[7] Docketed: The Indian | Kings address | to the King | and Parliam[t].

1. On 7 Oct. 1701 a number of Susquehannock and Shawnee chiefs appeared before the Provincial Council to take leave of WP. Orettyagh, Edward Shippen, and Caleb Pusey, among others, were present at that meeting, but the Council minutes do not mention this address. It was probably presented to WP at Philadelphia about this date, or possibly at Pennsbury, where another farewell meeting with the Indians took place in the autumn of 1701. *Minutes of the Provincial Council*, 2:45-46; John Richardson, *An Account of the Life of . . . John Richardson* (Philadelphia, 1880), pp. 132-36.

2. Shawnee.

3. There is no evidence that WP actually submitted this address to the English authorities, but he apparently hoped that it would help buttress his defense of Pennsylvania's proprietary government. In a letter of Apr. 1702 to the Board of Trade, WP noted that his colony had escaped Indian attacks for 20 years, asserting that this was "because we have not only been Just but very Kind to them, as I am ready to make appear from their own Testimonials." *Micro.* 10:112; also printed in *CSPC, 1702*, p. 282.

4. See doc. 11.

5. Connoodaghtoh, Wopechthah (Wopaththa), Orettyagh, and Shouwydaghow (Showydoohungh), or Harry, had all signed the treaty of 23 Apr. 1701 with WP (doc. 11). Tegoamaghsaw may have been the Conoy chief "Takyewsan" who signed the treaty. Possibly Moyonthguagh was the Methawennah who was a chief of the Shawnees above Conestoga in 1718. Charles A. Hanna, *The Wilderness Trail* (New York, 1911), 1:153. The Indians' marks are distinctive drawings, generally representing animals, except for that of Shouwydaghow, or Harry, who drew a large H.

6. Joseph Kirkbride (1662-1738), a prominent Quaker landowner of Bucks Co. and an active member of Falls Monthly Meeting, sat in the Assembly in 1698 and often

after 1712, in addition to serving frequently as justice of the peace from 1708 to 1726. Hinshaw, 2:962; *PA*, 2d ser., 9:762-64, 771, 773-77; Wilfred Jordan, ed., *Colonial and Revolutionary Families of Pennsylvania* (New York, 1948), 11:89-90.

7. Samuel Darke (d. 1723), a Quaker of Bucks Co. and a member of Falls Meeting, had emigrated from London in 1680. He served in the Assembly several times between 1682 and 1709, though he was not a member in 1701. Abstracts of Bucks Co. Wills, GSP, 1:30; *PA*, 2d ser., 9:769, 771-72; *PMHB*, 9:228.

26
CERTIFICATE OF REMOVAL FROM FALLS MEETING

[c. 8 October 1701][1]

To the monthly & Quarterly Meetings of friends {or other meetings whom it may Concern} in England or Elce where where this may Come

Deare friends

In the Covenant of Light life & Love whereby we are made neare & deare to one another So that we are therein as epistles writ upon one anothers hearts not to be forgotten wherein we do often remember you and ~~th~~at this time dearly Salute you

Hereby signifying to you that these Comes by our deare friend and Governor Wm Penn who whilest here was a member of our monthly meeting and therefore layd before us his occations to draw him away from us to England as also {of} friends in London pressing the necessity of his returning thither which hath given us occation of {Sorrow &} heavy{nes} ~~heartednes~~ but must sumit to the Lords ~~ord~~ will therein it being his Lot to Contend with Evil Spirits

And altho we know that a Certificate from us Cannot add to the knowledg you have of him in a more Spiritual relation then by these Lines we Can demonstrate yet he being willing in Complyance with the good order used amongst us to accept of one from us we think it our duty to Certefye Concerning him according to that Sence & experience the Lord hath given us of him dureing this his short Stay amongst us

His testemony hath been in the power & authority of truth from time to time and at all times when amongst us {hath laboured} to invite and perswade ~~friends~~ {us} to live the life of true religion and keep in the power thereof by an humble & close walking with the Lord and to beware of Looseing ~~of~~ our selves in the world & Cares thereof lest deadnes & drynes enter & only a form of religion remaine; his Conversation ~~&~~ deportment {& exemplary life} well agreeing with his Doctrine to the Comfort & edification of the honest hearted wch will remaine {& dwell} ~~amongst~~ {upon the ~~hearts of~~ spirits of} such as a good savor when he is farr {away} from us

And notwithstanding as our Governor he might {have} Claimed an authority beyond what he hath taken upon {him} with{out} any Just reflection yet he hath Chosen rather to rule as an elder not with rigour but in much love & brotherly kindnes being to the praise & comfort of those that do well but Sharp ~~to execute Justice~~ upon transgressors & Evilldoers

His ~~exercizes &~~ tryals {& exercizes} by false friends as well {as} open enemies have not been a few Considering the time he hath been here yet he hath been born over them with a steady mind knowing that its for the truths sake & its followers that such things happen to him other wise generaly loved & esteemed of most {for some of us have heard that} Some of his Cheifest opposits have~~ing~~ Said {he is too good a man to be a governor & others of them} they wold never desire a better Governor were he not a Quaker ~~therefore~~ its wherefore {not him but}[2] the Truth they ~~feight with~~ strive agt {and therefore the Controversie not meerly his own for its very evident to us there is a spt of Emnity {greatly strives} ~~Labours~~ here as well as with you to bring these American Churches into a suffering state of wch when you~~r~~ {are} made sensible we have hope that you will {not} stand unconcerned but assist him as much as in you lyes the which we shall be always ready to acknowledg as ~~an~~ acts of brotherly kindnes}[3]
And we earnestly desire that when he finds freedome in himself for his return to us againe you may not too much Consult your own and the truths intrest by reason of his services there and therefore use meanes to prevent him in his intentions but as you love and tender our well being forward him what in you ~~lyes~~ {can} to us againe remembering this province is of his begetting and that we the people thereof in a great degree through him were begotten to so great an under takeing as we have laboured under & under gone for want of his being more amongst {us} And that we may justly Claime his fatherly Care over us for our further and more Comfortable settlement in divers respects much whereof remaines yet to be done, Well knowing that his present and future peace and our satisfaction and Comfortable being is much Concerned therein

And {further} we ~~likewise~~ Certefie Concerning his deare wife and our ~~deare~~ {right ~~& much~~ esteemed} friend H P[4] {that} her {Conversation &} deportment amongst us hath been very discreet Shewing her self to be a Composition of tendernes & love nearenes and sweetnes in temper as well as {her being} well seasoned with the truth that thereby shee hath gained much love and esteeme amongst ~~the faithfull~~ {us} and that we are already {very} sensible ~~that~~ her absence will be ~~to us a~~ {our} Considerable loss ~~and emptynes~~ {Thus ~~in the renewednes of sincere love with hearty~~ with harty desires & supplications to the Lord that he wold be the safe Conductor and preservor of him and ~~all~~ his {in all his tryalls & exercizes whether by sea or by Land & in the renewednes of our sincere Love} ~~every way~~ we remaine your friends & bretheren in the {Truth} ~~fellowship of the Gospell of our Lord Jesus Christ who~~ [illegible deletion] ~~worthy of~~ [illegible deletion]

~~& praise~~[5]} ~~Thus in the renewednes of sincere love with harty desires & supplications for theire and all~~ [illegible deletion] ~~his~~ {~~that the~~ [illegible deletion] ~~Lord the will be his they~~[?]} ~~safe Conductor & preservor~~ {~~of him & all his every~~} ~~ways every way we remaine your friends & bretheren in the fellowship of the Gospell~~ from our monthly meeting neare the Falls of Delaware in the County of Bucks and Province of Pensylvania the [blank] day of the 8th month 1701
~~Signed by~~

Df. Quaker Scrap Book, Cox-Parrish-Wharton Papers, HSP. (*Micro.* 9:580.) Docketed: Rough draught of a | Certificate for W.P. | 8 mo 1701.

1. On 1 Oct. 1701 the Falls Men's Meeting directed Phineas Pemberton, Joseph Kirkbride, Richard Hough, and Samuel Darke to draw up a certificate for WP in anticipation of his departure for England. The certificate was read and approved at a meeting held on 8 Oct. Falls Monthly Meeting, Bucks Co., Minutes, 1683-1730, HSP, pp. 126-27.
2. In the manuscript this phrase is mistakenly inserted after "the Truth they."
3. The last lines of this page, from "and therefore" to "brotherly kindnes," are inserted sideways in the margin.
4. Hannah Penn.
5. This passage of five lines, beginning with "Thus," is inserted at the bottom of the page.

27
FROM ASSEMBLYMEN OF THE LOWER COUNTIES

[14 October 1701]

Reason's delivered to the Gouvournour from the members of the lower Counties against passing the Act of the Confirmacon of laws.[1]
Thatt the laws made att New Castle being ownd on both sides to be good in themselves must suppose some reason to re'enact or confirm them

butt the reasons menconed in a Certaine Petition[2] brought In by the Justices & officers of the Court of Phyladelpa have not Strenth, they haveing convicted none of Disafection to the laws past att New Castle nor performed the executione part of the law wch {in thatt case} was their Duty

In the bill brought Into the house from the Gouvournour noe reason Is aledged for the Confirmacion of laws butt this (Thatt {it} Is usuall & Customary.) butt the laws soe confirmed were only temporary, and a nessesity in those cases were the reason, wch cannot hold in this & wee know ~~noe~~ [illegible deletion] ~~Assembl~~ It becomes noe assembly to enact or confirm laws without reason

Further the consequence will be fatall to the lower counties For theire representitives cannot make laws in the territories butt must come Into the Province to make laws, wch must effect the Territories wch wee thinke very unreasonable

Further by the late Act of Union[3] the lower Counties were to have equall Priviledges in all things relateing to the Gouvourment with the upper, butt to say or own the laws past att New Castle want confirmacon here Is to discouridg New Castle to be the Seat of Assembly hereafter. and to humour some persons butt supposed to be Disafected wee shall Incur the Clamour of many hundreds in our own counties

lastly If the laws made att New Castle be not binding wee cannot conceive that their being confirmed here with the lower Counties in conjunction with the upper will add any force or strenth to them. unles they please to shew us what power they have more to make laws with us in the province then wee have to make laws wth them in the territories

Signed by us the Members of Assembly for the Lower Countys Att Philadelphia the 14th of october 1701[4]

John Brinckloe[5]
William Rodeney ~~Jr~~[6]
John Walker[7]
William Morton[8]
Luke Wattson Junr[9]
Jasper Yeates[10]
Richd Halliwell[11]
Adam pietersen[12]
John Donaldson[13]

DS. Miscellaneous Papers, Three Lower Counties, HSP. (*Micro.* 9:608.) Docketed: reasons given by the | members of the lower | counties in assembly | against the Act of | Confirmacon of | Laws | october 14 1701.

1. On 9 Oct. 1701 the Council had sent to the Assembly a bill to confirm the laws passed at New Castle in 1700, on the grounds that the Phila. Co. officials were unable to collect the £2000 levied at New Castle for the proprietor's use unless this tax was validated by the present Assembly. See the headnote to doc. 21; *Minutes of the Provincial Council,* 2:47.

2. This petition had asserted that Pennsylvanians objected to taxes imposed by the New Castle Assembly of 1700 because they were passed outside Pennsylvania's boundaries. *Minutes of the Provincial Council,* 2:47.

3. For the Act of Union that joined Pennsylvania and the Lower Counties, passed 7 Dec. 1682, see *Charter and Laws,* p. 104.

4. The signatories include all the assemblymen from New Castle and Kent Cos., but only Luke Watson for Sussex. The other Sussex members were William Clarke, a close adherent of WP; Joseph Booth, who missed the session because of illness; and Samuel Preston. *Votes and Proceedings,* 1:142.

5. John Brinkloe (d. c. 1721), of Dover Hundred, had served as clerk of the Kent Co. court, sheriff, and justice of the peace. In 1715 he was appointed associate justice of the Supreme Court. *PWP,* 2:554n.

6. William Rodney, or Rodeney (1652-1708), a Kent Co. attorney, had been a provincial councilor and register of the vice-admiralty court in addition to holding local offices. In 1704 he is reported to have been speaker of the first Delaware legislature. *PWP,* 3:574n.

7. John Walker (d. c. 1708?) served regularly as a justice of the peace for Kent Co. Leon de Valinger, Jr., comp., *Calendar of Kent County Delaware Probate Records, 1680-1800* (Dover, Del., 1944), pp. 28, 30; *PA,* 2d ser., 9:673.

8. William Morton (d. 1704), of Kent Co., sat in the Assembly for several terms from 1695 to 1701. De Valinger, *Kent Probate Records,* p. 26; de Valinger, ed., *Court Records of Kent County, Delaware, 1680-1705* (Washington, D.C., 1959), p. 316; *PA,* 2d ser., 9:679.

9. Luke Watson, Jr. (d. c. 1708), a landowner of Sussex Co., had served several terms in the Assembly since 1689 and in 1702 became a justice of the peace. De Valinger, comp., *Calendar of Sussex County Delaware Probate Records, 1680-1800* (Dover, Del., 1964), p. 22; *PA*, 2d ser., 9:683, 686-87.

10. Jasper Yeates (d. 1720), a wealthy merchant with property in New Castle and Chester Cos., served in both Provincial Council and Assembly and in 1701 was made a burgess of Chester; he sat as a provincial justice 1705-11. A staunch Anglican, he was active in attempts to separate the Lower Counties from Pennsylvania's Quaker government. Gregory B. Keen, "The Descendants of Jöran Kyn, the Founder of Upland," *PMHB*, 3:206-16.

11. Richard Halliwell (d. 1719), a leading New Castle merchant, served regularly in the Assembly and Provincial Council. Like Yeates, he was a leader among Lower Counties separatists. *PWP*, 3:302n, 492n; *PMHB*, 3:212.

12. Adam Pietersen, or Peterson (d. c. 1703), an Anglican of New Castle Co., sat frequently in the Assembly from 1696 to 1701. Phila. Will Bk. B, #105; *PA*, 2d ser., 9:671.

13. John Donaldson (d. 1702), a merchant of New Castle, had served three previous terms in the Assembly, beginning in 1690. *PA*, 2d ser., 9:670; *PWP*, 3:492n.

28
THE CHARTER OF PRIVILEGES

It was almost twenty years since WP had hammered out Pennsylvania's first Frame of Government, a document that was quickly revised to suit colonial conditions. The revised Frame of 1683 governed the colony for nine years, but many colonists were restive under the limitations placed on the Assembly and had gradually been advancing its powers. Under the two-year tenure of Benjamin Fletcher as royal governor, the 1683 Frame was set aside, and, though WP expected it to go back into effect on the restoration of his government in 1694, those dissatisfied with the Frame took advantage of the hiatus to question its legal status. In 1696 the Assembly induced Governor Markham to accept a new Frame that greatly expanded its powers, but this constitution never received WP's authorization. The proprietor's return to the colony in 1699 raised the constitutional question anew, but the Assembly of 1700 was unable to arrive at a settlement. By the fall of 1701 there was no longer any time for quibbling, and WP acceded to claims that he had long resisted. The Charter of Privileges signed on 28 October 1701 (doc. 28) gave official recognition to the powers that the Assembly had been accumulating over the years, and went further by completely eliminating the legislative role of the Provincial Council. The Assembly, now a unicameral legislature, would draft legislation, sit on its own adjournments, judge the qualifications of its members, choose its speaker and other officers, and exercise "all other Powers and Priviledges of an Assembly according to the Rights of the Freeborne Subjects of England and as is usuall in any of the Kings Plantations in America." In fact the Pennsylvania Assembly, in becoming the colony's sole legislative body, was claiming more power than any other colonial assembly. The Provincial Council became an administrative body appointed by the governor (see doc. 29). WP was unhappy with such departures from the original constitution, and he later complained to Logan of the colonists' ingratitude: "I acquiesced, having first shewed my Dislike: as at their disliking the model of an Elected Council to prepare, & an Assembly to resolve. & 2. as throwing away the use of the ballat wch their Children, as I told them, will have perhaps cause sufficient to repent of their folly therein" (doc. 97). Conflicts over the powers granted in this charter were to vex proprietary relations with the Assembly until the Revolution. On Pennsylvania's earlier frames of government, see *PWP*, 2:137-238; 3:456-66; Soderlund, *William Penn*, pp. 265-73. On the Charter of Privileges, see Andrews, *Colonial Period*, 3:319-21; Nash, *Quakers and Politics*, pp. 231-32; Shepherd, pp. 292-96.

[28 October 1701]

William Penn Proprietary and Governour of the Province of Pennsilvania and Territories thereunto belonging To all to whom these presents shall come Sendeth Greeting **Whereas** King Charles the Second by his Letters Patents under the Great Seale of England beareing Date the fourth day of March in the Yeare one thousand Six hundred and Eighty[1] was Graciously pleased to Give and Grant unto me my heires and Assignes forever this Province of Pennsilvania with divers great powers and Jurisdictions for the well Governement thereof **And whereas** the King's dearest Brother James Duke of York and Albany &c by his Deeds of Feofment under his hand and Seale duely perfected beareing date the twenty fourth day of August one thousand Six hundred Eighty and two[2] Did Grant unto me my heires and Assignes All that Tract of Land now called the Territories of Pensilvania together with powers and Jurisdictions for the good Governement thereof **And whereas** for the Encouragement of all the Freemen and Planters that might be concerned in the said Province and Territories and for the good Governement thereof I the said William Penn in the yeare one thousand Six hundred Eighty and three for me my heires and Assignes Did Grant and Confirme unto all the Freemen Planters and Adventurers therein Divers Liberties Franchises and properties as by the said Grant Entituled the **Frame of the Government of the Province of Pensilvania and Territories thereunto belonging in America**[3] may Appeare which Charter or Frame being found in Some parts of it not soe Suitable to the present Circumstances of the Inhabitants was in the third Month in the yeare One thousand Seven hundred Delivered up to me by Six parts of Seaven of the Freemen of this Province and Territories in Generall Assembly mett[4] provision being made in the said Charter for that End and purpose **And whereas** I was then pleased to promise that I would restore the said Charter to them againe with necessary Alterations or in liew thereof Give them another better adapted to Answer the present Circumstances and Conditions of the said Inhabitants which they have now by theire Representatives in a Generall Assembly mett at Philadelphia requested me to Grant **Know ye** therefore that for the the further well being and good Governement of the said Province and Territories and in pursuance of the Rights and Powers before mencioned I the said **William Penn** doe Declare Grant and Confirme unto all the Freemen Planters and Adventurers and other Inhabitants in this Province and Territories these following Liberties Franchises and Priviledges soe far as in me lyeth to {be} held Enjoyed and kept by the Freemen Planters and Adventurers and other Inhabitants of and in the said Province and Territories thereunto Annexed for ever **first** Because noe people can be truly happy though under the Greatest Enjoyments of Civil Liberties if Abridged of the Freedom of theire Consciences as to theire Religious Profession and Worship. And Almighty God being the only Lord of Conscience Father of Lights and Spirits and the Author as well as Object of all divine knowledge Faith and Worship who only {[can]} Enlighten the mind and perswade and Convince the understandings of people **I doe hereby** Grant and Declare that noe person or persons Inhabiting in this Province or Territories who shall Confesse and Acknowledge one Almighty God the Creator upholder and Ruler of the world and professe him or themselves Obliged to live quietly under the Civill Governement shall be in any case molested or prejudiced in his or theire person or Estate because of his or theire Conscientious perswasion or practice nor be compelled to frequent or mentaine any Religious Worship place or Ministry contrary to his or theire mind or doe or Suffer any other act or thing contrary to theire Religious perswasion **And** that all persons who also professe to beleive in **Jesus Christ** the **Saviour** of the world shall be capable (notwithstanding theire other perswasions and practices in point of Conscience and Religion) to Serve this Governement in any capacity both Legislatively and Executively he or they Solemnly promiseing when lawfully required Allegiance to the King as Soveraigne and fidelity to the Proprietary and Governour And takeing the Attests as now Establisht by the law made at Newcastle in the yeare One thousand Seven hundred Intituled an Act directing the Attests of Severall Officers and Ministers as now amended and Confirmed this present Assembly[5] **Secondly** For the well Governeing of this Province and Territories there shall be an Assembly yearly Chosen by the Freemen thereof to Consist of foure persons out of each County of most note for Virtue wisdome and Ability (Or of a greater number at any time as the Governour and Assembly shall agree) upon the first day of October forever And shall Sitt on the Fourteenth day of the said Month in Philadelphia unless the Governour and Councell for the time being shall See cause to appoint another place within the said Province or Territories[6] Which Assembly shall have power to choose a Speaker and other theire Officers and shall be Judges of the Qualifications and Elections of theire owne Members Sitt upon theire owne Adjournments, Appoint Committees prepare Bills in or to pass into Laws Impeach Criminalls and Redress Greivances and shall have all other Powers and Priviledges of an Assembly according to the Rights of the Freeborne Subjects of England and as is usuall in any of the Kings Plantations in America[7] **And** if any County or Counties shall refuse or neglect to choose theire respective Representatives as aforesaid or if chosen doe not meet to Serve in Assembly those who are soe chosen and mett shall have the full power of an Assembly in as ample manner as if all the representatives had beene chosen and mett Provided they are not less then two thirds of the whole number that ought to meet **And** that the Qualifications of Electors and Elected and all other matters and things Relateing to Elections of Representatives to Serve in Assemblies though not herein perticulerly Exprest shall be and remaine as by a Law of this Government made at Newcastle in the Yeare One thousand [Seven] hundred Intituled **An act to ascertaine the number of members of assembly and to Regulate the elections**[8] **Thirdly** That the Freemen [in Ea]ch Respective County at the time and place of meeting for Electing [th]eire Representatives to serve in Assembly may as often as there shall be Occasion choose a Double number of persons to present to the Governour for Sheriffes and Coroners to Serve for three Yeares if they Soe long behave themselves well out of which respective Elections and Presentments the Governour shall nominate and Commissionate one for each of the said Officers the third day after Such Presentment or else the first named in Such Presentment for each Office as aforesaid shall Stand and Serve in that Office for the time before respectively Limitted[9] And in case of Death and Default Such Vacancies shall be Supplyed by the Governour to serve to the End of the said Terme **Provided** allwayes that if the said Freemen shall at any time neglect or decline to choose a person or persons for either or both the aforesaid Offices then and in Such case the persons that are or shall be in the respective Offices of Sheriffes or Coroner at the time of Election shall remaine therein untill they shall be removed by another Election as aforesaid **And** that the Justices of the respective Counties shall or may nominate and present to the Governour three persons to Serve for Clerke of the Peace for the said County when there is a vacancy, one of which the Governour shall Commissionate within Tenn dayes after Such Presentment or else the first Nominated shall Serve in the said Office dureing good behaviour **fourthly** That the Laws of this Government shall be in this Stile Viz^{t} "By the Governour with the Consent and Approbation of the Freemen in Generall Assembly mett"[10] And shall be after Confirmation by the Governour forthwith Recorded in the Rolls Office and kept at Philadelphia unless the Governour and Assembly shall Agree to appoint another place **fifthly** that all Criminalls shall have the same Priviledges of Wittnesses and Councill as theire Prosecutors **Sixthly** That noe person or persons shall or may at any time hereafter be obliged to answer any Complaint matter or thing whatsoever relateing to Property before the Governour and Councill or in any other place but in the Ordinary courts of Justice unless Appeales thereunto shall be hereafter by law appointed[11] **Seventhly** That noe person within this Governement shall be Licensed by the Governour to keep Ordinary Taverne or house of publick entertainment but Such who are first recommended to him under the hands of the Justices of the respective Counties Signed in open Court which Justices are and shall be hereby Impowred to Suppress and forbid any person keeping Such publick house as aforesaid upon theire Misbehaviour on such penalties as the law doth or shall Direct and to recommend others from time to time as they shall see occasion[12] **Eighthly** If any person through Temptation or Melancholly shall Destroy himselfe his Estate Reall and personall shall notwithstanding Descend to his wife and Children or Relations as if he had dyed a Naturall Death[13] And if any person shall be Destroyed or kill'd by casualty or Accident there shall be noe forfeiture to the Governour by reason thereof[14] **And** noe Act Law or Ordinance whatsoever shall at any time hereafter be made or done to Alter Change or Diminish the forme or Effect of this Charter or of any part or Clause therein Contrary to the True intent and meaning thereof without the Consent of the Governour for the [time being and] six parts of Seven of the Assembly [mett] **But** because the happiness of Mankind Depends So much upon the Enjoying of Libertie of theire Consciences as aforesaid I Doe hereby Solemnly Declare Promise and Grant for me my heires and Assignes that the first Article of this Charter Relateing to Liberty of Conscience and every part and Clause therein according to the True Intent and meaneing thereof shall be kept and remaine without any Alteration Inviolably for ever **And Lastly** I the said William Penn Proprietary and Governour of the Province of Pensilvania and Territories thereunto belonging for my Selfe my heires and Assignes Have Solemnly Declared Granted and Confirmed And doe hereby Solemnly Declare Grant and Confirme that neither I my heires or Assignes shall procure or doe any thing or things whereby the Liberties in this Charter contained and expressed nor any part thereof shall be Infringed or broken And if any thing shall be procured or done by any person or persons contrary to these presents it shall be held of noe force or Effect **In wittnes** whereof I the said **William Penn** at **Philadelphia** in **Pensilvania** have unto this present Charter of Liberties Sett my hand and Broad Seale this twenty Eighth day of October in the Yeare of our Lord one thousand Seven hundred and one being the thirteenth yeare of the Reigne of **King William** the Third over England Scotland France and Ireland &c And in the Twenty first Yeare of my Government. **And** notwithstanding the closure and Test of this present Charter as aforesaid I think fitt to add this following Provisoe thereunto as part of the same That is to say that notwithstanding any Clause or Clauses in the above mencioned Charter obligeing the Province and Territories to Joyne Togather in Legislation I am Content and doe hereby Declare That if the representatives of the Province and Territories shall not hereafter Agree to Joyne togather in Legislation and that the same shall be Signifyed to me or my Deputy In open Assembly or otherwise from under the hands and Seales of the Representatives (for the time being) of the Province or Territories or the Major part of either of them any time within three yeares from the Date hereof That in Such case the Inhabitants of each of the three Counties of this Province shall not have less then Eight persons to represent them in Assembly for the Province and the Inhabitants of the Towne of Philadelphia (when the said Towne is Incorporated)[15] Two persons to represent them in Assembly and the Inhabitants of each County in the Territories shall have as many persons to represent them in a Distinct Assembly for the Territories as shall be requested by them as aforesaid[16] Notwithstanding which Seperation of of the Province and Territories in Respect of Legislation I doe hereby promise Grant and Declare that the Inhabitants of both Province and Territories shall Seperately Injoy all other Liberties Priviledges and Benefitts granted Joyntly to them in this Charter Any law usage or Custome of this Governement heretofore made and Practised or any law made and Passed by this Generall Assembly to the contrary hereof Notwithstanding.

Wm Penn

Edwd: Shippen
Phineas Pemberton
Sam: Carpenter
Griffith Owen
Caleb Pusey
Tho: Story
} Prop^ry^ and Governours Council

DS. Miscellaneous Manuscripts Collection, APS. (*Micro.* 9:741.) Endorsed: This Charter of priviledges being Distinctly read in Assembly & the whole & Every | part thereof being Approved of and Agreed to by us. Wee do Thankfully receive the Same | from our proprietary & Governour At Philadelphia this Twenty Eighth day of October | 1701. Further endorsed: Signed on behalf and by order of the Assembly | per Jos: Growdon Speaker. Further endorsed: Recorded in the Rolls Office at Philadelphia | in Patent Book A. vol. 2. page. 125 to 129 | the 31st 8mo 1701. | By me Tho. Story Mr ibim.[17]

1. 1681. See *PWP*, 2:61-78.
2. See *PWP*, 2:281-84.
3. See Soderlund, *William Penn*, pp. 265-73.
4. For records of the inconclusive deliberations on a new charter in the Assembly of May 1700, see *Minutes of the Provincial Council*, 1:602-5, 611-14; *Votes and Proceedings*, 1:119-22. The 1683 Frame was formally delivered to WP for revision on 7 June 1700,

with the understanding that he would govern under his royal patent and the Act of Union in the mean time.

5. *Statutes*, 2:39-42. WP is here repeating the provision for religious liberty enacted by Pennsylvania's first Assembly in Dec. 1682; see *Charter and Laws*, pp. 107-8.

6. For earlier variations in the number of representatives elected to the Assembly, see *PWP*, 3:449n, 465n. The times of elections and sessions are here changed from spring (Mar. and May) to fall (Oct.).

7. The Assembly is here granted extensive legislative rights, far beyond the restricted powers devised by WP in 1682-83; see *PWP*, 2:217-18; 3:465-66; Soderlund, *William Penn*, pp. 268-69.

8. *Statutes*, 2:24-27.

9. The 1682 and 1683 Frames had made similar provisions for election of sheriffs and coroners, but for one-year terms. *PWP*, 2:218; Soderlund, p. 270.

10. This repeats the style of the 1696 Frame, which similarly omitted specific mention of the Provincial Council. See *PWP*, 3:466.

11. See doc. 22, n. 6; doc. 24.

12. WP had called for such oversight of public houses by justices in a letter of 1697; *PWP*, 3:518. See also *Charter and Laws*, pp. 286-87; *Statutes*, 2:93-94.

13. Under English law the estates of suicides were forfeit to the crown, a right that in Pennsylvania belonged to WP as proprietor. Blackstone, 4:190.

14. WP is here relinquishing his claim to deodands, chattels that had caused the death of a human being and were thus forfeit. *Black's Law Dictionary*.

15. WP's charter of incorporation for Philadelphia, dated 25 Oct. 1701, was signed on 28 Oct. together with the Charter of Privileges. *Micro*. 9:682; *Minutes of the Provincial Council*, 2:60-61.

16. WP added this clause as a reluctant concession to separatist sentiment in the Lower Counties, but it did not prevent the Lower Counties from repudiating this charter in 1702. After years of wrangling, the two assemblies for Pennsylvania and Delaware separated completely in 1704. See John A. Munroe, *Colonial Delaware: A History* (Millwood, N.Y., 1978), pp. 116-21.

17. That is, master of that place, the rolls office.

29
COMMISSION TO THE PROVINCIAL COUNCIL

[28 October 1701]

WILLIAM PENN True and Absolute Proprietary and Governour in Chief of the Province of Pensilvania & Territories thereunto belonging To all to whom these presents shall come Sendeth Greeting **Know Yee** that I have Nominated Appointed and ordained my Trusty and Wellbeloved Friends Edward Shippen[1] John Guest, Samuel Carpenter, William Clark,[2] Thomas Story,[3] Griffith Owen[4] Phineas Pemberton Samel Finney Caleb Pusey and John Blunston[5] to be my Council of State for the Governm^t of the said Province of Pensilvania & Counties annexed, of whom any Four shall be a Quorum to Consult and Assist with the best of their advice & Council mee or my Lieutenant or Deputy Governour for the time being in all publick affairs & matters relateing to the said Government & to the peace, Safety, & Wellbeing of the people thereof, and in the Absence of mee and my Lieutenant out of the said Province & Territories or upon my Lieuten^ts decease or other Incapacity, I do by these presents give and Grant to the said Edward Shippen, Jno Guest, Samuel Carpenter,

William Clark, Thomas Story, Griffith Owen Phineas Pemberton Samuel Finney Caleb Pusey and John Blunston, or any five of them, to Exercise all and singular the powers Jurisdictions and Authorities whatsoever to mee and my Heirs by vertue of the Royal Charter or Letters patent[6] of King Charles the second given and granted that are or shall be Necessary for the well Governing of the said Province & Territories and for the Administring Maintaining and Executeing of Justice, and provideing for the safety and wellbeing of the said people dureing such Absence, They and Each of them the said Edward Shippen, John Guest Samuel Carpenter William Clark Thomas Story Griffith Owen Phineas Pemberton Samuel Finney Caleb Pusey & John Blunston to Continue in place till my Further order shall be known. and I doe further hereby grant to my Lieut Governour for the time being full power and Authority upon the Decease or Removal of any of the said Council to Nominate & Appoint others to serve in their place and Stead, also to Add to the number of Council now appointed and to appoint a president of the sd Council when and so often as my said Lieutenant shall see cause, and in case he shall not appoint a President then the First named or the next to him shall and is hereby Impowered to take the Chair.

Given under my hand & Great seal of this province at Philadelphia the Twety Eighth of October in the Thirteenth year of the reign of King William the third over England &c & the One and Twentieth of my Government Annoque Domini 1701

Wm Penn

DS. Penn Papers, Rawle-Cadwalader Collection, HSP. (*Micro.* 9:747.) Endorsed: Recorded in the Rolls Office at Philadelphia | in Patent book A. vol. 2. page 154:155. this 11th | 9th mo. 1701. | By me Tho: Story Mr ibim[7] | Seal 6s0d | Record 3 2 | box 1 3 | 10 5.[8] Docketed: Commission for the Council.

1. Edward Shippen (1639-1712), originally of Yorkshire, had accumulated a fortune as a merchant in Boston and converted to Quakerism in 1671. In about 1694 New England's persecution led him to remove to Philadelphia, where he quickly rose to prominence, building a large mansion and becoming speaker of the Assembly in 1695. In 1701 WP appointed Shippen mayor of Philadelphia as well as a member of the Council of State and a commissioner of property. In 1702 he became president of the council, and in 1703-4 he served as acting governor after the death of Andrew Hamilton. *PWP,* 3:325n; *PMHB,* 1:212-13; *DAB;* Raimo, *Governors,* pp. 326-27.

2. William Clarke (d. 1705), a Quaker attorney and landowner of Sussex and Kent Cos., served almost continuously on the Provincial Council from 1689 until his death, in addition to holding local offices. *PWP,* 2:313n; 3:110n.

3. Thomas Story (c. 1670-1742), a Quaker minister and former attorney who held a family estate near Carlisle, Cumb., lived in Pennsylvania 1698-1714. He had met WP in 1693 and accompanied him on his travels to Ireland in 1698. In 1701 WP appointed him keeper of the seal, master of the rolls, and recorder of Philadelphia. Story wrote a number of books and an autobiographical journal. Peare, pp. 354, 366, 413-14; *PMHB,* 72:285-86; *PWP,* 2:663; 3:557n; Smith, 2:636-39.

4. Griffith Owen (1647-1718), a Quaker physician of Philadelphia and First Purchaser of 5000 acres, served several terms in the Assembly and was a member of the Council continuously from 1700 to 1716. *PWP,* 3:306n; *PWP,* 2:662.

5. John Blunston (d. 1723), a Quaker landowner and J.P. of Darby, Chester Co., served regularly in the Assembly from 1682 to 1701 and in the Provincial Council from 1700 to 1710. *PWP,* 2:314n.

6. See *PWP,* 2:61-78.

7. See doc. 28, n. 17.

8. These figures, arranged in columns, list the fees entailed in recording this document.

30
LAST WILL AND TESTAMENT

New castle on Delaware 30. 8^{br} [October] 1701

Because it is appointed for all men once to dye, and that their days are in the hand of the almighty, thi~~s~~eir Creator, I think fitt upon this present voyage to make my last will & Testiment, which is as follows.

Since my estate, both in England & Irland are either Entailed or incumbred, my will is that w^{t} is Saleable, be sould for payment of my Just debts, and all my houshould Stuff plate & linnen, not given or disposed of to my Children by their relations. and if there should be any overplus, that it goe equally between my son william & daughter Lætitia, as to my estate in Europe, be it Land houses or moveables, except my Gold Chain & meddall,[1] wch I give to my son william; & except such estate as I had with or since I married this wife.

For my estate in America, It is also incumbred, but not with the tenth part of the true vallue there of, I mean ~~in~~off the Province of Pennsylvania & Countys annexed, when that incumbrance is discharged, I give my son william, all my sayd Province & Territorys, to him & his Heirs forever, As Proprietary & $Gover^{r}$. But out of {or rather in} the ~~sayde~~ soyle {thereof} I give to my Daughter Lætitia Penn one hundred thousand acres, Seaventy {of w^{ch}} out of {or rather [in]} the sayd Province, and ten thousand acres out of {or rather in} each of the Lower Countys of the territorys. I also give to my son John one hundred & fifty thousand acres, of wch one hundred thousand in the Province, & fifty thousand acres in the Lower Countys, and I also bequeath to him my tenth, or Proprietaryship of salem tenth or County in west new Jersy to my sayd son John {& his heirs forever;} with all rents Proffits & Interests therein. ~~as also~~

I also will that the Childe my Dr. wife, Hannah Penn, now goes with,[2] shall have one hundred thousand acres, if a boy, & Seaventy thousand if a Girle, in the Province aforesd. all which Land so given, shall lye between Sasquehanagh River & Delaware River, and to be taken up within twelve months after my death, If my encumbrances can be discharged in that time, or so soon as they are; but So, as that the sayd Lands be not above 80 miles above a due west line to be drawn from Philadelphia to Sasquehanah River. and to be layd out in the way of town ships, and to pay to my son william one Silver shilling for every town ship, or five thousand acres, when taken up, forever, {in lieu of all demands & Services.} hereby requireing my sayd son william, to erect all or any part of the aforesayd Lands into Mannors, with due powrs over their own Tennants, according to my sayd Childrens respective agreem[ts] with them, when they or any for them re{quire the same.}

I also give to my Dr. wife, five thousand acres of land, as a token of my love, to be taken up as before exprest, & upon the same acknowledgem[t] & within the sayd limits in my Province of Pennsilvania, to her & {her} heirs {& assignes} forever; & so I understand in my other aforementioned graunts to my Children, viz that I give it to them & their Heirs & assignes forever.

I also leave my Dr. Sister & her Children[3] some token of my love, such as my wife shall think fit, in memoriall of me. also to her father & mother[4] the like.

I give to my serv[ts] John & Mary Sachell[5] ~~two~~[?] three hundred acres between them. To James Logan one thousand acres, & my blacks their freedom, as {is} under my hand already,[6] & to ould Sam[7] 100 acres, to be his Childrens after he & wife are dead, forever; on common rent of one bushel of wheat yearly forever. for performance of which, I desire my loveing friends Edward Shippin, Sam[ll] Carpenter, Edward Penington & James Logan, in america {or any three of them;} & Benjamin Cool Thomas Callowhill, Henry Goldny {& Jos. Pike}[8] in england {or any three of them,} to be my excece[ts] trustees & overseers or any three of them, to see this my last will observed, and that I have right done me about my incumbran[c]es, that my family suffer not by oppressive demands, but {to} get me & myn righted in law or Equity. and I do hereby charge all my Children, as their loveing dying fathers last command & desire, that they never goe to law, but if any difference should arise, w[ch] I would hope will not, that they be concluded by the Judgement of frds to be chosen by the meeting of sufferings of the people called Quakers in England, for English & Irish Concerns, & In america to the Frds ~~named~~ of the quarterly meeting at Philadelphia in Pennsilvania for a finall decision.

I do further ordain by this will, that what estate I here give to either or any of my Children be never alienated from my family, for want of Heirs of their own body, but that de[bts] being payd they may owe, the rest to be inherited by the next of blood of my Body and discent, & for want thereof to my Dr. sister & her Blood, in such manner as she shall appoint.

and now, If ever I have done am[iss] to any, I desire their forgiveness, & for all the good offices I have ever done I give God, that Enabled me, the honour & thanks and for all my enimys & their Evil reflections & reports, & endeavours to ruine me, in name & estate, I do say, the Lord forgive them, & amend them; for I have ever from a Child loved the best things & people, & have had a heart, I bless the name of allmighty god, to do good, without gain, yea some times for evill, & and to confirme my own, to serve others, wch has been my greatest burden & infirmity; haveing a minde not only Just but Kinde, even to a fault; for it has made me sometimes hardly so Just, by means of debts therby Contracted as my integrety would have made me. and now for all my good friends, that have loved & helped me, do so still, in my poor Children, w^{t} you can, & God allmighty be to you & yours an ample reward. You have my hearty & gratefull acknowledgements & commemoration, who never lived to my selfe from my very youth, but to you & the whole world in love & service.

This I ordain to be (& accordingly is) my last will & $testam^{t}$ revoaking all other. Given under my hand & seale, the day & year above written

Wm Penn

Sealed & delivered
in the presence of
$Rich^{d}$ Halliwell
Jos: Wood
Rob Assheton
James Logan

The interliniations
were my writeing
they are twelve in
Number, { the pages 7.}[9]

ADS. William Logan Fisher Collection, HSP. (*Micro.* 9:812.) WP's signature appears at the bottom of each of the seven pages.

1. WP had inherited these from his father, Sir William Penn, who had received them from the Commonwealth in 1653 as a reward for his naval service against the Dutch. *DAB; PWP*, 1:150.

2. Thomas Penn (d. 1775), born at Bristol 9 Mar. 1702, managed proprietary affairs in Pennsylvania from 1732 to 1741. He then returned to England and became the chief proprietor of Pennsylvania after the death of John Penn in 1746 (*DAB*); on his role in Pennsylvania politics, see Joseph E. Illick, *Colonial Pennsylvania: A History* (New York, 1976), pp. 160-204.

3. Margaret Lowther had two surviving children: Sir William (c. 1670-1705) had been knighted in 1697 and served as M.P. for Lancashire 1702-5; Margaret (1668-1719) married Benjamin Poole of London. *PWP*, 3:262n, 435n.

4. Thomas Callowhill (c. 1640-1712) and Hannah Hollister Callowhill (d. 1712), prominent Quakers of Bristol. See *PWP*, 2:122n; 3:413n.

5. Apparently a slip of the pen for John Sotcher (d. 1730), also called Sacher or Satcher, and Mary Lofty Sotcher, who were steward and housekeeper at Pennsbury. They were married in Oct. 1701 at Falls Meeting, and WP persuaded the meeting to hasten its approval so that the wedding could take place before he left for England. John, a Quaker tradesman from Arundel, Sus., may have met WP at a quarterly meeting at nearby Warminghurst in 1687. Mary, originally of Bristol, had been a servant of Hannah Penn's there. The Sotchers remained at Pennsbury at least until 1709. See doc. 160; Hinshaw, 2:1024; Falls Monthly Meeting, Bucks Co., Minutes, 1:125, GSP; ACM, vol. 63; *PWP*, 3:427n.

6. This is the only one of WP's extant wills that contains such a provision. Neither his will of 1705 (doc. 107) nor his last will of 1712 (doc. 193) repeated this resolution, and, though WP freed some slaves during his lifetime, others passed to his heirs at his death. Pennsylvania Quaker meetings had shown some uneasiness about slavery before 1700, but the Quakers did not officially oppose it until the late eighteenth century. Peare, p. 415; Janney, pp. 422-24. See also doc. 59; James Logan to Hannah Penn, 11 May 1721, Penn Papers, Official Correspondence, 1:97, HSP.

7. Probably the slave Sam who, according to a letter of James Logan to Hannah Penn in 1721, "died soon after your departure hence." Penn Papers, Official Correspondence, 1:97.

8. Benjamin Coole (d. 1717), a merchant of Bristol, was active in Quaker affairs during WP's residence there in the 1690s (*PWP*, 3:422n). Henry Gouldney (c. 1657-1725), a Quaker merchant of London and a First Purchaser, was a close associate and

supporter of WP (*PWP*, 3:277n). Joseph Pike (1658-1729), a wealthy merchant and zealous Quaker of Cork, had traveled and worked with WP on Quaker business. His father, Richard Pike, had died in prison after being arrested with WP in 1667, and WP had maintained close ties with the family. Joseph bought a substantial parcel of land in Pennsylvania, part of which later became Pikeland Township in Chester Co. Myers, *Immigration*, pp. 150-51; *PWP*, 1:105, 133n; 2:662; *PMHB*, 42:92.

9. Beneath this line a section of paper has been cut out; it probably contained WP's initials or signature.

31
DECLARATION ABOUT THE CHARTER OF PROPERTY

In the following declaration, WP comments on the Charter of Property, drawn up by David Lloyd and hastily signed by the proprietor on 28 October. This charter confirmed WP's previous statements on land policy and on the land law passed at New Castle in 1700, and it also laid out a new administrative system for dealing with proprietary affairs. An elected body called a "General Court" would head an administration for property parallel to that of the government, with power to establish courts. The charter would have granted a good deal of popular control over land administration and assigned some of the powers of the Assembly to the General Court, possibilities that WP was perhaps willing to contemplate in face of the threat to his proprietary government. But he left the charter unsealed, and it seems probable that he never actually intended it to go into effect. Certainly he had not had time to explore all the implications of the changes it proposed, and on arrival in England he quickly sent instructions not to seal it; see *Minutes of the Provincial Council*, 2:62. The *Minutes* dismissed the charter with a brief note, attributing it wholly to the influence of David Lloyd and his faction. For the text of the charter and a discussion of its provisions, see Edwin B. Bronner, "Penn's Charter of Property of 1701," *Pennsylvania History*, 24:267-92.

Newcastle 31 8br [October] 1701

Because my time has been very short & many matters of moment Crowding at once upon me, I have not been able to digest & throughly Consider the charter of Property[1] in all the branches of it, especially in point of Courts & powrs therein expressed,[2] I have thought fitt for a common safety, to forbear the compleat passing of the Same, 1st, till I see the state of affaires at home, 2ly, because the Lower Countys are not ~~excl~~ Included, & till they either are included, or have a charter for their propertys also, I cannot safely do it, 3ly I shall, in the compass of 6 months, order the passing of the sayd charter under the great seale, if god give me life, unless affaires at home require us to change measures for generall good.

4^{ly} I do hereby declare, / graunt & confirm, the first part relateing stricktly to titles of land, as amply to be of force as if I executed the same, & only decline that of powrs, from necessary Caution, for a Common safety.

wherefore I do hereby order that my Honored friend, Gover^{r} Hamilton[3] keep the sayd draught in his Custody, signed by me, unsealed, till he heares from me, & In case he hears not from me to the Contrary, or my heirs, in 6 months time that than he suffer it to pass under the seal & not otherwise:[4] hereby promessing to all concerned that that, or such an Instrum^{t} as that, in the substance thereof, ~~with the advice of~~ as Council Learned in the Law in Eng^{d} shall advice to be safe for me and the people to pass, shall be by me executed there or here for our mutuall further security. In testimony of which I do here unto sett my hand & {seale} this 31. 8^{br} 1701.

Wm Penn

I do also promess to the Lower Countys a Charter of Property sutable to our relation to one another, if they require It from me

Wm Penn

ALS. Penn Papers, Letters of the Penn Family to James Logan, HSP. (*Micro.* 9:827.) Docketed: Proprietors Declaration | about the Charter of Property at | Newcastle 31 8^{br} 1701.

1. This charter of property, which was drawn up by David Lloyd and signed by WP on 31 Oct. 1701, survives incompletely in two sections. For a composite edition of the document, see Bronner, "Penn's Charter of Property," pp. 274-92. A partial draft appears in *Micro.* 9:754.

2. The charter provided for the establishment of a new elective body called a general court, which in conjunction with WP's deputy and six assistants would erect courts and oversee the administration of justice. In particular, the general court would supervise many property issues — probate of wills, settlement of estates, lawsuits over land ownership — and thereby encroach upon WP's proprietary powers. See Bronner, "Penn's Charter of Property," pp. 272-74; Nash, *Quakers and Politics,* pp. 234-35.

3. WP had commissioned Andrew Hamilton as deputy governor on 27 Oct. 1701; *Micro.* 9:716.

4. After returning to England, WP rejected the charter; his orders not to seal it arrived in Apr. 1702. *Micro.* 10:033; doc. 39, n. 1; *Minutes of the Provincial Council,* 2:62.

32
TO THE COMMISSIONERS OF PROPERTY

[1 November 1701]

Instructions To my Commissioners of Property
to be observed by them in granting of Lotts and Lands
in my Province of Pensilvania & Counties Annexed

Whereas I William Penn Proprietary and Governour of the Province of Pensilvania and Counties Annexed have by my Commission under my Great Seal bearing date the twenty eighth day of October last[1] / constituted and Appointed You my Trusty Friends Edward Shippen

Griffith Owen Thomas Story and James Logan my Commissioners of Property for the Granting and Confirming of Lands and Lotts in the sd Province and Territories thereunto belonging to the Purchasers Renters and Inhabitants thereof, Know therefore that for your better Direction and Guidance in the Execution of the said Commission I have thought fitt to Injoyn the following Instructions for your Observation

First) You shall Grant unto all persons who have right to take up any Lands in the Said Province by Purchase, all their whole Rights, and in such parcels and quantities as they can most conveniently Settle, and according to the Method of Townships appointed[2]

Liberty Land and Lotts You shall grant to first Purchasers according to their respective Rights[3]

Overplus Lands You shall Grant to the possessors according as the Law directs,[4] unless the possessor shall ~~part~~ agree to part with his right to compensate the Deficiency of his neighbour

Concealed Lands[5] You shall dispose of for the Value thereof in such manner as will most accommodate the people reserving such Tracts as you shall think fitt to be applied to any particular Uses for the Benefit of my Family.

After the same Manner dispose of Marshes Meadows & Cripples[6] according to the Necessity and Want of the persons desirous to take them up, reserving sufficient for the Accommodation of future Settlers

And for the better Accommodation of such as are willing to seat themselves on small parcels of Land and near other Inhabitants I am willing and doe allow That you dispose of out of my Mannor of Springetts bury[7] near Philadelphia fifteen hundred or two thousand Acres of that part chiefly most remote from the town or as you shall think most Convenient reserving for my Demesne at least one thousand Acres adjoyning on Fairmount and the City, at least one moiety of what you so dispose of to be upon Lease for a number of Years, and some smaller part, if you see cause, in Fee.[8]

For the same reasons and after the same manner You may retrench my Mannor of Pensbury[9] to five thousand Acres but not under

Also out of my mannor of Gilberts[10] you may dispose of three thousand Acres

Out of my Mannor of Rocklands[11] five thousand Acres & no more

Out of my Mannor of Highlands[12] three thousand Acres & no more

Out of my Mannor of Springtown[13] four thousand Acres & no more

All wch Lands to be disposed of out of my Mannors as aforesd, You shall subject to such Services as are customary in the Mannors in England[14] or as you shall otherwise see cause

The Reversions of the Bank Lotts of Philadelphia from the front

Street two hundred and fifty foot {into the River} I doe allow you to sell off for twenty shillings per foot reserving alwayes the Ground Rent[15]

The Yearly Rents of a penny per Acre You may reduce to one bushel of wheat for Six pounds per hundred or to an English shilling after the rate of twenty Years purchase[16]

After the same rate you may sell off the old Rents in the Lower Counties reserving one English shilling per hundred Acres[17]

All which Said Instructions being by you observed, I doe & shall from time to time ratify avow Justify Warrant and maintain all your proceedings in pursuance of the s^{d} Commission according to the full & true Intent & meaning thereof In Witness whereof I have hereunto Sett my hand and caused the lesser Seal of my Province to be affixed on board the Ship Dolmahoy[18] in the River or Bay of Delaware the first day of the ninth Month in the Year one thousand Seven hundred and one

Wm Penn

DS. Logan-Fisher-Fox Collection, HSP. (*Micro.* 9:842.) Docketed: Proprietors Instructions | to his Commissioners of Property.

1. *Micro.* 9:751. WP calls these officials his "commissioners of property," though previously he had usually referred to them as "commissioners of propriety."

2. According to WP's plan as set forth in the "Conditions or Concessions" to the First Purchasers, groups of purchasers were to be settled in townships of 5000 to 10,000 acres. *PWP,* 2:98; Shepherd, p. 48.

3. First Purchasers were granted 2 percent of their acreage in the Liberty Lands bordering on Philadelphia, in addition to proportionate lots in the town itself. *PWP,* 2:99; Shepherd, pp. 20-21n.

4. The land law of 1700 empowered WP to order resurveys within two years. Any overplus, after allowing 4 percent for differences in surveys and 6 percent for roads, belonged to the proprietor, with the possessor to have first refusal at reasonable rates. *Statutes,* 2:120; see also *PWP,* 3:111n.

5. Tracts whose existence was concealed by discrepancies in surveys. Shepherd, p. 58n.

6. Dense thickets in swampy or low-lying ground. *OED.*

7. The manor of Springettsbury lay northwest of Philadelphia at Fairmount (*PWP,* 2:576n, 361n). For the sites of this and WP's other manors, see *PWP,* 3:643-56.

8. That is, as an outright sale. *Black's Law Dictionary.*

9. Pennsbury Manor, WP's country estate on the Delaware River in Bucks Co., had been found on resurvey in 1700 to contain about 6500 acres. *PWP,* 3:262n.

10. The manor of Gilberts, on the north bank of the Schuylkill at Perkiomen Creek, originally consisted of 10,000 acres. *PWP,* 2:483-84n.

11. Rockland Manor lay along the Delaware River above Brandywine Creek in New Castle Co.

12. Highlands Manor consisted of 10,000 acres on the Delaware River above Pennsbury in Bucks Co. *PWP,* 3:177-82.

13. The manor of Springtown or Springton, in Chester Co., lay along Brandywine Creek north of the present town of Brandywine Manor. Futhey and Cope, pp. 153-54.

14. No manorial services were actually attached to Pennsylvania land grants. Shepherd, pp. 46-47.

15. In agreeing to sell bank lots along the Delaware, contrary to his original plan of a common riverfront, WP had reserved to himself a reversion of one-third of the improved value as rent after 51 years. He was now selling off the reversions in an attempt to gain ready cash. See Watson, *Annals,* 1:166-69.

16. WP here offers his tenants the opportunity to reduce their annual rents by buying them off in advance. The standard rent of 1d per acre came to 8s 4d for 100 acres. For £6, or about 14½ years' rent, tenants could reduce this to a bushel of wheat, which in 1701 was probably selling for 5s to 6s (that is, about 3s 4d to 4s in English money, which was worth about 50 percent more than Pennsylvania currency). Twenty years' rent, or £8 6s 8d, would further reduce the annual charge to 1s, which was the amount paid as quitrent by First Purchasers. *Statutes,* 2:62; Sung Bok Kim, *Landlord and Tenant in Colonial New York* (Chapel Hill, 1978), p. 195; McCusker, *Money and Exchange,* p. 183; Soderlund, *William Penn,* p. 63; doc. 52, n. 11.

17. The "old rents" in the Lower Counties were set at a bushel of wheat per 100 acres; WP here offers to reduce this annual charge of 3-6s to 1s on payment of 20 years' rent, or 20 bushels.

18. On 14 Oct. 1701 WP had signed an agreement with Capt. John Fitch, master of the ship *Dolmahoy,* for passage to England. WP and his family occupied the whole "great Cabin" of the vessel, which was specially fitted out by carpenters for the governor's use. See *Micro.* 9:606; ACM, vol. 119.

33
TO JAMES LOGAN

[3 November 1701]

Instructions to James Logan my Receiver & Secretary

I have left thee in an uncommon Trust with a singular Dependance on thy Justice and Care, which I expect thou wilt faithfully employ in advancing my honest Interest

Use thy utmost Endeavours in the first place to receive all that is due to me. Gett in Quittrents, Sell Lands, according to my Instructions to my Commissioners[1] look carefully after all fines forfeitures Escheats[2] Deodands[3] and Strayes[4] that shall belong to me as Proprietor or Chief Governour. Gett in the Taxes and Friends Subscriptions[5] and use thy utmost Diligence in making Remittances to me with all my Effects by Bills of Exchange Tobacco or other Merchandise ~~and~~ or by any means that in the best of thy Judgement or the Advice of my Friends skill'd in those affairs may be to my advantage, not only directly to London but by the West Indies or by any other prudent method whatsoever, but take Advice especially of Edward Shippen and Samuel Carpenter and others best experienced in Trade.

Thou may continue in the House I lived in till the year is up.[6] Pay off all my Notes and Orders on thee, Settle my Accounts Discharge all my Debts honourably but carefully. Make Rent Rolls Draw up an Estimate of my Estate, and of what may be raised from it[7] which send over to me as speedily as possible, for it may be of great use to me, and in all things else shew thy Self a careful & diligent Agent to justify my Choice of thee for so great a Trust.

Gett my two Mills[8] finished, and make the most of them for my Profit, but lett not John Marsh[9] putt me to any great Expence

Cause all the Province and Territories to be Resurvey'd in the most frugal manner with the Assistance of my Brother in Law Edward

Penington within the two years limited by the Law if possible, tho that Law ought not to be a bar upon me against doing it at any other time.[10] Carry very fair with my said Brother in law and prevail with him to be as easie as possible in that great work. I have Spoke to him about it.

Thou must make good to Coll Hamilton {my} Deputy Governour Two hundred p^{ds} per Annum of your Money till such time as I procure an Approbation for him, and afterwards three hundred pounds

Also to John Moore as Attorney General thirty pounds a year so long as he shall Serve me faithfully, but he is too much in Quary's Interest.[11] When my Cousin Parmyter[12] comes he must have forty pounds, but I hope the Assembly will take these Charges off my hands Pray use all your Endeavours to obtain it.

Judge Guest expects a hundred a year from me I would give him fifty Make him as useful and easie as you can I hope Coll Hamilton to whom I have recommended him will prevail on him

Lett not my Cousin Durant[13] want but be sparing to her.

Write to me diligently advising me of every thing relating to my Interest and Send Affidavits about Quary John Corsoe[14] &c

Send all the Houshold Goods up to Pensbury unless thou inclines to keep sufficient furniture for a Chamber to thy self for which thou hast my leave ~~but~~ & take care that nothing be damnified[15] or lost

Give my dear Love to all my friends who I desire may labour to soften angry Spirits and to reduce them to a sense of their Duty And at thy Return give a Small Treat in my name to the Gentlemen at Philadelphia for a beginning to a better Understanding [to] which I pray the Lord to incline their hearts for their own Ease [as well as mine] and my Friends.

For thy [ow]n Services I shall allow thee what is just and reasonable either by Commissions or a Salary ~~If th~~ But my Dependance is on thy Care and honesty Serve me faithfully as thou expects a Blessing from God or my favour and I shall support thee to my utmost as

Thy true Friend
Wm Penn

Ship Dolmahoy 3^{d} 9^{br} 1701

Remember
S Weaver's affidavits[16]
R. Stocktons Money[17]
S Jennings's Acco^{ts} [18]
Edward Gibbs Account[19]
Geo: Deacon in Newcastle[20]
Jos Carpenter[21] C Read[22] &c Affidavit
R Halliwell & his Land[23]
Newcastle Welch settlement[24]
J Sotcher & Pensbury
Blackwells Papers[25]

DS in the hand of James Logan. Penn Papers, Letters of the Penn Family to James Logan, HSP. (*Micro.* 9:856.) Docketed: Proprietors last Instructions | to me just at parting | Shipboard 3^{d} 9^{br} 1701.

1. Doc. 32.

2. Reversion of an estate to a superior lord in the absence of legal heirs. *OED.*

3. Personal chattels which had caused the death of a human being and were therefore forfeited to WP as governor. *OED.*

4. Stray animals were forfeited to WP if not redeemed.

5. The Assembly of Nov. 1700 had passed two taxes for support of the government, one of a penny per pound on property and one of £2000 for the proprietor. Their collection proved difficult; see doc. 35, n. 19. *Statutes,* 2:109-18. Local Friends' meetings had also subscribed £1000 to assist WP in defending his charter in England. *Micro.* 11:265; 9:870; doc. 67.

6. WP had been living in Samuel Carpenter's "Slate Roof House" on Second St. Logan was still there in 1702, for lack of other accommodation. Watson, *Annals,* 1:163-64; doc. 52, text at n. 38.

7. See doc. 36.

8. WP was building two mills, one on Cohocksink Creek in the Northern Liberties (later called the "Governor's Mill"), and the "Schuylkill Mill" in present West Philadelphia. Expenditures on the mills figure prominently in WP's cash books for 1701-2 (*Micro.* 8:591, 9:870). Neither venture proved profitable, and Logan repeatedly complained of them as a drain on WP's resources. The Governor's Mill was sold to Thomas Masters in 1714. Samuel H. Needles, "The Governor's Mill, and the Globe Mills, Philadelphia," *PMHB,* 8:279-87; *Micro.* 10:449; doc. 52.

9. John Marsh, miller of the Schuylkill Mill, abandoned the enterprise for New England in 1702; Logan had accused him of mismanagement and refused to pay his bills, arguing that the income from the mill should support him. In 1705 Logan reported to WP that the mill was in ruins because of Marsh's desertion. Doc. 52; *Micro.* 12:053.

10. See doc. 32, n. 4; *Micro.* 10:141.

11. Moore served as advocate of the admiralty court under Quary. See *PWP,* 3:512n.

12. Paroculus Parmiter (c. 1673-c. 1750), an attorney from Bristol and a kinsman of WP, served as naval officer of New York 1698-1702, but was described by Gov. Bellomont as a corrupt man who had formerly been convicted of forgery but pardoned. His New York law practice was marked by several suspensions and disbarments, and he was notoriously quarrelsome. WP commissioned him as naval officer for Pennsylvania on 1 Nov. 1701. Paul M. Hamlin and Charles E. Baker, *Supreme Court of Judicature of the Province of New York, 1691-1704: Biographical Dictionary* (New York, 1959), pp. 152-59; *Micro.* 9:839; *PWP,* 3:605n.

13. Martha Durant, widow of John Durant, was a poor relation of WP and of Robert Assheton, probably through WP's aunt Rachel Penn Bradshaw. In 1702 she appeared before the commissioners of property and was granted a warrant for 600 acres which WP had promised to her and her husband; despite this grant she was still impoverished in 1712, when she again appealed to the board for support. *PA,* 2d ser., 19:283, 351, 541; *PGM,* 25:127.

14. Juan Corso, a mariner described variously as Genoese or Spanish, was trying to recover debts for the building of the sloop *George* from the estate of the Philadelphia merchant Charles Sanders (d. 1699). On 22 Oct. 1701 Corso petitioned WP and the Council to appoint arbitrators, but the case remained unsettled, and Corso later carried his complaint to England. *Micro.* 9:639; *Minutes of the Provincial Council,* 2:52; Logan Papers, Documents of the Provincial Council, 3:26, HSP; Hinshaw, 2:416; doc. 56; *Micro.* 11:034.

15. Damaged. See doc. 37 for an inventory of goods left at Pennsbury and Philadelphia.

16. WP was expecting S. Weaver, who seems to have been a clerk, to provide details of the accounts of the late Robert Webb, marshal of the vice-admiralty court. Doc. 48; *Micro.* 8:128.

17. On 25 Oct. 1701 Richard Stockton, Jr. (c. 1645-1709), a wealthy Quaker of East New Jersey, purchased from WP a tract of 5500 acres on Stony Brook for £900. Logan complained in 1702 that he had received only £180 from Stockton; payment for the land had included a £450 bond, on which Stockton was still paying interest in 1703. Stockton's sister Mary had married Silas Crispin, WP's cousin, in 1697. *Micro.* 9:652; 10:141; *PA,* 2d ser., 19:386; *Morven and the Stocktons* (n.p., n.d.), pp. 70-72.

18. Samuel Jennings was receiver general in Pennsylvania from 1690 to 1693, and in 1697 he became WP's land agent for West New Jersey. Pomfret, *West New Jersey*, p. 127. For his accounts as WP's receiver general, see *PMHB*, 35:199-210; *Micro.* 6:494.

19. Edward Gibbs, a Quaker who owned land on St. George's Creek and had served as sheriff and assemblyman for New Castle Co., was collecting WP's rents in New Castle Co. *PMHB*, 35:210; Scharf, *Delaware*, 2:872, 833, 1017; *PA*, 2d ser., 9:662, 671.

20. In 1701 George Deakyne, or Dakayne, surveyor of New Castle Co., received from WP a grant of 600 acres in return for resurveying the lands along the Delaware River from Christina River to New Castle. *PA*, 2d ser., 19:247.

21. Joshua Carpenter (d. 1722), a Philadelphia brewer and the elder brother of Samuel Carpenter, was one of the founders of Christ Church; he held many offices, including justice of the peace (1693), alderman (1701), and assemblyman (1702, 1706-8, 1721). Edward Carpenter and Louis Henry Carpenter, *Samuel Carpenter of Philadelphia and His Descendants* (Philadelphia, 1912), pp. 35-38.

22. Charles Read (d. 1705), an Anglican merchant of Philadelphia, was named one of the city's first aldermen in 1701 and served in the Assembly in 1704. Read (and apparently Joshua Carpenter as well) had been one of the appraisers of the goods from the ship *Providence*, seized by the admiralty court in 1699, and WP was awaiting an affidavit from him that would testify to Judge Robert Quary's abuse of power. See doc. 38; *Micro.* 10:267; *PMHB*, 9:339-42.

23. WP had recently given Richard Halliwell a warrant for 400 acres in New Castle Co., which was surveyed in 1703. *PA*, 2d ser., 19:366, 531.

24. On 15 Oct. 1701 WP granted 30,000 acres to William Davis, David Evans, and William Willis for a new Welsh settlement in New Castle Co. The land was in Pencader Hundred along the present border with Maryland; part of it now lies in Cecil Co., Md. Scharf, *Delaware*, pp. 948-50.

25. John Blackwell (1624-1701), a Puritan from England via Boston, was deputy governor of Pennsylvania from 1688 to 1689. For his stormy relations with the Pennsylvania Quakers, see *PWP*, 3:215ff. For his papers, see Governor Blackwell's Papers, HSP.

34

THOMAS CALLOWHILL TO HANNAH PENN

Bristoll 4th of the 9th month [November] 1701

Deare Hannah

Thine of the 17th & 22° 6 month last[1] came to our hands & Gave us the Satisfaction of heareing of your health &c welcom to us. it signified Mary Loafty['s][2] Inclineation to Marriage there and of the want of a Certeficate of her Cleareness here the Inclosed therfore are & Intended by ~~the Ben & Hester~~ [blank] who are goeing hence on the Ben & Hester per way of Virginia ~~&~~ I have duplicate of the same which I intend per som other hand. wee continue in Indifferant good helth. I bless god. Many are in Expectation of your sudden comeing [over] which makes me dowbt whether this may find you at Pensilvania or noe[3] if it doth let it bring to thy Remembrance what I wrott in my former touching my Lands purchased there[4] of which I Expected thy Care & som answere to my satisfaction as also of wt thou have received from Thomas Roberts[5] or Thomas Paschall[6] thine of the 13th 2d month 1700[7] Said thou had received but 15l {pensilvania money}[8] from Tho. Paschall & none from Tho. Roberts & since have not said in any letter what is received from Either of them thy [le]tter hints Great uncertenty in your setlem^{t} and it is the opinion of B C[9] & other friends that you will com over sudenly soe that [o]therwise thy mother[10] would Incline to send over som Nessesaries which Now she omitts because of the Uncertenty of its finding thee there—wee arȩ now com to the 16th Instant & in prety good degree of helth, but not without weakenes & paines th[at] Attends our Age & decaying bodys our Coz Haynes[11] youngest daughter Lidia about 3 years of Age dyed in the small pox [yes]terday, & is to be buryed this day last 5 days past brought us news that [our?] p[arlia]ment was desolved and that the King would Isue out writts for a New Election to sitt 30th X^{m} next.[12]

Charles Jones[13] is not yet dead but very weak The swelling in one of his Leggs broake & voids much watter &c. This letter is now Called for with Deare love from myselfe & thy Mother to the Governour thy selfe Deare Jno Tishia.[14] & our~~s~~ friends in Generall I rest thy lo Father

Tho. Callowhill

phebe[15] desires to be kindly remembred to you

To our Friends & Brethren in the Province of
Pensilvania & whomsoever Elce it doth or may Concerne

Mary Loafty formerly of this Citty now of Pensilvania haveing Signified unto us her Inclineation to Joyne in Marriage there and requested a Certeficate of her Cleareness here—

whilest with us she lived soberly & was of orderly conversation and upon due enquery Doe not find but that shee is free and Cleare from all parties here in Relation to Marriage—which wee Certefy from our mens meeting in the City of Bristol this third day of the Nineth Moneth 1701

Signed in & on behalfe of the Meeting By

Richard Sneade
Thomas Callowhill
Charles Jones
Benj^{a} Coole
Joshua Cart
Jeff^{r} Pinnell
Arthur Thomas
Samuell Cox
Tho: Oade
Tho: Bayly
Walt^{r} Shippin
Alex. Arscott[16]

ALS. Dreer Collection, HSP. (*Micro.* 9:862.) Addressed: William Penn Es[q^{r}] | Proprietor & Governor of | Pensilvania for H. P. | or if Absent To James Logan | or Thomas Storie for M. L. Several parts of words worn through the page have been supplied by the editors in square brackets.

1. Not found.

2. The edge of the page has been clipped. Mary Lofty, a Quaker, probably was the daughter of Katherine and Thomas Lofty of Bristol. After accompanying the Penns to Pennsylvania, Mary became the housekeeper at Pennsbury and married the steward there, John Sotcher, at Falls Meeting on 16 Oct. 1701. See doc. 30, n. 5; *PWP*, 3:427n.

3. WP and Hannah were already on board the *Dolmahoy*, bound for England. Peare, p. 382.

4. Thomas Callowhill's earlier letter has not been found. He was a First Purchaser of 5500 acres in Pennsylvania. *PWP*, 2:639.

5. Thomas Roberts (d. c. 1703), a shoemaker, had rented a Philadelphia lot and house from Thomas Callowhill in 1692. Phila. Admins. Bk. B, p. 15; Roach, "Directory," p. 114.

6. Thomas Paschall (d. 1718), a pewterer from Bristol and First Purchaser of 500 acres in Phila. Co., had immigrated to Pennsylvania in 1682. Phila. Will Bk. D, #131; *PWP*, 2:650; Marion Balderston, "William Penn's Twenty-Three Ships," *PGM*, 23:41n.

7. Not found.

8. The inflated Pennsylvania currency was discounted at about 33 percent, with £150 Pennsylvania money equivalent to £100 sterling. McCusker, *Money and Exchange*, p. 183.

9. Benjamin Coole.

10. Hannah Hollister Callowhill.

11. Possibly the Bridget Haynes who signed the marriage certificate of WP and Hannah Callowhill; see *PWP*, 3:436, 437n.

12. Parliament was dissolved on 11 Nov. 1701; the new Parliament was summoned on 30 Dec. 1701 and dissolved on 2 July 1702. *Members of Parliament*, 1:586, 593.

13. Charles Jones, Jr. (d. 1701), a Quaker merchant of Bristol, died in Dec. His daughter Mary had married William Penn, Jr., in 1700. Digests of Quaker Records, Bristol and Som., GSP; Mortimer, 1:206; Jenkins, p. 108; *PWP*, 3:557, 558n.

14. John Penn and Laetitia Penn.

15. Phebe Harris (1686-1728), Hannah Callowhill Penn's first cousin, married Brice Webb (d. 1743), a Bristol Quaker linendraper, in 1706. Mortimer, 2:265.

16. Of these twelve Friends from the Bristol Monthly Meeting, Benjamin Coole, Thomas Callowhill, Arthur Thomas, and Charles Jones, Sr., are identified elsewhere in this volume. Richard Snead (d. 1712), mercer, was a non-emigrant First Purchaser of 1500 acres in Phila. Co. Joshua Cart (d. 1705), saddler, owned land between Springfield and Moreland manors in Phila. Co. Jeffrey Pinnell (d. 1713), merchant, and Thomas Oade (d. 1728), gloveseller, in 1708 joined Thomas Callowhill and others in granting WP a mortgage on Pennsylvania to help extricate him from his debts to the Fords. Samuel Cox (c. 1666-1733) was a soapmaker and tobacconist. Thomas Bayly (d. 1720), pewterer, lived in Peter's Parish. Alexander Arscott (1676-1737) had become the Bristol Friends' schoolmaster in 1699. No further information has been found on Walter Shippin. *PWP*, 3:56n, 419n; Mortimer, 1:194, 212; 2:xxx-xxxi, 233, 239, 255; Peare, p. 404.

35
FROM JAMES LOGAN

Philadelphia the 2 x^br [December] 1701

Honoured Governour

This tis hop'd will find thee through the Good Providence of God safely arrived on the English shore wch is the repeated Desires and Prayers of Thousands here.

By the Last Post from Newyork before this we were Informed next week would be Early Enough for the first ship to Sail from thence but by this we are Surprised to hear that Sam: will Scarce be able to recover[1] her in time wch wth Governour Hamiltons Absence who is now at Amboy[2] makes me unCapable of Sending all Designed by this Opportunity.

The Inclosed Letters came 10 dayes agoe (one Excepted) by way of Boston Some under the Cover of the agents[3] and some in D Zacharys[4] they were both thought fit to be opened on accot of what might be Contained of Publick Concern within.

In the agents was one from the Lords of Trade and plantations proving only a Duplicate of the Last thou recd at Pensbury and was read in Councill according to Order.[5] In Answer to one Clause in which requiring an accot of our Method of Court proceedings is Sent by order of Council under the Great Seal the Late Law past for that purpose[6] and in Answer to another Injunction in the same 'tis ordered that the whole Body of all the Laws in force be Sent over with all Expedition but they Could not yet be gott ready It was also thought fitt to Send an Authentick Copy of the Last Law of Marriage[7] the better to Obviate if there should be occation what Objections may arrise from the former. The two mentioned Covers are Sent open.

Inclosed also Comes a Copy of the Charter of Priviledges[8] one of the Intended Charter of Property[9] which I hope thou wilt take Early care Enough to prevent being perfected because Likely (if so) to be in many heads Injurious. Also one of the City Charter to be at hand in Case any Objection should be made upon that Clause appointing a Water Bailiff or A Morris's being named an Alderman[10]

I Intended Severall other Coppies but by the abovementioned Disapoint[ment] am too much Straightned.

The List of Inhabitants ordered to be sent over I can by no means Gett ready now that of Chester not being Sent up yet But Shall not fail to press & Hasten it.[11]

I can See no hopes of getting any Materiall Subscriptions from Those of the Church against the report of Persecution[12] they having Consulted together on that head and as I am Informed Concluded that not allowing their Clergie here what they of right Claim in England and not Suffering them to be the Superiour may Justly bear that name.

Colonel Quarry before his Departure gott & tooke Over with him Severall Subscriptions which I Doubt may prove Mischievous,[13] but all is kept so private among them there is no possibillity of knowing wth any with any Certainty what they are.

All things have gone very Smooth and Easy since thy Departure without the Least Obstruction or Emotion. Coming up from the Capes I Called W Rodeneys and Such others as were reconed Violent and Leading men & Left them Very Easy and good natur'd in appearance and when Come to town I made bold to give a Small Treat at Andrews to the Governour Richard Halliwell Jasper Yeats J Moore & some such others abot a Dozen Including T. Farmer[14] and the other owners of the small Hatch or Vessell the Family went Down to N Castle in[15] on ~~thy~~ thy behalfe & in thy name which being very well Tim'd and managed was I have reason to beleive of Good Service, 'Tis not that I would think it my place to take Such things upon me but at that time I ~~w~~Could not Easily have been Dissuaded from it.

There hapend however the very first day after I came to Town an Occation of some Clashing between the Admiralty & Civill powers by R Ashetons taking a Bond with the Governours Consent of William Righton[16] to produce a Certificate from Jamaica for a parcell of Indigoe the ratts having Eaten his papers at Sea I Fear it will make a Subject of Complaint but not by this Opportunity Par: Parm~~e~~yton who was the Cheif mover and adviser in ~~this~~ it I Suppose will advise thee by this Shipp at Large abot it with a full State of the Case and the Governour per next[17] Especially If J Moore should write[18] who has promised to do nothing on that head but wt he will first Expose here to veiw. Having done all that can be by Quarry he is very willing I perceive to Live ~~in~~ as quiet as possible and keeps in very Friendly with the Governour when here which 'tis thought will be the best Course on our Sides also till we see how affairs are Like to be Determin'd there which will be Earnestly Expected but The Court we fear will have other Bussiness of too great Importance to give this the Necessary Dispatch.

If any Disturbance arise 'tis Likely to be by Distreining for the Tax which is not begun yet Yesterday being the first day it could be Done for the Second payment and that being so high it was thought best to bring both together and prevent Exasperating the people too much by making two Distresses first for the one Moiety and again for the other.[19] They are goeing on in Chester County and I have good promisses from Bucks this Town alone is the unhappy place but I hope we Shall Resolutely break through it 'tis Generally Expected it must be paid but in Chester County Great Endeavours have been used ('tis Easily Guest by whom[20] to Scatter poison Especially by reporting thou hadst Left the Charters unsealed Andrew Job Came up upon't Very much Startled but return'd thorowly Satisfied for it was said the Assembly was mocked and thô that of priviledges was so often sent to them and their Speaker[21] as a mark of their Acceptance had Sign'd it yet thou would not finish it but made a Sham of the whole This was the Notion thô not Quite thus Represented by the Author Yet he is Really very Malicious & holds Little good Correspondence with any that I see.

There are none that I hear of Uneasy about the Charter of Property that know how things really were and there is no Ground as farr as can be yet seen to be gotten on that head but by Falce Representations.

The Susquahannah Subscriptions[22] goe not so briskly on as at first Chiefly through the undertakers want of time because of the

Fair[23] &c but 'tis Intended to be pressed forward with Vigour thô thy Absence is no small Damp to all things of that kind.

The Assistance money[24] is now one Moiety of it I Think become Due & will be forthwith Collected as farr as may be but the Scarcity of money in the Countrey and neither want of Substance nor Inclination makes many hold their hands The New Aldermen A: M:[25] and that begotted ass Pent: Teague[26] Last quarterly meeting utterly refused to Subscribe one farthing.

The Law for preventing abuses in Trade &c past at thy first coming and on which thou Vallued thy Self with the Crown is Utterly repealed by the Last Clause in the Last act of Confirmation and with it the Tunnage is Dropt[27] whether Designed by the Assembly or not I known not but 'Tis Unhappy none of the Councill took Notice of it. This must make me hold my hand in respect to the Buoys in the River 'twas to Continew in force only till Twenty Dayes after the rising of the Assembly in 1703. We have been threatned abo^t the Tunage and bid the persons Defiance having never Recovered the Repeal till Yesterday but now I beleive must Let it fall

The Thousand acres was Last week cutt off from the Tract in E Jersey on the West Side I gave Directions on the East having had 300^l bid for it if Laid there but upon Tryall we were obliged to take it so as would not accomodate the man though on the East Side and therefore the West was for Several reasons thought better.[28]

R. Stockton Cannot raise the money yet but offers Interest from the Date of the Bond[29] I Shall Oblidge him to it as soon as Possible but the Winter being more Set in and no acco^t of Bills from Maryland I would Rather it Lay in other hands upon Interest than Dead in mine though I Shall not forgett the Necessity of Remittance and use all possible Care and Dilligence therein

The Comm^rs Sett Every 2^d & 4 Day and Goe pretty regularly on the 19 Ult was the first Sitting[30] and we cannot yet say how things may proceed people as far as we can hear are Generally Easie and Quiet.

The Governour is not yet Sworn the Reasons I Leave to his own Pen[31] as also that abo^t W Righton with which I was no ways Concerned nor doe I by this Blame them that were in the own part for I think it was Reasonable and just But some fault I fear will be found

The Computation of what money may be Raised is the best we Could make up in the time[32] 'tis Wide to be sure in Severall particulars Some over and some under most of the Latter I believe that of Overpluss and Conceal'd Lands I hope is not above ⅓ and that of Newcastle Vacancies above one half of what may be raised in Some time but to make Even what we have given, Answer, It will be Necessary that there be care taken to Transport Families and if upon a Good Bargain thou Couldst thy self make a Speedy return it will be the only or best way to affect it I can make no Judgment of what there may be in the two Lower Counties[33] if good Collonies were brought into them as of the in N C[34] there might be Some Thousands of pounds Raised but the Post Staying Straightens me I must therefore with all Due Regards Conclude

Thy most Dutifull Servant
James Logan

We Intend to Sett abot Resurveys with all Expedition Pray be pleased to favour us with all opportunities of Writting.

LBC. James Logan Letterbook, HSP. (*Micro.* 9:896.)

1. Reach (*OED*). Logan may have been employing WP's slave Sam as a messenger to New York.

2. Perth Amboy, the capital of East New Jersey.

3. Charlwood Lawton, WP's London agent for Pennsylvania. His letter has not been found.

4. Daniel Zachary (1671-c. 1704), a Quaker merchant from Bucks, Eng., had settled in Boston and in 1700 married Elizabeth Lloyd in Philadelphia. His father, Thomas, had purchased land from WP in 1682. *PWP,* 1:237n; 2:657; Digests of Quaker Records, Bucks, GSP; Reuben J. Bates, comp., *The Zachary-Zachry Family* (Ann Arbor, 1960), p. 3.

5. This letter from the Board of Trade, dated 15 Apr. 1701, was read in the Provincial Council on 18 Nov. 1701. *Micro.* 9:201; *Minutes of the Provincial Council,* 2:63-64.

6. This law, drawn up by David Lloyd, had decentralized Pennsylvania's courts and increased the Assembly's control over them. *Statutes,* 2:148-59; Nash, *Quakers and Politics,* p. 230; Roy N. Lokken, *David Lloyd: Colonial Lawmaker* (Seattle, 1959), p. 116.

7. Anglicans had objected to Pennsylvania's marriage laws because their ministers were required to post public notice of intended marriages in addition to the church banns. The new law eased the publication requirements and reduced the fines for violations. WP was called upon to defend the law before the Board of Trade on 8 June 1702; see n. 12, below. *Statutes,* 2:161-62; *PWP,* 3:624; *CSPC, 1702,* p. 379.

8. Doc. 28.

9. See doc. 31.

10. WP's charter for Philadelphia empowered the sheriff to act as water bailiff (*Micro.* 9:682); on objections to WP's appointment of a water bailiff, see doc. 18, n. 32. Anthony Morris, one of the city's newly appointed aldermen, had infringed on admiralty jurisdiction as a J.P. in 1698; see *PWP,* 3:562n. In 1702 Quary complained to the Board of Trade about both these issues; See doc. 44; *CSPC, 1702,* pp. 248-49.

11. Lists of inhabitants were being drawn up for collection of the taxes levied by the New Castle Assembly of 1700; see *Statutes,* 2:109-18.

12. In Jan. 1701 the vestry of Christ Church had written to the Board of Trade, the archbishop of Canterbury, and the bishop of London to charge WP's Pennsylvania government with infringement of their religious rights. They were particularly offended by the newly passed marriage law, which they claimed violated the Anglican canon. Board of Trade Papers, Proprieties, 1701-1702, transcript at HSP, G13.

13. On 31 Mar. 1702 Quary appeared before the Board of Trade with a sheaf of papers containing charges against Pennsylvania's Quaker government. These included a memorial of 27 Oct. 1701 from the minister and vestry of Christ Church, alleging several miscarriages of justice, and an address from the Lower Counties of 25 Oct. 1701 complaining of the lack of a militia. *CSPC, 1702,* pp. 182-84; Board of Trade Journal, 1701-1702, transcript at HSP, p. 389; *Micro.* 9:669.

14. Thomas Farmer was sheriff of Phila. Co. by 1700 and served until 1703. Logan was entertaining these prominent Anglicans in hopes of mending relations with them. *PA,* 2d ser., 9:715; *Micro.* 8:493.

15. On their return to England in 1701, WP's family had evidently traveled down the Delaware in a smaller vessel to meet the *Dolmahoy* at New Castle.

16. William Righton (d. 1702), a Philadelphia mariner, was master of the brigantine *Hopewell,* which had arrived from Jamaica in early Nov. 1701 without its register and clearance certificate. Righton claimed that the papers had been destroyed by rats, and Robert Assheton took the case before the common pleas court and accepted a £1000 bond for production of a certificate from Jamaica within nine months. Quary complained of this to the Board of Trade as an infringement of admiralty jurisdiction. Phila. Will Bk. B, #84; *Micro.* 9:933; *CSPC, 1702,* pp. 248-49, 281-83. See also doc. 51.

17. Paroculus Parmiter had been commissioned naval officer and register of ships on 1 Nov. 1701. Neither his letter nor Hamilton's has been found, but see doc. 51.

18. Moore wrote to Quary, who produced his letter before the Board of Trade on 1 June 1702. *CSPC, 1702,* p. 370.

19. The New Castle Assembly of 1700 had granted WP a tax of £2000, to be raised out of the several counties in proportion to their wealth. Half of the assessment fell due on 10 May 1701 and the other on 1 Dec. 1701, but as both proved difficult to collect the government planned to resort to the distraint (seizure and sale of goods) provided for in the law. Even this expedient failed, for on 9 July 1702 Logan reported that officials were refusing to enforce distraints despite the fines imposed for such neglect. *Statutes,* 2:114-18; *Micro.* 10:360.

20. David Lloyd was opposing payment of the tax in Chester Co. on the grounds that WP had failed to seal the Charter of Property. See Lokken, *David Lloyd,* p. 116.

21. Joseph Growden. See doc. 28.

22. In 1701 WP had revived the Susquehanna land subscriptions of 1696, signing up additional subscribers and issuing a new set of concessions to purchasers on 25 Oct. (*Micro.* 9:672). Subscriptions had reached a total of £3000 by Dec. 1701, but they lagged after WP's departure, and by 1704 collection was problematic. WP finally dissolved the scheme in 1707, in hopes of selling the land for a higher price in England. See *PWP,* 3:671-78; docs. 36, 139; *Micro.* 11:240, 355.

23. The semiannual fair held at Philadelphia, 16-18 Nov. and 16-18 May. See *Micro.* 9:682; Scharf and Westcott, 1:153.

24. The first half of the Quakers' assistance money was due on 1 Dec. 1701 and the second on 1 Apr. 1702. See doc. 33, n. 5.

25. Anthony Morris.

26. Pentecost Teague (d. 1719), a wealthy Quaker merchant from Cornwall, had emigrated in 1694 and become an active member of Phila. Monthly Meeting. WP appointed him one of the city's first common councilmen in 1701, and he later served as an alderman. Phila. Will Bk. D, #157; *PA,* 2d ser., 9:748, 753; Phila. Monthly Meeting Abstract of Minutes, vol. 1, 1682-1707, GSP.

27. The confirmation act of 1701 had omitted the 1699 "act for the preventing of frauds and regulating abuses in trade"; the last clause of the confirmation act voided all laws not specifically confirmed. The trade act of 1699 had imposed a duty of 4d per ton on residents' vessels and 8d per ton on those owned by nonresidents, to be collected for WP's use for three years. Logan now had no legal grounds for its collection. *Statutes,* 2:142-48; Gail McKnight Beckman, comp., *The Statutes at Large of Pennsylvania in the Time of William Penn* (New York, 1976), pp. 242-46.

28. WP had reserved for himself 1050 acres of the 5500 acres in East New Jersey sold to Richard Stockton on 25 Oct. 1701; Logan as one of WP's agents for Jersey land was now looking for a buyer. See *Micro.* 9:652; 9:803; doc. 36.

29. See doc. 33, n. 17.

30. For this meeting of WP's commissioners of property, Edward Shippen, Griffith Owen, Thomas Story, and Logan, see *PA,* 2d ser., 19:185.

31. Gov. Hamilton should have sworn the oath prescribed for colonial governors before a group of royal commissioners, who included John Moore, Richard Halliwell, and Jasper Yeates, all staunch Anglicans and critics of the Quaker government. Moore, Halliwell, and Yeats refused to administer the oath unless they were granted possession of their commission, which lay in the provincial record office for safekeeping. On 21 Apr. 1702 the governor was finally sworn before members of the Council and the customs collector, an alternative sanctioned by the royal commission. See *Micro.* 10:169; *Minutes of the Provincial Council,* 2:62-63, 68-69.

32. Doc. 36.

33. Kent and Sussex Cos.

34. New Castle Co.

36
FROM THE COMMISSIONERS OF PROPERTY

[3 December 1701]

Whereas by thy Instructions under thy hand left at thy Departure[1] thou was pleased to order us thy Proprietary Deputies for this Province and Territories That upon the most Exact Survey {wee} in so short a time could take of the State of thy Revenue within this Government and of the Lands thou hast therein to Dispose of wee should Compute what sum or sums of money may in a short time be raised for thy Use out of the same

Pursuant there{un}to upon as Mature and Deliberate {a} Consideration as the shortness of time will Allow and upon the Most Modest and Reasonable C~~onsidera~~alculation wee do Compute that within the space of three years from the Date hereof the following Sums may be Respectively Raised out of thy Propriety and Governm^{t} of the said Province and Territories That is to say

Of the Tax Granted at Newcastle[2] payable forthwith We Compute there may be Depended on One thousand pounds	£1000:–:–
For Land sold by thy self in East Jarsey[3] before thy Departure the last payment to be made in 6: months:	900:–:–
For the Reversions of the Bank of Philadelphia[4] to be sold by thy order wee Compute 2000 foot at 20^{s} per foot	2000:–:–
From the Subscriptions for Land at Sasquehannah[5] Wee Compute at least five thous^{d} pounds there being a Moiety of that alr^{dy} Subsc^{d}	5000:–:–
For Land now Sold and Agreed for in New Castle County[6] the last payment to be made in 3 years	3500:–:–
For Land to be Disposed of by thy order out of thy Mannor of Springetbury at least 750 Acres at 40^{s} per Acre	1500:–:–
Out of thy Manner of Gilberts 2000 Acres at 20^{l} per Ct[7]	400:–:–
Out of thy Mannor of Rocklands 3000 Acres at 20^{l} per Ct	600:–:–
Out of thy Mannor of Pensbury 1000 Acres at 30^{l} per Ct	300:–:–
In the County of Newcastle wee Compute there may be at least 15000 A of Vacant & overplus Land to be disp^{sd} of at 10^{l} per Ct	1500:–:–
	16700:–:–

Brough over[8]	£16700:–:–
From thy Rents to be Collected at least	3000:–:–
Off Overplus and Concealed Lands[9] in the Province wee may Modestly Compute there will be sold in that time at least Ten thousand Acres at 20l per Cent	2000:–:–
Summ	£21700:–:–[10]

There are severall other heads might be Inserted as selling off the penny Rents selling off the Old Rents[11] Thy Estate in the Jersys and Divers Others But not being yet able to make a well Grounded Estimation wee at present forbear them. But the Abovementiond Sums being as wee have Good Reason to believe Computed within Bounds both as to Quantity of Land and Vallue Insomuch that wee Doubt not but if it please God this Province should Flourish for Three years longer as it hath since thy Arrival[12] in Respect to Improvements[13] there may be Advanced on severall of the preceeding heads at least One half and some may be Doubled Wee can see no Reason therefore to Doubt but the sum of at least Twenty Thousand pounds Money of this Province[14] may be Certainly raised within the time Expressed or thereabouts in Money or Countrey Produce to be Remitted Either Directly to England or by Way of the West Indies Unless some Great and Publick Calamity should Prevent the prosperity of this Colony together with the others of the Eng Domns in Ama

And this Estimation wee Give under our hands at Philada the 3d day of xbr 1701

Edwd Shippen
Griff Owen
Thoms Story
James Logan

Copy. Logan Papers, HSP. (*Micro.* 9:912.) Docketed: J L to the Proprietary 23d xbr 17[01] | wth the Commissioners Computation | of the Proprietors &c. A draft of this document partly in the hand of James Logan, with higher initial calculations of projected revenue, is also in the Logan Papers (*Micro.* 9:907).

1. Doc. 32 contains WP's instructions to his commissioners of property, Edward Shippen, Griffith Owen, Thomas Story, and James Logan, but it does not specifically call for this estimate of revenue.

2. On the £2000 tax for WP passed at New Castle on 27 Nov. 1700, see doc. 35, n. 19.

3. See docs. 33, n. 17; 35, n. 28. The draft adds under this entry: "For the Residue of that Tract if thou please to dispose of it forthwth 300:0:0."

4. See doc. 32, n. 15. The draft estimated 3000 feet selling for £3000, and then revised the figures downward—as with six of the other items on this list.

5. See doc. 35, n. 22.

6. See doc. 33, n. 24.

7. Twenty pounds per 100 acres.

8. Brought over from the previous page.

9. On overplus and concealed lands, see doc. 32, nn. 4-5; *PWP*, 3:111n.

10. The draft's higher estimates originally totaled £26,850, but were scaled down to £22,000.

11. See doc. 32, nn. 16-17.

12. In Dec. 1699; see *PWP*, 3:579n.

13. The draft here has a deleted passage, "~~and Money prove not too scarce.~~"

14. Pennsylvania currency was worth about ⅔ the value of English sterling. McCusker, *Money and Exchange*, p. 183.

37

CATALOG OF GOODS LEFT AT PENNSBURY AND PHILADELPHIA

A Catalogue of Goods left at Pensbury
the 3^{d} of the Tenth month [December] *1701*.

In the best Chamber

1 Bedd and bolster, 2 Pillows, 2 Blankets, 1 Silk Quilt, 1 Suite of Satin Courtins; one Table & pair Stands, 1 look{ing} glasse, 6 Cane Chaires, & 2 with Twigen[1] bottoms; 1 little black box, 1 Water Stand, 1 Close Stoole;[2] 1 pair of brasses, wth fire Shovel & Tongs: 1 little cane Stoole, 4 Satten Cushions.

In the Next chamber

One Bedd and Boulster, 2 Pillows, 2 Blankets, 1 India Quilt, 1 Sute of ~~white~~ Camblett[3] Curtins, wth white head cloath and Tester:[4] Six cane Chaires wth cushions, 1 Table, 1 looking glasse: One pair of brasses and a fire Shovle.

In the Next Chamber

One wrought Bedd, wth Bolster, Pillows, & Blanket and counterpane:[5] One Table & Standes, 6 wooden chaires & 1 Cane Ditto.

In the Nursery.

One Pallet Bedstid, 1 Table, 1 Skreen, 2 chaires of Master John's, & 2 Rushbottom'd chaires, ~~1 cane dit~~ One p^{r} of Brasses wth fire shovell and Tongs.

In the next Chamber

One Bedd and boulster, 2 Pillows, 1 Blankett, 1 Quilt, 1 Sute of Strip'd linnen Curtains: One Table 4 Rush bottom Chaires.

In the [blank]

~~Th~~ Two Chestes of Drawers, 2 Trunks, 1 Box.

In the Garrets

Fowr Bedd Stids, 2 Bedds, 1 Quilt, 1 Rugg, 2 Blanketts: Three Side Sadles one of them my M$^{rs's}$, 2 Pillions,[6] 1 Cloath

In the Lower Roomes

{Best Parlour}[7] Two Tables, 1 p^{r} Stands, 1 Couch 2 great cane chairs and 4 Small Ditto; 7 Cushions 4 of them Sattin, the other 3 green Plush: One p^{r} Brasses, Brasse fireshovel, Tongs & Fender, 1 Pr Bellows; 2 large Mapps

{The other Parlour} Two Tables, 6 chaires, 1 Great Leather chair, 1 Clock, {p^{r} brasses} 1 Tea Pot, 6 Saucers & cups, 2 Basins.

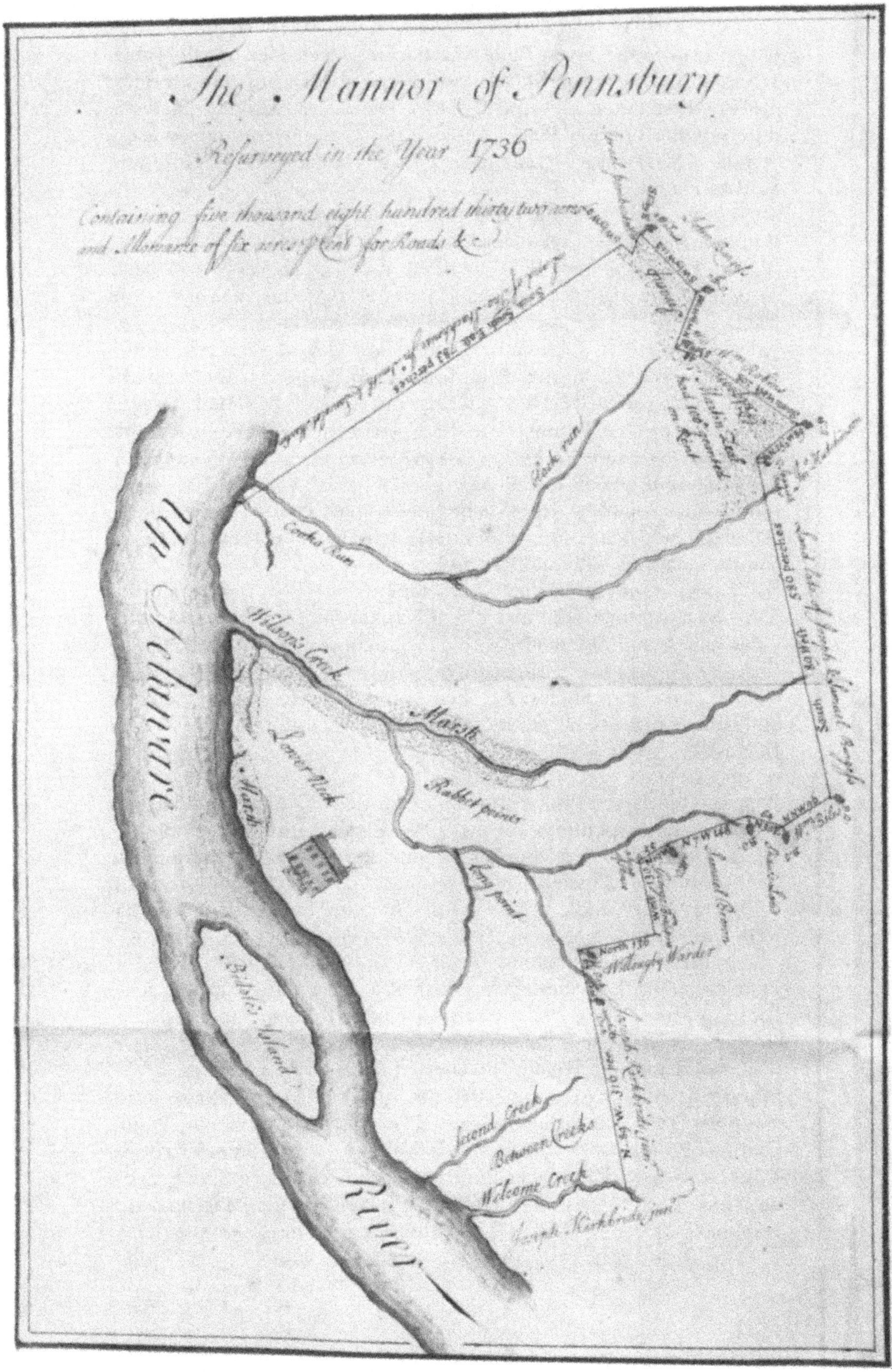

The Mannor of Pennsbury

Resurveyed in the Year 1736

Containing five thousand eight hundred thirty two acres and Allowance of six acres p Cent for Roads &c.

Delaware River

Bristoles Island

Cooks Run

Wilson's Creek

Marsh

Lower Neck

Rabbit point

Long point

Second Creek

Between Creeks

Welcome Creek

Willoughby Warder

Joseph Kirkbride junr

{In the little Hall} Six Leather Chairs and Two wooden ones 5 Mapps
{Great Hall} One Long Table & 2 Formes,[8] 6 chaires, 1 little Table, 1 Napkin Presse; Three very large ~~Putter~~ Puter Dishes, 6 lesser ones, 6 of the best Puter, 4 Soupe Dishes 2 Pye Plates, 2 cheese Plates, 2 dozen of the London Plates & 4 doz: & ½ of the common ones, 2 Stands, 5 Mazarins,[9] 1 Cullender, 2 Cisterns,[10] 2 Rings, 1 Doz^{n} and 10 Paté Panns.

Linnen & Plate in the great red Trunk

{Linnen, Damask}[11] 2 Pair of Fine sheets Marked WP, 2 p^{r} Pillows cases m^{rk}1 PC [blotted] {PC} the other WP, 1 p^{r} Sheets M^{rk} W^{P}H, 1 Table cloath and 1 Side board cloath, 18 Napkins, 2 Towells, all Damask m^{rk} P.

{Ireish Diap^{r}}[12] 1 Table and 1 Side board cloath, 12 Napkins M^{rk} W^{P}H, five Towells Mark'd P, all fine Ireish Diaper: 3 Table cloaths and Two long Towells m^{rk} P, 21 Napkins Mark'd 2^{P}4 {~~Huckabagg~~}[13] ~~in Oyletholes:~~[14] ~~1 Table cloath, 12 Napkins m^{rk} P in red,~~ [illegible deletion] ~~1 Side bord, & 8 Napkins m^{rk} P in red, 1 ditt^{o}, 1 Side Ditto 11 Napkins m^{rk} W^{HP} huckabagg~~

{Fine Dutch Diapar} ~~In all 2 p^{r} Sheets, 2 p^{r} Pillow cases, 9 Table Cloaths~~ 1 Side board m^{rk} P, all fine Dutch Diapar 1 Table cloath, 12 Napkins marked W^{P}H in Oylet holes.

{Hugabag} One Table cloath, 12 Napkins m^{rk} P in red, one other Table ~~bo~~ cloath and 1 Sidebord & 8 Napkins m^{rk} P in red and other Table cloath and Sideboard with 11 Napkins marked W^{P}H Háugaback

{Totall} In all 2 p^{r} Sheets, 2 p^{r} Pillowcases, 9 Table cloaths, 7 doz: & 10 Napkins, 5 Sidebord cloths, 9 Towells, 10 Callicoe courtins & ~~9~~ {4} Damask

Plate

{Plate} One large Tankard, 1 Bason, 6 Salts, 1 Skillet 5 Plates, 7 Spoons, 1 little Spoone, 2 forkes, 2 Porrengers, 2 little cups one m^{rk} J P the other H C. 1 p^{r} Snuffers, a small candlestick, 1 Chafing dish

In My M$^{rs's}$ Closset

4 Chayres with Needle work'd cases, 2 hanging Shelves, Some chinaware and Glasses

In the little closet below

Four large Dutch Dishes, 4 lesse dishes, 1 large white bason, 2 lesse Ditt^{o}, 16 white Plates, 10 blew Ditto, 4 Flower Basons, Some ordinary earthenware and the Suite of Turnbridge ware.[15]

{Chest of Drawers} Five p^{r} holland[16] Sheets large, 5 p^{r} lesse m^{rk} P in red 7 p^{r} Pillow cases, 9 m^{rk} P in red, 5 m^{rk} W^{P}H 4 p^{r} Corse Ditto, 3 p^{r} m^{rk} W^{P}H, 4 p^{r} little Ditto m^{rk} P in red. 1 Table cloath, 1 Side board 16 Napkins M^{rk} P in red, 1 Table cloath, 1 Side board, 11 Napkins, 2 Towels all markt P in red, 3 Table cloaths, 2 Side boards, 24 Napkins, 6 Towels, all hugabag, 1 Table cloath, 1 Side board, 8 Napkins, P in red, 2 Towels P in white, 2 lo~~g~~ng ones.

In all 6 Table cloaths, 5 Side boards, 12 Towells, 4 doz^{n} & 11 Napkins, 3 more old Table cloaths, 7 Napkins.
{In a great Box} Nine course Sheets m^{rk} W^{P}H in blew, 6 p^{r} whiter ditto m^{rk} mark as before, 2 p^{r} mr^{k} P in Blew, 7 p^{r} Pillowcases, 9 Cours Towels, 2 long ones, 3 huckabag Table cloaths, 2 doz: of Napkins course Huckabg 3 Table cloaths of Ozenbrigs[17]

Goods left at Philadelphia
The 20th of the 9th Month *1701*

{In the closet} One hanging Presse,[18] 1 Table and Stands
{best chamber} One Bedd and boulster, 2 Pillows, 2 Silk blanketts & white curtins, also 2 damask curtins for the Windows, 1 white Quilk, one great looking glasse, 1 Table and Stands, 1 Chest of Drawers 6 cane chaires, 1 close Stool, & Pann, 1 Water Stand, 1 [blank] Hearth, 1 p^{r} Brasses, fireshovell and Tongs, 2 chamberpots.
{Nursery} One Bedd and Bolster, 2 Pillows, 1 Blankett 1 Quilt, 1 Suite of Curtens, 1 chest of Drawers 2 cane chaires, 1 Fender[19]
{The other chamber} One Table and Stands and Bedd Stid
{Parlour} One great Table & a green Carpet, 1 Small Table, 6 Turcky work'd[20] chairs & 2 great ones the one a cane chair the other Leather Arm chair 1 clock, 1 p^{r} brasses, 1 brasse Fender, fireshovel and Tongs, 2 Sconces, 4 Mapps.
{The other Parlour} One great lookeing glasse Table & Stands, 1 Small Table 2 great cane Chairs, 4 lesser ones 1 Iron Fender, 2 Sconces, 6 Mapps.
{Hall} One great Table, 6 glasses, 1 p^{r} cruets, ~~x~~A case of Buckshors[21] knives and Forks.
{Kitching} Six Pueter Dishes, 1 {pye} Plate Ditt^{o} 1 Mazarin 2 Standes 1½ Doz: Plates, 3 Spits, 1 Grate Iron, 1 Pr Racks, 1 p^{r} greate Doggs,[22] 1 frying Pann, 1 p^{r} Pott hangers, 1 Hoock 4 Candle Sticks, 1 Powdering Tubb,[23] 2 Silver Spoons, 2 p^{r} of Holland sheets, 2 p^{r} Pillowcases, 1½ doz^{n} Napkins 3 Table cloaths.

Copy. William Penn's Cash Book, APS. (*Micro.* 9:918.) Docketed: Catalogue of Goods | left at Pen[n]sbury the 3^{d} | of the 10th Month, 1701. Docketed in another hand: Illa domi natas nostraque ex arbore ~~natas~~ {mensas} | Tempora viderunt:[24]

1. Wicker-worked. *OED.*
2. A chamber pot enclosed in a stool or box. *OED.*
3. Camlet, a fabric originally made in Asia of camel hair or angora wool, later in Europe of silk and wool. *OED.*
4. Canopy.
5. Bedspread.
6. Light saddles or riding cushions for women. *OED.*
7. This and succeeding notations appearing in the left-hand margin have been enclosed in braces and moved into the text.
8. Benches.
9. Deep plates, usually of metal. *OED.*
10. Large vessels or basins used at the dinner table. *OED.*
11. A fabric richly figured with woven designs. *OED.*

12. Diaper, a linen fabric with a simple woven pattern. *OED.*

13. Huckaback, a stout linen or cotton fabric used chiefly for toweling. *OED.*

14. Eyelet holes.

15. Inlaid wooden ware made at Tunbridge Wells, Eng.

16. A linen fabric originally made in Holland. *OED.*

17. Osnaburg, a coarse linen originally made in Osnabrück, Germany. *OED.*

18. A cupboard. *OED.*

19. A metal frame placed in front of a fire to keep the coals from rolling out. *OED.*

20. Covered with tapestry in the Turkish style. *OED.*

21. Probably buckhorn-handled.

22. Andirons.

23. A tub in which meat is salted and pickled. *OED.*

24. "Those times saw feasts born from our tree at home." The editors are indebted to Professor Myral Uhlfelder of Bryn Mawr College for this translation.

BATTLING THE BOARD THE TRADE

1702

WP and his family sailed from America in early November 1701 and reached England about a month later. On arrival, Hannah took John to her parents' home in Bristol to await the birth of her second child, and WP and Laetitia went to lodgings in London. He would spend the greater part of the year there, facing three interrelated challenges to his proprietorship: the Board of Trade's new attempt to get Parliament to pass a reunification bill; the charges against his government made by Robert Quary and others; and the opposition to his appointment of a non-Englishman, the Scot Andrew Hamilton, as deputy governor.

WP turned his attention first to Parliament, where the most serious threat lay. Slowed down by illness in January, he met the following month with Robert Harley, speaker of the House of Commons, and the earl of Manchester, principal secretary of state, to whom he entrusted his own plan for proprietary colonies (doc. 40). The Board of Trade rejected WP's plan, but its own bill never came to a vote in either house of Parliament, which was preoccupied with more pressing issues: the death of William III in March, the coronation of Anne in April, and the declaration of war against France and Spain in May. During his first months in England, WP deliberately slighted the Board of Trade, which he regarded as particularly prejudiced against proprietary government. By the end of March, the board members were becoming increasingly annoyed at his absence, especially after they received a barrage of complaints about Pennsylvania from Robert Quary. WP continued to put them off (doc. 43), hoping to receive the documents from Pennsylvania that he needed for his defense, but in April he attended three of the board's meetings to hear Quary's charges and deliver his own answer (doc. 44). The board's formal hearings on the case lasted nearly a month and required WP's attendance on at least eight occasions. When he heard that the board had approved Quary's return to the colonies and recommended that he be reimbursed for his expenses, WP went angrily to the Privy Council (doc. 50), which summoned the Board of Trade and ordered it to hear his charges against Quary. The board retaliated by challenging WP's title to the Lower Counties and by opposing Andrew Hamilton's appointment as deputy governor of Pennsylvania. Only after WP persuaded Queen Anne to his side in a two-hour audience with her at Bath in October (*Micro.* 10:530) did the board relent. Finally, after WP had made several important concessions — Hamilton's appointment was to be for one year only and would in no way prejudice the queen's title to the Lower Counties—the board gave its approval.

The long delays in Hamilton's official appointment aggravated the already troubled relations among political factions in Pennsylvania and the Lower Counties (docs. 51 and 52). Unsure of their land titles and chronically short of specie, colonists refused to pay quitrents or taxes. When WP vetoed the charter of property, he strengthened anti-proprietary feeling. Communication between proprietor and colonists was even more difficult than usual, with trade slowed by the impending war as well as by bad weather and epidemics in the colonies. By late June WP complained to James Logan that he was still ("after 7 months & more") waiting for the documents he needed to defend himself against Quary, "to my unexpressible trouble; & I fear Irreperable disapointm[t]" (*Micro.* 10:267). But Logan was unable to find witnesses who were both willing and able to testify, and he urged the proprietor, "Pray do not Expect more in thy Absence than could be done while thou wast present" (*Micro.* 10:538). The surviving documentation offers little evidence on whether WP seriously intended to return to Pennsylvania. He continued to assure officials there that William Penn, Jr., was coming over soon, but in fact his son did not arrive until February 1704. Married since 1699, WP's only surviving son by his first wife had developed habits of worldly extravagance that deeply worried his father. WP remained unrealistically hopeful about collecting substantial revenue from his colony, but this was an optimism born of desperation, as his financial troubles grew more serious. He was still unable to repay Philip Ford, to whom he had mortgaged the colony, and he probably sensed that Ford's death, on 8 January 1702, greatly increased the danger of his own exposure. The day after Ford's death and again in April 1702, WP signed new agreements with the widow, Bridget Ford (see doc. 117, n. 1). At the same time, WP had to provide a dowry for his daughter Laetitia, who by February 1702 was being courted by London Quaker merchant William Aubrey. Having no available cash, WP offered her Pennsylvania lands as a dowry but promised to pay interest on their estimated value of £2000 until they could be sold. In addition, he negotiated a separate loan of £3000 from Aubrey (see doc. 209). Naturally, this unorthodox marriage settlement resulted in considerable friction between the Penns and the Aubreys.

Apart from lobbying for his colony, WP resumed his leadership role in London Yearly Meeting during 1702 and did some electioneering for a parliamentary seat in Sussex (*Micro.* 10:377). His business concerns left little time for his family. He was in London when Hannah's second son, Thomas, was born in Bristol on 9 March 1702. In June he told Logan that he had been with his family only seventeen days out of the past five months. The family was able to gather only briefly during the summer at Warminghurst, where Laetitia was married to William Aubrey on 20 August.

Several of WP's letters to James Logan show a new level of disjointed phrasing and elliptical thinking, suggesting that the continuous whirl of events and rising financial and political pressures were exacting a psychic toll. Under these pressures, WP began in 1702 to talk of selling his governing rights in Pennsylvania to the crown (see doc. 48, n. 8)—a solution to his financial problems that would have repudiated everything he had been trying to accomplish in America since 1680.

38
TO JAMES LOGAN

Kensington 4th 11^{m} [January] 1701[/2][1]

James

Thou wilt hear, long ere this comes to hand, I doubt not, of all our safe arrivall through the great & continued mercys of God, save my leg,[2] that got a small rub about 4 days before our comeing to the Channel; wch by contrary applecations, in town has disabled me from haveing the benefit of my swift passage, as I might other wise have had. we were but 26 days from land to soundings, & 28 to the start[3] in Devonshire, & 30 to Portsmouth. N Puckle was but 34 days, ~~&~~ but J. Guy,[4] went north about after gaining within 200 leagues of the Lizard,[5] in less than 18 days, wch made his passage 11 weeks, & the letters but Just deliver'd before my comeing to London, but not before our arrivall at Portsmouth.

Nothing yet done in my affaires, but my comeing I do more & more see necessary, on divers acc^{ts} tho a troublesome & Costly Journy. My son has been very serviceable but Costly, & half given away [illegible deletion] {soy mesme}[6] for the Country, in some respects. I am not without hopes of a tollerable Conclusion, tho it will not be obtained without Charge & pains. They that seek the ruine of Propretors they say, will renew their Bill, but trye the Commons first, this time.[7] I shall say little of that affaire; only pray faile not {to send} wt I somuch need, & was so indiscreetly disregarded, viz, all requisit Cirtificats & affidavits that are yet behinde,[8] as to our conduct, & our foolish knavish enemys also, pray faile not to get in & returne wt monys were allotted for my supply in this affaire,[9] with all possible speed. And not only as to that branch, but the lands of E. Jer. & the other supply & Rents,[10] for there is a most absolute necessity to receive them wth all speed, & then returne them. For performing of which, lett no other business come in~~to~~ Competition, as thou wilt be a just man & recommend thy self to me & all that regard thee here. In order to which minde Tobacco, bright,[11] Bills in Maryland,[12] & flowr {(not bread)} to Barbadoes &c: Only know this, that Robt Egerton has never yet sent to S. vaus,[13] about that parcell {of flowr}; and that the ten hhds by N. Puckle, while all {else} he brought made Sterling, at least 3d⅝ ~~myn~~ that thou sent, made but 3d⅛ wch will loose the ½ of the whole it was payd at.[14] pray let not gratifying the unreasonable Importunity of the planters, hinder thy care of my languishing interrest, Since by my rents Lying out, I have lost that Interrest that would have payd the interrest of my debts, ~~fo~~ who have only the Principal (& that I Know not when,) to ballance both my Debts & Interrest.[15] James, let thy good sence & address in such matters, of Trade & accts, be religiously Imployd in my assistance & reliefe: I must expect it.

But wtever thou doest fail not to send me the probabilitys of the vallue of Rents, due, Supplys, Sasqr project,[16] lands saleable & Banck Lts [17] that I may make a Judgemt to my selfe, and a good argumt to others as occasion offers, for my service here.

Gett in all Debts due to me, as J. claypools Ch. Mar. &c:[18] according to Notes & bonds, In J. Harrisons time, & S. Jenings's.[19] be not hasty to end wth him, for reasons we discourst yet a while: However, my Daughters Banck lott[20] ought to be part of pay Since never Improved; & of all men never expected to have been so surprized. I greatly esteem him, but cannot bear to be greatly a looser by him. Rememberr G. Heathcots business, the date of his Pat. & surprize upon the Comrs.[21]

If the two Proprietys,[22] in right of wch J. Bass took up 20000 Acres in w. Jers. for me be not allowed, Gett them allowed, or an order to take up so much above the falls,[23] where is excellent land on that side as S. Jen: tould me, & wch Malen Stacy[24] tould him of; & wch the Indian that owns it, promessed me not to sell till I came, or with my consent, unless to me.[25] of wch Jos. Kirkbride & I think some others can informe thee. T. Fairman, can manage such an affaire well enough, & speaks that Indian Pretty well,[26] whose Bror Robt [27] was wth me t'other day, & so, so.

Colonel Q. comes on purpose to do us mischeife sent for hence by the party,[28] as well as to do himselfe wt good he can.

Let the council & w. Rodney, if can, be attested about those words, improved by Ignorance or Malice, about laying them by the heels, that should disown the Gover^{r}. There may be need of it—also, thine of Colonel Quarys professions to me, & that the reason of writeing that letter incloseing the sherrifs Commiss^{r} he took such pains to recover,[29] ~~&~~ was on acc^{t} of the affidavits I had sent, as he was assured, ags^{t} him {home} &c:

I must have the affidavits of the former appraisers ch. R. &c: about Lumbys Goods & the words that Induced them to Lowre them so much from their true vallue.[30]

I must have one of Bayling the Pyrats by Colonel Q. & Bass too,[31] as also the widdow Basnets not being pd by the first, ~~nor~~ tho the mony {was} kept by him for that purpose, as he tould me, & her also.[32]

The requisit affid^{ts} about Bonne's vessel & Perres Goods, wine, Iron & linnen, & w^{t} sould for, is essential,[33] as T. farmers about my commanding upon Col. Q, complaint that he proceeded no farther, & afterwards my ordering thee to take it up. likewise that There were but two, and that one of them was never executed, & tother but twice in indifferent Cases;[34] together with the occasion of their makeing, {viz,} Col. Q^{s} {almost} perpetuall absence, J. Moor's aversness to meddle with anything as his Dep^{ty} & that it was done by & upon the opinion of the Kings naval officer of New-york[35] of Ld. Bellom^{ts} prefering, & one of the Kgs Council {at law} for that province, that I might act safe. next, forget not the Spaniards case,[36] and suitable affidavits. his Counsil J. Moor sayd in my hearing I could neither say nor do more or otherways than I offered him, least any Brangle[37] follow on that acc^{t}.

Thou didst not gett the Bills of loading agst Capt Burford,[38] who insteed of satisfaction has most falsly spread storys agst us to his owners &c: & troubled frds therein, and all for want of {our early} care about it, to send over heither agst him, as I so often urged. pray lett it be done. one of his greatest storys was my Impr~~o~~is~~e~~oning his Mate & Doctor, & Forceing them to pay great sums of mony Phillip James & honest R. Bryants Daughter at Newcastle can informe thee fully whose attests would do well.[39]

whatever was forgot send, if not sent. But I hope the coppys of the charter of Prop^{ty} & the laws &c: are not (with severall of these things) now to be sent to me. I shall send a Coppy of the articles, & would have Colonel Markham[40] to clear his part & all else concerned, least there should be an occasion {here.}

There is a swamp between the falls & the Meeting house,[41] I gave the falls people formerly leave to Cutt timber in for there own use, which they have almost spoyled, Cuting for Saile, coopery[42] &c: wch now would have been worth some thousands, or in a while, (Phi: Pemb: Knows the business) lett all be for bid to Cutt there any more, & learn who have been the waisters of the timber, that here after they may help to Clear the rubbish parts, that will be fitt for use, or give me tree for tree, ~~if~~ wn I or my order shall demand it. That pyrattical latitude too many have, of thinking they can do me no wrong, and of makeing bold with other folks things, is a great dishonour to America, & makeing no returns in 7 years time, of wch I have heard enough & too much already. Some publick course must be taken therein or we shall be layd under mighty disgrace. There is 12 lb of good Chacolat sent us about 2 months agoe,[43] lett R. Ship. have 2 lb. Han Carp. 2 lb. Han. hill 2 lb. M. Norris 2 lb R. Prest. 2 lb. and Govr Ham. wife 2 lb.[44]

Consigne all thou sendst for me to ed. singleton[45] in Berbados. no need that R. E.[46] Knows of it; his presents poor man exceed his returnes. this to thy selfe.

Minde the sale of the wid. Calverts land, that both I & wid. Harris of Dub. may be payd.[47] faile not.

Search Bror Penngts office[48] if any returns are to be found for George shore of Irland. honest A. Strutle writes to Ed. Sing. to ask me of both. & let me Know if he is returned by Catalogue one of the first 100 Purchassers, that is in thy hands.[49]

Let Ed: Hopton[50] have a Patent for his land of Poquessin, if T. Fairman see good. be sure to use & secure him as we discourst loosing no time. Hop. is glad his son came not, talks of returning.

I hope thy eye is upon the mils to retrench expences. and see the utmost, at a leisure hour, of poor Marshes[51] project of navigating flats up scoolkill & sasquehanagh Rivers above the falls, he assureing me that he could make the experimt for 40ss, be it 50ss or 3l It were a mighty advantage.

I enclose a paper I found in my pocket of Eliz. Bennits;[52] if her request be reasonable, let her be considered. ~~I write~~

all Letters for me, wife or Daughter, or S. cl.[53] send back, except such as come from the Govermt here, for they are Endorst always, for the Kings service

I had a lettr Ld. Cornberry[54] sent me from Spithead that secretary vernon writt me by him,[55] to Bespeak my acquaintance & friendship & good ~~& intimate~~ Corrispondence in america, as Ld. Bell. and I had done before, which looks as if he came upon the same foot, & as if he had no thoughts of my being defeated of my Govermt. Sr H. Ashurst[56] tould me yesterday, there would be nothing done in it, he beleived, who lives in Kensington, & is Agent for New Engd; so says a lawyer used at Bottom[57] on that Side {but that is to thy selfe}. Divers tell me that Colonel Dudly[58] has been an enimy at bottom, & a flaterer to the attempt upon our charters; wch if true, I am sorry for it: But I shall, I hope, defeat all those designes, for I finde the greatest people of both houses tender in Conversation upon the state & Reason of the Case. I shall act the best I can for future safety to the people & my family, as one common Interrest. I know not of any more a~~s~~t present by this opertunity of the Messenger.[59] capt. Puckle follows in 14 or 20 days at most, as they say, by whom I purpose to write of all occuring as to us: and by this opertunity a General letter to Govr Ham. & Council.[60] but by the way send w^t thou Canst by Guy. Bear skins, & Buck skins, for they bear an advance,[61] & good Bright Tobacco. I hear but an ordinary Character of the Judge,[62] by Lewis M:[63] as formerly an husher of a writeing School, & not at all morall. more per next. If in the least he tricks, use him accordingly. my leg is better, wife & father & childe goeing this week for Bristoll,[64] my son & family well. a sweet Girle, & a sarazen of a Boy, his wife a good & pretty woman, at Bristoll on her fathers acc^t who is dead & buried.[65] J. Cosgarne marrys betty[66] — there is a letter for thee on acc^t of his business in Kent County wch put in as good away as thou canst pray, for my son is Interrested.[67] with my true love to all my Good frds, as If I named them, desireing the lord to be among you in wisdom, love & feare, I close & am their &

Thy assured Friend
Wm Penn

My love to my family[68] I writ by a N: eng ship last week to thee,[69] in short, not time to read it, that If John & Mary come, his bro^r leaveing him 150^l if he comes in two years for it,[70] that Hugh[71] be Steward & Gardiner, & old Peter[72] go to the Garden when needfull, & that P. Pembtons wife or Daughter[73] see to the beding & linnen once a month. minde that the leads[74] be mended. I pray god continue poor Phinias.[75] we all, remember you in your respective capacitys, with much love & regard & Pennsylvania will not be forgotton. Remember me to all officers in Goverm^t & to deserveing sweeds &c: a rumer within two days of the K. of sweedlands being lately in hazard in an Engagem^t but he resolves not to returne home till he has resetled Spahis over oginsky & the K. of Pol.[76] He has made a great begining. I send the Ks Speach, Lords & commons address, whence a warr, as wisely as they can, is like to ensue;[77] cutt you your coat according to your Cloath, & make hay while the sun shines, for Eng. & Irl. can not supply the Islands with Provisions.[78] a coppy hereof will goe by N. Puckle or some other Conveyance.
vale.
ought I to allow S. Jen. {a Sallery certain} for receiver, & he not receive, but must pay an other for Receiveing that he left behinde; poundage[79] is the fairest, unless all had been receivd. If he says I orderd him to let the Shrives receive, It was to save charges, being my officers, & could do it with the country Levys all at once, & who got by their places,[80] & not to pay 2^ss in the pound 1/10 of the whole, & he a sallery for only receiveing it of them, & useing it himself. But w. Rodney was no sherrif, nor B. ch^rs [81] nor did J. Hill[82] desist after out of the sherrifs place. If he says he did not receive all, because I forbad the Tennants to pay; why any, or more than I drew for? & why of the ablest, when I sayd only of the doubtfull or hazardous. and why suffer gibbs[83] to run 700^l in arrear, to live upon my rents, & yet charge

receivers sallery for the same time. why lett my goods his Inventory taken Says were at Pennsberry when he had the Charge be lost or Embezel'd, without a quarterly, or yearly survey. Never once done in 12 years runing. These things have sorrowfull & wounding touches in them; of all which make a wise use. & keep all as quiet as may be till, things here are over.[84] My son shall hasten,[85] possess him, goe with him to Pennsb^r advise him. contract & recommend his acquaintance; no rambling to N. york, nor mungrill corrispondence: He has promest faire, I know he will regard thee, but thou will see I have purchast the [illegible deletion] {mighty} supplys at a dear rate,[86] God forgive those wretched people that have misused me so, & preserve my spirit over it. Pennsylvania has been a dear Pennsylvania to me all over, wch few consider, and with me lay to heart. Be discreet. he has witt, kept the top company, must be handled with much love, & wisdom. & urgeing the weakness or folly of some behavours, & the necessity of another conduct from Interrest & reputation, will go farr. and get S. C. Ed. Sh. Is. N. P. P. T. Mas.[87] & Such persons to be soft & kinde & reaching, it will do wonders with him: he is conquerd that way, pretends much to honour, & is but over generous by half; and yet sharp enough to get to spend. He cannot well be put on. all this keep to thy selfe.[88] vale.

lett Bro^r Pennington Know his relations are well.[89] Ld Cornberry comes upon the Ch. favour, but wig Principles as people talk. pray desire Govr Ham. & our folks to carry a good Corrispondance wth him.[90]

ALS. Penn Papers, Penn Family to James Logan, HSP. (*Micro.* 10:013.) A signed copy of the letter, written in a hand other than WP's and sent via Barbados, follows the original in the same volume.

1. This letter was begun on 4 Jan. 1702 but must have been continued on about 11 Jan., since WP reports in his postscript here that he sent another letter (*Micro.* 10:008), also dated 4 Jan., "last week." See n. 69, below.

2. WP had complained of a sore leg several times during the summer of 1700. *PWP,* 3:609-10, 613-15; *Micro.* 8:548.

3. Start Point, WP's landfall, is ten miles south of Dartmouth on the Devon coast.

4. Like Nathaniel Puckle, John Guy, Quaker captain of the *Messenger* and later of the *Robert and Benjamin,* sailed frequently between Pennsylvania and England. While in Philadelphia in 1701, he received leave to marry Jemimah England. Hinshaw, 2:538; *PMHB,* 78:156; doc. 18, n. 17.

5. A peninsula in Cornwall at the southwestern extremity of England.

6. Himself [Old French]. As his father's agent (see doc. 1), William Penn, Jr., had evidently overspent in his lobbying efforts among members of Parliament.

7. For the 1701 Reunification Bill in the House of Lords, see the headnote to doc. 17. On 19 Jan. 1702 the Commons requested that the Board of Trade report on "their proceedings for the improvement of trade." The final section of that report, delivered 5 Feb., criticized the proprietary colonies. The House of Lords received the report 16 Feb. *Proceedings and Debates,* 2:v-vii, 398-401, 426-43; Michael G. Hall, *Edward Randolph and the American Colonies, 1676-1703* (Chapel Hill, N.C., 1960), pp. 205-13.

8. In his hurry to leave Pennsylvania, WP had not brought with him all the evidence he needed to counter the accusations against his government.

9. The Assembly had granted WP £2000 before his departure, and WP had

arranged for the sale of several pieces of his property in Pennsylvania and the Lower Counties. Docs. 32, 35.

10. WP had also arranged to sell some of his lands in East New Jersey as a means of raising money. See doc. 35, n. 28; doc. 36, text at n. 3.

11. Yellow-leaf tobacco — a high-quality variety produced in the Chesapeake region by the late seventeenth century — was prized in Europe for use as snuff. Lewis C. Gray, *History of Agriculture in the Southern United States to 1860*, 2 vols. (Washington, D.C., 1933), 1:218; G. Melvin Herndon, ed., *William Tatham and the Culture of Tobacco* (Coral Gables, Fla., 1969), pp. 338-39.

12. To transfer Pennsylvania assets back to England, Pennsylvania merchants frequently purchased Maryland bills of exchange, since Maryland merchants, with their regular tobacco trade, had steady credit with London merchants. Unfortunately, tobacco prices began to fall with the outbreak of war, and many of these bills were protested in England. *Micro.* 10:141; doc. 69; Gary B. Nash, "Maryland's Economic War with Pennsylvania," *Maryland Historical Magazine*, 60:240-43.

13. Samuel Vaus (b. 1648), or Vaux, the son of an early London Quaker, was WP's London factor until 1705 (*PMHB*, 78:151; Digests of Quaker Records, London and Middx., GSP). Robert Egerton was WP's agent in Barbados, but WP ordered Logan to use Edward Singleton from this time on (see text at n. 45, below).

14. WP's colonists were paying their quitrents with tobacco of the worst quality, which brought especially low prices in England. Logan promised to try to convert WP's income into other mediums of exchange. *Micro.* 10:634.

15. Besides WP's enormous debt to Philip Ford, he also had other, lesser creditors (see doc. 108; n. 49, below).

16. See doc. 35, n. 22.

17. On 1 Dec. 1702 Logan reported to WP that the sale of Delaware River bank lots had been discouraged by a statement of WP's cousin, Paroculos Parmiter, that the proprietor's rights extended only to the edge of the river, and that any landfill belonged to the crown. *Micro.* 10:634.

18. Both James Claypoole (1634-1687), a London Quaker who set up as a merchant in Philadelphia, and Charles Marshall (1637-1698), a Bristol Quaker physician who held property in Philadelphia, were long since dead. As late as Mar. 1704 WP was still asking about Claypoole's debt. *PWP*, 2:105n, 648; Mortimer, 1:209; *PA*, 2d ser., 19:397-99; doc. 76, text at n. 42.

19. James Harrison (c. 1628-1697), a Lancashire Quaker, had been WP's steward at Pennsbury. Samuel Jennings had been WP's receiver general but had not turned over any receipts to the proprietor and had moved to West New Jersey. *PWP*, 3:38-41; n. 77, below.

20. In a letter of 14 Aug. 1702, Logan wrote to Laetitia Penn that he had sold her bank lot and a small lot on High (Market) St. for £230. Logan Papers, 1:41, HSP.

21. George Heathcote (d. 1711), a Quaker merchant with ships sailing between England and the colonies, purchased 200 acres adjacent to Pennsbury in the early 1680s and disputed the amount of Delaware River frontage he had agreed upon with WP. In 1691-92, during WP's absence from Pennsylvania, Heathcote persuaded the property commissioners to grant him 304 additional acres adjacent to Pennsbury, for £30 at the "usual rent of a purchaser." WP wanted to contest Heathcote's claim by sending Logan a copy of the original deed, but he was never able to find it. *PWP*, 2:321n, 3:291n, 408-11; *Micro.* 4:598, 5:669; 10:634; doc. 48, text at n. 35; *PA*, 2d ser., 19:74-75, 87-88.

22. WP held two proprieties, or shares, of land in West New Jersey, which he purchased from William Haige and Daniel Waite in the 1680s. In 1697 he appointed Jeremiah Basse and Samuel Jennings as his agents to locate and dispose of his lands. Pomfret, *West New Jersey*, pp. 285, 286; *PWP*, 3:257.

23. The Falls of the Delaware River, at present-day Trenton.

24. Mahlon Stacy (d. 1704), a Yorkshire Quaker and West New Jersey proprietor, emigrated in 1678 and settled near the Falls of the Delaware. John E. Pomfret, "The Proprietors of the Province of West New Jersey, 1674-1702," *PMHB*, 75:123-25; *PWP*, 2:481.

25. The Indian who "owned" this property may have been Tammany (d. by 1701), chief sachem of the Unami Delaware in the 1680s and 1690s. WP reported that he bought the land from the "old King" who visited Pennsbury. Charles A. Hanna, *The Wilderness Trail* (New York, 1911), 1:98; *PWP*, 2:458n; 3:42n; *Micro.* 11:089; doc. 76.

26. Joseph Kirkbride (see doc. 25, n. 6) and Thomas Fairman had dealt with the Indians on WP's behalf earlier. The Indian language, which WP also claimed to understand, was the Unami Delaware tongue. Soderlund, *William Penn,* pp. 312-13; Trigger, *North American Indians,* p. 73.

27. Robert Fairman, a Quaker from Hertfordshire, bought land in Phila. Co. but apparently did not emigrate. *PWP,* 3:204n, 699-700; *PA,* 2d ser., 19:399.

28. Robert Quary was a leader of the anti-proprietary church party.

29. The commission, a copy of which Quary sent to the Board of Trade and later to the House of Lords, was for Philadelphia sheriff Thomas Farmer to serve as water bailiff. WP mistakenly wrote "Commiss^{r}" instead of "Commiss^{n}." *Micro.* 8:493; doc. 18, n. 32; *CSPC, 1700,* p. 839.

30. In 1699 the *Providence,* master, John Lumby, had been seized in Pennsylvania for violating the Navigation Act of 1696. Quary commissioned several men, including Charles Read, to appraise the ship's goods, which were to be divided in thirds and awarded to the proprietor, the informant (John Moore), and the crown. WP accused Quary of unlawfully seizing the ship and then ordering a low appraisal so that the owners could regain their property cheaply. He also asserted that Moore had split his third with Quary. Quary denied everything, and WP apparently never received the evidence he needed to support his charges. *CSPC, 1702,* pp. 95-96, 99, 104, 116-17, 397, 416-17, 516-17; *Micro.* 10:259, 267, 297, 431; 14:717; *PWP,* 3:624, 627-28; doc. 33, n. 22.

31. Quary had accused WP's deputy governor William Markham of allowing pirates to go free on bail, and WP wanted to bring countercharges that Quary and New Jersey Gov. Jeremiah Basse had permitted pirates to escape. In May 1702 Andrew Hamilton reported to WP that he had found several pirates at large in New Jersey, freed by Basse. *PWP,* 3:627-28n; *Micro.* 10:169.

32. Elizabeth Richards Frampton Bassnet (d. by 1712), a widowed New Jersey Quaker now married to Thomas Gardiner, was trying to recover a debt owed by John Eldridge, a convicted pirate. When Quary seized Eldridge's treasure on the pirate ship *Nassau,* he evidently promised to pay Bassnet but failed to do so. Hinshaw, 2:166, 197, 460; Phila. Will Bk. A, #30; *CSPC, 1700,* pp. 169, 278, 338, 761-62; *Micro.* 10:169.

33. Quary had accused Gous Bonin (anglicized as "Gousey Bunyan") and Samuel Peres of violating the Navigation Acts and presented the Board of Trade with a deposition from the mate of their ship, charging them with smuggling Dutch linen, claret, and iron from Curaçao into Philadelphia. Bonin, a Jewish surgeon, and Peres, a French Huguenot, both claimed to be naturalized Englishmen. In a letter of 2 May 1702 Logan reminded WP that before his departure for England he had given him a letter from Bonin, and he now enclosed a copy of Peres's accounts. *CSPC, 1702,* pp. 187, 328; *1708-1709,* p. 293; *1710-1711,* pp. 450-51; *1712-1714,* p. 74; Journal of the Board of Trade, 1702-3, transcript at HSP, p. 29; *PA,* 2d ser., 19:584; *Micro.* 6:048, 10:117. See also doc. 18, text at nn. 34-38.

34. WP had commissioned the sheriffs of Philadelphia (Thomas Farmer) and of New Castle (Joseph Wood) as water bailiffs in 1700. See doc. 18, n. 32.

35. Paroculos Parmiter, WP's cousin. *New York Col. Docs.,* 4:623, 664.

36. Probably Juan Corso. See docs. 33, n. 14; 56.

37. Squabble. *OED.*

38. Captain Burford, who had contracted to carry indentured servants from London to New Castle, had taken them to Maryland instead. *Micro.* 8:617, 627; 9:030; *CSPC, 1700,* p. 80.

39. Philip James (d. 1702), a Philadelphia merchant, was apppointed Philadelphia city councilman by WP in 1691. *Micro.* 10:117; Phila. Will Bk. B, #74; *PMHB,* 18:504. Robert Bryant (d. 1701) of New Castle had two daughters, Mary and Ann; WP probably meant Mary, who was married to New Castle justice of the peace John Cann. Phila. Will Bk. B, #60; *PWP,* 2:319-20n.

40. William Markham (c. 1635-1704), WP's cousin, had served as deputy governor of Pennsylvania in the 1690s until he was dismissed from office in 1699 for failure to enforce the laws against piracy. WP was now trying to defend him and other Pennsylvania officials against charges brought against the colony before the Board of Trade. *PWP,* 3:37n.

41. Falls Monthly Meeting erected a meetinghouse at Falsington in 1692.

42. Cooperage, or barrel-making. *OED.*

43. The chocolate arrived before this letter, but it was broken, Logan reported. *Micro.* 10:141, 634.

44. The first five of these women were the wives of leading Philadelphia merchants and prominent members of Philadelphia Monthly Meeting. Hannah Hardiman Carpenter (1646-1728), a Quaker minister, had emigrated from Wales in 1683 and married Samuel Carpenter the following year. Hannah Delavall Hill (d. 1726) married Richard Hill in 1700, soon after his arrival from London. Mary Lloyd Norris (d. 1748), daughter of Thomas Lloyd, married Isaac Norris in 1694. Her sister Rachel Lloyd Preston (d. 1716) married Samuel Preston in about 1688. Rebecca Howard Richardson Shippen (d. 1705), the widow of a New York Quaker merchant, had married Edward Shippen in 1689 and moved with him to Philadelphia in 1694. Andrew Hamilton's 1702 will gives his wife's name as Agnes, but nothing else is known about her. *PWP*, 2:614n; Hinshaw, 2:374, 400, 409, 549, 608, 626; Randolph S. Klein, *Portrait of an American Family: The Shippens of Pennsylvania across Five Generations* (Philadelphia, 1975), pp. 10, 13-14, 335; Isaac Sharpless, *Political Leaders of Provincial Pennsylvania* (New York, 1919), pp. 183-84; *NJA*, 23:203; *DAB*.

45. Edward Singleton, who was WP's relative by marriage, went to Barbados in about 1702 where he served as WP's agent. *PWP*, 3:404n; *PMHB*, 78:145.

46. Robert Egerton; see n. 13, above.

47. Judith Calvert (b. 1652) was the widow of John Calvert (1638-1699), an Irish Quaker who settled in Chester Co. in about 1683. After his death, she appealed to WP, through Robert Turner, to prevent the family lands from being sold by the sheriff to pay her husband's debts to WP and several Irish creditors, including Ann Harrison. The property was sold to Calvert's sons in Aug. 1702, but widow Harrison still had not been repaid by 1708. Myers, *Immigration*, pp. 317-18; Hinshaw, 2:442; *PA*, 2d ser., 19:66; *Micro.* 8:204; doc. 156.

48. Edward Penington, surveyor general.

49. George Shore, a Quaker merchant of Athlone, Ireland, was a First Purchaser of 5000 acres who never emigrated. Amos Strettle (b. 1658) and his brother Abel (d. c. 1708) were linendrapers in Dublin and landholders in West New Jersey and Pennsylvania, although not First Purchasers. Strettle was apparently trying to find out if he and Shore were eligible for grants of city lots and liberty lands guaranteed to First Purchasers. The Strettle brothers lent WP money, and Amos later accepted payment in the form of Pennsylvania land. *PWP*, 2:653; 3:545n; doc. 156; *Micro.* 14:190; James Logan to Amos Strettle, 25 Sept. 1717, Logan Letterbook, 4:53, HSP.

50. Edward Hopton (d. 1710), a London Quaker brewer, bought 250 acres on the north side of Poquessing Creek from WP for £130. His son Jeremiah, who married Thomas Fairman's daughter Abigail, obtained a patent for this land, although Benjamin Acrod asserted a prior claim, saying that he had bought it from Wollo Woolson, whose claim predated WP's proprietorship. Edward Hopton did not return to Pennsylvania, but his son continued to live on the family's city lot in Philadelphia. Digests of Quaker Records, London and Middx.; *PA*, 2d ser., 19:578, 614, 648, 675-77; *Micro.* 10:032.

51. John Marsh. See doc. 33, n. 9.

52. Elizabeth Bennett (d. 1707) of Philadelphia Monthly Meeting was the sole heir of her husband, Edmund, a First Purchaser and tobacco cutter from Bristol who died in Philadelphia in 1692. She may have asked WP to assist her in negotiating with Thomas Yardley, who had purchased 50 acres in Bucks Co. from her in 1696 and now was claiming the adjoining 6 acres of marsh land. In Nov. 1701 the commissioners of property had granted the additional land to him at 20s per acre. Phila. Will Bk. A, #83; Hinshaw, 2:336; *PA*, 2d ser., 19:195, 236, 409.

53. Sarah Clements had returned to England with the Penns after her ministry in America.

54. Edward Hyde (1661-1723), Viscount Cornbury and later earl of Clarendon, was commissioned governor of New York in Sept. 1701 and of New Jersey in Dec. 1702—positions he held until 1708. A cousin of Queen Anne and a strong supporter of the Church of England, Cornbury was one of the least successful and most corrupt administrators in colonial America. In a short note of 6 Dec. 1701, from on board his ship at Spithead, off Portsmouth harbor, Cornbury wrote to WP: "though our acquaintance has been but small in England, I did hope it might have been improved in Ammerica, and though I am not very fond of many Visitts here, yet I should have been very glad to see you" (*Micro.* 9:927). WP never became as friendly with Cornbury as he had been with the earl of Bellomont. Raimo, *Governors*, pp. 253-54; see also n. 90, below.

55. Secretary of State James Vernon's letter has not been found.

56. Sir Henry Ashurst (d. 1710), a baronet, served as agent for Massachusetts in

the 1690s and for Connecticut in the early 1700s. He had been instrumental in the defeat of the Reunification Bill in 1701. John Burke and John Bernard Burke, *Extinct and Dormant Baronetcies of England, Ireland, and Scotland,* 2d ed. (London, 1841), p. 18; Steele, *Colonial Policy,* pp. 69, 71, 79-80; Richard S. Dunn, *Puritans and Yankees: The Winthrop Dynasty of New England, 1630-1717* (Princeton, 1962), pp. 270-73, 277-79, 282, 332-333.

57. Secretly, or in reality, as opposed to superficial appearances. *OED.*

58. Joseph Dudley (1647-1720), who had repudiated the chartered Puritan government of Massachusetts in the 1680s and had been imprisoned during the Boston rebellion of 1689, was jockeying for appointment as governor of Massachusetts, which he received in Dec. 1701 despite all the exertions of Sir Henry Ashurst. Dudley served as governor until 1715. *PWP,* 3:475n; Dunn, *Puritans and Yankees,* pp. 278-79; Everett Kimball, *The Public Life of Joseph Dudley* (London, 1911), pp. 74-75.

59. John Guy's ship, the *Messenger.*

60. WP wrote to Gov. Andrew Hamilton and to the commissioners of property on 8 Jan. 1702 (*Micro.* 10:032, 033) and to the Provincial Council on 10 Jan. 1702 (doc. 39).

61. WP could receive payment for furs in advance from English buyers, but at this time Logan lacked goods to trade with the Indians and had no capital with which to buy them. *Micro.* 10:634; *PMHB,* 78:170-76.

62. John Guest. See doc. 10, n. 9.

63. Lewis Morris had arrived in England in July 1701 and returned to New Jersey at the end of April, after the surrender of New Jersey to the crown. *Micro.* 9:226; 10:267; Eugene R. Sheridan, *Lewis Morris, 1671-1746* (Syracuse, N.Y., 1981), pp. 35-48.

64. Hannah Penn and her son, John, went to Bristol to stay with her father, Thomas Callowhill.

65. Charles Jones, Jr., the father of Mary Jones Penn, was buried 25 Dec. 1701. WP's grandchildren mentioned here are Gulielma Maria and Springett. Jenkins, pp. 107-10, 126-29, 245; Digests of Quaker Records, Bristol and Som., GSP.

66. Joseph Coysgarne, Jr. (b. 1678), a Bristol Quaker merchant, married Elizabeth Jones (1679-1758?), the sister of WP's daughter-in-law, Mary Penn, on 22 Oct. 1702. Mortimer, 2:239.

67. Charles Jones, Jr., and his father had sold this property to Philip James in about 1688. James paid £36 and owed £64, which he had not paid as of Dec. 1702. *Micro.* 8:310, 9:634, 10:634.

68. The household staff left at Pennsbury.

69. *Micro.* 10:008, dated 4 Jan.

70. John Sotcher left for England in early May 1702 and returned to Pennsylvania on 20 Nov. 1702. *Micro.* 10:192, 241, 634.

71. Hugh Sharp (d. 1741), who served as gardener at Pennsbury, later became a leading member of Burlington Monthly Meeting. *NJA,* 30:428; *Micro.* 9:870, 12:005.

72. Peter (d. 1701 or 1702), whose surname is unknown, may have been a slave. See doc. 52, n. 35.

73. After the death of his first wife, Phoebe, in 1696, Phineas Pemberton married Alice Hodgson (d. 1711) of Burlington, New Jersey. After his death she married Thomas Bradford in 1704. Abigail Pemberton (1680-1750), the oldest surviving daughter of Phineas and Phoebe Pemberton, married Stephen Jenkins of Abingdon, Bucks Co., in 1704. Hinshaw, 2:249, 1021; R. C. B. Pemberton, comp., *Pemberton Pedigrees* (Bedford, Eng., 1923), chart 26.

74. Window leading.

75. Phineas Pemberton had been in poor health when WP left Pennsylvania. He died on about 1 Apr. 1702. *Micro.* 10:141.

76. In the early years of the Great Northern War, Charles XII of Sweden (1682-1718) occupied Lithuania in late 1701, seizing it from Augustus (1670-1733), the king of Poland and elector of Saxony. Charles was allied with the powerful Sapieha family in Lithuania against the Saxon-allied Oginski family. Luttrell, 5:116, 123; R. M. Hatton, *Charles XII of Sweden* (New York, 1968), pp. 178-79.

77. William III addressed the House of Lords on 31 Dec. 1701 (Luttrell, 5:125). After his death, Queen Anne officially declared war on France on 4 May 1702, initiating the War of the Spanish Succession, known in the colonies as Queen Anne's War.

78. WP anticipates that during the coming war Pennsylvania can provide the West Indies with staples normally shipped from England or Ireland. However, the war had

a generally dampening effect on trade because of increased freight and insurance rates. *PMHB*, 78:150.

79. A commission on each receipt of WP's revenue. *OED*.

80. WP is arguing that the sheriffs should not have been paid extra for collecting quitrents, since they were already employed to collect provincial taxes. Jennings had paid his assistants 10 percent of whatever they collected. *Micro.* 6:444; *PWP*, 3:408, 410n.

81. Benjamin Chambers (d. 1715) had been commissioned deputy receiver general under Samuel Jennings in 1690 and was acting receiver general during WP's second visit to Pennsylvania, 1699-1700. John H. Martin, *Martin's Bench and Bar of Philadelphia* (Philadelphia, 1883), p. 172; *Micro.* 6:444, 8:119.

82. John Hill (d. 1708), a prominent landowner and justice in Sussex Co., served several years on the Provincial Council between 1689 and 1706. *PWP*, 3:193n.

83. Edward Gibbs, Samuel Jennings's assistant for New Castle Co. See doc. 33, n. 19; *Micro.* 6:444.

84. Until the question of Pennsylvania's charter has been resolved.

85. William Penn, Jr., did not arrive in Pennsylvania until Feb. 1704. See doc. 76, n. 1.

86. WP is referring to his son's profligacy as one of the personal costs of the proprietorship. See Peare, pp. 383-84.

87. Samuel Carpenter, Edward Shippen, Phineas Pemberton, and Thomas Masters are all identified elsewhere in this volume. Isaac Norris (1671-1735), a Quaker merchant and member of the Assembly, had come to Philadelphia from Jamaica in 1693 and quickly became one of the wealthiest men in the city. He later served as mayor of Philadelphia and was on the Provincial Council for some 30 years. Sharpless, *Political Leaders*, pp. 181-85.

88. The copy of this letter sent via Barbados ends here. WP added in his own hand: "I have no time to compare it. vale." Penn Papers, Penn Family to James Logan, pp. 4,5, HSP.

89. Edward Penington, who died just a week after this letter was written, had two brothers and a sister still living in England: John Penington (1655-1710); William Penington (1665-1703) and his wife, Elizabeth; and Mary Penington Wharley (1657-1726), whose husband, Daniel Wharley (d. 1721), was a London woolendraper. All the Peningtons were First Purchasers, but Edward was the only one to come to Pennsylvania. *PWP*, 1:132n, 239n; 2:650; 3:436, 437n; L. V. Hodgkin, *Gulielma: Wife of William Penn* (London, 1947), chart preceding p. 223.

90. Gov. Hamilton met Cornbury at Burlington in June 1702 and invited him to visit Pennsylvania. Cornbury dined at Logan's Philadelphia house on 22 June, spent the night at Edward Shippen's, and the next day stopped at Pennsbury where Logan again entertained him and his party of 50. In July Logan reported that Shippen and Carpenter sent the New York governor madeira and beer, "wch has Engaged him in all protestations of Service possible in these parts." *Micro.* 10:241, 400.

39
TO THE PROVINCIAL COUNCIL

Kensington the 10th of the 11th month [January] 1701[/2]

Honoured & Esteemed Freinds

I have Joyned you in this, having writt allready from Portsmouth by the Jersey Frigott to Governour Hamilton.[1] I bless God this Leaves us all well Save my Sore Legg & Toe which yett are in a kindly way to be better. I have little news to write you; only am told the bussiness I came about is like to be dropt, and I am at some stand what to doe, I hope God will direct for the best. In the mean time for that Reason, if no other, I think fitt to forbid the putting of the Great Seale to the

Charter of Property, till I have had more room & time, to consult the nature & extent of those Powers, with Regard to my Patent. for as yett, as I could remember them, they are not approved {of} as Safe, especially in point of Prudence. Here has been villanous work against us, Such fallacy Malice, and Tricking, tis Contemptible as well as wicked; but I do not despond. East & West Jersey have weakly made hast to Surrender,[2] as if animated to it before my coming: It is not a Mistery to me. Keep all quiet, & be discreet, & yett Suffer not Government to be Trod upon. Affairs here are dubious, a war likely next Spring. Partys very warm & contesting, hard to say which may carry it.[3] I wish a discreet composure. I say no more than that I pray God Almighty to be with and among you in his fear & wisdom, & bring us once more together, which will be a Comfortable day I hope, to

Your {very} Affectionate
& Faithfull Freind WP

I send you an Instrument about not Sealing the Charter, & the Kings Speech.[4]
I want the whole Body of the Laws, as past at Philadelphia under the great Seale[5] WP

LBC. Penn Papers, William Penn Letterbook, 1699-1703, HSP. (*Micro.* 10:035.)

1. In this letter of 8 Jan. 1702 (*Micro.* 10:033) WP formally commanded Governor Hamilton not to affix the seal to the Charter of Property for six months or until further instructions.

2. On 6 Jan. 1702 the Board of Trade submitted to the king drafts of a surrender proposal unanimously endorsed by the proprietors of East and West Jersey. The surrender was executed on 15 Apr. Pomfret, *East New Jersey*, pp. 360-61; Pomfret, *West New Jersey*, p. 213.

3. Parliamentary debates over England's role in the European conflict split along party lines, with most Whigs favoring full-scale war and many Tories arguing that England should stay out of war or enter naval operations only. On 10 Jan., the date of this letter, William III and the Whigs overcame the opposition when the Commons approved the arrangements the king had made with the Dutch and the Hapsburg emperor, that England would contribute to the Grand Alliance 40,000 men on land and 40,000 at sea. David Ogg, *England in the Reigns of James II and William III* (Oxford, 1955), pp. 481-84; J. R. Jones, *Country and Court: England, 1658-1714* (Cambridge, Mass., 1978), pp. 288-290; Burnet, pp. 697-98.

4. See doc. 38, n. 77.

5. On 28 Oct. 1701 the Pennsylvania Assembly had confirmed the 96 laws passed at New Castle the previous year and passed 9 new laws. WP sailed for England before a copy could be made of the new laws, and he was unable to submit them for approval by the crown until 15 Dec. 1702. *Statutes*, 2:142-70; *Micro.* 10:704; *CSPC, 1702-1703*, p. 50.

40
PROPOSAL TO REUNITE PROPRIETARY COLONIES TO THE CROWN

During January and February 1702, when WP was trying to block the Board of Trade's continuing efforts to abolish the proprietary colonies in America, he met with other colonial proprietors and statesmen such as Robert Harley, speaker of the House of Commons, and the earl of Manchester, secretary of state, to discuss alternate proposals for reunification. Only a brief summary of WP's proposed reunification bill has been found; perhaps doc. 40 was all he ever put in writing. Manchester forwarded WP's summary, printed below, to the Board of Trade on 17 February 1702 without mentioning the author's name. The board recognized the source, however, and immediately concluded that, "the proposals made by Mr Penn which were enclosed in the Earl of Manchester's Letter of the 17th instt are no ways fit." WP's chief proposal — to unite the military command but leave the civil administration to the individual proprietors — was actually quite similar to the Board of Trade's own solution in 1697, when the earl of Bellomont was appointed "captain general" of all the colonies from New Jersey to New Hampshire. At that time, WP had unsuccessfully proposed a looser confederation; see *PWP,* 3:482–83. By 1702, however, the Board of Trade was satisfied with nothing less than the total resumption of proprietary colonies to the crown. The board vigorously promoted its new bill in Parliament, but it died without much debate. Parliament was preoccupied with more pressing concerns and discussed neither WP's plan nor the Board of Trade's. Steele, *Colonial Policy,* pp. 76–81; *Proceedings and Debates,* 2:427–42; *The Manuscripts of the House of Lords, 1699–1702* (London, 1908), pp. 436–63; Journal of the Board of Trade, 1701–1702, transcript at HSP, pp. 336–37; *Micro.* 10:043, 045.

[c. 17 February 1702]

Heads for a Bill for reuniting
to the Crown Severall Colonies
under proprietary Governments,
particularly that of Pensilvania

First — That the Military Government by Land and Sea, be Reunited to the Crown.[1]

2dly — That the Person the King deputes his Commander in Chiefe may have the Superintendency of the Officers of his Customes and Admiralty for the Security of his Revenue.

3dly — That the Civil Authority and Administration rest where they are, as they do in those Corporations in England, where the King has his Governours.

4thly — That nevertheless the proceedings in Case of Justice shall be in the Kings Name

5thly — That Appeales Ly to the King in all Causes above the Value of 300l Sterling; which hath been his Direction to other Colonys.[2]

6thly That the King has a Negative to any Law that shall be made in the Province.

whereby the King in Effect hath the Legislature and Jurisdiction Vested in him.

Copy. CO 5/1261, PRO. (Not filmed.)

1. WP had discussed similar ideas with Charlwood Lawton in 1701. See doc. 13.

2. The minimum amount required for appeals varied from colony to colony, from £100 to £500. WP had suggested in 1700 that one standard be set for all the colonies, either at £300, £400, or £500, but such a standard was not adopted until 1753, when it was set at £500. Joseph H. Smith, *Appeals to the Privy Council from the American Plantations* (New York, 1950), pp. 21–34; *CSPC, 1700*, p. 722.

41
FROM JACQUES LE TORT

De Londre ce 4e mar 1701/2

Monsieur

Jeay esté ches vous a Dessain dvoier Lonneur de vous voiar et ne vous ayans pas trouvé, Jeay apris que vous esties party pour Bristo, Jeay creu Monsieur que je devais vous Ecrire sur ceque jeay apris que Le Sr Coireay a presenté au Saigneurs quelque memoirs contre vous touchant Le Gouvernement de votre Province[1] et comme je ne Croy pas quil y ait de personne qui soit mieux Instruit que moy depuis saize a dix sept ans que La Perseqution de france mapoussé en votre province,[2] partiquliement pour cequi regarde Les affairs des Sauvages avec qui Jeay demeuré parmy eux et negociez depuis Le temps de mon arivee en Pensilvanie Jusque a present Je dit dont Monsieur que Le Sr Coiré est fort mal Instruit ou plutost fort malicieux de vous atribué un naigosse et un commerse avec des Sauvages cequi devroit Satribué a luy mesme plutost qua vous[3] estant entré dans La commission de charle Sandre et de Pigeon[4] qui ont toujours fait un grand Traficq avec ces Sorte de Jeans La, Je Luy ay mesme Payez sept a huit Pistolle[5] pour solde de Conte il ny a pas plus de sept a huit moyas pour marchandise Indiene et Pitre Bizaillon[6] viron deux sans quarante pistolle Louis Limosin[7] une autre somme considerable Le tout payable en peltrye a La reserve de moy, pour cequi est des Sauvages quil conte pour fransais[8] cest quil ce Lest Imagini car je nen Connais pas un et ausy ny en a nil point Je seay bien quil y a douze ou quinze Cabanne Indieni a Susquahana qui sont Le restant des Indiens que Les Irocoias aves de Depuis trante sinq a quarante ans detruits[9] et parse quils sont empetit nombre et Incapable de pouvoier entreprendre ny sur Les Irocoias ny sur autre nations il Leur ont donné La Liberté dy demeurez a La Charge de payez tribut comme Esclave, a Legard de votre province Je puis bien Dire avec Verité que dans tout Letans que [illegible deletion] gy ay demeuré Jeay toujours veu pratiqué La justice La concorde et Lamitié entre Les peuples et que Les Religions Sy sont toujours Professee avec toute Dousseur et bonne Intelligence Jusquace que Le Sr Coyré et Le Sr Jean More Son Jeandre yssons veneu qui ont toujours troubleé autant quils ons peu ce qui ne repont pas aux obligations et honnestetes que vous avez eiée pour Eux, et pour revenir encor aux Sauvages Jeay tres bonne connaissance quil vous Coute cher car outre quils ont toujours esté bien receu ches vous Beuvans et mangeans sans Conté toutes les autre Inquemodité que ces Sorte de Jeans La Donne cest quil ne vous ont Jamais fait de Presens que vous ne Leur en aye fait au Double, mais a dire Le vray ce nest pas tans Le mal que Le Sr Coyré vous veut comme votre Gouvernement car au precedent voyage quil a fait a Londre Il na pas peu Sempesché de dire quil vous feroit osté de votre Gouvernement et quil y Entreroit en effet il a[?] tans bersé Le peuple de cela quil Croyais que sela ce devoit faire a Cause de quelque Evesque qui estois parans de son Jandre[10] Je finiray en vous asseurant que je suis avec un profont respect

Monsieur
Votre tres humble et tres
obeissant serviteur
Le Tort

Japrans que Millord Petre Bareau[11] est un de vos amis et quil prens vos Interest dans Les ocasions qui ce presente

[Translation]

London the 4th of March 1702

Sir

I was at your house in order to have the honour of seeing you and not having found you, I learned that you had left for Bristol. I thought, Sir, that I should write since I have learned that Mr. Quary has sent several memorials to the Lords against you concerning the government of your province[1] and as I do not believe there is anyone better informed than I after the sixteen or seventeen years since the persecution of France drove me into your province,[2] particularly with regard to what concerns the savages, among whom I have lived and traded ever since I arrived in Pensilvania. I can thus say, Sir, that Mr. Quary is very ill informed or rather very malicious in attributing to you trade and commerce with the savages which should rather be attributed to himself than to you,[3] he being in the commission of Charles Sanders and Pidgeon[4] who have always had a great traffic with that sort of people. I even paid him seven to eight pistoles[5] on account not more than seven or eight months ago for Indian merchandise and Peter Bizaillion[6] about two hundred forty pistoles, Louis

Limoizin[7] another large sum, all repayable in pelts except for me. As for the savages that he considers French,[8] he has invented it; I do not know one, and there are none anywhere. I know indeed that there are twelve or fifteen Indian cabins at Susquehanna, which are the remains of the Indians which the Iroquois destroyed thirty-five to forty years ago[9] and as they are so few and unable to make war either on the Iroquois or on other nations they were given permission to live there and required to pay tribute like bondsmen. With regard to your province I can truthfully say that in all the time I lived there I always saw justice, peace and friendship practiced between the peoples, and religions were always professed there with complete calmness and good sense until Mr. Quary and Mr. John More his son-in-law came there, who have always made as much trouble as they could, which hasn't corresponded to the kindnesses and courtesy with which you have treated them. And to return to the savages again I know well that they cost you dear, for besides the fact that they have always been well entertained at your house with food and drink, let alone all the other trouble that these sort of people give, they have never given you presents that you have not repaid to them doubly. But to tell the truth this is not so much trouble as Mr. Quary wishes you and your government, for at his last trip to London he could not resist saying that he would have you deprived of your government and take it himself. In fact he deluded the people so much with this because he believed it would be done for the sake of some bishop who is a relative of his son-in-law.[10] I shall end by assuring you that I am with profound respect

Sir
Your very humble and very
obedient servant
Le Tort

I hear that Lord Peterborough[11] is one of your friends and that he promotes your interest whenever opportunities arise.

ALS. CO 5/1261, PRO. (*Micro.* 10:051.) Addressed: Monsieur | Monsieur Peen de present en La | Ville De Bristol | A Bristol. Docketed: Cap[t] Le Torts | lett[r] 1702.

1. The Board of Trade. For Robert Quary's letters to the board, see *PWP*, 3:570-74; *CSPC, 1702*, pp. 54, 64, 598. WP used Le Tort's letter as evidence in his defense against Quary in June 1702. See doc. 44; Board of Trade Journal, 1702-1703, transcript at HSP, p. 59. Le Tort's letter is incorrectly dated 4 May in *CSPC, 1702*, p. 290.

2. Capt. Jacques Le Tort (b. c. 1651), a Huguenot, had fled France with his wife, Anne, and son, James, when Louis XIV revoked the Edict of Nantes. After a brief stay in London, he went in 1686 to the Delaware Valley as an agent of the New Mediterranean Sea Company, and he later supervised the West New Jersey Society's fur trade with the Indians. He went to England on business in 1696 and seems never to have returned to the colonies. Charles A. Hanna, *The Wilderness Trail* (New York, 1911), pp. 165-66; *PWP*, 3: 191n; *Lancaster County Historical Society Publications*, 65:92-105; Francis Jennings, *The Ambiguous Iroquois Empire* (New York, 1984), p. 234.

3. Quary accused WP of monopolizing the Pennsylvania fur trade by requiring

traders to apply for a license from him. WP countered that, though he himself had made no profits from furs, Quary was one of the biggest traders. See doc. 44.

4. Charles Saunders (d. 1699) and Joseph Pidgeon were factors, or commissioned agents, of the New Pennsylvania Company, a joint stock venture formed in England in 1693 to control the English trade to Pennsylvania. Neither man was a Quaker; both settled in Philadelphia. *PWP*, 3:384n; Nash, *Quakers and Politics*, p. 141; Hinshaw, 2:416, 446.

5. Spanish gold pieces equal to four pesos, or pieces of eight, the universal money of the Atlantic trade. In 1702 a pistole was valued at 17s 2d sterling. McCusker, *Money and Exchange*, pp. 7, 11, 98-100.

6. Peter Bezaillion (1662?-1742), a French trader who probably came to Pennsylvania with Le Tort in 1686, began trading with the Indians at Conestoga before 1696 and eventually settled in East Caln Township, Chester Co. Bezaillion, like the Le Torts, was prosecuted and interrogated several times between 1693 and 1711 for conspiracy with the Indians and disloyalty to the English government. Hanna, *Wilderness Trail*, pp. 166-70; *PMHB*, 22:385, 24:17, 72:343.

7. Louis Lemoizin was another French trader under suspicion in Pennsylvania. He traveled to Canada with James Le Tort (Jacques's son) in 1701. Quary said he had run off with Canadian Indian "spies"; WP said it was more likely he had stayed with his Iroquois wife in New York. Besides, said WP, both Lemoizin and Bezaillion were employed by the Indian trading company of which Quary was the "chief Agent." *Micro.* 10:091, 112, 1002.

8. See doc. 44.

9. The Susquehannock Indians were dispersed in about 1675, but Francis Jennings asserts that their conquest by the Iroquois was a myth and that instead many of them sought sanctuary with the Iroquois when they fled from attacking Marylanders. In 1693, the few remaining Susquehannocks settled on their former lands at Conestoga, where they concluded a peace treaty with WP in 1701 (see doc. 11). *PWP*, 2:312n, 482n; Francis Jennings, "Glory, Death, and Transfiguration: The Susquehannock Indians in the Seventeenth Century," *Proceedings of the American Philosophical Society*, 112:15-53, esp. pp. 31-50.

10. Perhaps John Moore was claiming a relationship with John Moore, bishop of Norwich 1691-1707 and Ely 1707-14. *DNB*.

11. Charles Mordaunt, third earl of Peterborough, was an eccentric Whig, a religious freethinker, and a longtime friend of WP. After several years out of favor with William III, Peterborough regained his position at court and his ability to assist WP with the accession of Queen Anne in 1702. *PWP*, 3:418-19, 469-71; *Micro.* 7:304; *DNB;* Stephen B. Baxter, *William III and the Defense of European Liberty, 1650-1702* (New York, 1966), pp. 217-18, 230-31, 250, 257.

42
TO WILLIAM POPPLE

28th 1st m. [March] 1702.

Esteemed Fr.[1]
My own health & familys calling me out of Town[2] I send this to pray the favour that the Board may know I have received their Letter for proclaiming the Queen[3] in the Province of Pensilvania but no Territories being expressed to the King returned them so to me or as Counties annexed nor so much as an &c.[4] I know not how to order her to be proclaimed in the 3 lower Counties unless they think its being done at Philadelphia as Capital may serve for the whole wh I

begg to know. I admire at the Nicety if designed the matter being undetermined judicially.[5] And I Assure them for the Queens service I will take no Advantage of such a Superscription. I thought this fitt to be said And begg that my Agent[6] or Self may have a Line from Thee of the Mind of those Lds & Gentlemen. I return the Packett for the Addition. The Factious are to apt to take leave to throw of Obedience & treat Govmt rudely at such Examples wh I hope will for the Common Peace & Duty be at this Time avoided. I am heartily Thy Affectd & Real Fr.

W. P.

LBC. Penn Papers, William Penn Letterbook, 1699-1703, HSP. (*Micro.* 10:063.)

1. William Popple (1638-1708), secretary to the Board of Trade (1696-1708) and longtime advocate of religious toleration, had been WP's friend since about 1687. *PWP,* 3:520n; Steele, *Colonial Policy,* pp. 24-26; Caroline Robbins, "Absolute Liberty: The Life and Thought of William Popple, 1638-1708," *WMQ,* 3d ser., 24:190-223. Most of WP's letters to Popple are official in tone (for example, *Micro.* 10:691, 719); this document is a rare example of WP's more candid, personal correspondence with the secretary.

2. WP left London on about 29 Mar. 1702 and did not return until about 20 Apr.

3. Queen Anne (1665-1714), the daughter of James II and Anne Hyde, succeeded William III on 8 Mar. 1702 and was crowned on 23 Apr. In her early speeches to Parliament, she emphasized the continuity of her policies with those of William III but added, "I know my own heart to be entirely English,"—pointedly distinguishing herself from her Dutch brother-in-law. Edward Gregg, *Queen Anne* (London, 1980), pp. 151-53.

4. The Privy Council had circulated a printed form letter dated 18 Mar. 1702 ordering the queen proclaimed in the "most proper parts of her Majesty's Province of [   ]." Apparently the clerk had filled in the form to Penn with "Pennsylvania" only, not "Pennsylvania and the Lower Counties" (*Acts of Privy Council,* 2:396; *CSPC, 1702,* pp. 126, 147-48). WP seems to have suppressed the proclamation, which caused officials in his colony some difficulties; see doc. 51; *Micro.* 10:360.

5. WP's title to the Lower Counties was never settled in court.

6. Charlwood Lawton.

43

TO THE BOARD OF TRADE

7 2m (Ap) 1702.

Honble Frs

As I am much obliged to Your Justice that I shall not be Condemned unheard[1] so I must beg the Continuance of it to allow my Circumstances the Time requisit to wait upon You. I am 100 Miles of[2] with a weak Family & divided; my Wife in one place in the Straw;[3] a poor weak Child[4] in another whose languishing Condition occasioned my leaving the Town some days sooner than I intended tho I ha~~ve~~d been unprofitably as well as expensively there a whole Month.[5] And indeed

I admire at the present Alarum the Time considered for I thought all Attempts against Us over for this Session & had leave as I may call it of the Ld Manchester[6] to follow my Family-concerns.
I shall leave nothing to an Agent[7] being upon the Spot my Self & hope I shall not be surprised by hasty Commands. If I did not wait on You since my Arrival I both writt & told Your Secretary[8] why. It was no Fault but my Trouble. I was too Infirm to stand an hour or Two with leggs as feeble as mine are well Known to have been: Nor indeed could I think it necessary til You were pleased to make it so. I came but 3 Nights ago to my Family & neither the Condition of that nor my own Health allow me to post up. I hope the Malice of my Enemies & those of my deserving Country shal not have that power with You to hurry me away without some reasonable Allowance of Time. And in the mean time I pray for a Copy of the Accusations.[9]
I am Your respectfull Fr.

W. P.

LBC. Penn Papers, William Penn Letterbook, HSP. Superscribed: To the Lds Commissioners of Trade & Pls. (*Micro.* 10:082.)

1. On 2 Apr. 1702 the Board of Trade ordered a letter written to WP, requesting his appearance on 9 Apr. to answer charges brought by Robert Quary. At its next meeting, 4 Apr., the board revised the secretary's draft to make the summons more urgent and to signal its displeasure that WP had not contacted them since his arrival from Pennsylvania. *Micro.* 10:078, 079.

2. Off. WP had left for Bristol, where his wife was staying with her parents.

3. In childbed (*OED.*) Hannah Penn had given birth to a second son, Thomas, on 9 Mar. in Bristol.

4. John, Hannah and WP's eldest son, then one and a half, was reported to be "very ill; some danger of Life feared." He may have been staying at Warminghurst. S. F. Locker Lampson, *A Quaker Post-Bag* (London, 1910), p. 167.

5. WP had stayed in lodgings in Kensington while in London during Jan. and early Feb. He was back in London 5-28 Mar., at unknown lodgings. Ibid., p. 171; Janney, pp. 447-48; *Micro.* 10:045.

6. Charles Montagu (1660?-1722), third earl of Manchester, was secretary of state and a commissioner of the Board of Trade from Jan. to May 1702. He also chaired a select committee of the House of Lords assigned to study the issue of colonial trade in Nov. 1702. On 17 Feb. 1702 Manchester had presented WP's proposals for putting the proprietary colonies under the king's control to the Board of Trade (see doc. 40). *DNB;* Steele, *Colonial Policy*, p. 77; *Micro.* 10:048; *The Manuscripts of the House of Lords, 1702-1704* (London, 1910), pp. 73, 76, 81-92.

7. WP's agent, Charlwood Lawton, did attend the board twice on his behalf after this: on 9 Apr. he gave "several reasons in excuse" for WP's leaving town without seeing the commissioners; on 14 Apr. he reported that WP would attend the following week. Journal of the Board of Trade, 1701-1702, transcript at HSP, pp. 403, 409; *CSPC, 1702*, pp. 209, 219.

8. William Popple. WP wrote on 14 Jan. 1702 that new laws passed in Philadelphia "in my opinion will render this present inquiry not so necessary, to be sure the hast of it," and that he would have attended in person "if a sore leg had sufered me to have waited on them." Popple wrote back that the commissioners were willing to wait until they had seen the texts of the recent laws. *Micro.* 10:037, 039.

9. On 16 Apr. the board sent Lawton a copy of the accusations against Pennsylvania to forward to WP. *CSPC, 1702*, p. 226.

44
DISPUTE WITH ROBERT QUARY BEFORE THE BOARD OF TRADE

A
Abstract of Robert Quary's Complaint

[c. 16 April 1702]

Abstract of several Informations
relating to irregular Proceedings &
other undue Practices in Pensylvania

1st: That all illegal Trade is carried on there more than ever: Sloops are purposely imployed to go out of the Capes[1] and take on board Goods brought by other Vessells from Curaçao, which they land at Philadelphia or elsewhere, and then the Vessells that brought them come up to Philadelphia in Ballast, as if they had brought nothing.

2nd: The Acts past in pensylvania to prevent illegal Trade[2] are not put in Execution, as neither the Acts of Trade made here.

3rd: Mr Penn having appointed Water Bayliffs by his own authority,[3] has invaded thereby the Jurisdiction of the Admiralty established by the King.

4th: There is neither any Militia established, nor any Provision made of Arms or Ammunition; But the Country left Defenceless and exposed to all hazards both by Land and Sea; Of which the Representatives of the Lower Counties have several times complained to Mr Penn, but without obtaining any Redress.[4]

5th: Mr Penn endeavours all he can to invite foreign and French Indians, known to be Villains, and but lately come from Canada to settle in this Country,[5] Only for the benefit of a Trade with them; Which he takes care wholy to ingross to himself, by ordering the Indians not to permit any to Trade with them but such as produce an Indented Licence under his Seal[6]. What his profit may be thereby is not known, but it is apprehended this practice may tend to endanger the Lives of many Thousands of her Majesty's Subjects.

6th: Mr Penn prevailed with the Assembly at one Sitting to make a present to him of 2000lbs, and further to settle upon him 1000lbs per Annum and upwards in Taxes.[7] The Expence of their several Sittings whilst he was there amounts to above 600lbs;[8] But he has not disposed them to raise the small Quota of 350lbs which was signified to be requisite towards the Defence of New Yorke; They excusing themselves cheifly upon account of their Want of a settled Militia, Arms and ammunition for their own Defence. Nor has he disposed them to any Compliance with the Quota of Men for New York in Case of an attack, thô it be a Condition upon which the Government was restored to him.[9]

7th: The Representatives of the three Lower Counties, in an address to Mr Penn, have further represented, That instead of reaping the Security designed by the Laws past at New Castle, they find that the most essential of those Laws and which nearest concern them in their Estates have not been sent home for his Majesty's Approbation, especially those for Qualification of Magistrates and Juries, and those for establishing Property and raising Mony.[10]

8th: Those Representatives being doubtfull of Mr Penn's right to the Government of those Counties, they desired a Sight of his Deeds of Feofment:[11] But instead thereof were threatned with a Goal, without Bail, till either the King's pleasure should be known or Mr Penn's return into those parts: And by these proceedings being made more doubtfull of the Validity of the Laws past at New Castle, they refused to confirm the Same.

9th: In relation to the administration of Justice, Information has been given of three particular Cases very hainous. Vizt a Man committed for Bestiality with a Mare, for Want of {a} legal Method of proceeding, got off.[12] A Woman committed for murdering her Bastard Child, and confessing the Fact, was either acquitted or pardoned:[13] The Son of an eminent Quaker committed for a Rape, by several Shufling and irregular Practices, got off without Tryall.[14]

10th: Further Information has been given of a Jury, who not agreeing upon the Verdict in a Cause which they were charged with, determined themselves by Hustle Cap.[15]

11th: Appeals have not been granted from Sentences in Courts in Pensylvania to his Majesty in Councill here, particularly in the Case of Thomas Byfeild against John King.[16]

12th: The Deputy Governour left by Mr Penn is not qualified by his Majesty's Approbation or otherwise, as requisite by Law; Nor has Mr Penn ever given Security for any Deputy Governour, as directed by the Address of the House of Lords of 18th March 1696.[17]

Copy. CO 5/1289, PRO. (Not filmed.) Another copy is in the Logan Papers, HSP (*Micro.* 10:086).

B
William Penn's Reply

[c. 28 April 1702]

Answers to the Abstract of Complaints
agt Proceedings in Pennsilvania

{1.} This is more than I know. And wonder, if it be true, that Col. Quary (who I perceive presents these Informations to this Honble Board) never told me so before. For I never heard but of One Vessel that plaid us such a Trick;[18] and I wish that Col. Q. & his Officers had been more vigorous to prevent it. But for the Vindication of our Merchants, & of that Colony, I must desire Col. Q. to prove the

Charge; that due Course may be taken to punish the faulty, & prevent such things for the future.

{2.} I pray Proof of this also: For he never complain'd to me, that I can remember, of such Neglect. But this I know, that he told me, he thought I was too hard upon the Tobacco-planters, in making that Law; for by that Law the hh^{ds} of Tobacco were to be weighed at their Shipping, because they used to pass formerly at 400^{l} weight by Content, tho' perhaps they, or the Merchants crowded in 7. 8. or 900^{l} weight into a hh^{d}: By wch the King lost, at 1^{d} per pound, not less than 30, 40, or 50 Shillings, wch in a Thousand hh^{ds} comes to 1500 or 2000 Pounds.[19]

{3.} Col. Quary, in his Letter to this Board, laid the Charge, As if I had granted that Commission to all the Sheriffs. But of Six Sheriffs for the Six Counties, two only had them. They were granted of Necessity, to suppress great Disorders upon the Water, and in his Absence, and never disputed by his Deputy:[20] And when objected ag^{t} by himself, at his Return (after Six Moneths Absence,[21] upon his Traffick into other Colonies) I did immediatly command the Sheriffs to forbear acting by them, till further Order: One of them never had; and the Other but twice, & in Slight Occasions. However, 'twas drawn by one that Ld Bellamont had made a Council at New-York, & Naval-Officer therof,[22] well acquainted in Such Matters. And I offer'd to join with him,[23] to represent it Home to this & the Admiralty Board, to give Us our true Boundaries; as the King's Council in both Laws should advise.[24] Which he once promis'd: And best knows, why he did not perform it.

{4.} There's as much as was in Col. Fletcher's time. And the Same Governour I continued in Command, by the Queens Direction, all Commissions being, by Proclamation, to remain in force, till revoked; and they never were.[25] But it is a Mistake, That I had my Governm^{t} restor'd to me upon those terms: Let the Royal Instrument be consulted.[26] Nor was my Right ever dissolved; or that Interruption given me, to be by Law vindicated. And for the Country's being left Defenceless: 'Tis an Imposition upon the L^{ds}, to tell them a Militia can secure it: Since by Land, there's None to annoy it, and by Sea, the Position of the Countrey & the manner of our Settlements considered (our Distance from the Capes being 160 Miles, New-Castle 120, and the Shoals & Narrows so many, that a small Vessel of War would, under God's Providence, be the best Security.

{5.} I never, to my knowledg, invited or entertained One French Indian in my Life; but discouraged French-men, imployed by Col. Q. or his Customers,[27] from trading with our Indians (the Cause of that Restraint) that they might not debauch them from the English Friendship & Interest: All wch is notorious in those Parts; where the Truth can only be examin'd & found out. My Profit by the Indians was never Six-pence; but my known perpetual Bounties to them have cost me many hundreds of Pounds, if not some Thousands, first & last.[28] But this shews a necessity of a melius inquirendum[29] upon the Place.

{6.} I acknowledg the 2000^{l} that Money (wch makes not 1200^{l} Eng.)[30] but his 1000^{l} is not above 700^{l} that Money, nor 500^{l} this, & near expired.[31] But is that such a Recompence; when five times the Sum is less than my Due; having not had for 20 years One Farthing, but maintain'd the Deputy-Governor at my own Charge? And yet more than half of what they gave me is yet unpaid; and if Col. Q. & his factious Adherents can obstruct it, will never be paid me. Whereas, had the Law of Imposts,[32] given me in 83, been received by me, it had been 20000 Pounds & more Money in my Way; and wch was only by me waved for a few years, in our Infancy, upon Promises never performed to me. But for the 350 Pound the King writt to me about; I did not only endeavour to raise it, by calling an Assembly[33] (and wch helps up the Charge of the 600^{l} he talks of) but writt to the Governor of New-York,[34] That tho' I paid the 350^{l} my Self, he should not want such a Sum for the King's Service. Whose Answer was, That he neither wanted Men nor Money, but Col. Kremer the Engineer,[35] that the New-Englanders kept from him: Nor was it at the Same Session or Assembly that gave me that Supply, but more than a Year after.[36] Therfore, it cannot be justly concluded, That I preferr'd my own Wants to the King's Service. And it was Poverty, more than Defence, that was the Excuse of the Lower Counties for not contributing to it,[37] where a Ship only, as before, is their best Security; the Town of Philadelphia, at least the County, being, in reality, worth more than all the Inhabitants of the Lower Counties, who yet have equal Privileges with the Whole Province, on whose account he makes this Reflection upon us. However, they are not Singular; Virginia & Maryland, old & opulent, as well as King's Colonies, having declin'd their Quota's.[38]

{7.} It was then declared to them, and consented to, That the Imperfection of some Laws, in Matter & Wording, would require a Review another Session. And None were kept back, but those that were made towards the End of that Session, when the early Frost setting in so hard, and the Sickliness of the Place, made the Members impatient of further Stay. Nor am I (as I presume) obliged by my Patent to send them in so short a time:[39] However, I expect them daily.

{8.} They had the Sight of the Deed of Feofment; and were also told me,[40] it was upon Record at New-York. And for threatning them with a Goal; 'tis a most Abusive Perversion; for what was Said, was to a Member, but of One that was not a Member, that was suppos'd to have sowed such Reflections about the Town, by himself or Agents: And upon that I said, Tell me his Name, and prove it upon him, and I will take care to lay him where I shall prevent his Seditious Practices, till the King's Commands are known, or the Law release him. This is the Truth of the Case; and I am still of the same Mind, for the Preservation of the Common Peace; nor did I know how to preserve it otherwise: And, I thank God, it continues still, & hope will, till the Queens Pleasure shall be known: While our Neighbors at New-York are in such Confusion & Extremity;[41] tho' not only a King's Colony, but one of the most Importance.

{9.} For this foul Charge; I might refer the Board to the Records of the County.[42] However, I will say thus much; No body complain'd to me of it, nor appeal'd about the first of them: But I have heard, the Reason of his being clear'd was, that the Single Witness against him ran away, and was a fellow of no Credit into the Bargain: Upon w^ch^, after a long Imprisonment, he was discharged in Open Court of Quarter Sessions.

For the Woman; She is neither pardon'd nor acquitted; but the whole Case lies wth Secretary Vernon, to whom I sent it,[43] for the King's Mind, who only could pardon her: And, for want of a Sufficient Prison, is still in Custody (if living) of the Sheriff,[44] who waits for Directions therein. Which Representation was at the Instance and Address of the Swedish Minister[45] & Congregation, of wch She was a Member, that pleaded, 1st, That it was her own Discovery. 2^ly^, That it was five Years after the Fact. 3^ly^, Her extream Sorrow & Repentance, of wch the Discovery was an Instance.

As to the Rape; The Man challenged by the Woman, married her. And in the Opinion of the two only Lawyers of the Place, & one of them the King's Advocate of the Admiralty, & the Attorney-general of the Countrey, her Evidence was therby enervated.[46] But because the Marriage was not so regular as the Law required, I order'd the Prosecution of it with the utmost Rigour; as the Minutes of Council will shew.

For the Reflection upon our Profession, in stiling the Father An eminent Quaker; First, The Father was but a late Comer, and little known.[47] And 2^ly^, far from eminent There or Here; but of all held A quiet honest Man; who had been his Son's Security, the time he had [his Liberty to take in his Harvest, that had suffered consider]ably for want of him, before it was admitted; nor was it at last, without good Authorities in Law.

{10.} That was True; and they punish'd for it; or I had severely prosecuted them. But this was done some time before my Arrival.

{11.} This I must positively disown: For I never did deny One; nor was ever appeal'd or complain'd to. If any Court in my Governm^t^ presum'd to do so; I hope I know better things, in Justice & Prudence, than to countenance or endure it.

{12.} It was no fault of mine; Since I could not stay to receive it. But his Name was sent over by me to my Son, for that Service, above a Year before I thought of my hasty Return; but it was, it seems, omitted to be presented, because of the doubtful Issue of the Bill then in Parliam[t] against us.[48] However, I have the Opinion of Ch. Justice Attwood at New-York,[49] That being a Governor, in my own Right, till the King could be apprized of it, the Appointment I made was good. And Col. Quary cannot but know, That Necessity is ever a Commission; and that I was under an absolute One, both to come & to choose him; Seing there was not another person in either Province (not a Quaker) capable of it; unless my last Lieu[t] Governor, that I had displac'd upon the King's Commands in 99.[50] And I hope, whatever be Col. Quary's Point, the L[ds] will judg of my Proceeding, according to the Nature of Publick Exigencies.

Wm Penn

DS. Logan Papers, HSP. (*Micro.* 10:102.) Docketed by WP: answear to Coll | Quarys first | Memoriall. | N° 2. Marginal numbers have been moved into the text and enclosed in braces. Passages printed within brackets are torn or obliterated in the HSP copy and have been supplied from *CSPC, 1702*, pp. 226-28.

1. Capes Henlopen and May at the mouth of Delaware Bay. On the illegal trade with Curaçao, see doc. 18, text at nn. 34-37; doc. 38, n. 33.

2. An Act for Preventing Frauds and Regulating Abuses in Trade, passed in 1698 and reenacted in 1700; A Law for Regulating Traffic on Seas and An Act against Pirates and Sea-Robbers, both passed in 1700. *PWP*, 3:584n; *Charter and Laws*, pp. 268-74; *Statutes*, 2:100-104; Gail McKnight Beckman, comp., *The Statutes at Large of Pennsylvania in the Time of William Penn* (New York, 1976), pp. 242-48.

3. See doc. 18, n. 32; doc. 19, text at n. 9; doc. 38, n. 34.

4. Representatives from the Lower Counties sent at least three petitions to WP between Aug. and Oct. 1701, including complaints that French squadrons in the West Indies were ready to "fall on us naked & defenceless, being without Militia fort powder or shott tho' wee are the Frontiers of this River and heart of the main where the Enemy may land without blood Shed." The Lower Counties had earlier complained to Lt. Gov. Markham in 1699 about their defenceless condition. *Micro.* 9:361, 602, 622; *Minutes of the Provincial Council*, 1:563-64.

5. See doc. 41, n. 9.

6. The Law about Indian Traders, passed under Gov. Fletcher in 1693 and reenacted in 1700 under WP, prohibited nonresidents from trading with Indians in Pennsylvania. The law did not specifically provide for licenses, but WP did issue them. *Charter and Laws*, pp. 240-41; *Statutes*, 2:140-41; *Minutes of the Provincial Council*, 2:21-22.

7. On the £2000 granted WP, see doc. 35, n. 19. The £1000 probably refers to the expected income from duties on imported liquor and beer, to be paid to the proprietor. *Statutes*, 2:105-9.

8. This estimate of £600 was made by Lower County assemblymen in one of their protests to WP (*Micro.* 9:602). While the Assembly was in session, representatives received a salary of 4s a day, plus 2d per mile for travel expenses. The Assembly usually held one session a year, but WP summoned the Assembly five times during his two-year stay, including two sessions that lasted longer than a month each; they met 25 Jan.-10 Feb., 10 May-8 June, 14 Oct.-27 Nov. 1700; 1-6 Aug. and 15 Sept.-28 Oct. 1701. *Votes and Proceedings*, 1:112-64.

9. WP's government had been restored to him in 1694 on the condition that Pennsylvania help defend New York by sending either money or men, not both as Quary implies. WP had requested £350 for the defense of New York, but the Assembly, including the Lower Counties representatives, had refused to comply. See doc. 15; *Micro.* 9:361; *PA*, 2:28-31, 35, 40, 41.

10. This is an almost exact quotation from the Lower Counties assemblymen's letter to WP of c. 6 Aug. 1701. *Micro.* 9:602, 622.

11. See doc. 22, n. 11. WP had answered the Assembly that the deeds had been

recorded by Ephraim Herrman at New Castle and by Jonathan West at New York. *Minutes of the Provincial Council,* 2:42.

12. The editors have found no other reference to this case.

13. Probably Mary Hayes, who was summoned to the Court of Common Pleas in Kent Co. in Feb. 1701 on suspicion of "formerly makinge away with a bastard Child." Unable to make bail, she was ordered into the sheriff's custody. In Apr. 1702 she appeared with John Lawson and was ordered to appear at the next Court of Quarter Sessions, but no further records appear in her case. Leon deValinger, Jr., ed., *Court Records of Kent County, Delaware, 1680-1705* (Washington, D.C., 1959), pp. 198, 202.

14. In Sept. 1700 Elizabeth Henbury had accused William Smith, Jr., of raping her, and he was imprisoned to await trial. But Smith then persuaded Henbury to marry him secretly in prison. Since she could no longer testify against him, he was freed on bail in Dec. 1700. The case seems to have been dropped. *Minutes of the Provincial Council,* 1:589, 2:11.

15. In a Bucks Co. case, *White* v. *Allman,* the jury was divided 7 to 5 and decided to toss a coin. All 12 jurymen and the constable who tossed the coin for them were severely fined, and 6 of them were disciplined by Falls Monthly Meeting as well. Board of Trade Papers, Proprieties, 1701-1702, transcript at HSP; *Records of the Courts of Quarter Sessions and Common Pleas of Bucks County* (Meadville, Pa., 1943), pp. 353-55, 358-60; Miscellaneous Papers of Falls Monthly Meeting, 1696-1877, transcript by Gilbert Cope, item #3, GSP.

16. Thomas Byfield (d. 1707), a London merchant, had employed Quary to sue the estate of John King (d. 1698), a wealthy ship captain of Moyamensing, Phila. Co., for a debt of £343. Byfield complained that the jury, which decided against him, had been neither sworn nor affirmed, and that his efforts to appeal to England had been "Continually Delayed." On 8 June 1702 Byfield presented his case in person to the Board of Trade, and WP said he would produce witnesses from the other side. Byfield then said he was willing to submit to arbitration, and WP agreed. *PWP,* 3:133n; Hinshaw, 2:445; Phila. Will Bk. A, #169; Board of Trade Papers, Proprieties, 1701-1702, transcript at HSP; Journal of the Board of Trade, 1702-1703, transcript at HSP, p. 73.

17. On 18 Mar. 1697, not 1696, the House of Lords sent a message to the king requesting an order to require proprietors to give security "for due execution of the Acts of Trade and Navigation" by deputy governors. *CSPC, 1696-1697,* p. 402.

18. The *Deer* sloop. See doc. 38, n. 33. In hearings before the Board of Trade on 19 May 1702, Quary listed four other ships that had brought in foreign goods from Curaçao. WP replied that stopping illegal trade was the responsibility of admiralty officials like Quary, not the civil government. Journal of the Board of Trade, 1702-1703, transcript at HSP, p. 31.

19. On the tobacco law, see doc. 9, nn. 12-14. WP misunderstood which law Quary was accusing Pennsylvanians of ignoring. Quary meant the law against piracy; WP thought he meant the law laying taxes on tobacco shipping.

20. John Moore.

21. In Dec. 1700 WP reported to the Admiralty that Quary had been away from his post for about five months during the previous summer. *Micro.* 8:672.

22. Paroculus Parmiter, WP's cousin.

23. Quary.

24. For the attorney general's opinion on the boundaries between the admiralty and the civil government, see doc. 47.

25. Benjamin Fletcher (1640?-1703?), a staunch Anglican, was royal governor of New York 1692-98 and governor of Pennsylvania 1692-94. The 1694 order in council that restored WP's government to him required him to keep in office the deputy governor, William Markham, who had been commissioned by Fletcher. WP claimed that he had asked the militia officers appointed by Fletcher why they had never executed their commissions, but they had refused to answer. Raimo, *Governors,* pp. 249-50; Journal of the Board of Trade, 1702-1703, p. 58; *PWP,* 3:397-98, 400n. See also doc. 51.

26. WP is correct. The order in council of 1694 stipulated only that Pennsylvania assist New York with a quota of men or money when requested. *PWP,* 3:398, 400n.

27. For example, Charles Saunders and Joseph Pidgeon; see doc. 41.

28. For examples of WP's Indian bounties, see doc. 11.

29. A writ in common law commanding a further inquiry into a matter. *Black's Law Dictionary*.

30. In sterling, £2000 Pennsylvania currency actually would have been slightly more than £1300. McCusker, *Money and Exchange*, p. 183.

31. WP is saying that he expects the liquor duties to yield him only £700 Pennsylvania currency, which is less than £500 sterling—not £1000 as Quary claims.

32. In 1683 the Assembly passed this excise tax on liquor imported into Pennsylvania for the support of the proprietor, but WP consented to postpone its enforcement for one year. In 1684, when a new act was passed, the Philadelphia merchants proposed raising a voluntary subscription among themselves instead, and WP agreed. No money was raised, and in 1700 the Assembly passed the new tax that Quary is complaining about. *PWP*, 2:411-12, 558-59; *Charter and Laws*, p. 138; *Statutes*, 2:105.

33. The Assembly of 1-6 Aug. 1701. *Minutes of the Provincial Council*, 2:28-32.

34. John Nanfan (d. 1706) was acting governor of New York from Lord Bellomont's death in Mar. 1701 to Lord Cornbury's arrival in May 1702. His brief tenure was marred by political turmoil when he sided with the Leislerian faction. No letter of WP's has been found promising Nanfan that he would pay the £350 himself. Raimo, *Governors*, pp. 251-52; *Micro.* 9:306.

35. Wolfgang William Romer (1640-1713), a German military engineer who came to England with William III in 1688, was engaged in building forts in Albany, Schenectady, and Boston from 1697 to 1704. New York and Massachusetts complained frequently to the Board of Trade about his absence in the other colony. *DNB; New York Col. Docs.*, 4:881-82, 885, 888-89, 915-16; *CSPC, 1701*, p. 582; *1702*, p. 214; *1702-1703*, pp. 823-24; Cuyler Reynolds, *Albany Chronicles* (Albany, 1906), p. 163.

36. The New Castle Assembly of Nov. 1700 voted the £2000 for the proprietor; the Philadelphia Assembly of Aug. 1701 refused to approve sending the quota to New York.

37. *Micro.* 9:361, 622. See doc. 15.

38. The Virginia House of Burgesses refused to send men or money to aid New York, citing their own defense needs and lack of funds. Maryland's Gov. Blakiston had not called an assembly to discuss the issue. *New York Col. Docs.*, 4:921-22; *CSPC, 1701*, pp. 539-42, 585-87, 595, 668-69, 739; *CSPC, 1702*, p. 168.

39. WP's charter, section 7, required laws to be sent back for approval by the Privy Council within five years of passage. Soderlund, *William Penn*, p. 44.

40. The text printed in *CSPC, 1702*, p. 278, reads "by me."

41. See *Micro.* 10:096.

42. No records of the bestiality case cited by Quary have been found.

43. Not found. This is the Mary Hayes case.

44. Arthur Meston was sheriff for Kent Co. from 1694 to 1704. Scharf, *Delaware*, 2:1039.

45. Eric Björk was minister of Holy Trinity Church in Christiana, the only Swedish church in the Lower Counties. Jehu C. Clay, *Annals of the Swedes on the Delaware* (Chicago, 1914), pp. 71-74.

46. Attorney General David Lloyd argued for the defendant, William Smith, Jr.; the royal advocate for the plaintiff, Elizabeth Henbury, was John Moore.

47. William Smith "the elder," along with his wife and family, came to Philadelphia with a certificate of removal from Glastonbury, Som., dated 14 Aug. 1699. Albert Cook Myers, *Quaker Arrivals at Philadelphia* (Baltimore, 1957), p. 25. Quary may have confused him with other, more prominent William Smiths who had come to Pennsylvania or purchased land earlier. *PMHB*, 7:351; *PWP*, 2:614n; Walter L. Sheppard, Jr., ed., *Passengers and Ships Prior to 1684* (Baltimore, 1970), p. 42.

48. The Reunification Bill of 1701. No instructions to William Penn, Jr., to obtain approval for Andrew Hamilton as deputy governor have been found.

49. William Atwood (c. 1652-d. after 1709), an English lawyer, served as chief justice of the New York Supreme Court from July 1701 to June 1702, when he was forced out by Lord Cornbury because of his activities on behalf of the Leislerian faction. *DNB;* Paul M. Hamlin and Charles E. Baker, *Supreme Court of Judicature of the Province of New York, 1691-1704: Biographical Dictionary* (New York, 1959), pp. 11-18; *Micro.* 8:660.

50. William Markham.

45
FROM GRIFFITH OWEN

Philadelphia the 8t of the 3d Moth [May] 1702

Dear & much Esteemed Governour

We have lately received the wellcome & comfortable News of thy safe arrivall with thy dear wief & family; which we have long waited for.[1] Some of us expected you should have a short passage, the wind continueing in the North west severall weeks after your departure from hence. We began to sit about thy property the 19th of the 9th Moth last & I thinke have Sate two dayes in every week since, excepting 3 weeks; and we commonly have as much buisness as we can compass or goe through: things have gone on pretty well hitherto, and I do not remember that we have hitherto mist to decide or put an end to any matter; although some have been difficult & required severall hearings.[2] There is a prospect of raiseing a considerable summe of money; from Lands in few years. we sould some parcells of the upper end of the Mannor of Rockland & about Brandiwine & Christeena[3] {& lower} ~~in~~ in New Castle County for good price: to be paid some in 6. Moths Some in 12th Moths & Some in 18 Moths. we have as yet sold but litle of the Mannor of Springfield: & of the Mannor of Gilberts: & none of the Mannor of Springetts. I thinke the less we now sell of the Mannor of Springetts & of the Mannor of Springfeild the better:[4] soe that a supply may be raised otherwayes: for they are like to advance considerably and to let any part of them (Especially Springetts for rents to Tennants; I thinke will not be to thy advantage: for they will destroy the Timber which is valuable so near the Towne & plow out the heart of the ground & give it up barren to thee.[5] We have alsoe sold some parcells here & there of overplus Land & conceald Lands:[6] and I hope we shall find pretty much of that before the Latter end of the year; if the Resurvey goes on well;[7] Cornelius Empson[8] with some others of New Castle & Chester Counties have Requested a Graunt for 15000 or 16000 acres upon Octeraro the south side of it within 8 or 9. miles of the head of Maryland Bay; we were at a stand about it & desired them earnestly to stay till we knew thy mind. But they plainely told us if we would not graunt it presently to them they would goe to Maryland & purchase it from Talbot[9] being formerly surveyed to him & a part of his Mannor & they would settle it forthwith. soe we did let them have it at the Rent of 2 bushells of wheat per every 100 acres to be delivered at Cornelius's Mill at Christeena reserving 1000 acres in every 5000 for thee. If thou couldest procure a place ~~a place~~ for a Towne & shiping at the head of that Bay, it might be of great advantage to thee; more then any man now can immagine, thy Country about Sesquahannah would be a brave place.[10] few as yet have purchased of their Bank Lotts.[11] There are many that have not as yet paid their taxe The money towards assistance comes in.[12] James Logan may give a full account of particulars[13] he haveing the minutes of our proceedings which to the best of my Understanding are honestly & fairely ~~kept~~ stated (if he can get time) he is very diligent and Labourious. As to the Goverment: I must referr to the Governours account Secretary[14] & others who may do it more ample & Satisfactory then I can.

The smallpox hath much reigned here since thou went & still doth it has been much in Chester County, New Castle County & this Towne & County, and I hear it begins in Bucks County & the upper parts of Jersey.[15] it has not been very mortall considering the number of people that had it: Edward Pennington dyed of it in the hardest time of winter,[16] his wief[17] downe of it the same time, his was the fluxing Sort & hers the distinck: he had it very thick with a great Salivation his Mother in Law[18] was with him all the time & tended him very carefully his Child[19] had the same sort & thick & recovered: Samuell Carpenters youngest boy Abraham dyed of it.[20] Samuell Preston[21] was very near death but now is recovered, his Children & R: Johns boyes[22] had it & recovered. George Claypooles wief dyed of it.[23] her sister Thomas Masters wief & Child[24] has it now favourably: Mary Norris & her eldest daughter[25] has it alsoe favourably. Samuell Buckleys wief[26] has it very thick the fluxeing Sort yet I hope will recover: John Jones' wief[27] has them just comeing out I think they will {not} be very thick: Jonathan Dickinsons wief[28] had them & recovers, my Eldest boy[29] had them very thick the ~~f~~ fluxing sort & now is recover~~y~~ing but very weak, I have four more that never had it: I believe it will goe through the Country, before it leavs it; there are many as yet in the Towne that never had it as they Say Jon Moore & his wief and Children,[30] Wm Trent & Children,[31] Joseph Pidgeon & his,[32] with many more. Thomas Chakley[33] & Josiah Langdale[34] are safely returned here frm Barbadoes by the way of Burmudos have had good service in both Islands: & do report that they found great openess among the people: Jon Salkeld[35] is now here goeing to the Yearly Meeting in MaryLand. & frm thence if conveniency presents for England; John Estoe[36] has had the Small pox at New Towne in Jersey, & they say is like to marry a young woman that came frm London, came in when we were at NewCastle hath a plantation in Jersey I thinke her name is Haddon. Thomas Thompson[37] is gon towards Virginia and Carolina: I am at the writeing of these lines at Samuell Buckley he & his wief desires to be kindly remembred to thee, thy wief & family; my time is now spent in goeing from house to house to visit the Sick, which I should be heartily glad was over, It is more out of Love & Charity & to avoid reflections then any profitt or advantage to me or mine.

Dear Governour I desire thee to excuse my prolixity in writeing with the salutation of my endeared ~~Love~~ and unfeigned love in that which will abide to thee, thy dear wief & all thine, hopeing & earnestly desireing (if it be the Lords will) to See thee againe I rest

Thy true friend who desires the
prosperity of thee & thine
Griffith Owen

ALS. Cliveden Manuscripts, Chew Family Papers, HSP. (*Micro.* 10:180.) Addressed: For | William Penn | Proprietor & Governor | of Pennsylvania | At Henry Gouldneys | In London | These. Docketed: Griffeth Owen | 8th May 1702.

1. WP's letter of 4 Jan. 1702 to Logan (doc. 38) did not arrive in Philadelphia until Apr. 18. The long interval with no news had led to rumors that his ship had been lost at sea. *Micro.* 10:117.

2. The minutes of the property commission's meetings, beginning 19 Nov. 1701, are found in *PA*, 2d ser., 19:192ff.

3. Christina River runs into the Delaware River below the Brandywine.

4. Springfield and Springettsbury, as the closest of WP's manors to the city of Philadelphia, held the land most likely to appreciate in value.

5. The destruction of valuable timber was a persistent problem for WP: see doc. 38, text at n. 42.

6. See doc. 32, nn. 4, 5.

7. The resurvey of proprietary lands did not proceed as rapidly as hoped, because of the death of Surveyor General Edward Penington (see n. 16, below). *Micro.* 10:141.

8. Cornelius Empson (d. 1701), a New Castle Co. justice of the peace, headed a group of 20 families who wanted to settle on Octoraro Creek, which flows into the Susquehanna in present-day Cecil Co., Md. They offered to buy it at £5 per 100 acres, or to rent at 1 bushel of wheat a year per 100 acres, but settled with WP's commissioners for £8 or 2 bushels. *PWP*, 3:616n; *PA*, 2d ser., 19:240, 245; *Micro.* 10:360.

9. George Talbot, an Irish Catholic and first cousin to the third Lord Baltimore, Charles Calvert, was surveyor general of Maryland and proprietor of Susquehanna Manor in Cecil Co. *PWP*, 3:30n; Clayton Colman Hall, *Narratives of Early Maryland* (New York, 1910), pp. 437, 439; John Bailey Calvert Nicklin, "The Calvert Family," *Maryland Historical Magazine*, 16:54-56.

10. See doc. 35, n. 22.

11. See doc. 32, n. 15.

12. See doc. 33, n. 5.

13. Logan gave a full account of the property commission's proceedings in a letter of 7 May 1702 (*Micro.* 10:141).

14. James Logan.

15. A physician, Griffith Owen here gives WP a clinical account of the smallpox epidemic of 1701-2. He distinguishes between the "distinct," or milder, form of the disease in which the eruptions are separate from each other, and the more severe "thick," or "fluxing," form in which the pox have thickened and run together. *OED*.

16. Edward Penington died 11 Jan. 1702, at the age of 34. Hinshaw, 2:405.

17. Sarah Jennings Penington (b. 1679), the daughter of Samuel and Ann Jennings, immigrated to West New Jersey with her parents in 1680. Hinshaw, 2:249; Digests of Quaker Records, Bucks, GSP.

18. Ann Olliffe (or Olive) Jennings, a Quaker minister who married Samuel Jennings in 1672. *PWP*, 3:36n.

19. Isaac Penington (b. 1700) was the only son of Sarah and Edward. Hinshaw, 2:405; DQB.

20. In a letter of 10 May 1702, Samuel Carpenter told WP of his son's death. Abraham Carpenter died 9 Feb. 1702, at age 5 or 6. *Micro.* 10:192; Hinshaw, 2:344; Edward Carpenter, *Samuel Carpenter and His Descendents* (Philadelphia, 1912), p. 39.

21. Samuel Preston (1665-1743), a Quaker merchant from Maryland, married Rachel Lloyd and settled in Sussex Co., Del. Their children living in 1702 were Margaret (b. 1689), who married Richard Moore in 1709, and Hannah (b. 1693), who married Samuel Carpenter, Jr., in 1711. *PWP*, 3:300n; DQB.

22. Richard Johns (1645-1717), a prominent Maryland Quaker, had five living sons: Abraham (1677-1707), Aquilla (1684-1709), Richard (1687-1719), Kinsey (1689-1729), and Isaac (1692-1733). Edward C. Papenfuse, *A Biographical Dictionary of the Maryland Legislature, 1635-1789* (Baltimore, 1979—).

23. Mary Righton Claypoole, daughter of William and Sarah Righton of Burlington, N.J., married George Claypoole (1675-1730) in 1699. She died 28 Apr. 1702. Hinshaw, 2:346, 487; *PWP*, 2:373n.

24. Sybilla Righton Masters, Mary Claypoole's sister, was an inventor, the first American to receive patents from the English patent office. She and her husband had five children living as of 1715: Sarah, Thomas, William, Mercy, and Joseph. DQB; Hinshaw, 2:393-94; Edward T. James, ed., *Notable American Women, 1607-1950* (Cambridge, Mass., 1971); Phila. Will Bk. D, #302.

25. Mary and Isaac Norris had 14 children; their eldest daughter was Mary (1694-1751), who married Thomas Griffiths. DQB; Wilfred Jordan, ed., *Colonial and Revolutionary Families of Pennsylvania* (Baltimore, 1978), 1:82-85; Phila. Will Bk. G, #239.

26. Anne Jones Bulkley married Samuel Bulkley (d. 1703) in 1693 and, later, married Joseph Growden. Hinshaw, 2:342, 477.

27. Probably Ann Pritchard Jones, who married Quaker master carpenter and trader John Jones in 1700. Hinshaw, 2:383, 567; *PWP*, 3:384n

28. Mary Gale Dickinson (d. 1719), the wife of prominent Quaker merchant Jonathan Dickinson (1663-1722), who was in Jamaica at this time. She joined him there after recovering from her illness, and by 1710 they were both back in Pennsylvania to stay. DQB; Hinshaw, 2:354; Maria Dickinson Logan Family Papers, HSP.

29. Probably Griffith Owen, Jr. (d. 1732). Two other known children were Robert (b. 1679) and Sarah (b. 1682). Griffith Owen, Sr.'s first wife, Sarah, died 22 Dec. 1702. Hinshaw, 2:401; Digests of Quaker Records, Lancs., GSP.

30. John Moore was married to Rebecca Axtell of South Carolina. The children listed in his will of 1732 were John, Thomas, Rebecca Evans, Mary Evans, Richard, William, and David. Phila. Will Bk. E, #272.

31. William Trent (d. 1724), a Philadelphia merchant and later chief justice of New Jersey, was a widower with five children: James (d. 1705), John (d. 1725), Maurice (d. 1730), William, and Mary French. *PMHB*, 3:217n; 72:346; Eli F. Cooley, *Genealogy of Early Settlers in Trenton and Ewing* (Lambertville, N.J., 1883), p. 283.

32. In 1702 widower Joseph Pidgeon had at least three living children: Richard (d. 1703), Isabel (d. 1707), and Rebecca (d. 1714). Hinshaw, 2:446.

33. Thomas Chalkley (1675-1741), a Quaker minister who emigrated to Philadelphia in 1701 with his wife, Martha Betterton, made several visits to other colonies and died on the island of Tortola. DQB; Rufus Jones, *The Quakers in the American Colonies* (London, 1911), p. 124n. For his own account of the 1702 trip to Barbados, see *The Journal of Thomas Chalkley*, 2d ed. (London, 1751), pp. 33-37.

34. Josiah Langdale (d. 1723) of Bridlington, Yorks., had come to America in 1701 with Thomas Thompson for an extended visit with Friends. DQB.

35. John Salkeld (1672-c. 1739), of Coldbeck, Cumb.—a Quaker minister, farmer, and maltster — came to America in 1700, visited Barbados, and then settled near Chester, Pa. DQB.

36. John Estaugh (1676-1742) of Kelveden, Essex, came to America in 1701 as a Quaker minister. After visiting New England and the southern colonies, he came to Philadelphia and married Elizabeth Haddon (1680-1762), a London Quaker who had come to manage her father's property in present-day Haddonfield, N.J., on 1 Dec. 1702. DQB; James, *Notable American Women.*

37. Thomas Thompson (1673-1727), born in Skipsea, East Riding, Yorks., visited America in 1701 and again in 1715 with Josiah Langdale. DQB.

46
ADDRESS TO QUEEN ANNE

A
Proposal to Address the Queen

[30 May 1702]

This meeting[1] agrees that a Gratefull acknowledgmt be drawn up on behalfe of this meeting unto the Queen for her further Renewed Assurances in her late Speech to preserve and Maintain the Act of Tolleration.[2] And that it be drawn up by the Friends following agst next meeting 2d day sixth hour, and Signed by the Members of this meeting that are appointed, and on the meetings behalfe at the Meeting for Sufferings,[3] wch is adjourned to that time.

George Whitehead
Wm Penn } & Benja Coole

The Friends following are appointed to deliver it

Wm Penn
Geo Whitehd
Richd Davis
Nichs Gates
Rt Haddock
Arthur Cotton
Joseph Heall
James Baines
John Roads
Jno Vaughton
John Taylor
Joshua Middleton
Ambros Crowley
James Dickinson
Saml Hunt
~~and~~ Jon Peacock
Arthur Thomas
Hen: Cane
and Thos Taylor
or any 12 of them.[4]

MBE. London Yearly Meeting Minutes, FLL. (Not filmed.)

B
Address to the Queen

[c. 3 June 1702]

Here follows a Coppy of the Yearly meets Address to the Queen [illegible deletion] wch was Delivered to the Queen at Windsor the 3d 4mo 1702 by Wm Penn and the Friends that signed it, and it was kindly Recd:

To Queen Anne over England, &c

The Humble and Thankfull Acknowledgemt of the People commonly called Quakers, From their Yearly Meeting in London the 30th day of the Third Month called May 1702.

May it please the Queen

Wee ~~thy~~ thy peaceable and Dutifull Subjects mett from most parts of thy Dominions at our Usual Yearly Meeting (for the Promotion of Piety and Charity) being Deeply affected with thy free and Noble Resolution in thy late Speech at the Prorogation of the Parliam[t] to Preserve and Maintain the Act of Tolleracion for the Ease and Quiet of all thy people: could not but in Gratitude Esteem our selves Engaged both to Thank Almighty God for that favourable Influence, and to Ren~~d~~e~~r~~w and Render our humble and hearty acknowledgem[ts] to the Queen for the same assureing her (on behalfe of all our Friends) of our Sincere affection and Christian obedience.

And we beseech God the Fountain of Wisdome and Goodness soe to direct all thy Counsells and Undertakings that Righteousness which exalts a Nation and Mercy and Ju~~d~~stice, that Establish a Throne may be the Character of thy Reigne and the blessings of these Kingdomes under it.

Signed by the appointm[t]
and on the behalfe
of the Said Meeting by us.

Rob[t] Haydock
James Baines
Jn[o] Vaughton
Thos[s] Taylor
Joseph Heale

W[m] Penn
Jn[o] Taylor
Richard Davies
Ambrose Crowley
Joshua Middleton
Jn[o] Peacock
Sam[l] Hunt
Nicholas Gates

To w[ch] the Queen was pleased to answer.

I am very glad you are So well pleased with w[t] I have said, and you may depend upon my Protection.

Copy. Book of Cases, Meeting for Sufferings, FLL. (Not filmed.)

C

Nicholas Gates's Report to the Kent Quarterly Meeting

3 4m [June] 1702

I have Long desir'd to Speake to the Queen to acknowledge with Gratitude the many Favours we have rec[d] from her shee Reply'd I accept of it. I am the man who was Father to the Nurse who nursed thy Son[5] And I desire the Lord to bless the Queen and Continue her Reign long over us she Reply'd I thank you M[r] Pen I am {so} well pleas'd that what I have done is to your Sattisfaction that you and your Frinds may be assured of my Protection

MBE. Minutes of the Kent Quarterly Meeting. (*Micro.* 10:224.) Kent County Archives Office, County Hall, Maidstone, England. Docketed: The Freinds that Carried the Adres to the quene the 3d of the 4m 1702 | William Penn Samuell Hunt | John Taylor Nicholas Gates | Ambrose Crawley Jos Heale | John Vaughton Richard Daves | Robert Haydock Joshua Middleton | Tho: Taylor | James Baines | John Peacock.

D

Report to the Meeting for Sufferings

[5 June 1702]

Cases of Sufferings

Wm Penn acquaints the Meeting That the 3d Instant he with the other Friends appointed attended the Queen at Windsor with the Yearly Meetings Address and were kindly Recd and It's left to Wm Penn and John Vaughton to take care to get the Queens Answer to sd Address Incerted in the Gazet,[6] if it be thought adviseable.

And Benj: Bealing[7] is directed to enter the said Address in the Book of Presidents.[8]

An Account of the Delivery of the Address Is as follows:

London the 3d 4mo 1702

Dear Friends and Brethren of the Meeting for sufferings

Our very dear love in the Lord Salutes you with the Wishes of peace and prosperity.

Know that according to the Agreement and appointmt of the Yearly Meeting we the under Written went with their Humble and Thankfull acknowledgement to the Queen then at Windsor, and for your better Information we let you know that we had a Ready access & a favourable Reception and Answer.

For after the Introduction by Word of Mouth W. P. Presented her with the Meetings Paper, shee took it and then Returned it to him to Read, wch he did and upon it she answere'd as followeth vizt

I am very glad you are so well pleased with what I have said; and you may depend upon my Protection.

MBE. Minutes of Meeting for Sufferings, FLL. (*Micro.* 10:230.) Docketed: 1702 | 4 mo 5 | the | delivery | of the | Address | to the Queen. Further docketed: Queens Answer.

1. The London Yearly Meeting, held 28-30 June 1702. This was the final piece of business at that meeting.

2. In a speech dissolving Parliament on 25 May, Anne announced, "I shall be very careful to preserve and maintain the Act of Toleration [of 1689], and to set the minds of all my people at quiet," although she also said that her personal loyalty would always be firmly attached to the Church of England. Edward Gregg, *Queen Anne* (London, 1980), pp. 151-59.

3. The Meeting for Sufferings, held annually since 1675 to discuss how to deal with persecution against Friends. *PWP,* 1:354n.

4. George Whitehead (c. 1636-1723) was a longstanding Quaker leader who had been instrumental in the passage of the Affirmation Act in 1696. The other represen-

tatives to the London Yearly Meeting named here were Richard Davies (1635-1708) for Wales; Nicholas Gates (c. 1633-1707) for Hampshire; Robert Haydock (1660-1737) for Lancashire; Arthur Cotton (1627-1708) for Essex; Joseph Heale (1663-1722) for Middlesex; James Baines (c. 1654-1705) for Westmorland; John Roades for Derbyshire; John Vaughton (c. 1644-1712) for London; John Taylor (c. 1637-1708) for Yorkshire; Joshua Middleton (1647-1720) for Durham; Ambrose Crowley (1657-1720) for Worcestershire; James Dickinson (1659-1741) for Cumberland; Samuel Hunt (1666-1707) for Nottinghamshire; John Peacock (c. 1659-1718) for Huntingdonshire; Benjamin Coole and Arthur Thomas (d. 1720) for Bristol; Henry Cane (d. 1724) for Devonshire. There were two Thomas Taylors at the yearly meeting, one from London and one from Herefordshire. *DNB;* DQB; Digests of Quaker Records, GSP; *PWP,* 2:130n, 641, 648; 3:93n; Mortimer, 2:238, 263; Braithwaite, *Second Period,* pp. 177-84.

5. Nicholas Gates's daughter Lydia Pack (d. 1694) had served as wet-nurse to Anne's son, William Henry, duke of Gloucester, the only one of her 5 children (of about 17 pregnancies) to live beyond infancy. Gloucester died of smallpox in 1700, just after his eleventh birthday. Gregg, *Queen Anne,* pp. 72-73, 98, 120-21; Jenkin Lewis, *Memoirs of Prince William Henry, Duke of Gloucester* (London, 1789), pp. 5-6, 33-35; Digests of Quaker Records, Dorset and Hants., London and Middx., GSP.

6. *The London Gazette,* the official newspaper which carried all ministerial printed matter and was the most widely circulated paper in England. J. A. Downie, *Robert Harley and the Press: Propaganda and Public Opinion in the Age of Swift and Defoe* (Cambridge, 1979), pp. 1, 12.

7. Benjamin Bealing (d. c. 1739) was recording clerk of the London Yearly Meeting 1689-1737. Mortimer, 2:234.

8. Doc. 46B, above. Official Quaker documents such as this were filed in the Book of Cases, to be used later as precedents.

47
SIR EDWARD NORTHEY TO THE BOARD OF TRADE

In a letter of 11 June 1702, in the midst of its hearings on Quary's charges against WP, the Board of Trade addressed four questions to Attorney General Edward Northey: (1) Was a governor or deputy governor legitimate without crown approval? (2) Was the Court of Admiralty set up in 1696 the proper court for trial of infringements of the navigation acts? (3) Could other courts try such cases? and (4) Had WP interfered with admiralty jurisdiction by appointing water bailiffs? The last three questions were also sent to Advocate General John Cooke, whose response of 13 June was unfavorable to WP. Northey's answers, far more friendly to WP, were based in part on a brief drawn up by WP's lawyers, John Dodd and Mr. Rutter. Northey found that WP's deputy governor did need crown approval and that the admiralty courts had legitimate authority in the colonies, although the Navigation Act of 1696 was in his opinion "confused and darke" on the matter of jurisdiction. The attorney general agreed with the lawyers that WP's appointment of water bailiffs for enforcement on inland waterways did not infringe on the admiralty courts, thus clearing WP of one of Quary's chief charges. This was a major victory for the proprietor, who enclosed a copy of the attorney general's vindication in a letter to Pennsylvania (doc. 48). *Micro.* 10:235, 345; *CSPC, 1702,* pp. 383, 388–89, 451–52; Root, *Relations of Pennsylvania,* pp. 10–11; Charles M. Andrews, "Vice-Admiralty Courts in the Colonies," in *Records of the Vice-Admiralty Court of Rhode Island, 1716–1752,* ed. Dorothy S. Towle (Washington, D.C., 1936), pp. 63–69.

[c. 7 July 1702]

As to the First Question, the Words of the Act[1] of Parliam^t^ fol 509 are Express, That every Govern^r^ Nominated and Appointed by any Proprietor who shall be Intituld to make such Nomination shall be Allowed and Approved off by the King his Heires and Successors and take the Oathes to be taken by the Governours of his Ma^ts^ Plantations before their Entring on their Governm^t^ Therefore its plain her Ma^ts^ Approbation must be had before such Govern^r^ can do any Act whatsoever as Governour; For the Act makes the Queens Approbacion necessary to the being of the Governour, and without which, and till it be had, the Proprietors Appointm^t^ is as if it had not been made

To this Mr Penn Objects, that he as Propriet^r^ is Govern^r^, and therefore not within the Act, And I am of Opinion he is not within the Act, but his Deputy Lieuten^t^, or Substitute, is within it, but in this he Excuses himself from the Necessity of his return to England which Obliged him to leave a Deputy in his Absence, and that his late Ma^tys^ death prevented his Applying to him, but he is now Applying to her present Majesty for her Approbation of him[2]

As to the Second I do not find the Act of the 7th & 8th of King William Directs the Settling an Admiralty Court in the Plantations, but Supposes them already Settled there[3]

The Practice of the Plantations since the makeing the Act of the 7th & 8th of the late King hath been to Sue for Forfeitures by this Act in the Admiralty Court in the Plantations, And many Unregistred Shipps have been there Condemned, and Appeales have been to the late King in Councill from such Sentences, And the Jurisdiction of the Admiralty Courts hath never been there denyed though the Act is confused and darke, yet the Clause fol 497 giveing Liberty to Sue in any Court in the Plantations, And the Admiralty being Expressly mentioned fol: 502 I am of Opinion the Parliam^t^ intended that Court among others in the Plantations under the Generall words[4]

As to the Third Q I conceive if a Suite be first properly begun in the Court of Admiralty Pending such Suite, no proceeding ought to be in any other Court, and if there be a Judgm^t^ given in such Court of Admiralty it determines the matter in Suite, and that determination is finall unless altered on an Appeale from the same, But the Common Informer who is to have a Third part of the Forfeitures[5] may Sue for unlawfull Trade either in Westm^r^ Hall or in any Court in the Plantations and is not restrained to the Admiralty[6]

As to the 4th I conceive the Commission Granted by Mr Penn to the Water Bayliffes doth not interfere with the Admiralty Jurisdiction for it doth not grant them any {Admiralty} Jurisdiction, nor to Execute Process on the High Seas but within the Rivers wch is within the Jurisdiction of the Common Law Courts, And is only Constituteing a Sherriffe of a County, which Mr Penn calls a Water Bayliffe,[7] and he is to Execute Process to be directed to him, wch the Admiralty Process is not, but to the Marshall of the Admiralty, And on View of the Grant made by King Charles the Second the 4th of March in the 33th Year of his Reigne whereby the King gives his full power and Authority to Appoint and Establish any Judges and Justices Magistrates and Officers whatsoever for what Causes soever for Probate of Wills and granting Administrations within the Precinct granted to Mr Penn as to him should seeme convenient,[8] I conceive Mr Penn hath not power to Erect an Admiralty Court there, The power to Constitute Judges being to determin all causes within that precinct which must be causes there and not on the High Sea of which the Admiralty Courts have Cognizance.

Ed. Northee[9]

Copy. Penn Papers, Penn v. Baltimore, Pennsylvania Miscellaneous Papers, HSP. (*Micro.* 10:338.) Endorsed in WP's hand: A True | Coppy | Wm Penn. Docketed: Attorney-general's | Report to the Queen, upon | the Queries sent to him by | the Lds of Trade, &c.

1. The Navigation Act of 1696, officially known as An Act for Preventing Frauds and Regulating Abuses in the Plantation Trade. Northey uses the references provided by WP's lawyers, Dodd and Rutter (*Micro.* 10:345), from the text by the king's printer, Charles Bill, included in *Anno Regni Gulielmi III Regis . . . Septimo & Octavo: At the Parliament begun at Westminster the Two and twentieth Day of November, Anno Dom. 1695* (London, 1696). An abridged text appears in Merrill Jensen, ed., *English Historical Documents: American Colonial Documents to 1776* (London, 1955), pp. 359-64.

2. WP to Queen Anne, c. 22 June 1702 (*Micro.* 10.289). The brief by WP's lawyers addressed only the issue of whether or not the proprietor himself needed royal approbation to serve as governor and ignored the question of proper qualification for his deputy governor. *Micro.* 10:345.

3. Dodd and Rutter wrote, "No Courts of Admiralty are directed to be Settled in the Plantations by this Act, as this Query supposes, there being no Clause or Words in the said Act implying, much less, expressing, any such Direction." Ibid.

4. Dodd and Rutter came to the opposite conclusion, that "the Courts of Admiralty in the Plantations have no Power, and are very improper Courts to try Causes relating to the Breaches of the Several Acts of Trade." They based their argument on several contradictory clauses in the act, including a mention of jury qualifications, implying that trials of infringements would be by jury, which admiralty trials were not. This argument had been made by Roger Mompesson in a treatise written on WP's behalf in 1699. Ibid.; *PWP*, 3:629n; Andrews, "Vice-Admiralty Courts," p. 67.

5. The 1696 act provided that penalties and forfeitures arising from the execution of the act were to be divided, one-third to the crown, one-third to the local governor, and one-third to the local officer or informer.

6. This argument follows that of Dodd and Rutter, who held that informers could take cases to other courts besides admiralty courts. *Micro.* 10:345.

7. Advocate General John Cooke at first disagreed with Northey on this issue, saying that WP could no more appoint a water bailiff than he could an admiralty judge. Cooke later reversed himself, however. *CSPC, 1702*, pp. 388, 451; Andrews, *Colonial Period*, 4:256.

8. Jensen, *English Historical Documents*, p. 95; *PWP*, 2:66.

9. Sir Edward Northey (1652-1723) was attorney general 1701-7 and 1710-18. In Jan. 1702, soon after his arrival in England, WP had seen Northey, who obligingly delayed consideration of the Pennsylvania laws until a copy of the new laws arrived. Northey's "signature" in this copy is in WP's hand. The actual document was signed by John Cooke as well as by Northey. *DNB; Micro.* 10:037; doc. 39, n. 5; *CSPC, 1702*, p. 451.

48
TO JAMES LOGAN

London 28th 5^{m} [July] 1702

James Logan

Thy letters ~~by~~ both by Capt Miller[1] & J. Sacher, with Box of Packets &c: I have received,[2] But any thing of an answear in perticuler must not now be expected, for want of time to digest so much writeing. yet some things I will hint at.

1 I have writt by N. Puckle at large, & so by young Tregenes ship,[3] Hen. Childe[4] the person to deliver it; an honest man.

2 C. Quary is gone, I suppose run away from my prosecution & and the Mer^{ts} & owners of the Providence, for at Notingham there is a Tryall this assize on that acc^{tt}, likely to goe agst him for 2000^{l} tho there are endeavours usd to putt it by till the records of the Tryall in the Province arrive.[5] He is an artfull knave, & so govern thy selfe towards him.

3 I beleive P. George[6] will be your viceroy, & the Council of Trade his Council, with a change of members; wch may better things there, he being an honorable & worthy man; and I hope so will his Lt Gen^{ll} & Admirall[7] be, that will superintend wth a fleet for those parts of the world. but of this only informe the Gover & a few discreet Persons upon discretion.

4 I beleive this Parl. will not meddle with our Graunts, but I am willing to settle things, w^{ch} ~~some~~ would please some people, for whose sake, & because we will first be Justified agst^{t} Quarys vile & base informations, I have refused to comply as yet wth terms, tho I know they are advanced agst us for that reason.[8]

5 By all means hasten Kebles Cirtificat authentick,[9] & Urge Govr Hamil. or the Magistrates to oblige Ch. Reed to give his evéidence about that knavery.[10] Q. has huddle up[11] his acc^{ts}, by Blathwaits means, with the Ld^{s} of the admiralty, unknown to the Drs Commons,[12] but all will be overhal'd. what ever you do, load him wth truths insteed of the falshoods he has loaded us with. He has so basely used Govr Ham. that there is[13] Peace with such a villain; his Perry[14] & others, saught to me for it; but I could not be such a Culle[15] & senseless Creature, as to accept of it. I will sooner loose all than be at peace with a forger of lyes to ruine me.

6. By my son, (and family I think)[16] at least by ~~my~~ the Messenger (that if it stays not for him thinks of sayling in 10 or 12 days) I shall be more perticuler. However, I hope by this to send the answear Q. gave to my Complaint, & my reply;[17] by wch you will have an hint of things, how close I strike. Malitia is all they have to hitt us with.[18] Govr Ham., the D. of somerset[19] tould {me,} was not refusd by the K. or Q. on any acc^t But a charge of indulgeing of scotch Traders & Ships, wch that founder'd[20] fellow Randall took his oath of,[21] & offer'd to repeat it, and that being [illegible deletion] {a main point} he feard would hardly suffer the Q. to allow him us. But the D. of Queensborough[22] being upon the roade, I shall apply to him (with the D. of somerset, now Master of the horse) so soon as arrived, to encounter that difficulty, & send the event with the first opertunity; for his name lyes before the Queen for her approbation, & has a great while. I am just come from the Lord high Treasurer & Ld Privy Seal,[23] who promess to recommend him to the Queen the next Cabinet, or have her reasons; also an order to hear the Lords of Trade & me upon Quarys Impostures & visions. I yet hope a tollerable Issue.

7. nothing will hinder my Sons family, & him Consequently more than the visitation wth the Small pox. The Lord cleans the poor Country of it.

8 I want advice for those scraps of bills. they ask for you, Mundy[24] especially. capt^t Hyde[25] takes time for the 15^l to accept or not, the 40ss he has accepted. pray hasten more.

9 I had hopes to have writt thee my daughter was married,[26] but a messenger is come from chichister to call away John,[27] so that I must press. but 2 days hence, (5th d. this being 3^d) the solemnity will be over. I leave to John the story of ould & young Marks[28] to save time & room.

10. pray quiet ed. Farmer, J. Growden &c:[29] till my son comes, unless I should have more time to {be} perticuler now, wch is doubtfull, the winde being faire, after long westerly winds.

11. Gover^r Ham. is to have 200^l per annum made good by me, if fines & perquisits[30] amount not to it. I am no other wise Concern'd. here is a settled annimosity ag^st him, wch would I but connive at, not 14 days agoe I was offer'd w^t I would for a new deputy. But I dispaire not yet of him.

12. Tho: Fairman, Since thou Knowest his abilitys, good will to me &c treat him accordingly,[31] till thou hast myn per my son.

13. Things within doors move with an unspeakable delatoriness here, but seem vigilent ab^t forraign affaires; or we had come to an issue longe agoe.

14. pray let us have affidavits of Sneads frauds, moors saying, so he might get mony, he cared not how, nor of whom.[32] also w^t betty web & weaver can remember of her husbd^s acc^ts w^t mony R. Web pd Quary, and compare it with the Inclosed acc^t.[33] I want the last appraisem^t of Lumbys goods;[34] faile not to send it, authentick.

15. I send thee a coppy of G. Heathcots agreemt & by that his baseness will be better seen.[35] also the atturny Genlls opinion as to admiralty Jurisdiction & the outcry of Quary about the water balyifs Commissn.[36]
16. pray lett wm. Hall[37] have full powr abt my interest, & if can secure S. Hedge[38] agst one of the falsest of men Dr. Cox. I have his fathers Interest, that if I had nothing else I take it to be sufficient. young Cox[39] sent to me to wait upon me, I answeard wn he pleasd wn in town, but never come at me; if there use him as he deserves. Kit after Kine. Thy caracter of T. F.[40] is the Docs to an haires breadth.
17. There is no need of Holding any assembly, & I had rather it were putt by till the laws are confirm'd, at least till a depty be approved wch shall be the same if fair or hard words can prevale.[41]
18. C. Quary denys he ever sayd he was to have the Ks ⅓d for his Sallery. or that he ever writt to york to T. wenham[42] for that lettr back that Inclosed the Comis. to T. F. & J. W.[43] for water Balifs; & that he sent it, on the provocation of affidavts sent by me for Eng. agst him. or that he ever urged under appraismts upon C. Reed &c: in favour of owners. in all wch methinks thou mayst be able to contradict. some things thou hast already, as to thy affidavit, & wt thou sayst of Ch. R. discourse.[44] Q. horrid prevarications & most audacious untruths & denials of Truths. more in both those respects would do good here; Since wt distroys his Credit disapoints our enimys here as well as there, who use him for a toole agst us.
19. He has confidently told the Lords & Queen in Council he was deny'd an appeal in Byfields case, & therefore pray'd an order to have the Cause over to be heard before the Queen, but Bif. & he Crosing one an other before the Comrs of Plantations, one saying that J. Moor refus'd tryal because his Clyent Bifd order'd him to have a Jury upon oath, & B. deny'd he gave any such Instruction, or even to appeal it self upon a Judgemt receiv'd, hobbles Quary & his matters extreamly.[45] In short the Bp. of Lond.[46] & Comr Blathwayt are Sayd to have Sent for him over to prejudice us & the Govermt and the Bp. being one pro prop. fide,[47] I apply to an higher bord, where I now am, viz, a Committe of the Ministers.[48] yet about the months publication before marriage, he seem'd reasonable.[49] I have, because I must have done. only R. Janny.[50] &c: fell into the french hands, wch I refer to J. Sacher, as I do him to my Comrs to encourage him, for I will have John[51] rewarded well.
[20.] I bless the Ld. we are pretty well, & all our Dr. Loves to Frds as if named, the Govr & Council & Comrs of P. and pub. Frds in perticuler. the Hopewell I am not free to ensure, but hear nothing of her.[52] pray see wt thou Canst do to detect Quarys acct herin Sent,[53] by him given in to the Comrs of the Customs & Lords of the admiralty; it is of great moment. but wtever is done, one or two witnesses viva voce, out way 100 affidavits. the Parl. & Judges rejectg them. But

the wise Com[rs] of T. & P. need none, but can Judge ex parte;[54] for w[ch] they are growing rediculous: However affidavits are better than nothing & goe a great way wth them w[n] they can perswade themselves to be indifferent. remember me to J. Bewly, tell him I never made use of the Cirtificat he signed;[55] he is well esteem'd at the Custom house. 21. pray let me have a clear acc[t] of the remainder of orr & T. & L[s] debts about Gillams Good[56] to finish here, w[ch] I cant for want of it. 22. tell T. Fairman, I din'd tother day wth his Bro. & Sist.[57] in Southwark, where I did him some service; & his Bro[r] is hearty, & for comeing too. I must conclude for this time, & am

Thy reall Friend
Wm Penn

let S. Carpenter know how well I take his love,[58] tho by reason of J. G.[s] [59] being at the Bath I have done nothing in it as yet. also salute me to Is. Norris whose love & respect by his lett[r] I was pleasd with & acknowledge.[60] W. & Jane Biles come now, she has a request to the Com[rs], if reasonable favour her else keep tite to your rules.[61] I cannot Just now find G. H. paper.[62] may perhaps ere the ship goes [illegible deletion]

For my cos. ashton,[63] I am willing to be as kinde as I can, & am sorry the Town Clashes wth the Country; Let the Gover[r] be desired to mediate that affaire. for the land, It is asking me so much mony out of my ~~Company~~[?] pocket. nor will I let it goe for 4 or 500 acres, but to reduce his other pretentions, & give security for the overplus of the vallue, if any. and in case it ever was a part of the Mannor of Springfield, I can part with such a quantity. but more of this per my son; only tell ed. Farmer no body else, if not he, shall have a foot of the land he requests of me.[64] vale.

ALS. Penn Papers, Penn Family to James Logan, HSP. (*Micro.* 10:382.)

1. Perhaps James Miller, master of the *Callipatch*, whom Quary and Randolph called "an old pirate." *CSPC, 1702*, p. 328; *Micro.* 6:671, 8:128; *PMHB*, 78:146.

2. John Sotcher brought WP letters from Logan dated 2 May, 7 May, and 12 May, along with letters from several other Pennsylvania officials, including doc. 45, and mail from England and Holland that had arrived after WP's departure. *Micro.* 10:117, 141, 169, 192, 197, 202, 205.

3. Henry Tregeny (d. 1704), a Philadelphia merchant and master of the *Canterbury*, had transported WP to Pennsylvania in 1699.

4. Henry Child (b. 1684), the son of first purchaser Henry Child, Sr., of Coleshill, Herts., arrived in Philadelphia on the *Canterbury*. Digests of Quaker Records, Bucks and Herts., GSP; *PWP*, 2:640; *Micro.* 10:354.

5. See doc. 38, n. 30.

6. Prince George of Denmark (1653-1708), husband of Queen Anne, was appointed lord high admiral on 20 May 1702. The two peers on the Board of Trade, Lords Stamford and Lexington, were replaced by Lords Weymouth and Dartmouth. R. D. Merriman, *Queen Anne's Navy* (London, 1961), pp. 2-3, 355; Steele, *Colonial Policy*, p. 86.

7. WP probably means the earl of Peterborough, whose appointment as commander of English forces in the West Indies was rumored as early as Jan. 1702. Luttrell, 5:129. See doc. 53, nn. 2, 7.

8. WP means that he is willing to sell his rights to govern Pennsylvania to the crown, an option he first hinted at in a letter of 21 June 1702 to Logan (*Micro.* 10:267): "I have had the wisest men in Eng; & of the Greatest, to advise with about a bargain, that love me; & all say stay a while, be not hasty, yet some encline to a good Bargain."

9. John Keble, an Anglican merchant, had been convicted of aiding an Anglican minister in an illegal marriage of servants at his house on Duck Creek in Kent Co., where he lived from about 1700 to 1709. Quary produced Keble's deposition to the Board of Trade on 8 June 1702; WP contended that Keble and the minister were "scandalous persons" and that the marriages were performed with no prior publication and "in a drunken frolic." *CSPC, 1702*, pp. 378-79; *1706-1708*, pp. 736-77; *1708-1709*, pp. 29, 35-36; Perry, *Historical Collections*, 2:55.

10. See doc. 33, n. 22.

11. Concealed.

12. The admiralty court sat in Doctor's Commons. WP means that Quary had obtained Blathwayt's assistance in concealing his records from the admiralty court.

13. WP carelessly omitted "no" here.

14. Probably Micajah Perry. See doc. 81; *Micro.* 12:251.

15. Dupe or simpleton. *OED.*

16. Although WP stated in Jan. 1702 that William Penn, Jr., was hastening over, he did not go to Pennsylvania until Feb. 1704. His family did not accompany him. See doc. 38; Jenkins, pp. 109-11.

17. Doc. 44.

18. See doc. 44, nn. 4, 25, 26.

19. The duke of Somerset had supported Andrew Hamilton's appointment as royal governor, which was blocked. *Micro.* 10:267.

20. Sunken, as with a ship. *OED.*

21. In June 1702 Edward Randolph charged that Hamilton had permitted William Righton to carry tobacco to Scotland and to import coal from there into Pennsylvania. He also complained of WP's and William Markham's illegal practices. Robert N. Toppan, ed., *Edward Randolph: His Letters and Official Papers* (1899; reprint, New York, 1967), 5:284-87; *Micro.* 10:237.

22. James Douglas (1662-1711), second duke of Queensberry and duke of Dover, was royal commissioner for Scotland. *DNB.*

23. John Sheffield, first marquess of Normanby, was keeper of the privy seal; Sidney Godolphin, first Baron Godolphin, was lord high treasurer.

24. Probably John Munday (d. by 1719), a London Quaker mariner. Digests of Quaker Records, London and Middx., GSP.

25. Probably John Hyde, a London Quaker merchant with whom Logan continued to do business into the 1730s. *Micro.* 10:400, 14:190; *PMHB*, 12:10, 75:143.

26. Laetitia Penn married William Aubrey on 20 Aug. 1702. Jenkins, p. 63.

27. Probably John Sotcher.

28. Perhaps London Quaker Nathaniel Markes and his eldest son, William (b. 1687). Digests of Quaker Records, London and Middx., GSP.

29. Edward Farmer (d. 1745) had wanted WP to confirm his ownership of 100 acres in the proprietary manor of Springfield and to sell him an additional 100 acres for £100, a request not satisfied until 1713. *Micro.* 10:188; *PA*, 2d ser., 19:304, 553, 559. Joseph Growden claimed 14,000 acres between Poquessing and Neshaminy Creeks, but WP had agreed to a total of 10,000 acres if Growden could find his father's deed, and only 5000 acres if not. Phila. Will Bk. H, #43; *PA*, 2d ser., 19:250-51, 254, 301-2, 380, 403.

30. The deputy governor derived part of his income from fines for trading with the Indians or operating a tavern without a license, and from taxes collected on liquor. *Statutes*, 2:105-7, 140-41; doc. 191.

31. In a letter of 12 May 1702 (*Micro.* 10:205), Fairman had reminded WP that "Thee was pleased to forgive me the Quittrents in arrears," and asked him to relay this to Logan. He also wanted to be surveyor general but complained years later that Logan and the proprietary commissioners did not appreciate his past services. *Micro.* 14:588.

32. Robert Snead, an Anglican justice of the peace in Philadelphia, had arrested suspected pirates in 1697 when, according to his testimony, other Pennsylvania officials refused to act. John Moore had been accused of conspiring with Quary to seize ships unlawfully for personal profit. Logan could neither find anyone who had heard Moore's

damning statements firsthand nor persuade anyone to testify against Snead or Moore. *PWP,* 3:516-17, 525-26n, 528-29n; *Md. Archives,* 25:561-81; *Micro.* 10:259, 634; *CSPC, 1702,* pp. 396-97.

33. Robert Webb, an Anglican, had been the customs collector in Philadelphia in the late 1690s, and Elizabeth Songhurst Barber Webb (d. 1727), a Philadelphia shopkeeper, was his widow. A Quaker herself, she later married Samuel Richardson. "Weaver" may be Thomas Weaver (d. 1708), the New York collector from 1700 to 1702; see also doc. 33, n. 16. Logan could not find Webb's accounts, which he said Webb had given directly to WP, and he doubted that Webb paid any gold to Quary; perhaps WP meant Edward Randolph, to whom Webb would have been accountable. *PWP,* 3:39, 41n, 548n, 613; Hinshaw, 2:633, 680; *Micro.* 10:634.

34. See doc. 38, n. 30. Logan was unable to find the final appraisement and was asking the Coutts brothers to send it. *Micro.* 10:634.

35. See doc. 38, n. 21.

36. See doc. 47.

37. William Hall (d. c. 1713), a merchant of Salem, N.J., was also a Pennsylvania First Purchaser. *NJA,* 23:202; *PWP,* 2:644.

38. Samuel Hedge (d. 1709) had come to New Jersey with John Fenwick in 1675 and was married to his daughter Rebecca. *PWP,* 2:357n.

39. Daniel Coxe, Jr. (1673-1739), came to New Jersey in 1702 and became a leader of the anti-Quaker faction there. He received lands from his father, Dr. Daniel Coxe (1640-1730), which made him the largest single shareholder in West New Jersey after WP. *PMHB,* 7:326; John E. Pomfret, *The New Jersey Proprietors and Their Lands* (Princeton, 1964), pp. 88, 93, 99, 102; *PWP,* 3:86n.

40. Thomas Fairman. Logan had noted, in a letter of 7 May 1702 (*Micro.* 10:141), that Fairman's loyalties were divided between WP and the London Company, which had purchased 60,000 acres, and "to do his Duty he halts between two."

41. WP hoped to have the Pennsylvania laws confirmed and Andrew Hamilton approved as deputy governor at the same time. See doc. 52, text at n. 19.

42. Thomas Wenham (d. 1709), a New York merchant and member of the governor's council under Bellomont and Cornbury. *New York Col. Docs.,* 3:749; 4:624, 1137, 1180; 5:102, 123.

43. Thomas Farmer and Joseph Wood. *Micro.* 10:259, 634; doc. 18, text at n. 32.

44. See doc. 38, n. 30. Logan had reported on 2 May 1702 that Charles Read told him he had been suspicious of the low appraisement of the *Providence,* but Read refused to testify unless summoned by a court of law. *Micro.* 10:117.

45. See doc. 44, n. 16.

46. Henry Compton.

47. Literally, "in favor of their own belief." The more usual legal term is *in propria causa,* "in his own cause." On 23 June 1702 the bishop of London was appointed an ex officio member of the Board of Trade. Had the board been a court of law he would thereby have been prohibited from serving in cases that concerned the church. *Black's Law Dictionary; CSPC, 1702,* p. 409.

48. The Privy Council committee studying the colonial situation.

49. Compton had objected to Pennsylvania's Act for the Preventing of Clandestine Marriages, passed by the Assembly 28 Nov. 1701, which specified that members of all religious societies intending to marry must publish their intentions a month before the marriage and have a certificate signed by a justice of the peace. Anglicans protested the requirement of a civil certificate. On 8 June 1702, when WP and the bishop of London appeared before the Board of Trade, WP conceded that the publication of the banns as required by the church would be sufficient, which satisfied the board. *Statutes,* 2:21-23, 161-62; *CSPC, 1702,* pp. 314-15, 322-23, 370, 375, 379.

50. Randall Janney (1677-1715), a Quaker merchant from Cheshire, had settled in Philadelphia about 1699 and traveled frequently to England. Miles White, Jr., *The Quaker Janneys of Cheshire and Their Progenitors* (Harrisburg, 1904), pp. 23, 27, 35; *Micro.* 10:709, 1031; doc. 61.

51. John Sotcher.

52. The *Hopewell* was a brigantine in which James Logan bought a 3/8 share on WP's behalf. He urged WP to insure the ship, but WP was unable to afford the high rates in effect because of the war. The *Hopewell* arrived safely in England, although much later than expected, but its profits were disappointing. *PMHB,* 78:145-51.

53. Doc. 44A.

54. For the benefit of one party, in this case, the English government. *Black's Law Dictionary.*

55. John Bewly (d. 1704), the Philadelphia customs collector and a member of the Christ Church vestry. *PWP*, 3:586n, 623n. See doc. 51, n. 5.

56. William Orr, George Thompson, and Peter Lewis—all former pirates now living in the Lower Counties — had obtained goods from James Gillam, who was captured and executed in England for piracy. WP had recovered the goods still in their possession and had taken bonds for the goods they had disposed of. Logan managed to collect some of the property, which legally belonged to the crown, but reported that he could do no more because they were impoverished. *PWP*, 3:598-99n; *Micro.* 8:372, 647a, 738; 10:634, 1002.

57. Robert and Mary Fairman; Robert died in 1716, and Mary married Richard Hawkins in 1718. Digests of Quaker Records, London and Middx., GSP.

58. Carpenter had sent WP a bill of exchange worth £100 drawn on Joseph Grove. As of Sept. 1703 Carpenter had not been able to make good on the bill and was asking WP to pay Grove himself. *Micro.* 10:192; doc. 67.

59. Joseph Grove (c. 1652-1714), a Quaker of Rotherhithe, Sur., had lived for many years in Barbados. Smith, 1:875; Besse, 2:316, 332, 338, 341.

60. Isaac Norris's letter has not been found.

61. William Biles (d. 1710) of Bucks Co. served nearly every year in either the Assembly or Council from 1682 to 1709. In 1701 his second wife, Jane Boyd Atkinson Biles (d. 1709), received the permission of Falls Monthly Meeting to travel as a minister to England and Ireland, and her husband accompanied her. After their return in 1703 he became active in the anti-proprietary party. *PWP*, 3:454n; *PMHB*, 26:58-70, 192-206, 348-59.

62. See doc. 38, n. 21.

63. Robert Assheton was asking for land according to his father's patents, which he could not produce. In Mar. 1702 the commissioners of property granted him a tract of 314 acres but required him to post a bond in case WP disallowed the grant. *PA*, 2d ser., 19:282-83, 320; *Micro.* 10:634.

64. See n. 29, above.

49
TO JAMES LOGAN

warm.[1] 19 6^{m} [August] 1702

James Logan

There is a Gentlewoman[2] comes over in the Canterbury,[3] as I suppose, that, upon the Credit of my cosin Rooth,[4] thou art to Supply as farr as 60^{l} or 70^{l} {of your mony} ~~sterl~~[?] yearly, {as my next on this subject shal advise} [illegible deletion]. She has been unhappy, & Changes the aire for retirem^{t}. her husb. liveing, but an ill Choice, & that her misfortune; of wch be discreet. any Civility thou showst her will be acknowledged ~~here~~. She is recommend to my Cos. Ashton[5] to be boarded; if he takes in none, advise together for a sober & reasonable family. I never saw her, but have had her Character from him, as a person seeking solitude. I add no more but my good wishes, and that If w^{t} my Cos. Mark. writt to my Sister & selfe, about, wch he will tell Thee, be practicable, I would oblige him at last,[6] tho he might have given less occasion to our malicious & watchfull enimys. I am

Thy Loveing Friend
Wm Penn

ALS. Princeton University Library. (*Micro.* 10:463.) Docketed: Propr to JL | Worminghurst 19.6.02 | per Mary Philips | 1mo 1702/3.

1. Warminghurst, WP's estate in Sussex, was his primary residence from 1676 to 1707. *PWP,* 1:287, 366n; doc. 210.

2. Lady Mary Newcomen, who came to Philadelphia under the pseudonym of Mary Phillips, was the wife of Sir Robert Newcomen, sixth baronet of Mosstown and an M.P. for Co. Longford, Ireland, in 1731. She was the youngest daughter of Arthur Chichester, second earl of Donegal, and Jane Itchingham. *PWP,* 3:90, 92n, 123, 137, 141n.

3. The *Canterbury* was the ship on which WP and his family sailed to Philadelphia in 1699. Jenkins, p. 71.

4. Richard Rooth of Epsom, Sur., was the son of Sir Richard Rooth (d. by 1688), Admiral Penn's cousin and frequent companion while they were both serving in the navy. The younger Rooth had married Lady Newcomen's mother after Lord Donegal's death in 1678. *PWP,* 1:137n; Burke's *Peerage; Peerage,* 4:390; Robert Latham and William Matthews, ed., *The Diary of Samuel Pepys* (Berkeley, 1970-83), 2:110, 3:91, 4:205, 10:356.

5. Robert Assheton.

6. William Markham had apparently asked WP and his sister, Margaret Lowther, for the position of surveyor general of Pennsylvania. Logan replied in a letter of 24 June 1703 that the appointment would be impractical, since the resurvey was already costing hundreds of pounds out of WP's own pocket. A month later, Markham was appointed register general. *Micro.* 10:1002; *Minutes of the Provincial Council,* 2:97.

50
TO THE EARL OF NOTTINGHAM

Warminghurst 22 6m (Aug) 1702

Noble Friend[1]

I was yesterday favour'd with a letter from thy own hand, I wish it had been upon an other subject.[2] But this I will say, the Queens Commands, Immediately, or by her ministers, will ever finde a reverent regard from me. I married my only daughter but the day before yesterday,[3] and as soon as I can reach the town I will waite upon lord Notingham, and the rest of those noble lords that Constitute the Committe of Council,[4] where I think my affaires more properly ly than with the Commissrs of Trade & Plantations, after the Partiality those Gentlemen, but too plainly, exprest in favour of the Common Enimy of our poor Country:[5] But that must have, also, its reasonable submission and I humbly take leave to hope, that I shall I[6] appear so in Judgements less lyable to a byass than that of

Thy very Respectfull Friend
Wm Penn

ALS. CO 5/1233, PRO. (*Micro.* 10:467.) Docketed: Mr Pen | Augt: 22: 2: 26: 1702.

1. Daniel Finch (1647-1730), second earl of Nottingham and a staunch Tory, served as secretary of state from Mar. 1702 to May 1704. He greatly enlarged the secretary of state's role in colonial affairs, which was to WP's advantage in the fight against Quary. *DNB;* Steele, *Colonial Policy,* p. 87.

2. Nottingham's letter of 19 Aug. 1702 (*Micro.* 10:460) reminded WP that the Board of Trade was still waiting for answers to its questions of May and June 1702 (see doc. 54).

3. Laetitia Penn was married to William Aubrey at Dorking and Horsham Monthly Meeting on 20 Aug. 1702. Digests of Quaker Records, Sur. and Sus., GSP.

4. Nottingham had told WP that his case against Quary would be heard by the Privy Council committee for colonial appeals. *Micro.* 10:460; *Acts of Privy Council,* 2:vi-xi.

5. Robert Quary, on whose behalf the Board of Trade had written to Nottingham and the customs commissioners asking that he be reimbursed for the expenses of his trip to England. Root, *Relations of Pennsylvania,* pp. 353-54; Journal of the Board of Trade, 1701-1702, transcript at HSP, pp. 92, 98, 100.

6. WP added this word by mistake.

51
FROM ANDREW HAMILTON

[19 September 1702]

Sir

The last I had from You was by Mr Morris of the 24th of April.[1] This is the first Opportunity I have had since to write by. I wrote severall letters of the 7th & 9th of May[2] by John Satchell[3] whoe came by Guy[4] & several since as opportunities offered wch I hope are all come to your hands. in one of mine I sent you a certificate from Jamaica & attested by Mr Barley[5] to be a true Copy of the Original in his hands that the Indico[6] for wch Wm Roydon's sloop[7] was seized (wch I mencioned to you in mine of Decr last)[8] had paid the duties & bond given pursuant to the directions of the Acts of Parliamt. I hope then I shall not be blamed for haveing admitted him to baile to produce this certificate.

As to the State of Your Country in generall filthy foul practices are used to run the Inhabitants into Confusion but as yet both Province & territories keep Courts at their Seasons appointed by Law except the Court at Bucks wch by a Stratagem of D: L:[9] was adjourned without doeing any thing wch I shall put {out} of his power next time.

Since I proclaimed the Warr by Order of the E: of Nottingham[10] I have appointed Officers for the Province & territories Noe body can Imagine wt ungentleman-like practices are sett a foot by those whoe to the scandall of their profession call themselves Churchmen to discourage those whoe have inlisted themselves to Continue they cause their wives to fall upon them for leaveing their business as they call it & those that Want they busily dissuade them to appear any More in Armes for say they the Chief argument we have to defeat the present Governmt under Mr Penn is to have it to Complaine that we are without a Militia & your Appeareing will remove that Complaint[11] however the Cavalier part of the Church despise those Mean devices & take Commicions & industriously encourage the inhabitants to Inlist themselves.

The Small pox has run thro' your Country & West Jersey & by the extream variety of Weather fevers & agues are very frequent but praise to God he carried off but few. Poor New York lies under a sorer affliccion for after the Small pox had run over the towne a Malign^t fever ensued wch has carried off several Hundreds among others Colonel Menville[12] & the Secretary[13] & rages at present at that rate that all Communicacion is broke up with them but by the post Most families left the Towne & Settle in the Jerseys & Long Island & My Ld Cornbury forced to keep at Albany I hope the cold Weather will abate it, it is farr More terrible than that Sickness wch happen'd at Philadelphia the fall before your arrival.[14]

My humble Duty to his Grace the D: of Hamilton[15] I humbly make my Acknowledgm^ts for the honour you tell me he doth me in remembring Me I designe next post to write to his Grace. I thank God all our family[16] are in good health & begg you & your Lady Accept their humb[le] regards & soe doth in great sincerity

S^r
Your Most obedient servant
And: Hamilto[n]

Burl:[17] 19th Septr 1702

Copy. CO 5/1262, PRO. (*Micro.* 10:502.) Docketed: To Mr Penn. WP enclosed this transcription of part of Hamilton's original letter (not found) in a letter to William Popple of 10 Dec. 1702 (*Micro.* 10:691). *CSPC, 1702-1703,* pp. 26-27.

1. Lewis Morris, the representative of the East New Jersey proprietors, left England in late Apr. 1702 and landed in Boston June 11. WP's 24 Apr. letter to Hamilton has not been found. Pomfret, *West New Jersey,* p. 262.

2. The letter of 7 May is *Micro.* 10:169; that of 9 May has not been found.

3. John Sotcher. See doc. 38, n. 70.

4. John Guy.

5. John Bewley. Hamilton enclosed a copy of Righton's Jamaica certificate (see n. 7, below), signed by Bewly, in his letter of 7 May 1702. *Micro.* 10:169.

6. Indigo.

7. William Righton's brigantine, the *Hopewell.* See doc. 35, n. 16. In June 1702 Edward Randolph had repeated his 1696 accusation that as attorney general of New Jersey Hamilton had earlier overlooked illegal trade by Righton and his associates. *Micro.* 10:697; *CSPC, 1696-1697,* pp. 213-14; Robert N. Toppan, ed., *Edward Randolph: His Letters and Official Papers* (1899; reprint, New York, 1967), 5:157-58, 283, 286-87.

8. Not found.

9. David Lloyd.

10. When Hamilton received Nottingham's directive to proclaim war against France and Spain in the name of Queen Anne (*Micro.* 10:178), Pennsylvania had not yet received the order to proclaim the new queen. WP had held up that order (see doc. 42), and the Provincial Council was forced on 5 July 1702 to proclaim the queen without it. *Micro.* 10:544; *Minutes of the Provincial Council,* 2:69-70.

11. See doc. 48, text at n. 18.

12. Col. Gabriel Minviele (d. 1702) had served as mayor of New York and as a member of the New York Council. *Collections of the New-York Historical Society,* 25:339-40.

13. Matthew Clarkson (d. 1702) had been secretary to the New York Council since 1691. Ibid., p. 349; Paul M. Hamlin and Charles E. Baker, *Supreme Court of Judicature of the Province of New York, 1691-1704: Biographical Dictionary* (New York, 1959), p. 308.

14. A severe epidemic of yellow fever had struck Philadelphia just before WP's arrival in Dec. 1699. Watson, *Annals*, 1:23; *PWP*, 3:579.

15. James Douglas (1658-1712), fourth duke of Hamilton and earl of Arran, had been a friend of WP's since the 1680s. *PWP*, 3:52n, 277, 455, 474n, 606.

16. Hamilton had one son by his first marriage, John Hamilton (d. 1735), who later became postmaster general of America. For his wife, Agnes, see doc. 38, n. 44. *DAB*.

17. Burlington, N.J.

52
FROM JAMES LOGAN

Philad^ia the 2^d 8^br [October] 1702

Honoured Governour

My 2 Last[1] were by our ship Industry Robt Trowbridge m^r [2] who sailed hence for York 17 6 month to put himselfe under the Convoy of the Advise Man of War[3] and much beyound Expectation has staid there till this week but now believe is sailed by our Last advices from thence; the occasion of his stay was Lord Cornbury's keeping at albany & Aesopus[4] for fear of the sickness which is still furious there. Copies are Inclosed the first was Delivered to the master the Last sent to N Y after I had been Ill for some weeks of a feaver of which I am not yet Recovered so as to be fitt for business[5] after the date of the s^d Letter it fixed in my head wth a Violent Pain almost to Distraction Reducing me to an Exceeding weakness but blessed be God those pains have Left me but the Dreggs of the Distemper remain as in this Epedemicall Disease it Generally does, (Especially with Those that have been severly visited as I have) for a Long time after, frequently returning to the same Person with relapses but now I hope with the help of the Lord I shall soon regain Strength, thô at this time scarce able to do 2 hour's business in a day it so weakens my Brain.

Since the sailing of the s^d Vessell there has been no opportunity of shipping Returns the first we Expect is N Puckle whom we Daily Look for, Captain Cumly[6] being Arrived at N York who sailed with him and the Grand Fleet if he return this Season it will answer well otherwise being Disapointed of the Ship Experiment[7] Intended Last Spring for these parts wth the Correspondents of whose owners (W Crouch and T Eccleston)[8] I Engaged for Freight, it will ~~be~~ {prove} Exceeding Troublesome. I have if the Weight hold out 11 Tun of Logwood yet to ship and should have 50 or 60 hogsheads of Tobacco having already shipt [blank] Tun of the First and 90 hogsheads of the Latter,[9] Bills I cannot procure if my Life Lay at stake there is no purchasing them without Dollars wch are by no means to be had, all kind of money being scarce beyound beliefe. I hope the Distempers among us as Small pox &c have been the Cause of the Great Damp on Trade this year and may recover, but at this time tis Extream Dull;

We have scarce any Trade to the Indies; our Goods that are bought here for 20. sell there for 15, which will by no means answer. so that though that business be the Easiest, for shipping off beyound Comparison of any other: Yet, I Design to send no more that way, till there be more Encouragem^{t}. Wheat bears no price, the Bolters[10] universally refusing to buy: the Planters Expect 5^{s} per Bushell, but cannot Gett it; 'tis Expected to be much Lower.[11] Skins are Extream hard to be gott without Goods;[12] but I have some, at first Designed by the Industry, but could not {to} p{ur}pose. What I can this Winter {coming,} and the spring shall Endeavour to my utmost; in both those and Bills. And am Exceedingly Troubled, The Circumstances of Things would not suffer me to Answer Expectations better. But I have done all in my Power, as many here can Wittness. Wheat not Selling makes the Countrey people uncapable to Answer their Engagements.

I am sorry my Letters cannot be more pleasant; tis with regret ~~that~~ I write them; and am sure, take no pleasure in Melancholy stories but I must act the part of a true Historian, whose subject, if Displeasing, the fault is in that, and not in him: and therefore believing my self obliged, to give Impartial Relations, of what passes: After the preceeding, must give the Following.

Our Corporation of Philadelphia, have of Late, ~~Exerted~~ so highly Exerted their power; Especially, in Claiming a right to all the Aldermen, to sitt Justices, in the Court of Common Pleas; for both City and County: which some Considerable Lawyers, as well as the Govern^{r} & others; think they have no right to; ~~and~~ that {it} has bred Confusion, between them & the ~~Justises~~ Justices {by} ~~By~~ Commission: J Guest and Capt Finey, the Cheif Opposed it highly: the Latter refusing to sitt any more; and the Former {un}Easie to the utmost, whither he will sitt, or not, I know not: his Love to a place, perhaps may prevail.[13] The Courts have been strangely adjourned, upon it; but at Length, the Mayor and Aldermen,[14] Carried it, *I may say by force,* Declaring, thou hadst given a Charter,[15] (that was their Explication of it) and none whatever, should hinder them. And proceed accordingly they have held their Mayors Court, in which they use the same Methods; and Claim the whole fines, for all offences, within their Cognizance, among which, those of the Publick houses, for selling without Licenses;[16] wch is the only I have been able to get a farthing by: touches me the nearest, the rest I think they have mostly a right to. Of These, I have gott as many Imposed as the Juries would Let me, and Gott them also Levied this summer; but if they can have their way; have been taking pains for others, this I Doubt will Cost me a Dispute with them: which I shall Enter on rather than Lose them, thô it will be one ~~means~~ means more to Expose me to Ill will

A fortnight agoe, a Councill being held; the Election of Representatives for assembly: Granted to be yearly 1st of 8^{br} to sitt 14 by the Charter of ~~Pl~~ Priviledges, was Discoursed of, wch not being by

Writt, and therefore not the Gov^{rs} Act.[17] He was of opinion ~~with me~~ {with but few others} ~~who am~~ {among whom my self being} admitted freedome of speech in Councill[18] (for that day with much adoe I gott down Stairs and was present) that by all means an Assembly at this Juncture, the Governour not being approved, was to be avoided Especially (beside the afores^{d} reason wch would occasion Disputes when it Came to Legislation) because in all probability it would be a means of Disuniting the Lower Counties from this Province,[19] which was rec{k}oned very unfitt now, and that all our Study should be only to preserve peace and good orders and prevent occasions of Complaint as much as ~~may~~ {might} be wch attempting matters of that moment might suggest: and it was thought that as the Lower Counties who have absolutely Denied the Charter would not take any notice of it so the Province might slip it over not Remembring it, but some being of opinion this would forfeit their priviledges and others who had got it by the end thinking this the only time to Disunite and serve them {selves} with Laws for their purpose took care to publish it so that Yesterday being the day an Election was made, Fr^{ds} Cheifly appear~~ing~~ed. the members of this County are, David Lloyd in the first place Then Anthony Morris, S Richardson & Gr. Jones[20] the stiffest men they could Chuse. The paper was presented to the sherrif by that worthless man N Waln. I forgot to mention[21] when speaking of the Charter that 'tis the Opinion of most Indifferent men of Sense that the whole management of the Corporation Especially their Contending wth the Countrey Justices; those being so Called who are Such by thy Commission, is an Intrigue of D Lls & J M's (who are now most strictly united)[22] to Confuse all our Courts and their proceedings that a stop being Put to the administration of Justice such Complaints may be now sent home as were upon the Convulsions of this Government when the King took it into his hands before.[23] but what Fr^{ds} Intention in Choosing the first Member could be is yet a Mistr{e}y.[24] He is now made J M's Deputy Judge of the Admiralty advocate of the s^{d} Court and is now at N Castle upon a Trial in it Notwithstanding his oposition to it before thy arrivall occasion'd ~~thee~~ thee so much Trouble.[25] He and the s^{d} J M are the City advocates and Daily blow them up to such Mettle, ~~'tis therefore thought that the Town being so much in Love with the Priviledges suspecting the force of it as the Charter only would have it Confirmed by Assembly. for my own part I have reason to apprehand the Charter of Property D's mighty Darling, of the not passing of which he represents me the very Cheif reason Instrument according to his Custom of Blackning me all he can because in thy service. The Governour I know by Intimation will do all in his power to prevent their Sitting, and Especialy their Disuniting But their means of doing that by the Charter being only a Remonstrance and Petition to the Governour I fear it cannot be avoided but there are some means Still Left to perplex it wch I believe will be taken David will~~

~~Doubtless be stiff for it & the whole manager, as for his father~~[26]~~and John Swift~~ [illegible deletion] ~~but ill affected. I hope I have taken Effectual means to prevent their being elected.~~[?] ~~I have not yet heard the Names of Either for that County or Chester.~~[27]

I really know not what to make of the Face of things among us this Town's Charter which should ~~blind~~ {bind} ~~a&~~ the people to thee sett them so much for themselvs that there is too Little regard p^{d} thee and scarce any to thy Interest for my own part I have Endeavoured to Deal as Equally to the people as possibly can Consist with thy Interest Yet having so few (I may with much Justice say scarce any) to stand ~~firmly~~ by me, firmly; Especially in Consultation for thy Interest that I am Left Exposed rendered Severe and Cruell by Exacting of Prices, wch yet I know are Still too Moderate and Low, were it in my Power to Doe better thô in the Generall Thou hast no ~~Cause~~ {reason} to Complain If the Examination be not Left till 7 or 10 years hence when prices may be Doubled, This I know, I am universally found fault with by the Common Vogue of the Countrey, thô reasonable men think more favourably and ballance it with that of my discharging but my Duty in it I speak not a syllable of this I can boldly Declare it to gain favour but as the Matter Offers wch if not believed will be a real Injustice for I can Safely say there is Generally so great a Disregard of thy Affairs among the People that to Carry them on Vigourously is to sail against wind & Tide, They are very Considerable in this Province as I have shewed before, and if things go well in Europe and the W Indies Give Encouragement may Extricate me of all my Trouble I mean from C^{rs}[28] thô that Calculation was too Large for buyers are very Dull now to what they were just before thy going off no Strangers having this year come amongst us nor any ship from England but the Messenger. I say thy Affairs however are so Considerable that they not only Deserve thy high regard but Imediate presence as I have often Mentioned before. The Load now Lies so much upon me that notwithstanding I have but Little befriended my self since my coming into the Province by all my Trouble and this year {by reason of} my Charge, Less than Ever and therefore might want a Support yet I had better go Into the woods than perpetually undergoe the fatigue wch in a little time for want of more {true} Friends to thee should things Continue as they are will grow wholly unsupportable nor can I name one here fitt (for want of Either Capacity or Inclination) to take off any share of the Burthen, the Commissioners in that business sitt pretty Duly but E S[29] is much Throng'd in his own affairs and has the Faculty of understanding Little but those, yet ~~those~~ {he} has been true and well Inclined according to his Ability and hope will Continue so but the Corporation has done him no kindness. I wish thine by any art could be made his own business and then none would Equall him. T S[30] with a Resolution taken up not to give any Offence besides his Naturall Inclination avoids as much as possible any Trouble of that kind being Exceeding uneasie to him and Desirous to be released as I suppose thou wilt shortly hear from his own hand. Honest G O[31] is steel to the Back were he very Capable, but none will Concern themselves any further than that bare Commission; Except in some few things I force on them. Nothing can be Expected from any thou canst send from thence for they never proved well yet. Thy self therefore it is that must stand the main wheele & I Doubt not but it will prove worth while. Pray write nothing from ~~from~~ my Letters to any here as the Corporation or others for then I must fly the Province, Pray write Joyntly to the Commissioners.[32] if thou Suspect any thing in my Letters be pleased to Consult any from hence 'tis an unhappiness Puckle is not arrived before the Departure of this ship (who is bound to Milford from Wm Trent &c: Wm Burge[33] comes in her John Guy is mr) that I might Answer thy Letters which I Expect will be angry for those things sent by John Sotcher (who we hear is arrived) not coming sooner, But however the unhappiness of affairs may have rendred things I did all that with any shew of reason was in my Power and am sure no Backwardness of mine was the Cause of it but I have there Given the Reasons wch I hope will be satisfactory My Trouble is that Puckle sailed from London before his[34] arrival.

Att Pensbury they are now in Indifferent health Peter I Informed before is Dead[35] & both Hugh and Barras[36] the only 2 white servants have been Ill of the Distemper but are recovered. Hugh is going to be Married and Leaves us as soon as his place can be suplied, Mary[37] is so Lonesome that she is resolved in Winter, if her husband come not before to come Live in Town.

Having some time after thy Departure to Live in S Carpenters house[38] I Continued Longer Resolving not to Leave it till Spring but then receiving in thy Letter an account of mr Wms Design to come over[39] and finding no Conveniance to be had in Town for the Councill, Commissioners of Property Reception of the Govr &c: and willing that some appearance of Govmt should Continue by having a fixt place for that and all other Publick affairs and ~~believing~~ {thinking} by that thy coming wch I cause to be believed as much as possible, would be the more firmly Depended on I have still Continued & kept house in it till this time being the only Suitable place to be thought of in Town. but now hearing nothing more of thy sons Coming and I finding things bear too hard upon me, I Design Speedily to goe table my self and a man abroad and shorten my Charges wch I have hitherto been at Cheifly for Publick Considerations

I fear I am, not only now but Generally too prolix thô now I have but small reason to be so for I much doubt the sense of what I have wrote, but think it my duty to be particular, If I offend by it please to Notifie and it shall be mended.

John Marsh run away Last Spring from Sk: Mill[40] and believe will scarce return the reason I suppose was because I would not pay his bills to maintaine him after the Mill went and ground. I then thought if she was not sufficient to maintain him after 150^{l} Charge in stead of 70 she was not worth Expending more upon her and Especially not to maintain her Millar, I Ordered some rents to be Carried in to her in wheat wch he presently Spent and then shewed the Villian, The Mill I rec{k}on is Lost for none will take to her should we give her for Nothing

The Town Mill[41] goes well but will not Yeild much profitt (thô she cost above 400^{l}) without a pair of Black stones or Cullens[42] which I wrote for before, The millar next week Leaves her for that on Naamans Creek[43] we have not yet gott another. I will not add but that I am with due respects & service to the Family

Thy Faithfull and Dutiful Servt
J L

LBC. Logan Papers, Logan Letterbook, HSP. (*Micro.* 10:514.) Docketed: n^{o} (9). WP sent an excerpt of this letter to the Board of Trade on 7 Dec. 1702 (not filmed); see nn. 21 and 24, below; doc. 55, n. 1.

1. Logan's two previous letters were dated 13 Aug. and 11 Sept. 1702 (*Micro.* 10:449, 493).
2. The *Industry,* also known as the *Cantico,* was a ship in which Logan had bought a quarter-share on WP's behalf. The ship was never insured and was captured by the French; see doc. 56. Robert Trowbridge and his brother Daniel were both ship captains. *Micro.* 10:360, 400, 449, 493.
3. The *Advice* was a 48-gun ship under the command of Capt. Calwell. R. D. Merriman, *Queen Anne's Navy* (London, 1961), pp. 112, 335, 383; *Micro.* 10:634.
4. Esopus, a town on the Hudson midway between Albany and New York.
5. On 11 Sept. (*Micro.* 10:493) Logan wrote that he had been sick for three weeks.
6. Perhaps John Comly (b. 1661) of Bedminster, Som., and Barbados, who was probably the half-brother of Bucks Co. First Purchaser Henry Comly, or Comby. Phila. Will Bk. C, #280; *PWP,* 2:641; G. N. Comely, *Comly Family in America* (Philadelphia, 1939), pp. 2, 15; *New York Col. Docs.,* 4:917, 921.
7. The master of the *Experiment* was a Capt. Watson. Docs. 69; 74, n. 6.
8. William Crouch (1628-1710) and Theodore Eccleston (1650-1726) were both prominent London Friends. Fox, *Short Journal,* pp. 299-300, 340.
9. Logan sent 40 hogsheads of tobacco and 11 tons of logwood on the *Industry,* making WP's total investment on the voyage worth more than £600. *Micro.* 10:241; *PMHB,* 78:149.
10. Millers. *OED.*
11. By Mar. 1703 wheat had fallen to 4s or 4s 6d but was still not selling. *Micro.* 10:782.
12. English goods, such as blankets and coats, used to trade with the Indians for furs.
13. John Guest was chief justice of the Provincial Court; the associate justices were Samuel Finney, William Clarke, and Thomas Masters. John Hill Martin, *Martin's Bench and Bar* (Philadelphia, 1883), p. 14.
14. The Philadelphia mayor was Edward Shippen; the recorder was Thomas Story; the aldermen were Joshua Carpenter, Griffith Jones, Anthony Morris, Joseph Willcox, Nathan Stanbury, Charles Read, Thomas Masters, and William Carter. *Micro.* 9:682.
15. The charter for the City of Philadelphia, granted 25 Oct. 1701 (*Micro.* 9:682), stated that the mayor, recorder, and aldermen were to be justices of the peace and justices of oyer and terminer, but it did not specify whether they should serve on an existing court or set up a separate mayor's court.

16. A law passed in 1700 prohibited selling liquor without a license and set a fine of 4d per gallon, with proceeds to go directly to the governor. *Statutes,* 2:107.

17. Doc. 28, text at n. 6. The Provincial Council met on 17 Sept., but the minutes contain no mention of the discussion about elections. *Minutes of the Provincial Council,* 2:70-71.

18. Logan was admitted as a member of the Provincial Council on 21 Apr. 1702. *Minutes of the Provincial Council,* 2:68.

19. See doc. 48, text at n. 41.

20. Samuel Richardson (d. 1719) and Griffith Jones (d. 1712) were both prominent Philadelphia Quaker merchants who had often opposed proprietary interests. *PWP,* 3:54n, 112n.

21. WP omitted several lines in his excerpt to the Board of Trade; he wrote, "I forgot to mention an Intrigue of D: Loyd's" and ended with "so much Trouble." See doc. 55, n. 1.

22. David Lloyd and John Moore, previously antagonists, were now united against the proprietary.

23. William III put Pennsylvania under royal authority 1692-94. See *PWP,* 3:347-48, 358-59, 393-99.

24. WP omitted the clause from "but what Frds Intention," in his excerpt to the Board of Trade. See n. 21, above.

25. WP had been ordered by the Board of Trade to remove David Lloyd from the office of attorney general in 1700 because he was undermining the authority of the admiralty courts. *PWP,* 3:592-93, 598n.

26. Probably a reference to Joseph Growdon, David Lloyd's father-in-law.

27. Jeremiah Langhorne, Joseph Growden, John Swift, and William Paxson were elected from Bucks; Andrew Job, Nicholas Pile, John Worrall, and John Bennett represented Chester. *Votes and Proceedings,* pp. 118, 123, 142, xxii.

28. Creditors.

29. Edward Shippen.

30. Thomas Story. No letter has been found from him to WP requesting to be released from his responsibilities.

31. Griffith Owen.

32. The property commissioners.

33. William Burge (d. 1745), a Philadelphia merchant. Phila. Will Bk. H, #19.

34. John Sotcher arrived in England in July 1702, a few days after Nathaniel Puckle left for Pennsylvania. On 21 June WP wrote Logan that he had only received one letter from his secretary "after 7 months & more" and that Logan's failure to send documents WP needed for his defense against Quary was "to my unexpressible trouble; & I fear Irreperable disapointmt." *Micro.* 10:267, 329; doc. 48.

35. See doc. 38, n. 72. Logan told WP of Peter's death in a letter of 29 July 1702 (*Micro.* 10:400).

36. For Hugh Sharp, see doc. 38, n. 71. John Barras, or Barwis (d. 1749), a Quaker indentured servant who was "good for nothing" according to Logan, left Pennsbury at the end of 1702 and married Jennet Skilton in 1705. By 1742 he was living in Bristol, Bucks Co., where he was assessed at £10. Hinshaw, 2:977; Bucks Co. Will Bk. 2, #188; *Micro.* 10:449, 634; Terry A. McNealy and Frances W. Waite, comps., *Bucks County Tax Records, 1693-1778* (Doylestown, Pa., 1982), p. 8.

37. Mary Sotcher, whose husband, John, returned to Pennsylvania in December 1702.

38. Logan had been living in the so-called Slate Roof House owned by Carpenter and used by WP as his Philadelphia residence 1700-1701. By 1703 Logan was living in Isaac Norris's house. Docs. 33, n. 6; 69, text at n. 44.

39. William Penn, Jr., did not actually sail for Pennsylvania until late 1703.

40. For Schuylkill Mill and the miller, John Marsh, see doc. 33, n. 9. On 13 Aug. Logan reported that he heard Marsh was "skulking around" in New England. *Micro.* 10:449.

41. The Governor's Mill on Cohocksink Creek in the Northern Liberties. Doc. 33, n. 8.

42. Logan had requested the millstones in letters of 7 May and 13 Aug. 1702 (*Micro.* 10:141, 449). Cullen, or Cologne, plates were made from an alloy of copper and zinc (*OED.*).

43. Naaman's Creek ran along the boundary between Chester and New Castle Cos.

53
FROM THE EARL OF PETERBOROUGH

Oct the 3th 1702.

My Friend I have received yours[1] & thank you for your compliment because I know it is sincere, if I had not heard from you this week, I had writt to you the next, then I should have been att Liberty to have inform'd you of what you heard from my Ld Godolphin,[2] I intended to doe itt the first moment it was in my power, that I might offer you my best services, & tell you how much I desired to see you, to receive your advice, I hope you are coming to London,[3] The Time for my departure Drew neere for in my way I had brought the Duke of Ormond[4] a considerable reinforcement but we have this very moment received the unlucky advice, that he is returning home unsuccessefull, unlesse in a few rapes & some plundering att Port St Maryes,[5] I allways foretoald the event of that undertaking when engaged inn so late in the yeare, but our misfortune is that when coffee houses have formed a design, & The waygerers have engaged, the poor ministry is forced to attempt, however any thing is better then allways riding in Torbay.[6] The Honour the Queen hath done mee is very great, in giving me the command of her Fleet, the command of her Troops, and the authority & directions in all her American Colonies,[7] The best hopes & expectations I can give you of my self, is to lett you know how sensible I am of my unfitnesse for so great a Trust, which will certainly perswade you, I shall seek, & make use of all the assistance I can gett, yours I depend upon & know I shall not be dissapointed of itt, neither shall our friend Clement[8] of what service I can doe him, the mannor & way with which the Queen & her ministers have used mee, adds to the obligation, it is sett off by the practise of late dayes, & the Turn hath been entirely english,[9] which shall be requited by {my} most zealous & diligent endeavours, now S^r^ I should Lament with you, but why trouble you with complaints I am Sure we both grieve, & I am Sure there is no remedy I had not the satisfaction of seeing a Dying Friend, Ld Nottingham[10] kept me in such subjection, tho I went post I came to Northampton too late, a few hours after my Ld Sunderlands death,[11] I have found of late the ease of acquiescing, a pleasure I have not allways been acquainted with, but without which there is no tollerable quiet in this world, you may guesse the hurry I am in yet my inclination carryes mee to writt you such a letter, that I ought to excuse its Lenght, pray send me in your next the name & abode of the Sea officer you once recommended to mee. I liked him very well, and it will now be in my way to make use of him & to lett him see he obtain'd an effectuall recommendation, when he procured yours.

your affectionate Friend
Peterborow

ALS. Penn-Forbes Collection, HSP. (*Micro.* 10:532.) For Mr William Pen att his | House | In Bristoll.[12] Docketed: Peterborow | Oct. 3. 1702.

1. Not found.

2. Godolphin apparently told WP that Peterborough had been appointed governor general of Jamaica, something the Board of Trade did not learn until 17 Nov. 1702. *CSPC, 1702,* p. 733; Stephen S. Webb, *The Governors-General: The English Army and the Definition of the Empire, 1569-1681* (Chapel Hill, N.C., 1979), pp. 481-82.

3. Peterborough repeated his desire to see WP in a second letter of 6 Oct. 1702, but WP does not seem to have gone to London until Nov. *Micro.* 10:536; Journal of the Board of Trade, 1701-1702, transcript at HSP, p. 259.

4. James Butler, second duke of Ormonde (1665-1745), was commander of the English and Dutch forces that attacked Cadiz in Aug. 1702. *DNB.*

5. Ormonde's forces failed to capture Cadiz but ransacked Puerto de Santa Maria, north of Cadiz. The fleet set sail for England on 30 Sept. and, on 12 Oct. (after this letter), retrieved success by capturing part of the Spanish treasure fleet in Vigo Bay. *DNB;* George M. Trevelyan, *England under Queen Anne: Blenheim* (London, 1930), pp. 262-72.

6. The fleet had been at Torbay, Devon, on the English Channel before sailing for Cadiz. *CSPD, 1702-1703,* p. 192.

7. Along with the governorship, Peterborough had been appointed admiral and commander-in-chief of the British navy stationed in Jamaica. He was supposed to lead an Anglo-Dutch invasion of the Spanish West Indies, but the expedition was cancelled when the Dutch pulled out, and Peterborough never went to Jamaica. Webb, *Governors-General,* pp. 481-82; *CSPC, 1702,* p. 733; *DNB.*

8. Simon Clement (d. c. 1735), Hannah Penn's uncle and a Quaker wool merchant, had done business with WP since the 1670s. WP may have been trying to get him a position as secretary to Peterborough, whom Clement was working for by 1710 (see doc. 175). Clement was later employed by Robert Harley to write propaganda tracts and, after WP's illness and death, as an agent for Hannah Penn. Penn Papers, Private Correspondence, 1:249, HSP; Mortimer, 1:196; *PWP,* 1:581, 590-96, 620; J. A. Downie, *Robert Harley and the Press: Propaganda and Public Opinion in the Age of Swift and Defoe* (Cambridge, 1979), pp. 121-22; *Micro.* 14:190.

9. Peterborough is contrasting his employment by the "entirely english" Queen Anne with his disgrace during the reign of the late Dutch King William.

10. As secretary of state, Nottingham would have been consulting with Peterborough on the West Indies campaign.

11. Robert Spencer, second earl of Sunderland, died 28 Sept. 1702 at Althorp, the Spencer family seat in Northampton, after a month-long illness. Sunderland had long been a friend of both Peterborough and WP. *DNB; PWP,* 3:52n; J. P. Kenyon, *Robert Spencer: Earl of Sunderland* (London, 1958), pp. 327-28, 334.

12. Probably Thomas Callowhill's house.

54
TO THE BOARD OF TRADE

[c. 30 November 1702]

AN ANSWER TO FOURE QUERIES SENT ME BY THE Lds COMMISSIONERS FOR TRADE AND PLANTATIONS.[1]

MAY IT PLEASE THE BOARD.

I Say to the first and Second Query, the People chiefly engaged with me, and that Setled the Province, were those called Quakers, and the Constitutions, and Laws were framed, & made accordingly, and Solemn attestation was generally the way of pledging fidelity to the

Crown, & Obedience to me under it, as also of giveing of Evidence: Yet even as early as in 83, when an Oath was desir'd of such as could Swear, an Oath was given, and so it Stood till Gov^er Fletcher's time, and I remember no alteration Since. but that those that were call'd Quakers were Solemly attested according to the Law, & custome of the Province,[2] & those that were of the Church of England, or other Professions, that could take an Oath, were Sworn,[3] as required, whether in Evidence, or entring on Offices, wch is all I can say to the first and Second head.

To the Third,

Heavy Pieces of Eight go for 7^s 8^d and Leight ones in proportion, Dollars {at 8^s} 6:[4] the Motive doubtless to bring into, or keep Money in the Country. But I frequently discountenanc'd it, as much as I could, and expected directions from hence for a Standard for that and the rest of the Colonies, upon the Continent at least, according to my Letters to you upon that Subject,[5] and did no otherwise Confirme it, than I did all the Laws promiscuously in the hurry of my Comeing away; referring to the Kings Negative, in Order to the regulation as afore Mentioned.

To the Fourth,

I answear that my Title to the Lower Countys is by Deeds of Feofment from the Duke of York, and his letter of Attourney to his President {& Surveyor General & Clark of the Peace}[6] to give me possession, and Submission, wch they readily did by Turf and Twig, and Water;[7] as also by a ready acknowledgm^t of me as Govern^er in open Court of Sessions,[8] and w^ch (as Covenanted to do in the Said Deeds) he intended a Confirmation, & further Grant by Letters Patent, when King; as appears by Sr Wm Williamses draught,[9] by his Order in 88; but Obstructed by the disorder the Court was in a little before the Revolution, & wch I humbly hope, for the Reasons therein exprest, will not be refused to be perfected by our Gracious Queen:[10] In which, I would take leave to hope I shall not want Your Mediation.

Wm Penn

DS. CO 5/1262, PRO. (*Micro.* 10:627.) Docketed: Pennsylvania | Mr Penn's answer to the 4 | Queries sent him in May & | June 1702. | Rec^d 30th Nov^r | Read 1st Dec^r | 1702. A copy of the answer to the fourth query appears in CO 5/1290, PRO.

1. WP had received two letters from William Popple with specific questions from the Board of Trade. The first, of 19 May 1702, asked: (1) Do all Pennsylvania and Lower Counties officials either take an oath or make the prescribed affirmation? (2) Is anyone who wants to take an oath permitted to do so? (3) What is the rate for pieces of eight in Pennsylvania, and why is it higher than that of other colonies? The second letter, dated 23 June, asked: (4) On what basis did WP claim title to the Lower Counties? By 9 Sept. 1702 the board was threatening to hold up the order in council approving Andrew Hamilton as deputy governor until WP answered their questions. When he finally did, Popple reported that "they do not think it altogether satisfactory, yet in order to the dispatch of your affair, they are willing at present to acquiess with it." *Micro.* 10:213, 314, 491, 632. Journal of the Board of Trade, 1702-1703, transcript at HSP, pp. 37, 259, 279, 297.

2. The Fundamental Laws of Pennsylvania (1683) provided Quakers with the right to make an affirmation but did not mention the right of others to take an oath. In 1693, under Gov. Fletcher, the oath became the standard, with the affirmation an acceptable alternative; this provision was re-enacted in Markham's Frame of 1696. In 1700 the Assembly again made the affirmation the standard form. The Pennsylvania law provided for a simple promise to tell the truth, with no mention of God, whereas the English Affirmation Act of 1696 (7 & 8 Will. III, cap. 34) specified the wording: "I, A.B., do declare in the presence of Almighty God, the witness of the truth of what I say." Pennsylvania also permitted the affirmation in all cases, criminal as well as civil, while the English law permitted it only in civil law. Soderlund, *William Penn,* p. 131; *Charter and Laws,* pp. 247-49; *Statutes,* 2:39-42; Root, *Relations of Pennsylvania,* pp. 234-53.

3. WP ignores the problem that arose when the officials eligible to administer the oath were all Quakers, whose conscience would not allow them to do so. In such cases, a potential witness or officeholder was forced to make the affirmation or refuse to participate in the proceedings. *PWP,* 3:448n.

4. The Pennsylvania Assembly raised the value of Spanish coin in a law passed on 27 Nov. 1700, with pieces of eight of full weight ("heavy") set at 7s 10d, slightly higher than WP's figure, with 4d subtracted for every pennyweight below the standard weight in "light," or clipped, coins. The Assembly openly declared that its purpose was the "bringing in of money to promote trade and make payments more easy," but neighboring colonies complained that Pennsylvania's inflated rates were draining their supply of specie. *Statutes,* 2:87-88; Root, *Relations of Pennsylvania,* pp. 180-88.

5. In 1700 WP had joined Governors Bellomont and Nicholson of Virginia in proposing a standard of coin in America. See *PWP,* 3:618. In 1704, prompted by the Board of Trade, the crown did establish tables for proclamation money, rating the piece of eight at 6s, but Pennsylvania continued to ignore the new rates. Root, *Relations of Pennsylvania,* pp. 180-88; doc. 67.

6. John Moll and Ephraim Herrman were the duke's officers who surrendered the Lower Counties to WP in Oct. 1682. See *PWP,* 2:283-84.

7. In the common law ceremony of livery of seisin, a grantor transferred possession of property to the grantee by giving him a symbol of possession, in this case, a piece of turf with a twig on it and a porringer of water (*Black's Law Dictionary*). For Moll's account of the ceremony, see *PWP,* 2:305-8.

8. WP attended the court in New Castle in early Nov. 1682. Ibid., p. 299.

9. Sir William Williams (1634-1700) was appointed solicitor general in 1687 by James II; he left office in 1689 after the Glorious Revolution (*DNB*). His incomplete draft for James II's confirmation of WP's title is *Micro.* 5:900; an additional copy is in Penn Papers, Three Lower Counties, 15:31-33, HSP.

10. Neither Queen Anne nor any subsequent monarch ever confirmed WP's title. In 1717 George I nearly approved the competing claim of John Gordon, the Scottish earl of Sutherland. Doc. 204; John A. Munroe, *Colonial Delaware: A History* (Millwood, N.Y., 1978), pp. 131-34.

55

DECLARATION ON THE CROWN'S CLAIM OF RIGHT TO THE LOWER COUNTIES

On 11 November 1702, after WP had personally appealed to the queen at Bath, the privy council provisionally approved Andrew Hamilton as deputy governor of Pennsylvania. WP had succeeded in overriding the Board of Trade's objections against Hamilton, but the board was successful in attaching several conditions to the royal approbation, including a requirement that the proprietor admit the crown's challenge to his title in the Lower Counties. On 2 December

WP composed a loosely worded statement referring to the queen's "Pretentions" in the Lower Counties (doc. 55A). His revised version (doc. 55B), perhaps drawn up with William Popple's assistance, kept "Pretentions" but added "or Claime of right." In the end, the board insisted on the wording, "her Majesties Claim of Right," (doc. 55C), and WP — still unwilling and procrastinating — finally signed the board's version on 10 December.

A

First Draft

whitehall 2 10br [December] 1702

I do hereby declare & Promess that I will take no advantage of the Queens Royall approbation of Colonel Andrew Hamilton to be my Lieut Goverr of Pennsylvania & Countys annexed, in reference to the Queens Pretentions to the Govermt of the sayd lower Countys, after the expiration therof;

Wm Penn

ADS. Society Collection, HSP. (*Micro.* 10:678.) Endorsed: my Declara | tion the Lds of | Tr. & Plant.

B

Second Draft

4th Xber 1702.

I do hereby declare and promise I will take no advantage of the Queens Royall approbation of my Deputy Governour Colonel Andrew Hamilton, for one year, to elude or diminish her pretentions or Claime of Right to the Government of the lower Counties upon Delaware, now under the administration of the said Hamilton in Conjunction with the Province of Pennsylvania

Wm Penn

Copy. CO 5/1262, PRO. (*Micro.* 10:683.) Endorsed: Copy.

C

Declaration Required by the Board of Trade

[8 December 1702]

Sir

Your Letters of the 4th & 7th Instant with the Papers there inclosed,[1] have been laid before the Lords Commissioners for Trade and Plantations; And upon Consideration of your Declaration relating to her Majesties Right to the three lower Counties upon Delaware

River, (which was inclosed in the first of your said Letters) Not finding the same so conformable to her Majesties Order in Councill[2] as they conceive it ought to be, Their Lordships have directed me to return it to you, and therewith also to send you (as I do here inclosed) the form of a Declaration prepared by themselvs in Conformity to her Majesties said Order, which they desire you to dispatch accordingly, upon fair large Paper;[3] And I am further to assure you that upon the Receipt thereof they will make no delay in what remains to be done by them, in pursuance of her Majesties aforesaid Order.[4] I am &c.

W: P:[5]

I under written do by these presents declare and promise, that the Queens Royal approbation and allowance of Collonel Andrew Hamilton to be Deputy Governour of Pennsylvania and the three Lower Counties upon Delaware River, for one Year only, shall not be construed in any Manner to diminish or set aside her Majesties Claim of Right to the said three lower Counties. In Witness whereof I here unto set my hand and seal, this [blank][6] Day of December 1702.

Copy. CO 5/1290, PRO. (*Micro.* 10:688.) Superscribed: To William Penn Esq[r]. Docketed: 1702 | Dembr 8th. Further docketed: Letter to Mr Penn | in answer to his | of the 4th Instant, | relating to her | Majesties Title to | the 3 lower Counties.

1. On 4 Dec. 1702 (*Micro.* 10:681) WP sent the board his declaration (doc. 55B) and wrote, "I have sign'd a paper that I hope will please you, and Can signe no other without signeing away those dear bought Countys that 20000l will not reprize me as well in soyle as Govert." His letter of 7 Dec. (*Micro.* 10:685) enclosed excerpts (liberally edited by WP) of three recently received letters from James Logan urging dispatch in Gov. Hamilton's approval. *CSPC, 1702-1703*, p. 20; *Micro.* 10:400, 449; doc. 52, nn. 21, 24.

2. The Order in Council of 11 Nov. 1702 specified that the queen would approve Hamilton for one year only provided that: (1) WP gave security of £2000 sterling, (2) Hamilton obeyed the Navigation Acts, (3) WP gave direct answers to the Board of Trade queries, and (4) the approbation of WP's deputy did not "diminish or set aside" the queen's "right and title to the Three Lower Counties." *CSPC, 1702*, pp. 715-16; Board of Trade Papers, Proprieties, 1702, transcript at HSP.

3. WP asked Popple to send him a copy of the declaration to sign because he had "neither so good paper nor so good a hand" and he wanted "to avoide giveing occasion to any of the Lords to think I delay with designe to triffle with them." *Micro.* 10:691.

4. The final approbation was delayed until WP had submitted a copy of Pennsylvania laws to the Board of Trade and had given security for Hamilton's good performance. It finally was signed on 21 Jan. 1703. *Micro.* 10:704, 707, 717, 719, 724.

5. William Popple, secretary to the Board of Trade.

6. The final document, in a clerk's hand and signed by WP, was dated 10 Dec. 1702. *Micro.* 10:694.

FIRST PROPOSALS FOR SURRENDER

1703

During 1703 the Board of Trade relaxed its efforts to take away WP's proprietary authority in Pennsylvania, but the long and bitter dispute was undermining WP's ability, and even his desire, to hold onto the governmental powers granted by his charter from Charles II. In May and June he began to negotiate for the sale of his colony's government to the crown. Obviously this was a dramatic turnabout from his previous strong arguments for charter colonies. But the influx of non-Quaker settlers, added to the quarrels among Quaker factions, had destroyed all traces of Pennsylvania's early consensus; royal officials were pressing hard for increased centralization of control; the advent of Queen Anne's War pointed up the Quakers' limitations as governors of a frontier colony; the colony continually failed to provide tangible support for its founder; and WP's personal financial woes were reaching an unprecedented pitch. Under these circumstances, the prospect of a surrender upon favorable terms, including guarantees of constitutional freedoms for the colonists as well as a large financial settlement for the proprietor himself, could seem attractive —especially when set against the threat of an act of Parliament that might dispossess him outright. On 6 June 1703, in doc. 61, he told James Logan, "I beleive it repents some [of Queen Anne's ministers] they began it; for now, tis I that press it, upon pretty good terms, as well for the people as selfe." For further discussion of these negotiations, see the headnote to doc. 60.

WP's lengthy suit for royal approval of Andrew Hamilton as deputy governor, which finally succeeded in January 1703 (docs. 55–56), was rendered futile by Hamilton's death on 26 April, before the document certifying his approbation even reached Pennsylvania (*Micro.* 10:908). His replacement, John Evans, obtained surprisingly quick acceptance from the Board of Trade, despite his evident lack of qualifications (see doc. 63). The new governor came over in company with William Penn, Jr., an undisciplined young man who was unlikely to settle comfortably into a Quaker colony; see WP's guarded remarks on his son in doc. 67. In February 1704, after a very long voyage, Evans and Penn arrived in Pennsylvania to find the colony's government in serious disarray. The Anglican party, under the tutelage of Robert Quary and John Moore, had launched a well-organized campaign to cripple the Quaker government and thus promote a royal takeover. Hamilton's death, leaving the proprietary administration without a head, encouraged efforts at disruption. By denying the legality of courts held without oaths, refusing to administer oaths or affirmations to provincial councilors, and discouraging enlistment in the militia established by Gov. Hamilton, Quary's adherents managed to prevent or delay many of the normal procedures of government (docs. 66 and 69; *Micro.* 10:985, 1002). One of them boasted that they had "laid the Government on its back, & left it Sprawling unable to move hand or foot" (doc. 66; see also Nash, *Quakers and Politics,* pp. 248–55).

WP's hold on Pennsylvania affairs was more tenuous than ever as communications, always slow, suffered the hazards of war. Several ships were captured by the French, while others were delayed waiting for convoys. WP complained in late August of Logan's silence (doc. 67), having received none of the eight letters the agent had written him since December 1702. In December 1703 Logan had just received WP's letter of the previous June. If his grasp of Pennsylvania politics had loosened, however, WP had solidified his position in the world of courtly maneuvering at home. He freely complained to the lord treasurer about the Board of Trade's incompetence (doc. 58), and he did not feel bound by a request from the House of Lords that he keep secret an impending change in colonial currency values (doc. 67). Quary charged in July that WP thought he could ignore the Board of Trade, "haveing a greater Interest then all of them" (Nash, *Quakers and Politics,* p. 246; *CSPC, 1702–1703,* p. 571).

As in 1702, WP spent most of his time in London. In August he reported that he had spent less than three months away from court since his return to England. His family was in Bristol, where he spent two weeks on the occasion of the birth of his daughter Hannah Margarita in August 1703. His long residence in London not only displeased his wife (docs. 68 and 70) but also entailed heavy expenses. The settlement of his older children's fortunes caused a further drain on his resources. In May WP signed a complex set of indentures to provide a marriage settlement for his daughter Laetitia, resorting to extensive mortgages and trusteeships for some of William Penn, Jr.'s lands in Ireland as well as Penn lands in Pennsylvania (see doc. 209F, G, K, M). The Penns found their son-in-law, William Aubrey, both grasping and ungrateful, as evidenced by Hannah Penn's outburst against "that muck worm" in doc. 70. WP's hoped-for income from Pennsylvania was extremely disappointing, as colonial trade was entering a long slump brought on by the war, and the colonists had no money — as well as no inclination — to pay taxes and rents. Logan's strenuous efforts as both trader and receiver brought scanty results; WP complained at the beginning of the year (doc. 56) that he "never was so low & so reduced," and by the close of the year (doc. 71) he described himself self-pityingly as an "Old, Kind & Abused Land Lord."

56
TO JAMES LOGAN

24th 11^{m} [January] 1702[/3]

James Logan
Lo^{g} Friend
I have thy Packet by the Messeng^{r};[1] thyn per Cantico & the Mary being gone for France,[2] to my great disapointm^{t} & straights; nor indeed would they have amounted to the vallue thou mentionst,[3] they only geting or makeing a saveing voyage, that Get well upon English goods, that can spare to loose upon returns {of Tobacco}, and yet gain upon the whole. I & others wonder'd thou wouldst send the best & most of goods by the dullest & worst ship, and entitle me to half of her too, w^{n} thou wast doubtfull of her in all thy former letters to me, least she should fall into their hands that have her.[4] Ensure I cannot, but S. V.[5] I think might have done it, knowing my tenderness[6] & haveing (I suppose) thy intimations, that are a sort of orders in trade. But he tells me, besides my mony to ensure, the ensurers never pay above the rate the same qualitys pay here, & then the Gain had been small, upon the whole, the Customs Consider'd. for our Tobacco is in poor request, now the Zarr has broak his word wth our Mer^{ts} especially;[7] and for Log wood,[8] Cales & Vigo[9] ha~~s~~ve so much sunck the vallue of it, that the Lady Bellomont has lost 9^{l} ~~out of~~ {out of the} 15^{l} that it cost her per tun. That by the first ship,[10] sould pretty well, logwood I mean. I observe thy hint ab^{t} my Tobaccos to Hamburg.[11] I shall prye into it per first, for that would be very unfaire, if not dishonest & fraudulent; But hope it is a mistake.
Thou must change thy Method of returns; I am satisfyed that of Flowr & bread & Bear[12] to {Barbados} Virginia Antigo,[13] Nevis {Jamaica} &c: rather than Barbados, (& S. V. {says} that way also) would outdo Tobacco. In the mean time send me all the silver thou canst gett any where or of any thing, as plait[14] &c: rather than leave me destitute. for such expences as I am putt to (& small presents too) cannot (with my family) be supported without supplys, & speedy ones

too. I never was so low & so reduced; for Irland my {old} principall verb,[15] has hardly any mony, Eng. severe to her,[16] no trade but hither, & at engs mercy for prizes, saveing Butter, & meat to Flanders, & the west indias, that we must goe & eat out half our rents, or we cannot enjoy them. and I have great Interest, as well as my sons settlemt to Deduct,[17] wth 3ss or 4ss per 1l Tax here,[18] & 20l & 24, 5 & 6l per cent for exchang from Irland to Eng. to answear.[19] I therefore urge earnestly supplys, & by the best methods, & least hazardous. I know thy ability, doubt not thy integrety; I desire thy application & health, & above all Growth in the feeling of ~~under~~ the powr of truth; for that fitts & helps us above all other things, {even} in business of this world, clearing our heads, quickening our spirits & giveing us faith & Courage to perform. I am sorry to finde by thyn, thou art so much opprest in thy station, and wish I could make it lighter. If my son (whose delay, was {from} your sickness & N. yorks,[20] aggrevated here, & Just now his wifes being within 6 weeks of her time)[21] will apply himselfe to business he may by the authority of his relation, & a little pains, render thy post easier to thee. I know the baseness of the temper of too many of the people thou hast to do with, wch calls for Judgemt & great temper, with some authority, but I hoped that wn gone, Ed. Sh.[22] & T. Story would have been helpfull, & I. Norris & S. Carp.[23] now & then as volunteers. If T. Fairman were of Credit with the people he might ease thee; he has capacity, but not wt he thinks. I must referr the managemt of him to thee. He most basely injur'd me {wn} here, by his suggestions to the Purchassers, as he confest at parting tho deny'd it on bord [the] Canterbury,[24] and in righteousn[ess] owes me reparation, wch he has promest me, & I have no scruple of Conscience that it be made me at their cost that made him their toole for my abuse & hardship. I send a lettr at the Companys request abt their land,[25] &, except half of Gilberts, I I think they will submitt {for the rest,} & that is under Consideration too. T. Fs. Brors wife[26] is a little sharp upon him to me, & waits for an afternoon at her house upon that subject; I am sorry all his papers will be ineffectuall, for they are gone to France; For Tho' a Corrispondence is not yet clos'd, I hear nothing of my packet. The Commander is at Dinant,[27] has writt for 5 pounds to me,—it came 3 days agoe to hand, but have made him no answear. I think I ~~shall hardly~~ [?] must fling good after bad. No Cartell[28] settled yet. The Newspapers I think to send, & some poems & pamphlets,[29] that will acquaint thee &c: with the state of things both at home & abroad, so shall not load my lettr with News. only Lord Cornbr at Council, had the better of Atwood, who has printed his case & left one at my Lodgeings;[30] and that there will be no Bill this year agst us; and I may add, that the next year {warr} (in Europe) is like to be the greatest that has been these hundred years, for action.

I am sorry the foolish Capt. of the Cantico[31] did not sinck my packet, as other ships formerly did that have been taken

Pray minde to let me know by all opertunitys Quarys Conduct & Carriage, and Moors among you. for the latter, I shall turn him out of all within my Commission for a sawcy ungratefull fellow. and shall write to Govr Ham. about it.[32] and If he shall refuse to surrender the Records off his office of Registry, that forth with the Gover^{r} order the proper officers to seize & remove them by force. For I will henceforth make open head agst those Inveterate villans to me & my poor Country. I hope to furnish you with a man of sence[33] & [illegible deletion] & law in a while, & to lett the Com^{rs} & Govr know.
Pray let Rakestraw Brewster[34] &c: have thy care to answear. Keep off appeals all thou canst, & things will do well, or perticulers from vexing me here. I will referr all back to you again, whoever complains, but if they apply to the Queen, It may be much more troublesome, as the old spanierd;[35] of whom I have nothing from thee, as to my Conduct & trouble to Issue his matter, & wish for the Minuts & history {of it,} well attested wth w^{t} speed may be, & where I left it, & the business pitcht & pincht. [illegible deletion]
I could wish the officers of the Citty of Philadelphia would be carefull not to strive nor strain points, to make their Charter more than it truly means, & so a Burden to the County & the Goverm^{t}. for if they take that Course, I shall enquire into it, & put a period there unto, as lawyers tell me here I may very easily do, and the Goverm^{t} here would Countenance the attempt. I therefore desire an accommodation may be found out to ease that Controversy between Town & County.[36]
[illegible deletion]
Wm Hall of salem writes to me[37] for ampler powr about my concerns there, wch you {have} & can give him & of wch I write to thee some time agoe.[38] p[ray] minde it.
I have had 2 nameless letters from your parts or Boston,[39] the last was from Philad. 5 10^{m} intimateing a quarrell between Coll. Q^{s} wife & Mr[?] Thomas Jones,[40] Mr. of the Societys ship, & that he is both able & wiling, be secured his wages, viz 70 pounds or thereabouts, that he is gone to Boston, & there might be treated with. I would have thee writ (& gett his relations of that place to write) to D. Zachery to enquire after him, & secure him his wages on my acc^{t} to gett the truth {out} of him, of Q. Knavery to the Company, twould slacken him here in his surveyorship, & render it easier for me to get him discarded; for If I live I will & shall be able to do it.
This year the Customs upon goods from Pennsylvania amount to 8000 pounds, the year I arrived there 1699, but to 1500 pounds at the most. a good argum^{t} for me & the poor Country. It has a greater regard {here} & made the care of an officer as well as Virg. & MaryLd. {at the Custom house}: N. york not the half of it.
But o that we had a furr Trade insteed of a Tobacco one, & that thou wouldst do all that is possible to master furs & [s]kins for me; but Bares more especially; [torn] hadst thou sent me two or three Chests

of them, I could have sould them almost for wt I would. 16ss, ay 20ss a skin at this Juncture, & thou promest me, 2 if not 3 chests in thy last packet. I earnestly press thee upon this one point as thou desirest to assist me in the readiest & surest way.
I hope thou mindest my land, {especially} where the wood carrier & seller by Ed. shippens, used to cutt down my wood, to stop {his} further mischief, & that my purchass of w. Southby,[41] goe not to decay for my eye (tho' not my heart) is upon poor fairemt [42] unless the unworthiness of some spirrits in your town drive me upp to Pennsberry or Sasquehanagh, for good an all: God will, in his time, rebuke their baseness.
Also the 50000 ~~pounds~~ Acres of land that belongd~~s~~ to Sr John, & now to Sr Robt Fagg,[43] that It be taken up as I order'd when there; & If that taken up by T. F.[44] in chester County & Newcastle will answear it, pray let it; else I am content that the one half at least be taken up at this New Discovery of T. Fairmans, if his swan do not prove a Goose. O that it [shall ans?]wer but as true [as faire,?] ay [several words torn]t thy Loosere [one line torn]
That business depen[di]ng between W. Biddle and me,[45] should come to some Issue while I am here; and I wish S. Jen.[46] Memory is not decayd, & Govr Ham. do[es] not lean too much that way; but my Cos. Markham can't forgett the agreemt that they & son & Daughter should have their lives in ~~it~~ {half of it,} & then revert to me, & that their halfe should be from end to end on their Side the River & that next Pennsberry to belong to me. try a faire issue on that Side the water, & if can end it there, do, else I can best Issue it while here my self, and I lay great ~~wait~~ weight upon it. Note, 1o, that Frds on that side forbad them buying it, 2 'twas out of rule attempted by her[47] wth our Indians, to treat wth them for wt we claim'd without leave: 3. she was forbad by Colonel Mark. then my Dep. Goverr so that arbitrarily & clandestinly {(or surreptiously)} as well as rudely & Injuriously she (Sarah Biddle) obtaind possession; yet in Ja: Harrisons time our Stock was putt on it. pray min[d]e it: I hope my son will contribute to it if [n]ot too eager; his greatest ~~fault~~ in[torn]. He comes with [the] messenger[48] [two lines torn] Him, and in order to it Immediately take him away to Pennsberry, & there give him the true state of things, & ~~lay~~[?] weigh down his Levitys, as well as temper his resentmts, & inform his understanding, Since all depends upon it, as well for his future happiness ~~&~~ as in measure the poor Countrys. I propose Govr Hamilton, S. Carpenter, I. Norris, yo{u}ng shippens,[49] & the easiest & most Sencible & Civiliz'd for his Conversation; and I hope Coll. Markham, & Cos. Ashton, & the Farmers may come in for a share, but the first cheifly. watch him, outwitt, & honestly overreach him—for his good. Fishing, little Journys, as to see the Indians, &c: will divert him. and pray Frds to bear all they can, & melt towards him, that they may melt & gain him; at least Civilly if not religiously. He will empty himself to thee. If S. Carp, R. Hill, & Is. Norris could gett within him, & honest

& tender Gr. Owen, not the least likely (for he feels & sees) I should rejoyce. Pennsylvania hass cost me dearer in my poor Childe, than all other Considerations.[50] the Lord ~~yet~~ pitty & save in his great love. I yet hope.

I have writt to Coll. Ham: wch deliver, & Inclosed the Queens approbation,[51] wch if not upon the spott open & read, & send an express for him, that he may feel life in his Duty. I would also have Colonel Markham have the Registry & Probat of wills, but the Records lye as they do, if most advisable; that you may see I dare reward that base man[52] according to his villany; and I will not have thee pay him one penny more, let what will be due, as att. Genll wch will be in the hands of an other shortly,[53] from hence, & in the mean time; if moor Flings up, Constitute who you will, I mean the Govr & Council. Give Judge Guests letter[54] as he deserves, 'tis Kinde. and encourage all, for I hope you will in a while see cause more & more: one thing at a time, the Carriers pace is the safest.

23: 12m [February 1703]

Here is a Mighty complaint of a secreet Corroco trade by an understanding wth Road {Island,}[55] illustrated by Coll. Q. ~~with~~[?] after his usuall manner, sweling it to a mighty mountain, the perticulars I have not, but because all must be known to thee & Govert that has any truth or fact in it, be preperad per next to advertise me. 'Tis like his Swish Swash Bounces abt the Comss I gave T. Farmer & J. Wood, that he thought to shake all by, wch after all proves just; & is approved by that very great man of the law they hoped ~~to~~ {would} have reported against me.[56] why do you not Rub him for it, & fling his Craks in his face & humble him; but I hope you will finde a learneder & reasonabler Judge in a while in that post. keep cleare of Frauds, & punish them to their merrit, and all will do well; but as some offences of that Nature, (tho much less than wt are committed by other Colonys, more immedately under the Queens Govermt & Cognisance) are the strength of our Common Enimys, so do you watch carefully that such faults be either prevented or effectually punisht, & we shall do well enough. I have discourst some of our Chiefest Ministers upon a Composition, in which the ratification of our Constitution & Laws is the first article; wt it will issue in I cant yet give any account.[57]

I was yesterday to visit the widdow Groom[58] who employs Capt Hans[59] as her factor in the Furr Trade; she says she sends him a 1000l worth of Goods at a time, & that he is very Just to her, & Confesses he makes Good return, & that she makes more than cent sterling per cent by them; especially of Bear Skins, seling them for above 20ss sterl. per skin. How happy should I be if the people did but in lieu of other maintenance, ~~would~~ confine the Indian trade to me, wch w[ere] nothing out of the[ir] Pocket, tho it were but for 7 or eleven years, more would still be better,[60] I should be able by such returns to Clear my heavy Incombrances. pray lay this before the Govr & a few of the best to be trusted, if this could be obtained, for Tobacco's will not do, Since these 25 hogsheads will hardly Clear so many pounds.

I must press thee to lay before the Comrs the preservation of my trees, & cedar swamp, & Black walnut, both up Scoolkill & Delaware, of wch great Havock & Spoyle have been, & I fear is still but too much made.

Thou hast sayd nothing about T. Bifields Jury,[61] wch Quary sayd he order'd to be sworn & Bifield deny'd to the Lords of Trade & Plants to Qs face. ~~but he denyd that~~ [illegible deletion] He also sayd the name of God was not used in our attestations. an authentick acct of that whole proceeding & J. Moors most false allegations of his lettr of atturny for a sworn jury & an appeal else for Eng. with an acct of that tryall, as also the tryals {lately} about fals Tr[ad]e in our Civil Courts, & [half a line torn] would be of Signal [service?] [torn]

they Imagin you wont right the Queen there, or you might put the Nose of an admiralty {one} out of Joynt.

A: Paxton at last has taken his leave of me {(the first time I saw him)} has been very ill, & his letters from Coll. Ham: came but the day before yesterday, as I take it, to hand, so that wt I writt by him to Gor Ham:[62] was before I had his Packet; but I have since its receipt, improved it for his advantage. Pax. chest was wth the ship, & the packet in it, I suppos'd Cover'd to Jos. Ormston,[63] an unhappy delay. I am forc'd to break off here, time calling me away, that none can refuse yet if more fall in, will Improve this to severall perticularitys. However take notice.

1 I will have no lands in the Mannors layd out to the company. for my lettr to the Comrs of Property for them, was on that Condition.[64]

2 press to get the Asembly to limitt the fur t[ra]d[e] [torn] [y]ears at least to my assignes or order, in order to make returne, & insteed of any levy, excise or tax for my acct, if possible.

3 Get some allowance {from the Inhabitants} for Goverr Hamilton now he is approv'd of by the Queen till his year is out at least. for the time he has been & is Govr.

The Lds of Trade have promest me to receive no Complaints wthout the Partys sending them, give them to the Partys they are sent agst, upon the spot, ~~& the~~ for their answears, in the nature of Bill & answear in Chancery, that nobody may be murder'd in the dark. a great reformation & relief, & for wch american Govermts owe me their Good will.

The mony will be forthwith by the Q. proclamation reduc'd to sterl. or 25 pounds per cent at most,[65] of wch make the best use for me, & [on?] secrecy intimate it to S.C. I.N. R.H.[66] The lawyers say the Q. can do it here, therfore there.

also a summary way of Justice under ten[?] pds is like to [fo?]llow cum aliis.[67]

I will add no more, [b]ecause I cant, but that I am taken up in our European, family & american Pennsylvania settlements,[68] in wch I hope to make some thing of the latter. I wish Johnne had upon his town lott,[69] a small mansion built of 100l or 150l, 'tw[o]uld lett; and the rest lett out profitably, saveing a Garden plott & fruit trees. we are through mercy well, send our love to all our frds of all sorts, p[e]rticulerly the best affected, & our own immediate dependents & family. I am

Thy assured Frd.

I desire thee, by the Messenger ~~pray~~ to send me {at least} a pipe or 2 hhds of the best Madera wine, & one of St George,[70] for that barrell I had of Ed. Sh:[71] has excell'd here.

I hope youl have one shortly that will be a safer Guide, & surer footing in law, than ever yet was there, an able, grounded Lawyer, & a Good temperd & honest so[b]er Gentleman.[72] this to thy self; but [torn] [be?]leive hele deliver [torn] be resp [rest of line torn]

28 1 [March]—1703

vale. I am solicited about G. Foxes Gift.[73] In deed it was myn to him; & therfore must take the liberty to say, that for the request of the meeting I a little admire at it; the considerablest of them that signe it, must know it was so. I shall willingly allow a field of twenty acres, if it were 25 acres for frds use, out of liberty lands neer any meeting but to allow any out of the Citty lots, is wt I will never do, unless I were upon the Spot. I Still remember the Collops[74] Cutt out of myselfe & my son & daughters concerns in my former absence, & will suffer none of those things to be acted again. I have not forgot the Lott n. n.[75] where our meeting house stands, that was reserv'd for Tishe,[76] who as per list appears, is without any High street lott at all, now that is gone. I know who urge these difficultys upon me, but alas they are in the powr of one greater than I am to humble & distress them. one would think that the hand of God has been so legible upon them, one in the loss of an only, lovely Jewel, & tother of his xtian & Civil reputation,[77] wch ought to so mark him as never to be employd in either Civil or Church capacity till a pure repentance & purgation had restored him. In short make this matter as easy as may be. the Land graunted from the Mill at towns end [would have done] [torn] [the bu]siness [torn] of wt they aske. however I will honour his name that honoured truth above all men, & loved me, but in my own way & time. I can satisfy thee I have writt to nobody anything that can give them the least occasion agst thee.

The Gentleman that Brings this,[78] is Constituted Judge of the Admiralty of Pennsylvania, the Jersys & New york, & is yet wiling to be my att. Generall, to rectify matters in law, & to putt you into better methods, in wch respect he is by the Judicious here thought to be very able. gett him a sober, suitable house to diet in as well as Lodge. If, you were together twere for thy advantage in many respects. He is a moderat Churchman, knows the world here, has been in 2 severall Parliam^{ts} [79] & Recorder of southampton; only steps abroad to ease his fortune of some of his fathers debts he was early, unwarily engaged for. He is a favorite of Ld. Cornberrys Father Ld Clarendon.[80] I have graunted him a Commiss. for Chief Justice, in case the people will lay hold of such an opertunity, as no Goverm^{t} in america ever had before, for an English lawyer, and encourage him by a proper [stipend?] of at least 100 pounds if not 150 pounds per annum. for [three or four words torn] more for their service, than [most of line torn] ing, because his business Chiefly relates to their property, & the other to state & warr. My son, haveing life, resolves to be wth you, per first.[81] his wife this day week deliverd, where I came in the evening, of a fine Boy, which he has Call'd william, so that now we are Major, Minor & Minimus. I bless the Lord I & myn are pretty well, Johnne Brisk, my wife Bigg,[82] Tomme a lovely large Childe; and my Grandson springet a meer Saracen, his sister a Beuty.

For news, domestick & forraign, besides the pamphlets, I referr thee to the Bearer, above all books & persons that goe~~ne~~ hence to you, only upon truths acc^{t} we are generally well & easy. Jer. Hignal, T. Gilpin —Perrin, deceas'd.[83] give my Dr. love to all Frds, & to the officers in Goverm^{t} my remembrance. also J.S. & Mary.[84] of whose care & faithfullness I have no doubt. My wife joyns with me in the same, & to thy selfe, with a frequent remembrance of thee & dilligence for us, & concerne that nothing is now sent thee as a token thereof wch yet shall be if possible. only I have sent some hats, one for Gr. owen, & tother intended for Ed. Shippen, wch thou mayst take, wth this Just excuse, that the Brim being to narrow for his age & heighth, I intend him one wth a larger brim & [so?] soon as I saw it, told the frd so that m[a]de it. neith[er?] [torn]ing profitable [torn] I thought it handsom tho I pinch here, to be sure. If my son send hounds, as he has provided 2 or 3 couple, of Choice ones, hounds that will follow a man as well as deer, foxes & woolves; pray let great care be taken of them, & J. So[tc]her quarter them about, as wth young w. Biles[85] &c: I also recommend Randal Janny[86] about the sasquehanagh purchass to us[e] him kindly and easily therin: of all wch more by my son, but if that should prove within Balt[87] bounds I should make a Count[r]y for him, but I think to fasten that matter wth ant. sharp.[88] I add no more but my good wishes, & leave all to the secreet wise ordering of my good God, & close

Thy reall Friend
Wm Penn

Alexand: [blank] and [blank] Milner married last week at Bristoll[89] poor Mic. Russel sen^{r} dyed by an apoplectick stroak last month.[90] vale.

ALS. Penn Papers, Letters of the Penn Family to James Logan, HSP. (*Micro.* 10:735.) Docketed: Proprietor to J L London 24 11mo 170[2] | & 28 1mo 1703 | per the Messenger received 1 5mo 1703. Six of the eleven pages of this letter are torn at the bottom edge, causing awkward gaps in the text.

1. The *Messenger* had left Philadelphia on 5 Dec. 1702 with a shipment of tobacco and letters for WP. Among them was Logan's letter to WP of 1 Dec. 1702 (*Micro.* 10:634). Albright G. Zimmerman, "James Logan, Proprietary Agent," *PMHB*, 78:149.

2. The *Cantico*, or *Industry*, and the brigantine *Mary* of Barbados had both sailed for England from Pennsylvania in the summer of 1702 and had been captured by the French. For the letters Logan sent by these ships, see *Micro.* 10:400, 449, 493; doc. 52, n. 1.

3. Logan had estimated the value shipped on the *Cantico* at £400 or more and that of the *Mary* at £200. *Micro.* 10:241, 360.

4. Logan had bought WP a share in the *Cantico*, but in a letter of 18 June 1702 he reported: "She is a Dull Sailor & therefore if war will Require the better Insurance for it will be Very unfitt to trust her without it" (*Micro.* 10:241). He later told WP that the ship's speed had been improved before sailing and the voyage planned by experienced merchants. Zimmerman, "James Logan," pp. 152-53; *Micro.* 10:891.

5. Samuel Vaus, WP's agent.

6. WP's language here suggests a conscientious scruple, but Quakers in general seem to have had no objection to insurance, and WP was not troubled by the idea that Vaus, another Quaker, might insure the vessel.

7. A group of English tobacco merchants had contracted with Czar Peter I for the sale of colonial tobacco to Russia. The outbreak of Queen Anne's War plunged the tobacco trade into a deep depression and intensified efforts to exploit the Russian market, but the czar was not fulfilling his end of the bargain. See Jacob M. Price, "The Tobacco Adventure to Russia: Enterprise, Politics, and Diplomacy in the Quest for a Northern Market for English Colonial Tobacco, 1676-1722," *Transactions of the American Philosophical Society*, n.s., vol. 51, pt. 1 (1961); Lewis C. Gray, *History of Agriculture in the Southern United States to 1860* (Washington, D.C., 1933), 1:253.

8. Heartwood of the American logwood tree, used in dyeing. *OED*.

9. In the fall of 1702 the English navy had failed to engage the enemy at Cadiz but had destroyed or captured the whole of a large French and Spanish fleet at Vigo. The seizure of cargo from these vessels glutted the market for colonial logwood. See doc. 53, nn. 4-5; Zimmerman, "James Logan," *PMHB*, 78:153.

10. The *Rebecca*, which left Philadelphia on 11 July 1702, had carried a cargo of eight tons of logwood. Ibid., p. 149.

11. In his letter of 1 Dec. 1702, Logan had relayed a report that Samuel Vaus was "borrowing" WP's tobacco for shipment to Hamburg. *Micro.* 10:634.

12. Beer.

13. Antigua.

14. Silver plate.

15. The chief, or most important, thing. *OED*.

16. 10 & 11 Will. III, cap. 10, passed in 1699, restricted the Irish wool trade to England. For WP's views on Anglo-Irish trade, see *PWP*, 3:548-52.

17. WP had mortgaged some of his Irish lands to pay for his daughter Laetitia's marriage settlement with William Aubrey and had settled others on William Penn, Jr., before the latter's marriage in 1699. See *Micro.* 10:407; Jenkins, p. 107; doc. 209A, B.

18. Probably the land tax of 4s per pound, levied to finance the War of the Spanish Succession. Stephen Dowell, *A History of Taxation and Taxes in England* (London, 1884), 2:71.

19. This statement is difficult to decipher. In calculating the exchange rate from Irish to English currency, par was set at 8⅓ percent, with actual rates varying from 5 to 10 percent according to the season. McCusker, *Money and Exchange*, pp. 34, 39.

20. See doc. 51, text at nn. 12-14.

21. Mary Penn gave birth to William Penn III on 21 Mar. 1703; see text at n. 81, above.

22. Edward Shippen.

23. Samuel Carpenter.

24. WP had traveled to Pennsylvania on the *Canterbury* in 1699; see doc. 49, n. 3. WP had previously expressed dissatisfaction with Thomas Fairman's surveying; see doc. 14, n. 24.

25. This letter has not been found. On 11 Aug. 1699 WP had sold 60,000 acres in Pennsylvania for £2000 to the "London Company" of Tobias Collett, Michael Russell, Daniel Quare, and Henry Gouldney. The land included 5000 acres each in WP's manors of Gilberts, Highlands, and Rocklands. *Micro.* 8:089; *PMHB*, 31:436; doc. 110, text at nn. 31–32.

26. See doc. 48, n. 57.

27. Perhaps Robert Trowbridge, master of WP's captured ship the *Cantico*, had written to WP from Dinant, now in southern Belgium. His letter has not been found.

28. Agreement for the exchange or ransom of prisoners. *OED*.

29. These enclosures have not been found.

30. Lord Cornbury had suspended William Atwood (c. 1652-post 1709), chief justice of New York, for his high-handed and irregular judicial procedures, particularly in the prosecution of Nicholas Bayard and John Hutchins in 1702. An Order in Council of 21 Jan. 1703 confirmed Cornbury's action. Atwood published his side of the matter in *The Case of William Atwood* (London, 1703). *New York Col. Docs.*, 4:1024; Paul M. Hamlin and Charles E. Baker, *Supreme Court of Judicature of the Province of New York, 1691-1704: Biographical Dictionary* (New York, 1959), pp. 11-18.

31. Robert Trowbridge.

32. On 29 Mar. 1703 WP wrote to Hamilton to appoint William Markham as register general, replacing John Moore. *Micro.* 10:821.

33. Roger Mompesson, who ultimately carried this letter to Logan; see above, text at n. 78.

34. William Rakestraw (d. 1719), a Philadelphia Quaker, had complained to WP that Thomas Holme had cheated him out of his city lot. Either Abraham or John Brewster (d. 1719), of New Castle Co., had also written to WP with "a mighty Complaint" about his land. WP forwarded Brewster's letter, together with two from Rakestraw, to the commissioners of property on 10 Jan. 1703. *PWP*, 3:112n; *Micro.* 10:197, 709; *PA*, 2d ser., 19:230, 264; *Calendar of Delaware Wills, New Castle County, 1682-1800* (New York, 1911), p. 23.

35. Juan Corso; see doc. 33, n. 14.

36. For Logan's report of the Philadelphia government's contention with the county courts over jurisdiction, see doc. 52.

37. Not found.

38. See doc. 48, n. 37.

39. Not found.

40. Sarah Quary (d. 1717), wife of Robert Quary, was evidently at odds with Thomas Jones, but the nature of their quarrel is unknown.

41. William Southerby, or Southeby (d. 1722), a prominent Philadelphia Quaker landowner and politician, held land along the Schuylkill River. *PWP*, 3:110n.

42. Fairmount, site of WP's Springettsbury Manor.

43. Sir John Fagg (d. 1701), a civil war parliamentarian who later supported the Restoration, had joined WP in campaigning for Algernon Sidney in 1679. Sir John, and later his heir Sir Robert (d. 1715), held 50,000 acres of Pennsylvania land in trust for the children of WP's first marriage. A smaller tract later known as "Fagg's Manor" was laid out in Chester Co. and allotted to Laetitia Penn Aubrey, while other portions of the land went to William Penn, Jr. *PWP*, 1:553-54n; Burke's *Peerage* (1883), 1:499; Society Collection, HSP; *Micro.* 11:240.

44. Thomas Fairman. His "new discovery" was a tract of about 80 square miles. See doc. 91, text at n. 3.

45. On WP's dispute with William Biddle (1634-1711) of Burlington, West New Jersey, over the title to "Biddle's Island," see *PWP*, 3:36n, 139, 141n.

46. Samuel Jennings.

47. Sarah Smith Kemp Biddle (1638-1709), the wife of William Biddle. *PWP*, 3:141n.

48. William Penn, Jr., did not sail on the *Messenger*, as his trip was delayed until Oct. 1703. See doc. 61, nn. 4-5.

49. Edward Shippen, Jr. (1678-1714), Boston-born son of the wealthy Philadel-

phia merchant was no longer a Quaker by the time of his death. Elise W. Balch, *Descendants of Edward Shippen* (Philadelphia, 1883), pp. 48-49; Hinshaw, 2:447.

50. WP believed that his long absences from home in attending to Pennsylvania's affairs had damaged William Penn, Jr.'s character by removing him from his father's influence. See also docs. 38, n. 86; 91, text at nn. 1-2.

51. For Queen Anne's approbation of Hamilton, see *Micro.* 10:728. WP's letter to Hamilton has not been found.

52. John Moore, whom WP was replacing as register general.

53. Roger Mompesson; see above, text at n. 78.

54. Not found.

55. Robert Quary had charged that in June 1702 a brigantine had illegally imported European and East Indian goods from Curaçao to Pennsylvania, then run off to Rhode Island to unload the rest of its illicit cargo. Quary claimed that Pennsylvania's government had failed to cooperate with royal officials in seizing the ship. *CSPC, 1702-1703*, pp. 15-16. William Popple forwarded this charge to WP in doc. 57.

56. For Attorney General Northey's approval of WP's commissions for water bailiffs, see doc. 47.

57. WP's negotiations with the ministry for the surrender of his government of Pennsylvania were to produce a formal proposal by 18 June 1703; see doc. 62.

58. Sarah Moore Groome (c. 1658-1705), widow of the Quaker mariner Samuel Groome (d. 1698) of London. *PWP*, 3:489n; Digests of Quaker Records, London and Middx., GSP.

59. Capt. John Hans Steelman.

60. In a letter of 9 July 1703, Logan quashed this naive hope of WP's that he might be given a monopoly of the fur trade: "to expect to have the Ind. Trade Secured to thee is as vain as to expect they will make Offerings of their whole Estates to thee the Merchants will never bear it." *Micro.* 10:1031.

61. On the charges against Pennsylvania's handling of Byfield's case, see doc. 44A.

62. Alexander Paxton had carried Hamilton's letter to WP of 21 Oct. 1702 (*Micro.* 10:544); Logan later accused him of purposely delaying its delivery (*Micro.* 10:1031). Paxton (d. post 1709), a well-to-do resident of Philadelphia, was probably an Anglican. *PMHB*, 99:16; Phila. Will Bk. C, #11.

63. Joseph Ormston (d. post 1719) was a Quaker merchant of London. Digests of Quaker Records, London and Middx., GSP.

64. WP's letter about the London Company's land has not been found, but he evidently had arrived at an understanding with them that they would waive their rights in the manors in exchange for land elsewhere. See n. 25, above.

65. A royal proclamation of 18 June 1704 limited the colonial value of the standard piece of eight to 6s, an advance of about ⅓ over its sterling value. Pennsylvania joined other colonies in failing to comply with this order. Curtis P. Nettels, *The Money Supply of the American Colonies Before 1720* (1934; reprint, Clifton, N.J., 1973), pp. 232, 242-44n.

66. Samuel Carpenter, Isaac Norris, and Richard Hill.

67. With the rest.

68. Probably a reference to the property settlements WP was making with respect to the marriages of Laetitia and William, Jr. See doc. 209.

69. Probably the lot on High St. mentioned in the will of John Penn. *PMHB*, 32:214.

70. Portuguese wine from São Jorge Island in the Azores. Wine from Madeira and the Azores was exempted from the Navigation Acts' restrictions on colonial trading. A. D. Francis, *The Wine Trade* (London, 1972), p. 261.

71. Edward Shippen.

72. Roger Mompesson; see text at n. 78, above.

73. George Fox (1624-1691), the most prominent of early Quaker leaders, had bequeathed to Phila. Monthly Meeting the city lot and liberty land that went with his 1250 acres of Pennsylvania land, a grant from WP. Fox's land and lot had never been laid out, however, and Samuel Carpenter, David Lloyd, and Anthony Morris had written to WP on behalf of the meeting after failing to obtain satisfaction from the commissioners of property. WP here refuses to give up more of the city land allotted to himself and his children; the commissioners eventually gave the meeting part of a lot formerly assigned to Thomas Brassey. *PWP*, 1:132n; *PA*, 2d ser., 19:405, 437, 616; Phila. Monthly Meeting Records, Abstracts of Minutes, GSP, 1:334, 374; *Micro.* 10:823.

74. Slices. *OED.* For WP's previous complaints about this, see *PWP,* 3:408.

75. Not named. Walter T. Rogers, *Dictionary of Abbreviations* (London, 1913).

76. Laetitia Penn had originally been assigned a large lot stretching from Front to Second along High St.; the meetinghouse stood at Front and Second. *PMHB,* 80:197.

77. The first reference here is to David Lloyd, whose only son had died in June 1701, and the second is to Lloyd's father-in-law, Joseph Growden, to whom Thomas Lower had written about Fox's legacy. Growden had created a scandal by impregnating the daughter of a respectable Quaker and then marrying her off to one of his servants. *Micro.* 10:141; Roy N. Lokken, *David Lloyd: Colonial Lawmaker* (Seattle, 1959), p. 96; *The Friend,* 39:93-94 (1865).

78. Roger Mompesson, who was traveling to Pennsylvania aboard the *Messenger.*

79. Mompesson had sat in 1699 and again in 1701 for the borough of Southampton. *Members of Parliament, Part I, Parliaments of England, 1213-1702* (n.p., 1879), pp. 583, 590.

80. Henry Hyde (1638-1709), second earl of Clarendon, was the brother-in-law of James II; he had served as a privy councilor under Charles II and as lord lieutenant of Ireland under James. After the Glorious Revolution he had been arrested as a Jacobite. *PWP,* 2:39n; 3:61n, 208n; *DNB.*

81. William Penn, Jr., ultimately reached Pennsylvania in Feb. 1704. See docs. 73, 74.

82. Hannah Penn gave birth to Hannah Margarita (1703-1708) on 30 July 1703. Jenkins, p. 73; doc. 67.

83. Jeremiah Hignell (d. 1703) was a cooper and longtime Quaker sufferer of Bristol; Thomas Gilpin (1622-1703) was an active Quaker minister and sufferer of Warborough, Oxon.; Edward Perrin (d. 1703), a Quaker merchant of Bristol, had sent his children to the Bristol Friends school when Logan was schoolmaster there. Mortimer, 1:203-4, 211; Braithwaite, *Second Period,* p. 359n; Smith, 1:846; Besse, 1:566, 572.

84. John and Mary Sotcher.

85. William Biles, Jr. (1671-1739), cooper of Falls Township, Bucks Co., later became a J.P., assemblyman, and speaker of the Assembly. His land lay near Pennsbury. *PMHB,* 26:352, 356-57.

86. Randall Janney was returning to Philadelphia from a visit to England. Part of his large Pennsylvania landholdings lay in territory disputed between WP and Lord Baltimore, now in Cecil Co., Md. Miles White, Jr., *The Quaker Janneys of Cheshire and Their Progenitors* (Harrisburg, 1904), pp. 23, 27, 35.

87. Lord Baltimore's.

88. Anthony Sharp (1642-1706) was a prominent Quaker merchant and clothier of Dublin and a large New Jersey landholder. Sharp had been offered a chance to purchase Talbot's Manor, which included the proposed Pennsylvania settlement at Octoraro, then in dispute with Maryland. See doc. 45, n. 9. *PWP,* 1:134n; 2:89n; 3:292n.

89. On 24 Mar. 1703 Alexander Arscott, the Quaker schoolmaster of Bristol, had married Ann Milner (1659-1728). Mortimer, 2:233.

90. Michael Russell, Sr. (c. 1648-1703), of White Hart Court, Lombard St., was a Quaker weaver of London and an investor in Pennsylvania land; see n. 25, above. WP's son Thomas was apprenticed to Michael Russell, Jr., a mercer, about 1716. Digests of Quaker Records, London and Middx., GSP; Jenkins, p. 90.

57
FROM WILLIAM POPPLE

[28 January 1703]

S[r]

The Lords Commissioners for Trade and Plantations do Order me to send you the inclosed Copy of a Paper which they have lately received from Pennsylvan[a], being the Answer of the Members of three Upper Counties to the Lieutenant Gov[r] and Councill, signed by David Lloyd, John Swift and others, and to desire you to explain the meaning of a Expression therein, Signifying the Willingness of those Members to Act as an Assembly *in a Charteral way.*[1]

They have also Ordered me to desire you to let them have Copies of the several Grand Charters which they understand were lately granted by you in Pennsylvania;[2] And they have further directed me to send you the inclosed Paper of Queries, drawn by their direction, unto which they desire your Answer.

I am likewise Commanded to acquaint you, that upon consideration of your Letter of the 25th Instant and of a Draught of her Majesties Order in Councill therein referred to,[3] their Lordships see no reason for any Alteration to be made in that Order, the Matters therein contained being such as relate equally to the due Administration of Justice and to the good Government of the Province of Pennsylvania I am &c.

W: P:

Whitehall January 28th 1702/3.

Queries proposed to Mr Penn by the Lords Commissioners for Trade and Plantations. January 28th 1702/3.

Who is the present Naval Officer in Pennsylvania?[4] By what Authority does he Act? What are his Instructns or directions for the Execution of his Office?

Whether there be any Court in Pennsylvania, (other than the Court of Admiralty established by the Authority of the Lord High Admiral) wch takes upon them to hear and determine Informations upon Seizures for breaches of the Acts of Trade and Navigation, and other Admiralty Causes? And by what authority any such Court Acts?

What information have you received from Pennsylvania of ships coming thither directly from Curasao with European and East India Goods; And of other ships designed for Curasao with Tobacco from Pennsylvania?

Whether any of those ships have been Tryed and Condemned; And in what Court?

What Information have you received of ships going from Pensylvania to Rhode Island, with Illegal Trade?[5]

Copy. CO 5/1290, PRO. (*Micro.* 10:774.) Addressed: To Wm Penn Esqr. Docketed: January 28th 1702/3 | Letter to Mr Penn | in Answer to his of | the 25th instant, Also | inclosing some Que= | ries relating to Pen= | sylvania.

1. This declaration of the Philadelphia, Chester, and Bucks Co. assemblymen had been made to the Provincial Council on 19 Nov. 1702. The Board of Trade had just received a letter from Robert Quary of 7 Dec. 1702, which enclosed a copy of this minute, though with different wording and order of signatures from the version in the Council minutes. The Upper Counties representatives were insisting that they would join in an Assembly with the Lower only according to the provisions of the Charter of Privileges of 1701 (doc. 28). Quary complained that WP had never shown this charter to the Board of Trade. *CSPC, 1702-1703*, p. 18; *Minutes of the Provincial Council*, 2:82.

2. The Charter of Privileges and the Charter of Property. See docs. 28; 31, n. 1. WP does not seem to have complied with this request until 1705; see the headnote to doc. 63.

3. In his letter of 25 Jan. (*Micro.* 10:770) WP argued that the approval of Gov. Hamilton (*Micro.* 10:728) should be issued separately, instead of being tacked onto an order in council that dealt first with Pennsylvania's currency, WP's title to the Lower Counties, and the administration of oaths in Pennsylvania courts. For his further complaint about the board's refusal to change this, see doc. 58.

4. WP had commissioned Paroculus Parmiter as naval officer on 1 Nov. 1701 (*Micro.* 9:839). Quary's letter of 7 Dec. 1702 had charged that Parmiter, a relative of WP's, was taking cases of seizures of ships to the civil courts instead of the admiralty court. *CSPC, 1702-1703*, p. 16.

5. See doc. 56, n. 55. Quary claimed that a regular import-export trade was secretly being carried on between Pennsylvania and Curaçao, with the connivance of Rhode Island (*CSPC, 1702-1703*, pp. 15-16). For previous charges of illicit trade with Curaçao, see doc. 19, text at nn. 14-18.

58
TO LORD GODOLPHIN

3 12th M. [February] 1702/3.

To the Ld Treasurer[1]

Lett me not look Impertinent or Presumptuous Noble Friend that I have inclosed a Paper[2] I received from the L^{ds} Commiss^{rs} of Trade & Pl^{s} that confirms thy Opinion of the Reasonablenes & Judgement of the ablest of the Board who instead of charging or Accusing Me or the Province would have me answer their Questions under my hand ex Officio that would do both at w^{h} my Lawyers laugh.

They have also cram'd the Queens gracious Approbation[3] of my Deputy Govr with so many things that were no part of my Petition & of w^{h} I never heard one word instead of making the Law of the 7th & 8th of the late King[4] the Preamble of the said Approbation being the Reason for the Power in the Crown that of 3 sides of a Sheet of large Post paper closely writt It makes but 4 or 5 lines w^{h} closes the Order of Council Instead of giving so considerable an Act of State the form & Dignity of a distinct one.[5]

Nor is this all they have adventured to lead the Queen to extend a Law of Eng^{ld} to all & limited to Eng^{ld} into America & there to alter a Law not only made in Our Province but w^{h} was confirmed by the late King above 8 years ago.[6] A stretch of Prerogative somewhat Extraordinary since a Law there confirmed here cannot be altered but by the same steps & Degrees of Authority. All w^{h} proves in my Opinion (with an Overplus) that Quality & Clarkship[7] without Judgement wont do Busines for nothing exposes ~~a~~ M~~a~~en more than to affect a part & a place their Understanding cant fill.

I most humbly begg three Minutes some time to Morrow forenoon or by Two after it to prevent if possible my Busines coming again before the Qu. in Councill w^{h} Ld W.[8] seems for ought I see of the Opinion to do I am with great regards Thy very Respectfull Fr.

W. P.

LBC. William Penn Letterbook, 1699-1703, HSP. (*Micro.* 10:779.)

1. Sidney, first Lord Godolphin, had held the post of lord treasurer several times since 1684.

2. Doc. 57.

3. For the royal approbation of Hamilton, see *Micro.* 10:728.

4. The Navigation Act of 1696 (7 and 8 Will. III, cap. 22) required royal approbation of the governors of proprietary colonies.

5. See doc. 57, n. 3.

6. A Pennsylvania law passed in 1693 and confirmed in 1694 had provided for the giving of evidence in Pennsylvania courts under a solemn promise to tell the truth. The order in council approving Hamilton called for the administration of oaths to all who would have been required to take them under English law. *Charter and Laws*, p. 228; *PWP*, 3:401n; *CSPC, 1693-1696*, p. 321; *Micro.* 10:728.

7. Mere record keeping; a dig at William Blathwayt, the leading member of the Board of Trade. WP is complaining that the board is made up of nobles like Weymouth (see n. 8) and bureaucrats like Blathwayt with no understanding of colonial affairs.

8. Sir Thomas Thynne, first Viscount Weymouth (1640-1714), an adherent of the high Tory party, was president of the Board of Trade. *DNB*.

59
TO JAMES LOGAN

Lond. 1 2m [April] 1703

James

I have writt at Large, 6 sheets if not 7, and sent per Roger Mompesson esqr. to wch referr thee.[1] I here enclose R. Janny's Bond[2] for two of his best servts, one a Carpenter t'other an husbandman, that the outhouse, in part, may be perfected within, & a moderate stable built, for 8 or 10 Horses, & a shelter for Cattle or sheep, neer the Barn as formerly. wch I refer to J. Sacher.[3] Yaff[4] is also gone, in the room of one that cant goe for weakness, & I have resolvd after four years faithfull service he shall be free. yet I have left it to him to returne, if {he} may passage free (wch he will more than deserve in any ship) in the Messenger; nay I leave it for him to return from Deal if he will. thou art to allow R. Janny nothing for him; that goes into the 20 pounds for the other two; {also} ~~& besides,~~ he wants 3, of his compl~~i~~ement, and must have payd as much had he not gone; besides, I have otherwise been kinde to him Yaff is an able planter, & good Husbandman {& promesses faire,} & Sam has but one year more to serve, I think, by my note, if he has serv'd well.[5] I hope Randall Carrys a Hatt for Ed. Sh.[6] of a Mayorall size. I orderd one to him.

See if the Town would be so kinde to build me a pretty Box, like Ed. Ship. upon any of my Lots in town or Liberty-land, or purchass Grif. owens, or T. fairmans,[7] or any neer healthy Spott, {as} wicoco,[8] or the like; for Pennsberry will hardly accommodate my sons family & myn, unless enlarged. Let wt is there, be kept up, but only substantiall

Improvments to be {now} followed. I should like fruit at the distance of forty or 50 in fields, as also peach trees, that shall neither hurt corn nor grass. Now is the time to make earnings in the Islands,[9] wherfore faile not {to use} the opertunity, & lett me see some Chests of Furs per Messenger. If thou canst, send me per her, a coppy of the Laws to lye by me. Churchill cals oné me for his mony.[10] pray write & returne w^t is sould, & w^t I must say to him. I send 2 or 300 Books ags^t G. K.[11] per R. J. wch may be disperst as there is occasion & service. If I have more time I shall write again. So take my leave for this time, Randall goeing in an hour and this has 3 or 4 miles to goe to him

Thy Loveing Friend
Wm Penn

My Dr love to all frds, & salutes to all that deserve it. take care of my mills, remember me to my family & let them be kinde to poor Lucy & Dutch.[12]

ALS. Penn Papers, Letters of the Penn Family to James Logan, HSP. (*Micro.* 10:828.) Addressed: For James | Logan. Docketed: Proprietary Governour to J L. 1 2mo 1703 | Inclosing R Janneys Bill of | Sale for 2 Servants & a Receipt | received per the Messenger 1 5mo 1703.

1. Doc. 56.
2. Not found.
3. John Sotcher, WP's steward at Pennsbury.
4. Yaff, a slave, had been bequeathed to WP in 1691 by Lewis Morris, a wealthy Quaker planter of Barbados and New York. Yaff was evidently with WP in England and was traveling to Pennsylvania. Robert Bolton, *History of the County of Westchester, from its First Settlement to the Present Time* (New York, 1848), 2:292; Harry Emerson Wildes, *William Penn: A Biography* (New York, 1974), p. 324.
5. Probably the "ould Sam" mentioned in WP's will of 30 Oct. 1701 (doc. 30). The slave Sam evidently did not live to gain his freedom; see doc. 30, n. 7.
6. Edward Shippen.
7. Griffith Owen owned an estate in Merion. Thomas Fairman's house at Shackamaxon had served as a lodging and headquarters for WP during his first visit to Pennsylvania in 1682-84. *PWP,* 2:336n; *PMHB,* 92:32; *PGM,* 23:124.
8. Wicaco, now part of Philadelphia, lay south of the city along the Delaware River.
9. The West Indies.
10. WP had imported to Pennsylvania a shipment of books on consignment from the Churchill brothers; see doc. 76, n. 37. In 1721 Logan reported to Hannah Penn that they still had not been sold. Penn Papers, Official Correspondence, 1:97, HSP.
11. George Keith (1639-1716), a leading Scottish Quaker minister and writer, had challenged the rule and theology of the Delaware Valley Quaker elite in the 1690s, instigating the Keithian schism. After his condemnation by Quakers in both America and England, Keith turned to Anglicanism and toured the American colonies from 1702 to 1704 as a missionary. *PWP,* 3:357n; Ethyn Williams Kirby, *George Keith, 1638-1716* (New York, 1942), chaps. 9-10; Edgar Legare Pennington, "Keith the Quaker and Keith the Anglican," *Historical Magazine of the Protestant Episcopal Church,* 20:346-483.
12. Not identified; possibly WP's dogs or horses. Hannah Penn mentioned Lucy in a letter to Logan written in Pennsylvania about 1701: "My husband is much consern'd that John has forgot Lucy, pray let Ja^c Streeter take care of her." Logan Papers, 1:24, HSP.

60
TO THE BOARD OF TRADE

Doc. 60 represents WP's formal entry into negotiations with the crown for the surrender of his proprietary government. His proposed terms, in doc. 62, sought to preserve most of the advantages of a charter government while shedding its responsibilities. He asked for confirmation of the colony's constitution and laws, which he hoped would protect the Quakers in their freedoms; £30,000 in payment for the crown's debt to his father and his improvement of the colony; the right to nominate candidates when the colony's governorship fell vacant; and confirmation of his proprietorship of the lands of both Pennsylvania and the Lower Counties. In many ways, surrender on such terms would offer WP the best of both worlds. The Board of Trade was unimpressed, however, and in a report to the House of Lords on 16 December 1703 it commented that WP was "demanding not only a great sum of money, but in effect much larger powers from her Majesty than what he offers to yield, and likewise a new and positive grant of the three lower counties. . . . " All in all, the proposal was deemed "very unreasonable." (*The Manuscripts of the House of Lords, 1702–1704* [London, 1910], p. 314.) The negotiation dragged on for years with no results (see below, docs. 96, 98, and 136; headnote to doc. 187). Meanwhile, in Pennsylvania, rumors that WP was about to relinquish the government caused uneasiness and discouraged payments of rents and taxes (see doc. 69). Quakers especially were worried less by surrender itself than by uncertainty about the protection of their privileges. Otherwise many, including Logan, were ready to dispense with the charter government. As Logan wrote to WP in Sept. 1703, "In this State of warr Friends cannot Possibly hold it" (*Micro.* 11:034).

11th 3m (May) 1703

Honble Friends
Since I observe your bent is extreamly strong to bring all proprietary Goverments more immediately under the disposition of the crown, and the disadvantage they are, & must be under, on that acct, I thought fitt to lett you know, that upon a Just {regard for} the security ~~to~~ of me & the people, in our Civil Rights, according to the Laws & Constitutions of the Country, I shall, upon a reasonable satisfaction, resigne to the Crown, the Govermt thereoff, saveing some few previledges that will not be thought, I beleive, unreasonable.[1] I could say

abundance to vallue my pretentions upon this head, but will not anticipate yr Inclinations to be Kinde as well as Just to

Your respectfull Friend
Wm Penn

ALS. CO 5/1262, PRO. (*Micro.* 10:951.) Docketed: Pennsylvania | Lre from Mr Penn of 11th May | 1703, signifying his willingness | to resign the Govnt of Pennsylva | to the Crown. | Recd: | Read | May the 11th 1703.

1. For WP's formal proposals of surrender, see doc. 62.

61
TO JAMES LOGAN

Lond. 6th 4m [June] 1703

James Logan

I have had none from thee since the tenth month last,[1] which I am surprized at, so many opertunitys, from new y. & N. Eng. presenting, tho not from you. I bless the Lord we are all yet in the land of the liveing, my son, has another Boy, myn & his name, & my poor wife goeing down to morrow to Bristoll to lye in, being within Six weeks of her time;[2] my Daughter aubrey[3] not with childe that I know of.

I have writt fully by the messenger, as also by Randall Janny in the Jolly Gally,[4] which I hope are come well to hand; & will be considerd & followed.

For my rents, debts due to me, publick ~~of~~ or private, as also saleable lands, as per last, I do earnestly press their returns, but much rather in furrs & skins, than Tobacco, ay per Barbados; but by Bills, were best; for the Load I am under must be too heavy to bear without large supplys. wherfore avoide all expence unneccessary.

My Son is now in Earnest to be with you by the Virginia Fleet that sayls by order, the 1o of the Sixth month (2 months hence)[5] and so thence up the Bay, unless better Conveniency offers more directly in the mean time, as early as that.

I am actually in Treaty with the Ministers for my Govermt.[6] and so soon as it beares, you shall be informed of it. I beleive it repents some they began it; for now, tis I that press it, upon pretty good terms, as well for the people as ~~I~~ selfe, in the {judgemt of the} wisest & best of my Frds ~~Judgement~~. But that shall never weaken my love to & residence in Pennsylvania, & so I command by will my posterity. you will have an Encrease of Frds among you to support the superiority (or Ballance at least) in the Province. for after I have done wth the Govermt & call'd upon Irland, if the Lord give me life, I purpose to Fly to you as fast as I can

I have been much prest by Jacob Telner about Rebecca Shippins business in the town.[7] I desire that truth & rightiousness may take place, & that it may be done at any rate, Impartially.

Also pray minde S. Carpenter of his promess about ending the business of the widdow Lloyd, that regards poor Tho: Hart & Ed: Man,[8] by whome I am Spoaken too very often, wth Griefe as well as resentment—faile not.

B. Chambers is much call'd upon by the poor adventurers in the old society,[9] & some of them are truly so, even to the want of Bread; they are not satisfyed with his acct & think he should let them know wt is left upon a moderate estimate; for want of wch none will buy where some would sell their shares; ~~of~~ In wch be perticuler {to him}, for tis a dishonorable business to the Country.

Perhaps I may have an other, larger opertunity by the Same way, so shall {now} say no more but that we send thee our loves & good wishes, & desire the same may be made perticuler to all or town & Country frds, as if named, & other folks as they deserve it, and that I am

Thy affect. reall Frd
Wm Penn

7th—

I have sent a Duplicat by R. Janny or Guy,[10] of the Queens approbation of Govr Ham.[11] of whose Conduct I desire an acct. His Country men at this minute under the Greatest Ferment, & Let him know that D: Hs party prevail'd to have grievances & Priviledges preferr'd to the sess[12] that the Commissr D. Q. prest.[13] no notable thing, but the alliance wth Portugal, shrewdly manag'd by Methuins negotiation, who is yet Ld chancellor of Irland.[14] I have sent a letter, sent me from the Lords for Td & Ps about the old quota business, wch is Inclosed to Colonel Hamilton,[15] to act or recommend as he sees reason. He obtains a better Credit here; and for poor Bass, he is the most miserable wretch liveing: sonomans has his place, who is run away, left the Commissn for secretr of the Jerseys, for want of mony to take it out,[16] & has left his poor Bror Loiflin & one wilcox[17] in the Lurch, breaking all faith with them at goeing away; so that his Credit is at an end. Pray minde my 2 proprietys in west Jersey, taken up by Bass for me, & his frd Danll Leeds,[18] of wch the Collector at Burlington[19] is able to give an acct for I think he was Surveyor & I left the draught when there, in my Closet I am Confident. Jos. Grove has payd me tother fifty pds, when I never wanted more a Guinia being less to me a year since than a Crown is now,[20] therefore remember me by all opertunitys. my love to the Comrs of Propty & Magistrats. vale.

ALS. Penn Papers, Letters of the Penn Family to James Logan, HSP. (*Micro.* 10:971.) Docketed: Proprietary to J. L. 6 4m | Viâ Boston | received 4th 9br.

1. WP refers to Logan's letter of 1 Dec. 1702 (*Micro.* 10:634); see doc. 56, n. 1. Logan had written since then on 3 Mar. and again in Apr. and May (*Micro.* 10:782, 891, 908, 948, 958).

2. See doc. 56, n. 21, text at n. 81.

3. Laetitia Penn Aubrey.

4. For WP's letters sent via Roger Mompesson on the *Messenger* and Randall Janney on the *Jolly Galley* (Robert Fry, master) in late Apr. and early Mar. 1703, see docs. 56, 59; *Micro.* 10:815, 821, 835.

5. That is, 1 Aug.; on 4 June the Board of Trade urged the admiralty to dispatch the Virginia fleet at the end of July or beginning of August (*CSPC, 1702-1703*, p. 483). But William Penn, Jr., actually did not sail to Pennsylvania until early Oct. 1703, arriving in Philadelphia on 2 Feb. 1704. See doc. 73.

6. See docs. 60, 62.

7. Jacob Telner (d. post 1712), a wealthy Quaker merchant from Amsterdam, was a large Pennsylvania landholder and former resident of Germantown who had moved to London in the late 1690s. Rebecca Shippen's town business may have been related to the lot at Walnut and Second Sts. held by her late husband, Francis Richardson. *PWP*, 2:567n; *PMHB*, 80:184.

8. Patience Story Lloyd (d. c. 1724) was the widow of Thomas Lloyd (d. 1694). Thomas Hart (c. 1629-1704), a Quaker of Enfield, Middx., formerly of Barbados, had been a proprietor of East New Jersey. Edward Mann, a prominent London Friend and hosier, also had a country house in Middlesex. The nature of their business is not known. *PWP*, 2:278n; 3:35n, 38n; Fox, 2:422.

9. Benjamin Chambers had become president of the Free Society of Traders on Nicholas More's resignation in 1685. On Chambers and on the society's failure, see *PWP*, 3:53n, 58, 200; Gary B. Nash, "The Free Society of Traders and the Early Politics of Pennsylvania, *PMHB*, 89:170-71.

10. Randall Janney on the *Jolly Galley*, or John Guy, master of the *Messenger*. See n. 4, above.

11. *Micro.* 10:728.

12. Tax. *OED*.

13. In the Scottish parliament of 1703, the duke of Hamilton was leading nationalist opposition to the policies of his arch-rival, the duke of Queensberry, who was royal commissioner for Scotland. *DNB*; George M. Trevelyan, *England Under Queen Anne: Ramillies and the Union with Scotland* (London, 1932), pp. 232-35.

14. John Methuen (c. 1650-1706), lord chancellor of Ireland, had negotiated an alliance with Portugal, concluded by his son Paul (1672-1757) on 16 May 1703. Methuen the elder was appointed ambassador extraordinary to Portugal in Aug. 1703 and went on to negotiate a more extensive treaty covering trade relations in Dec. *DNB*.

15. The Board of Trade's letter of 21 May 1703 (*Micro.* 10:964), reminding WP of the £350 Pennsylvania owed as its quota for the support of New York's defense, was enclosed in his letter to Gov. Hamilton of 7 June 1703. The Pennsylvania Council read it on 29 Jan. 1704. *Minutes of the Provincial Council*, 2:114-15.

16. Jeremiah Basse had been unable to raise the money needed to pay for his commission as secretary of New Jersey, and Peter Sonmans had applied for the place in his stead. *CSPC, 1702-1703*, p. 921.

17. Not identified.

18. Daniel Leeds (1652-1720), of Burlington Co., N.J., former surveyor of West New Jersey and a member of the first New Jersey council, had left the Quakers to follow George Keith and join the Anglican church. Pomfret, *West New Jersey*, pp. 123, 214, 235; *NJA*, 23:289; Lord Collection, 1:149, GSP.

19. Capt. John Jewell, customs collector at Burlington, had been an anti-Quaker adherent of Basse, who named Jewell to his council in 1697 and appointed him a surveyor general of West New Jersey. Pomfret, *West New Jersey*, pp. 195, 207; *NJA*, 1:302.

20. A guinea was worth 21s, a crown 5s.

62
PROPOSALS FOR SURRENDER OF THE GOVERNMENT OF PENNSYLVANIA

[18 June 1703]

Proposalls to the Lords Comm[rs] for Trade & Plantations About the Surrender of the Goverm[t] of my Province of Pensilvania.

{1} That the Goverment of the Province of Pensilvania & territorys

Continue to be the same distinct Govermt under the Crown that it hath always been & now is.

{2} That the Laws & Constitutions thereof be Confirm'd by the Queen, Except such few as I shall object Against

{3} That a Patent pass to me & my heirs, for the three Lower Countys of Newcastle, Kent, & Sussex, Called the Countys annexed, or Territorys of Pensilvania, according to a Grant begun by the Late King James, & had been finished ~~s~~had he stay'd one week longer att White hall, as may appear by a Bill drawn in persuance of his Warrant signed William Williams attorney or solicitor Generall.[1]

{4} Since my first Expedition Cost me 10500l, & that My Govermt has stood me in {twice} as much, & since that Govermt was the best part of the Consideration I had from the Crown,[2] having bought the Land of the natives over & over, & that the Soyle is only made of any value to me upon my own Interest, & their & & my Charge that Ingaged, & that from hence forward my shop windows will be shutt down, & my [markett] over (my case & that of my Province hav[ing Peculia]ritys Distinct from all others) The motive [to treat] being over by my surrender of my Gover[ment, and since] that will disable me to Pay the Debts the wh[ole has] Contracted upon me & my Estate, by loosing [the benefitt] & that Prospect of return the Poeples Just[ice might] afford me & my posterity as their Goverr [and since my] property as it is Called & distinguisht [by an] English Scale, While but a wild & other wise unculted one and never to be otherwise butt att my Cost wch is 99 parts in 100, besides the fall twill Give to our present settlements (that rise 50 per Cent on my Last arrivall there) & an abundance of Seen & unforeseen prejudices, that may follow to me & myn, & those Engag'd on My Account, & that the Custome of Goods imported here from thence, directly, Amounting ~~to~~ from 1500l since my arrivall)[3] to 10000l per ann: to the Queen, and by circulation of our trade by the Ilands[4] In their Commoditys hither, to not less than as much more, wch before it was myn Never Return'd any thing, I hope it will not be thought hard that I ask t~~wen~~hirty thousand pounds pd, & one half the penny per pounds upon tobacco in the Country, as well as of wt sum or sums the poeple shall Give & Grant the Goverr for the time being for his salery ~~for~~ {by} my assistance.

{5th} ~~Lastly~~ having so great a stake there, & the Inhabitants thereof, & to distinguish my self & family as the founders of the Country, that I & my Heirs shall have power to present as often as a Governour is wanting, 2 or more persons, to the Queen or King for the time being Qualify'd for that station, for her or him to appoint & commission one of them to be Goverr & vice Admirall thereof.

{6} That noe appeals shall Lye to the Queen In personall Actions, where the Cause of Action is of Less value than 200l

{[7]} That all Rights, Priviledges Jurisdictions, Power & Preheminences, Granted unto me & my Heirs by Patent as Lord of the Soyl {&

waters} & Proprietor of the Country, with all Incident Courts & offices thereunto belonging, be in the amplest manner Reserved & Confirm'd, & that all such further priviledges franchises & libertys as upon Consideration shall be found necessary to the Good & prosp[erity] of the said Province &c: & {in} augmenting the {trade} & further poepling there of may be granted & Confirmd to me & my posterity wch is submitted b[y]

Wm Penn

18th 4m (Jn) 1703

DS. CO 5/1262/33, PRO. (*Micro.* 10:995.) Docketed: Pennsylvania | Mr Penn's Proposals for | surrendring the Govnt of | Pennsylvania. | Recd 18th | Read 22th | June 1703. The editors have enclosed marginal numerals in braces and moved them into the text. Words torn away in the original text have been supplied with the aid of the version printed in *CSPC, 1702-1703*, pp. 509-10.

1. Solicitor General Sir William Williams had drawn up a grant to WP from James II of the three Lower Counties on 10 Dec. 1688, but the king fled from London the next day and the document was never sealed. See doc. 54, text at n. 9.

2. The crown had granted WP's charter to Pennsylvania in consideration of a debt to his father, Sir William Penn (*PWP*, 2:30-31). For WP's previous comments on the cost of his colony, see docs. 13, text at nn. 10-12; 20, text at nn. 3-4.

3. The opening parenthesis is missing. In 1705 WP submitted to the Board of Trade accounts of duties on goods imported from Pennsylvania, showing that customs revenues had risen from about £1600 in 1701 to over £8500 in 1702. Board of Trade Papers, Proprieties, 1704-1705, N52-54, transcript at HSP.

4. The West Indies.

63
TO THE BOARD OF TRADE

Faced with the immediate need for a new Pennsylvania governor, WP hit on an unlikely candidate: John Evans, the twenty-six-year-old son of an old friend, a young gentleman from Wales with no governmental or administrative experience. A sharper contrast can scarcely be imagined between this and one of WP's earlier appointments, the Puritan veteran John Blackwell (see *PWP*, 3:183, 195n); but Evans proved an equally unfortunate choice. He was an impeccable Anglican — a feature WP particularly emphasized to the Board of Trade in doc. 63. WP told Logan that Evans was "Intirely in my Interests" and had provided his own bond of security, saving WP considerable trouble and expense (doc. 67). The Board of Trade approved Evans at once, and the young governor sailed for Pennsylvania together with WP's son in October 1703, arriving in February 1704.

WP's instructions to Evans (doc. 65) were general in character and must have given him very little help upon the spot. In matters of government WP referred Evans to his original royal charter and to "the Laws & Constitutions of the Country made in persuance thereof by & with the Early Unanimity of the Country." This was strange advice from the proprietor who had just negotiated a major new constitution for the colony in 1701. Here and in his December letter to the Provincial Council (doc. 71), WP wrote as if the Charter of Privileges did not exist. He did not submit the new charter to the Board of Trade until 1705, despite its request in January 1703 (doc. 57), possibly because he thought it would complicate his negotiations for surrender of the government. But his silence provoked resentment among the Pennsylvanians, who were living under its provisions. WP's commission to Evans (*Micro.* 10:1069) gave the governor power to prorogue and dissolve the Assembly and reserved a final veto to WP — issues that provoked howls from the Assembly about WP's violation of the charter (see doc. 83).

8 5m (Jul) 1703

Honble Friends
The Gentleman[1] named in my Petition to the Queen and Letter to you,[2] is a Person that has had a Liberal Education, been abroad & know's the world very well, is sober discreet and of a good understanding. No Merct & So no temptation that way. No Souldier but hath been in Flanders and observ'd the Discipline of the Troops frequently, and Penetrates more than I Presume our Poor Colony wants. He will give unquestionable Security as Colonel Hamilton did, and has more than enough to Secure them that are his, & is not in debt, but lives like a Gentleman upon his Estate here. He is a Single Man, neither voracious nor extravagant, & is a known zealous member of the Church of England; And I Presume will be recommended by Gentlemen of undoubted Reputation; I am in hopes this may Satisfie your Enquiry, and the Gentleman that gives this for me, being his Acquaintance Char: Lawton Esquire may be more perticular if you think it Necessary. I am

Your Respectfull Friend
Wm Penn

LS. CO 5/1262, PRO. (*Micro.* 10:1028.) Docketed: Pennsylvania | Lre from Mr Penn in | answer to one writ him[3] | abt Mr Jno Evans proposed | by him to be Depty Govr | of Pennsylvania. | Recd | Read | July 9th 1703.

1. John Evans (c. 1678-c. 1743?) was a Welsh gentleman and reputedly the son of Thomas Evans, a mariner of London. WP described the father as an old friend who "vallu'd me not a little" (doc. 67). If Thomas was the father, however, it is puzzling that in a letter written to Peter Evans in the 1680s, Thomas omitted mention of this son while asking to be remembered to his wife and mother. ACM, Penn Manuscripts, box 2, file 10; Raimo, *Governors*, pp. 327-28.

2. *Micro.* 10:1022, 1024.

3. *Micro.* 10:1026.

64
FROM DANIEL DEFOE

In July 1703 WP interceded in the case of Daniel Defoe, who was in Newgate prison for writing *The Shortest Way with the Dissenters,* a satire in which he impersonated a high churchman calling for harsh treatment of dissenters. High Tories like the earl of Nottingham were incensed at what they saw as Defoe's libel against the church, and he received a harsh sentence, including three days' standing in the pillory, a fine of 200 marks, and imprisonment during the queen's pleasure. WP evidently admired Defoe's support for toleration, and he attempted unsuccessfully to mitigate his punishment. On 18 July WP wrote, probably to Nottingham, asking for Defoe's reprieve or pardon (*Micro.* 10:1056), and apparently obtained a postponement of the sentence. But on 29, 30, and 31 July Defoe appeared in the pillory, where he was greeted by the London crowd with warmth rather than abuse. Eventually he was released through the agency of Robert Harley in Nov. 1703. William Freeman, *The Incredible De Foe* (London, 1950), pp. 152–58; J. A. Downie, *Robert Harley and the Press: Propaganda and Public Opinion in the Age of Swift and Defoe* (Cambridge, 1979), pp. 62–63; *CSPD, 1703–1704,* pp. 53, 66; *DAB.*

July 12th, 1703.

Sir

Tho' a Long Appology Suites Neither yor Own Temper, Nor my Condicion, yet I Can Not but Let you kno' wth all The Thankfullness I am Capable The Sence I have of your Extraordinary kindness:—Concerning yor Self For me So Much a Stranger to you, Nor Can I Doubt whether To One who Appeares So much my Friend as to attempt being my Saviour From This Distress, I should Scruple to use the uttmost Freedome with Relacion to the Present Case

Sr The Proposall you are pleas'd to hint By yor Son from My Ld Nottingham, of Discovering Partyes is the same which his Lordship has often Put upon me before[1]

Sr In Some Letters wch I have Sent his Lordship I have Answer'd him with the Same Assurance I did to the Privy Council, Vizt That in the Manner which they Proposed it I really had No person to Discover: That if my Life were Concern'd in it I would Not Save it at the Price of Impeaching Innocent Men, No More would I Accuse my Friends for the Freedome of Private Conversacion[2]

It has been my Character Sr among those who kno' me, That I Scorn to Lye, and by Gods Grace Ile preserve it while I live. I Take the Freedome to give you the Trouble of repeating it, Onely To affirm to you with the More Confidence the Protestacion I make. I Sollemnly Affirm that Other than what Passes in Conversacion, and perhaps There is ill blood among people of my Opinion More than Enough, but other Than that I have no Accomplices, No Sett of Men, (as my Lord Call'd Them) with whom I used to Concert Matters, of this Nature, To whom I us'd to show, or Reciev hints from them in Ord^r to These Matters, and Therefore to Put it upon Condicion of Such a Nature is to Offer me Nothing Attall

But S^r My Case is this, I came in upon the Honour of the Govornment, being Under Baile that (at least Some of them) Consented to Let me go away and presst me to it. I agreed to give the Court No Trouble but to plead Guilty to the Indictment,[3] Even to all the Adverbs, the Seditiously's, The Malitiously's, and a Long Rapsody of the Lawyers et Ceteras; and all this upon promises of being us'd Tenderly and Treated like a Gentleman: — and with Submission to yor Judgement, I Think that the honour, of the Govornm^t is Concern'd in it, and No Man will Venture to Thro' himself upon their Mercy again, if I am made the Example of their Tenderness in This Manner I am like a Prisoner of Warr yielding upon Discrecion and afterwards Cut in Peices in Cold blood wch Tho' they may Indeed do by Law yet No Man will Trust Them after it

As to the Church of England as I Never Meant to Insinuate That those of England as a Church did Design So to Treat the Dissenters, So Tis plain There are Members of or Rather in the Church who have Declar'd their Resolucion to do it if it was in Their Power and as these are the Men I Aim'd at So I am Ready To do the Church of England any justice by Vindicateing her in the Same Publick Manner They Suppose her affronted I mean in Print

This is what I Tho^t Fitt to give you the Trouble of, For which I ask yor Pardon, and Entreat the Continuance of those Kind offices you have So Generously undertaken for

An Unknown Captive
Yo^r Distress'd Servt
Daniel De Foe

July 12

Copy. FLL. (*Micro.* 10:1038.) Addressed: For William Penn. Esqr | Humbly Presented. Superscribed: From Mr Daniel De Foe to William | Penn. Esqr.

1. Nottingham had evidently promised leniency on condition that Defoe reveal his accomplices. See John Robert Moore, *Defoe in the Pillory and Other Studies* (Bloomington, Ind., 1939), pp. 8-9.

2. A few days after receiving this letter, WP told officials that Defoe was ready to name his accomplices. George Harris Healey, ed., *The Letters of Daniel Defoe* (Oxford, 1955), p. 7n.

3. Defoe had been induced to admit authorship of the tract, throwing himself upon the queen's mercy, rather than force the prosecution to prove the fact. Moore, *Defoe in the Pillory*, p. 7.

65
TO JOHN EVANS

[9 August 1703]

William Penn. Proprietary & Governour of the Province of Pensylvania & Territorys;
To his trusty & well beloved Friend John Evans Esq: Deputy Governour
Instructions for Government & Conduct therein

{1} Take care in all things, to keep within the compas of & to keep up the Powrs of my Graunts from King Charles the Second & his Bro^{hr} the Duke of York;[1] & the Laws & Constitutions of the Country made in persuance thereof by & with the Early Unanimity of the Country;[2] & in no wise suffer them to be broaken in upon by any refractory or factious Persons what ever; that as I would not have thee Exert the Rigour of thy authority, so neither to endure it to be Con~~s~~temned or Encroacht upon.
{2} That thou hast an Especiall care strictly to observe the Laws relating to Trade & the Plantations & to give the Queens officers all due Encouragement therein & discountenance every appearance of unlawfull Trade, & that without the Least respect to Persons or Partyes.
{3} That thou doest dilligently Superintend & Nicely watch ov[er] the Magistracy to the end there may be no Defect or obstruction of Justice, more especially in the Cases of poor people, & Absentees. In order to this that thou doest sometimes, att Convenient seasons, visit the Courts of Justice, to observe pro~~s~~ceedings, by which thou mayest be the better directed in thy Advice to the respective Magistrates & officers in the Governm^{t}
{4} That noe Corrupt, Uncapable or Negligent officers be kept in or put in to any Employm^{t}, & that the Dilligent, Knowing ~~are~~ & faithfull be Encouraged, Especially among the Old Planters that hasarded all to Engage with me in makeing that a Colony.
{5} That thou Usest thy utmost Endeavours to qualify things & make the people easy under their differing Perswasions & Interests, both by wisdom & Authority, & ~~there unto~~ in order {there unto} that all heats, reflections, & reports, to the Contrary, be discountenanced.
{6} That thou takest care to suppress all vice & Irregularitys by Land or ~~ſ~~Water, & all such practises as the Laws of the Governm^{t} have forbid; & perticolarly that Publick Houses keep good hours, which will raise an Esteem of thee with the best & most sufficient of the inhabitants; & this thou wilt doe, if thou doest but remember thou ~~wastest~~ {warest}[3] my character, & that thy Conduct will be chargable upon me there, & here too.

{7} In all cases of Moment, wherin~~s~~ thou art Con~~s~~cern'd in the Government, as signeing any orders or delivering thy Judgemt, Consult the Atturney Genll [4] {& the oldest Counsellers} that thou mayst act safely.

{8} Never interpose between a sentance & an Execution, ~~unless the case be hard, & that~~ where the Judgemt is Legall, ~~&~~ {unless} Circumstances make it fitt to mittigate or pardon, nor yet, then if it be disagreeable to the minds of the most prudent Mag~~e~~istrates & is unpopuler.

{9} Have a close Eye upon Cll Quary & J Moore; by shuch Church men (& s~~h~~uch theire are) as are of a moderate spirit, & would doe as they would be done by. & what thou Canst learn & prove aganst them, spare them not there, & send over the Informations & Proofs hether allso; & never trust to their most sollemn promises, for thay are as falls men as can live, Q: Espes~~c~~illy. but perticulerly any pertiality or Corruptions of Quary in his own Office of surveyer of the Customs; ~~for it will root him out of that Governmt, whither mine or the Queens, if it be possible~~

{10} I recommend Samll Carpenter, Edward Shipppen, Richard Hill, Griffith Owen, Isaac Norris, & James Logan in perticuler, of the side of our friends, to thy esteem & Conversation for Knowledg & Counsel; & of those that Goe to the Church of England, Coll Markham, Capt Finne, Robert Ashton, ~~&~~ the 'Collector Beuley, Thomas Farmer sherrif, William Trant[5] merchant, Charles Reed, a shopkeeper. &~~c~~ {such moderat church men}[6] as those ab~~s~~ove, & J: Logan {(of our frds)} Especially, shall inform thee, of whose good Capacity to advise & give measures, I am perfectly satisfyed; & in point of Improvemt of thy self in the business of Governmt, & generall Book Knowledg, thou canst not find an abler; but manage thy inward regards to him, without raiseing Jealousys upon him {as if he was a favourite},[7] & there are many good & unsuspected occasions between a Governour & a secretary: he knows the factious, the frindly, the sincere, the Hollow, the Bold, the Timid, ~~&~~ the able, & the week: who to Countenance, who to be ware of, & who to gain; & use, but not trust without good Reason

{11} And that nothing may lye att my door in reference to the Defence of the Country, so much the Pretence & Clamour of Q: M[8] & their disaffected Gange; know, that thou art as amply Impowrd as any of my former Liuetenants were, or my self if upon the spot. & that the Commissions granted by Coll Markham for a Milisia, are still in being,[9] & should not be altred, but to change some disaffected officers. but if Coll Markham that was their Coll before, remains so, he will modell them for the best, Knowing well & haveing had the Handling of them all from the first of the Colony, in all which J: Logan will safely advise thee. but never Consent to any Law perticulerly, for raising trainning & paying that may be penal or affect the {Persons &} ~~Libertyes of~~ estates of ~~any~~ our Friends, that when they went &

venturd themselves with me into amerrica, hoped to be rid of those encombrances: else my own Friends, & the originals of the Colony, will have the Governmt turnned aganst them, & their & my Principels, by my Deputy & authority, which God forbid; & is forbid already in my Conscionce. Wherfore, all I can agree to is a Law that those that are desirous that a Militia & a military defence m~~y~~ay be raised trainned & regulated as is Customary may be gratifyed; but none that profese a Concientious tenderness therein Complelled in Person or purse ore the worse used because thereof, & which is all those Malitious folks desired of me when I was amongst them. Niether Lett there be att those times any vaine or unnescesary Expences Countinanced, nor affronts to others permitted, or any m{a}deness, {or} Loosness; for so the pretended Defence would become a reall [illegible deletion] {Greivance} to the Governmt, & which will be apt ~~to~~ insensiblly to creep in, without a severe & vigorous discipline, which may bring them into more order & moderation towards those that have heitherto succesfully trusted God, ~~be~~ or {be} Less troublsom, with their Zeal for their Defence; which I know, & time will Let thee see, is more to pinch us in a tender place, than from any true grounds of fear or Dainger, as we ~~ar set~~[?] ar scituate[d.][10]

{12} There is another point in which the Enimies of our profesh~~i~~on or rather of our posseson (for it is to get the Governmt out of our hands; which we have allwayes offered them to share with us in) & that is the solemn affirmation, they knowing our friends are tender in ~~a~~ Calling god to wittnes, which is the form in England. but not there by our Laws, & if that should be practis't by compulsh~~i~~on, which Q: &c {may} press the ablest people in the Governmt in all respects will be Excluded, which to them will be a persicution for [illegible deletion] {Conscience} sake, in a Country of our own makeing, & for our own ease. In this case, observe well the Law, & take the best advice, & I shall endever to modarate matters here

{13} The Chefe of our Enimies are Rbt Qua: J: More, Josh: Carpenter att Philadelphia: Jasper Yeates att Chester, a hot & a haughty man, whom~~e~~ I have Endevered to ablidge in vain;[11] Richard Hallowell att new Castell, & Wm Rodney, Clarke of the County of Kent; & J: Logan will informe thee of others. have a watch over thy self, as well as them in relation to their behaveour about the publick

{14} By all means open to those friends, to whose good Sence & Integrety I have allready recommended thee in the tenth Instruction, the Absolute Necesity of Establishing a Revenue forthwith, for the Governmt. & that unless they show a franckness towards a Competent Provision, by a small Custome & Excise, or otherwise, in some proportion to other Governmts; It is to be feared their Laws will meet with difficulty here, ~~to~~ tho' some of ~~it~~ {the Supply}[12] were not Heriditary, but from three years to three years. & without it I fear, I shall make the Poorer Bargain for them, as well as my selfe; ~~I~~ Thou hast enough to say to induce them from my vexations & fateigus as well as Expensive attendance upon the Ministers, to gain points. In this, ~~be~~ {as I would have} as discreet in the manner, so be most Earnest in the matter, {I mean}[13] of a publick supply.

In the rest, I must Commend thee to those on the Spot, for a further & [mor]e perticular [acco]^{t}, & the measures proper for thee. and in Generall referr my own Interest, in both Capacitys, as Govr & Proprietor to thy care & Integrity. Given at Bristoll This 9th day of the 6 month Call'd August, 1703.[14]

Wm Penn

DfS. Penn Papers, Granville Penn Book, HSP. (Not filmed.) Docketed: Instructions to | Lieut. Colonel Evans. | 1703. The editors have enclosed marginal numbers in braces and moved them into the text. A signed copy of this document is in *Micro.* 10:1077.

1. See *PWP*, 2:281-84; *Charter and Laws*, pp. 81-90.
2. WP here refers Evans to the Frame of 1683 (Soderlund, *William Penn*, pp. 265-73), ignoring the Charter of Privileges (doc. 28) that superseded the earlier constitution in 1701.
3. *Micro.* 10:1077 reads "bearest."
4. WP evidently means Roger Mompesson (see doc. 56, text at nn. 78-79), but it is not clear whether he actually took up this post.
5. William Trent.
6. Insertion in WP's hand.
7. Insertion in WP's hand.
8. Quary and Moore.
9. As lieutenant governor under Benjamin Fletcher, William Markham had evidently issued commissions for a militia, but these commissions have not been found. See doc. 44, n. 25.
10. WP's comments to Evans here become ironic in light of Evans's later actions: in 1706 he spread false rumors of a French invasion to impress Quakers with the need for defense, and in the process caused dangerous disorders. See Nash, *Quakers and Politics*, pp. 259-60; doc. 129.
11. WP had appointed Yeates a burgess of Chester in 1701. See doc. 27, n. 10.
12. Insertion in WP's hand.
13. Insertion in WP's hand. *Micro.* 10:1077 reads, "In this, as I would have thee Discreet in the Manner, so be most Earnest in the Matter, I mean, of a publick Supply."
14. The final paragraph is added in WP's hand.

66
FROM THE PROVINCIAL COUNCIL

[26 August 1703]

May it please our Proprietary & Governour

The mournful Account of our late Lieutenant Governours decease, having by this time we hope reached thee as well from the Secretary as others,[1] We think our selves obliged to acquaint Thee with our Circumstances and Proceedings thereupon.

Soon as a Council could meet after the Governours Interment We published our Commission on the 4th 3^{d} Month[2] with a Resolution to act in all things absolutely necessary for the present Support of Government in pursuance of the Powers of the Sd Commission till further Provision could be made.

But not long after viz on the 17th of the Same Month Colonel Quary produced to us then Sitting an Order of the Queen in Council requiring all Magistrates & Officers in this Government to take the Oath directed by the Law of England, or the Affirmation allowed by the Said Law to Quakers, and that no Judge be allowed to Sitt upon the Bench, who Shall not first take the Oath of a Judge or in lieu thereof the aforementioned Affirmation as directed by the Law of England Also that all persons who in England are obliged and are willing to take an Oath in any publick or Judicial Proceeding be admitted so to doe, or otherwise all their Proceedings are declared to be null and Void.[3]

With this Order by directions from the Lords of Trade & Plantations (as Coll Quary declared) all the Courts in the Government were Served successively as they came, from wch Some among us who too much make it their business to obstruct all our Affairs for their own Sinister ends took occasion to endeavour a Stop to the Proceed[ings of the] Courts at that time, notwithstanding all the Magistrates of {this &} most of the [Counties had] really taken all those Oaths or Affirmations as directed by the Said Order [upon their] admission to their respective places

But because in two of our Counties of the Province viz Chester and B[ucks it will] be very difficult, and in Bucks almost impossible to find a sufficient Num[ber of fit] persons to make a Quorum of Justices that will take or administer an Oa[th it will] be a very great hardship there to have none on the Bench but such as c[an Swear] for our friends can no more be concerned in administring an Oath than they [can take one] And in all Actions where the case pinches either party, if they can fro[m any Corner] of the Government bring in an Evidence who demands an Oath the cause m[ust Either Drop] or a fitt number of persons must be alwayes there to administer it, tho' only [perhapps upon] the Account of Such an Evidence, a Hardship upon a People consisting chiefly of those that cannot Swear at all, that we presume had never been putt upon us in these cases if fully understood.

The Order however appearing positive Several Powers or Writts of Dedimus Potestatem[4] for the Qualification of the Magistrates were necessary which must be Issued by the Council but we our Selves not being qualified, it was objected that there was a Necessity for us first to take what the Law required, and especially that Injoyned by the 7th & 8th Wm 3 for the Security of Trade[5] for Administring of which to the Governours of this place a Dedimus under the great Seal of England is directed to Colonel Quary R Halliwell John Moore & Jasper Yeats and two more absent or deceased.[6]

For Answering this, Letters were Sent by us to the persons named desiring them to attend the Council on the 29th of the 4th Month[7] (to wch time it was delaid by Colonel Quary's Absence) in Order to discharge what was Injoyned by the Said Dedimus and Order of the Queen.

Accordingly they came and first for some time insisting on the Surrender of the Dedimus into their hands which before had been kept with the Records of the Government, Upon their ~~Promise~~ {Engagement} to return it, it was delivered to them and they withdrew to consult what was proper for them to doe.

About an hour after returning they delivered up the Dedimus again, as they had ~~promised~~ engaged, but told the Council that unless five of us which Number makes a Quorum would take the Oath in express words as directed they could not administer it to fewer.

It was insisted on that it should be administred to such of the Council as could Swear who were only two,[8] and that if nothing else did, yet the Queens Order which Colonel Quary had produced gave Liberty that an Affirmation Should be taken in all cases of Magistracy where the persons could not take the Oath, and therefore that if Such Should Swear who could, and others who in Conscience could not, took the Affirmation as required by the Law of England to the Same effect it might fully Answer. To this, that there might be no Obstruction in business and the Administration of Justice, they were urged [but] constantly refused and thereupon withdrew After which one of them viz Rd Halliwell Insultingly made his Boast that they had now laid the Government on its back, & left it Sprawling unable to move hand or foot.

But the Said Dedimus being also directed to five of the Council & Collector of the Customs for the Port of Philadelphia as well as to the others beforenamed, We called the Coll[ector][9] and required of him upon the others refusal to discharge his Duty in this case, [But Co]lonel Quary having some Influence over him by reason of his Office as Surveyor Genl [of] this River had Sent for him before and warn'd him not to meddle, upon which he [al]so at that time refused.

But not only some of our own Lawyers but One in the Neighbourhood viz J. Re[gnier[10] Em]inent for his Skill taking some pains to Inform him that it was indispensably his Duty to administer the Said Oath when required, to as many as would take it, being [Se]nt for again he complyed and on the 16th of the 5th Month[11] administred it in Council [to] Judge Guest and Captain Finney and the rest of us who could not swear generally [too]k and Subscribed the Same by an Affirmation according to the Law of England and [the] Queens Order which was the Utmost we could doe.

This Obstruction being Surmounted much to the Disappointment of our Adversaries we proceeded to transact what was of immediate Necessity before us, but through these Mens restless

Endeavours find it extreamly Difficult fully to discharge the Duties of Government Incumbent upon us, they taking all Advantages of throwing in our way whatever may perplex or be a hardship to Us by reason of Oaths or such other things as are Inconsistent with the Principles of most of us. Besides that many things occur in the Administration of Government according to the Laws of England, If no Immunities by our own Laws must in these cases be allowed us, that cannot well be executed by Men of our Profession.

We doubt not but that according to the Custom of these Men they have been exhibiting [Comp]laints against us, Occasions for them being what they daily court, and when by [their] Endeavours by any means brought to bear they greedily lay hold on them

Governour Hamilton last winter Issued a Commission of Oyer and Terminer and G[aol] Deliv[ery] for the County of Philadelphia to ~~Captain F~~ Judge Guest Captain Finney and Edward Farmer[12] The trials were by the Commission required to be wholly by Oaths, because some of the Provincial Judges had been tender of trying them otherwise, Some of the Prisoners being upon their Lives, But the Attorny General that thou left us (J. Moore) instead of discharging his Duty in prosecuting for the Queen rode out of town, and such effectual Endeavours had been used with the persons Impannell'd for the Juries (being chiefly those called Church men & such as could take Oaths) that not one of them would Serve but positively refused. The Same Methods had also been used in Philadelphia to prevent all persons from Listing themselves in the Militia under the said Governours Commissions last Year, And yet we are credibly Informed that they have complained as well of the Small Appearance of Men in the Militia, as of People being tried only by Affirmation, tho' these Complainants themselves were the Cause of both.

Their Plott is to have the whole Government represented to the Ministry to be in Confusion And that thereupon it will be absolutely necessary to be taken into the Queens more immediate care, to this end they magnify every Small Occurrence where they can have the least Grounds and Scruple not to make where they find none, as Colonel Quary has lately done to the Lord Cornbury in a Letter, as that Nobleman himself declared, Affirming that we were reduced to such Confusion that we had no Government at all, or to this effect with a Design to induce that Lord (who we presume has more honour) to represent it home upon Quary's Information that it may there gain the greater Credit,[13] but should it be so represented, we affirm 'tis positively false, and Shall take Occasion [to] acquaint the Lord Cornbury accordingly.

It is also intended, we are informed, to be made the Subject of a Com[plaint that] one Burgess Lieutenant to Captain Pulleyn Commander of the [blank] Captain Dampiers Co[mpanion in] his intended expedition to the South Seas, lately brought in a prize that the

S[aid Ship had] taken in the Canaries loaden with wheat, into our Capes, and that the said Bu[rgess going] on Shoar {at Lewis} was not seized with his Ship.[14] She had 12 Guns & 15 Men mostly [English &] tho' there was no reason to discredit the Masters or Mens report Yet it was [believed] they had left Captain Pulleyn upon some unfair Design. An Account of [this being] brought to Philadelphia in the worst dress while the Ld Cornbury was here in his [Visit to us] from Burlington at his Accession to his Government there. Upon a Consultation [with the] said Lord Cornbury, it was thought fitt, That He as Vice-Admiral of Jersey [Should Issue] his Commission for seizing and bringing her up, and a Vessel and Men [for that End] be furnished from this place, in order to which preparations were forthwith [made but] another Vessel coming up the River brought Advice that the Prize had [Sailed &] we Since hear by the Post from N York that the Said Captain Burgess has [Carried her in] thither, and is to have her legally condemned as his Prize.

One would admire what Consequence could be drawn from hence, but [we understand] the Complaint is, that she might as well have proved a Rogue as honest [& therefore] the County Should have Seized her, according to the Advice of the Collector th[ere[15] who being] Youthful and Active was very brisk in endeavouring it, but mett not with [so ready a] Concurrence as desired from the Inhabitants, who perceiving her to be no [Enemy & of] some force were unwilling (as we are informed) to expose themselves in a hazardous Undertaking without Seeing any reasonable cause for it, or any Probability of Advantage or Safety from it. We indeed of Philadelphia upon the first Information feared it might prove worse, for it was represented to us under Some Surprize which caused those preparations Our readiness towards which the Ld Cornbury promised he would duly acknowledge to the Queen or Ministry, but the whole proving better than expected and the Vessel being gone, it dropt, Only we have thought fitt to turn out the Sherif of that place[16] upon Complaint of his refractary Behaviour to the Collector in this and some other cases But if he or any other there Should be found deficient in their Duty, We hope it will be considered that these are some of the Men who employed Colonel Quary in their behalf to complain against thee and this Government, and therefore will not be imputed to the Quakers here, there not being at that time above one in the place for W Clark was then (as now) at Philadelphia.

However because Occasions are continually taken from our Circumstances chiefly upon our late Governours decease, all which might have been we hope effectually stopt upon the Arrival of his Approbation by the Queen had he Lived, We most earnestly request thee, that thou would procure some fitt person of Moderation and Temper who can fully comply in all points of Government with the Law of England to be approved by the Queen and take the Government wholly upon him that Such Men as these (Colonel Quary and John Moore especially we mean) who have no Interest nor one foot of real Estate that we know of in the place, but Seek the Overthrow of the first Adventurers here for their own Sinister ends may no longer insult over us, nor be suffered to make continual [War]r upon the just Rights and Privileges of both thy Self and the People. And we [bese]ech thee more effectually to represent our case with thy own to our Sovereign the [Qu]een whose Justice and Tenderness to all her loving Subjects, we are well Assured [wo]uld lead her of her Innate Goodness if acquainted with our Circumstances, to [pr]otect us from the Designs of those Men who for the Sake of aggrandizing them[se]lves by Offices without any regard to the true Interests of Her Colonies endeavour [to] deprive us of our just Rights, and injuriously become in a great measure the [Ma]sters of the Toil and Labours of an Industrious People who first embarqued in [a] Design of Settling this Colony in a full expectation of enjoying the Privileges first [prop]osed to them without Infraction. None are willing to pay a more entire Obedience to [the] Crown in all things in our Power, None can acquitt themselves with more Fidelity [&] therefore we would in all Humility hope that We shall never be excluded from any [Share] of our royal Mistress's benign Influences that others of her Subjects happily enjoy [&] that thou wilt also be favourably pleased to use thy Endeavours for th~~y~~e obtaining [it n]ot only for thy own just Interests but those also of the People who have embarqued [with] thee and among the rest of

Thy most faithfull friends
Griffith Owen
Edwd: Shippen
Sam: Carpenter
Wm; Clark
Caleb pusey
Tho: Story

DS. CO 5/1262, PRO. (*Micro.* 10:1087.) Docketed: Pennsylvania | Letter from M[r] Penns Council to | himself, relating to their Proceedings | in the Government of Pennsylvania | after the Death of Colonel Hamilton | Deputy Governor thereof; Dated the | 26 August 1703. | received: with M[r] Penns | Lettre: of 22 December 1703[17] | Received the 11th January | Read 3[d] March | 1703/4. | Entred D. fo: 449 | M: 19. Words in brackets have been supplied from a letterbook copy in James Logan Letterbook, 1:104, HSP.

1. Logan had written to WP of Gov. Hamilton's death on 29 Apr. and again on 6 May, but WP had not yet received these letters. *Micro.* 10:908, 948; doc. 67.

2. 4 May 1703; see *Minutes of the Provincial Council,* 2:87-88. For WP's commission to the Provincial Council, see doc. 29.

3. See *Minutes of the Provincial Council,* 2:89. The royal order requiring the administration of oaths to all who desired them was issued on 21 Jan. 1703, at the same time that Gov. Hamilton was approved by the crown (*Micro.* 10:728).

4. Writs empowering one who is not a judge to act in place of a judge (*OED*). In this case, to enable magistrates to administer oaths to judges.

5. The Navigation Act of 1696.

6. The men thus empowered to administer oaths to Pennsylvania's governors had

also refused to administer the oaths to Gov. Hamilton in Nov. 1701; see *Micro.* 10:169; *Minutes of the Provincial Council,* 2:62-63.

7. 29 June; see *Minutes of the Provincial Council,* 2:92-93.

8. John Guest and Samuel Finney.

9. John Bewley.

10. Jacob Regnier (c. 1672-1714), an English-trained lawyer of New York, married into the family of William Markham and made frequent trips through Pennsylvania. Paul M. Hamlin and Charles E. Baker, *Supreme Court of Judicature of the Province of New York, 1691-1704* (New York, 1959), 3:172-75; *PMHB,* 33:361.

11. 16 July; see *Minutes of the Provincial Council,* 2:95-96.

12. See *Minutes of the Provincial Council,* 2:86.

13. On 29 May 1703 Cornbury wrote to the Board of Trade about letters he had received from Pennsylvania that reported the conduct of trials there without oaths. On 23 July the board ordered WP to see that this practice stopped. *CSPC, 1702-1703,* pp. 467, 566.

14. The ship *Fame,* under Capt. Henry Pullen, had gone as a privateer to the South Seas and had captured a French prize ship. Pullen's first lieutenant, Samuel Burgess, sailed with the prize ship to the American colonies and put in for water at Lewes in Aug. 1703. Quary reported the incident to the Board of Trade, claiming that the ship should have been seized on suspicion of piracy or mutiny. *CSPC, 1702-1703,* p. 741.

15. Henry Brooke (d. 1736), a younger son from a family of Cheshire gentry, emigrated about 1702 to become customs collector at Lewes. He went on to become a noted poet and a prominent citizen of Lewes, serving as a J.P. and a justice of the Supreme Court. In 1722 he was appointed to the Provincial Council. *Micro.* 11:312; *PMHB,* 52:310; C. H. B. Turner, comp., *Some Records of Sussex County Delaware* (Philadelphia, 1909), pp. 45, 46, 206.

16. Jonathan Bailey (d. 1748?), a miller of Lewes, was sheriff in 1702-3. He also served as a J.P. and later as associate justice of the Supreme Court. Scharf, *Delaware,* 1:536; 2:1210, 1211, 1256; Leon deValinger, Jr., comp., *Calendar of Sussex County Delaware Probate Records 1680-1800* (Dover, Del., 1964), p. 54.

17. When WP received doc. 66, he sent it to the Board of Trade on 22 Dec. 1703, protesting against the actions of the Anglican faction in Pennsylvania. *Micro.* 11:121.

67
TO JAMES LOGAN

Warmingst 27 6m [August] 1703

James Logan

I have heard by two letters[1] from my Cos. Parmiter from New york, one of the 3d the other of 23 of the last 3m of the Death of Colonel Hamilton, and by the last that he dyed at Amboy. That being an affaire which much affects me & the Province, I hoped to have heard from thee abt it[2] per first opertunity, any where upon the Continent. Next, the Lords Comrs for Trade & Plantations took notice to me, of the present Insufficiency of the Govermt in Pennsylvania because the first of the Council, was not able to Register Ships, administer an oath, or perform some other requisits in Govermt. I told them this could not hinder Govermt while three or four of the Council, were church men, & of age & experience in affairs, & no matter who of the Council transacted them so that they were qualifyed to do it; and that by our Constitution our frds were so for the administration of our Goverment. It went over, till a lettr came from Ld Cornberry, your *great friend,* importing a representation from the Church of England with you, to him, Complaining of a mans being lately sentenc'd to Death ~~by~~ upon a Jury of Quakers, not only not sworn, but not attested according to the act of Parliamt in England;[3] To which I answeard I had heard nothing of it; & so soon as any advices came should inform them ~~of it.~~ In the mean time, It was not to be thought that a Colony & Constitution of Govermt made by & for Quakers, would leave them{selves} & their lives & fortunes out of so essentiall a part of the Govermt as Jurys. That there & here differ'd much, or we had never gone thither wth our lives & substance to be so precarious in our security as not to be capable of being ~~a~~ Jurym~~a~~en. If the comeing of others shall overrule us that are the originals & made it a Country, we are unhappy. That it is not to be thought we intended no easier nor better Terms for our selves in goeing to America than we left behind us. As yet this has allay'd the Spirit of the Objecters. But of none of this have I a word, wch has been some Concerne to me; pray let me hear oftener. I have not had one Penny Consequently towards my Support Since the takeing of the 2 ships I advised thee of;[4] and liv'd in town ever Since I came over, at no small expence; haveing not been 3 months of 20 that I have been in England absent from Court, Puting all the times together that I have been at this place & Bristoll. from whence I came three weeks agoe, & was their but abt 14 or 16 days, on occasion of my wifes lying in, who this day month has been brought to bed of a Daughter, whom we call Hanna Margarita. They with my Two sons[5] were lately well, and so am I, I bless god at present. I did upon the news of the Death of Colonel Hamilton Immediately {apply} to the Queen for an other Goverr and Named one here,[6] as a Disinterested Person, which she referr'd, by Ld. Notingham, to the Lords of Trade ~~that~~ who lost no time in reporting in his favour, so that he quickly obtaind the Queens Approbation, & is now ready to Embark, with his Commission & Instructions from me,[7] & Instructions from the Lds about the Acts of Trade only.[8] He is a young man, not above Six & Twenty, but solid, & Sencible; Intirely in my Interests as farr as he may goe; and the Son of an old Frd of mine, that vallu'd me not a little. He will be discreet, adviseable, & especially by the best of our frds, & thyselfe, as the most verst & knowing in my affaires, as well as engag'd in my Interest.

He will early apply to S. Carp. Ed. Ship. Is. Nor. R. Hill & honest Grif. owen,[9] his Country man, but especially to thee, in the first place, for the reason aforesd, even how to demean towards them, least there should be any alteration in the tempers or inclinations of them. His name is Jon Evans, & welchmen are mightily akin, perhaps it may have some Influence upon the Parson.[10] I also recommend him to Colonel Mark. Cos. ashton, T. Farmer &c: in which give him thy Hints. He will hear Frds, & goes possest with the Justice & reason of their Case: & the rest I must leave to you upon the Spot. But my son will tell the[11] more of the Motives to this Choice. He has been at all

the Charge I bore for Colonel Hamilton, & gott his own security,[12] & gave me no trouble on that acct. He shows not much, but has a good deal to show, & will grow upon the esteem of the better sort. He has Travell'd, & seen armys, but never been in them. Book learning, as to men & Govermt, he inclines to; Carrys over some {good} Books, & expects among mine & thyn to help himselfe wth {more.} Give him, as soon as he comes, a hint of Persons, & things; & guide his Reading. I wish him to my Cos. ashtons, or Cos. Markhams to borde, unless he, {my son,} R. Mompesson (his Friend) & thou should take a house among you. I allow him two hundred pds that mony per annum wch will be sterl. or at most at the New England Starling,[13] by that time the Queen returns from the Bath. I gave thee a hint of the designe of altering the Coyne, in some of my last letters.[14] pray act therin for the best advantage.
Now I am to tell thee, that when I told the Lords Colonel Hamilton was dead, Secretr Blathwayt answeard me, then there is dead the man of all the rest, that hath writt agst Proprietary Govermts the most neatly & strongly ~~upon that subject~~; I replyd, and yet with wt difficulty, besides charge, did I obtain that enimy of my Interest, & frd to yours, to be my Dept Goverr? But his moderation about the affaires of N. york,[15] renew'd a good opinion of him, & I beleive, had he liv'd, by the help of his frds here, he had been favourd in his Concerns. But of this passage of Comrs Bla. say nothing, unless under secrecy to S. Carp, or S. Jenings, or Fr: Davenport;[16] but those two may remember at Gover. Hams house at Burl.[17] I told them this, as my Jealousy, at least to Davenp. & Gardner,[18] & else where to Sam. Jen. more than once, {I suppose} to Ingratiate {himself} agst they became Ks. Govermts. but I could as soon have pickt a pocket, or denyd my friend or name, Considering the Bread he eat was, for 15 or 16 years runing by Proprietary Governours.[19] But what shall a man Say of this wretched world. I am wth Counselr West[20] endeavouring to serve his Creditors & family about the Post however. I wrott to thee thrice since the receipt of any from thee, one by a ship Directly to New England, directed to Dan. Zachery an other by Colonel Usher,[21] but that ship touches at newfoundland, inclosed also to Dan. Zachery; an other by way of New york, Directed to the Postmr of that place, as I remember; If not one to John[22]
The story of the Mony will be told thee by the Dept Goverr and more fully by my son, who comes to see how he likes, & so to stay, or returne to fetch his wife, or settle here.
I referr thee to my former letters for wt Concerns him, & thy respect & care of him every way. He aimes to improve his Study this winter wth thee, as well as to know the Country, the laws & people therof, & his Interest & mine therin: Use thy utmost Influence upon him to make him happy in himselfe & ~~I~~ me in him. Watch over him pray for Good; qualfy his heats, Inform his Judgemt, encrease his knowledge,

he has a more than ordinary Opinion of thee. advise him to proper Company, give him fitting hints, how farr to goe, he being naturally but too open, & prevent his quarreling with our Ennimys, an advantage they may improve to our Common prejudice. In short, keep him Inoffensively employd at those times that he is {not} proffitably Concern'd. Let the first thing be the Country, its Laws & Constitutions—the settlemt of the town & Countys. In short the true State of the case; then Study; with intervals in the woods, & upon the waters, where I should be ~~gld~~ Glad such Company as I. Nor. S. Prest. and sometimes S. Car. & R. Hill,[23] as well as the young shippys,[24] would be so kinde as to [obliterated]. Cos. Ashton, {Mompess.} & T. Farmer if not worse {than forme[rly?]} would be well enough sometimes also. I hope I need not Bid thee take care to lay thy hand upon some Choice discovery of land, where there is water, Meddow {Timber} & riseings,[25] to to clap some {old} purchasses upon, that some of my Frds are buying of first undertakers. a word to the wise.

I am now to tell thee, that I am to make my Daughters Lots & lands up 2000 pounds sterl to wm Aubrey,[26] & w^{t} ~~that~~ is wanting, ~~if it will wanting,~~ [?] a farm in Eng. is to supply that deficiency, tho I hope her Interest is better worth there. and tell the Trustees sell (for so it is to be Call'd) as thou wilt heare from him,[27] as I suppose, or his atturneys, R. Hill & his poor hones[t] Bro^{r} in law,[28] but advise th[e]m [t]o secrecy. Thou a[r]t to pay them at the rate of one hundred & [twenty?] pds yearly, sterling vallue, w^{ch} [is I sup]pose, 160^{l} your present mony; in wch be [ex]act.

Let me per first have thy sence of my Interest of the Lowring of mony to [E]ngs Standard, or New Eng^{ds} at leas[t, w]hether it will be better [obliterated] [circum?]stances, or thy reasons why not. I think to send thee, the Queens repeal of the mony law,[29] but that is to be a secreet; for tho the Lords brought it to that, without my knowledge, yet upon my Memoriall to the Queen for a standard,[30] or all would be in confusion, the Lords desired me, after hearing me,[31] to keep the Repeal by me, till they had made their general Representation, which is at the Standard of Boston, because their law was confirmed by King William else would reduce it to Eng^{h} Standard.[32] What obstructs the delivery of it to the Queen in Councill, is the nicety of two of their Board, one would give 3 or 6 months, to the end pre-contracts may have time to be paid off. The other, would have them exempted in general, without nameing any time. the rest think the objection trivial and have sign'd without regard to precontracts: and argued from none being provided for in our own Laws upon raising the Coin three times, nor in England at the rise & fall of Guineas, nor in other nations, as Ireland, France & Holland, where it varies most of all. In case it be for my advantage and no detriment to the Public, publish the repeal, if not, keep it by thee, & unknown; I have a duplicate by me if askd for, and no Obligation upon me to answer their request after doing this thing without my Knowledge.

For my Government, I refer thee to the Deputy Govr & my Son more Inwardly, entreat our Friends to gain him all they can, and never speak or report any thing of him to his disparagement behind his back, but tell him of it, and he has that reasonableness & temper in him to take it kindly. Be as much as Possible in his company for that reason & suffer him not to be in any Public House after the allowed hours.

I shall write to the council to represent how it is taken that there is no settled Revenue in the Province to answer the exigencies of the Govern^t especially for a Gover^r and a Judge and an Attorney General. Without this be gone in hand with, I fear our Enemies there will have but too plausible a pretence against us here, especially in war time. Pray represent this to E^d Shippen, S. Carp^r R^d Hill, Grif Owen &^c We shall have none of our laws, I am afraid, that we most desire, and but an ordinary bargain shall I be able to make for them or myself, if they will not goe to a small Custome on Imports & exports and an excise. I can't bear the burden, as I have done these twenty two years, save when I was last there. That foolish Covetousness of theirs, is so far from good husbandry, that it will be found mony ill saved at long run. I fear Laws will be made here to rule us there, if we are so stout & stingy. But I'le say no more of this, save if we had done like men, we had not been in precarious circumstances as we are.

I hope by this time thou hast got in the £1000, of S. Carp^r subscribed by the people for my support, as also the 2000[33] & the remainder of the Custom & excise, and if so, send it not over unless in valuable goods, and minde pray and get me clear & easy in my private capacity as well as the Publick affairs of Gov^t for *I have been involved by my Public Spiritedness* both there and (to be sure) here. once more pray expedite the Sale of my Daughters lands & lotts to disengage me from the Interest I am to afford till payd. If it be delayd I shall think myself wrongd.

The wind is come about and I must break off but before I do, pray let me have no more money laid out at Pennsbury, and see that its produce at least defrays its charges; and since my Son aims at thy Company more than any other thing, pray let him be constant[34] with thee, and not keep any expence at Pennsbury, as entertainments.[35]

AL and transcript. Penn Papers, Letters of the Penn Family to James Logan, HSP. (*Micro.* 11:005.) The last part of the manuscript letter is missing and has been supplied from a manuscript copy by Deborah Logan in the Logan Papers, Selections from the Correspondence of the Honourable James Logan, HSP. Deborah Logan produced two variant transcripts of this letter; the editors have used her earlier version, which seems likely to contain fewer editorial emendations. Significant differences between the two versions are noted below.

1. Not found.

2. Logan had written to WP twice about Hamilton's death, on 29 Apr. and 6 May (*Micro.* 10:908, 948).

3. Cornbury had written to the Board of Trade relaying reports from Philadelphia that courts there had condemned people to death even though neither judges nor

jury had been sworn. There was no mention of the attestation prescribed for Quakers. Logan warned WP of Quary's complaints on this issue in his letter of 24 June (*Micro.* 10:1002); the courts had proceeded with trials based on affirmations when the Anglicans refused to swear oaths in order to obstruct Pennsylvania's courts. In the two capital cases tried, a man was burnt on the hand for manslaughter, and a woman was con demned to death for murdering her child but was not executed. *CSPC, 1702-1703*, p. 467.

4. The *Cantico*, or *Industry*, and the *Mary;* see doc. 56.

5. WP's two young sons by Hannah Penn, John and Thomas.

6. WP petitioned the queen to approve John Evans as Hamilton's replacement on 6 July (*Micro.* 10:1022). The petition was referred to the Board of Trade, which approved him on 9 July. *CSPC, 1702-1703*, pp. 531, 546.

7. For WP's instructions to Evans, see doc. 65. His commission is *Micro.* 10:1069.

8. See *CSPC, 1702-1703*, pp. 563, 587.

9. Samuel Carpenter, Edward Shippen, Isaac Norris, Richard Hill, and Griffith Owen.

10. Evan Evans (d. 1721), a Welsh minister, was rector of Christ Church and head of the Anglican church in Philadelphia. *PWP*, 3:624n.

11. Thee.

12. Evans had given the Board of Trade a bond for £2000 security for his observance of the Navigation Acts. *CSPC, 1702-1703*, p. 563.

13. See n. 32, below.

14. See doc. 56, n. 65.

15. Probably a reference to Hamilton's willingness to act as deputy for the Jerseys under the New York administration of Sir Edmund Andros. *DAB*.

16. Francis Davenport (d. c. 1707), a prominent Quaker of Burlington, had served as speaker of the West New Jersey assembly and president of its council, in addition to his long tenure as a justice. Pomfret, *West New Jersey*, pp. 147, 180, 186; *NJA*, 23:129.

17. Burlington, N.J.

18. Thomas Gardiner (d. c. 1712), another leading Quaker of Burlington, served as a justice, president of the West New Jersey council, and king's attorney. Pomfret, *West New Jersey*, pp. 183, 186, 202; Hinshaw, 2:163; *NJA*, 23:178.

19. WP is evidently counting from 1686, when Hamilton was first appointed to examine the administration of East New Jersey. Raimo, *Governors*, p. 325.

20. Robert West (d. 1718), a London lawyer and a former proprietor of East New Jersey, was a partner with Hamilton in the establishment of a colonial postal system. Pomfret, *East New Jersey*, p. 249; *PWP*, 3:628n; ACM, vol. 106; *DAB*.

21. John Usher (1648-1726), an Anglican born in Massachusetts, was traveling to New Hampshire to take up his post as lieutenant governor there. He had formerly served in the administration of Massachusetts and as lieutenant governor and commander in chief of New Hampshire from 1692 to 1697. Raimo, *Governors*, pp. 166-67.

22. John Sotcher. For WP's letters to Logan, see doc. 56; *Micro.* 10:835; docs. 59, 61.

23. Isaac Norris, Samuel Preston, Samuel Carpenter, and Richard Hill.

24. Edward Shippen, Jr., and Anne (1684-1712), children of Edward Shippen. Shippen's other son, Joseph (1679-1741), lived in Boston until 1704. Elise W. Balch, *Descendants of Edward Shippen* (Philadelphia, 1883), pp. 49-50, 52.

25. Hills. *OED*.

26. William Aubrey (d. 1731), originally of Brecknockshire, Wales, was a merchant of White Lion Court, Cornhill, London. On 20 Aug. 1702 he married Laetitia Penn; his first wife, Mary Davis, had died in 1694. The marriage settlement guaranteed Aubrey at least £2000 from the sale of Laetitia's Pennsylvania lands. See doc. 209B, M; Howard Williams Lloyd, comp., *Lloyd Manuscripts* (Lancaster, Pa., 1912), pp. 12-13; Jenkins, pp. 63, 244; Digests of Quaker Records, London and Middx., Sus. and Sur., GSP.

27. William Aubrey.

28. Reese Thomas (c. 1665-1742), a leading Welsh Quaker of Merion, served as a J.P. and assemblyman, had married William Aubrey's sister, Martha, and was now serving as Aubrey's attorney along with Richard Hill. Lloyd, *Lloyd Manuscripts*, pp. 291-96.

29. On 30 July 1703 the Queen in Council repealed Pennsylvania's law of 27 Nov. 1700, which regulated the values of coins according to weight. *Statutes*, 2:87-88; *Acts of Privy Council*, 2:441-42. See also doc. 56, n. 65.

30. See doc. 54.

31. From this point the text follows Deborah Logan's transcript. See provenance note, above.

32. A Massachusetts law of 1697 had set the value of the 17-pennyweight piece of eight at 6s; this had been approved by the crown. The Pennsylvania values were more inflated, allowing 7s 8d for the piece of eight of 17 pennyweight. Curtis P. Nettels, *The Money Supply of the American Colonies Before 1720* (1934; reprint, Clifton, N.J., 1973), p. 243n; *Statutes*, 2:87-88.

33. See doc. 33, n. 5.

34. Deborah Logan's second transcript reads "constantly."

35. The second transcript adds "&c."

68
FROM HANNAH PENN

Bristoll 13th 8br [October] 1703

My own dearest

because I am ready to hope thou wilt put an end to this way of convers, ere, another can come to thy hand, I am therfore willing to make use of this post to carry thee my dearest remembrances, and to tell thee, I cannot with any Satisfaction endure thy absence much Longer; and therfore I hope thy next will bring me the Joyfull acct: of thy coming {to me,} since I am so constrain'd to abide from thee; or {else} we would not have lived so long apart as already we have done and yet the many mercys I do InJoy I must not forget; but desire to be reverently thankfull for that of our health, wch through the goodness of our great preserver is continued, in a good measure to us all. my Mor [1] has not her ague as we fear'd, nor our little Girle[2] any fit since the first, but pretty well again, Johnne well & hearty, so Tomme wn I last heard[3] & my selfe pretty well, as is my father[4] Cousens &c, all desire to salute thee, but none so dearly as her that with Great Patience, as well as great satisfaction, is

Thine own HP

ALS. Penn Papers, Penn-Forbes Collection, HSP. (*Micro.* 11:085.) In Jan. 1705 WP wrote a draft fragment of a letter to Hannah Penn on the bottom of this document.

1. Hannah Penn's mother, Hannah Hollister Callowhill.
2. Hannah Margarita Penn.
3. Thomas Penn, then about 18 months old, had evidently been sent to a nurse or relative. See also *Micro.* 10:354.
4. Thomas Callowhill.

69
FROM JAMES LOGAN

Philadelphia 5 December 1703.

Honoured Governour

Two Posts agoe I received thine of the 6 ~~the~~ 4mo Ult[1] via Boston by wch percieve None of Mine Since that of the 10 Mo Last per the

Messenger[2] was then come to Hand But Seeing tis owing to the Misfortune of the Conveyance & no Remissness of Mine I doubt not but I shall be acquitted By the Cornbury from York Capt Symmonds Comr [3] I was very Large in one of Several Sheets accompanying a Pacquett directed to the Secretaries Office dat 3 1st Mo Last[4] In that I Sent a full Answer to CQ's Articles[5] with all the Minnutes of Council at Large Relating to our ~~Asse~~ Assembly[6] and Many other Papers & Minnutes of the Govrt considerably Exceeding in Bulk the first Mention'd per Guy (vizt of 10br)[7] wch I now wish had Never gone the Vesseles we hear being carried into France. By the Same also Staying at York Much longer than Expected I wrote again 20th 2d Mo & again 26 Ditto[8] of wch also Sent Coppies via Boston and again 29 from Amboy[9] Informing of Governour Hamiltons Death wth Bills for £100:18:— Sterling again 6. 3d Month[10] both by Barb. & Jamaica again by way of Yorke & Boston 13 of the Same Month[11] By Capt Buckle[12] & the Experrimt [13] I have also been Large Dated 14 4 Mo [14] the Same also by way of Boston and again 24 of the Same Month[15] by the Same Opportunities I sent Pacquetts wch I also did by the Messenger 2d 7br and again on the 8th do[16] by Capt Dykes[17] and by Way of Virginia again 29. 7br & 2d 8br [18] besides another Letter wch I have Omitted dat 9th 5 Mo [19] both by York & Boston all wch in the Single Coppies besides the Many Duplicates Make above 50 Pages in folio Close Writt In my Book of Copies[20] and Many of them I hope by this time are arrived Since the Last of these this place affords {very} Little New More than that of[21] the 15 of 8br the Representatives chosen by the Province for Assembly for Each County 8 together with 2 for this Corporation according to Charter[22] Mett & Chose D Lloyd Speaker who appeared in General to the people & the Members Chosen Very well Affected for the Publick good Whatever he Might Cover underneath and Earnestly prest to proceed to Business with the Council but the Latter Wholly refused Wch I believe they would Scarcely have done had the Report been then as Currt as Now of the Surrender of the Govrmt

This accot is Confidently given us by one Usher Govr (I think) of New Hampshire lately come over who Affirms that the Queen has agreed to pay £15000 due to thy father in Consideration of her ~~Res~~ Reasuming it but Mentions Nothing of any Terms Obtained for the people wch I wish had accompanyed the other for their Genl Satisfaction for Money without Any other Conditions would give too Great occasion for Discourse to the Ill affected but by what thou hast been pleased to hint in thy Last Mention'd of 4mo Ult[23] I take upon Mee to Assure them they May be Secure in that point Tis an Unhappiness We are No better aware of it if true for the Want of an Approbation to Govr Hamilton While living & the Expectation of thy Success in those Affairs from thy Letters from Ju Mompesson[24] wth the ~~C~~uncertain posture of our Affairs Since his[25] said Decease has Occasion'd thy Dues from the Govt to be Much in arrears for Property ~~Business~~ Conserns I can be Answerable but for the others it has Not been in My Power

From thy frequent Pressing Instances in thy Letters for Returns I have Strain'd to My Utmost this Year & have Sent & Shipt off according to the Inclosed Schedule[26] Why I could not Send More Bills and Furrs I have before given the reasons at Large.[27] I wish those I have Sent may be to Satisfaction Abt the Bear Skins I was not fairly dealt with by E Farmar Some of the Bills Indorsed by J Regnier will I doubt Meet the Same fate with at Least one half (as 'tis thought) of those Sent this Year from Maryland there being this Last Summer Sent back protested to that Province according to an account taken of them (as is affirm'd) to the Vallue of 30000 £ which will be 6000 £ dead Loss to the Countrey upon the Allowance of 20 per Ct given in Such Cases by their Law as well {as} ours[28] ~~and~~ the 10 hogsheads Tobacco and 8½ Tun of Logwood will I Doubt come but to a poore Markett but having purchased it long before thy Advices came[29] was Obliged to Ship it Tobacco however will this Year yield a great price by being as tis Computed they Say Moderately one half of all Made in Virginia & Maryland lost by the Most Violent Storm that was Ever known in these parts in the Memory of Man on the 6th or 7th of 8br last[30] Nor was it less Severe upon York and our two Lower Counties where Near one half of the Timber Trees (Many Say a Much greater proportion) being destroyed by it & the Roads so Blocked up that three Years will not be Sufficient (as the Most Credible persons of these Parts Affirm) to Clear them. When I Shipt on the 3 last Gallys gone for Barbados We had accot of good Markets but Since hear that Bread & Flower is Much Fallen Beer is Tollerable & Tobacco of wch Sent 19 hogsheads by them was Lately very High there but I wish the Jolly Gally on whom R Janney came may be Safe having Left the Capes but the day before the Storm[31]

Of the Robt & Benjamin Brigantine[32] Jno Guy Master I purchased ⅓ Joyntly with Wm Trent and Isaac Norris in Order to make returns in Rice from Carolina this River Now Affording nothing that's Encouraging there being Little Tobacco and What there is will not doe Bills doubtfull and Scarce for now in Maryland the place of our Supply they will not draw and Money Scarcer and the West Indies Very uncertain and at present low Our Design as Laid was to Send a Loading of our Goods upon an Information of a Tollerable Market which we have done in twenty tun of Beer abot 12 Tun of Flower 4 Tun of Bread with Apples Cheese &t to the Vallue of 686 £ in the Whole Besides the Vessell fitted out at 560 £ Jno Crapp[33] is gone factor and with this is to purchase Rice but in the Mean time the Vessel Returns hither wth a Load of Salt wch 'tis hoped will clear one half of her and forthwith to Return With More goods to Compleat her Loading of Rice to England which may be abot 1000 £ to Joyn the Virginia

Fleet Next Spring & then if She will but Sell at a price that will pay her Wages We Expect No more if the Rice will yield but 24/per C[34] this is as well Laid as any Voyage can be but Success is all it May Many wayes Miscarry for Trade is a Lottery but I think I cannot be better Justified than by Acting in Convert[35] with the Most Industrious thriving & Intiligent Traders here Whatever the Event May prove I honestly doe My Endeavour the rest Must be left to the great disposer of all things.

Had I known thy Bargain[36] Should have Been more Sparing for now hope the Necessity [illegible deletion] in a great Measure is over in Straining and Shall be so for the future the only Way to gain here is by Importation The Revenue of this Province will doe best to be Spent here allowing alwaies Some to Ship off to Import by it other Necessaries Returns from hence can Seldome Make Profitt

I Impatiently Expect thy son's arival[37] and Should be Extream glad Could we firmly Depend on seeing thy selfe & whole Family this a place of Ease (thô not to Me) Compar'd wth that Buzzing Theatre thou may live truly happy as Propry here. For the future I design Wholly to Apply My self ~~of~~ to the Settling of thy Affairs for thy Ease & untill Fresh Orders come Except the accot of the Surrender prove falce Shall Trouble My self abot Returns but little More. I hope to be Able to perfect Compleat Rent Rolls wch hitherto I could not because of Resurveys But Now in thy Absence & Since Govr Hamilton's Decease I much want Some Support for because I cannot be of Every ones Speed there are those I would fain have Expected better things from that give not all the Countenance they Might. In thy Next to the Council I request thee to give Some Small Injunctions for the More Easy furtherance of thy Affairs the Burthen as well as Frowns of wch are here too well known to lay some weight on me. I hope an Easie Access to the Rolls Office for thy Service and all the Patent Books will alwayes be accounted thy Receiver Genls Due. I nevr Yet would Clash with any Man ~~could~~ If I could avoid it and hope Shall Ever keep Clear in those Cases Pray be Very Plain and full to Me remembring My Engagements have been & are Wholly in thy Affairs. This place is healthy and frds Genrly well Honest Saml Carpr finely Recovered and has almost Finisht his works at Bucks[38] he~~r~~is daughter dangerously Ill of her late Delivery of a 2d Son, the first is dead,[39] She was 2 Nights agoe Dispaired of and her Frds Called to See her departing but Since there are Some Small Better Hopes. He dear G O & E S[40] also give their kindest Salutations. So My Landlord [illegible deletion] I Norris[41] & all the Families vizt R Hill &t. Tho Masters has ~~built~~ built another Stately house the Most Substantial Fabrick in the town on Lætitia's Bank[42] wch for the Improvemt of the place was Sold him for 190 £ Including the Reversion abot 18 Months agoe & is thought could not be Better disposed off for if her husband[43] Should Ever desire it again if Tho keep his

Humor he May have it again in all Probability for less than it cost him by all his Labour and Most of the Ground Samuel Carpenter has Sold the house thou liv'd in[44] to Wm Trent for 850 £ & the Coffeehouse[45] to Capt Finney for £450 towards paying his Debts & so designs to Continue to the last foot he has in the Province if nothing less will doe by these two he Affirms he has Lost above £300 I add Nothing here that have Mention'd in My former not doubting but they with the Virginia Fleet May arive. Our Trade to the W Indies in Genl has been prosperous this Year I am wth due respects &t

J L

LBC. James Logan Letterbook, HSP. (*Micro.* 11:105.) Endorsed: Sent Inclosed to Danl Zachary to be | Sent by the Ship Centurion[46] in Boston.

1. WP's letter to Logan of 6, 7 June 1703 (doc. 61).
2. See doc. 56, n. 1; for Logan's letter to WP of 1 Dec. 1702, see *Micro.* 10:634.
3. The *Cornbury* was captured by the French, and Capt. Symonds threw all letters overboard. See doc 74.
4. For Logan's letter of 3 Mar. 1703, see *Micro.* 10:782.
5. Logan had enclosed *Micro.* 10:839, the Provincial Council's extensive answer to doc. 44A.
6. See *Minutes of the Provincial Council,* 2:71-85.
7. *Micro.* 10:634.
8. For Logan's letter of 20, 21, and 26 Apr. 1703, see *Micro.* 10:891.
9. For Logan's letter of 29 Apr., see *Micro.* 10:908.
10. For Logan's letter of 6 May, see *Micro.* 10:948.
11. For Logan's letter of 13 May, see *Micro.* 10:958.
12. Nathaniel Puckle, master of the *Philadelphia.* See doc. 13, n. 1.
13. For the *Experiment,* see doc. 52, n. 7.
14. For Logan's letter of 14 June, see *Micro.* 10:985.
15. For Logan's letter of 24 June, see *Micro.* 10:1002.
16. For Logan's letters of 2, 7 Sept. and 8 Sept., see *Micro.* 11:034, 022.
17. Not identified.
18. For Logan's letter of 20, 29 Sept., see *Micro.* 11:063; the letter of 2 Oct. has not been found.
19. For the letter of 9 July, see *Micro.* 10:1031. Logan also wrote to WP on 14 June (*Micro.* 10:985), 11 Sept. (*Micro.* 11:026), and 13 Sept. (*Micro.* 11:031).
20. James Logan Letterbook, vol. 1, HSP.
21. Evidently an error for "on" 15 Oct.
22. The Charter of Privileges of 1701 (doc. 28) provided that, in case the Lower Counties separated from Pennsylvania, the Assembly should consist of eight representatives from each of the counties of Philadelphia, Chester, and Bucks, and two from the city of Philadelphia.
23. See WP's letter of 6, 7 June 1703 (doc. 61), text at n. 6.
24. Judge Roger Mompesson had carried doc. 56 and other letters to Pennsylvania.
25. Gov. Hamilton's.
26. This enclosure has not been found, but for Logan's shipping schedules, see Albright G. Zimmerman, "James Logan, Proprietary Agent," *PMHB,* 78:154-56.
27. See, e.g., doc. 52, text at nn. 9-12; *Micro.* 10:782.
28. Laws in both Maryland and Pennsylvania stipulated a penalty of 20 percent on protested bills of exchange. Curtis P. Nettels, *The Money Supply of the American Colonies Before 1720* (1934; reprint, Clifton, N.J., 1973), pp. 57-58; *Statutes,* 2:86.
29. See doc. 56, text at nn. 8-10.
30. Despite the storm, a deep depression in tobacco prices prevailed from 1703 to 1713. Lewis C. Gray, *The History of Agriculture in the Southern United States to 1860* (Washington, D.C., 1933), 1:268-69.
31. The *Jolly Galley* survived the storm and was still operating in 1705. ACM, vol. 120.

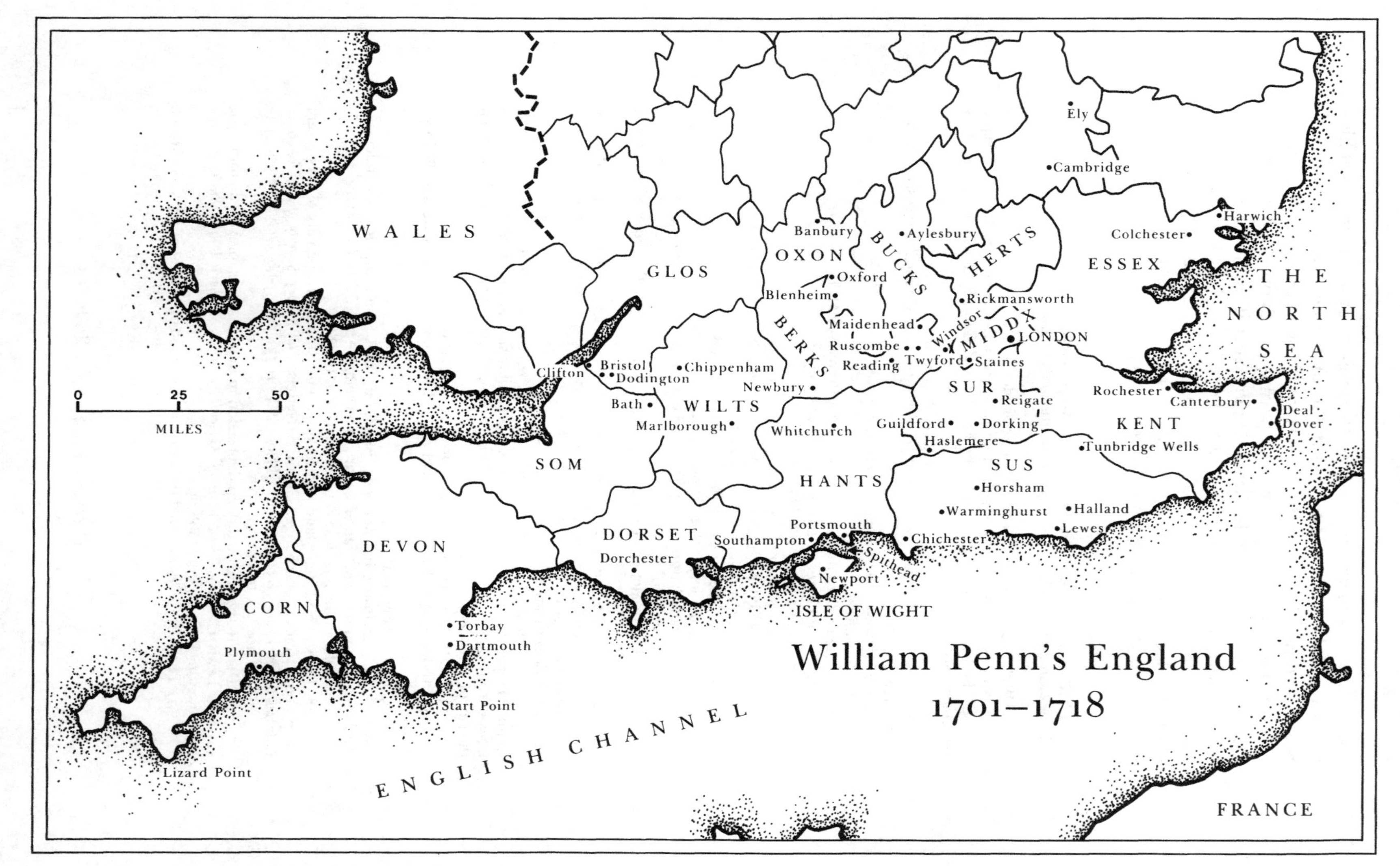
William Penn's England
1701–1718
WALES
GLOS
OXON
BUCKS
HERTS
ESSEX
BERKS
MIDDX
WILTS
SUR
KENT
SUS
HANTS
SOM
DORSET
DEVON
CORN
ISLE OF WIGHT
THE NORTH SEA
ENGLISH CHANNEL
FRANCE
Ely
Cambridge
Harwich
Colchester
Banbury
Aylesbury
Oxford
Blenheim
Rickmansworth
Maidenhead
Windsor
LONDON
Ruscombe
Reading
Twyford
Staines
Clifton
Bristol
Dodington
Chippenham
Newbury
Rochester
Canterbury
Deal
Dover
Bath
Marlborough
Reigate
Guildford
Dorking
Whitchurch
Haslemere
Tunbridge Wells
Horsham
Warminghurst
Halland
Lewes
Portsmouth
Southampton
Chichester
Spithead
Dorchester
Newport
Torbay
Dartmouth
Plymouth
Start Point
Lizard Point
0
25
50
MILES

32. The brigantine *Robert and Benjamin*, John Guy, master, sailed from the mainland colonies to both England and the West Indies. Ibid.

33. John Crapp (d. 1712), a surgeon of Philadelphia, later set up a public slaughterhouse in the city. J. Granville Leach Collection, Genealogical Data, 1:327-29, GSP.

34. This was a conservative estimate, even though the price of rice was falling in these years; navy victuallers in London were paying about 42s per hundredweight in 1703. Sir William Beveridge, *Prices and Wages in England from the Twelfth to the Nineteenth Century* (London, 1939), 1:565.

35. Evidently an error for "concert."

36. WP's negotiation with the crown for the sale of Pennsylvania's government.

37. William Penn, Jr., arrived in Pennsylvania together with Gov. John Evans on 2 Feb. 1704. See doc. 74.

38. Carpenter had been troubled by financial setbacks, but was completing a large complex of sawmills and other shipbuilding facilities on Mill Creek in Bristol, Bucks Co. *Micro.* 10:782.

39. Carpenter's daughter, Hannah Carpenter Fishbourne (1686-1728), had given birth to her second son, Samuel (d. 1721), on 8 Nov. 1703. Her first child, Abraham, born 18 Oct. 1702, had died on 28 July 1703. Edward Carpenter and Louis Henry Carpenter, comps., *Samuel Carpenter and His Descendants* (Philadelphia, 1912), p. 161.

40. Samuel Carpenter, Griffith Owen, and Edward Shippen.

41. Logan was boarding at the house of Isaac Norris. Frederick B. Tolles, *James Logan and the Culture of Provincial America* (Boston, 1957), p. 42.

42. Thomas Masters's three-story brick house, on the southeast corner of Front and High Sts., was finished in 1704. *PMHB*, 53:6-7.

43. William Aubrey.

44. WP had stayed at Carpenter's slate-roofed house, at the southeast corner of Second St. and Norris's Alley, during his visit to Pennsylvania in 1699-1701. See Carpenter and Carpenter, *Samuel Carpenter*, p. 17.

45. Carpenter had owned a coffeehouse at the northeast corner of Front and Walnut Sts. Carpenter and Carpenter, *Samuel Carpenter*, p. 17.

46. H.M.S. *Centurion*, commanded by Capt. John Herne, was to sail for England from Boston but was delayed until March 1704. See doc. 78; R. D. Merriman, ed., *Queen Anne's Navy* (London, 1961), p. 331.

70
FROM HANNAH PENN

Worminghust 27th 10br [December] 1703

My Dearest

Thine I had by last & the former post[1] and herwith send thee the best Doe we have, as Parham[2] keeper tells me, at least as good as any; but tis so very Indifferent that could I have sent thee an answer any other way I would not have been at theis charge, doubting twill not answer thy expectation at last, if for any extraordinary occasion. I hope {nothing} (will by next post) alter thy intentions of setting out 5th day,[3] at wch time I purpose the horses shall meet thee at Darking[4] & hope it will please the Lord to bless us at last, wth a comfortable meeting. we are at presant all pretty well I shall not be very long now, hoping in a few days to have the happyness of a more intimate Conversation; I hope Johnes briches at least, are done, & that thou will bring the coat body for hanna, both wch are very much wanted, as also a firkin of butter, for none is yet come to hand, the sugar, wine, &c is come; but no German Bull.[5] I am consernd that thou should order me to draw on w^{m} Aubrey, but more, that he should be so disrespectfull as to return the bill, I hereby also send him a letter of resentment,[6] & another bill {goes from Tho: Woolnen} the other has been hence 10 days & more, & now returnd to his great disapoyntm^{t}, & will be to our dishonour if th~~e~~is is not punctually payd, wherfore ~~if~~ pray wherever the mony is borrow'd, let 30^{l} be Layd in Wm Aubreys hands, to save that muck worm harmless. I am forct to draw at sight or five days, it being from him already due. & on Wm Aubrey again, tho against the grain, that ~~the~~ it may not be known here, he esteems our frdship so little; & {would} rather have it thought twas some mistake, or oversight, {than slight,} & hope it so too, or ~~I~~ else I think twas very unkind. Now my dearest {accept my truest} love, & heartiest wishes for thy health & safe return. pray give my dr love to relations, & our landlord & wife, with ~~resp^{ts}~~ respects to Lady Barnerd,[7] to whom I own my selfe obliedgd for the favours already bestown, & hope to deserve her friendship, & [illegible deletion] should {be} sorry to purchase her displeasure; I think think her advise kindly intended, & almost resolve to take it, if my husband will live so long and oft in London, but if I could with him, Live a retired, as well as country Life, I should wish well to my frds there, but say happyer still am I. since the above T. W. was wth me for the bill & says the carrier will be in early 4th day by whom I incline to send the Venson[8] [illegible erasure] directed to W: Weston,[9] to whom I inclose this, and remain in dearest Love and deepest Ties

Thy own aff^{t}
H Penn

dr love to sister Lowther[10] &c
Daugh^{r} & {the 3} children[11] desire their duty & cous Rebecka[12] her respects, she & w L.[13] are of opinion that could he be cleard of the Q^{s} [14] part that wade[15] will assuredly forgive his. E Blackfan is fully perswaded of it.
we very much want a pillion & cloth having none but S H^{s} [16] & but one side sadle for all these servants; but pray let not this take up thy time or hinder thy return in the least from thine own HP.

ALS. Dreer Collection, HSP. (*Micro.* 11:126.) Addressed: For Wm Penn Esqr | at his Lodgings near | Hidepark Gate | or elswhere. | London.

1. Not found.
2. Parham Park, a manor house four miles from Warminghurst.
3. Thursday, 30 Dec. 1703. WP was still in London on 31 Dec. (see doc. 71), so his departure must have been delayed.
4. Dorking, Sur., 22 miles SSW of London.
5. A drink made by flavoring water with spirits. *OED*.
6. Not found.
7. Possibly the widow of Sir Edward Barnard (d. 1688) of Yorkshire, a distant relative by marriage of WP. She had evidently advised Hannah Penn to move to London. Burke's *Landed Gentry* (1879).
8. Venison.

9. William Weston was a vintner of Leadenhall St., London, and a member of Devonshire House meeting. Digests of Quaker Records, London & Middx., GSP.

10. WP's sister, Margaret Penn Lowther.

11. Mary Penn, wife of William Penn, Jr., and their three children, Gulielma Maria, Springett, and William, III.

12. Rebecca Crispin Blackfan (d. post 1736), a cousin of WP. Her husband, Edward Blackfan (1653-before 1713), had visited Pennsylvania before their marriage in 1688. Rebecca and her son William became caretakers of Pennsbury after Edward's death, about 1713. In 1725 Rebecca married Nehemiah Allen of Philadelphia. *PWP*, 3:141n; Hinshaw, 2:466; Phila. Will Bk. E, #450.

13. Possibly WP's nephew Sir William Lowther, the son of Margaret Lowther. Jenkins, pp. 24-25, 183.

14. The queen's. Blackfan had evidently incurred a fine or debt due in part to the crown and in part to Nathaniel Wade or the city of Bristol.

15. Nathaniel Wade (d. 1718), a lawyer and town official of Bristol who had signed the marriage certificate of WP and Hannah Callowhill. *PWP*, 3:437n.

16. Sarah Hersent, housekeeper of Warminghurst. *PWP*, 3:427n.

71
TO THE PROVINCIAL COUNCIL

Lond: 31 10m [December] 1703

Esteemed Friends.

I heartily salute You, wishing You & Yours true Happines. I perceive by divers Letters, as well as that I received from most of You,[1] the restless Endeavours of a few Mal-Contents to throw the Gov^mt into Confusion, that they might have the better Excuse & Pretence for changing the Gov^mt & Shifting Hands in which now it is. As for Instance, That You are Careless about the Laws of Trade & Navigation because You are not Cruel & Extortious, where Facts relating thereunto have happened through Ignorance or undesigned Omissions, as in the Case of poor Lumby, Kirle & Righton,[2] to say nothing of the Barbarous treatment of Geo. Claypole & Th. Masters, for w^h Qu. & Moor[3] deserve the Aversion & Scorn of all Honest Men, & I doubt not but they will find it in due time. The next Instance is their Outcry for want of a Militia to defend them in times of Danger, & then strenuously endeavour to defeat the Means of obtaining & setling It.[4] 3dly. After all their Aggravations about trying for Life without an Oath, they have discouraged the Methods taken by my L^nt Govr Ham^n to the Obstruction of Justice which might accomodate that Matter,[5] then w^h hardly anything can appear more disingenuous. 4^thly. I was astonished at the Account of the Address, delivered by Qu. in the Name of the Vestry in Philad^a to the Ld Cornb.[6] at his last being there, & I admire almost as much at Your Extreme Patience under so Impudent an Affront & Injustice, I suppose it was out of Respect to that Noble Lord; otherwise I think, had I been there, I should have made those Gentlemen sensible of the Smart of that Power they have so often abused in Your hands, & for that reason now would have wrested out of them: But His Answer[7] I confess (as it comes from thence) shews His Prudence & their Folly, & with the Addition of what his Father the Earl of Clarendon told me t'other Day, upon my mentioning to Him the Unaccountablenes of that Passage in their Address, as well his great Justice; for (says He) I will never solicit the Q^{n} or any Body else for that w^{h} is the Property of another Man. 5^{thly}. I also understand that these open Defiances to the Gov^{mt}, they have got their Bread under, have excited many of my Renters in the Lower Counties to refuse the Payment of my Quitrents; An Unhappines, poor People, to themselves at long runn; for I am determined to shew them they are in the wrong, & forgive them when they have submitted to their Old, Kind & Abused Land Lord; But perhaps their Leaders may have Cause one time or other to wish they had not misled them from their Duty & Common Justice. My present Indisposition (which they say is the beginning of the Gout) makes writing uneasy to Me, or else You had had all this from my own hand. I shall conclude when I have said I expect from You that You maintain my just Rights & Priviledges both in Gov^{mt} & $Prop^{ty}$ granted to me by K: Ch. the 2^{d} under the great Seal of Eng^{ld} & by J: Duke of York his Royal Brother,[8] & the Constitutions Laws & Customs Unitedly [&] Universally fixt & established in that Gov^{mt}, long before the Coming of those Troublers of our Peace amongst Us;[9] for You cannot think that I shall support them here, if You submitt them there to the unjust Clamours & Insolent Practises of those Notorious Enemies to our publick Peace. I am Your very

Loving Friend
Wm Penn

LS. Logan Papers, HSP. (*Micro.* 11:131.) Endorsed: Duplicate.

1. See doc. 66.
2. On Lumby, see doc. 38, n. 30; on Righton, see doc. 35, n. 16. Joseph Kirle (d. 1704) was a Quaker mariner of Philadelphia and a former cooper of Bristol. *PWP*, 3:469n.
3. The nature of Quary and Moore's barbarous treatment of George Claypoole and Thomas Masters is not known. Masters had signed a bond for William Righton together with several other Philadelphia merchants (*Micro.* 9:933).
4. See doc. 66.
5. Ibid.
6. James Logan had reported this incident to WP in his letter of 2 and 7 Sept. 1703. Quary had presented Lord Cornbury with an address from the Philadelphia vestry soliciting his patronage and urging him to ask Queen Anne to extend his government over Pennsylvania as well as New York and New Jersey. *Micro.* 11:034.
7. According to Logan's report, Cornbury "Spoke what was Proper from a Churchman," answering that it was up to the Pennsylvanians to petition the queen, but that he would be ready to obey her commands if required. Ibid.
8. On WP's grants from Charles II and James II, then duke of York, see *PWP*, 2:61-73, 281-84.
9. Here, as in his instructions to Gov. Evans (doc. 65), WP ignores the new Pennsylvania constitution of 1701 and harks back to the earlier settlement of 1683.

GROWING CONFLICT IN PENNSYLVANIA

1704

The year 1704 was one of false hope for WP. The proprietor expected his opponents in Pennsylvania to be quiet after the arrival of his new deputies, Lieutenant Governor John Evans and William Penn, Jr. Supposing his colony's administration in good hands, WP spent much time lobbying for Pennsylvania. He pressed the Board of Trade to reprimand Robert Quary (doc. 77), he urged the attorney general to complete his review of Pennsylvania's laws, and he defended the right of Pennsylvania Quakers to affirm rather than swear the oath prescribed by Queen Anne in 1702. And he continued to negotiate toward the surrender of Pennsylvania's government to the crown for £30,000 — though WP told Robert Harley (doc. 72) that he would settle for £20,000. But his plan to sell the colony's government proved to be another false hope.

Meanwhile, developments in Pennsylvania reflected a mounting anti-proprietary sentiment. Only the unusually long delays in communication between the colonies and England kept WP from knowing sooner about the extent of opposition his new deputies faced. James Logan, the provincial secretary, provided the proprietor with detailed reports about the political situation and WP's financial affairs in the colony (docs. 78, 82, 86). This news was seldom good. Economic conditions in the colony worsened despite the opening of the trade with Spain in the West Indies, and WP was especially hard hit as all the ships and cargos he had invested in were lost at sea. Once the colonists learned (doc. 74) that WP was trying to sell his government, they were less willing than ever to pay quitrents and taxes, or even to buy land from him. Lieutenant Governor Evans found himself without an adequate salary or administrative revenue. Even more damaging to WP's negotiations with the crown was the breach between the Lower Counties and Pennsylvania, which Evans was unable to mediate. In the Pennsylvania Assembly, the representatives met in two sessions but failed to pass a single law because they could not gain firm assurances for their legislative privileges. "I believe in the whole Assembly there are not three men that wish ill to thee — and yet I can expect but little good from them," wrote Logan in September 1704

(*Micro.* 11:369). As described in the headnote to doc. 83, the speaker of the Assembly, David Lloyd, spearheaded a campaign against WP both in Pennsylvania and among weighty Friends in England (see also docs. 84 and 86). Lloyd pushed for changes in the colony's legal system that would weaken the proprietor's authority; he devised three bills designed to strengthen the colonists' independence against the proprietary prerogative; and he prevented Evans from executing WP's instructions to reunite the Lower Counties with Pennsylvania, to establish a militia, or to limit the Assembly's powers of self-government. John Evans was ill prepared for this massive attack on proprietary rights, but he held his ground in the battle with the Pennsylvania Assembly and refused to accept Lloyd's interpretation of the charters of Privileges and Property, or the charter for Philadelphia.

The biggest blow to WP in 1704 was his son's misconduct in Pennsylvania. William Penn, Jr., seemed at first to like the colony and especially his father's country seat at Pennsbury, where he could keep horses and hounds in the style of an English gentleman (doc. 73). But he found his political role as proprietary heir-apparent awkward and ambiguous, and he found it hard to make friends among the Pennsylvania Quakers. Frustrated by his lack of income or real estate (see doc. 82), and having no adequate place to stay when in Philadelphia, William Penn, Jr., soon began to follow his own inclinations, straying more and more from the sober ways his elders and most Quakers considered proper. The problems facing WP's son are candidly described by James Logan in doc. 86. Young Penn's disenchantment with his lot in Pennsylvania became spectacularly apparent when he chose to get involved with the training of the militia. This act of open defiance of Quaker tenets was followed by his involvement in a tavern brawl in Philadelphia, which resulted in proceedings against the proprietor's son in the mayor's court. This incident so upset William Penn, Jr., that he quit the colony and sailed home from New York in early November 1704—barely nine months after his arrival.

72
TO ROBERT HARLEY

Warminghurst 9th 12m (feb) 1703/4

Much Hond Friend

If I keep no better distance to thy great post,[1] & greater Qualifications, thou must impute it to the easiness thou hast long indulg'd me in. Nor at this time do I think I ought to be in paine for an Apology,

Since I write upon a Subject agreed, & by an Authority allowed of, & long after the time exspected.

I need not tell so knowing a Person that the Colonys in America have been almost all made by privat undertakers; Some to enjoy their Consciences more quietly, others out of necessity, & lastly Some Involuntarily, as being Delinquents. New-England[2] Conneticot, Rhoad-Island, Jersys Pennsylvania, & virginia & Maryland too, in part, were begun on the first foot, but the two last (virginia especially) have been frequented by the necessitous, & much Stockt with Criminalls. wch Compar'd with New-england &c: for the time of planting, shows evidently how much better the Colonys thrive in Proprietary hands than under the immediate Govermt of the Crown; so that wt tis Suggested the Crown looses by Trade, through the over indulgence of Proprietary Governours, is (if that were true) much more than answeard by the greater improvemt (& trade, that in proportion follows upon Such improvemt) in Proprietary Govermts, to Say nothing of their better Regimt as to manners, & common Conversation. Now this is our unhappiness, that though we in N. England, Rhoad-Island, Plymouth, Connecticot, New Jersey, and Pennsylvania went thither to be quiet, by ample Graunts from the Crown, to make & keep ourselves easy & Safe in our Civil & Religious Priviledges, yet we are made extreamly uneasy by officious & turbulent Persons, who to recommend themselves to the Bps. & especially of L.,[3] here, do us all the d~~i~~esspight they can, in the name of the Church, & the Revenue; tho, the church enjoys the Same Liberty they do that made these Colonys. and tho the Queens officers, both in the Revenue & Admiralty are in those Respective Colonys, and may as freely exercise their powers as if they were in the Kingdom of England. So that there is nothing more to do or desire but to have the Govermt that they may be Lords of our Labours, have all the Employmts in their hands, & make us Dissenters in our own Countrys; a Designe Barbarous as well as unjust, Since it was to be Free of her {(the churchs)} pow'r & out of her reach we went so farr, & not to make Colonys for her, but from her, for ourselves. And as we are a People not over & above in the interest of the clergy, too many of them Seem Engag'd to undermine us even there: I wonder wt they would be at, where they think we will or can go next. Now I humbly conceive, this work is very dishonorable to the Govermt & extreamly disserviceable; for it Sowrs the People, disheartens them in their Improvemts & Trade, for one is the Spring of tother, and the Colonys must, & I assure thee do dwindle yet I will venture to Say that we have done more to make a Country in 23 years than any of the Colonys Cal'd the Crowns, hath done in 100 years; for Virginia has not a town bigger, if half so big as Knightsbridge,[4] while we have Severall bigger, & one as large as Windsor,[5] N. Eng. as Reding or Shrowsberry,[6] & twenty as big as Maidenhead;[7] So Plymouth & Conetticut; and for New york (a Dutch Proprietary improvemt (the West-india Company) one as bigg as Bath.[8] to say nothing of Severall pretty little towns in the Jerseys.[9] where converse, education & traffick are to be had, the way to make a Country & Civilize mankind, as well as for preservation. Now for my own immediate affaire, ~~from~~ I have waited these two years to be off or on, about my Govermt: To be confirm'd in it after the shake given in a former Parliament[10] or Since it was & is so great a part of my Graunt, & much of the reason of my Undertakeing & vast expence, as well as many Toyles & Hazards, & consumption of the best share of my life, that I may have an equivolent or some Sutable Consideration. I askt of the Comrs for Tr. & Pl. 30000l [11] of wch I ~~was~~ am contented to take one moity ~~there~~[?], in things to be found there. not thinking the summe a proportionable Satisfaction for what it has cost me, to Settle & support the Govermt, & Colony, & what I may reasonably expect by it to me & mine in the present & after time

First the Undertakeing was Chiefly encourag'd by the Graunt of Govermt, wch cost me 10557l in less than three years time, wch was many thousands more than I receivd for land (which my own Interist made so valluable & not the Crowns)

2ly I have payd the Dept Goverr of my privat estate, as well as supported my Selfe in Govermt and here also to maintain & preserve it agst the attempts of our Enimys from 1681, to 1703.

3ly I never had but 2000l eng. Starling & that but 3 years agoe,[12] wch did not pay my last voyage thither, liveing 2 years there, & my returne, much less my attendance in town two years more, to obtaine some favorable issue upon the reason of my hasty returne.

4ly my case is very Singular in two respects, one that I had a debt upon the Crown of abt 16000l of mony lent by my father for the victualing of the Navy 1667. which was shutt up in the Exchequer. The other is, that I have sown largely, as the Crop upon the Ground shows, but I never reapt one yet. which is not the Case of the most of the other Colonys, so that insteed of Enjoying it for a Satisfaction, It becomes a perfect ruine to me & my family as well as an Irreparable disapointment of the People that made it a Country, who were neither Criminals nor Necessitous, if there be not a due Consideration to confirm the Laws & Constitution I have Settled them under, and Reprise me & mine, for the present & future loss that must accrew to us by the resignation of the Govermt. I askt indeed some {meer} honorary mark, as a Founder of the Colony viz, as the first (Hereditary) Privy Counselr or chief-Justice, or the like, wch I shall not insist upon, contenting myselfe with the Rights of Landlord & Lord of the mannor of the Country. But in a lettr to our great Frd the Ld. H. Treasr [13] I would accept of 20000l.

AL. Loan Manuscripts 29/191, BL. (*Micro.* 11:145.) The letter is written on the eight sides of two folded sheets; the closing page or pages have not been found.

1. Robert Harley was speaker of the House of Commons from 1701 until May 1704, when he became secretary of state. *DNB*.

2. WP means Massachusetts.

3. The bishops of the Church of England, especially the bishop of London, Henry Compton.

4. In WP's day, Knightsbridge was a hamlet on the western edge of London on the highway to Berkshire. Peter Cunningham, *A Handbook for London: Past and Present* (London, 1849), 2:463.

5. The market town of Windsor, Berks., seems to have had a population of about 2500 at this date, which was the size of Philadelphia. Daniel Lysons and Samuel Lysons, *Magna Britannia; Being a Concise Topographical Account of the Several Counties of Great Britain* (London, 1806-22), 1:435; Gary B. Nash, *The Urban Crucible: Social Change, Political Consciousness, and the Origins of the American Revolution* (Cambridge, Mass., 1979), pp. 4, 54, 409.

6. Boston, the chief town in New England, had a population of about 7500 in 1704. Reading, Berks., and Shrewsbury, Salop., were both county seats and among the larger English provincial towns. As WP indicates, Reading seems to have been much the same size as Boston, Mass., in 1704; it had a population of 8000 in 1761. Lysons and Lysons, *Magna Britannia,* 1:338-39; Nash, *Urban Crucible,* pp. 4, 54, 409.

7. Maidenhead, Berks., was a small market town with a population of 949 a century after this date, according to the first British census of 1801. Lysons and Lysons, *Magna Britannia,* 1:209.

8. In 1703 the population of the City of New York was reportedly 4436 inhabitants—a total WP claims to be comparable to Bath, Som., the fashionable spa 12 miles east of Bristol. Evarts B. Greene and Virginia D. Harrington, *American Population Before the Federal Census of 1790* (New York, 1932), p. 92.

9. In 1680 the population figures for Perth Amboy, Elizabeth, Shrewsbury, Middletown, Woodbridge, Piscataway, Newark, and Bergen in New Jersey were estimated to range from 350 to 750. Peter O. Wacker, *Land and People* (New Brunswick, N.J., 1975), p. 130; Greene and Harrington, *American Population,* pp. 109-10.

10. For the move to bring the proprietary colonies under royal government, see headnote preceeding doc. 17.

11. For WP's request to the Commisssioners of Trade and Plantations, see doc. 62; for his calculations of expenses for and income from Pennsylvania, see *Micro.* 11:221, 14:693.

12. A reference to the New Castle Assembly's grant to WP of £2000, payable in 1701; see doc. 35, n. 19.

13. WP's letter to Lord Godolphin has not been found.

73
FROM WILLIAM PENN, JR.

Phila: 15: feb: 1704

Dr Father

Wee are at Last Arriv'd after Sixteen weeks out of Sight of Land & seventeen to Ground[1] a Long & tedious passage & full of Violent storms; but I am Extreamly well Pleas'd wth the place now I am here, I have been att Pensbury & like itt well, beleive If thee wouldst allow me a Good Gardiner I could make it one of the pleasantest places in the world. Wee have been here so little a time & have been so much taken up that I have not been Able to write much, wch I hope thee will Excuse, for I suppose James Logan will supply my Defect,[2] but per next I hope to Give a full Account of all things that Relate to any publick matters.

I have writ to my wife[3] about some things wch she will Let thee know,

I begg I may have some more hounds sent over for they will do mighty well here.

That Stalion two that I Spoke off My Bro[r] Abereys[4] freind Puseley has, thee promest to Gett for me, he is a fine horse & well worth Sending, & would be of Great value here, wherefore I begg he may be sent. The Vessell is upon sailing, wherefore I shall only add My Duty & Dear Love to Thee my Mother Brothers & Sisters, Desiring the Lord to Preserve us all to meet againe, I am

Thy Most Dutyfull son
Wm Penn J[r]

ALS. Division of Archives and Manuscripts, Pennsylvania Historical and Museum Commission, Harrisburg. (*Micro.* 11:153.)

1. William Penn, Jr., and Gov. John Evans landed in Philadelphia on 2 Feb. 1704. Doc. 74.
2. For James Logan's letter to WP, see doc. 74.
3. Mary Jones Penn.
4. William Aubrey, brother-in-law of William Penn, Jr.

74
FROM JAMES LOGAN

Philad[ia] 15th 12[mo] [February] 1703/4

Honoured Governour

Thy son by this Same Opportunity informing thee of his arival,[1] to his pen, as he most able & proper I leave the Acc[t] of his tedious Voyage Gov[r] Evans also would write, but because he can not So fully, nor to so many as he thinks himselfe Oblidged, when to any, he craves to be Excused to thee in particular, nor indeed will time allow any of Us to be large.

By thy Son who arived wth the Governour 2[d] Inst[t] I received thine of 27th 6th month[2] And Shall observe the Contents as far as possible, tho' Unable now to be particular in answering any part of it, more than this, that from the blame I lie Under for My infrequency (as 'tis thought) in writing I desire the perusal of the Inclosed[3] may acquitt me, the Original was Sent by the Man of War Centurion[4] from Boston, and recites My Lett[rs] with the greatest fidellity.

'This a great Unhappiness that so many of mine had the fortune to goe by such unprosperous Vessels. Directing to York to one Interested in the Cornbury Cap[t] Symonds m[r] [5] they were all I find putt on board her, but by this dayes post am informed that the Captain happily threw all his Letters & therefore some dangerous Packetts of Mine overboard, I am troubled for many papers there & Especially for some Bills of Exchange for 100[l] Sterling, for to our great trouble we have by the same post some Advices to day that give us apprehensions of Ed Shippens in the Experim[t] Cap[t] Watson M[r],[6] by whom I Sent the 2[d] of the same, being also unfortunate & tis probable Cap[t] Puckle

also both in the Virg^{ia} fleet. If true I doubt of 1600^{l} wch I have sent off by ~~the~~ severall wayes this year, nothing will as yet have Come to hand, for that to Barb: & Carolina I know is imposible. I hear of Nothing to Barbados yet that has miscarried.
Thy Son's Voyage hither I hope will prove to the Satisfaction of all & to his, & there fore thy happiness, It is his Stock of excellent good Nature that in a great Measure has led him out into his youthfull Sallies, when too easily prevailed on, and the same I hope when seasoned with the Influences of his prevailidg better Judgem^{t}, with which he is well stored, will happily conduct him into the Channell of his Duty to God, himself, & thee, He is very well received and seldom fails of drawing Love where he comes & hope it will be encreased, tis his good fortune here to be withdrawn from those temptations that have been too successfull over his Natural Sweetness & Yielding temper with his Associates.

The Governours arivall was Extreamly Seasonable for thy Interst here for, as by the Inclosed Copy[7] thou wilt find we thought all positively gone the report was owing to Colonel Usher[8] who Confidently reported & persists in it, but has not been so fair as to send me thy Letters by him wch perhaps might have contradicted it, nor have I ever received thy other sent to the Postmaster of York, the Vessell I suppose Never having arived, so that since Judge Mompeson I have Never received more than one by D Zachary.[9] I Shall Undertake to say Nothing as yet of the Governour only that he has Enlarged the Councill by adding Ja: Momp:[10] W Trent R Hill & my Self and for the Territories J Yeats W Rodney, & Intends to add R French[11] & perhaps J: Coutts[12] as Newe, Whither he intends to morrow, thy son also whom I should have first Mencioned takes a Place at the Board when he thinks fitt next to the Govr The onely difficulty we now labour Under is the S~~a~~eparation of the Prov: & Territories by Means of that Unhappy Charter of Privileges wch I doubt is Unavoidable, thô all Endeavours to the contrary will be used. I Informed thee of this by the Messenger 10^{br} 1702[13] wch thou received, & there fore Admire, as the Governour does wth much trouble that thou hast never taken notice of it. I much fear the consequence notwi~~k~~thstanding all Endeavours that can be Used for the Terrs will not own the Charter Nor the Prov: quitt it or I believe ever more hear of as Union if to be prevented, I sent the Minutes of Councill[14] in Many Sheets att large by the York Vessel. having first by my said Letter given thee a Summary of the whole.
Pray send over a fresh Commission to the Councill with power to succeed the Governour in Case of Absence or Mortallity Agreable to his Choice (if thou thinks fitt) wch was made by the Advice of Others, reciting the Powers as in the Governours Commis^{n} both from the King & Duke, that should he be removed the Govm^{t} may be at no loss as before, I sent a Copy of the present Commission wth the other Papers.[15] And either And either in that or in the Governours[16] there

ought to be a power continued to add Members or suspend, as there is Occasion, tis now in that to the Councill, but in the Governours there is one Clause that will much disgust viz Saveing to thyself a final Assent to all bills & wch I Must Confess I think is too Much in any but those relating to thy Property, & will be a Check Against granting publick Supplies Seeing they cannot be Sure that any thing besides will pass. and 3 Negatives to the Assembly will be thought too much: It might be Advisable Also perhaps to oblidge the Governour to act in Legislation by Advice & Consent of the Councill as in all the Qu's Governments, wch would be thy greater Security. But what must the Territories doe if the Prov: proceed to Act without them? for I doubt there is no foundation there sufficient for An Assembly. tho I believe it will be tryed.[17]

The present Governour Will not be rash I suppose, but a ₵good Councill adds to the Dignity of Govmt. the present is W P Junr R. Mom: [E: Sh: J Guest: W: Cla: S Carpr T. St Gr: O. S. Fin: C Pas: J: Bl:] J L: W: Trent, R: Hill W. Rodeny J Yeats & J L. & R. Fre. & J Coutts[18] I supose must be added for the Territories. C Qua[19] makes his Court to the Governr, and this day entertain'd him att diner with Judge Momp: &c at his house, he now declares an Entire satisfaction ~~with Judge Momp:~~ And would be Inclinable I suppose to have all old things done away, There is no danger I think of the Governours being wrought upon by Any of them, for he seems very true to thy Interest in all respects, yet is Inclinable to make as fair wheat{h}er in the Government as he can, which doubtless will not be Unadvisable, but exceedingly troubled that he Understood Nothing of this Difference between the Upper and lower Counties before he left Engld.

The Adress to the Qu.[20] shall be prepared with all Expedition as desired, but whether it can be carried to Answer the End I Know not. And shall observe thy other Direction thô I cannot here mention them. Only must Againe tell thee as I have often before That we have Not been able to doe Anything Almost in the Tax of 2000l [21] since thy Departure, but now hope we shall be Able to press it to better purpose. I have often been large on this head before tho this be the first time thou hast mencioned it to me since. The Subscriptions by friends A Mounting to about 300l has been mostly paid in flower according to their Tenour[22] and what remains will now be gott in wch had not a Governour come could not have been, but tHis the worst pay almost in the Country & in Bucks Especially. The Tax Excepted The Incredible Scarcity of Money makes all things of that Kind difficult, what is now demanded in relation to the Tax is a Confirmation of the Laws and an Other Unhappiness is, that none among Friends can be gott to distrain, & others, are generally to much disaffected for it. I Admire What thou Meanes by desiring the promised Copy of the Laws having Sent it by J Sotcher twenty months Ago And doubtless came Safe toe hand wth the rest As to lowring of our Monney[23] if I might advise I would by all Meanes perswade thee Not be Concerned in it for thy proffitt by it Considering the Rents are sterling will be but very little, but the Dissatisfaction of the people in generall great for most Certainly, Unless we find some Trade Againe wth the Spanish Indies we shall Shortly have none left whether raised or lowr'd or Not touched with, yet if it be lowered the exportation of it will be wholly Imputed to this, whatever else the cause May be And those concerned in it bear the blame, besides that Unless Provision be made for Debts contracted before, it will be the greatest Injustice & some mens Especially S Carpenters ruine who is almost irrecoverably plunged[24] Unless times here mend Pray inform further What thou Means by ordering me to pay what I receive into Sa: Carprs hands, he has already 200l of Letitias Money on Interest,[25] which he Knows not how to pay But of these points shall be more full by a better opportunity, in the meantime though through the unhappy Circumstances of Affairs of Trade in generall thou must meet with Many Disappointmts Yet thou may rest Assured I shall leave Nothing Undone for thy Interest, that Considering all Circumstances can reasonably be Expected.

New Castle 18th 12mo [February 1704]

We are now here Conferring with those of the Lower Counties the Govr is handsomely received And the People seem not dissatisfied he has Published his Commission & the Qus aprobation here also for their greater satisfaction Upon a Conferrence this Day t'is agreed that Not withstanding the Assembly of the Prov: hath thrown them of by doubling their own Numbers of Representatives according to the Close of the Charter, yet Upon the Govrs Writts they will meet at Philadelphia 4 for each County According to law, and if by Conferences with those of the Province it can be done that they proceed to an Union if not, that they continue Separate as they now Conceive themselves to be, wch I Supose will be the result of the whole.
Thy Son is also Here And carries it well But the Tide hastening the Vessell away (for Barbados) I must at this time break of & Close

Thy most dutif. Servt

LBC. Logan Papers, James Logan Letterbook, HSP. (*Micro.* 11:156.)

1. Doc. 73.
2. Not found.
3. Not found.
4. The H.M.S. *Centurion* did not leave Boston until early March. *CSPC, 1704-1705*, pp. 11, 66, 99, 189, 381.
5. The *Cornbury*, with Capt. Symonds at the helm, had been in New York in Apr. 1703 and was captured by the French. *Micro.* 10:891.
6. See doc. 52, n. 7.
7. Not found.
8. John Usher, lieutenant governor of New Hampshire, had been spreading the rumor that WP had surrendered the government of Pennsylvania to Queen Anne for £15,000. See doc. 69, text at n. 23.
9. Logan had received WP's letters of 24 Jan.-28 Mar. 1703 (doc. 56) and 1 Apr. 1703 (doc. 59) on 1 July 1703; he received WP's letter of 6 June 1703 per Daniel Zachary (doc. 61) on 4 Nov. 1703. Seven other letters from WP to Logan in 1703 have

survived but they reached him later or not at all (*Micro.* 10:835, 1017; 11:005, 031, 083, 089, 136).

10. Copyist's error for Judge Roger Mompesson.

11. Robert French (d. 1713), a non-Quaker landowner in New Castle and Kent Cos., was elected provincial councilor in 1700 and was commissioned as an associate justice of the provincial court of Pennsylvania in 1701. In the dispute between Pennsylvania and the Lower Counties, French was one of the proponents of establishing an independent assembly in New Castle, and he subsequently served as a legislator of the Lower Counties. *PMHB,* 3:208, 212-14, 217-20; 18:27; 22:104.

12. James Coutts, a merchant of New Castle Co., was elected to the General Assembly of Apr. 1704; when the legislators from Pennsylvania and the Lower Counties refused to cooperate, Coutts became speaker of the separate assembly that met in New Castle in Nov. 1704. James Logan Letterbook, 2:39; Miscellaneous Papers, Three Lower Counties, Delaware, 1655-1805, pp. 127, 129, HSP; *PMHB,* 3:212; 54:236, 238, 239; 86:146; Scharf, *Delaware,* 1:128, 130, 131.

13. See *Micro.* 10:634; doc. 56, n. 1.

14. For the dispute between Pennsylvania and the Lower Counties late in 1702, see *Minutes of the Provincial Council,* 2:72-86.

15. This enclosure has not been found, but for WP's commission of 1701 to the Council, see doc. 29.

16. *Micro.* 10:1069.

17. A separate assembly for the Lower Counties met in Nov. 1704 in New Castle after Gov. Evans's attempt to mediate in the dispute between Pennsylvania and the Lower Counties had failed in Apr. 1704. *PMHB,* 54:236-39.

18. Edward Shippen, John Guest, William Clarke, Samuel Carpenter, Thomas Story, Griffith Owen, Samuel Finney, Caleb Pusey, and John Blunston were the councilors for Pennsylvania when Evans arrived; William Penn, Jr., Roger Mompesson, James Logan, William Trent, Richard Hill, William Rodney, and Jasper Yeates had been added by Evans; Robert French and James Coutts were prospective councilors from the Lower Counties. The brackets in Logan's list of councilors are in the manuscript; he mistakenly listed his own initials twice. *Minutes of the Provincial Council,* 2:116-19.

19. Colonel Quary.

20. The address to congratulate Queen Anne on her succession to the throne had become an issue of contention in the Delaware Valley because the orders for her proclamation in the province had failed to make specific mention of the Lower Counties. The Pennsylvania Assembly formulated its congratulatory address to the queen on 25 May 1704. *Votes and Proceedings,* 1(pt. 2):6; docs. 42, n. 4; 51, n. 10.

21. See doc. 33, n. 5.

22. See ibid.

23. See doc. 56, n. 65.

24. Samuel Carpenter had overextended himself with a 30-acre complex of gristmills, sawmills, and shipbuilding facilities in Bristol, Bucks Co., at a time of political and economic instability. Carpenter had to sell off much of his land and many of its improvements at a great loss in order to pay his debts. E. Carpenter and L. Carpenter, *Samuel Carpenter* (Philadelphia, 1912), p. 15; *PMHB,* 9:66; 20:321-22; *Micro.* 10:782, 11:034; doc. 69, text at n. 38.

25. On 14 Aug. 1702 James Logan wrote to Laetitia Penn that he had lent Samuel Carpenter £200 of the £300 proceeds from the sale of her lots in Philadelphia. Logan Papers, 1:41, HSP.

75
TO AMBROSE GALLOWAY

Lond. 19th 12m [February] 1703[/4]

Dear Friend

My Dr. love salutes thee & thine.[1] I was somewhat disapointed at our last interview, when I promessed myselfe more time with thee, of a serious & weighty nature. this only comes to entreat thee {to} inquire If any milch asses are in yr parts, as Glyne, the Broyle, Awland[2] &c: and if thou canst borrow one for my family, or if they will unwillingly lend, then Sell one, that is not too old, the youngest being best, intimate it to my wife, who will send for it on loane or pay, & the sooner thou obligest us herein, the better. the{ir} milck is beyond all Doctrs skill, for sweatening of the blood. perhaps Doctr White could informe thee where to borrow, or else purchass one reasonably. I use this freedom with thee, because I take thee for my old & true Frd, & that I am sure I shall always be glad of an occasion to return thy love, who with a great deale to thee & Kinde Ruth & yr children, & Fs also, am

Thy assured Frd
Wm Penn

ALS. AMC. (*Micro.* 11:167.) Addressed: For Ambrose | Galloway in | [illegible deletion] Lewis | Sussex.[3]

1. Ambrose Galloway (1659-1718), a Quaker from Lewes, Sus., married Ruth Hobbs (d. 1723) in 1679. They had three children: Ambrose (b. 1680); William (1683-1710); and Elizabeth (b. 1689). Digests of Quaker Records, Sus. and Sur., GSP.

2. Glynde is a Sussex village three miles east of Lewes; Broyle Place at Ringmer (three miles northeast of Lewes) was the residence of the Springetts; Awland may be Halland, a village seven miles northeast of Lewes. Thomas Walker Horsfield, *The History, Antiquities, and Topography of the County of Sussex* (Lewes, Eng., 1835) 1:343-45, 350, 416.

3. Lewes, a town in Sussex, is 43 miles south of London and 18 miles east of Warminghurst.

76
TO JAMES LOGAN

London 10th 1m [March] 1703/4.

James
I hope ere now, my Son & Lt Govr are arrived.[1] This comes, by Ed: shippin & N. Puckle, To whom I referr thee, as to Generalls, & common news, & the Prints that come with them.[2] And in the first place know, that I have received none from thee since I writt largely to thee, by way of Barbados & Antego ~~& Ne England~~, and Since that, a shorter to the Council & so to thee {by way of new England},[3] duplicats of wch goe now — and I hope & please my Selfe to think, you will be quicken'd to show your selves men in that affaire, to witt of Quarys & his few venommous adhearants proceedings agst the Govermt. for if you Could longer endure thos contempts, which I take to be a betraying of the rights of the people, as well as mine & my Posteritys. I have made good use of the Defence thou sentst me, the Councils Letter, & of passages out of thine, much to the purpose;[4] & the very Lords Commrs are at last come to dislike his busy & turbulent proceedings; & I hope for a lettr (next week, to send by this, or the next oportunity to N. york, in 14 or 20 days time) from

that borde, to repremand his behaviour;[5] haveing Convinc'd them by the Instances you gave me, of his disingenuous practices as well as injurious; as also that I have shown them, that the Countys he has seduc'd from their duty, are the only Tobacco folks, & that the only enumerated Commodity in our Country; as also, that the People of the Territorys purg'd, by their address to the {late} King anno 1699/700[6] the Colony from Col: Quarys imputations upon {us about} Trade, & who also anno 1684, did by their addresses to the Kg & Duke[7] highly express their Satisfaction in me & their Union with the upper Countys (& wch was indeed their seeking) ~~and long so continnued~~, returning their humble thanks to both for sending them so kinde a Landlord, & so good a Governour and therfore to Quarrys foul treatm^{t}. & the Protection he brags ~~of~~ there, he has here, I owe that great defection, thos poor people have been lead into of late. In short, I am more likely to keep my Goverm^{t} than ever, or to have some equivalent for it; and take this from me, *that if you do but the Queen Justice in her Revenue & discountenance illegall Trade, and allow the admirallty their jurisdiction so farr as agrees with the atturny Generall*^{s} Opinion, I sent you,[8] ~~&~~ you will not be molested hence, but protected; this the *Ministery* assures me here. and I do *require* it of the Lt Govr the Councill & Magistrates, that they maintaine, to the utmost, the powrs of my Graunt, & the authority of the laws; and iff Quary or any of his rude & ungratefull Gang, offer to invade or affront them, that they feel the Smart of them. His being an officer {in the Revenu} shall not exempt him from Correction, or support him in his seditious & factious practices with *Impunity.* I have perusd thy letter to Ld. Cornberry,[9] & bateing[10] thy Conformity to S. J.^{s} [11] ill example (tho he more Justifyable, ~~Let~~ being under his Goverm^{t}) I like it well, & thy *Zeale* as well as *argum*^{ts} and I say, *Goe on.* I am to send a Coppy of Q.^{s} & his packt Vestrys address,[12] to the Ld^{s}, wch Ld Clarendon gives me from his Sons, if not that ~~he had from~~ his son sent him,[13] for they are asham'd at hearing of so impudent a thing. I could almost send orders to have him prosecuted with the utmost Rigour, & if I can finde encouragem^{t} from the learned in the law here, that I{t} may be done to purpose, I think to do it per this or next oportunity. wch keep to thy Selfe till thou hearst more of it. ~~The~~ My Duplicat to the Council of the 31. 10^{m} [14] that is enclosed with thine, is not directed to the Council, through hast, being ready to take horse upon a journy; do thou supply {it,} & write for the Council of Pennsylvania & Territorys, & give it them as from me.

For w^{m} Rakestraws affaire,[15] If I can finde time, I will write to him, however; positively lett the Case be heard fairly, & See where & how it comes to pinch; {1.} if it was done by my Order? if not, by whose? & let them make him Satisfaction. {2} for that I must {ever} do it, for other mens injustice & partiality is {hard;} ~~If I am to do something, I did through oportunity, I should very hardly be brought to it.~~ I leave it to the Borde of Propriety to quiet him from further noize & Squabble: but one thing take with thee, That l~~and~~ott, my Cos. Markham has almost agst his house,[16] I will not allow him nor any body else, & had rather pay Rakestraw the vallue of his Claime as worth, when I gave it him (or the mans in whose right or place he came)[17] & the Interest of it, to this Day; {tho} [illegible deletion] Colonel Mark. & he once agreed it; look into that. & keep minutes of all that passes, that your offers & carriage to him may Justify you, if he comes hither to ~~b~~Clamour as, he threatens or employs a Relation he has here. Casper Hoodt & John Warder[18] have writt to me about their thirds; I am content to return them, takeing a little now & a little then; I forgot the quantum.[19] pray call to minde Richard Bainhams[20] Sale to me of 300 acres of land he bought of wm. Biddle; The writeings I left with thee and I desire a Claime may be made of it upon wm Biddle; a good Support of mine upon the Island:[21] That out of that I may be Satisfyd for the half I allowed him for his, wifes, & sons & daughters life.[22] make the best, Since those 300 acres, where they were sold, (& w. B.[23] was one of the Com^{rs} of allotment) viz, Rancocus Creek,[24] would now {be} worth 2 if not 300^{l}. Make all the returns thou canst to me, but of my own, not my daughters, as unhappily {thou} Sentst them word; but withall, pray see that the atturneys there[25] do {returne} discreetly & expeditiously—or I may pay the reckoning of their weakness. lessen interest as thou payst, with them pray, I have a good opinion of their honesty & love to me. I hear not a word about land improvem^{ts} at Pennsberry but of divers, of the declineing condition of {it}, notwithstanding the mony I layd out, w^{n} there, to help it. Also that John[26] works to his Trade, & yet has great wages of me; w^{t} {if} 20, or 30 Servants were under him at the hard labour of Tobacco planting in Maryland or Virginia, would be an exceeding Sallery. but this may be only noize, & illwill. for I love him & Mary. I am at a loss till I hear from you, How my Dep^{t} Govr [27] is received, as also my poor Boy: for methinks their arrivall ought to give you quiet, & Silence the objections of your base enimys for {an} approved Gover^{r} I offerd the Lords Com^{rs} tother day, either that we might be bought out, or have Liberty to buy out our *turbulant* churchmen, & they wish it were so, the latter they sayd. I desired them to forward it, & I assured them I would finde 4 among {us} that could & would do it. They are throughly apprised of your hardship[s] & so are greater Persons, & Quarry will have a rebuke by this oportunity or wth the new york Convoy from that bord, as before noted.[28] I have further Enquired about the hatts sent to honest Gr. owen & thy selfe,[29] and they were the best of Beavers now worne, & I remember to have open'd the Box on purpose to see them & w^{t} Hats he sent for Serv^{ts}, and I ware[30] no better than they appear'd to me to have been; and I am Satisfyed there has been foul play, wch is an abominable thing, whereever it has been.

I had a Letter from the Lds Com^{rs} for Trade &c: upon occasion of one from Sr Tho: Lawrence,[31] that vox et preteria nihil,[32] complaining of Contemptuous expressions us'd by T. Story in publick meetings agst Baptisme & the Lords Supper {in Maryland last Generall meeting}; a Silly knight, tho I hope it comes of officious weakness the Talent of that Gentleman, with some Malice, rather than an unnecessary attack, or in irreverent terms. I never heeded it, only sayd, if that Gentleman had sence enough for his office, he might have known his Tale was no part of it: & that the Rudeness & perpetual Clamour {& revileing} of G. K.[33] and the rest of the drunken Crew of Priests in those parts, in their Pulpits, with publick Challenges besides, gave occasion for w^{t} past. that he was a Discreet, & temperat man, & did not use to exceed in his retorts or returns. But tis childrens work to provoak a Combat & then Cry out that such an beats them. I hopt they were not a Committe of Conscience, nor Religion, & that it showd the shallowness of the Gentleman that playd the busybody in it. However, let Gr. Owen mention this to Thomas, least time faile me. tho I took phisick to day, & hop't for privacy twenty people of quality have broak in upon me, & they say the ships will sale in 2 days. If I can send the newspapers I will. J. Ash I have been extreamly Civil to, but the Lords Proprietarys will do nothing without hearing first from tother side; so that he is under a distracting disapointm^{t}. He is an ingenuous man, very sharp & for that reason quick, & too Strickt, nice & uneasy. poor man, he was yesterday a dying; but hope he is better tonight. I wish him well through this world to a better. Ben. Furley[34] writt lately to me from Holland as if difficulty were made about assigning him his front & high street lott, wch if any, was on Schoolkill Side. was his purchass before the 2^{m} 1682; if so, aright else not, for the 100 lots or shares, were up, to whom only the town lots were Graunted. also I promest him or his wife rather lying in at that time, that each of her Boys should have a lott;[35] let them so soon as I send their names, a lott of 25 or 30, or 40 foot, next them already entituled by purchass among the five hundred acres purchassers. Forget not Tace Sowle,[36] our only Stationer, now, as well as printer, to countenance her atturny in takeing up her land, in right of her father, wch was his Gift to her. also pray Say something to the Churchills about their forty pd. Cargoe.[37]

there is one J. Lask or Lisk[38] thy Countryman, or Fathers, Highly recommended by Robert & David Barclay,[39] & their Uncle Gilbert Mollison,[40] a solid frd in town, as are the other two for their time, as an ingenious man, somew^{t} of a Scholler, a Civilian[41] too, but a Good writer & bred much of a Merchant, I would have him in thy office, or in the [rece]ipt of quitrents, or what may be worth him fifty pds per annum & Countenance to boot. He may be usefull. pray be regardfull to him, & direct him as to persons & things being a Strainger. pray w^{t} comes of James claypoles debt,[42] my Cosen Silas's Bro^{r} in law in East Jersys purchass.[43] pray be very mindfull of my Jersy lands, & remember my last ab^t the old Kgs[44] Graunt to me at Pennsberry. Inquire of Bass & look over a paper in the nature of a Cirtificat of Survey Dan. Leeds gave or sent me, or the Capt the Collector that was at Burlington, about my two Proprietys. What did young Cox[45] at Salem; be full pray on these points. we hear nothing of the Pennsberry Gally yet.[46] I earnestly desire our folk would make their Tobacco more Correctly, or give it over, for we loose intollerably by it, besides the great dishonour to our Country—Remember poor Johnne, the little american, according to w^t I writt both of his Grandfathers lott & land & w^t I gave him, in my former lett^rs.[47] I will have no more Banck lotts dispos'd off, nor Keys yet made into the river, without my speciall & fresh leave, for reasons Justifyable. Tell my son I mett my wife & his at young S. Tillys[48] marriage near Guildford[49] & then they were well, & by 2 lett^rs since their returne [Guily] & Sprg^t [50] are well from their agues, & little bille so too, & the Spark of them all; & my poor little ones also well, & great love among the Children. I beseech God encrease it every where more abundantly, for the want of it will Smite the Earth with a Curse, if People will not fear love & obey. Jacob Simcock[51] writt to me about mony due, or Interest. His Father ne[v]er desired, but plainly & positively before him [&] others, he expected nor would have any Interest, & therfore let Jacob know it. wth my l[ove to] him & his & Mo^r & Fa^r George Meris. Salute me to all Frds as if named, the {Council &} Magistrates & officers & Inhabitants that behave discreetly. I send thee a Coppy of my Memorial the Lords Com^rs desired of me & w^t I would have them write to C. Q.[52] a Duplicat of all this to thee & Lt Govr & my son, will Goe by Cock or Robertson.[53] If I have time, may add more, but for fear of loosing the opertunity, N. Puckle lying at Portsmouth[54] for a wind, Close this, with hearty good wishes for thy true prosperity, & that wisdom may guide thee, that wisdom wch is Gentle & easy to be Entreated, for it comes from above, & will outlive all the false wisdom of this low & miserable world, being

thy reall Friend.
Wm Penn

The Friend that made the seals says that he will prove before the most Skilfull that there is no manner of fault in them thô he fears some in the manner of Impressing. Therefore look well to that[55]

Lond. 8 2^m [April] 1704[56]

I am grieved to think that ever You gave way to any other Affirmation than that appointed by Law in the Province[57] by which You have given away a most tender point not easily recoverable My regard to this Q^n is Known almost to a Partiality; but I shall never obey her Letters against Laws unto w^h She may be drawn by Interested Persons or those that would make their Court at other Mens Cost & go upon private Piques. But the great Blower up of these Coals the Bp. of L.[58]

is himself under humiliations. However pray use thy utmost Wits to get Intelligence of the Motions of our Enemies there in their Designes & what Correspondencies they hold at N. Yk. Virg: & Maryld & communicate them to Me with the quickest & safest Opportunities.

10 5m [July] 1704[59]

I am larger by this opertunity by another hand.[60] I hear no thing From Bar[bado]es, Jamaica, or Carolina &c: n[o]r had a penny thence Since [t]hyn of 10br [61] nor any lettr from thee. a letter goes from the Council o[f] Trade &c: to Colonel Q.[62] to Quell his fury & exhort to moderation at large, & perticulerly to respec[t] the Govermt & Magistracy. I have nothing else new. see wt I have w[r]itt to S.C. & E.S.[63] & my son will show thee his & so the {Dp} Goverr.[64] vale.

ALS. Penn Papers, Penn Family to James Logan, HSP. (Not filmed.) Docketed: The Proprietor to J. L. | dat. 10 1 month 1703/4 per E Shippen. The postcripts of 8 Apr. and 10 July have been taken from a copy in the Logan Papers, HSP (*Micro.* 11:178), which is docketed in Logan's hand: Proprietor 10. 1 month 1703/4 | 8. 2 month & | 10. 5mo. 1704.

1. William Penn, Jr., and John Evans arrived in Pennsylvania on 2 Feb. 1704. Docs. 73, n. 1; 74.

2. See also WP's letter to Nathaniel Puckle, 8 Apr. 1704. *Micro.* 11:221.

3. Probably WP's letters of 31 Dec. 1703. Doc. 71; *Micro.* 11:136.

4. For the Council's letter to WP, see doc. 66; for "An Abstract of Divers Letters received from Pensilvania, giving a Account of the uneasy and uncomfortable Circumstances of the People & Government of that Province, through the Practices of Robrt Quarry, Surveyor of the Customs there, & some Adherents" (22 Dec. 1703), see *Micro.* 10:839 and *CSPC, 1702-1703*, pp. 897-902.

5. Council of Trade and Plantations to Col. Quary, 11 May 1704 (*CSPC, 1704-1705*, p. 123); doc. 92, n. 18; see also James Logan's comment on this (*Micro.* 12:005).

6. WP is probably referring to the address of the General Assembly in Feb. 1700. *PWP*, 3:584.

7. These addresses to Charles II and the duke of York have not been found. Possibly WP is referring to the petition he received from the Lower Counties for union with Pennsylvania in 1682. *PWP*, 2:318-19.

8. See doc. 47.

9. This letter has not been found.

10. Abating or excepting. *OED*.

11. Samuel Jennings became councilor to Lord Cornbury, royal governor of New York, and first governor of New Jersey after that colony had fallen to the crown. Pomfret, *West New Jersey*, pp. 214-15.

12. See doc. 71, n. 6.

13. On Lord Cornbury's father, the earl of Clarendon, see doc. 56, n. 80; see also Clarendon's letter to Quary, 17 Feb. 1704, Chew Family Papers, HSP.

14. See doc. 71.

15. See doc. 56, n. 34.

16. William Markham's lot, fronting Market and Second Sts., was very close to William Rakestraw's lot in the same block, fronting Chestnut St. between Second and Third Sts. *PMHB*, 80:198.

17. Rakestraw had purchased from Philip Ford 2500 acres in Pennsylvania that had originally been assigned to Robert King, who also had been assigned a 51-foot city lot. Unaware of Rakestraw's purchase, WP mistakenly sold most of the city lot. In 1690 the property commissioners had granted Rakestraw a 100-foot bank lot at the northern end of town. *PA*, 2d ser., 19:488.

18. Caspar Hoodt's and John Warder's letter to WP has not been found. Hoodt (d. 1732) of Helmershausen in Hesse, Germany, immigrated to Pennsylvania, where he became a Quaker and was naturalized in 1701. Warder (d. 1711) was a Quaker clay

pipemaker from Philadelphia. Hinshaw, 2:376, 432; *PMHB*, 18:121; 54:105; *Micro.* 9:333; doc. 165; Phila. Will Bk. E, #301.

19. Amount.

20. Richard Beaumont alias Bainham, a weaver of London, had purchased 300 acres on Rancocas Creek, N.J., from William Biddle. WP bought this land, valued at £25, with £10 or £15 as downpayment. Beaumont's widow asked WP to pay the remainder, and he in turn asked his secretary to find documentation of the transaction. Logan only found Biddle's lease, and the matter was left unresolved. *Micro.* 12:229, 535; docs. 97, 156; William Nelson, ed., *Patents and Deeds and Other Early Records of New Jersey, 1664-1703* (1899; reprint, Baltimore, 1982), p. 400.

21. For the ongoing dispute about Biddle's island, see doc. 56, n. 45; 154, text at n. 50.

22. Sarah Smith Kemp Biddle was the wife of William Biddle, whose children were William Biddle, Jr. (1669-1743), and Sarah Biddle Righton Plumstead (1678-1705). *PMHB*, 14:365-66, 369, 374-77.

23. William Biddle.

24. Rancocas Creek flows into the Delaware from the Jersey side, about midway between Philadelphia and Burlington.

25. James Logan and Samuel Carpenter acted as William Aubrey's attorneys in Pennsylvania.

26. John Sotcher and his wife, Mary, formerly maid to Hannah Callowhill Penn, were stewards at Pennsbury. For Logan's positive report on Sotcher's land improvements at Pennsbury, see *Micro.* 11:369.

27. John Evans.

28. See n. 5, above.

29. See doc. 56, text at n. 85.

30. Wear.

31. See William Popple, Jr., to WP, 12 Jan. 1704 (*Micro.* 11:143); and Sir Thomas Lawrence (c. 1645-1714), secretary of Maryland, to the Board of Trade, 25 Oct. 1703 (*CSPC, 1702-1703*, p. 767). Edward C. Papenfuse et al., eds., *A Biographical Dictionary of the Maryland Legislature, 1635-1789* (Baltimore, 1985).

32. "A voice and nothing more," a windbag.

33. George Keith.

34. Benjamin Furly, an English Quaker merchant in Rotterdam, was WP's agent in promoting Pennsylvania on the continent; he bought 5000 acres in the colony in Nov. 1682, too late to entitle him to the privileges granted to the First Purchasers. Furly's letter of complaint to WP has not been found. *PWP*, 2:30n, 566-67, 597n; William I. Hull, *Benjamin Furly and Quakerism in Rotterdam* (Lancaster, Pa., 1941), pp. 30-31; *William Penn and the Dutch Quaker Migration for Pennsylvania* (Swarthmore, Pa., 1935), pp. 339-40.

35. Benjamin Furly's first wife was Dorothy Grainge, who had three sons before she died in 1691: Benjohan (b. 1681), John, and Arent. Hull, *Benjamin Furly*, pp. 30-31.

36. Tace Sowle (d. 1749), daughter of the London printer Andrew Sowle, married London printer Thomas Raylton in 1706. In 1730 she conveyed to her nephews a deed for 1000 acres purchased by her father in 1682. *PMHB*, 62:478-79; *JFHS*, 50:103; Smith, 2:475; Digests of Quaker Records, London and Middx, GSP.

37. Awnsham and John Churchill had sent books to Pennsylvania for sale in 1700. When WP returned to England in 1701, he entrusted James Logan with the sale of the remaining books. Logan corresponded with the Churchills about the sale and payment in 1704 and 1706. Doc. 86, text at nn. 44-48; James Logan Letterbook, 2:41, 82, HSP; Edwin Wolf II, "A Parcel of Books for the Province," *PMHB*, 89:428-46.

38. John Lisk, or Leske, the son of a Quaker merchant in Aberdeen, went instead to Arkhangelsk (Archangel), the Russian seaport; he probably came to Pennsylvania later, but Logan never employed him. Doc. 91, text at n. 44; *Micro.* 12:005; Hinshaw, 2:445.

39. David (b. 1683) and Robert (b. 1673) Barclay were the sons of Robert Barclay, the leading Scottish Quaker of his day and a friend of WP. Their mother was Christian Molleson Barclay (1648-1690). The young Robert Barclay became an important voice in the discussion about oaths among Quakers in England and Scotland. *PWP*, 2:25n; Braithwaite, *Second Period*, pp. 189, 198, 204, 448; Digests of Quaker Records, Scotland, GSP.

40. Gilbert Molleson, the brother of Christian Molleson Barclay, had moved to London by 1697. Braithwaite, *Second Period*, p. 446; Digests of Quaker Records, Scotland; London and Middx., GSP.

41. An expert in civil or Roman law.

42. See doc. 38, n. 18.

43. Richard Stockton, Jr. See doc. 33, n. 17.

44. Probably Tammany. See doc. 38, n. 25.

45. Daniel Cox, Jr.

46. James Logan had shipped flour, bread, tobacco, and beer in the *Pennsbury Galley* to Barbados in Nov. 1703. *PMHB*, 78:155.

47. Thomas Callowhill had designated John Penn as the heir to his Pennsylvania properties. See *Micro.* 11:240; doc. 199, n. 10.

48. Samuel Tilly, or Tully, of Shipley, Sus., married Jane Constable (d. 1719) at Guildford Monthly Meeting on 8 Mar. 1704. Digests of Quaker Records, Sus. and Sur., London and Middx.

49. Guildford, Sur., 28 miles southwest of London.

50. Gulielma and Springett Penn.

51. Jacob Simcock of Chester Co., the second son of John Simcock (d. 1703) and his wife, Elizabeth, married Alice Maris (1660-1726), eldest daughter of George Maris (1632-1705). Family notes, GSP.

52. For WP's memorial to the Board of Trade about accusations by Col. Quary, see doc. 77.

53. The duplicates apparently carried by Capt. Cock, since WP sent a later letter to James Logan (12 Aug. 1704) with Capt. Robertson. *Micro.* 11:324.

54. Portsmouth, a seaport on the English Channel.

55. This postscript is not in WP's hand on either the Penn Papers copy or *Micro.* 11:178 (see provenance note, above).

56. This postscript, which is not in WP's hand, is taken from *Micro.* 11:178.

57. See doc. 54, nn. 1-3.

58. The bishop of London, Henry Compton.

59. The rest of the document is not in WP's hand.

60. Probably doc. 81.

61. For James Logan's letter of 5 Dec. 1703, see doc. 69.

62. See n. 5, above.

63. Samuel Carpenter and Edward Shippen.

64. WP's letters to Samuel Carpenter; Edward Shippen; WP, Jr.; and John Evans have not been found.

77
TO THE BOARD OF TRADE

[13 March 1704]

A brief Memorial of several Matters of Complaint against Col: Quarry & Others, more largely exprest in the Pacquet laid before You,[1] & my humble Request thereupon.

{1.} That He has aggravated Divers Things against Us in reference to the Laws of Trade & Navigation, either where the Attorney Gen[l] & Judges of Engl[d] have given Their Judgments for Us,[2] or where We, for the Encouragement of Trade, & Preventing of Ruin to the Parties, have forbore an immediate confiscation of Ships, meerly upon Clearings or Registry by Them undesignedly left behind, They giving sufficient Security for Ships & Cargo[s,] with all Demands & Damages.

{2.} That, when upon His Complaint of the want of a Militia, & that People were tried for Life without Oaths, Coll: Hamilton, to accommodate that Matter, gave Comission for raising a Militia, & to such Judges as could take Oaths to try by Juries that were of the same Sentiments, He or His Adherents as strenuously discouraged what they had before complained of, least that Occasion they took against the Government should thereby be removed.
{3.} That He has manifestly endeavoured to disaffect the Lower Counties with the Upper, thô they first desired the Union, to the great Disorder of the Publick & unspeakable Prejudices to me & my Family, since they generally refuse to pay their Quit-rents, thô some are very many Years in Arrear; Who, no longer since then 99, were the People that in an Address to the late K: William vindicated the Province against Col: Quarys Suggestions of Illegal Trade,[3] & among whom (if any) it must needs have laid, they being the great Tobacco-planters under that Government. But I must own that when I prest the Law we made at that time against Illegal Trade,[4] so much aggravated by that Gentleman, they began to sowr to me, which was heightenend by him, saying, I was too strait to Trade, for he even told me so himself on that Occasion; thô there was no other way to prevent what he had complained of, in so wilde a Bay & so full of Creeks as that of Delaware.
{4.} Nor is this enough to content Him & his Secret Agent Moor,[5] who in good Measure has had his Bread from Me, & that at the Instance of Col: Qu[y] too; but not having the Patience of staying till he received an Account how Matters went between this Board & My self relating to the Government, by way of Anticipation at the head of his pack'd Vestry complemented the L[d] Cornbury with an Address,[6] wherein they hope by their Applications they shall prevail with the Queen to extend the Limits (as they phrase it) of his Government over them, that they may enjoy the same Blessings with others under his Authority. A Passage One would not exspect from those that pretend to be lights & Examples of Obedience & Submission to Government.
These Things I complain of, & I hope You think I ought to do so. Redresse is in Your Power, & therefore I beseech You effectually to apply It, be it for Reprehension or Advice or both, that We may no longer be troubled with their little Spites to serve Privat Turns; Of which I desire a Dupplicate; I am in all Sincerity

Your Respectfull Friend
Wm Penn

Lond: the 13 1m (c. March) 1703/4

LS. CO 5/1262, PRO. (*Micro.* 11:199.) Docketed: Pennsylvania | Memorial from M[r] Penn | Containing matters of Complaint | against Col[o] Quary and | others | Rec'd | Read 13th March: 1703/4. The editors have moved the marginal numbers into the text and enclosed them in braces.

1. This packet probably contained the memorials that WP had submitted to the Board of Trade in 1702 when he countered Quary's charges that Pennsylvania mismanaged its government, violated the navigation laws, and defrauded the crown of revenue. See docs. 43-44; *Micro.* 10:091, 112, 259, 293, 297, 319, 325, 431. WP reactivated his criticism of Quary after receiving reports from Pennsylvania about Quary's performance as judge of the admiralty court. See, for example, doc. 66.

2. See doc. 47. Attorney General Edward Northey later submitted a complete review of Pennsylvania's laws in Oct. 1704. *CSPC, 1704-1705*, pp. 276-81.

3. WP is probably referring to the Assembly's letter of 9 February 1700, which was signed by representatives of the Lower Counties as well as Pennsylvania. *PWP*, 3:584.

4. See doc. 44, n. 2.

5. John Moore.

6. See doc. 71, nn. 6-7.

78
FROM JAMES LOGAN

14 1st mo [March] 1703/4

The Original of the Above[1] is Sent by Way of Barbados with a Copy of a former by the Centurion via Boston[2] by Whom returning to Boston having Struck on a Rock going out this is Intended if it can Possibly reach wch I must Suspect and therefore Shall not Enlarge. This Morning John Guy Whom I mention'd in my former per Said frigat is come in from Carolina and he Shall be dispatched thither with all Expedition again to get a Loading (according to former Advices) and Sail With the Virginia Fleet for England. I am Every day more out of heart through the Great discouragemts we Lie under here the Countrey has no Money What little there is The Traders in town have it Wheat the Farmars dependance bears no Price and bread & flower is a very drugg Notwithstanding so high in demand 3 Years agoe Things are now at Such a Stand that I know not Whethers to Receive thy dues or not Seeing they can by no means be had in Money this Morning We have also the account of the great Storm in England[3] and the Losses by it, another Blow! Last Week Thy Son, J Momp.[4] and My Self went to Pensbury to Meet 100 Indians of wch 9 were Kings Oppewounumhook the Chief with his Neighbours[5] Who came thither to Congratulate thy Sons Arival presenting 9 Belts of Wampom for a Ratification of Peace &t and had Returns accordingly he Staid there with the Judge Waiting Cl Plumsteads[6] Wedding with Sarah Righton formerly Biddle I am as before

Thine &t
JL

by way of Boston with a Copy of the former

LBC. James Logan Letterbook, HSP. (*Micro.* 11:207.)

1. Logan is referring to doc. 74, a copy of which he enclosed with this letter.
2. See doc. 69.

3. On 27 Nov. 1703 a storm hit England, Wales, and Holland particularly hard; see Luttrell, 5:363-64, 366, 367, 369, 376.

4. Judge Roger Mompesson.

5. No official account of this meeting with the Indians has been found. Oppemenyhook was a Delaware Indian chief at Lehigh. *Minutes of the Provincial Council*, 2:26; Charles A. Hanna, *The Wilderness Trail* (New York, 1911), 1:93, 100.

6. Clement Plumstead (1680-1745), merchant of Philadelphia, served repeatedly as assemblyman for Phila. Co. in the 1710s and as councilor in 1720; he was elected mayor of Philadelphia in 1723, 1736, and 1741. He married the widow Sarah Biddle Righton in 1703. *PMHB*, 14:226, 274-76; Phila. Will Bk. G, #163.

79
TO THE HALF-YEARLY MEETING IN DUBLIN

[26 April 1704]

My dearly beloved Friend's & Brethren
In the Covenant of light & life I very dearly salute you, remembring the sweet fellowship the Lord gave Us togather when I was last in that Kingdom,[1] both in the famous Meetings of worship & discipline, & also in our ordinary Conversation, for it was a time of times, never forgoten by me, Neither will I hope to the End, this has Made Me desirous in the Will of God to se your faces once More, & did Not Many Excercises Interpose, you had seen Me Instead of this Epistle at your Next half yearly Meeting, for I Can truly say I love you in that devine love w[ch] hath Made us a people, that were No-people, & hath gathered us into the Communion of saints the Nearest & dearest of all relations, where I pray God preserve us to the End, & As we hould the head C{h}rist Jesus the fountain & fulness thereof, there will be No fear of our Endureing to the End, O! my breathren If we hould the head we shall all hould our places in the living body to his praise & our Edification, & Comfort Mutually, there will be No Envy, hatred, surmises or self seekings among us, & truely where C{h}rists yoke Burthen & Cross are born there Can be No roome for such things, but humility, Love, & holiness will prevail, the heavenly Ornaments of the Redeemed & begotten of God, w[ch] In the End will outshine All the Glory of this World, & will distinguish & Dignifie God's people in the Earth, wherefore My Dear Friends & Brethren wait Dayly to feel the power of the pretious truth that you proffess that you May be preserved from the Evill of the World, & Also from Inordinate desires after the good things thereof, that you May have Dominion & raign In the Kingdom of God over all sublunary things, for there is safety No where Elce; the Brethren of this Nation Are Generally well, & truth May be said to prosper in divers places, Many Come to hear, & Not A few Are Affected & some stay With us, so that we have Caus to say the harvest is great, & I wish I Could say the labourers were Not A few, but why should It be so, sence that w[ch] Makes ~~a~~A good Friend will Make A good Minister, I Cannot well

forbear saying that I believe the time is At hand, that the Lord will raise More Preachers, & yet perhaps there May be Less preaching, for I waight for the Day that the Meetings of the Lords people shall Be filld with his Prophets by the Growings of the Word in the hearts of his Children, & babes shall tell of his Goodness, the Lord be good & great in the Midst of you severall places with shewes of Joy & peace In your bosoms, saith My soul who Am

Your Friend & Brother in the faith Love
& patience of the Kingdom of Christ.
Willm Penn

London 26th 2mo 1704

I know Many Brethren here[2] would be glad to se some of your Meeting at ours.

My dear love in A particular manner to Publick friends & Elders More Especially to My Antient Worthy Friend & Brother Wm Edmundson.[3]

Copy. Dublin Yearly Meeting Historical Collection, Friends Library, Dublin. (*Micro.* 11:227.) Docketed: Coppy of Wm Penns | Epistle to Friends in | Ireland 26th 2mo 1704. Further docketed: Wm Penn's Epistle | to Friends in Ireland | 2-26-1704.

1. WP had spent the summer of 1698 in Ireland. See *PWP,* 3:543.
2. London.
3. William Edmondson, or Edmundson (1627-1712), a prominent Irish Quaker, lived at Rosenalles, about 50 miles from Dublin. *PWP,* 3:292n.

80
TO SIR WILLIAM TRUMBULL

Worminghurst 3d 3m (May) 1704

Honored Friend[1]

I venture this to ask how poor Lady Trumbol[2] does, in whose wellfaire I take the share & concerne of a friend, if that be not too free a term to one that has been, & they say may be secretary of State if he will: but others say, tis H. Boyle,[3] & then I guess easily who will be Chancellor of the Exchequer. for our Forraign affaires, some will have it they are not so shineing as we wish; that the Duke of Savoy[4] will at last play an other game, & that Portugal is too unprovided for our forwardness,[5] & so the Spanish K.[6] has time by the foretop. a Clowd is riseing in Scotland, the Queen refuses all addresses from any of that nation in Town, till Seafield [the] Chancellor[7] returns, or Sends her an acct of some instructions she gave him to gage the council & members of the Parl of [that] Kingdom, as to the Succession & a Sess,[8] as they call it; which I Suppose will be wth her quickly, if not arriv'd. The Plag[ue] of Lampoons walks by night, & fresh arrows dayly fly the Streets; what sha[ll] we end in? No further removes, at present, talkt of. H. St Johns[9] has not Bl. house,[10] but a new & fine house is prepareing, at the Qs cost. I mett him at H. Boyls tother morning, where I Congratulated his humility, that ⅕ part of Bl. contented his youthfull ambition well, It is all a fool to east hamsted[11] & worminghurst, & wch is worse tis a lye & a fatal Snare; Farewell dear friend, lett our originall, B[eing] duty & end, be the first & last of our meditations, & lett the middle Corrispond with both ends, & we shall be in our lives {all} of a piece. I am with due re[g]ards to Lady & selfe

Thy Faithfull Friend
Wm Penn

ALS. Trumbull Miscellaneous Correspondence, A.R.I. Hill, Esq., and the Trustees of the Downshire Settled Estates, Berkshire Record Office, Reading. (*Micro.* 11:235.)

1. Sir William Trumbull (1639-1716), formerly lord of the treasury in 1694 and secretary of state in 1695, retired from active political life in 1698 and declined offers to serve on the lord high admiral's council (1702) or to become secretary of state again (1704). *PWP,* 3:76n; *DNB.*

2. Lady Katherine Trumbull, daughter of Sir Charles Cotterell, died in July 1704. *DNB.*

3. Henry Boyle (d. 1725)—baron Carleton of Carleton, Yorks., after 1714—had been appointed lord of the treasury in 1699, chancellor of the exchequer in 1701, and lord treasurer of Ireland in 1704. He became principle secretary of state in 1708-10. *DNB.*

4. Victor Amadeus (1665-1732), duke of Savoy and later king of Sicily (1713), had joined England's allies against France in Oct. 1703. The English feared that because his allegiance to their cause was highly opportunistic he was likely to change sides again. George Macaulay Trevelyan, *England Under Queen Anne: Blenheim* (London, 1930), pp. 116-17, 304-7, 342.

5. In May 1703 Portugal had joined the Grand Alliance against France, and Secretary of State Nottingham wanted to take advantage of this alliance by sending an English army to invade Spain. WP seems to be unaware that by May 1704 the English had decided to put their chief effort into defending Leopold I of Austria from French attack, and that the duke of Marlborough was on his way to Germany, where he would fight the French at Blenheim in Aug. 1704. Ibid., 1:298-304, 335-36, 344-46.

6. Philip V (1683-1746), grandson of Louis XIV, had ascended the Spanish throne in 1700 and was supported by the French. The Grand Alliance supported the Austrian archduke Charles (1685-1740) as King Carlos III of Spain; he was now in Portugal, preparing to invade Spain. Edward Gregg, *Queen Anne* (London, 1980), pp. 124-26, 172.

7. James Ogilvy (1664-1730), first earl of Seafield and later (1711) fourth earl of Findlater, was the secretary of state in Scotland when Anne ascended the throne and subsequently served as the Scottish lord chancellor. Ibid., pp. 151, 201, 475.

8. Queen Anne's ministers were trying to make the Scots accept a Protestant Hanoverian succession, while the Scottish Jacobites were actively plotting to collaborate with France. In the summer of 1704 the Scottish Parliament proceeded to pass a bill of security, which separated the Scottish succession from that of the English and excluded Scotland from supporting England's wars. Ibid., p. 185.

9. Henry St. John (1678-1751), later first viscount of Bolingbroke (1712), was a protégé of both Robert Harley and the duke of Marlborough. He became secretary at war in Apr. 1704. *DNB.*

10. St. John had hoped to acquire the estate of Bucklebury, near Reading, Berks., through his marriage to Frances Winchcombe. Walter Sichel, *Bolingbroke and His Times* (New York, 1901), p. 145.

11. Easthampstead Park, Berks., was Trumbull's residence. Ibid., 3:608-9.

81
TO JAMES LOGAN

Lond. 11th 5^{m} [July] 1704

James Logan
Since thine of the 10^{m} last,[1] now 7 months agoe, not one Scrip of paper has [illegible deletion] come from thee to me, nor indeed any else, Save that {~~by w^{ch}~~} Dan: Zachery was so kinde as to intimate to me my sons & Lt Gover^{r} [2] safe arrival, by one from Is. Norris, & by Isaacs to Jo^{n} ascew;[3] wch tho very obligeing in him, & joyfull to us, yet we sowr'd a little at thee, that any body should write, & not the secretary of the place, be present enough to him selfe, to write to his principal, under th~~ose~~at extrordinary Circumstance, & upon such an occasion. But I (other ways both troubled and asham'd) & John Ascew, told them thou, as well as my son, & Lt. Gover^{r} had sent by way of Barbado's, no ship goeing from our parts, where the Pacquet boat is lookt upon the best way of conveyance, the lett^{rs} of Is. Norris being but {a} duplicats and were sent by way of Boston, where they Imagined something might prolong the man of warrs Stay, tho very Small hopes of it. In short the Silence has been so longe, by means of winter also, that it is uneasy and gives a disrepute to the Country.
I have little to say more than former letters express.

1 Conduct.

Give no just occasion for exceptions or reflections, & vallue them not where made, or thrown without a cause. but command thy temper all that is possible, in doing thy business: for in Jos. Pikes case,[4] thou hast been hardly represented to him, & sorely he is provoakt at thee, & displeas'd wth me; of which more by another hand upon the Spott. I know whence the arrow came, 'tis provoaking, but this is the Cross we are to bear, to approve ourselves xtians indeed. w^{t} ever thou doest, give no offen[ce] & be not high minded, but feare. I take the lesson to my selfe we all need an holy & dayly remembrance of it.

Col. Quarre

Letters are gone to him From the Councill of Trade & Plant^{s} [5] as also Little Perry,[6] his Support, to moderate his conduct, & carry respectfully to the Goverm^{t} & Magistracy, only being careful ab^{t} his Station. I promest to write to you to be as discreet on y^{r} part, & carefull not to winck at forbidden trade. wch I have done to Gover^{r} & Council, & perticuler members, and renew my Caution by this to thee.

Banck Lotts.

Till further orders, I will have no Banck Lotts sold. & never the 20^{ss} per lott, on any acc^{t}. pray minde this. I have good reasons for it at present.

Jo: Lumby & owners

There is one John Pecket & Company concerned with or in Lumbys ship & Cargoe, that want some mony there in prosecution of Colonel Quarre, that will pay me here. furnish them there, twill be but a small matter, perhaps 20—or thirty pds. be it wt it will; remembring {upon Bills} that the Queen by these Proclamations now Sent thee,[7] has Settled the [illegible deletion] Coyne, at 25l per Ct according to the New-England Standard, & would have done it to Eng. Starling, but for the late K. Ws confirming of their law of rates for mony, wch extends to all our america.

Rent Role.

I am at so great a want for a Rent-Role[8] that I must press it; that if not Sent already, as in thy last thou promest me, per thy next, faile not to send it me per first vessel that comes away from those parts.

Goverrs Spannel Dog.

Consellor Panel, & Docr Hedgberry, almost Clamour on Peter Evans,[9] the Govrs Cosin & Clark, ~~which~~[?] Who Stole him away, that I desire thee to advise them to Send him over, or to make a good apology for not doing it.

open trade

I am assured of an open trade wth the Spaniards as much as ever in the west indias, if not already opened: not that Risks are not run as before the warr, but that there Shall be none on our parts from our Selves. I read the draught.

Skins & Furs

I have also been perticuler abt the Furs.[10] pray be not So ill used by any Body. the Skins last Sent were Sold to advantage.

Supplys.

I desire the utmost care to get a reasonable Revenue Settled for the Gover~~r~~mt & perticulerly for the Goverr &c: Our laws lye for a good Fee to the atturney Genll [11] 50 Guineas at least. I have told thee that nothing is come of the Bills of Laden[12] but wt came directly, and I wish the death of w. R. & J. M.[13] proves not a loss to me tho poor J. Mils sent me word, the goods sold pretty well, & would take Speciall care of remiting me the effects per first abt 14 days after W: Ragers's death, & dyed {himself} in 14 days I think after the date of his to me. write, as I shall, to Jonathan Dickeson[14] abt it pray.

Laws.

Be sure, the very next assembly, to lett the laws pass with the Queens name, tho under my Seal, according to Charter, the att. Genll makeing the want thereof an ugly objection agst the Confirming of them tho a good Fee will goe a great way to Clear the Scruple, if I had it to give him; for wt with the decay of Irland, half in halfe at present, & the loss of 2 ships,[15] nothing comeing from the Islands & Carolina wth 4s in the pound {here},[16] my Sons part of the estate, &, [illegible deletion] the Interest mony I have to pay,[17] I live but from hand to mouth, and hardly that.

Returning to america.

Thou pressest my returne; but alas how? tis good Sence, to save my estate here to discharge debts, & eat up wt I have there, as the best returns; but I want water to launch my vessell. Think of that; as also, if I am not worthy of a house in or neer the Town, as Gr. owens, {T. Fairmans, or Dan. Peggs,}[18] or the like (that 500^{l} that mony {or 600^{l} at most perhaps} may purchass) for my reception, & at least 500^{l} per annum to live there, besides my own rents, I have Spent all my days, mony, and pains, & Interest to a mean purpose. think of this, & impart it. They will all gett by it as well as I.

churchills Books.[19]

pray write to him, & give him some acctt of them, that he may not have reason to reflect, tho his own act, not ours.

T. Brocks wife.[20]

my father Callowhill wishes thy care would not lett him be an entire looser by his wifes death. He has been a great one upon the acc^{t} of the Country. Remember w^{t} I writt about Roberts's lott.[21]

Pennsbury

Let me not {be} put to more Charge there, but only to keep it in repaire, & that its produce may maintaine it.

Woods

I hope there is an effectuall care taken of my woods, that they be not devoured near the Citty, Especially.

Resurveys

Lett me Know pray, w^{t} is done therein, & if there has not been time enough, I hope the assembly will be so reasonable as to prolong [the] time to perfect them.[22]

{our Health}

I bless god, I and mine, are all well, or were lately so, includeing my Sons. I have writt to him, & two {L^{trs}} goe by this opertunity from his wife.[23] I Send no news. But except Germany, things Look but ill as to the warr: But the D. of Marlb. is in a great way to preserve the Empire,[24] that before was very low. I hope {my} son, in some measure, answears my okations,[25] & those he gave at parting, m[or]e especially. Do thy endeavour, I desire thee, that he may be my Comfort & honour while I live.

Seale

The engraver will Send directions, that will render that wth thee sufficient; he says it is for want of better understanding it. so with my deare love to all Frds, & the moderate of others, wth thy Selfe, & the family, I close

Thy affectionate & reall Friend
Wm Penn

my wife Salutes Frds & thee & our family

12. 5m [July] 1704

Last night came to hand thine of the 12. 12^{m} [1]703/4, & a postscript of 14. 1^{m} [26] following wch made some atonem^{t} for the long Silence we have uneasily bore, & ~~Silence~~ {reasons} for it. all that time & winde will allow me to say is, first, that I only desire to hear from thence as often as others. 2 that my heart is glad at the news of my poor Childes arrivall safe among you, & more that he does not offend, & {is} likely to be discreet. 3 that he had not only one but divers lett^{rs} for thee, single, besides Packets, one Joshuah[27] had, if not more. 4. I desire the Gover^{r} & Judge mompesson would be very large & perticuler to me in their ~~particuler~~ proper Stations, & w^{t} aimes & hints they think proper for me to take my measures by. I am glad my son sometime attends, to learn business; & pray let me know if he enclines to Stay till I come & have his wife & children to goe to him, or returne to them.

5 Keep the 2500^{l} that I order'd to S. Carp.[28] in thy own hands, if in danger there, because I would assigne it for paying off of Debts to such as {C}h~~e~~oose to have it in his hands, of wch more per next.

6. I am sorry that our people Stoop not to the Queen that Stoops so much & so kindly to me. They will I fear provoak a ruine to me & mine by the loss of the Goverm^{t} without a Proportionable Satisfaction {to me}, & a yoak upon themselves too. Those Sturd~~y~~ees, will never leave till they ketch a Tartar;[29] and must come hither to be lost in the Crowds of taller folks, to be humbled, or made plyable; for what wth the distance, & the Scarcity of mankinde {there}, they opine too much; & I am under great dissatisfaction at w^{t} thou writest {of their aversness to the union}. Since, I know their aversion to an union, now the Queen has order'd {the means of} it, will sett an ill complexion upon them towards her, at my Cost at last {& recommend their enemys}. Nay, were I better fixt in the Lower Countys, I would finde a way to dissolve the Charter so farr, but in no reall priviledge. 7 Pray let me Know why thy 2 Packets were dangerous that {were lost}? also Supply my Son Aubrey to his atturneys there.[30] 8. I fear my letters & thine have been lost by interception rather than other miscarriages. 9. I am glad the Indians were so regardfull to me, absent, as to come down to congratulate my son & present him.[31] I hope you were good Husbands towards them. 10 I hope the Gover^{r} will cure the disaffected as to Seizure, where any are so refractory as to refuse. did they think to be exempted from charge, or that I was to come thither & Spend more than they ever gave me, and returne at my own charge; for all they gave by assembly, equalls not w^{t} It cost to goe, Stay there & returne; and to maintain common right above 3000^{l} Since I came back, from a yoak the basest of them would not long suffer without Clamour.

11. I told thee ~~before~~ of opening of a Trade wth the Spanierds,[32] before thine came to hand, & thou mayst depend upon {it.} I am now goeing to Ld. Treasurer[33] about it, & Sr. P. Meddows;[34] and if {I hear} any more about it, will intimate it before I Seale; Though the Mer^{ts} & M^{rs} are gone down {& the winde faire}. Here are 7 proclamations of the Queens, Sent me by the Lords, wth a letter about the Coine,[35] wth a salvo to thy objection of precontracts too. 'tis Gen^{ll}: none of my doing, nor indeed {my} opposeing, for your Practice is

Run down by all the men of good Sence or good morralls at this Side or end of the world. My Deare Embraces to my poor Childe, the Lord direct & preserve him. my Salutes to the Govr Judge, Council, Frds, & Magistrates, and I hope the Lord will bring us to you before or by this time twelve months. I am

Thy Lovg Friend
Wm Penn

my wifes Dr. Love to my Son & rejoyces at his Safe arrival. She salutes Frds & the Goverr. thy lettr came by Portugall. a coppy Save if in thy own hand. Johnne[36] Says respects {Duty} & love to Brother.

15. 5m 1704

the 13th came thine of the 15. 3m & my Dr sons,[37] Seperate, to my Great Comfort, wch I have Sent to my Daughter,[38] tho I doubt not but she was not forgotten. we also heare the virginia fleet is in the chopps[39] of the Channell.

{20. 5m.}

I herwith Send a Coppy of the Instruction to Govrs about opening of a Trade with the Spaniards.[40] and perhaps a letter may come formally to me to send to the Goverr & Councill, as I do this abt mony.

vale WP.

pray lett not Flowr[41] send us over any news letter but wt thou makest Correct, & fitt to be publisht, wch we have made this in some measure. Vale WP.

22. 5m

Tell my Cos Markham I have his,[42] & take it very kindly from him; Its a good generall (& of some, a perticular) Vew, that is instructing. He has good sence, & I see it does not leave him. I am sorry he is not in his place. Herewith comes a fresh commission, as also a blanck Commission for an atturney Generall for I would have that virulent fellow[43] out of all places in my Govermt and dispise his frowardness, Since in vain I have so long suffer'd it. His Carriage about Capt Dun[44] is sufficient & his disputeing of my Commission to my Cosin Markham: I must say I take ill the Govrs not writeing; tis hardly Credible wth those that ask me of his Frds, and more, they think it unpardonable. my Cosin is very just to him in a discreet character, & so he is to thee also. pray consult him sometimes, & tell Colonel Evans, I would have him do so too; & in honour to him, have offerd him to be of the Councll. I shall write no more to him {(Ev)} haveing writt already twice,[45] till I hear from him. This business of the disunion Sticks with me Still. I fear twill lead to a worse thing, unless we had adjusted the matter here. wt will the Queen think after all my memorials to preserve the Govermt without a seame, to finde, & that on our Side, it is torn into. O the weakness of men! Use the utmost of thy address with the wise, the honest & the weake to accommodate things, & dont lett them make use of a charter agst me, now I keep the Govermt, at unspeable[46] charge, & att evidence, that I only graunted in the extent it has, agst our Enimys when they & I feared I should loose it. This thought, one would immagin, well layd before them, should prevaile wth them. I doubt not but I could have made disunion one branch of my Bargain to have kept the rest, had they gon into an union for the present. But—

Here is a long lettr of J. Mump. to Ch: Lawton, inclosed in a less, design'd for the vew of Ld Clarendon[47] who show'd it me {(& was the reason of his retrenchmt at last)} but not a word of me in it; as well as your newsmonger;

not a very respectfull omission, after my Civilitys, & tenderness. the last might have Sayd somthing that had lookt thankfull to me for the Care I had over them in sending over a Goverr to them. according to the Poet, If Tom such praises have—nor has he sayd any thing of my son by way of distinction, either in respect, or to denote him my Son, wch I have endeavour'd to Supply, by the word *young* in this print. for from the imperfect mention of Colonel Evans's goeing over Goverr; those two (or one of them) the Post boy & flying Post,[48] gave occsion[49] to the Nations to think the Queen had solely made him, & I lost my Govermt. but the Postman[50] handsomely Corrected it. and people might have thought without *young,* It had been so indeed, & that I was gone with him, *a blanck,* He being Call'd Goverr but I have added Lt to prevent such a Construction. I have no other letters yet from thee than wt I have mentioned. I hope by the Virginia Fleet you will all make us amends. those news papers, will come to you.

Be punctuall in my son aubreys business[51] to keep thy Credit with my poor Girll. tell my son all were well at worm. tother day.

I inclose a lettr from Ld Clarend. to his Son the Neighbour Govr [52] about Samll Bonos;[53] that if he is not yet at liberty, will, I hope, procure it. But I admire at his permissions if not proceedings at this time of day, when the Queen & Ministry show so moderate a Side towards dissenters here; & on complaint in this affaire would be very ready to resent & reprimand Such a differing Conduct. Send it to him by a discreet Frd if needfull.

I think to chide S. Vaus for his unnacctble Silence to thee abt so many accts between you. Nothing yet come Since I begun this, now 11 days agoe. the ships are ready to Saile, & the winde at North, so that I conclude with my Kinde love to all the deserveing, & dear love to my Childe (who, I hope, Studys, at least reads & takes notice of some of my excellent (as well as thy) Historys, & wt relates to Govermt). I close

Thy Loveing Frd
Wm Penn

ALS. Logan Papers, HSP. (*Micro.* 11:273.)

1. See doc. 69.

2. William Penn, Jr., and John Evans.

3. John Askew, a London merchant, was a partner of WP, Isaac Norris, and James Logan in a number of mercantile endeavors involving the transatlantic shipping of tobacco and other colonial products. Isaac Norris had written to him on 15 Feb. 1704, while James Logan's letter to Daniel Zachary is dated 14 Mar. 1704. *PMHB*, 78:156, 163-65; Isaac Norris Letterbook, 5:119-20; James Logan Letterbook, 2:39, HSP.

4. WP had granted Joseph Pike a patent for 10,000 acres of land formerly held by Mathias Vincent in Chester Co. Pike believed that this grant included ⅘ of the mining rights, which was contrary to the ⅗ customarily held by the First Purchasers. James Logan corresponded with Pike in 1705 explaining the division of the mining shares among king, proprietor, and purchasers. *PMHB*, 42:92; *Micro.* 7:696, 761; 10:782; 12:156; 14:021; doc. 30; James Logan Letterbook, 2:61-62, HSP.

5. See *CSPC, 1704-1705*, p. 123.

6. Micajah Perry.

7. See *CSPC, 1704-1705*, pp. 123, 147, 168-69, 175, 177, 188, 643.

8. Logan did prepare a new rent roll in about 1705. See Logan Papers, 2:76½, HSP.

9. Peter Evans (d. 1745), a lawyer, was elected sheriff of Phila. Co. in 1708 and was commissioned as register general in 1713. When moving to Pennsylvania, Evans—as did William Penn, Jr.—brought a dog from England that WP's associates wanted back. *Colonial Records*, 2:237, 391, 397, 473; *PMHB*, 34:254; 49:188; 57:245; *Micro.* 14:411; Drinker, *Hannah Penn*, p. 37.

10. See doc. 69.

11. Sir Edward Northey, the attorney general, completed his review of Pennsylvania's laws in Oct. 1704. *CSPC, 1704-1705*, pp. 276-81.

12. Lading, i.e., lists of goods shipped.

13. William Rogers (d. 1703) and James Mills (d. 1703) were Quaker merchants in Jamaica to whom James Logan had sent a consignment of "our Country Goods" for the account of WP in 1703. Logan Papers, James Logan Letterbook, 2:40-41, HSP; see also doc. 127, n. 19; *Micro.* 10:948; 11:236, 240; 12:005; 13:156.

14. WP's letter to Jonathan Dickinson has not been found.

15. Probably the ship *Industry* and the brigantine *Mary*. See doc. 56, n. 2.

16. See doc. 56, n. 18.

17. For WP's indebtedness to his son and son-in-law, see doc. 209.

18. For Owen's and Fairman's houses, see doc. 59, n. 7. Daniel Pegg (d. 1703), a brickmaker, had built a brick house on his 200 acres in the Northern Liberties. *PWP*, 3:325n; *PMHB*, 53:8-10.

19. See doc. 76, n. 37.

20. Joan Brock of Bristol, Bucks Co., had made an agreement with Hannah Penn in 1701 to repay a debt owed Callowhill by her previous husband, Michael Huff, who died before 1694. In 1683 Callowhill had agreed to pay the passage of Huff and Philip Russell; in return they were to take up his Pennsylvania lands and sell goods on consignment for him. They failed to settle his lands and never returned any money to him. In 1706 Callowhill granted Logan power of attorney to settle the issue. Maria Dickinson Logan Papers, HSP; Phila. Will Bk. A, #116; C, #149; *Micro.* 11:240.

21. Thomas Roberts rented Callowhill's Front St. lot. See doc. 139, n. 23; *PA*, 2d ser., 19:66.

22. In Aug. 1704 the Assembly did not consider an extension of the period for resurveying WP's land grants, but the legislators discussed a bill for regulating the actions and proceedings of the commissioners of property, surveyor general's office, and secretary's office in an effort to end some of the confusion connected with property transactions. *Votes and Proceedings*, 1(pt. 2):9.

23. WP's letter to his son and Mary Jones Penn's letters to her husband, William Penn, Jr., have not been found.

24. In 1704 the Grand Alliance was threatened militarily by French and Bavarian victories in northern Italy and on the Danube. To rescue Leopold I of Austria, John Churchill (1650-1722), first duke of Marlborough, led an allied army into Germany, joined the Austrian general Eugene of Savoy, and won a spectacular victory over the French at the battle of Blenheim on 13 Aug. 1704. David Chandler, *Marlborough as Military Commander* (New York, 1973), pp. 124-50.

25. A mistake for "expectations."

26. For those two letters, the first of which is actually dated 15 and 18 Feb.—not 12 Feb. as WP reports—see docs. 74, 78. In the following paragraphs, WP comments on these letters point by point.

27. Probably the London Quaker ship captain Joshua Guy. Digests of Quaker Records, London and Middx., GSP.

28. Probably a mistake for £200, a reference to the sum Carpenter held as a loan from the sale of Laetitia's lots. Doc. 74, n. 25.

29. An opponent too formidable to escape from or conquer. *OED*.

30. Samuel Carpenter and James Logan. William Aubrey's power of attorney was not entered in Philadelphia until 1706. See doc. 209.

31. See doc. 78, text at nn. 4-5.

32. The queen had issued instructions permitting English privateers to trade with the Spanish West Indies after 1 June 1704, in spite of the war. *CSPC, 1704-1705*, pp. 49-50, 113-114.

33. Sidney Godolphin.

34. Sir Philip Meadows (1626-1718), commissioner for taking public accounts and a member of the Board of Trade since 1696. Steele, *Colonial Policy*, pp. 20-21.

35. See *CSPC, 1704-1705*, pp. 168-69.

36. WP's son John, who was born in Pennsylvania in 1700.

37. For Logan's letter of 16 May 1704, see *Micro.* 11:236; William Penn, Jr.'s letter to his father has not been found.

38. Laetitia Penn Aubrey.

39. Entrance.

40. This enclosure has not been found. See n. 32, above; *Micro.* 11:324.

41. Probably Henry Flower, a Quaker barber, who immigrated to Philadelphia in 1683 together with his father, Enoch Flower, and uncle Seth Flower. *PWP*, 2:601n; Hannah Benner Roach, "Philadelphia Business Directory, 1690," *PGM*, 23:123-24.

42. William Markham's letter to WP has not been found. On WP's orders the Provincial Council had commissioned Markham as register general in 1703, but John Moore had refused to surrender the seal and files belonging to that office. *Minutes of the Provincial Council*, 2:121-22.

43. John Moore had served as Pennsylvania's attorney general after Paroculus Parmiter left the post in 1703. Scharf and Wescott, 2:1560.

44. Capt. John Dun was committed to jail in 1701 and held a prisoner in Philadelphia on suspicion of murder at sea. According to James Logan, the death of Lt. Gov. Hamilton in 1702 made it impossible to have the captain tried in Pennsylvania. *Micro.* 11:034; Logan Papers, 3:59, 104, HSP.

45. See *Micro.* 11:172, 174.

46. Unspeakable.

47. The letters from Roger Mompesson to Charlwood Lawton and to the earl of Clarendon have not been found.

48. Abel Roger's *Post Boy* and George Ridpath's *Flying Post* were rival newspapers: *The Post Boy*, with a circulation of 3000, was directed to Tory country gentlemen, and *The Flying Post* circulated among a Whig readership of 400. J. A. Downie, *Robert Harley and the Press: Propaganda and Puplic Opinion in the Age of Swift and Defoe* (Cambridge, 1979), pp. 7-10.

49. Occasion.

50. Jacques de Fonvive's *Post Man* appeared three times a week with a circulation of about 4000 and was therefore more successful than both *The Flying Post* and *The Post Boy*. Downie, *Harley and the Press*, pp. 7-10.

51. For WP's obligations to his son-in-law, William Aubrey, see doc. 209.

52. This enclosure has not been found.

53. The Quaker Samuel Bownas (b. 1676) was convinced when he was an apprentice in Westmorland. In the decade following 1698, he served as a traveling minister in England, Scotland, America, and Ireland. While traveling in New York, Bownas became a victim of a more tightly controlled legal system under the governorship of Lord Cornbury; he was arrested in Jamaica, Long Island, in Oct. 1702 and not released from prison until a year later. The circumstances of his imprisonment are detailed in *Account of the Life, Travels, and Christian Experiences in the Work of the Ministry of Samuel Bownas* (London, 1756; reprint, Stanford, N.Y., 1805), pp. 100-152; Braithwaite, *Second Period*, pp. 519-21.

82
FROM JAMES LOGAN

Philadia 14th 5mo [July] 1704

Honoured Governour

Opportunities now proving rare, I shall embrace all Appearances of them to inform thee of our Circumstances, thô because of their great Uncertainty I shall be brief.

Third Month last I sent per Al: Paxton in the Virginia Fleet a Pacquet,[1] with Minutes of Council and Several Papers at Large, which I hope will Come to hand, Since that time the Assembly has mett again,[2] but done nothing besides presenting to the Governour[3] a Bill for Confirmation of the Charter of Privileges, upon the Separation of the Territories, explaining all things that appear'd doubtful, their own Way, making the Annual Assemblies to Continue from Ellection to Ellection with the Power of Adjournments, new Elections upon false Returns, or Ejectmt of Members, to be intirely Within them Selves, Excluding the Governour from any Power or[4] Dissolution or Prorogation, and Prescribing the Qualifications of their Members to be by taking the Declarations directed by the Law of England to be taken by such as can not swear at all,[5] and upon this they Adjourned to the first of the 6th Month[6] after Harvest, and are in the Mean time to Proceed by Committees upon other Affairs of Importance. They have voted to raise a thousd Pounds for Publick services,[7] but Intend I doubt to sell it very dear—Judge Momp: has been here during their late sittings, and of great Service in Council but going to N York, as he Said for a few Days, has not returned yet, nor I fear intends it, to stay wth us, Bridges[8] the Chief Justice there being lately Dead, whose Place t'is Expected he will Supply. He Seems to be tired of us as we have reason to be of our selves, all things Considered In short I see little to be Expected here that Should Incline thee to defer Accepting of good Terms one hour After they are Offered. This People think Privilleges their Due, and all that can be Grasped to be their Native Right but when dispensed wth too Liberal a hand, may proove their greatest Unhappiness. Charters here have been or I doubt will be of fatal Consequence, Some Peoples Brains are ~~So~~ As Soon intoxicated with Power as the Natives are wth their [illegible deletion] Beloved Liquor and as Little to be Trusted wth it they think it their business to secure them selves against a Qu's Governour but then their Privileges could they obtain them, may prove as troublesome and Opposite to the publick Good as now: ~~a~~A well temper'd mixture in Government is the happiest, the greatest Liberty & Property & Common wealth Men invested wth Power have been seen to prove the greatest Tyrants.

The Governour is at present very ill with the dry belly ach in no wise Owing I believe to what is commonly accounted the cause of it: Intemperance.

There are three good Companies of the Militia in town Under Capt Roche[9] late of Antigua, young Captain Finney & Capt Lowther,[10] but the Old Party Still use all Endeavours to discourage it, for now great part of the Church are become of the Loyal side, and t'is hoped will Shortly Address the Qu;[11] no way to the Advantage of the Uneasy Gentlemen, thy Son hopes to Carry it over and see it Presented, Were all our own People as reasonable as Some others might be induced to be, we might live much more Easy.

The Governour at present lodges at Sd Captain Finney's the Sherif of this County, but intends if he can accquitt himself of an Engagement with Robert Assheton to make one of our Family in Wm Clark's house in Chesaut[12] street, which we were forced to take, the whole Town not Affording any Suitable Accommodation to thy Son as a Boarder, those that were Able declining the Trouble, and others not being fitt to Accept it. We have now been in it a Month having Continued till than at Is: Norris's, whose Wife thô very Obliging could not bear So Considerable an Addition to the Burthen of her Family especially that of her Tender Children now Six in Number & all Small[13] Samll Carpenter is retired wholly to his Plantation. E. Shippen's Wife[14] is too humoursome, and it Suited not his Sons Circumstances to be with him.[15]

I lie under a great hardship for want of a more full Adjustmt of matters in relation to his Supplies here before he left England, he threw himself he sayes intirely upon thy Generosity, and therefore resents it the more Nearly when I am not able to come up to his expectations, which thô far from extravagance, are yet much above the Limitts sett me, the Directions given me can by no means Satisfy him, nor Answer what is thought Suitable to the Presum{p}tive heir of the Province upon his first Appearance in it even by the most reasonable, He Expresses himself dutifully to thee, but notwithstanding it, forces him on thoughts that render his Visit of Less Service to him, It proves a hardship upon me between both, but I shall endeavor the best, thô in so nice a point I doe not expect the success of pleasing Either.

We have lately received Advice that the Qu: has granted her Subjects Liberty to trade with the Spa: W: Indies[16] wch 'tis Possible if it Succeed, ~~pr~~ may prove of Advantage to these parts. All depends on the Arch Dukes' Success[17] from which According to Appearance I doubt there is but little to be Expected. and if that comes to Nothing, so I fear will the English Dominions in America, I wish they may stand Else where. As things are now we lie under the greatest Discouragments. The Countrey has Scarce any thing to Pay, and all means of Returns could we receive Effects, are cutt off except it be by Sending our Goods to Barbados to be Sold at Less than half cost here & returned in Rum to purchase Bills in Maryland wch now also are dangerous & Require great Caution, but t'is the onely Trade now

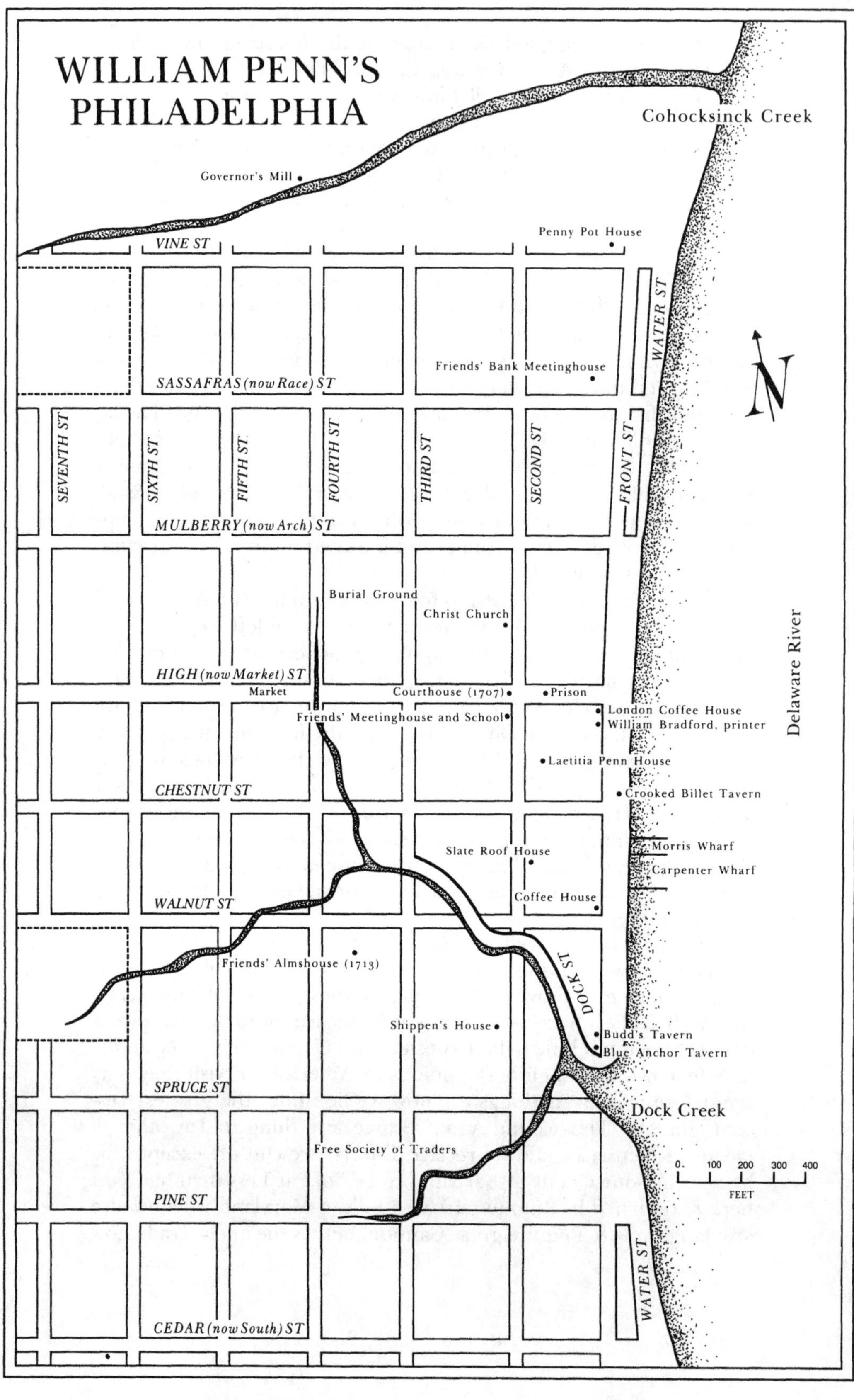
WILLIAM PENN'S
PHILADELPHIA
Cohocksinck Creek
Governor's Mill
Penny Pot House
VINE ST
WATER ST
Friends' Bank Meetinghouse
SASSAFRAS (now Race) ST
N
SEVENTH ST
SIXTH ST
FIFTH ST
FOURTH ST
THIRD ST
SECOND ST
FRONT ST
MULBERRY (now Arch) ST
Burial Ground
Christ Church
Delaware River
HIGH (now Market) ST
Market
Courthouse (1707)
Prison
London Coffee House
William Bradford, printer
Friends' Meetinghouse and School
Laetitia Penn House
CHESTNUT ST
Crooked Billet Tavern
Morris Wharf
Slate Roof House
Carpenter Wharf
WALNUT ST
Coffee House
Friends' Almshouse (1713)
DOCK ST
Shippen's House
Budd's Tavern
Blue Anchor Tavern
SPRUCE ST
Dock Creek
Free Society of Traders
0 100 200 300 400
FEET
PINE ST
WATER ST
CEDAR (now South) ST

left us to purchase English Goods by, and when Successfull has been profitable, their goods being very low, there & bearing some price here but the Risque is great through the great numbers of Martinice Privateers,[18] they have this War taken Above 150 Sail of English 4 of ours, Another large sloop belonging to Is Norris Samuel Carpenter &c (the last stick that Samuell was concerned in at Sea) was taken in her return hither by a large Privateer of St Maloes[19] coming from the Havanána called the Duke of Orleans and being bought off again for 800l Sterling came a few dayes agoe into Maryland Captain Puckle we believe is lost the Vessels that came out in Company with him being arived at Boston & Virginia some weeks agoe, if so, it will be the greatest blow this Countrey has received of the Kind She is deep Loaden and rich we are told & Goods have not been known Scarcer here, there being nothing Arived this year from England.

I have Lately wrote four several Wayes to John Askew to insure 300l on thy Account on John Guy from Carolina Some of wch must needs come to hand.

Is Norris has done the Same, as W Trent also to his Correspondent, T Coutts.[20] I know not now what to Say of that Vessel,[21] when that Voyage was projected Nothing Could Promise Better, there being a great Probability of Making out Money Sterling but instead of that, nothing could have happen'd worse In her Return to Carolina she met with Southerly Winds. Which Kept her long on her Voyage, and the Commandore of the Virginia Fleet through an Unaccountable humour sailing much sooner than Expected and by that means leaving many of the Vessels under his Charge behind him. Our Vessel could not fail of the same Unhappiness, We then had hopes the other two Men of War intended to be Sent to Joyn and Strenghten the Virginia Convoy Missing the other might arive and prove a Second for the Vessels left behind, but meeting the fleet about ten leagues from the Capes at Sea, the Commadore Obliged them to return without the Privilege of refresshing them Selves wth Wood or Water or landing Any of their Passengers except Eight who bought one of their Pinaces[22] & in that Ventured a shoar. By this Means there is no probability of any Convoy from these Parts Again this Year & It was upon this We Wrote for Insurance As before but Now We much Fear Whether it will be Possible to Perswade the Master to Sail or to gett Men to goe home, and that instead of Sailing directly from Virginia According to our Orders Which there Wait him, he will Come {in} hither. We have Advices from our Factor, that there is Loaded on the joynt Account 150 barrels of Rice & 200 of Pitch—& some goods We believe taken in upon freight, Were it Not for that, and that the Rice is a perishable Commodity, it might be better she Came in hither & unloaded her Pitch, wch at home we believe is of more Value than the Rice & proceeded on some other Voyage till a better Opportunity offered of shipping for England. We Shall rather however endeavor to Send her away directly and trust to Insurance wch if not made I Request may be yet done with a Proviso In case she proceed on the Voyage, otherwise the Premium to be returned wch is very Common or if the Insurance be Made before this comes to hand. the premium may be drawn back Again if it be proved she did not proceed the Voyage But by all Meanes I Request Insurance may be made, leaving it at Large whether her Place of Departure be Carolina, Virginia or Pensilvania. I ~~Intended~~ Hinted in my Letters to J. Askew, of which he must doubtless Receive some, that I feared John Guy would scarce goe Master, to which also Regard must be had in the Insurance. I know J A will be very careful in this being himself concerned in her joyntly with I Norris. and when About it for himself, will not begrutch so much Trouble for thee. I have been large here as well for thy own full Information, as that I may perhaps be disappointed of writing to him per this Opportunity (thô I shall endeavor it) & there for~~e~~ intreat thee to communicate it and press it upon him. The Voyage will prove bad at the best but I can not bear to think that from so good a Prospect it should become an intire Loss these things Must needs prove very Melancholy to thee, nor are They Without a Large share of the same to me, I Act for the best & with the best Advice and Concurrence, but against Providence there is no contending. Business of all Kinds is so discouraging that I am quitte dispirited and shall venture no more till there be a better prospect & the Face of Affairs Alters unless commanded. But in that point I have too great reason to be Easy, for as things now are, I can receive nothing to Enable Me to it, We can sell no Lánds nor receive for those sold, my present engagements are as much as I can deal With The Governour not having received Any thing yet from the Countrey, expects as well As thy Son his Supply from Me.

I have not yet answered the Interest due to W Aubry,[23] but besides Expences is now the~~s~~ first payment I have to Make, the Charge of that Unhappy Brigantine[24] having lain long upon me, the Interest I Shall Shorten as fast As Possible by means of the Town Lotts as far as they Will goe (for the Land Will not sell now) but the Trustees have sent so very Lame a Power of Attorney[25] That we can make no Titles by it to Satisfy those that would Purchase. People There believe Any thing will serve Us. but they are much Mistaken we are but too Exact We must have an other Instrumt with much Stronger Clauses than Her: Springett[26] usually putts in those he Sends hither, obliging the Constituents to ratify and give further Assurance and this must be Signed before two Evidences who can personally prove it here, We have a Law for this made at Newcastle,[27] & nothing Short of it will doe If this be Neglected so must the whole business, for we have no Power but what is given us, and this we have Will extend no further than to enable Us to Agree wth the Buyers till a Title can be made I have wrote to the Trustees them selves, by the Virginia fleet wch whether received or not be pleased to Press this, thy self being nearest concerned in it. I wrote also by the Same to Robert Fairman and Several others by a latter Opportunity from hence to Virginia which I fear may Miscarry the Fleet having sail'd so disorderly, and Many fine Ships are left behind which is likely to Prove a great loss to the Countrey.

I am securing what convenient pieces of Land I can but find Faggs and the 50,000 Acres of which thy Son claims one Moiety by his Mother[28] are both the Same, how ever [illegible deletion] I shall lay out some convenient Tracts, at least the best I can, but there is very little now to be found. Samll Carpenters great Unhappiness in the World by means of the Countrey Sinking & his debts growing Yearly, has greatly Altered him, his being concerned with the Sasquehannah business has been a Retardement to it[29] tho~~u~~ thou hast not a heartier friend in the Count{e}ry. But how We Shall get in that Money Seems untelligible to me, the circumstances of Times between Subscription and Payment So widely differ, I shall however doe What I possibly can in it But we grow Weak in Property Affairs. Th. Story has now been Absent near five Months, upon wch the Corporation has made D Lloyd Recorder in his Stead. Gr: Owen is weak in business and E Shippen in health, he is much brooke of Late by the Advances of that wch Admitts no cure, and 'tis hard for me Alone to press affairs of Importance as they ought to be

I before Advised of Colonel Markham's decease on the 11th {last month}[30] ~~Ult~~ he died of one of his Usual fitts and was buried very honourably like a Soldier with the Militia &c. I have received all the Papers from the Widow And we are to have the Accts view'd & examined but J Reignier the Councellor, her Son in Law Stands very Firm to her, and they Plead Debts due to them for Services, over and Above all that can be pretended Against them. He is now gone to York but at his Return we are to inquire into it. The Old Gentleman made a Will but has left his own Daughter very little thô wth him. The Register's Office is now in the Governours own hands. We are healthy and poor a good Crop & harvest, but the most hot dry weather that has not been in my Time. I shall not now add but that with due respects & sincere Love to the family I am

Thy faithful & Obedient Servant
J L

LBC. James Logan Letterbook, HSP. (*Micro.* 11:297.)

1. See James Logan's letters to WP of 16, 25, and 26 May 1704 (*Micro.* 11:236, 238, 240).
2. After adjourning on 23 June 1704, the Assembly met again from 1 to 26 Aug. 1704. *Votes and Proceedings,* 1(pt. 2):9-16.
3. John Evans.
4. Mistake for "of."
5. In an address to Queen Anne (25 May 1704), the Assembly petitioned that the Quakers in the colonies might have the same legal right as their brethren in England

to an affirmation instead of the prescribed oaths, and they went further and asked that anybody in Pennsylvania — irrespective of religious affiliation — might be allowed to affirm rather than swear. *Votes and Proceedings,* 1(pt. 2):6-7.

6. August.

7. *Votes and Proceedings,* 1(pt. 2):7.

8. Dr. John Bridges (c. 1667-1704), an English lawyer, had been appointed by Cornbury as chief justice of the New York Supreme Court and a member of the provincial council in 1703. Paul M. Hamlin and Charles E. Baker, *Supreme Court of Judicature of the Province of New York, 1691-1704: Biographical Dictionary* (New York, 1959), pp. 26-29.

9. Capt. George Roach, or Roche (d. 1739?), moved to Pennsylvania from Antigua and became a prominent member of the Philadelphia municipal corporation. He was admitted to the Provincial Council on 9 May 1704. *PMHB,* 40:263; 90:196; 99:17; Family Notes, GSP; *Minutes of the Provincial Council,* 2:140.

10. John Finney, son of Capt. Samuel Finney, was appointed provincial councilor in 1702 and sheriff of Phila. Co. in 1703 (*PMHB,* 22:54n; docs. 65, 139; *Micro.* 10:958, 1002; 13:148, 243; Family Notes, GSP). George Lowther (d. 1706) of Nottinghamshire was a lawyer who arrived in Philadelphia in 1701 (*Micro.* 10:400; 13:468).

11. This address has not been found.

12. A mistake for "Chestnut."

13. In 1704, the six children of Isaac Norris and Mary Lloyd Norris were: Mary, Hannah (1696-1774), Joseph (1699-1733), Rachel (1700-1711), Isaac (1701-1766), and Elizabeth (1704-1779). They lived in the Slate Roof House, which Norris had purchased from Samuel Carpenter. Wilfred Jordan, ed., *Colonial and Revolutionary Families of Pennsylvania* (Baltimore, 1978), 1:83; *PMHB,* 5:9.

14. Rebecca Shippen.

15. In 1704 Edward Shippen's sons were Edward (1678-1714) and Joseph (1679-1741). Randolph S. Klein, *Portrait of an Early American Family* (Philadelphia, 1975), p. 326.

16. See doc. 81, n. 32.

17. Archduke Charles of Austria, who claimed to be King Carlos III of Spain, was invading Spain from Portugal in 1704. See doc. 80, nn. 5-6.

18. French privateers from Martinique in the West Indies.

19. St.-Malo, a seaport on the northwest coast of France, was headquarters to many privateers in the seventeenth and eighteenth centuries.

20. Thomas Coutts, the brother of James Coutts, was a merchant in London. *Micro.* 10:891; 11:409; 12:535.

21. The *Robert and Benjamin,* John Guy, master. Isaac Norris, William Trent, and Logan, acting on WP's behalf, were the investors in the ship. *PMHB,* 78:156-57; James Logan Letterbook, 2:44, 46.

22. Pinnaces, small light vessels. *OED.*

23. For the terms of WP's financial commitment to his son-in-law, William Aubrey, see doc. 209.

24. Probably the brigantine *Mary.* See doc. 56, n. 2.

25. William Aubrey's trustees in England were Henry Gouldney, Samuel Waldenfield, and David Wharley. James Logan and Samuel Carpenter acted as Aubrey's attorneys in Pennsylvania. *Micro.* 11:369; see also doc. 2091.

26. Herbert Springett (d. 1724), a cousin of Gulielma Penn and son of Sir Herbert Springett, a non-immigrant First Purchaser, was WP's lawyer in London; his chambers were in St. Edmund parish, Lombard St. *PWP,* 3:182n; doc. 124; *London Inhabitants Within the Walls, 1695,* pp. xli, 276.

27. An Act for the Effectual Establishment and Confirmation of the Freeholders . . . in Their Lands and Tenements (cap. 87, sect. 11-12), passed in Nov. 1700 in New Castle. *Statutes,* 2:123.

28. See doc. 56, n. 43.

29. For Samuel Carpenter's financial problems, see doc. 74, n. 24.

30. William Markham died on 11 June 1704. In his will (13 Dec. 1703, probated 3 July 1704) he named his wife, Joanna, sole executrix and main beneficiary. His daughter, Anne Brown, was to receive £50 whenever his widow sold their Philadelphia home, and the residual land of his estate was to be divided among his two grandsons, James and William Brown, and his wife's daughter, Elizabeth, who was married to Jacob Regnier. Phila. Will Bk. B, #137; *PMHB,* 33:361; James Logan Letterbook, 2:56.

83
FROM THE PENNSYLVANIA ASSEMBLY

On 25 August 1704 the Pennsylvania Assembly adjourned without having resolved the heated debate between the governor and the representatives about the Assembly's right of dissolution and prorogation. Just before adjournment the assemblymen did agree, however, to draw up an address to the proprietor detailing the main points of their concern. They appointed David Lloyd, Joseph Willcox, Isaac Norris, John Wood, Griffith Jones, Anthony Morris, William Biles, and Samuel Richardson to form a committee to draft the address, but only Willcox and Lloyd seem to have worked on the draft. Without further communication with other committee members or the Assembly, Lloyd—as speaker of the house—then signed the letter that he and Willcox had written, which is printed below. Although the remonstrance is dated 25 August, the last day of the first 1704 session of the Assembly, Lloyd probably signed and sent the address only in October — together with his letter to George Whitehead, William Mead, and Thomas Lower (doc. 84)—when he was, according to the Charter of 1701, no longer the Assembly's speaker. We know about the particular circumstances of Lloyd's authorship through James Logan's report to WP on 27 October 1704 (*Micro.* 11:402). Logan claimed that Lloyd had tampered with the minutes of the Assembly so that they would reflect both the points made in the address and the Assembly's mandate that its speaker write and send the remonstrance. Lloyd's bold move in launching this attack on the proprietor upset the governor and Council and even Philadelphia Monthly Meeting, none of whom could obtain a copy of Lloyd's representation. WP was particularly hurt by Lloyd's public criticism, and in 1705 he instructed Logan and Evans to have Lloyd prosecuted for forging an address of the Assembly (doc. 95).

[25 August 1704]

TO WILLIAM PENN Proprietary and Governour in Chief of the Province of Pensilvania &c

THE REPRESENTATION of the Freemen of the said Province in Assembly Mett the Twenty fifth day of the Sixth Month 1704

SHEWS & Remonstrates

THAT to Encourage thy First Purchasers & Adventurers to Embark with thee to Plant this Colony And to Transport themselves their Familys and Estates from their Places of Abode into this Province (then an Uncultivated Wilderness) thou wast Pleased to Promise them divers large Priviledges And Amongst other things (Upon the Objeccions made against the Quitrents reserved which with the Purchase money were thought too Severe[1] and Indeed without President or Example in any new Settlement of English Colonys in America) Thou Gave them to Understand thou must be at Considerable Expences & Charges as Governour which as Proprietary only thou wert not Lyable to, And That therefore to Continue them a People free from Taxes (so Grievious & Offensive to them in their Native Countrey) It was necessary the Quitrents Should be as proposed in order to Support the Dignity of the Governour who must keep a free Table And be Generous in Entertainment &c which would be very Chargeable.

THAT these Argum^ts Accompanied with the Charter of Priviledges thou Granted under thy hand and Seal in the Second month 1682[2] Prevailed upon thy Friends, who Reposed very great Trust and Confidence in thee and thy Engagments to them And Accordingly Promised themselves under thy Government All the Temporall Felicity and happiness Mortalls could be Capable of Enjoying in this Life Especially they being to have So Great a Share in it themselves As by that Charter (where thou hadst but a Treble vote in Legislacion)[3] they really had, To Acquiesce with the Quitrents thou reserved upon their Lands in the Countrey, Expecting it to be in liew of all Taxes that might be proposed for the Support of thee or thy Lieutenant And Many who came here Severall Years after from the Fame of the Priviledges granted by the Said Charter and thy Printed Papers Spread over the Nation of England were Introduced to Purchase and Settle here, But Instead of having their Expectation Answered thou Disappointed them in those very Things, As here after Appears.

THAT We find by the Minutes of Assembly & other Papers As well as Living Witnesses That Soon after thy first Arrivall here thou having Obtained the Duke's Grants for the Three Lower Counties, Prevailed with the People of the Province to Unite in Legislacion & Government with them of the Lower Counties And then by a Subtil Contrivance And Artifice layd Deeper than the Capacities of Some could Fathom Or the Circumstances of many could Admitt them time then to Consider of, A way was found {out} to Lay Aside that And Introduce Another Charter Which thou Compleated in the Year 1683.[4]

The Motives which We find upon Record Inducing the People to Accept of that Second Charter were Chiefly Two, vizt, That the Number of Representatives would prove Burdensom to the Countrey[5] And the other was That In Regard thou had but a Treble Vote[6] The People through their Unskillfulness in the Laws of Trade and Navigacion might Make Some Laws over thy head Repugnant thereunto which might Occasion the Forfieture of the Kings's Letters Patent[7] by which this Countrey was Granted thee, And wherein is a Clause for that Purpose, Which we find very much Relyed upon and Frequently Read or Urged in the Assemblys of that time And Security Demanded by thee from the People on that Account, A Third Motive

(As we Gather from the Severall Petitions & Messages concerning the said Union)[8] was the Great Conveniency & Advantage it would be to the Province in Point of Trade & making Returns for England.

As to the First Motive We know That the number of Representatives might have been very well Reduced without a New Charter. And as to the Laws of Trade We Cannot Conceive That a People So fond of thy Self for Governour And who Saw much with thy Eyes in those Affairs Should against thy Advice and Cautions Make Laws Repugnant to those of Trade and So bring Trouble & Disappointment upon themselves by being a Means of Suspending thy Administration The Influence wherof And hopes of thy Continuance therein Induced them (as We Charitably Conclude) to Imbark with those in that Great & weighty Affaire more than the honour due to persons in those Stations Or any Sinister Ends Destructive to the Constitution they Acted by Therefore We See no Just Cause thou had to Insist upon Such Security Or to have a Negative upon Bills to be past into Laws in Generall Assemblys Since thou had by the Said Charter (Pursueant to the Authority & Direccion of the King's Letters Patent aforesaid) Formed those Assemblys And {thereupon} Reserved but a Treble Vote in the Provinciall Councill which could not be more Injurious to thee than to the People for the Reasons aforesaid.

AND as to the Conveniency of the Union of the Province and Lower Counties We Cannot Gainsay {it} If the King had Granted thee the Government As the Duke had done the Soil[9] But to our Great Grief and Trouble We Cannot find that thou had any Such Grant And if thou had thou would not Produce it though often requested so to Do Therefore we Take it the harder that thou, who knew how precarious thy Power was to Govern the Lower Counties, Should bring thy Province into Such a State and Condicion That Whenever the Crown had Assumed that Government Or the People there Revolted or Refused to Act with us in Legislation, As they often did, That then the Said Second Charter Should become Impracticable & the Priviledges thereby granted of no Effect to the Province Because the Representatives of the Lower Counties were Equall in Number with those of the Province And the Charter Required a greater Number than the Province had or by Charter could Elect for Members of Councill and Assembly And our Numbers by that Charter could not be Encreased without the Revolters Consent So that the Inconveniencys that has Attended the Union has Out-ballanced all the Advantages that the People of the Province have or Could Reap thereby As thou hast managed it.

THUS was the First Charter laid aside Contrary to the Tenor thereof And true Intent of the first Adventurers And the Second Charter Introduced and Accepted by the Generall Assembly held at Philad[a] in the First and Second Months 1683 where thou Sollemnly Testifyed That what was incerted in that Charter was Solely by thee

Intended for the Good & Benefit of the Freemen of the Province And Prosecuted with much Earnestness in thy Spirit towards God at the time of it's Composure Nevertheless in the Year 1686 thou Gave Orders to thy Five Commissioners of State As also to Captain Blackwell to Dissolve the Frame of Government Constituted by that Charter[10] But what thou and they could not Effect in that behalf was Performed by Colonel Fletcher in the Year 1693 And then We were brought under the Immediate Direccion of the Crown but with Commands for him to Govern us by the Laws of the Countrey And although both the Laws and Charter had been long before Transmitted to thee in order to get the late Kings[11] Approbacion thereof which we Insisted upon And Urged that they were Laws 'till Disapproved Yet thou having Sent No account whether they were approved or not We were forced to Comply with him And Accept of Such as he Pleased But the Charter he totally Rejected.[12]

THAT upon thy being restored to the Government thou required thy Lieutenant[13] to Govern us according to the Charter which by reason of Fletcher's Interruption became Impossible before thy Orders reached us And So the Government fell under great Confusion again; Nor was the Administration of thy Propriety much better mannaged Because thou put some in that Commission with whom the rest would not Act And at last the offices of Property & Surveyor Generall Came to be Shut up And thou kept them So whilest thou Sold Land to the value of 3000l [14] Sterling And Gave thy Warrants in England for Surveying the Sd land And also Got great Tracts of Land layd out or Secured for thy Self and Relations besides severall valuable Parcells which should have been layd out for the Purchasers But were reserved by thy Surveyors whether for thee or themselves We know not However thou Appropriated those Lands to thy Self by the name of CONCEALED LANDS, Whereas in Truth they were Concealed from the Purchasers, who were to have their Lands layd out Contiguous one to Another And no vacancys left between them And thou was to have only thy Tenth as it fell According to the Concessions thou made with First Adventurers, And if thou took it not up so, 'twas thy own (not their) fault; But the other a manifest Injury to many of them as above Declared.

THAT upon thy last Arrivall[15] here after all the Hardships and Disappointments we had Laboured Under We hoped to Enjoy the Fruits of thy former Promises & Ingagments But Instead of that we found thee very full of Resentment And many of our Applications and Addresses about our Just Rights and Properties were Answered by Recriminations or bitter Invectives And We found That the Falce insinuations & Reproaches that our Adversarys had Cast upon the Province with respect to Falce Trade And harbouring Pirates had made so great an Impression upon thee that thou rather believed them than thy honest Friends And when thou Entred upon Legislation thou was pleased to Repeal all the Laws that were made in Fletcher's time which were Approved by the King or Queen As we were Informed And as Some of us gathered by the Account thou gave of them vizt That Chancellour Somers[16] had sent for thee to know what thou had to Object against any of those Laws, And if it had not been for thee none of them had past Or words to that Effect And not only So But the People being minded to Surrender the Said Second Charter upon thy Promise to Give them a better in Liew of it,[17] And under Pretence of Passing an Act for Confirming and Securing their Lands &c,[18] Thou Obtained Liberty to Resurvey all the Lands in the Province And bring the People to Terms for the overplus So that by this Strategem The Warrants Surveys and new Patents Cost the People as much and to some more than the First Purchase of their Lands besides their long attendance upon thy Secretary & Surveyors to have their Business done But before thou would Pass that Act It must be Accompanied with an Impost or Excise And a Two thousand pound Bill besides.[19]

AND all this thou Esteemed but Inconsiderable when thou Compared it with the vast Charge thou had been at in the Administracion & Defence of this Government Since the Year 1682, though We know thy Stay here at first Coming was not above Two Years[20] But Went home about the Difference betwen thee & Baltemore concerning the Bounds of the Lower Counties And Did not Return 1699 Excusing thy Stay by thy Service to the Nation of England in Generall And to thy Friends there in particular (As Appears by thy Letters from time to time) Whilest the Interest of this Province was Sinking which might have been Upheld by many Wealthy persons that were Inclined to Transport themselves here after the Rout of Monmouth[21] If thou had then come over According to thy repeated Promises. And how farr thy Stay has either Effected what thou went about or Contributed to the Establishment of the Inhabitants here in their Just Rights Liberties and Properties We Leave thee to Demonstrate And the World to Judge In the mean time We Desire thee to Consider better what to place to the Account of this Province And Do not forget That No part of thy pretended Charges was Expended in Paying Some of those who Acted under thee in the Administracion here One of whom, to witt, Thomas Lloyd Served thee in that Stacion about Nine Years of thy Absence which thou Leaves, It Seems, for the Countrey to Discharge.[22]

THAT after thou had Managed these Points And wast Sent for to England thou granted the Third Charter of Priviledges,[23] by which We are now Convened As also a Charter to Incorporate the City of Philadelphia[24] And Signed a Charter of Property[25] But Refused to order thy Seal to be Affixed thereunto till thou had Advised upon it in England Nevertheless thou Promised under thy hand that thou would Confirm the First part of it Relating to Titles of Land BUT thou sent thy order Under thy hand & Seal Dated within Six months after, to Countermand the Sealing thereof.[26]

THAT after the Laws were Compleated for Raising all the Said Taxes and Imposts Thou proposed That if thy Friends would Give thee a Summ of Money thou Promised to Negotiate their Affairs at home to the best Advantage And Endeavour to Procure the Approbacion of our Laws And a Generall Exemption from oaths; We find That Considerable Sums have been Raised by way of Subscription & benevolence for that Service[27] Part thou Received before thou went And more has been Received Since by thy Secretary BUT We had no Account that our Laws are Approved Nor had We as much as a Letter from thee nor any other Intimacion But by thy Secretary's Letters which he Thought fitt to Comunicate by peicemeal Whereby We understand thou hast been Making Terms for thyself & Family And by what We Gather thou hast been upon Surrendring the Government NOR are thy Friends here Eased of Oaths But on the Contrary An Order from the Queen Requiring oaths to be Administred to all persons who are willing to Take them in all Judicatures Whereby the People called Quakers are Disabled to Sitt in Courts.

THAT By the last Charter of Priviledges thou Established an Annuall Eleccion of Representatives for Assembly And that they Should Continue And Sitt upon their own Adjournments;[28] YET By thy Commission to thy present Deputy John Evans[29] thou Did in a Direct opposition to the said Charter Give him Power not only to Call Assemblys by his Writts But to Prorogue & Dissolve them As he Should See Cause AND also Reserved to thy self (tho' in England) Thy Finall Assent to all Bills passed here by thy Deputy; We Suppose thou hast not forgot That what rendred the Former Charter Inconvenient, if not Impracticable was Chiefly That Colonel Fletcher's Interruption had Extinguished the Rotacion of the Councill And next to that The Proposalls of Laws by the Councill in presence of the Governour as also the Instabillity of the Lower Counties which We had before Experience of and whose Revolt was then Doubled As hath since happened But That Annual Standing Assemblys lyable only to the Dismission and Call of the Governour as Occasion Required was never found an Inconveniency nor Assigned as a Reason for Changing the said Former for the present Charter; And Should that of Dissolucion be Introduced It would Frustrate the Constitution Because If a Dissolucion Should happen the Province might be a great part of the Year without an Assembly And the Governour of power to call one whatever Commands from the Crown or other Occasions may happen FOR THAT the Eleccion being fixt by Charter which is in Nature of a Perpetuall Writt And has the Authority of a Law; If it could be Superseded by the Governours Writt which is but an Act of State & merely Temporary It would be of pernicious Consequence to the Province as well as thy self, And of this thou Seem'd very Sensible when being Desired by the Assembly upon the Close of the Session in the Year 1701 to Dissolve them (being then called by Writts) Thou told them thou wouldst not Do it for that thou couldst not Answer to the Crown to Leave the Province without a Standing Assembly.[30]

THAT as the Exemption from any Dissolution or Prorogation Seems to be an Inseperable Consequent of thy Grant As well as our Constant Practice upon the former Charter, Which, This, was by thy Promise to Exceed, So upon an Attempt made by the Councill to Prorogue us in October last[31] We have thought it our Duty to Prepare a Bill for Ascertaining Explaining and Settling our present Constitution[32] Which we having Presented to thy Deputy for his Assent, He finding that the Power of Dissolucion & Prorogation is not in Express words Granted away by Charter As also the Inconsistency thereof wth his said Commission, After Severall Conferrences thereupon had with him & his Councill He thought fitt to Advise us to Forbear farther Pressing it 'till wee Should hear from thee,[33] Therefore he being unwilling to Pass the said Bill by us Judged So necessary And the Very Foundation of our Constitution We could not Think it proper to proceed to Perfect any other Business whilest that Remained Unsettled Nor Do We Suppose any thing will be done in Legislacion Either by the present or Succeeding Assemblys 'till the Difficulty We Labour Under herein be removed Either by thy Speedy Order or by thy Deputy without it; Seeing to Proceed upon other matters would be to raise a Superstructure before the Foundation were well layd; Nor Do We look upon it very Advisable for us to Proceed Farr in Legislation untill thou Repeals those parts of thy Lieutenant's Commission relating to Prorogation & Dissolucion of Assemblys for the reasons before given; As also concerning thy Finall Assent to Laws; Which We Conceive to bery unreasonable in it Self, And a great Abuse and violation of our Constitution that thou Should offer to Put three Negatives upon our Acts whereas by our first Charter We had none but that of the Crown And how thou Gained Another to thyself we have before Shew'd thee, But Now to bring us under Three, Seems a Contrivance to Provoke us to Complain to the Queen That thou art not Effectually Represented here And make that a Motive for her to Take us under her Immediate Care & Protection Which would make thy Surrender in Some measure our Act which if thou Should Do without the Consent of the Proprietors and Inhabitants of this Province First obtained would Look too much like Treachery.

THAT It appears by Severall Petitions now before us[34] That very great Abuses have been and are put upon the Inhabitants And Extortions Used by thy Secretary Surveyors & other officers concerned in Property as well as Courts, Which might have been prevented or Sooner Remedied had thou been Pleased to Pass the Bill proposed by the Assembly in the year 1701 to Regulate Fees[35] As also the Want of a Surveyor Generall which is a great Injury and Dissatisfaccion to the People; as is likewise the want of an Established Judicature for Tryalls between thee and the People For if We Exhibit our Complaints against thee or those who Represent thee in State or Property, they must be Determined by or before Justices of thy own Appointment By which means thou becomes in a Legall Sence, Judge in thy own Case which is against naturall Equity Therefore we Propose That a Man learned in the Laws of England may be Comissionated by the Queen to Determine all Matters wherein thy Tennants have Just Cause to Complain against thee, thy Deputies or Comissioners Or Esse Restore the People to the Priviledge of Electing Judges Justices and other officers According to the Direccion of the First Charter[36] And Intent of the First Adventurers And as the People of New-England have by King William's Charter.[37]

THAT thy Commissioners of Property are very Unwilling to make Good the Deficiencys of those Lands thou hast been ma{n}y Years ago paid for (though thou Gave them Power So to Do) AND So Great is the Difficulty & Trouble to Get Satisfaccion in this particular That 'tis better for one to Forego his Right than Wait on & Attend the Commissioners about it unless the Quantity wanting be very great.

WE have many other Things to Represent to thee as Grievances, As thy unheard of Abuses to thy Purchasers &c In Pretending to Give them a Town, And then by Imposing Unconscionable Quitrents makes it worse by Ten fold than a Purchase would have been; Also the Abuse about the Bank, And want of Common to the Town; And not only So But the very Land the Town Stands on is not Cleared of the Sweads Claims.[38]

These are the Chief heads which We thought Fitt at this time to Lay before thee, Earnestly Entreating thy Serious Consideracion of them And that thou wilt now at last (after we have thus long Endured and Groaned under these hardships which of late seem to be multiplyed upon us) Endeavour as far as in thee Lies to Retreive thy Credit with us thy poor Tennants & fellow Subjects by Redressing these Aggrievances, Especially in Getting our Laws Confirmed,[39] And also to be Eased of Oaths,[40] And Giving possitive Orders to thy Deputy to unite heartily with us upon our Constitution, And That the Charters thou granted us for City and Countrey may be Explained Settled and Confirmed by Law; AND We farther Entreat That Effectuall Care be Taken for the Suppressing of vice Which, to our great Trouble we have to Acquaint thee is more Rife and Comon amongst us, Since the Arrivall of thy Deputy and Son, Especially of late than was ever known before, Nor are we Capable to Suppress it whilest it is Connived at, if not Encouraged by Authority, The Mouths of the more Sober Magistrates being Stopt by the said late Order about Oaths, And the Governour's Lycencing Ordinarys not Approved by the Magistrates of the City of Philadelphia,[41] And the Roast[42] Chiefly Ruled by Such as are none of the most Exemplary for vertuous Conversations; Thy possitive Orders in the premises will be Absolutly necessary to thy Deputy, Who thinks it Unreasonable And a great Hardship upon him to Give Sanction to Laws Explanatory of thy Grants Or to Do anything by way of Enlargment or Confirmacion of ought Save what is particularly & Expressly granted by thee It being by Some of his Councill Urged as an Absurdity in us to Expect, And We Desire That thou would order the Lycencing of ordinarys & Taverns To be by the Justices According to thy Letter dated in September 1697,[43] And We hope We need not be more Express in Charging thee as thou Tenders thy own honour and honesty or the obligations thou art under to thy Friends & particularly thy first Purchasers & Adventurers into this Province That thou Do not Surrender the Government whatever Terms thou may, by so Doing, make for thy Self and Family, Which we Shall Deem no less than a betraying us, And at best will Look like First Fleecing than Selling But rather Use thy utmost Interest with the Queen to Ease us in the promises And if after thy Endeavours Used to keep the Government It be perforce Taken from thee thou will be Clearer in the Sight of God and us the Representatives of the People of this thy province Who are thy Reall Friends & well Wishers, As We hope is Evident in that we have dealt thus plainly with thee.

Signed by order of the House
Da^d^ Lloyd Speaker.

DS. Cliveden Manuscripts, Chew Family Papers, HSP. (*Micro.* 11:332.) Docketed in WP's hand: Representation of the | assembly 1704 | for J. Logan.

1. WP had conceded this point and postponed the collection of quitrents until 1685.
2. The Frame of Government & Laws Agreed Upon in England, c. May 1682. *PWP,* 2:211-27.
3. The 1682 Frame, article 6. *PWP,* 2:216.
4. The Second Frame of Government (1683). Soderlund, *William Penn,* pp. 265-73.
5. Article 1 of the Second Frame reduces the number of representatives in the Assembly from 200 to 36. Ibid., p. 267.
6. See n. 3, above.
7. See the Assembly debate of 15 Mar. 1683 on this point. Soderlund, *William Penn,* p. 236.
8. See, for example, Petition for the Act of Union, *PWP,* 2:318-20.
9. See *PWP,* 2:90-91, 103-4, 281-84; *Micro.* 6:132, 161.
10. Lloyd is probably referring to *PWP,* 3:209.
11. Probably James II.
12. See *Votes and Proceedings,* 1:66, 68.
13. William Markham.
14. This is a reference to the sale of Susquehanna lands to subscribers in the 1690s. *PWP,* 3:679.
15. WP visited Pennsylvania last from Dec. 1699 to Oct. 1701.
16. John Baron Somers (1651-1716) served under William III as solicitor general (1689), attorney general (1692), lord keeper of the great seal (1693), and lord high chancellor (1700); under Queen Anne he became president of the council (1708). *PWP,* 3:620.

17. See *Votes and Proceedings,* 1:119-21; *Minutes of the Provincial Council,* 1:602-5, 611-14.

18. See *Statutes,* 2:118-23.

19. See docs. 35, n. 19; 44, n. 14.

20. WP's first stay in Pennsylvania lasted from Oct. 1682 to Aug. 1684.

21. Monmouth's rebellion in 1685.

22. See *PWP,* 3:386.

23. See doc. 28.

24. See *Micro.* 9:682.

25. See *Micro.* 9:770.

26. See *Micro.* 10:033; doc. 39, n. 1.

27. See docs. 35, n. 26; 44, text at n. 10.

28. See doc. 28.

29. See doc. 65.

30. On 27 Oct. 1701 the Assembly voted its own dissolution. *Votes and Proceedings,* 1:164.

31. See *Minutes of the Provincial Council,* 2:110.

32. For the bill confirming the Charter of Privileges, see *Votes and Proceedings,* 1(pt. 2):5, 7, 9, 11, 13, 15.

33. See *Votes and Proceedings,* 1(pt. 2):14, 15; *Minutes of the Provincial Council,* 2:152-58.

34. See *Votes and Proceedings,* 1(pt. 2):9, 16.

35. Ibid., p. 16.

36. See *PWP,* 2:218.

37. The Massachusetts charter of 1691; see Louise Philips Kellogg, ed.,*The American Colonial Charter* (New York, 1904; reprint, 1971), p. 47.

38. Lloyd's complaints about the bank lots, the lack of a common, and the land claims of the Swedes focus on well-known features of WP's plan for Philadelphia: bank lots were not part of the original grid, the grid design included four squares but no common, and the city was situated on land held by the Swedes. Gary B. Nash, "City Planning and Political Tension in the Seventeenth Century: The Case of Philadelphia," *Proceedings of the American Philosophical Society,* 112:55-73. *PWP,* 2:334, 337-39; 515.

39. For WP's complaint about the expense involved in having the laws confirmed, see doc. 81, text at n. 11.

40. WP was much concerned about the problems Pennsylvania Quakers experienced as a result of the queen's orders concerning oaths. See doc. 76, text at n. 57.

41. The Charter of Privileges stipulated that the governor would issue tavern licenses to persons first recommended to him by the county justices. Doc. 28.

42. Roost.

43. See *PWP,* 3:518.

84

DAVID LLOYD TO GEORGE WHITEHEAD, WILLIAM MEAD, AND THOMAS LOWER

Philadelphia the 3d of 8br [October] 1704

Honoured Friends
G W
W M
T L[1]

This comes along wth a Representation or Remonstrance from the Generall Assembly of this Province To Wm Penn;[2] And I am Requested on the behalfe ~~of the behalfe~~ of the Inhabitants here, To Intreat That you would Lay these things before him, and get such Reliefe therein as may be obtaind from him; And if you find him Still Remiss in Performing his Promesses and Ingagemts towards us; or

Making Terms for Himselfe as he Calls it, We desire you will be pleasd by such Christi[an] Measures as you shall see meet, to Oblige him to Do the People Justice in those things wch this Represantation shews he has been Deficient [in.] Here also is Inclosed a Coppy of a bill wch this Last Assembly[3] prepared to be past into a Law That the Affirmation should Pass instead of an Oath, Be pleased to Consider the Reason & Nescesity of {our having} such a Law, and Solicit the Queen about it, For we cannot find that Wm Penn has done any thing for our Reliefe in that Perticular, But his Deputy here has given forth a Proclamation to Declare the Proceedings of our Courts Null & Voyd in all Causes where the Proceedure is wthout Oath.[4] Tho the ~~Generallity~~ Affirmation is Lookt upon by the Generallity of the People, who are not of our Perswasion, to be as binding as an Oath: This Proclamation as ~~well~~ Also Another ~~for~~ Proclamation for Raising a Militia[5] are Pretended to be made to recomend Wm Penn's administration to the favourable Notice of the Queen; But, to our Sorrow We find they prove ~~as~~ Skreens to the most abominable Wickedness as well as to weaken the hands of friends in the Suppressing Vice & debaucherys, And not only so, but the sayd Proclamations, especially the Last ~~Leaves~~ abt Oaths, Leaves a Dore open~~ed~~ for the greatest Malefactors to Escape unpunished and Shuts out friends from being Magistrates, And by Consequence Lets in the Vilest of Men to the admin~~d~~ist~~a~~ration of Justice. We desire your utmost assistance in this thing.

Here are also Inclosed Duplicates of our addresses to the Queen[6] they have been sent severall Ways I hope Some will come safe to hand.

Our assembly have agreed to rayse 100l for this year and I presume will at their next Meeting Make it an Annuall Fund[7] to defray the Charge of a Corrispondance wch they desire to have setled for Negotiating th[e] affairs of the Province For you now see ~~how~~ [torn] we have been Abused Trusting to WP.

We have Sent an Address to him (along wth these to the Queen) dated in the 3d month last,[8] since wch we found that he had not got our Laws aproved of by the Queen Nor Obtain'd any reliefe for us against the Inconveniencys We Labourd Under by reason of her late order about Oaths which we expected from him and also we have had reason Since that Address to Change our Opinion of his Deputy,[9] Who has much a~~f~~ltered his Measures in Governmt: from what he then & all along before that time gave us assurance of. The Tokens we had of his Closing wth our Enemys & pla~~y~~in Demonstration of his Masters Wm Penn's neglect toward us before the assembly ended[10] Moved us to deale thus pla~~y~~inly with W.P. and if he shall Endeavour to make this Representation Inconsistant wth the Address, I hope you will Consider that the Representation is three Months after {that} Address In wch time Observing all Passages that Occur'd to our Notice, We found Sufficient Cause to alter our Opinion & fall upon These Measures and the Address being Signed 3 months before the Representation by order of the house it could not be recalled Else I believe it Would.

Friends Its the Publick Cryes for your assistance which I hope will Excuse me (Who am Unknown to you)[11] thus far to trouble you, I suppose you will have a more ample account by others of the Condition this poor Province is brought to, by the late Revells & Disorders which young Wm Penn & his Gang of Loose fellows he Accompanys[12] with are found in to the great Griefe of Frds & others in this Place.

If there were an able Counseler at Law That were a person of Sobriety & Moderation (But not in W: Penns Interest) Comisionated by the Queen to be Judge of the Province & Lower Counties, as also of the Jerseys wch they as well as we extreamly want and are [a]ll willing to support I doubt not but his place may b[e worth f]our or five hundred pound per Annum, besides fees & {m[any?]} [per]quisites & the buisness of these [illegible deletion] Provinces may be easily perform'd by one Chief Judge wth Certain associates that the respective Countys as he goes his Circuit will Supply. I desire you may use your Endeavors to get such a Man. Here was one Roger Mompesson, Who we thought to Ingage in that affair, but he being Judge of the Admiralty & Cheife Judge of the Supream Court at New York, he could not stay here, Besides he was too much in Wm Penns Interest & given to drink so that he did not suit this place so well. This with Unfeigned Love is all at presant from

Your frd to serve you in what I can
Da^d Lloydd

Copy in Hannah Penn's hand. Logan Papers, HSP. (*Micro.* 11:392.)

1. Like George Whitehead, William Mead (1628-1713) and Thomas Lower (1633-1720) were prominent English Friends; both were sons-in-law of Margaret Fell. Mead, a linendraper of London and Romford, Essex, had been a co-defendant with WP in the famous trial of 1670, but since then he had become a sharp critic of WP, particularly in the ongoing controversy over the affirmation. Lower, a Cornwall physician, was another early Quaker sufferer who had become critical of WP. *PWP,* 1:132n, 174n, 515n; 3:394, 451n; Fox, 1:440.

2. Doc. 83.

3. See *Votes and Proceedings,* 1(pt. 2):7.

4. Issued 23 Sept. 1704. See *CSPC, 1704-1705,* pp. 285-86.

5. Issued 18 July 1704. See ibid., pp. 270-73.

6. The Assembly's address congratulating the queen on her succession to the throne of 25 May 1704, and the petition concerning the prescribed oath of the same date. *Votes and Proceedings,* 1(pt. 2):6-7.

7. The Assembly voted a special fund to support its own lobbying efforts in England. Ibid., pp. 10-11.

8. For the Assembly's address to WP, 26 May 1704, see *Micro.* 11:258.

9. John Evans.

10. The Assembly adjourned on 25 Aug. 1704 and reconvened on 14 Oct. 1704. *Votes and Proceedings,* 1(pt. 2):16.

11. David Lloyd did not personally know the prominent Friends he addressed here, but he had previously corresponded with Thomas Lower. *The Friend,* 49:93-94.

12. For further comments on the bad company William Penn, Jr., kept in Pennsylvania, see doc. 86, text at nn. 37-38.

85
TO JOHN EVANS

Bristoll. 6. 9^{br} [November] 1704

Esteemed Friend

I cannot let this Bearer[1] goe without a salutation, for it is by another hand (in the Same ship),[2] that I have writt to thee already, but tis about 6 weeks if not two months agoe.[3]

First thy relations were lately well, to whom I took care to deliver thy letters;[4] thy uncle is now, or lately was on his Circuit, & in Cornhill.[5] I have given thy Salutes to Ld Clarendon &c; and the character I have had of thy conduct, since there, has done thee Service. I can make no Judgem^{t} of our affaires, only that the adverse Interests[6] struggle mightily, & tis thought this Session of Parliament will issue it one way or other. our affaires in Germany in a secure condition,[7] not so in Portugall, & yet worse in savoy;[8] but the other successes more than Ballance that; & some think that the war is but begun. vast preparations on both Sides. I have both thine,[9] as in a former to thee I intimated.[10] I only desire thee to Stand legally by my Just interest, & w^{t} room there is for favour, to be on the Side of my affaires; for If I keep my Goverm^{t} thou keepest my Lieftenancy; & if I resigne, one article will be to Continue thee there. for it will be hardly done but by Consent. as I would have the just to all, so discreet to our enimys, but kinde to the Friends of the Country & of my honest Interest. I have hinted at large my minde to the secretary[11] about the division of the upper and lower Countys; and Let James Coutts know, that what ever they can desire of thee as by Dep^{t} I shall ~~upon~~ acquiess in what thou does upon thy ~~approbat~~ best consideration, & those of the Province that are of the worthiest mindes, [seven words illegibly deleted] & further confirm the same notwithstanding the ungratefull & unworthy behavour of Robt French and John Hill.[12] Lett w. Clark know pray that I have his,[13] per last opertunity, & had his {2} former, & writt an answear. Tell him I shall complain to the Com^{rs} of Trade & Plantations ab^{t} the Marylanders proceedings,[14] & consider of the rest he writt of. I need not bid thee respect my son, & yet I would not carry that too farr; and I hope there will be no need of it. Thy Frds remain Such I wish I could Say the Same. If it lays in thy way to help the bearer, pray do, he is a poor kinsman of my wifes', who Salutes thee, as does with a true regard

Thy assured & affect Friend
Wm Penn

my Salutes to the Council, & Majest^{rs} & the well enclined at large.

ALS. ACM. (*Micro.* 11:423.)

1. Samuel Hollister (b. 1679), son of Bristol grocer Samuel Hollister (d. 1696). His grandfather William Hollister was the brother of Hannah Penn's maternal grand-

father, Dennis Hollister. See doc. 91, text at n. 22; Mortimer, 1:204; 2:248; Digests of Quaker Records, Bristol and Som., GSP.

2. The *Biddeford Factor*, or *Biddeford Merchant. Micro.* 11:409.

3. This earlier letter has not been found.

4. Not found.

5. A street in the City of London between Poultry and Leadenhall St. Peter Cunningham, *A Handbook for London: Past and Present* (London, 1849), 1:234-35.

6. Col. Quary, the "church party," and others who lobbied for Pennsylvania to become a colony of the crown.

7. Marlborough's victory at Blenheim. See doc. 81, n. 24.

8. The duke of Piedmont-Savoy, Victor Amadeus II (1666-1732), was beset on all sides by French armies, and only in 1706 were his territories freed from this threat. Geoffrey Symcox, "Britain and Victor II," *England's Rise to Greatness, 1660-1763*, ed. Stephen B. Baxter (Berkeley, Calif., 1983), pp. 160-62.

9. Not found.

10. See n. 3, above.

11. James Logan.

12. Robert French and John Hill supported the separation of the Lower Counties from Pennsylvania.

13. WP's correspondence with William Clarke in 1704 has not been found.

14. There is no evidence in the journals of the Board of Trade that WP presented Clarke's complaint to the Lords of Trade.

86
FROM JAMES LOGAN

Newcastle 22nd 9m [November] 1704

Hond Gov:
Duplicate to be read
S. B. O. f.[1]

By thy Son in the Jersey and John Guy in the Brigantine[2] who sailed from York about 14 days agoe, I wrote several letters of which 3 inclosed to John Askew[3] were designed more private than the rest, informing as fully as I then could of the fate[4] of our affairs, all which I hope will arrive safe before this can come to hand, I cannot without the deepest regret consider how little satisfactory some of them & especially their bearer[5] on some Account may prove, but as I have had & still have my share of trouble at the thoughts of it, & can truly Sympathize with those more nearly concerned, Yet as I have endeavoured to acquit myself with a good conscience to the utmost of my power, were even the whole unhappiness to lie at my own door, this still would yield me the greater ease,[6] and to that I doubt must thy chief recourse be for comfort, I have undergone I am sure, the deepest pangs of trouble in my own Soul for several Months past, ~~p~~but hope it will please the Lord to give a greater dawn of consolation to those whose whole dependence is upon him,

The return of thy Son and the representation he brings[7] with the unhappy effects these have had upon him accompanied at the same time with that unparalelled piece of business from D.L.[8] will soon put thee (I doubt not) upon measures for thy ease from such an Accablemt[9] of troubles, The Govr has positively demanded a Copy of that remonstrance from the Assembly, but that Vilian[10] under pretence of answering the Govr demands in a proper method by the basest Artifice endeavoured to pursuade the House, that they ought first to make it by a Recognition or Amendmt, as they should think fitt the Act of the House, and then they might properly send a Copy, but this being too gross to pass (notwithstanding the great influence he has over the Majority composed of Knaves and fools,[11] for of the latter they got as many as they could, that they might the easier be led by the Rattle of Rights and privileges)[12] he as I am credibily informed by some others of the Members owned it as his own proper Act & therefore as such pleaded that it was not Subject to the house or any other power He pretended indeed to send for it again from York when it was too late but upon the whole he denies a Copy either to the Govr [13] or the Meeting of Philada which has also Sued for it,[14]

We are now in such Circumstances, that I cannot by the best lights I am master of[15] foresee any probability of being regularly brought into Order again till under the Crown, and it seems all owing to those unhappy Charters,[16] which being designed as favours, are made use of by ill men as tools for mischief there is a general Infatuation got amongst us as if we were preparing for destruction, everything however innocently & well designed seems to close in an unhappy event, & the most unexpected incidents daily arise to perplex us we are too much in the same Circumstances here as in England in regard to public affairs, and perhaps tis as much the falt[17] of the Nation as our particular Sins, but I am too subject perhaps to run upon such Melancholy reflections[18] The Govr and Assembly have clashed so far[19] notwithstanding all endeavours have been used on our side to keep matters easy, that there seems nothing or at least very little to be expected from them, they will not allow him the power of dissolving Proroguing, dismissing for a time or adjourning them, but claim the privilege of setting at all times as they shall see occasion like the Parl in 1641[20] which they nearly imitate, they are all for setling Constitutions & privileges without any regard to the Public present safety or making any provision for the Government That rediculous Old man W. Biles frequently affirms they will never grant one penny on any Acct, till they have all their privileges explained and confirmed, that is till they have 5 times more granted then ever they claimed before, Witness the City Charter Bill,[21] and then tis alledged the Govr knows the terms how he may have money,[22] & if the Public suffers for want of it it will be at his door,

We are now come hither to hold a distinct Assembly for the Peers[23] designed only to keep them in some order, and to shew they are regarded, but each County being represented only by four members[24] little will be done this time, some endeavour to keep in upon the foot of the Charter, not through any great liking to it but that the whole might continue more like one Government, But Judge Guest with the designing men of this place seem to endeavour an utter Seperation, and that this alone may be made the Mart for all the People below, The consequence of this thou wilt easily see, and how inconvenient a distinct Assembly will be when taken notice of at home, and how injurious to thy interest, but what is done now could not be avoided unless we would wholly lose the Obedience of these Counties, it depends therefore the more upon thee (on whom the burthen always too heavily lights) to hasten a suitable provision I wish Public affairs at home may be in a Condition to afford thee an Oppertinity The Prov: & Peers[25] can scarce ever agree together, but asunder they will never doe anything, and therefore should be joined on equal privileges, and all Charters destroyed, for our friends are unfit for Government by themselves and not much better with others, We are generally in these parts too full of ourselves and empty of sense to manage affairs of importance & therefore require the greatest Authority to bend us, If thou surrender the Government & keep the propriety[26] as I doubt thou must the ~~better~~ {latter} of necessity, the naming of the Council as well as the Governor will be worth thy Consideration and then of most I know, I doubt[27] there is scarce any[28] more unfitt or less a friend to thy Property than that weathercock Judge Guest. A Desire to be somebody and an unjust method of craving and getting seems to be the rule of his Life he has often been ~~wrought to be~~ of great Service, wch should of it self be acknowledged but 'tis owing to litle good in his temper It was[29] his failings that were laid hold on to lead him to it, and upon the whole I must give it as my opinion that he is not to be trusted. {He is remarkable in one unhappy talent of abusing every past government & seems fixed to no man} I should prefer even John Moore to him {in the main}. poor old Captain Finney too is {grown} somewhat dotish and very weak, Jasper Y.[30] has as much honor, thô he has been an Enemy, as any I know. ~~The Judge because I cannot gratify him in new Grants of Land according to his unsatiate Desires takes all occasions of abusing me in the grossest manner without any other provocation whatever and seems to have Inclinations very obstructive to thy private Interest, thô he is much for the support of Govmt, to wch by his own Interest he is chiefly led, but his natural failings and especially his indulging himself in Liquors and exposing himself by his excesses in it disables himself in a great degree to doe either the good or hurt that he might otherwise be capable of.~~ {But thy Son will be very capable of giving thee the later accounts of men besides Captain Roche who is but a weak man though generous, and a West Indian in his Life, there is one Rd Sleigh come lately from Jamaica a very sober good Ch. man[31] and Colonel Cressy very lately from virginia and Antigua Men of Note & Substance & more daily expected. but our Corporation gives all[32] strangers great offence and will make us odious. Ja: Coutts is a good man & thy

Friend[33] R[34] Halliwell if presented by others need not be much feared, and would be as good perhaps as R French W Rodeny holds with Ja: Coutts against all men John Hill is honest[34] Jos. Growdon very much mended & directly opposite to David[35] in the house}

As I told thee in my last[36] I used some freedoms in some of my Letters especially the private ones wch I hope will {not} be taken amiss they are the Result ~~,~~of my closest thoughts and when thou art pleased to consider what I wrote concerning thy Propriety ~~here~~, and the state of thy family thou wilt find {it} ~~cause~~ I believe ~~to judge them~~ but too well grounded ~~for as things are like to goe in general I can see but litle hopes of thy settling a regular Estate here for thy younger Children, but it is to be feared that should thou be willing to part with all it will be difficult to find any to take it off thy hands for a suitable consideration. This would~~. {It will} be no grateful Doctrine I believe to thy son[37] but I must ~~believe it is what~~ {be of opinion it} would best suit thy Circumstances ~~in general~~ {& perhaps} not be to his disadvantage for should thou goe off the stage I know not what would be made of it} I have ~~been very hard putt to it~~ {had some difficulty} to carry even between my duty to thee, and my Regards to him, but hope I have not ~~quite~~ miscarried in either. Lett me take the freedom to request thee to be very tender towards him in thy Resentments, lest those he has already conceived {from the abuses putt upon him} should by any addition precipitate him into ~~his~~ Ruine, he has much good Nature, wants not very good sence, but is unhappy {chiefly} by indiscretion, ~~he should not have been sent over without~~ {tis a pity} his wife {came not with him} ~~for her presence would have confined him within the bounds that he was not too regular in observing~~,[38] there is ~~nothing~~ {scarce any thing} has a worse effect upon his mind than the belief thou hast a greater regard to thy second children than thy first and an emulation ~~that seems fixed in him~~ between his own and thy younger rivets him in it {~~which ought to be obviated by the best~~} ~~but one irremediable unhappiness (unless he himself would resolve to take up) is, that his Inclinations and way of living lead him too far beyond the bounds of what any Estate he can at present enjoy will afford him. Thus I give my thoughts and Observations freely as I think my self in Duty obliged, not that I take any pleasure (for it is far from me) in making remarks so litle grateful in their Nature but that thou may the more fully know how things have past here. It is not but that I might be capable of acquitting my self more courtly in my Informations, but it neither suits my place nor Inclinations, & I hope & earnestly request thou wilt alwayes be pleased to remember that I write to thy selfe alone.~~ which ought to be obviated by the best means it can for he is and must be thy son, and thou must be either happy or unhappy in him The tie~~s~~ is indissoluble What I write I hope will be taken as designed and as the Result of an affectionate concern remembring tis only to thyself.

29th 9br The Assembly (as it is called) here[39] have past two acts only[40] & intend no more the first is for the Confirmation, and the other for encreasing the number of Representatives from 4 to 6[41] the Governour is very earnest for an Act to establish the Militia but they seem resolved not to touch with it till their next meeting wth advanced numbers I doubt I sha'nt have time now to send thee any Copies They have made provision in the latter to come in next time upon the Charter[42] but for no other reason than to keep more like one Government for they hate it as other good men doe We have had no Accounts for some Months from Europe, we fear 'tis owing to some great Embargoe upon the Account of Portugal[43] Pray excuse my repeating the same things in several Letters, they are either such as have great place in my own thoughts or that I am desirous should have some in thine. I am wth Love & Duty,

Thy faithful & Obedient servant,
J L

PS

I have found the Catalogue of thy Books[44] thrown in among the Jersey Deeds Deeds in the litle Trunk & have examined them there is Sr Waltr Rawleigh His. and Purchas's Pilgrims[45] wanting of the folios and by the black lead Marks in the Margin made at examining them when first brought from Col. Markhams they seem never to have been there since thy last Arrival, if they were I shall recover them or others in their stead there is no other folios missing but Braithwaits Engl. Gentleman[46] wch with the rest shall be made good, there was never a greater Villain known than he that plaid the trick,[47] yet was never discovered nor suspected till the day after he left me ~~that~~ by a remarkable Providence that the Innocent might be cleared. His father made me promise to be private in it engaging to make full satisfaction and hoping it would be the last of the kind but he is mistaken I doubt {take no notice &c.}[48] We cannot by any Deeds left here make out thy Title to thy Proprieties in the Jerseys & S: Jennings sayes that the Council of Proprietors there admitt of none to take up land without producing their Deeds or Authentick Copies of them The Deeds here relate only to Salem and they want explanation for there seems something yet wanting to clear that matter fully. This will require a Speedy Answer I mean about the Proprieties wch I intreat thee send us ut ante.[49]

J. L.

I hope this following Spring to clear off Wm Aubry's interest but we must have a new Power[50] & should have one likewise for the 15500 Acres[51] in Newc County the Patent for it is dated the 27 or 28th of 8br 1701 as I remember[52]

Transcript, Logan Papers; LBC, James Logan Letterbook, HSP. (*Micro.* 11:432, 434.) The editors have correlated two flawed transcripts with a partial rough draft in trying to establish the text of this important document. The transcription in the Logan

Papers (*Micro.* 11:434) is complete but unreliable; it is our preferred text for the first 40 percent of the document. Deborah Logan prepared a far looser transcript of the opening three paragraphs (not filmed) which in a few places seems preferable to the Logan Papers transcript. James Logan's letterbook contains a rough draft of the closing 60 percent. This letterbook copy (*Micro.* 11:432) is our preferred text from n. 27 onward.

1. The meaning of these initials is unclear; for Logan's duplicate, see doc. 92, text at n. 1.

2. William Penn, Jr., took passage in the H.M.S. *Jersey;* John Guy was master of the brigantine *Robert and Benjamin.*

3. Excepting Logan's letter to WP of 27 Oct. 1704 (*Micro.* 11:402) and Logan's letter to John Askew of 5 Oct. 1704 (James Logan Letterbook, 2:50-51), these letters have not been found.

4. Deborah Logan reads "state."

5. William Penn, Jr.

6. Deborah Logan's transcript here is quite different: "as I have endeavoured to acquit myself to the best of my power, and have left nothing unessayed which I could think of for his benefit, my conscience yields me the greater ease."

7. The corporation of Philadelphia had initiated proceedings against William Penn, Jr., in the mayor's court in response to his participation in a brawl at Enoch Story's tavern. *Micro.* 11:369; *Minutes of the Provincial Council,* 2:160.

8. Deborah Logan reads "baseness." The reference is to David Lloyd and doc. 83.

9. "Accumulation" in Deborah Logan's transcription.

10. Probably "villain"; Deborah Logan read it as "David."

11. "Designing and weak men" according to Deborah Logan.

12. This phrase omitted by Deborah Logan.

13. *Minutes of the Provincial Council,* 2:176-77; *Votes and Proceedings,* 1(pt. 2):30.

14. Omitted by Deborah Logan.

15. On 27 Oct. 1704 the Phila. Monthly Meeting elected several Friends to inquire about a "paper" sent to England concerning the reputation of Truth and Friends. Phila. Monthly Meeting Records, Abstracts of the Minutes, 1:427, GSP.

16. The Charter of Privileges (1701) and the Charter of Property. See doc. 28; *Micro.* 9:770.

17. Deborah Logan reads "fate."

18. Deborah Logan's transcription ends here. Her reading of the passage "there is a general infatuation . . . upon such Melancholy reflections" is totally different from the wording here and appears to be her own invention.

19. See *Votes and Proceedings,* 1(pt. 2):23-29; *Minutes of the Provincial Council,* 2:173-75.

20. This refers to the Long Parliament elected in 1640 which refused to acknowledge Charles I's order to dissolve.

21. *Micro.* 9:682; *Votes and Proceedings,* 1(pt. 2):20.

22. Possibly a reference to John Evans's proposition to use the licensing of taverns as a way to defray the costs of government. *Minutes of the Provincial Council,* 2:159-60.

23. Copyist's error for "Terrs.," i.e., the Territories or Lower Counties, which held a separate Assembly at New Castle on 14 Nov. 1704. *Minutes of the Provincial Council,* 2:178.

24. The 1701 Charter of Privileges allowed for the election of eight representatives per county in case of separate assemblies for Pennsylvania and the Lower Counties. See doc. 28, text at n. 15.

25. "Terrs."

26. The property rights of soil and revenue in Pennsylvania, which WP planned to keep, just as Lord Baltimore had retained his property rights in Maryland after surrendering the government of that colony to the crown in 1690-91.

27. Here begins Logan's letterbook version.

28. Logan Papers adds "Man of sence."

29. Logan Papers adds "generally."

30. Jasper Yeates.

31. Churchman, i.e. Anglican.

32. The Logan Papers transcript reads "many."

33. Logan Papers adds "(the first talks of returning, and the last meddles with no

kind of business, nor seems altogether fitted for it; the other is a merchant, as Roche is) but."

34. The Logan Papers transcript adds: "but weak & sometimes Silly."

35. David Lloyd.

36. Logan's letter to WP of 27 Oct., the one preceding this one, does not contain the passage referred to here. *Micro.* 11:402.

37. The Logan Papers transcript reads "to M^{r} W^{m}."

38. Apparently many colonists did not approve of the company William Penn, Jr., kept. Together with John Evans and other restless young men he frequented taverns of ill repute and seemed to have lived in a style considered inappropriate for his station and position. See text at nn. 5-7, above.

39. See n. 23, above.

40. The minutes of this New Castle Assembly have not been found.

41. The Logan Papers transcript adds: "for each County."

42. The New Castle Assembly was called by the governor's writ, not according to the Charter of 1701. See *Minutes of the Provincial Council,* 2:129-31, 134, 164.

43. Probably a reference to the opening of the Peninsular War in 1704, when English troops were committed to fighting France and its allies on the Iberian peninsula. George Macaulay Trevelyan, *England Under Queen Anne: Blenheim* (London, 1930), pp. 402-7.

44. The catalog of a consignment of books WP had brought to Pennsylvania in 1699; one of Logan's servants had stolen some of these books. For more detail, see Edwin Wolf, II, "A Parcel of Books for the Province," *PMHB,* 89:428-46.

45. Samuel Purchas, *Purchas his Pilgrimage* (1626); Walter Raleigh, *An Abridgement of Sir Walter Raleigh's History of the World* (1698) [Wing, R151].

46. Richard Braithwaite, *The English Gentleman and the English Gentlewoman,* 3d ed. by John Dawson (1641) [Wing, B4262].

47. The book-stealing servant.

48. The Logan Papers transcript adds: "I request thee to take no notice of it there if thou imagine who the Person is which is not difficult."

49. As before.

50. See doc. 82, text at n. 25.

51. The Logan Papers transcript reads "15000."

52. The Logan Papers transcript reads: "is dated 23rd 8^{m} 1701 the Quitrent to thee one Beaver Skin but I wish thou couldest have that in thy own hands, Yet now there is an absolute Patent for it upon Record." This patent has not been found.

ANTAGONISTS CLOSING IN

January–October, 1705

By 1705 a storm that had long been brewing—over WP's unpaid debt to the late Philip Ford and his heirs—was about to burst. Although WP may not have realized that the Fords were preparing to take him to court, he must have known that his position was precarious, especially as his eldest son, William Penn, Jr., was living well beyond his income, and his son-in-law, William Aubrey, was pressing him to pay large obligations. The Fords were certainly contemplating hostile action as early as January, and by July word of their claim to Pennsylvania had reached the colony (doc. 101). The Fords' suit against WP was to occupy most of his energies for the next three years, ultimately taking him to debtors' prison in 1708.

Early in the year, with this threat still in the background, WP wrote to James Logan (doc. 91), imploring him with renewed urgency to collect and remit more proprietary revenue from the colony. Actually, Logan was doing quite a bit: between 1701 and 1705 he had remitted more than £4000 to WP in England and paid an additional £3000 on WP's account in Pennsylvania (see doc. 100). But this was by no means enough. Hence in January 1705, WP renewed his negotiations for the sale of Pennsylvania's government to the crown, after a hiatus of a year and a half. Pressed by debts and discouraged by the colonists' ingratitude—both political and financial—WP must have seen surrender as a more attractive option than earlier. In a series of exchanges with the Board of Trade (docs. 87–90), WP laid out his new position: he was prepared to waive many of the powers he had sought to reserve in his 1703 draft (doc. 62), and he would now insist mainly on religious and civil freedoms for the Quakers and on certain proprietary privileges for himself and his heirs. In his new draft surrender (doc. 96) and patent (doc. 98), WP sought to solidify these points: Pennsylvania laws and customs were to be confirmed, yearly assemblies held, and liberty of conscience guaranteed. At the same time, WP would be granted exemption from taxes and the erection of a county palatine, in which he would hold quasi-royal power. The Board of Trade objected to WP's palatinate and to the clauses on government and toleration, arguing that these were matters to be left to the queen and the Toleration Act. Although WP sought to answer their objections (doc. 99), by 1 September he was submitting a more modest list of requests (doc. 105). WP's efforts to win concessions bore little fruit. More than half of the Pennsylvania laws submitted by WP to the crown for review—55 out of 105—were objected to either by the attorney general or by the Board of Trade (doc. 104). Negotiations on the colony's government lapsed until early in 1707, when the board demanded unconditional surrender (doc. 136).

Ironically enough, just as WP was most vigorously pursuing his surrender negotiations, Logan was writing to report that Pennsylvania's political climate was improving markedly (docs. 92, 100). Embarrassed by David Lloyd's fulminations against WP in the name of the Assembly (doc. 83), both Quakers and non-Quakers seemed inclined to a new civility. WP was predictably outraged at Lloyd and his cronies and hurt by the colonists' disregard of his efforts and sacrifices on their behalf. Still, he was buoyed by the failure of Lloyd's efforts to distribute the remonstrance among English Quakers. Despite a bout with illness in February, WP responded authoritatively to challenges from Pennsylvania. He rebuked the colonists as disobedient children, called Lloyd an "ungrateful Hypocrite" and Griffith Jones a "false Jew," and threatened to vacate the charters he had granted (docs. 93–95, 97, and 106). He applauded Governor Evans's rejection of the Assembly's presumptions and urged him to press charges against Lloyd's ally, Assemblyman William Biles: "fall on him or any other Such unruly People at once, and make Some one Example to terrifie the rest. Thou hast not only my leave, but liking and encouragement whether call'd Quakers or others" (*Micro.* 12:251). WP was evidently feeling that his political position was strong; after all, he wrote, he could "Dispose all to the Crown, Soile as well as Governm^{t}" (doc. 94). But all this suddenly changed in July 1705 when his English and American adversaries—the Fords and David Lloyd—made common cause; see the headnote to doc. 101.

87
TO THE BOARD OF TRADE

2 11^{m} (Ja) 1704[/5]

Honorable Friends

Since my last proposall[1] Seemed to you to clogg the practicableness of the thing desired by you, to witt, the Resignation of my Goverm^{t}

to the Queen, because of the reservations made by me upon it, I write this to let you know, that Since [i]t is made So difficult to me [to ho]ld, I shall wave those Conditi[on]s that were in my own favour, [an]d shall be satisfyed with my Seigniory and Proprietary Priviledges, with {this} only Saveing to me & my Successors, that we shall be exempted from troublesom offices & the Publick Taxes; and that the Inhabitants, may have their entire Liberty of Conscience, & be continued, as Capable & eligible to any Civil employments, as hetherto they have {been}, the People called Quakers especially, because of their Number & wealth, & that they Chiefly made it a Country; which I desire you to report to the Queen, with a just regard to my vast expence & Fateigu[e]s these 30 yeares, employd to ge[t] & make it & maintain it to the present Unpresidented Progress [the] place is arrived at, and you will much oblige

your respectfull Friend
Wm Penn

I propose an other Lt Governour to be approved, to succeed the present Gentleman in case of Death, that there may be no disorder, or failure in Goverm^{t} on such an accident.

ALS. CO 5/1263/3, PRO. (*Micro.* 11:458.) This letter is torn along one edge; the editors have supplied conjectural readings of the missing text within brackets.

1. Doc. 62.

88
TO THE BOARD OF TRADE

3 11^{m} (Jan^{r}) 1704[/5]

Hon^{bl} Friends

To explain my Selfe upon the termes, offices [&] Taxes in my letter [o]f yesterday.[1] I mean by offices, any one under the Governour wch is not of our own seeking, Civil or Military. and by Taxes, not to pay pole mony, or any land or mony Tax, I mean not Customs, or tradeing Impost[s] I begg your dispatch in this affaire, being as I Conceive, come to the poin[t] you exprest to Satisfy yo[u] when my first & large memoriall[2] was presented to you; takeing this with you; that your Bill in Parliament gave me no time to settle a Revenue[3] to my own great expence for these 3 years in defraying the charges there, & so long expensive attendance here to issue m[y] Languish[ing] affaires: as also that the first year after my arrivall there, the Queens Revenue augmented from 2 or 300^{l} per annum to ~~17~~2000^{l} per annum, & the year 1700, 8000^{l} and odd monys per annum.[4] as I have {cirtificats} to show out of the Custom house books here, wch I think is a present advantage to the Queen, & she will have it more in her own Powr to augment them by the care of her own officers & Gover^r. I am wth a just esteeme

Your Respectf^ll Friend
Wm Penn

ALS. CO 5/1263/2, PRO. (*Micro.* 11:462.) This letter is torn along one edge; the editors have supplied conjectural readings of the missing text within brackets.

1. Doc. 87.
2. Doc. 62.
3. When WP rushed back to England in 1701 to oppose a parliamentary bill for reuniting proprietary colonies to the crown, the only direct revenue he had obtained from the Pennsylvania Assembly was a tax of £2000 for the proprietor's use levied in 1700—which was not fully collected by 1705. See doc. 33, n. 5.
4. See doc. 62, n. 3.

89
FROM WILLIAM POPPLE, JR., AND THE BOARD OF TRADE

[11 January 1705]

To Mr Penn.

S^r

The Lords Commiss^rs for Trade & Plant^ns having had under Consideration your Propos^ls for surrendring your Right of Governm^t of Pennsylvania to her Majesty,[1] they have Commanded me to send you the inclosed Queries, unto which they desire your particular & distinct answer in writing tomorrow morning. I am &c.

Wm Popple jun^r[2]

Whitehall Jan^ry the 11th 1704/5.

Queries for Mr Penn.

Quer. What is meant by *Seigniory and Proprietary Priviledges?*
A full and distinct Account is desired what those Priviledges are, and how far they are understood to extend.
Q. Who is to be understood by the word *Successors* that are to be exempt^d from publick Offices and Taxes?
Q. Whether by *intire Liberty of Conscience* any thing else is meant, than such a Toleration as is allowed by the Act of Parliament past here.[3]
Q. What is meant by *the People called Quakers being continued as Capable and eligible to any Civill Imployments?* {What are those Employments.} Is it intended such people shall be admitted to Imployments without taking the Oath directed by the Law of England or the Affirmation allowed to Quakers; And will such People allow such persons as in England would be obliged and are willing to take an Oath in any publick Proceedings to do the same?

Copy. CO 5/1291/87, PRO. (Not filmed.) Docketed: January the 11th. | Letter to Mr Penn, wth | Severall Queries upon | his Proposalls for the | Surrender of his Right | of Governmt to the Crown. Another copy of the queries appears in *Micro.* 11:466.

1. Doc. 87.

2. William Popple, Jr. (d. 1722), served as his father's assistant until May 1707, when he took over as secretary to the Board of Trade, a position he held until his death. Steele, *Colonial Policy*, pp. 115, 167: *CSPC, 1706-1708*, p. 436.

3. The Toleration Act, passed in 1689 (1 Will. & Mary, cap. 18).

90
TO THE BOARD OF TRADE

My Answear to the four Queries[1] sent me by the Lds Comrs for Trade & Plantations

11 11m (Jan) 1704[/5]

To the First, I mean all the Royaltys that can belong to ~~to~~ Paramount[2] Courts, as fines Forfeitures deodands,[3] &c: wth Jurisdiction of Courts Leet & Barron,[4] & erecting of mannors &c: as exprest in my Graunt[5] ~~R~~Mines, Minerals, Royall mines & Fishes

To the second Querie, I mean by Successors, my Blood, discending from me, my Children, & Posterity.

To the 3d Querie {abt Liberty of Conscience} I mean, not only that relating to worship, but education, or Schools, a Coercive Ministeriall maintainance the Militia

To the fourth Querie I say, I meane, that they may be capable of any Civill employmt but Goverr takeing the Legal affirmation of the Country according to Custom, from Counsellor to Constable, as they have been from the begining: wch is but just & reasonable in my opinion, & every bodys else I have ta[lked] with on that subject, being a Country & Govermt made by them, for their own ease in points where they found themselves pincht here; & will very uneasily be made Dissenters in their own Country, where also, they never excluded or abridg'd any, but only claim equall priviledges & Prefermt with others, even when twenty to one and that they may Continue so is wt I desire as a most reasonable saveing, & wch I hope will seem so in your opinion.

12 11m (Jan) 1704 — Wm Penn

ALS. CO 5/1263/3, PRO. (*Micro.* 11:468.) Docketed: Pennsylvania | Mr Penns Answer to the | Queries Sent him the 11 Instant | upon his proposals for the Sur- | render of his Govt to the Crown. | Recd 12 January | Read Ditto | 1704/5.

1. Doc. 89.

2. Higher or superior. *Black's Law Dictionary.*

3. Deodands: personal chattels which had caused a person's death and were thus forfeit. Ibid.

4. Manorial courts; the court leet oversaw the presentment of crimes and punishment of misdemeanors, while the court baron dealt with manorial services and personal actions. Ibid.

5. WP's grant of Pennsylvania from Charles II; see *PWP*, 2:63-73.

91
TO JAMES LOGAN

London 16 11m [January] 1704[/5]

James Logan
I think I may say I have all thy letters as well privat as publick, from my Son, John Askew &c:[1] a Melancolly sceane enough allways; religiously upon my poor Childe: Pennsilvania begun it by my absence {here} & there it is accomplisht, with *expence, disapointm*t, ingratitude & *poverty.* The Lord uphold me under these sharp & heavy burdens, wth his Free Spirit. I should have been glad of an acct of his expences, and more of a Rent Role, that I may know wt I have to Stand upon, & help my selfe with. He is my greatest affliction for his Soul's & my posteritys or familys Sake. I say once again let me have a Rent-Role, or I must Sinck with gold in my vew, but not in my Powr. To have neither Supplys, nor a reason of Credit here, is certainly a Cruel circumstance. I want to know wt has been sold, wt Bonds taken & mony received, Since I arrived in the Country; wch I desire thee to send most expeditiously {as also Duplicats of Bonds, attested by authority}; & that all other business may give way to it, be it of wt kinde it will. I am also sorry to hear there is no land left to be taken up for me or my abused Posterity.[2] The Game must be then up indeed. But I can hardly let it enter my thoughts. Is all T. Fairmans discovery taken up, & I & mine no sharers in it, forty miles from Philadelphia, & 12 miles by six,[3] Surrounded by rocks, of wch he Seem'd so pleas'd when I was there or soon after I left you. I have 100 German familys, prepareing for you, that buy 30, or 40000 Acres;[4] & no longer than yesterday Sr Charles Hedges,[5] discourst me upon a Swiss Colony,[6] intending thither, by the request of our Envoyee in the Cantons;[7] but keep this close for many reasons; only look out, & keep it in remembrance. I also want the Propriety acctts, what & to whom, & when, & for wt. Thou must pay twenty five pds, to the Gentlewoman Phillips[8] for twenty pds I receiv'd here upon her acctt by remittall of the Bishop of Cloyn,[9] by Ed. Hastwell;[10] according to the late standard of value.[11] The Barbado's Fleet, comeing home so late, mett both wth Stormes of winde & Guns, the french faling in among them, ~~&~~ so that of 120 sale, not above 80 & odd got in, where ~~I am~~, out of forty odd Hogsheads of Sugar, I have lost 30. & Ed. Singleton carryed into France. They frieghted upon five vessels; one burnt wch Ed. came out in, had 10 hhds & two {were} taken, that had ten hhds each. one of 5 & {an other} of 6 hhds come in. one at Sea, a Brigentine, she has 7. no news of her. and as for Guy[12] no news yet, but my son, who is come safe, tho neer foundring in the Jersy, Says, he beleives she is lost, for after the Storme they saw her no more. J. As. ensured one hundred pds upon thy letter,[13] but the ensurer broak, & the 20 guineas[14] lost. this done upon the former intimations. Ensurers faile much.

I have not a word abt the East Jersy Frd that was to have payd 900l N.Y. mony. I think his name is Stockins; Cos. Silus's wifes bror.[15] nor of Ricd Beumont~~s~~, of whom I bought 300 Acres in west Jersey, as the writeings I left wth thee {show}, bought of Biddle, by him, & might be applyed to secure the Island before Pennsberry.[16] 'twas to have been upon Rancocas Creek, his widdow clamours me much abt it, this is the Sixth time at least that I have writt thee abt it:[17] nor didst thou Send me word wt my Son Sould his Mannor for;[18] but after all, he drew a bill for ten pds at his arrivall, to ride 200 miles home, wch he perform'd in 2 days & a night. I mett him by apointmt between this & worm.[19] Stayd but 3 hours together, See, how much more the bad frds treatmt of him Stumbled {him} from the blessed truth ~~&~~ than those he acknowledges to be good ones, could prevaile to keep him in the profession of it; from the prevailing ground in himselfe to wt is loose[20] more than to wt is retired, Circumspect and virtuous. I have writt very copiously to thee by severall Packetts, 2 by Ed: Lane,[21] but a great Ennimy to Frds, a rev~~o~~iller, 2 or 3, by Samll Hollister,[22] one of my wifes kinsmen both upon the Biddeford Factor, or Mert via Maryland, of wch pray take notice. Now for your Govermt. Depend upon it shall part Speedily from it, & had I not given that ungratefull & Conceited people that charter,[23] & {gott but 400 per annum fixt for Govr & no[t]} made but too good Conditions for them, I had had twice as much as I am now likely to have. If I dont desolve it the Queen will, that Charter I meane, wch after all DLs [24] craft & malice dispis'd for its Craziness. as for him, he will perhaps be constrain'd to Change the aire & his Blackbird too. M—.[25]

For Selling all, If I can Clear my Incumbrances, [illegible deletion] without it, I shall do so. If not, then, Pro. or Ters shall goe. But alas I can neither Sell, or Borrow till I know wt I have to do either. pray minde this, & lett it not be sayd, that after 5 years time I know not wt I have to sell or mortgage If I would do either. I heartily acknowledge to the Govr J. Evans his quietness, good distinction & integrity & Courage. had he past those Laws[26] he had disstroy'd me & him Selfe too. I shall Stick close to him in those methods he has taken. For Bewlys place[27] whose death is a loss indeed—the Gang here [Paxton[28] &c. with the Bp of London got Moore in before thine[29] came to my][30] hand, [almost a month, if not 6] weekes[: a wonderful thing: That pack]et that g[ave me the {first} notice of the poor] mans de[ath, came viâ Lisbon, & the] Milford, that put [in there, & cost me] 1l-11ss-6d. No Bill, nor Cargoe, [& wch] Crowns all, Guy carryed also into France. But besides commission mony at Phil. the {commission at the} receipt & returne at Barb. &c: & then once here, reduces it to next nothing.[31] In short {Bills there or goods} to Jamaica, if can get mony, now the Trade is open wth the Spanierds,[32] to returne, or Bills {thence,} and the Maderas, ~~is~~ are all the Returns I would have made. pray Carefully penetrate to the bottom of the Designe of affronting my Son.[33] Had I not orders to turn out D. L. from the Lds Justices, & to prosecute

& punish him, & Send word wt Punishmt I inflicted, & that part of it should be that he were never Capable of any employ in the Country?[34] & does {he} endeavour my ruine for not obeying, but offering him to cover himself in the proffits, under any tollerable name? did I {not} do almost as much for A. M.[35] who had orders to treat him {sharply} for his Barrels of Tobacco, in lieue of Flowr? and has he forgott how I gott Q.[36] to drop it &c: & has Gr. J.[37] forgot my Boons I have done for him, many a day; well. als well that ends well.
[But if those illegitimate Quakers think their unworthy treatment no fault towards me, they may find I can upon better terms,][38] take [their Enemies by the hand, than they can mine. and unless the honest] will by [Church discipline, or the gover]mt whilst [it is mine, take these Korah's[39] to t]ask, & make them sensible of [their] baseness, I must & will do so. In short, upon my knowledge of the Conclusion of this winters assembly, I shall take my last measures. when the Prosperity that attends the Country is talkt of, & wt they have done for me or Deputys, that have Supported them agst their neighbours Envy, & Church attempts here & there, they show Struck with admiration & must think me an ill man, or they a base People. That wch I expected was 3, or 400l per annum ~~that money for~~ {for} the Govr & {to raise for} other Charges as they saw occasion. and If they will not do this wilingly, they will finde, before they are a year older, they must give a great deale more, whither they please ort not. I, only {by my interest,} have prevented a Scheam, drawn to new moddell the Colonys, told so by a Duke, & a Minister too.[40] For indeed, If our folks had Settled a reasonable revenue, I would have returned to Settle a Queens Goverr & the people {together,} & have layd my bones {wth them,} for the Country is as pleasant to me as ever; and if my wifes Mor should dye,[41] who is now very ill, I beleive, not only my wife & our young Stock, but her Father[42] too, would encline thither, who has been a Treasure to Bristoll, & given his whole time to the Service of the poor; Frds first, till they make 8 per Cent of their mony; & next the Citty poor, by act of Parl. where he has been kept in beyond form;[43] he has so managd to their advantage, that the Citty members gave our Friend[s?] & my Far in perticular, an encomium much to their honour {in the house}. well! God almighty forgive, reclaim, amend & preserve us all, amen.
The young man John Lisk I writt of,[44] goes for Archangel. methinks of those that goe hence thou mayst finde one Suitable for thee. Here Came the Book theif, dada's own Image,[45] That there should ever be such a succession of incomparable— He came for a letter to thee, I took no notice of past offences, us'd him Softly enough. per next a Catalogue, but I would have one thence.
I want a distinct knowledge how the business of the Resurveys goes, & wt it comes to. That law & ⅔ of the rest are reported Blanck by the Atturney Genll [46] so that they must to work again, & give mony or

noe Laws nor Govermt for Ile maintain none; & for their Address,[47] Ile use them for Pyes,[48] insteed of affrontg Royall hands, wth that mans name for Speaker,[49] that is the aversion of the ministry, most if not all of whom, where Lds Justices, or in office when his degrading punishmt & disability were commanded agst him.[50]
my son speaks well of Q:[51] as most Civil to him, & that Moor[52] Promest him he never more would Vex or Cross grain my Interest—expound this. For the three Bills[53] they are the scorn of Lawyers & men of sence that have seen or hear of them, as was DLs Hedgeing in of the Cucko, by the new castle charter.[54] did I give them a charter for fear I should loose the Govermt to secure them herafter, & when I have at my great trouble & charge preserv'd it, & them in authority, and Send them a milde, discreet & couragious Goverr approved by the Queen, in Spight of Q. M.[55] &c: to give him no Sallery, to pay me none of the Subscription mony,[56] but turn my own Charter against me & my posterity, & make head agst my officers, as if I & they were their greatest Ennimys, insteed of Q. M. J. Car. J. W.[57] &c: who ever was so treated? The Lord forgive them their great Ingratitude, as well as Prophainness, to quit me to Follow such a self-interested tool, as D. L.[58] that owes his bread to me too: surely Such a people dwell not upon the face of the Earth. God I hope will deliver me from them If they are not {delivered} from so absurd & sordid a behavour & Conduct. and this I command thee to Communicate to the Guilty, as well as the innocent of that assembly, who profess the blessed Truth—and I desire the Goverr & my officers, will take a little more Spiritedness and quickness upon them; & curb their Insolences as Stricktly, as they pretend to do irregularitys in the Corporation.
S. V.[59] takes great exception to J. Gro[ve's][60] Consigning the Sugars to Ed. Singleton, & so he would the goods on Guy, if knew it. wherfore, forbear giveing him offence, who has been friendly to me. But if no goods come that will naturally follow. wt mony did Cr Bierly[61] Lend my son? Direct thy letters to John Elys[62] Esqr at the secretarys office at whitehall, wch I have often told thee, & that would save me the heavy Postage, & let the Goverr know as much; for they come Safely to hand & Speedily. writeing {on them} *for the Queens Service.* I have Sometimes thought, if thou didst change the Property of the Bonds due to me, it might be safer, & pass better in pay. I have a minde also to Sell off ½ the quitrents, if could have Bills, or mony there to returne hither according to the regulation of Coyn,[63] except wt is due upon Eng: Standard, as all those of the Province are. I beleive, the Fee farmers wo'd give 20 years Purchass. and that would ease me here. Consider of these things, & cast about how to do Something that may ease me of my ~~great~~ Heavy Burdens here, that have been great & long, & dayly encrease. Ed. Ship.[64] &c. may ketch at[65] Such a proposall; so some N. yorkers. Would ~~that~~ our people {be} brought to know their Interest & help me ~~to them~~ parting with the

Govermt should never part them & I, but to them I would yet come, & be a protection to them under it, & settle my younger brood wth them. but I dispaire of their recovery, & {beleive} that a Tite & Rigorous hand must first teach them how to vallue my Company[66] & give me a better entertainmt. I Justify not my sons folly, & less their provocation; but if his regards to your Govern~~ment~~our does not hinder him, he has a great interest to obtain it, wth Persons of great quality & in the Ministry too ~~obtain it~~, & he is of a temper to remember them;[67] tho I fear they did designe the affront to me more than to him, wch renders the Case worse.
In short, Sell nothing but to returne as I Sayd just now, neither one thing nor an other {in cash or bills}; I will rather Sell here to the Govermt — I expect that Frds and the assembly will do me Justice upon D. L. If wt thou writest {be true} of his forgery & clandestine work after the assembly was up.[68] 'Tis an intollerable abuse & wt deserves his Eares &[69] all he is worth in the world; & ~~I do desire that Judge M~~ (unless they will make {him} a publick example for his villainy, forthwith, & turne him out from being Recorder, or a Practitioner at any of my Courts; I {say I} herby desire Judge mompesson, as he has exprest {he can,} would show them the force of their Charters, as well as they have basely the use of them. I say again, I desire that he would evacuate, both that to the towne & that to the Province,[70] Since I finde more Justice & mercy from my enimys than some of my profest Frds, I mean as to the Profession {such}. Let no time be lost, & I shall loose none here. I am a[nxi]ously greiv'd at thy unhappy love,[71] for thy sake & my own; for T. S.[72] & thy discord has been of no service here any more than there, & some say, that come thence, that thy amours have so alter'd or influenced thee, that thou art grown Tuchy & apt to give short & rough answears, wch many call haughty &c: I make no Judgement but caution thee, as In former letters to lett truth preside, & bear impertinences as patiently as thou canst. Others would insinuate farther, {as if} thy Complacency[73] {was} for thy own interest, att my damage; but I turn a deaf eare to that: The best conducts draw often the greatest Envy or reflection sometimes. I own I am unspeably[74] disapointed in not knowing how my Interest lyes, as to Bonds, Rent-Roles &c: wt received & wt payd, & faile not of it by the first. I had a lettr from the Judge; [&] packets from the Goverr, a lettr from S. C. I. N. & Gr. owen,[75] wch Ile answear If I can, but my incomparable difficultys press me; & one is two German Gentlemen[76] that are come hither to pass to you, to fix a Colony in the Province, of Germans, & the ship's [re]ady to saile. But I purpose to write [to] the Goverr. My Dr love to the above [named] & all others [that are right minded.]
For Barbers letters,[77] they are safe, by the ships being taken &c. — O that some of our People would read the Book of Numbers from the 20th to the 30 & see their Condition.[78] But I must be brief, so desireing

thee to send me a full acct of all things, & to be lively, & dilligent in my business, wch succeeding, so shalt thou, I end

Thy Log Friend
Wm Penn

I had John Sachers letter,[79] & desire him to goe on as he has done, & send me their history by all opertunitys, wth my love to him & her, & the family.[80] I was pleased wth his acct but would have it yet more exact myn are well, & Salute Frds & thee. vale.

ALS. Logan Papers, HSP. (*Micro.* 11:474.) Missing text has been supplied in brackets from a partial duplicate in Logan Papers, 1:57, and from a manuscript copy by Deborah Norris Logan in Logan Papers, Selections from the Correspondence of the Honourable James Logan, HSP.

1. See doc. 86, n. 3.
2. For Logan's views on WP's efforts to settle an estate for his younger children in Pennsylvania, see docs. 82, text at n. 28; 86, text at nn. 36-37.
3. See doc. 56, n. 44. The location of this land has not been determined.
4. Johann Henry Kersten (or Kersen, Kirsten, Kursten, Kuirson) and Lawrence Christopher Nohren appear to have been the agents for this group; they were Saxons who between them had bought 1000 acres of Pennsylvania land from Col. Frederick de Redegeldt in England. The two traveled to Pennsylvania in 1705, but Logan complained that they were only looking, not preparing to buy large tracts as WP believed. Kersten (d. 1726), a woolendraper from Langensalza, settled in Pennsylvania in 1709. *Micro.* 12:368; *PA*, 2d ser., 19:468, 686; Phila. Will Bk. D, #358.
5. Sir Charles Hedges (d. 1714), secretary of state 1700-1701 and 1702-6, was Tory in his politics. He had been a privy councilor since 1700 and an M.P. since 1701. *DNB*.
6. Georg Ritter of Bern was promoting a plan to settle 400-500 Swiss Protestants in Pennsylvania or Virginia under the protection of the English crown. Hedges sponsored the proposal and submitted Ritter's petition to the Board of Trade. After an abortive expedition in 1710, Ritter's group ultimately founded New Bern in North Carolina. *CSPC, 1706-1708*, pp. 61-62, 79-80; Albert Bernhardt Faust, *Lists of Swiss Emigrants in the Eighteenth Century to the American Colonies* (Washington, D.C., 1920), 1:2-3.
7. Dr. William Aglionby (d. 1705), diplomat and author, had served in Spain and Savoy before his appointment as envoy to the Swiss cantons in 1702. Ritter had enlisted his aid in promoting a Swiss colony. D. B. Horn, *The British Diplomatic Service, 1689-1789* (Oxford, 1961), p. 227; Luttrell, 2:333, 3:105, 5:214; Faust, *Lists of Swiss Emigrants*, 1:2.
8. Lady Mary Newcomen, alias Mary Phillips; see doc. 49, n. 2.
9. Charles Crow (d. 1726), appointed in 1702 as bishop of Cloyne in Co. Cork, Ireland.
10. Edward Haistwell (c. 1658-1709) was a London merchant and Quaker lobbyist at Parliament. *PWP*, 3:92n.
11. WP refers to the inflated Pennsylvania currency, whose value had been reset by royal proclamation in 1704; see doc. 56, n. 65.
12. John Guy, master of the brigantine *Robert and Benjamin*, in which WP owned a share. The ship had been seized by the French. Albright G. Zimmerman, "James Logan, Proprietary Agent," *PMHB*, 78:158.
13. Logan had written to John Askew asking him to insure the vessel for £300. See doc. 82.
14. £21.
15. Richard Stockton, whose sister Mary had married Silas Crispin, WP's cousin; see doc. 33, n. 17.
16. On WP's purchase from Beaumont and his dispute with Biddle, see doc. 76, nn. 20-21. Beaumont's widow seems to have been applying to WP for additional payment on his purchase; see *Micro.* 12:535.

17. See *Micro.* 11:409; doc. 76.

18. William Penn, Jr., had sold his manor of Williamstadt to William Trent and Isaac Norris for £850; this 7482-acre tract included the site of the present Norristown. Jenkins, pp. 114-15n; Townsend Ward, "The Germantown Road and its Associations," *PMHB*, 5:9.

19. Warminghurst, Sus.

20. The word "loose" in the manuscript has been changed to "levity" by a modern hand.

21. Edward Lane (1664-1710), son of a Quaker grocer of Bristol, had settled in Pennsylvania by 1683, where he accumulated large landholdings in Phila. Co. Lane embraced Anglicanism in the wake of the Keithian schism among Quakers in the 1690s. For WP's letter carried by him, see *Micro.* 11:355; the second has not been found. Mortimer, 1:207; Digests of Quaker Records, Bristol and Som., GSP; A. J. Barrow, "St. James's, Perkiomen," *PMHB*, 19:89-90; Phila. Will Bk. C, #160.

22. For letters carried by Samuel Hollister, see doc. 85; *Micro.* 11:409.

23. The Charter of Privileges (doc. 28).

24. David Lloyd's.

25. "Blackbird" was later used as a slang term for black slaves, but the *OED* lists no examples of this usage before the nineteenth century. It might be an oblique reference to the devil, "blackbeard" (see Bartlett Jere Whiting with Helen Wescott Whiting, *Proverbs, Sentences, and Proverbial Phrases: From English Writings Mainly Before 1500* [Cambridge, Mass., 1968], p. 44). "M — " may stand for John Moore, a close associate of Lloyd's, or for "mum," meaning that Logan should keep silent. Roy N. Lokken, *David Lloyd, Colonial Lawmaker* (Seattle, 1959), pp. 119-22.

26. The 1704 Assembly had passed three bills to confirm and explain the Charter of Privileges, the Charter of Philadelphia, and the province's laws of property. As Logan reported to WP, the Assembly's recasting of these laws attacked WP's prerogatives, including the veto he had reserved on laws passed by the Assembly and deputy governor. Gov. Evans urged the Assembly to defer its claims, citing the need to consult authorities in England, particularly on the issue of the dissolution and prorogation of the Assembly. Since the Assembly refused to proceed in legislation without these fundamentals of the constitution settled, none of the bills became law. *Minutes of the Provincial Council,* 2:149, 153-54; *Votes and Proceedings,* 1(pt. 2):14-15; *Micro.* 11:369.

27. The collectorship of the port of Philadelphia had fallen vacant on the death of John Bewley in 1704. John Moore was appointed to replace him. See *Micro.* 11:312.

28. Alexander Paxton traveled from Pennsylvania to England in 1704 and probably carried a letter from John Moore to Henry Compton, bishop of London, which announced Bewley's death and asked for the post. *CSPC, 1704-1705,* pp. 223, 132.

29. *Micro.* 11:312.

30. Missing text here has been supplied from a partial duplicate in Logan Papers, 1:57, HSP.

31. WP is complaining of the charges that reduced his profit on the trade via Barbados.

32. See doc. 81, n. 40.

33. William Penn, Jr., had been cited by a Philadelphia court for disorderly behavior; see headnote to doc. 72; *Micro.* 11:369.

34. See *PWP,* 3:576-77. WP's orders from the Lords Justices required him to remove Lloyd from all public offices and to punish or discourage all offenders but did not specifically mention prosecution of Lloyd.

35. Anthony Morris; see *PWP,* 3:573, 576-77.

36. Robert Quary.

37. Griffith Jones.

38. Missing text here has been supplied from Deborah Logan's transcript; see provenance note, above.

39. Korah, leader of a rebellion of Israelites against Moses and Aaron, was swallowed up by the earth with all his followers. Num. 16.

40. Probably a reference to WP's lobbying against the plan to reunite the charter colonies to the crown.

41. Hannah Hollister Callowhill lived until 1712.

42. Thomas Callowhill.

43. An act of Parliament had established the Bristol Corporation of the Poor in 1696, and Callowhill had become one of its first members, serving a term of six years

instead of the usual four; during his tenure he held the offices of treasurer and deputy governor, each for a year. Callowhill also served as treasurer for the Bristol Men's Meeting. E. E. Butcher, ed., *Bristol Corporation of the Poor: Selected Records, 1696-1834* (Bristol, 1932), pp. 33, 174; 7 & 8 Will. 3, private act cap. 32; Mortimer, 2:188.

44. See doc. 76, n. 38.

45. See doc. 86, text at nn. 40-44.

46. Attorney General Edward Northey had raised objections to 38 out of 105 Pennsylvania laws. WP later had to answer additional objections from the Board of Trade; see doc. 104. *CSPC, 1704-1705*, pp. 276-81.

47. Doc. 83.

48. The word "Pyes" in the manuscript has been changed to "Piles" by a modern hand.

49. David Lloyd, who had been chosen speaker of the 1704 Assembly.

50. WP's memory is faulty here; only one of the 1705 ministers, the earl of Pembroke, was in office when the Lords Justices issued their instructions about Lloyd in Sept. 1699. *Handbook of British Chronology*, 2d ed. (London, 1961).

51. Robert Quary.

52. John Moore.

53. See n. 26, above.

54. Using a hedge or wall to restrain a cuckoo was proverbial behavior of fools, and WP is implying that David Lloyd's legal sallies against his proprietary powers were equally ineffective. The "new castle charter" was the abortive charter of property, drawn up by Lloyd and signed by WP at New Castle, but never sealed; see doc. 31. Burton Stevenson, ed., *The Home Book of Proverbs, Maxims and Familiar Phrases* (New York, 1948), p. 1012.

55. Quary and Moore.

56. Probably a reference to the unpaid subscriptions for Susquehanna land. See doc. 92.

57. Quary, Moore, Joshua Carpenter, and Joseph Willcox.

58. David Lloyd.

59. Samuel Vaus.

60. John Grove (d. 1717) was a Quaker merchant of Barbados. Joanne McRee Sanders, ed. and comp., *Barbados Records: Wills and Administrations: Volume III, 1701-1725* (Houston, 1981), p. 147.

61. Thomas Byerly (d. 1725), collector and receiver general of New York and later a member of the New Jersey council, had lent about £175 to William Penn, Jr. *NJA*, 4:62, 13:482, 14:23, 30:81; *New York Col. Docs.*, 5:768; *Micro.* 13:729.

62. John Ellis (1643?-1738) served as undersecretary of state 1695-1705 and M.P. 1705-8. At this date he worked under Secretary of State Sir Charles Hedges. *DNB*.

63. See doc. 56, n. 65.

64. Edward Shippen.

65. Catch at, or seize on eagerly. *OED*.

66. The word "Company" in the manuscript has been changed to "Kindness" by a modern hand.

67. WP is hinting that his son might obtain the governorship of Pennsylvania and use the post to avenge himself.

68. See headnote to doc. 83.

69. The words "his Eares &" have been deleted from the manuscript by a modern hand.

70. The 1701 charter to Philadelphia and the Charter of Privileges (doc. 28).

71. Logan had been disappointed in his courtship of Anne Shippen, who later married Thomas Story. See doc. 92, n. 35; Frederick B. Tolles, *James Logan and the Culture of Provincial America* (Boston, 1957), pp. 76-77.

72. Thomas Story.

73. This word reads "Complaining" in the duplicate.

74. Unspeakably.

75. These letters, from Judge John Guest, Gov. Evans, and Samuel Carpenter, Isaac Norris, and Griffith Owen, have not been found.

76. See n. 4, above.

77. Robert Barber (d. 1708), a Chester Co. cordwainer, carried docs. 83 and 84 on board the brigantine *Robert and Benjamin*, which was captured by the French. *Micro.* 11:402; Phila. Will Bk. C, #100.

78. Num. 20-21 tells of grumbling against Moses by the Israelites, but chapters 22-25 focus on the efforts of the Moabites and Midianites to enlist Balaam's aid against Israel, and chapters 26-30 deal with the establishment of the Israelites' laws of inheritance, offerings, and feasts. The relevance of these chapters to WP's case is tenuous, and he may well have been thinking of chapters 16-17, dealing with Korah's rebellion; see n. 39, above.

79. Not found.

80. John and Mary Sotcher had two small children, Hannah (b. 1703) and Mary (b. 1704). Hinshaw, 2:968.

92
FROM JAMES LOGAN

Philadelphia 11th 12mo [February] 1704[/5]

Honnoured Gover

The Inclosed is much of what I wrote from New castle when the Assembly was held there, but were ever Duplicates come wrote in my own hand, I request that the first may be destroyed and the latest only kept,[1] Since that Time Capt Robinson[2] arived with thine of the 5th moth last[3] by wch I am extreamly troubled to perceive the apprehensions our Separacion of the Prove & Territories give thee, and that it may prove a hindrance in thy Treaty with the Crown, All possible measures as has been largely said have been taken to prevent it, but there was no Remedy, However if thou canst not find thy acct in treating wth the Ministry by as much more pacifick temper for this Winter among the People than we were blest with some time before, I am in hopes that it may not prove impossible to Carry on Affairs for some further time with so much ease that it may be no great hardship to thee Still to hold the Government. Matters have been much Smoother of late & all things very quiet, whether it may be in some measure Owing to the hopes we have of better days from that great Action on the Danube[4] I know not, & of our Trade reviving, but this Govmt has never been more calm than of late Quary & all the rest are very good frds in appearance the present Mayor G: Jones (the direct contrary of wch was expected) acquitts himself with the greatest moderation & most Temper, that any in the place has done; only that lurking Snake D LL.[5] keeps and is kept at a Distance, what the Assembly will be prevailed on to doe when they meet, wch is to be the 3d Month next,[6] I know not but it is to be hoped time by degrees will open the Misled Members eyes & that if this year produce no good effect, it may as little ill, & then perhaps Davd may be disappointed in the next Election, wch we could not bring to bear in the last because of some advantages that by an unlucky occasion he took & improved, his base Letter[7] I hope has fallen into thy own hands only, and then the damage will be small, & will but serve to give thee a Portraiture of the Hell that some Men carry in their Breasts. He is much abhorr'd by most good Men that hear of it, but as I have said in my last we Can by no means Come at a Copy of it. Upon the whole I humbly offer it as my Opinion, that if thou canst not come to advantageous Terms wth the Crown for the Government the best Way would be for thee to settle Affairs there the best thou canst, and make a trip over thy self (for thou canst never in my Judgm^t be safe altogether here while the Govm^t is in thy own hands) and endeavour to gett back these Charters[8] granting others at the same time equally beneficial to [th]e People & so once more sett matters on a Right foot wch I doubt will [never?] be while that Charter of Privileges in[9] in force as it now stands. I have [torn] been[?] of Opinion, that in all Respects it would be most for thy advantag[e] to reside amongst us, but then it was wth this Suposal, that thou [would]st also find it for thy Benefit to disengage thy self of the fatigues attending the Government If otherwise could we once surmount these difficulties wch I believe can scarce be but by the Aforemencioned measures, the Govm^t by thy Interest wth the Ministry at home may be ma[in]tain'd to thy Credit & Reputation, and free from the Charge to thy self [that] thou hast hitherto un[ha]ppily laboured Under, for if that [blotted] (D LL) were once [blotted] we might fitt very easie in time I gave my thougts before freely in [re]lacion to a surrender & now doe the same in case that should not prove faisible[?]. But before thou leaves England there is a necessity of procuring the Laws to be past at some rate or other, for thence arises the peoples greatest Objection, & by that means they might be the most Succesfully wrought upon. There is a no less necessity also of having the Lines run between thee & Baltemore for it now Occasions great Confusion, we sold Jos: England[10] 1000 Acres near Black Birds Creek in New C.[11] ~~&~~ & after he had p^d part of the Money & was seating it he was drove off it. The Welch settlers also in that County positively refuse to pay their Money because of the Claims made on great part of the Lands survey'd to them, & we can find no possible means here to remedy it. Thy sons Interest with Baltemore's son young Calvert[12] may facilitate this matter, It may be very Adviseable also, I believe, to settle the whole business of the Lower Counties wth the Crown for whatever this Reign be, perhaps no other can be depended on to be more favourable to thy Affairs, & should it be left to be settled by thy Heirs. 'tis not difficult to imagine what Advantages the Crown might see Occasion to take, this is of the highest Importance being sorely complain'd of by the Inhabitants, & redounds no less to thy own private loss. I must also again press for transcripts of the Deeds for thy two Proprieties in Jersey,[13] otherwise thou wilt loos[e] the Advantage of a Survey as S. Jen: tells me I have p^d Richd Hill 180^l in silver Money for W Aubry being one years Interest, & hope to clear the rest this Spring & make the Trustees some remittances to shorten it, but we want the Powers I wrote for I dessign to write to Læt^ia per this opp^ty.[14] This having been the hardest winter & deepest Snow that has been known by the oldest amongst [us] We have had but one Post all this season, whose quick Return & sho[rt] notice Allows not enlarge, the River is still fast[15] & likely to continue, I hop[e] the next Post will reach D Zachary & the Mast fleet by whom this comes. [I] would willingly hope also, that the uneasiness M[r] Williams[16] Return may have Occasion[d] is by this time blown over, & some measures taking for his own & thy Comfort, w[ch] is most heartily desired by

Thy faithful & most Obed[t] Serv[t]
J L.

The Proclamation for the money[17] was duly published but the people doe not as yet regard it, there is not a Man in the Prov: but takes money at the old Rate

I [torn] thought to have at this time confined my self to [the] forego[ing,] And because I expect the next Post will also reach this opport[unity of?] C[onvey?]ance I shall not much exceed my intended Bounds But I thought fitt to add that notwithstanding the Orders of the Lords of Trade to C Q[18] and his Civil Behaviour in Appearance towards the Gov[mt] yet the Gov[r] who by his strict frequen~~cy~~ting of the Church & his being partner in name as well as Nation with [blank][19] is of Opinion from the lights g[ive]n him that there is yet still as much Malice & [blotted] Machinations as ever [blotted] his [In]terest w[th] and letters to the B[shp] [20] & fo[men]ting of some divisions among the Clergy in these parts he seems to be secure in his thoughts from any injury they can offer & that the more they stir the more effectually they will draw ruine on their own heads Q is exceeding busy in his negociations & leaves no stone unturned to have J: M: fixed in the office[21] of whom I have largely wrote before but if not yet disposed of C: Eden[22] who (before this time thou hast heard I supose) is among us, seems to have some assurance of an Interest that could be made for him by his Brother Roderick Floyd[23] & Hen: Graham[24] wth the L[d] Treasurer,[25] I wrote before for Hen: Brooke & therefore shall not medle wth it. Ch:[26] is at present my bedfellow as it happens & thy Son his great friend I shall not now enter into the Detail of thy Private Concerns only must take notice that the susqueh. Subscriptions[27] will be managed wth great Difficulty. I may be bold to say it It was some unhappiness that I was never Entrusted nor had any Charge of that matter (w[ch] I do not all Mencion through a Desire only to excuse my self) but it is most certainly true that I alwayes thought samuell Carpenter & some others of those thou convened at his house before thy Departure had wholly taken the Trust upon them and taken Care to have all things relating to them as effectually done, as those were for thy Assistance,[28] but when after thy Sons Arival I called on Sam[l] for the subscriptions he had not one by him but that of this Town and two other small ones not worth regarding the first amounts not to 2000l & the other two are very insignificant. I have applied to the other meetings for the rest but some who by Common report I thought had subscribed considerably deny that they ever did any thing, and those who are too well known to have done better have laid such Injunctions on the persons in whose custody they are, that is very difficult to wrest them out of their hands, but I have taken such measures wth some of them [th]at I doubt not but were[29] I can prove there are any I shall oblige them to surrender [On?] the whole my Opinion is that unless the summ will amount to above 5000l [to]lerable good Pay, the advantages parted wth are so great, that it will be scarce [wor]th while to make a survey, Unless there be some better encouragment to the [far?]mers & Countrey in general ~~but~~ {than} for these two last years has been it will be [exc]eedingly difficult to gett in the subscriptions for we may depend upon it, all manner [of] tergiversations will be used & if better times should come, more might be made of it how~~bei~~ever if we can make up much abt that Sum We shall proceed the best we can, but if thou canst reconcile it to thy own Conveniency to visit us before [this?] winter it would turn to much better Account I believe to defer it but in the mean time I shall do all that lies in my Power.

I have mencioned in the first sheet our Greater ease in the Government and a more pacifick temper that seems growing on the People so that this winter has past the most smoothly of any time I have known in this Government nor is it owing I believe wholly to the season & its severity that has bound up most men in their habitations but there seems to be growing on the Inhabitants in the main much better Inclinations wch could we have the same success in Portugal as in Bavaria[30] I believe would greatly increase upon us for tøis spain that must support us[31] and easy Circumstances seldome fail of superinde~~ni~~ucing good Nature Yet one thing creates to me still no small uneasiness which is the Charge of our house keeping, & the thoughts that all the present Emoluments of the Govmt will by no means defray {it} ~~the Charge~~, thô we endeavour to make the best of it, but a good Assembly may in some measure make amends for it if thou still thinks fitt to continue it as it is.

I can not possibly finish a Rent Role as desired[32] 'tis a mighty work as I carry it on & will make many Quires of paper. I never promised it that I know of thou art pleased to mention, but I shall drive it on to my utmost. tho the want of good writers is a hardship & fitt hands to be assistant of which I have great reason to Complain, as well as that the matter it self will by no means afford encouragment by Next Post if there be a Probability of its reaching the fleet of wch I doe not despair, I dessign to write to Joseph Pike[33] that haughty as well as angry Man, by wch the Author of those heats[34] may gain no more than he has by some other of his equally base Attacks upon me, I shall be very moderate, but must doe my self Justice, he courts A.S.

still,[35] & still to the same purpose, tis he that knows the heart gives success & I believe both are alike wth him. But I must close — ut suprâ[36]

JL

LBC. James Logan Letterbook, HSP. (*Micro.* 11:499.) The postscript to this letter, starting, "I [torn] thought to have . . . ," has not been filmed.

1. See doc. 86.
2. David Robinson, master of the ship *Elizabeth.* Albright G. Zimmerman, "James Logan, Proprietary Agent," *PMHB,* 78:159.
3. Doc. 81.
4. The duke of Marlborough, commanding allied forces against the French, had won a decisive victory at Blenheim on the Danube in Aug. 1704.
5. David Lloyd.
6. May 1705.
7. Doc 83.
8. The Charter of Privileges and the Charter of Philadelphia; see docs. 28; 52, n. 15.
9. An error for "is."
10. Joseph England (d. 1732), a leading Quaker of Duck Creek, represented New Castle Co. in the Assembly several times between 1692 and 1700, and served as a New Castle J.P. before moving to Philadelphia in 1729. Phila. Will Bk. E, #291; Hinshaw, 2:359; *PA,* 2d ser., 9:667, 670-71; 19:414, 442; Minutes of Duck Creek Monthly Meeting, GSP.
11. New Castle Co.
12. Benedict Leonard Calvert (1679-1715), later fourth Lord Baltimore, son of Charles Calvert, third Lord Baltimore. John Bailey Calvert Nicklin, "The Calvert Family," *Maryland Historical Magazine,* 16:57.
13. On WP's lands in West New Jersey, see docs. 38, n. 22; 86, text at nn. 48-49.
14. Logan wrote to Laetitia Penn Aubrey about her Pennsylvania property on 12 Feb. 1705. Logan Papers, 1:55, HSP.
15. Solid, or frozen. *OED.*
16. William Penn, Jr.'s.
17. See doc. 56, n. 65.
18. WP had expected the Board of Trade to rebuke Quary for his behavior (see doc. 76), but its instructions were actually quite mild. On 11 May 1704 the board wrote to Quary, praising his efforts in Jersey affairs and noting that since the Pennsylvania government now promised not to obstruct the admiralty courts, "we will not doubt but that on your part you will do everything that may tend to the composing of differences, avoiding unnecessary disputes, and quieting the mindes of H.M. subjects in that Province." *CSPC, 1704-1705,* p. 123.
19. Gov. John Evans, a Welsh Anglican, shared the same last name with Evan Evans, the Welsh rector of Christ Church. See doc. 67, n. 10.
20. These letters to Henry Compton, bishop of London, have not been found.
21. Quary had actively promoted the confirmation of John Moore's appointment as collector of the port of Philadelphia. See doc. 91, nn. 27-28.
22. Charles Eden (1673-1722), an Anglican from Durham, became governor of North Carolina 1714-22. Raimo, *Governors;* Marshall DeLancey Haywood, "Governor Charles Eden," *North Carolina Booklet,* 3 (1903).
23. Eden's sister Anne had married a Welshman, Roderick Lloyd (d. post 1724). Haywood, "Governor Charles Eden."
24. Probably Henry Graham (d. 1707), M.P. for Westmorland, the eldest son of Col. James Graham. *DNB;* Luttrell, 5:189, 6:66; *PWP,* 2:538n.
25. Lord Sidney Godolphin.
26. Charles Eden.
27. See doc. 35, n. 22.
28. On the subscriptions raised by Quakers for WP's aid in 1701, see doc. 33, n. 5.
29. Where.

30. England and her allies were engaged in a campaign against Spain along the Portuguese border; in this Peninsular War the English captured Gibraltar in July 1704, but otherwise scored no successes comparable to Marlborough's victory at Blenheim in Bavaria. See n. 4, above; George Macaulay Trevelyan, *England Under Queen Anne: Blenheim* (London, 1930), pp. 402-13.

31. Of all the mainland English colonies in the early eighteenth century, Pennsylvania with its wheat and flour trade could benefit most from trade with Spain and its dominions.

32. See docs. 81, 91.

33. Joseph Pike had become incensed against Logan for his alleged role in obstructing a patent for 10,000 acres of Pennsylvania land purchased by Pike from Sir Mathias Vincent. On 26 May 1705 Logan wrote to Pike to explain the affair and rebuke Pike for his invective against him. James Logan Letterbook, 2:61, HSP.

34. Thomas Story, with whom Logan had quarreled over Anne Shippen in 1703. See *Micro.* 11:034; doc. 91, nn. 71-72.

35. Anne Shippen, the daughter of Edward Shippen, married Thomas Story in 1706, bringing him a large amount of property. Elise Willing Balch, *Descendants of Edward Shippen* (Philadelphia, 1883), p. 49.

36. "As above."

93
TO ROGER MOMPESSON

[17 February 1705]

Honour[d] Friend.

It is a long time, since I have been Oblig'd with any Letter from thee;[1] and then so short, that had not others furnisht me with thy American Character, I had been at a Loss to have Answer'd the Inquiry of thy Friends. But by my Son I received one,[2] more Copiously Informing me of those Affairs, that so nearly Concern both the publick, and my personal and Family Good. And for Answer to the greatest part thereof I desire thee to Observe, First, that I am Determined (with God's help) to stand firmly to both; and for that Reason will neither turn an Enemy to the publick, nor suffer any under the {stile of the} publick Good, to Supplant mine. And as I take thee to be a man of Law, and Justice and Honour I do Intirely Refer my Concerns, both as to the Legality and prudence thereof (not only in Governm[t] but property) To thy Judicious and Judicial Issue; So as it may hold water with thy Most-Learned & Hon[ble] Friends here of both parties. I went thither to lay the Foundation of a free Colony for all Mankind, that should go thither, more especially those of my own profession; not that I would lessen the Civil Liberties of others, because of their perswasion; but skreen and Defend our own from any Infringement upon that Account. The Charter I granted,[3] was intended to shelter them against ~~the~~A violent or Arbitrary Governour Impos'd upon us, but that they should Turn it against me, that Intended their Security thereby, has something very unworthy & provoking in it; especially, when I alone have been at all the Charge, as well as Danger & Disappointment in Coming so abruptly back, and defending ourselves against our Enemies here, and Obtaining the Queen's Gratious Approbation of a Governour of my Nominating & Commissioning, the Thing they so much seem'd to Desire. But as a Father dos not use to knock his Children on the head, when they do Amiss, so I had much rather, they were Corrected, & better Instructed, than Treated to the Rigour of their Deservings. I therefore earnestly desire thee, to Consider, of what Methods Law & Reason will Justify, by which they may be made sensible of their Incroachments & presumption, that they may see themselves in a true Light, in their Just proportions and Dimensions, according to the old Saying, Metiri se quemque suo modulo ac pede, verum est.[4] No Doubt, but their Follies have been frequent and big enough in the City to Vacate their Charter;[5] but that should be the last thing, if any thing else would do. I would hope, that in the Abuse of power punishing the Immediate Offenders, should Instruct them to use it well: But doubtless the Choice of D L. both for Speaker and Recorder,[6] after the Affront he gave in open Court, to the Authority of the Crown in the late Reign; which he own'd, but never Repented of; and for which the Lords Justices of England Commanded me to have him Tryed & punishd, and to send them word, wt punishmt I Inflicted; as also that he should be made Incapable of ever being any more Employed in the Governmt.[7] As also the Choice of A M to be Mayor, that Confessed himself to have sent Flower instead of Tobacco to N. England, to Defraud the King of his Customs (for wch he is punishable to this Day; since Nullum tempus occurrit Regi)[8] are ugly Flaws in their Charter. There is an Excess of Vanity, that is Apt to Creep in upon the people in power in America, who having got out of the Crowd, in wch they were lost here, upon every little Eminency there, think nothing taller than themselves, but the Trees, and as if there were no After-Superior Judgmt to wch they should be Accountable; So that I have sometimes thought, that if there were a Law to Oblige the people in power in their respective Colonies, to take Turns in coming over for England, that they might lose themselves {again} amongst the Crowds of so much more Considerable people at the Custom-house, Exchange and Westminster hall, they would exceedingly Amend in their Conduct at their Return, and be much more Discreet & Treatable, & fit for Governmt. In the mean time pray help them, not to Destroy themselves. Accept of my Commission of Chief Justice of Pensilvania and Territories;[9] Take them all to Task for their Contempts, presumption and Riots: Let them know and feel the Just Order and Decency of Governmts and that they are not to Command, but to be Commanded, according to Law & Constitution of English Governmt. And till those unworthy people, that hindred an Establishment upon thee, as their Chief Justice,[10] are Amended, or laid aside, so as thou art Considerd by Law to thy Satisfaccion, I freely allow thee Twenty pounds each Session, which I take to be at Spring and

Fall. And at any Extraordinary Session thou mayst be called from N. York unto, upon Nice or weighty Causes, having also thy Viaticum[11] discharged. Let me Intreat this, as an Act of Friendship, & as a Just and honourable Man. More particulars Expect by James Loggan:[12] for I perceive Time is not to be lost.

Now I must Condole thy great Loss in thy wife & own brother[13] the particulars of wch I must refer thee to her own brother, & our Common Friend C. Lawton. Thy Letters enclosed to me, I deliver'd, & was well enough pleased to see, that one of them was directed to Ld S.[14] I write no news; only I find, that Moderation on this side the water, is a very Recommending Qualification; neither high Church nor Violent Wig, neither seeming to be the Inclinacion & Choice of the present Ministry: I wish, our people on that side had no worse Disposition.

I cannot Conclude this Letter till I render thee, (as now I do) my hearty Acknowledgmts for all the good Advices thou hast given for the publick & my private Good; Especially thy Sentimts to the Govr upon those 3 preposterous bills, foolishly as well as Insolently presented him by D L.[15] the last Assembly: Let him part with Nothing that is Mine: For had he past them, they would never have been Confirm'd here; but he might have Spoild himself. What a Bargain should I have made for my Governmt with the Crown, after such a bill had taken from me the very power I should Dispose of?[16] I will say no more at this time, but that I am with Just Regards

Thy Very Affectionate
and Faithful Friend
Wm Penn

Hyde-Park
17 12mo.(February)
1704/5.

PS. Since writing the foregoing I am Assured by thy Friends, there is no prevailing for the Salary formerly Allowed to the Chief Justice of York;[17] And I fear, that Governmt under the present Managemt is under a very Ill Circumstance with the Ministry at home.[18] I shall order James Loggan to Consider thy Services to ours, since thy Arrival.

WP

P.S.

The Reason why I use another hand, is my late Indisposition, which hath left my head uncapable of allowing me to write myself; but I bless Almighty God, I am something better.

WP

Ld. Cornberry writt for Col. Quary abt the admiralty business, in thy disfavour, to his father, who followed his sons desires to thy disadvantage;[19] of whom we hear the worst of things, be they true or false

LS. Penn Papers, Letters of the Penn Family to James Logan, HSP. (*Micro.* 11:512.)

1. No letters to WP from Mompesson have been found.

2. Probably a reference to James Logan's letter of 28 Sept. and 3, 6 Oct. 1704 (*Micro.* 11:369).

3. The Charter of Privileges, doc. 28.

4. A quotation from Horace's *Epistles:* "It is right that each man should measure himself by his own foot." Burton Stevenson, ed., *The Home Book of Proverbs, Maxims and Familiar Phrases* (New York, 1948), p. 860.

5. On Philadelphia's charter and the extensive prerogatives claimed by the officers under it, see doc. 52, text at nn. 13-16.

6. David Lloyd had been chosen recorder of the Philadelphia city court in 1702 and speaker of the Assembly in 1704. Scharf and Westcott, 2:1567.

7. See doc. 91, n. 34.

8. Anthony Morris was elected mayor of Philadelphia in 1703 (*PA,* 2d ser., 9:747); on his shipping of tobacco, see *PWP,* 3:573. "Nullum tempus occurrit regi" is a legal maxim meaning "no period of time runs against the king." W. Gurney Benham, *Putnam's Complete Book of Quotations, Proverbs, and Household Words* (New York, 1929), p. 604.

9. Mompesson was sworn in as chief justice of Pennsylvania in Apr. 1706. *Minutes of the Provincial Council,* 2:239.

10. The Assembly had refused to vote Mompesson a salary as chief justice, and by 1706 Logan despaired of obtaining one for him. See doc. 133.

11. Travel expenses.

12. See doc. 91.

13. This brother, Edward Mompesson (c. 1664-1705), had lived in London. Roger Mompesson had two sons, Thomas and Henry; his wife has not been identified. *Publications of the Harleian Society,* 31:285; 117:48.

14. Perhaps Charles Spencer, third Lord Sunderland. See doc. 136.

15. David Lloyd. On the three bills, see doc. 91, n. 26.

16. Lloyd was attempting to eliminate WP's veto power over Pennsylvania laws; see doc. 91, n. 26.

17. In 1704 Mompesson had been appointed chief justice of New York but was unable to obtain the salary formerly paid by the crown. Paul M. Hamlin and Charles E. Baker, *Supreme Court of Judicature of the Province of New York, 1691-1704: Biographical Dictionary* (New York, 1959), p. 135.

18. New York's government under Lord Cornbury was proving corrupt, arbitrary, and ineffective. See *DAB;* Michael Kammen, *Colonial New York: A History* (New York, 1975), pp. 155-58, 221-22.

19. This postscript is in WP's hand. In Apr. 1703 Mompesson had been appointed judge of the vice-admiralty court for the northeastern colonies from Pennsylvania to Massachusetts, but by early 1704 Robert Quary was reinstated in the office. *New York Col. Docs.,* 5:423n; *CSPC, 1702-1703,* p. 651; *1704-1705,* p. 50.

94
TO FRIENDS IN PENNSYLVANIA

[26 February 1705]

Deare Friends,[1] I Salute you in that Love which is Mingled wth the Feare of God whose awfull power and presence are in measure with mee at this time; tho not well able to write with my owne Hand (as I could wish) through the Present weakness of my head and Eyes,[2] the fruit of many weights & Burthens, Griefs & Sorrows I have met withall and indeed, it is wth an unexpressible Trouble that I have any accation to write as Follows, to you, viz[t], the unworthy treatment (I am informed) I have mett with there, after all I have hindred here, that was adoeing to our prejudice, and all I have done For our Common good, to See that after all the paines Hazzards vast Expences and the Employments of my whole Interest and the best part of my Life which Pensilvania has Cost me, Soe many of those For whose Sake~~s~~ I have done and Sufferred Soe much, Should Either actually designe the ruin of me and mine, or Suffer themselves to be Drawne away by those that Notoriously do soe, Considering, how much the people in generall, & our friends In perticular were desirous of me before my Last arrivall; and how unwilling to part with me when I Came Last away, perticularly friends, as by their Letters and Cirtificates to friends in England doth appeare.[3] You know I came on the Errand of the publick good (to Save the Goverment) wch I have done hitherto at a tempestious time, in a Crazy and doubtfull Ship[4] and with a very feeble Family; and are they Now for that, wch they were Soe willing I should Come heither to hinder, to witt a Queens Governour to be Sett over them? or at Least to make me weary of being theirs? had they told me this upon the Spot, where I was so perpetually accessible, and So Ready to Comply with Every Reason[able] Request, they had Sav'd me Some thousands, & I had Enjoy'd a Comfortab[le] Scociety wth the best among you to this verry day: for Nothing of my private Concerns at home Should have pravaled with me to have Left You, and the pleasure I had of Liveing in pensilvania at Least For Some yeares to Come. Nor Can I take Less Ill, Since I have prevented what they feared (and what some of their Neighbour's feel)[5] that the precautions I took (Least I Should not prevaile or Succeed here when I was arrived) For the preservation of the Goverment, are Rigorously Employed, and Even beyond the Letter thereof against mee;[6] and Ingratitude and treatment So Sordid and base, as hardly Ever fell to the Share of any person under my Circumstances, to my Greife, the ~~C~~Scandall of worthy minds, & Triumph of our Enemies as well as to the Shame of our profession. But what will not an Inplacable & Stubbourn Envy ~~never~~[?] doe, to {have} his unjust revenges, acting the partriot against the partriot, Making it an argument against any Man to be trusted by the publick, because he is Intrusted by me, or hath a Just regard to my honest Interest, Dividing that Interest in my absence, which I Left united and in a good Condition at my Parting.[7] And what have I done Since to Change that apprehention? is it, Lying here at Stake at a most troublesome and Chargeable Rate, neglecting the Comfor~~s~~ts of wife & Children, and a most pleasant habitation, more then halfe the time Since I Left you o friends I Pray hartily that god may not ~~soe~~ too publickly avenge My Righteous Cause against those wicked koraths![8] for Cirtainely, if Justice and Moderation doe not take place, I know not, what Judgments god will please to Inflict upon the please.[9] he has already been angry, and drawn his Sword, & wounded Deeply; Lett him not be provoked to Second his Stroake:

~~for if~~ I therefore Earnestly desire you to use Your Endeavour's as men and Christians, both as Pensilvanias and men in the truth, to moderate all Extreames to Satisfye and Quiet the people with Reasonable Securityes not to be blown up by Evill Instruments to Intemporate Desires and unjust Expectations; lest Seeking all, they Lose all; their three Laws[10] had been Dissolved here if they Could have past there, and the Governour Emediately displ[ac]ed for doeing of it. what Can be sa[id] to Satisfye any Reasonable man, why they have Left the Charge of Governour upon me? because my deputy would not Joyne wth Some there to ungovernour his Cheife Governour and violate the ~~Cheife~~ the Constitution of England, as well as that of the place where he Comands. had they been ask'd before I Came heither, that In Case I would wave the bill for Ennex~~ting~~ing the proprietary~~s~~ Governments to the Crown and Continue the administration and Goverment as it was? would they Establish a moderate maintanan~~an~~ce upon the governour, [illegible deletion] and Raise a requisite Supplyes to defray publick Charges? I doubt not but one and all would answered yes, with all our harts. and when It was twenty to one, a Queens Governour would be sent, to find to the Great disapointmt of all their Enemies, & to their own Surpriseing Satisfacti[on] a Governour Sent according to our Letters Pattens, and him approved by the Queen; and to Refuse him Even Subsistance money,[11] unless he will betray and Expose me that Sent him, hath Someting in It Soe enormiously base that noe profaine person could give it soe deep a dye; Hypocrisy alone, which is the abuse of Religion to ~~to~~ wor[ldly] purposes, being only able to tinge it Soe black, as that action m[ust] appeare to all that Considers it.

I Could Make one Conclution of this whole matter, and that is to Dispose all to the Crown, Soile as well as Governmt and be rid of them once for all and Leave them to Inheritt the fruites of their owne dowings But I must not forgett the hand that brought that Country to me; the Sealeing Engagements, and Sealing of his goodness in those Solitary Countrys and unless he hinder me nothing Else I hope shall prevent me from Spending the best part of my Life there, or there away though I am 20 Thousand pounds the worse man, than when I began that Colony, as I am able to make appeare; Love, feare and Solitude was my aime: and the Lord in his due time give those Excellent things more Credit with the Inhabitants of that place. I am a Suffering and Mournfull man In the Senses of Spirrits and things I write to you, as my Friends In truth, and as men of Significancy where you are: Help the Government against the ungovernable; ~~all~~ And all you can, quiet Friends under faire and R[easonable] Enjoyments. Councill them, not to Straine points, [illegible deletion] nor halt before a Cripple;[12] Lett them not Suffer themselves [to] be disquieted and blown about wth the windy and Emty Suggestions of Sinister and designing persons; but lett the antient Love and feare and faith, that ware our alpha be our omega; and we may yett Live to see happy Days, before we dye the Lord if it be his blessed wi[ll] Grant this to us! Soe with Deare Love to You and Yours, and others that are worthy (wherein my wife Joynes heartily ~~herein~~ with me) ~~I Clude~~ I Conclude

Your Faithfull & Loveing Friend
Wm Penn

Hide park the 26th 12 mo: 1704/5

Abstract. Penn Papers, Penn Family to James Logan, HSP. (*Micro.* 11:524.) Headed: An abstract of a Letter Lately Sent from | Governour Penn to Divers friends in Pensilvania. Endorsed: Govenour Penn's Letter to friends | an Abstract. This document was abstracted by Griffith Owen and others; see doc. 122, text at n. 2. The Penn Papers copy has been folded and torn; missing words and letters have been supplied within brackets from another copy in the Society Collection, HSP.

1. WP addressed this letter to Quakers in Pennsylvania whom he considered proprietary supporters, probably including Samuel Carpenter, Richard Hill, and Isaac Norris. See David Lloyd's complaint that WP had not addressed all Friends alike (doc. 102).

2. WP had recently suffered "a stroke of illness that has much affected my hed." *Micro.* 11:520.

3. See doc. 26.

4. The *Dolmahoy*. See doc. 32, n. 18.

5. I.e., a royal takeover of the colony's proprietary government, a fate that had befallen Maryland, New York, New Jersey, and Massachusetts.

6. WP is complaining about the colonists' attempts to assert the Charter of Privileges against his interests; see also doc. 91, text at n. 55.

7. The union between Pennsylvania and the Lower Counties was shaky at WP's departure, and he was induced to insert a clause in the Charter of Privileges permitting their separation; see headnote to doc. 21; doc. 28.

8. Korah was an Israelite rebel; see doc. 91, n. 39.

9. "Place."

10. See doc. 91, n. 26.

11. The 1704 Assembly had failed to pass a supply bill that would have granted Gov. Evans a salary. See doc. 91, text at n. 56.

12. The English proverb against halting, or limping, before a cripple was a warning against trying to deceive an expert. Burton Stevenson, ed., *The Home Book of Proverbs, Maxims and Familiar Phrases* (New York, 1948), p. 455.

95
TO JOHN EVANS

Knights-Bridge 26 12mo. (February) 1704/5.

Honrd Friend

I have Received thine of the 5th 6th & 8th Month;[1] of the former I have already Advised:[2] And thô I now write by another hand, I can Assure thee, it is with the same Mind. First of all I am sorry for thy late troublesome Indisposition; but hope, these will find thee better, as it leaves me, from a troublesome Swimming in my head,[3] that for sometime hath disabled me, from writing; the Fruit of troublesome Attendances here, and Anxious thoughts about your Welfare there;

And for want of that sweet Air and fitting Exercise, my own Habitation would have given me. *My son is come safe hither, but in some respect not to my satisfaction: However, I leave it with God and Time to Rectify.* I am so far from Discountenancing thy Care, to preserve my Just Authority, that I return thee my Acknowledgmts for all thy Demonstrations thou hast given thereof. And do hereby Desire and Strictly Charge thee at no rate to Comply with any Importunities to lessen it. For since some people have shewen themselves so unworthy of the Condescensions I have made in their Favour, I am determin'd with God's Strength, to stand by all my reasonable and Just points to a Tittle. And when they come to know themselves better, that have Attempted to Invade them, they will have Cause to think as Ill of themselves, as they have obliged me to do. In rejecting those bills[4] thou didst thy Duty as became a wise and honest Man: For had they been past there, they had been vacated here, and thyself in Danger of missing the future Favours Intended thee.

But that after sending a Governour according to our Charter, of a quiet and Discreet Temper, with the Queen's Royal Approbation to Countenance his Administration (which at their request, as well as for my own Interest I came hither to obtain) They should basely Huxter about a Maintenance, unless thou woulds betray thy trust to me, their benefactor, as well as they Principal (under the Queen) and violate the very Constitution of the English Governmt, making themselves the whole Legislative, shews a supreme Weakness, as well as Ingratitude: Concerning which the few Leaders may in a little while meet with their Match. In the mean time I desire thee to go on Cheerfully and resolutely; suffer no Incroachmts nor Indignities to pass without a Just Resentment and Correction. If D L's former offence,[5] that gave Occasion for my last Costly Voyage to Pensilvania, more than any one thing Charged upon us, viz His Affront to the late King's Commissions {To Quarry & Moore} can yet be prosecuted, then let it be done with all Expedition; of which have Judge Mompesson's Opinion: *And Also Anthony Morris {for} defrauding the Crown of its Customs, by knavishly Exporting Tobacco instead of Flower to N. England, be speedily and throughly prosecuted; since Nullum tempus occurrit Regi.*[6] Also that any Extravagant Use of the powers of the City Charter[7] be called in question & the Committers thereof Fined according to the Nature of the Crimes: Which Judge Mompesson can easily Inform thee of, upon whose Judgment I dare Rely before the Queen and her Council. *[8] I have also writ to the Secretary to have D.L. prosecuted for his late Misdemeanour of forging an Address or passages therein to my Dishonour & Dis-service, upon the Rising of the Assembly;[9] according to the proofs that shall Arise: For I would have the worst of men have Justice; *and such an one I take him to be.* I also desire, a most strict Inquisition may be made into his Court-books during the time he was Clark of the peace of the Town & County of Philadelphia:[10] For divers have told me (and J. Moor in particular) of his base Razures and Interlineations therein. Likewise to have the Roll's-office Examin'd during the Time he held it, upon that Account: As also, that he be prosecuted, for Usurping that Eminent Office of Trust several Years without a Commission.[11] And thô he was my Attorney General, he Register'd several Deeds Conveying away the Lands of me and my Children, that had been already Surveyed and Set out, instead of Entring Caveats, as his duty required. These things I Earnestly Refer and Recommend to thy Care, and Inspection, and Prosecution. *

Thy Friends were lately well; thy Uncle[12] with me, the day I was taken Ill of the Swimming of the head, and he looks well. Many ask kindly of thee, and of thy performances, to whom I have given an Agreeable Account, both of thine and thy Fathers[13] Acquaintance. And remember if I part with my Governmt, thou needst no other Interest to Recommend thee as the Queens Governour, than my own. My Son hath done thee Justice, and divers more; as well as Exprest his Resentment of the Hypocrisy, Ingratitude and Affronts of some others, which have taken but too great a place upon his Mind: but Time and providence will, I hope, set all things Right. Incourage Judge Mompesson to fix among us, *for he is denyed here the Salary of Chief Justice of N. York,*[14] *which his predecessor enjoyed; which I hope, will help towards it.*
pray, prevail with those that are our Friends of the Church-party, not to give any Advantage against the{ir} good Affections by any Irregularity of Life; but a little Consider, what are the Circumstances of him, that was the Founder of the Colony; for their weakness will be the Strength of their and my Enemies, as well false Quakers as false Church-men. Many Eyes are upon thee, and the most of them for good: Let the same Temper and prudence Conduct thee, that hath hitherto Recommended thy Administration: But if fair Means will not prevail, Currat lex.[15] Thus much for this Time; which shall be Inlarged, if it be True, what is said, that there will be an Imbargo.[16] So with my good wishes to thyself, and all our Friends of all Kinds, both in the province and Territories, I Conclude Theirs and

Thy Assured & Affectionate Friend
Wm Penn

PS. Thy Letter & Kinsman's about honest Bewley's Death came not to hand,[17] *till J M's Commission had gone through all the Offices, and I fear, they were detain'd with that Design: but perhaps thou may* hear of an Alteration shortly. A neighbour Governour's Affairs are under a Malevolent Influence at this time.[18] Things in Europe look favourably on the Confederates side,[19] and it is expected this next Campain will make an End of the War. The bill of Occasional Communion was Thrown out of the Lord's house by 22 Voices; and tacking of it out of the house of Commons, by 55 or 6 voices.[20] The D. New Castle receives the D. Buckingham's white staff;[21] more Alterations at Court are expected. Vale.

WP.

LS. Penn Papers, Tempsford Hall Papers, HSP. (*Micro.* 11:531.)

1. Evans's letters to WP have not been found.
2. WP had written to Evans on 6 Nov. 1704 (doc. 85).
3. See doc. 94, n. 2.
4. See doc. 91, n. 26.
5. In 1698 David Lloyd had allegedly ridiculed the royal commission granted to the officers of the vice-admiralty court; see *PWP*, 3:573n.
6. See doc. 93, n. 8.
7. See doc. 52, text at nn. 13-16.
8. This asterisk and the one at the close of this paragraph appear in the manuscript; their meaning is unclear.
9. See the headnote to doc. 83.
10. Lloyd had served as clerk for Philadelphia county and city courts in 1686-89. Scharf and Westcott, 2:1566, 1573.
11. Lloyd had served as deputy master of the rolls under Thomas Lloyd beginning in 1689-90 and again exercised the office in 1698-99, after Thomas Lloyd's death. Patrick Robinson had been commissioned Thomas Lloyd's successor in 1694. Ibid., 3:1738.
12. See doc. 85, text at n. 5.
13. Probably Thomas Evans; see doc. 63, n. 1.
14. See doc. 93, n. 17.
15. "Let the law run"; or WP might have meant *curat lex,* "the law provides."
16. On 20 Feb. 1705 the House of Commons had passed a bill prohibiting commerce with France. Luttrell, 5:521.
17. These letters have not been found. On the death of John Bewley, collector of Philadelphia, see doc. 91, n. 27.
18. Probably a reference to Lord Cornbury's administration in New York; see doc. 93, n. 18.
19. The allies of England in the War of the Spanish Succession. WP is overly optimistic here; despite the allied victories, Louis XIV continued to fight until peace was finally arranged in 1713.
20. The occasional conformity bill, aimed against dissenters who took Anglican communion once a year to evade restrictions on their officeholding, had been rejected by the House of Lords on 15 Dec. 1704 by 71-50, or 21 votes. WP understates the division in the Commons vote, in which a move to tack the conformity bill's provisions onto a land tax bill was defeated by 251-134, or 117 votes, on 28 Nov. 1704. Luttrell, 5:492, 498.
21. John Sheffield, first duke of Buckingham and marquis of Normanby, a leading Tory, had been lord privy seal since 1702, but was now being replaced by John Holles (1662-1711), duke of Newcastle, a prominent Whig. *DNB.*

96

PROPOSAL FOR SURRENDER OF THE GOVERNMENT OF PENNSYLVANIA

[April 1705][1]

Know all men by these presents that I Wm Penn of [blank] in the County of Sussex Esqr for & in consideration of the summ of [blank] pounds of good & lawful money of England to me in hand ~~payd~~ at & before the ensealing & delivery of these presents by order of her most excellent Majty Ann by the Grace of God of England Scotland France & Ireland Queen Defender of the faith &c well & truely payd & Satisfyed & for divers other good causes & considerations me thereunto especially moveing Have for my self & my heirs surrendered resigned released & quit claimed & do by these presents surrender resign release & quit claim unto her sayd Majty her heirs & successours all & all manner of power & authority to ordain make constitute & enact within the Province of Pensilvania in North America & the Territories thereof or thereunto reputed to belong any laws or ordinances whatsoever & to make erect & constitute Sea Ports & Harbours as also to ~~establish~~ appoint & establish wthin the sd Province & Territories any Judges Justices Magistrates & Officers for any cause or causes whatsoever as also to remise release pardon & abolish whether before or after judgment all or any crimes or offences whatsoever as also by my self & my heirs or Captains or other Officers of me or of my heirs to levy muster & train all or any sorts of men & to make war together with all the estate right title interest property claim & demand whatsoever of me the sd Wm Penn & my heirs of in & unto all & singular the sayd powers & authorities as also of in & unto the government both ecclesiastical civil & military of or wthin the sd Province & Territories enjoyed or claimed by from or under any Letters Patent from the Crown of England or otherwise howsoever Excepting allways the office of surveyor General of the sd Province & Territories as also saveing & reserving unto me my heirs & assigns the Palatinate or Jurisdiction of a Palatine of & in the County of [blank] wthin the sd Province {as such jurisdiction is now held & enjoyed by the Bisp of Durham {in the county of Durham} in the Kingdom of England}[2] as also all the property right title claim & demand of me my heirs & assigns in possession reversion remainder or expectancy of in & unto all & singular Lordsps Manours & Royalties within the sd Province & Territories together wth the severall & respective rights members & appurtenances thereof or therewith used occupyed or enjoyed or thereunto incident or annexed by any grant or grants from the Crown of England or otherwise howsoever other than power & authority to hear try & determine causes (in any Court besides the Court of the sd County Palatine) {not} exceeding the value of tenn pounds sterling & particularly excepting Saveing & reserving unto me my heirs & assigns the Royalty of Fishing & all Royall Fishes Wrecks of the sea Flotsam Jetsam Lagan[3] Royall Mines & Mineralls & all Quitrents Escheats Fines Forfeitures Deodands[4] & Profits of Courts allready due or hereafter to arise or grow due unto me my heirs & assigns in respect of or relation unto the sayd County Palatine & my respective Manours any or either of them within the sayd Province & Territories As also excepting saveing & reserving the proportion of & in Escheats of Persons dying intestate wthin the sd Province & Territories to me as Proprietary Governour thereof before the makeing of this surrender actually due incurred & accrued In witness whereof to this my deed hereby concluded on & agreed to be enrolled I have set my hand & seal this [blank] day of [blank] in the [blank] year of the Reign of her sd Majty Annoque Dni [blank]

D. CO 5/1263/19, PRO. (*Micro.* 11:546.) Endorsed: M[r] Penn's Surrender. Docketed: Pennsylvania | M[r] Penns Draught of a Surrender | of his Government of Pennsylv[a] | to her Majesty. | Received | Read | June 5th 1705.

1. For the dating of this document, see doc. 97, text at n. 4.

2. The lord of a palatinate or county palatine had *jura regalia,* rights and privileges like those of the king in his palace. The bishop of Durham held these privileges, which included power to pardon felonies and appoint justices. WP had unsuccessfully sought to gain palatinate jurisdiction over Pennsylvania in his original charter from Charles II. See *PWP,* 2:40-42.

3. Wreckage of ships or their cargo: flotsam designates wreckage found floating on the surface; jetsam, goods thrown overboard and washed ashore; and lagan, goods or wreckage lying on the seabed. *OED.*

4. WP's feudal privileges included escheats, the reversion of estates in the absence of legal heirs, and deodands, the forfeit of chattels that caused the death of a human being. WP had relinquished his right to deodands in Pennsylvania in the Charter of Privileges of 1701; see doc. 28, n. 14.

97
TO JAMES LOGAN

Hyde Park 30th 2m [April] 1705

James Logan

I wrote by Burman[1] giveing an acc[tt] of the receipt of thine from time to time according to thy own, & a Duplicat therof goes now by Guy that was taken;[2] but receiveing another lett[r] from thee dated the 22 of 9[br] last from New castle,[3] I was willing to lett thee know it; and that in the main I am not dissatisfyed with thy Hints, & as to my family Interest I shall Consider of things, tho hardly to be brought to turn my back entirely upon a place the Lord so specially brought to my hand, & has preserv'd agst the Proud Swelings of many waters {both} there & here. My Surrender of Gov[t] is before the Lords,[4] a Coppy of w[ch] & Conditions, as also of the Report of the att. Gen[ll] as to the 37 laws he excepts agst[5] {I send now} that you may obviate them before ~~Rayd~~[?]efused by the Queen. The rest shall be confirmed. I can do no more, & w[t] with the load of your unworthy Spirits there, & some not much better {here, with} my poor sons goeing into army or Navy, as well as getting into Parl[6] through so many checks & Tests upon his morals, as well as Education, wth the Loads of debts, hardly to be answeard from the difficulty of getting in w[t] I have right to, of twice their vallue, (which is Starveing in the midst of bread) my head & heart are filled sufficiently wth trouble. yet the Lord holds up my head & Jobes over righteous & mistaken Friends[7] have not Sunck my soule from its Confidence in God.

I therefore urge thee to gett under bond all that is due (I think a Bond to me is of the Nature of a Judgem[t]): and gett in pay the best thou canst, on the oldest, for I shall appropriate {most of} all the Bonds thou hast to paym[t] of Debts to people here paying there first, & so from time to time, by w[t] comes in be it of Bonds or quitrents. In order to which I shall send my orders by Guy that commands a new Messenger wch will be ready in a month, 40 Tun bigger than the Former, built to run.

But forgett not the direction of mine by Sam^{ll} Hollister & Edwd Lane,[8] nor that Burman brings. If the Countys of the Province are not bounded westward Lett them be orderd to run to Sasquehanagh River; and likewise if that of Bucks be not bounded upward ~~&~~ or Northward, that it run 5 times the Breadth of the other Countys, & I would have the [illegible deletion] sayd County to be marked northerly by trees or stones monumentally, and that this be done forthwith. I also desire that a Bill I send now to make bonds assignable & Currant pay,[9] whether the Assigner live or dye, be past in your First assembly, since mony is so scarce; and I wish you had a land banck[10] that so paym^{ts} might be made easier to all partys. not over rateing the Lands to be made the funds therof.

The act of Parliament past here to encourage navall Stores to be raised in america,[11] I hope you will take notice of, as far as flax & Hemp goe; for Pitch & Tar you have not the means of ~~in~~ in our Country. But I wish extreamly well to potashes, & that It may be Encouraged, as I hinted once before, & should like that an hundred or 2 of pounds went that way for my poor Children, If valluable, and I tould John Jones, so, who is now here, but not otherwise.

Thou hast forgott w^{t} I writ; 1 of a Rent role to my unspeakable prejudice, for {I} know not w^{t} I have, I loose the Credit here that would make me easy. 2, Richard Beamont^{s} [12] 300^{l} acres on Rancocoss Creek in W. Jersey, bought of Wm Biddle. See my former letters.[13] 3^{ly} The writeings of Dan: waite {[illegible deletion]} are there,[14] for I saw them there, or Wm Hages,[15] each selling me a Propriety. wch forget nott. 4^{ly} about Evans the Pyrats affaire,[16] being Teiz'd here by the people Concernd, I mean {his} relations.

10 3^{m} [May] 1705

I hope since my sons leaveing those parts[17] he is less under the Temptation of Unseasonable Discourses; for that's, what will undo all. pray let him know, his Friends are generally well, and ask kindly after him, and that I have writ amply to him by this Fleet already, and by Burman too, as I remember.[18]

Barber is a Sneeking presbyterian Q.—a Contented C. of D. K.'s à parte antè, as well as â parte pòst:[19] But he is watch'd and rubb'd by several. He knows nothing of the Packet sent by him being wth me.[20]

All that is possible, make that ungrateful Hypocrite D K.[21] as uneasy as can be, and let the Governour Know, I would have him Snub and discourage him all he can, and watch proper Opportunities to make him sensible of his villanous practices {till he bows or breaks}[22]

Ld Cornberry is so Far (poor man) from gaining points upon us, that there is no Argument left here to keep him there; but the Aversion they have here {~~to him~~} to have him home. We are in a great Strife between Whiggs and High-Churchmen, and never more struggle at Elections, than just now: 3 Tackers left out, and 5 or 6 chosen: A Duel already fought in Cheshire.[23] {less Tackers by 40-50 added to the whigs as they say of their number in last parl.}[24]

War like to be fierce this Summer. My Friend Ld Peterborough & Sr C. Shovill are just going upon a great Expedition by Land and Sea.[25] The K. of Portugal very ill;[26] News last night of the King of France's Death,[27] but so we had 14 days ago of the Emperour's,[28] and Kg. Augustus of Poland,[29] but no Confirmation. Watch over my Just Interest; encourage the Govr to be Couragious for all reasonable things. Keep in with the best of our Friends, & by them work upon the rest, and undermine Knaves and hypocrites of all sorts. I shall add no more now, but remember to let me have a Rentroll per first, and an Acco^t of what bonds are in hand, my son says, to the value of 14000^l that money. Also w^t has been received in money, & for what, & what the overplus lands come to, & w^t received, & w^t upon bond, & w^t in money, & w^t in any thing else. This is requisite for my knowledge of my Condicion {& for the bettering of it.}[30]

Robt Barber owns the Packet, & that D. LL. read most of it to him, & said, it was the Act of the Assembly, wch he now pretends to have been his own: that very villany should be punisht in a signal manner. And unless he visibly shifts his Course, I would have him Indicted for it, as an high misdemeanour. For bow him I will, if I can; if not, break him to peices in that Colony. {NB I take the shuffle of this assembly in covering the forgery wors than any act of the last.}[31] Thy last letter was sealed with a large & dull Coat of Arms, & wax, not like thy usual Seal & wax, thô the superscription thy hand, or well imitated. My son has lost his Eleccion, & Ld Keepers son in Law;[32] but both hope to recover it, by proving Bribery upon the 2 that have it, thô they had the majority: Lord Windsor, & Sq^r Arsgell.[33] I wish it may turn his face to privacy & good husbandry, if not nearer to us. To enable you in Authority to call D. LL. to Acco^t I have sent the Letter pretended to be writ by Authority of the Assembly, onely signed by David Lloyd,[34] wch you must wisely get him to acknowledge, that you may either bow him to better manners, & gain him, or prosecute him to the utmost rigour of Law.

Next I have sent thee that false Jews impudent, knavish as well as ungrateful letter.[35] The greatest wrong I ever did, was, to let him have GF's Lot in the Front,[36] that he got more by Importunity than by money, as also the liberty-land near his own, promising to be Zealous for my Interest to pay quitrents & taxes, & to encourage all others to do so too, & what not. If any of his Lies can be turn'd upon him to the utmost rigour, fail not, for he is a false & ungrateful person; I would only briefly observe his & D LL's falshoods.

1. The Charter made in England[37] was but probationary, as the Conclusion shews: & when the real one was executed, 'twas with all

the solemnity of an Interior & exterior presence, unanimously, as ever any Act could be performed. That wch was the great Stick at first was, that I would not stand with my Grant & Estate, a security to the Crown for their use of the negative voice (I by that in London, having but a treble voice in all Cases)[38] unless they & theirs would be a Counter, security to me & mine: wch after 2 or 3 days Consideration agreed rather to leave that Powr, ~~&~~ than be ~~liable~~[?] {liable} to answer for the use of it, ~~than them & theirs~~.

2. That Charter was never alter'd by me, but by the suggestions of his present Confederate D LL. to my regret,[39] as my letters before, & conduct after my arrival plainly shew'd; and truly, they have not prosper'd since.

3. For the last Method establisht at my Arrival it was by so great a Majority carried, that I see no blame. And being nearer to English (Methods, they called for so often) I acquiesced, having first shewed my Dislike: as at their disliking the model of an Elected Coun~~se~~cil to prepare, & an Assembly to resolve. & 2. as throwing away the use of the ballat wch their Children, as I told them, will have perhaps cause sufficient to repent of their folly therein {in time to come, &c.}[40]

4. I have not in the province so many Mannours as my Tenths[41] come to, viz ~~for every 100000~~ 10000 Acres {out of every 100000 acres taken up therin};[42] & for my Children, & S^{r} J Faggs (for my wife)[43] they bought dearly what they had, their Mother lending her Estate in Land to the value of at lest 3000^{l} or thereabouts, to Answer my debts, that was raisd by Seling, her hereditary land, or being mortgaged, which is all one.

5. If any are deficient it is their own fault for they had 2 years before my returning,[44] & 3 years & ½ since, to have taken it up, & all cann't have it ne~~a~~er. I have not any ~~good~~[?] {neer} I'm sure {but as liberty land}; I was defeated of my land {by Capt Holmess}.[45] Charles Ascom[46] laid out in the County of Chester 10000 Acres of land {but the people had it}, great part of the mannour of Springetsberry, Gilberts and Highlands {is} taken up by Encroachers, as he well knows {& would not endure if his case}. And for the lands of my Children thou canst Answer upon the spot, how Will's & Tishes have been encroached upon, thô all first purchasors, viz {they are ~~of~~} of the 100^{l} share-men.[47] And pray, let the old surveyor Gen^{lls} books be examined, & there will be found War^{ts} for at least 40000 Acres of land never Executed for them ~~&~~ wch was T. H.^{s} unfaithfulness

6. He nor any else ever once, in the 2 years I was there, ~~ever~~ accused me, or apply'd to me on any of these clamorous Acco^{ts}, wch shews w^{t} spt[48] has exercised them since those days. {Tho I came back so dangerously & suddanly to secure & serve them.} I having lain at stake with purse & pains these 3 years & ½, without {any sallery} ~~half a Crown~~ to support me, & gain so many points for them, & held up their Credit. For were it not for me, to morrow we should be Sacrificed

to the Envy of New York & her enrichment; wch these poor wretches think not of. He appears in that spirit Friends always told me {he was of,} & my kindness being unable to change his Character, {there} will soon come ~~colr~~[?] {over} by some old acquaintance of his, by what Frauds he got, w^{t} he had with him to America. For the Incomparable villany of D L's Lying & sawcy Letter. It speaks itself out also, & I desire, nay Command, that the Governour call a select Council, & view the enclosed, & see under the greatest secrecy w^{t} is fit & practicable to be done, to Crush these Varlets. But if not to be done to purpose, then to expose them w^{t} you can, or make them knock under. I think, if they own their Letters, you have room enough to deal with them to purpose: of wch let me hear per first.

My son says he had but 20ss. your money weekly, & that he spent all over that allowance out of his own money he sold his land for. If thou thinkest, that confirming the present Governour if I can get it, or getting one, that will be fit to settle me & mine in our property, will do, & is preferrable to selling all here (considering a peace is like to be this winter, & that many will remove to you to settle among you) pray let me have thy best digested and clearest thoughts. for I cannot tell, how to leave America. Thô the Scene those ill men have opened to me, after my Chargeable 2 voyages to them, & stay among them, & never leaving them by choice, but compulsion, & being always at stake here for them & Country, without a Groat, for 20 years or thereabouts, & by it sunk in my Estate above 20000^{l} & might out of 1500^{l} per Annum have saved 700^{l} a year besides, wch is as much more: I say, after my hazzards, expences, Interest & pains, & absence from my own dwelling to attend that service, to be treated as a Lurcher of the people, & one that had an Interest against them, as D LL. expresses it, is more, one would think, than any poor mortal man could bear. I say, without any byass, but on {an} Intrinsick weight, give me, upon thy utmost observation, by Converse or recollection, thy sense of it; Sell or not wth the rentroll & ballance in gen^{ll} at least, that I may know, w^{t} I may call my own, by the first safe opportunity, directed for me, as ~~I have before exprest At~~ {~~or rather~~} ~~for Jno Ellis Esqr at Sr Charles Hedges's office at Whitehall, or~~ for R^{t} Harley Esqr secretary of State at Whitehall, and take a Receipt for it, and within direct for me; or rather to John Tucker[49] esq^{r} in Sr C. Hed. office ~~than either of them~~. I shall only add place my Father Callowhils {& Johnnes}[50] R. Sneads, Jo^{n} Nelsons, Jo^{n} Blayklings[51] &c: of wch I writt formerly, wch Father Cal. buys upon some good overplus lands—vale. we are all pretty well, & Salute thee & our true Frds & family. Thy reall Frd.

WP.

AL and signed copy. An incomplete autograph of pages 1-4 of this letter, ending at n. 17, is in Penn Papers, Letters of the Penn Family to James Logan, HSP. (Not filmed.) The remainder of the text has been supplied from a copy of the document, with insertions and closing in WP's hand, in the Cliveden Manuscripts, Chew Family Papers, HSP. (*Micro.* 12:029.) Endorsed: WP to J: Logan.

1. Probably a reference to doc. 91, carried by Benjamin Burman, master of the *Hopewell.* See *Micro.* 12:053.

2. John Guy and his ship, the *Robert and Benjamin,* had been captured by the French in 1704. Albright G. Zimmerman, "James Logan, Proprietary Agent," *PMHB,* 78:158; doc. 102.

3. Doc. 86.

4. See doc. 96.

5. Actually 38 laws; see doc. 91, n. 46.

6. William Penn, Jr., lost his bid for Parliament; see n. 32, below. On his efforts to obtain a post in the army or navy, see also *Micro.* 12:792.

7. Job's friends believed that his many afflictions were a divine punishment for his own sins; see Job, chaps. 4-31.

8. See doc. 91, nn. 21-22; doc. 85.

9. This bill has not been found, and it apparently was not considered by the Pennsylvania Assembly.

10. Unsuccessful attempts to establish land banks had been made in Massachusetts and Barbados. See Andrews, *Colonial Period,* 4:351.

11. 3 & 4 Anne, cap. 10, offered premiums for the importation of tar, pitch, turpentine, hemp, and timber from the American colonies.

12. The Cliveden copy here adds in WP's hand, "or Baynams." See docs. 76, nn. 20-21; 91, n. 16.

13. The Cliveden copy here adds a marginal note in WP's hand: "NB wt I payd for sayd land send over the original lease or release."

14. The Cliveden copy here has a marginal insertion by WP, "in my scriptore."

15. The Cliveden copy here has a marginal insertion by WP, "I send a perticuler of." In the 1680s WP had purchased two West Jersey proprieties: one from Daniel Waite (d. 1728?), a Quaker bodicemaker of Westminster, and one from William Haige (1646-1688), a prominent Quaker merchant, landowner, and officeholder in Pennsylvania and the Jerseys. *PWP,* 2:114n; 3:259n. See also docs. 38, n. 22; 126, n. 25.

16. David Evans (d. by 1704), a Welshman, had been arrested in Philadelphia on suspicion of piracy and sent back to England. His family was now trying to recover the remainder of his Pennsylvania estate in order to pay his debts. See *PWP,* 3:598n; *Micro.* 10:267; 11:409.

17. Here the autograph manuscript ends and the text follows the Cliveden copy.

18. This paragraph is oddly worded; the opening sentence clearly refers to William Penn, Jr., while the second sentence seems to refer to Gov. John Evans. For WP's recent letter to Evans, see doc. 95.

19. WP here charges Robert Barber with being a "presbyterian Quaker" and a creature of David Lloyd's, both before and after the fact.

20. Barber had carried doc. 83, David Lloyd's remonstrance written in the name of the Assembly.

21. Copyist's error for David Lloyd.

22. Insertion in WP's hand.

23. "Tackers" were high church M.P.'s who had voted for the proposal to tack the occasional conformity bill onto the land tax (see doc. 95). In the hotly contested elections of 1705 they drew opprobrium not only from Whigs and tolerationists, but also from patriotic Tories who were appalled at their endangering the nation's supply in time of war. At the Chester election a Whig mob had rioted, breaking windows in the cathedral. George Macaulay Trevelyan, *England Under Queen Anne: Ramillies and the Union with Scotland* (London, 1932), pp. 15, 27-31.

24. Insertion in WP's hand. The Whigs gained from the split among the Tories and claimed a majority of 40 in the new Parliament, while only 80 of the 134 original Tackers were re-elected. Trevelyan, *Ramillies,* p. 31.

25. Lord Peterborough and Sir Cloudesley Shovell were embarking as co-commanders on a major naval expedition to the Mediterranean, where they captured Barcelona in Oct. Shovell (1650-1707), an eminent naval commander, had served at sea since 1664 and become an admiral in 1696. He served as M.P. for Rochester from 1698 until his death. Trevelyan, *Ramillies,* pp. 66-68; *DNB.*

26. Peter II (1648-1706), king of Portugal, was in poor health throughout 1705 but lived until Dec. 1706. Luttrell, 5:507, 558, 586, 618.

27. Louis XIV was suffering from gout in 1705, but he did not die until 1715. Ibid., 5:549.

28. Emperor Leopold I (1640-1705) died in May 1705, to be succeeded by his son Joseph I.

29. King Augustus of Poland (1670-1733), elector of Saxony, had been expelled from Poland by the Swedes in 1704 and was fighting to regain his crown, which he ultimately achieved in 1709.

30. Insertion in WP's hand.

31. This insertion in WP's hand appears in the margin; the insertion point is not clear.

32. William Penn, Jr., and Samuel Sambrooke had lost their bid for election to Parliament for Bramber. Penn, Jr., filed but later withdrew a petition charging his opponents with bribery. Sambrooke, the son of a wealthy London merchant, was married to the daughter of Sir Nathan Wright (1654-1721), lord keeper from May 1700 to Oct. 1705. *The Journals of the House of Commons,* vol. 15 (London, 1803), pp. 13, 56; George W. Marshall, ed., *Le Neve's Pedigrees of the Knights* (London, 1873), pp. 361, 457; *DNB.*

33. Thomas Windsor (c. 1669-1738), a Tory viscount of Tardebigge, Worcs., was elected M.P. for Bramber in 1705; he represented Monmouthshire between 1708 and 1712. John Asgill (1659-1738), a writer and barrister, had been expelled from the Irish Parliament in 1703 for writing a satirical pamphlet. After representing Bramber 1705-7, Asgill was expelled from the next Parliament and was imprisoned for his Irish debts. *DNB;* Basil Duke Henning, *The House of Commons 1660-1690* (London, 1983), 3:744.

34. Doc. 83.

35. Griffith Jones had written to WP complaining of abuses, but his letter has not been found. See *Micro.* 12:156; Deborah Logan and Edward Armstrong, eds., *Correspondence Between William Penn and James Logan* (Philadelphia, 1872), 2:57.

36. Jones had been granted a part of George Fox's city lot that lay contiguous to his own, in exchange for part of another lot. *PA,* 2d ser., 19:405, 437.

37. *The Frame of Government* and *Laws Agreed Upon in England* (*PWP,* 2:211-26) were revised by WP and the Pennsylvania Assembly in 1683 to create the Second Frame of Government of 2 Apr. 1683; see Soderlund, *William Penn,* pp. 267-73.

38. While the original Frame gave WP only a treble vote in the Provincial Council, the Second Frame gave him a veto, since otherwise either WP or the colonists would be liable for security to the crown for violations of the Navigation Acts. Nash, *Quakers and Politics,* p. 71.

39. WP refers to Lloyd's role in revising Pennsylvania's constitution by the 1701 Charter of Privileges, doc. 28.

40. Insertion in WP's hand.

41. WP had reserved for himself 10,000 acres out of every 100,000 in his "Conditions or Concessions to the First Purchasers" of 1681. *PWP,* 2:99.

42. Insertion in WP's hand.

43. See doc. 56, n. 43.

44. That is, the two years (1699-1701) that WP spent in Pennsylvania before his return to England.

45. Thomas Holme (c. 1624-1695) had been surveyor general of Pennsylvania from 1688 to 1695. *PWP,* 2:127n; see also vol. 3.

46. Charles Ashcom (d. 1727), deputy surveyor for Chester Co. *PWP,* 3:89n.

47. Pennsylvania's original First Purchasers were sold "proprietary shares" of 5000 acres for £100 each. *PWP,* 2:81.

48. Spirit.

49. The manuscript's conclusion, from the words "or rather to John Tucker," is in WP's hand. John Tucker was undersecretary of state to Sir Charles Hedges. Luttrell, 3:468, 4:705.

50. John Penn.

51. John Elson, also called Nelson (c. 1624-1701), a Quaker carpenter of Clerkenwell, London, and John Blaykling (1625-1705), Quaker minister of Yorkshire, were non-emigrant First Purchasers of Pennsylvania land. Thomas Callowhill had purchased Elson's 500 acres and Blaykling's 1000 acres for the benefit of WP's younger children, and WP is instructing Logan to have them surveyed on lands that had fallen vacant as overplus. Fox, 2:457; *PWP,* 2:377n, 642; *Micro.* 11:355; doc. 159.

98
DRAFT OF A NEW PATENT FOR PENNSYLVANIA

[23 May 1705]

Anne by the Grace of God of England Scotland France and Ireland Queen Defender of the Faith &c. To all to whom these presents shall come Greeting. Whereas Our good subject William Penn of [blank] in the County of Sussex Esqr late Proprietary Governour of the Province of Pennsilvania in North America, *and the Teritories thereunto belonging,*[1] hath by his Deed {Poll} of even Date with these presents,[2] surrendred, resigned, released, and quit claimed his S^{d} Gov^{r}m^{t} to us our Heirs & successors as in & by the said Deed enroll'd among the Records of Our High Court of Chancery, relation thereunto being had, it ~~doth~~ may & doth more at large appear. Know ye that for the Securing unto the said William Penne his heirs & Assigns & to all the Freeholders Inhabitants and Resyants[3] of and within the said Province *and the Territories thereunto belonging or appertaining or reputed to belong or appertain*[4] all his and their *rights, properties, Liberties, priviledges & imunities.*[5] We of Our Speciall Grace certain knowledge & Meer Motion, *have Accepted of the said surrender resignation, release & quitt Claim with & according to the Exceptions, Savings, reservat*^{ns} in & by the s^{d} Deed Mentioned and expressed & no otherwise, and do for Us our Heirs & Successors ratify & confirm all & every the Laws & Acts at any time or times before the Date of these our Letters Patent made & passed in every or any Gen^{ll} Assembly & Assemblies or reputed Gen^{ll} Assembl~~ies~~y and Assemblys of the said Province not before this time revoked, repeal'd, alter'd or disallowed,[6] and doe likewise hereby ratify and Confirm all & every the Laws *Legal Customes, Constitutions and Usages now observ*^{d}[7] or to be observed within the Said Province & Territories. And moreover we do of Our Special Grace certain knowledge and meer Motion, for Us our Heirs & successors, grant unto the said Wm Penn his Heirs and Assigns, and unto all the Freeholders, Inhabitants & Resyants of & within the said Province and Territories, that the Sole power of making Laws for the Peace wellfare & Governm^{t} of the s^{d} Province & Territories laying imposing and raising publick Taxes & Contributions for erecting, repairing & Maintaining places for Religious worship, Schools & other publick buildings as also for maintaining or paying Preachers Ministers & Teachers in Religious Assemblies and Schools, excepting only such Contributions as shall be freely & voluntarily made & given by any Body or Bodys publick or Civill, or by the respective Freeholders Inhabitants or Resyants of or within any County, Hundred, City, Town, Parish, Townships or other Division or Precinct within the said Province & Territories to which no person or persons shall be bound by the Act or Acts, Vote or Votes of any Majority but only by his her or their own free Consent, shall for ever be, reside and continue in the Govr for the time being and upon the Death, absence or incapacity of the Governor in the Lt or Deputy Governor, and in the Genll Assembly of the said Province & Territories, but that it shall be Lawfull for any particular person or persons, Bodies Politick or Civill to build maintain & provide for places of or for his her or their way of Religious Worship & Discipline and Schools for the Instructn and Education of Children and youth, and to maintain or pay Preachers, Teachers & School-Masters at his her & their proper Charges & Expences, as to them any or either of them, shall seem good & Convenient. And we will & by these presents Grant that all Members of or for the General Assembly of the said Province & Territories, excepting only such as shall at that time be of the Councill, shall be Chosen by Freeholders, according to the Constitution, Law & practice of the said Province & Territories, and that the Number of Representatives shall not at any time or times be altered otherwise than by Act of the said Generll Assembly, And that a New Assembly of Representatives of & for the said Province & Territories shall be chosen Yearly and every Year at the time & in the manner appointed as aforesaid, and shall once at the least in every Year be holden Sit and Act under the Governor or the Lt or Deputy Govr & with the Councll from time to time appointed by Us our Heirs & Successors, according to the powers wch they had or were Entituled unto with & under the said William Penn as aforesaid,[8] And further that untill the forms of the *Declarations & Oaths required by the Law of the said Province*[9] shall be altered by Act of Genll Assembly all they who are or shall be Freemen of or within the said Province or Territories as the Laws there now stand, shall have & enjoy all the Rights Liberties & priviledges of Freemn in the Electing Representatives to serve in any Generall Assembly, or being Elected thereunto; And further we have granted and by these presents, do grant for Us Our Heirs & successors unto the said Wm Penn his heirs & Assignes, and unto all & every the Freeholders Inhabitants and Resyants of & within the said Province & Territories, That *it shall not be in the power of any Gen*ll Assembly, Governor Lt Govr Deputy Governor & Councill {*any*} *or either of them, to defeat abridge or lessen the liberty of Conscience & free use & Employing of persons and places for Religious Worship* & Discipline,[10] and of Schools & persons for the Instructing of Children & Youth now setled, allowed or enjoyed within the said Province or to render any person or persons who do or shall Scruple the taking any Oath incapable of being a Member or Members of the said Genll Assembly or serving upon Juries or of holding & Exercising any Office or Employment, or Enjoying any Liberty or priviledge whatsoever, ~~they~~ they making and giving such or the like *Solemn Affirmation* and legal Assurance as is now required *by the Law of the said Province,*[11] or to impeach or make void any Marriage formerly had & solemnized {or hereafter to be had & Solemnized} within the said Province or Territories after the way, manner & Usage of the people Called Quakers, or to subject or expose any person or persons of that perswasion, to any Fyne, Forfeiture, Penalty, *reproach*[12] or abuse, for or by reason of his her or their usual and Accustomed way of speech gesture or carriage, or to Compell them or any of them to serve in the Militia within or without the said Province and Territories, or directly and expressly to contribute thereunto; and we have Granted & declared & do hereby grant and declare, that all & every such Marriage & Marriages as aforesaid within the Said Province & Territories shall be deemed taken & adjudg'd to be good & Valid to all intents and purposes any Law, Canon, Custome or usage to the Contrary thereof in any wise Notwithstanding; And that the People called Quakers while continuing of that perswasion, shall be freed & exempted from all fines, forfeitures, penalties, reproaches & abuses, for or by reason of such their perswasion, or of their usual and accustomed way of Speech, Gesture & Carriage, and from being compelled to serve in the Militia or Directly and expressly to contribute thereunto; And we do hereby Oblige our Selves our Heirs & Successors for ever to Maintain the said Liberty of Conscience, Freedoms, Priviledges, Immunities and Exemptions inviolable & declare, that if any Governor L^{t} or Deputy Governor or Memb^{r} of the said Councill, shall Violate the same or promote or Encourage the Violation in others by any overt Act, It shall be cause of forfeiture & A moveall of and from the said Governm^{t} and Office or Offices, and upon due proof, it shall be adjudg'd and declared accordingly by Us Our Heirs and successors. **And** we further Ordain & Will, that every Govr L^{t} & Dep^{ty} Govr of the said Province & Member of the said Councill, shall before the Entring upon his & their Office & Offices respectively swear upon the Holy Evangelists or make a Solemn Assureance according to the Law & Custome of the said Government,[13] that he will to his power observe and Maintain and Cause to be observed & maintained throughout the said Province and Territories, Liberty of Conscience and freedom of worship & discipline & Schools, and all other the Liberties, freedomes, Priviledges, Immunities & Exemptions in and by this our Charter Mentioned express'd granted or Confirmed, and all the Laws & Legal Customes & usages of the said Province & Territories which Oath or Solemn Assurance, any two or more of the said Councill, are hereby Authorized and impowered to Administer.

And Whereas the said Province hath been Cultivated and improved Cheifly by the great expence Application & Interest of the said William Penn, and divided into *six Counties,*[14] in Consideration thereof, as well as of the said Surrender & for perpetuating the Memory of a work so beneficial ~~w~~We do further of Our Special Grace certain knowledge and Meer Motion for our selvs our Heirs and successors erect the County of [blank] where the Said Wm Penn hath been at the greatest expence in buildings and Emprovements into a County Palatine or Palatinate perpetually to endure, and hereby make & Constitute the said William Penn his Heirs and Assignes Palatines thereof with all Regalities, powers, Jurisdictions and Authorities to Palatinates and Palatines usually belonging & Appertaining as the same have at any time heretofore been used and Exercised in Our County Palatine of Durham[15] within this Our Realm of England, with full power and Authority to name app^{t} and Constitute, Judges, Justices of the Peace, Sheriffs, Registers of the Grants and Titles of Lands Tenements & Hereditaments wthin the said County Palatine, and all other Officers proper for the same and to settle & Establish the times for the sitting and holding of Courts and sessions, And the Supream Court of Justice of and for the said County Palatine, is hereby Authorized and Empowered to hear Try & Finally determine all Actions or Causes of Action, and all Murders, Robberies, Felonies Crimes, Offences, Matters things & Causes Tryable at Common Law (other than high Treason) arising within the said County and to Cause Execution to be had and made thereupon. And it is hereby further grant^{d} that there shall be no Appeal or removall by Habeas Corpus or ~~other~~ otherwise of any person, Action, suit, Judgement or Execution that shall be awarded adjudged or determined in the said Court to the value of [blank] pounds or under not including Costs of suit. And for the taking away all Doubts which do shall or may arise touching or concerning the Erecting of the said County, into a Palatinate or County Palatine, as also touching or concerning any the Mannors or reputed Mannors of the s^{d} William Penn within the s^{d} Province & Territories, We do hereby for Our Selvs Our Heirs and Successors, Coven^{t}, promise and grant [illegible deletion] to and with the said William Penn his Heirs and Assigns, that at any time or times up^{n} the Petition or Petitions and at the Costs and Charges of the s^{d} William Penn his Heirs & Assigns, We our Heirs and successors shall and will grant to the s^{d} William Penn his Heirs & Assigns one or more Charter or Charters or Letters Patent under Our Great Seal of England or Seal of the said Province for the full legall and Effectual erecting the said County into a Palatinate or County Palatine {as also for the granting to the said Wm Penn his heirs & Assignes, all Fin[es] forfeitures Deodands} Waifs Strays and Wrecks hap'ning & arising within the said County Palatine, and for making such and so many Mannors of other the now Lands of the said Wm Penn within the said Province and Territories or any particular Tract or Tracts thereof or Corporations within the same, with power of holding Courts and Acting in Bodies Corporate, and all other legall powers and priviledges, perquisits and Emoluments to any Mannors Lordships or Corporations belonging, as by the s^{d} Wm Penn His heirs and Assigns, or his or their Councill, Learn'd in the Laws of England, and of the said Province shall be reasonably advised and desired, upon which Letters Patent

Charters or Grants or any of them the said William Penn his heirs or Assignes, shall in no wise be obliged or required to pay or render to Us Our Heirs or Successors any Acknowledgement or prestation[16] by reason of Tenure or otherwise further or other than Yearly and every Year if demanded [blank] for the said County Palatine and one [blank] for each Mannor to be paid at Our Fort at New York. And we doe hereby grant unto the said William Penn his Heirs and Assigns full power & Authority in any the Courts of his severall and respective Mannors w^th^in the said Province & Territories other than the said County Palatine by him or themselvs, or by his or their Steward and Stewards and the Deputy or Deputies of such Steward and Stewards, to hear Try and finally determine all personall Actions, Suits and Trespasses arising or to arise within the limmits and precincts of the said respective Mannors, not Exceeding the Value of Tenn Pounds sterling, from which finall Determinat^n^, there shall not be any Appeal or removall of any person, Action, Suit, Judgement or Execution where the princip^ll^ demand and Judgement thereupon (not including Costs of Suit) shall not exceed the said value of Tenn Pounds.[17]

And further wee doe of Our Especial Grace certaine knowledge and meer Motion, for Us Our Heirs and Successors, Remise Release, acquitt and discharge the said William Penn his Heirs and Assignes for ever, *off and from all forfeitures, Rents, Quit Rents, Arrearages*[18] of Rent, Services and Dues whatsoever, at any time heretofore incurr'd, accrewed & grown due and which ought by the said William Penn to have been paid done and perform'd to Us or any of Our {Royal} Predecessors, for or by reason of the said Province and Territories or reputed Territories thereof or any part of the Same.

And further we doe of Our Especial grace certain knowledge and meer Motion for Us our Heirs and Successors, Covenant and Grant to and with the said William Penn and his Heirs that the said Wm Penn and the Heirs Male of his Body Lawfully begotten, shall for ever hereafter be Exempted and freed off & from all Taxes, Impositions, Customes and Dutyes whatsoever w^th^in our said Province,[19] and that we our Heirs and successors, when any Act of the Assembly of the said Province shall for that purpose, be made, shall and will give Our Roy^ll^ Assent thereto and pass the same, as also Our Royall Assent to such other Law or Laws as shall be agreed on in any Generall Assembly or Assemblyes of the said Province for ratifying and Confirming all and every Clause and Clauses, Matter or Matters thing & things in this our present Grant and Confirmation mentioned or conteined according to the true intent and meaning thereof.

And further we do of our especial grace certain knowledge & Meer Motion, Ratify & confirm unto all the People of and within the said Province & Territories the severall & respective grants at any time or times to them respectively made by the said William Penn, they duly paying or causing to be paid unto him his Heirs and Assignes, their severall Quit Rents in and by such Grants reserved and made payable.

To quiet the Minds of people and to avoid all Occasions of Animosities & disputes, a Generall pardon to all people formerly concerned in the Administration.

Copy. CO 5/1263, PRO. (Not filmed.) Docketed: Pennsylvania. | Copy of the Draught of a New | Patent, upon the Granting of wch | Mr Penn is willing to Surrender the | Government of Pennsylvania to Her | Majesty | Recd | Read | 23 May 1705. The Board of Trade's marginal comments and criticisms are indicated in the notes, below.

1. Marginal note: "These words to be left out; for that in the Patent for Pennsylvana there is no mention of Territories belonging thereunto."

2. A marginal note has been deleted here: "~~Touching~~[?] ~~the Draught of the Deed of Surrender~~.

3. Residents.

4. Marginal note: "These Words to be left out al over for the reason aforesd."

5. Marginal note: "Q: What are those Rights &c ment by these Words? This ought to be especially exprest."

6. Marginal note: "The Board cannot propose a general Approbation of the Laws till they have been particularly considered, & then they are to be confirmed each by its particular Title. The Board are ready to enter upon the consideration thereof."

7. Marginal note: "These Words are unintelligible & too general."

8. Marginal note: "The Govnt being once surrendred to her Maty this whole Clause (to the end of pa: 7) is unnecessary. For that her Maty will provide for the same by her Commissn & Instns to her Govr, as is don in all her other Plantns. Besides this Clause surrenders nothing." The Board is here referring to the long clause on rights of government and religion, ending here.

9. Marginal note: "The Board cannot agree to this Clause, not knowing what the Declarations & Oaths required are."

10. Marginal note: "The Act of Tolleration provides for this, wch is judged sufficient."

11. Marginal note: "Instead of these words, insert *required, according to the Law of Engld.*"

12. Marginal note: "The Queen ought to be trusted wth the Protection of her Subjects. Besides it is not easy to determin wt will be accounted a Reproach; Nor wt Words and Gestures will be judged punishable."

13. Marginal note: "The Govr can not be obliged to take any other Oaths than wt is required by the Law of England, until some new Law be made for that purpose ither here or in Pennsylvania."

14. Marginal note: "Q: Which are they?" The Board probably realized that WP was here including the three Lower Counties as well as the three counties of Pennsylvania.

15. WP had attempted unsuccessfully to obtain the extensive powers of the palatinate of Durham in his original grant of Pennsylvania, including the power to pardon treasons, murders, and felonies, and the power to appoint all judges and justices of the peace. See *PWP*, 2:40, 42n. WP probably intended to locate this palatinate in Bucks Co.; see also doc. 97, text following n. 8.

16. Payment. *OED.*

17. Marginal note: "This Clause is very large & contains more power than Mr Penn has already by his Patent: Besides that the Board is not well informed of the ~~exact~~ Extent of the Power of a Pallatin of Durrham; And they cannot propose to her Maty the parting wth her Power & Prerogative in the Plantations."

18. Marginal note: "This is proper for the previous Consideration of the Ld H: Treasurer, as immediately relating to the Revenue."

19. Marginal note: "This likewise is proper for the previous Consideration of the Ld H: Trr as immediately relating to the Revenue."

99
TO THE BOARD OF TRADE

6 4m (Jun) 1705

Hon:ble Frds

I returne your remarks wth my answear, as my Counsll has drawn it, & pray your consideration of it I am

Your Respectfll Friend
Wm Penn

{Mr Penns} Observations upon the objections made by the Lords Commissioners of Trade & Plantations to the Charter[1] humbly desired by him.

{f. 1.}[2] Tis concievd Territories ought to be named since by virtue of a subsequent grant & several declarations of the Crown by Proclamations & otherwise[3] besides the submissions of the People he had a Governmt over them & since he is named late Proprietary Governour it can be no prejudice to the Crown but to omit it would be very hard for the People of those Territories if they may not be assured of the same privileges wth others.

{f. 2.} This shews the reason for reteining what concerns them in the 2d page[4] The Q.[5] tis supposd is groundless the Charter being onely a guard to their present Rights &c

{f. 3} Tis conceivd the clause confirming the laws ought to stand it implying that such as ought to be disallowed are so before the Charter passes[6]

{f. 4.} Tis conceivd there's a plain difference between laws wch are supposd to be positive & legal customes, wch grow by tacit consent of the Governours & Governed, & Constitutions may be legal tho not wth the formallity of laws in a full exercice of the Legislature.[7]

The next clause being excepted agst only as unnecessary[8] & what will be provided for {by} her Majties' Commissn & Instructions since there's no reall objection against tis hopd may stand that such Provision may be perpetual it being more than is usual for other parts but highly expedient for ease of that People

{f. 8} That of allowing the present Declarations & oaths till altered by Act of Assembly is of great importance to their security for otherwise most of the Freemen of the Province may be renderd incapable of enjoying their privileges.* [9]

{f. 10.} The Act of Toleration dos not reach all the particulars requisite to secure the liberty of that People in religious matters;[10] nor as tis conceivd ought it to depend upon the continuance of that Act wch possibly may be repeald or alterd upon the future dispositions of Parliamts {neither dos the Act in Strictness extend thither.}

{f. 11.} The variation in the form not being in anything essential but such as has satisfyed the scrupulous there tis hopd no form new to them will be insisted on.[11]

{f. 12.} Since this Charter is cheifly in relation to future times, as the desireing the guard against Reproaches argues no distrust of her Majty tis hoped that clause may stand.[12]

{f. 15.} That of the Governours oath is not insisted {on} tho tis conceived the Prerogative in Relation to foreign Plantations, as it has several powers for the benefit of the subjects there wch cannot be exercisd in England may justify the imposeing such an oath.[13]

{*f. 8.9.} If it cannot then certainly it removes the objection agst allowing the old oaths till alterd by Act of Assembly[14]

{f. 17.} For the Crown to grant such Jurisdiction holding of the Crown was never thought a parting wth its Prerogative[15]

If this might be in England much more in the Plantations nor can there be mischeif by it when confin'd to a small district.

Since the two last exceptions referr to the Lord Treasurer it seems a naturall ground for a Letter to him from the Board as Mr Penn has formerly requested.[16]

ALS and D. CO 5/1263/20, PRO. (*Micro.* 12:066.) Docketed: Pennsylvania | A Lettre from Mr Penn with | his Answer to the Observations | of the Board {~~returned~~} upon the Draught | of a New Charter desired by | him wch were delivered to him | the 5th ~~of June~~ Instt | Recd | Read | 7 June 1705.

1. The Board of Trade had raised a series of objections in the margins of WP's draft charter of 23 May 1705, doc. 98.
2. These references to folios in WP's draft appear in the margin. The editors have enclosed them in braces and moved them into the text.
3. WP's title to the Lower Counties was based on deeds from the duke of York and on the crown's subsequent de facto recognition of his jurisdiction there. A formal patent for the territories had been drawn up under James II, but the Glorious Revolution intervened before it could be sealed. See *PWP*, 2:281-84; doc. 62, n. 1. For the board's objection, see doc. 98, n. 1.
4. Another reference to the board's objection to inclusion of the Lower Counties; see doc. 98, n. 4.
5. Question; that is, the second question raised on fol. 2 of WP's draft, asking for specific explanation of the rights to be confirmed. See doc. 98, n. 5.
6. See doc. 98, n. 6.
7. See doc. 98, n. 7.
8. See doc. 98, n. 8.
9. The asterisk here draws the reader's attention to a similarly marked passage at n. 14, below, reinforcing WP's argument on the issue of oaths. For the Board of Trade's objection see doc. 98, n. 9.
10. See doc. 98, n. 10.
11. See doc. 98, n. 11.
12. See doc. 98, n. 12.
13. See doc. 98, n. 13.
14. See n. 9, above.
15. See doc. 98, n. 17.
16. See doc. 98, nn. 18-19. Letters from the Board of Trade to Lord Treasurer Godolphin on this issue have not been found.

100
FROM JAMES LOGAN

Philadia 4th 5th moth [July] 1705

Hond Governour

I wrote largely by way of Barbados 5th 2mo & again by Fial[1] & Maryland 17th & 30th of the 3d Month last,[2] Some of wch I doubt not but will come to hand.

At writing the last of these I had no knowledge of C Quary's design for England So Soon, but he is gone from hence in order to it about 3 weeks agoe and will doubtless be mischievous there. I suppose the Account that Blaithwait sent the Secretary of York[3] of thy being about Surrendring the Govmt has hastned him; At his going off the Governour took him aside at W. Tonges[4] house at Newcastle & after some short discourse he made all the Protestations of friendship that were possible declaring he would doe the Governour all the Service that lay in his power and that he had nothing in the World to complain of or Object against him.

We all know however how far he is to be trusted, he made Colonel Hamilton the same when he last went over, and broke them all as Soon as there, But could a certain person here,[5] who having business in England is Extremely desirous to goe over by the same Opportunity, but find wayes to effect it, he might prove Such a rub in his way, as might render his Journey very furuitless by destroying that Interest wch has been so Serviceable to him and his party, the Bishop of London's if he can possibly bring his matters to bear he will doe it wthout dalay. if not he will find means I suppose to weaken him in a cause where it will not be Suitable for thee to appear or be be concerned. In the mean time as he promised me at parting at Newcastle to wait upon thee immediately after his Arrival hoping (he said) there would be no further cause of Difference, So I would humbly offer it as my Opinion that it would be most adviseable to hold it fair with him, without seeming to understand or Suspect any Cause of Dissatisfaction, at the Same time guarding thy Self as much as possible & Obser~~b~~ving his Designs. If that Gentleman cannot gett over by this opportunity, yet there will be such an Interest I suppose made with the Bishop as will very much Stagger his.

What is mostly to be feared is, least he should come upon the nick of thy Surrender and making terms, but I have this to offer, that in case it be not over nor the chief Terms concluded on, so as to putt it out of danger, thou may safely I believe stand off and resolve to hold it till a better opportunity, for I am of Opinion the Govmt here in a little time may be in as good Order in all respects as can almost be wished for or desired. The Assembly running upon unexampled extravagancies is now dismised for this Year, And friends are generally so uneasy at their Proceedings that they have drawn up the Letter to thee I mencioned before in my last[6] to which almost all the Proffession sign declaring their abhorrence of that Letter Sent to thee by R Barber[7] and assuring thee of their readiness & perfect willingness to Support all the charges of Govm[t] without any burthen to thee, and they are making the strongest Interest they possibly can to carry the next Election and will take care to choose the best and ablest men in the Govm[t]. Indeed I could wish that now their eyes are fully opened, it might not prove too Late but that they might have one opportunity more, w[ch] I doubt not but would redound to thy Interst and honour. But if the Surrender be already over I could heartily desire that Letter as it is drawn, had never been Attempted, for 'tis wrote so friendly and with the Expression of so much Duty notwithstanding they fail not to putt thee in mind of all things that they take to be honnestly their Due, that should nothing at all be done in the surrender to Answer it, it might be turned to an ill Use by thy enemies thô wrote by thy heartiest friends. It was drawn up in great haste at the rising of the Assembly that the honest Members of it might sign {it} before they went out of town (among whom thou wilt think it Strange that Jos: Growdon should be the first) and is managed by Doctor Owen, Caleb Pusey and R[d] Hill. I had no hand at all in the draught of it whether well or ill. It will come perhaps with this, or the first Virginia Ships. I Send copies of the last proceedings of the Assembly inclosed, Such as goe before these were sent in my last two wayes. thou wilt be startled I believe to hear it alledged, that the Quittrents were reserved for the Support~~ed~~ of Govm[t].[8] but in case we have an other Assembly, the more these men offer of this Kind it is the better, for it still exposes them the more.

When the Assembly had adjourned on the 23[d] 3[mo] last[9] the Governour the same evening summoned W[m] Biles in an Action of 2000[l] for saying these words in the 11th month last[10] "He is but a boy he is not fitt to be our Governour we'll kick him out" we'll kick him out. and at the ensuing Court himself not appearing and D. LL. his attorny demurring upon a Plea of Privilege as an Assembly Man w[ch] was over ruled he was ordered to plead over & come to an issuable plea but this he refused & therefore Judgem[t] went against him Yesterday a Jury of Inquiry Sate upon the Damages & found 300[l] to the Governour w[ch] was much Less than was excepted,[11] this 'tis possible may come before the Queen by Appeal for Will[m] is stiff in it besides that he denies the words, but a great many fr[ds] are fully Satisfied that he spoke them (besides the positive evidence that he said them to) being now largely convinced of the baseness and folly of his temper his medling talkative conceited humour and the strange Shortness of his memory in forgetting & denying this Minute what he said the next before. yet he very much influences that debauched County of Bucks in which there is now Scarce one Man of worth Left, Phineas its father

& honest Rd Hough[12] being gone, but Samuel Carpenter I Suppose will be prevailed on to stand for it next election, whose Interest {joyn'd} with Jos: Growdons & Jer: Langhorns[13] (which two last were the only that Stood for thee of that place this Last Assembly) 'tis hoped will be able to carry it, but we have the Least hopes there of any part of the Government. In Philadia County there was but one on the right side Reece Thomas,[14] and in Chester five as thou wilt see by the Letters.[15]

The Governour as I wrote before from Newcastle,[16] held an Assembly there recommending to them only the Defence of themselves and support of the Govmt, for the first they agreed on an Act for the Militia wch the Governour happened to pass that morning C: Quary was there, being the day they Arose, but thô they were amused and given to expect other things, he would pass nothing else of what they had prepared, thô Several of their Bills were not amiss. The holding an Assembly there is only a [blank] to Carry on Such things with the greater shew of reason & Strength that are of Absolute & immediate necessity but certainly they can make no Laws that are binding. The Governours own Command is of much more force; only while they Acknowledge it to be their Own Act and to have consented to it, there is the less room to complain, this was necessary upon the Account of a Militia and what they would contribute for the Support of Govmt, but I am of Opinion 'tis best to wave all other kind of Laws Untill they have fuller Powers. for thô they Acted in Conjunction with the Province upon the foundation of the Kings Charter,[17] yet Separate I see not how they can Pretend to it. As for the support they declared their Willingness and readiness, but Excused themselves for their Poverty till they should be better enabled, a plea that we must Own is but too well Grounded for these Counties were never in so wretched a Condition ('tis declared by all that ~~we~~ have known them) Since this was a Govmt I Send thee the Governours Speech the Militia Act, and their Answer to that of the Support when press'd upon them Just before their rising.[18]

Wm Clark was Speaker, he and three friends more enter'd not only their Dissent but Protest against it, yet Wm was Speaker (as Peter footwell was also at Burlington)[19] was obliged to sign it {~~th~~ the same night he sickned as he thought of a Surfeit of Cherries} and in two dayes dyed at Newcastle the Govr and most of the Company being come away. We were all extremly Surprised at the Acct of his Death and for my Own part I am not a Little grieved, for I think notwithstanding all the faults alledged against him, he was the best Man in these parts a Credit and Support to them, and I am Confident will be greatly miss'd I have alwayes been very Sharp upon him for what he received,[20] and therefore believe he had but very little in his hands, and gave him frequent directions about his Accounts. so that I hope we shall not suffer, I intend down thither in the fall, but cannot before.

His Son was engaged to one Rebecca Curtis[21] of Barbados, by his fathers dextrous management, a young woman at that time of a very good reputation, much esteemed, of about 1500^{l} to her portion, She came over with one John Hunt[22] her own Sisters Husband last fall by way of Maryland where by means of their Relation he fell into too great a familiarity with her, wch at 9 months end after all her demure carriage here, made known their Shame to the world, not only to their own eternal Scandal but greatly to that of friends. this broke out at Philad^{ia} the same day Wm Clark Sickned at Newcastle; but I suppose he never heard of it. some are of Opinion he did & that it broke his heart, for he was perfectly proud of the Match before, but I doe not believe it ever reached his ears, the foolish Youngman designs to have her Still 'tis thought, they had been before one meeting[23] and the Old man had settled the House we now live in[24] on him & her Joyntly, So that we must I supose turn out, her brother hunt, We heard Yesterday, is gone in to Virg^{ia} capes for Maryland with his whole family from Barbados & above 100 Negroes as 'tis s^{d} in Order to come here & Settle, if not taken by a Privateer[25] that very lately lay off there, and took Severall Vessels bound in, She lay off N York before and took some there & threatned Our Capes as Lord Cornbury who Sent out 4 Privateers after her advised Us by an Express, but she pass'd them and went down to the Southw^{d} So that she happily took her Station at the two Chiefest Govm^{ts} immeditately under the Queen upon the Continent. that very week she Lay at sandy hook more of our Vessels went out of the Capes than was usual in a month before Yet all escaped her and since that Several have come in, and indeed the fortune of the place seems to have been indifferent good for these 3 Months past, but last Year and Winter it was Extreamly Severe I wish it may hold and mend, or we shall be extreamly reduced as for my own part, whatever it proves, I adventure noting.[26]

By the Latter End of Next Month the time that the 3^{d} Year is up I Shall have cleared off all the Interest Money to R^{d} Hill thy Son Aubry's Attorn{e}y,[27] So that I hope he will have no further Cause to Complain. I shall also very Speedily Send about 150^{l} Sterling in Bills which will be full one half of all that I have received of theirs & perhaps may Clear it all by the Virg^{ia} Fleet, which when done will render me very Easy. I Suppose by Your Neglecting to send other Powers by burnam[28] & by Will^{ms} taking a small business with Randal Janney out of mine and putting it into such a Little Tool's hands as Tho: Lyfords[29] a Shop boy to Sam: Bulkly,[30] it is not intended that I shall be further concerned in Lætitia's business. I acted an honest and perhaps no injudicious part for Willm wth Randal, and whether blamed or praised I have been faithfull to Lætitia (if She can pass by my converting between 4 & 500^{l} of her Money to thy Use upon a pinch in 1702 wch I hoped presently to repay & if not done she has Interest for it, & now shall have the Principal) but if she cannot take it so, I have done, employ whom she pleases, I shall readily resign, only once more I must advise thee on thy Own acc^t to take care that Some fitt Person be impowred to make Titles for what I have agreed for, and to receive the Money that the Load of Interest may be taken off thee wch wert thou still to pay it all, would I believe be ⅓^d of the Yearly quittrents that the Province Yields. I have sent all things necessary in Order to this, wch were received in 10^br last & in the 12th Mo^th following,[31] 2 months after the Receipt of the Other, a good Opportunity offered by whom we received other packets thô that was neglected, I can but discharge my Duty in advising at such a Distance, in the mean time I have here made the best Contracts I could to secure Interest for as much as I could dispose of, Since the last Powers came, but unless better are sent all will be void, that's past I fear The people will not pay Mon{e}y without being secured, nor will they pay Interest long for what they dare not venture to improve.[32] My own Security that they Shall have a title, should I Offer it, it is not sufficient, and I am sure no body will be bound wth me that Wm Aubry Shall make one Samuel Carp^r who is Joyned wth me, as he has good reason, refuses it, thô as hearty as any man to serve thee or thine. I have now mentioned this in every Letter (as I remember) for these 12 Mo^ths past and can doe no more.

As soon as I have discharged these Incumbrances of Wm Aubrys I shall doe what I can to make remittances to thy Self 'Tis a mournful consideration to think what thy fortune has ~~has~~ hitherto been, I have shipp'd off and remitted since thy Departure above 4000^l this money as thou wilt find by my Acc^ts Bills of Lading &c and I have paid here on thy Acc^t above 3000^l more wch I Suppose will startle thee at first view as it did my Self in Casting it up, yet there is none of it, I believe upon a full Inquiry that Can be found fault with, however to avoid all hard thoughts Seeing I have mencion'd so much I shall draw out the chief of those heads that make up that sum, as they Stand in my Leidger[33] as near as I can Settle them on a Short view, and yet reckon nothing of thy Sons or Governours charges or the Interest paid Wm Aubry for 3 years at 180^l per Annum, wch as I s^d before in 6 weeks time I hope will be fully discharged.

I call all these, paym^ts, because by one means or other I have Answered them, & they stand all Charged for them in my Books in their Proper Respective Acc^ts, I send also an Acc^t of my several Returns & Remittances because easily drawn out, & thou shalt have a scheme of all my Acc^ts as well what I have received as paid, if desired before I make up the whole. Thy Daughter is Sharp upon me for making thee turn Merch^t but I think I have done nothing of that Kind, but what I have Express Orders for, & in Pursuance of these Orders have acted by the best directions, & in the best company, however as Success must be accounted the Standard of Merit, and thy Affairs have had no great Share of it, I expect no more favour from the world for my want of it than if I fell as far short in honesty upon the plainest discoveries, but my happiness is that with thy Self I am secure, where I am well Satisfied than an honest and punctual Discharge of an incumbent Duty with a hearty Zeal & affection will fully alone[34] for the want of the other that lies in no human Power besides that the ill fortune, if we may call it So, lies not at my door. I follow orders, contrive for the best, and more can not be expected.

I sent a List of Bonds by way of Fial & should send a Duplicate now would time Allow it but since that I have received B: Chambers's and 70l of Richard Stockton wch I have paid mostly to Richard Hill, and thus Some of them will alwayes be discharging.[35] of them as are not good will be no Loss because if the Persons bound pay not the mon{e}y they will have nothing for it, and thou wilt still have thy Own.

We are not yet come to observe the Queens Proclamation about the Money[36] and plead Ld Cornbury's example in it they say, he has made some representation home in the matter[37] 'tis an unhappy perplexed regulation and will certainly Sooner or later prove to thy Loss unless reduced to Sterling wch if it can be procured to be done by Act of Parliament is to be Advised on many Accts for all other changes are hurtfull.

I know nothing Colonel Quary can find to Complain of at home unless it be Ralph Fishbourns business[38] wch I sett fully out in mine of the 2d month last, & have Sent 2 Copies Since of that part of the Letter & now send a third, but I suppose the Original may be come to hand the vessel being arrived at Barb: that carried it thither. I am hard putt to it for a good Copyist, yet now shall do with those I am furnished with, and desire no other for some time at Least.

A Shallop of Wm Fishbourn's[39] was here lately Seized by the Collr [40] and released by the Govr of wch he writes fully to the Commissioners.[41] inclosed is a Copy of one he designed to them, but upon second Thoughts judged it more proper to forbear while Quary is there therefore that part only relating to Fishbourn is sent, but the whole may be worth thy perusal and consideration, it was finished and I was Obliged to Copy it my Self from the rough Draught. Pray be Pleased to read the Paragraph in the Copy of 2d Moth last[42] now sent that has the hand to it

I continually propose to my self to apply to nothing but thy Affairs of Property but in vain. for Still there is Occasion for my hand in other matters, however these are not nor shall be neglected. for I hope punctually to make good what I proposed

I refer to the Governour to be full about Quary the Parson[43] &c in whose way it best lies

Rd Hill has sent ~~in~~ one of the Letters from friends it has only the hands of those about the town yet I suppose, but it will be carried round the whole Countrey & others sent afterwards I am wth all dutiful affection to thy self & family

Thy faithfl & obedient servt

J L

LBC. James Logan Letterbook, HSP. (*Micro.* 12:087.) Endorsed: Sent by Tho: Graham[44] to Virginia on board | the Strombolo[45] inclosed to J Ellis at Whitehal.

1. Fayal, the westernmost island of the central group of the Azores.

2. For Logan's letters of 5 Apr. and 17 May 1705, see *Micro.* 12:005, 053; the letter of 30 May has not been found.

3. George Clarke (1676-1760), originally of Somerset, Eng., was a relative of William Blathwayt, who helped him obtain the secretaryship of New York in 1703. After serving on New York's council 1716-36 and as lieutenant governor 1736-43, Clarke retired to an estate in Cheshire purchased with his large American fortune. Raimo, *Governors,* p. 262.

4. William Tonge (d. post 1709), clerk of New Castle Co., had formerly lived in Philadelphia and served as deputy sheriff and tax collector there. Miscellaneous Papers, Three Lower Counties, 1655-1805, p. 115, HSP; *PA,* 2d ser., 9:715, 717; *Micro.* 9:870.

5. Probably Evan Evans, who had been appointed rector of Christ Church by Henry Compton, bishop of London. Quary was at odds with Evans and a group of Anglican ministers who, as Quary later complained, were trying to do away with vestries in the colonies. Evans was back in England by 1707, urging the bishop of London to appoint a colonial bishop. Perry, *Historical Collections,* 2:20-21, 30, 40-41. See also text at n. 43.

6. In his letter to WP of 17 May, Logan mentioned that this letter from Friends was planned, but the letter itself has not been found. See *Micro.* 12:053; doc. 122.

7. Doc. 83.

8. On 23 May 1705 the Assembly presented an address to Gov. Evans, claiming that the original Pennsylvania purchasers had agreed to pay quitrents to WP "upon Communication had between him and them, concerning the extraordinary Charge which he should be at in the Administration of the Government." *Votes and Proceedings,* 1(pt. 2):41; see also *PWP,* 2:81-82.

9. 23 May 1705.

10. Nov. 1704. On 8 May 1705 the Council resolved that Biles should be prosecuted "for his scandalous and seditious words against the Government." Biles was an assemblyman, and, though his words were not spoken in the house, the Assembly objected strongly to his arrest as a breach of its privilege. *Minutes of the Provincial Council,* 2:186; *Votes and Proceedings,* 1(pt. 2):43-44, 46.

11. Copyist's error for "expected."

12. Phineas Pemberton had died in 1702, and Richard Hough (d. 1705), a First Purchaser from Macclesfield, Ches., who settled in Bucks Co., had been an active member of Falls Meeting and served in the Assembly for many years. *PWP,* 2:645; 3:40n; Hinshaw, 2:961.

13. Jeremiah Langhorne (1673-1742), a Quaker from Kendal, Westm., came to Pennsylvania in 1684 and settled in Middletown Twp., Bucks. A frequent assemblyman 1700-1741 and twice speaker, he became chief justice of the Supreme Court in 1739. Digests of Quaker Records, Westm., HSP; William J. Buck, "Jeremiah Langhorne," *PMHB,* 7:67-87.

14. In addition to Reese Thomas, the members for Phila. Co. were David Lloyd, Everard Bolton, Joseph Willcox, Joshua Carpenter, Edmund Orpwood, John Roberts, and Francis Rawle. *Votes and Proceedings,* 1(pt. 2):17.

15. Nicholas Pile, Nicholas Fairlamb, Joseph Cobourne, Isaac Taylor, and John Bennett, members for Chester Co., had absented themselves from the Assembly after it was dismissed by Gov. Evans on 23 June 1705. The other proprietary supporters—Joseph Growden, Jeremiah Langhorne, and Reese Thomas—had done the same. The remaining members, including Chester representatives John Hood, Richard Hayes, and Joseph Wood, met despite Evans's dismissal and adjourned themselves after condemning the behavior of the absent members. *Votes and Proceedings,* 1(pt. 2):48.

16. Not found; probably the letter of 30 May referred to in n. 2, above.

17. WP's royal charter gave him authority to make laws with the consent of the freemen of Pennsylvania, but did not apply to the Lower Counties. The 1682 Act of Union had extended the legislative privileges of Pennsylvania to freemen of the Lower Counties when the two acted in conjunction, but Logan doubted that these powers could legitimately be exercised by the Lower Counties independently. See *PWP,* 2:63-77, 339n; *Charter and Laws,* p. 104.

18. The Council's minutes for the period of this New Castle Assembly are missing from the published records. *Minutes of the Provincial Council,* 2:198.

19. Peter Fretwell (d. 1719), a Quaker tanner of Burlington, was speaker of the New Jersey Assembly in 1704, when Lord Cornbury and his faction pushed through a militia bill that levied a £1 fine on those who refused to serve. *NJA,* 23:175; Paul A. Stellhorn and Michael J. Birkner, eds., *The Governors of New Jersey, 1664-1974* (Trenton, 1982), p. 37; *Proceedings of the New Jersey Historical Society,* 1st ser., 5:20.

20. William Clarke had been collecting quitrents for WP; see Penn Papers, Accounts, 1:7, HSP.

21. William Clarke, Jr. (d. 1758?), married Rebecca Curtis, daughter of Emanuel Curtis of St. Philips Parish, Barbados, and became a member of Phila. Monthly Meeting. Joanne McRee Sanders, ed. and comp., *Barbados Records: Wills and Administrations: Volume II, 1681-1700* (Houston, 1981), p. 83; Hinshaw, 2:486; Phila. Admins. Bk. G, p. 128.

22. John Hunt (d. 1706), merchant of Philadelphia, Barbados, and Virginia, seems to have married Rebecca Curtis's eldest sister, Mary (d. by 1706). In 1705 he moved to York Co., Va. Sanders, *Barbados Records: Wills and Administrations: Volume III, 1701-1725,* p. 92; Phila. Will Bk. C, #108.

23. On 30 Mar. 1705 Rebecca Curtis and William Clarke appeared before Phila. Monthly Meeting to declare their intention to marry. Hinshaw, 2:500.

24. Logan and Gov. Evans were lodging in William Clarke's brick mansion at Chestnut and Third St.; see doc. 82, text at n. 12; Watson, *Annals,* 1:374.

25. This was a French privateer; see *CSPC, 1704-1705,* p. 562.

26. Copyist's error for "nothing."

27. On WP's debts to his son-in-law, William Aubrey, see doc. 130, n. 32.

28. Benjamin Burman, master of the *Hopewell.*

29. Thomas Lyford, a Quaker, seems to have traveled often between England and Philadelphia. Hinshaw, 2:587; doc. 146; *Micro.* 13:468.

30. Samuel Bulkley or Buckley (d. 1703), a First Purchaser from Plumbley, Ches., was a Quaker merchant of Philadelphia. *PWP,* 2:639; Hinshaw, 2:342; Phila. Admins. Bk. B, p. 22.

31. Dec. 1704 and Feb. 1705.

32. See David Lloyd's complaint about this in doc. 102, text at n. 11.

33. For Logan's ledger, see Logan Family Papers, "Accounts of the Proprietor of Pennsylvania, 1701-1704," Library Company of Philadelphia, on deposit at HSP.

34. Copyist's error for "atone"; similarly, "than" two lines above is an error for "that."

35. The passage that follows does not make sense; the copyist probably omitted a line or phrase.

36. See doc. 56, n. 65.

37. On 19 Feb. 1705 Lord Cornbury wrote to the Board of Trade, complaining that the queen's proclamation setting currency standards had caused an instant flight of coin from New York. He noted that other colonies were not complying, citing New England in particular, and reported that since strict enforcement of the proclamation would ruin his colony, he was delaying compliance pending further word from England. *CSPC, 1704-1705,* pp. 378-81.

38. Ralph Fishbourne (d. 1708), a Quaker from Talbot Co., Md., who lived in Chester, had imported wool into Pennsylvania from Maryland, apparently in ignorance of the English wool act forbidding such trade (10 & 11 Will. III, cap. 10). The goods were seized by the New Castle collector, but Fishbourne refused to appear at the New Castle court, and the New Castle sheriff had no authority to cross over to the province and compel him. In his letter of 5 Apr., Logan pointed to this as a flaw in Pennsylvania's law regulating courts. *Micro.* 12:005; *PWP,* 3:330n.

39. William Fishbourne (1677-1742), a Quaker merchant of Philadelphia, later served as assemblyman, provincial councilman, mayor of Philadelphia, and J.P., among other offices. Hildeburn Manuscripts, 1:27, GSP; *PA,* 2d ser., 9:642, 718-22, 736-37, 747; Hinshaw, 2:523.

40. John Moore.

41. Not found.

42. Apr. 1705; apparently a reference to the paragraph in *Micro.* 12:005 that deals with Ralph Fishbourne; see n. 38, above.

43. Evan Evans, rector of Christ Church. See n. 5, above. Gov. Evans did write to WP in May and July 1705, but these letters have not been found. See doc. 106.

44. Probably Thomas Graham (d. 1710), a merchant of Anne Arundel Co., Md. Phila. Will Bk. C, #169.

45. H.M.S. *Strombolo*, commanded by Capt. Matthew Teate, was convoying a fleet bound for England from Virginia in July 1705. *CSPC, 1704-1705*, p. 596.

101
FROM JAMES LOGAN

WP's efforts to sell Pennsylvania's government to the crown were probably intensified by his need to satisfy the Fords, who held a strong legal claim to the ownership of his Pennsylvania land unless he repaid his debts. The Fords began to assert their own public claim to Pennsylvania on 24 January 1705, when Bridget Ford first drew up a power of attorney to David Lloyd, Isaac Norris, and John Moore. On 29 March Philip Ford, Jr., wrote to these agents, claiming ownership of Pennsylvania and urging the colonists to cease paying quitrents to WP. David Lloyd quickly made Ford's claim public, causing an uproar among Pennsylvania landholders (doc. 101). WP evidently did not learn of this development until late in the year: as Logan noted in doc. 101, "it must needs startle thee," and WP later complained that Ford had written "in the midst of an amicable treaty" (doc. 123). Lloyd lost no time in renewing his direct assault upon WP's pretensions to benevolent patriarchal rule. His letter of 19 July (doc. 102), remarkable for its fluent venom, probed all the deficiencies in WP's absentee proprietorship. In Lloyd's view, WP was a grasping landlord who did not deserve the rents and taxes he claimed because he had performed few services for the colonists in the past twenty years: he had failed to capitalize on James II's patronage, he had failed to protect the Quakers' property rights and political and religious liberties under William and Mary and Queen Anne, and now he was flouting the fundamental constitutional liberties agreed upon in 1701. Even WP's friends were upset by the claim that he had actually conveyed the colony to Ford, a possibility that made Pennsylvania land titles alarmingly insecure (docs. 101 and 103). On 4 October Bridget Ford probated Philip Ford's will, taking the case decidedly into the public arena. By 20 October, when WP himself wrote a new will (doc. 107), he admitted that his estate was sadly encumbered, not by "Projects, or Riotous liveing," but by "liberality to the needy," by service to Pennsylvania and the Quakers, and by "the extortious treatm[t] I have had by some I entirely trusted." For documentation and discussion of WP's legal struggle with the Fords, 1705–8, see docs. 108–21.

13th 5mo [July] 1705

Honoured Governour

My Pen has been but too much accustomed of late to entertain thee with melancholy Subjects, of wch the following I fear will prove none of the least.

{On} The 10th Instant in the Morning Edward Shippen Doctor Owen[1] & my self Commissioners of Property {(TS[2] being absent)} were desired to meet David Lloyd Isaac Norris & John Moore upon a business they had to communicate to us wch proved to be a Letter from Philip Ford[3] to them {dated 29th of 1mo last arrived} by way of Bardados informing them that in March 1697 his father had purchased of thee the Province of Pensilvania and Territories {in fee,}[4] and on the first of April following had granted thee a Lease[5] {of it} ~~for the same under the Ye~~ for three Years ~~under~~ {at} the ~~Yearly~~ Rent of 630l per Annum wch term expired the first of April 1700 and that since that time thou hadst been but Tenant at Will He ~~further informed~~ {added} that Since his fathers Death thou hadst paid thy Rent but very dully (I use his words in the whole) and that now there was above 2500l Sterling due, that therefore they {(meaning I suppose himself & sisters)}[6] were resolved to take the~~ir~~ Countrey into their own hands and appointed the sd persons their Attorneys that by the Virginia Fleet wch would sail the {then} next ~~ensuing~~ Month (viz April) they would send Powers that were then preparing[7] in the mean time he desired them to give notice to the Inhabitants not to pay thy Agents any Quittrents for if they did it would be ~~to~~ {in} their own wrong This ~~to the best utmost that~~ as far as I could charge my Memory (for they ~~refused~~ {thought not fitt to give} a Copy) is the true Contents of the Letter, At Shewing it to us ~~it was~~ {the worst of them} pretended ~~to be done~~ {it was} in Good will ~~and~~ that we might from thence take a caution not to proceed in {sales} ~~business~~ and it seemed to us to be fully agreed on among them ~~not~~ to conceal it from all other persons, {at least} till the powers should arrive but David presently after made it publick I Norris thou may depend on it ~~as far as honour will goe~~ is thy {hearty} friend.[8] JM pretended ~~a great deal of Honour in the case yet~~ {~~something of the Same~~ to be very honourable in the case, yet I believe} is not displeased at it but to David it is doubtless as agreeable as it is at this conjuncture unhappy to be in his hands {for it is to be expected he will press it both by Letters to Philip[9] & here to an extremity that he may gett by it}

This {unusual method of ~~taking~~ {giving} Security} is strangely Surprizing to all kinds of Men, ~~not so much that thou should be in debt or that thy Creditor should have Security but that thou should leave no room for any~~ {the} ~~equity of Redemption by the written Instru~~ Our Enemies make reflections upon it very disadvantageous that after passing such an Instrument thou should still proceed to sell {& impower others to do the same}, and thy friends who were rallying now more than {for a long time before} ~~ever~~ are extreamly grieved notwithstanding we all know it is no more than Security given for the payment of 10500l and that what he calls the Rent is the Interest of that sum. {but the granting it away in fee ~~is what none can understand~~ wthout any Defeazance[10] but a Lease is (if true) what none can understand.}

If this step was made by Philip without thy knowledge ~~it m~~ the account of it must needs startle thee, but if so I humbly crave leave to move that all gentle Methods may be used to retrieve him out of the hands of those that seem~~ed~~ to have been his Counsellors ~~in this matter~~, and that he may be brought to hearken to reason, but thou may assure thy Self ~~all~~ {after the Instruments & Powers are once produced} Payments will be stopt in general till this {great incumbrance} is taken off wch I heartily desire thy Surrender {of the Government} may enable thee to doe, and as far as that falls short that Th: Call:[11] would be prevailed on to contribute ~~according to his Ability~~ and take Some equivalent for it here especially seeing he is inclinable to remove hither. I shall for my own part hasten to finish a Computation of the {value of the} Rents ~~and~~ Overplus Lands &c & ~~bring it~~ {intend to come} over with it with all expedition in case I can gett in enough to clear Wm Aubry's[12] and {some} other ~~Incumbrances~~ {~~Debts~~ Incumbrances} wch ~~will be~~ {I fear will prove} somewhat difficult, for even Bonds that are for Lands will now be disputed seeing what they bought (as it will be ~~said~~ {alledged}) was granted ~~before~~ away to another before. the Confusion {& unhappiness both to thy self & others} that will arise from this is so obvious that I need not note it especially the Resentments as well of the London Company as other purchasers unless it is timely remedied Some would hope thou art privy to it but by the Language of the Letter it seems not probable {for it ~~seems~~ {appears} to have been done in a pett & upon ill natured advice}. However it be I have a kind of Confidence that {its coming to light may} with good Management ~~it may turn no way~~ {prove not much} to thy Disadvantage, because it will both oblige thee to bring matters to an issue wch otherwise might have been long delaid {to thy ~~great~~ {irreparable} Loss} & further will excuse thee for what thou art obliged to doe upon such a pinch of necessity, but I hope thou wilt alwayes be pleased to remember thy friends who have resolved of late upon the base proceedings of others to exert more courage in thy behalf & make it manifest that thou art not ~~so~~ {yet} abandoned by theý People.

I cannot enlarge here having three of these to write by so many several wayes of Conveyance {that offer today} viz Fial Madeira & Jamaica & shall continue {Copies} by ~~all~~ {some} others.

My presence here will ~~be useless~~ {not be of much use} till matters are settled and may be of Service there in the doing of it wch alone will induce me to undertake the Voyage. it will be 4 Months ~~at least~~ {I doubt} before I can be ready ~~and~~ {but} if thou disapproves of my

Intention pray use all opportunities ~~immediately~~ to acquaint me with it[13] of wch the Pacquet boat to Barbados in Summer time ~~pr~~ may prove none of the ~~best~~ worst.

I sent a Large Pacquet last week to Virginia to be conveyed by the Strombolo frigat informing of Colonel Quary's coming over &c {of} wch I cannot possibly gett copies now ready {nor can I add but that} I am with all du~~l~~ti{ful} respect & ~~sincere~~ affection

Thy faithful & Obedient Servant
J. L.

P.S. 18th 5mo
What putts me upon resolving to come over is the belief that nothing can be of more Service to thee there (but Mon{e}y it Self) than an exact Acc^{t} of the whole value of the Province & Territories in Rents Arrears & Lands wch I would labour to bring over Compleat enough to form any proposal upon it, thô it Should not be exact to the greatest Nicety, but the great Streight I am under is, how to reconcile this to the haste that is Necessary in dispatching it, however thou may depend upon it, I shall Use all the Dispatch I Can, & stay no time after I can finish it but for an Opportunity wch I would take by any safe way, for I should not so much Value going into Fra: my self as the losing of Papers & Accounts.

LBC. James Logan Letterbook, HSP. (*Micro.* 12:103.)

1. Dr. Griffith Owen.
2. Thomas Story.
3. Philip Ford, Jr., son of Philip Ford, WP's former steward. This letter has not been found.
4. That is, in fee simple — to Ford and his heirs and assigns forever without limitation. This was identical to the original grant made to WP of Pennsylvania and the Lower Counties. *Black's Law Dictionary.*
5. See *PWP,* 3:661.
6. Bridget, Anne, and Susanna Ford.
7. Philip Ford's widow, Bridget Ford, drew up a power of attorney to Lloyd, Moore, and Norris, dated 24 Jan. 1705, but did not send it to Pennsylvania until Oct., when the Fords had decided to prosecute WP in Chancery (see doc. 108). On 12 Dec. 1705 Logan reported to WP that the power of attorney had arrived. Bridget Ford also sent a letter, dated 18 Oct. 1705, promising to send her title to Pennsylvania by way of Col. Robert Quary, which, Logan concluded, "seems to shew she acts in Concert with him and is the more probable beca{u}se the Lett^{r} is directed to D. Ll. & J. M. only leaving out I. N. for being thy Friend I suppose." *Micro.* 12:442.
8. In fact, Norris wrote to Philip Ford, Jr., on 29 Aug. 1705. While agreeing that the debt should be paid, Norris asked Ford to pursue the issue with "as much Temper & respect" to WP "as the thing will bear, remembering that thy father was his friend from the begining & he his." Norris also became involved in subsequent negotiations with the Fords to reach a financial accommodation with WP that would prevent Pennsylvania from falling into their hands. Norris Papers, Norris Letterbook, 6:91, HSP.
9. Not found.
10. A collateral instrument which defeats the force or operation of another deed or conveyance (*Black's Law Dictionary*). See WP's effort to explain the terms of his grant to Ford in doc. 110, esp. text at n. 17.
11. Thomas Callowhill, WP's father-in-law.
12. On WP's debts to William Aubrey, see doc. 130, n. 32.
13. In March 1706 WP encouraged Logan to return to England, but he eventually told him not to come, in a letter of 10 June 1707. *Micro.* 12:647, 13:214.

102
FROM DAVID LLOYD

Philadelphia 19th 5thm [July] 1705.

Governour Penn

Thine Dated from Hyde-Park the 26th of the 12th month last[1] Containing Divers personall Undeserved Refleccions and false Charges Against me And Some other Friends therein named As well as against other Representatives of the Freemen of this Province in Assembly arrived {But} That part ~~of thy Letter~~ {~~thereof~~} wherein those personall Refleccions are, has been hitherto Concealed from me Tho' Whispered about by some of them to whom thou Sent it, But that part which Came to my hands As well as what I understand of the rest I hold my self Obliged in Conscience to Answer Desiring thee to ~~D~~Receive the same, As I intend it, Not only to Allay the Opinion thou Seems to have of thy Services for this Countrey by holding the Administration of thi~~se~~ Government in thy own hands Or by what thou did or Suffered on that Account But also to Convince thee That thy Resentments Against the Assembly are grounded Upon False Suggestions.

As to the Unworthy Treatment thou mencions (which I Understand by those who Expound thy Letter to be the Representation I Sent thee by R: B:[2] in J^{on} Guy Who was Taken by the French) I shall only referr to the Inclosed Copy of the Votes and Proceedings of the Assembly on that Account And Lett the Impartiall Judge how farr it Tends to the Ruine of thee and thine.

Remember thy own Cautions Not to Strain points Nor halt before a Cripple[3] And Do not Endeavour to Insinuate As if thou has not had Suitable Returns and Compensations from the People here for all thy Pains Hazards Expences and Imployment of thy Interest And the best part of thy life which thou Sayst Pensilvania has Cost thee, As for thy Pains and Expences upon the Account of this Province, If what thou Did or art to receive by the 2000^{l} Tax and the Imposts which I am Informed Amounted to Severall thousand pounds more And Some Thousand pounds besides which thou hast had or art [illegible deletion] to have by Voluntary Subscriptions[4] be not Sufficient to reimburse thee I know the people are willing to make thee further Satisfaccion when thou Exhibitts thy Account of the particulars properly Chargeable upon them And as for thy Hazards and Hardships &c I ~~do not see~~[?] understand that they bear but a very Small Proporcion to what the first Adventurers here Underwent thou knows that many of them as well as the after purchasers came for thy Sake into this Countrey Where they Exposed themselves & Tender Families to the danger of a Savage Nation As well as of an howling Wilderness And at Such time too as severall of them who could not Get Provision for mony were reduced to such Extremity That they had no food for many Days but Herbs and Green Corn And many of them have layd down their heads that were as likely to live as some that Did Survive the Difficulties & hardships of this New Settlem^{t}. The Sence of these things And thy Dealings with the people I believe Made that Good man G: F:[5] a little before his Death Charge thee To mind poor Friends here.

It would have been much to the Purpose had thou particularly Demonstrated what thou hast done for our Common Good; It is well known That thy promises of Residing here And of Establishing the people ~~here~~ in their Properties Rights and Liberties Adding Such peculiar Priviledges & Immunities as might render them more free and Easy than they were in their Native Countries Were Great Motives to Induce them to Adventure upon the Settlement of this Colony And Give thee Such great rates for Land and ~~to~~ Prevaild Upon them to Submitt to a perpetuall Quittrent not only Upon their land in the Country but upon their City lotts Which thou promised to Give them Gratis as no part of their purchase And yet made them pay 5^{s} or 10^{s} Sterling per Annum[6] for what in proporcion of their other purchase was not worth Three pence Nor Stood thee in so much According to what pay thou made the Sweads for it And yet the Swead's Claim to the whole Town plat Still remains.[7]

Which Quitrents (As was made appear to this and the last Assembly by living Witnesses) thou reserved towards the Extraordinary Charge thou should be at as Governour & promised That thy Tennants Should purchase the same at a Certain rate Set in some of thy Printed Papers[8] So that it might be reduced to a pepper-Corn or ~~so~~[?] Some Such Small Acknowledgment to thee as Lord of the Soyl Therefore how Could thou Sell the Rents to Philip Ford And not Give thy Tennants here the Offer of them And now to Tell us of Selling the Government Which those Rents were in part to Support And throw the Load wholly upon the people Who have been or it seems must be at most If not all the Charge of Carrying on the Government both Legislatively & Executively during about Sixteen Years of thy Absence When thou went from hence to Defend Baltemore's Claim to the Lower Counties Which through thy Neglect, as I am Informed, Remains Yet Unsetled[9] To the great Discouragement If not Ruine of the Inhabitants of those Controverted places Besides the great Loss & hindrance thy Stay has been to this Countrey in Generall Especially Considering how precarious thou then made the powers of Government And what Confusion the Propriety fell into by reason of thy Commissionating Some as thou knew or was Informed would not Act in Conjunction wth the rest[10] And in the mean time thou Sold Lands and Gave Speciall Warrants to Survey them While many of the former Purchasers could have No Warrants to Lay out their Lands and none Could have their Locations Settled by Patents And Yet thy Secretary[11] Makes them Pay Rent from the Begining

And when thou went last over thou knows thou Gave Friends here an Expectation that thou would Gett the Royall Sanction to our Laws Or at least to so many of them as might Secure us in the Charterall Priviledges thou Granted {us} as well as our other Rights & Properties In Case thou could Divert the Bill then moving in Parliament for Annexing this Government to the Crown. But If not then thou promised to Use thy Endeavours for Procuring Some Grant or Publick Instrument to secure us, our Charters, Laws, & Liberty of Conscience As also to Defend us from Tithes and other Exactions of the Priests And That the People called Quakers might not be rendred Uncapable to have their Share of the Government Because of Oaths or to that Effect

This thou pretended to be thy Chief Errand home at that time which thou recommended to {the Consideracion of} Friends at the House of Samuel Carpenter wth So much Indifferency That If they had any other whom they thought fitt to Send as their Agent in that Affair Thou would Ingage thy Interest at home to Assist him If not thou would Undertake it thy Self And Assured Friends thou could Save them {some} Scores If not Hundreds of pounds in the Charge of that Negotiation Whereupon they Accepted of thy offer And a Voluntary Subscription was Carried on in order to Furnish thee wth ready Money to Defray the Charge of thy Voyage & Service because a Competency of the 2000^l^ Tax could not be Collected soon enough to Answer those Exigencies, A great part of wch Subscription Money thou rece^d^ before thou went And most If not all the rest has been payd Since Therefore It's very Odd That our Laws had layn so long before the Attorney Generall for want of a Large Fee as thy Lieu^t^ Tells us,[12] And That an Order should Come from the Queen in the mean time requiring Oaths to be Administered Whereby Friends are Disabled to Act in Courts.[13]

I Do not Complain by reason of any Charge I have been {at} upon that Account For I Did not believe that thou could be an Extraordinary Agent for the People in these times Since thou Neglected in the Reign of King James when it lay in thy power to do them Good; Nor Could I rationally Conclude from the Examples thou Gave & Allowed or Connived at Under thy own Administracion Since thou Came last to this Country that thou would do much for our Relief ag^t^ Oathes being thou by thy Comission Under thy own hand and Seal Called Dedimus Potestatem Gave to thy then Secretary[14] power to Qualify thy Judges and Justices which he did by Swearing them upon the Bible And when thou was Acquainted therewith thou sayd thou did not Commissionate him to Administer Oaths But I remember very well thou was not willing he should be prosecuted for Administring Oaths without an Express power for so doing. The like Example has been follow'd after Colonel Hamilton's Death & before the present Govr Arrived Nor did thou Exert thy Authority for the just relief of Friends who were Builders or Owners of vessells here in Allowing them to Register Upon their Sollemn Affirmacion or Attest which was then Allowed instead of an Oath in Maryland and other Governments[15] So that to prevent their Vessells to be layd up by the Walls they were forced to make such as Could Swear to be part Owners of their Vessells And thou Subscribed That the Oath was Administred in thy presence as the Statute of the 7th & 8th of Wm the Third requires[16] Nor could I see That thou wast Clear to Do much against the priest since thou had Granted Lycences for him[17] to Joyn people in Marriage Some of them being Under very Ill Circumstances. Of which thou was Advertized before their Marriage. Nor Did I Expect much better Success to our Laws being they were made in Conjunction wth the Representatives of the Three lower Counties Where I thought thou had not the like right to Govern as thou had in the ~~Govern~~[?] Province And since I have seen the Reserve which the Queen made in her Approbacion of thy present Lieutenant[18] I am Confirmed in my Opinion.

Thou Rightly Observes that the people in Generall & our Friends in particular were desirous of thee before thy last arrivall, And I believe and am well Satisfyed That Friends and most of the Churchmen and all or most of the Baptists Independants & other Professors would rather thou should Continue Governour in Chief And Come to live amongst Us than that thou should Sell or Surrender the Government. Nevertheless I think it will be more Satisfaccion to the Generality of the People that thou should Committ the Adminnistration of thy Government to another And keep the Nomination only to thy self as now it is And I question not but they will Do what may be fitting on their parts to be done towards the Support of such Lieutenancy Therefore It is a very wrong Insinuacion That the People here desire a Queens Govr to be set over them Or to Make thee Weary of being their Governour Unless the Asserting of their rights due by thy Grants and Promises should make thee so But they Gave the Queen and thy Self their hearty Acknowledgments for Supplying thy absence by thy present Lieutenant As appears by severall Addresses Sent thee from the last Assembly[19] Of wch we have no Account tho' they were Sent Severall Ways. Nevertheless thou may perceive by the Assembly's Address to thy self last Year[20] As also by the other proceedings of that and the present Assembly That though the Queen's Approbacion of thy Lieut was (as thou says) to our Surprizing Satisfaccion Yet We find That the Branch of his Commission[21] wch Impowers him to Call Assemblys by his Writts & to prorogue & Dissolve them is directly Contrary to the Charters thou granted us As well as our former Usages & Constitutions Which thou by thy Letters dated the 4th of December 1703 & the Eighth of the 2nd Month 1704[22] bids us Assert and not Tamely resign; But that Branch wherein thou reserves thy finall Assent to all such Bills as he should pass into Laws here put

Such a Check upon the Queens Approbacion That it proves rather a Satisfaction than a Disappointment to our Enemies And raises a Materiall Doubt in some of our Friends whether thou art fully & Effectually represented here Tho' thou had sufficient Cautions by the Earnest Applications of the people whilest thou was last Upon the Spot That If thou left us thou should be fully represented in thy Absence to prevent the Confusion {we} ~~w~~had formerly laboured under by reserves in thy Commissions of State & propriety.

Thou says thou wast Accessible when here And ready to Comply with every reasonable Request, It may be so, But I am Sure That the Delays and Disappointments many people met with made their access of little Service And those things which thou Complyd with and was very desirous to Grant and Establish by Charters and Laws to the people, Especially when thou thought the Government would be Taken from thee, have been since in a great Measure actually Violated by thee and thy agents And in the main rendred ineffectuall to Frds in particular As well as to the people in Generall And yet thou sayst thou prevented what we feared And what some of our Neighbours feel; Now lett it be Examined what it is they have felt which {we} have not or are like to feel, If thou does not perform thy Engagements to the people & Alter the Measures lately Taken. Had our Neighbours their Proprietors at home to Surrender their Rights to the Government?[23] So We have One that Says he can Dispose of all to the Crown Soyl as well as Government Had our neighbours their Laws Stitched up and Sent out of their Government and were they left to the Courtisies of their New Governour how farr they should be rul'd by their former Laws and Constitutions?[24] So are our Laws left It seems before the Councill & no account Given us wch of them are approved & wch rejected So that We now Labour under the like Inconveniencies and Uncertainties as they do. Have they Oaths Imposed upon such Who for Conscience Sake Cannot Swear? So have We For this County Magistrates lately Fined Jos: Yard & Thomas Rutter[25] for refusing to Swear tho' willing to Take the Affirmacion And Committed them to the Sheriffs Custody till they payd their Fines And not only so but our Lieutenant Governour Issued forth his proclamacion Under thy Seal to Declare Null & void the Court-proceedings of this City agt Certain persons for Disorders & Breach of the peace For that the Witnesses produced upon Tryall were not Sworn[26] tho' there was none upon the Bench but Quakers And the Witnesses declared they held themselves as much Obliged by the Affirmacion As by an Oath upon the Bible. Have our Neighbours made a Law for raising a Militia & to make Distresses upon the Quakers? Yes. And So have thy Lieutenant & Assembly of the Three lower Counties[27] And No Doubt but when they are Annexed Again to the Province We shall have the Same In the mean time here is a Militia Authorized by thy Lieut under thy Seal And thy own Coat of

Arms in Some of their Ensigns And those that are Inlisted are by proclamacion Exempted from their Dutys of Watching and Serving as Constables[28] Which No Law nor Custom as I ever heard of in England can Warrant By which Means the City Watch is much Weakened And Vice greatly Encouraged And not only so But Some of the Captains and Officers say They Cannot Command their Soldiers to appear upon Duty unless they please which occasions some to Conclude That the Queen is not well dealt wth When she is Inform'd That here is a Militia made up of so many men well disciplined And Yet If their Service were required they are Under no Sufficient Ingagement to Appear in Arms. Have our Neighbours been Disturbed in their free Eleccions of Representatives to serve them in Assembly? Yes, And So have We at our last Eleccion[29] when the Militia with their Arms Drums and Colours March'd through the place where the Freemen of this County were Gathered together at the time Appointed to make their Eleccion Where the Militia Rushed in Upon the Electors and Treated them very rudely Severall of them having their Swords in their hands to the Great Terror & Disturbance of the peaceable people there present.

As to our 3 Bills wch thou says had been dissolved there If they could have past here And thy Lieu^{t} immediately displaced for doing of it: If so, then our Condicion is farr worse than our Neighbours And this makes us feel what We feared was the Intent of the Reserve of thy finall Assent wch by this Rule may prove to be of much worse Consequence to thy Lieutenant than If he were Under the Immediate direction of the Crown, And is one of the Strongest Arguments I have Yet heard ag^{t} Prop^{ry} Governments.

I Do not remember that the Govr had ~~h~~ Any {more than} 4 Bills before him that Assembly, To witt, One for Confirmacion of the Charter of Priviledges One for Confirmacion of the City Charter The Third for Confirmacion of Property And the Fourth for the Affirmation to pass instead of an Oath But which of these are the Three thou means We are left to Guess:[30]

The Two first are but Confirmacions of thy own Grants past under thy hand & broad Seal with great Solemnities, Both of them requiring Some Explanations The First by reason of an Attempt that the Councill made in 8^{br} 1703 of Proroguing the Assembly And the Disagreement of the lower Counties Whose Representatives refused to Act wth us by Charter[31] And the Second by reason of the Inroads that the County Justices ha~~ve~~d made upon the Powers there by granted to the City Magistrates:[32] As to the Third I know nothing in it but what is very Consistent wth thy Grants Promises & Ingagem^{ts} particularly the Charter of Property[33] which I Drew by thy Express Order & Direccion And which thou Signed at New Castle But by reason of Some powers Contained in the later part of it thou delayd the Sealing thereof Nevertheless thou Did by an Instrument Under thy hand & Seal then and there in the presence of thy then Lieutenant[34] and

Severall of thy Councill Declare Grant and Confirm the first part thereof relating to Titles of Land as amply to be of Force as if thou Executed the same[35] And only declined that of powers Though thou may remember That When thou gave me direccions to Draw somthing that might Secure the People in their properties And Friends in the Executive part of the Governmt I Desired it might be done in Two distinct Instruments Which thou positively refused Saying That what related to property would be a means to make the other about powers pass the better And So I proceeded upon the Draught And brought it over to thee for thy Correction And thou Ordered thy Cozin Parmiter to peruse it which he did And thou and he approved of every part thereof before it was Ingrossed Therefore It's hard to Conceive how thou can have a hand in Dissolving any of those Three Bills Nor can thou Justly Charge us for Employing the said Charters beyond the Letter or Naturall Consequence thereof.

But What is very Astonishing to me and others is That those Charters which thou so Sollemnly granted and made the people believe they were for the perpetuall Security of the Inhabitants of this province in their Rights Priviledges and properties Should be by thee now Diminished into meer Precautions Which thou took for the preservation of the Government least thou should not prevail or Succeed when thou arrived there I know not what thou Aims at by this part of thy Letter Unless thou intends to Make the Reader believe That If a Queen's Govr was sett over us We should Contend wth him for those Rights & Priviledges thou Granted us as aforesd But If thou Succeeded well and wert Established in the Government Then what thou Granted Should ipso facto be reduced again to thy Unconstant Will & pleasure.

As to the Fourth I am not Willing to believe that thou would Displace thy Deputy (for I am well Satisfyed the Queen would not) for passing a Law to Exempt the People called Quakers from Swearing And Allowing them to be Qualified for publick offices and Trusts As well as give Evidence in all Cases upon their Sollemn Affirmacion in the Same Form as prescribed by Acts of parliament which thou Allowed when here to be Taken by Friends And Suffered Oaths to be Administred to others, {Therefore I hope this is not one of the Three.}

That Strange Flight of thine which Suggests That Some here (meaning the Assembly for none else can regularly give Supplies) ~~r~~Refused the Governour Subsistence Money Unless he would betray and Expose thee that Sent him, Is so Void of Truth And so Enormously Base (to Use thy own Words) That no {person} ~~other~~ but thy Informant or some other so Tinged with Hypocrisy (Which, as thou rightly observes is the Abuse of Religion to Worldly purposes) could be so False and Wicked as to Say So, For Upon the 25th day of the Third Month 1704 The Assembly Agreed Nemine Contradicente That a Tax not less then 1000l should be raised for Support of Government.[36] And on the 21st of the 4th month following The Assembly Agreed to appropriate to the Govr 400l of the sd Tax & 100l to Maintain a good Correspondence with the Indians &ct.[37] And on the 9th of the 6thmo following The Assembly Resolved That 100l thereof should be Transmitted to Certain Persons in London pitched upon as Agents for this province to Attend the Attorney or Solicitor Generall & Board of Trade in order to Obtain the Queen's Royall approbacion to our Laws,[38] And afterwards a Draught of a Bill was prepared for that purpose, But the Governour for reasons best known to himself refused to Concurr with that Assembly in Establishing those Things which they thought reasonable and fitt for him to do as he was thy Lieutenant For they Expected nothing from him but what they apprehended very Consistent wth thy Charters Which I hope thou never designed to be Contrary to the Constitution of England For had they been so thou might have took a Shorter and better Course to Lay them Aside than after thou had granted them to find out So many Ways to Elude or render them of no Effect to the people as they have been hitherto. Nevertheless the present Assembly went upon the Consideration of the Supply And on the 19th of the Third Month last Resolved to raise Twelve hundred pounds and an Impost upon all Wines and Cyder Imported in Bottoms not belonging to this Province And That Six hundred pounds of the said Tax with the Impost should be appropriated to the Governour. And for his more Speedy Supply The Assembly Agreed That 20s per pipe should be paid him for all Wines sold by retaile With Severall other Duties That would have Furnished him With Present Money And This the Assembly declared themselves willing to do Without any other reserve but the Governour's Concurrence to Redress the Grievances of the people & Confirm them in such Things as were Agreeable to thy promises and Ingagments to them according to Equity & Justice And with due regard to thy Just Interest.[39]

Thus the People are ready to Support thy Government Tho' thou hast given no true Demonstracion yet that thou wilt Support the Constitucions by which they Act But leaves them at Uncertainties About the Laws which Cost the Country many Thousand pounds besides what thou had So That the Magistrates Cannot Act Safely by them further than for the Conservacion of the peace which might be done without them And not only So but thy Talk of Selling Resigning & Surrendring the Government & the Intimacion lately had from others to that purpose proves a very great Disheartning to the people in Generall

Many Grievances were Complained of But the Assembly thought the best Way of Redressing them was to Make Suitable Provisions to prevent the like for the Future Which was Endeavoured by the Bills now before the Governour[40] And some more that were Agreed to be Drawn but Cannot as yet be ready And for all this the Governour~~'s Lieutenant~~ Undertook to Dismiss us Contrary to Charter,[41]

And thou Endeavours to Render us as the Vilest of men And We are Called Rogues Rascalls & Villains by thy Secretary Whose Insolent behaviour to the people in Generall and his Cruell hard Usage under pretence of pursuing thy Int{er}est has Cooled their Affection to Such a degree That unless thou does them Justice And not Give Credit to such false Informacions as thou seems to have done against those that truely love thee & heartily Wish the prosperity of this province, thou wilt find it of little Effect to Talk of the Ancient Love, Fear, & Faith Especially to Recommend Such a Composure as thy Letter appears to be ~~of~~.

Thou Directed them to whom thou sent it to Use their Endeavours to Moderate all Extreams to Satisfy & quiet the people &c But they took the wrong way to do it by reflecting & misrepresenting, as they do, the proceedings of the Assemblys And Set up the Minor of those Assemblys (Some of whom have been the Chief Obstructors of Publick Business And at last deserted the house)[42] over the heads of the Major Who faithfully Discharged their Duty to thee & the people And prepared Such Bills as might have been of Extraordinary Service to thee and them had thou Suffered the Governour to Concurr with them. I Cannot See what Advantage It will be to thee in the End thus to Leave us Uncapable of Enjoying the Benefit of our Laws and Charters Unless it be That thou thinks the more Uncertain thou Leaves us in that respect the more Money thou may Get for the Government. And he that Comes Governour Immediately from the Queen will be better Able to bring us to his own Terms For thy Charters will then be of little Service to us for want of the Confirmacions which We proposed & thou rejected But the Wise and Just God (Who knows with what Simplicity the first Adventurers Settled this Colony And very much Gave up their Understanding, in matters of Government As well as their Estates to thy direction) will plead the righteous Cause of them and their posterity, And I hope will order all things to Work together for their Good in the End.

How Canst thou pretend to be a man of peace & Truth when thou Acts So Contrary thereunto As is Evident by thy Letter which is filled with bitter Invectives against Some particulars, And false Suggestions agt the Assembly Whom the people deemed to be (as the Charter Requires) Men of most note for vertue Wisdom & ability to represent the Country in Legislacion Which {is a} part of the Governmt ~~is~~ granted to them by the Royall Charter[43] And ought to be preserved as free from Refleccions & Indignities as the Ruling or presiding part Which thou cannot pretend to Claim but by the same Grant

Thou will find the Assembly were Unanimous That a Representacion Should be drawn and Sent thee as ~~I~~ Observed before And though Some of them that then Voted for it And others that never Saw it nor knew the Contents thereof Were Prevailed Upon to Subscribe a Letter which has been of late in a Clandestine manner handed among Friends in Town and Country Inveighing ag^{t} those particular persons & proceedings which I suppose thou points at,[44] Yet I doubt not but when the Subscribers are (As Severall of them Since our Votes were published have been) Undeceived And Come to a right Understanding of what the Assembly Did concerning the Said Representacion as well as the before mencioned Bills and for Support of Government they will clearly perceive the Wicked designs of such as misinformed thee And Resent thy rash & unwarrantable Expressions in thy Letter Whereby thou Renders those that Act the Patriots ag^{t} thee as so many Wicked Korahs Whereas there were not above 4 of the last Assembly & 6 of this but what were Friends in Unity,[45] And above a Quorum Which is Two thirds of the whole Agreed to what past the house Therefore Consider what thou hast done And what Discord it may Cause amongst Friends And how Unchristianlike it is that thou should Write such things of Some Friends And direct it to others Who Concealed it from me and those Who were Traduced by it.

As this thy Treatment of Such as are of the same Community wth thee is very Unfriendly & Offensive to the Church of Christ as not being Agreeable to Gospell-order So If thou ~~wilt~~ duely Considers it thou wilt find That So farr as thy Letter has prevailed wth any of the Members of this or the last Assembly to Subscribe and Assent to any thing that Oppugns what they Voted or reflects upon that wherein the Majority Overrule~~s~~d them Or has Excited other people to Entertain wrong Conceptions of the proceedings of their Delegates It will prove of Ill Consequence to the State And perhaps Exasperate those Members not of our perswasion (Who were very kind & Condesce{n}ding to Friends in these Assemblys) to Influence the rest of their Communities to renew those Animosities against {Friends} which ran High when thou wast here And have been very much Allayd Since they had these opportunities to See & Observe how the Generality of us Aime at the publick Good.

But when they Understand how disingeniously thou hast dealt wth them and the rest of our Assemblys by Exposing to others what thou Conceived Amiss in our proceedings And not Write at all to us concerning those Things Nor Shew us thy particular Objections against the Three Bills before mentioned Nor wherein the same or the other Bill or any of them were Absurd or Inconvenient Nor what thou would have Altered or Incerted therein, It will be very Obvious to them as it is to others That thou has both Abused and Neglected the said Assemblys.

I would not have thee be ~~angry~~ {offended} with me for my plain dealing And do not wrong thy own soul to Insinuate that this proceeds from any Malice or Revenge For I can sincerely say That I bear thee none Nor do I desire that th~~is~~ou should be exposed by what I write But that thou {may do} the people of this province Justice And perform thy grants & promises thou made them or {at least shew ~~thy~~}

~~give them~~ thy willingness to compensate their Loss {& disappointment} ~~Disappointment where~~ wherein thou art not able to perform And that will give thee Ease & ꝑLasting peace which ~~is th~~ I heartily wish who am

~~Thy~~ {~~abused~~} ~~Freind~~
[illegible deletion]
Thy abused though reall Freind
Dad Lloyd[46]

LS. Franklin Papers, Van Pelt Library, University of Pennsyvania. (*Micro.* 12:109.) Docketed: A Letter | To | Wm Penn.

1. Doc. 94.
2. Robert Barber, who in 1704 carried doc. 83 in the *Robert and Benjamin,* John Guy, master.
3. See doc. 94, text at n. 12.
4. See docs. 33, n. 5; 35, n. 27.
5. George Fox.
6. For complaints about quitrents in Philadelphia, see doc. 22, n. 8.
7. On WP's purchases from the Swedes and grants to them in compensation for their lands at Philadelphia, see *PWP,* 2:577n; *PA,* 2d ser., 19:498; doc. 83, n. 38.
8. See doc. 22, n. 17.
9. WP had left Pennsylvania in 1684 to defend Pennsylvania's boundaries against the claims of Lord Baltimore; see *PWP,* 3:25. WP's title to the Lower Counties had never received royal confirmation and was being questioned by the Board of Trade; see doc. 55.
10. Probably a reference to WP's unsuccessful attempt in 1687 to balance factions on the Provincial Council; see *PWP,* 3:144-46, 162; Nash, *Quakers and Politics,* p. 106.
11. James Logan. See Logan's similar comment about the people's unwillingness to pay without secure titles, doc. 100, text at n. 32.
12. On 16 May 1705 Gov. Evans reported to the Assembly that Pennsylvania's laws had long waited in the attorney general's office for lack of a large fee to obtain his report. WP had first presented the laws to the Board of Trade on 15 Dec. 1702; the board relayed them to Attorney General Northey on 28 May 1703, but he did not return his report until 13 Oct. 1704. The board, in turn, did not read and consider the report until 18 July 1705. *Minutes of the Provincial Council,* 2:193; *CSPC, 1702-1703,* pp. 50, 463; *1704-1705,* pp. 276-81.
13. This order was issued with the queen's approbation of Gov. Hamilton in Jan. 1703, *Micro.* 10:728.
14. Not found; the secretary was probably Patrick Robinson, who was serving as secretary of Pennsylvania in 1699-1700, during WP's second visit. *Minutes of the Provincial Council,* 1:589.
15. In 1700-1701 WP had sought to obtain permission for Pennsylvania Quakers to register ships upon attest rather than oath, a privilege that was granted to English Quakers by the Affirmation Act of 1696 and was practiced in other colonies, but had been forbidden in Pennsylvania by Edward Randolph. See doc. 4, n. 9; *PWP,* 3:585, 589; *Micro.* 8:305; 7 & 8 Will. III, cap. 34.
16. The Navigation Act of 1696, 7 & 8 Will. III, cap. 22.
17. Either Edward Portlock, who was the Anglican minister in Philadelphia on WP's arrival in 1699, or Evan Evans, who replaced him in 1700. *PWP,* 3:635.
18. The queen's approbation of Gov. Evans sanctioned his appointment as deputy governor of Pennsylvania without limitation, but as deputy for the Lower Counties only during her majesty's pleasure. WP was also required to make a formal declaration that the approval of Evans would not damage the crown's claim to the Lower Counties. *Micro.* 10:1045, 1066.
19. On 25 May 1704 the Assembly approved an address to Queen Anne, thanking her for her favor to WP and her approval of Evans. *Votes and Proceedings,* 1(pt. 2):6.
20. Doc. 83.
21. *Micro.* 10:1069; see headnote to doc. 63.
22. In his letter of 4 and 7 Dec. 1703 (*Micro.* 11:089), WP chided Pennsylvanians

for obeying the queen's order requiring oaths in courts, urging them not to "resigne the Laws customs & Usages tamely." He echoed this in doc. 76, text at n. 55.

23. The proprietors of New Jersey had surrendered their governmental rights to the crown in 1702.

24. A reference to the plight of New Jersey under the administration of the anti-Quaker Lord Cornbury, starting in 1703. See Paul A. Stellhorn and Michael J. Birkner, eds., *The Governors of New Jersey, 1664-1974* (Trenton, 1982), pp. 36-37.

25. Joseph Yard (d. 1716), bricklayer, and Thomas Rutter (d. c. 1729), blacksmith, were both Quakers who had lived in Philadelphia since the 1680s. Phila. Will Bk. D, #65; E, #145; Hannah Benner Roach, "Philadelphia Business Directory, 1690," *PGM,* 23:111; Hinshaw, 2:642, 1024.

26. On 23 Sept. 1704 Gov. Evans issued a proclamation voiding a Philadelphia city court judgment against Enoch Story because the bench, made up of Quakers, would not administer an oath to the witness against him. In Oct. the mayor and aldermen of Philadelphia addressed to Gov. Evans a remonstrance against this proclamation. Board of Trade Papers, Proprieties, 1704-1705, transcript at HSP, N7; *Minutes of the Provincial Council,* 2:161.

27. See doc. 100, text at nn. 16-18.

28. On 18 July 1704 Gov. Evans, with the concurrence of the Council, issued this proclamation exempting militiamen from duty on the city watch and service as constables. The mayor and aldermen complained of this in their remonstrance of Oct. Board of Trade Papers, Proprieties, 1704-1705, N4; *Minutes of the Provincial Council,* 2:151-52, 161.

29. The last election had taken place on 2 Oct. 1704.

30. WP was referring to the three confirmation acts. See doc. 91, n. 26; *Votes and Proceedings,* 1(pt. 2):39.

31. For the dispute over prorogation of the Assembly in 1703 and the breach between the assemblymen for Pennsylvania and the Lower Counties, see *Minutes of the Provincial Council,* 2:110-11, 82-83, 128-34.

32. On quarrels over jurisdiction between city and county justices, see doc. 52.

33. See doc. 31.

34. In margin: "Col Hamilton."

35. Doc. 31.

36. On 25 May 1704 the Assembly resolved that a tax of not less than £1000 should be raised for the support of government, but a bill to that effect was never passed. *Votes and Proceedings,* 1(pt. 2):7.

37. On 21 June 1704 a grand committee of the Assembly resolved to allot £400 for the governor and £100 for the Indians from the £1000 tax. Ibid., p. 8.

38. On 9 Aug. 1704 the Assembly agreed to allot £100 of the £1000 tax for Pennsylvania's agents in London. Ibid., pp. 10-11.

39. On 19 May 1705 the Assembly resolved to raise a £1200 supply for the government, along with an impost on foreign wines and cider, on condition that Gov. Evans confirm the colonists' political and property rights. Ibid., pp. 40, 42.

40. A reference to the bills passed in 1704; see doc. 91, n. 26.

41. Evans dismissed the Assembly on 23 June 1705, after the Council had agreed that "there appeared no manner of Disposition in a majority of them to doe any Business." *Minutes of the Provincial Council,* 2:201.

42. The proprietary faction had responded to Gov. Evans's dismissal by leaving the house, contrary to Lloyd's order, while the rest of the Assembly, led by Lloyd, adjourned itself. See doc. 100, n. 15.

43. See *PWP,* 2:65-66.

44. See doc. 100, n. 6. In margin: "See the Appendix to Rush: Col 2 pt 2 vol 263." A reference to John Rushworth, *Historical Collections,* pt. 2, vol. 2 (London, 1680), p. 263. The passage here refers to a group of judges in Richard II's time who were led by royal pressure to subscribe to an unjust verdict but immediately regretted it.

45. Of the assemblymen of 1703-4, Charles Read and Joseph Wood were Anglicans; Griffith Jones and Joseph Willcox were out of unity with Philadelphia Friends. In 1704-5, Charles Read, Joseph Wood, and Joshua Carpenter were Anglicans; John Swift, Joseph Willcox, and Francis Rawle were former Quakers. The other members seem to have been Quakers in good standing. *Votes and Proceedings,* 1(pt. 2):1, 17; *Micro.* 13:021; Phila. Monthly Meeting Minutes, GSP.

46. The last paragraph and closing are in David Lloyd's hand.

103
FROM THOMAS FAIRMAN

Philadelphia the 27th of the 6 moth [August] 1705

Honor Proprietor and Governor

We have had of late very amuseing discourses of a Chainge in property affaires, by a Letter sent by P: F[1] unto persons heare adapted the best for such a purpose agst thy Interest But thine of later date[2] Noteing nothing of the affaire we hope its not of weight to be feared. If it may be, And thee thinke fitt to order it, I can soone furnish thee with Drafts of surveyes to make up the forty thousand acres for thine and Childrens use above a hundred ~~thousand~~ thousand acres[3] and that without any Noyse or come to the knowledg of any but my selfe & James Logan If this may be of service signifye thy pleasur, In the meane time I will be doeing If nothing come of it: for I see a Letter in Samll Carpenters hands from Tho: Lower[4] abot George Fox his Lott & Liberty Land blameing friends delay in secuering the premises, eare it be to Late: wch Expression I take to be significant especially from such a hand, The may assuer T: L: I have surveyd & Returnd the Lott & Liberties late George Foxes unto Anthony Morris &c appointed by the meeting As to the Land Compas affares[5] because of theire Importunancy I have fixed them in all theire Lands Except a thousand and odd hundred acres which I must use my skill to befriend them in In consideration of some of theires too remote, I have Not surveyd theire proportion in the Mannor of Rocklands to waite the utmost result of an accomadation If it may be; yet to secure from others I have surveyd the front to Delaware by Namans Creek. I have not returnd the 5000a In Gilberts nor the 5000a In Highlands My reason is because greate part of that claimed by P: Fords shamm returne, falls to them since thy son William (agst my minde) prevaild wth the Commissenors and got 7000a for his 5000a [6] I have settled Jo~~h~~nathan Hayes[7] to his Content tho farther, remote to any settlers But I can not finde by the Compas Letters that any thing short of theire bargaine will Content them: thee has yet an opportunety If thee can prevaile; I have sent them Drafts of what is now Pattented and am so farr Easd in my minde I can assuer them and thee I have dealt uprightly to my power between the Proprietarie & Purchasor. Many such Tracts may yet be had and not much felt in the Province, for a good {consideration} dont Feare to sell a hundred thousand acres more I know I can finde the Land to Content and sufficent for the old purchasors. I have almost perfected a Draft of all the Liberty Lands as they lye Contiguous: also the Mannor of springutts Berry with the former Incroachments and the latter Cansels, I thinke thee had better allow the old vine Dressers widdow & Children[8] a Consideration for her Husbands service then part wth that Land I see the Comissionrs (as Generous as they were) have Incerted in the Pattent that he should maintaine and keep up the vinyard wch is not done, besids theire swarveing from thy Instructions makes the Grant Cyrupticious[9] nevertheless let the Laborer have his hier in Land or &c: elce-where.

I heare nothing of thy proceedings to a partition wth my Lord Baltamore I observe his Commission^rs continew to Grant Lands in oure Province But both ~~are~~ have discouragements to settle as they would for that reason; I take that wch they Call thy confines, for almost the Navel of thy Province. since Latitud hath breadth as its known heare to containe neare 70 miles And my Lord by his Pattent comes UNTO the 40th degree, that must needs terminate Instantly over 39 And since the Pattent to thy selfe Commences at the Begining of the 40th degree It must be Instantly over 39 which Degree will be found within 6 or 8 miles of Annopeles[10] as I have lately convinced severall of the Cap^ts & Collo^ls in Maryland particularly one King at Langfords Bay in Chester river[11] who showes his likeing that it be Insisted for In hopes that oure settlers will form a Towne altho theires can not. I intreate thee to Consider me, that I have a son Capable of busines, yet out of Imploy[12] I beg not for my selfe yet I grudg to see fresh hands that have never served Proprieto^r or Contrey jump into Offices of proffitt and Eate the bread due to others by a kinde of birth right. Sam^ll Carpenter or Nathan Stanbury will be my sons Securety If thee please to Conferr an office upon him, he is known to be proficient and I doubt not of his vigelency. Tho: Storey upon the acco^t of his Testamony is sometimes absent from the Province halfe a yeare together and hath had a good shaire. Merchantdizeing is now so hazardous (If I could) tis not prudence to advance a stock as times goe there is timber at Samuels Mill to build him a house on that Lott next Lætitias as per her Consent[13] Governo^r I earnestly Expect to receive thy favour to my son. for my selfe, I finde it hard to gitt my bread, yet I am not so solicitous: Because busines is a nessesary divertion to youth and proper to prevent visscious occurrances I have not Cause to Complaine of my son as such, for his moderation is much Commended, and the best master of his pen in the Proince.[14] I can not thinke of any thing further to Inform of Therfore give my Love to thy selfe wife and famely & take leave to subscribe my selfe

Thy friend & servant Tho Fairman

ALS. Cliveden Manuscripts, Chew Family Papers, HSP. (*Micro.* 12:201.) Docketed: Tho: Fairman | 27th Aug: 1705. Further docketed: Tho: Fairman.

1. Philip Ford, Jr., had written to David Lloyd, John Moore, and Isaac Norris on 29 Mar. 1705; see doc. 101, n. 3.
2. Probably doc. 97.
3. Fairman later wrote to WP claiming that he could find not only 100,000, but 300,000 acres. James Logan was skeptical, however, as he wrote to WP on 5 Jan. 1708: "I have not yet discoursed T F about those great Tracts of Land, thou fully knows my Opinion of the man & time does not alter it, his Letters perhaps may be of Service to thee, but there's little more than Wind in him." Doc. 139, text at n. 29; *Micro.* 13:362.

4. Lower had written to Carpenter about George Fox's bequest on 17 Apr. 1705. *The Friend*, 39:115. See also doc. 56, nn. 73, 77.

5. The London Company; see doc. 56, nn. 25, 64.

6. William Penn, Jr.'s manor of Williamstadt, originally allotted 5000 acres, contained 7482 acres when Penn sold it in 1704. The commissioners of property granted him a warrant for its resurvey on 2 May 1704. Penn Manuscripts, Warrants and Surveys, HSP; doc. 91, n. 18.

7. Jonathan Hayes (d. 1714) of Chester Co. had bought 1100 acres, originally laid out in William Penn, Jr.'s manor of Williamstadt; at WP's urging he had accepted 1100 acres elsewhere in exchange for the Williamstadt claim. Phila. Admins. Bk. B, p. 112; *PA*, 2d ser., 19:208-9, 368-69.

8. The widow and children of Andrew Doz, a Huguenot who had established a vineyard in WP's manor of Springettsbury, on the east bank of the Schuylkill, in 1682. In 1690 WP's commissioners of property issued Doz a patent for 200 acres there provided he "keep up and Improve the Vineyard so long as he shall live." *PWP*, 2:458n; 3:68n; *PA*, 2d ser., 19:32.

9. Surreptitious.

10. Fairman's novel interpretation of WP's southern boundary line would have reduced Maryland to half its present size. For discussion of the Pennsylvania-Maryland boundary controversy, see *PWP*, 2:111-13, 256-58.

11. Langford's Bay was the broad lower portion of Chester River, in Kent Co., Md. Col. or Capt. King has not been identified. Frederic Emory, *Queen Anne's County, Maryland* (Baltimore, 1950), p. 532.

12. Fairman had two sons: Thomas, Jr., who later joined the army of the duke of Marlborough, and Benjamin (d. 1740), who inherited his estate at Shackamaxon. Phila. Will Bk. D, #22; Hinshaw, 2:360.

13. A warrant of Nov. 1701 directed the survey of a 24½-foot lot for Fairman on Front St. adjacent to that of Laetitia Penn, who endorsed the document, "I refer this to my father." Fairman seems to have built on the lot in the 1690s, but his son Thomas was still trying to get a patent confirming his title in 1717. Penn Papers, Penn Family to James Logan, 2:79, HSP; *Micro.* 14:588.

14. Province.

104
ON THE LAWS OF PENNSYLVANIA

A
The Board of Trade's Objections

[26 July 1705]

Objections made by the Commissioners of Trade and Plantations upon severall Acts of Pennsylvania.[1]

Page 8[2] An Act against Menacing and Assault and Battery.[3]

The words Menace write or speak slightingly or carry themselvs abusively, are too General and uncertain and lyable to be construed according to the humour of the Courts. The penalty in that Act is too General.

An Act against Sedition, spreading false News and Defamation.[4]

In this Act it is said, That if if any person shall speak Act or write any thing tending to Sedition or dissafaction to this Goverment[5] such Person is to be fined at the discretion of the Justices of the respective County Courts, not less than five pounds or three Months Imprisonment. instead of the words **Sedition** and **disaffection to this Government** ought to have been against her Majesty or this her Majesty's Government,[6] for there cannot be any Sedition, but against her Majesty.

Page 11. An Act of Priviledges to a Free Man.[7]

This Act Ordains **that no Freeman shall be hurt damnifyed, distroyed, tryed or condemn'd, but by the Lawfull Judgment of his 12 equalls or by the Laws of the Province,** This we think interferes with the Act for preventing Frauds and Regulating abuses in the Plantation Trade pass'd in the Seventh and Eighth Years of the late Kings Reign, whereby Admiralty Courts are Settled in the Plantations.[8]

11. An Act for the names of Days and Months.[9]

Every Man may call the Days and Months as he pleases, this Act is insignificant and not fit to be laid before her Majesty.

Page 13 **An Act** to ascertain the Number of Members of Assembly, and to Regulate the Elections.[10]

In this Act **Advertizem**ts for the day of E{l}ections are to be posted upon some Tree or House in the way leading from every hundred or Precinct to the Capital Towns, and upon the Court Houses and publick meeting Houses, It ought to have been **Churches Chapples & publick Meeting houses.**

Page 24th **An Act** directing the Attests of severall Officers and Ministers.[11]

If the Government be Surrendered to her Majesty, this Act ought not to be Confirmed, because Judges, Justices, Sherriffs &c, are hereby required to promise Fidelity to the Proprietary.[12] Besides none of the Officers mentioned in this Act, are obliged to take an Oath for the due Execution of their Places and Trusts, but only to make an Attestation in the Form therein set down, which we think not Sufficient. the Words **Master of the Rolls** are not used in any other of her Majestys Plantations, and is peculiar to her Majestys Officer in Chancery here.[13]

{Pag: 27 An Act against speaking in Derogation of Courts.[14]

This Enacts that if any Person shall speak rudely any thing in Derogation of any sentence or Judgement given in any Court or shall misbehave himself in the said Court, such Person shall be Fyn'd &c. These words we think too general and lyable to Arbitrary Constructions.}

Page 31. **An Act** for the preservation of the Person of the Proprietary and Governour.[15]

We think this Act not proper to be laid before her Majesty, the Proprietary and Governour having already the same protection by Law as other her Majesty's Subjects.

Page 49. **An Act** requiring all Masters and Commanders of all ships and vessells to make Report at the Town of New Castle, that are or shall be bound to and from the Sea.[16]

This Act Establishes the Town of New Castle as a Port: Whereas the power of settling Ports is by Act of Parliament vested in the Commissioners of the Customes[17] under the Direction of the Lord High Treasurer or Commissioners of the Treasury. Besides if the Government be surrendred to her Majesty; This Act must not be Confirm'd, because part of the Penalties herein, are appriated to the Propriet{ar}y.

Page 51. **An Act** for the Levying of Fines.[18]

This Act cannot be confirm'd for the same reason, The Fines being appropriated to the Proprietary.

The Law against scolding.[19]

The words if any Person shall be Clamorous with their Tongue are too Generall, and want Explanat[n] and the Penalty of standing Gagg'd, in some publick place or five Dayes imprisonment at hard Labour is too great; It is not said how long the Person shall stand gagg'd.

Page 54. **An Act** to prevent the sale of ill Tann'd Leather, and working the same into shoes and Boots.[20]

It cannot be expected that encouragement should be given by Law, to the making any Manufacturys made in England, in the Plantations, it being against the advantage of England.

55. **An Act** that no publick house or Inn within this Government be kept without Lycense.[21]

If the Government be Surrender'd to her Majesty This Act cannot be confirm'd because these Lycenses are to be Granted by the Proprietary or his heirs, or his or their Deputy Governour; and the Penaltys are in part appropriated to the Proprietary.

Page 59. **An Act** against Pyrats and Sea Robbers.[22]

This Act cannot be Confirmed because a late Act of Parliam[t] past in England has provided for these Cases,[23] And Commissions have been issued by her Majesty accordingly.

77. **An Act** for Erecting a Bridge over the Creek at Chester in the County of Chester.[24]

The first Enacting Clause begins Be it Enacted by the authority aforesaid, Whereas there is only the Governor and Councill mentioned before

79. The Law about Tryalls by Twelve Men.[25]

This Act as it is Worded interferes with the abovemention'd Act, for preventing Frauds & Regulating abuses in the Plantation Trade.

102 **An Act** against swine running at Large in severall of the Townships within this Government.[26]

This Act also cannot be confirm'd if the Government be surrender'd to her Majesty, because the Forfeitures in this Act are to the Proprietary.

We observe besides the above particular objections upon all the Pennsylvania Acts in Generll, that in most of them it is said Counties or Territories annex'd Whereas we know of none Annexd.[27]

Her Majesties name or the year of her Reign are not mentioned.

In all the said Acts it is said This Government. Whereas it ought to have been this her Majestys Government.[28]

The stile of Enacting is in all the Acts to be redressed.

An Act for Establishing Courts of Judicature in this Province and the Counties annexed.[29]

Vid: Mr Penns objection.

Minutes 9th October 1705.[30]

Copy. CO 5/1291, PRO. (*Micro.* 12:140.) These objections were forwarded to WP in a letter from William Popple, Jr., on 26 July 1705.

B

The Proprietor's Answer

[c. 31 August 1705]

The Objections Considered about Some Pennsilvania Laws

To the first Objection	It's Agreed that Law be returned, but let the Simplicity of the times in that Wilderness excuse inexpertness. Pray word it better for us, or give us directions how to do it.
2d Obj.	Agreed to be returned, and Amended.
3d Obj.	No need of using her Majesty's name, when the names used Stand upon the Queens Authority.
4th Obj.	I cannot help it, 'tis the great Charter that all English men are entituled to, and we went not So far to loose a tittle of it.
5th Obj.	Agreed to be mended.
6th Obj.	I think a word no reason to lay by, or delay So material a Law; when there are words enow besides to Answere the end, nor have we yet Church places to Authorize it.
7th Obj.	I am of Opinion my Surrender will best repeal that part, which regards fidelity to me.
8th Obj.	I cannot see any reason to out the People that made it a Country from the Governmt of it; for their tenderness about an Oath, that went thither to avoid it with other things. And for Stiles of Officers they were under no Obligation to Symbolize wth England. Carolina dos not, And that wch is called Mayor in one place is a Bayliff in another, and in Ireland in divers places Soveraigne.
9th Obj.	Agreed to be mended.

10th Obj. When the Governmt is Surrendred, to be Sure it becomes useless.

11th Obj. Under favour you will find {the} power of ports in me, Since 'tis one of the clauses {to be} Surrendred by me,[31] Nor dos the Act reach but to Colonies in the Queens immediate disposition, nor dos the Act undo wt is done, nor compell the Queen to it.

12th Obj The Same Answere Serves

13 Obj Agreed to be mended.

14th Obj. It is not to be wholy hindred, and if done, then to {be} done not fraudulently, nor can any reason of State in prudence or justice, put one mans commodity, as this will, upon another at the Sellers price, as this dos. As good forbid wearing Shoes at all.

15th Obj. I desire only the priviledges truly Proprietary, or as Lord of the Mannour of the Country; Except the Queen pleases at the inst[ance] of the board to make a farther distinction.

16th Obj. I presume they are not inconsistent.

17th Obj. But that implys the Crowns Authority, under which they claime the Same in Palatinats and Corporations here.

18th Obj. I must Submit to Lawyers, but the Nature of that Act and it's extent, deserves to be explained and Settled.

19th Obj. A clause in the Surrender as aforesaid may regulate it, till the Surrender is perfected tis good, and that I pray wth expedition

20th Obj. Since So Stiled by the Kings and Queens, It must be no fault to use it, nor is there inconveniency in it

21t Obj. It is in our Courts and Acts of Court, and in the Rolls, *by the Queens Authority, and name of the Propiatary,* ~~is~~ {being} the old forme and it must be an undesigned Omission, but the by Laws of our great Towns here; I Suppose do the Same thing.

Wm Penn

DS. CO 5/1263/28, PRO. (*Micro.* 12:211.) Docketed: Pennsylvania | Mr Penns Answer to the Obser- | vations made by the Board upon | the Pennsylvania Laws. | Received | Read | Augt 31st 1705.

1. Attorney General Edward Northey had reported on Pennsylvania's laws on 13 Oct. 1704, objecting to 38 of the 105 submitted. The Board of Trade here raises objections to 17 additional laws and echoes WP's objection to one, the law about courts (nn. 29-30, below). All the laws criticized by Northey and the Board of Trade were disallowed by the Queen in Council on 7 Feb. 1706. *CSPC, 1704-1705,* pp. 276-81; *1706-1707,* p. 47; Copy of Order in Council, 7 Feb. 1706, Cliveden Manuscripts, Chew Family Papers, HSP.

2. The editors have moved marginal page numbers into the text. These numbers probably refer to the copy of Pennsylvania laws submitted to the Board of Trade by WP (not found).

3. *Statutes,* 2:13-14. The board's criticism of this act is labeled as the first objection in WP's Answer (doc. 104B).

4. *Statutes*, 2:14-15.

5. The board's second objection in doc. 104B.

6. The board's third objection in doc. 104B.

7. *Statutes*, 2:18.

8. The Navigation Act of 1696, 7 & 8 Will. III, cap. 22, which provided for trial without jury; on juries and admiralty courts in Pennsylvania, see *PWP*, 3:469-70, 553-54, 595-96. This is the board's fourth objection in doc. 104B.

9. *Statutes*, 2:19-20. The board's fifth objection in doc. 104B.

10. *Statutes*, 2:24-27. The board's sixth objection in doc. 104B.

11. *Statutes*, 2:39-42. A revised law regulating attestations was passed 12 Jan. 1706. *Statutes*, 2:212-21.

12. The board's seventh objection in doc. 104B.

13. The board's eighth objection in doc. 104B.

14. *Statutes*, 2:45. The paragraph on this act appears sideways in the margin. This is the board's ninth objection in doc. 104B.

15. *Statutes*, 2:52-53. The board's tenth objection in doc. 104B.

16. *Statutes*, 2:81-82. The board's 11th objection in doc. 104B.

17. The Navigation Act of 1696 empowered the lord treasurer, commissioners of the treasury, and commissioners of the customs to appoint customs officers at any location in the colonies.

18. *Statutes*, 2:83. The board's 12th objection in doc. 104B.

19. *Statutes*, 2:85. The board's 13th objection in doc. 104B.

20. *Statutes*, 2:90-91. The board's 14th objection in doc. 104B.

21. *Statutes*, 2:93-94. The board's 15th objection in doc. 104B.

22. *Statutes*, 2:100-104. The board's 16th objection in doc. 104B.

23. An Act for the More Effectual Suppression of Piracy (11 & 12 Will. III, cap. 7), passed in 1700, directed that special commissioners be appointed to try piracy cases.

24. *Statutes*, 2:124-26. The board's 17th objection in doc. 104B.

25. *Statutes*, 2:128-29. The board's 18th objection in doc. 104B.

26. *Statutes*, 2:164-65. A revised law was passed on 12 Jan. 1706 (*Statutes*, 2:261-63). This is the board's 19th objection in doc. 104B.

27. The board's 20th objection in doc. 104B.

28. The board's 21st objection in doc. 104B.

29. *Statutes*, 2:148-59.

30. *CSPC, 1704-1705*, pp. 633-34. On this date the board read WP's commentary on this act; he objected to the phrasing of the act's clause about ejectments and suggested that it not be approved by the crown.

31. WP's royal charter of 1681 entitled him to establish ports; see *PWP*, 2:69. See also the 5 Apr. 1705 draft of WP's surrender, doc. 96.

105
REQUESTS TO QUEEN ANNE

[1 September 1705]

Pray'd from the Queen at the Surrender

1t To Confirme our Constitutions and Laws not excepted against by the Attorney General,[1] and Such when amended to be confirmed alsoe.

2d To Grant Liberty of Conscience both as to Faith Worship and Discipline and by publick and private Meetings relateing thereunto when and where they please in their own houses or places built or to be built for that purpose by them.

3d Liberty for our own Educacion by Schools of our own and Such Masters Mistresses and Ushers as we Shall appoint.

4th To Marry according to our way and method, and Such Marriages to be allowed and held good and valid to all intents and purposses.

5th To be exempted from forced maintenance to any Clergy wtsoever and from building and repairing any Meeting houses, or houses for religious Worship under any name or pretence whatsoever.

6th To be exempted from Militia Services and charges thereof So as we watch & Ward in times of trouble. ~~or~~

7th I and my Male Issue to pay no Taxes for our Mansion or chief Plantations

8th The Queen to pass these by grant and to confirme the Same by giving her Royal Assent to Such a Law when presented to her from the General Assembly of the Province

Copy. CO 5/1263, PRO. (*Micro.* 12:221.) Docketed: Pennsylvania | Mr Penns Paper containing | the Heads of what he desires | from Her Majesty upon his | Surrender | Recd: | Read | Sep: 1st 1705.

1. Sir Edward Northey. On his report about Pennsylvania's laws, see doc. 104, n. 1.

106
TO JOHN EVANS

Lond. 22. 7br [September] 1705

Honred Friend
I have had thine of the 12th & 3d month,[1] since those I receiv'd before my last {to thee;}[2] & am glad thy distemper has abated, & thy health is restored. a seasoning some wt ~~rest~~ Extrordinary for our Country, wch I hope will make no more insults upon thee. Thy Labours above & below,[3] are gratefull to me, & keeping a good decorum in the mannors of the Country, as becomes my Character, & moderation otherwise through out, will defeat our domestick enimys of severall objections. we are hurried, so must be short, but 1st pass no laws without an establishmt for the Govermt secondly shew pow'r sparingly, yet properly, & mercy with distinction. Keep in wth the most serious & best spirited people, pittying & informing the rest. I had thine of July too, abt Colonel Qs voyage[4] but hear nothing of him. Here are divers waite for him that will treat him but indifferently. they think he will hardly venture. Colonel RNickolson 'tis thought Engages him. be aware of his motions. once more fear not whether I keep or Surrender, for thou hast a good reputation here, & frds. of Jon Moor, expect to hear shortly & of Q. too. 3. wt can be made appear agst D. L.[5] Fail not to use effectually, for he is the greatest of Vs. Thy Frds are well, & are glad to hear so well of thee & thy managemt. Keep the Lower Countys in hopes of good days, but had they not turn'd aside

from me on Q[s] acct[t] they had never been seperated; theirs to the Lords Com[rs] did the business,[6] to our Common prejudice. Those Ld[s] kept me so late in hopes of their letter of rebuke ab[t] our assemblys backwardness ab[t] Supplying the Goverm[t] & the Laws they have past,[7] being broak loose into the Country (but Sett next week)[8] that I am surprizd by the fleets sailing, w[ch] makes me abrupt. I enclose one from my son to thee,[9] who is well & grown great at Court, & I hope Considerate, of w[ch], per next, I may be more particular. 6 weeks hence we expect an other Fleet sailes, by w[ch] may be larger. I writt fully per the last ships, w[ch] I hope are come safe. I bless god we are pretty well, & send thee our good wishes. I write no news, and at present we are a little in the Dark from all parts. a peace is talked of, but that is all. Farewell, and do for me, as thy own Just sence & Principall shall on all occurrances direct. I am

Thy Faithfull Frd.
Wm Penn

ALS. Penn Papers, Tempsford Hall Papers, HSP. (*Micro.* 12:245.)

1. Not found.
2. Doc. 95.
3. That is, in Pennsylvania and in the Lower Counties.
4. Not found; on Quary and his voyage, see doc. 100.
5. David Lloyd.
6. On 21 Nov. 1702 the members of the Assembly for the Three Lower Counties had sent an address to the Board of Trade, complaining of WP's government and asking to be taken under the queen's immediate protection. Robert Quary used their address to support his attack on WP. *CSPC, 1702-1703*, pp. 19-20.
7. No such letter was written; on 22 Feb. 1706 WP urged the board to express satisfaction that the most recent Assembly had finally granted a supply. *CSPC, 1706-1708*, p. 57.
8. The Board of Trade had last met on 4 Sept. and was to meet again on 25 Sept. Journal of the Board of Trade, 1705-1706, transcript at HSP, pp. 41-42.
9. Not found.

107
LAST WILL AND TESTAMENT

[20 October 1705]

My last will & Testam[t] made & writt in my own hand this twentyth day of the 8[m] 8[br] 1705 in the 61 year of my age.

Because of the assurance of death & the uncertanty of it, I make this last will of mine, revoaking all others.[1] and first. It is my unhappiness & sorrow to be indebted, but I bless god it never was from Projects, or Riotous liveing or any secreet ways, But liberality to the needy, Supporting Pennsilvania here & there, without gratefull & sufficient supplys, and being solicitor Generall for my Friends in Particular, & all sorts of sufferrers & my Country of England at large, at my own charges, to the injuring of my estate & poor Family (whom the Lord Support) as also the extortious treatm[t] I have had by some I entirely

trusted, & therefore did any thing they desired to satisfy them, without any examination or knowledge till of late, when they have prest me for mony.[2] This was indeed my great indiscretion & Credulity but [no]t any unjust or evill designe, & I this say, in my own hand, & that in the truth & integrety of a christian man, and I hope {my friends calld Quakers whom} ~~those~~ I have so long loved & served, & that in the high places of the earth, ~~my Frds called Quakers,~~ will take notice ~~of it~~ & do my memory ~~& my poor wife & Children~~ Justice in; yea, I desire, press & expect It at their hands.
Next, my Just debts being payd, I give ~~my~~ {the} overplus {of my Estate} thus; If my Son william will lett my younger children, his half Blood, into my Fathers estate in Ireland, viz, the lands west of Cork in Ibaune & Barriroe,[3] to enjoy that part of their Grandfathers estate, by me, that then I give him two thirds of my [illegible deletion] {Pennsilvanian} estate, and to be Styled the chief Proprietary, & but one third of the sayd estate called the Province of Pennsylvania & Countys annexed or Territorys, to my children by my present Dear wife, to be sett out by my Trustees hereafter named; but if he refuse to settle (by act of Parliam^{t} or otherwise, the sayd Irish estate upon, & to the use of my younger {children}, than I give herby ⅔ two thirds of my sayd Province & territory rents & lands, to be divided among my sayd younger Children, always observing, that both of the Irish & american estate, my eldest son John Penn, by this vent~~ure~~er,[4] shall have the preferance, by a double portion of the Same. and my son william but one third of my sayd Province & Territorys, ~~I~~ being at {or upon} my Death in the full possession of ~~the estate~~ the estate of Sr Wm Springet his D^{r} mothers Father,[5] & Sr Wm Penn, my Father, to w^{ch}, a third is a great ad[d]ition.
Thirdly I make my D^{r} wife Hannah Penn her father Thomas Callowhill {Thomas Cuppige[6] &} Jos. Pyke of Irland, & Sam^{ll} waldenfield[7] my executors. Leaveing the education of my poor children to their D^{r} & Tender mother. I also pray my Good Frds John vaughton, Henry Goldney, Nathaniell Marks,[8] Edward Hacket[9] & ambrose Galloway {here & in America ~~here~~ Sam^{ll} carpenter & James logan} my Trustees or overseers to see this my will executed. Leaveing them, w^{n} all is payd each a large Bible. also I bequeath to Frds that are poor of the County of Sussex {in pensylvania}[10] in the first place, & other poor Frds, ten thousand acres of land in Pennsilvania for a Township that is half to sussex poor, & the other to such other as the Frds above named shall direct. ~~chargeing all & my children to live in fear~~ chargeing all my children to live wth fear towards God & love towards one another   this is all writt in my own hand

Wm Penn

A Codicell to my last will & Testam^{t} dated 8 of 8bre 17056
I do herby confirm my foregoing will, and add, that my Dr Childe Lætitia aubrey, I count one of my Children, & so farr as w^{t} she has already, shall be short of an equall share with my younger children

(John Penn, my Pennsilvanian, & first born of my present wife, excepted) that it be made up ~~by~~ to her by my Sayd executors, & in case she has equall, yet I give to her my Piece of Gold, my mother Penn gave her Dr Mother,[11] I wore ever since her death abt my neck, of ferdinando & Isabella, an old Spanish piece wth my good wishes for her temporall and eternall happiness. when my Debts are payd, I would have an Alms-house for 6 poor captains or Masters of ships, built neer Ratcliff hill {in Bristoll} in commemoration of my Honored Father, whose eminency in that vocation & element, Was the ground work, wth my honest & sensible mothers substance, of all my familys prosperity, wch I own, and charge all mine to do so too, as the engage{g} Good providence of God. I Leave my prayers for you all, that God may be with you, in his holy Love & fear to the end, & that you may keep to & walk in truths way in the Simplicity & plainness & humility of it in wch I {end}, with Glory to God on high, Peace on earth, & good will to all men. amen saith my Soule, who have lived a lover & servt of all mankinde, and that at my own charges, to my familys present outward loss above 50000l.

Wm Penn

executed in the presence of the following wittnesses, in full health & understanding, this 21 of the Sixth month call'd August 1707.
Tho: Cuppage
Cha: Willcocks

ADS. Penn Papers, Granville Penn Book, HSP. (*Micro.* 12:263.)

1. For WP's earlier wills, see *PWP,* 2:585-86; doc. 30.
2. A reference to the heirs of Philip Ford.
3. On WP's lands in the barony of Ibaune and Barryroe, Ireland, see *PWP,* 1:570-73. WP inherited this estate from his father, Sir William Penn (1621-1670), a leading admiral under the Commonwealth. See *PWP,* 1:30n; 2:29n.
4. Wife, i.e., Hannah Callowhill Penn.
5. Sir William Springett (c. 1620-1644), the father of WP's first wife, Gulielma Maria Springett Penn (1644-1694), had left her substantial estates in Kent, Sussex, and Ireland. *PWP,* 1:68n, 71n.
6. Thomas Cuppage was an Irish Quaker and attorney for WP's Irish lands; see doc. 156, n. 2.
7. Samuel Waldenfield (c. 1652-1715) was a London merchant and Quaker minister. Fox, 2:497.
8. Nathaniel Markes (c. 1655-1709) was a Quaker glover from Northamptonshire who lived in Cheapside, London. Digests of Quaker Records, London and Middx., GSP.
9. Edward Hacket (d. 1721) was a Quaker grocer of Bristol and a distant relative of Hannah Penn. Mortimer, 1:202; 2:245.
10. Apparently inserted in the wrong place, as WP no doubt meant Sussex Co., Eng.
11. Margaret Jasper Vanderschuren Penn (1610?-1682), mother of WP, and Gulielma Penn, mother of Laetitia Penn Aubrey. See *PWP,* 1:30n.

AT LAW: FORD v. PENN

October 1705–July 1708

From 1682 to 1699 WP had signed a substantial number of accounts and instruments that showed him to be heavily indebted to his steward, Philip Ford, and made Ford, from 1696, both the legal proprietor of Pennsylvania and WP's landlord (see *PWP*, 2:290–95; 3:656–663). These facts had not been made public. On 8 January 1702 Ford died, having named in his will his widow, Bridget, and two Quaker merchants, John Hall and Thomas Moss, as trustees for Pennsylvania, with allowance to WP to redeem his proprietary within six months of the testator's death on payment of £11,134 8s 3d and all arrears of rent. If WP failed to take advantage of this offer within that period, the trustees were permitted to sell Pennsylvania in order to pay several specified legacies.

If Ford's will were probated and executed, it would bring to light WP's embarrassing financial and political arrangements with his late steward, which, in turn, could complicate his efforts to surrender the government of Pennsylvania to the crown, arouse further antagonism toward him by the anti-proprietary forces in the colony, and deplete his personal resources. An anxious WP persuaded the executor of the estate, Bridget Ford, to forego probating the will, as long as he showed a willingness to pay the debt. However, after the matter had dragged on inconclusively for another three years, on 4 October 1705 Bridget, apparently to WP's surprise, probated the will in the Prerogative Court of Canterbury. Any remaining hope by WP that the matter could be solved quietly and an equitable compromise worked out was soon shattered. On 31 October 1705 Philip Ford, Jr.; his sisters Anne, Susanna, and Bridget; and Bridget's husband, James Ayrey, filed a Bill of Complaint in Chancery against WP; his son William, Jr.; and the three trustees named in Philip Ford's will (see doc. 108).

Despite the seeming complexities of the case, the central issues were quite simple. The Fords claimed that WP had borrowed large sums of money from their father, that he had not repaid these loans, and that he had persuaded their father to accept Pennsylvania and the adjoining territories instead. When Ford allowed WP to rent Pennsylvania for £630 per annum from 1697 to 1700 and to have a limited right of repurchase, WP failed to take advantage of this right and yet attempted to keep control of the colony. Since the trustees had not performed their duty by evicting WP and selling the province, the complainants now asserted their legal rights by filing a Bill of Complaint in the court of Chancery, where disputes over land were adjudicated.

WP, on the other hand, countered that Philip and Bridget Ford had conspired to deceive and defraud him (see docs. 109–11). He argued that the various instruments that he had signed were generally mortgages for debt based on Ford's accounts as his steward. Admittedly he had conveyed Pennsylvania to Ford in 1697, which subsequently led to the three-year lease whereby he became an apparent tenant of his steward, but WP asserted that the real reason for that conveyance was to assist Ford in avoiding the payment of taxes on interest-bearing loans. This subterfuge was continued by Ford in his will when he claimed to be the legitimate owner of Pennsylvania. In any event, the accounts upon which all these instruments were founded were wildly extortionate. The Fords, knowing that WP trusted them, had always presented him with accounts when he was in a hurry and had never given him any copies to peruse at his leisure, although they agreed that he could later amend them if any errors were discovered. WP did not deny that he owed the Fords money, but he stressed that he was willing to pay only what was legitimately owed. It was imperative for WP's defense that the numerous Ford accounts be treated as one continuous account from 1682 to 1696, that they be scrutinized in order to determine the proper debt, and that the various instruments signed by WP be ruled either mortgages for debt or tax evasion schemes based on that underlying debt. The Fords would then be compelled to recognize WP's legal right to Pennsylvania once he paid the legitimate debt.

The issue was thus joined. What remained were procedural and technical questions, with the two sides responding in writing to each other's bill and response, and with legal counsel also arguing the merits of the respective cases before the lord chancellor, who was the ultimate judge (see docs. 112–14). Matters did not go smoothly for WP. On the advice of counsel, he dropped his initial Bill of Complaint on 14 December 1706, agreeing to pay the defendants' legal costs (*Micro.* 13:023). Yet WP was not about to admit defeat: on 23 December 1706 he filed a new Bill of Complaint against the same defendants (see *Micro.* 13:036), to which the Fords responded in late spring 1707. WP's counsel drew up a brief (see doc. 115) of this response in an effort to devise a counter-response, or replication, which was given on 14 May 1707 (*Micro.* 13:165). At that time the lord chancellor, after hearing counsel for both sides, effectively refused to reopen the accounts. He apparently hinted, however, that the various instruments signed by WP amounted only to a mortgage (see Norris Papers, 7:82, HSP). WP's lack of success should not have been surprising, since his second Bill of Complaint was remarkably similar to the first. Although a final decree had not yet been issued, WP seems to have been prepared to appeal an adverse decision to the House of Lords (see Norris Papers, 7:122, 162), which prompted his counsel to prepare another summary of the case (doc. 116). To make matters worse, WP was the target of a number of other legal actions brought against him by Bridget Ford, either alone or with others (see *Micro.* 13:185, 187, 190, 194, 196, 199). Although WP had successfully obtained a Chancery injunction (see Penn Papers, Ford vs. Penn, p. 54, HSP) against an Exchequer suit for £20,000 for breach of covenant, he was bailed to appear for trial at several Common Pleas actions at the Guildhall, in London, in May 1707. It appears, however, that only an action for £3150 back rent allegedly owed by WP was tried at that time. WP's lawyers drew up a brief for his defense (doc. 117), which proved to be unsuccessful. WP chose confinement in the Fleet prison as a debtor instead of paying the alleged debt.

This success encouraged the Fords to anticipate victory in Chancery, but they unwisely preempted a final decree by petitioning Queen Anne on 22 January 1708 (doc. 118) to grant them letters patent for the proprietorship of the province of Pennsylvania. Their demand for the government of the colony, as well as for the lands, was based on their belief that as long as WP controlled the appointment of offices there, they would be perpetually thwarted as landlords (see Norris Papers, 7:156, 160). WP replied to this petition (doc. 119) and gained the support of the lord chancellor (doc. 120), who administered a sharp rebuke to the petitioners for assuming a Chancery victory that had not yet taken place and for attempting to make the government of Pennsylvania "ambulatory" (see Norris Papers, 7:157). Although they had committed a strategic blunder, the Fords' impatience was understandable. As long as WP remained a prisoner in the Fleet and as long as the lord chancellor delayed his final decree, the Fords would be unable to collect their debt from WP in either money or land. A compromise solution seemed inevitable. Yet a major impediment, despite WP's desire to get out of prison, was his reluctance to settle on a figure remotely approaching the £14,000 claimed by the Fords (see docs. 121A–C). Nonetheless, with members of the London Meeting for Sufferings playing a critical role in negotiations, both sides ultimately settled on £7600 as the amount WP would pay to redeem his colony. The issue was legally settled in October 1708 (see doc. 211).

108
THE FORDS' BILL OF COMPLAINT

[31 October 1705]

To the Right honourable William Cowper[1] Esquire Lord Keeper of the Great Seale of England

Humbly complaineing shew unto your Lordshipp your Orators and oratrixes Phillip Ford the younger[2] of London Merchant James Ayrey[3] of London Merchant and Bridgett his wife[4] Eldest Daughter of Philip Ford the Elder late of London Merchant deceased Anne Ford & Susanna Ford youngest Daughters of the said Phillip Ford the Elder[5] That William Penn of Worminghurst in the County of Sussex Esqr being seized in his Demeasne as of Fee[6] or affirming himselfe soe to be of and in all that {the} Province or tract of Land commonly called or known by the name of Pensilvania Scituate lying and being in America in partes beyound the seas and also of and in all that the Town of Newcastle otherwise called Delaware in America adjoyning or bordering upon or near unto the said Province of Pensilvania And also of and in all that Tract of Land lying within the Compass or Circle of Twelve miles about the same Town of Newcastle and of and in a Certaine River there called Delaware River and of and in the soile thereof and of and in all Islands within the same Respective premisses And of and in diverse Royaltyes and hereditaments within the said parts beyond the seas as the same are sett forth and described in Certaine Deeds for that purpose herein after referred unto and being so seized and haveing a designe for Improveing the same but not haveing a stock of money to Accomplish such his Designes he the said Mr Penn did about Twenty three yeares since upon his First Entrance upon the said premisses or very soon after prevaile with the said Phillip Ford the Elder to lend him three Thousand pounds or some other great summe of money upon a Mortgage of some part of the said premisses[7] and haveing soe Engaged him did afterwards from time to time sollicite and prevaile with him to give him further helps and Creditts with severall other great summes of money even to a Continuall draining him the said Phillip Ford and diverting from his more proffitable Trade in Merchandising Whatever money his Estate or Creditt could raise which he yeilded to doe out of the great respect Frendshipp and Esteeme he had for the said Mr Penn and out of an intire beleife of his Justice and Integrity and that the premisses were of vallue much beyond his Debt All which moneys so advanced by and due to the said Phillip Ford upon a faire Computacion in or about the Month of September One Thousand six hundred and ninety were agreed betweene them to be and did amount unto the summe of six Thousand and nine hundred pounds which he the said Mr Penn from time to time promised he would satisfy and pay and as an Evidence of his reallity and to quiett the said Phillip Ford the Elders feares who was then growne aged and sickly and very uneasy under the Apprehensions that his Estate (which he had preserved for the support of and provision for his Children and Family should lye so remote and and inconvenient and out of his power hee the said Mr Penn did perswade and impose a beleiffe upon him (who he knew would not suspect any thing that he should solemnly affirme) that the said premisses were really worth Thirty Thousand pounds or some such great summe And offered that he would mortgage all the said premisses unto him for the money he then owed him which your Orators Father thorowly Crediting Assented thereunto and thereupon and pursuant thereunto he the Said Mr Penn by his Deeds of Lease and Release bearing date the second and third dayes of September in the yeare of our Lord one Thousand Six hundred and Ninety[8] or by some other Way did Well and Sufficiently convey unto your Orators and Oratrix's said Father Phillip Ford the Elder and his heires All that the Province or Tract of Land commonly called or known by the name of Pensilvania with the Islands therein Contained and thereunto belonging and therein described to be bounded on the East by a Certaine River called Delaware River from twelve miles distance Northwards of Newcastle Town to the three and Fortieth degree of Notherne Latitude and Extendeth Westward Five Degrees in Longitude and is bounded on the south by a Circle then drawne at twelve miles distance from Newcastle aforesaid northwards and Westwards to the begining of the Fortieth degree of Notherne Latitude and then by a streight line westwards to the limitt of Longitude above mencioned And all and singular the Islands Rivers Feilds Woods Mountains Hills Fenns Isles Lakes Rivers Waters Rivuletts and Bays together with all Edifices and buildings thereupon Erected and built and all and all manner of Rents Issues and proffitts thereof and of every part and parcell thereof And all that the Towne of Newcastle otherwise called Delaware And all that Tract of Land lying within the Compass or Circle of twelve miles about the same scituate lying and being upon the River Delaware in America and all Islands in the said River Delaware and the said River and soyle thereof lying north on the southernemost part of the said Circle twelve Miles about the said Towne together with all Rents services Royaltys Franchises Dutys Jurisdiccions libertyes and priviledges thereunto belonging And all the Estate right Title Interest powers property Claime and demand whatsoever of him the said William Penn of in or to the same or to any part or parcell thereof And also all that Tract of Land upon Delaware River and Bay ~~being~~ begining twelve miles south from the Towne of Newcastle otherwise

Called Delaware Extending south to the Whore Kills otherwise called Capen Lopen Together with Free and undisturbed use and passage into and out of all harbours Bays Waters Rivers Isles and Inletts belonging to or Leading to the same together with all sorts of Minerallss and all and singular the said premisses And all the Estate Interest Royaltyes Franchises powers priviledges and immunityes whatsoever of him the said William Penn therein or in or unto any part or parcell thereof And the Revercion and Revercions Remainder and Remainders of all and singular the premisses with their and every of their appurtenances To have and to hold unto your Orators and oratrixes said Father Phillip Ford the Elder his heires and Assignes to the only Use and behoofe of him his heires and Assignes for ever Subject nevertheless to a provisoe therein specifyed to be voyd upon payment of the summe of ~~one~~ {six} Thousand and nine hundred pounds and interest for the same unto the said Phillip Ford the Elder att a Certaine day therein sett downe and long since past And your Orators and Oratrixes further shew that that the said summe of six Thousand ~~pounds~~ and nine hundred pounds or any part thereof was not paid att the time Limitted by the said provisoe or at any time after but instead thereof hee the said William Penn after such his Default wanting more money prevailed with your Orators and Oratrixes said Father to supply him with the Further summe of Three Thousand Four hundred Forty and seven pounds and for secureing the same by his Indenture of Release and Confirmacion bearing date the nine and Twentieth Day of September in the yeare of our Lord one Thousand six hundred ninety and six[9] Reciteing therein to the Effect aforesaid and for and in Consideracion of the Further summe of three thousand Four hundred Forty and Seaven pounds then in hand paid unto him by the said Phillip Ford the Elder over and besides the said summe of six Thousand and nine hundred pounds principall money as aforesaid Did Release Ratifye and Confirme unto the said Phillip Ford the Elder your Orators and Oratrixes said Father his heires and assignes the said severall recited Indentures of Lease and Release and the said Tract or parcell of Land called Pensilvania together with the said severall other Tracts or parcells of Land above mencioned and all and Singular other the Lands Hereditaments & premisses in and by the same Indentures Mencioned or intended to be granted and released as aforesaid together with all and every the Rents services Royaltyes Franchises Dutyes Jurisdiccions libertyes and priviledges thereunto belonging and also all the Estate right title Interest power property Claime & Demand Whatsoever of him the said William Penn of into or out of the said premisses and of in to or out of every part and parcell thereof and the Revercion and Revercions Remainder and Remainders Rents Issues and proffitts of all and singular the said premisses with their and every of their appurtenances together with all Grants Deeds and Writeings whatsoever touching or concerning the premisses or any part or parcell thereof then had or obtained or then after to be had or obteyned in any wise howsoever To have and to hold unto the said Phillip Ford the Elder your Orators and Oratrixes said Father and his heires To the only Use and behoofe of him and his heires and Assignes forever Freed and Discharged of and from the Agreement and Intencion for Redempcion aforesaid and of and from all right and benefitt of Redempcion {in} Law or Equity by meanes thereof in any manner of wise whatsoever And your Orators and Oratrixes likewise shew that afterwards by Indenture of Defeazance bearing the same date[10] and mencioned to be made betweene the said Phillip Ford the Elder of the one part and the said William Penn of the other part It is in and by the said Indenture of Defeazance Declared and Agreed between the said partyes that if the said William Penn his heires or Assignes should pay unto the said Phillip Ford the summe of Ten Thousand Six hundred Fifty and seaven pounds of Lawfull money of England on the Thirtieth day of March then next ensueing att or upon the Royall Exchange in the Citty of London that then and thereupon the said Phillip Ford should upon the reasonable request and att the Costs and Charges of the said William Penn his heires or Assignes Reconvey or Surrender unto him and them all and singular the said Landes Hereditaments and premisses herein before mencioned or Intended to be Granted and Released unto the said Phillip Ford the Elder as aforesaid and all his Estate Title and Interest therein Freed from all Incumbrances by him done or Committed or the same was so limitted and Agreed by some provisoe or Covenants in the said Mortgage Deed And your Orators and Oratrixes Further shew that the said summe of Tenn Thousand six hundred Fifty and seaven pounds or any part thereof was not paid att the time Limitted or att any time after and that the said William Penn being sensible of the great and long forbearance of that great summe and of his inability to discharge the same and that he was subject to be sued on his Covenant for his Default therein and being sensible that the said premisses were not near of such Value as by [blank] had been Imagined and not being able to sell or dispose the same premisses Whereby to raise money for the discharge of that great summe wherewith the said premisses were too heavily burthened and being then in a just and full apprehension of those insuperable Difficultyes was desireous to be att Ease from the same which he wisely foresaw could not be procured by any other purchaser and therefore to Ease himselfe and putt Your Orators and Oratrixes {said Father} in rest who was in great Trouble of mind that his Estate was under such doubtfull Circumstances hee the said Mr Penn Freely agreed once more to Release all Equity of Redempcion and accordingly in pursueance thereof did by his Deed bearing date the First day of Aprill one Thousand six hundred ninety and seaven[11] after reciteals of the aforesaid Mortgages for and in Consideracion of the Further summme of Twenty shillings to him paid by the said Phillip Ford over and besides the Respective summes aforesaid Did Release Ratify and Confirme unto the said Phillip Ford the said severall Recited Indentures of Lease and Release and Confirmacion aforesaid and the said Province Tract and parcell of Land called Pensilvania together with the said severall other Tracts and parcells of Land and premisses above mencioned and every part and parcell of them and every of them And all the Estate Right Title Interest property Claime and demand whatsoever of him the said William Penn of in to or out of the said premisses or any part or parcell thereof and the Revercion and Revercions Remainder and Remainders Rents Issues and profitts of all and singular the premisses with their and every of their appurtenances together with all writeings touching or concerning the premisses or any part thereof To have and to hold all and singular the said premisses with their and every of their appurtenances unto the said Phillip Ford his heires and Assignes to the only use and behooffe of the said Phillip Ford his heires and Assignes for ever Freed and absolutely discharged of and from the said recited Indenture of Defeazance Provisoe and Covenants for Redempcion and of and from all right and benefitt of Redempcion in Law or Equity by vertue or reason thereof or by any other meanes ways or pretence whatsoever And your Orators and Oratrixes {~~also shew~~ also shew that your Orators & oratrixes} said Father after the premisses were so absolutely and Indefeasably ~~in~~vested in him, hee your orators and oratrixes said Father Att the Request of the said William Penn did by his Deed dated the second day of Aprill in the yeare of our Lord one Thousand six hundred ninety and seaven[12] and made betwixt your Orators and Oratrixes said Father of the one part and the said William Penn of the other ~~part~~ Demise and Lease all and singular the said premisses unto him the said William Penn for the Terme of three yeares from the first day of the same month of Aprill ~~one~~ under the Rent of six hundred and Thirty pounds per Annum And your orators and oratrixes likewise shew that after makeing ~~such~~ the {said} Lease of the premisses for three yeares unto the said Mr Penn hee the said Mr Penn knowing your Orators ~~and oratrixes~~ {said Father} was a man of Candor and would not suspect that Mr Penn would ensnare him to any Inconveniency to Weaken his Title soe well Established and discharged of all Equity he the said Mr Penn with a private designe to create a New Equity without mencioning any desire thereof only desired from your Orators said Father that in Case he should part with the premisses and not otherwise) that he the said Mr Penn might have the same in such a rate as your Orators said Father then rated the same att which he absenting[13] unto the said Mr Penn drew him {in} to Execute a Deed poll or some other Deed dated on or about the Tenth day of Aprill one Thousand six hundred ninety and Seven[14] reciteing his absolute purchase of the premisses and also reciteing the last mencioned Lease thereof to the said William Penn and likewise reciteing his purpose to sell the same premisses and that the said William Penn haveing declared unto him his hopes to be in a Condicion to repurchase the same within three yeares and desireing him to give him the preference in the said purchase and that he might not be streightned in time for raiseing the money to perfect the same your Orators said Father did by the same Deed poll declare that if the said William Penn or his heires should before the End and Expiracion of three yeare's then next ensueing the date of the said Deed poll pay or Cause to be paid unto the said Phillip Ford the summe of Twelve Thousand seven hundred Fourteen pounds and Five shillings for the Full and absolute purchase of the said Lands and premisses that then he the said Phillip Ford his heires and Assignes should and would Reconvey unto the said William Penn his heires and Assignes to his and their only use all and singular the said premisses Freed of all Incumbrances done or comitted by him the said Phillip Ford his heires or Assignes And your Orators and Oratrixes further shew that the said William Penn not haveing made any step towards the payment of the said repurchase money and after his Failure therein and the severall transaccions aforesaid your Orators and Oratrixes {said father} not suspecting but that the said premisses had been absolute in himselfe without being subject to any Equity unto the said Mr Penn (who was not subject by any Covenants whatsoever to make such payment but {was} wholly Free) did on or about the Twentieth day of January one Thousand six hundred ninety and nine make his last Will and Testament in writeing[15] and therein and thereby did recite to the Effect following (Vizt) That whereas he made an absolute purchase from the said William Penn to him and his heires for Ever of the Whole Tract and province of Pensilvania the Town of Newcastle alias Delaware and two other Tracts of Land there one of them lying within the Circuit of Twelve miles about the said Towne and the other near to the same together with All Islands Lakes Rivers & hereditaments whatsoever within any of the said premisses he did by his said Will devise the same and all other the Tracts of Land which he had purchased from the said William Penn and all the Estate and Interest of him the said Phillip Ford therein unto Bridgett Ford his then wife[16] mother of your Orator Phillip Ford and of your said Oratrixes and unto John Hall[17] Cittizen and Draper of London And Thomas Moss[18] of London Merchant his approved Freinds and their heires and Assignes upon Trust that they and the survivors and survivor of them and his and their heires should within six months after his death or assoon as they could sell the same to such person and persons as should and would be the best purchasers for the same But if the said William Penn would in his life time within the said six months pay unto his said Trustees the summe of Eleven thousand one hundred thirty ~~one~~ {four} pounds Eight shillings and three pence together with all such summes of money as should be in Arreare for Rent of the premisses upon the First day of Aprill next after the date of the said Will upon a Lease then before to him made att the Rent of six hundred and Thirty pounds per Annum together also with all such other debts as should be due from him the said William Penn to him the said Phillip Ford att the time of his death That then his said Trustees and the survivors and survivor of them should in Consideracion thereof sell and Convey the said premisses unto him the said William Penn and his heires and Assignes for ever which said Appointment was neverthelesse under a provisoe in the said Will sett downe and specifyed in the words or to the Effect Following (Vizt) Provided alwayes and my Intent and meaning is that this kindness of mine to the said William Penn ~~which~~ which is my own voluntary Act shall not in any wise give him much less his heires any Title or Equity of Redempcion[19] And the said Phillip Ford did in and by his said Will direct appoint and devise that Fifteene hundred pounds part of the purchase money soe to be raised should be for a porcion for your Oratrix Bridgett his Eldest Daughter now the wife of your Orator James Ayrey and that Three Thousand pounds another part of that money should be for ~~the~~ porcions for your Orator Phillip Ford his son and heire and of his two other Daughters And did by the same Will devise all the residue of the money which should be raised by such sale to his said Wife[20] whome he made his Executrix as by the said Respective Conveyances Deeds Lease counter parts of Conveyances and Leases writeings Will and books of Account of them the said William Penn and of your Orators and Oratrixes said Father and Mother all remaineing in their power had your Orators and Oratrixes the same to produce it doth and would more fully appeare And your Orators and Oratrixes further shew that soon after the death of their said Father your orator Phillip Ford together with the said John Hall and Thomas Moss two of the Trustees aforesaid did Attend the said William Penn and Acquaint him with the Will as before settforth upon which he declared it was true and that he was noe other then a Broker for your Orators Family and promised to raise money to pay off the Legacyes and desired your Orators and Oratrixes patience and be Assured that their money was as safe as if in a Chest in their own possession or to that Effect And your Orators also shew that they did hope that the said William Penn would have gratefully accepted of the Condescencion of your Orators and oratrixes said Father in giveing him by his said Will the preference for the repurchase of the said premisses within the time Limitted and that your Orators should have bee[21] paid their Respective Legacyes out of the same or at least that after such Failure that your Orators and Oratrixes said Mother and the said Mr Hall {and Mr Moss} her Co-Trustees in the said Will named for the sale of the said premisses should have absolutely sold the same premisses according to the direccion of the said Will that so your Orators and Oratrixes might have been fully paid as by their Father was appointed and Intended But so it is may it please your Lordshipp the said Mr Penn prevailed with your Orators said Mother not to prove the said Will untill very lately[22] and the said Mr Hall and Mr Moss being fearfull of Trouble and loth to doe any thing that may be displeaseing to the said Mister Penn decline to Joyne with her in sale of the premisses and in the meane time the said Mr Penn haveing been in possession of the premisses by vertue of the said Lease for three yeares dated the second day of Aprill one Thousand six hundred ninety and seaven hath Continued in the possession of the same ever since by Colour thereof and takeing advantage of the above recited Deed Poll which was Freely and voluntaryly granted by your Orators and oratrixes said Father unto him the said Mister Penn, that he should have the premisses Reconveyed unto him the said Mr Penn and his heires soe as he paid unto your Orators and Oratrixes said Father the said recited summe of Twelve Thousand seaven hundred fourteen pounds and Five shillings within the limitted time in the said Deed Poll and alsoe takeing advantage of the Clause afores^d^ in your Orators and Oratrix's said Father's will (made long after the limitted time for his repurchase) That if the said William Penn should within six months after his death pay unto his Trustees the summe of Eleven Thousand one hundred Thirty Four pounds Eight shillings and Three pence together with all arreares of Rent that should be due on the first day of Aprill next after the date of the said Will Hee the said Mr Penn doth {now} very unreasonably deny his Release of the Equity of Redempcion and farther insists that in Case he had Executed such Releases yet that now he hath a new Equity created to him by the said Will and that the said Trustees have noe power to sell the same unto any other persons whereas it is expresly declared by the said Will that the priviledge given to the said Mr Penn (by your Orators and Oratrixes said Father) to give him preference and convenient time for the Repurchase was out of his good Will only and not to give him any Equity or to dissettle his said Estate after the Equity of Redempcion so often and so solemnly Released and for soe great a Consideracion And the said m^r^ Penns now insisting thereon is very unkind to hinder the settlement of the Children of a person so much his friend who had stretched and Exahausted his Estate in assisting him to Establish that Province and plantacion and by whose money the same was Effected and the said Mr Penn as a further instance of unkindness hath Influenced the said Mr Hall and Mr Moss to refuse to Joyne in any sale for raiseing the said porcions and the said Mr Penn threatens that in Case your Orators and oratrixes said Mother and the said Mister Hall and M^r^ moss do sell the said premisses that he will avoid the same in this honourable Court in Equity and in the meane time he continues to receive the Rents Issues and proffitts of the said premisses to his own Use and hath not paid any Rent for the same for a long time

Whereas in truth he att first Entred by and under the Lease aforesaid and hath since the Expiracion thereof been only a Tennant by Sufferance And he likewise takes Advantages of the Remoteness of the said province and plantacion and the Difficulty of the said Trustees to obtaine the possession or to make any sale or proffitt thereof by reason of his power and Interest in the said province and thereby and by other the Difficultyes and pretences by him raised he not only discourages purchasers but hopes to Compell your Orators and Oratrixes to yeild their Interest in the premisses to him on some meane and unreasonable termes And he sometimes pretends that your Orators said Father never paid him the ~~said~~ purchase money aforesaid and that he will question the Title and keep the possession of the premisses altho he very well knowes that he had the possession only by Lease from the said Phillip Ford as aforesaid and that he himselfe paid the Rent thereon reserved untill the date of the ~~said~~ {last} Will of the said Phillip Ford before settforth and very lately proposed and Came to an Agreement with your Orators and Oratrixes said Mother For the repurchase of the Mannours of Pensberry and Highlands parcell of the said premisses and within the said province att the price of Two Thousand pounds[23] and since the death of your Orators and Oratrixes said Father and before such Agreement last mencioned that is to say the second of Aprill one Thousand seaven hundred and two he Came to Account with your Orators and Oratrixes said Mother touching the premisses and Rent thereof upon the ballance whereof there was due to her as Executrix to their said Father the summe of Five hundred ninety one pounds Eight shillings and tenn pence for Rent[24] and after he had the same Account in his Custody to Consider above a Month he gave his Assent thereunto and subscribed the same in these words I William Penn of Worminhurst in the County of Sussex Esquire doe hereby declare that I have Considered and Examined the Accounts here above written which I find to be Just and true and doe Acknowledge that the ballance thereof being five hundred ninety one pounds Eight shillings and Tenn pence sterling lawfull money of England is by me the said William Penn really and bona fide due and owing to Bridgett Ford Widdow as she is intituled thereto by the last Will and Testament of her late husband Phillip Ford deceased And do promise to pay the said summe of Five hundred ninety one pounds Eight shillings and ten pence sterling to her or her Order at Demand Accordingly att her now dwelling house in Water lane London, alsoe I doe hereby Acknowledge that the Rent of the premisses is six hundred and thirty pounds sterling per annum as is here above (in the particulars of this Account) mencioned witness my hand and seale in London this second day of Aprill And in the first yeare of the Reigne of our soveraigne Lady Queen Anne Anno Domini One Thousand seaven hundred and two which he now would avoyd under pretence he had not Considered thereof altho he had the same in his Custody for the space aforesaid and att other times pretends that he hath made some settlement of the premisses upon William Penn the younger his son and heire apparent and made other Incumbrances prior to his Conveyance to your Orators said Father[25] And the said William Penn his son threatens that he will Enter on the premisses after his said Fathers death or sooner so that the dealings of the said Mister Penn the Elder not to purchase himselfe but hinder all others soe to doe and create such Incumbrances are very Injurious unto your Orators and Oratrixes and the forbearance of your Orators and Oratrixes said Fathers Trustees and their Indulgence to the said Mr Penn and his Dilatory promises and their not raiseing and paying your Orators and Oratrixes said Legacyes tend to their great wrong and Damage against which they are noe way releiveable save only in this honourable Court in Equity In tender Consideracion whereof and for that the said Will and other the Deeds writings and Evidences aforesaid and counterpartes thereof are in the Custody of the said confederates or some or one of them and the truth of the premisses is very well known unto them and not discoverable by your Orators other then by the oaths of the Confederates their Wittnesses being beyond the seas and for that the matters aforesaid are proper for Releife in this Court To the End the End therefore that the said Mr Penn the Elder And his said son may on their Corporall Oathes settforth and discover whether he the said Mr Penn the Elder had not very many and great summes of Money From your Orators and Oratrixes said Father on his Creditt or Mortgages sometimes of part and at last of all the said premisses and whether he did not Release all his Equity as aforesaid and whether he hath not held and Enjoyed all and singular the premisses and the Rents Issues and proffitts thereof by Vertue or Colour of the Lease thereof to him made by your Orators and Oratrixes said Father by his Indenture dated the second day of Aprill in the yeare of our Lord one Thousand six hundred ninety & ~~nine~~ seaven for the Terme of three yeares under the Rent of six hundred and Thirty pounds per Annum and ever since as Tennant at sufferance And whether he hath not paid unto your Orators and Oratrixes said Mother since their said Fathers death severall summes of money and how much towards and in part of Rent for the premisses after the rate aforesaid and whether he did not signe and Execute unto her under his hand and seale such stated Account as aforesaid And Wherefore he now refuseth to give up the possession of the premisses to the End the same may be sold according to the direccion of the said Will but inverts the Clause thereof to give him preference in the purchase to Create in him an Equity of Redempcion Whereas he knows in his Conscience it was only intended to shew what your Orators and Oratrixes said Father had given a full value for the same and did not covet the premisses but only to sell the same to make good his Damages and reiumburse the great summes by him

Expended and thereout to make provision for his Family and not to Embarrass his Title by giveing the said Mr Penn any handle to hinder the s~~e~~ale thereof to any other in case he should not thinke fitt to Repurchase the same within the time given him soe to doe And that the said William Penn the younger and other the Confederates when discovered may discover and settforth their pretended Titles with the true dates and Consideracions of the same and reall times of makeing and Executeing thereof for as much as your Orators and Oratrixes are by the delay and practices of the said William Penn the Elder and by the tenderness of their mother and other the Trustees (to Attend the dilatory and delusive promisses of the said William Penn the Elder) kept Out of their said Legacyes and in Danger of Loosing the same therefore that your Orators and Oratrixes said Mother may settforth the said Will verbatim and produce the same to be Examined unto in perpetuam rei memoriam[26] And that the said Mr Hall and Mister Moss and your Orators said mother may Joyne in the sale of the premisses and makeing a Conveyance thereof according to the direccion and Intent of your Orators and Oratrixes said Fathers Will and may out of the purchase money pay unto your Orators and Oratrixes their respective Legacyes with Interest for the same or in default thereof that your Orators and oratrixes may hold and Enjoy the same in leiu of their said Legacyes and that the said Mr Penn after his failure of complying with and abuse of the favour offerred and Granted by your Orators and Oratrixes said Fathers Will may not be suffered to obstruct the sale of the premisses to any other but his pretence of Equity may be forever Extinguished And to the End that all the said Confederates may make true Answer to all and singular the premisses as if here againe repeated and Interrogated and that all the said premisses may be held and Enjoyed agt the said Mister Penn and his son and the Rents and proffitts of the premisses may be Accounted and satisfyed to the Estate of your Orators and Oratrixes said Father And that all Deeds counterparts of Leases and other writeings relateing to the premisses in the hands or power of any of the Defendts may be discovered by them and may be delivered to Attend the Inheritance of the premisses and to Assist and Encourage the sale thereof and that all reasonable further Assureances may be made of the premisses for the purposes aforesaid And that your Orators and Oratrixes may be therein releived according to Equity and good Conscience May it please your Lordshipp to Grant unto your Orators and Oratrixes her Majestyes most gracious Writt or Writts of subpena to be directed to the said William Penn the Elder William Penn the younger Bridgett Ford Widdow John Hall and Thomas Moss thereby comanding them and every of them at a Certaine day and under a Certaine paine therein to be limitted personally to be and appeare before your Lordshipp in her majestyes most high and honourable Court of chancery then and there upon their Corporall oathes true and perfect Answer to make to all and singular the premisses and further to stand to and abide such further Order and Decree herein as to your Lordshipp shall seeme meet And your orators and oratrixes shall pray &c

Per P. King[27]

Copy. Penn Papers, Ford vs. Penn, HSP. (Not filmed.) A copy of this document, also in the Penn Papers, Ford vs. Penn, HSP, is in *Micro.* 12:275.

1. William Cowper (d. 1723), first Earl Cowper, a Whig barrister of the Middle Temple, became lord keeper in Oct. 1705. On 9 Nov. 1706 he was raised to Baron Cowper and on 4 May 1707, after the Act of Union between England and Scotland, he became the first lord chancellor of Great Britain. He later supported the Tories and became a lord justice under George I. *DNB.*

2. Philip Ford, Jr. (b. 1677), son of Philip Ford, WP's former steward. He had been a landholder in Pennsylvania since 25 Aug. 1682 when he received 2000 acres from WP. Digests of Quaker Records, London and Middx., GSP; Wynne Papers, DDWY/750, Bedfordshire Record Office.

3. James Ayrey (c. 1661-1712), a Quaker of Southwark, Sur., had married Bridget Ford, Jr., daughter of Philip Ford, on 16 Mar. 1704. He died eight years later of a fever and convulsions and was buried in Bunhill Fields, London. Digests of Quaker Records, London and Middx., GSP.

4. Bridget Ford, Jr. (b. 1676), eldest daughter of Philip and Bridget Ford, had received 1000 acres in Pennsylvania from WP on 25 Aug. 1682 (ibid.; Wynne Papers, DDWY/753). See also n. 3, above.

5. Anne Ford (b. 1678) and Susanna Ford (b. 1682) were the younger daughters of Philip and Bridget Ford. Each received 1000 acres in Pennsylvania on 25 Aug. 1682 from WP. See Digests of Quaker Records, London and Middx.; Wynne Papers, DDWY/759, 753.

6. WP had been granted Pennsylvania and the Lower Counties in fee simple, that is, to himself and his heirs and assigns forever without limitation as to disposition. *Black's Law Dictionary.*

7. See *PWP,* 2:291-92. The agreement of 24 Aug. 1682 was for 300,000 acres, but the £3000 mentioned here as a loan was not paid to WP by Philip Ford but was instead a rounded approximation of the £2851 owed at that date by WP to Ford. WP believed that Ford had intentionally enlarged the amount in this agreement to give an impression that money had been loaned. See doc. 110, text following n. 12.

8. On 2 and 3 Sept. 1690, by indentures of lease and release, WP sold Pennsylvania and the Lower Counties to Philip Ford forever for £6900. See *PWP,* 3:659-60.

9. See ibid., 3:660.

10. See ibid., 3:660-61.

11. See ibid., 3:661.

12. See ibid., 3:662. WP in his Bill of Complaint (doc. 110) claimed that Philip Ford requested this.

13. Mistake for "assenting."

14. See *PWP,* 3:662.

15. See Probate 11/484, PRO.

16. Bridget Gosnell Ford (c. 1636-1710), originally of Shropshire, married Philip Ford in 1672. They settled in Bow Lane, London, where Bridget played an active role among London women Quakers. Although disowned by Friends because of her actions against WP, she was interred in the Quaker burial ground at Bunhill Fields. Fox, *Short Journal,* p. 321; Devonshire House Monthly Meeting minutes, vol. 2, FLL; Digests of Quaker Records, London and Middx., GSP.

17. John Hall, a Quaker, was the son of John Hall, of Warwick. He is listed in Quaker records as a citizen and dyer of London and may be the merchant listed in London Record Society, *London Inhabitants Within the Walls* (Chatham, Kent, 1966), p. 133, as a widower, residing in St. Mary Colechurch, with an estate valued at more than £600. See Digests of Quaker Records, War., Leics., and Rut., GSP.

18. Thomas Moss (b. 1658), a Quaker, was the son of Isaac and Mary Moss of Manchester and brother of Benjamin, who became a Bristol merchant. Thomas married Elizabeth Monke at Manchester in 1685 before moving to London. It is probable that he is the merchant mentioned in *London Inhabitants*, p. 209, as residing in St. Mary Bothaw, with an estate valued at more than £600. See Digests of Quaker Records, Lancs.; London and Middx.; Mortimer, 2:253.

19. Equity of Redemption: the right of the mortgager of an estate to redeem that estate after it has been forfeited by a breach of the condition of the mortgage, upon paying the amount of the debt, interest, and costs. *Black's Law Dictionary.*

20. Bridget Ford.

21. Mistake for "been."

22. Bridget Ford probated the will on 4 Oct. 1705 in the Prerogative Court of Canterbury. See doc. 113, text at n. 38.

23. Drafts of this agreement indicate that alternative sums were discussed. One draft provides for a payment by WP of £2000; another provides for a payment of £2500, while a third leaves the payment blank. The date of the discussions is unknown, but no settlement was reached. See *Micro.* 12:487.

24. On 1 Apr. 1702 Bridget Ford drew up an itemized five-year account of WP's debits and credits as lessee of Pennsylvania since 1 Apr. 1697. She stated that WP's rent of £630 per annum, plus small additional charges, totaled £3233 7s 1d. She credited WP with £2641 18s 3d in payments, leaving a debit of £591 8s 10d. This account, with WP's acknowledgment of 2 Apr. 1702 in the wording as given in doc. 108, above, is in *Micro.* 10:074.

25. In WP's will of 6 Aug. 1684 he settled the proprietorship of Pennsylvania on his eldest son, Springett, and conveyed lands and rights there to other members of his family. In his will of 30 Oct. 1701, WP settled the proprietorship of Pennsylvania on his eldest surviving son, William Penn, Jr., and conveyed extensive lands and rights to other members of his family. *PWP,* 2:585-86; doc. 30.

26. In perpetual memory of the matter.

27. Peter King (1669-1734), later Baron King, seems to have prepared the Fords' case. A devout Presbyterian and Whig, he entered the Middle Temple in 1694, was called to the bar in 1698, and had a successful practice at Westminster and on the western circuit. At this time King was an M.P. and recorder of Glastonbury; he later became recorder of London, lord chief justice of Common Pleas, speaker of the House of Lords, and lord chancellor. Edward Foss, *The Judges of England* (London, 1864), 8:132-37.

The following three documents provide a detailed synopsis of WP's case against the Fords. When he learned of the Bill of Complaint filed against him in Chancery (see doc. 108), WP and his counsel began to prepare his defense (doc. 109), a time-consuming process leading him to petition the court for more time to respond. This was granted until 12 January 1706, the first day of Hilary term (*Micro.* 12:459). His answer was given, probably in that month; at about the same time his counsel also prepared a cross Bill of Complaint against John Hall, Thomas Moss, and the Ford family (doc. 110), which was filed on 23 February 1706. The Fords responded to this bill on 5 June 1706, at about which time WP and his lawyers drew up a concise draft of the case (see doc. 111) probably in preparation to rebut the Fords' response.

Docs. 109–111 make it clear that WP relied on the classic Chancery defense — claiming fraud, deception, extortion, and conspiracy. In addition, by focusing on the need to study and revise the accounts kept by Philip Ford, WP could hope to drag the case out for years, a common occurrence in Chancery suits involving questionable accounts (see Blackstone, 3:453). The crux of WP's argument was that Ford charged usurious interest and commission rates, often more than once for the same amount. WP claimed that Ford's salary of £40 per annum precluded any right to charge a commission; he rejected the charges Ford debited to his account for stock in the Free Society of Traders; and he alleged that Philip and Bridget Ford conspired to trick or coerce him into signing various accounts and legal instruments, particularly in 1697 and 1699, when he conveyed Pennsylvania to his former steward after releasing all equity of redemption and without demanding a defeasance. The critical witness for WP's version of events, however, was Bridget Ford, who was under coverture (see doc. 113, n. 46) at the time these events took place and was therefore not bound to testify.

109
DRAFT DEFENSE TO THE FORDS' BILL OF COMPLAINT

[c. 1–19 November 1705]

That when WP return'd from Pennsylvania in the year 1684 PF[1] told WP that notwithstanding the great summs of money arising from Land sold in Pennsylvania as well as in England with all the Rents of WPs Irish Estate which the said PF received that he was indebted to PF some 1000s £ since his departure for Pennsylvania which was in 1682[2] and althô the said PF was very well satisfyed with the security[3] the said WP had given him at his said embarqing for Pennsylvania yet his Wife[4] was not Contented therewith but led the said PF her Husband an uneasy life till he should procure a fresh and larger security from the said WP for the pretended sume due Whereupon the said PF proposed to the said WP to renew the said Mortgage and grant him one of the whole Province But the said WP refused upon the Acct of his continual selling and disposing of parcells of the same to new Comers being the Circumstances that a new Colony was under above a settled Estate To which the said PF answered that it should make no alteration but lye only as a private security for the money until the same could be raised as oppertunity offer'd out of the Province by the sale of Lands and that it should never alter the property of the said WPs right thereto or be any prejudice to him or his Heires which is well known to ~~the~~ Bridget Ford his said Wife she being present at most if not every security WP executed and the real cause as her Husband said of repeating and renewing the securitys for WP well knew That the same was then 3 times and now ten times the value that the then pretended Debt required neither was that all which the said PF engaged for before his Wife when WP refused to Execute the Mortgage which was in Essex street[5] unless he would solemnly promise three things one whereof is as before expressed at Which the said PF gave the said WP his hand and solemnly promised as that before so these should be sacredly observed by him and his Wife with whom he said he intended (if he died before her) to leave the whole disposition of his affairs and that all things between them should lye as secret as they were before (viz) That it should lye only as a dorment security and should never be to the prejudice of the said WP or his Heires, and that he would not at all urge or press the said WP for moneys but would be contented to receive the same in such manner as the said WP could raise it out of the premisses from time to time —And also that whenever the said WP should pay the said PF the summe of 500 or 1000 £ of the Principal money that then he would lessen the security proportionable and so from time to time all which is alsoe well known to the said Bridget Ford and she assented thereunto.

And forasmuch as we cannot come to the perfect knowledge of the particulars of several great summs of money inserted in the Accts {and referr'd to ~~to be mencioned~~ in certain Invoyces} that the said PF pretended so suddenly to advance for the use of the said WP viz 1400£ at one time[6] and [blank] at another for want of {the said} Invoyces that are now in America in the respective storekeepers hands and forasmuch alsoe as there are other great sums of moneys charged to the Acct as laid out for the use of the said WP Or his Children in the name of the Pennsylvania society[7] It's pray'd that the said B Ford be obliged to bring the Books ~~and Copies or Duplicates of the said Invoyces~~ wherein the said great summs {relating to and in the name of the Pennsylvania society} are particularly mencion'd ~~or else that the~~ and that the said WP may have sufficient time allow'd him for the sending for the said Invoyces or true Copies thereof he having sufficient reason to suspect the Truth of the said great summs being expressed severally {each} in one single line ~~each~~ in the said Accts and believing that there are several things therein charged without the order or direction of the said WP to his great loss and abuse on purpose to advance the private gains of the said PF by an extravagant interest and poundage

Draft. Penn Papers, Ford vs. Penn, HSP. (*Micro.* 12:362.) Endorsed: Penn Mr Jefferyes[8] | writeing being a | Caste or [?] by WP.

1. Philip Ford.

2. According to Ford, WP owed him £2851 7s 10d when he left for Pennsylvania in Aug. 1682. Between 23 Aug. 1682 and 21 Mar. 1685, Ford received £8198 on WP's account and expended £8549. When £1090 was added in commission and interest, WP's debt to Ford had risen to £4293 3s ½d by 21 Mar. 1685 (see *Micro.* 12:544; doc. 111, text at n. 14).

3. WP had mortgaged 300,000 acres of Pennsylvania land to Ford before leaving for the colony. See *PWP*, 2:291-93.

4. Bridget Ford.

5. In London.

6. The accounts for 6 July 1682 to 23 Aug. 1682 included an expense of £1448 12s 7d for goods shipped on the *Welcome*. See *Micro*. 12:544.

7. The Free Society of Traders. Philip Ford had been an original subscriber of £400 to the society and had acted as either its bookkeeper or treasurer (see *PMHB*, 11:175, 179; doc. 121C). The original subscription list for the Free Society indicates that WP subscribed £1000 for his three children, Springett, Laetitia, and William, Jr. (*PMHB*, 11:175). Here WP claims that Ford overcharged him. In his cross Bill of Complaint (see doc. 110), WP accused Ford of charging him £500 and £712 10s as half-subscriptions to the society, without providing him with any tangible evidence of such a stock purchase. The matter was finally resolved late in 1708 (see doc. 211A).

8. Probably John Jeffreys, who calculated Philip Ford's overcharges in order for WP to arrange an equitable out-of-court settlement (see doc. 121C). This may be the Quaker schoolmaster, formerly of Corsham, Wilts., but now of Ealing, Middx. See Digests of Quaker Records, London and Middx., GSP.

110
CROSS BILL OF COMPLAINT AGAINST THE FORDS AND OTHERS

[23 February 1705/6]

To the R^t Honourable Sr William Cowper Barronet Lord Keeper of the great Seale of England.

Humbly Complaining shew unto your Lord^pp your Orators William Penn of Worminghurst in the County of Sussex Esqr and Wm Penn his Sonn That your Orator Wm Penn the elder about the yeare 1668 {did} take into his Service to manage his Affairs one Phillip Ford late of London deceased at a Sallary of 40^l per annum onely which he thankfully Accepted,[1] And Continued in your Orators Service as aforesaid from the said yeare 1668 untill the 24th day of June in the year of our Lord 1694 At the Sallary of 40^l per annum And your Orator never Agreed to Allow nor did the said Phillip Ford Ever pretend to aske {or} demand Any further advantage from your said Orator during all that time but Seemed very well Contented and Satisfyed therewith And untill the Sixth day of July 1682 the said Ford made and Cast up his Accounts before that time and then depending betweene {him} and your Orator Wm Penn the Elder for the most part three or four times in the yeare and when ever he brought the Same to be Signed by your Orator the Same was mencioned to be with Errors Excepted and he allways delivered to your said Orator at the Same time a part thereof Signed by the said P Ford himselfe,[2] And the said Phillip Ford hath not in any part of the said Account to the said Sixth day of July 1682 charged your Orator with Commission money for the buying of any goods by him bought for your Orator before that time, alltho in {that} part of the said Account which was delivered to your Orator the said Sixth day of July 1682 and Carryed on to that day there are goods Charged to be before that time by the said Ford bought for your said Orator Amounting to the Summe of twelve hundred pounds and upwards[3] because the said Phillip Ford {well} knew that it was your said Orator's Agreement to allow him only 40l per annum Sallary. And that where a Sallary is allowed there can never be any pretence for Comission money: *And* your said Orator the said Wm Penn the Elder never Suspected till very lately that {he} the said Phil: Ford ~~ever~~ demanded of or charged him in his Account depending between them Since the said 6th day of July 1682 with any further Demand then the said Summe or Sallary of 40l per annum and a reasonable allowance for money really advanced by him for your Orator. *And* your Orator the said Wm Penn the Elder further Sheweth that about the month of July 1682 he being very ~~much~~ busie in making preparacion for a Voyage which he intended to make to the province of Pennsilvania in America whereof he was the proprietor and Governour, he gave direccions to the said Ford to buy {for} him Severall parcells of goods for his accomodacion in the said province amounting to the Summe of 2800l or thereabouts which the said PFord bought[4] upon the Creditt of your Orator Wm Penn the Elder and had Six months time or more given him for paying for the same by the respective Sellers of the said Goods, And that the said Phillip Ford might be Enabled to pay for the said Goods according to the times soe agreed on for paying for the Same Your Orator Wm Penn the Elder left an Authority with the said Phillip Ford about the time of his embarking for Pennsilvania (which was in the month of August 1682) for receiving All such moneys as was then due to your Orator Wm Penn the elder or as should become due unto him upon any Account whatsoever[5] And by vertue of the said Authority or otherwise the said Philip Ford did receive of the money of your said Orator before his returne from the said province into England which was about the month of January 1684[6] the Summe of 8198l 10s 7½d and particularly the said Philip Ford did receive the Summe of 5000l and upwards part of the said Summe of 8198:10:7½ long before the time given by the said Sellers of the {sd} goods for paying for the Same was Expired.[7] And the said Philip Ford so paid or might have paid for the said goods with your {sd} Orators owne money soe received, And the Severall and respective Contracts for the said goods soe bought, and the respective prizes they were bought for and when they were respectively to be paid for, and of whome the same {were} respectively bought and the respective times when they were bought and the Severall times; and ~~by~~of what persons by name the said Philip Ford received the said 5000l of your Orator {the sd} Wm Penn the Elders money And by what Summes your Orator Wm Penn the elder expressly chargeth appears by the ~~books~~ Invoyces of the said Goods and the books papers and Accounts of the said Philip Ford now or late in the possession Custody or Power of Bridgett Ford his relict and

Executrix. *And* your Orator Wm Penn the Elder offers to be Concluded[8] by the said Books invoyces and papers if produced without any un/due and unjust Alteracions of any of them as to the said matters concerning the said goods so bought for him by the said Philip Ford, *And* your Orator the said Wm Penn the Elder further sheweth that Soon after the said Sixth day of July 1682 {he} the said Philip Ford and Bridgett his wife contriveing together to make an unjust advantage of the Confidence your Orator Wm Penn the Elder gave them in his Affairs and apprehending that ~~a~~ greater Summes of your said orators money would come {to} the hands of the said Phillip Ford During your Orator Wm Penn the Elder's Stay beyond the Seas were desirous that the said Phillip Ford should be Continued as Agent as aforesaid at the said Sallary only of 40l per annum without any more or other Allowance from your said Orator. *And* the said Bridgett well knoweth that the said P Ford did agree and was well Satisfyed to continue in your ~~said~~ Orators said Service at the {sd} Sallary of 40l per annum upon your Orators Consenting to such continueing of him at 40l ~~said Orators Se~~ per annum Sallary and no more and that it was a competent and large allowance for such service, *And* your Orator Wm Penn the elder further Sheweth that the said Phillip Ford and the said Bridgett his wife being Sensible that in the months of July & August 1682 your ~~said~~ Orator Wm Penn the Elder was in a great hurry of business in preparing for his said Voyage for the said Province he being to imbarque the latter end of the Same month of August,[9] they tooke that oppertunity of imposing upon & of Circumventing & Surprizing your Orator Wm Penn the Elder and therefore on or about the 23th day of Augst 1682 (which was the same day your Orator Wm Penn the elder went from London to *Deale* in order to his goeing the said Voyage)[10] they {or one of them} brought your Orator Wm Penn the Elder a part of the Account then depending between your Orator Wm Penn the Elder and the said Phillip Ford begining the said Sixth day of July 1682 and Ending the 23th day of August following upon the casting up whereof by the said Phillip Ford only and not by your Orator Wm Penn the elder the Sa~~me~~id Phillip Ford pretended the Summe of 2851:7:10 was due to him. *and the said P: Ford affirming to your Orator Wm* Penn the Elder {that} the goods contained in that and a former part of the ~~said~~ {same} Account betweene your said Orator and the said Phillip Ford amounting together to the Summe of 2850l were Actually paid for at that time by the said Philip Ford. *And your* Orator ~~the said~~ Wm Penn the Elder at that time Crediting the integrity of the said P Ford and being {then} in a Great Hurry and Confusion Subscribed to the said part of the said Account with Errors excepted without perusall or having any Coppy thereof, *whereas* the truth is and so your Orator expressly chargeth that the said Bridgett Ford knows beleives or hath heard from her said Husband or Other persons She creditts that the said Summe of 2850l or any Considerable part thereof was not paid by the said Philip Ford at the time of your Orator's Subscribing to the s^{d} part of the said Account of the said 23th day of Augst 1682 nor untill or about Six months {or more} afterwards and that the said goods were bought upon the Creditt of your Orator Wm Penn the Elder. All which appears by the Invoyces of the said goods and the books papers and Accounts of the said Philip Ford and which now {are} or lately were in the custody or power of the said Bridgett Ford as your Orator expressly chargeth But notwithstanding the said Philip Ford had not paid the said Summe of 2850^{l} on the said 23th day of August 1682 and before payment of of the said 2850^{l} had received moneys of your said Orator Sufficient to pay the said 2850^{l} or the greatest part thereof, Yet the said Phillip Ford hath in the next part of the said Account to the Wrong and injury of your said Orator charged him with Interest for the whole 2850^{l} from the said 23th day of August 1682 to the said 29th day of September 1696 which is the End of the said Account soe begining the 6th of July 1682, *And* your Orator Wm Penn the Elder further Sheweth that the said Phillip Ford in further prosecucion of his designe of circumventing and Surprizing your said Orator and unjustly to gaine great Summes of money from your Orator the said Phillip Ford Did accompany your said Orator to Deale aforesaid and there without any previous notice given ~~him~~ to your said Orator brought unto him ready ingrossed[11] two Deeds of Lease and release Dated the 23th and 24th days of August {1682} whereby your Orator Wm Penn {the Elder} findes he~~re~~ is mencioned to Convey to the said Phillip Ford and his heires 300000 Acres of Land in the said Province for the Consideracion of the Summe of 3000^{l} And also then brought him a Bond bearing date the said 24th day of the same month of August Condicioned for the payment of the Summe of 3000^{l} on the 26th day of the same month.[12] Which Lease Release and bond the said Phillip Ford prevailed on your said Orator to Execute without peruseall and without ~~a~~ having any Counterparts or Coppys of any of them by pretending to your Orator Wm Penn the Elder that the said part of the {sd} Account Bond and Deeds of Lease and release were all for the same Summe and that by his Signing to the said part of the said Account with Errors Excepted the Summe mencioned in the said release and bond would be Subject to the Errors which should Appeare in that part of the said Account soe Subscribed and the Words —Errors Excepted in the said Account so Subscribed—would Subject the same to be rectified, and that the Consideracion in the said deeds of Lease and release being noe fresh money but only what the said Ford demanded upon such pretended Account would be Subject to the Event of the said Account Alltho the designe of the said Phillip Ford and Bridgett his wife was to charge or to have it in theire power or at their pleasure to Charge your said Orator ~~both~~ with the said Summes of 2851^{l}:7:10 mencioned in the said part of the said Account and 3000^{l} mencioned in the said Release and bond as Separate and destinct Summes and Demands And therefore the pretended ballance of the said part of the said Account and the Consideracion of the Deeds of Lease and release were made to be different Summes Viz^{t} the said Summes of 2851:7:10 and 3000^{l} *And* your Orator the said Wm Penn the Elder further Sheweth That in the said Account betweene him and the said Phillip Ford Carryed On from the said Sixth day of July 1682 to the said 29th {day} of September 1696 the Severall Errors heerin after mencioned Do plainly Appeare upon the face thereof And that although the said Phillip {Ford} pretended to make severall Castings up and ballances at severall times of severall parts of the said Account yet the Same Account was never at any time Closed or any of the ballances paid off but from time to time carryed on to the said 29th day of September 1696 and the severall ballances Subscribed to by your said Orator were Allways so Subscribed to ~~be~~ by him with Errors Excepted. And by the Originall thereof in the Custody of the said Bridgett Ford it appeareth *That* the {s^{d}} whole Account was carryed on from the said 6th day of July 1682 and continued and ended the said 29th day of September 1696 and was carryed on and Continued In severall parts as followeth. Viz^{t} the first of the said parts of the said Account beginneth the said 6th day of July 1682 and endeth the 23th day of August following. the Second of them begins the said 23th day of August 1682 and Ends 21th day of March 1684 the third of them begins the Same 21th day of March and ends the 11th day of Aprill 1687 the fourth of them begins the same 11th day of Aprill and Ends the 11th day of October 1689. the fifth of them begins the same 11th day of October and ends the 24th day of January {1694} {the 6th of them begins the same 24th day of January} and ends the 1~~2~~1th day of June 1696.[13] ~~At~~ {to} which time the ballance of the said severall parts of the said Account is ~~then~~ computed to be and amount to the Summe of 10202:8:7½ by the unjust and unreasonable Articles appearing in the said Severall partes of the said Accounts Soe as aforesaid Carryed on and continued by the said Philip Ford from the said Sixth day of July 1682 to the said 1~~2~~1th day of June 1696 and the Seaventh and last part of the said Account begins the said 1~~2~~1th day of June 1696 and ends the 29th day of September then next ~~Ensueing~~ {following} by which said last part of the said Account Your Orator is only charged with the said ballance of 10202:8:7½ and the interest thereof from the said 1~~2~~th day of June 1696 to the said 29th of September following and on the said 29th of Septem^{r} 1696 the said Phillip Ford pretended that from All the said severall parts of the said whole Account from the said 6th day of July anno Domini 1682 to the said 29th day of September 1696 there was due to him the Summe of 10347:15:5½ *And* According to the nature of Accounts where transaccions of Affairs are Carryed on and Continued Notwithstanding there may be at Severall times Severall castings up and severall ballances, and Such Castings up and ballances are from time to time carryed on to the End of the Account and the said Castings up and ballances ~~are from ti~~ noe otherwise Signed then with Errors Excepted Such Account of transaccions cannot be divided into Severall Accounts but as Esteemed one Entire Account. And the said *Phillip* Ford knows or beleives {that} in all the castings up ballances and Subscriptions to the said severall parts of the said Account excepting the last part thereof the sd Phillip Ford never pretended to aske for any release or discharge from your said Orator or any receipt or Acquittan[ce] to be written on the said Severall parts of the said Account or any of them but the said Phillip Ford and Bridgett his wife having by faire promises of opening the said entire Account drawn your Orator Wm Penn the Elder into signing the last part of the said Account on the said 29th day of September 1696 the said Phillip Ford to Strengthen Such Stateing and Closure of the said Account workt your Orator into giving him a generall release and also to Sign a Subscription at the foot of the said ballance of 10347:15:5½ in the words or to the effect following[14] vizt Wee do acknowledge to have Adjusted and Agreed the Account hereabove written and do Allow and approve of the same as Settled and adjusted betweene us and there is due from the said Wm Penn to the said Phillip Ford the ballance of this Account being 10347:15:5½ In testimony whereof we have both of us heerunto put our hands in London the twenty ninth day of Septemr Ano Domini 1696. Which allthough your said orator did so Signe with {out} the words Errors Excepted contrary to what he had allways done at the severall castings up of any parts of the said account from the 6th of July 1682 to the 29th of Septemr 1696 Yet your Orator Wm Penn the elder reserved the liberty of inspecting the said entire Account from the ~~3~~6th day of July 1682 to the said 29th {day} of September 1696 and to Examine the same and to have the Errors therein rectified and an Allowance for the same and therefore your Orator Wm Penn ~~the Elder~~ required and had the Promise of the said Phillip Ford to give your said Orator {~~Wm Penn the Elder~~} such writings as is heerin after mencioned ~~for~~ and accordingly he the said Phillip Ford did After your Orator {Wm Penn the Elder} had Executed the said generall release and Signed the said Subscription Signe Seale and duely Execute unto your Said Orator a Writing or Deed in the words or to the Effect following, **Whereas** upon Settling Accounts between Wm Penn and my selfe he hath not only Allowed the said Account to be true and Signed the same Accordingly but hath likewise given me a generall Discharge bearing even date heerwith, Now I for the said Wm Penn his Satisfaccion doe Agree and Promise that if heer after any materiall Error shall be found in the said Account to his prejudice and be cleerly made appeare then and in such Case the Same shall be made him good notwithstanding ~~of~~ the said generall Discharge witness my hand and Seale the 29th of Septemr 1696[15] to which said writing or deed your said Orator for more certainty referrs himselfe he having the same in his Custody ready to produce as this honoble Court shall Direct. And the said Phillip Ford and {the sd} Bridgett his wife well knowing tha~~d~~t your said Orator Allways Signed the said severall parts of the {sd} Accounts upon the producing them by the said Phillip Ford without ever perusing or Examining them or any of them and indeed without ever having any Oppertunity so to doe by reason the said Phillip Ford & {the sd} Bridget his wife never lett your Orator Wm Penn the Elder have any Coppie or Copies of the said Account or of any of the parts thereof or {the} Originalls of any parts thereof, and your said Orator chargeth That At the time when the Same Deed or writing of the said 29th day of Septemr was given by the said Phillip Ford to your ~~said~~ Orator Wm Penn the Elder, Your said Orator never had any Copies or Counterparts {of any of the sd parts of the sd Account}, but All the parts of the said Account and the severall Castings up and ballances thereof from the said 6th day of July 1682 to the 29th day of Septemr 1696 and All the Copies of them were kept from ~~being~~ {& not} left with your Orator Wm Penn {the Elder} untill he had Signed the Said Account and Executed the Said release bearing date the 29th day of September 1696, But sometime after the said 29 ~~of~~Day of Septemr 1696 the said Phillip Ford and Bridgett his wife delivered to your Orator Wm Penn the Elder Copies of all the parts of the said account ~~begining the said 6th day of July~~ and of All {the} castings up and ballances ~~of~~ thereof Signed by your Orator Wm Penn the Elder from the said 6th day of July 1682 to the 29th of Septemr 1696 the Copies so delivered to your Orator Wm Penn the elder being of the sd Phillip Ford's owne hand writing and by him Signed with Errors Excepted *And* your Orator Wm Penn the Elder hath left the said Copies so delivered with Mr Samuell Browning[16] his Clarke in Court that the said Bridgett Ford and the ~~other~~ {rest of the} Confederates heerin after named may view and peruse the same {&} Sett forth whether the said Copies are not of the said P: Ford's owne hand writing and whether according to the Originall Account~~s~~ to which the said Coppies relate the said Account ~~with~~ was not Carryed on between Your Orator Wm Penn the Elder and the said Phillip Ford from the 6th day of July 1682 to the said 29th Day of Septr 1696 And whether any other Accounts then what the said Coppys relate~~s~~ to and are Copies of where ever kept cast up or any way ballanced during the said time Vizt from the said 6th of July 1682 to the said 29th of Septemr 1696 betweene your Orator Wm Penn the Elder and the said Phillip Ford. And that the said Phillip Ford looked upon All the parts of the said Account beginning the said 6th day of July 1682 and ending the said 29th day of Septemr 1696 to make up one entire Account the same ~~being~~ {are} in the said writing by him Sealed to this yr orator the 29th day of September 1696 for inspecting the same Account mencioned to be but one Account. *And* your Orator the ~~said~~ Wm Penn the Elder further sheweth That he the said Philip Ford and Bridgett Ford his wife did at Severall times before the said 29th of September 1696 by circumvention and Surprise prevailed on your {sd} Orator to execute to the said Phillip Ford Severall deeds of severall parts of the said province ~~of~~ and Severall and destinct Summes of money are mencioned to be the severall Consideracions of such deeds and in particular in the Yeare 1690 a Deed of the whole province[17] upon pretence that such deeds were only Collaterall Securitys for what money should justly Appeare to be due to the said Phillip Ford upon Examining the said Account the said whole Province of Pennsilvania to which your Orator was then entituled being worth to be Sould 60000l {Sterling} and upwards[18] ~~Ster~~ And to Induce your said Orator to Execute the Same Deeds the said Phillip Ford and the said Bridgett his wife did from time to time pretend to and Assure your said Orator that the Consideracion money mencioned in the said Severall Deeds and what he the said Phillip Ford demanded by the said severall parts of the said Account were both the same and that therefore your Orator Wm Penn the Elder's Executing the Deeds would not barre him from having the Liberty of Examining the said severall parts of the said Account and of having the Severall Errors in them rectified, for that your said Orator had Allways Signed them with Errors Excepted. *But yett* such Deeds were so drawne as to have no relacion to any parts of the said Accounts nor to Each other nor was there any writing Signed by the said P Ford purporting that the said Deeds related {to} any parts of the said Accounts nor to Each other So that according to the Artifices and contrivance of the said Phillip Ford and Bridgett his wife Your Orator Wm Penn {the Elder} Appeared to be Debtour for and his Estate Charged with many more Summes then he really owed or {then} there was any pretence was owing by him to the said Phillip Ford. *And* your said Orator Wm Penn the Elder further Sheweth and so chargeth that the said Bridgett ford knoweth That the said Deeds by your Orator Executed before the said 29th of September 1696 were all brought to him ready ingrossed without any Instruccions given by yr said Orator for the making such deeds and without any previous notice or without any drafts of them tendred to or Left with your Orator for his perusall. And that they were all Executed by your said Orator upon the Confidence and trust~~ing~~ of the honesty and integrity of the said Phillip Ford without ever looking upon any of the Same Deeds or having any ~~Coppys~~ Counterparts or Coppys thereof other then and Except that concerning one of the said Deeds purporting to be an Absolute Conveyance of the said province to the said Phillip Ford and his heirs in Fee and which bears date in Septemr ~~1696~~ {1690} About which Conveyance only the said Phillip Ford did Consult your Orator who was then under the displeasure of the Government,[19] and to induce your said Orator to make that absolute

Conveyance to the said Ford he pretended that he was informed your said Orator had many Enemies and that Allthough he {was} never ~~was~~ so innocent he might be in danger ~~from~~ {from} theire malice, and Advised him for the preservacion of the said Province for his Family to make the said absolute Conveyance thereof to the said Ford and his heires and your Orator Wm Penn the Elder had then so great Confidence in the said Phillip Ford and Apprehended the Representacion of the said Phillip Ford to be so Sincere and So much for your Orators benefitt that your Orator Suffered the said absolute Conveyance to remaine with him the said Phillip Ford without taking any Defeazance[20] thereof from him untill the said 29th day of Septem^r^ 1696.[21] *And* your said Orator the said Wm Penn {the Elder} further Sheweth that he the said Phillip Ford knowing that by his giving the said Deed or writing of the said 29th of September 1696 for inspecting the said Account and the said Defeazance after the said Estate had for the time aforesaid remained absolute in him he had now confirmed and Established himselfe in the good Opinion of your said Orator he the said Phillip Ford together with the said Bridgett his wife did consult and Contrive how they might further defraud your said Orator and gaine from him another Deed that might purport an Absolute Conveyance of y^r^ Orators said province to him the said Phillip Ford and his heirs and for that purpose in the month of Aprill 1697 When a Tax was laid on money att Interest[22] the said Phillip Ford applyed himselfe to your {s^d^} Orator and Acquainted him that he advised with Severall Councels[23] and produced to your said Orator theire Opinions in writing[24] that notwithstanding the Security given for the Summe pretended to be due to him was forreigne yet the parties living in England it was Subject to pay Taxes and therefore entreated your said Orator to make and Convey {to} him the said Ford an Absolute Estate in the said Province & Territoryes telling your Orator that his Councell w~~as~~ere of Opinion that Since noe more money was advanced then what was mencioned in the {said} Defeazance of the 29th of Septem^r^ 1696 ~~frequently~~ {& the interest thereof[25] an Absolute Conveyance so quickly} after the said 29th of September 1696 would keep it Still to be a mortgage and ~~an Absolute Conveyance would~~ not make it other and by these pretences the said Phillip Ford with the privity and knowledge of the said Bridgett his wife prevailed on your ~~said~~ Orator Wm Penn the Elder to execute a release bearing date the 1st day of Aprill 1697[26] being within 2 days after the Sixth months from the s^d^ 29th of Septem^r^ expired[27] whereby (reciting the former Mortgages made in the years 1690 & 1696) Your Orator in Consideracion of 20^s^ is mencioned to Release All his right tytle and Interest in the said Province to the said Ford and his heires, {And} under pretence that the said Phillip Ford Estate in the said Province and Territories might looke the more absolute and by that means he might be the more Effectually Secured against the payment of taxes he the said Phillip Ford and the said Bridgett his wife prevailed on your said Orator to accept a Lease of the Same premisses from him the said Phillip Ford Dated the 2nd day of Aprill 1697 for the terme of 3 years at 630l per annum Rent,[28] And the said Phillip Ford and Bridgett his wife the better to Conceale from your Orator his reall Designe by such Release and Lease of grasping Your said Orators Estate pretended to give your Orator a writing or Deed Poll dated the 10th of the said month of Aprill[29] which the said Phillip Ford called and represented {it} to your Orator Wm Penn the Elder to be a Defeazance of the said release of {the 2nd of} Aprill 1697 and to Declare the Same remained Still a Mortgage, {& that it could not be otherwise construed Whereas after} ~~for thereby~~ reciting that your Orator had Conveyed the said Province to Ford and his heirs and that he had leased it to your Orator for 3 years It is thereby mencioned to be agreed ~~that~~ in Consideracion of the trouble in raising ~~the~~ money That in Case your Orator Wm Penn {the Elder} or his heirs Should pay to the said Phillip Ford for the purchase of the premisses at the house of Samuell Carpenter in Philadelphia 12714:5:0 with the allowance of the Exchange to London before the End of three years next Ensueing then the said Phillip Ford would reconvey the said premisses to your said Orator & his heires which said writing of the {sd} 10th day of Aprill 1697 your said Orator accepted beleiving the Same to be a Defeazance as the said Phillip Ford and his {sd} wife Alledged it was. And that the word Purchase was only inserted to keep the Summe from taxes and the said Bridgett Ford beleives in her Conscience the Same was given only to Fence against taxes *And your Orator* Wm Penn the Elder further Sheweth That the said Release and the Lease and Defeazance of Aprill 1697 were all drawne and ingrossed by the said Phillip Ford and at his Direction and not by any direction from your said Orator who never Saw the Same or any of them or any draft Coppy or minutes of them or any of them untill they were produced by the said Phillip Ford and his said Wife at the Ship Taverne in Gracechurch Street London At the very time they were Sealed and Executed by your Orator Wm Penn the Elder At which place Assoon as your Orator had Executed the {sd} release and a Counterpart of the said Lease and of the said writing or Deed Poll the said Bridgett Ford being present and observing {he} her said husband in a Seeming Extasie of Joy embraced your said Orator and looking on his said wife said to her Law you now (which was his usuall way of expressing himselfe) You thought he would not Doe it or used words to that Effect and also at the same time continuing his Embraces said to your Orator in the presence ~~of~~& hearing of his said wife that what he your said Orator had Done should be noe prejudice to him but he should be in the same Condicion as if he had never Executed the Same Deeds or used words to that or the like effect and did then and at Severall times afterwards owne & Acknowledge to and in the presence and hearing of the said Bridgett Ford that the said last menconed Deeds were made unto him the said Philip Ford in Trust and onely for the purpose aforesaid To Save Taxes {&} that the premisses remained only a mortgage~~d~~ to the said Phillip Ford. *And* your said Orator the said Wm Penn the Elder further Chargeth that the truth is and the said Bridgett Ford knoweth or hath heard & verily beleives that there never was at any time any Summe of money {whatsoever} advanced by the said Phillip Ford to make the Consideracion money Expressed in the said Deeds or any of them but what is mencioned in the said Account and that {All} the Deeds bonds and writings which the said Phillip Ford hath obtained from your {s^{d}} Orator are only for what money should Appeare to be justly due and owing upon an Examinacion of the said Account and rectifying thereof, and relate only to what the said Phillip Ford pretended upon the severall Castings up and ballances of the said Account were at the times of such castings up due to the said Phillip Ford as the then ballance and not for any ~~other~~ Summe or Summes lent or paid your Orator not included in the said Account from the 6th of July 1682 to the 29th Septem^{r} 1696. and yet the said Bridgett Ford though she knows of her owne knowledge how the Consideracion of {all} the said Deeds to the 29th of Septem^{r} 1696 are made and Can Assigne no other Consideracion of them then what is included in the said Account refuseth to discover the Same. *And* your Orators the said Wm Penn the Elder & Wm Penn the Younger further Shew that to prove that the {s^{d}} Deeds and writings made in the ~~said~~ year 1697 were only a mortgage your said Orator the said Wm Penn the Elder did after the making the Same Deeds to the said Phillip Ford, Sell and Convey to divers persons Severall parcells of Land part of the said Province and particularly a Considerable part thereof to your ~~Son~~ Orator {the s^{d}} Wm Penn the Sonn and to Others in Trust for him[30] which was done with the knowledge and privity of the said Phillip Ford deceased and the said Bridgett his wife and neither of them ever pretended to Oppose the Same or {to} Shew the Least dislike thereof as they ought to have done if the said P: Ford had before Such Sales an Absolute Purchase of the lands so Sold by your Orator Wm Penn the Elder for that they knew the Sales and Conveyances of the same were made to purchasers for good and Valuable Consideracions really and truly paid to your Orator Wm Penn the Elder and amongst the rest to your ~~said~~ Orator Wm Penn the Younger for just and Valuable Consideracions who is well Satisfied that your Orator Wm Penn the Elder would not have pretended to have made Such ~~a~~ Sale & Conveyance ~~an~~had he not knowne he had a power (as in truth he *had*) soe to Doe *And* particularly your Orator Wm Penn the Elder further Sheweth that about the month of July 1699 he did not only with the knowledge {& consent} of the said Phillip Ford & Bridgett his said wife but at the Instance and encouragement of the said Phillip Ford (as the said Bridget Ford well knows) treat with Tobias Collett Citizen & haberdasher of London, Michael Russell of London Weaver, Daniell Quiare of London Watchmaker[31] and Henry Goldney of London Linnen draper and Severall other persons for the Sale of a considerable parcell~~s~~ of Land lying in the said province of Pennsilvania and about the 11th day of August 1699 came to an Agreement with them for the same for as much money as {in} the whole amounted to 2000l (of which the said Phillip Ford received only the Summe of 820l or thereabouts) and by the Consent and Privity of the said Phillip Ford your Orator Wm Penn the Elder made and Executed to the said Tobias Collett Michaell Russell Daniell Quiare and Henry Gouldney and their heirs Conveyances of the said parcell of Land[32] part of the said province which was by them soe contracted and Agreed for with your Orator Wm Penn the Elder {as aforesd} And your Orator Wm Penn the Elder {allways ~~having~~} ~~allways~~ Acquainted {the sd} Phillip Ford of the Sale of Such Lands in the said Province As he from time to time sold after the {sd} Conveyance in the yeare 1697, {And} the said Phillip Ford in the said month of July 1699 At his Desire received from your Orator Wm Penn the Elder a list of {the} Severall Sales and Conveyances Your Orator Wm Penn the elder had so made of the Lands part of the said Province And the said Phillip Ford did never pretend to Contradict Such Sales or Conveyances but only desired to know the particulars of them that he might not render his said Mortgage Deficient. And there~~a~~fore the said Phillip Ford ~~said~~ {did Send} to your Orator Wm Penn the Elder a Note of his owne hand writing dated the 11th of August 1699 which is left with your Orators said Clarke in Court, Which your Orators pray the said Bridgett Ford may look upon and Answer whether it is not all the said Phillip Ford's handwriting and which is in the words following, Deare Freind Cannbury[33] the 11th 6mo 99 Please to give my Sonn an Note to Harbtt Springett to add the rest of ~~the~~ Deeds Land ~~I~~ sold by thee that I have not in my List that I had ~~with~~ {from} Harbtt Springett, this with true Love concludes Thy Lo: Friend Phillipp Ford[34] the said Phillip Ford being well Satisfied your Orator Wm Penn might Sell and that the said Phillip Ford had only a Mortgage, and what was Sufficient to Secure All that would appeare due for his said mortgage money *And* your Orators the said Wm Penn the Elder and Wm Penn the Younger further Shew that the said Phillip Ford being Sensible {of his incapacity} of making ~~any~~ Conveyances of any part of the said Province notwithstanding such ~~Con{v}eyey~~ Conveyance to him in 1697 And that by the {sd} Conveyance made in 1697 he was not in truth an absolute Purchaser of the matters therein mencioned and that he Still {in reallity} continued a Mortgagee he the said Phillip Ford did about the 23th day of august 1699 (your Orator the said Wm Penn the Elder being {then} upon taking a voyage for the said province) request your Orator Wm Penn the Elder to Execute to the said Phillip Ford a Letter of Attorney[35] and Leave it with him whereby to impower the said Phillip Ford to Sell any part of your said Orator's Lands Plantacions tenements or ~~h~~ hereditaments whatsoever lying beyond the Seas in the said province of Pennsilvania and East & west new Jersey or any of them which in the Same Letter of Attorney are called your Said Orators Lands and the Authority thereby given is for Sale of them in the name of your ~~said~~ Orator Wm Penn the Elder {&} at the instance of the said Phillip Ford as the said Bridget well knows your ~~said~~ Orator Wm Penn the Elder caused the Same Lettre of Attorney to be made and Sealed and delivered it in the presence of Charles Bissell[36] and George Hinsh[37] who Subscribed theire names thereto as witnesses and afterwards delivered it or caused it to be delivered to the said Phillip Ford who Accepted thereof from your said Orator as the said Bridgett Ford {very} well knoweth. And your Orators further Shew that the said Phillip Ford is lately dead[38] but that before his Death as the said Bridgett Since pretends he made his last Will and testament in writing and thereof the said Bridgett his wife Executrix who hath Since his Death proved the Same in the Prerogative Court of Canterbury[39] *And* he the said Phillip Ford being Conscious of the truth of what is before Sett forth but designing as he did by the said release in 1697 to keep what was due on the said mortgaged premisses from taxes Did by his said will Declare your Orators right of redempcion by mencioning that he did give your Orators said province and Territories to the said Bridgett his wife and to John Hall and Thomas Moss and their heirs upon trust that they and the Survivor of them should within 6 Kallender months next after his Decease or Assoon {after} as they could Sell the Same and in his said will did direct that in case yr said Orator the said Wm P~~a~~enn the Elder should pay to the said trustees the Summe of 11134:8:3 with All Such rent as Should be in Arreare for the premisses and All other debts which should be due to the said Phillip Ford in Such {case} the said Trustees should Convey the Same premisses to the said Wm Penn & his heirs.[40] *And* your Orator Wm Penn the Elder further Sheweth that he was allways ready in the life time of the said Phillip Ford to come to a fair Account with him & to pay him what should ~~j~~appeare to be justly due unto him thereon, So as your Said Orator might have had a reconveyance of the said Province and other the premisses mencioned in the said Deeds & All the Deeds writing bonds Securitys and papers whatsoever which were obtained from yr said Orator by the said Phillip Ford delivered up to him And your said Orator hath oftentimes made the like Offer to the said Bridgett Ford and by this his bill doth Offer to come to a fair Account with her and to pay her and the said John Hall and Thomas Mosse what shall ~~justly~~ appear {to be} justly due by the Said Account of the said Phillip Ford, he your said Orator having an Allowance made him of Such Summes as have been by him paid the said Phillip Ford in his life time Since the said 29th day of September

1696 and to the said Bridgett his Executrix and the rest of the Confederates heerin after named Since his Decease And So as an Allowance & Abatement be made unto your said Orator of All Such Summes of money as Appears upon the face of the said Account betweene your Orator and the said Phillip ~~Ford~~ {Ford} from the said 6th of July 1682 to the said 29th of Septemr 1696 to be unjust and overcharges on your said Orator According to the Liberty given him by the said writing made by the said Phillip Ford Dated {the sd} 29th day of Septemr 1696 for inspecting the Same Account and rectifying All Errors appearing therein *And* your ~~said~~ Orator the said Wm Penn the Elder further chargeth That Since the said Account of Septemr 1696 he hath paid to the said Phillip Ford deceased in his life time and Since his death to the Deft Bridgett Ford and her Trustees and Children or Some of them or Some other of the Confederates heerin after named divers great Summes of money Amounting in the whole to the Summe of 4000l and upwards[41] towards the Discharge of what could be pretended to be due upon the same Account over and besides which your said Orator the said Wm Penn the Elder Soon after the making the Said Deed Poll or Defeazance of the 10th day of Aprill 1697 paid the said Phillip Ford deceased the Summe of 157l in part of the said Mortgage monys[42] in the said Deed Poll of Aprill 1697 mencioned & tooke a receipt for the same under the hand of the said Phillip Ford deceased indorsed on the Same Deed Poll. *And* your Orator WmPenn the Elder further Sheweth that he hoped the said Bridgett Ford & the said other Confederates would have rectified the Errors appearing upon the face of the said Account from the 6th of July 1~~8~~682 to the said 29th day of September 1696 which are amongst others th~~ings~~ese which follow Vizt in that part thereof begining the said 6th day of July 1682 and Ending the 23th Day of August following the Severall Summes of 70l therein mencioned to be Comission money at 2l10s0d per Cent paid the said Phillip Ford himselfe for 2845l ~~but~~ {Sent} in Six Ships to Pennsilvania and of 712l10s therein mencioned to be paid for the halfe Subscription {money} to the Society[43] and 2850:15:1 charged therein for goods not paid for are Overcharges on your Orator Wm Penn the Elder. And in that part of the said Account beginning the said 23th day of August 1682 and ending the said 21th day of March 1684 the Severall Summes following Vizt the Summe of 2851:7:10 therein mencioned to be the ballance due the 23th day of August 1682 for that it Appears by the books and papers of the said Phillip Ford now or late in the Custody or Power of the said Bridgett Ford that the Same or any part thereof was not then advanced by the said Phillip Ford or any way then Due to him and the further Severall Summes of 112:11:0, 101:11:7, and 116:7:4 and 113:11:7 and 134:5:7 Amounting in the whole to the Summe of ~~583~~ {578}:7:1 as Computed by your Orator which in this part of the said Account is charged every Six months by the name of Interest or

Consideracion and the further Summe of 500^{l} therein mencioned to be paid for your Orator for halfe Subscriptions in the Societys Stock, and the further Severall Summes of 48^{l} and $86^{l}3^{s}$ mencioned to be paid for John Songhurst,[44] and the Summe of $500^{l}7$:0 mencioned to be paid for advance money according to the Custome of Merchants and Salary at 6^{d} in the pound are All of them likewise overcharge~~d~~s on this your said Orator Wm Penn the Elder[45] And in that part of the said Account beginning the said 21th day of March 1684 and ending the said 11th day of Aprill 1687 the Severall Summes following are Overcharges on your ~~said~~ Orator Wm Penn the Elder Viz^{t} the Summe of $4293^{l}3^{s}0½^{d}$ therein mencioned to be the ballance due the said 21th day of March 1684 for that the whole or greatest part thereof is made up of the Severall Summes overcharged as aforesaid in the precedent part of the said Account and the further Severall Summes of 18:19:3¼[46] charged for one months Interest of $3792^{l}16^{s}0^{d}$ with $9^{s}6^{d}$ being 6^{d} in the pound for allowing the said Phillip Ford that Summe and the further Severall Summes of $172^{l}10$:0 and of 179:12:1 and 186:18:4 and of 4:12:8 and 194:11:7 and 3:18:6 and 25:7:2 Amounting in the whole to the Summe of 786:19:1½[47] as your Orator Compute~~d~~s in this part of the said Account charged for interest at 8^{l} per Cent per annum computed every 6 months and made principall and the Summe of 200:2:6 mencioned to be paid or allowed to the said Phillip Ford at 6^{d} in the pound for 8004:17:1½ by which computacion the said Phillip Ford hath Reckoned your said Orator 6^{d} in the pound for the whole Debet of the said Account many times And in that part of the said Account beginning the said 11th day of Aprill 1687 and ending the said 11th day of October 1689 the Severall Summes following are overcharges on your said Orator Wm Penn the elder Viz^{t} the Sume of 5282:9:8½ therein mencioned to be the ballance due the said 11th day of Aprill 1687 because that Sume is made up of the severall {Summes} overcharged as aforesaid in the foregoing parts of the said Account and the further severall Summes of 211:6:4½ and 219:15:0½ and 228:10:10:¼ and 237:13:8½ and 247:3:0¼ (amounting in the whole to the Summe of of 1144:9:9½[48] as computed by your Orator) in this part of the $\{s^{d}\}$ Account charged for interest or Consideracion at 8^{l} per cent per annum computed every 6 months and made principall and the Sume of 193:0:6 charged to be paid or allowed to the said Ford himself at 6^{d} in the pound for 7720:19:0¼ for the greatest part whereof the said Phillip Ford hath reckoned 6^{d} in the pound severall times over in the preceding part of the said Account, And in that part of the said Account beginning the said 11th day of ~~Aprill~~ of October 1689 and ending the said 11th day of January 1694 the Severall Sumes following are overcharged on your said Orator Viz^{t} the Summe of 6333:19:2 therein mencioned to be the ballance due the said 11th of October 1689 because it is made up with the Severall Sumes overcharged as aforesaid in the former parts of the said Account: and the further severall sumes of 253:7:2 and 263:9:10 and 274:0:8 and 284:19:10½ and 296:7:10½ and 308:5:0 and 320:11:7 and 333:8:0 and 346:14:9 and 360:12:0 and 187:10:4 Amounting in the whole to the Summe of 3229:7:0½[49] as computed by your Orator in this part of the said Account charged for interest or Consideracion {at} 8^{l} per cent per annum computed every 6 months and made Principall and the Summe of 300^{l} in this part of the said Account charged as due from your said Orator to the said Phillip Ford for Land in Pennsilvania sold by your said Orator[50] and 54^{l} for 2 years and one quarter of a years interest of the said 300^{l} at 8^{l} per cent {per annum} and 10^{l} more for other Land in Pennsilvania sold[51] by your said Orator Wm Penn the Elder And in that part of the said Account beginning the said 11th day of January 1694 and ending the said 1~~2~~1th day of ~~Jan^{r}~~ {June} 1696 the severall Summes following are overcharged on your said Orator Wm Penn the elder Viz^{t} the Summe of 9016:12:5 mencioned to be the ballance due the s^{d} 11: day of Jan^{r} 1694 and the Summe of 1060:16:8½ for the interest or Consideracion thereof for 17 months at 8^{l} per Cent {per annum} and the Summe of 1385[52] for Land in Pennsilvania sold by your Orator And in that part of the s^{d} Account beginning the said 1~~2~~1th day of June {1696} and ending the 29th day of Septem^{r} 1696 the two Sumes following are overcharg[ed] on your s^{d} Orator Viz^{t} the Summe of 10202:8:7½ therein mencioned to be the ballance ~~of~~ due the s^{d} 1~~2~~1th day of June 1696 for that the whole or the greatest part thereof is made of the severall Summes overcharged as aforesaid in the preceding parts of this Account & the Summe of 245:6:10 for the interest thereof at 8^{l} per Cent per Annum from the said 1~~2~~1th day of June to the said 29th day of Septem^{r} 1696. *And* your Orator Wm Penn the Elder expressly chargeth that the particular Summes before Sett forth & charged in the s^{d} Account to be Errors do all Appear upon the face of that part of the s^{d} Account which next preceeds the s^{d} 6th day of July 1682. And of the s^{d} severall other parts of the said Account from the said 6th of July 1682 to the s^{d} 29th of Septem^{r} 1696 & in the s^{d} Coppies of them of the Said Phillip Fords own hand writing & it Appears by the same Coppies that the said fraudulent designe of the said Phillip Ford and Bridgett his wife was carried on & continued to the said 29th of September 1696 and that the same Errors are All of them Such overcharges which ought to be rectified as your Orator is advised in this honourable Court notwithstanding the severall Acts and Conveyances the s^{d} Phillip Ford & Bridgett his wife have obtained from your Orator Wm Penn the Elder to Disguise Shelter and Support them. And that your Orator Wm Penn the Elder ought to have {an Allowance &} an Abatement made unto him for the same upon a faire State and Settlement of the said Account according to the said writing for that purpose given him by the s^{d} Phillip Ford dated the said 29th day of Septem^{r} 1696 and for that (in ~~the~~ a Court of Equity) matters of fraud soe Apparent as the sd Overcharges are in their own nature ought to be Sett aside and releife had against them Especially when the same Errors before mencioned Do Appear upon the face of the said Account which is written and Signed by the said Phillip Ford with his owne proper hand and the sd Errors & all the Evill practices that have been made use of to Shelter and fence against them ought to be discovered and detected by the Oath of the sd Bridgett Ford and the other Confederates and by the inspeccion of the sd Coppys and books of Account of the sd Phillip Ford without any further Evidence or entring into other Examinacions And your Orator Wm Penn the Elder to prevent any pretence that the sd 8l per cent {per annum} charged in the said Accounts ought not to be answered unto by reason of the Penalties in the severall Statutes against usury Doth heerby declare that he will {not} because of the sd unlawfull interest of 8l per cent impeach the sd Securityes obtained from him by the said Phillip Ford ~~deceased~~ but is willing the same Securitys Shall Stand good for so much money as shall upon an Examinacion of the said Accounts Appeare to be justly due only your sd Orator humbly hopeth and insisteth that he be not liable to pay any larger interest then 6l per cent per annum for any Summe which shall Appeare justly owing by him as aforesaid on the said Account *And* your sd Orator Wm Penn the Elder doth particularly insist that an Allowance be made unto him upon the said Account for the said Severall Summes of 712:10:0 & 500l mencioned to be paid as Subscription money to the said Society and for all interest or consideracion your said Orator is charged with for the same for that the said Phillip Ford having procured himselfe to be Treasurer[53] for the said Society being a company or Society of Men trading to and from the said Province of Pennsilvania (who by Articles of Agreemt amongst themselves were formed into a Company and were called the Free Society of traders in Pennsilvania) he the said Phillip Ford under colour of his office received all money paid by any person or persons who were willing to become Adventurers in the said Society and to have an interest therein, And upon receiving the same the said Phillip Ford gave receits for such money as he received under his hand and the Seale of the {sd} Company which receipts gave the persons paying in their money a Title to a Share and interest in the Stock of the said Society and of the proffitts thereof according to the Summe of money paid in And the said Phillip Ford was Entrusted with all books papers and Accounts and Also with the moneys and goods belonging to the said Society and with Severall Title Deeds of Land which were part of the Stock of and belonging to the said Society or Company All which said books papers and Accounts and alsoe the said tytle Deeds and the writings or receipts by which your said Orator ~~was~~ should be entituled to an Interest in the Stock and Trade of the said Society She the said Bridgett Ford now hath or lately had in her hands Custody or Power and retaineth and keepeth them under pretence that She is entituled so to do by reason She is Executrix to her said husband and will not Suffer your said Orator to inspect or peruse the same books papers Accounts and Deeds nor did the s^{d} Phillip Ford in his life time nor hath the said Bridgett his Executrix Since his Decease delivered to your said Orator any writings or receipts Whatsoever to Entitle him to any interest in the Estate Stock and trade of the said Society according to the said Severall Summes of 712^{l}10^{s} {& 500^{l}.} *And* in Case by the books of the said Society it should appeare that the said Phillip Ford deced did advance for your said Orator the said Severall Summes of 712^{l}10^{s} and 500^{l} She the said Bridgett Ford ought to deliver unto your said Orator Wm Penn the Elder such receipts or instruments as may entitule him to a Share or interest in the Stock and proffitts of the said Society in proporcion to the same Summes and to produce the said books papers accounts and writings belonging to the said Society whereby the Value of your Orators interest in the Estate and Stock of the said Society (if he hath any therein) and in the proffitts thereof ~~it~~ doth Appeare and to the intent that ~~she~~ the said Bridgett Ford as Executrix to her s^{d} husband may Account with your said Orator for his part and Share (if any he hath) of the proffitts & advantage arising from the ~~said~~ Stock of the s^{d} Society ~~of~~ {Of} which your said Orator never yet received one penny nor any Allowance for such proffitts in the said Account or otherwise howsoever Altho the said Phillip Ford at the time of his death had and the said Bridgett Ford ~~or~~ & Some of her Children now have in theire or some or one of theire hands 3000^{l} and upwards or some other very great Summe of the Estate Stock and proffitts belonging to the said Society a Share whereof according to the said 712^{l}10^{s} and 500^{l} belong to your Orator Wm Penn the Elder. But now Soe it is may it please your Lordship the said Phillip Ford being Dead the said Bridgett his relict Phillip his Sonn James Ayrey and Bridgett his wife one of the Daughters of the said Phillip Ford deceased Anne Ford and Susanna Ford two other of his Daughters and the said John Hall and Thomas Mosse confederating together amongst themselves and with the rest of the Confederates heerafter ~~mencioned~~ {named} and with divers other persons to ~~other~~ {your} orators unknowne to defraud your Orator the said Wm Penn the younger of his interest in the said province and alsoe to defraud your Orator Wm Penn the ~~younger~~ Elder and to gaine from him th~~ise~~ {s^{d}} whole province of Pennsilvania and the Lands and Territories thereunto belonging and alsoe unjustly and fraudulently to establish the pretended ballance of the said Account Stated the said 29th day of September 1696 and {all interest for the same from the time of ~~the~~ Stating thereof {&} over & besides} the pretended ballance of the said account of the {s^{d}} 29th of Septem^{r} to claime and Demand from your Orator Wm Penn the Elder and his Estate in the said Province the Severall Sumes of 3000^{l} 5000^{l} & 6000^{l} on the severall Mortgages for the same heerafter mencioned and alsoe the said Severall Summes of 6900^{l} & 3447^{l} and 20^{s} being the pretended Consideracion of the said Ind^{r} of release Dated the s^{d} 29th day of Septem^{r} 1696 and ~~the rest of~~ the Severall other Summes heerin after mencioned though all the said Severall Consideracions and Summes of money of the said mortgages are Comprehended and included in the said account from the 6th of July 1682 to the said 29th of September 1696 they the said Bridgett Ford James Ayrey and Bridgett his wife Phillip Ford the Sonn Ann Ford Susanna Ford John Hall and Thomas Mosse doe refuse to come to a fair Account with your ~~said~~ Orator the said Wm Penn the Elder and to take what shall justly Appeare to be due (if any thing) upon an Examinacion of the said Account Stated the said 29th day of September 1696 with the interest thereof and doe insist upon the said Summe of 10347:15:5½ the ballance thereof and interest ~~thereo~~for the same Since that time and also upon the said Mortgages All or Some of them and will not distinguish which of them they claime and which of them ~~therein~~ they wave and which are and which they pretend are not included in the said Account and pretend alsoe that the said Province of Pennsilvania was absolutely Conveyed to the s^{d} Phillip Ford deceased and his heirs in his life time by the said Deed in 1697 for a Summe of 12000^{l} and upwards by him the said Phillip Ford deceased really advanced to your {s^{d}} Orator Wm Penn the Elder besides the {s^{d}} Sume of 10347:1~~6~~5:5½ and the Interest thereof *and* Sometimes they clayme 10000^{l} and upwards as Due to the said Bridgett Ford upon a Stated Account as Executrix to her s^{d} husband, and Sometimes 12000^{l} and upwards as due from the s^{d} province upon One or more mortgages thereof and Sometimes that the said Phillip Ford was a Purchaser of the s^{d} province but whether the ballance {of the s^{d} Account} from the 6th of July 82 to the 29th of Septem^{r} 1696 were a part of such Mortgages or a part of such purchase money or how particularly and distinctly such pretended mortgage monies were made up or the said pretended purchase money the {s^{d}} Bridgett Ford though She was privy and Acquainted with all the Dealings between your Orator Wm Penn the elder and the said Phillip Ford deceased relating to the Said Account and pretended mortgages and purchase~~s~~ she refuseth to Discover, the iniquity of Such her demands being ~~left~~ {best} protected by making them Various and uncertaine *and* therefore your Orator Wm Penn the Elder ought in Equity to have and prayeth~~eerin~~ {a very} destinct discovery {of} what is demanded from him ~~only~~ or his Estates by the said Confederates & how Such demands are founded and really & truly made out *especially* Seeing the s^{d} Confederates pretend that your s^{d} Orator hath from time to time for severall Summes of money pretended to be advanced by the said Phillip Ford deceased besides what is mencioned in the said Account made & Executed to the s^{d} Phillip Ford {deceased} the Severall Deeds heerin after mencioned as mortgages for securing the severall Consideracions therein Expressed and the interest thereof (that is to say) the said Indrs of Lease and release dated the 23th and 24th days of August 1682[54] for Securing the said Summe of 3000l (mencioned to be the Consideracion thereof) and interest with a bond dated the sd 24th day of Augst in the penalty of 6000l Condicioned for performance of the Covenants in the sd Indre of Release and Also an Indre of Demise dated the 10th day of June 1685 of the other part of the said Province for the terme of 5000 Years for Securing the sd Summe of 5000l (mencioned to be the Consideracion thereof) and interest with another bond of the same date in the penalty of 10000l with Condicion for performance of the Covenants in the sd Indre of demise mencioned,[55] And also one other Indr bearing date the 11th day of Aprill 1687 pretended to be a demise of the whole Province for the terme of 5000 Years for Securing the said Summe of 6000l (menconed to be the Consideracion thereof) and interest with another bond of the Same date In the Penalty of 12000l Condicioned for the performance of the Covenants in the sd last recited Indenture of Demise mencioned[56] And alsoe one Deed Poll bearing date the 30th day of August Ano Domini 1690 being as is pretended a release from your sd Orator Wm Penn the Elder of his Equity in ~~his said~~ {the} last mencioned terme of 5000 Years which is pretended to be Assigned by the sd Phillip Ford to One Thomas Ellwood in trust to Attend the Freehold of the sd province[57] And also Indrs of Lease and release bearing date the 2d & 3d days of Septemr 1690 whereby the inheritance of the said Province & other Lands therein mencioned is pretended to be by your sd orator released and Conveyed to the sd Phillip Ford deceased & his heirs for Securing the paymt of {the Summe of} 6900l (mencioned to be the consideracion of the sd Indr of Release) and interest for the same with a bond of the same date with the last mencioned release in the Penalty 13800l with Condicion for performance of the Covenants in the sd last Indr of release mencioned.[58] And Also One other Indr of Release[59] bearing date the 29th day of Septemr 1696 whereby it is pretended Your orator Wm Penn the Elder in Consideracion of the Summe of 6900l and 3447l and 20s hath released All his Equity of redeeming the sd premisses which he had by the last mencioned Indentures of Lease and release made in the sd Yeare 1690 which sd release of the 29th Day of Septemr 1696 is by a Defeazance of the same date[60] mencioned to be a Security for the said severall Summes of 6900l and 3447l & 20s and the interest for the same. And also the sd Confederates pretend your said Orator Wm Penn the Elder did likewise on the 29th day of Septemr 1696 execute to the said Phillip Ford deceased another bond in the penalty of 20000l Condiconed for paymt of the Summe ~~of~~In the said Defeazance Condicioned to be paid,[61] and alsoe a generall release dated the sd 29th day of Septemr 1696.[62] *And* the sd Confederates doe now demand of your sd Orator Wm Penn the Elder and insist that there is due to the s^{d} Bridgett Ford as Executrix as aforesaid the said principall sume of 3000^{l} 5000^{l} and 6000^{l} with theire respective Interest as ~~is~~ mencioned in the aforess^{d} severall Deeds And Alsoe the s^{d} severall Summes of 6900^{l} 3447^{l} and 20^{s} principall money and the interest thereof by vertue of the s^{d} mortgage defeazance and bond bearing date the s^{d} 29th day of Septem^{r} 1696 and pretend that the same mortgage defeazance and bond have no referrence to the said Account stated between your said Orator and the said Phillip Ford deceased And Insist that your said Orator did by the S^{d} Lease and release in the Year 1697[63] convey to the said Phillip Ford in his life time and to his heirs an absolute Estate in the said Province and the Lands and hereditaments therein mencioned for the ~~s^{d}~~ Summe of 12000^{l} or thereabouts advanced for the s^{d} Phillip Ford dec^{d} over & besides the s^{d} Summes before mencioned and further insist upon a great Summe of money pretended to be due for rent of the said province by vertue of the s^{d} Lease[64] *Whereas* the truth is and so your ~~s^{d}~~ orator Wm Penn ₵the Elder chargeth it to be that Altho the said severall Summes before mencioned to be the Consideracion of the s^{d} Severall Deeds are in Such deeds mencioned to be received by your s^{d} Orator yet the s^{d} deeds were given for no other Summe {of money} whatsoever than Such as should Appeare to be justly due to the s^{d} Phillip Ford dec^{d} on the s^{d} account Stated the 29th of Septem^{r} 1696 on a fair Examinacion thereof and that on the same 29th of Sept: 1696 Your Orator Wm Penn the Elder was not indebted unto the s^{d} Phillip Ford deceased in any Summe of money whatsoever other then what should Appear to be justly due on the said Account Stated on that Day and so the said Bridgett ford knows & beleives in her Conscience or hath heard from her said husband Phillip Ford deceased *Yet* he the s^{d} Phillip Ford dec^{d} that he might have an Advantage against your Orator to ~~opprese~~ {opresse} him allways made the s^{d} Deeds without referrence to the s^{d} Account and the severall ballances or castings up thereof and Consideracions of the s^{d} severall deeds allways to disagree except upon the Stating the said whole Account the 29th of Septem^{r} 1696 at which time the s^{d} ballance Of the {s^{d}} whole Account then Stated and the time of Stating the same Account agree with the date of the said Indenture of release then given (which is dated the same 29th day of Septem^{r} 1696) and the consideracions thereof vizt the time of Stating the same Account and the date of the same Ind^{r} of release are both of them the s^{d} 29th day of September and the ballance of the s^{d} Account then Stated and the Consideracion of the same Indenture of release are ~~then~~ brought up to agree in the same Summe which was so contrived & done by the s^{d} Phillip Ford deceased and the s^{d} Bridgett Ford because they then beleived the said Phillip Ford Secure against any Advantage that might be taken agst him by reason of the aforemencioned unjust and usurious charges for that the said Phillip Ford & the said Bridgett Ford had then gained from y^{r} said Orator the s^{d} Wm Penn the Elder the said generall release of All Accions accounts claims & demands. *And* your Orator the s^{d} Wm Penn the Elder further sheweth that the said Phillip Ford dec^{d} in all his transaccions with y^{r} s^{d} Orator being conscious to himselfe that his notorious usury of 8^{l} per cent may make him Lyable to some Penalty by means of the Statutes agst usury in All the writings & deeds he gained from your orator as aforesaid tooke care to cover his said usury with the word Allowance money and never tooke any Covenant from your s^{d} Orator for payment of any Summe of money untill by the s^{d} Defeazance dated the 29th of Septem^{r} 1696 from which time by the same Defeazance he pretends to demand only 6^{l} per cent {per annum Interest}. *And* the s^{d} Wm Penn the Elder further Sheweth that the said Confederates to justifie and maintaine what they so unreasonably insist upon as afores^{d} and to Avoid coming to an Account with your said Orator according to the said Deed or writing dated the s^{d} 29th day of Septem^{r} {1696} and executed by the s^{d} Ford to your Orator which is for Examining the s^{d} Accounts & making an Allowance to your s^{d} Orator for the Errors Appearing upon the same they the said Confederates doe insist that your s^{d} Orator hath released the same deed or writing of the s^{d} 29th day of Septem^{r} 1696 by a Deed or writing under your said Orators hand and Seale in the beginning whereof they pretend is a true Coppy of the same writing of the 29th of Sept. 1696 and that afterwards such release is in the words following Viz^{t} Whereas the above named Philip Ford hath desired me to Deliver him up his originall note whereof the Coppy is here above or else to Assign error if I have found any in the s^{d} Accounts to which the s^{d} Note relates I William Penn do heerby acknowledge that noe Error hath hitherto Appeared in the s^{d} Account and therefore Doe by these presents release & discharge the s^{d} Phillip Ford from the s^{d} note which being mislaid I Cannot at present deliver up as it ought to be but doe promise that when ever the same shall come to my hands I will deliver it up to the s^{d} Phillip Ford or order to be cancelled Witness my hand & Seal in London the 10th day of August 1699[65] which s^{d} writing your Orator Wm Penn the Elder on his parte to Acknowledge & admitt everything that in justice he ought to admitt beleives he did Execute to the s^{d} Phillip Ford deceased about the time of the date thereof but doth insist that the same ought not to be of any force or Effect against your Orator to prevent his having the benefitt of the said writing given him by the s^{d} Phillip Ford {deceased} Dated the s^{d} 29th day of Sept. 1696 for Examining the {s^{d}} Account for that as your Orator Wm Penn the Elder sheweth his Affairs in the s^{d} Province of pennsilvania very much requiring his presence there And the s^{d} Phillip Ford the Elder having often pressed & urged him to goe thither Your s^{d} Orator did in the Year 1699 sometime before the month of August agree with Henry Tregany (master of the Ship called the Canterbury) for the Carrying your Orator his wife daughter severall Servants and a Considerable Cargoe of Goods to the s^{d} Province and that Pursuant to Such Agreem^{t} Your Orator sent his goods ~~to the s^{d} Province~~ and Servants on board the said Ship which according to Agreem^{t} made between him & the s^{d} Master was to Sayle from Portsmouth about the 24th day of August 1699 directly on her Voyage to Pennsilvania afores^{d} And your s^{d} Orator further Sheweth that he & his wife and Daughter being in London about the 16th day of the said month of August 1699 and under an Obligacion to See the s^{d} Phillip Ford the Elder before he went the said Voyage (which the s^{d} Phillip Ford and his wife very well knew) your Orator did about the s^{d} 16th day of Augst goe to the Lodgings of the said Phillip Ford dec^{d} at Islington in the County of Middlesex (he the s^{d} Ford being ille) And After your Orator Wm Penn the Elder had been for sometime entertained by the s^{d} Phillip Ford and his said wife with great Seeming friendship Upon your Orator Wm Penn the Elders ~~goeing way~~ taking Leave of the said Phillip Ford & just upon his goeing {a}way the Same Phillip Ford after some whispering with the s^{d} Bridgett his wife applyed himselfe to and told your Orator in her presence and hearing that he {the s^{d} Phillip Ford} must have up the paper writing he gave your Orator bearing date the 29th of Septem^{r} in the year 1696 whereby the s^{d} Phillip Ford Agreed that All Errors that Should be found in the s^{d} Account before that time between him & your Orator should be rectified ~~and~~ {or} Allowed or to that or the like {or some such} Effect the Phillip Ford {the father} expressed himselfe to your Orator Wm Penn {the Elder} in the presence of the s^{d} Bridgett Ford his wife and in her presence & hearing And your Orator Wm Penn the Elder being at Such demand greatly Surprized and telling ~~him~~ the same Phillip Ford that it was unreasonable for him to require it and that it was impossible then to find such writing it being as your Orator beleived at his house in Sussex he the said Phillip Ford {the father} thereupon declared that your {s^{d}} Orator must give the same Phillip Ford a writing to release the Same paper writing of the s^{d} 29th of Septem^{r} 1696 and the s^{d} Phillip Ford {the father} likewise in the hearing ~~of the said L~~ and presence of his said wife told your Orator Wm Penn the elder that the ~~s^{d}~~ {same} Phillip Ford had prepared and then produced such writing of release And your Orator Wm Penn the Elder replying that by such release the s^{d} writing of the 29th of September 1696 would become of noe use for your Orators examining & inspecting the s^{d} Account And that it was reasonable that the Same writing should continue in force forasmuch as your Orator Wm Penn the Elder had not inspected and perused the said Accounts {or} replyed in words ~~or~~ to that or the like Effect upon which the said Phillip Ford in the presence and hearing of his said wife declared it Should be All One and the same thing if your Orator did not Execute such writing of release And that your Orator Wm Penn the Elder notwithstanding such writing of release should have liberty to Examine the s^{d} Entire Account as afores^{d} begining in ~~2~~1682 and Ending the 29th of Septem^{r} 1696 and to rectifie any Errors therein or to that or the l~~e~~ike effect, And the said Phillip Ford dec^{d} further declared to your s^{d} Orator in the hearing of the said Bridgett his wife that he required such {re}Lease only for Caution without any design thereby to prejudice or conclude yor s^{d} Orator ~~from Wm Penn the Elder~~ from rectifying any Errors in the same Account~~s~~ or to that or the like Effect. And your Orator Wm Penn the Elder upon perusing the s^{d} writing of Release soe produced objected in the presence and hearing of the said Bridgett Ford that the same contained a fallacy and might imply that your Orator ~~Phillip Ford~~ {W^{m} Penn} the Elder upon ~~the~~ {Examining} the said Account had found no Errors or undue Charges therein in mencioning that ~~th~~ noe Errors had appeared to your {s^{d}} Orator in the said account Whereas in truth your Orator Wm Penn the Elder had never Examined inspected or perused any part thereof And that Such Expression might turne to your s^{d} Orators prejudice or to that or the like Effect whereupon the said Phillip Ford declared in the presence and hearing of his s^{d} wife that your Orator might & must trust him and his wife And that as the s^{d} Phillip Ford the Elder had been trusted with the s^{d} absolute Conveyance to him in the year 1690 and notwithstanding such Absolute Conveyance had declared the same 6 years after according to the truth thereof to be only a Mortgage so he and his wife might be trusted with the s^{d} writing of release. And that they would take no advantage of such Release or of any Expression therein or to that or the like Effect And Also Assured your Orator Wm Penn the Elder that as the s^{d} Mortgage or conveyance of the s^{d} Province had been to that time kept private he the s^{d} Phillip Ford the father had taken Care in the making his ~~wife~~ will that the Same should not be known to any person but his s^{d} wife and that if the s^{d} Phillip Ford had dyed between the s^{d} {year of} 1690 & 1696 he had taken Care that contrary to the import of the s^{d} Absolute Conveyance the Lands thereby mencioned to be Conveyed should be only a mortgage {so} he would take ~~up~~ {Care} that notwithstanding such release the s^{d} Account should remain still Subject to have the Errors and undue charges thereof rectified or to that or the like effect but your Orator Wm Penn the Elder Still insisting that it was unreasonable to require him to Execute such release the s^{d} Phillip Ford & his s^{d} wife being Sensible of the Advantage {they had} agst your Orator and the Awe they had over him by its being in the Power of the S^{d} Phillip Ford to have Stopt your Orator from proceeding on his said voyage and to Expose him both here and in Pennsilvania thereby and by publishing the Mortgage of the said Province (which was then Concealed & only knowne to the s^{d} Phillip Ford dec^{d} & Bridgett his wife) he the s^{d} Phillip Ford and his s^{d} wife or the said Phillip Ford in her presence and hearing declared & peremptorily insisted that he the s^{d} Phillip Ford must have the said writing of release So produced by the s^{d}

Phillip Ford ~~deceased~~ to be Executed and Signed by your Orator Wm Penn the Elder. And Declared that your sd Orator Wm Penn the Elder should not goe to Pennsilvania without Executing the Same And Alsoe Declared to your Orator that unlesse that were done he would divuldge the sd mortgage or used words to that or the like Effect Upon which threatnings your Orator Wm Penn the Elder Considering that his goods and Servants were then Shipt on board for the said voyage and the great Losse as well as Disgrace he should undergoe by being hindred from proceeding on the sd Voyage as also ~~o~~If the sd mortgage should be then disclosed, Your Orator Wm Penn the Elder was forced to Signe the said writing of release soe produced by the sd Phillip Ford whereby the said Bridgett Ford now pretends the sd writing of the said 29th day of Sept. 1696 Executed by the said Ford {deced} is discharged[66] And that your {sd} Orator cannot {now} have the Errors in the said Account~~s~~ from the 6th of July 1682 to the 29th day of Septemr 1696 rectified *Whereas* your Orator doth expressly charge & so the truth is that the sd Deft Bridgett {Ford} knoweth that the sd writing of the 10th day of Augst 169~~6~~9 was prepared by her said husband or his Councill And that your Orator was not made Acquainted with it nor was it offered to your Orator or produced untill the very hour it was required by the sd Phillip Ford deced to be Executed And when your said Orator had provided for and {was} ready to Enter upon his ~~said~~ Voyage to Pennsilvania (which he begun About the 25th day of the said month of August 1699) And that the sd Bridgett Ford & her sd husband had contrived the sd writing & that the sd Phillip Ford deceased to enforce the Execucion of the said writing of the 10th of Augst 1699 Did use Such or ~~t~~the like Expressions promises and threats as aforesaid and doth verily beleive in her Conscience that your Orator Wm Penn the Elder executed the Same upon the Promise and Declaracion of the sd Phillip Ford deced that it Should not prejudice or Conclude him from ~~having~~ rectifying the Errors in the sd Account or having an Allowance made him of All Errors therein And that all matters should be in the same Condicion as if your {Orator} Wm Penn the Elder Did not Execute the same And that the threats of the sd Phillip Ford deceased to hinder your sd Orator from goeing to Pennsilvania and to Disclose the said Mortgage unless he Executed the sd writing of the 10th day of Augst 1699 & the fear your {~~sd~~} Orator Wm Penn the Elder was under thereby of ~~the~~ losse as well as Disgrace compelled & prevailed on him to Signe & Execute the Same writing And for these reasons your sd Orator humbly Hopes the Same shall not be made use of or Sett up agst him ~~to~~ {to} hinder him from releife against the sd Extravagant Account & the Errors & undue charges thereof but that the same writing of release being gained by the threats circumvention Surprize & ille practices aforesd shall be Sett aside. *And your* ~~sd~~ Orator Wm Penn the Elder further Sheweth that the sd Confederates further to colour &

Strengthen their most unjust and unreasonable claims & to avoid coming to {a} fair ~~End~~ and reasonable account ~~that~~ insist that an Account Of rent was Stated between your Orator & the sd Bridgett Ford as Executrix to the sd Phillip Ford begining the 1st day of Aprill 1697 & ending the 1st day of Aprill 1702 and that a writing or instrumt under the same Account was reciprocally Signed & Sealed between your sd Orator & the sd Bridgett Ford & witnessed by the sd Jno Hall & Thos Mosse ~~a~~which as they pretend is in the words or to the Effect following[67] Vizt I William Penn of Worminghurst in the County of Sussex Esqr Do heerby declare that I have Considered & Examined the Accounts here above written which I ~~said~~ {find} to be just and true and Do acknowledge that the ballance thereof being 591:8:10 Sterling Lawfull money of England is by me the sd Wm Penn really & bona fide due & owing to Bridgett Ford widdow as She {is} entituled thereto by the last will and testamt of her late husband Phillip Ford deceased And doe promise to pay the said Summe of 591:8:10 Sterling to her or her order at Demand ~~at her~~ Accordingly at her now dwelling house in Water Lane London Also I do heerby acknowledge that the rent of the premisses is 630l Sterling per annum as is here above (in the particulars of this Account) mencioned Witness my hand & Seal in London this 2d day of Aprill And in the first year of the reigne of Queen Anne Ano Domini 1702 Which said writing your Orator beleives he might Execute about the time of the date thereof and the sd Confederates insist that the word rent hath Established the sd Account & turned All the sd mortgages into a Purchase of the province of Pennsilvania. *But your* sd orator expressly chargeth as the truth is that the sd Bridgett Ford Jno Hall Tho: Moss and the rest of the sd Confederates well know that the said Writing was drawn by them or by Some of their Procuremt & that before the sd Account of 1702 & the writing under it was Signed & Sealed by your sd Orator Wm Penn the Elder he made many Objeccions Against doeing thereof & particularly agst Signing ~~of~~ it as an Account of rent & did insist that the sd Conveyance made in the yeare 1697 & the Lease then Accepted by him from the sd Phillip Ford the Elder were made only for the Saving taxes to the sd Ford {the father} & that it would be very hard if what your Orator intended as a kindness to the said Ford deced for Saving him the Tax & complying wth him for that Purpose only should be made use of as an Absolute Conveyance {or to that or the like Effect} & therefore your Orator Wm Penn the Elder refused to Signe & Seale the sd writing but upon Condicon that the same should not Conclude your sd Orator or be a barr unto him from Examining into and having the Errors in All the severall parts Of the said Account rectified & that the word rent mencioned in the Same account should not be construed to make the sd Confederates Estate in the ~~sd~~ premisses absolute or otherwise prejudiciall to yr Orator And the sd Confederates Bridgett Ford John Hall and Thomas Mosse some or One of them know that your sd Orator Signed and Sealed the Same account of 1702 upon the Condicion aforesd or upon some Condicon or provisoe to that or the like Effect & not otherwise And that they some or One of them know that he did at the time of his Sealing the said Account and writing under it & before he Signed the Same declare that he Executed it with a reservacion to himselfe to make ~~the~~ {his} Objeccions to all former Accounts between him & the sd Ford deceased & that all Errors in them Should be rectified and that he should not become a Tennant to the sd Bridgett Ford John Hall & Tho. Mosse or any of them or any other person for the sd province and premisses {as having an Absolute Estate therein wthout yr Orator redempcion} or used words to that or the like Effect & before your Orator Wm Penn the Elder executed the same Writing that he Expressed a very great disatisfaccion at the Same account and writing {&} utterly refused to Execute the same unlesse the sd Bridgett Ford would accept {it} on such or the like Condicions as aforesd And that the sd Bridgett Ford was very well contented therewith & upon Such condicions & not otherwise Accepted from yr sd orator {Wm Penn} the Elder the Same account & writing under it And that She the sd Bridgett Ford at the same time executed a Counterpart or Duplicate thereof to your sd Orator And the sd John Hall knoweth your sd Orator executed the Same Account and writing under it noe otherwise {then} on the Condicions as aforesd upon the Advice of the sd Hall & upon the sd Halls Saying that he would do the Same thing himselfe as your Orator had done if guarded and defended by the said Condicions agst prejudice to himselfe or used words to that or the li~~f~~ke Effect. And your Orator the Sd Wm Penn the Elder further Sheweth That the sd Bridgett Ford and the rest of the said Confederats Do Also Sett up the said will of the said Phillip Ford deceased in Opposicion to your Orator & pretend that since your Orators said Estate is by the said will given and disposed of as aforesd the Same Shall be Sold & the money thereby raised shall be paid as the sd will directs without any hindrance from your orator or any Account to be given him of the money which they intend to raise by Such Sale *And* further to entangle your said Orator & his sd Estate the said Confederats pretend that a Comission of Bankrupty hath been awarded agst the sd James Ayrey directed to Francis Atterbury & Osborne Fish Esqrs Joshuah Hattfeild Thomas Clendon Wm Collyer and John Cole Gentlemen who have declared the sd Ayry to be a bankrupt within {the} Severall Statutes made concerning Bankrupts Some or One of them and have Assigned over his Estate to Wm Moore Samuell Rose Wm Clarkson and Edward Woodcock and particularly a Legacy of 1500l pretended to be given to the sd Bridgett his wife by her sd Fathers will which they demand of your sd Orator Wm Penn the Elder his sd Estate of Pennsilvania being as they pretend charged by the sd Will of the said Ford deceased with such Legacy and Sometimes threatnen ~~him~~ to Compell him to pay the Same for the benefitt of the Creditors of the sd James Ayrey Altho the truth is as your Orator Expressly charged that your said Orator long time before the sd Ayrey became a bankrupt Did by the direccion of the sd Bridgett Ford John Hall and Thomas Mosse pay unto the sd James Ayrey the Summe of 500l and upwards[68] in part of the sd Legacy given by his sd wife by her said fathers Will which your Orator craves may be allowed him as paid towards the Discharge of such money As Shall Appeare to be justly due On the said Account of the 29th of Septemr 1696 and for which mony so paid the sd John Hall on your sd Orators behalfe hath taken receipts or other notes or discharges from the sd James Ayrey which are now in the hands or Custody of the sd John Hall or some of the rest of the sd Confederates. *And the* sd Comissioners & the sd Wm ~~Rose~~ Moore Samuel Rose Wm Clarkson and Edward Woodcock Do Absolutely Refuse to Suffer your said Orator to redeem his sd Estate upon paymt of what on a just Account Shall Appear to be due from him And do intend thereby to defeat your Orator Wm Penn the younger of his Interest in the said premisses *And further* to Entangle & vex your ~~said~~ orator the sd Wm Penn the Elder the sd Bridgett Ford notwithstanding the sd pretences that the sd Province of Pennsilvania was absolutely sold to the sd Phillip Ford deceased in Hillary terme last[69] caused your Orator Wm Penn the Elder to be arrested in an Accion at the Common Law for the Summe of 20000l in the Court of Exchequer in Westminr at the Suit of the sd Bridgett Ford Executrix[70] to her said husband as if the Same were only mortgaged by one or severall mortgages and ~~Still~~ holds him to Bayle And as a further pretence that the same is mortgaged in Michaelmas Terme 1705 by the contrivance of the said Bridgett Ford and the rest of the sd Confederates a Bill was Exhibited into this honourable Court[71] in the names of the sd Phillip Ford the Son ~~of~~ James Ayrey and Bridgett his wife Anne & Susana Ford Complainants in which bill the said Bridgett Ford John Hall & Thomas Mosse are all made Defts by their owne Direccions with design to compell a Sale of your sd Orators Estate & interest in the Sd Province of Pennsilvania & to Extinguish your Orators right & Equity of redempcion of the sd premisses To which Bill your Orators have put in their Answer[72] and thereby Asserted their right and title to the sd Province & premisses & setting forth {the} said manifest frauds & injurys done to your Orator Wm Penn the Elder & how he was imposed on by the sd Phillip Ford the Elder with the Contrivances of the sd Bridgett Ford And as the sd Phillip Ford {deceased} greatly injured and Oppressed your Orator by the repeated & multiplyed Errors in the sd Account and by the multitude & Variety of the sd Conveyances *soe the* sd Confederates & Especially the sd Bridgett Ford {& Phillip Ford her sonn} Endeavours to Oppresse and vex your Orator as much as Possibly with multi~~d~~tude & variety of Accions thereby to force him to comply with their unreasonable Demands have caused your Orator Wm Penn the Elder to be Arrested and held to bail in foure Severall Accions in the Court of Common Bench at Westm^r^ by processe returnable in Hillary terme next One of which Accions is at the Suite of the s^d^ Bridgett Ford for 8625^l^ debt[73] another at the Suit of her & the s^d^ Jno Hall and Thomas Mosse for 4000^l^ debt[74] and Another at the Suit of the said Bridgett Ford only for 1890^l^ debt[75] And the fourth {is an} Accion of Covenant at the Suit of the s^d^ Bridgett Ford Damage 2000^l^ [76] All which All Accions as well that in the Exchequer as those in the Common Pleas the said Confederates threatnen to prosecute and recover from your Orator the severall Summes for which the s^d^ Accions are brought and besides that to Sell & dispose of your Orators s^d^ Province for their owne benefitt {~~and~~And the s^d^ Bridgett Ford & Phillip her Son or one of them have or hath very lately given out in Speeches that is no other ways to force your Orator Wm Penn the Elder to comply with them then by having him ~~a~~ in Goale or {have used [?] Speeches} to that or the like Effect} And your Orators Expressly Charge that the s^d^ Bridgett Ford the Executrix in her s^d^ husbands life time was privy to all the transaccions between her s^d^ husband & your Orator Wm Penn the Elder & privy to and contriving ~~of~~ all the unjust charges in the s^d^ Severall parts of the s^d^ Account betweene them as is before particularly mencioned And that She assisted her s^d^ husband in making his s^d^ Account and in contriving to charge your s^d^ Orator the s^d^ Wm Penn the Elder with the Severall usurious and unreasonable Charges contained therein & was very instrumentall in perswading your Orator the said Wm Penn the Elder to sign the s^d^ Account and to Seale the s^d^ writings & Deeds and especially the s^d^ writing of the 10th of Aug^st^ 1699 and very well knows that your {s^d^} Orator was never indebted to her said husband in any Summe whatsoever besides such as may Appeare to be due on a fair Stating of the said Account & {that} the s^d^ severall Deeds and Securitys were given by y^r^ s^d^ Orator & so Accepted by the s^d^ Phillip Ford deced ~~wh~~ only for Securing what Should on Examining the s^d^ Account Appeare to be justly due and that alltho the s^d^ Severall Summes before mencioned are Expressed to be the Consideracion of the s^d^ respective Deeds or Securitys yet At the Sealing such deeds or at any other time no Summe of money whatever was ever p^d^ by the s^d^ Phillip Ford deceased to your s^d^ Orator or for his use as the Consideracion of such Deeds or any of them then what is mencioned in the s^d^ Account between them And that your s^d^ orator Signed the said Severall parts of the s^d^ Account & Executed the s^d^ Severall deeds out of the great confidence he had in the~~e~~ {~~s^d^~~} pretended honesty of the s^d^ Phillip Ford & without perusall examinacion or seeing any Vouchers touching the matters in the s^d^ severall parts of the s^d^ Account Specified and that her s^d^ husband in her hearing often declared that he would take no advantage of what your s^d^ Orator {So} Signed or Sealed being Subscribed Condicionally only & with an Excepcion of Errors to be at any time rectified and open and that the s^{d} writings were to be a Security for the ballance which on an Examinacion should Appeare to be justly due on the said Account And the s^{d} Bridgett Ford also very well knows that the s^{d} release given & the Lease Accepted by your Orator Wm Penn the Elder in the year 1697 were only under colour & a trust & were prepared by the said Phillip Ford & Executed to Save him from Paym^{t} of taxes for the money pretended to be due to him and were never intended to be a badge of the s^{d} Phillip Fords Purchase or to bring your s^{d} orator under the disadvantage of being a reall Tennant to & for his own Estate & Inheritance which your Orator chargeth is of tenn times the Value of any Sume of money {ever} pretended to be due to the s^{d} Phillip Ford deced And what money your s^{d} Orator at any time paid to the s^{d} Phillip Ford ~~to the s^{d} Phillip Ford~~ Since the 2^{d} day of Aprill 1697 in his life time or to the said Bridgett his Executrix {Since his decease} amounting in the whole to the s^{d} Summe of 4000^{l} and upwards & the s^{d} Summe of 500^{l} paid to the s^{d} James Ayrey was to be deemed as part of what should be found justly due to the s^{d} Phillip Ford deceased or to the s^{d} Bridgett or any person Since his death on the s^{d} whole Account ending the s^{d} 29th day of September 1696 with such reservacion to your Orator as afores^{d} And that your s^{d} Orator entirely trusted the said Phillip Ford {deceased} with the transacting & making up the s^{d} Severall parts of the said Account of 1696 without reading or examining the same and Sealed the s^{d} Writings on presumpcion the s^{d} Account was true and on her & her husbands Affirmacions that if any Errors miscomputacions wrong demands mistake or overcharges Should thereafter Appeare (Errors being Excepted) both the s^{d} account and the s^{d} Deeds were all Lyable to be rectified And Also She well~~s~~ knows and the rest of the s^{d} Confederates beleive that your Orators Estate in Pennsilvania was no otherwise Lodged in the s^{d} Phillip Ford dece^{d} by all or any of the s^{d} Writings or Deeds but as a Security redeemable on payment of what Should Appear justly due on the s^{d} Account And as an Evidence that the s^{d} Estate of the s^{d} Province vested in the s^{d} Phillip Ford deceased was only a Mortgage *the s^{d}* Confederates Some or One of them knew that your Orator Wm Penn the Elder in the s^{d} Account of 1702 is charged the Summe of 13:15:0 Quitt rent for Newcastle part of the s^{d} Province or the territoryes thereunto belonging All which or the greatest part thereof did accrew or become due since the said Conveyance made to the s^{d} Phillip Ford deceased in the year 1697 {And the s^{d} Bridgett Ford Bridget Ayrey & Phillip Ford the Sonn do know} and the rest of the said Confederates Do beleive that your s^{d} Orator was forced to Execute the said writings or release Dated the s^{d} 10th day of August 1699 by the threats and undue practices of the s^{d} Phillip Ford deceased and his Said wife as is before Sett forth & that the s^{d} Phillip Ford deceased at the Executing thereof promised yr sd Orator that it should not prejudice him & that yr your sd Orator {should} notwithstanding such release have the liberty of Examining the sd Account according to the ~~sd~~ liberty given him by the sd Phillip Ford deceased under his hand & Seale dated the sd 29th of Sept. 1696 and that the sd Mortgage or Conveyance of the sd Province should be kept private And they the sd Bridgett Ford Phillip Ford the Son Bridgett Ayrey and the rest of the sd Confederates well know that the sd Phillip Ford deced accepted from yr sd orator the sd Letter of Attorny dated the sd 23th day of August 1699 or Some other such like authority from yr sd orator Wm Penn the Elder All which ~~writings~~ {Actings} and doeings of the said Bridgett Ford & the sd other Confederates are contrary to Equity & good Conscience In tender Consideracion of all which matters and forasmuch as your Orators Witness to prove all and every the Allegacions and charges before sett forth are either dead or in parts beyond the Seas remote {&} unknown to your sd Orators So that they cannot have the benefitt of their Testimony nor are your orators releivable in the premisses but in a Court of Equity before your Lordpp where frauds breach of trust unjust Accounts oppressions & evill practices are discoverable & remediable To the ~~the~~ End therefore that the sd Confederates & particularly the sd Bridgett Ford may {sett forth &} discover All the {sd} matters and charges of your Orator's {sd} bill as it particularly repeated {& interrogated}[77] and more Specially {th~~ate~~ sd Bridgett Ford may Sett forth & discover} or produce upon Oath before the one of the Masters of this honourable Court[78] All and Singuler the books papers accounts memorandums bills of parcell invoyces receipts & papers whatsoever which concerne or relate to any Accounts and Dealings between your sd Orator & the said Phillip Ford deceased And alsoe All Such as doe any way relate to the ~~sd~~ persons now or formerly called the Free Society of Traders in Pennisilvania and may produce and Shew forth the Same for your sd Orator Wm Penn the Elder to peruse and Examine & especially to see if there were any Such Summes as 712:10:0 and 500l in the said Account before mencioned paid by the sd Phillip Ford deceased for your said Orator or o~~r~~n his Account to the said Society that thereby your sd Orator may discover what interest he hath in the Stock Estate and Effects of the said Society and if any Appeare that the sd Bridgett Ford & the rest of the sd Confederates may either deliver to your sd Orator All such receipts Deeds writings and Papers which may intitule your sd Orator Wm Penn the Elder to the said 712l 10s & 500l or that She & the rest of the sd Confederates may Answer & pay your sd orator the sd moneys with interest for the Same as this honourable Court shall think meete And that the sd Confederates & especially the sd Bridgett Ford Phillip Ford & Bridget Ayrey may Sett forth and discover whether the sd Phillip Ford deceased did not Execute unto your sd Orator Wm Penn the Elder Such writing dated the 29th day of Septemr 1696 whereby your sd Orator had a liberty of Examining the s^{d} account then Stated and whether your Orator Wm Penn the Elder was not forced to give Such ~~a~~ release thereof dated the 10th day of Augst 1699 by the threats and Contrivance of the said Phillip Ford {dec^{d}} imediately before your orators last voyage to Pennsilvania & in particular if the same was not gained from your s^{d} Orator at Canbury house in Islington or where Else & by what means And if the said Phillip Ford deceased did not threatnen your s^{d} Orator that unless he Executed the s^{d} release he the said Ford would hinder your Orator from going his s^{d} Voyage & would divuldge the incumbrances of the said province which he had gained from your said orator or used the like threats to induce your s^{d} Orator Wm Penn the Elder to Execute the Same And that they the s^{d} Bridgett Ford Phillip Ford {&} Bridgett Ayrey may and the rest of the s^{d} Confederates may Sett forth and discover whether the s^{d} Phillip Ford deceased did not Accept from your s^{d} Orator a Letter of Attorney dated the said 23th day of August 1699 or wh^{t} other letter of Attorny for Selling ~~goods~~ your ~~s^{d}~~ Orators {s^{d}} Land in Pennsilvania and transacting his Affairs during Your Orators absence there[79] {& that the s^{d} Confederates may} Sett forth and Discover all Such Deeds as they or any of them have in their hands which your Orator {W^{m} Penn the Elder} hath Executed to Severall Persons for Severall parcells of Land in the s^{d} Province who have not paid their purchase money & deliver the Same Deeds to your orator Wm Penn the Elder which Deeds were intrusted with the s^{d} Phillip Ford deced for him to deliver ~~on~~to ~~p~~the Purchasers on paym^{t} of their Purchase money & in case of their not paying thereof to returne the same back to your said Orator And that All the s^{d} Confederates may Sett forth & discover their Severall Titles claims & demands of in to and out of the s^{d} premisses & how & for what Consideracion the same was ~~p~~made contrived or created And that the s^{d} Confederates may come to fair {& just} Account wth your s^{d} Orator Wm Penn the Elder touching all the matters afores^{d} And that on your s^{d} Orators paym^{t} of what money Shall upon such Account Appeare to be justly due to them or any of them your orators may be decreed to redeeme~~d~~ the premisses and that the s^{d} Confederates & all others claiming under the s^{d} Phillip Ford deced may be compelled to reconvey to your said orators & their heirs according to their respective Estates tytles & interests therein or to Such person~~s~~ or persons as {they} shall Appoint All & Singular the said premisses freed & discharged of & from ~~all~~All and every the incumbrances aforesaid & all claime ~~of~~ {&} pretence of them or any of them And that the said Bridgett Ford may Answer if she was not Consenting that the s^{d} Bill should be brought Agst her & your s^{d} orators for ~~theire~~ {her} owne benefitt and if the said Severall Suites commenced against your Orator Wm Penn the Elder at Common Law are not for money or Some Cause of Accion pretended to Accrew ~~pretended to Accrew~~ unto her or Some other of the Confederates for ~~making~~ matters and things contained in the s^{d} account and Deeds or Some of them and which of them in particular And that all & every the said Confederates may true and perfect answer make to all and Singular the sd premisses & matters before Sett forth and Charged in this your Orators Bill of Complaint and that there may be an Injunccion awarded to Stay the sd Proceedings at Law commenced against your sd Orator Wm Penn the Elder at the Suit of the sd Bridgett Ford John Hall and Thomas ~~or~~ Mosse or {any or} either of them.[80] May it ~~thereof~~ please your Lordship the premisses Considered to grant unto your ~~said~~ orators her Majesty more gracious Writt or Writts of Subpoena to be directed to them the Said Bridgett Ford Phillip Ford the Younger James Ayrey and Bridgett his wife Anne Ford Susannah Ford John Hall Thomas Moss Francis Atterbury Osborne Fish Thomas Clendon John Cole Joshuah Hattfeild William Moore Samuell Rose Wm Clarkson Edwd Woodcock [blank] and the rest of the said Confederates when discovered thereby Commanding them and every of them at a certaine day and under a certaine pain therein to be limitted personally to be and Appeare before your Lordpp in this honourable Court then and there to answer to All and Singuler the premisses And further to Stand to Abide performe & fullfill such order & Decree therein as to your Lordpp shall Seeme meet and just.

And your orators shall Ever pray &c.

G Pauncefort[81]

D. Penn Papers, Ford vs. Penn, HSP. (*Micro.* 12:602.) The document also contains numbers from 1 to 237 in the margin which mark folios at every 72 words.

1. In a draft Bill of Complaint (*Micro.* 12:544), WP describes Ford as a man of "little or noe estate or meanes to maintain himselfe or family haveing formerly been a schole Mar." At another time, WP claimed that Ford's original annual salary was £12. *Micro.* 13:273.

2. Twelve of Ford's early accounts with WP have been found. Accounts nos. 1-6 (19 Apr. 1672-7 July 1674) and nos. 12-17 (27 Apr. 1677-9 Mar. 1680) are printed in *PWP,* 1:577-645. Unfortunately, except for an account of expenditures towards revoking Gov. Fletcher's commission (4 July 1694-23 Jan. 1695), printed in *PWP,* 3:666-70, all of Ford's accounts itemizing debits and credits from Mar. 1680 onward are missing. Each of the surviving 13 accounts is in Ford's hand, with the closing notation "Errors Excepted" and his signature.

3. In the draft bill (*Micro.* 12:544), WP lists the amount of the purchases and the ships in which they were sent: £524 13s 1d in the *John and Sarah;* £292 15s 5d in the *Hester and Hannah;* £307 17s in the *Amity;* and £75 10s 3d in the *Samuel.*

4. In addition to the items listed in n. 3, above, Ford also purchased goods worth £201 6s 9d, sent by Robert Hopper, and goods worth £1448 12s 7d sent in the *Welcome* (*Micro.* 12:544). According to WP, Ford charged an illegal commission on goods he purchased on WP's behalf.

5. See *PWP,* 2:293-95.

6. Actually Oct. 1684 (ibid., 2:604).

7. In the draft bill (*Micro.* 12:544), WP states that "all or the greatest part" of the £8198 was paid to Ford by the end of Dec. 1682.

8. That is, WP would put an end to the enquiry and agree to pay what he owed based on the Ford accounts "with errors excepted."

9. WP embarked on the *Welcome* during the week of 27 Aug. 1682. See *PWP,* 2:290-91; *Micro.* 3:584, 595.

10. In fact, WP did not leave London for Deal until 26 Aug. 1682. WP's meeting with the Fords almost certainly took place in London, not Deal. See *PWP,* 2:292n.

11. In final form, ready to be signed.

12. See *PWP,* 2:291-93.

13. None of these accounts has been found.

14. See ibid., 3:661.

15. This document has not been found.

16. Unidentified.

17. See *PWP,* 3:659-60.

18. It is difficult to determine how WP arrived at this figure, which varies from estimates he gives elsewhere. In doc. 108 the Fords claim that WP valued Pennsylvania at £30,000.

19. In 1690 WP was suspected by the government of William III of plotting the return to England of James II. See *PWP,* vol. 3.

20. An instrument which defeats the force or operation of some other deed or estate (*Black's Law Dictionary,* p. 376). In this instance, the lack of a defeasance enabled Ford to have absolute control of Pennsylvania without providing WP with the right of repurchase.

21. See *PWP,* 3:660-61.

22. Late in 1696 parliament passed an Act for Granting an Aid to His Majesty (8 Will. III, cap. 6), part of which called upon all persons who had interest-bearing loans outstanding to pay 25s for every £100 loaned in 12 monthly installments beginning 25 Feb. 1697. The act did not include arrears of rent.

23. Apparently, the lawyers who provided the opinion were John Darnall and Sir Creswell Levinz. See *Micro.* 13:194.

24. This has not been found.

25. By the defeasance, WP was to pay Philip Ford £10,657 on 30 Mar. 1697.

26. See *PWP,* 3:661.

27. See ibid., 3:660-61.

28. See ibid., 3:662.

29. See ibid.

30. The editors have not located any conveyances of Pennsylvania land to William Penn, Jr., after 1697, until WP's 1703 conveyance of Pennsbury to his son (see doc. 209D, G, I). For sales WP did make 1697-1702, see *Micro.* 8:070 and n. 32, below.

31. Daniel Quare (1648-1723) was a prominent London Quaker clockmaker, who became a master of the Clockmaker's Company in 1708. Fox, *Short Journal,* p. 339.

32. See *Micro.* 8:089. The purchasers were known collectively as the London Company. See doc. 56, n. 25.

33. Canonbury, now part of the north London borough of Islington.

34. This has not been found.

35. See *PWP,* 3:662.

36. Unidentified.

37. Unidentified.

38. Philip Ford died on 8 Jan. 1702.

39. Bridget Ford did not probate the will until 4 Oct. 1705.

40. Here WP conveniently omits any mention that Ford also insisted that this clause was not to be construed as giving him any equity of redemption beyond this six-month period.

41. The Fords, in their answer to WP's second Bill of Complaint (see *Micro.* 13:147), conceded that he paid at least £3800. See Chancery, Reynardson's Division, bundle 183, #40, PRO.

42. See *PWP,* 3:542-43. The exact payment was £157 10s, representing one-quarter of the annual rent.

43. The Free Society of Traders. See *PWP,* 2:246-56.

44. John Songhurst (d. 1689), a carpenter from Chiltington, Sus., was a First Purchaser who immigrated to Philadelphia. See *PWP,* 2:336n.

45. In his draft Bill of Complaint (*Micro.* 12:544), WP provides the dates on which Ford charged these amounts and the manner in which the interest rates were calculated: £112 10s, charged on 23 Feb. 1683, was six months' interest on £3765; £101 11s 7d, charged on 23 Aug. 1683, was six months' interest on £3386; £116 7s 4d, charged on 23 Feb. 1684, was six months' interest on £3879; £113 11s 7d, charged on 23 Aug. 1684, was six months' interest on £3786; £134 5s 7d, charged on 23 Feb. 1685, was six months' interest on £4476. The £500 was charged on 2 Apr. 1684, the two payments by John Songhurst were charged on 14 Mar. 1685, as was another £56 5s; the advance money of £500 7s was charged on 21 Mar. 1685.

46. In his draft bill (*Micro.* 12:544), WP has £19 3s 9½d.

47. In his draft bill (ibid.), WP provides the dates on which Ford charged these amounts and the manner in which the interest was calculated: £172 10s, charged on 23 Sept. 1685, was six months' interest on £4312 11s; £179 12s 1d, charged on 21 Mar. 1686, was six months' interest on £4489 19s 8½d; £186 18s 4d, charged on 21 Sept. 1686, was six months' interest on £4677 18s 9d; £4 12s 8d was consideration money for six months; £194 11s 7d, charged on 21 Mar. 1687, was six months' interest on £4864 9s 9d; £3 18s 6d was consideration money for six months; £25 7s 2d, charged 9 Apr. 1687, was consideration money for 21 days on £5062 19s 10d; £200 2s 6d, charged 11 Apr. 1687, was advance money based on 6d in the pound on £8000 17s 1/2d.

48. In his draft bill (ibid.), WP provides the dates on which Ford charged these amounts and the manner in which the interest was calculated: £211 6s 4½d, charged on 11 Oct. 1687, was six months' interest on £5282 9s 8½d; £219 15s 9½d, charged on 11 Apr. 1688, was six months' interest on £5493 16s 1½d; £228 10s 10¼d, charged on 11 Oct. 1688, was six months' interest on £5713 11s 2d; £237 13s 8½d, charged on 11 Apr. 1689, was six months' interest on £5942 2s 1/4d; £247 3s 10¼d, charged on 23 Aug. 1689, was six months' interest on £6179 15s 8¾d; £193 6d, charged on 11 Oct. 1689, was advance money based on 6d in the £ on £7720 19s 1/2d.

49. In his draft bill (ibid.), WP provides the dates each sum was charged: £253 7s 2d on 11 Apr. 1690; £263 9s 10d on 11 Oct. 1690; £274 8d on 11 Apr. 1691; £284 19s 10½d on 11 Oct. 1691; £296 7s 10½d on 11 Apr. 1692; £308 5s on 11 Oct. 1692; £320 11s 7d on 11 Apr. 1693; £333 8s on 11 Oct. 1693; £346 14s 9d on 11 Apr. 1694; £360 12s on 11 Oct. 1694; and £187 10s 11d on 11 Jan. 1695.

50. Land sold during the years 1691-93. See ibid.

51. For 300 acres purchased by John Everet. See ibid.

52. In his draft bill (ibid.), WP has £979 15s. In his later complaints of Ford overcharges, WP states that he sold £2000 worth of Pennsylvania land, and paid Ford £615 of this. Ford then charged him the remaining £1385. See doc. 121C.

53. The Fords later denied that their father had ever acted as treasurer of the Free Society of Traders. See Chancery, Reynardson's Division, bundle 183, #40, PRO.

54. See *PWP*, 2:291-93.

55. See ibid., 3:658.

56. See ibid.

57. See ibid., 3:658-59.

58. See ibid., 3:659-60.

59. See ibid., 3:660.

60. See ibid., 3:660-61.

61. See ibid., 3:661.

62. See ibid.

63. See ibid., 3:661-62.

64. In 1707 Bridget Ford, John Hall, and Thomas Moss were awarded a special verdict in the court of Common Pleas against WP for back rent amounting to £2908 2s 2d. See doc. 118, text at n. 9; *Micro.* 13:291.

65. This has not been found.

66. For a detailed version of this meeting, which took place in Aug. 1699 at the Fords' house in Islington, see *Micro.* 12:831.

67. See *Micro.* 10:074.

68. The Fords, in their answer to WP's second Bill of Complaint, alleged that Ayrey received only £300 from WP, who implied that it was a loan. See Chancery, Reynardson's Division, bundle 183, #40, PRO.

69. Hilary term normally ran from mid-Jan. to mid.-Feb.

70. This action was based on WP's failure to honor the bond for £20,000 which he had given to Philip Ford on 29 Sept. 1696 (see *PWP*, 3:661). WP, however, was able to obtain an injunction against this action until the suit in Chancery was adjudicated. See Penn Papers, Ford vs. Penn, p. 54, HSP.

71. See doc. 108.

72. This has not been found.

73. This has not been found. Bridget Ford, in the Fords' answer to WP's second Bill of Complaint, denied that she had brought an action for this amount. See Chancery, Reynardson's Division, bundle 183, #40, PRO.

74. An action for this amount has not been found. However, Bridget Ford, Thomas Moss, and John Hall did sue WP for £3150 back rent and £100 damages. See headnote to doc. 117.

75. This represented three years' rent. The Fords also asked for £10 damages, but the suit does not appear to have come to trial. See *Micro.* 13:196.

76. See *Micro.* 13:199, which implies the action was for £3000 damages. In any event, this suit does not appear to have come to trial.

77. Witnesses in Chancery were questioned by means of written interrogatories. For example, see *Micro.* 13:375.

78. The lord chancellor was assisted in the court of Chancery by 11 masters.

79. See *PWP,* 3:662.

80. WP was able to obtain an injunction for only one of Bridget Ford's actions. See n. 70, above.

81. Grimble Pauncefort (d. 1729), originally of Clater Park, Heref., now resided in the parish of St. Andrew, Holborn. Admitted to the Inner Temple in 1672 and called to the bar in 1680, he became a master of the bench in 1706. See *Masters of the Bench of . . . the Inner Temple, 1450-1883* (London, 1883), p. 60; F. A. Inderwick, ed., *A Calendar of the Inner Temple Records* (London, 1901), 3:147, 399, 421.

111
STATEMENT OF ACCOUNTS WITH PHILIP FORD

[c. June 1706]

WILLIAM PENN ESQ D^r^ TO PHILIP FORD

	£ s d
To Cash due to Philip Ford on 23^d^ of Augt 1682	2851.07.10
To Cash paid per Philip Ford as per Acc^t^ from [the 23^d^] of Augt 1682 to 21^t^ of March 1684/5	8549.05. 2
To Cash paid as per an Acc^t^ from the 21^t^ of March 1684/5 to the 11th of April 1687	3006.10.10¼
To Cash paid as per an Acc^t^ from the 11th of April 1687 to 11th of 8^br^ 1689	1293.19. 6
To Cash paid as per an Acc^t^ from the 11th of 8^br^ 1689 to 11th of January 1694/5	498.18.11
To Cash paid as per another acc^t^ from the 4th of July 1694 to 11th of January 1694/5	94.17. 8
To Cash paid as per Acc^t^ [from the 11th] of January 1694/5 to 11th of June 1696	1.11. 7
To Cash paid per Philip & Bridget Ford as per Acc^t^ from 11th of June 1696 to 24th of April 1700	82.08. 4
To Cash paid per Bridget Ford as per Another Acc^t^ from 24th of April 1700 to 1^t^ April 1702	18. 9
	16379.18. 7¼[1]
The Ballance to William Penn	1581.10. 8¾[2]
	17961.09. 4

Note this Abstract has no regard to Interest or Commission money, but only to moneys Simply paid and Received.

PER CONTRA Cr

	£	S	d
By moneys Receiv'd per Philip Ford by the same Acct	8198.	10.	7½
By moneys Receiv'd by the Same Acct	2922.	09.	1[torn]
By moneys Receiv'd by the Same Acct	1580.	00.	4½
By moneys Receiv'd by the Same Acct	1045.	12.	9
By moneys Receiv'd by the Same Acct	98.	19.	1[torn]
By moneys Received as per another Acct on or before the 11th of January 1694/5	350.	00.	[torn]
By moneys Received as per Acct from the 11th of January 1694/5 to 11th of June 1696	866.	18.	4
By moneys Received as per Acct on 13th of June 1696	100.	00.	0
By moneys Received on the 10th of April 1697	157.	00.	0
By moneys Received per Bridget Ford from the 10th of April 1697 to 24th of April 1700	1571.	18.	3
By moneys Received per Bridget Ford from the 24th of April 1700 to 1t of April 1702	1070.	00.	0
	17961.	09.	4³
By the Ballance	1581.	10.	8¾

WHEREAS in the year 1669 William Penn Esquire did on the good Character and recommendation given him of Philip Ford deceased imploy him in his Fathers[4] business, in which (as far as the said William Penn knew) he behaved himself just And afterwards made him his own steward, and entirely rlying on his good name & hon[esty] committed the whole management of his Affairs to him. AND WHEREAS it appears b[y] this ABSTRACT (that is truly drawn out) of the several Accts Between the said William Penn and Philip Ford deceased from the year 1682 which were written and signed by the said Philip Ford's own hand, and not either made up, or kept by the said William Pe[nn] And of two other Accts since his decease Between the said William Penn and Bridget Ford Relict of the said Philip Ford; that the said Philip Ford and Bridget his Relict hav[e] had and Received of the said William Penn's money 1581l 10s 8¼d more than what they ever paid for him or his use, allowing several considerable summs to be true, which the said Philip Ford setts down as paid (Vizt) {such as} 622l to one man at one payment, and above 700l to another, for which the said Philip Ford never gave the said William Penn any Testimon[y] or Receipts for the paymt thereof. And also supposing that the said Philip Ford gave the said William Penn Credit for all the summs he Received of his moneys (Except one summe of 157l that the said Philip Ford Received of the said William Penn himself and for wch he gave him his Receipt without bringing the same to the Acct or giving the said William Penn credit therefore,[5] althô there is reason to doubt the Contrary, inasmuch as the said Philip Ford well knew that the said William Penn kept no Acct between them, but only relyed on the honesty and fair dealing of the said Philip Ford AND WHEREAS the said William Penn never had or Received any moneys from the said Philip Ford or Bridget his [relict?] neither did they pay any moneys for him, since the year 1682 (at wch time the said Philip Ford was in the said William Penn's debt) other than what are mencioned in the said Accts; Yet the said Bridget Ford, together with Philip her son and other her Children do demand now of the said William Penn above the summe of 12,000l [6] arising from those Accts and for the Recovery thereof have unjustly and very ungratefully preferr'd a Bill in Chancery against the said William Penn,[7] (laying hold of several securitys wch the said William Penn gave to the said Philip Ford deceased for the moneys pretended to be due to him on the Ballances of the said Accts [two lines illegibly erased] (and particularly of a Grant[8] that the said William Penn made to the said Philip Ford upon his importunity and earnest request, only as he said, and so intended by the said William Penn to save to the said Philip Ford the duty or Tax of the moneys due to him fon the said Securitys (there being then a Duty or Tax laid on moneys at Interest)[9] which said securitys were intended and declar'd by the said William Penn and so accepted and acknowledged by the said Philip Ford deceased in his life time to be only Collatoral security for such moneys as should appear to be justly and bonâ fide due to the said Philip Ford who alsoe promis'd and agreed that they should be never otherwise used (as appears by Letters under his own hand)[10] but should only lye as a security for the moneys justly appearing to be due to him Untill the same could be raised out of the premisses, and accordingly pursuant to his promisses & agreemts the said Philip Ford made his Will, and expresst to the said William Penn his satisfaccion in so doing, but when the said William Penn was gone to Pennsylvania, the said Philip Ford being afterwards otherwise perswade[d] by the said Bridget his Wife, he made another Will[11] (as she has since confessed)[12] wherein he violated his promisses and agreemts made to and with the said William Penn & endeavoured thereby to Barr the heires of the said William Penn from having any Equity or right of Redempcion of the said premisses) on purpose to foreclose the said Willm Penn's Estate, and to stifle the notorious Errors and Extortions of the said Accts and that the same should not be examined into and rectifyed, wherefore the said Bridget Ford, Philip her son and other her Children did several times refuse to accept of a Referrence of the said Accts to indifferent persons to be equally chosen as well by them as by the said William Penn thô often by him desir'd thereto;[13] which said summe of above 12,000 (together [w]ith several other Errors and Overcharges too tedious here to insert) was made up & raised chiefly by the ways and methods herein after mencioned.

On the 6th of July 1682 Philip Ford deceased was Indebted to William Penn Esquire in the summe of 521^{l} as appears by an Acc^{t} then stated Between them; But the said William Penn being then about to make his expedicion to Pennsylvania, had occasion of diverse considerable quantitys of goods, for the better accommodacion of so extraordinary an undertaking, and imployed Philip Ford to buy the same, which he accordingly did. And on the 23^{d} of Augt then following [illegible erasures] the said Philip Ford delivered to the said William Penn an Acc^{t} of goods bought &cetera amounti[ng] in the whole to 4000^{l} £01^{s} 6^{d} wherein he makes the said William Penn [debtor?] the Ballance in the summe of 2851^{l} 07^{s} 10^{d} for which the said William Penn gave him a sufficient security,[14] And on the 23^{d} of February then following (being 6 months) the said Philip Ford charges the said William Penn for 6 months Interest of the said sume of 2851^{l} 7^{s} 10^{d} and also for 6 months Interest of above 800^{l} more which he paid not 3 weeks before the time he charged 6 months Interest for it, in the whole the summe of 112^{l} 11^{s} (althô it may be reasonably suppos'd, that the goods the said Philip Ford bought more than the value of the moneys of the said William Penn's, which he had then in his hands, were on the credit of the said William Penn and for which the said Philip Ford had 6 months time for the paym^{t} thereof or ha[d] an allowance or abatem^{t} on prompt paym^{t}) And 6 months after that he reckons the Interest as well of the said 112^{l} 11^{s} as of the said summe of 2851^{l} 07^{s} 10^{d} together with 6 months Interest of what other moneys he had since pretended to advance (yet in this Acc^{t} the said Philip Ford did {not} sett down any the days months or year on wch he Received above 6000^{l} of the said William Penn's money) And after this method the said Philip Ford proceeds by reckoning Interest upon Interest every 6 months at 6^{l} per Cent per Annum unto the end of this Acc^{t} which was on the 21^{t} of March 1684/5 And by the last Article thereof the said Philip Ford setts down 500^{l} paid himself for advance money[15] according to the Custome of Merchants and Sallary at 6^{d} per £ (for so he calls it) althô the said Philip Ford in this whole Acc^{t} did not pay above 8549^{l} 5^{s} 2^{d} which at 6^{d} per £ comes to but 213^{l} 14^{s} 7½^{d} of which the goods he bought by this [torn] did not amount unto more than 2990^{l} 16^{s} 1^{d} whereby to deserve 6^{d} per £ sallary, but paid the remainder (Viz^{t}) 5558^{l} 9^{s} 6^{d} to certain persons per William Penns order, and not for goods bought in which he deserved according to Custome but 10^{s} per Cent, so tha[t] his sallary or Commission money justly reckon'd amounts to but 102^{l} 11^{s} 2^{d} instead of the said 500^{l} And upon the Ballance of this Acc^{t} he makes the said William Penn Debtor in the summe of 4293^{l} 3^{s} when by this Acc^{t} he paid but 350^{l} 14^{s} 6½^{d} more than w^{t} he Received as appears thereby (save to himself his Interest & Commission money) not inclu[ding] the said sume of 2851^{l} 7^{s} 10^{d}.

And by another Acc^{t} begining the said 21^{t} of March 1684/5 the first Article thereof the said Philip Ford charges the said William Penn for the Interest 3793^{l} 16^{s} for 1 month thô it wanted 2 days of it (being only 26 days) 18^{l} 19^{s} 3¼^{d} and 6^{d} per £ (vizt) 9^{s} 6^{d} (for tis so mencioned in the Acc^{ts} in two distinct summs) for paying himself the said 18^{l} 19^{s} 3¼^{d} his simple Interest, being too much too, because the Interest did not come to above 16^{l} 4^{s} 3½^{d} althô he charged 19 six pences for paying of it, but he chosed to Err on that hand rather than on the other, And at the end of 6 months following the said Philip Ford charges the said William Penn with two articles the one 4^{l} 11^{s} 10^{d} for the Interest of the moneys he had disburst that 6 months (over and above the Ballance of the last Acc^{t}) thô he paid the greatest part of it not 2 weeks before, and the other Article 172^{l} 10^{s} for the Interest of the said Ballance 4293^{l} 3^{s} with the first Article of 18^{l} 19^{s} 3½^{d} and the 9^{s} 6^{d} added thereto and computed at 8^{l} per Cent per Annum and 6 mon[ths] after that he again setts down the Interest of what moneys he had ~~laid~~ {advanc'd} in that time (w[ch] were not paid a fortnight before and the Interest of the said last Ballance together with the Interest of his Interest ~~money~~ and Commission money added to it at 8^{l} per Cent per Annum and according to this method the said Philip Ford proceeds by reckoning Interest upon Interest every 6 months and once sooner at 8^{l} per Cent per Annum unto the end of this Acc^{t} wherein he makes the said William Penn Debtor on the Ballance in 5282^{l} 9^{s} 8½^{d} althô the said Philip Ford did not pay in both those Acc^{ts} above the summe of 434^{l} 15^{s} 5¾^{d} more than w^{t} he thereby Received by which and the good improvem^{t} of the said summe of 2851^{l} 7^{s} 10^{d} in ab^{t} 4½ years time he brings it to the summe of 5282^{l} 9^{s} 8½^{d} And in the last Article of this Acc^{t} the said Philip Ford setts down 200^{l} 2^{s} 6^{d} paid to himself 6^{d} per £ for 8004^{l} 17^{s} 1½^{d} in which he again reckon'd 6^{d} per £ for paying himself his principal that he Reckon'd 6^{d} per £ for paying of it twice before, once in the last Acc^{t} and once in another preceeding that, also 6^{d} per £ for paying himself his interest that he charged in the last Acc^{t}, and therein reckon'd 6^{d} per £ for paying of it too, And also 6^{d} per £ for paying himself his Interest that he charges in this Acc^{t} Together with 6^{d} per £ for paying himself the said 500^{l} his Sallary or Commission money of 6^{d} per £ as before, Now the said Philip Ford did not pay by this Acc^{t} more than the summe of 3006^{l} 10^{s} 10¼^{d} (save to himself his Interest and Commission money) which at 6^{d} per £ would have come to only 75^{l} 3^{s} 3^{d} but the goods he bought and sold per this Acc^{t} amounted to but 942^{l} 17^{s} 7¾^{d} the Remainder of the said sume of 3006^{l} 10^{s} 10¼^{d} he paid Bills of Exchange &c whereby his Commission money justly reckon'd had been but 33^{l} 17^{s} 9^{d} instead of the said 200^{l} 2^{s} 6[d]

And by another acc^{t} begining the same day the last ended which was the 11th of April 1687 in 6 months after the date thereof the said Philip Ford setts down the summe of 211^{l} 6^{s} 4¼^{d} paid himself for 6 months Consideracion of the Ballance of the last Acc^{t} which was the Interest thereof at 8^{l} per Cent per Annum (and althô he calld it consideracion he used but little in these Acc^{ts}) and 6 months after that he setts down as well the Interest of the said 211^{l} 6^{s} 4¼^{d} (his Interest money) as of the said Ballance of 5282^{l} 09^{s} 8½^{d} at 8^{l} per Cent per Annum and according to this method the said Philip Ford proceeds by making [t]he Interest Principal every 6 months and computing it at 8£ per Cent per Annum unto [t]he end of this Acc^{t} which was on the 11th of 8^{br} 1689 wherein by the last Article thereof the said Philip Ford setts down 193^{l} 0^{s} 6^{d} paid to himself 6^{d} per £ for 7720^{l} 19^{s} 0¼^{d} when by this Acc^{t} he did not pay above 1293^{l} 19^{s} 6^{d} (save to himself for Interest & Commission money) of which not above 445^{l} 1^{s} 10^{d} was for goods bought and sold, but the rest for moneys paid Bills of Exchange &cetera whereby his Commission truly reckon'd had been but 15^{l} 7^{s} 6^{d} instead of the said 193^{l} 0^{s} 6^{d} wherein the said Philip Ford again charges 6^{d} per £ for paying himself the same summe that he charged 6^{d} per £ for over and over, thrice so for before, and 6^{d} per £ for paying himself his own Interest which he charged 6^{d} per £ for twice before, and alsoe 6^{d} per £ for paying himself his Interest arising by this Acc^{t} Together with 6^{d} per £ for paying himself his said Commission money, part of which he Reckon'd 6^{d} per £ for once before, And although the said Philip Ford did not pay in all those 3 last Acc^{ts} above 149^{l} 1^{s} 9¼^{d} more than what he Received yet he thereby and by his way of calculating the Interest of the said 2851^{l} 7^{s} 10^{d} with the principal and his Comission money and the Interest of that too, in about 7 years time, now makes the said William Penn Debtor on the Ballance of Acc^{ts} in the summe of 6333^{l} 19^{s} 2^{d}.

And by another Acc^{t} begining the 11th of 8^{br} 1689 in the first Article thereof he setts down the aforesaid summe of 6333^{l} 19^{s} 2^{d} being the pretended Ballance of the last Acc^{t}, and in the next article, being 6 months after (for in that time he paid no moneys for the said William Penn) he charges 253^{l} 7^{s} 2^{d} for 6 months consideracion or Interest of the said Ballance at 8£ per Cent per Annum and 6 months after that he setts down 263^{l} 9^{s} 10^{d} that is, the Interest as well of the said 253^{l} 7^{s} 2^{d} as of the said 6333^{l} 19^{s} 2^{d} when at the same time the said Philip Ford had a sufficient security given him by the said William Penn by a Mortgage[16] for the said summe of 6333^{l} 19^{s} 2^{d} And althô in several other spaces of 6 months he did not pay 20^{s} in either of them for the said William Penn; yet Nevertheless the said Philip Ford makes the Interest Principal every 6 months and Sometime Sooner, and computes it at 8£ per Cent per Annum throughout this whole Acc^{t}, without having any regard to his said security or Mortgage, and without making any deduction for the several summs of money which the said Philip Ford Received in the mean time, (until at the end of the Acc^{t}) [a]mounting in the whole to 1045^{l} 12^{s} 9^{d} And at the end of this Acc^{t} which continued 5 Years and 3 months, and contained in one sheet of Common paper, wherein the said Philip Ford did not pay above 498^{l} 18^{s} 11^{d} of which 354^{l} was to himself on the sam[e] day that the Acc^{t} ended: so that in the 5 years and 3 months, the said Philip Ford p[aid] only for the said William Penn (save to himself) the sume of 144^{l} 18^{s} 9^{d} in which t[ime] he Received of the said William Penn's money the said sume of 1045^{l} 12^{s} 9^{d}, Neverthele[ss] the said Philip Ford by his industry and great skill in computing of Interest (althô [he] Received more money than he paid by this Acc^{t}) now advances the said summe of 6333^{l} 19^{s} [2^{d}] on the Ballance of this Acc^{t} to the summe of 9016^{l} 12^{s} 5^{d} and made the said William Penn Debtor therein.

And by another Acc^{t} begining the 11th of January 1694/5 and continuing 17 months (wherein the said Philip Ford paid only 1^{l} 11^{s} 7^{d} for the said William P[enn)] at the end thereof the said Philip Ford charges 1060^{l} 16^{s} 8½^{d} for the 17 months Interest of the said summe of 9016^{l} 12^{s} 5^{d} (wherein was included the several summs of Inter[est] and Comission money before mencioned) which he computed every 6 months at 8^{l} per Cent per Annum and so makes the whole summe to be 10,079^{l} 00^{s} 8½^{d}.

And by another Acc^{t} in the same folio the said Philip Ford makes the said William Penn Debtor in the summe of 1385^{l} which were the moneys for the said William Penn's own Land,[17] which the said William Penn sold, part whereof the said Philip Ford received for his own use, so that the said summe of 138[5]^{l} was altogether charged in the said William Penn's wrong.

And by this Last Acc^{t} the said Philip Ford having Received several other considerable summs of the said William Penn's money on the 11th of June 1696 the said Philip Ford brings the Acc^{t} to a Ballance and makes the sa[id] WIlliam Penn Debtor on the Ballance in the summe of 10,202^{l} 8^{s} 7½^{d} whereas the Principal and Interest of the said summe of 2851^{l} 7^{s} 10^{d} at 6^{l} per Cent per Annum simple Interest, and alsoe the Principal and simple Interest thereof of what moneys were due to the said Philip Ford on the Ballances of the several Acc^{ts} to 11th of June 1696 together with his Commission money justly computed (deducting the moneys he had then Received) would not have amounted to at that ti[me] above the summe of 3837^{l} 10^{s} 1¼^{d} instead of the said summe of 10,202^{l} 8^{s} 7½^{d} [since] which time the said William Penn has paid unto the said Philip Ford and B[ridget] his Relict the summe of 2815^{l} 11^{s} 2^{d} more than what they have since laid out [for?] him, which was not 100^{l} as appears by the said Acc^{ts}.[18]

D. Penn Papers, Ford vs. Penn, HSP. (*Micro.* 12:691.) Docketed: State of Accounts & Case | with P Ford, a Narrative at large | Received 4mo 1706.

1. These figures actually total £16,397 8s 10¼d.

2. If the sum in n. 1, above, is correct, this figure should read £1564 5¾d in order to total £17,961 9s 4d. For slightly different figures, see *Micro.* 13:273, 622.

3. The overall total indicates that the pence column should add up to 40.

4. Admiral Sir William Penn. Ford was initially hired by WP to help manage his father's properties in Ireland. See Richard S. Dunn, "Penny Wise and Pound Foolish: Penn as a Businessman," in Richard S. Dunn and Mary M. Dunn, eds., *The World of William Penn* (Philadelphia, 1986), p. 38.

5. See *PWP*, 3:542-43.

6. See ibid., 3:662, where the total given is £12,714 5s.

7. See doc. 108.

8. See *PWP*, 3:661-62.

9. See doc. 110, n. 22.

10. These have not been found.

11. See Probate 11/484, PRO. The alleged previous will has not been found.

12. Any firm evidence that Bridget Ford "confessed" to this has not been found.

13. On 14 Nov. 1705 WP had complained to Devonshire House Monthly Meeting in London about the Ford's Bill of Complaint and asked Friends of that meeting (to which Bridget Ford belonged) to intervene. Despite protracted efforts by the meeting, the Fords refused to drop their lawsuit or refer the matter to an impartial panel of Friends. They were subsequently disowned by Friends and WP was given permission to take legal action to defend himself. See Devonshire House Monthly Meeting minutes, vol. 2, FLL.

14. See *PWP*, 2:291-93.

15. Payment on security of future reimbursement (*OED*). It appears that Philip Ford was charging a commission for advancing money on WP's behalf for the purchase of goods. Although this was not illegal, WP would protest that he had paid Ford sufficient funds to make such purchases within the prescribed time for payment.

16. See *PWP*, 3:660.

17. See doc. 110, n. 52.

18. WP is here referring to the debits and credits tabulated at the beginning of this document, which indicate that during the period 11 June 1696 – 1 Apr. 1702 he paid £2898 18s 3d to the Fords, while they paid £82 19s 1d on his account, leaving by his reckoning a balance of £2815 11s 2d (actually £2815 19s 2d) in his favor for this period.

112
ANSWER OF JOHN HALL AND THOMAS MOSS

The following document is the answer of two of the trustees for Pennsylvania — appointed by Philip Ford in his will — to the Bill of Complaint brought by Philip Ford, Jr., his sisters, and his brother-in-law (see doc. 108). Forcing Hall and Moss to be defendants, along with Bridget Ford, was really a ploy by the plaintiffs to make it appear that Pennsylvania obviously belonged to them, but that the trustees had been negligent in performing their duty. In fact, Bridget Ford admitted that she was made a defendant on the advice of her lawyer (see *Micro.* 12:698). In addition, this tactic would force Hall and Moss to answer in detail concerning the events surrounding a critical document signed in April 1702 by WP and Bridget Ford.

[14 June 1706]

The Joint and Severall Answers of John Hall and Thomas Moss two of the Defendants to the Bill of Complaint of Phillip Ford the younger, James Ayrey and Bridgett his Wife Ann Ford and Susannah Ford Complainants.

The said Defendants severally saveing unto themselves all benefitt and advantage by way of Exception or otherwise to the manyfold Incertainties Insufficiencies and other Imperfections in the Complainants said Bill of Complaint contained For Answer thereunto or unto such part thereof as they are advised to be materiall for them to make answer unto doe severally answer and say That they beleive that Phillip Ford the elder did make such last Will and Testament as in the Bill of Complaint sett out, and that he did therein and thereby make such Devise to these Defendants and to his Wife Bridgett Ford on such trusts and for such purposes as in the Bill of Complaint sett out, however these Defendants doe for greater certainty herein referr themselves to the said last Will and Testament when produced, And these Defendants doe severally further Answer and say That soon after the death of the said Phillip Ford the elder These Defendants went with the Complainant Phillip Ford the younger to William Penn the elder one other of the Defendants to the said Bill of Complaint and acquainted him with the Will of the said Phillip Ford the elder And thereupon and after some debate the said William Penn proposed to raise or procure a considerable summe of money and therewith pay some of the legacies in the said Testators Will And that sometime afterwards the said William Penn proposed and offered to pay the summe of Two thousand Five hundred pounds or two thousand pounds in consideration of a Reconveyance of some part of the Estate soe devised[1] And these Defendants doe further severally say That they beleive it to be true that the said William Penn had the account ending the First of Aprill one thousand seaven hundred and two in the Bill of Complaint mencioned to be to him to delivered by the said Bridgett Ford in his custody about three Weekes at least to peruse And these Defendants saw him afterwards signe seale and deliver what is thereunder subscribed bearing date the second of Aprill one thousand seaven hundred and two[2] and these Defendants severally subscribed their names as Witnesses thereunto And this Defendant Thomas Moss read to the said William Penn the said subscription at the bottome of the said account before the said William Penn signed sealed and delivered the same And these Defendants doe further answer and say That they are willing to act in the Trust reposed in them by the Will of the said Phillip Ford the elder deceased soe as they may be indempnified in soe doeing And these Defts severally declare they have noe moneys nor writeings of the said Complainants in their hands And deny all Combinacion and Confederacy in the Bill of Complaint alleadged Without that that any other matter or thing in the Complainants said Bill of Complaint contained materiall or effectuall in the Law for these Defendants or either of them to make answer unto and not herein and hereby well and sufficiently answered unto confessed or avoided traversed or denyed is true all which matters and things these Defendants and each of them are ready to averr maintaine and prove as this Honourable Court shall thinke fitt to Award And humbly pray they may be hence dismissed with their reasonable costs and charges in this behalfe susteyned.

Peter King

DS. C5/332/16, PRO. (Not filmed.) Docketed: Affirmatio et declaratio per Ambos Defendentes secundum formam statuti 14to Die Junii ~~1706~~ 1706 coram Richard Holford[3]

1. WP negotiated for the purchase of his manors of Pennsbury and Highlands from the Ford family and trustees Hall and Moss, but the transaction was never completed (see *Micro.* 12:487). WP did arrange to borrow £3000 in Aug. 1702 from his future son-in-law, William Aubrey, and may have intended to use some of this money to pay the Fords. See doc. 209 B, G; *Micro.* 10:455.

2. For the wording of WP's acknowledgment of his debt to Bridget Ford, 2 Apr. 1702, see doc. 108, text following n. 24.

3. Affirmed (Hall and Moss were Quakers) and declared by these two defendants according to the form of the statute, 14 June 1706, in the presence of Richard Holford. Holford was a master in Chancery, 1693-1711. See Edward Foss, *The Judges of England* (London, 1864), 7:295, 376.

113
BRIEF OF THE PLEA AND DEMURRER BY BRIDGET FORD AND OTHERS

The Fords answered WP's Bill of Complaint (doc. 110) on 5 June 1706 (see *Micro.* 12:698). In Chancery there were several options available to defendants preparing what was technically known as an "answer." First, they could simply answer the bill in all its points. Second, they could demur to the bill, that is, they could argue that it lacked sufficient matter of equity, thereby precluding any right of the plaintiff to succeed in the court of Chancery, or that the bill sought to discover something that could cause a forfeiture by the defendants or criminal action against them, which was not permissible in a court of equity (see *Black's Law Dictionary*, p. 389; Blackstone, 3:446). Third, they could plead in bar to the bill, that is, they could try to prevent, or bar, any further prosecution on the grounds of an act of parliament, a previous release, or a former decree (see Blackstone, 3:446). Finally, defendants could combine all three options in one answer. The following document is a brief of the Fords' answer drawn up by WP's counsel in order to prepare another document, know as the "replication," which was the plaintiff's response to the defendant's answer. The brief clearly indicates that the Fords chose to combine all three options.

For a plea in bar, they cited the numerous deeds and releases signed by WP, along with the account of 1 April 1702, where WP admitted that he was a tenant of the Fords and that he owed back rent. They also pleaded the statute of limitations and the marriage agreement between James Ayrey and Bridget Ford, Jr. The Fords hoped to prevent the court from reexamining the accounts in question by arguing that WP had fully accepted them, that he had conveyed Pennsylvania and the Lower Counties to Philip Ford without equity of redemption, and that in any event the statute of limitations had been exceeded. On the accusation of exorbitant interest charged by Philip Ford, the defendants demurred, arguing that, if true, it might cause a forfeiture of their principal and therefore was unacceptable in Chancery. The Fords answered the rest of the bill, endeavoring to show that WP had acted in bad faith and that Pennsylvania belonged by right to them. They failed, however, to address the matter of WP's stock in the Free Society of Traders.

[c. July 1706]

Ford ad^{s} [1] Penn Answer

As to any thing to lessen the consideration in any of the Deeds after pleaded or how much ought to stand secured or to draw in question the Accounts before the 29th Sept 1696[2]

fo:[3]4

PLEA[4]

~~pl~~ plead Lease & release 23: & 24 Augt 16~~9~~82 {of 300,000 acres land in Fee} cons 3000^{l} receipt under hand and seale 24 Augt 1682 for the 3000^{l} bond for paym^{t} of 3000^{l} & Int 26 Aug: 1682.[5]

15 Mortgage {for 5000 yeares} 10th June 1685 cons 5000^{l} Provisoe for paym^{t} of 5000^{l} the 21th March 1686 with usuall allowances in the Province — receipt for the 5000^{l} under hand & seale & bond to perform Covenants.[6]

21 Ind^{r} [7] 11th Ap: 1687 in cons 6000^{l} mortgages for 5000 yeares All the Province. receipt under seale, bond to perform Cov^{ts}[8]

27 Deed Poll release 30th Augt 1690 Penn releases in cons of 5^{s}: the Terme of 5000 yeares—set forth full[9]

34 Ind^{r} of Assignm^{t} 1st Sept 1690 reciting &c Philip Ford Assigns to Elwood[10] the Tract &c for 5000 yeares to attend the revercion.[11]

37 Lease & release the 2^{d} & 3^{d} Sept: 1690 in consideration 6900^{l} releases the Province to Ford & his heires, set forth full a Receipt under seale for 6900^{l}, bond to perform Covenants.[12]

50 Release & confirmacion 29th Sept 1696 reciting &c that the 6900^{l} was not paid in cons of the further summe of 3447^{l}: {tot 10347^{l}} releases & conf~~e~~irmes &c free of all Equity receipt indorsed[13]

58 Ind^{r} of Defeazance 29th Sept 1696. Ford to reconvey on paym^{t} of 10657^{l}—bond to pay the money[14]

62 That the 29th September 1696; they settled accounts under their hands ballance 10347:15:5:½[15]

65 Generall release the s^{d} 29 Sept[16]

67 Ind^{r} of Release & confirmacion 1st Aprill 1697 in consideration of 20^{s} ~~ra~~ & of the s^{d} summes—ratifyes &c free of all redempcion Cov^{t} for further Assurance—receipt indorsed for the 20^{s}.[17]

75 Ind^{r} 2^{d} Aprill 1697 Ford Lease to W Penn for 3 yeares at 630^{l} Sterling, set forth largely[18]

86 That Penn by his Answer to their bill admitts that by Deed Poll 10th Ap: 1697 reciting &c the absolute conveyance & the Lease at 630^{l} Ph: F: give 3 yeares time to purchase at 12714:5:0[19]

90 writing under the hand and seale of Wm Penn Dat 10th Augt 1699 which referrs to a note dat 29th Sept 1696 which was given by Ford to lett Mr Penn into the Accounts, whereby Mr Penn accknowledges noe error to appeare in the Accounts & releases the s^{d} recited note[20]

95 Plead Fords will 20th Jan: 1699 & Codicill 15 March 1700[21]

112 That the 1st Aprill 1702 an acco^{t} the ballance due to Bri: Ford 591:8:10[22]

120 Plead the Statute of Limitacions & that six yeares is past by the Plaintiffs own shewing.[23]

122 farther Plead That 25 January 1703 they signed articles of Agreem^{t} on Ayryes marriage[24] relating to her portion given by old Fords will, and all this they plead ag^{t} drawing the accounts in question.

DEMURRER[25]

139 as to Interest of 8^{l} per Cent or any above 6^{l} & as to 6^{d} in the pound & all exorbitant allowances because ~~by~~ it would endanger the losse of their principall[26]

ANS^{r}:[27]

143 All say they claim nothing by vertue of the accounts in case the Co^{rt} shall judge a redempcion[28] they claime the 10347: & Interest[29]—& they alsoe claime the rent of 630^{l} in arreare[30] had rather have the 10347 & the interest and arreares of Rent but don't offer it but insist~~g~~ the Estate wa~~g~~s not redeemable

149 beleive old Ford did nothing after 10th Ap: 1697 to give Equity[31] ~~on~~ unlesse the Receipt on that deed for 157^{l} which they submitt to the Court but insist the Plt prove that receipt and then they'l explain it.[32]

150 Philip & his mother[33] admitt severall summes p^{d} after the acco^{t} of the 1st of Aprill 1702 amounting to ab^{t} 800^{l}

159 theres due for rent 2293:2:2.[34]

160 the Plaintiff P^{d} Ayrey 300^{l} 28th June 1705[35]

163 B: ford insists that the acco^{t} of ~~2^{d}~~1st Ap^{ll} 1702 ought to stand[36] — knowes of noe condicion for examining acco^{ts} then declared,[37] if it was tis not materiall

169 proved the will 4th octo: 1705, staid at the Plts importunity[38]

168 a great ~~will~~ {while} after P. Fords death never imagind [the?] accounts were to be questioned.

171 Severall passages betweene Plt & defts, that he would make them easy — that he had not made over the Province.[39]

172 by their Cov^{ts} the Plaintiffs ought to exonerate the premisses from any incumbrances[40]

173 Bridget & Philip threatened to publish the purchase & the Plaintiff entreated their silence[41]

174 P. Ford[42] was in Pensilvania in May 1701 demanded the rent of Plaintiff & threatened to publish the lease but the Plt pacifyed him[43]

176 Susanna and Philip Say the Plaintiff threaten'd them, ~~and~~ to keep them out of their money and hang up the cause 10 or 20 yeares[44]

181 Bridget Ford was privy to the first Bill ~~as~~& by advice of Councill was made a Defendant[45]

186 tis not materiall w^{t} Bridget knew under Coverture[46] her husband never was a schoolmaster but the 28 Sept 23 Car primi[47] was bound to a merch^{t} at York for 8 years to be free[48] of the old Hance & Eastland Company[49] & that he was a Merch^{t} in good circumstances & never wronged the Plt or any body else

Note they say nothing as to the businesse of the Pensilvania Co:[50]

D. Penn Papers, Ford vs. Penn, HSP. (*Micro.* 12:484.)

1. Abbreviation for "ad sectam," meaning "at the suit of." *Black's Law Dictionary*, p. 47.

2. The central issue for the Fords was to avoid lessening the amounts mentioned in any of the deeds because of inflated interest. Therefore, they were determined to avoid having the accounts opened before Sept. 1696, at which date WP conveyed Pennsylvania to Philip Ford.

3. Folio, a unit of measure consisting of 72 to 90 words used to determine the text length of a legal document. The numbers in the margins of doc. 113 refer therefore to the folios in the Fords' answer. *Black's Law Dictionary*, p. 579.

4. This begins the Fords' plea in bar (see headnote).

5. On 23-24 Aug. 1682 WP conveyed 300,000 acres in Pennsylvania to Philip Ford ostensibly for £3000, for which WP gave Ford a receipt. In fact, Ford was owed £2851 by WP and was apparently accepting this land as a mortgage for debt. It was

accompanied by a bond in which WP promised to pay Ford £3000 with interest on 26 Aug. 1682, subject to a penalty of £6000. If WP paid the money on time, the land would revert to him (see *PWP*, 2:290-93). This matter was never settled.

6. On 10 June 1685 WP leased 300,000 acres in Pennsylvania, along with several of his manors and his city lot in Philadelphia, to Philip Ford for 5000 years ostensibly for £5000, for which WP gave Ford a receipt. Once again, this was a mortgage for debt (see n. 5, above). WP gave a bond to pay the £5000 by 21 Mar. 1686, on pain of £10,000. See *PWP*, 3:658.

7. Indenture.

8. On 11 Apr. 1687 WP leased Pennsylvania to Philip Ford for 5000 years ostensibly for £6000, for which WP gave Ford a receipt. As it was really a mortgage for debt, WP also gave a bond to pay Ford £6000, on pain of £12,000. See *PWP*, 3:658.

9. On 11 Apr. 1687 WP agreed by deed poll to pay Philip Ford £6000 by 11 Apr. 1688, which would void the indenture of 11 Apr. 1687 (see n. 8, above). However, on 30 Aug. 1690 WP admitted he had not paid the £6000 and therefore he released for 5s all equity of redemption and confirmed the 5000-year lease to Ford. See *PWP*, 3:658-59.

10. Thomas Ellwood.

11. On 1 Sept. 1690 Philip Ford assigned Pennsylvania in trust to Thomas Ellwood for the remainder of the 5000-year lease (see n. 8, above) formerly granted by WP to Ford. See *PWP*, 3:659.

12. On 2-3 Sept. 1690 WP conveyed Pennsylvania and the Lower Counties to Philip Ford forever, ostensibly for £6900, for which WP gave Ford a receipt. As this was probably a mortgage for debt, WP also gave Ford a bond to pay the £6900 on pain of £13,800. See ibid., 3:659-60.

13. On 29 Sept. 1696 WP admitted that he had failed to pay the £6900 he owed Ford (see n. 12, above); consequently, for an additional £3447 from Ford, WP confirmed the conveyance of Pennsylvania and the Lower Counties made by him in 1690 and agreed that Ford was now free to enter upon these American possessions. See *PWP*, 3:660.

14. On 29 Sept. 1696 WP and the Fords signed an indenture of defeasance whereby Ford agreed to reconvey Pennsylvania and the Lower Counties to WP upon payment of £10,657 on 30 Mar. 1697; in the interim WP could peacefully enjoy those lands. WP also gave a bond to pay the said amount on the prescribed date, on pain of £20,000 (see *PWP*, 3:660-61). Bridget Ford later sued for the latter amount.

15. See ibid., 3:661. The amount agreed upon in the accounts differed from that agreed upon in the bond (see n. 14, above), a potentially serious problem for WP in his claim that the accounts underlay the various deeds he gave to Ford. This was also the case, for example, with the 1682 conveyance of 300,000 acres to Ford (see n. 5, above). In effect, the Fords could claim that WP owed them both the total in the accounts and the various totals in the deeds.

16. On 29 Sept. 1696 WP released Ford from all claims or demands either in law or equity since "the beginning of the world." See *PWP*, 3:661.

17. A critical document in the case. On 1 Apr. 1697 WP released his right of redemption to Pennsylvania and the Lower Counties, confirming them to Philip Ford for 20s. However, neither the covenant nor receipt mentioned here has been found. Neither the Fords nor WP mentioned that this document also gave WP the right to administer Pennsylvania for the next ten years and provides the names of his attorneys there. See *PWP*, 3:661.

18. Another critical document. On 2 Apr. 1697 Philip Ford leased Pennsylvania and the Lower Counties to WP for three years at an annual rent of £630. At the end of three years, the property reverted to Ford. See *PWP*, 3:662.

19. See ibid.

20. Probably the most important document in the case relative to the accounts. This note of 10 Aug. 1699 has not been found but is discussed in doc. 110, text at n. 65.

21. See Probate 11/484, PRO. The Fords would plead in bar that Philip Ford left Pennsylvania and the Lower Counties to his heirs and granted WP only a limited right of repurchase.

22. That is, WP acknowledged that he was a tenant of the Fords, and that he still owed back rent of £591 8s 10d. See doc. 110, text following note 67. See also Penn Papers, Ford vs. Penn, fol. 80, HSP.

23. The statute 21 Jac. 1, c. 16, entitled An Act for Limitation of Actions, and for Avoiding of Suits in Law, limited the right to bring an action against accounts to six years after the cause of the action (*Statutes at Large*). In this case the Fords argued that WP's claim against Philip Ford's accounts exceeded the statute of limitations. See doc. 115, text at n. 32.

24. On 25 Jan. 1703 James Ayrey, having proposed marriage to Bridget Ford, Jr., entered into articles of agreement with her; Philip Ford, Jr.; and Peter Briggins, a London tobacconist, disposing of the late Philip Ford's legacy to Bridget of £1500 to be raised from the intended sale of Pennsylvania. The Fords contended that Ayrey entered into this agreement on the belief that Bridget's legacy was secured, thus precluding any right of redemption assumed by WP. See doc. 115, text at n. 33.

25. For the nature of demurrers in equity, see the headnote to this document.

26. Chancery practice permitted a demurrer in cases where a Bill of Complaint sought a discovery which might result in a forfeiture of any kind. In this instance, the defendants were seeking to avoid any reduction of principal as a result of errors in the accounts. See Blackstone, 3:446.

27. This begins the Fords' answer to those parts of WP's Bill of Complaint which they had not pleaded in bar or demurred against.

28. That is, if the court of Chancery decided that WP could legally redeem his colony.

29. See the text at n. 15, above. The Ford argument that they claimed nothing by virtue of the accounts is specious, since the £10,347 mentioned here was a settlement of the accounts in 1696.

30. WP would argue that all rent payments should have gone towards reducing the debt owed Ford, for they were not separate from the accounts but were interest payments disguised as rent.

31. That is, equity of redemption to WP.

32. See n. 18, above, and *PWP*, 3:542-43. There is no evidence that WP was called upon to prove this receipt, or that it represented anything other than one-quarter of the annual rent.

33. Philip Ford, Jr., and his mother, Bridget Ford.

34. That is, by June 1706 WP owed £2293 2s 2d in back rent. However, the Fords in their answer specified that another £300 would be added if WP refused to honor a payment of that amount by John Hall to Bridget Ford. In June 1707 a Common Pleas jury ruled that WP owed the Fords £2908 2s 2d; this implies that he had protested the £300 and also now owed another half-year's rent of £315. See doc. 117; *Micro.* 13:194, 291.

35. Apparently as part of the legacy left by Philip Ford to his daughter, Bridget, wife of James Ayrey. See n. 24, above.

36. See text at n. 22, above.

37. In fact, WP was not disputing this account, which dealt with back rent from 1697 to 1702, but was anxious to reopen the earlier Ford accounts.

38. That is, Bridget Ford did not prove her husband's will until three years after his death, because WP had continued to insist that he would pay what was owed.

39. That is, WP would pay what he owed and had not conveyed the province to anyone else.

40. That is, because of the various covenants WP had given to Philip Ford, he had no right to diminish the value of Pennsylvania by conveying large parts of it to others, such as his son or other heirs. This right resided only in the Fords as legitimate owners.

41. A reference to the meeting between WP and the Fords in 1699 just before WP's departure for Pennsylvania. In his Bill of Complaint (doc. 110), WP cited this incident as an example of the coercion and deceit practiced against him by the Fords. Here the Fords use it as an example of WP's purported willingness to pay the debt rather than have it publicly known that he was no longer the proprietor of Pennsylvania.

42. Philip Ford, Jr.

43. Another two-sided example of coercion versus willingness to pay. See n. 41, above.

44. WP did indeed try to delay judgment, as when he filed a second Bill of Complaint after withdrawing his first. See headnote to doc. 115.

45. Bridget Ford's lawyers seem to have advised her that if she and the other trustees were made defendants in the Bill of Complaint against WP, it would imply

that the other members of the Ford family viewed ownership of Pennsylvania as an established fact and that the trustees had failed to perform their duty of selling it. Although an interesting tactical device, it probably had little effect on Lord Chancellor Cowper's deliberations.

46. The legal condition of a married woman vis-à-vis her husband. In this case, whatever Bridget Ford witnessed between her husband and WP was immaterial because she could not be forced to testify about it.

47. That is, 1648, when Ford was about 18 years old.

48. That is, admitted to the privileges of that trading company. *OED*.

49. The Eastland Company was chartered in 1579 and controlled the Baltic trade.

50. The Free Society of Traders. Thus the Fords' answer did not address itself to WP's claim that Ford illegally charged his account for stock in the Society, and that Bridget possessed the requisite books which should be produced in court.

114
LORD KEEPER COWPER'S REPORT ON THE DEFENDANTS' PLEA AND DEMURRER

The following document represents a major setback for WP in his Chancery prosecution of the Fords, who had answered his Bill of Complaint in June 1706 (*Micro.* 12:698). Because they had pleaded in bar and demurred to significant parts of the bill (see headnote to doc. 113), the matter had to be argued by counsel for both sides before Lord Keeper Cowper. If Cowper accepted the pleas in bar and demurrer as a legally valid answer, he was highly unlikely to reopen the accounts for scrutiny. He might agree that the documents which WP signed represented mortgages for debt and an elaborate tax evasion scheme (for which WP would be criminally liable), but the best that WP could then hope for was the right to redeem Pennsylvania at the amount requested by the Fords. Unfortunately for WP, as doc. 114 makes clear, the lord keeper accepted the plea and demurrer, although allowing WP to except for want of a direct answer to the question of errors in the account, no doubt referring to the failure by the Fords to address the question of WP's stock in the Free Society of Traders.

[8 November 1706]

Lord Keeper. Veneris Octavo Die Novembris Anno Regni Anna Regina Quinto Inter Gulielmu Penn Seniorem Armiger et alia Quer Bridgetta Ford Vidua Executricem Philippi Ford nuper Viri sui Defuncti Philippu Ford Anna Ford Susanna Ford et Jacobu Ayrey et Bridgetta Uxorem ejus et alia Defendentes[1]

The matter upon the Plea's and Demurrers putt in by the Defendants to the Plaintiffes Bill[2] coming to be argued on the second day of July last before the Right honourable the Lord Keeper of the Great Seale of England[3] in the presence of the Defend^ts^ Councell

~~and~~ none then attending for the Plaintiffes[4] and the said Plea and Demurrer being then opened It was Ordered That the same should be allowed with which Order the Plaintiffes not resting satisfyed peticioned his Lordship to have the said Plea and Demurrer reargued which being granted on the said plaintiffes depositing three pounds six shillings and eight pence with the Register and the matter upon the said Plea and Demurrer~~s~~ coming this present day to be reargued accordingly before his Lordship in the presence of the Councell learned on both sides And the said Plea and Demurrer being again opened Upon debate of the matter and hearing what could be alleadged by Councell on both sides His Lordship doth Order That the said Plea do stand ~~for an Answer~~ allowed but that the Plaintiffes have liberty to except for want of an Answer to the severall Errors if any in the Bill alleadged to be Errors ~~appearing~~ {appearing} in the body of the accompts pleaded And It is further Ordered That the said Demurrer be allowed as to any discovery touching the matter of the plaintiffes Bill demurred unto[5] and the three pounds six shillings and eight pence deposited with the Register on obtaining this [Rehearing are] to be paid unto the Defendts

AD. Penn Papers, Ford vs. Penn, HSP. (*Micro.* 13:008.) Endorsed: [illegible erasure] Penn v Ford | 8o Nov: 5o Ra Annæ | order for allowing plea | 1696.[6]

1. Friday, 8 November in the fifth year of the reign of Queen Anne, between William Penn, Sr., gentleman, and others, complainants, Bridget Ford, widow, executrix of Philip Ford her late husband deceased, Anne Ford, Susanna Ford, and James Ayrey and Bridget, his wife, and others, defendants.

2. For WP's Bill of Complaint, see doc. 110. The Fords responded with their plea and demurrer on 6 June 1706. See *Micro.* 12:698.

3. William Cowper.

4. No reason has been given for this failure of WP's counsel to attend. WP had delayed a final decree in Chancery by filing a second Bill of Complaint in Dec. 1706. Quite possibly, this was another delaying tactic.

5. The defendants demurred to any discovery of overcharges in the accounts on the grounds that it would reduce their principal, would make them liable to criminal charges, and would put their security from WP in jeopardy. See headnote to doc. 113. Although Cowper permitted the plaintiffs to except against the plea for lack of any answer about errors in the accounts, his acceptance of the demurrer made it unlikely that he would permit the accounts to be reexamined.

6. A mistake for 1706.

115

BRIEF FOR AN ANSWER TO THE DEFENDANTS' SECOND PLEA AND DEMURRER

On 23 December 1706 WP filed a second Bill of Complaint in Chancery against John Hall, Thomas Moss, and the Ford family (see *Micro.* 13:036). This bill was virtually identical to his first bill, which he withdrew in December 1706 after the lord keeper accepted the Fords' plea and demurrer. The Fords answered this second bill on 21 April 1707 (see Chancery, Reynardson's Division, bundle 183, no. 40, PRO). The following is a brief of that answer drawn up by WP's counsel in order to form a replication to the answer (see headnote to doc. 113). As doc. 115 makes clear, the Fords' second answer differed from their previous answer (see *Micro.* 12:698) only by including a response to WP's charges relating to the Free Society of Traders. WP replied to this answer on 14 May 1707 (see *Micro.* 13:165). These documents are an excellent example of the way in which plaintiffs or defendants with time and resources could drag out proceedings in Chancery for years. By putting in a new bill, WP was apparently hoping that he could outlast the Fords' willingness to accumulate high legal costs without their having received money from either WP or his colony. WP's tactics persuaded the trustees of Phillip Ford's estate to bring an action against WP in the court of Common Pleas; see doc. 117.

[c. April 1707]

Penn v. Ford

BILL[1]	
fo:[2]5	Pl^{ts} [3] 1st voyage to Pennsilvania in July 1682 goods bought for him by old Ford, Pl^{t} left Authority to receive money to pay for them
12	Fords Salary at 40^{l} per Annum to doe the Pl^{ts} business
14	Pl^{t} signed an Acco^{t} begining 6: July 1682 & Ending 23 Augt 82 in a hurry at Deale[4] ballance to Ford 2851:7:10
17	Goods not paid for till 6mo after bought[5]
19	Lease and Release signed by the Plaintiff at Deale[6] 23: & 24 Augt 1682 for 3000^{l}
26	one Account from 6: July 1682 to 29: Septem^{r} 1696[7]
36	Account settled in September 1696 between Pl^{t} and Ford ballance to Ford 10347:15:5–1/2
38	Ford gave Pl^{t} a writing 29: 7^{ber} 1696 to give him Liberty to look into Accounts and rectify Errors
42:45	Pl^{t} never had any Coppies till then. hath left those Coppies with his Clerk in Court for Def^{ts} to see and sett forth if they are not old Ford's hand
47	Ford got an absolute Conveyance in 1690 (for 6900) of the province[8] which is worth 60,000^{l}
51	The Deeds differ in the Consideration[9] so the Pl^{t} is Lyable to pay all the Consideracions. Ford tendred the Deeds ready ingrossed, Pl^{t} under Displeasure of the Government in 1690 noe Defeazance of the Deeds in 1690 till 1696[10]
58	Ford's Lease to the Pl^{t} in 1697, and Agreement for Sale to Plaintiff[11] absolute Conveyance to ford then, Ford advised with Councill about Saving the Tax on money.[12]

66 Plt Executed Deed at Ship Taverne in Gracechurch street. Ford's expression at Execucion,[13] no other money advanced then in the Accounts, Deeds a Collaterall security[14]

75 Plt by Fords Direction sold Land to Collett and others in 1699[15]

79 Plt Acquainted Ford with his Sale of Lands who sent a note to get a Catalogue of Mr Springett,[16] this note Left with Plts Clerk in Court for Defendants to see.

81 Plt gave Ford Letter of Attorney to Sell Land in 1699[17]

84:87 Ford by his will gave the Estate to be sold: Plt is ready to Account & pay on allowance of Errors:

93:113: Errors in the Account Appeare on the face thereof being 8l per Cent. and 6d in the pound for paying the Plaintiffs money.

118 Plt waves the Adavantages of the Defendants usury[18]

119 Plt insists on Allowance of money mencioned in the Account to be paid to Pennsilvania Company,[19] Defts have all the books of that Company.

128 Defts Endeavour to gain the ballance of the Accounts in 1696 & consideration of all the Deeds[20]

134 Plt prays a Discovery of their Demands.[21]

137 to 145 Defts have gained from the Plt the Deeds following[22] vizt

Lease & Release Augt 1682 Consideration 3000l and bond

Demise June 1685 for 5000 years Consideration ~~6~~5000l and bond

Demise Aprill 1687 for 5000 yeares Consideration 6000l and bond

Release and Assignemt of the Terme, Aug: 1690 to Attend the Inheritance

Lease & Release 7ber 1690 Consideration 6900l and bond

Release 29: 7ber 1696 consideration 3447l besides the 6900l in the Last Deed

Defeazance of the same Date for payment of 1065~~3~~7l

Generall Release from Plt to Ford.

148 The Deeds are for no other Summes then the Accounts & made without reference to the Accounts

153 Interest is called Allowance in the Deeds, & no Covt [23] for paymt because 'twas 8l per Cent.[24]

156 Release of Augst 1699 of note of 1696 for rectifying Errors in the Accounts, the indirect means of obtaining it[25]

181 Account of 1702 between Plt and Bridgett Ford with the manner of obtaining it[26]

193 Ayrey Bankruppcy[27]

197
201 Defts Accions at Law & Bill in Canc.,[28] & talk of Laying Plt in Gaole

204
214 Bridgett privy to all Concernes in her husbands life

219 Prays the Defts may produce all papers {relating} to Pennsilvania Company, that the plt may see what Interest he hath therein.

PLEA[29] As to so much as tends ~~th~~ to lessen the Consideracion of the Deeds or Draw the Accounts in Question, PLEAD[30]

5 Lease and Release 23: & 24: Augt 1682 consideration 3000l of 300,000 Acres of Land and bond to pay the money

15 Mortgage 10: June {1685} of 300,000 Acres and 3 Mannors & all the Quittrent for 5000l to be paid with Allowances, receipt, bond to performe Covenants

23 Mortgage 11: Aprill 1687 in Consideration 6000l sells all the Province for 5000 yeares. receipt and bond to performe Covenants

27 release of the Equity 30: Augt 1690

33 Assignemt of the same date to Attend Inheritance

37 Lease & release 2: & 3: 7ber 1690 Consideration 6900l of all the Province to Ford

48 Release and Confirmacion 29: 7ber 1696 of the premisses discharged of all Equity Consideration 6900l and 3447l

56 Defeazance the same day for the Plt to repurchase in 6mo for 10657l bond in 20,000l for payment of the money

61:63 Plt and Ford settled Accounts in writings, Plt gave generall Release

65 Indr of Release & Confirmacion of all the premisses 1: Aprill 1697

~~6~~73 Lease from Ford to the Plaintiff 2: Aprill 1697 for 3 years at 630l rent.

84 Deed Poll 10: Aprill 1697 to Purchase in 3 years at 12714:5:0 to be paid in Pennsilvania with Allowance of Exchange to London.

88 Release 10: Aprill 1699 of the note to inspect Accounts

92 Will of Ford 20: January 1699,[31] gives all to be sold

110 Account in 1702 with writings under it

117 Stat. 21: Jac. primi of Limitacions[32]

120 Plead Ayrys Articles of marriage[33]

DEMURRER[34]

136 As to more then 6l per Cent. and 6d in the pound &c Demurr

Ansr[35]

141	Deny all the Circumstances at Executing the Release Lease and Deed Poll of Aprill 1697 at the Ship Taverne, Bridgett saith she never heard her husband owne the Deeds in 1697 were made to save Taxes
147	Deny the indirect Circumstances of obtaining the Release
160	Have not the Letter of Attorney
16[3?]	If redeemable claim the 10347l and interest and rent had rather have the money
167	Deny they have incumbred[36]
~~16~~170	Know not that the Plt sold land to T: Collett &c. in 1699, 'tis not worth while to see the note left with Clerk in Court.
176	Several Summes paid Since Aprill 1702
185	Do not remember any direccion to pay Ayry 300l
188	Circumstances of obtaining Account 1702 denyed
200	Plt protested he had not conveyed away any part of the Province
202	Bridgett proved Ford's will October 1705
205	Demanded money at Plaintiffs Lodgings
207	Phillip[37] in Pennsilvania in 1701 & demanded the money of the Plaintiff
210	Anne and Susann Say the Plt promised payment
212	Plt threatened to hang up[38] the Suite & keep them out of their money
214	Accions at the Defendants Suite & Bill agst Plt
218	As to Account left with Clerk in Court, will not see it because it is Covered by Plea and Demurrer
224	It is not materiall what Bridgett Said or did under Coverture[39]
225	Account of the Affair of Pennsilvania Company. Defts have none of the books[40]

D. Penn Papers, Ford vs. Penn, HSP. (*Micro.* 13:349.)

1. The first part of the Fords' plea, demurrer, and answer recapitulates WP's second Bill of Complaint (*Micro.* 13:036). To enable readers to grasp quickly the points at issue, the editors refer to WP's first Bill of Complaint (doc. 110), which is virtually identical.

2. Folio. See doc. 113, n. 3.

3. Plaintiff's.

4. WP contended that Philip Ford took advantage of his impending trip to Pennsylvania to surprise him with this account. See doc. 110, text at n. 11.

5. WP insisted that Ford did not loan him the money necessary to purchase the goods for Pennsylvania but had actually bought them on six months' credit, by which time WP had paid him the required cash. See doc. 110, text following n. 10.

6. Another "surprise" for WP (see n. 4, above) at the time of his departure for Pennsylvania.

7. WP claimed that what appear to be separate accounts were, in fact, one continuous account within these dates. See doc. 110, text at n. 13.

8. See *PWP,* 3:659-60.

9. That is, they differed from the total in the accounts at the time the deeds were executed.

10. Therefore Ford had an absolute conveyance from 1690 to 1696, which he did not take advantage of. WP claimed that this bolstered his confidence in the integrity of Philip Ford, which made him an easy and unsuspecting target for fraud and extortion.

11. See *PWP,* 3:661-62.

12. See doc. 110, nn. 22-23.

13. Ford, in a "Seeming Extasie of Joy," embraced WP, and "looking on his said wife said to her Law you now . . . You thought he would not Doe it." See doc. 110, text following n. 29.

14. In other words, mortgages for debts.

15. WP argued that a tenant (as the Fords alleged him to be) would not have the right to sell any part of his tenancy.

16. See doc. 110, text at n. 34.

17. Once again, WP alleged that a tenant could not grant a power of attorney to the alleged proprietor (Ford) to sell part or all of his tenancy. See n. 15, above.

18. That is, WP would not bring charges against the defendants nor would he disavow the securities which he had given. He simply wished the amount of the securities reduced in proportion to allowances and abatements he claimed on the accounts.

19. WP wished to have diminution of the charges against his account for stock in the Free Society of Traders. See n. 40, below.

20. Once again, WP insisted that the various securities he signed were based on one continuous account and were not separate transactions.

21. An ascertaining of what the defendants could legally claim from the plaintiff.

22. The deeds can be found in *PWP,* 2:291-95; 3:658-63. See also doc. 113.

23. Covenant.

24. That is, the amount charged was extortionate, leaving the defendants liable to prosecution for usury; therefore, WP claimed that Ford had disguised it as "allowance," or, in other words, a commission.

25. Although the background to this release is discussed at length in WP's first Bill of Complaint (doc. 110, text at nn. 65-66), a more detailed account can be found in *Micro.* 12:831.

26. See doc. 110, text at n. 67.

27. See ibid., text at nn. 67-70.

28. See ibid., text at nn. 71-73.

29. Here begins the defendants' response to WP's Bill of Complaint. This section contains the pleas in bar. See headnote to doc. 113.

30. The documents cited here can be found in *PWP,* 2:291-95; 3:658-63. See also doc. 113.

31. See Probate 11/484, PRO.

32. See doc. 113, n. 23.

33. See ibid., n. 24.

34. See headnote to doc. 113.

35. Here the Fords directly answer points in WP's second Bill of Complaint.

36. This is unclear but may refer to WP's allegation that Phillip Ford had conspired with him to avoid taxes. An encumbrance often refers to taxes which are still owed on a property. See *Black's Law Dictionary,* p. 473.

37. Phillip Ford, Jr.

38. To delay.

39. As the wife of Phillip Ford. See doc. 113, n. 46.

40. The Fords stated that WP had subscribed to the Free Society in 1682 in the names of and for the benefit of his children — Springett, William, Jr., and Laetitia — and for William Markham, William Haige, Silas Crispin, Rebecca Crispin, Richard Penn, and John Darby. The Fords also insisted that any receipts or certificates for such subscriptions were signed by the president and treasurer of the Free Society, but that Philip Ford had never been treasurer. The books, they added, had long since been taken to Pennsylvania, except for some private books kept by the Society's agents, who were under an obligation of secrecy (See Chancery, Reynardson's Division, bundle 183, no. 40, PRO). It appears that the books held by Bridget Ford were subsequently turned over to Chancery where further "errors" in the accounts were discovered. See doc. 116, n. 35.

116
STATEMENT OF THE CASE AGAINST BRIDGET FORD AND OTHERS

The following document, drawn up by WP and his counsel, is difficult to date precisely. It mentions (text at n. 32) that "My Lord Chancellor" has allowed the Fords' plea, a reference to Sir William Cowper, who became lord chancellor on 4 May 1707. WP's counsel, on 14 May 1707, argued his replication (*Micro.* 13:165) before Cowper, who essentially denied their efforts to reopen the Ford accounts. Doc. 116 differs considerably from this replication and seems to have been drawn up for another purpose, most likely as the basis for an appeal to the House of Lords. On 10 June 1707 WP indicated to James Logan (see doc. 139) that the case would be appealed in the Lords in an effort to reopen the accounts. Thus doc. 116 probably dates from the summer of 1707. Despite continuing talk of an appeal to the Lords (see Norris Papers, 7:104, 127, 162), the case was resolved out of court. Doc. 116 contains two notable differences from previous documents in this case. First, it admits that WP's case has numerous serious disadvantages, a point clearly enunciated by Lord Chancellor Cowper at the 14 May 1707 hearing. Second, the appended accounts represent WP's contention that at most he owes the Fords only £5413 as of 1 April 1706, and that the figure was more likely £2263. This amount would be totally unacceptable to the Fords.

[c. summer 1707]

William Penn Esqr Ag^t^ Bridgett Ford Widow Executrix of Philip Ford her late Husband deceased & Philip Bridgett Susan & Anne her Son and Daughters with John Hall & Tho. Mosse

About the year 1669[1] Philip Ford the deceased being then in mean Circumstances[2] applyed himself to Mr Penn that he might be employed by him as his servant, Mr Penn as such did accept his service and Agreed to allow him a sallary of 40£ per Annum.[3]

The said Ford continued the service from that time to the year 1682 and performed it faithfully and from time to time gave in his accounts under his hand to Mr Penn once in 6 months or oftner.

Ford continued his service until about the 29: of September 1696[4] but instead of charging Mr Penn with the sallary alone he hath as appears by his Accounts added thereto most Exorbitant Charges.

Mr Penn in the year 1682 having a Grant of the Province of Pennsylvania; and the Country in order to the improvement thereof requiring his presence there, Mr Penn was wholy taken up wth matters relating thereto and in preparing for his voyage, And was under a necessity of depending upon the Integrity of Philip Ford as to all matters between them; Note Mr Penn went his voyage in Augt 1682.

Ford by his former service (when indeed he wanted the oppertunity of imposing upon Mr Penn) having Established himself in the good Opinion of Mr Penn took now the advantage of him, went with him to Deale where he Embarqued for the said province, and offered Mr Penn there an Account (the Ballance of which due to the said Ford as he had made it amounted to 2851:7:10) which Mr Penn in that hurry he then was at the Instance of Ford Signed with Errors Excepted.

{4 Augt 1682}[5] Ford at the same time tendred a Deed being a Mortgage for the Terme of 500[0] years of part of the Province for securing to him 3000l wch Mr Penn also executed[6]

NOTE Mr Penn being at this time (as may reasonably be supposed) uncapable of advising with others, or looking into these matters himself with that care which the case required, he upon the Confidence he then had of the integrity of Ford implicitly Signed and Executed the Account and Deed without peruseal or having any parts or Coppies of either: And that he did not observe what he was to doe plainly appears.

For the 24: of August 1682 he signes an Account by which he makes himselfe Debtor to Ford 2851:7:10 And the same day Executes a deed[7] whereby he makes himself Debtor to Ford 3000l to be paid the 26 of the Same month without reference of one to the other, or observing the difference between the Account and Deed.

In October 1684 Mr Penn returned from Pennsylvania to England and continued here till August 1699

Mr Penn upon his returne being very much Engaged and taken up about the Affairs of his Country and other publique matters Ford observed It, and took his oppertunity when Mr Penn was most busy, to get him to signe his Accounts and Execute his Deeds, which he had allways ready ingrossed[8] wthout previous Notice given to Mr Penn and when Ford mett him accidentally his way was to perswade him to goe to a Coffee house, Alehouse or Taverne and there tender his Accounts and Deeds which Mr Penn too readily signed and Executed, allways believing Ford to be honest And that the Deeds were a Collateral security for the Ballance of the Accounts And that by his signing the Account with Errors Excepted, both the one & the other were thereby subject to an Examinacion not observing the Variance between the Ballance of the Accounts and Consideracions of the Deeds.

{21 Mar:1684} Mr Penn signed an Account whereupon a ballance of 4293:3:0½ is made Due to Ford which begins the said 24 of August 1682 And the first Article therein charged is the said Ballance of 2851:7:10.

{10 June 1685} Mr Penn gives him a Mortgage of other part of the Province for 500 Years with Provisoe to be void upon payment of

5000l the 21: of March 1686 and usual allowances in the said Province.[9]

{Note} To make the last Ballance 5000l he reckons more than 8l per Cent for two years[10]

{11 April 1687} Mr Penn signed an Account whereupon a Ballance of 5282:9:8½ is made due to Ford which begins the said 21: of March 1684 And the first Article therein charged is the said Ballance of 4293:3:0½.

{11 April 1687} Mr Penn Gives a Mortgage of the whole Province for the Terme of 5000 Years with a Provisoe to be void upon payment of 6000l the 11: of April 1688 and usual allowance in the said Province.[11]

{Note} To make the last Ballance 6000l he reckons more than 8l per Cent. for one Yeare

{11 Octor 1689} Mr Penn signed an Account whereupon a Ballance of 6333:19:2 is made due to Ford which begins the said 11: of April 1687 And the first Article therein charged is the said Ballance of 5282:9:8½.

{Note} It plainly appears that the said Mr Penn signed and Executed the said Accounts and Deeds upon entire confidence in the Said Ford for none of the Said Deeds have any reference to the other or to the Accounts So that he now stands charged by the Account, debtor to Ford the summe of 6333:19:2 And by the several Deeds as in the Margent amounting in the whole to 20333:19:2 when the said Ford did not pretend any more than 6333:19:2 due to him.

{30 Augt 1690} Mr Penn released to Ford his Equity of Redempcion in the Said Mortgage of the 11 of April 1687.[12]

{1 Septr 1690} The Mortgage of the 11 of ~~Septemr~~ {April} 1687 was assigned to one Thomas Ellwood for the remainder of the said Terme of 5000 years in trust for the Said Ford.[13]

{2 & 3 Septr 1690} Mr Penn by Indenture of Lease and Release in Consideracion of 69000l conveys the whole Province to Ford & his heires without any Defeazance.[14]

{11 Jan. 1694} Mr Penn signed an account whereupon a Ballance of 9016:12:5 is made due to Ford which begins the said 11 of Octor 1689 and the first article therein charged is the said Ballance of 6333:19:2.

{11 June 1696} Mr Penn signed an Account whereupon a Ballance of 10202l 8:7½ is made due to the Said Ford which begins the Said 11 January 1694 And the first Article therein charged is the Said Ballance of 9016:12:5.

{Note} That the Conveyance before mencioned of 2 & 3 of Septr 1690 was made when Mr Penn was under the displeasure of the Government which was the reason it was made absolute to the said Ford, And it is an undeniable Evidence that Mr Penn put entire Trust & Confidence in him, and his Confidence was so great that he suffered the estate to continue absolute till 29 Septr 1696.

That the said Ford for sometime before the 29: of Septr 1696 having quitted the service of the said Mr Penn he the said Mr Penn then desired a Defeazance of the absolute Conveyance of the said Province in 1690.

Ford insisted upon stating the Accounts in a more formal manner than had been done formerly and prevailed on Mr Penn to signe an Account stated in method following.—

William Penn D^R^

1696		
11 June	To Ballance then due at stating Accounts	10202:8: 7½
29 Sept^r^	To Consideration Dr Ballance	245:6:10
		10447:15: 5½

Per Contra Cred^R^

1696		
13 June	By Cash received of thy self	100: 0:—
	By Ballance then due to Philip Ford	10347:15: 5½
		10447:15: 5½

We do Acknowledge to have adjusted and agreed the Account hereabove written and do allow and approve of the same as settled and adjusted between us And there is Due from the said William Penn to the said Philip Ford the Ballance of this Account being 10347:15:5½ In Testimony whereof we have both of us hereunto put our hands in London the 29: of Septr 1696.

Signed in the presence of

P Whinnick[15] William Penn

W Whinnick[16] Philip Ford.

At the same time this Account was stated Ford prevailed with Mr Penn to Execute a General Release bearing date the said 29 of Septem^r^ 1696 of all Accounts claims and Demands &c.[17]

{29 Sepr 1696} Mr Penn Executed to the said Ford alsoe at the same time a Release of all Equity of Redempcion[18] in the said Province reciting the said Lease & Release of 2 & 3 of Septem^r^ 1690 And declaring that allthough it was absolute yet it was intended only as a security for the 6900^l^ Consideracion therein expressed

{Note} the Consideracion of this Deed is the same with the Ballance of the Account stated at the same time.

Mr Penn at the same time had a Defeazance[19] from Ford (reciting the last mencioned Deed) whereby Ford agrees with Mr Penn to convey the Estate back again to him upon payment of 10657 the 30: of March following which is the said Ballance of 10347:15:5½ and interest thereof from 29 of Septem^r^ to the 30th of March following.

☞ What is to observed here is that it plainly appears By the date of the Account and ballance thereof, they agreeing with the date of the Deed and Consideracion thereof, that the Deeds and Accounts are for the same money. At this time Mr Penn had Ford's promise for giving him Coppies of what he had signed and Executed which 'tis supposed he was then the more easily satisfied with, though he had them not at that time, because he thought himself safe in the Writing given him by Ford at the same time which is as Followeth.

Whereas upon settling accounts between William Penn and myself he hath not only allowed of the said account to be true and signed the same accordingly but hath likewise given me a General Discharge bearing even date herewith Now I for the said William Penn his satisfaccion Do Agree and promise that if hereafter any material Error shall be found in the said Account to his prejudice and be clearly made appear Then and in such Case the same shall be made him good notwithstanding the said General Discharge Dated the 29: of Septemr 1696.

Signed and sealed in the presence of
P Whinnick　　　　　　　　Phillip Ford
W Whinnick

{Note} About 6 months after, Ford according to his Promise gave to Mr Penn all the before mencioned Accounts which are by carrying the Ballances from one to another made one Entire Account And upon the whole the Ballance pretended to be due is the said sume of 10347:15:5½ These accounts delivered to Mr Penn by Ford, are all of his own hand writing and all severally signed by Ford with Errors Excepted.

{Note} Mr Penn by his Bill in Chancery[20] prays relief against the Errors appearing in the Body of the Accounts which are therein particularly sett forth & amount to about 10000.l He alsoe makes the Accounts part of his Bill and Leaves them in the hand of his Clerke in Court for the Defts to View, and answer whether they are not the hand writing of Ford; But the Defts give noe Answer to anything relating to the Accounts other than that they say they claime nothing but by the Account stated in 1696 if the Estate in Ford be deemed a Mortgage.

As the Case now appears it seems reasonable that the account should be examined, for notwithstanding all Acts done blindfold by Mr Penn before and on the 29: of Septemr 1696 he is to have all Errors appearing in the Account to be allowed him by the said Writing under the hand and seal of Philip Ford of the 29 of Septemr 1696. And as to the Acts done by Mr Penn at {this time} and before, they are by the same Writing wholly made ineffectual and no part of his Case, But since that time he has done the Acts following which makes the difficulty of his Case.

About the begining of Aprill 1697, {~~being~~ abt 6 mo. after the said mortgage} it being when there was a Tax upon money at Interest;[21] Ford applyed himself to Mr Penn with the Opinion of Counsell,[22] that moneys due upon the Province would be lyable to be Taxed the

Parties living in England, And that it could be prevented noe Other way then by Mr Penn's making to Ford an absolute Conveyance of the Province, and his making a Lease thereof to Mr Penn at an Annual Rent {to preserve his possession}.

{1 Aprill 1697} Mr Penn still retains his Opinion of Ford and by Indenture absolutely releases and Confirmes the said Province to Ford and his heires.[23]

{2 Aprill 1697} Ford demises the same to Mr Penn for 3 years at the Rent of 630l per annum payable one halfe in Pennsylvania and the other half in London[24] wch 630l per annum was Exactly the Interest of the money pretended to be then due.[25]

{10 Ap. 1697} Instead of a Defeazance Ford enters into an Agreement with Mr Penn (reciting the last Conveyance & Lease) whereby he Agreed that in Consideracion of trouble of raising money and of Mr Penn's desire to purchase the Province; To sell the same to him upon payment of the summe of 12714:5:0 in the said Province at any time within three Yeares with allowance of Exchange.[26]

{Note} it may reasonably be supposed that Mr Penn was the more easily induced to these last Acts, by Fords giving the Defeazance in 1696 after the Province had been absolute in Ford above 5 years as believing it to be an Act of integrity tho there was nothing in it because as hereafter appears the Deft chooses the money rather than the Country.

Mr Penn in his Bill setts forth that these Acts in 1697 were done at the desire of Philip Ford for the purposes aforesaid, and that he was by the said absolute Conveyance a Trustee for Mr Penn except as to what should appear due to the said Ford upon examining the said Account, and charges that the Deft Bridgett Ford was privy to this Circumvencion, that she knew the Deeds were only a Trust as aforesaid, and that she was present at the Execucion of them and charges that Ford assured him at the same time that it was the Opinion of Counsell that the contract would be construed a Defeazance, and several other Circumstances, But she denys all Except that she was present at the Execucion of the Deeds at the place suggested and there is indeed so Little proofe of it's being a Mortgage that Mr Penn must for that purpose chiefly rely upon the said Agreement for sale of the Povince back to him and the Circumstance of the Rent reserved being Exactly the Interest of the money pretended to be due.

{Note} In the month of August 1699 Mr Penn with his Wife & Daughter being then bound out on a Voyage for Pennsylvania, And under an Agreement with the Master of a Vessell to be aboard his ship[27] about the 28 of the same month and the goods and servants of the said Mr Penn being all on board, And he having taken his Leave of all his Friends at Court, The said Mr Penn about the 20: of August went to Ford at his Lodgings at Islington[28] to take his Leave of him, and the said Ford and his Wife knowing the advantage they had of him the said Writing given the 29 Septem^r 1696 for allowing to him the Errors appearing in the said Account, which Mr Penn not having, but it being at his house at Worminghurst in Sussex, they produced a Writing ready ingrossed, and told him he must Execute that, or else he should not goe to Pennsylvania, and threatned to divulge the Country's being made over to Ford (which was a Secrett, only in the breasts of Ford and his Wife and Mr Penn) And by other Threats, and by assureances given him, that it should not be made use of to hinder the Examining the Accounts, or otherwise to His prejudice, prevail'd with Mr Penn to Execute the same Writing a Coppy of which is as followeth, The said Writing of the 29: of Septem^r is sett forth verbatim after which the said Writing now given is in these words WHEREAS the abovenamed Philip Ford hath desired me to deliver up his Original Note whereof the true Coppy is hereabove, or else to assigne Errors If I have found any in the said accounts to which the said Note relates. I WILLIAM PENN Do hereby acknowledge that no Error hath hitherto appeared in the Said Account And therefore do by these presents Release and Discharge the said Philip Ford from the said Note which being mislaid I cannot now deliver up as it ought to be; But do promise whenever the same shall come to my hands I will deliver it up to the said Philip Ford or order to be Cancelled Wittness my hand and seale in London the 10: Augt 1699.

All the Circumstances by which this Release was obtained are suggested by the Bills But denyed by the Def^ts And all the Proofe Mr Penn hath is that by the date of the release it appears that it was Executed about the time he Embarqued for Pennsylvania.

{Obs:} That Philip Ford by his Will[29] (reciting that he had purchased the said Province) gives the Same to John Hall Thomas Moss and Bridgett Ford & their heires in Trust for them to sell and dispose of the same, and out of the money that shall be raised by sale thereof to pay the summe of 4500^l to and amongst his Children and the remainder he gives to his Wife Bridgett, But declares if Mr Penn in 6 months time shall pay the summe of 11134:8:3 with all Arrears of Rent, and all other Debts, That then his said Trustees should convey the said Province to Mr Penn and his heires with Provisoe that this kindness shall not extend to his heires, in Case of his death, or to give him or his heires any Equity of Redempcion, he makes the said Bridgett Ford his Executrix That which seems still harder on Mr Penn is the Account next following which is a Stated Account of Rent between him and the Execut^x of Ford.

WILLIAM PENN ESQ^R D^R

1697 April 1: To rent due for the Province of Pennsylvania as by Lease dated 2: April 1697 for 3 years at 630^l per Annum to be paid half yearly one half the 1: of April and the other 1: Octo^r in every year	£ 1890

To Rent due from 1: of April 1700 to 1 April 1702 is 2 years	1260
	3150

PER CONTRA CRED[R]

1697 Novem[r] 13 By Cash of Samuel Vaus for the account of W P.	£	30: 0:
And of himself and several persons for his account		2528:11:2
amounting in the whole to		2558:11:2
Ballance due to Bridget Ford 1: April 1702		591: 8:10
		3150: 0:0

I WILLIAM PENN of &c. Do hereby Declare That I have considered and Examined the Accounts hereabove written which I find to be just and true and Doe hereby acknowledge that the Ballance thereof being 591:8:10 is by me the said William Penn really and bona fide due and owing to Bridgett Ford Widow as she is Entitled thereto by Vertue of the last Will and Testament of her late husband Philip Ford deceased and do promise to pay the said summe of 591:8:10 to her or her order at demand accordingly at her new dwelling house in Water Lane London, also I do hereby acknowledge that the Rent of the premisses is 630[l] per Annum as is hereabove in the particulars of the Account mencioned

WITTNESS my hand and seal in London this 2: of April An[o] Domini 1702.

Sealed and delivered in the presence of John Hall
Thomas Mosse

{NOTE} For Relief against the last Account of M[r] Penn in 1702 It is suggested in the Bill that he executed it condicionally, that it should not be construed to ratifie the Conveyance of the Province in 1697, or to make him Tennant thereof or to obstruct or hinder his Examining the said Accounts, And that notwithstanding his Executing thereof he reserved to himself the Liberty of having the Accounts between him and Ford examined, And that upon these Condicions and Termes the said Bridgett Ford accepted the said Writing in 1702.

Bridgett by her Answer denys all and says she would not have accepted upon these Condicions, And that M[r] Penn had the Draft thereof 3 weeks in his Custody to consider of, and believes he Executed it freely.

{NOTE} M[r] Penn hath no other Wittnesses of what is suggested in his Bill but Hall and Mosse who will say That before he Executed the said Writing he was very unwilling to do it And declared he had not read or examined one Item of the Account, And that he did it with a Provisoe of saving to himselfe a further Examinacion of that Account, as he had heretofore done when he signed former Accounts, And that he particularly objected against the Word Rent in this Account.[30]

{Obs:} That the Defts have pleaded all the before mencioned Deeds and also the settlement of the Account the 29: Septemr 1696 But say by their Answer that they claime nothing by any of the Accounts before the date of the Lease in 1697 (if any such Accounts there be) which Fact they do not intend to put in issue. But if the Court adjudge the Estate redeemable, they claim that the sume of 10347:15:5½ the Ballance of the Account in 1696 ought to be the Principal money on such Redempcion And by their Answer choose to accept the Same[31] with the Interest thereof and Rent due rather than the Country but say that they dare not make such offer, therefore insist that the said Estate is not redeemable.

This is truly the Case of Mr Penn with all the disadvantageous Circumstances in it.

My Lord Chancellor[32] upon arguing the Plea hath allowed it,[33] But it is hoped that upon hearing the Cause the Conveyance in 1697 will be Decreed only a mortgage.

It is true that Mr Penn by the Confidence he had in Ford by the Awe and Command Ford had upon him least he should discover the Conveyance to him of the Country, and his beliefe that all Acts done by him would be subject to the Justice of the Account, hath been inadvertantly prevailed upon to do so many things before and since the Account settled the 29: of Septemr 1696 (which is a settlement of the whole Account from 1682 it being nothing but a Ballance of the whole and the Interest of that Ballance) that it seems very difficult to come at an Examinacion thereof especially since Ford is dead.[34]

But That which gives hopes for Reliefe in this Case is

{1} That by the Instrument given by Ford to Mr Penn the 29: of Septr 1696 (which was the time of settling the last Account, and indeed the whole Account between them from 1682) for having all Errors in the Account allowed, it appears that all Acts done before that time were to be subject to what should appear justly due upon Examining the Accounts.

{2} That Mr Penn hath the whole Account in several parts from 1682 to the 29: Septemr 1696 All of the hand Writing of Ford and by him several times subscribed with Errors Excepted for proofe of which he made it part of his Bill and left them in the hands of his Clerk for the Defts to View, and his hand is so remarkable and so well knowne that it cannot be a Question whether the Accounts are Ford's.

{3} It appears plainly in the pleadings that the Ballance of the Account of the 29: of Septemr 1696 and the Consideracion of the Deed dated the same day, that they are one and the same summe And it further appears that the Defts Demand springs from the said Account because by their Plea they have pleaded the settlement of the Account 29: of Septemr 1696 and by their Answer they claime the Ballance thereof and interest if the Estate be deemed a mortgage As for their claiming Rent besides; that unreasonable Demand Answers it self for it appears that the Rent is exactly the interest of the money pretended due when the Lease was made.

{4} The Errors appearing in the Account are particularly sett forth in the Bill and amount to 10,000^{l} and upwards[35] And what Mr Penn prays Relief against, are only the Errors appearing in the body of Philip Ford's owne Account which cannot be supposed to be a hardship upon the Execut^{r}. The Errors appearing in the Account are reckonings of Interest at 8£ per Cent. every six months, and interest every 6 months at 8^{l} per Cent for the Interest and 6 pence in the pound for the whole Debet of every Account which is made up mostly of Ballances brought from former Accounts and interest carryed to the Account, besides Commission at 2^{l} 10^{s} per Cent. and interest at 8^{l} per Cent. every 6 months for the six pences and Commission, and making these reckonings several times over for the same summes which cannot be so intelli~~b~~gibly expressed as seen by the accounts, This Account hath been examined by a very good Artist[36] who hath given Ford more than the usual advantages, (Viz^{t}) 6^{l} per Cent Interest for all money advanced, and made the Interest principal Every year, 2^{l} 10^{s} per Cent. for all goods mencioned to be bought and sold in the Account, and 10^{s} per Cent. for all money received and paid and his sallary of 40^{l} per Annum and interest thereof annually and so made principal And the whole Ballance comes to but 5413:17:0½ as appears by the Account following when the Def^{ts} demand is about 14000^{l}.

An Abstract of the several Accounts Between William Penn Esquire Philip Ford deceased and Bridget his Relict, from the 23^{d} of Augt 1682 to 1^{t} April 1706 with the Interest of the first Ballance (said to be due to the said Philip Ford) made Principal at the end of every year, and sometimes sooner at the end of the Acc^{ts} and the Interest of the several Ballances following made principal as aforesaid; Together with his sallary reckon'd every year, and his Commission money & the Interest thereof annually added thereto, and all Computed at 6£ per Cent per Annum.

		£ s D
23 Augt 1682	Cash due to Philip Ford	2851:07:10
To 23 Augt 1683	For the Interest thereof for 1 Year	171:01: 8
	For one Years sallary for Philip Ford	40:00
		3062:09: 6
To 23 Augt 1684	For the Interest of the Total or last sume for 1 year	183:14:11½
	For one Yeares sallary	40:—:—
		3286:04: 5½

Date	Particulars	£ s D
To 21 Mar 1684/5	For the Interest of the last summe for 7 months wanting 2 days being the end of this Acct	112:12: 7¼
	For P Fords sallary for the same time	22:16:11¾
	Cash paid by Philip Ford	8561:04: 7
	For Commission money at 6d per £ for 422:6:11 being what the Goods came to that were bought in this Acct And	10: 11: 2
From 23 Augt 1682 to the 21 March 1684/5	For Commission money at 10s per Cent. for 8138:17:8 being the moneys paid Bills of Exchange &c in this Account	40:12:11
		12034:02: 8½
	Cash Received by Philip Ford	8198:10: 7½
21 Mar 1684/5	The Ballance due to Philip Ford	3835:12: 1
	The Interest of the Ballance for 1 Year	230:02: 8½
to 21 Mar 1685/6	For one Years sallary	40:—:—
	Carried over	4105:14: 9½

Date	Particulars	£ s D
	Brought from 'tother side	4105:14: 9½
To 21 Mar 1686/7	For the Interest thereof for 1 Year	246:06:10¾
	For one Yeares sallary	40:—:—
		4392:01: 8¼
To 11 Aprill 1687	For the Interest of the last sume for 21 days being the end of this Account	15:02: 0¾
	For P Fords sallary for the same time	2:06: 0¼
	Cash paid by Philip Ford	3006:10:10¼
From 21 March 1684/5 to the 11 of Aprill 1687	For Commission money at 6d per £ for 214:5:2½ being what the goods came to that were bought in this Acct and	5: 7: 1½
	For Commission money at 10s per Cent for 2892:5:7¾ being the moneys paid Bills of Exchange &c in this Account	14:09: 2½
		7435:16:11½
	Cash Received by Philip Ford	2922:09:11
11 April 1687	The Ballance due to Philip Ford	4513:07: 0½

Date	Item	£ s d
To 11 April 1688	The Interest of the Ballance for 1 Year	270:16: 0¼
	For one Years sallary	40:—:—
		4824:03: 0¾
To 11 April 1689	The Interest of the last summe for 1 Year	289:08:11½
	For one Years sallary	40:—:—
		5153:12: 0¼
To 11: 8br 1689	For the Interest of the last summe for six months being the end of this Account	154:12: 1¾
	For the sallary of the same time	20:—:—
From 11 April 1687 to 11 of 8br 1689	Cash paid by Philip Ford	1293:19: 6
	For Commission money at 6d per £ for 142:3:4 being wt the goods came to that were bought in this Account—	3:11: 1
	and For Commission money at 10s per Cent for 1151:16:2 being the moneys paid Bills of Exchange &c in this Account	5:15: 2
		6631:09:11
	Cash Received by Philip Ford	1580:00: 4½
11: 8br 1689	The Ballance due to Philip Ford Carried Over	5051:09: 6½

		£ s D
	The Ballance brought from 'tother side	5051:09: ½
To 11: 8br 1690	For the Interest thereof for one Year	303:01: 9¼
		5354:11: 3¾
To 11: 8br 1691	For the Interest of the last summe for 1 year	321:05: 5½
		5675:16: 9¼
To 11: 8br 1692	For the Interest of the last summe for 1 Year	340:11:—
		6016:07: 9¼
To 11: 8br 1693	For the Interest of the last summe for 1 Year	360:19: 7¾
		6377:07: 5
To 11: 8br 1694	For the Interest of the last summe for 1 Year	382:12:10
		6760:00: 3

Date	Item	£ s D
To 11: Jan. 1694/5	For the Interest of the last summe for three months being the end of this Account	101:08:—
From 11: 8br 1689	Cash paid by Philip Ford	134:18:11
		6996:07: 2
To 11 Jan. 1694/5	Cash Received by Philip Ford	1399:14: 2
11 Jan. 1694/5	The Ballance due to Philip Ford	5596:13: 0
To 11 Jan. 1694/5	For the Interest of the Ballance for 1 Year	335:15:11½
		5932:08:11½
To 11 June 1696	For the Interest of the last sume for 5 months being the end of this Account	144:11: 2½
From 11 Jan 1694/5 to 11: June 1696	Cash paid by Philip Ford	1:11: 7
		6078:11: 9
	Cash Received by Philip Ford	866:18: 4
11 June 1696	The Ballance due to Philip Ford	5211:13: 5
To 11: June 1697	The Interest thereof for 1 Year	312:14:
		5524:07: 5
To 11 June 1698	The Interest of the last summe for 1 Year	331:09: 3
		5855:16: 8
To 11: June 1699	The Interest of the last summe for 1 Year	351:07:—
		6207:03: 8
To 24 April 1700	The Interest of the last summe for 10 months 13 days being the end of this Acct	324:07:11¾
	Carried over	6531:11: 7¾

Date	Item	£ s D
	Brought from t'other side	6531:11 7¾
From 11: June 1696 to 24: Ap. 1700	Cash paid by Philip or Bridgett Ford	82:08: 4
		6613:19:11¾
	Cash Received by Philip & Bridget Ford	1828:18: 3
24: April 1700	The Ballance due to Philip or Bridget Ford	4785:01: 8¾
To 24: April 1701	The Interest of the Ballance for 1 Year	287:02: 1
		5072:03: 9¾

To 1: April 1702	The Interest of the last summe for 1 Year wanting 23 days being the end of this Acct	285:03: 0½
From 24: April 1700 to 1 Ap: 1702	Cash paid by Bridget Ford	18: 9
		5358:05: 7¼
	Cash Received by Bridget Ford	1070: —: —
1: April 1702	The Ballance due to Bridget Ford	4288:05: 7¼
To 1: April 1703	The Interest of the Ballance for 1 year	257:05:11
		4545:11: 6¼
To 1: April 1704	The Interest of the last summe for 1 year	272:14: 8
		4818:06: 2¼
To 1 April 1705	The Interest of the last summe for 1 year	289:01:11
		5107:08: 1¼
To 1: April 1706	The Interest of the last summe for 1 year	306:08:11¼
1t April 1706	Due by this Acct to Bridget Ford	5413:17: 0½

NOTE that in this Account there is allowed to Philip Ford the summe of 712l 10s (said to be paid by him) on 23d Augt 1682 and of 500l on the 2d of April 1684 to the Pennsylvania Society[37] for the use of William Penn. The Truth of which is questionable he not having any demonstracion of the payment thereof: For Bridget Ford refuses to discover the Books of the Society by which it ought to appear that Ford hath given Credit for the same sumes,[38] and if they with the Interest included in this Account (which amount in the whole to 3150l and upwards be taken out of the said Ballance of

	5413:17: 0½
	3150: —: —
There remains due to Ford but	2263:17: 0½

D. Penn Papers, Ford vs. Penn, HSP. (*Micro.* 12:470.)

1. Ford began working for WP on 20 Sept. 1669 (*PWP*, 1:103); his first assignment was to accompany WP to Ireland and help him manage Admiral Penn's property in 1669-70.
2. For WP's patronizing description of Ford's occupation immediately preceding his hiring, see doc. 123, text at n. 25.
3. Although £40 is normally cited by WP as Ford's salary, a state of the case drawn up about Sept. 1707 notes that Ford "Sold Threat laces in the Streets of London But a Little Time before the sd W Penn Took him into his Service for £12 for Annum." See *Micro.* 13:273.

4. The date at which Ford ceased his tenure as WP's steward is unclear. In his Bill of Complaint, WP claims that Ford continued in his employ until 24 June 1694 (doc. 110, text at n. 1). Elsewhere (doc. 111, text at n. 18), WP implies that Ford continued as his steward until 11 June 1696 when he presented WP with a balance on the account. According to the abstract of the Ford-WP accounts stated here, Ford performed few services for WP after 1689. Between 23 Aug. 1682 and 11 Oct. 1689, Ford expended £12,861 14s 11¼d on WP's account, but between 11 Oct. 1689 and his death on 8 Jan. 1702, Ford expended only £219 17s 7d.

5. In margin. The editors have placed marginal citations within these {brackets}. The correct date is 24 Aug. 1682.

6. See *PWP,* 2:291-92.

7. See ibid., 2:292-93.

8. See doc. 110, n. 11.

9. See *PWP,* 3:658. The term was 5000 years, not 500.

10. The legal limit for interest on loans was 6 percent a year. See doc. 125, n. 11.

11. See *PWP,* 3:658.

12. See ibid., 3:659.

13. See ibid.

14. See ibid., 3:659-60. The correct figure is £6900.

15. Unidentified.

16. Unidentified.

17. See *PWP,* 3:661.

18. See ibid., 3:660.

19. See ibid., 3:660-61.

20. See doc. 110.

21. See ibid., n. 22.

22. See ibid., n. 23.

23. see *PWP,* 3:661.

24. See ibid., 3:662.

25. Although WP appears to be correct in equating the interest owed and the amount charged for "rent," the matter is not as clear as he implies, for the precise sum of £10,500 was not stated in any of the documents which WP signed. WP could claim that the £10,347 owed by him on 29 Sept. 1696 (see *PWP,* 3:662) remained fully unpaid until 2 Apr. 1697, by which time at 6 percent interest the debt amounted to £10,657. On that date he signed the lease with Ford, and paid him £157 (although Ford dated the receipt 10 Apr. 1697), which left the debt at £10,500. There are two difficulties, however, with this scenario. First, the receipt is dated later than the lease, implying that WP was not reducing the debt to £10,500 and then leasing Pennsylvania for an annual rental equivalent to the interest rate. Second, in May 1698 (see *PWP,* 3:542-43), WP angrily inquired of Samuel Carpenter why his bills of exchange for £157 10s and £315 had been protested. These, along with the above-mentioned £157, represented (less 10s) the annual rent payable by WP to Philip Ford, and therefore indicate that the £157 paid in Apr. 1697 was not intended to lessen the debt to £10,500 but was a rental payment.

26. That is, a deed poll. See *PWP,* 3:662.

27. The *Canterbury,* with Henry Tregeny as master.

28. Islington is at present a north London borough.

29. See Probate 11/484, PRO.

30. The response of Hall and Moss to interrogatories about this matter have not been found, but in their answer (doc. 112) to WP's Bill of Complaint they state that WP had the account three weeks, and they imply that he signed without protest.

31. Rather than rely on the £11, 134 with interest and back rent mentioned in Philip Ford's will.

32. Sir William Cowper, who became lord chancellor of Great Britain on 4 May 1707.

33. See doc. 114.

34. Ford died on 8 Jan. 1702.

35. Estimates of the overcharges vary according to the time when they were calculated. In the summer of 1708, John Jeffreys estimated the overcharges as £9697, not including the questionable charges relating to the Free Society of Traders (see doc. 121C). In July 1708 WP wrote to Nicholas Gates (*Micro.* 13:505) that the Free Society charges were also erroneous, raising the alleged overcharges to £12,946.

36. Unidentified, although it may be John Jeffreys. See n. 35, above.

37. The Free Society of Traders.

38. In fact, Chancery caused the books in question to be "forced out of the Fords hands" (*Micro.* 13:505), whereby further errors were discovered (see n. 35, above.).

117
BRIEF FOR THE DEFENSE IN SUIT FOR ARREARS IN RENT

By filing a second Bill of Complaint in the court of Chancery against the Fords, WP had been able to forestall their efforts either to take possession of Pennsylvania or to secure a substantial cash payment. However, the Fords had other legal options. In 1707, in a civil suit filed against WP for arrears of rent for his tenancy of Pennsylvania, Bridget Ford, Thomas Moss, and John Hall demanded £3150 back rent and £100 damages. The trial was scheduled for 20 May 1707 in the court of Common Pleas at the Guildhall (see *Micro.* 13:187) and was postponed until 28 June 1707. Unlike Chancery, the court of Common Pleas was not interested in the circumstances surrounding these deeds, e.g., fraud, deception, blackmail, but simply whether WP was in possession of Pennsylvania as a contracted tenant of the Fords, and how much rent he owed. The lawyers who prepared the following brief on behalf of WP were hoping to limit the amount of back rent owed by WP; they predicated his defense on differences in wording between the declaration, an account of 1702 between WP and Bridget Ford, and the 1697 lease between WP and Philip Ford. They requested and obtained a special verdict, that is, the jury was to state the facts as it saw them but leave the complex legal questions to be settled by Lord Chief Justice Trevor, who would pronounce the final verdict after hearing counsel from both sides. The jury found that WP had signed the demises in the declaration, that he owed £2908 2s 2d in back rent, and that he should pay 12d damages and 53s 4d in court costs (see *Micro.* 13:291). Lord Chief Justice Trevor on 23 November 1707 sanctioned this award (Norris Papers, 7:127). On 7 January 1708, when bailiffs attempted to arrest WP on a writ of execution at Gracechurch Street meeting, he voluntarily submitted himself to the Fleet prison rather than pay the debt (ibid., 7:147).

[c. 28 June 1707]

IN THE COMMON PLEAS
for the Deft Bridgett Ford Widdow John Hall & Thomas Mosse Plaintiffs — Agt Wm Penn Senr Esqr Defendant

DECLARATION The Plts declare that on the 2d of Aprill 1702 they lett to the Deft the Province of Pennsilvania in America & two other

Tracts of Land neer the same & all Islands Mines &c. And all other the Land of the Plt in America aforesaid (Except 5000 acres in Pennsilvania) To hold for one year & so from year to year as long as all parties should agree at 630l per annum rent so long as the Deft should hold the premisses payable on the 1: day of Octor & the 1: of Aprill & for 315l for halfe a years rent due 1: of Aprill 1707, the plts bring their Accion.[1]

The Deft hath pleaded Nil Debet[2]

PLEA[3] The Deft employed Phillip Ford deceased as his Steward from 1682 {1669} & Ford from time to time made up his Accounts & pretended great Summes due to him & gained from the Deft severall Conveyances of the Province of Pennsilvania & two Tracts of Land adjoyning & in the year 1697 gained an absolute Conveyance thereof as a meanes for Saving Taxes for the summe of 10500l {pretended} to be due to him and to secure the Interest[4]

Ford made a Lease to the Defendant of the sd Province & the sd two Tracts of Land for 3 yeares at 630l per annum (being the interest of the said 10500l) to be paid on the 1: of October & the 1: Aprill halfe yearly One halfe at the Exchange in London & the other halfe at Mr Carpenter's house in Pennsilvania[5]

Ford made his will[6] {January 170[blank]}[7] and gave the premisses to the Plts to be sold and Soon after dyed

The Plt [8] and Bridgett Ford made up an Account & therein the Plaintiff is charged for rent of the Province of Pennsilvania and Territories thereunto belonging to be paid at the dwelling house of Bridgett Ford in Water Lane in London and under this account is a writing dated the 2: of Aprill 1702 Sealed by the Deft wherein the Deft accknowledges the summe of 591:8:10 as the ballance of the Account & the rent of the premisses to be 630l per annum as in the Account. Vide the Account.[9]

The ~~plt~~ Deft hath brought a Bill in Chancery[10] to be releived agt the Mortgages & Conveyances obtained by Ford

This Account is the Evidence the Plts have to prove their demise[11] & insist that the Conveyance in 1697 was Absolute & not redeemable.

Note the Account does not mencion the two Tracts nor all other the Lands of the plts as in the Declaration but only the Province of Pennsilvania & Territory.

QUER[12] If this Account will Support their Declaration as to the parcells in the demise

Tis true One part of the Account dos referr to the Lease,[13] but therein the Parcells are not the same as in the Declaration For the Lease is of All other the Lands purchased by Ford of the Deft but the Demise in the Declaration is of the province &c and all other the Lands of the Plts without Saying which were purchased of the Deft by Phillip Ford deceased therefore the Lease and the Demise laid in the Declaration may be of different parcells because Ford might have other Lands then what he purchased of the Deft And the Rent reserved by the Lease is to be paid One halfe in London and the other halfe in Pennsilvania And in the Declaration the Plts only say Rendring 630l per annum generally which must be intended on the Lands unless they can ground their demise on the Accot of 1702 which mencions the Rent to be paid at Water Lane then for the same Reason that there was a Speciall Verdict[14] in a like ~~case~~ accion brought last Terme there must be one now, And it is Supposed the plts cannot for the Explaining the Account of 1702 referr to the Lease in writing unless they make the Agreement by this Account In all respects {the same} with the Lease and then they cannot maintaine their Action because their demise in their Declaration so much differs from the Termes in the Lease if they insist upon the Agreemt by the Account in 1702 without reference to the Lease (which they cannot well doe because it dos referr to the Lease) Then the Parcells in the Declaration are not the same in the Account For the Account mencions nothing but the Province of Pennsilvania and Territories therunto belonging. The Demise in the Declaration is of the Province and two Tracts of Land distinct from the Province all mines mineralls &c. And of all other the Lands of the Plts in America which will comprehend all Lands the plts may have in New Yorke Barbadoes or any other part of the West Indies. But the agreement by the Account Expressing noe more then the Province and Territories thereunto belonging it cannot Extend to Land out of the Province. And if the Plts goe upon the agreement without reference to the Lease the Excepcion[15] in the Declaration makes a Variance from the Agreement in the Account So likewise doth the mencioning a place of payment in the Account & not in the Declaration as is before observed.

Tis hoped this Account cannot look Forwards and respect anything future but is only a Stating of matters to the time 'twas made And so no ~~more~~ {new} demise cann be proved by it, And at most it cann only be an Evidence of a Tenancy att Will[16] and not of such a Special demise[17] as the plts have Laid which is for one yeare certaine and soe from yeare to yeare &c. which Amounts to a certaine Interest for two yeares.

The plts about a year agoe (which is long since the Account of 1702) sent their Orders & direccions to Isaac Norris and others in the Province of Pennsilvania to forbid payment of any Rent to the Deft & to Enter on the premisses & receive the Rent thereof for the plts use and at the same time adviced that by the next Oppertunity they would give them fuller Powers to sell lett &c[18] Norris came away soon after the said Orders and directions came to his hands & did not Act anything and cann give no further Evidence then that he received such orders and direccions for the plaintiff Bridgett And that those orders were so publickly made knowne before he came away by One LLoyd[19] who was one of the persons to whome the same were directed that it put a Stop to the payment of any Rent to the Defts Agent[20] And that he beleives no Rent hath been Since paid but Phillip[21] the plts Sonn is not only privy to these orders sent whilst Norris was in Pennsilvania ~~but~~ but also to the fuller powers afterwards sent[22] According to the Advice before intimated.

QUER If proofe to these matters above will not at least Amount to a dissolving the Agreement laid in the Declaration if any such Agreemt had been.

To prove the matters above. ISAAC NORRIS. PHILLIP: FORD

Put the Plt upon Proving the Deft hath the possession of the premisses.

D. Penn Papers, Ford vs. Penn, HSP. (*Micro.* 13:237.) Docketed: Penn | ads[23] | Ford | Briefe To be tryed on | Satturday 28: Instant[24] | at Guihald[25] In the Common pleas | SPRINGETT.[26]

1. There is confusion over the rent period covered by this action. According to a previous brief prepared by WP's lawyers for the trial on 20 May 1707 (see *Micro.* 13:194), and another brief of the jury's finding for a special verdict (see *Micro.* 13:291), the plaintiffs declared that on 9 Jan. 1702 (the day after Philip Ford's death) they demised, or leased, to WP the province of Pennsylvania and two other adjoining tracts to hold from that date until 1 Apr. 1702 for rent of £315. On 2 Apr. 1702 the Fords then demised the same premises to WP for one year definite and then from year to year for an annual rent of £630. They were claiming £315 for the initial contracted period (9 Jan.-1 Apr. 1702) and £2850 for the period 2 Apr. 1702-30 Sept. 1706, that is, 4½ years at £630 per annum. This present brief, however, fails to mention the contract of 9 Jan. 1702 and indicates that the period being covered was 1 Apr. 1702-20 Sept. 1707, that is, 5 years at £630 per annum. The Fords' petition to Queen Anne in Jan. 1708 (see doc. 118) states that the verdict in this case covered arrears of rent due to 30 Sept. 1706.

2. He owes nothing.

3. This is the elaboration of WP's plea of "nil debet."

4. See *PWP,* 3:661. For WP's contention that the conveyance in 1697 was part of a tax evasion scheme, see his Bill of Complaint, doc. 110., text at nn. 24-30.

5. See *PWP,* 3:662. See also doc. 110, text at nn. 29-30.

6. See Probate 11/484, PRO.

7. The date is entered in the margin; the correct date is Jan. 1700.

8. A mistake for "Deft."

9. "See the account." It can be found in *Micro.* 10:074 and is discussed in doc. 108, n. 24.

10. Doc. 110; *Micro.* 13:036.

11. Their lease.

12. "Query." What follows is the essence of WP's defense and resulted in the special verdict. See n. 14, below.

13. The lease granted in 1697 by Philip Ford to WP. (*PWP,* 3:662.)

14. A special verdict normally occurs when the matter in question involves issues beyond a jury's competence; it states the facts as it finds them, leaving the final verdict to the judge or judges.

15. That is, the clause "Except 5000 acres in Pennsilvania." See text at n. 1, above.

16. A tenant at will possessed premises by permission of the owner or landlord, but without a fixed term. The lessor could put him out at whatever time he wished. *Black's Law Dictionary,* p. 1314.

17. Presumably a reference to the implied tenancy from year to year (see declaration, above), where no certain term has been mentioned, but an annual rent has been reserved. Ibid.

18. The letter from Philip Ford, Jr., to David Lloyd, Isaac Norris, and John Moore, dated 29 Mar. 1705, which conferred these powers, has not been found. However, James Logan, writing to WP in July 1705, describes the contents of the letter. See doc. 101, text at nn. 3-7.

19. David Lloyd.

20. James Logan.

21. Philip Ford, Jr.

22. Bridget Ford apparently sent a power of attorney, dated 24 Jan. 1705, to David Lloyd, John Moore, and Isaac Norris, enclosed in a letter of 18 Oct. 1705 to Lloyd and Moore; neither of these documents has been found. See *Micro.* 12:442.

23. See doc. 113, n. 1.

24. The only Saturday in 1707 which was on the 28th of the month was in June.

25. The Guildhall, in east London, north of Cheapside, was the seat of the courts of Exchequer, King's (or Queen's) Bench, and Common Pleas for several days each law term. Peter Cunningham, *A Handbook for London, Past and Present* (London, 1849), 1:362-63.

26. Herbert Springett, WP's attorney.

118
PETITION TO QUEEN ANNE BY BRIDGET FORD AND OTHERS

[c. 22 January 1708]

TO THE QUEEN'S MOST EXCELLENT MAJTIE IN COUNCILL.

The humble Peticion of Bridgett Ford Widdow of Phillip Ford late of London Merchant deceased & of Phillip Ford Sonn and Heire & Alsoe Devisee of the last named Philip, James Ayrey & Bridget his wife & Anne & Susanna Ford Daughters of the said Deceased Phillip.

SHEWETH

That his late Majtie King Charles 2d by his Letters patent of 4th of March in the 33d yeare of his reigne Did Grant to William Penn Esquire & his heirs a Tract of Land therein particularly described & called Pennsilvania in America, with severall Powers for {the Governmt of} the people and for the Erecting & Supporting Courts of Justice there[1] And by proclamacion of the 2d of Aprill 1681 Did Declare his royall will & pleasure That all Persons Settling or Inhabiting within the Limitts of the said Province of Pennsilvania should yeild a due obedience to the said Wm Penn his heirs & assignes as absolute proprietors & Governours thereof & alsoe to the Deputy or Deputies agents or Lieutenants Lawfully Comissionated by him or them according to the Authority granted by the {sd} Letters Patents.

And by other Letters patents of the 22d of March in the 35: year of his reigne Did grant to his Late Majtie King James the 2d (then Duke of Yorke) & his heires the Towne of Newcastle in America and the Tract of Land Lying within the Compasse or Circle of 12 miles about the same Towne, and Another Tract of Land called Delawarre being 12 miles South from the said ~~South~~ {Town} together with severall Powers ~~from~~ {for} the Government of the people of those severall Tracts of Land, which powers & Lands are perticularly sett forth in those Letters Patent.

That his s^{d} late Maj^{tie} King James (then his royall Highness Duke of Yorke) did by 2 severall deeds of Bargaine and Sale Inrolled & dated the 24: August 1682 grant and Convey to the s^{d} Wm Penn & his heirs the premisses Comprized in the last mencioned Letters Patent Together with all the rights & powers of his then royall Highnesse of in & to the same.[2]

That the s^{d} Wm Penn afterwards (For Severall Summes of money amounting to 10658^{l}) Did by severall Deeds (the last of which bears date the 1st day of Aprill 1697)[3] grant Transferr & Convey all the before mencioned Lands and premisses {and all his rights & powers} of in & to the same unto the s^{d} Deceased Phillip Ford & his heirs together with the s^{d} severall Letters Patents & all other Charters & Patents obtained & to be Obtained relating to the premisses & did deliver to him the said Letters patent & deeds from their s^{d} Late Maj^{ties} which your Peticioners have in their Custody ready to produce And he did alsoe release all right of Redempcion[4] & afterwards tooke a Lease of the premisses from the s^{d} deceased Phillip Ford for 3 years at the rent of 630^{l} per annum.[5]

That the s^{d} deceased Phillip Ford by his last Will in writing bearing date the 20th day of January 1699[6] did Advise & dispose of All the premisses unto & for the benefitt of your petitioners ~~respet~~ respectively Viz^{t} 5000 Acres to your peticioner Phillip & his heirs & all the rest to your petitioner Bridgett Ford and to 2 Trustees (John Hall & Tho: Moss) & their heirs upon Trust to make sale thereof & to dispose the money thereby arising unto & among your petitioners the Widdow & children of the said deceased Phillip Ford in such parts as by his s^{d} Will is directed & made your petitioner Bridget Ford Sole Executrix and Dyed 8: January 1701.

That the s^{d} Lease for 3 yeares ended on or about the 1: Aprill 1700 & the s^{d} Wm Penn hath ever since held the premisses without Lease[7] & now refuseth to Deliver Possession or to pay any rent Altho by an Account under his hand & seale dated 2: Aprill 1702[8] he hath {not onely} charged himselfe ~~not only~~ with the said 3 years rent of 630^{l} per annum but alsoe with the like rent for the 2 following yeares, & having allowance of all he had paid since he took the s^{d} Lease He acknowledgeth himselfe Debtor to your peticioner Bridgett Ford to ballance the summe of 591.8.10 And your peticioners in the names of their Trustees did in Michaelmas Terme 1707 Obtaine Judgement in your Maj^{ts} Court of Common Pleas Against the s^{d} Wm Penn Senior for 2908.2.2. for the arrears of the s^{d} Rent due to the 1st Octo^{r} 1706[9] & there is now another yeares rent in arreare and your peticioner Can obtaine no Satisfaccion of the said Wm Penn for the said arrears the s^{d} William Penn having disposed of his Estate here and being a prisonner in the Fleet prisonn.[10]

That in Michaelmas Terme 1705 the said William Penn & his Sonne Wm Penn the Younger did Exhibite a Bill[11] into your ~~K~~Maj^{ties}

{high} Court of Cancery[12] Against your Petitioners & the said Trustees that they might redeeme the premisses & might pay noe more for the redempcion of the same then what should appear to be due upon a Generall Open Account to be taken from the begining of all Dealings betweene the sd Deceased & the sd Wm Penn the Elder, without Regard to the said deeds & writings, To which Bill your Petitioners by answer Submitted to the Judgemt of the Court Whether upon Consideracion of all Circumstances the Plaintiffs ought to be admitted to any Redempcion and Insisted by plea[13] that they ought not ~~that they~~ to draw your petitioners into any Accot nor be Admitted any way to Lessen or impeach the said Consideracion~~s~~ moneys Amounting to 10658l which plea was allowed (upon Solemn Debate by Councill on both sides) by the present Lord high Chancellor[14] and afterwards in Decemr 1706 the sd Wm Penn & his Sonn Exhibited another Bill[15] (for the like purpose differing very little from their said other Bill) whereto your peticioners likewise Answered and pleaded to the same Effect as before,[16] And the Lord Chancellor upon Solemn Debate also Allowed that plea.

That notwithstanding the sd severall deeds & proceedings the sd Wm Penn & his Sonn by their Influence over the Magistrates and Officers upon the place (Who are put in by & depend upon the said Wm Penn the father) Keep the Possession of the premisses & receive the Quittrents thereof, and the said William Penn the father has (Since he absolutely Conveyed the same to the Testator) made several Sales & Conveyances of Severall parts thereof to others (and as your peticioners are informed Continues so to Doe) both here by himselfe, and in America by his Deputies and Agents, to the great Deceipt of severall of your Majesties Subjects.

By which & other means your Peticioners & those that shall Claime under them are now kept and (Without your Majties Aid) are likely heerafter to be kept from the possession and Injoyment of the premisses Altho they have an undoubted Tytle thereto which Difficulties hinder your Petitioners & the said Two Trustees from making Sale of the premisses according to the Direccion of the said Will: and from receiving the profitts in the meanetime, Soe that your petitioners (the said Widdow and Children) are kept from their provision & Subsistance.

Therefore and Forasmuch as the sd Wm Penn hath divested himselfe of the property of the premisses, and of the powers granted by the said severall Letters patent, by aliening and Transferring the same as aforesaid, And in regard some doubt arise whether those powers (tho now out of the said Wm Penn) are soe vested in your petitioners or any of them, that they cann by & under the said Letters patent Give sufficient Commissions & Authority for the Administracion of Justice & other the parts of Government upon the said Lands, And for that by reason of the power and Interest of the said Wm Penn upon the place while persons in his Interest and Dependance are in the Magistracy & Government thereof Your Petitioners cannot get Into and be protected in the Quiet possession and Receipt of the Rents thereof without the Influence of your Maj^{ties} power and authority.

Your peticioners therefore humbly pray your Maj^{tie}~~s~~ To Grant to them or some of them or to such other persons as shall be most proper such powers by your Royall Letters Patent as shall be effectual for the purposes in the aforemencioned Letters patent Specifyed. ~~And that your Maj^{tie}will please~~ And that your Maj^{tie} will please (In such manner as you shall in your great Wisdome and Justice think proper) to assist your petitioners in the putting Quieting and protecting them and those that shall Lawfully claime under them In the full and Free possession and Enjoyment of the premisses.

And to Order for preventing the Inconveniencies that may happen to many of your Maj^{ties} Subjects by purchasing Lands of the said William Penn whereto he hath noe Tytle.

And your petitioners (as in duty bound) shall ever pray &c.

Her Majesty having by her order in Councill of the 22th of January last been pleased to referr to me the Petition of Bridgett Ford Widdow of of Philip Ford and of Philip Ford Son and heir and other the Children of the said Philip Ford deceased touching William Penn Esqr and the Title and possession of the Province of Pennsilvania and other lands in America to the end I may Examine the Allegations of the said Petition (a Copy whereof is hereunto and alsoe to her Majesties said order annexed) and Report to her Majesty a State of the Peticioners Case with my opinion what is fitt for her Majesty to doe therein I doe appoint to consider of the matters to me referred by the said order on monday the ninth day of February instant at five of the Clock in the afternoone at my house in Lincolns Inne Feilds[17] And the partyes and their Councill then and there to Attend Dated this Second day of February 1707

Cowper C

D. Penn Papers, Ford vs. Penn, HSP. (*Micro.* 13:371.) Docketed: Penn ad^{s} Ford | Copy of Fords Peticion to | the Queene | referred to Ld Chancellor | to be heard before him at | his house 9th Feb: at 5 | afternoone | for Mr Penn.

1. See Soderlund, *William Penn*, pp. 39-50.
2. See *PWP*, 2:281-83.
3. See ibid., 3:661.
4. WP, of course, denied that he had released his equity of redemption, citing the deed poll of 10 Apr. 1697, which allowed him to repurchase the province. See *PWP*, 3:662.
5. See ibid., 3:662.
6. See Probate 11/484, PRO.
7. This was not true, as the Fords themselves testified in their action against WP for back rent. See doc. 117, n. 1.
8. See *Micro.* 10:074; doc. 110, text at n. 67.

9. See *Micro.* 13:291 for the jury's verdict, later confirmed by the Lord Chief Justice Trevor of Common Pleas.

10. On 7 Jan. 1708, when the Fords attempted to have WP arrested at Gracechurch Street Friends meetinghouse on an execution for nonpayment of rent, WP had himself incarcerated in the Fleet prison by writ of *habeas corpus,* although he later secured lodgings in the Old Bailey. See Norris Papers, 7:147, 157; doc. 147, n. 6.

11. Doc. 110.

12. A mistake for "Chancery."

13. See *Micro.* 12:698.

14. See doc. 114.

15. See *Micro.* 13:036.

16. See Chancery, Reynardson's Division, bundle 183, no. 40, PRO.

17. An enclosed square bordering Lincoln's Inn, one of the Inns of Court, adjacent to Chancery Lane. See Peter Cunningham, *A Handbook of London, Past and Present* (London, 1849), 2:480-84.

119
BRIEF IN RESPONSE TO BRIDGET FORD'S PETITION

[c. 9 February 1708]

Bridgett Ford Philip Ford James Ayrey & Bridgett his wife Anne Ford & Susannah Ford Peticioners to the Queene in Councill ag^{t} Wm Penn Esqr for the possession of Pennsilvania[1]

To be heard before my Lord Chancellor[2] the 9th Feb: at 5 afternoone

My Lord Chancellor is to examine the allegations of the Peticion and to Report a State of the Peticioners Case

The Peticioners Sett forth their Title as if absolute which is not true for altho Mr Penn did the 2^{d} of Aprill 1697[3] Release unto Philip Ford deceased the Equity of Redempcion and particularly the Covenant for Redempcion given by Philip Ford to Mr Penn in a defeazance dated the 29th of September before[4] Yet the said Philip Ford did at the same time though dated Eight dayes after execute to Mr Penn a writing bearing date the 10th day of the same month of Aprill[5] whereby he agrees upon payment of a Summe of money therein expressed at the end of three yeares to reconvey the Said Province &c to the s^{d} Mr Penn & his heires

Though this writing be Soe Artificially contrived as if it were intended to signifie that Philip Ford had an absolute Estate and that out of respect to Mr Penn Philip Ford doth thereby pretend to give him the preference to repurchase, Yet Since it gives a liberty for Redemption It is hoped (notwithstanding Such extraordinary contrivance) that this writing will Undoubtedly be deemed a Defeazance.

And altho this writing be dated Eight dayes after the pretended purchase Deed yet they being sealed both at the Same time as will appeare by the Same witnesses being to each of them if they'l produce their Deed, It's hoped the distance of time in the dates will not be construed to the disadvantage of Mr Penn but meer art to deceive him

It is an odd circumstance in this Case That Philip Ford Six months before vizt the 29th Sept should look upon the Province &c to be a good mortgage for 10657l (for then he gave a formall Defeazance) and That Six months after when 157l thereof was paid off[6] (as appeares by indorsement on the said writing of the 10th of Aprill) and the summe reduced to 10500l That Mr Penn should then give an absolute conveyance, And it seems a strong presumption that the Conveyance given in Aprill 1697 was only a mortgage for that the Rent of the Lease then accepted by Mr Penn was 630l per Annum which is exactly the Interest of the 10500l then due And in truth it was only a mortgage for the absolute conveyance was made to save the Tax on money at Interest[7] and the Lease was a contrivance of Philip Ford the better to deceive the Comrs [8] if there had been occasion

By other proofs in the cause Mr Penn will alsoe prove the Estate redeemable, And the Peticioners Doe by their Answer (fo: 165)[9] in effect admitt the Estate to be onely in Mortgage for they Say they had rather have their principall money and the Interest thereof than the Country

By the will of Ford there is 6 months time allowed to Mr Penn to redeem which the Peticioners have omitted Setting forth in their Peticion[10]

As to what is Suggested in the Peticion of Selling lands in the Province by Mr Penn he saith he alwayes took himself to be onely a Mortgageor & therefore did beleive he might doe it but what he sold (as will be proved in the cause) was known to Philip Ford who took an account thereof from time to time and never opposed the same in England or Pennsilvania he knowing his Title to the Province was only a mortgage

As to what is Suggested That by the influence Mr Penn hath on the Magistrates in the Country they are kept out of the possession It is beleived to be imaginary and that the Peticioners never tryed them for by the Deed in Aprill 1697 as appeares by the Plea (fo: 71) Mr Penn hath given Power to Samuel Carpenter and Severall other persons therein named[11] to deliver possession of the premisses to Philip Ford and the Said Ford hath never required from them the delivering him the possession there And if he did & it was denyed Philip Ford had his remedy at Law in the Courts of Justice in the Said Province[12] which he never made use of but ought to have done first before any application can be made to the Queen in Councill And if Justice be denyed in the Country then the Peticioners come properly before the Queene &c by way of Appeale but not before

As to what is Suggested That the Governmt is conveyed to Ford and his heires, if the Governmt be assignable it is Supposed the words Powers Jurisdiccions in the Conveyances to Ford will not transferr it

{Quer} If the Governmt be assignable by one Subject of England to another especially Since by the Patent from the King as Sett forth in the Peticion all Power of Governmt is granted to Mr Penn and his heires onely without the word Assignes

As to what is Suggested That by an account signed & settled with the Petr Bridgett Ford in 1702[13] wee have charged our Selves with the Rent of the Said Province we Say That account was signed Condicionally that noe advantage should be taken from the word rent and that notwithstanding our signing thereof wee should have liberty of inspecting that and all former accounts betweene us and Philip Ford deceased and hope to prove it by persons present at Signing it[14]

But what Mr Penn Cheifly insisteth on is That the matter of this Petition is not properly before her Majesty in Councill till Justice be denyed the Petrs in the Province and till the cause yet depending before my Lord Chancellor be heard For the Plaintiffs may impeach the Plea and my Lord may see cause on the hearing to break into the Accounts[15]

{Note} The Plaintiffs have replyed to the Plea and Answer last Terme[16] and Served the Defendants with a Subpoena to rejoyne[17] they have alsoe filed their Intryes[18] and are willing to consent to heare the cause assoon as it may be and to consent to any thing with the Petitioners for expediting thereof

Copy. Penn Papers, Ford vs. Penn, HSP. (*Micro.* 13:386.) Docketed: Penn | ads | Ford | Breife to be heard | before Ld Chancellor | 9th Feb: 1707 at 5 | afternoone. Endorsed: for Mr Penn.

1. See doc. 118.
2. Sir William Cowper.
3. See *PWP,* 3:661.
4. See ibid., 3:660.
5. See ibid., 3:662.
6. This is a critical element in WP's defense, but is not as clear as he implies. See doc. 116, n. 25. For WP's abortive attempt to pay a further £157, see *PWP,* 3:542.
7. See doc. 110, n. 22.
8. The commissioners of the treasury.
9. See Chancery, Reynardson's Division, bundle 183, #40, PRO.
10. Here WP is somewhat disingenuous, for he neglects to add that Ford's will specifically rejected any effort by WP to construe this clause as establishing an equity of redemption in the province. See Probate 11/484, PRO.
11. The others were John Goodson, William Markham, Robert Turner, and Arthur Cook. See Chancery, Reynardson's Division, bundle 183, no. 40, PRO.
12. The Fords, of course, would argue that the courts in Pennsylvania were dominated by WP's allies.
13. See *Micro.* 10:074; doc. 108, n. 24.
14. Here WP is referring to John Hall and Thomas Moss. See doc. 116, n. 30.
15. Although Lord Chancellor Cowper had not yet issued his final decree, there was little likelihood that he would reopen the accounts, since he had denied WP's previous effort in this direction. See Norris Papers, 7:58, 64, 156-57, HSP.
16. See *Micro.* 13:165.
17. This has not been found.
18. That is, interrogatories. See *Micro.* 13:375.

120
LORD CHANCELLOR COWPER'S REPORT ON THE PETITION BY BRIDGET FORD AND OTHERS

[9 March 1708]

In obedience to your Maties Commands to me by your Maties Order in Councill of the 22th Day of January Last made upon the Petition of Bridgt Ford widdow of Phillip Ford late of London Merchant deceased, and of Phillip Ford Son and heir and alsoe divisee of the {last} named Phillip, James Airey and Bridgett his wife, Ann and susanna Ford Daughters of the said deceased Phillip hereunto annexed,[1] praying that your Majesty would assist the petrs in the recovery of the possession of Pennsylvania to wch the Petrs Claim a Title by a Conveyance from Mr William Penn: I most humbly Certify your Majesty, that haveing fully heard the partys concerned on both sides by their Councill and Agents to the Matter of the Said peticion I am humbly of Opinion that it being a Question yet depending and undecided in the Court of Chancery, whether the Estate of the Petrs in the premisses be redeemable by mr William Penn or not and if it Should prove redeemable and mr Penn Should redeem the Same, it would be inconvenient to your Maties Subjects in those parts that the possession Should be Soe often Shifted, and that therefore the petrs have craved your Maties Assistance too Soon, The said Petrs not being yet certainly intitled to an Absolute and indeafeasable Estate, wth wch opinion the Agents for the Petrs Seem for the present well Satisfied, and when the Petrs Shall be Soe intitled if that Should ever happen, whether your Majesty Should extend your Assistance to the Petrs for the recovery of the possession in the manner prayed, or leave them to the ordinary Course of Justice will be a point very questionable & deserving further Consideration. and Since it is possible the Same may never come in question. I forbear at present to trouble yr Maty wth my opinion therein.

Mar 9th 1707 Cowper C

D. Penn Papers, Ford vs. Penn, HSP. (*Micro.* 13:406.) Endorsed: Report from Ld Cha[ncellor] | abt Ford and Penn | ~~Baltimore.~~ Further endorsed: Report of the Lord Chancelor | Cowper to the King on the | Petition of the Fords to ob | tain the Province of Penn | sylvania from Wm Penn.

1. No longer with the document. For the petition, see doc. 118.

121
ALLEGED OVERCHARGES IN THE FORD ACCOUNTS

The following document represents three attempts by WP and his advisers to prove that he did not owe the heirs of Philip Ford the full

£14,000 claimed. Since the Ford accounts for the period 23 August 1682–1 April 1706 have not been found, we are forced to rely on WP's various reconstructions of those accounts. In account 121A, WP reckons that he owes the Fords £4559 18s 1½d, including commissions and interest at 6 percent for nearly twenty-four years. But this calculation conflicts with a parallel account in doc. 116 for exactly the same time span computed at the same interest rate, where WP reckons that he owes them £5413 17s ½d. In account 121B, WP reckons that Philip Ford overcharged him in advance payments, errors, and extortionate interest a total of £5841 13s 10½d in the 1682–96 accounts, which with 6 percent interest added would amount to £9346 14s 2d by September 1706. And in account 121C, he reckons the overcharges at £9697 1d. Since all of these calculations focus on interest and commission rates charged and do not provide adequate details of the transactions that make up the accounts, it is impossible to determine if WP was correct in his allegations about Ford's extortion. After the failure of their petition to gain possession of Pennsylvania (see docs. 118–20), the Fords were apparently prepared to entertain cash offers from WP. Generally, WP admitted that he owed between £4500 and £5500, but this included the "rent" for which he had been convicted as well as charges for the Free Society of Traders which were discovered in 1707 to be excessive. Just why the Fords finally agreed to a settlement of £7600 is unclear. Probably they insisted upon the rent due to October 1708, amounting to about £4200, and agreed to deduct some of the Free Society overcharge and accept £3400 for the remainder of the debt.

A

[c. April 1706]

AN ABSTRACT of severall accounts betweene William Penn Esq[r] Philip Ford deceased and Bridgett his Relict from the 23[d] of Aug[t] 1682 to the 1st of Aprill 1706 with the Interest of the severall ballances of the said Accounts including Comission money and the Interest made Principall at the end of every the said Accounts & computed at 6[l] per Cent per Annum

from 23[d] Aug[t] 1682 to 21 March 1684/5

Cash due to Philip Ford on the 23[d] Aug[t] 1682	2851:07:10
for the interest thereof	440:11:10¾
Cash paid per Philip Ford	8549:05: 2
For Comission money at 6[d] per pound for 2978: 16: 8 being the moneys of the goods bought & sold by this account	74: 9: 5

For Comission money at 10s per Cent for 5570:8:6 being the moneys paid bills of Exchange &c per this account	27:17: 0
	11943:11: 3¾
Cash received by Philip Ford	8198:10: 7½
The ballance due to Philip Ford 21st March 1684/5	3745: 0: 8¼

from the 21st Mar 1684 to 11th Aprill 1687

For the Interest thereof	462: 6: 1¼
Cash paid per Philip Ford	3006:10:10¼
for Comission money at 6d per pound for 942:17:7¾ being the moneys of the goods bought & sold by this account	23:11: 5
for Comission money at 10s per Cent for 2063:13:2½ being the moneys paid bills of Exchange &c by this Account	10: 6: 4
	7247:15: ¾
Cash received by Philip Ford	2922: 9:11
	4325: 5: 5¾

turn over

The ballance brought from t'other side	4325:05: 5¾

from the 11th Aprill 1687 to the 11th October 1689

For the Interest thereof	648:15: 9¼
Cash pd by Philip Ford	1293:19: 6
For Comission money at 6d per pound for 445: 1: 10 being the moneys of the goods bought & sold by this Account	11: 2: 6
For Comission money at 10s per Cent for 848:17:8 being the moneys paid bills of Exchange &c per this Account	4: 5: 0
	6283: 8: 3
Cash received by Philip Ford	1580: 0: ½

from the 11th of 8ber 1689 to the 11th of January 1694

The Ballance due to Philip Ford 11th octo: 1689	4703: 7:10½
For the Interest of the ballance	1481:11: 2½
Cash paid by P: Ford as per Account	498:18:11
Cash pd P: Ford as per another accot	94:17: 8
	6778:15: 8
Cash received by Ford as by severall accounts	1494:11:10
Ballance due to Philip Ford 11th January 1694/5	5284: 3:10

from 11th January 94/5 to 11th June 1696
for the Interest of the ballance 449: 3: 1
Cash paid by Philip Ford 1:11: 7

5734:18: 6
Cash received by Philip Ford 866:18: 4

The ballance due to Philip Ford 11th June 1696: 4868: 0: 2

from 11th June 1696 to 24th Aprill 1700

For the Interest of the ballance 1130:14: 2
Cash pd by Philip or Bridgett Ford 82: 8: 4

6081: 2: 8
Cash received per Philip & Bridgett Ford as per Account & Receipts 1828:18: 3

The ballance due to Philip or Bridgett Ford the 24th Aprill 1700 4252: 4: 5

The Ballance brought from t'other side 4252: 4: 5

from 24 Ap: 1700 to 1st Ap: 1702

The Interest of the Ballance 494: 3: 9
Cash paid by Bridgett Ford 18: 9

4747: 6:11
Cash reced by Bridgett Ford 1070: 0: 0

Ballance due to Bridgett Ford 1st Aprill {1702} 3677: 6:11
To the Interest of the Ballance to the 1st Aprill 1706 882:11: 2½

4559:18: 1½

Note in this account there is allowed to Philip Ford the summes of 712l 10s od said to be pd by him on the 23d Augt 1682 and of 500l on 2d Ap: 1684 to the Pennsilvania Company for the use of Wm Penn Esqr, The truth of which is questioned

Copy. Penn Papers, Ford vs. Penn, HSP. (*Micro.* 12:664.)

B

[late 1706?]

The overcharges in several Accounts of Philip Ford Between William Penn and him, which were kept and written by Philip Ford's own hand; with the Interest thereof computed at the same rate & time as in Philip Fords own Accts vizt every 6 months & sometimes sooner at 8l per Cent.

PHILIP FORD DEB^{R}

In folio			
34	21 Mar: 1684/5	To an Overcharge of 500^{l} 7^{s} said to be paid to himself for Advance money according to Custome of Merch^{ts} and sallary at 6^{d} per £ which with the Interest thereof to 29:7^{br} 1696 amounts to	1235: 0: 5½
In another acc^{t}			
8	21: 7^{br} 1685	To an Overcharge of 48^{l} 4^{s} Interest money, which with the Interest thereof to 29 7^{br} 1696 amounts to	114:10: 1
14	21: Mar 1685/6	To an Overcharge of 48:4:3¾ Interest money; which with the Interest thereof to 29:7^{br} 1696 amounts to	110:02: 8½
20	21: 7^{br} 1686	To an Overcharge of 51:7:3 Interest money: which with the Interest thereof to 29: 7^{br} 1696 amounts to	112:16: ¾
	21: Mar 1686/7	To an Overcharge of 52:11:¾ Interest money And	
25	11: April 1687	To an Overcharge of 6:6:9½ Interest money: which in the whole with the Interest thereof to 29: 7^{br} 1696 is	123:04: 9¼
25	11: Ap: 1687	To an Overcharge of 200:2:6 for Cash paid himself 6^{d} per £ for 8004:17:1½ which with the Interest thereof to 29: 7^{br} 1696 amounts to	420:14: 3
In another Acc^{t}			
5	11: 8^{br} 1687	To an Overcharge of 52:16:7 Interest money: which with the Interest thereof to 29: 7^{br} 1696 amounts to	106:15: 2
7	11 April 1688	To an Overcharge of 54:18:9 Interest money: which with the Interest thereof to 29: 7^{br} 1696 amounts to	106:14:11¾
		Carried over	£2329:18: 9¾

In folio		DEB^{R}	
		Brough over from 'tother side	2329:18: 9¾
8	11: 8^{br} 1688	To an Overcharge of 47:2:8½ Interest money: which with the Interest thereof to 29: 7^{br} 1696 amounts to	106:15: 8¼
10	11:8^{br} 1689	To an Overcharge of 61:15:11½ Interest money, and of 193:0:6^{d} paid himself 6^{d} per £ for 7720^{l} which b[eing] in t[he] whole 254:16:5½ with [Inter]est thereof to 29th 7^{br} 1696 amounts to	440:04: 2½

Dit^{o}	11 April 1689	To an Overcharge of 59:8:5 Interest money: which with the Interest thereof to 29: 7^{br} 1696 amounts to	106:14: 9

In another Acc^{t}

1	11 April 1690	To an Overcharge of 63:6:9½ Interest money: which with the Interest thereof included to 29: 7^{br} 1696 amounts to	106:11: 9¼
Dit^{o}	11: 8^{br} 1690	To an Overcharge of 65:17:5½ Interest money: which with the Interest thereof to 29: 7^{br} 1696 amounts to	104:12: 0
Dit^{o}	11 Ap: 1691	To an Overcharge of 68:10:2 Interest money: which with the Interest thereof to 29: 7^{br} 1696 amounts to	105:04: 7¼
Dit^{o}	11: 8^{br} 1691	To an Overcharge of 71:04:11½ Interest money: which with the Interest thereof to 29: 7^{br} 1696 amounts to	105:05: 5
Dit^{o}	11: Ap: 1692	To an Overcharge of 74:1:11½ Interest money: which with the Interest thereof to 29: 7^{br} 1696 amoun[ts] to	104:18: 6½
Dit^{o}	11: 8^{br} 1692	To an Overcharge of 77:1:3 Interest money: which with the Interest thereof to 29: 7^{br} 1696 amounts to	105:05: 7¾
Dit^{o}	11:April 1693	To an Overcharge of 80^{l}:2:10¾ Interest money: which with the Interest thereof to 29: 7^{br} 1696 amounts to	105:05: 4
		Carried over	£3720:16: 9¼

In Folio PHILIP FORD DEB^{R}

		To the Summe brought from 'tother side	3720:16: 9¼
2	11: Octr 1693	To an Overcharge of 83:7: Interest money: which with the Interest thereof to 29: 7^{br} 1696 amounts to	105:05: 5½
Dit^{o}	11: Ap: 1694	To an Overcharge of 86:13:8½ Interest money: [which] with [the] Interest thereof to 29: 7^{br} 169[6 amounts to]	105:04: 8½
Dit^{o}	11: 8^{br} 1694	To an Overcharge of 90^{l} 3: Interest money: which with the Interest thereof to 29: 7^{br} 1696 amounts to	105:04: 7
Dit^{o}	11 January 694/5	To an Overcharge of 46:17:7 Interest money: which with the Interest thereof to 29:7^{br} 1696 amounts to	53:13: 1¼

In another Acc[t]

11 June 1696	To an Overcharge of 265:4 for Interest money: and by an Error of 1385[l] for Land Sold in Pennsylvania of William Penn's being in the whole 1650:4: which with the Interest thereof to 29: 7[br] 1696 amounts to	1690: 2: 6½
29: 7[br] 1696	To an Overcharge of 61:6:8½ Interest money	61: 6: 8½
		5841: 13:10½
	To the Simple Interest of the Total 5841:13:10½ from 29: 7[br] 1696 to 29: of 7[br] 1706 at 6£ per Cent. per Annum is	3505:00: 3½
		£9346:14: 2

Note the figures on the outside of the Margin respects {only} the the folios or pages of the Several Acc[ts] of Philip Ford in which these Overcharges are contained.

Copy. Penn Papers, Ford vs. Penn, HSP. (*Micro.* 13:060.) Endorsed: The Overcharges in Philip | Ford's Acc[ts] between him | and William Penn.

C

[c. July 1708][1]

The Case of W[m] Penn

Whereas W: Penn hath, upon an intire confidence under his hand, Sign'd sundry Acc[ts] Depending betwixt him and his late Steward, Philip Ford Deceased, and one with his Widdow and Executrix, very much to his own prejudice as can be made to appear by many undeniable instances, and objections, yett for Peace sake, and in order to an accomodation of the whole matter in difference, W: Penn will confine himselfe, and only insist upon Three Articles in which he expect releife without unraveling the whole Account, and doubts not but that all men of Honour, Conscience, understanding and Judgm[t] will think them to be most just and reasonable.

	Over Charges £ s d
1 PHILIP FORD Charges his old Master and Freind for mony advanced 8 per cent Interest, w[ch] is 2 per cent beyond what the Law allows, W: Penn is willing to allow 6 per cent and desires the abatem[t] of the 2 per cent, which amounts to	4040: 4: 6
2 He Charges W: Penn with 6[d] in the Pound or 2½ per cent provision or Commission for Receiveing and paying even himself his own Intrest mony w[ch]	

he adds to the Principal every 6 Months, makeing him to pay 6[d] per pound 6 or 7 times over for the same mony, and charges 8 per cent Intrest upon that also w[ch] mounts it to a vast Summe in the whole Account and that being very unreasonable and severe, W: Penn desires releif therein amounting to 3302: 1: 1

3 And Whereas W: Penn Mortgaged the Province of Pensylvania to the said Ford for his Security, Reserving a Liberty to sell Lands untaken up in the Province, and had his consent thereto, and having sold Lands to the value of Two Thousand Pounds, of w[ch] he paid him Six Hundred and odd Pounds to Lessen his Debt with him, because P: Ford did not Receive the whole Two Thousand Pounds he makes W: Penn Debt[r] for the remaining part, which is 1385[l] w[ch] he adds to his former accounts as if he had advanced Soe much more mony and Charges W: Penn 8 per cent Interest makeing Intrest Principal every 6 Months, How unjust and unreasonable this is lett all honest men Judge 2354:14: 6

9697:00: 1

The Charging of 8 per cent Intrest upon Intrest from almost the beginning of his Acc[ts] and allowing little or no Intrest att all for greater Sums for W: Penns Acc[t] nor abateing any Intrest upon his own Acc[t] under that Equitable Consideracion, w[ch] to have done would have reduc'd the Intrest on his Acc[t] to a Ballance at least.

Note That by P: Fords receiveing an overballance of one Thousand Six hundred Fifty nine Pounds by his Order and for his Acc[t] W: Penn hath over paid him all the Principal mony he did ever advance for him, and what they now demand of W: Penn, and for w[ch] he's now under Confinem[t] is only for the abovesaid unlawfull and unreasonable Intrest and Provision or Consideracion for Receiveing and Paying, and Intrest upon that as abovesaid, together with the Article of One Thousand Three hundred and Eighty Five Pounds, upon the Sale of Land as above, and Intrest of 8 per cent upon that also. If W: Penn coud be releiv'd in these wrong Charges and agrevations, he is ready and willing to pay even more then the just ballance due to him. Philip Ford has received as appears per his own Acct[t] 17859[l] and Charges as paid for W: Penns Acct[t] in the whole but 16200[l], so that he has indeed received more then paid by 1659.[l]

	£	
P.F.	17859	rec[d]
	16200	paid
	£1659	Ball[a]

To Conclude The reason why W: Penn submitted himself so readily to their unnaturall Confinem[t] of him to the Fleet, is not that he is not uncapable or unable to pay all just demands to the full, But the Demands upon him from his Prosecutor being Three times the value justly due, he cannot with any Regard to his Family comply with it since the validity and verity of what is here asserted he can affirm to be true and made appear by divers of his Freinds and others of Eminency who have inspected and Scrutined the accounts,[2]

	£
The Fords Demand above	14000
The Over Charges	9697
Ballance	4303

Which and more he is willing to pay for accomodating the matter.

Farther Note that Whereas P Ford Charges W Penn in his Ac[t] wth 1200[l] put into the society stock for his Children and Relations w[ch] by Intrest att 8 p Cent and Intrest Principall every 6 mos {am[ts] to 3300 & odd Pounds} It Does appear that upon the late [illegible deletion] Examination of the society Books that he hath Givn him Creditt but for 600[l] [3] so that there is another Overcharge of the One half of the s[d] 3300 & odd Pounds

Copy. Penn Papers, Ford vs. Penn, HSP. (*Micro.* 13:626.) Docketed: W[m] Penns Exceptions | to: P: Fords Account.

1. Although this document is undated, it states that WP is in prison, which places it between Jan. and Sept. 1708. On 19 July 1708 WP wrote to Nicholas Gates (*Micro.* 13:505) reporting a "late discovery of 3249 pounds upon the Pensylvania Society's Books being by chancery forced out of the Fords hands, wherein he gives me credit but for 500 pounds insteed of 1200 he charges me with." Since doc. 121C makes this same point, the account probably dates from about July.

2. In July 1707 a group of English Friends, including Edward Haistwell, John Freame, Joseph Wright, and Joseph and Silvanus Grove, examined the accounts and reported that "they never Saw nor heard of the Like Extortion" (Norris Papers, 7:82, HSP).

3. Apparently a mistake for £500. See n. 1, above.

DESPERATE FOR MONEY

November 1705–December 1706

On 14 October 1705 WP turned 61. At an age when he should have been peacefully enjoying his growing family, WP was faced instead with the gravest threat to his proprietorship and patrimony since the early 1690s. On 31 October 1705 the Fords initiated their lawsuit against him in Chancery (see headnote to doc. 108), and this suit was to dominate WP's thoughts and actions for the next three years. It also played a large part in the thinking of his friends and foes in Pennsylvania and the Lower Counties who had learned of the Fords' claim in the summer of 1705 (see docs. 101, 122). WP at first tried to stall the Fords' suit (see docs. 124, 128), and then—when he realized that his large debt to the Fords was public knowledge — he finally explained his side of the story in letters to his allies in Pennsylvania (docs. 123, 125, 127), claiming at one point that he had taken care to secure all land grants in the colony (doc. 125). This does not appear to have been true. Wary colonists wisely adopted a wait-and-see attitude, refusing to pay any more quitrents until the suit was formally adjudicated (see doc. 129). Both James Logan and Samuel Carpenter warned WP that he had a very poor defense against the Ford claim and was likely to lose (docs. 130, 131). Logan also recognized that WP's bargaining position for surrender of the colony government to the crown had been weakened. No progress was made during this period on WP's negotiations for royal reimbursement, but he continued to revise upward his estimate of how much he had lost financially by founding Pennsylvania. Employing a mode of calculation reminiscent of Philip Ford's, he reckoned that the colony had cost him £76,000 (see doc. 135). This estimate omitted altogether the very sizable proprietary income he had received since 1681.

The dual pressures of the Ford case and the continuing proprietary expenses in Pennsylvania focused WP's attention, as never before, on his financial insolvency. In February 1706 he proposed that 200 of his allies in Pennsylvania loan him £100 per person, but he was bluntly informed by Logan and Carpenter that this was impossible:

the War of the Spanish Succession had destroyed Pennsylvania trade, harvests were poor, money was short, and merchants were floundering in debt (docs. 123, 129, 130, 131). If WP were going to procure a new loan to pay off the Fords, he would have to do it in England. His correspondence in this period is filled with contentious discussion about money owed to Deputy Governor John Evans and money spent by William Penn, Jr., during his visit to Pennsylvania in 1704 (see docs. 127, 129, 130). Although Evans was more poorly paid than other colonial governors, WP kept trying to reduce his salary, perquisites, and living expenses chargeable to the proprietor. His desperate search for money even led him to join Lord Fairfax and others in a bizarre and fruitless scheme to salvage shipwrecks in the West Indies (docs. 127, 132).

While WP saw a surrender to the crown as the last solution to his financial woes, this panacea was not at all attractive to many of the colonists. His political foes in Pennsylvania and the Lower Counties seemed determined to prevent any settlement beneficial to his interests. The embittered proprietor vainly called upon Logan to prosecute David Lloyd, leader of the anti-proprietary forces, for illegal activities since the late 1690s (docs. 127, 130). In fact, Lloyd's leverage against WP was enhanced when the Fords empowered him to act as their agent in Pennsylvania. This became obvious in November 1706 when the Pennsylvania Assembly, dominated by Lloyd's allies, drafted a bill that gave the colony courts authority over proprietary land titles and gave the Assembly control over the courts. When Evans rejected this bill and attempted to erect courts by ordinance, the Assembly began impeachment proceedings against Logan, a direct challenge to the proprietor. The following month, the Assembly decided to write letters to WP and to prominent English Quakers complaining of their grievances (see doc. 133). Meanwhile the Assembly of the Lower Counties, meeting at New Castle in November 1706, introduced a bill to erect a fort in that town, at which all vessels coming into the Delaware River would be forced to stop and pay a duty. This Assembly also demanded the right to legislate independently. It was clear to James Logan that the New Castle representatives were spearheading a drive to oust WP as their proprietor and to establish New Castle as a rival port to Philadelphia (doc. 133).

WP's proprietorship was not helped by the antics of his deputy governor, John Evans. Two of Evans's actions particularly outraged Pennsylvania Quakers: the false alarm of a French attack on the colony and the imprisonment of William Biles (doc. 129). Within WP's own family, his errant son, William, Jr., openly demonstrated his contempt for Quakerism and failed to obtain any meaningful employment (see docs. 123, 125, 127, 129). WP's wound was partially salved by the arrival of another son, Richard, born in January 1706 (doc. 123). A rare moment of wistful reflection appears in WP's letter to Dr. Edward Baynard, in which he looked back to early days in America to describe how Pennsylvania Indians cured their fevers by alternating steam baths with ice-cold baths (doc. 134). This pleasant reminiscence of times past should have been the rule, not the exception, for a man of his years.

122
FROM GRIFFITH OWEN

Philadelphia 9th 9th Moth [November] 1705

Dear Governour

We received noe letter from thee since that dated at Hyde Park the 26t 12 Moth last[1] about the ill treatment of some persons here, we drew an abstract of it leaving out some few lines touching D: Ll:[2] wch we thought might be some hinderance to the service of it. we drew an answear to it[3] & went with thy Letter & our answear to friends in & about this Towne, we read both to them, & they generally signed the answear (excepting very few) 2 or 3: we went with them to Merion & after the Meeting they were both read & after some debate they all signed it but one person as I remember, then a conveniency presenting, before we could get more hands we sent what we had to thee: wch we hope is come safe to thy hands, & since it has gone through the three Counties, & severall hundreds of hands to it: wch I beleive will be sent to thee by this oppurtunity. D: Ll: Gr: Jo:[4] Jos: Willcox & that party did muster up their forces & did use all their interest against us, and had two letters[5] from young Phillip Ford directed to D: Ll: Is: Nor:[6] & Jon Moore to stop all selling of Land & paying of Quitrents as if the Country was his,[7] & that he would send them orders & full power by the fleet, wch they did spread abroad to weaken the hands of thy friends & to strengthen themselves by drawing the peoples affections from thee. & they seem'd to threaten the people that signed the letter to thee. and they usd all their interest with the Country to carry the Election.[8]

and they did prevaile with many, some for fear joyned with them, others being tinctured with their prejudice & revenge. Soe that there was such striveing & shouteing at our Election as was never before here. D: Ll. lost it for the County by 4 votes, but got it for the Citty.[9] however the Election was carried on pretty well in thy favour & I thinke, it may be hard to get a better. The Assemby are now sitting & are goeing on with buisness, & I understand that D: Ll: is quiet amongst them, amending the Laws rejected at home,[10] & about a supply, I hope things will be carried on pretty well, they looke with a good aspect hitherto, although nothing as yet brought to perfection, as concerning Ph: Fords buisness nothing comeing with the fleet its all silent. I admire the prejudice & malice of these men without any ground for it, they have increasd their Estates considerably in this Country, & live full & plenty. it seems as if nothing would satisfie them but to have thee out of the Goverment. and how they have infusd it into many others who can hardly bear to hear well of thee, Gr: Jones is shewing his Letter, & other things conteined in the remonstrance sent by R: B:[11] to persons that they thinke that they can prevaile with,[12] & they have perswaded many that all is truth & that they will prove it. & stand by it. I never had such difficulty to keep up my reputation, & affection in the hearts of the people as since I have been concerned for thy interest & property. those that were very warme in their affection towards me are [illegible deletion] much cooled because I stand for thy just rights & the good of frds & the Country. and they say that Thomas Storey & I do hold the stirrops for James Logan to mount & Ride. I must say that as farr as I can understand he is true to thy Interest & I know not where thou might have another ~~that~~ So capable to manage thy buisness, yet for all that he has not a pleasing way to gaine the love of the people. he has a slighting & provoking way of expression by nature, wch the people cannot bear, wch is the reason that soe few speaks well of him and makes it harder for us that are concerned with him. the property buisness is pretty well over,[13] we met with great hardships, & hard thoughts from some of our best friends to get through soe farr. I am glad to hear that many Germans are about buying ~~th~~great tracts of Land of thee[14] I heartily wish they may come forward with their designe, whereby thou mayest clear thy debts, & stand over the heads of thy Enemies. I syncerly & heartily wish that thou & all thy family were well over here. I beleive it would be much for the service & promotion of truth, & to remove Jealousies evill surmisings, & reproaches that are in the hearts of many here. and I fear nothing short of thy presence & company will do it. The bearer hereof young Rowland Ellis[15] ~~is~~ comes over about buisness who may acquaint thee more at large about affaires here, & therefore shall conclude with sure {Love} & hearty well wishes to thee & to thy dear wief & Children, To thy son Wm Penn & his & to frds as free & remaine

Thy faithfull & Loveing friend
Griffith Owen

My wief[16] remembers her dear to thee & all thine G.O.

ALS. Cliveden Manuscripts, Chew Family Papers, HSP. (*Micro.* 12:391.) Addressed: For | William Penn Esqr | Governour of Pennsylva | nia To be Left at | the Admiralty | Coffy house[17] near | Charing Cross | These | London. Docketed: Griffeth Owen | 9th Novr 1705. Endorsed: Gr. owen.

1. See doc. 94.

2. David Lloyd. The abstract printed as doc. 94 is not in Owen's hand.

3. This has not been found.

4. Griffith Jones.

5. These have not been found, but see doc. 101, text at n. 3.

6. Isaac Norris.

7. On 31 Oct. 1705 Philip Ford, Jr., with several others, filed a Bill of Complaint against WP in the court of Chancery in an effort to gain title to Pennsylvania and the Lower Counties. See doc. 108.

8. Elections for the Assembly had taken place on 1 Oct. Despite concern over opposition attempts to control the election, James Logan considered the new Assembly "one of the best choices this Government ever had." *Micro.* 12:272.

9. According to James Logan, Lloyd's victory in the city of Philadelphia was the result of "unfair play." *Micro.* 12:272.

10. In May 1705 WP sent James Logan a copy of Attorney General Northey's report citing objections to 38 Pennsylvania laws. The Assembly was now attempting to meet these objections. See *CSPC, 1704-1705*, pp. 276-81; doc. 97, text at n. 5.

11. Robert Barber. For the remonstrance, see doc. 83.

12. The remonstrance of Aug. 1704 (see n. 11, above) had been sent by David Lloyd to William Mead, Thomas Lower, and George Whitehead, three prominent members of Meeting for Sufferings. See doc. 84.

13. Owen, a commissioner of property, is probably referring to difficulties the commissioners encountered with resurveys in Pennsylvania and the Lower Counties, as well as the prickly question of overplus lands, a matter in dispute between WP and the Assembly. See docs. 24, 32.

14. In Jan. 1705 WP mentioned that 100 German families had purchased 30-40,000 acres of Pennsylvania land. See doc. 91, text at n. 4.

15. Rowland Ellis (d. 1726), son of Rowland Ellis, of Bryn Mawr, had come to Pennsylvania from Wales with his father in 1686. By 1700 he had moved to Philadelphia and sat in the Assembly in 1700, 1703, and 1705. Thomas A. Glenn, *Welsh Founders of Pennsylvania* (1911; reprint, Baltimore, 1970), p. 163; *Votes and Proceedings*, vol. 1.

16. Sarah Songhurst Owen (1664-1733), daughter of John Songhurst and widow of Zachariah Whitpaine and Charles Saunders, had become the second wife of Griffith Owen on 30 Nov. 1704. Digests of Quaker Records, Sur. and Sus., GSP; Phila. Monthly Meeting Records: Marriages, 1672-1871, pp. 19, 32, GSP; Phila. Will Bk. E, #333.

17. The Admiralty coffee house stood next to the Admiralty offices from about 1698 to 1714. Bryant Lillywhite, *London Coffee Houses* (London, 1963), p. 73.

123
TO SAMUEL CARPENTER AND OTHERS

Lond. 18: 9br [November] 1705

My Deare Frds
S.C. E.S. G.O. R.H. T.S. C.P. I.N.[1] &c:
Yours, with many more, my Kinde Frds, is come to my hand[2] & I could not but say it was some Comfort to me in the midst of my manifold afflictions, the Neerest, my poor sons goeing off from truths way,[3] *& the occasion;* next the malevalent Spirts wth you, that in the name of Truth & Frds persecuted & oppressed me, my affaires & reputation, whilest the Body & best of Frds were otherwise minded. and wt wth paying Deptys *for twenty years there,* my own expences upon the 2 Journeys or voyages I made thither, & wt It hath cost me here in 20 years attendance, & 7 more before I gott it; one to gett, the other to Keep, & that I have never seen besides the last time, before

nor since 3000l sterling from that Province & Territorys in 24 years time that it has been in my possession (tho I have given the best time of my life from 3~~8~~0 to Sixty to gett & keep; all my Interest, in fine the bent of Spirit, person, powr & purse), you must, dear Frds, think, wth my late losses, I must be exceedingly reduced to difficultys. This is at least one half of the true reason of my Surrender,[4] unless I could have been by you releived from my debts here, tho' I had repayd you by Lands, nay mannors & rents too, rather than lie under my present loads, & then you should have had me & my family among you; so I intended last time, but how soon prevented? the ennimys here & there, takeing turns; & wt with the incumbrances I have here, & the Cry off my Frds & Station & interest there, I am broaken & divided. but were my Debts here answeard, or secured, I would not stay 6 months {longer} in this kingdom & my poor wife submitts readily to such a resolution. Dr. Frds think of these things in a serious manno~~e~~r, & lett me hear from you upon this only subject of my stay from you. For wt you are willing to do in that regard, by way of loane, my Comrs [5] have powr to engage wt is Fitting, to assist me & make my returne easy & Expeditious. Could you agree a proposall to me, both for supply & security for the repaymt. I could work off my chains & encombrances here.[6] think of this pray, &, as before, wth all Speede. I have not yet surrendred, & should I 'twill be unavoidable necessity compells me.

Mine are through the Lords mercy all well, with an encrease of 3 pretty Children since I left you.[7]

Mine must have been long since with you that I sent per J~~os~~. Guy; by wch you will see the exceptions to the Laws,[8] & by the last opertunity wt I require for all our security if I Surrender; & so satisfy your selves: I will never leave {yo} exposed in your Rights & Priviledges; Nor shall you ever be left by me, unless you leave me first. the Lord preserve us all in fear & love Continually, that he may hear our prayers, & encompass us about agst the Cuning & mighty works of the Prince of darkness, who desires & seeks to winnow us; and let us not tempt the Lord, least he be left to do it, and we Fall. The lord god of our glorious day & dispensation uphold us & ours & continue his blessings amongst us, and make us all glad in his holy house of Prayer; amen. so with Dr love from me & mine to you & yours, & to all honest Frds & the well affected of others, I end,

Your Faithfull & affectionat Friend
Wm Penn

Hyde Park 3. 12m [February] 1705/6

Dr. Frds.

I haveing heard that young P. Ford in the midst of an amicable treaty[9] writt to I. Norris Jon Moor & D. LLoyd of his fathers {pretentions} on my Country,[10] & as a purchass absolutely, know that besides the baseness of the act, {*& unworthiness*} ~~&~~ *in D. LL to publish it before its time,* It is utterly false; for at the best that can be made of their Pretentions (his widdow & childrens)[11] it is but a mortgage. And no more can, or do they make of it in Chancery, where their obstinacy has carried it, after 3 years agitation, & 2000l lyeing dead (for the most part) to pay them, would they {have} sufferd a revew of their accts & Sinck, ~~as in~~proportion to the paymt, an equall proportion of the security,[12] that I might have had my hands more at liberty & my posterity in measure out of danger of them; which at my Executing the deeds they vallue themselves upon, old Phillip solemnly prommessed, as he did, to take the mony that should appeare due as it could be raised out of the country ({So} never to seize it from me & mine, but only for a security) and I to have ½, or at least ⅓ of such monys; & lastly, that it should never goe farther than among us, & that he would in his will so leave it ~~by will~~. and indeed he had so made his will,[13] & rejoyct to me one day {that no body could Know any thing by it;} but his wife made him break all bounds a little before his death, as she has done since, known to & confest by her own Trustees[14] ~~ess~~ in favour of her *sawcy,* insolent, *&* *Idle* son, whom she all along has had in her eye to make Proprietary of Pennsilvania as I now heare; suitable to the mothers excessive vanity, avarice & Cruelty, so well Known here, in three other Cases,[15] [Here follow eight lines illegibly deleted].[16]

I must also lett you know, that they are all denyd by Frds for refuseing to referr our difference to~~e~~ frds To be equally chosen between us, wch they ma~~k~~de slight of, in a most Insolent manner, after monthly repeated meetings advice upon adjournmts on purpose to induce them;[17] wch every honest professor of truth must dislike *& never touch with them there.* In short, their Bill is in, & my answear,[18] & I am now puting in a Cross bill,[19] wch will show & expose some of the blackest & most extortious actions that any Court ever had before it, as well as my Confid~~e~~ing, foolish temper of relying & trusting those that have used me so ill. The first generall act of mine to settle the Province & Territorys was about the year 1690,[20] when I was in my troubles, on purpose to Cover & secure them from the Govermt as well as I could; & that upon my own thoughts as ~~at~~ {well as} at his instance, & advice; and after all was over, truly he held me to it, & I must quarrell (~~& I~~ when {I} could not pay, nor {did I} know of his extortion, never perusing his accts wch generally he kept) or be quiet & waite some happy providence to deliver {me}; ~~hope~~ hopeing at my arrivall in Pennsilvania upon Purchasses & Loans I might Clear it off, & be easy. The pretended release of equity,[21] was another vile breach of Trust; for, as by his own letters & papers I have show'd, & have to show, that I only Consented to it, to save him the tax upon mony at mortgage, wch came to about 300^l, nor did I do that wth out a deed Poll[22] to return it upon paym^t in some years time, the Release & lease for 4 years[23] being only the Blind, contrived by his Lawyer to palliat the mortgage & cover the mony ~~in~~ from the Tax. yet wickedly did this old woman,[24] gett the poor old man to make this his Title in his will, bare faced, tho ~~made a~~ {a plain} lye, under his own hand in lett^rs & papers afore sayd; & when she was askt by me before her Trustees, children & Counsil why she would sett up such a pretence Contrary to knowledge, & make my {kinde} Condiscention to save them 300^l, my snare, & prejudice, she sayd she was advised ~~sed~~ to it as best for her & family. This is the man I took from Taging & makeing of laces for womens bodies & teaching children to read & write in alisberry,[25] that has (if they could gett it) by me, & the intrest he had {on my acct} for his wifes Trade of hoods & scarfes, & his own mercery[26] in Eng^d (till their Deare & extortious rates lost it them) together & above all by the factory of those that went to america, left an estate of two or three & twenty thousand pounds 23000^l. The Lord forgive them & convirt them. I hardly ever heard of a poor M^r & a rich steward that was an honest man, & as my Counsel calls him, {such} a Man-eater, & {say} that in their whole practice they never Knew such an Instance for repeated oppression & extortion. upon a Just calculation, as a runing Cash, he has receiv'd above 160^l [27] more than payd. 2^ly at a fair six per cent I ow~~e~~d him or his {in 1702} but about 2300^l which, with allowance for Factorage,[28] & interest to this time, (a legal one I mean) will not mount it to above 4500^l by a reasonable Computation, and that a Security so large & valluable, should be snapt by any person of Common justice, and by so scandalous a treachery or betraying of trust {is abominable; especially} when w^t I did was at their Importunity & to serve them & not my selfe. Thus have I told you in my own hand, my sorrowfull story, & if it may finde a due impression upon your Spirits, & that you will sensibly sympathize wth me, and afford me your Speedy relief & assistance, you'l redeem me & mine from a Burden, that shall be an *perpetuall* obligation upon me & my posterity *to you & yours upon the Records of time, to all succeeding Generations.* This will bring us & keep us together, *unite and fasten our Knott of relation, Religious, & Politica[l]* and w^t you finde in your hearts to do, Pray ~~do &~~ {do quickly} *& encourage thos subscribers, to the Gen*^ll letter I have received on acc^t of Publick & Goverm^t matters.[29] Methinks 100 persons lending me 100^l a peice, or 200, fifty pds each, your mony, {to be} payd here at 3 months, or 6 months sight (takeing your interest in land) & I repaying the Principall as fast as land [illegible deletion] can be sould, & quitrents rais'd, to repay the same {might not be impossible}; and w^t can be raised here, & w^t I have here shall be the care of my self & Frds to apply to release the mortgage or En[cu]mbrance that is upon the Country in case they should be awarded the whole

12000l they sett up for as yet due; for they have received since 84. my first returne, above ~~7~~8000l and if I{'ve} justice ~~be~~ done me, It will sinck the debt more than halfe, & you there & some here may master it more [e]asily. For the lettr you w~~r~~ith others Subscribed, take it under my hand you shall {have} all further reasonable security, for I shall secure you to secure my selfe {& Posterity}. my love in the truth salutes you & yours, & Frds: my family, through mercy is pretty well; & my wife ~~a~~ was the 17 of last month safely delivered of the largest son she has had yet,[30] so that our stock ~~a~~is now advanc'd to 5. 3 sons & 2 daughters.[31] the Lord preserve them & give them an inheritance in their poor abused Fathers dear bought Country. so the Lord be with us all, & give us a blessed & comfortable meeting once more. amen. so prays

Your truly affectionate Friend
Wm Penn

excuse bad Tools

P.S.[32]

I long to hear of the progress and Issue of your last Assembly. Since I Received your Letter, I had one from D. Lloyd of 19th 5mo 1705.[33] which intimates that your Letter was handed among Friends in a clandestine manner, inveighing against certain persons and proceedings; and that he doubted not but when the Subscribers (as Several of them Since have been) are undeceived and come to a right understanding of what the Assembly did, they would, clearly perceive the wicked designs of Such as misinformed me, and, resent my rash and unwarrantable Expressions in one of my Letters.[34] These for the most part are all his own express words.

WP.

ALS, except for the postscript. Penn Papers, Granville Penn Book, HSP. (*Micro.* 12:397.) Docketed: From | Govr Penn 28 9mo | 1705 | to | Samuel Carpenter | and others | Philadelphia. This document, which combines two letters written two and a half months apart, was apparently sent to Pennsylvania in Feb.; it arrived between 25 July and 14 Aug. (see doc. 130, text at n. 3; *Micro.* 12:812).

1. Samuel Carpenter, Edward Shippen, Griffith Owen, Richard Hill, Thomas Story, Caleb Pusey, and Isaac Norris.

2. This letter has not been found. It supported WP's proprietorship, in contrast to the Assembly remonstrance composed by David Lloyd (doc. 83). See docs. 100, text at n. 6; 122.

3. William Penn, Jr., partly in reaction to his treatment by Quakers in Philadelphia, had renounced Quakerism. See doc. 91, text at nn. 1-2.

4. Of the government of Pennsylvania; see docs. 62, 96.

5. Commissioners of property.

6. The Fords had opened their Chancery suit against WP on 31 Oct. 1705, which WP makes no mention of in this letter. Apparently he was still hoping that his chief supporters in Pennsylvania would remain ignorant of the Fords' claims. By the time he wrote his next letter of 3 Feb. 1706, WP knew that he had to talk about the Ford case; see the text at nn. 9-11.

7. Thomas, Hannah Margarita, and Margaret (1704-1751).

8. This is the report of Attorney General Northey's exceptions against 38 Penn-

sylvania laws which WP sent to Logan in May 1705 via Capt. John Guy. See *CSPC, 1704-1705*, pp. 276-81; doc. 97, text at n. 5; *Micro.* 12:156.

9. WP's claim that negotiations had been amicable between himself and the Fords is not borne out by the rest of this letter.

10. This letter has not been found. For more on its contents, see doc. 101.

11. The widow is Bridget Ford, wife of Philip Ford; the children are Philip, Jr., Bridget, Anne, and Susanna.

12. Despite WP's apparent willingness to pay them £2000, the Fords (minus Bridget, Sr.) filed a Bill of Complaint on 31 Oct. 1705 against WP (see doc. 108); they were not prepared to lessen the amount they believed was owed to their father and themselves, either in the accounts or in the securities which WP had signed.

13. This first will of Philip Ford's has not been found.

14. John Hall and Thomas Moss. For the will, see Prob. 11/484, PRO.

15. It is uncertain to which cases WP is referring. However, from 14 Feb. 1705 to 9 May 1705 Devonshire House Monthly Meeting to which Bridget Ford, Sr., belonged, minuted her refusal to show the books of the Pennsylvania Society to its members. Finally on 9 May it was reported that she was "likely to come to an accommodation with those persons." See Devonshire House Monthly Meeting Minutes, vol. 2, FLL.

16. These lines, referring to a dream WP had about Philip Ford, appear to have been overwritten, probably by James Logan and Samuel Carpenter, who then blotted them out. They regarded the initial passage as unsuitable for public consumption. See *Micro.* 12:812.

17. On 14 Nov. 1705 WP complained to Devonshire House Monthly Meeting (to which the Fords belonged) that he had been served with a subpoena to appear to a Bill of Complaint filed against him in Chancery by Philip Ford, Jr., and others. The meeting now attempted to bring about an amicable accommodation of the differences, requesting that the legal proceedings be terminated and the matter, if unresolved, go to arbitration by neutral Friends. The issue dragged on until 26 Dec. 1705, when the meeting declared that it could not "have unity with the said Bridget Ford, Philip Ford, Ann Ford and Susanna Ford until they have complied with the tender advice and judgment of this meeting in these matters." The meeting also gave WP the liberty of making "his defence in the law as he shall see meet." See Devonshire House Monthly Meeting minutes, vol. 2.

18. WP probably answered the Fords' bill in Jan. 1706. See headnote to doc. 109.

19. WP filed his Bill of Complaint on 23 Feb. 1706. See doc. 110.

20. See the series of documents, 30 Aug.-3 Sept. 1690, in which WP conveyed Pennsylvania to Ford and Ford leased the colony to Thomas Ellwood. *PWP*, 3:659-60.

21. On 29 Sept. 1696 WP effectively surrendered his right to repurchase the colony. Ibid., 3:660.

22. On 29 Sept. 1696 WP signed what he claimed was a defeasance—an instrument that essentially nullified any absolute ownership of Pennsylvania by Philip Ford. Ibid., 3:660-61; doc. 110, text at n. 21.

23. The time span was, in fact, three years, not four, as stated here by WP. See *PWP*, 3:661-62.

24. Bridget Ford, Sr.

25. Aylesbury, Bucks.

26. A shop that deals in textiles, particularly silks, velvets, and other costly materials (*OED*). The Fords' shop was in Bow Lane, London.

27. Presumably a mistake for £1600. In doc. 111 WP claims that Ford paid out £1581 less than he had received.

28. The buying and selling of goods on commission (*OED*); in effect, Ford acted as WP's factor in England.

29. See n. 2, above.

30. Richard Penn (d. 1771), born on 17 Jan. 1706.

31. The three sons were John, Thomas, and Richard; the two daughters were Hanna Margarita and Margaret.

32. The postscript is in the handwriting of someone other than WP.

33. See doc. 102.

34. See doc. 94.

124
TO SIR WILLIAM COWPER

Sandy lane wilts 30th 9br [November] 1705

My old & Honored Frd

I this night am told by my Kinsman & atturny[1] greater things did not blott me out of thy thoughts, for wch I returne my hearty acknowledgemts and must pressingly begg the continuance of thy Friendship, being the most unworthily treated that ever man was, my Kindness, trust & entire confidence being turnd against me by my own servt & steward[2] to distroy me after a Barbarous as well as scandalous manner. I earnestly desire the leave given, till next term[3] may not be lessen'd since the matter is of that moment, & length of time, & I absent & unprepared presumeing upon the time given me Lett me owe that favour to our old & Free friendship, and be assured, as the cause will not dishonour it, neither shall it be forgotten by

Thy obliged & Faithfull Friend
Wm Penn

ALS. Hertfordshire Record Office, Hertford, England. (*Micro.* 12:431.) Addressed: For Sr wm Cowper | Bart neer Bedford | Row neer Greys Inn[4] | London. Endorsed: From William Pen | Quaker. Docketed: Will. Penn | Nov 30th 1705.

1. Herbert, or Harbert, Springett of Mayfield, Sus., was a lawyer with chambers in Lombard St., London. A cousin of the proprietor's first wife, Gulielma Springett, he is not to be confused with Gulielma's uncle, Herbert Springett (d. 1687), also a lawyer, who had been employed by WP in the 1670s and 1680s. Penn Papers, Will of Harbert Springett, HSP; doc. 82, n. 26.

2. Philip Ford.

3. On 19 Nov. 1705 WP had petitioned the Master of the Rolls seeking more time to put in his answer to the Bill of Complaint brought against him in Chancery by Philip Ford, Jr., and others. WP was given until after Christmas. Consequently, when Hannah Penn became ill, WP traveled to Bristol to see her, but while he was gone the plaintiffs obtained an order from Chancery agreeing to void the previous order of additional time on 15 Dec., unless WP could show good cause. WP was now hoping that Cowper would confirm the original order. In fact, on 15 Dec. 1705 the court allowed an extension until 12 Jan. 1706, the first day of Hilary Term. See *Micro.* 12:434, 451, 459.

4. Gray's Inn, one of the Inns of Court in London.

125
TO JAMES LOGAN

London 28th 10th mo [December] 1705

James Logan

Lo. Friend

I have received of thine of this years date 1 of 2mo and of 3mo of the 5mo, 6mo[1] and last ~~th~~ night thine of 26th 8mo[2] to my great satisfaction. I will not now undertake to answerr 'em distinctly by this Pacquet boat that goes away to night, and the rather because Several of them have been Answer'd by mine, Sent by the new Messenger Joshua Guy Commander,[3] with whom honest and faithful John Saltkill[4] is gone and his Wife; and also by reason thine of 6mo ult. is so volumenous and came but of late to my hands, I do not mention its largeness out of dislike, but am pleas'd thou was so particular therein. As to P. F's [5] business the first subject of thy large Letter, as well as of my present Exercise and expense, Know in short that the Same is only a Mortgage, and that I offer'd upon adjusting the Acct (agt which I have great and equitable Exceptions) that the one half Should be then presently paid, and the other reasonably Secur'd, and that I desir'd not to be a judge in my own Case, I propos'd to referr it to Friends of their and my choosing, both which (after three years agitation) they refus'd, on which I complain'd to the Meeting they belong'd unto,[6] and had it not been for the young man's late illness[7] which hindered their Attendance on the Meeting, that adjourned from week to week mostly on that acct: they had been disown'd by them, or had stopt their proceedings in Chancery. These People have been very dilatory false and changeable as well as insolent & unmannerly, and their strength is not their cause, But their Abettors Some of the Worst among you,[8] and of Such here, that have long laid a design to Supplant both me and mine. I hope the Lord will disappoint them to their Shame. The reason why they will not referr their case is Suppos'd to be the blackness and injustice of the Acct which by Chancery they hope to Stifle and have the oppressive Sume allowed, being upon a security: But my Councell, esteemed the top of that Court[9] assure me otherwise, and then their 12000£ pretence must bear a considerable abatemt whose Acct thô so volumenous have been by providence more than my carefullness preserv'd entire, having never open'd them Since the Family deliver'd 'em Seal'd to me till on this Occasion. Some of the Exceptions thereunto are these. 1t he received more moneys of mine than ever he paid for me as appears by the Acct inclosed.[10] 2d that the pretended Sume amounted to that highth by an unreasonable and voracious Computation of Compound Interest every 6 months and Sometimes Sooner, at 6 but oftner at 8l per Cent.[11] 3d His unusual and extravagant sums he Setts down as Sallary money for paying himself out of my money And 2½ per Cent for money advanc'd when the Custom here is but ½ per Cent. 4th That he did not set down any the times on which he Received 8000£ of my money whereby one might bring the Acct to a Ballance, but continued the first Sume advanced which was 2800l [12] and the Compound Interest thereof reckon'd every 6 mo. with other demands as aforesaid. There are many things more which I cannot here insert by reason of the Shortness of time, which expect by Colonel Quary who is just upon his returne to you, and I hope with a moderate issue in the Business of the Wool Offence and that of the Vessel at Philadelphia,[13] The Commissioners of the Customes with whom I was and Colonel Quary call'd in Shewing great tenderness upon both cases, so that Colonel Quary assured me he would follow their Example, and let those Matters drop easily. We are all thrô mercy well, and Salute all our Friends. my Father Callowhill[14] intends an Answer to thy last,[15] my Wife and all her Children there,[16] my Son and his Family also pretty well, likely to be preferr'd under Lord Treasurer in Some post relating to the Treasury.[17] Let the Governour know I had his of 6mo[18] and Shall write to him per next.[19] Friends Letter with the many Subscriptions are come to hand,[20] my dear love to them all. And let none be concern'd ab^t the Lands they purchas'd either before or Since my last being among you for care was taken therein.[21] And let them know that I neither have, nor willingly Shall Surrender,[22] Since they desire I Should not.

Tis very late and for fear there Should be no other Pacquet after to night go ~~to~~with this Pacquet boat bound for Barbados I must abruptly end. I am

Thy Lo. Friend
Wm Penn

Lett[23] S. Carp^r Know I have his,[24] & shall answear it per next occasion.[25] wth my Dr. Love to him & his also tell T. Fair. I had his to whom I intend to write[26] pray take care that P. Fs Bond for his agency in the society[27] be well kept for I & children have 700^l in as his acc^ts say. vale

no list of Bills & Bonds yet come.[28] as I always told thee, want of their credit has been very hurtfull.

WP

LS. Penn Papers, Letters of the Penn Family to James Logan, HSP. (*Micro.* 12:463.) Docketed: Copied | date 1705.

1. For James Logan's letters of these months, see *Micro.* 12:005, 053, 061, 087, 103, 156.

2. This letter has not been found. WP may have the date wrong, for Logan did write to him on 24 Oct. See *Micro.* 12:272.

3. See doc. 81, n. 27.

4. John Salkeld.

5. Philip Ford's. See headnote to doc. 108.

6. Devonshire House Monthly Meeting. See doc. 123, n. 17.

7. Devonshire House Monthly Meeting on 19 Dec. 1705 minuted that Philip Ford, Jr., was "much out of health" and was unable to attend the meeting that day to choose impartial Friends to arbitrate between his family and WP.

8. David Lloyd, John Moore, and their supporters.

9. Several lawyers represented WP at this time: Thomas Vernon (1654-1721) of the Middle Temple, whose practice in Chancery would span 40 years, was considered the ablest lawyer in that court; Spencer Cowper (1669-1727), lawyer, parliamentarian, and later judge of Common Pleas, was the younger brother of Lord Keeper Cowper; Roger Ackerley (1665?-1740) of the Inner Temple, brother-in-law of Thomas Vernon, was best known for his political, legal, and constitutional treatises, including *The Jurisdiction of the Chancery as a Court of Equity Researched;* Henry Poley (c. 1653-1707), lawyer and parliamentarian, was considered one of the best common lawyers in England.

DNB; Basil D. Henning, ed., *The House of Commons, 1660-1690* (London, 1983), 3:257. A list of WP's counsel appears in Lord Keeper's Order for Injunction, 18 Oct. 1706, Penn Papers, Ford vs. Penn, p. 54, HSP.

10. No longer with this letter. However, in doc. 111, WP stated that, exclusive of interest and commission money, he had paid to the Fords £17,961 9s 4d for debits totalling £16,379 18s 7¼d, leaving a balance in his favor of £1581 10s 8¾d.

11. The statute 12 Chas. 2, cap. 13, restricted interest on loans to 6 percent; this remained in force until 12 Anne, cap. 16, which reduced the rate to 5 percent. See *Statutes at Large.*

12. The exact sum was £2851 7s 10d, WP's debt to Ford as of 23 Aug. 1682. See doc. 109, n. 2.

13. Here WP is referring to the wool-smuggling charge against Ralph Fishbourne, whose shallop, captured at Philadelphia, had been released by Gov. Evans. It appears that Col. Quary had asked the commissioners of the customs for advice on the case but had not formally complained about Evans's failure to bring the matter before the vice-admiralty court. WP believed that the Board of Trade would not prosecute Fishbourne. See doc. 100, n. 38; *Micro.* 12:251.

14. Thomas Callowhill, WP's father-in-law.

15. Logan had written to Thomas Callowhill on 30 May 1705 and again on 9 Nov. See James Logan Letterbook, 2:60, 69, HSP.

16. At Bristol.

17. No record has been found of William Penn, Jr., holding any office in the Treasury.

18. Gov. John Evans's letter has not been found.

19. WP wrote two letters to Gov. Evans in Feb. 1706. See *Micro.* 12:505, 531.

20. See doc. 122, text at n. 3.

21. In fact, it is unclear what steps, if any, WP had taken to protect landowners from the Fords' claim to Pennsylvania.

22. Surrender the government of Pennsylvania to the crown.

23. This postscript is in WP's hand.

24. Samuel Carpenter's letter has not been found.

25. Perhaps doc. 123.

26. Thomas Fairman wrote to WP in Aug. 1705. See doc. 103. No response from WP has been found.

27. The Free Society of Traders. WP claimed that Philip Ford had acted as its secretary and treasurer and had erroneously charged WP and his children for shares that had never been received. See doc. 109, n. 7.

28. In Jan. 1705 WP had written to Logan (see doc. 91) for an account of lands sold in Pennsylvania, and bonds taken and money received on his behalf. On 17 May 1705 and again on 4 July, Logan claimed to have enclosed a list of the bonds (see *Micro.* 12:053; doc. 100), but the ship carrying it had been captured and Logan had failed to send the promised duplicate (see doc. 129, text at n. 37).

126
TO JAMES LOGAN

Lond[n] 7th 12mo [February] 1705[/6]

James Logan
Lo. Friend.

Since my last of 28th 10mo[1] which I sent Via Barbados, and expect 'twill come to hand before this, whereof the inclosed is a Copy. I Receiv'd one of thine of 9th of 9[br] [2] and was very glad of the Contents thereof and shall be to hear those prospects thou hadst of the happy Issue of the sitting Assembly, fully answer'd, for thence it is we must date the begining of our future Comforts: or living there would be a perpetual carefullness if not war within our selves. I hear by Colonel Quary there is a pacquet come for me by the Nonsuch, but is not yet come to hand, of which which the Colonel had a Letter, the ships also being arrived above a fortnight, which shews an over Carefullness to deliver it to me, or that it sticks by the way which am sorry for being willing to have answer'd it by this oppertunity

I promis'd in my last to be more particular ab^t P F's[3] business, but the large Acc^t I have given in the inclosed Letter sent to Friends[4] (which have left open that thou mightst read it and make thy remarks thereon, and after to seal it with the lesser seal of the Province the [half of line illegible] so deliver it) will shorten this and [half of line illegible] 1690 in the time of my troubles by [two words illegible] advice as [well] as my own inclination the better to [save?] the Province from [what?] might ensue, I made an absolute Grant thereof.[5] but as soon as the [illegible] were a little [improved?] I began to [rest of line illegible] Released from the said Deed which he seem'd unwilling to do, but at Last made me a Defeazance thereof.[6] And the Parliam^t having laid a Tax on moneys at Interest the said P F under a Pretence as he said only of saving the money from being Taxed which would have amounted to about 300£ did frequently urge me to save him that money by a shew of releasing the Equity of Redemption[7] according as Counsell had advised, whose Opinions I have by me and have produc'd,[8] and that it might look of the better face, of taking a Lease of the premisses for 3 yeares (thô upon his urgent request I made him a Mortgage of the whole in usual forme with Condition of Redemption about of 6 mo. before which was in the year 1696[9] I then not so much suspected the baseness and Extortion of the acc^t) which for a long time I refus'd; But at last consented to it,[10] on Confidence of the performance of these three things which he solemnly promis'd in the presence of his Wife. 1^t that Notwithstanding whatever was or should be done or executed between us that the Premisses should still continue only as a Mortgage and that it should never be otherwise us'd by him or his. 2dly that it should always be kept privately between our selves and never hinder or obstruct the sale and Confirmation of Land, and that he would never urge or press me for moneys but as I could raise it out of the Province. And 3dly that he would Execute to me a [D]eed Poll containing a Clause for the Redemption of the premisses and reducing the same on the foot of Mortgage, thô not by the name of a Defeazance the better to blind the business upon his affirmation, the~~e~~is he accordingly executed bearing date about 10 days after the Release[11] within which I suppose was the Time appointed by the Commissioners for Examination.

Now these ungrateful persons (worse than the Wolfe in the stable) lay hold of the Crutch that I gave them to help them along, and do unjustly fight against me herewith, And his Wife still pleaded on the force of that release untill she was otherwise advis'd by her own Counsell, and perswaded her husband to alter his Will that he made according to our agreem^ts and to make another which was his last and therein laid hold of the said Release that I granted (for their favour) as an absolute title and not a condescention to serve them: than which nothing can be more villanous which and more are larger set forth in my Bill in Chancery.[12]

I hope I shall be able with the Assistance of my Friends there and here together with what moneys may be raised by Forreign Purchasers (viz) the Saxons and Swissers &c.[13] to pay off the just debt due to P F. But in Case the Court of Chancery should order him his unexampled and extortious sume (having sufficient reason to think the Contrary) then I must sell part of my Mannours and w^t else I can to raise the same. I have wrote to Friends (as thoul't see in my Letter) about their Assistance in this matter what they will do therein would have thee send me an Acc^t by the 1^t Oppertunity.

Am sorry that there should be any persons among you so ungrateful as to Act still in despite of me, who endeavours their good, and Admire that there should be such Considerable Factions now raised when you have so moderate and Friendly an Assembly, and matters seem to look of a better Aspect. However as it happens I have not any Acc^t that such Representations are come to the Lords for Trade & Plantations concerning my property, and I hope your good offices will obstruct them.[14]

As to the Provision of my younger Children on that side the Water I would have thee as oppertunity offers, and a good Bargain presents, to buy some pretty Tracts of Plantations there of the first Purchasers for my Childrens use and shall not be unmindfull of those young ones so dear to me.[15]

I will not part with any Land in Gilberts to P Ford and am not ignorant what he meant when he said he would in time find a way to make himself easy,[16] but shall endeavour to disappoint him therein. I hope that the great successes in Spain by the prudent Conduct of the Earle of Peterborough[17] my very good Friend will contribute much to the Opening a Trade with the Spaniards and furnishing you with money.

As to the London Company I will accomodate that matter the best I can,[18] several of them being very ready to offer me their Assistance as far as they can, if things should press me in this present Conjuncture.

The neglect of the Division of the Boundaries[19] lys not at my door, I have already press'd the Lords for Trade about it, and will again: tho I had rather it was done while I was on the spot.

I have spoken to M Philips her Relations ab^t her, but she must wait a little longer with patience, there will come for her by this Fleet if possible a Box and 2 Umbrellas, Robt Ashton has got the returne of her moneys, which is very like Robert.

William Warren[20] assures me that Tobacco and Logwood would be of a great value here, at least of as much more as the prime Cost.

The Germans have been with me and talk of buying of about 2 or 3000£s worth of Land, The Doctor a Saxon is now return'd to his own Friends with an Acct thereof. Let the two Germans that are left behind Johann Henry Kirsten and [blank] Nohr[21] have the 500 Acres of Land between them they giving sufficient security therefore until their pretensions appear clear, The Germans incline most to have the Susqueh. Lands[22] and will give more for 'em here in ready money than what's proposed there of which send me thy private thought.

I have sent the Governour[23] a Commission without the frightful reservation to that tender Brittain and Patriot D LL,[24] trusting upon the Governours honour and Integrity in the use thereof, have only sign'd it and do desire th~~at~~ee to take care that the Mar of the Rolls seal it with the great seal of the Province.

William Hages Mortgage to old P. F on my behalf[25] is so well known to his son that is in those parts, that for 10£s he offer'd me to release the Equity of Redemption some years since in this Town, and pray make an end with him by the first oppertunity, and suffer me not to be a looser on that side the Water as I have been of our own, hoping they will allow me that Land I bought of the old Indian King[26] at Pennsbury as part of my proportion, or let me have the goods again, for which he sold it me for a seat for my self.

I am sorry thou didst not take Beaumonts business[27] by The right end, tis 300 Acres upon Cancocrass Creek[28] a Navigable place, it was put up in my Scriptore with divers papers relating to it as to Location delivery and seizin. Beaumont bought it of Wm Biddle as the paper show, and he or his heires must make me Satisfaction for it since it is of more real value than 5000 Acres in the Woods. Pray think of my West Jersey Interest both above and below the River, of some value to me and my poor Children: as also of my East Jersey Propriety. I took care of thy Letters as I do one from one of thy Relation in Ire[lan]d come by this oppertunity. I am with unf[eigne]d Love

Thy Assured Friend
William Penn

Copy. Penn Papers, Letters of the Penn Family to James Logan, HSP. (*Micro.* 12:512.) Endorsed: Copied | 1705. Docketed: Proprietor [7th 1]2mo 1705 London | Du[p]lic[ate] viâ Boston. | wth a Pa[cquet?] [inclu?]ded, not in the other. On the first page of this letter, six lines are badly faded and partially illegible.

1. See doc. 125.
2. Not found. Logan failed to keep a copy of this letter. See doc. 130.
3. Philip Ford's. See headnote to doc. 108.
4. Doc. 123.
5. On 2-3 Sept. 1690 WP conveyed Pennsylvania and the Lower Counties to Philip Ford for £6900. See *PWP*, 3:659-60.

6. The indenture of defeasance, which gave WP the right to repurchase Pennsylvania and the Lower Counties from Philip Ford for £10,657, was executed on 29 Sept. 1696. See *PWP*, 3:660-61.

7. That is, WP's right to repurchase Pennsylvania. See doc. 110, text at n. 22.

8. These have not been found. See doc. 110, nn. 23-24.

9. WP confirmed Philip Ford's ownership of Pennsylvania and the Lower Counties on 29 Sept. 1696. See *PWP*, 3:660.

10. WP leased Pennsylvania and the Lower Counties from Philip Ford on 2 Apr. 1697 for £630 annual rent. See ibid., 3:662.

11. Ford's deed poll, which allowed WP to repurchase Pennsylvania and the Lower Counties for £12,714, was executed on 10 Apr. 1697. See ibid.

12. Doc. 110.

13. See doc. 91, text at nn. 4-7.

14. WP here refers to Logan's warning in Nov. 1705 (*Micro.* 12:368) that the Lower Counties' Assembly had prepared an address to the Board of Trade, which reflected badly on WP's proprietorship.

15. Here WP is reacting to Logan's advice of Aug. 1705 (*Micro.* 12:156) that WP could best provide for his young children by selling Pennsylvania and putting the money into trusts, rather than keeping the colony and providing them with lands there.

16. Philip Ford, Jr., was claiming the right to 5000 acres in Gilberts manor, originally laid out for his late father. The commissioners of property had referred the matter to WP. According to James Logan, Ford had warned that if the commissioners refused to grant his request, he would "in time find a way to make himself easy," i.e., he would gain title to all of Pennsylvania through his suit in Chancery. See *PA*, 2d ser., 19:464-65; *Micro.* 12:156.

17. Charles Mordaunt, third earl of Peterborough, commanded the English expeditionary army that captured Barcelona in 1705. *DNB*.

18. See doc. 101.

19. For the problem of the boundary between Maryland, the Lower Counties, and Pennsylvania, see doc. 12, n. 5.

20. William Warren, an English Quaker, had been one of the Meeting for Sufferings committee delegated late in 1701 to distribute the French edition of WP's *A Key Opening the Way* "among the French People." *Micro.* 9:937.

21. Lawrence Christopher Nohren; see doc. 91, n. 4.

22. WP was still hoping to establish a large settlement in the Susquehanna River Valley. See *PWP*, 3:671-78.

23. John Evans.

24. David Lloyd. The new commission, dated 7 Feb. 1706, reappointed Evans as governor. While leaving out WP's right to veto new legislation, it failed to address Lloyd's other objection (see doc. 102) to Evans's original commission: the governor's right to call, prorogue, and dissolve the Assembly at his discretion.

25. WP had purchased a proprietary share in West New Jersey from William Haige in the 1680s, through the auspices of Philip Ford. One of Haige's sons, either Obadiah or Francis, questioned the transaction and claimed the share for himself or demanded payment for releasing the equity of redemption. Logan reported to WP in Sept. 1707: "I can say nothing of . . . Haigs Mortgage to Ford on thy Account for there is nothing of it here." See Pomfret, *West New Jersey*, pp. 90-91; *PMHB*, 24:96-99; Penn Papers, Letters of the Penn Family to James Logan, vol. 1, fol. 25, HSP; *Micro.* 13:274.

26. See doc. 38, n. 25.

27. See doc. 76, nn. 20-21.

28. Rancocas Creek, N. J.

127
TO JAMES LOGAN

James Logan London 9th 12mo [February] 1705[/6]

Lo. Frd

I this [day re]ceived thy Pacquet by Jno Hamilton who had been a week or 10 days in Town and never Sent it me, or left it for me at any place. but as it happens Colonel Quary by whom this comes, goes not till the 11th and So have time to Answer it briefly. I'll begin with thy lesser and last letter before of 9th 9br.[1] I am glad with all my heart this Assembly considers the Load that Governmt is to me, but I hope it is not intended by thine, it should be continued upon me in any branch of it, wherefore pray know that I pay not one doit[2] or farthing after a Revenue establisht.[3] Next, it was but two hundred pounds per Annum that I allowed your money, and if I must make it Sterling, that is 350£s a year as your rates goe, if not more, by thy reckonings in thine of 22d of 6mo Ult.[4] And as I only promis'd 200£ per Annum your pay it will be tite enough upon me, that I make it if thou wilt 300£ your money, but thou Shouldst have inform'd me first, what rate thou hast paid at hitherto; thou canst not be Sensible of my great needs, and plead for Sterling, and an advance, and perquisits; I can't reach thy meaning in it. I hoped to have come in for Snacks[5] in the publick allowance to the Governr, ⅓ at least of the peoples gift, Especially if he has a Share of the Fines: for that I should have neither Share in the Sallary of the Governmt and loose all my Fines too, is too much in my Opinion, as well as Circumstances to be abated, or to run by the Mill.

I Grant if he must treat all Strangers, as at a constant Table, or live like Lord Cornberry or Colonel Seymeur,[6] he had need of great Supplies; but then let the Country give them, I can't; nor dos So Small a Colony and infant too, require Such an Expence, as well as it cannot pay it. Had the Law T Ll[7] gave up, of which I have ere now informed thee to get a [copy?] [several words obliterated] there had been no need of this tedious work, there had been enough for us all. It is a very weak Argumt that because I Spent 1000£ per Annum that had a Family as a Wife, childe, Nurse, 3 Maids and 3 or 4 men, a Single man must Spend 600£ per Annum. Colonel Wintrop[8] Governr of Connetticut is not so allowed, nor Colonel Cranston[9] Governr of Rhoad Island, that were Collonies threescore years before us, have not more than I allowed Colonel Evans. Ad to this, that Lord Cornberry had but 600£ per Annum for Sallary besides his Command of a Company and Generall Codrington[10] the same or but 700£ per Annum at the most, till the Queen augmented to the first. And for Colonel Dud.[11] with his great Command, they have not allowed him more, or very little, and the Carolinian Lords not So much (I think) as I do him, thô there are 8 pockets to pay it;[12] but of all this thou art Sensible. I desire thy utmost good Husbandry, and the Governrs contentmt in doing what I can, and believe, that I both love and have honour'd him in great Company, and made him known to People of Note, with a valuable Character; and if I Surrender he may depend upon my Friendship. I am glad I hear he is a provident and discreet Governour; but I cannot learn why he must needs keep house. He might as honourably have boarded, Especially before a publick Revenue, and I would do So Still. Tis the pest and Folly of the World, that State prevails, without considering the differences in ranks and Circumstances; and that the Same Words Do not signifie the Same things for that very reason. Governrs Mayors Colonels Counsellors and Justices of the peace are not of the Same import or Significancy every where or alike, though the Same Letters Spell those words.

Well, thou desiredst an Express Answer to thine, being the Total of it, and of so much weight with thee, wherefore I issue it for the time past at 300£ your money per Annum but none for time to come, if the Country has provided for a Governr. I have had a Complaint of his taking 8l per License[13] Sent me over by those that wish him and me well. Now if there be but 30 such houses, they make 240£ per Annum, besides many lesser ones, and what fines I know not, and then there is the Registers place![14] I do again a little Complain of thee, to thee; for thou hast Shifted thy Judgment about Selling the Governmt, one time with all Speed, and another time keep it; one time Sell all, perplexitys in property Staring us in the face as well as those in Governmt, another time Governmt only, and go thither and enjoy my self quietly in the Evening of my time with my Family and Friends, and it would much advance my propriety, and thou advisest me to sell Governmt and the Millions of Rough Lands remaining, being about 30 Millions of Acres, unless the lakes divide with me.[15] Now the Opinion I have of thy Abilitys (as is well known to our Secretarys and great men here) makes me Stagger under diversity of directions. Know also thou hast two or 3 good heads there in thy intimacy, and that I make my self believe, love me, and wish me well; that are good Assistants to thee, and I wish I had your solemn final resolve, what I shall do. Clear off the Fords,[16] and I fly to you, and I believe Some here will advance half; at least ⅓; did Friends there do the like, and thou out of mine own in thy hands, or due to me, help to Crown all, be the Summe 6 or 12,000£ to be paid. I have not yet had a list or Inventory of what Bonds and Bills and Mortgages &cetera as thou promis't me,[17] and would have been of a Surpassing Credit to me in my Streights; Especially with Some Friends in profession and friendship, had I only had a Certificate of their Value or Total, it had been kind; thou must take all in good part from a loaded mind, and a Sore Spirit. I do by M. Austell, Joseph's Brother,[18] who is Nathaniell Markes's Agent, going over in 6 weeks to Jamaica, intend directions abt what Effects were in the hands of the Executors of W Rogers and J Mills[19] whom Dr Dover gives an ill Character ~~of~~: I have not yet read thy long letter, but hope to do it, and answer it before the Fleet is clear off the Channel. Contract Expences all that's possible, be as Sharp and diligent as time and health will let thee, and if Friends there will help to keep me my property: I'll endeavour to keep the Governmt among us. My paper is Scanty, and time more so, and therefore with true Love to thee and Friends and Servts I Close

Thy Sincere Frd
William Penn

P.S.

If Ja. Dickerson or Brother[20] should draw upon thee or any by my order to Assist Lord Fairfax and Company about fishing for a Wreck near Jamaica,[21] to the value of 300£, Credit me. Why do you not prosecute D Ll[22] on the points I hinted to the Governr, and thee? And why dos not Judge Mompesson answer my desires in that and other matters? Compound with all that will Show they are in earnest, or prosecute Such as will not.

If they will not part with D Ll. from the City,[23] I will part with them, or part them. the D. of Shrewsberry being come over,[24] I Shall apply my self to him, upon the old Score; but pray forget not the hints I long Since gave of his Acting as Mar of the Rolls without Commission, his forgery of the Sessions orders, and those of the Assembly; which he has now renewed to W. Mead and T Lower &cetera.[25] A perfect Rebbell to Gratitude and most malicious. Pray let my son have justice agt the Authors of that barberous affront committed upon him, and Company.[26] first he was my Son: 2dly he was the first of the Council, and not rightly wthin their order (or orb) of power, or their reach: They might have Complain'd to the Governr only his Superior there, who with the Council might have had Cognizance thereof being no Assembly Impeachmt. And I take it as done to my Self thô I blame his giving any handle to those people to reflect upon him. He wants money and therefore pray remit the Effects of his imprudent hasty Sale,[27] by the first oppertunity, by Such methods as he desires: deducting his Extraordinary Charges, and allowing what I allowed him in my order to thee (viz) his Common accomodacion and 20s per week for Pocket Expences, and his passage home. I forget to mention another of D. Lloyd's Crimes (viz) that while he was as Generall Mar of the Rolls, and Clerke of the peace, he suffer'd Encroachmts upon my Lotts in the City, and Mannours in the County and recorded them without one Caveat enter'd in favour of his Mar [28] and Patron, or my poor Children. Am

Thy real Friend
William Penn

Copy. Penn Papers, Letters of the Penn Family to James Logan, HSP. (*Micro.* 12:520.) Docketed: Prop 9th 12mo 1705 | Coll Evans Allowance at large my | [illegible] advices to clear him off | James [obliterated] to Credit Ja: Dickerson 300. Son's abuse. Prosecute D Ll | Duplicate via Boston. Endorsed: A Copy.

1. Not found. See doc. 126, n. 2.

2. A Dutch coin valued at half an English farthing, or an eighth of an English penny. *OED.*

3. Logan had informed WP that the Assembly had voted a tax to raise about £200 to support the government (see *Micro.* 12:368). WP was now insisting that he was not obliged to pay Gov. Evans once a revenue was established. For Logan's further concern over the issue of Evans's salary and expenses, see doc. 129.

4. WP had agreed to pay Evans a salary of £200; he is now contending that this pay is in Pennsylvania currency, not sterling. Logan had indicated (*Micro.* 12:156) that Pennsylvania's currency had weakened against sterling.

5. Receive a share. *OED.*

6. John Seymour (d. 1709) had become royal governor of Maryland in Feb. 1705, a post he held until his death. Raimo, *Governors*, pp. 97-98.

7. Thomas Lloyd. See doc. 44, n. 32.

8. John Winthrop (1638-1707), grandson of the founder of Massachusetts, was governor of Connecticut 1698-1707. *PWP*, 3:474.

9. Samuel Cranston (1659-1727) had become governor of Rhode Island in 1698 and held the post until his death. Raimo, *Governors*, p. 392.

10. Christopher Codrington (1668-1710) held the post of captain general and governor of the Leeward Islands from 1697 to 1703. *DNB*.

11. Joseph Dudley was royal governor of Massachusetts Bay and New Hampshire, a post he held from 1702 to 1715. Doc. 38, n. 58; Raimo, *Governors*, pp. 130-31.

12. There were eight proprietors of South Carolina.

13. The governor had the right to issue licenses for ordinaries and taverns upon nomination by the justices of the appropriate county. However, David Lloyd had complained that Evans was feathering his nest by approving ordinaries not recommended by the justices. See doc. 28, text at n. 12; doc. 83, text at n. 43.

14. In July 1704 Logan had informed WP that Gov. Evans had assumed the post of register general. See doc. 82, text following n. 29.

15. Logan regarded these remarks as unfair and unreflective of his advice. For his reply, see doc. 130.

16. That is, pay off what was owed to the Ford family.

17. See doc. 125, n. 28.

18. Moses Austell (b. 1684) and his brother, Joseph (b. 1672), were sons of William Austell, a Berkshire Quaker. Moses became a London merchant and member of Devonshire House Monthly Meeting, while Joseph came to Pennsylvania, where in 1706 he opened an ordinary in the home of Alice Guest. See *Micro.* 8:505; Digests of Quaker Records, Berks.; London & Middx.; John William Wallace Collection, p. 34, HSP.

19. William Rogers and James Mills, two deceased Jamaica merchants, had received £50 worth of goods from James Logan, which they had sold for £30 before their deaths. Logan was endeavoring to get this money from the executors and had sent a power of attorney to Ezekiel Gomersall in Jamaica, who was to have the money sent "in some proper goods" to London for WP. See doc. 81; James Logan Letterbook, 2:53-54, 75, HSP; *Micro.* 13:156.

20. Jonathan and Caleb Dickinson, of Jamaica, sons of Francis and Mary Dickinson, of "Barton," Jamaica. See Maria Dickinson Logan Family Papers, HSP.

21. Thomas Fairfax (1657-1710), fifth Lord Fairfax of Cameron, had received a patent from the queen to fish all wrecks in the West Indies between the 6th and 36th degree of latitude north. Among those involved in financing this venture were Richard Rooth, Robert West, William Russell, and WP. See Basil D. Henning, ed., *The House of Commons, 1660-1690* (London, 1983), 2:293; *CTB, 1709*, p. 236; *Micro.* 12:659; 13:226.

22. David Lloyd. WP had previously expressed his desire to have Lloyd prosecuted for past "crimes." See doc. 91, text at nn. 68-70.

23. Lloyd had been elected to the Assembly for the city of Philadelphia. See doc. 122.

24. Charles Talbot (1660-1718), duke of Shrewsbury, had returned in Jan. 1706 from a five-year sojourn in Europe. Dorothy H. Somerville, *The King of Hearts* (London, 1962), p. 224. For his earlier connection with WP, see *PWP*, 3:235-36.

25. David Lloyd had written on 3 Oct. 1704 to George Whitehead, William Mead, and Thomas Lower, prominent members of the Quaker Meeting for Sufferings, attacking WP's actions as proprietor. On 16 Aug. and 4 Dec. 1706 he renewed these accusations in letters to the same men. See doc. 84; Dreer Collection, David Lloyd, HSP; Fallon Scrapbook, no. 6, HSP.

26. In Sept. 1704 William Penn, Jr., while at Enoch Story's tavern in Philadelphia, became involved with others in a "fray" with the night watch. No action had been taken against any of the participants. See *Micro.* 11:369; *Minutes of the Provincial Council*, 2:160; Watson, *Annals*, 1:114-15.

27. In Oct. 1704 William Penn, Jr., had sold his 7000-acre manor of Williamstadt, above Plymouth Township near the Schuylkill River, to William Trent and Isaac Norris for £850, a transaction, according to James Logan, they were initially "unwilling to touch . . . but he was resolved to sell and they careless of buying" (*Micro.* 11:369). See Norris Papers, 6:43, HSP.

28. Master, that is, WP.

128
TO SIR WILLIAM TRUMBULL

17 2^{m} (ap) [April] 1706

My Good Friend

What I would say is this, the acc^{ts} are open & plain & all in the Persons own hand,[1] I meddle with no new thing, and w^{t} I object is w^{t} that acc^{t} allows to be true. I have indeed obliged him wth mortga~~res~~cs[2] but they were gott by surprize or on trust to pay reasonably, not extortiously: & takeing off the extravagant mixt & compound Interest & consideration, repeated, I shall be ready to pay, & prevent the extream charges of Law, and I shall leave that adjustm^{t} to him[3] & little Pooly[4] to fix & determine: I hope this will reach thee before thou seest him. I am wth true respect

Thy Faithf^{ll} Frd
WP

If I am poor it is by him (F)[5] if he be rich it is by me.

ALS. Trumbull Miscellaneous Correspondence, A.R.I. Hill, Esq., and the Trustees of the Downshire Settled Estates, Berkshire Record Office, Reading, Eng. (*Micro.* 12:671.) Addressed: For my Hon^{d} | Friend S^{r} Wm | Trumbol.

1. The accounts kept by Philip Ford as WP's steward, which were entered as evidence in the Chancery suit between WP and the Ford family.
2. For WP's mortgages to Philip Ford, see *PWP*, 3:656-63.
3. Probably one of the lawyers representing the Fords.
4. Henry Poley, one of WP's legal counsel.
5. Philip Ford. WP claimed that Ford left an estate worth £23,000 (see doc. 123). Since no inventory of Ford's estate has survived, the editors are unable to verify this sum.

129
FROM JAMES LOGAN

Philad^{ia} 28th 3mo [May] 1706

My last large Letter was by the Jamaica Fleet in 9^{br} [1] and before that by the Virg^{ia} Fleet,[2] to none of which I have Received any answer, Since those I wrote again 9^{br} the 18th [3] by Captain Palmer[4] directly For Plymouth and 10^{br} the 12th [5] several Duplicates by way of Barbadoes &c informing of the arrival of Br. Fords Power of Attorny,[6] but Fear the Loss of the Pacquet boat cast away in the Gulf, has occasion'd them to miscarry, I wrote again by Barbados 29th 11th month[7] wch I doubt had the same fate, and since that in the 2^{d} moth a very short Letter by the same way.[8] We expected the Virg^{ia} Fleet would have sailed long e're this, but now the Time is uncertain, I send in the mean time to hint what is most necessary, but shall refer to Is: Norris who designs over himself wth the Fleet[9] For Fuller Notice of our affairs.

The Assembly rising the 2d of the 11th Moth after they had past about 50 Leaves[10] sate againe the 18th of the 12th Moth, but did no more than make a Few Orders For regulating their own matters. I was absent at the time in the two Lower Counties settling business there, after Wm Clark's death,[11] where I found things left in too great Confusion: Sussex is very deeply in Arrears, but what they paid was to good hands, but in Kent they have paid much, but great part of it into such bad hands that it has been Lost, wch severely taxes the Negligence of those at the head. The Inhabitants are poore than ever they have been since the Countrey was thine, yet they are Generally all willing to pay except those to the Southward of Lewis, who absolutely refuse till the Line is run,[12] alledging that according to the Order of Council they in all probability will fall into Maryland, and therefore that till they more certainly Know their Landlord they are in danger of paying in their own wrong In the first month I returned to Philadelphia, and made what Progress I could about Quittrents, in all the three Counties, and in some little time hope to be able to bring them into a very good order.

You will doubtless have heard, before this can arive, of the Powerfull Fleet the French have in the West Indies & the damages they have done We have heard yet only of the utter Ruine of St Christopher & Nevis,[13] but DeCasse[14] having (as 'tis said) joyned that Fleet that did that Mischief with 15 sail more of great ships of War, wch makes their Number now 27 great ships, besides all their Privateers and small craft 'tis reasonably apprehended that much more must follow. This has generally alarmed all the English Dominions in America and put almost an intire stop to all manner of Trade & intercourse wth them wch reduces us into a miserable condition, the Continent here is generally very much alarmed, N York especially being informed from St Thomas's a Danish natural[15] Port that D: Breville[16] the Commander of the Squadron that took Nevis, being the same who coming to N York 5 years agoe in a French man of war from Mechasippi[17] to wood & water took an opportunity in the night to sound their whole harbour designs this Summer to Visit them, & therefore they are fortifying with the utmost application. Our Lieutent Governour[18] upon this thought himself alsoe obliged to doe all in his power, and having gained Credit to an acct, he caused to be brought, that there was a Fleet upon the Coasts, he published a proclamation[19] requiring all persons without fail to furnish them Selves wth arms and ammunition, and caused Regular Guards to be Kept by the Militia For a Night or two, after wch on the 16th Instant in the morning being the first day of our fair, an alarm was brought by the Sherif & Clerk of Newcastle[20] that 6 French Vessels were in the River & 4 of them had actually past that place upon wch the sd officers had hastned up to give Notice to this Town.[21] the Govr immediately Spread & inforced the Report acting as vigourously as if the matter had been real, and pressing all that would bear arms to society Hill[22] where there appeared about 300 but the whole Town & great part of the Countrey was in the deepest Confusion, Neither I nor any other person here, I believe was Privy to the design besides the Govr, but soon coming to the Knowledge of it, I thought the Fittest part for me to take was to Endeavour to allay it as soon as possible, & accordingly I hastened a little way down the River wth a light boat & 4 oars & Fortunately meeting a shallop returned wth an acct that there was no such thing & so undeceived the People who were in as Miserable a Consternation & Confusion as if an Enemy had really been in the midst of them. This has left Such an Impression on the minds of great Numbers of Frds Especially that it will not be easily gott over but what is like to Follow will I doubt make them much more uneasy Some dayes after this, the Members of Council who are not Frds waited on the Govr and represented to him that the late Alarm made it evidently appear how naked & defenceless the place would be found in case of a real attack by an Enemy, and therefore it was absolutely necessary that some Provision should be made by a Law to Establish a Militia & oblige all persons that can fight to serve, & that money should be raised by the Publick to build a Fort &c that in order to this the Assembly should be forthwth called as in the Neighbring Govmts, to find some way to Effect it, that in Case they Failed all in the Govmt that are not Quakers would think themselves obliged to address the Queen to take some orders about it in Engld that they well Knew the Quakers would not fight themselves, nor did they desire it of them only that all others that can Fight should be compelled to it & that all persons should contribute to the Publick Charge. Upon wch adress the Govr meeting with Tho: Grey[23] who is under me in my Office ordered him Forthwith to draw out writts or Preceipes[24] to the sherif to sumon the Members to Town, this was done abroad at a Publick house, but when I had Notice of it and an opportunity, I Laid the Consequences before the Governour of wch he seemed at that time to be made sensible, & next day I Further urged that the matter should be first laid before the whole Councill, accordingly a Councill was Called but being thin & the Govr being obliged to goe to day to N: Castle to view the Militia there it, it was concluded to adjourn the business till his Return that a full Councill might be held upon it (vizt to Consider whether an assembly should be called or not) upon wch the Govr Resolved to return againe wth all possible Expedition to hold such a Council, and wch way 'tis Like to be Carried these steps too fully demonstrate as the whole business Largely Shews what the Consequences must Necessarily be those Members who advise to this several of them at least, are not apprehensive I believe that it will be much to thy Injury, only think it indispensably incumbent upon them to take this care for their own Preservation, & the Govr I believe really thinks he is Dischargeing his duty in it, so that how We shall be able to stave it off is what I can not yet see, but unless thou canst fully Settle all matters with the Crown before such an address comes, it must needs be unhappy. The assembly neither will nor can doe any thing, and the Address of persons that only desire to be better enabled to defend themselves & preserve a Colony in the heart of the Queen's Dominions here From Falling into her Enemies hands, and this without any Charge to the Crown, will doubtless be readily heard, after a Sumer too that I doubt will prove so very fatal to these Dominions, Upon all wch I assure thee all that Lies in my Power at present is thus to represent The matter to thee, and Give thee Notice before hand, if I can doe anything more as matters Advance I shall use all the Address I am Capable of, but the difficulty is that the Govr of Late has been inclinable to Change his former measures and rely upon his own Strength, I can say no more, But fr^ds^ look upon themselves to be in as ill Circumstances as if thy bitterest Enemies here had obtained all their desires, and are ready to think there is like to be no difference as to the Treatm^t^ they are to meet wth between thy Fr^ds^ and foes, the Countrey has raised Money and given the last Stroak to Perfect a Governour,[25] and now in so dangerous a Time of war, he must shew himself Active some way or other wch makes him & them of very different Sentim^ts^. So that upon the whole the intire Body seems disgusted and are piqued to the heart at the Contrivance of that alarm wch they Think served only to Expose them to their Enemies here, from whom they were apprehensive of as much mischief, had the Confusion continued as from the French themselves, but if they look on the Govr as their Enemy, I think they really wrong him.

But I shall leave this and must Lay before thee another particular that much Troubles me & I shall greatly want to be directed in, wch is this, after Mr William[26] had been here a few months lodging at Is: Norris, we became so troublesome to his Numerous Family that we were obliged to Remove & (as I have largely wrote before) to take a house the Lt Govr first took Lodging at Al: Paxsons where his wifes condition (being soon ready to lie in) rendring his Stay inproper, he removed to John Finneys[27] whose wife being also in a Little time in the same Condition, he was obliged to look out again but finding no place and I considering that we were already at the Charge of house Keeping and that where ever he went till Money were otherwise Raised I must answer it on thy Account, wch would still make it deeper and much heavier to me, concluded therefore to invite him to the same house, as it was in Gen^ll^ thought most proper, upon wch to give way to him I turned up into the Garratt, Thy son Departing in a Few months after, We were left to Keep house by our selves, When we first entred on it, I told M^r^ W^m^ I could bear no other part of it, than to pay as a Boarder that at Is: Norris I paid 30^l^ per Annum and at another place 20^l^ for a serv^t^ that here I would allow 60^l^ per annum but could no more, wch was then thought very reasonable, thy Son as I said being gone we could not pretend to break up, the Govr would want Accommodation as much as ever, and it must be found him by me, till by some other means money could be raised, and so to this Time We have Continued, the Assembly of the Province hath granted thee 800l (as thou wilt see by the Laws) payable to the Lt Govr For suppt of Govmt besides half of an Impost for three years. the Lower Counties have given him a penny in the pound wch makes about 200l more, part of this being raised & the Treasurer having money in his hands Last Night I told the Governour that I had now for so long as time answered all the Charges of House Keeping, but that money being Scarce I was Much dun'd, that it would very Proper now to give me an order To the Treasurer to pay off and reimburse past Charges, but much contrary to Expectation he seem'd not to Understand what I meant by the demand, but told me, he was to have a Salary of 200l sterling per Annum of thee till Such time as the Countrey should raise a support that I had not paid him this & that it ought at Least to goe for the Charges. I told him I understood it that the Proprietor was to make it up to him 200l per Annum in case what he might Receive fell short, that this 200l was now by the Assembly Fully made up and Therefore whatever I advanced on thy Acct till such Time as other Provision could be made, ought to be refunded, for thou was obliged to no more than to make good Such a sum, as I understood it, and not to pay him such a Certain Salary, and that all Perquisites and Profits ought to be brought into the Acct, this startled him againe, for none could think it reasonable, he thought, that he should acct For money Recd for Licenses Registers &c. We differed widely in our sentiments upon the whole, I insisted on it that every farthing I had Expended or advanced For him should be repaid me out of the Publick money now raised, and that he ought to give me an Order for it; that whatever he received above the 200l a Year I should not think myself concernd in the Acct of it, but would leave that to thee, if the Countrey allowed more it was reasonable he should have it (For certainly nothing less than 500l this money Yearly will give a Governour a Competent Subsistence) only there was no reason the Propr & Countrey should both pay, he said he did not desire it: when the Countrey paid he would rely upon it, but that thou was Obliged to pay till the Country did, and as For reimbursing he could not understand it. Our house Keeping For these two Years past has Stood in above 600l, When thy Son was here, it was highest but that was not quite Five months of the Time but the Governour has been 22 months & the Charge Chiefly on his Acct, For I should never have Kept it my Self, having lived much easier before, nor indeed could I afford it, But of this besides 60l per annum Allowed by me & 20l more for Jacob Taylor[28] in the Surveyors office, there ought to be some Further Allowance made by thee on Account of thy Publick

Affairs Transacted in the house, Upon the whole I desire thy full and Positive Order and be very plain to the Lt Govr {himself} about it, as well as to me, he is very diligent about getting the money in, but the Arrears {of thy} ~~being 200~~ 2000^{l} lie still most Scandalously behind, notwithstanding the Strict Law past For Collecting them,[29] nor can I can make it otherwise, I can neither putt in nor turn out an Offier,[30] and I Assure thee thy Interest is very Little regarded there are Few that think it any sin to have what they can from thee, yet there are still some truly Honest but none look upon it as thir business and therefore still all thrown upon me While the World stands thy Interest is like to be Unworthily served [illegible deletion] {here}, every man is for himself & so in the Close thou wilt find it, as for my own parts my ~~heart~~ Spirits are often ready to fail me Publick Calamities, Maladminestration among ~~is~~us no success in thy affairs but Disappointments from all quarters, and none to assist often give thought too heavy to bear up against, & deprive me of that vigour that thy business Requires, This from the Govr Exceedingly Troubles me, I depended on 800^{l} from him at least besides 112^{l} I advanced for him in money to supply his Necessities the first Six Months after his arrival, but thou sees what I am likely to gett, I shall Endeavour to prevail on him to something more Reasonable but after what is past, and Knowing how very Loath he is to part with any thing {of the kind} I have very Little hopes Pray consider the matter Fully and be pleased to write expresly about it. In my Judm^{t} 20^{l} [31] sterling a year if the Countrey will grant more is not sufficient, but I doubt they are so disgusted they will hold their hands till what is done be pretty well dereined [?], the first Occasion of dislike that he more reasonable took was from his Imprisoning that Foolish Old man W Biles upon a Judgm^{t} obtained (formerly mentioned)[32] For 300^{l} Damages, after that upon an application From the Assembly who in Pity to his years and Circumstances had interceeded For him he had given them an Expectation That he would not injure him, but when he had lain a month in Goal[33] & all Solicitations were thought to be utterly vain, he very handsomely released him.

Judge Mompesson has accepted the Commission to be chief Justice & for last Provincial Court I have p^{d} him 20^{l} & about 10^{l} more For what thou calls his Viaticum or expences in thy Letter to him.[34]

We have scarce any trade this year at all Our Crops failed as last harvest so that many are like to want bread before the next, & we have not had one vessell from the west Indies but a small one from Antigua & but one gone all this season thither, perhaps into our Enemies hands. Rum can not be had under 10 or 12 shillings a Gallon, thô sold most of Last sumer for 2s 6 or 3 shillings in short if the west indies Fall, as we much Fear it, we are ruined whether an Enemy come hither or not.

If it be not already as I hope it is, I earnestly desire my Long Letter of the 6th Moth last by the Virg^{ia} Fleet[35] may be closely consid-

ered, there is a Rumour here spread by some lately arived in Maryland that Colonel Nicholson is coming over to the Govm^t of N: York and thy son to an other neighbouring one,[36] but we can Credit nothing. I design by the Virginia Fleet to be Larger.
Postscript Copies of this I have sent ~~to~~by Jamaica & by a Vessell from hence bound to the West of England wth Considerably more added wch I shall not now stand to Transcribe

This is now intended by a Vessell That runs without Convoy to Newcastle, wch may Serve for a Conveyance, if she Escape. I send also in her a Copy of the Laws last past, having two fair Draughts, and have Committed the Care of them to Wm Burge who goes wth a Charge of Tobacco in the s^d Vessel, & hope will find some way to Convey it to London, I shall send also wth the Lawes an Account of what Bonds I have, & of thy Debts here wch is what thou most wants I suppose, but the Extracts of the Rent rolls design'd by the Fleet are too tedious to draw Duplicates of them now Considering the small service they can be of there. As for the acc^t of Bonds not arriving last year,[37] I find since that the Vessell by which they were sent was taken, & when making up the Duplicate Pacquet wch arrived, the second draught of that appeared Unfitt to send, so that it was laid aside. If thou intends to assign these Bonds, Be pleased to Remember that before any Assignment comes there will doubtless be some part of them paid by next Spring I hope to make some more remittances, but shall forbear being particular here till I. Norris comes. I have received thy Letters about P Ford's business viz that by Barbados & Owen Thomas,[38] but not the other,[39] a strange and unhappy Acc^t between the greatest villany on the one hand & unheard of easiness on the other, but after all this, wilt thou still Keep the Government to be ruined both there and here, will nothing perswade thee to make thy self easy? Next Assembly I suppose will once more convince thee of the Necessity.

LBC. James Logan Letterbook, HSP. (*Micro.* 12:676.)

1. *Micro.* 12:368.
2. Penn Papers, Penn Family to James Logan, 1:25, HSP, filmed in part, *Micro.* 12:229.
3. *Micro.* 12:416.
4. Anthony Palmer (c. 1675-1749) was a prominent Barbados merchant and ship captain who, by 1709, settled in Philadelphia, where he became a provincial councilor, justice of the peace, and acting governor of Pennsylvania (1747-1748). Raimo, *Governors,* p. 333.
5. *Micro.* 12:442.
6. According to Logan (*Micro.* 12:442), Bridget Ford had sent a power of attorney, dated 24 Jan. 1705, to David Lloyd, Isaac Norris, and John Moore, along with a letter, dated 18 Nov. 1705, to Lloyd and Moore, promising to send her "title" to Pennsylvania. For the Ford case, see the headnote to doc. 108.
7. *Micro.* 12:495.
8. Not found.
9. After numerous delays, Isaac Norris sailed from Virginia on 17 Sept. 1706 aboard the *South River Merchant.* See Norris Papers, 1:133, HSP.

10. Error for "Lawes." Fifty-one laws passed this session are listed in *Votes and Proceedings*, vol. 1, pt. 2, pp. 80-81.

11. William Clarke had died in mid-June 1705. See doc. 100.

12. The boundary between Maryland, the Lower Counties, and Pennsylvania. See doc. 12, n. 5.

13. In Feb. and Mar. 1706 a French fleet burned and plundered the English plantations on St. Christopher and Nevis, in part as retaliation for English destruction of French sugar plantations on Guadeloupe in 1703. See Richard S. Dunn, *Sugar and Slaves* (Chapel Hill, 1972), pp. 136-37; *CSPC, 1706-1708*, pp. 75-78, 83-88, 117-19, 254-55.

14. Jean Baptiste Ducasse (d. 1715) was a squadron commander in the French Royal Navy. In Aug. 1702 his squadron had bested an English squadron commanded by Vice-Admiral John Benbow in a bloody six-day engagement off Riohacha in the Caribbean, when four of Benbow's seven ships failed to join the fight. *Biographie Universelle, Ancienne et Moderne* (Paris, 1852), 11:381-82; *CSPC, 1702*, pp. 576-80, 673-78, 744-45; *1702-1703*, p. 360.

15. Error for "neutral." St. Thomas and the other Danish Virgin Islands were virtually the only noncombatants during the Anglo-French-Dutch-Spanish warfare in the Caribbean, 1702-13.

16. Pierre Le Moyne, Sieur d'Iberville (1661-1706), a French-Canadian soldier and colonizer of Louisiana, had commanded the squadron which attacked St. Christopher and Nevis (see n. 13, above) in the spring of 1706. *Encyclopedia Britannica* (1947), 12:31.

17. Mississippi. In June 1700 d'Iberville, commanding a 50-gun man-of-war, *La Renomée*, bound for France, had stopped near Staten Island and spent the next month sounding the harbor from New York City to Sandy Hook. D'Iberville died suddenly in Havana in July 1706 while outfitting a squadron to attack the Carolinas. *New York Col. Docs.*, 4:684, 686, 701, 877, 969; *Encyclopedia Britannica* (1947), 12:31.

18. John Evans.

19. Not found. At a Provincial Council meeting on 14 May 1706, Evans produced a letter purported to be from Gov. Seymour of Maryland, containing information on two French privateers and numerous other enemy ships off the Virginia Capes. Evans and the non-Quaker councilors ordered the proclamation. The letter was later discovered to be a forgery, and Evans's behavior was viewed by James Logan as "Exceedingly boyish." *Minutes of the Provincial Council*, 2:240-41; *Micro.* 12:721.

20. The sheriff of New Castle was John French (d. 1728), who later became commander of the fort at New Castle, justice of the peace, and chief justice of the Lower Counties. The clerk at New Castle was William Tonge. Scharf, *Delaware*, 130, 133-35, 526, 933, 939; Maria Dickinson Logan Family Papers, HSP; *Minutes of the Provincial Council*, 2:97.

21. John French brought a letter apparently from the sheriff of Sussex Co. "informing that Lewis [Lewes] was burnt" (*Micro.* 12:721). The letter was a forgery by Gov. Evans.

22. See map of Philadelphia, p. 290.

23. Thomas Grey was James Logan's assistant and a clerk for the Provincial Council. It appears that he concerned himself primarily with financial matters. See *Minutes of the Provincial Council*, 2:160, 205; *Micro.* 12:796.

24. *Præcipes* are writs requiring something to be done or demanding a reason for its nonperformance. *OED*.

25. On 12 Jan. 1706 the Pennsylvania Assembly had passed an act to raise money for the support of the government, from which £800 was to be given, on the proprietor's behalf, to the lieutenant governor for his salary and administrative expenses. *Statutes*, 2:280-91.

26. William Penn, Jr.

27. John Finney (d. 1728), son of Capt. Samuel Finney of Chester Co., had been a provincial councilor in 1702 and served repeatedly as sheriff of Philadelphia, 1703-7. He later returned to Cheshire, Eng., where he died. His wife was Jane Latham, daughter of Thomas Latham, of Ireland and Cheshire, Eng. *Minutes of the Provincial Council*, 2:68; Scharf and Westcott, 3:1737; Howard Finney, Sr., *Finney-Phinney Families in America* (Richmond, Va., 1957), pp. 219-20.

28. Jacob Taylor (d. 1746), of Chester Co., a surveyor, astronomer, mathematician, Quaker schoolmaster, and publisher of numerous almanacs, was surveyor general

of Pennsylvania from 1706 to 1733. *PMHB*, 4:441-42; 21:130-31; Scharf and Westcott, 3:1767.

29. On 12 Jan. 1706 the Pennsylvania Assembly passed an act for collecting the arrears of £2000 granted to WP in 1700 and 1701. The new act permitted collectors to levy distraints on those who refused to pay. *Statutes*, 2:263-66.

30. "Officer."

31. A mistake for £200, the salary WP wished to pay Evans as governor. See doc. 127.

32. See doc. 100, text at n. 10.

33. Despite William Biles's refusal to pay the £300 judgment, Evans had implied that he would forgive him. On hearing this, Biles came to town, only to be imprisoned for one month on Evans's command. According to James Logan, the resultant outcry over this incident cost Evans "his own Interest with the Country & his frds" (*Micro.* 12:721).

34. See doc. 93, n. 11.

35. *Micro.* 12:156.

36. Neither rumor was correct. Francis Nicholson had been recalled in Aug. 1705 as royal governor of Virginia and did not hold another governorship until that of South Carolina in 1721 (Raimo, *Governors*, p. 482). Despite WP's repeated efforts, William Penn, Jr., does not appear to have gained employment. For example, see doc. 125, text at n. 17; doc. 97, n. 6; *Micro.* 12:792.

37. See doc. 125, n. 28.

38. Possibly Owen Thomas, a mercer and ship captain of Carmarthen, Wales, and owner of the *William Galley* (*PMHB*, 1:330-32). For the letters from WP mentioned here, see docs. 125, 126.

39. Probably WP's letter of 14, 21 Sept. 1705 which responded to Logan's letters of Feb., Apr., and May 1705. See Penn Papers, Letters of the Penn Family to James Logan, 1:25, HSP, filmed in part, *Micro.* 12:229.

130
FROM JAMES LOGAN

Philad^ia^ 25th 5mo [July] 1706

Honoured Governour

Last night I received two Packets by Boston one from J Jeffries[1] inclosing the Order of Councill about the Laws[2] the other containing Duplicates or Copies of 4 Several Letters, 3 of which being the first I have received of them (for C Quary is not yet arived) I shall take Notice of here, as far as the shortness of my Time will allow me, but must first observe that the Letter mentioned to be sent to Friends inclosed in the same pacquet & left open for my Perusal is not there[3] but perhaps it comes by C Quary, So D LL's Letter to W M &c.[4] in the name of the Assembly was mentioned in thine per C Dunster[5] as inclosed but it never came either that or any other way, wch proved a great Loss to us.

Two things in thine I shall now take the opportunity to speak particularly viz thy trouble at my incosistency with my self in my Advice as to parting with the Government, & my unreasonable Desires in behalf of the Lt Governour.[6]

To The first I have Examined the Copies of most of my last Year's Letters and find that in my Large one of 22^d^ 6mo last[7] after a large discussion of the matter I Concluded my opinion that 'tis by all meanes most adviseable to surrender at least the Government &c for a valuable consideration if to be obtained, for that should be the Chief Inducement &c. and I think the whole Strain of that Letter Runs intirely that way, and the Motives that led me to advise to this were, because I could by no means see any other probable Method of clearing thy Debts wch I take to be the first great thing thou art to labour. In my next of the 24th of 8^{br} [8] I told thee the assembly Resolved to doe all in their power for thine & the Countries' good & would Endeavour to putt things in the best condition for a Surrender if thou must be obliged to it, tho *they desire* the Contrary, wch last expression I suppose it is that thou takes particular Notice of.

As it has alwayes been my opinion that nothing concerned thee more than to find a Method to Discharge thy Incumbrances, & it has generally (I believe I may say always) been my Thoughts, that it is not worth thy while to undergoe the fatigue the Government gives for all the Advantages 'tis attended with, so by compounding these two opinions I am sure it never entred me but that it was altogether adviseable to sell the Government at least, thô in that Letter I told thee the Assembly rather desire thou should Keep it, And 'tis Certainly true that were I firmly settled in this place, and had nothing but my own Interest to Regard I would rather that thou should Keep the Govm^{t} & lett me still be Secretary or in some other better post, and thus thinks the Assembly, No wonder if thy, wholly made up Friends would not Rather enjoy places of Trust & Credit & live easily under thy administration than run the Risque of hazarding such enjoym^{ts} by a Change, the Effects of ~~of~~ all Changes in State affairs being uncertain, & they being the Representatives of the people think for them & themselves in this point, not for thee, I never Sent one of their sentiments as is related to thee or thy Concerns, I only said what might certainly be Known before, that they desire not to see a Change Nay very few of thy greatest Enemies desire to see it, for they well Know they Live easier now than they can hereafter. But what is this to the Discharging of thy Burthens? I have largely shewn that I can see no other way to make thee easy than to sell, and when I write so, I doe it purely in regard to thy Circumstances, & nobodies Else, my own as little as any man's. In my next of the 6th Moth [9] & added that I had no reason to recede in my opinion from what I then wrote, nor can I find that I have said one Syllable differing from this any where, unless I dropt something (wch I doe not believe) in that short one of the next day, viz of 9^{br} the 9th,[10] wch thou mentions relating to the Govr & of wch I Kept no Copy, I have indeed at some times said that if thou could make thy self easy upon other Scores, the Govm^{t} might perhaps as well be Kept as parted with, wch was wrote at such times as things promised best, but I am sure that of clearing off has alwayes with me preponderated all other considerations, and thou wilt never find a Syllable interfering with that, But if there should be such a thing as I am Confident there is not, can that come in competition wth solid Argum[ts] a Case stated & brought to the ballance, wth the Weights of each scale calculated and compared, this I Endeavoured in a slender measure to perform, after w[ch] I should think that no man's opinion ought to weigh much, as to determining thy Thoughts, unless it be[11] discover an Error in the Computation, and that if after this I should Ever so much alter my advice it would be of no Importance, unless I at the same time demonstrated the Nature of the thing to be otherwise than was at first Laid down, Reasoning Seems to me to be the art of Comparing things rightly & Judgement to consist in the skill of preferring the most Valuable, And I am so great an Admirer of Al~~e~~gebra w[ch] is wholly employed in discovering Equations, that I take it to be the best Rule to be transferr'd to the Conduct of Life. So that I think I have said full enough upon that head, and thou may assure thy Self I neither have nor ever can change my Opinion that thy Debts must be discharged, & that the only way that I can see for it is to Obtain a Consideration from the Crown for the Govm[t], and that if thou canst receive such a Sum as has been mentioned[12] thou wilt Receive a Thing of great value for an other of a very small one w[ch] is accounted good Marketting. On the other hand if thou didst not want money or could have it an other way w[th]out Damage to thy Self, as I believe thou canst not I look upon thy holding or parting w[th] the Govm[t] to be a thing almost in Æquilibrio, but rather as thou now stands in favour, to preponderate on the side of holding it, & some times I am more of this Opinion some times less according as the scale is made lighter or heavier by our Circumstances and administration, and if my Sentim[ts] in that case seem to vary 'tis no more to be admired than that the same person here in winter can scarce gett Cloathes thick Enough, or in sumer thin Enough or that the Sailor crowds Sail sometimes on one side, & sometimes on the other, 'tis owing to no Inconstancy in the person but to causes out of his power, to w[ch] he must accommodate.

I write not this so much to Justify my self as to state the matter more clearly, & to give a trutine[13] to all that I have wrote on the head in w[ch] I was alwayes more plain (because of the necessity there seems to be in it) than I had a Full Freedom in myself to appear, I thought if I stated the Case and furnished the Materials to Judge by, it would be both better manners & more prudent to stop there than to proceed to advise, as those Historians are often most approved of, that barely relate the matter with all Circumstances that can furnish out a Judgement and then leave that to the Readers themselves. But I was Commanded to give my Opinion & therefore did it, Yet would rather choose to see The Government sold (thô I desire to see it done, for thy Interest but against both my own & that of many Friends) upon any other person's advice than mine, 'tis a point I am as loath to advise in, as I would be in {a} [illegible deletion] case of Marriage, but

I have done it, & I think steadily, As for considering others here 'tis in vain, the 3 ablest that I Know of my Acquaintance are S: Carp: I Nor: & Rd Hill & his wife[14] for one, the first says 'tis a pity, but if thou holds it thou'l be ruined, the 2d is wholly a Trader and will not advise in the matter, he thinks as I doe, that 'tis best for him thou shouldst hold it, but for thee {to} part with it, the Last heartily wishes any other means could be found to discharge thy Incumbrances, but if there be a Necessity (as I think that point is fully proved) all good people must acquiesce. What I said for thy parting with thy Property, also, had relation to thy Younger Children whose Interest it would doubtless prove, but as that seems to me impracticable as things now stand, thy next best method would doubtless be to come hither and settle, that is, as to thy Self, but I question whether it would prove so for thy Children, after Age has struck the last {of} time to thee & summoned thee to part from them, Upon the whole these several distinct considerations ought to be fully compared one wth the other & that wch is found of the greatest weight to be adhered to. I think they all Stand in Full view and scarce need any further Light to Manage them. for my part I take my self to be so far from being uncertain in my advices that I much rather blame my self for taking so much upon me in matters of such importance; but my Excuse to my self is, that 'tis required of Me.

The Next point is the Governours Allowance. I am heartily troubled I Kept not a Copy of that Letter[15] for of all my Letters there is not one I should be now more desirous to see, however I think I can pretty well Remember the tenour of it, being I presume consonant to the Course of my thoughts in general on that head, And then I say that I must still think that 200l of this money is to[o] slender an Allowance for a Govr of this place, that is, in case he were to have nothing more {of} ~~mor~~ any Kind, and were to Account for all his Perquisites & still believe that Unless a Governour can by one means or other make 500l or near it, 'tis not worth his while, and that out of all manner of Proffits 200l Sterling wch According to the common reckoning I accounted 300l of this money was little enough & I believe I mentioned something of Perquisites, but if I did, I never understood that they should belong to him above his Salary, I was of Opinion that thou design'd he should be Accountable for every farthing he received and that thou was only to make up, what that fell short, 200l wch I thought should be Sterling & he sayes it was agreed it should be such, And that if the Countrey raised enough or if by any other means he should receive so much out of the Government, thou ought not to advance a farthing whether by License money fines or any other Method, but of these there are few, the Corporation[16] taking to themselves all those of the City & in the Countrey there are but very few, & these not at all collected. I must be of Opinion 'tis the Governours imediate business to see they are duly Collected, Seeing 'tis all done by the Officers of the Govm^{t} who are more im{m}ediately under him, & have but a secondary relation to me but there has been very Little Care taken of them, or anything of the Kind. I have not been wanting to speak but our Officers are very Careless.

If Thou Conceived any hard Thoughts of me upon this business thou wilt find by the first inclosed (wrote at the time of it's date & of wch I have already sent away 2 Duplicates & design a 3^{d} now ready besides this) that my Intentions were mistook, and whatever may be apprehended from what I have wrote I never altered my sentiments about it one tittle. I am sure I have never been partial agst thy Interest, whatever I have been for it, and I should think my self egregiously so, if I proposed anything like what thou seems to apprehend from my Letter for the Difference between him and me now is, whether into the Money thou allowes, all Perquisites are not to be reckoned, and whether what the assembly allowes, it being given to thee,[17] thô payable to him, ought not to extend backwards for the Time past, as well as forward, wch I take to have been their Intention, So that thou wilt find me as Carefull for thy Interest on that head, as can be desired, yet at the same Time I am for a more reasonable Allowance than 200^{l} but would not have thee pay it As for what is said of other Govm^{ts} [18] I think it does not hold (with submission) for there is not one of them but has double their Salary by other Proffits and the point here is, whether there should be anything more than barely the salary or whether into that Salary also should be accounted all perquisites whatever.

Thy Computation of the Amount of Licenses[19] in a year is grounded on an Error The Taverns in Town 'tis true paid for these 2 years past 8^{l} for a License, wch was a Contrivance of mine at the Council Board to save thee money & not to put it in his Pockett, thô now he reckons otherwise, for I could not bear to be alwayes advancing Money to him as I had been for 6 Months after his Arival, and from that time I never paid him a penny but had advanced before that above 100^{l}, & what he has had since is in the Charges of the house Keeping, of that 8^{l} 10 shillings comes to my office, and of such houses there are but about 7 or 8 in town, the rest paid from 40 shillings to 4^{l} my Office Fees included however the whole came to above 100^{l} per annum. I suppose near 150 Th: Grey who does all the business of course in the Secretarie's office received the Money for him, and alwayes was his Cashier so that I never received it, Pray settle this Matter Fully between us, for I shall suspend it till I have an answer, but shall still continue my Claim, as for his Keeping house, I have given a full Acc^{t} of it before[20] there was no place in town that could & would accommodate him, and I found those wth whom he had ben at first reckoned at least 5^{l} a weak as much more than it would Cost him at a house where he might have a perfect Freedom & call it his own, besides that it would look much more reputable and be much more convenient. We lived as Cheap as possibly I could Contrive it, had Just two Dishes of Meat a day, unless upon some few occasions, & no more but everything is so Chargeable here, that it self drew high. Jos: Chessman[21] was our Providore Caterer Butler & everything only one maid to cook, but when thy Son & he were both here, it was higher, Joshua by thy Letters to me I Know needs No good word to recommend him for a very good Servant & yet he {&} I very often differed about our Expences, till I gott my self an ill Name by it, I am sure I had a very great fatigue by it but expect no other returns for the whole than blame, I never that I Know of, paid money so Unwillingly on my own Acct as I all along did for the house, till such time as the assembly gave money, & now they have done it, there is none like to Come, it seems where I Expected, As for thy coming in for a Share of what the Countrey gives,[22] I see nothing unreasonable in it, so far as it may pay for the Expences thou art {at} for the service of the Government. but that the Lt Govr Should have any share of the fines I see no reason if he is Sufficiently paid otherwise, But upon the whole I think that you Should be upon a Certain Agreemt wch in my Judgemt would be reasonable thus, that in Case the Proffits of Govmt amounted not to 300l this money thou should make it up that sum that if they exceed 300l he should still have them as far as 4 or 500l Provided always that thou art at no manner of Expence, and that all that Exceeds that sum should come to thee, By the Proffits of the Government I understand all moneys whatsoever that arise from the Government whether grants of Assembly Fines Forfeitures or whatever it be, and that he should be obliged either to Keep an Exact Account or else that such & & such perquisites should be valued at such a Certain Rate, or that they should be all paid to a certain person who should Keep an Exact Account of them as to me or my Deputy, for a Govr Seldom or never Receives money himself and this I believe would be a very Equal way, for I think 'tis as reasonable that the Govr in Chief should gett by his Govmt & agree with his Lieutent as 'tis for me to agree with with Th: Grey in my office nor doe I see the Difference but in degree. These are truly my sentimts between both and neither better nor worse than I should have given them last 12th Moth when that Letter was wrote,[23] Tis his Cousin[24] has the Registers place who I think may well Enough deserve it. What I mention'd of the amount to Licenses will not hold now, the assembly having reduced them to 40 S: in town & 20 out of it.[25]

Before I quite leave this Subject I cannot but observe that I Expect a Severe censure for the discrepancy between what I wrote formerly of the Govr & the Account given in my Last Letters,[26] but I cannot avoid it, If I be Just, I am Obliged to Relate things as I find them & think I'm no more to blame than if I were to give an account of the Several Phases of the Moon for a Month together I should say, that when I first saw her She appeared only like a C inverted at 7 dayes like a Semicircle at 14 like a whole Circle ~~at 14~~, and so back againe, I might be answered that the Body of the Moon was certainly the same all this Time & had been so for thousands of years, wch thô true yet argues not but that what I said was true, and that I ought to give That acct & no other, And 'tis to be remembred that all men are compounded of variety of Passions, of the worst of men some good may be said and of the best some ill, we call good or bad not considering men absolutely so, but as the one or t'other is predominant and the Character of any Man exactly drawn will require variety of Colours In everything I have said I at this Minute believe I have been very Just and were I to write again should neither add nor diminish, any otherwise than as I might be disposed to use a greater or less Freedom in expressing myself.

These last words further lead me to beg an Allowance for that I take the Lt Govr used to write to thee after the same manner he would to any other Superiour, but for my part, I take the Weight of business that lies on me to be an Intire Dispensation from any manner of Ceremony, there are Certain Rules and degrees to be Observed in accosting a great Man but his Domesticks are Admitted wthout any, besides common good manners, wch priviledge I desire may be allow'd me in distinction from those that Claim it not. I must.

I sent a Duplicate of the first 3 sheets by John Guy to Whitehaven[27] wth 4 or 5 more[28] in wch I was large about the Govr the Jersey Lands[29] and some other heads, what there is about T: S:[30] I wish were unwritt, for I shall not meddle to make any such Request, only I think that as the Assembly has past an Act requiring all Deeds to be recorded, wch will mightly increase his Business, So if both Sealing and Recording of Patents belong'd to my office as well as drawing them, it would be very Just and reasonable, for positively my whole Profits out of the Secretarie's Office amount not to much above £50 or 60l a year

There has been but 435 Patents issued ever since thy Departure, for they stand all numbred, & the business of Warrants wch never Yielded much seems quite over yet because I have the management of thy Concerns I am look'd on as somebody but want a support or bottom to answer the figure (Thomas was married 15 dayes {agoe})[31] Besides I must Consider Life is like the seasons of the Year; wch has a time to sow, a time to reap, & a Time to doe neither but spend if we have it. As I take it, I am so far from deserving to be upbraided, for endeavouring to gett something, that I think I can never answer it to my Self, if in these Years I Provide not for another day, and I hope thou canst not blame me, while I seek not to strain upon thee, or take any thing out of thy Pocket, but as it is Indisputably my due. I have secured Wm Aubry his money by Bonds here,[32] but have unhappily abused some very honest men, who have bought parts of the great Lott[33] and built brick houses on them wthout a Title, they have paid no money 'tis true but their whole Improvements are in danger, &

they are ready to pay if they Could have a Title, they were drawn in by me; believing I was safe and that I had men of Sincerity to deal with, but if those Deeds[34] I So often wrote for & wch thou sayes, he promised by Guy last year, arrive not with these Virg^ia Ships in wch C Quary comes I shall certainly conclude something else than what's fair is designed. vizt after he has Security for the Portion there, to Keep that and the Lands here too in his own hands, he has made over only 5000 Acres of Land, and The Appurtenances granted to her by thee by some old Deeds we Know nothing of, & the Persons to whom it is made over have sent us a blind Letter of Attorny[35] witnessed only by two Persons there and no otherwise certified wch thou canst not but Know as well as I that it will not doe Her 5000 Acres are Patented {& called 7800} wth out Relation to those old Deeds that were never seen here nor heard of. her great Lott is also Patented wth out Relation to them & therefore must be conveyed by recital of the Patents. but besides these there are 15000 Acres of valuable Land in Chester & Newcastle County also firmly Patented to her of wch there is no manner of mention made in any Deeds sent over. I sent by thy Son Full Accounts of this wth Copies of all the Patents or Sufficient Acc^ts of them. The Portion agreed on was 2000^l and Interest till paid and they were to Release all their Rights here to thee if thou expects this it ought effectually to be done without further dependance, P F[36] may be one Instance more to thee that mankind is not to be Trusted where their Interest is concerned, if they can have any pretence for it; & how far W.A.^s Character will exempt him from the Level of mankind for Generosity I shall leave, especially if it come to be tried in a case where 'tis only taking from the father to give the Daughter, for my own part, I have nothing to interpose ag^st her having all the Lands design'd for her, at first, unless it be fully agreed otherwise, but that he shall have these Lands and the 2000^l secured to him besides Seems barbarously unjust, I must upon this say it Seems Nothing Strange to me that thou art so plunged into difficulties, for such a management must produce unhappy Effects, and we cannot so reasonably complain of being abused when there is no Care taken to Prevent it I had ordered the matter so at first, as that thou needed not to have gone to ask for this, I gott Pattents drawn and signed for all her Lands, and told her I had taken very good care for her, as I am sure, I had, wch was all she Knew of the matter Yet because she was a Maid & undisposed of, I Kept them from the seal all but One, because I Knew there could be no service while a father is living in making an Unmarried Daughter absolute M^rs of 5 or 6000^l, and yet least any thing should happen, I had it Secure for her. I hinted this to thee when I wrote also about Joh~~a~~nne's Patents[37] viz that one of the Trustees was dead but I had very quickly a positive Order to pass them all, wch appeared then some what strange for Lætitia was married, & thou hadst contracted otherwise wth her husband and I thought it lookt Odd to make a Dead man vizt Edwd Pen:[38] a Trustee, however the Order was observed immediately. I Know not whether I shall be thought to take too much upon me here, but I would venture a Small imputation, if it would but Contribute to rowse thee to think thorowly of thy Interest in Such weighty points

I have Bills for 100l Sterling {for W Aubry} to send by The Fleet, & have bought & Paid for the Like sum more but shall scarce receive them in time to send by the Same Conveyance, I suppose they must come to the Trustees, this makes 300l & I have good Bonds for 570l more wch makes up what I have received of hers besides the 100l Sterling Bill she carried with her, & Charges. I have Sold to the value of 700l more wch would come in and pay Interest, if I could make the People's Titles, however whether their Lands pay thee or not thou payes them, there will be due next Month in the whole 720l this money for Interest, of wch I have Actually paid 600l (or 590 I am not now certain) & shall be punctual with the rest, 180l per Annum here is certainly Some part of thy Yearly Revenue when the Rents of The whole Province are not 400l Sterling a Year, and The Rents of the Lower Counties are alwaies so miserably paid. I hope to remitt this Year to Mr William 2 or 300l this money, but can not be positive, I shall write to him[39] by The Fleet. I am concerned with Wm Trent in building a ship[40] of 400 hogsheads to be L[o]aded home in the spring, before wch I believe I shall remitt thee nothing but the Inclosed or a few Bills for Rent. Pray oblige R: Rooth to pay this Bill; for she[41] has had it of me, & be pleased to deliver him the Inclosed[42] Sealed if thou thinks fitt, tis at her Request, R Assheton must not have the Return for her money, 'tis base in him, & like him, & Shews him a true Cousin. I Designed to ship 20 hogsheads Tobacco by Is: norris but being absent from Town most of the 12th & 1st Moth, he was loaded before I could gett it ready. but I believe 'tis no damage for going with the Fleet Tob: must be Low at its' Arrival.

As to what relates to the Assembly I need say little, they mett the Govr made a Speech & had an Answer,[43] copies of which are inclosed either in this or The Governours. They were ordered to adjourn to some time in the 6th Month, but would not agree to any other time of themselves but the 20th of 7br 10 dayes after wch a New Election comes on, they are all disgusted, & I expect the next will be as bad As any we have {ever} had yet, We have all lost our Interest by the late Proceedings, and thou wilt certainly suffer.

As to Ford's business[44] I wish thou may not be disappointed, and thy Council deceive thee Security given generally ends all Accts and thy paying the Interest of the Ballance for some years Strenghtens them against thee, I much fear the Result in Chancery & am apt to believe thy Relief must be from the house of Lords, if to be Obtained anywhere. I can scarce forbear falling to Extasies of hatred (if I may use the Expression) against the whole world we live in that it should ever produce such monsters of hellish baseness and Ingratitude, Sure Hell itself is transplanted hither or those infernal Powers have a Commission to Equip thy Enemies Capapie[45] with the blackest or most flaming Villanies of all their Stygian Stores, for there can {not} goe ~~no~~ less to compound those wretches & such as their Accomplices here particularly D LL.[46] as for J: M:[47] the other attorney I have that opinion of him still, that his blood will turn at it as from poison, at least I hope so, of the other I expect nothing but the very Extract & quintessence of Baseness {towds thee}. But as for prosecuting him[48] I Know not how we shall goe about it That Letter wch he sent in the assemblies name[49] & wch thou said in the Letter per C Dunster was Inclosed there, would have been the only foundation to have gone upon this last Assembly, but that ~~Letter~~ never came (as many things are mentioned in thy Letters to be sent that are not) & now the opportunity is slipt I fear as for the other Charges against him they will not hold, 'tis in vain I Believe to attempt it he Carries so fair with our w{e}ak Countrey People, and those that lo~~g~~ng lookt on him to be [illegible deletion] the Champion of friends' Cause in Govmt Matters in former times that there is no possessing then, In the Assembly the most Judicious were for having business done first least quarrelling with him should prevent doing it and throw them into Confusion, for his party ~~be~~ is Strong as that of the wicked and Foolish The Toolls of the other is every where in this World, but now as I said before our Interest is unstrung & we can doe very little, Nothing remaines that I Know of, but terms with the Crown, in wch if possible pray either Destroy or humble the Corporation thy most backward Friends in the Governmt but of the two rather the Latter for it will prove more honourable because after the Change they will Endeavour to Defend thy Grant, wch will still Reflect some honour, & more, then, to thee perhaps than now ~~'tis against thy self~~, for it will then be thy Grant disputed with the Queen, wn now 'tis against thy Self. but they are altogether unworthy. J Wilcox is Mayor his father in Law was Last year,[50] his brother that is to be in a few dayes viz E: Shippen[51] was first & 2d & his Brother A: Morris[52] 3d so that it has still been in that family, And by the Conjunction of E S wth that family they are now very strong, & grow more so every day as the Government grows weaker. that poor Unhappy man last mentioned has lost himself beyond reparation, he has committed Folly in his almost decrepit age to an extremity, At two monthly meetings he was Kept off from proceeding, at the 3d he was at length admitted, since wch Such things have been discovered in his converse with that woman (Esther James[53] Jos: Wilcox' Sister) that last night, he was warn'd not to appear at meeting to day wch was the last of asking, and now all his honour is tumbled in the Dirt and he has made himself scandalous and contemptible to the last degree, of wch Is. Norris may give Fuller Accts 'tis time now to end mine.

At beginning this I expected not the vessell would have allowed me more time than to have wrote a sheet or two, but I have proceeded to a length that I am Ashamed of. If it be expected that I should write to thee as to others about common business I Know my prolixity is intolerable, but if many write large Volumes to instruct only in a Science, & others buy & read them, seeing no Studdy comes nearer than our own Interest and Concerns, I hope my pains in writing will not be ill received, I cannot think it becomes me when I write about thy business to give it by hints & touches as a Superiour may to those below him, & therefore I indulge my pen, sometimes I own to excursions & reflections that might be lett alone, but w^{n} they're wrote, I desire they may be all favourably taken together.

Some things in this will not be so fully understood without the last 5 Sheets per John Guy wch I hope will be come safe to hand before this arrives wch is intended by Newcastle with a Body of the Laws, as I hinted in my Potscript of the other. the Letter I design to Order by Post from thence, but the Lawes by a good hand by Sea or otherwise.

Before I conclude I would observe that if thou canst Sell the Sasquehannah Lands[54] there for 3^{l} per Cent Acres or even 50 shillings thô that's much too Cheap, it will be as good or better than 5^{l} here of our Subscriptions but pray remember the Indian Settlements.

J. Jeffreys writes a singular good hand & I am glad so honest a man is with thee; but being unable I suppose to read the Original, from wch he wrote, his Copy is perfectly unintelligible in what I suppose may be the most important part of th~~at~~e Account of the mortgage,[55] thô I understand enough to discover the baseness, but not sufficient to make others conceive the whole, as I would doe.

Pray be prevailed on to issue that business or drive {it} at least towards a period with the utmost Endeavours, that thou may once see thy self Easy. and Lett me once more Request that {as} I am thy Secretary my Letters may be to thy self alone, & no part that concerns others be communicated, however near they are Related. I have not yet heard anything further of the Adress mention'd in my other inclosed. I wish thy proposing C Quary to be of the Council may not prove a Snare, it may both be unsafe & disgust thy Fr^{ds}. But now I at length Conclude

Thy most Faithful & Obed^{t} Servt
J: L.

LBC. James Logan Letterbook, HSP. (*Micro.* 12:796.)

1. John Jeffreys.
2. On 7 Feb. 1706 the Queen in Council repealed 53 Pennsylvania laws. See Cliveden Manuscripts, Chew Family Papers, HSP.
3. Here Logan is referring to WP's letter of 18 Nov. 1705-3 Feb. 1706 (doc. 123), which he claimed to have enclosed with that of 7 Feb. 1706 (doc. 126).
4. For David Lloyd's letter to William Mead, George Whitehead, and Thomas Lower, dated 3 Oct. 1704, see doc. 84.

5. Charles Dunster (d. 1727), a merchant of Perth Amboy, East New Jersey. See *Micro.* 12:156; *NJA,* 1st ser., 23:146.

6. John Evans. For more on WP's concern over Logan's attitude towards the surrender of Pennsylvania and the lieutenant governor's salary, see doc. 127, text above n. 15.

7. *Micro.* 12:156.

8. *Micro.* 12:272.

9. Here Logan erroneously writes "6" for "9." See his letter of 8 Nov. 1705 (*Micro.* 12:368), which WP did not receive until Mar. 1706 (see *Micro.* 12:647).

10. Not found.

11. Here Logan omits "to."

12. See doc. 135, n. 5.

13. Balance. *OED.*

14. Samuel Carpenter, Isaac Norris, Richard Hill, and Hannah Delavall Hill.

15. See *Micro.* 12:156. For previous discussion of Evans's salary and perquisites, see docs. 127, 129.

16. The city government of Philadelphia.

17. See doc. 129, n.25.

18. WP had compared the earnings of other colonial governors with that of the governor of Pennsylvania. See doc. 127.

19. See ibid., text at n. 14.

20. See doc. 129.

21. Josiah Cheesman was an indentured servant sent to Pennsylvania by WP in 1703, preferably to work at Pennsbury. See *Micro.* 11:031.

22. WP had complained that the Assembly did not give him a share of the revenues for support of the government in Pennsylvania. See doc. 127, text at n. 5.

23. Doc. 127.

24. Peter Evans was appointed deputy register general on 11 Dec. 1704. Gov. John Evans held the register general's position. See Scharf and Westcott, 2:1571.

25. See *Statutes,* 2:291.

26. Initially, Logan had high praise for the new lieutenant governor, remarking, for example, in May 1704 (*Micro.* 11:238) that Evans "acquitts himself beyond what could possibly be expected from his Years."

27. A port town in Northwest England.

28. Not found.

29. WP was endeavoring to clarify his property rights in New Jersey. See docs. 91, 126, n. 25.

30. Thomas Story, the master of the rolls.

31. Thomas Story had married Ann Shippen on 10 July 1706. Randolph S. Klein, *Portrait of an Early American Family* (Philadelphia, 1975), p. 24.

32. As part of the marriage settlement for his daughter Laetitia, WP had agreed to pay William Aubrey £120 a year until Laetitia's 5000-acre manor of Mountjoy and her lands in the northern liberties and the city of Philadelphia were sold. This debt, as well as 6 percent interest on £3000 loaned by Aubrey to WP, were secured by lands in Ireland. See doc. 209.

33. Probably Laetitia Penn's lot on High St. between Front and Second Sts.

34. William Aubrey was obliged to send Laetitia's deeds on her various properties to James Logan and Samuel Carpenter in Pennsylvania, who were acting as her attorneys to dispose of her properties. He had not yet done so. See doc. 209.

35. This power of attorney, dated 24 Sept. 1703, was sent to James Logan and Samuel Carpenter; signed by the English trustees for the lands, Daniel Wharley, Henry Gouldney, and Samuel Waldenfield; and witnessed by Herbert Springett and John Page (London law partners). See doc. 2091.

36. Philip Ford.

37. John Penn. On 25 Oct. 1701 WP had confirmed a grant of 12,000 acres on the Schuylkill River to his son John, appointing Samuel Carpenter, Isaac Norris, and Edward Penington as trustees until he came of age (see Plumstead Papers, HSP). Logan had been anxious to draw out patents for this and other properties given to John (see *Micro.* 12:053, 156).

38. Edward Penington, who had died in Jan. 1702, was a trustee for some of John Penn's land. The patent for that land was not recorded until 12 Dec. 1702, almost

a year after Penington's death, but still included him as a trustee See doc. 45, n. 16; Plumstead Papers, HSP.

39. Logan wrote to William Penn, Jr., on 12 Aug. 1706. See Logan Papers, 1:62, HSP.

40. Launched officially on 4 May 1707, the ship was registered as the *Diligence* but was renamed on that day the *Happy Union* in celebration of the union between England and Scotland. See *Micro.* 13:148.

41. Mary Newcomen, alias Phillips. For her connection with Richard Rooth, see doc. 49.

42. No longer with the document.

43. For Gov. John Evans's speech of 25 June 1706 and the Assembly's response the following day, see *Votes and Proceedings,* 1:85-86.

44. See headnote to doc. 108.

45. From head to foot. *OED.*

46. David Lloyd.

47. John Moore.

48. See doc. 91, text at nn. 68-70.

49. See doc. 83.

50. Joseph Willcox's father-in-law, Griffith Jones, had been mayor of Philadelphia 1704-5. Willcox was married to Jones's step-daughter, Ann Powel. Scharf and Westcott, 3:1736; *Passengers and Ships,* p. 35; Phila. Monthly Meeting Records, Marriages, 1672-1871, pp. 65, 67, GSP.

51. Edward Shippen was about to marry the widowed sister of Joseph Willcox; he had been mayor of Philadelphia 1701-3. Scharf and Westcott, 3:1736.

52. Anthony Morris had been mayor of Philadelphia 1703-4 (ibid.). He was a brother-in-law of Edward Shippen, whose first wife — like Morris's — was a daughter of John Howard of Yorkshire. Robert C. Moon, *The Morris Family of Philadelphia* (Philadelphia, 1898), p. 59.

53. Esther Willcox James (d. 1724), sister of Joseph Willcox and widow of Philip James, was about to marry Edward Shippen, when Phila. Monthly Meeting refused to approve the match, having "unhappily discovered her apron to rise too fast," that is, she was pregnant. Despite lack of approval, Shippen and James married, "one of the darkest Weddings that ever I Knew in the place," commented James Logan (Logan Papers, 1:62).

54. See doc. 126, n. 22.

55. John Jeffreys was assisting WP in assessing the exact amount of "overcharges" in the Ford accounts. See doc. 121C.

131
FROM SAMUEL CARPENTER

Chester the 15 6 mo: [August] 1706

Dr Freind and
Govr Willm Penn

I have writ to thee by this oppertunity about a Grant for the Schoole[1] and the Businesse of the Land Company[2] to which Refferre thee, I Came heather with Isaac Norris and his Wife and my Sonne Jno [3] their Servt who are hastening Down to Virginia to goe with the Fleet,[4] Soe that I have very Little time Being Now Past midnight and ab^t^ halfe Flood and they are for Goeing at high water, and I have Severall to Writte Yesterday I Received thy Generall Letter to freinds[5] and Last night gott Some freinds together unto whome Directed and opend It I sent to Edw^a^ Shippen to Desire him to be at the opening of It but he Being Some what undisposed In Body (but: worse In

Mind)[6] sent word that he Could not Come and Desired that wee would open It without him. the Contents thereof gave Matr of Sarrow on thy Behalfe And on our Owne In that thy freinds that are Willing are Not able to Answer thy Expectations, Money Being Scarce Tradeing Dead and people Poore and those that have good Estates In the Countrey many of them Cannot Pay their owne Debts but Lye upon Intrest which Is Like to Ruine Many It Cannot Be thought how much the Nature of Trade and Business [i]s Altred soe that many that have Lived well, made good Pay & have Done much many Ways Cannot Doe for them Selves, nor keepe their Credit and are Some of them I may Say Many Lyable to Be torne in Peeces for Debt and Severall of the Traders In towne Breake and Cannot pay their Debts I Cann truley Say ~~& Id~~I Really and Truley Sympathize with thee and Am sorry for thy sake that I am not able to help thee Being Really Willing as I know are Many more who would Doe for thee but wee have Neither money nor Butt Little Corne or other Produce of the Countrey, or Goods and Less Crdt and People Are not Able to Pay what was Granted the Last Assembley.[7] soe that If thou hast a Dependancy from hence I feare thou will Wholey be frustrated, I Cannot Express My Sorrow and Trouble abt these things and I have often wished, that I were able to help thee but I Cannot Being much yet In Debt and I Cannot Sell. If such A proposall had Been made 8: or 9 Yeares agoe, here then was a Number of freinds In the Countrey I Beleve Both Able and Willing to have Done a great Deale towards It If not the Whole upon good Security—but Its now far otherwise with the Generall Edwa Shippen If he were Willing is able to Doe· Considerabley but his Money Is out of his hands att Intrest and Will not act butt upon Good Security but I feare he will Doe Little If Any thing, he has Married Joseph Willcox sister the Widdow of Phillip James deceased,[8] and Is pretty much Influenced by her Brother. Dr Govr I Cannot Easily Leave this Although halfe Asleepe and some times alltogether, thou hast a Many Freinds In England who are Able to Lay Down Money (there whare It Must be paid) Upon Good Security. which I Take thy Province & Territorys to be Also Rich Relaetions who If Secured I Thinke would Lay Down the Money If thy Father[9] would settle any thing upon thy Children It might Be Done by th Same security when thats Cleared off and soe gett time to ~~Cleare~~ Raise Money to Cleare It off Whereby the Purchasers of Land Since that mortgauge[10] would Be Secured and made Easey and thou the oppertunity of Makeing the Most of thy Lands that are to Be Sold. I have Understand there May Be Another way to Doe It by Surrendring to the Q.[11] Which Being A Right & Privilidge In Government that the People have a Share In. I Dare not advise to sell It of, though I feare the keepeing of It will [illegible deletion] ~~will~~ Indanger to Ruine thee by the Contingent Charges In Defending It not Doubting {but} that has helpt to Sinke thy Estate

With payeing off Intrest for the Same. on the Other hand If thou sell; the People will thinke them selves and their Posterity Wronged. As I Cannot say or Doe any thing that will availe in this Troublesome Affaire yet I heartley wish thee a good And Speedy Issue to It and as God his Been Pleased to Deliver thee out of Many Troubles I hope he will out of this which Seemes to me to Be the Greatest of Any outward Exercise Considering the Persons Manner Curcomstances and Consequences in all Respects, though (they should Never gaine their Expected Ends) ~~besides~~ Besides that It Doth Expose Both Partyes to the $Censure of Frds & Enemyes and Causes a great Reproch. I Shall Conclude With Dr Love to thee and thy Wife and Children.

Thy Reall Freind
Sam: Carpenter

for thy further Satisfaction I Reffer the to James Logan & Isaac Norris.

Dr Govr   Ditto the 18th day

The foregoing ~~is~~ Coppy by Isaac Norris. this followes by {Wm Burge In} a vessell yet In this River bound to Millford[12] or Bristoll & goeing to Joyne the Fleet, In which I Suppose James Logan or thou art Concerned.[13] And notwithstanding what I have writt as fearing litle can be done here, to assist thee by reason of our want of abillity that thou may not depend on It upon such an urgent Occasion; yet I would assure thee that my Endeavours shall not be wanting to Serve thee what I can, wth all Expedition but I foresee soe many difficultyes & obstructions ~~that~~ as well as our Incapacity to performe that I feare all Endeavours will be frustrated.

1st wee have not money, nor Corne & other Product to answer publick debts & Supply private necessityes besides our private debts (our two last Cropps haveing failed Exceedingly)

2d Many of those that are well affected to thee as well as others are In debt which they Cannot pay & are much Streightned

3d Those that have anything before hand {or out of Debt} their Substance lyes in Land & ~~Si~~ Stock or ~~In money~~ out at Intrest & It may be observed that {most} such have been very wary, Close & Reserved {& true} to their owne Intrests, but not very open hearted, And therfore litle hopes from most of them

4 The Towne grows poor as well as the Countrey, & unlesse It be Edwa Shippen Isaac Norris Richard hill & Tho: Masters, I know none that can doe anything Considerable, & E.S. can doe more then all the rest, tho his money Is out of his hands at Intrest & is now building a house for his Sonne In law Tho: Storey will Cost near 1000l, & his daughters portion & Reb: Morreys[14] portion to pay quickley which will be 1000l Each I suppose or thereabouts

5 Thy ~~money~~ debt being {Speedily} to be pd In England Its allmost Impossible (as things are here with respect to paymts

& Returnes) to transmitt any Considerable vallue, in a short time unlesse wee had money to send In Specie, as thou knows by Experience to thy losse

6 {Therfore} Although ~~though~~ thou has a great Estate here In Lands Rents & debts & Cannot wth thy Owne Effects here Answer thy obligations there (notwithstanding thou has a Steward[15] Can & I believe doth doe whats possible). Soe heres many Friends well wishers to thee & would assist to their power whose Estates lyes in Lands & Stock & Improvements which are of great vallue here but are not In any Capacity for want of moneys or proper Effects for Returnes to pay money In England

7th The next thing to be Considered is {our} Credit In England upon the assurance of our Estates [illegible deletion] {here} in Land Improvements & Stock ~~here~~, & how farr that might answer if our Friends were willing to Engage themselves Considering ~~the~~ Our Remoteness & how wee & our Estates In america / are lessened & undervallued by moneyed men in England; who can put out their money at home upon good Security & whether they would not a soone take thy province for Security & pay thee the money there rather then take some persons here upon a worse Security {~~from~~ their Circumstances being unknowne} ~~persons not knowne~~, which seemes very Improble, For I Cannot see but thy Province will be better Security then all ours added together as ~~&~~ being a noble & Intire thing and growing and brings in a Yearly profit

8th If {Such} personall Security {here} were to be had as ~~co~~ Could answer ~~the~~ those ~~as~~ {who} would lay downe the money In England to pay off P: F:[16] In part, for thats the most that Is proposed by thee or can be thought of here. There arises from thence another difficulty which is how such persons Can be Secured Thy Lands and Rents being pre Engaged, {I feare} there can be no Act of thine or thy Commissioners here can Secure Such persons who must be Involved {there} In Bonds to Each Other here {beforehand} In order to Such Security to be given In England untill the mortgauge be paid off which ~~Cannot be done~~ will fall naturally after{wards} ~~Such~~ soe that there will of necessity be a time or Space betweene the Executing the one here In order to a Supply or Credit & the Executing the Other there In order to a Security for the Same which will be hazardous by thy Death or otherwise or ~~be~~ seemes to be soe which may deter some persons from being deeply Concerned, but If this difficulty could be got over, Another followes which seemes greater. That Is If thou take up part of the money there to Cleare the morgauge wee suppose they will also Expect a Security by the premises ~~also~~,

& how that Can be done Either Joyntly or Seperately & If Seperately how It will be Divided or proportioned to the Satisfaction & Security of both partyes Seemes a difficulty

9 If all this Could be done to Satisfaction or made practicable, The distance wee are at ~~Time to be Spent~~ & difficultyes In Effecting Such a designe Considering our Circumstances as before and the many persons to be Consulted ~~&~~ to Concurr ~~In~~ & Joyne therin I feare will Spend too much time, For It seemes to me by what I have seen & heard Concering the matter that the decree[17] will be positive Either to pay such a Summe of money In a time Limitted or thou wilt be foreclosed from the Equity of Redemption, there will therfore be an absolute necessity of speedy Supply there ~~or~~ {but} a Considerable time to perfect any thing here that might be a Reliefe from hence unlesse the Sute can be prolongued untill assistance can be had or meanes used to Raise soe great a Summe of money as they demand, if decreed them.

Govr by the above which is the Result of many Carefull thoughts Since I writt at Chester, Thou may see that If anything can be done here It will be wth great difficultyes & time. Yet I doe not raise these Objections to trouble thee but that ~~by~~ thou may not too much depend upon what seemes soe Impro{ba}ble by reason of the difficulty of Effecting whats desired. Thy Occaisions requireing what is Certaine & Speedy and what may be had there upon the Spott, & If I am mistaken pray Excuse me for I wish It prove soe & that what is desired from us might be according to Expectacon answered. wth due Respects & Esteeme & true sorrow for thee & desires ~~to he~~ and Endeavours to helpe thee If I can I remaine Thine to serve thee according to my power

Sam: Carpenter

mine & my wifes dear love to thy~~ee &~~ wife & Children.

Copy and ALS. Cliveden Manuscripts, Chew Family Papers, HSP. (*Micro.* 12:823.) Endorsed: Coppy. Docketed: Samuel Carpenter | 15th Augt 1706. The text dated 15 Aug. is a copy signed by Carpenter; the postscript dated 18 Aug. is in his hand.

1. In 1701 Phila. Monthly Meeting had received a charter from WP for a free public school, which met in the Bank Meetinghouse, Front St. near Arch. In 1705-6, when the monthly meeting attempted to secure land and convey deeds for a new building for the school, the former charter was discovered to be insufficient. David Lloyd drafted a new grant and the meeting ordered Carpenter, Thomas Story, Anthony Morris, and Griffith Owen to write to WP to confirm it, which they did on 7 Aug. 1706 (*Micro.* 12:806). See *PWP,* 3:535-38; Phila. Monthly Meeting Records, Abstracts of Minutes, 1682-1707, pp. 451-54, 456-57, 463-66, 468, 471, 484, GSP.

2. Probably the London Company (see doc. 56, n. 25), whose subscribers were in dispute with WP over the extent and location of their Pennsylvania lands. See doc. 101, text following n. 12; doc. 103.

3. John Carpenter (1690-1724) had been placed by his parents with Isaac Norris in order to learn the mercantile trade. Edward Carpenter and Louis H. Carpenter, *Samuel Carpenter and His Descendants* (Philadelphia, 1912), pp. 49-50.

4. Isaac Norris, Mary Lloyd Norris, and John Carpenter were preparing to embark for England. See doc. 129, n. 9.

5. See doc. 123.

6. A reference to Shippen's recent controversial marriage to Esther Willcox James, which had brought him into severe disfavor with Phila. Monthly Meeting. See doc. 130, text at n. 53.

7. In Jan. 1706 the Assembly passed two revenue-producing laws: chap. 159 for collecting the arrears of £2000 formerly granted to the proprietor, and chap. 164 for raising a supply to support the government. See *Statutes,* 2:263-66, 280-91.

8. See n. 6, above.

9. Thomas Callowhill.

10. The mortgage by WP of Pennsylvania and the Lower Counties to Philip Ford in 1697 (see headnote to doc. 108), which had become the focal point of the Ford-Penn legal dispute.

11. Queen Anne.

12. Milford Haven, in Pembrokeshire, Wales.

13. James Logan had a one-eighth share in the brigantine *Evans* of Philadelphia (Josiah Harwood, master) and its cargo. William Burge, who was delivering this letter, was supercargo of the vessel. See James Logan Letterbook, 2:78, HSP.

14. Edward Shippen's daughter Ann had recently married Thomas Story; his stepdaughter Rebecca (b. 1685), through his marriage to Rebecca Richardson, had married Thomas Murray in Jan. 1704, and her daughter Rebecca had been born in Shippen's house on 11 June 1706. Presumably, the second portion mentioned came from the estate of Rebecca Richardson Shippen, who had died in April 1705 (*Micro.* 12:053); it may also have been Edward Shippen's gift for his new step-granddaughter. See Mary T. Seaman, *Thomas Richardson . . . and His Descendants* (New York, 1929), pp. 36, 223.

15. James Logan.

16. Philip Ford.

17. The final decree from the court of Chancery in the Penn-Ford case. Carpenter was predicting that WP would be required to pay the Fords or lose his proprietary title to them.

132
FROM JONATHAN DICKINSON

Jamaica 7br [September] 17th 1706

Honoured Frd

Thine of 6th {first} Month[1] we received on the 29th 5 Month And all thine since[2] per Capt Smith[3] & Benja Lopdell[4] on the 16th Instant. We shall answer thy Request in Prossicuting the Designe,[5] if its possible such a sume can do it, wch we doubt it will not. To buy a Vessel we are Certain that sume cannot, there being not Vessels Enough to answer the Trade of the Island: to hire [a Ve]ssel to search such Difficult places (is wt we doubt) she must be well man'd & provided wth Navil & Victualing stores all which runs high. We are full Intended to seek for a little small Sloope wch will require a small Charge, and Endeavour to gett some Divers; if we can Accomplish this, he may goe seek for the Wreck—wch if he finds, may Encourage a fur~~d~~ther progress—But what Capt Smith Enformes me of Capt Braholt,[6] makes me doubt his Informacion. for as I remember Capt Braholt was upon the quest of a wreck & meeting with disappointments became a Pirate. And Capt smith seem'd surprised at the {sum} ~~sume~~, he depend it had been greater when I first acquainted him that I doubted the sume would not answer the Intenciones of Search — as to the Mans Charecter, so far as I can Learne from others, he seems to be both sober and solid and very Intent upon this adventure.

Our Residence is a hundred Miles {of} our Marts wch is Kingston & port Royll[7] But to Encourage this Designe, we have a Bror in Law a Mercht[8] & man of good repute whome we Ingaged to our Assistance on this Occassion to do the outmost that may be, which by next Packet we may {be} able to render a more ample accot. I find Capt Smith wants money to support him; the place of business is greatly Expencive to a good husband wch by what I can learn from Benjamin Lopdell he seems to deserve the Carecter hithertoo.

As to Benja Lopdell I shall take Care of him [and?] prefer him to such business as his Genius & [torn] may acquire, if this Island may Suite thereto wth his Inclinations, at present he is with me until the bussiness he came upon may require him. he seems to be out of order having had one brush of a Feavor allready wch went off with bleeding, I shall use my Endeavors to support him.

The Unity & Wellfare of Frds is Acceptable to us being joyed to hear thereof at all oppertunities. also the wellfare of our Aged Uncle[9] whome I salute wth Dutifull Respect. As to my thoughts of returning to Philadia, Its so Imprinted that I cannot put it out, as soone as I may have settled my Affairs in this Island if the Lord permits me so to do, am fully designed to returne & hope it may be next spring or summer;[10] I have left two of my sons there;[11] one we brought with us[12] and my Wife[13] hath about a Month to reckon for a fourth Child[14] — Thy last was with Inclosed order on thy Secretary James Logan[15] w~~e~~ch we doubt not, and the power against the Executors of Willim Rogers and James Mills[16] we shall pross~~ie~~cute, and Advise of our proceedings therein.

Worthy Frd please to Accept mine & Wifes Salutation of pure Love to thee and thine. I am thi~~ne~~y Faithfull and Affectionate Friend

Jonata Dickinson

ALS. Logan Papers, HSP. (*Micro.* 12:850.) Docketed: Jamaica 7br 17. 1706 | Copy To William Penn Esqr.

1. *Micro.* 12:659.
2. See *Micro.* 12:688, 732.
3. Capt. Edward Smith. See n. 5, below.
4. Benjamin Lopdell, a scribe and accountant, was a son of Daniel and Anna Howard Lopdell, of Deal, Kent, who were both dead by this time. WP had recommended him to Jonathan and Caleb Dickinson in Mar. 1706 "for his Excellent Fathers sake" (*Micro.* 12:659). Digests of Quaker Records, Kent, GSP.
5. In Mar. 1706 WP had asked Jonathan and Caleb Dickinson to pay £300 on his account to any honest ship captain who would agree to search for shipwrecks off Jamaica and salvage their treasure (*Micro.* 12:659). WP's colleagues in this venture (see doc. 127, n. 21) had already written the Dickinsons (see Maria Dickinson Logan Papers,

HSP) asking them to hire Capt. Edward Smith, who they supposed was already "gone in quest of the wreck." As this letter indicates, the search had not yet begun.

6. Capt. Braholt told Smith that he had found a shipwreck and had taken from it "some dollars and a pig of silver" (Maria Dickinson Logan Papers).

7. Jonathan and Caleb Dickinson resided in Western Jamaica at Pepper plantation, about 12 miles from their father's plantation at Barton, in St. Elizabeth's parish. Evangeline W. Andrews and Charles M. Andrews, eds., *Jonathan Dickinson's Journal* (New Haven, 1945), p. 125.

8. Ezekiel Gomersall, a Kingston merchant, was married to Jonathan and Caleb Dickinson's sister, Mary. Ibid.

9. Edmund Dickinson (1624-1707), of London, had been personal physician to Charles II and James II (*DNB*). His nephews had learned from WP previously that although in declining health, he was "yet alive" (*Micro.* 12:659, 688).

10. Dickinson removed permanently to Philadelphia about 1709. See Maria Dickinson Logan Papers.

11. Jonathan (1696-1727) and Joseph (b. 1698) Dickinson were boarding in Philadelphia with Samuel and Rachel Preston. Ibid.; Phila. Monthly Meeting Records, Births, GSP.

12. John Dickinson (b. 1701), although born in Philadelphia, had been taken by his parents back to Jamaica. See Maria Dickinson Logan Papers.

13. Mary Gale Dickinson.

14. Mary Dickinson was born in Jamaica in Oct. 1706. See Maria Dickinson Logan Papers.

15. See doc. 127, text at nn. 20-21.

16. See doc. 127, n. 19.

133
FROM JAMES LOGAN

Philad^ia 9^br [November] the 26th 1706

Hon^d Governour

Inclosed is a Copy of my last but one,[1] wch one was but a few Lines[2] hinting a small part of the other. Since that I can only inform thee that both Assemblies are sitting. that of the Province have been till this time upon a Law for Establishing Courts but are Likely to make very little of it.[3] In the Bill they proposed to the Govr they were for making all Judges & Justices to continue dum se bene gesserint,[4] or to be displaced only at the Request of the Assembly & for giving Fines directly to the Queen for the support of Govm^t all forfeited Reognizances especially except those that went to the use of the City Philad^ia whose Powers they enlarged to a very great degree, almost as much as by that Bill thy Son brought over.[5] This Bill is all we have as yet seen from them, and at length we believe the matter must be settled by an ordinance,[6] For they seem not of a temper to agree to anything of that Kind that's reasonable. What made us mostly incline to have it done by Act of Ass. was the hopes of procuring a Salary For Judge Mompesson[7] but that we now see is in vain. We have had no quarrel with them yet, only sent them the Gov^rs & Councill's Objections. but how the whole will issue cannot be Fully foreseen, thô we have reason to expect very little that's Favourable. In the other at Newcastle they are for reenacting all those that are repealed by the Queen[8] at least as many as please them, with many new ones added. they have prepared a Bill For Building a Fort at Newc:[9] to wch all Vessels coming into the River shall pay a quarter or half a pound of Powder per Tun. for our own Vessels a quarter and for strangers half a pound, of wch the practice with us is 4 per sh {pound}[10] by the Barrel but by Retail in the cheapest shops 5 sh per pound. Their Assembly is violent upon it, & they use the same language there the Scots doe in relation to England, that if their Govr will not agree to such Acts as are for their Interest least he should disoblidge those of the Province, they must take care to provide themselves with such as shall be under no hardship. At a Conference appointed last 7th day between some Membrs of Council & the Representatives of Newcastle County I very strenously insisted on it but there was none to back me that the King's Grant for the Province was so Absolute and all Passages into and out of it so fully granted that nothing less than an Act of Parliament or their own Consent could lay any imposition upon them, and that they had as good tax the Merchts of Philadia to pay for the Goods in their stores, as their vessels that only pass'd by them, but 'tis all in vain, unless they can obtain all they desire, they think themselves heinously wrong'd, & the Govr is severely pinch'd on both sides. they are carrying on some other unaccountable Acts of wch one is, that all their ~~officers~~ offiers shall live among themselves even the Council Secretary & Attorney General. thus they drive on as furiously as a true Scotch humour can make them 'tis managed by some of the Chief ~~of~~ at Newcastle, who hope to make that town the center of Trade for these 3 Counties, who were it possible, would even lay the penny per pound on all Tobacco coming from thence to Philadia. Both these Assemblies will be mischievous, the [blotted] Consequence of that Act for the Fort & Powder money will be either to bring the matter to a perfect war between Philadia & Newc: or if the Govt assents not to it, to send over the Act to the ~~C~~Lds of Trade with a Complaint that they cannot be allowed to secure themselves in the way that all other Govmts take, and how odd an Act pass'd by those who never had any such power granted them from the Crown will appear at home, may be easily judged, and I request thee to Consider. We are told here that some proposals P. F.[11] has made, have putt a stop to thy Treaty wth the Lords,[12] but I can never believe that any Minister much Less the Queen would hearken to anything on so vilainous {a} foundation but 'tis much to be feared thy backwardness to make Known thy case will hurt thee as it has formerly been the greatest disadvantage. I hope that this will be the last good opportunity of writing this Winter, that so there may be none of sending home such things either from Newcastle or this place, as may be Injurious till thou canst have time to settle matters better with the Crown, wch if thou dost not now, I much fear the opportunity will be wrench'd out of thy hands, It seems to be the One thing that requires thy whole Intention and application, for when once our Case comes to be thorowly Known, we shall be found scarce worth the accepting, & I am really of opinion that the thing now drove at by the Assembly is to Disable thee to make any terms to thy own Advantage, I once more shall give it positively as my Opinion, that thou wilt daily find more and more Inconveniencies to arise from hence that will grievously obstruct thy Proceedings And that if thou defers a Treaty thou wilt ~~grievously~~ be in great danger of quite losing the Opportunity. I do really think the present Assembly is mischievously bent against thee, and in the Lower Counties 'tis in vain to plead thy Interest for they take that to be always repugnant to theirs. Ours here contend For the whole Power & have the Govr only a name, & they cry 'tis their Right From thy first Charter granted them in England, wch should be still Obligatory upon thee, These are melancholy stories, but as they are most true so they may serve to putt thee upon the only Remedy wch if not applied before next summer, I much fear the Consequence, I am fully fixt upon coming over. for we have nothing now in Property affairs to doe.

9^br the 30th [13] We have this afternoon received the Inclosed Address from the Assembly wch will sufficiently shew thee their temper,[14] the first of the two Articles exhibited ag^st me, is that I conceal'd the L^ds Objections to some of the Laws,[15] I received them the day they mention[16] wch they came to Know by my Indorsem^t on them. I presented them immediately to the Govr & some Members of Council that were of the Assembly, but they were not thought very Fitt to be communicated however when the Repeal came,[17] the Assembly were so very earnest to Know all the objections that they could be detain'd no longer & they were at Length presented to the Last Sessions of the last Year, but no further notice then taken of them, the other of advising the Govr to an Ordinance[18] wch undoubtedly is thy Right to doe is no more to be Fix'd on me than any other Member of the Council who were all Unanimous in the Opinion and I believe is not to be disputed, for the Charter is exprest in it. Two Opportunities of Conveyance immediately present to send these by, but the Papers that have past are so prolix that 'tis impossible to have been copied. the Inclosed[19] with what I have mentioned in this Letter will be Sufficient to inform thee. The last House and I were Entirely F^rds because they were thine, & because the present is not so, is the only reason they treat me Thus, for I have given no other occasion. Upon the whole I can say [no mo]re but this, that I firmly believe if thou uses not without any mann[er of] delay the warmest endeavours to bring matters to an Issue & put it out of their power to hurt thee, they will long before their Year is over disable thee to serve thy self with the Crown. I really apprehend an Address to the Q[ueen][20] begging their Priviledges may not be make a market of, but if sh[e] thinks it Fittest that the Govm^t should be in her own hands, to [take?] them Freely, for what is treated for is theirs & not thine, & thou hast already made more of the grant than was thy due. The very Recital of this seems so heinous that I could scarce perswade myself, to mention it in my Ink, yet 'tis better to be thought of before hand & prevent the effects, than by a dangerous Security or postponing it find them when 'tis too late.

Thou hast many Friends here that should be Considered, but pray Consider thy self First, and then they may come in, what I've mention'd in the Inclosed Copy of the 15th of 7br [21] may perhaps be well worth thy thoughts. I mean as to the Queen.[22] I give thee the best of mine, & must say I scarce expect after this to be Capable of serving thee, For what I write hereafter will I fear come too late if even this it self doe not so. If all thy Interest at Court can afford thee a speedy & Full opportunity with the Queen it should be Forced, & gett her Royal word for something or other that cannot be recall'd. as For my own part I value them all not one Farthing, besides 'tis not me they strike at.

I will only only add that in the worst of our Former Assemblies we had 7 or 8 honest men of good sence who were thy Friends that we could advise wth & that retarded their Proceedings but in the Present we have not one left us so that we can Know nothing & I fear Mischief is done already. I shall now conclude

Thy most Obedt Servant
J. L.

LBC. James Logan Letterbook, HSP. (*Micro.* 13:015.)

1. *Micro.* 12:838.
2. *Micro.* 13:005.
3. The Assembly was attempting to gain direct control over the colony's court system and to grant the courts final jurisdiction over land titles. Disagreements between the Assembly and the governor on this issue prevented passage of a law to establish courts in Pennsylvania until Feb. 1711. See *Statutes,* 2:301-31.
4. *Quamdiu se bene gesserit:* during good behavior. *Black's Law Dictionary.*
5. In 1704 the Assembly had passed a bill confirming the charter of Philadelphia, which Gov. Evans vetoed (see doc. 91, n. 26). Evidently William Penn, Jr., took a copy of this bill to WP when he returned to England in late 1704. For the new bill of 1706, see *Votes and Proceedings,* 1(pt. 2):98, 100.
6. On 22 Feb. 1707 the Provincial Council, concurring with Gov. Evans, ordered the preparation, engrossing, and sealing of an ordinance establishing courts in Pennsylvania. See *Minutes of the Provincial Council,* 2:337; James Logan Letterbook, 1:274, HSP.
7. Roger Mompesson had been commissioned as chief justice of Pennsylvania on 17 Apr. 1706. Scharf and Westcott, 2:1558.
8. See doc. 130, n. 2.
9. Newcastle.
10. A mistake for "4 sh per pound."
11. Philip Ford, Jr.
12. Despite this rumor, the Ford lawsuit does not seem to have completely blocked WP's negotiations with the Board of Trade for the surrender of the government of Pennsylvania.
13. In the margin.
14. On 29 Nov. 1706, in a lengthy message to Gov. Evans, the Assembly strongly defended its proposed bill for establishing courts in Pennsylvania and sharply criticized James Logan for his malevolent influence over Evans. They demanded Logan's dismissal. See *Votes and Proceedings,* 1(pt. 2):113-14.

15. The complaint was that Logan delayed reporting these objections until after the Assembly had voted to collect WP's quitrents and to raise a revenue for Gov. Evans.

16. The Assembly reported that Logan had received the Board of Trade's objections on 10 Dec. 1705. *Votes and Proceedings,* 1 (pt. 2):113.

17. See 130, n. 2.

18. See n. 6, above.

19. No longer with the letter.

20. Queen Anne. Instead, the Assembly in Dec. 1706 decided to write two letters: one to WP and one to George Whitehead and other leading English Quakers, complaining of their grievances. See *Votes and Proceedings,* 1(pt. 2):115. Logan warned WP that the Assembly was aiming at "putting a stop to the surrender upon any terms that shall be advantageous to thee" (*Micro.* 13:021).

21. *Micro.* 12:838.

22. Logan had counseled WP to throw himself on the queen's favor regarding the surrender of the government of Pennsylvania, rather than relying on the Board of Trade or Lord Treasurer Godolphin. Ibid.

134
TO DR. EDWARD BAYNARD

[c. 1706][1]

As I find the *Indians* upon the Continent more incident to *Fevers* than any other Distempers, so they rarely fail to Cure themselves by great *Sweating,* and immediately plunging themselves into *Cold Water,* which, they say, is the only way not to catch *Cold.*

I once saw an Instance of it, with divers more in Company. For being upon a Discovery of the back part of the Country,[2] I called upon an *Indian* of Note, whose Name was *Tenoughan,*[3] the *Captain General* of the Clans of *Indians* of those Parts. I found him ill of a *Fever,* his Head and Limbs much affected with Pain, and at the same time his *Wife* preparing a *Bagnio* for him: The *Bagnio* resembled a large Oven, into which he crept, by a Door on the one side, while she put several *red hod Stones* in at a small Door on the other side thereof, and then fastned the Doors as closely from the Air as she could. Now while he was Sweating in this Bagnio,[4] his *Wife* (for they disdain no Service) was, with an *Ax,* cutting her Husband a passage into the *River,* (being the Winter of 83 the great Frost, and the *Ice* very thick) in order to the Immersing himself, after he should come out of his *Bath.* In less than half an Hour, he was in so great a *Sweat,* that when he came out, he was as *wet,* as if he had come out of a *River,* and the *Reak* or *Steam* of his Body so thick, that it was hard to discern any bodies Face that stood near him. In this condition, *stark naked* (his Breech-Clout only excepted) he ran to the *River,* which was about twenty Paces, and *duck'd* himself twice or thrice therein, and so return'd (passing only through his *Bagnio* to mitigate the immediate stroak of the *Cold*) to his own House, perhaps 20 Paces further, and wrapping himself in his woolen Mantle, lay down at his length near a long (but gentle) *Fire* in the middle of his *Wigwam,* or House, turning himself several times, till he was dry, and then he rose, and fell to getting us our Dinner, seeming to be as easie, and well in *Health,* as at any other time.

This tradition was in great measure, however, the loss of one of the bravest of the Nations of *Indians* (remembred by *Capt. Smith,* in his History of the Setllement of *Virginia*)[5] called the *Sasquenahs.*[6] For having, after the coming of the *Europeans* among them, learned to drink *strong Liquors,* and eat freely of Swines Flesh (mostly without *Salt*) it brought the *Small Pox* among them; they took the same Method to cure themselves of it when they were come out, which struck to their Heart, and prov'd more mortal than the Plague, few escaping the Disease, by reason of that improper Practice; tho' one would think that before they came out, it might have moderated their Venom, and Impression.

I am also well assur'd that they wash their Young Infants in cold Streams as soon as Born, in all Seasons of the Year.[7]

W.P.

Printed transcript. Sir John Floyer and Dr. Edward Baynard, *The History of Cold Bathing* (London, 1706), pp. 103-5. (*Micro.* 13:065.)

1. Although undated, this letter was probably written about 1706, since it is included in Dr. Edward Baynard's portion of *The History of Cold Bathing* (see provenance note, above). Baynard (b. 1641), physician and poet, was a fellow of the College of Physicians of London; he practiced medicine there and in Bath. *DNB.*

2. Albert Cook Myers concluded that WP, about Jan. 1684, traveled along the Schuylkill River from the Falls to Monocacy, in present-day Amity Township, Berks Co. See Myers, *William Penn, His Own Account of the Lenni Lenape or Delaware Indians, 1683* (Moylan, Pa., 1937), pp. 53-54.

3. Tenoughan was one of the Delaware chiefs who sold WP lands between Chester and Pennypack Creeks, from the Delaware to the Susquehanna River, in the 1680s. Ibid.; Deed from Shakhuppo and Others, 30 July 1685, Pennsylvania Historical and Museum Commission, Harrisburg (not filmed).

4. In another account of this incident, WP added that while in the bagnio, the chief sang to divert himself from the heat and also pondered aloud why the Indians were sick but the strangers were not. See John Oldmixon, *British Empire of America* (London, 1708), pp. 161-62.

5. John Smith, *The Generall Historie of Virginia, New England and the Summer Isles* (London, 1624).

6. Susquehannocks.

7. Compare WP's earlier account of this practice in his *Letter to the Free Society of Traders* (1683), *PWP,* 2:448-49.

135
ESTIMATED COST AND CHARGES OF PENNSYLVANIA

[c. 1706?][1]

	£
The Interest of the Exchequer Debt of Sr William Penns,[2] at the Shuting up of the Exchequer,[3] Supposing it to be 10,000^l^ from the year 1670 to 1706 at 6 £s per Cent.	21,600

The Interest of the Charge of the Expedition to AMERICA, to Settle a Colony there, being 10,500 and odd pounds,[4] for 24 years.	15,120
The Interest of 11,000l being for the Maintenance and Support of Government, ~~in~~Excluding the charge of the last Voyage there.	7,924
Principal 31,500l — Interest	44,644
	31,500
	£76,144[5]

D. Penn Papers, Official Correspondence, HSP. (*Micro.* 13:063.) Docketed: An Estimate of the Cost, | and charges of Pennsilvania | to be mended.[6]

1. This document is impossible to date precisely. WP seems to have made this calculation in 1706, although he may be responding to the Board of Trade's query of May 1707 about his charges (see doc. 140A). WP pressed the board in Jan. 1707 to hasten its report on his surrender (*Micro.* 13:086), and the board responded on 5 Feb. (see doc. 136).

2. WP appears to be ignoring the fact that he received the proprietorship of Pennsylvania as payment for the crown's Exchequer debt to his father (see *PWP,* 2:30-33). Apparently, in emulation of the Fords, WP now reckoned that he was entitled to claim 37 years of interest on this debt.

3. In Jan. 1672 Charles II suspended for one year all payments on assignations in the Exchequer, including payment on the debt owed to Admiral Penn. See *PWP,* 2:32-33; C. D. Chandaman, *The English Public Revenue, 1660-1688* (Oxford, 1975), pp. 114, 224-28.

4. Here WP seems to base his cost of settling Pennsylvania on a figure provided by Philip Ford. In 1697 WP had leased Pennsylvania from Ford for £630 a year, a figure WP claimed was calculated on 6 percent interest on a debt of £10,500 (see doc. 116, n. 25). Yet during WP's legal proceedings in Chancery with the Ford family, he would attempt to refute that figure as highly exaggerated. See, for example, doc. 110.

5. Wisely, WP never attempted to recoup this amount from the crown. He had initially asked for £30,000, but the Board of Trade did not take this figure seriously (see headnote to doc. 60). In Feb. 1707 the board recommended that while WP deserved some recompense upon surrender, the actual amount should be left to the discretion of the queen; WP later settled for £12,000. Docs. 136, 198.

6. "To be mended" appears to be in WP's hand.

DEBTORS' PRISON

January 1707–August 1708

On 7 January 1708 WP entered the Fleet prison in London as a debtor and lived for the next nine months or so under loose arrest at lodgings in the nearby Old Bailey prison. It had been more than thirty-five years since he had last been imprisoned, but the circumstances were significantly different. In 1671 he had suffered for his faith (see *PWP,* 1:192); in 1708 he suffered for his carelessness. His legal case against the Ford family was weak, and, although he battled throughout 1707 in both Chancery and Common Pleas, all indications were that he would eventually lose. On 23 November, with the Chancery suit still unresolved, Lord Chief Justice Trevor confirmed a jury's finding that WP owed the Fords almost £3000 in back rent. WP refused to pay, partly because he had no money and partly because he was trying to make the Fords settle for much less than their overall claim of £14,000 (see the headnote to doc. 108). He entered prison in 1708 as a martyr to his ungrateful steward's cupidity. With WP incarcerated, and Lord Chancellor Cowper continuing to delay his final decree in chancery, the Ford case was at a stalemate. By May 1708 (doc. 147) WP thought the Fords might settle out of court for £7000 — a figure not far from the final settlement of £7600 reached five months later. But where was this money to come from?

WP had already sold Warminghurst Place in Sussex, his principal English property, in November 1707. The sale price was £6053, over £1500 more than he had paid for it thirty-one years earlier, and he received about £2300 in addition for timber and stock (see docs. 145, 148). But WP could not pay off the Fords from these proceeds; Warminghurst had been sold to redeem other heavily mortgaged family property in Kent and Sussex. Nor could WP get the cash he needed by surrendering the government of Pennsylvania to the crown. In February 1707 the Board of Trade recommended that WP's surrender be accepted, although it was to be "absolute and unconditional" and had to include both Pennsylvania and the Lower Counties (doc. 136). But the amount to be paid WP was left to the queen's discretion. In May 1707, when the board approached WP with further queries about his terms of purchase, and his charges and profits, WP replied that he wanted £20,000, but offered no solid figures to justify such a payment (doc. 140B). There the matter rested for the next three years, until July 1710 (see doc. 179). WP grasped at other possible sources of income: salvaging treasure from shipwrecks in the West Indies (doc. 137), or mining silver and copper in Pennsylvania (doc. 149). But the only tangible help he received came from the Quaker community in England. Friends were embarrassed and scandalized that WP, the most venerable and prominent of living Quakers, was entangled in debt, prosecuted in the courts, confronted by bailiffs at Gracechurch Street Meeting, and imprisoned in the Fleet. By October 1707 the English Quaker merchants to whom he was indebted were giving him six months' sight on bills of exchange from Pennsylvania at a reasonable rate (doc. 144). After he entered prison, a consortium of nine Quakers from London, Bristol, and Ireland—most of whom had covered for him financially before—pledged to raise the money WP needed. Between May and October 1708 they negotiated a final out-of-court settlement with the Fords (see doc. 211).

WP was still nominally the overlord of Pennsylvania and continued to feel the effects of political upheaval there. David Lloyd, speaker of the Assembly, had found a useful stick with which to beat WP—letters to George Whitehead, William Mead, and Thomas Lower, three prominent English Quakers. Having already written a scurrilous attack on WP to them in 1704 (see doc. 84), Lloyd proceeded to write to them again in August and December 1706, complaining of WP's proprietorship (see doc. 143). From the opposite side of the political spectrum, the Anglicans in Pennsylvania were agitating against an act passed by the Assembly in January 1706 permitting officers, judges, and jurors to subscribe an affirmation rather than take an oath in public or judicial proceedings. They hired an English attorney, George Wilcox, to lobby the Board of Trade against this law. WP replied to Wilcox's charges, citing his concern that the Anglicans were trying to bar the Quakers from the colony's legal and political establishment (see doc. 142B). This struggle over the Quaker right to affirm would continue for years, particularly as the English government generally opposed its use for officeholding and for most legal proceedings. Although WP regarded David Lloyd as his greatest enemy in the colony, his deputy governor, John Evans, actually did him greater harm. In May 1707 (doc. 138) WP warned Evans that he was unhappy about the false alarm of May 1706 (see doc. 129), distraints levied on Quakers in the Lower Counties for refusing to bear arms, the apparent growth of vice in Pennsylvania, and the excessive licensing of public houses. By July 1707, according to Isaac Norris, WP was intent on removing Evans, "but Whither it be from any other Reason then putting his Son in I must not determine." When asked his views, Norris suggested that William Penn, Jr., was an inappropriate candidate, an opinion "not well taken" (Norris Papers, 7:82). Another possible contender was Chief Justice Roger Mompesson (ibid., p. 96), but with both the Ford case and the surrender negotiations lingering, WP's ability to find a suitable candidate willing to accept such a tenuous undertaking was limited. In the spring of 1708 Whitehead, Mead, and Lower visited WP in prison and told him that unless he dismissed Evans they would appeal to the queen (see docs. 147, 148). This forced WP to action. He appointed Charles Gookin, a professional soldier in his mid-forties who received Queen Anne's approval on 18 July 1708 (see docs. 149, 150). Pennsylvania was about to receive another strangely chosen and undistinguished deputy governor.

136
THE BOARD OF TRADE TO THE EARL OF SUNDERLAND

Whitehall February 5th 1706/7.

My Lord[1]
Her Majesty having, Some time past, directed us to treat with William Penn Esqr in order to his Surrender of the Proprietary Government of Pensylvania,[2] and his other Claims and Pretensions of Government to the adjoyning Territories, and to report the Same to Her Maty for Her further Directions thereupon;[3] We have accordingly been attended from time to time by Mr Penn, and received from him divers Proposals,[4] and having endeavoured to bring him to Such Terms as Should be most advantagious to Her Majesty's Service; Upon the whole We humbly offer, that whereas in regard to the Memory & Merit of the Father of Mr Penn in divers Services, and (as Mr Penn alledges) in consideration of a Debt of Sixteen Thousand pounds due to him from the Crown, at the Date of his Letters Patents, a Charter of the Proprietary Government of Pensilvania was granted by King Charles the Second to the Said William Penn, and his Heirs,[5] containing many large and ample Priviledges, Immunities and Liberties, which in Our humble opinion are capable of being extended to the Diminution of the Royall Prerogatives of the Crown, and which if reunited to the Crown, from whence they were originally derived, by a Voluntary Surrender of the Said Charter, would be of great use and benefit, and conduce to the obtaining of these ends following.

To the Establishment and Maintenance of Her Maty's more immediate Authority in that Province.

To the more Speedy and impartiall Administration of Justice to all Persons, thô under different perswasions in religious Matters.

To the more regular carrying on of a legal Trade in those parts conformably to the Severall Acts of Parliament made in that behalf.

To the better Security, Protection and Defence of Her Maty's Subjects in that Province as well against intestine Dissentions as against a Forreign Enemy.

And finding in Mr Penn a ready Concurrence and Disposition upon fit Encouragements to make Such Surrender, We take leave to represent, that upon consideration of his Case it appears to us, that Mr Penn with great Expence, many Risques & Dangers, both to his Person & Fortune, with continued pains and Industry, and by the help of his own personal Interest, has in great part accomplished a very difficult Undertaking, by cultivating & improving what before was a desolate Wilderness, into a well peopled Colony, which by an increase of Trade, as appears by the Accounts of the Custom house, do's yearly add a considerable Revenue to Her Majesty;[6] for effecting of which Publick Work, he has much impaired and diminished his own private Fortune, not having had time enough hitherto to reap the Profits of his forepast charge and Labour, and the Returns which have been made him not countervailing in any reasonable Degree his many Expences.

And Whereas Mr Penn has often attended Us with certain Proposals of Terms & Conditions previous to his Surrender, Some of which We could not approve of;[7] And thô We are Satisfyed that he has deserved an equitable Consideration of his Expences and Services; and that his Surrender as is before mentioned, may be a valuable benifit to the Crown, yet We are humbly of Opinion, that Such Surrender ought to be absolute and unconditional, including a Renunciation of all Right, Claim and Pretension, as well to the Government of Pensylvania, as to that of New Castle & the Two Lower Counties; the whole be Stated and drawn up in Such Form and Manner as by Her Majesty's Councill learned in the Law Shall be advised.

~~But as to the Measure or Quantum of the Consideracion to be given, We are further humbly of Opinion that a matter of this nature will be carryed on, as with more Decency, So with less inconvenience by the way of Bounty than of Bargain; And We have therefore advised Mr Penn that by way of Petition, he intimate his readiness to make a Voluntary & absolute Surrender without any previous Stipulations or Conditions, intirely referring himself to her Maty's Royall Grace and Bounty. We are~~

As to the Quantum to be given Mr Penn in consideration of the Surrender of his Government, and in recompence of his Services, We humbly conceive it will be best to Submit both to Her Majesty's Royal

Grace and Goodness, And we find in Mr Penn a ready Disposition So to do.

My Lord

Your Lordship's Most humble Servants
Dartmouth
Rob: Cecill
Ph: Meadows
Wm Blathwayt
John Pollexfen
Mat: Prior[8]

D. Penn Papers, Official Correspondence, HSP. (*Micro.* 13:097.)

1. Charles Spencer (1674-1722), third earl of Sunderland, of Althorp, Northants., a prominent Whig connected by marriage to the duke of Marlborough, had been appointed secretary of state for the southern department in Dec. 1706. *DNB.*

2. WP had first approached the Board of Trade with an offer of surrender on 11 May 1703. See doc. 60.

3. For the queen's letter of 8 June 1703 ordering the Board of Trade to negotiate with WP, see Board of Trade Papers, Proprieties, 1702-1704, transcript at HSP, L35.

4. See docs. 87, 88, 90, 96, 105; *Micro.* 12:217.

5. See Soderlund, *William Penn,* pp. 39-50.

6. For WP's calculations of the increase in custom revenue, see doc. 88.

7. See headnote to doc. 60; doc. 98.

8. William Legge (1672-1750), first earl of Dartmouth, a moderate Tory, sat on the Board of Trade 1702-10; Robert Cecil (d. 1716), younger son of James, third earl of Salisbury, and later M.P. for Wotton Basset, sat on the Board of Trade 1702-7; Sir Philip Meadows (1626-1718), noted diplomat and author, sat on the Board of Trade 1696-1714; William Blathwayt sat on the Board of Trade 1696-1707; John Pollexfen, merchant and author, sat on the Board of Trade 1696-1705; Matthew Prior (1664-1721), poet, diplomat, and moderate Tory, sat on the Board of Trade 1700-1707. *DNB;* Steele, *Colonial Policy,* pp. 173-76; *Burke's Peerage,* 2:2175.

137
TO JONATHAN AND CALEB DICKINSON

London 14 12m [February] 1706[/7].

Dr. Friends

It would have been a great satisfaction to my Frds, in whose interest I earnestly wrott to you,[1] had they, by me, received a few lines from you, or either of you, in relation to the Wreck affaire;[2] for you must, by your commerce wth your Brother Gomersone[3] & his in the town, have learnt the probability of the undertakeing, & it would be yet a favour to hear from you & the Success of it ~~the undertakeing~~. And because they hear that their Credit wth you was, as Capt Smyth[4] Says, too Scanty, I wrott in my first, that much was left to your prudence, & prospect to Enlarge the Summ: as I also did by Moses austell, a little more expressly for it were pitty a good sheep should be lost for an half penny worth of Tarr[5] I will own to you, I am concerned ultimately ~~concerned~~ in it haveing indeed a pretention of above 40000l upon the Spaniard; & I am of opinion, Wrecks found wth the leave of Crowns, are a faire propriety, being under water, & by neglect of pretenders, theirs that are at the pains & charge of findeing them. We have heard that your Bro^r^ Gom. gave Capt Smyth great encouragem^t^ that there was such a wreck & that it {had} been actually begun to be Fisht, & that some thousands of Pieces of 8, had been taken up, & brought into that Island;[6] & that he had seen some of them. This being so, or otherwise probable, I entreat you to supply wth requists, those entrusted, that a hopefull designe may not Sinck by an Insufficiency to Succeed & accomplish it; and pray take the Same way to reprize your selves, as in my former letters unless you Succeed, & do it there on the Spott.

your old uncle[7] yet lives, wth whom I was 2 nights agoe, but has {had} a long Flux upon him, that putts him to his utmost skill to help himselfe, but is now some w^t^ amended.

Isaac Norris is now here, but the Length of time he has been upon the way from Philad. (6 months) & puting in at KingSaile[8] in Irland, & his wife[9] being neer her time, she wth Mary, their Daughter, Stayd among Frds in Cork, where she is well brought to bed of a large son, called Thomas.[10] I & mine are in a pretty good state of health (my wife dayly expecting to be in the same Circumstances)[11] &, with me salute you & yours. with our best Philadelphian love, desireing your true happiness, & that we may meet once more (as we once comfortably did) in poor Pennsylvania, if god please I have only to add, that {being encouraged by your good news thence &} the time of the Former graunt being spent,[12] the Queen, upon our fresh application, has gruanted the same [illegible deletion] time by a fresh Graunt to Ld Fairfax & Partners {of} wch pray advise the Govr [13] & Capt smyth & such as are or may be Concernd. so with my best wishes & the respects of the Concerned to you, I close

Your very affec^t^ & assured Friend
Wm Penn

Salute me to Capt Smyth & poor Benjamin,[14] & tell them I had their letters[15] wth satisfaction. vale.

ALS. Boston Public Library. (*Micro.* 13:110.) Docketed: Jonathan & Caleb Dickinson. Endorsed: rec^d^ the 4th May 1707 per Nath: Herring.

1. See *Micro.* 12:659, 688, 732.
2. For Jonathan Dickinson's response to this scheme, see doc. 132, which WP had obviously not yet received.
3. Ezekiel Gomersall.
4. Edward Smith; see doc. 132, n. 5.
5. To risk failure for a trifling reason; tar was used to protect wounds on sheep from destructive attacks of flies. *OED*.
6. Jamaica. For the Dickinsons' account of the alleged wreck, see *Micro.* 13:156.
7. Dr. Edmund Dickinson, who was 82 years old. Despite WP's optimism about his recovery, Dickinson died on 3 Apr. 1707. *DNB*.
8. Kinsale, a seaport in Co. Cork.
9. Mary Lloyd Norris.
10. Thomas Norris was born on 29 Jan. 1707. Hinshaw, 2:400.

11. Hannah Penn gave birth to a son, Dennis, at Ealing, Middx., on 26 Feb. 1707. Jenkins, p. 77.

12. The queen had granted a patent to Lord Fairfax and others to fish wrecks in the West Indies, and this patent had expired. See doc. 127, n. 21.

13. Thomas Handasyd, lieutenant governor of Jamaica.

14. Benjamin Lopdell.

15. Not found.

138
TO JOHN EVANS

Eling[1] 15 3m [May] 1707

Esteemed Friend

As my dependance was upon thy honour, so I never thought my selfe unsafe wth it. But three reports, strenuously improved to my disgrace, in these parts, (for so I account every thing that affects thee & thy Conduct in wch I am so much Concerned) makes me very uneasy. The first is, the allarme,[2] given the people, by thy Knowledge, if not contrivance, wn at the same time, thou ~~Kno~~ Knewst there was no reality in the pretended reason of it, & gav'st those {persons} the privat hint of the falicy, that perhaps could not more deserve the whisper, than others that were left to be frighted, as the very best & most obligeing of our friends in town & Country {were}; & this Just after they had shown their distinguishing regards for thee & me, by the provision they had zealously made for Goverr & Govermt & for wch Singula[r] token of Wisdom & Kindne[ss] they have been neglected in th[e] last election,[3] that being improved by mine & our Frds implacable enimys, to misguide & blow up the present assembly to fall upon things, either impracticable, or inconvenient, as well as enflameing agaist us. I am truly Sorry for these things.

The 2d Report, is the Suffering our Frds lye under, as well as {are} exposed to, in the lower Countys, on acct of not Bearing armes;[4] a thing that Touches my Conscience as well as honour. He must be a Silly Shoemaker, that has not a last for his own Foot. That my Frds should not be easy & secure under me, in those points that [r]egard our very Characteristick, [b]ut that fines, or a forced disowning of their own Principles {they must stoop to} for one Brewster[5] says in his letter, to one Childe[6] (come to my hand) that ~~one~~ {Oliver Matthews} was plunderd of no less than six pounds for fifteen {shillgs} when the very fine is a violation of our Constitution, & custom {too} since my Interest {was} there. all wch I desire may be rectifyed forth with, or I must take up {a complaint} with the whole Body of our Frds, represented in our next Genll Assembly, to the Queen, agst such a persecution. And how they come {by themselves} to make laws,[7] {that refused to do so wth the Provin{ce} (unless the Queen has given that powr to thee under the great seal {they objected to me}) I cannot tell. Pray Speak to the best disposed of them {as wm Rod.[8] &c:} that so every Tub may stand upon its own bottom & that they do not lay their separation {from the Province} (*the~~ir~~at fatal day,* as they will finde at last, I feare) in persecution of those that have made New castle so Consederable, & must do, if they would have a little patience. Envy has risen too soon for any bodys {good} among some of both partys perhaps, wch I hoped thy quitere & equaller Temper would have prudently over come.

The 3d Compl[ain]t is the encouragemt of the Growth of Vice for want of powr {& countenance} ~~& encouragemt~~ to Suppress it. Now this Touches my reputation that so fairly begun, in both good laws & good examples too. and as one instance of it, solomon Cressens Story[9] is Sent over by the present Speaker,[10] as I take it, &c: Severely aggravated, both as to the house, the time of night, & thy Caneing of him, while ~~wth~~ the very Badge of authority {was} in his hand, & doing his duty therby required; & they say he is an honest, sober, inoffencive man, & was gone, & calld back by one of the family, wth a designe to provoak thee agst the sd Conestable Cressens. Another Instance they [give is the] more than [e]nough of publick houses, especially in Philadelphia, that ar[e] lice{n}sed by thee, & the unfitt persons that are so, being not of sobriety & good order, required in such as keep Taverns &c: also the unreasonable Summs required from some of them {for licenses,} & that yearly,[11] even after so full a provision has been made by {the former} assembly for the Govr [12] in all wch I desire thy answear, & utmost caution on one hand, & Care on the other, to Suppress vice, {as} by a pro~~c~~clamation now sent,[13] & takeing advice of the most eminent Frds, & other sober people of that Citty, who are most deserveing or best qualified to Keep publick houses, there especially.

[a]s I desire that [Vice] may be supprest, one great end of Govermt, so I desire that care may be taken that no just offence maybe [g]iven to the Crown officers there in refference to the Revenue therof; and I hope Colonel Quarry came to you last with a disposition of liveing easily & fairely among you;[14] & pray let no occasion be given him to change his resolution; for that has hithe[r] to been the pretence to fall upon Pro[pr]ietary Govermts tho none so [d]eserveing of the Crown, being made & Governed at their own Charge. Give no occasion to the Inhabitants, nor yet court any Selfish spirits at my cost, & my suffering familys. Distinguish tempers & pleas; & let realitys & not meer pretences engage thee. Redress real Grievances, Suppress vice & faction, & encourage the Industrious & sober; & be an example as well as a com[m]ander & [thy] authority w[il]l have the greater force & acceptance with the people.

I am far from lending my eares agst my own officers, it is neither wise nor Just; nor is it so to refuse to hear wt is sayd by way of complaint, wn the nature of the thing calls for it, & the exegency of affaires requires it: But there is, I Kno[w], a just caution to be observed i[n the] use to be made therof on all hands.

Thy Frds, of which mine are not the least, (my relations I mean) enquire of thy wellfaire, & these & other storys comeing to their eares, have troubled them, as not savouring of the Character that they had before apprehended to have been thine, & sutable to one employed by me & mine. I earnestly desire thy utmost[15] honour prudence and Justice, yea Courage in my affaires, and don't dispond of a hapy providence and success in them at last, wch hither to has not failed to attend me in the close of various and hazardious adventures in the World and for a Conclusive Paragraph upon these things what thy honest & friendly father and Mother would advise thee, if living to doe for my service and honest (thô abused) Interest that doe with all thy might I desire thee.

For Publick Affaires here they will come by the Prints of Course onely at present the affaires of Spain look a little dark[16] — some Wish for peace & some fear it. — Be wise and Tite to the last for I hope a Tollerable Issue ~~will~~ at least will succeed Remember me to the deserving

Thy &c
Wm Penn

AL. Chester County Historical Society, West Chester, Pa. (*Micro.* 13:177.) Addressed: WPrGr | For Colonel John | Evans Lieut Goverr | of my Province of | Pennsylvania & Terrrs | at Philadelphia. Letters and words torn in the original, as well as the text of the final missing page, have been supplied from a copy in Penn Papers, Letters of the Penn Family to James Logan, 1:34 (not filmed), HSP.

1. Ealing, a borough in west London.

2. See doc. 129.

3. WP had probably received James Logan's critical assessments of the new Assembly elected in Oct. 1706. See doc. 133; *Micro.* 12:838; 13:005, 021, 026.

4. Under the terms of the Militia Act numerous Quakers in the Lower Counties had suffered distraints of their goods for refusing to serve. See doc. 102; Dreer Collection, David Lloyd, HSP.

5. Probably John Brewster, a New Castle innholder and later associate justice of the Lower Counties, who held land in Christiana Hundred, where the persecuted Quaker Oliver Matthews lived. See Scharf, *Delaware,* 1:562, 868; Logan Papers, Quit Rents, Three Lower Counties, 1701-1713, p. 24, HSP.

6. Unidentified. The letter has not been found.

7. The Assembly of the Lower Counties had taken upon itself the right to enact legislation for those counties.

8. William Rodney.

9. Solomon Cresson (d. 1746), a Philadelphia constable, had been allegedly beaten by Evans in Nov. 1704 while trying to disperse a tavern crowd. The resulting "fray" included the city's mayor and recorder, along with alderman and future mayor, Joseph Willcox. See *Votes and Proceedings,* 1 (pt. 2):184; *Minutes of the Provincial Council,* 2:171; Phila. Will Bk. H, #106.

10. David Lloyd. He wrote on 16 Aug. 1706 to George Whitehead, Thomas Lower, and William Mead. Dreer Collection, David Lloyd, HSP.

11. See doc. 127, n. 13.

12. Ibid., n. 3.

13. Not found.

14. In fact, Robert Quary had become friendly with James Logan and implied his willingness to assist WP's interests in the colony. In June 1707 he completed negotiations with Logan to rent Pennsbury for seven years or until WP came over to reside there. See *Micro.* 12:812, 837; 13:121, 135, 148, 233.

15. From this point the text follows the HSP copy; see provenance note, above.

16. By May 1707 the news had reached England that an Anglo-Portuguese army in Spain had been overwhelmingly defeated by a French army led by the duke of Berwick. See Luttrell, 6:168-70.

139
TO JAMES LOGAN

Lond. [10th 4th (June) 1707]

James Logan

Michell[1] being taken, our letters are gone wth him f[or] France. The requisit I g[ive] minutes of [by Capt] John Hamilton,[2] wth who[m] I have entrusted divers hi[nts] for measures to thee. I [was] to have had a present for help[in]g him [to] 1650l here, but forty [o]dd pounds of thy acct with [h]is father is all I am to hope [for]; so mea[n] is my service. and I would h[ope] thou hadst cleared accts before no[w] wth his mor [3] of wch I remembr thou writst to me above a yeare Since.[4] He returns Depty post mr Generall, & has 200l per annum a noble post, & a sensible man. next, Know that our chancery suit[5] is like to goe to the house of Lords, not because Ld. Chancelor[6] dos not repute it a a mortgage, & not a fee, for that he has already done, but because I have great hopes to have the accts reduced to at least a moyty.[7] Frds are {engaged} very warmly [up]on it; S. wal[e] Jo. Frame, ed. Hastwe[ll] Jos. wright, Jos. & Silv. Grove &c.[8] and if the ships are not gone in 4 or 6 days, expect wt is done in order to engage a Genll ~~attack~~ report [?] of Frds upon that Barberous family & the Govermt {here} too, if that take not effect, & wth s[uc]h demonstration as no man, that would not hazard all [cr]edit in this world & his salvation in the next, would Oppose. they are stopt till the next mic[h] terme,[9] when the first & great Britanick Parliament[10] meets, to wch it will goe. Many Great men interpose for the ending it by reference, or lumpeing it, to prevent Scaning these enormious accts & certainly that must be a base & wretched acctt that cannot stand the inquiry of an honest & able accountant. But my son Aub.[11] grows very troublesom because he getts nothing thence; almost to an open breach, did I not bear extreamly. all his last Bills are protested, at wch he has no patience; and truly tis provoaking. Cos. Rooth[12] is yet behinde 36l not as yet receiveing it. Renires[13] Bill of nine pds is protested. so those upon Ch: Eds:[14] Frds. neither are the Rent Bills accepted, but more per next[15] of th[is]. As thou bidst me be stout; be thou so. cherrish & threaten tennants as they give occasion for either, & gett the Govr [16] & the best of my Frds (wch I bless god are of the best) to bestirr themselves & browbeat that villanous fellow D. Ll.[17] who sent his letters to w. M. g. w. T. L.[18] &c: {& the remonstrance too} from the assembly & Citty[19] (I shall send a coppy in a {few} days [illegible deletion] if can) inclosed to P. F.[20] to show the Corrispondence. But I bless the Lord I am yet upon my Rock & lasting foundation; and had I supplys from thee, that I could beare up my head, till matters Issue wth the Fordds, I should hope for a comfortable & easy conclusion of my present troubles, & days too, in gods time. I desire thee to hasten all the relief thou canst, both to me & son Aubrey, of whom I would be clear, of all men; he has a bitter tongue, & I wish I had nothing to do with ~~them~~ him in mony matters.

8. 5^{m} [July]

Make the best of my Jersey Concern{s} e. & w.[21] pray; & particularly of Jo. Fenwicks Interest in Salem tenth,[22] for my poor younger Children. Canst thou not b{u}y out Robertss interest in Father callowhil's ~~interest~~ Lot,[23] 'twere valluable. Lett me know if any body has atturned to Loyd on Fords acc^{t} or refused to pay thee & who,[24] under publick authority, & [illegible deletion] send notice per first. Had our law of Registry,[25] repeald by me at New castle, been in being, tho I had regranted rather, de novo, every mans title, It had invalida[te]d these Deeds of {96,} 97 & 99[26] I hereby order thee to desolve the sasq^{r}hanagh purchess,[27] hopeing to make twice the vallue of it. But the rest, I desire all care ab^{t} geting in. Frds are takeing in to their hands my concerns in europe & Pennsil. & clear me from the Fords &c: & pay themselves gradually & allow me 500^{l} per annum wch I incline too. & if Frds there will come in, tho but for 5000^{l} sterl. Ile come to them & live among them to death for ought I know. I take the sasq^{r} purchass to be as bad for me as that of the company[28] was; an other method may do better. T. Fairman, to whom remember me, ~~&~~ has writt me (a 2^{d} time, as the first)[29] about 100000 acres of land) [illegible deletion] {so now} of 300000 acres, he has found out that is good land, & fitt to deale out to purchassers. a word from thee of that pray. Think not of comeing, for tis there I want thee most, to head the Craft & designes of D. LL. J. Moor J. wilcox &c:[30] for here ~~are~~ divers able men, as S. Walling^{d} [31] Jos. & Sil. Grove, H: Goldney, N. Marks, John Frame, Jo. Field[32] are engaged to my assistance both heads & hands, ay & pursus[33] also: but if they press thee too hard, & the Gover^{r} be {not} stout to browbeat LL. &c: wth the Courage I expect from him, thou mayst make a Trip hither. wert thou here I would not spare thee, but being there, till we see an Issue here, thou must bestirr thy selfe, & urge the Gover^{r} on all occasions to e[xtend] his powr to help my affai[res and] discountenance them. I have thine of 2^{d} 1^{m} & 12. 2^{m}.[34] I wish thou hadst been larger about Coxes business;[35] fearing you wanted my Knowledge of fact to help my Interest therin. I like the Gov^{rs} Commiss^{r} for a court & Courts of Justice at the present,[36] Since the more priviledge the more presumption [illegible deletion] & untowardliness. The insolence of LL is Such that had he done it to me, I would not have proceeded to do any thing, till they had proposed an other speaker & punisht this. I am ashamed these things should be Known to mankinde. once more press the Gover^{r} to persue all advantages agst those three or 4 men, LL. will. Jones, & Biles.[37] I have writt him,[38] upon their complaints ~~to~~ ags^{t} him; sent to G. W. W. M. T. L. W^{m} Cr. & Wal. Mires,[39] to be Layd before the Queen &c: agst me, him &c: for so I count every thing that {they} complain of agst you.

But C. Finne, J. More, w. Trent, J. Pidgeon & Jasper y[eates][40] have employd one wi[lcox[41] an a]tturny & Colonel Quarrys, to complain upon your Law of Qualifications,[42] & I have been before the Lords com^rs once or twice {about it} & must be again a week hence. Is. Norris seems unwiling to part easily with it. I think to Send a Coppy, & thou wilt finde the first article a plain bespeaking of the whole Goverm^t out of Frds hands;[43] the language of the old Petition in Cosin Mark^s time,[44] ab^t the year 89 wch Col. Q. gave to Gr. Jones, the welch atturny in the lower Countys, to form into a formidable petition or Remonstrance agst Frds haveing goverm^t {as he told me}.[45] I am Glad Col. Q. carrys so well, encourage it, & lett him have Pennsberry upon pretty good terms, & for w^t time he will, surrendring at the arrivall of me or my order, or assigne;[46] be sure of that. the Coll Liveing so long; for depend upon it, if god favour me, & my son,[47] with life, one, if not both of us come as soon as possible. worm: he has at last resignd for sale,[48] so that haveing conquer'd himselfe & wife[49] too, who has cost me more mony than she brought, [illegible deletion] by her unreasonable, & for that reason, imprudent obstinacy for dweling there, to wch she could have no pretence, ~~by~~ either by family or portion, but by being my sons impetuous inclination; I wish she had brought more wisdom since {she} brought so little mony to help the family; w^ch, wth some land to be sould in Irland, 45^l per annum will lighten his loade, as well as mine, for his marriage & my Daughters[50] too have not helpt me; his to be sure more especially. we are entering or {it} seems likely we should into neerer friendships than before, he Knowing, I hope, the world & Duty {to} a fa^r better. for he has been of no use, but much expence & Griefe to me, many ways, & years too; loosing him before I found him, being not of that service & benefitt to me that some sons {are}, & 'tis well Known I was to my father before I married.[51] But O! if yet he will recommend himselfe, & show him selfe a good childe, & a true friend, I shall be pleas'd & leave the world with less concern for him & the rest also.

For the Gover^rs Salary, I expect to be reemburst out of w^t the people have given,[52] & if he has 400^l per annum your mony ~~be~~ payd, the rest I expect, both of the peoples Gifts as well as my own fines & forfeitures.[53] &c: I cannot add more and shall think it a mercy if thou getst this Safe considering the wickedness of men. I yet hope for an other post, the winde comeing ab^t & is to night at N. W. in their teeths. All our loves are to thee, But W. A.[54] a Tyger agst thee for returns; come not to him empty as thou valluest thy credit & comfort. I am opprest too much prospects dark for the publick, yet a good peace hoped for.[55] Give honest & wise S. Carp. Cal. Pews. T. Mas. G. owen, & I hope T. S. too[56] my D^r love, not forgeting Capt. Hill & {his} Sweet wife.[57] Indeed all that love the truth in the si[mplicity {my love &} & a f~~ig~~or{give} for] the re[st my God has not forsaken] nor yet forgotten me, in all respects, blessed be his name. Is. Nor. & wife & children are well, much respected for his own merrit, & a little for my sake. a masterpiece for his education. I could not correct the coppy, being in hast, nor have I coppy of this in my own head (tho I may pretty well remember it my love to all that deserve it from me, Frds or others on both Sides the water—begining wth Gov[r] & Council, &c: I am

Thy reall Friend
Wm Penn

ALS. Penn Papers, Letters of the Penn Family to James Logan, HSP. (*Micro.* 13:214.) The editors have established the text of this document from two copies. The first (*Micro.* 13:214) is mainly in WP's hand and concluded by a copyist; the second (unfilmed, also in Letters from the Penn Family to James Logan) is mainly in the copyist's hand and concluded by WP. When combined, these two copies constitute an ALS. The filmed copy is damaged; missing letters and words have been provided within brackets from the second copy, which concludes in WP's hand at the point where he left off in the filmed version (see n. 53, below). This second copy is endorsed: Proprietor 10th 4[mo] 1707 | per Captain Hamilton received | 28th 10[br] 1707.

1. Capt. James Mitchell and his ship, the *Elizabeth,* had been captured by the French. See *Micro.* 13:233.

2. Son of the late Gov. Andrew Hamilton.

3. Agnes Hamilton, widow of Andrew Hamilton and step-mother of John Hamilton.

4. Not found.

5. For WP's lawsuit with the Ford family in the court of Chancery, see headnote to doc. 108.

6. Sir William Cowper.

7. WP's claim that the lord chancellor had agreed that the documents signed by him and Philip Ford were mortgages for debt is an overstatement, for a decision had not yet been rendered (see headnote to doc. 115). For WP's efforts to reduce the amount claimed by the Ford family by at least a moiety or half, see headnote to doc. 121A.

8. Samuel Waldenfield, John Freame (d. 1745), Edward Haistwell, Joseph Wright (b. 1669), and Silvanus Grove (1674-1717) were London Quaker merchants and members of Meeting for Sufferings. Joseph Grove was a Quaker merchant of Barbados and London. See Smith, 1:706-7; doc. 211; Digests of Quaker Records, London and Middx., GSP.

9. Michaelmas term, one of the four common-law court terms, was generally held in Oct. and Nov.

10. The first Parliament of Great Britain met on 23 Oct. 1707, about six months after the union of England and Scotland.

11. William Aubrey. For his financial arrangements with WP, see docs. 130, n. 32; 209.

12. Richard Rooth.

13. Jacob Regnier.

14. Charles Eden.

15. See doc. 144.

16. John Evans.

17. David Lloyd.

18. David Lloyd had written letters complaining of WP's proprietorship to William Mead, George Whitehead, and Thomas Lower, three prominent members of Meeting for Sufferings, in Oct. 1704 and in Aug. and Dec. 1706. See docs. 84; 143, n. 2; Dreer Collection, David Lloyd, HSP; Fallon Scrapbook, p. 6, HSP.

19. Doc. 83.

20. Philip Ford, Jr.

21. East and West New Jersey. Logan summarizes the state of WP's Jersey property rights in *Micro.* 13:274.

22. John Fenwick (d. 1683), an English Quaker, had started a colony at Salem, N.J., in 1675. Fenwick held title to one-tenth of West New Jersey; his tract was known as the Salem tenth. Much of it he sold to the Salem colonists, and the remainder to WP. However, it was not surveyed for WP until 1706 by which time Col. Daniel Coxe claimed that he was the lawful owner of WP's share. The matter had been settled with Coxe by James Logan and Thomas Story early in 1707, but WP had not yet been

notified of the settlement. See Pomfret, *West New Jersey,* chap. 5; *Micro.* 12:253, 721, 837, 838; 13:121, 135, 148.

23. In 1692 Thomas Callowhill had leased a large lot on Delaware Front St. to Thomas Roberts, a shoemaker, for 50 years at an annual rent of £50, provided that Roberts also build two houses on the property. In 1706 Callowhill appointed James Logan as his attorney in Pennsylvania, and Logan was trying to collect arrears of rent, either from Thomas Roberts's assignee, Thomas Tress, or from his son, Robert Roberts. Logan was having difficulty obtaining the money, prompting WP's query. See Logan Papers, 1:61, 64, HSP; James Logan Letterbook, 2:60, 70, 77, 106, HSP.

24. Here WP is referring to those who had refused to pay quitrents to James Logan after learning of Philip Ford, Jr.'s power of attorney to David Lloyd,

25. Presumably, WP is referring to the Charter of Property, part of which confirmed the law of property enacted at New Castle in Oct. 1700. WP's refusal to permit the sealing of the Charter of Property effectively nullified it (see headnote to doc. 31). It is unclear, however, what effect that charter would have had on the deeds in question.

26. See headnote to doc. 108.

27. For WP's unsuccessful efforts to establish a settlement in the Susquehanna River Valley, see *PWP,* 3:671-78.

28. The London Company; see doc. 131, n. 2.

29. Thomas Fairman had written to WP on 27 Aug. 1705 (doc. 103) proposing to set aside 100,000 acres of Pennsylvania land for the use of WP and his children. Fairman's second letter mentioned by WP has not been found.

30. David Lloyd, John Moore, and Joseph Willcox, WP's leading antagonists in Pennsylvania.

31. Samuel Waldenfield.

32. John Field (c. 1647-1724) was a London Quaker schoolmaster, preacher, and writer. *PWP,* 3:558.

33. That is, "purses." English Quakers, particularly those involved with Meeting for Sufferings, were attempting to raise funds to help WP settle his financial dispute with the Ford family. See headnote to doc. 108.

34. See *Micro.* 13:121, 135.

35. See n. 22, above. Logan responded at length on this matter in Jan. 1708. See *Micro.* 13:274.

36. See doc. 133, n. 6.

37. David Lloyd, Joseph Willcox, Griffith Jones, and William Biles.

38. See doc. 138.

39. See n. 18, above. No letters from Lloyd to William Crouch and Walter Miers (c. 1633-1724), two London Quaker merchants and members of Meeting for Sufferings, have been found. Fox, *Short Journal,* pp. 299-300; Fox, 2:475.

40. Capt. Samuel Finney, John Moore, William Trent, Joseph Pidgeon, and Jasper Yeates were all Pennsylvania merchants. WP has erroneously named Yeates instead of George Roche as one of those who hired the London attorney. See *CSPC, 1706-1708,* p. 320.

41. George Wilcox, or Willcocks, Robert Quary's London agent. Root, *Relations of Pennsylvania,* p. 245; Doc. 142.

42. An Act Directing the Qualifications of all Magistrates and Officers, as also the Manner of Giving Evidence (see *Statutes,* 2:266-72) permitted Quakers to hold office in Pennsylvania by substituting the affirmation allowed in restricted circumstances in England in place of the oath of office.

43. On 6 Nov. 1706 the Board of Trade received a memorial from George Wilcox against the Pennsylvania Law of Qualifications; in the first article, Wilcox claimed that sufficient non-Quakers lived in the colony to permit only those willing to take an oath to hold offices there, which (as WP says) would eliminate Quaker participation in that government. Doc. 142.

44. William Markham, deputy governor of Pennsylvania in the 1690s.

45. WP's memory is faulty on the date in question, for he is referring to the Anglican petition to William III about 1695-96, written by Griffith Jones. See *PWP,* 3:443-45.

46. Quary had agreed to rent Pennsbury for seven years, or until WP arrived to live there. See doc. 138, n. 14.

47. William Penn, Jr.

48. The sale of Warminghurst by WP and his son to James Butler took place in Nov. 1707. See docs. 145, 210.

49. Mary Jones Penn.

50. Laetitia Penn had married William Aubrey, whose financial dealings with WP were increasingly acrimonious.

51. WP remembers the business he did for his father in Ireland, 1666-70, but seems to have forgotten the anxiety he caused his father when he was expelled from Oxford and when he converted to Quakerism. See *PWP*, vol. 1.

52. See doc. 127, n. 3.

53. From this point WP's hand is found on the second copy of this letter; see the provenance note, above.

54. William Aubrey.

55. Despite WP's optimism, the War of the Spanish Succession continued until 1713.

56. Samuel Carpenter, Caleb Pusey, Thomas Masters, Griffith Owen, and Thomas Story.

57. Richard and Hannah Delavall Hill. WP inserted "his" in *Micro.* 13:214.

140
QUERIES CONCERNING THE SURRENDER OF PENNSYLVANIA

A
From William Popple, Jr.

[12 May 1707]

S[r]

The Lords Commissioners of Trade and Plantations having had your affair under Consideration, the better to enable them to proceed therein; They have Commanded me to desire your particular Answer in writing, to the following Queries, Viz[t]

First. The Charges you have been at on Account of the Settlement of Pennsylvania &c[a]

2[ly] What are the Profits you have made thereof, computing the Value of the Property remaining to you.

3[ly] How the said Charges and Profits have arisen

4[thly] What advantages the Crown will receive from that Colony, by purchasing the Propriety, more then it now hath, and how the same may arise.

5[thly] What is the Annual Charge of that Government

6[thly] What Revenue is Settled for the Support thereof; the Yearly value of such Revenue, and for what time Granted.

7[thly] The Terms of purchase, that is, the Quantum demanded & times of Payment

8[thly] Lastly, what Priviledges and Immunities you have Granted by Charter or otherwise, to the Citty of Philadelphia, or other Towns or Corporations in the Province of Pensylvania. I am

S[r]
Your most humble Servant
W[m] Popple jun[r]

Copy. CO5/1291/472, PRO. (*Micro.* 13:162.) Addressed: To M[r] Penn. Docketed: May the 12th | Letter to M[r] Penn | with severall | Queries relating | to his Government | of Pennsylvania. Further docketed: Whitehall May the 12th 1707.

B

To William Popple, Jr.

2 Instant July 1707

Esteemed Fr[d]

Pray, Let the Lords forgive me, that I Say I am not a little Surprized that the Lords put me upon Answering Quærys that have been So fully answer'd So long agoe, at least those that are proper to the Surrender.

As for the first, 2[d] & 3[d] Quæry, I gave in an Estimate above 4 Years ago,[1] with as Exact an Acc[t] of what I Sold as I could do here; But I cannot comprehend how my Gains by the Land comes before that Board, They may be Sure I never Received ¼ of my Charges, nor dos this relate to the Governm[t] the Sole thing in Treaty; and which was all the Crown gave me for making a Colony to it, having bought the Land of the Natives at dear Rates.

The 4th Qu. is Answer'd very particularly in the Report made by the Board to the Lord high Treasurer[2] to which I refer.

To the 5th & 6th Quæ. I cannot be exact as to the Charge: But it's what the Assembly of 1706 took care to Supply for 3 Years.[3]

I Ask 20000£ of which 5000£ to be paid there, and 15000£ here;[4] which I propose to be paid 8 in money and 7 in {English} Copper with a Patent for the Coynage of it into Small money, as pence, half pence & farthings: for the Colonys in those parts, which they Stand in need of.

To the last Quærie, The Charters lye in that Office which the Lords may peruse; but they were long considered by that Board before their report was made; And I am extreamly concerned that after almost 6 Years Attendance and the necessary great Expence thereof, with a Family in Town, that what has been done Should be to be ~~g~~done over again, like a man that being ready to Enter his Port, is blown back again to that he left; But I must Submit, and therefore have Sent this Letter to thee, to be communicated to them, with all respects, This had come Sooner, but for being out of Town, and extraordinary business. I am

Thy assued Fr[d]
William Penn

D. CO 5/1264/9, PRO, (*Micro.* 13:238.) Addressed: William Popple Junior. Docketed: Pennsilvania | Letter from M[r] Penn in answ[r] | to one writ him the 12 ~~Instant~~ {May} | with Several Queries relating to | his Surrender &[ca] | Recd | Read | 2 July 1707.

1. See doc. 62. See also WP's more recent estimate of his charges, doc. 135.

2. WP may be referring to the letter of 5 Feb. 1707 from the Board of Trade to the earl of Sunderland, secretary of state for the southern department (See doc. 136). A copy of that letter was later circulated to the treasury. See *CTP, 1708-1714*, pp. 128-29.

3. See doc. 129, n. 25.

4. Initially WP had asked for £30,000. See doc. 62.

141
TO RICHARD HILL

Lond 22 5m [July] 1707

Dr. Friend R. Hill

The Kindeness of thyn, of the last Six month,[1] well deserved a quicker acknowledgemt but I can truly say it was not through the least Slight or forgetfulness. There are very few I am so much indebted to on that Side the great waters; {except} Samll Carpenter & Griff. Owen, who sometimes are so Kinde as to remember me. The lord have you all in his Keeping, for your provocations are many & great, & only his wisdom & oyle of life can preserve you to the end of your day & service.

I have Complained of the foolish as well as Malicious practi~~s~~ce of ~~m~~Maryland,[2] to ~~Colonel~~ Colonel Blacston,[3] a reasonable man, who assures me does not only dissent to such proceedings, but has writt agst them as indiscreet as well as unneighbourly, & I hope to get a lettr from the Lords Comrs to that Goverr agst those practices.[4] I now wth my wife (the distance allowing the mention of it) condole wth thee & thy good wife your great & sensible loss, the male of your Flock.[5] But why do I say loss; Since no childe can be lost to a right Friend, because he findes him again in the eternall, as Dr G. Fox sayd once in my hearing to a tender mother of a [young?] son. The lord sanctify [torn] an exercise to your enlarg[e]mt as of resignation, so of his future favours & enjoyments. yet I would hope to see you ere my s~~o~~un is sett & head is layd. I leave all to the lord, & in his lasting love salute thee & thy Dr Companion, wth honest Frds S: C: C: P: T: S: Gr. O:[6] &c: as if named. to wch my wife says amen. we are well, so your relations goeing to morrow for Dolabron.[7] I referr to J. L.[8] for other things & close

Thy assured Friend
Wm Penn

ALS. Gratz Collection, Governors of Pennsylvania, HSP. (*Micro.* 13:246.)

1. Not found.
2. In 1704 the Maryland Assembly had levied a heavy duty on liquor imported from Pennsylvania and prohibited the importation of other colonial products from that colony. In 1707 these acts were renewed. See Gary B. Nash, "Maryland's Economic War with Pennsylvania," *Maryland Historical Magazine*, 60:240-43.
3. Col. Nathaniel Blakiston, London agent for Maryland.
4. Despite WP's optimism, no letter has been found on this subject from the Board of Trade to Gov. Seymour of Maryland.
5. Richard Hill, Jr. (1701-1705), son of Richard and Hannah, died on 12 Nov. 1705. Hinshaw, 2:374.
6. Samuel Carpenter, Caleb Pusey, Thomas Story, and Griffith Owen.
7. Dolobran, in Montgomeryshire, Wales, home of the Lloyd family, to whom Richard Hill was related by marriage.
8. James Logan.

142
TO THE BOARD OF TRADE

A
George Wilcox's Memorial

[6 November 1706]

REASONS humbly Offered to the Right honourable the Lords Commissioners for Trade and Plantations against Confirming An Act passed at An Assem[bly] of the Province of Pensilvania Entituled An Act for Directing the Qualifications of All Magistrates and Officers, as also the Manner of giving Evidence.[1]

IMPRIMIS. 'Tis presumed that the Preamble is grounded upon a falsity in fact,[2] for though the Major part of the Freeholders and Inhabitants of the province were Such who pretend Scruple of Conscience in taking Oaths or Administring of them (which is denyed) yet it does not follow that Inevitably there will[3] a failure of Justice without this Act, there being A Sufficient Number of Such who are well qualifyed to Execute All Trusts and Offices that are requisite for the Government of the Said Province, and who do not Scruple to take and Administer Oaths.

2dly 'Tis conceived that the First Clause in this Act as it must be intended to Establish Quakerism in the Said Province So it will destroy the present Settlement both Ecclesiastical and Civill, any persons being here Authorized to be Qualifyed for, and capable of Acting in All Offices and Trusts whatever without taking the Oaths of Allegiance in the Solemn Form required by the First of Wm & Mary[4] or Oaths for the due Execution of their Offices, And Although it is mentioned in the Said Clause that the Affirmations and Declarations in One other Act of the First of Wm & Mary Entituled An Act for Exempting their Majties Subjects Dissenting from the Church of England from the Penalties of Certain Laws[5] shall be taken and Subscribed as requisite to Such qualification. It is humbly proposed that though there was Indulgence So farr given to Scrupulous Consciences as to Exempt them from Penalties they would otherwise have Incurred and by permitting them to take and Subscribe Such Affirmations and Declarations as aforesaid instead of the Oaths of Allegiance required by the Said other Act upon tender of the Said Oaths as a Testimony of their fidelity to the Government, yet it was not thought fitt by that Act or any other to Admitt the taking Such Affirmations to be a Sufficient Qualification for the being part of the Government by Acting and Executing any Office of Trust of the least Importance whatever. And the Parliament of England in One other Act of Indulgence to Quakers[6] by permitting their Affirmation to be taken instead of An Oath in Civill Cases Seems to have a regard in that Act Cheifly to the Rights of other Subjects which might frequently be prejudiced if Such Affirmations of Quakers as is therein mentioned Should not be taken as An Oath, yet in that very Act (which was but Temporary) It is Expressly Provided that Such Affirmation shall not Qualify to be a Witness in Criminal Causes or Serve on a Jury or make Capable of Executing any Office or place of proffit in the Government Whereas this Act is perpetual and this Clause expressly includes them all which may be of very ill Consequence to the Lives and Properties of the Subject and directly tending to the Unhingeing the Present Establishment both in Church and State by letting in persons into the Government who under the Notion of Quakers and persons Scrupulous to take Oaths may defeat and Evade that Security intended by the Said Act requiring Oaths of Allegiance, and may enjoy Offices of the highest Trust without being bound to Execute them faithfully in the Solemn manner that all others are obliged, nor does there Seem any Occasion for this Extraordinary Act for all the preamble Says as a Mischeif (if it were true) is only that there will be a failure of Justice for want of Persons Qualifyed to Administer An Oath to which Single Supposed Mischeif it is endeavoured to provide this Unsuitable and Unnecessary Remedy.

3dly The Clause Enacting the Form of the Affirmation Seems not to be with Solemnity or Propriety Sufficient for a Matter of that Importance for that it is not An Express Declaration of the Party that he sayes the Truth but declares in the presence of God the Witness of the Truth of what he Sayes wch gives too much room for Equivocating the Sence of it, being taken One way that God is Witness of the Truth if he Sayes Truth, but otherwise not, And therefore 'tis only an Implyed Declaration of Speaking Truth & not Express.

4thly The Clause Impowering Such who Scruple to Administer Oaths, to Administer the Affirmation instead of it, even to persons willing to take Oaths may be of ill Consequence and tend to the Subversion of Justice Since many persons may esteem themselves bound more Solemnly by an Oath than by Such Affirmation.

5thly The Clause Enacting that the tender of An Oath by One Magistrate in the presence of a Bench of Magistrates shall be esteemed his Act only and yet as Valid as if done by the whole will extend the Power of any One Magistrate too much, Since One Man may take upon him to do that which is intrusted only to a Number of Men for divers reasons and by their Silence and not concerning themselves in it may be as effectual as if with all their Consents.

6thly As for the Clause to Salve Objections against Such Affirmations that the Persons Shall be as lyable to Punishment for Perjury as if Sworne upon Oath, though that may deterr where a Man may have but a Small interest as to Serve a Friend in private Civill Cases yet where Offices of Proffit may be Attained and where the detection of Wilfull Perjury cannot be easy, but in those Cases must be very difficult Men may be induced to take this Affirmations especially Since the tenor of breaking a Solemn Oath may be thought to be Evaded which Oath in these Cases would be wanting.

7thly The last Clause relates to the Deposition or Affirmation of a Witness being taken before A Judge or Justice of Peace after Summons of the Adverse Party and Sayes it shall be as Valid as if they had Sworne in the Presence of a Court where A Witness has Occasion to go out of the Province or is Sick. This may be very inconvenient not only to the Properties but to the Lives of the Subjects for that a Witness designing to be Absent may pretend Occasion to go out of the way or be Sick whereas in England in those Cases Oath is required of Such Necessity even before a Tryal shall be put off, but in no Such Case the Deposition to be read if the party alive unless upon Convenient Notice to the Adverse party and upon Motion in Publick Court and upon hearing of Councell on both Sides and Affidavit of the Necessity of Such absence and this only in Civill Cases; But this is never allowed to be done by any Single Judge of his Own private Authority without Such Application as aforesaid. and this with great reason because of the known benefitt of Cross-Examining A Witness who very often by An Unexpected Question reveals the Truth which might otherwise by Secret Examination have been Concealed, And Sometimes by the manner of delivering his Testimony a Jury has not beleived a Witness. And for the Summons of the party there is no time Sett, So that may be So Short as to be impossible to be there.

All which Reasons are humbly offered to Your Lordships against having the Said Law Confirmed.

By My Lords
Your Lordships
most Obedient humble Servant
Geo: Willcocks

DS. CO 5/1291/XP7117, PRO. (Not filmed.) Endorsed: Pennsylvania | Meml from Mr Wilcox containing | Reasons agt an Act of Pensilvania | for directing the Qualifications of all | Magistrates & Officers, as also the | manner of giving Evidence. | Received | Read | 6 November | 1706.

B
The Proprietor's Reply

14. 6m (Augst) 1707

Esteemed Friend

The inclosed Answers to G. Willcoxes Reasons has been ready above a weeke Since, but my wifes great illness in the Country disabled me from waiting upon the Lords Comrs with it. I hope the Lords will upon perusall of it be of an Opinion they are frivolous, not to say malicious to our perswasion,[7] Since the drift of that Memoriall is to unquallify us for Shares in our own Govermt a most improper as well as {an} unreasonable thing; and that since they came Dwarfs into the

Province, whatever they are now, Is it not very hard that these Gentlemen Should make us Dissenters in our own Country? and in effect themselves our Lords & masters, for life, Liberty & Property. I will in a few dayes (God willing) wait upon the Lords both upon this and the other Subject[8] before them.
I am

Thy assured & affect[t] Friend
Wm Penn

Answears to the Reasons offerd by Geo Willcox to this Hon[ble] Board ag[st] confirming an act past at Philadelphia Entitled an Act directing the Qualifications of all Magistrates & Officers, and alsoe the manner of giving Evidence.
To the first
Tis evident that the preamble of the Act is grounded on {a} reality, for in the Countys of Chester and Bucks 2 of the 3 that Compose the Province, there are at least 4 of the people called Quakers to one that can Swear, and in the later they are not only 5 to one but there are not able and Sufficient men enough other than those called Quakers to Execute Justice among them, therefore there would be a failure of it if those people were Excluded. Besides this very Law in question was fully Debated in a free conference, between the Councill and Assembly, before the Gov[r] a Chur[ch]man,[9] at w[ch] Councill there were 5 or 6 Churchmen and but 3 Quakers[10] and not one of those Gentlemen Soe much as offerd to deny the Superiority of Number when urged by the Quakers, insomuch that the Governour declared himself and the rest too, satisfied of the plurality and necessity of thier being concerned in the Adminstration of the Goverm[t] the denying therefore that the Majority of the freehold[rs] of the Province of Pensylvania are such who are Scuplous of take[ing] Oaths is at least a mistake, but certainly this Article carrys apparent Exclusion in the very face of it, in alleadging that there are a Sufficient number of Such who are well quallified to exe[cute] all Trusts and Offices in the Goverm[t] of the s[d] Province, who doe n[ot] Scruple to take and Administer Oaths: thereby doubtless intending totally to devest and discharge our friends from haveing any Share in the Administration thereof, tho of a Province or Colony of their ow[n] making, at the known hazard of their lives and fortunes and a va[st] Expence and Labour for 26 years past, by w[ch] means a meer wilde[r]ness is converted into a usefull and beneficiall Colony to the Crow[n] a poore returne for the favours Shown them by the people cal[led] Quakers
To the 2[d]
As before Soe I must Say its highly reasonable and according [to] naturall right, that a people which made a Country Should be Esta[blish]ed therein, neither will their Establishm[t] therein destroy the pres[ent] Setlem[t] as is Suggested in this Article, when the Greater part [of] the Ministers are Quakers, and the Legislators almost all,

and the Sec[uri]ty of an affirmation wth them is certainly as valid as that of an [oath] with those that are free to take it, their incomparable And Constant Sufferings for not swearing considerd, the expression of leting in Quakers into the Goverm^{t} of that Province is ridiculous they haveing had the whole Goverm^{t} there, and by their humanity and free Principles admitted others to a participation wth them that show now they doe not deserve it from them.

To the 3^{d}

What is Said agst the forme of Affirmation there tis presumed may be alleadged agst the Affirmation here, wch seemes a reflection on the wisdom of Parliam^{t} the Affirmations being worded alike

To the 4th

This Clause is only where there is no proper officer on the Bench that can Administer an Oath, and where almost the whole are the people called Quakers. Besides the greatest part of the people of the Province are as well Satisfied wth the Affirmation as wth an Oath, and hold themselves as much obliged thereby, and therefore there is no Shew of any ill Consequence from this Clause. And further I must Say the whole Province and Territorys had an agreeable distribution of Justice free of Oaths for many years wthout any Complaint or Address to the Crown in respect of the mode or manner of the Administration thereof untill these Complainants and their few adherents began to make those people uneasy who made the Province, wch has in a great measure made them w^{t} they are.

To the 5th

The Clause enacting that the tender of an Oath by ~~a~~ {one} Magistrate in the presence of a Bench of Magistrates shall be esteemed his act only, yet as valid as if done by the whole, Cannot too much extend the pow'r in any wise of any one Magistrate, as is here Suggested, because the same is limited to the administration of an Oath only.

To the 6th

Tis presumed that the Quakers hold themselves as firmly bound by an affirmation, as others in Generall by an Oath as before at large, and therefore this reason Seemes to Carry no weight in it

To the 7th

There is a great deale of reason for that clause relating to the depos[i]tion or affirmation of a wittness, being Sick or necessitated to goe out of the Province; for the people having often occasion, there being many of them Traders, to goe to new York, New England, Maryland Virginia, Jamaica, Rhoad Island, Barbadoes &c as well as to Come to England: and the Judge before whome Such deposition is to be made is Certainly thought to be Capable of knowing whether there is a necesity of Such deposition or not, and if he finds none, then tis conceived he will not admitt of it; who is also to summon the Adverse party to appear before him & will undou[bt]edly give them Sufficient time to appear, else Such deposition 'tis presumed would be laid aside by the Court: Besides this appears only to have a relation to property and not to the life of the subject however it seemes to have been Coppyed after a Barbados Law that has long Since had the Royall Sanction, for so I have been Informd

all wch is humbly Submitted to the Consideration of this Honrble Board in behalf of the people called Quakers of the Province of Pensylvania.

LS & D. CO 5/1264/13,13i, PRO. (*Micro.* 13:260.) Addressed: For wm Popple | esqr secretary to | the Lds Comrs for Trade | & Plantations at | Whitehall. Docketed: Pennsylvania | Lettre: from Mr Penn enclosing his | Answers to Mr Wilcox his reasons | against an Act past in Pensylva | relating to the Qualifications of | Magistrates &ca | Received: 16 Augt | Read 20th Octr | 1707. Docketed by WP: My answear | to G. Wilcoxes | Memoriall | WP.

1. See *Statutes,* 2:266-72.

2. The preamble asserted that "in some of the counties, unless an affirmation be allowed instead of an oath . . . there will inevitably be a failure of justice." Ibid., 2:267.

3. The clerk has omitted "be."

4. 1 Will. and Mary, cap. 8.

5. Ibid., cap. 18.

6. 7 & 8 Will. III, cap. 34.

7. The Quakers.

8. Here WP is referring to his offer to surrender the government of Pennsylvania. See doc. 140B.

9. John Evans, an Anglican. The conference took place on 9 Jan. 1706. See *Minutes of the Provincial Council,* 2:225-28; *Votes and Proceedings,* 1 (pt. 2):78-79.

10. For a nearly identical account, see Isaac Norris to Joseph Pike, 30 July 1707, Norris Papers, 7:91, HSP. The Quaker members of the Council present on 9 Nov. 1706 seem to have been James Logan, Griffith Owen, and Thomas Story. The Anglican members were John Guest, Joseph Pidgeon, William Trent, and Jasper Yeates, as well as Gov. Evans and Attorney General George Lowther. See *Minutes of the Provincial Council,* 2:224-27.

143
TO SAMUEL CARPENTER AND OTHERS

London ~~1~~7 8th [October] 1707

Dear freinds & Brethren[1]

In the Antient tender Love that long Since hath Engagd, Our hearts to the Lord, & in him to one another, I Salute you.

And where as there hath been Communicated to me by George Whitehead Wm Mead, & Thos Lower the Coppey of an Addres made to me from the last Assembly of Pensilvania, held 1706.[2] Containing Complaints of Divers unfaire & Injurious things in the Administration of the Goverment. I have at the Request and out of a Desire to Satisfie the Inhabitants in theire Just and Reasonable Expectations writ to my Deputy Governour[3] to Exert the utmost of his Authority to punish vice and in order to it, to Reduce the Number of publicke houses, and that Such ~~that~~ as are Allowed with in the City be recommended to him by the Magistrates of the City and for the Counties, by the Justices thereof in open Sessions I have alsoe Severely Checkt his treatment of the Constable at Philadelphia,[4] and likewise the

Countenance he seemed to give {~~to~~} [illegible deletion] to that false and Reproveable Alarme that Soe much Disturbed the people.[5] I have alsoe Shewn my Great Disatisfaction, Indeed Abhorance of the Leate treatement of my friends in the Lower Countys by the Militia Law[6] (and fare beyond it) which I shall take all possible Care here to prevent, being Confirmed; And in the meane time I have ordered, him to Stope all proceedings, & Prevent them for the future and in other matters wherein the Inhabitantes are Realy Agreived, and which is in my power to Red~~uce~~ress I shall not be wanting there in, of all which I Referr you to my Deputy Governour Councill, and Assembly as you shall find Occasion, to make youre Address and Application unto them Shall add noe more but my best wishes for you, and your~~se~~ whole peoples prosperity being their and youre

Loving Friend in truth
Wm Penn

LS. Penn Papers, Letters of the Penn Family to James Logan, HSP. (*Micro.* 13:288.) Addressed: To Samuell Carpenter | Grifith Owen | Thos | Storey | Caleb Pusey | Rowland Ellis | Richd Hill. Endorsed in WP's hand: a coppy of my | lettr to S.C. C.P. | T.S. R.H. G.O. | R.E. &c.

1. Griffith Owen, Thomas Story, Caleb Pusey, Rowland Ellis, and Richard Hill.
2. This address, prepared by the Pennsylvania Assembly on 4 Dec. 1706, called on WP to dismiss Dep. Gov. Evans and Secretary Logan and appoint more suitable proprietary administrators. The text of the address has not been found. On 4 Dec. the Assembly also wrote to Whitehead, Mead, and Lower, enclosing the address and empowering them to appeal to the queen or to the Meeting for Sufferings for help in redressing WP's misgovernment. See Fallon Scrapbook, p. 6, HSP; *Votes and Proceedings,* 1 (pt. 2):115.
3. John Evans. For WP's letter, see doc. 138.
4. For Evans's treatment of Solomon Cresson, a Philadelphia constable, see doc. 138.
5. See doc. 129.
6. See doc. 138, n. 4.

144
TO JAMES LOGAN

Lond. 16. 8br [October] 1707

James Logan
I have writt by Capt Hamilton, & Rd Townsend.[1] one I hope is there, the other in the {Boy of the} Nore,[2] for the first {faire} windes. This goes by the west india packet boate Inclosed by Silvanus Grove to his Bror John to send thee per first conveyance.
Now Know that divers of my Friends, to whom I am Indebted, as well per Bonds, as notes & Book debts, clear me here for Bills at Six months Sight upon wt is oweing me there & that is in thy hands, the ~~coppy~~ account of wch is on the other si~~ugh~~de. A great relief to me from clamour & charge here, & the greatest benefit that place has yet yeilded me. pray comply there with, & that ~~&~~ in a respectfull manner;

& w[t] thou canst not doe in time, haveing So copious a fund, to be sure my Frds there will assist thee, upon Credit thereof to comply handsomly wth the sayd Bills. I have drawn them at sixty percent.[3] I can say no more [bu]t that if the compremise take not, the Lords this session will hear of us, if not releived at the hearing of the cause finally in chancery, w[ch] is not yet done.[4] And do you all, {that are} in my service & Interest Keep your Ground, & advise wth Judge Mompesson in every point of law. they Stickle for possession,[5] but foolishly; & pray give no just occasion & stand firm. Thine of the Fifth month came first,[6] the 17[ss] 5[d] packet came via Irland,[7] perhaps per T. Grey, w[ch] thou mightest have hindred if superscrib'd to J. Lewis[8] member of Parliament at the secretarys office at white-hall. He is under secret. [to] R. Harley Principal secret[r] of State.
Remember the lotts by Hugh Derb[ry] [9] &c: & quiet Rabsh. Rakestraw[10] that Poor restless man. my Dr. love to Frds really so. & salutes to the Gov[r] councill &c: vale.

Thy reall Frd
Wm Penn

Remember to clear off Hages pretentions;[11] he offered for 10 pounds a release of the equity, get one at any reasonable rate, I mean at twenty pounds rather than fail. next, pray quiet Jacob Simcock that threatens me with laying his grievance before Friends, if not complied with.[12] I send thee a Letter also from Father Callowhill in his affairs,[13] which pray observe, as also about the lott. quiet and keep in good humour T Fairman, and be easy to all in general, and Just also to all, not leaving me out of that direction. 9[br] 6th vale. Thy real Friend
Wm Penn

P.S. I desire those who take the growth may be accomodated to content. at current price

WP.

The Bills[14] drawn are as followeth

		£	s	d
To	Richard Richardson	219	7	–
	John Willmore	204	–	–
	Joseph Buckley	079	1	–
	W[m] Weston	043	10	–
	Tho. Raylton	048	–	–
	Henry Thompson	044	–	–
	Jacob Franklin	084	8	–
	Rich[d] Berry	032	–	–
	Abel Wilkinson	117	–	–
	Rich[d] Champion	087	6	–
	Isaac Jennings	060	13	–
	W[m] Lickfield	608	–	–
	John Jefferys[15]	112	–	–
		1739	5	–

ALS. Penn Papers, Letters of the Penn Family to James Logan. (*Micro.* 13:311.) Addressed: [torn] To | Jam | of the | Penn | Phi. The postscript of this letter is missing from the ALS and is supplied from Deborah Norris Logan's manuscript copy in Logan Papers, Selections from the Correspondence of the Honourable James Logan, HSP.

1. Richard Townsend (c. 1644-1732), a London Quaker carpenter and First Purchaser, had arrived in Philadelphia with WP in 1682. He built a sawmill in Chester Co. and a corn mill near Germantown. See George E. McCracken, *The Welcome Claimants Proved, Disproved and Doubtful* (Baltimore, 1970), pp. 496-503; Phila. Will Bk. E, #311. The letter sent via Capt. Hamilton is doc. 139; that sent via Richard Townsend is *Micro.* 13:243.

2. Presumably the buoy marking the Nore, a sandbank in the center of the estuary of the Thames River.

3. That is, £1 sterling would be worth £1.67 Pennsylvania money.

4. Here WP is referring to the Ford case (see headnote to doc. 108) and his plan of appealing to the House of Lords if a compromise could not be worked out before a final decree was issued in the court of Chancery.

5. The Fords hoped to gain possession of Pennsylvania by decree from the court of chancery and were therefore unwilling to make a money settlement on WP's terms out of court.

6. No letter from Logan of July 1707 has been found. WP seems to be speaking of doc. 130, sent in July 1706.

7. Possibly *Micro.* 12:812, a sizable letter written by Logan in Aug. 1706.

8. Probably John Lewis (c. 1660-1720), of Cardiganshire, member of a prominent Welsh family and a former parliamentarian. See Basil D. Henning, ed., *The House of Commons, 1660-1690* (London, 1983), 2:739-40.

9. Hugh Durborow (d. 1741), a Philadelphia Quaker bottler, owned land on Second St. adjoining some vacant lots. In Feb. 1702 the Board of Property, apparently unbeknownst to WP, divided these lots among several purchasers, including Thomas Callowhill. Logan apprised WP of this development in July 1708. See *PA.*, 2d ser., 19:260-61; *Micro.* 13:507.

10. William Rakestraw was embroiled in a dispute with WP over property rights in Philadelphia. Rakestraw ultimately complained to Phila. Monthly Meeting but lost in arbitration and was forced to write a paper of self-condemnation for abusing WP. Here WP sarcastically refers to him as Rab-shakeh, meaning "chief of the nobles," the title of the Assyrian official who failed to gain the surrender of Jerusalem. See doc. 56, n. 34; *Micro.* 13:392; J. D. Douglas, ed., *The New Bible Dictionary* (Grand Rapids, Mich., 1962), p. 1073. In doc. 154 WP calls Rakestraw, "one of wicked Loyds tools of clamour."

11. See doc. 126, n. 25.

12. See doc. 76, text at n. 51.

13. Not found. For Logan's response to Callowhill's letter, see James Logan Letterbook, 2:106, HSP.

14. These are the bills described in the second paragraph of WP's letter.

15. Richard Richardson (c. 1653-1718), John Wilmer, Joseph Buckley (c. 1647-1711), William Weston, Thomas Raylton (c. 1658-1708), Jacob Franklin (c. 1661-1710), Abel Wilkinson, Isaac Jennings, William Lickfold (c. 1644-1714), and John Jeffreys were all Quakers of London and Middlesex. Richard Champion (c. 1676-1748) was a Quaker of Bristol, while Richard Bury (d. 1731) was a Quaker of Bristol and London. Henry Thompson has not been identified. Digests of Quaker Records, London & Middx., GSP; Smith, 2:475; Mortimer, 2:236-37.

145
THE SALE OF LIVESTOCK AND EQUIPMENT AT WARMINGHURST

[27 November 1707]

Know all men by, and Witnesse these presents That I William Penn late of Worminghurst[1] in the County of Sussex Esqr for and in consideracion of the summe of three hundred thirty & four pounds eighteen shillings & six pence of good money to me paid by James Butler of Michelgrove in the same County Esqr [2] Have bargained and sold And Doe hereby bargaine and sell unto the said James Butler to his own Use and benefit Sixteen Bucks eighteen Soares[3] eight & twenty Soarells[4] Forty pricketts[5] & eighty six Does & Five & forty Fawnes or thereabouts being in the parke late of {me} the said William Penn in Worminghurst aforesaid And also Fower Cowes Four heifers, One ~~Bo~~ Bull Two Calves Eight Ewes Three Rams Four Working Steeres One Mare with a plow and two chaines thereto belonging two Yokes and harnesse a Stack of Faggotts Four more Horseharnesse & Wipps, a Mare called the Garton Mare and a horse called the Doctors horse, One Sow, one Boare, one hog, Four Shots[6] two sowes more and Five piggs One horse Rowler,[7] sixteen acres of meadow hay in the barne being about thirteen load, {and the Ferne in the same Barne} about twenty load of hay in the Stable barne {being all the hay therein} the hop poles in the hop garden and the Stant[8] two Waggons with Wheeles, Cartladders & wheele ladders[9] and one pair of ropes and a dung pott Six Racks, One long ladder One plow without irons and a harrow Five ~~pairs~~ pair of Old horse harnesse with Thillers[10] harnesse and some old blindfolds, and in the Milkhouse One Cheese presse, One hand Churne Four Cheese Vants[11] two Cheese Racks Four leads[12] and stands, two Milk bucketts and a dresser with Leggs a Cheese Salter or trough, In the syder house, a Steel Malt Mill and bin one Cyder Mill and wheeles with a Shed over and trough underneath With a Cyder presse and trough All which are in and about the house and grounds late of {me} the said William Penn in Worminghurst aforesaid And all the right title & interest of ~~him~~ {me} the said William Penn {in and to the same} in Worminghurst aforesd and also the Dung in the Yards To have and to hold the said Deer Stock and other the premises Unto the said James Butler his executors administrators and assignes To his and their own use and benefit And I the said William Penn for ~~him~~ {me} and {my} ~~his~~ heires do~~th~~ hereby Warrant unto the said James Bulter and his heires the said Deer Stock and other the premises against {me} ~~him~~ the said William Penn {my} ~~his~~ heires executors & administrators. Witnesse my hand and seale this seven and twentieth day of November in the year of our Lord Christ One thousand seven hundred and seven.

Wm Penn

Sealed and delivered (the same being first stampt) in the presence of (the words [& the Ferne in the same Barne,] & the Words, being all the hay therein, being first interlined

H Springett
Peniston Lamb

DS. Society Collection, HSP. (*Micro.* 13:338.) Endorsed: Received by me the within named William Penn | of and from the within named James Butler | the summe of three hundred thirty & four pounds | eighteen shillings & six pence within mencioned | to be paid by him to me Witnesse my hand the | day and year first within written | 334l 18s 6d | Wm Penn | Witnesse | H Springett | Peniston Lamb. Docketed: 27th Novr 1707 | Assignmt of the | Deer Stock &c to | Mr Butler.

1. Five days previously, on 22 Nov. 1707, WP had sold his house and lands at Warminghurst to James Butler for £6053 15s. He had held this property since 1676, when he bought it for £4450 (see *PWP,* 1:648-49). For the terms of sale in 1707, see docs. 210B-C.

2. James Butler (d. c. 1742), son of parliamentarian James Butler of Amberley and Patcham, Sus., was himself a member of Parliament for Arundel, 1705-8, and for the county of Sussex, 1715-22 and 1728-1742. Basil D. Henning, ed., *The House of Commons, 1660-1690* (London, 1983), 1:754-55; *Sussex Archaeological Collections,* 33:97-98, 100; 35:130, 138, 144, 150, 153, 156.

3. Sores: bucks in their fourth year. *OED.*

4. Sorrels: bucks in their third year. Ibid.

5. Prickets: bucks in their second year, having straight, unbranched horns. Ibid.

6. Shoats: young, weaned pigs. Ibid.

7. Roller: a broad, paded girth for a horse. Ibid.

8. Stent: a stake for stretching fishing nets upon in a river. Ibid.

9. A cart-ladder was a rack or framework at the front, back, or sides of a cart, to increase its carrying capacity; a wheel-ladder was a rail for the back part of a wagon, having a small roller or windlass attached, by which the ropes for binding the load could be strained tight. Ibid.

10. Tillers.

11. Cheese vats used in cheese-making. *OED.*

12. Leaden milkpans. Ibid.

146
TO HENRY CANE

28 12m [February] 1707[/8][1]

Dear Frd

please to send this, because it is too late for me to write, to my secretary[2] & Frds In Pennsylvania, to let them Know, that my adversarys Petition {to the Queen}[3] to be put into possession of my Country, before a decree obtain'd in chancery {& the cause heard in ~~Eng therein~~[?]} was last night dismist, as improper & unreasonable; wch perhaps may putt thos furious Ingrates to think of an accommodation, wch is much desired by Frds. please to direct this To James Logan secretary of Pennsylvania, & entrust it wth Ricd townesend (to whom my Dr love) or poor Tho: Liford, by whom I have allready writt to thee.[4] we are all pretty well, through mercy, the Lord has left among us. Farewell dear Frd wth all thine & honest Frds, says

Thy Faithfull Frd & Bror in
the Truth
Wm Penn

ALS. ACM. (*Micro.* 13:399.) Endorsed: Henry Kane by Thomas Lyford.

1. This is WP's first surviving letter written from debtors' prison. He had entered the Fleet prison on 7 Jan. 1708 but was actually living in Old Bailey, one street away. See doc. 147, n. 6; Peter Cunningham, *A Handbook for London, Past and Present* (London, 1849), 1:310-13; 2:603-4.

2. James Logan.

3. For the petition of Bridget Ford on behalf of her family against WP, see doc. 118.

4. Not found.

147
TO JAMES LOGAN

Lond 3 3m [May] 1708
Lord Treasurers[1]

J. Logan
Log Frd

I have had none from thee since the last 6m [2] wch gives me great uneasiness, Since the virulent treatmt of D.L.[3] &c: can much sooner finde its way to P. Fod [4] & by him, to G.W. W.M. & T.L.[5] who have been wth me at my Lodgeings in old baly,[6] to represent the state of the province, & render it very Lamentable under the present Lt Goverr [7] and unless I will discharge him, & putt in a man of virtue, yeares & Known experience, & of a moderate Spt they cannot avoide layg the assemblys Complaint before the Queen & Council in wch they have enumerated all the faults if not imprudences, they can lay to his conduct. The alarm,[8] the refusal of the Law for Courts &c:[9] the Newcastle law to pay Toll goeing {from} & comeing to Philadelphia,[10] & the violent struggle upon it; His geting young Sus. Harwood with Childe, & conniveing at the escape the old one made from Justice,[11] & accompanying them into an other province for avoiding shame & punishmt. To wch they {add} a lewd voyage to sasquehanagh with the vilest character of his & his retinues practices with the wives & daughters of the people at Conostogo. My Soule mourns under these things, for the very fame of them, but musth more if true, ~~after advanceing him from so little a Station as I found him to goe before & be governour over such a great & professing people of the Stricktest way~~[12] I doubt not his regards for my interest in the main, but this disjoynts all, & cutts me down at once, so that I have been forc'd to think, much agst my desire, of looking out another to putt in his place; & at last I have found one,[13] of whose morrals, experience & fidelity I have some Knowledge, & of his family 40 years; and has a recommending Character from persons of great Ranck; & he assures me, he intends to center wth us, & end his days in that Country;[14] being 46 years of age,[15] single, & sould his estate in Europe to lay out his mony there & be a good Freeholder among you. Highly commended by Lewt Genll Earle[16] & Major Genll Cadogan[17] & the Igoldsby[18] Family, as well as by Major Morris, my Steward,[19] & some Frds in Irland. & if he goes, it will be as one resolv'd to retire, & absolutly disposed to commend himselfe to you by sobriety & thriftiness rather than Luxury or rapaciousness. wch I thought fitt to communicate, & pray break it to him; and that the reason why I choose to change, rather than contest wth the Complaints before the Queen in Council, is that he may stand the fairer for an employmt elsewhere, wch would be very

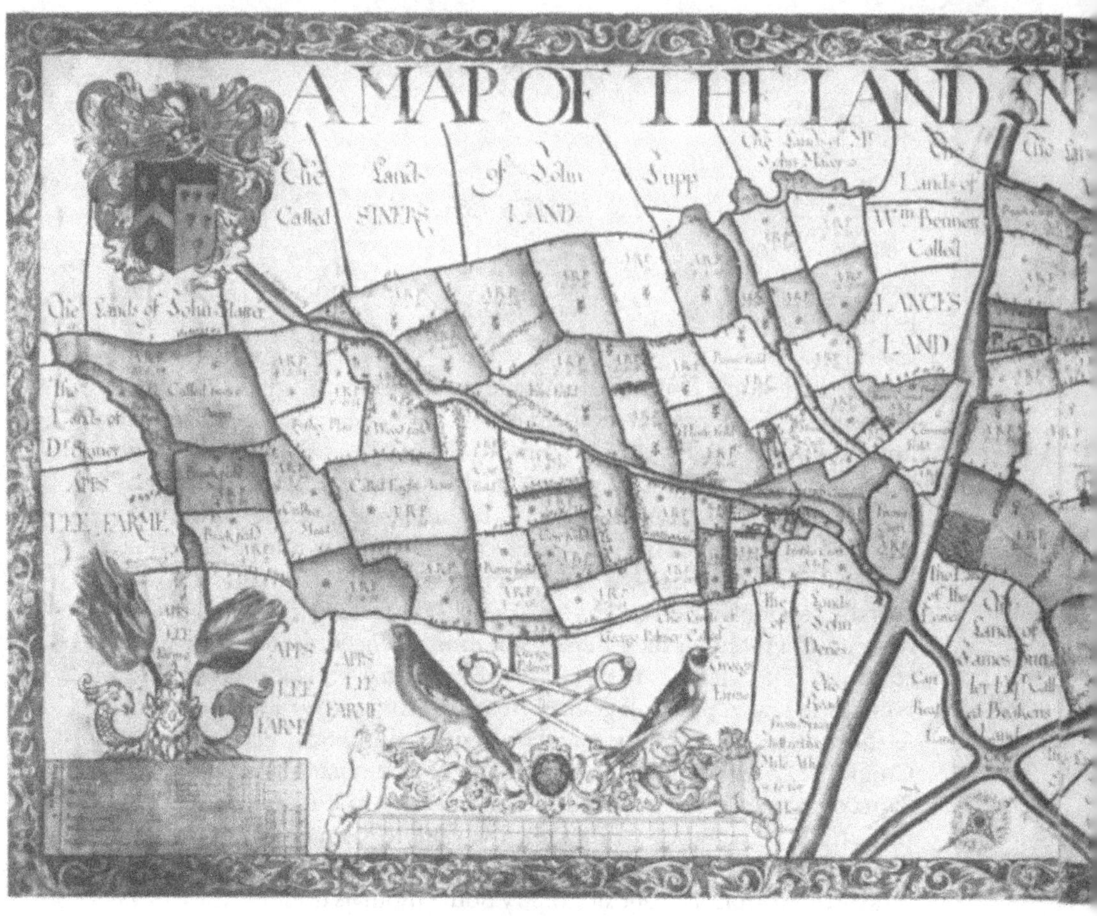

doubtfull, if those blemishes were agrevated in Such a presence. so much for that. The Person that will give this is a long & full espistle himselfe, to wch I must referr my Selfe for thy ampler instruction & knowledge. The Fords seem to embrace an accommodation,[20] & severall Frds & others not of our profession interpose to mediate it. 7000l Looks to be the summ. to be sure that or 8 will do it effectually, & tho I dont like my Frds method, yet it will do, I hope at last, in wch my poor recovering Father Callowhill comes in for 1000l for his share. so that I hope to regain my property, & pay them by the way of the Govermt or wt arizes there. Ld Treasr I hope will lend me 7000l & receive it at new york for the service of the Governmt or forces, & give me 7 years to pay it in.[21] and I finde secretary Lownds[22] enclinable to encourage it as a practicable thing; and then I may ~~yet~~ still keep the Govermt or at least for a time.

to the Frds before mentiond I read thy Defence thou sentst me upon the Margen of the Impeachmt[23] stopt their mouths, & Is. Norris adding his own Knowledge to fortify some parts of it, rais'd a character for thee insteed of confirming of the ill character they had conceiv'd of thee. some fear least Col. Q.[24] had a designe in takeing my house[25]

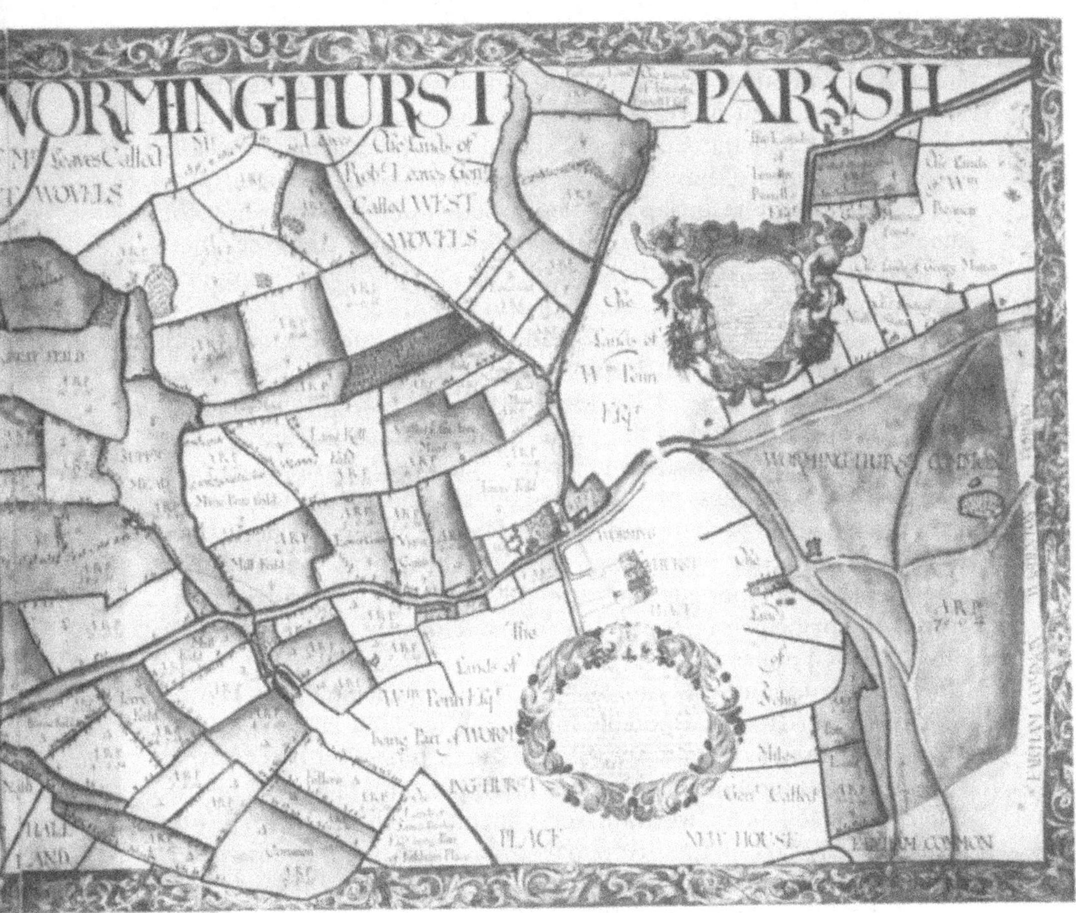

to recommend himselfe to the Fords by giveing them possession wch they are confident enough to pretend to goe over to gett, upon hopes of peoples readily atturning Tennants upon their Mortgage, especially, if the Queen had graunted them her letter to them to that purpose, as they had the presumption to ask her; but they were denyed & their Silly & sawcy petition dismist.[26] Since wch the Company[27] here have prevail'd upon the Mr of the Roles to oblige them to produce the companys books, wch they have conceald so closely, that their own Trustees, *Hall* & *Moss,* have ~~not to disting~~ [?] never seen or lookt into them; & tis thought that this affaire will consinderably assist my case, at least to render a fair Issue. I shall enclose the order of ~~Counsel~~ {Reference from the Queen & Councill} ~~&~~ to the Ld chancellor, & his report, as also D. Loyds letter to P. Ford agst me & my honest Interest.[28] I also here with enclose my original letter of advice upon severall Bills[29] drawn upon thee at 6 months Sight in country produce to a Considerable vallue.

I hope mine[30] by Capt. Hamilton is safely arrivd thy hands, as also mine to the Lt Goverr [31] wch Contained some account of complaints, wch must give him aime of wt must follow. I am glad T. Firman[32] has fo[u]nd out an other Tract of about 120,000 a[cr]es of good land & fitt for settlem^{ts} but more that mines so rich are so certainly found, for that will Clear the Country & me of all other encombrances & enable me to reward those that have approved themselves Faithfull to me & my Just Interest. clap some ~~body~~ body upon them as serv^{ts} for me; & per next send me some of the Oare to gett it tryed by the ablest of seperators here. I send thee a coppy of a lett^{r} [33] upon my application to get over such a person, that is ingenious & prudent, who is chief operator for the Copper & lead company[34] (mostly among our Frds) & I send thee & M. (Lofty) Sacher {each} a token of the silver ~~by~~ extracted out of the welch ~~lead & Copper~~ {mines} about 3000^{l} tother day being coyn'd in the town, & the mark of the union on it all, ~~&~~ the first mild or stampt since it was made.[35] And pray, if you are assured of the goodness of your oare, send us some Barrels of it, wch may be better, & perhaps more expeditiously seperated here than there, wch would be a good and a much cheaper as well as better Cargoe than any other you can raise. this is w^{t} Dr. Right[36] advises me, who is the principall of those that follow & directs the so profitable Silver Leaden mines afore mentioned.

The Black sand mine that came wth Is. Norris in a leather Bag proves no better than Iron as a notable melter tels me, Jo^{n} Haddon whose Daughter is married to old Ant. Sharps son in Jersey.[37] I had 2 letters from differ~~ent~~ing hands as sending me tryals but Isaac gave me no other, & so tell them w^{n} thou seest them. encourage Searches & dispatch Semplars of the divers oares per first. w^{t} is that Mitchell[38] that thou fearest is insincere?

I send thee a Crown piece of the welch Silver, wth the union Stampt. I enclose the Report containing the petition ~~&~~ in it.[39] cos. Spring^{t} [40] being down the river could not have it; but hope to write again before the fleet goes out of the channell But Moses Austell goeing send this not finisht by ⅓, with a Coppy of the Report where all Sticks at present, an accommodation being in hand, & the mony raised at least subscrib'd by able hands to pay the agreem^{t}. we are all pretty well, thro mercy. Jo^{n} carpenter has divers tokens, from Johnne & his mother.[41]

ALS. Penn Papers, Letters of the Penn Family to James Logan, HSP. (*Micro.* 13:421.)

1. The Treasury office was in Whitehall; the lord treasurer was Sidney Lord Godolphin.

2. Possibly *Micro.* 13:274, which was written in the summer of 1707, although not sent until Jan. 1708.

3. David Lloyd.

4. Philip Ford, Jr.

5. George Whitehead, William Mead, and Thomas Lower, to whom the Pennsylvania Assembly had previously complained in 1704 and 1706 (see docs. 139, n. 18; 143, n. 2). On 10 June 1707 the Assembly sent a further remonstrance to WP via Whitehead, Mead, and Lower, repeating their call for the dismissal of John Evans and James Logan and threatening to appeal to the queen (see *PA*, 8th ser., 1:768-73).

6. Although WP was technically a prisoner for debt within the jurisdiction of the Fleet prison, he was allowed to lodge at the Old Bailey. WP reported in Mar. 1708 that

he was "under restraint" and could not attend the Board of Trade (*Micro.* 13:418), but the fact that docs. 147 and 149 were both written at other locations in London implies that WP was permitted out of the confines of his lodgings. See headnote to doc. 117.

7. John Evans.

8. See doc. 129.

9. See doc. 133, nn. 3, 6.

10. See ibid., text at nn. 9-10.

11. Susanna Harwood, Sr., a Quaker widow and Philadelphia shopkeeper, had been imprisoned for debt but was released by Evans and allowed to abscond. See doc. 149, text at n. 6; Hinshaw, 2:372; *Minutes of the Provincial Council,* 1:578; *Micro.* 8:128; Philadelphia Monthly Meeting, Abstract of Minutes, 1:472, GSP.

12. This passage seems to have been written over in part and then crossed through, probably by James Logan, who at one point added the words "his Mistaken Notions."

13. Charles Gookin (b. c. 1662), an Anglican Irish soldier, was approved by Queen Anne as lieutenant governor of Pennsylvania in July 1708. Raimo, *Governors,* p. 328.

14. It did not take long for Gookin to reassess his position. See doc. 165.

15. Yet see doc. 149, text at n. 19.

16. Thomas Erle (1650?-1720), of Charborough, Dorset, was a parliamentarian and soldier. He worked for the accession of William III and had a distinguished military career under William and Anne. *DNB;* Basil D. Henning, ed., *The House of Commons, 1660-1690* (London, 1983), 2:268-69.

17. William Cadogan (1675-1726) of Dublin, later first Earl Cadogan, was a parliamentarian who had a lengthy political and military career under William III, Anne, and George I. *DNB.*

18. Ingoldsby, a prominent military family of Buckinghamshire and Ireland. *DNB.*

19. Possibly a relative of William Morris (d. 1680), who had served as WP's land agent in Cork, Ire. *PWP,* 1:133n, 564, 575.

20. See headnote to doc. 108.

21. Contrary to WP's hopes, this offer never materialized.

22. William Lowndes.

23. Outraged by Logan's belligerent opposition to its policies, the Pennsylvania Assembly had drawn up articles of impeachment against him in Feb. 1707. These articles and Logan's answers are printed in *Minutes of the Provincial Council,* 2:344-47, 353-56. Logan evidently sent to WP a combined version of articles and answers; this has not been found. The impeachment proceedings foundered in May 1707 when Gov. Evans refused to try the case (ibid., 2:364-72).

24. Col. Robert Quary.

25. Quary had agreed to rent Pennsbury for seven years (see doc. 139, n. 46). At this time, however, matters were at an impasse because of developments in the Ford case. See *Micro.* 13:362.

26. See docs. 118, 119, 120.

27. The Free Society of Traders.

28. David Lloyd's letter to Philip Ford, Jr., has not been found.

29. See doc. 144.

30. See doc. 139.

31. WP's letter to John Evans is doc. 138.

32. Thomas Fairman. See doc. 139, n. 29.

33. Not found.

34. The Quaker, or London, Lead Company, chartered in 1705, was involved in the commercial production of lead and silver in England and Wales. The company was providing the English government with most of the silver it needed for the new coinage issued under Sir Isaac Newton. See Arthur Raistrick, *Quakers in Science and Industry* (New York, 1950), chap. 5.

35. The Act of Union between England and Scotland had been formalized in May 1707.

36. Dr. Edward Wright (d. 1728), a London Quaker physician, chemist, and inventor, was a charter member of the Quaker Lead Company and a major contributor to the invention and perfection of the reverberating furnace for smelting lead ores with coal. See Raistrick, *Quakers in Science and Industry,* pp. 163, 166, 168-72.

37. John Haddon (c. 1654-1724), a Surrey Quaker blacksmith and anchor maker and a charter member of the Quaker Lead Company, gave numerous properties in West New Jersey to his daughter, Elizabeth, in 1701. Contrary to what WP claims, she

did not marry a son of Anthony Sharp; rather she married John Estaugh. See Raistrick, *Quakers in Science and Industry*, p. 167; doc. 45, n. 36.

38. François Luis Michel (1675-1720), of Berne, formerly in the French Army, had come to Pennsylvania to explore for mines. Logan later reported to WP on 18 June 1708 (*Micro.* 13:468): "Mitchel {the Swiss} that has been chiefly employ'd in search of the Mines is not . . . I doubt to be depended on by us." In 1709 Michel settled in New Berne, N. C. See Leo Schelbert and Hedwig Rappolt, eds., *Alles ist ganz anders hier* (Freiberg, 1977), pp. 33, 39-40.

39. That is, the report of Lord Chancellor Cowper noting the petition of Bridget Ford. See doc. 120.

40. Herbert Springett.

41. John and Hannah Penn.

148
TO JAMES LOGAN

Loveing Friend Lond. 18 3m [May] 1708
James Logan

My last promest this.[1] Know then that I enclose the coppy I promest of D. Lds letter to PF[2] by wch thou wilt be furnish'd with an infallible profe ~~of the~~ of the conspiracy agst me, & whether such a Traiterous Person ought not to be expell'd a Country as well as be made uncapable of any Trust & employ, as he was declared by the Lords Justices of Engld, & the Lds Comrs for Trade & Plantations;[3] If the Proprietary & Goverr of any Country can look well upon or ever oblige such a people as doth, in defiance of the Crown here & me & my Interest & authority there & here, show such respect to a Delinquent, & a vile Ingrate. one, that wont do right & obstinately maintain the wrong thing, witness his folly that provoaked the Govermt & his perversness before 12 Frds one evening at my house that would not Suffer him to bow so farr as to acknowledge it a fruit of passion, or anger to Colonel Quarry {&c:} rather than disrespect or undutifullness to the late King, & therfore to beg his Pardon, & I would do my best to make Such a submission.[4] I Say again, wt Proprietor & Goverr would care one jot wt comes of such a foolish (if not wicked) people. The Lord turn them & forgive them their deceivableness (& blind I hope) disaffection & defection from their poor Frd & Govr that has made them & their prosperity hundreds of times yea, ever Since they were a people, my care & expence of time mony & Interest, well Known to the Lord, & my many packets both before & Since I return'd from thence, bear witness therunto; & as they use me (who have been of the riseing & geting Side, & I & mine of the Sincking & loosing) God, that brought me thither, & that place to me (and which {has} made the most of them wt they are) will use them & theirs. And so soon as my bonds are broak & I have visitted Frds in a Generall meetg way, in Each County (wch fifty days will do) the Lord wiling) I goe to Bristol, & thence for Irland, whence I determin for you, if it please God, and I hope next Spring if not next fall to sett forth. for I am bent so comfort & confirm the Good, Satisfy & pleas the moderate, & convince the unreasonable, or expose them as enimys of the Common peace & publick good.

I Send thee a Coppy of my letter to S. C. T. S. Gr. O. C. Pew. R. H. & R. ellis[5] to be communicated as in wisdom they may see Good for quietness Sake wch wth one I think to the Govr[6] I satisfyed G. W. W. M (not the least pleas'd with it) & T. L.[7] who were contented to only Take notice of D. LLs work as from Frds & not as from a Spea{ker} of an assembly.[8] & they were pleasd wth thy Defence as in my last, abt a week Since, Is. Norris reading both, & commenting usefully upon the same, J. Fd Hen. G. Sil. Grove,[9] &c: present as I remember; also I send thee my exceptions to the Fords acctts & demands after the best method,[10] wch promote as may be needfull. I farther Send thee a Duplicat of a former letter, adviseing of Bills of exchange drawn on thee,[11] & accepted for debts owing here, & Six months tim Given, & payable in the country produce; wch ends this lettr hopeing for a farther occasion, the windes being at present out of the way & I hear Is. N. is Still at Portsmouth.[12]

Frds of Bristoll have Subscribd 2000l of wch my Far Call. 1000l, finely recover'd. Here[13] they have writt 3000l and 2000l from Irland, of wch I pay one makeing in all, the compromise as we hope & take for graunted. and if honest Frds there will help to discharge some of this debt, to receive it leisurely there, I shall take it kindly; but Such as shall help me at my cost, for their own unreasonable advantage, I shall ever look upon them wth a mean regard. I am to have 7 years time to pay it in, & at 6l per Cent Carry it kinde to capt Finey,[14] to whom I intend a favour all I can & as soon as possible. Give my Dr. love to all Frds wth my wifes, especially the right minded, & remember me to all in & out of authority that deserve it, & that of all nations & perswasions. Thou must needs excuse my poor wife to H. Hill[15] for not writeing to her, so weary of her Journey, & so much to do upon her arrivall from Bristoll; but intends it, if can per this opertunity. Jo. Fothergill & w. Armsteed[16] now in town, & from whom I have had the best acctt of Persons & things. No news of the union[17] yet, wch looks clowdy. It cant come in a better time; for my Cos. Rooth ows me 16l of the first, & all the last Bill. wt comes of the Jamaica business,[18] I fear that will be a loss. I have to the full Kindly treated parson Evans,[19] who has succeeded mightily in his busine{ss} & his enimys will feel it. New York will be happy in their New Governour Ld Lovelace,[20] the reverse of to'ther of that name;[21] being a sober, good temper'd man, & honorable. He came with Esqr Blaithwaite[22] to see me first. let them use him well, & friends be sure to be of the first that congratulates his arrivall, & recommend themselves by a just regard to his good qualitys. so with all our true love, I conclude at present

Thy assured Friend
Wm Penn

I am teized with Churchill abt his Books,[23] makeing me his Debtor would a Stopt the summs in Esqr. Butlers hands for Stock he bought of mine when he purchassed worminghurst.[24] He is a Parlm[t] man. I gave 4500[l] for it, & sould it for 6050[l] after I had cutt down 2000[l] of Timber

Direct to w[m] Popple secret[r] to the Lords of trade &c: at whit hall or J. Addison esq[r] [25] at Lord Sunderlands office there, & the Inclosed for me. Jo. Sanders is in Bedlam.

ALS. Penn Papers, Letters of the Penn Family to James Logan, HSP. (*Micro.* 13:434.) Endorsed: My lett[r] to J.L. Docketed: Proprietor 18. 5[mo] 1708 | per I Norris received 2/9 7 Aug. 708. Further docketed: copied 1708.

1. See doc. 147.

2. David Lloyd's letter to Philip Ford, Jr., has not been found.

3. In 1699 the Board of Trade learned that David Lloyd had ridiculed the king's authority in a suit brought by Robert Quary as judge of vice admiralty. The board recommended to the lords justices that Lloyd be removed as attorney general of Pennsylvania and never be allowed in future to hold public office. When William III concurred in this decision, the board ordered WP to dismiss Lloyd. See *PWP,* 3:576-78; Roy N. Lokken, *David Lloyd, Colonial Lawmaker* (Seattle, 1959), pp. 85-86.

4. The meeting described here took place in 1699 or 1700 when WP, having returned to Pennsylvania, was trying to reach an accommodation with Lloyd. By Apr. 1700 he had removed Lloyd as attorney general and in May suspended him from the Council. See *PWP,* 3:592; *Minutes of the Provincial Council,* 1:604; Lokken, *David Lloyd,* pp. 81-82.

5. Samuel Carpenter, Thomas Story, Griffith Owen, Caleb Pusey, Richard Hill, and Rowland Ellis. See doc. 143.

6. John Evans. See doc. 149.

7. George Whitehead, William Mead, and Thomas Lower.

8. Lloyd had written to the English Friends in his guise as speaker of the Assembly. See doc. 139, n. 18.

9. John Field, Henry Gouldney, and Silvanus Grove.

10. Possibly doc. 121C.

11. Doc. 144.

12. Isaac Norris and his family, who had been visiting England, were being delayed by unfavorable winds in their return to Pennsylvania. They finally embarked from Portsmouth on the *Mary Ann* on 24 May 1708. Norris Papers, 7:172, HSP.

13. In London.

14. Probably Capt. Samuel Finney.

15. Hannah Hill, wife of Richard Hill, whose son had died in Nov. 1705. See doc. 141.

16. John Fothergill (1676-1745), of Wensleydale, Yorks., and William Armitstead, or Armistead (b. 1675), of Giggleswick, Yorks., were traveling Quaker ministers. About 18 June 1707 they had embarked from Pennsylvania to England via Barbados and were thus able to give WP news from his colony. Digests of Quaker Records, Yorks.; *Micro.* 13:233.

17. Here WP is referring to the *Diligence,* or *Happy Union,* which apparently did arrive by Sept. 1708. See doc. 154.

18. See docs. 132, 137.

19. Evan Evans, who had come to England in 1707 to respond to claims by Col. Robert Quary that he was too friendly to Gov. John Evans, WP, and the Quakers in Pennsylvania. He brought back silver communion pieces from Queen Anne for Christ Church. Charles P. Keith, *Chronicles of Pennsylvania* (Philadelphia, 1917), 1:342-43.

20. John Lovelace (d. 1709), fourth Baron Lovelace, a colonel of the horse guards, had been recently commissioned captain general and governor-in-chief of New York and New Jersey, arriving in New York about the end of the year; he died in May 1709. *DNB;* Raimo, *Governors,* p. 254.

21. Here WP is referring either to John Lovelace (1638?-1693), third Baron Lovelace, a cousin of the new governor of New York, and a notorious drinker and gambler (*DNB*), or to Gov. Francis Lovelace (d. 1675), of New York, 1667-73, who lost his colony to the Dutch in 1673 and was imprisoned by the duke of York for debt (see Raimo, *Governors,* pp. 240-41).

22. William Blathwayt had been dismissed from the Board of Trade in 1707; he was now an M.P. and auditor general of plantations. Basil D. Henning, *The House of Commons, 1660-1690* (London, 1983), 1:667.

23. See doc. 76, n. 37.

24. See doc. 145.

25. Joseph Addison (1672-1719), essayist, poet, parliamentarian, and statesman, was under-secretary of state to Sir Charles Hedges and his successor, the earl of Sunderland, 1706-9.

149
TO JOHN EVANS

London Thy honest frs [1] house
27th 3 moth [May] 1708

Esteemed Frd

since my Last to thee 15th 3 moth 1707[2] by Capt Hamilton, I have not till 2 days agoe of the 28th 7br 1707[3] reced one title from thee tho soe necessary to both our affairs, as well to my Enemies Contrivances agst my Property, as the Seditions agst the Govermt by that Letter thou wilt perceive the Objections to thy Conduct, since wch by other folks Letters, I have heard of an Extream false step abt a Law made at N. Castle[4] to the prejudice of the fundamentall Right and Claime of the Province; vizt free and undisturbed passage to and from the Province in my Patent most Pathetically[5] worded, wch Seemes to have united the Sevll Partys agst thee and me, in Consequence upon a Common Intrt wch Indeed Looks like a finishing Stroke to thy unhappiness, however that is not all, for the Charges of a Lewed Deportmt at Conostogoe is mightily aggravated wth thy Journey Incognito to bring the mor and Daughter[6] on their voyage or at least Journey to the Ship after Soe much freedom with the [illegible deletion] Later,[7] at Least knowing of the formers escapeing out of Prison to the Loss of her Credrs, two such Capitall breaches of God's Commandmts, and that of the Debtoress, directly in the very eye of the Govermt that all I have been able to prevent some of our friends from goeing to Queen and Councill, with the Complaints from the Assembly there and rather quietly to lay thee aside after Soe many years being in, wch is Customary wth [the Queen or] Councill to doe as in the Case of the [Duke of Ormond,] Ld Cornberry[8] &c than by an obstinate dispute to have such things exposed, as must have disabled thee from other services or Employmts that yet thou mayst Stand fairly for this I thought the best way and so Some of thy truest and kindest friends to prevent the mallice of Some ill Spirits, So that thou must give Such a Prooff of thy discretion as may bespeake thy Prefermt in Some Station not Less beneficiall.

Esqr Lawton,[9] Parson Evans,[10] Netervill[11] thy uncle[12] & Mor have been acquainted wth the reason of this, for no Longer agoe than the begining of this Month 3 Persons[13] who had received the Last as well as former assemblys Invectives agst thee, Came with a Sort of Impeachmt from them there agst thee to the Queen and made me their last Complem[t] and if rejected to proceed to Queen and Councill; so that w[t] we have done was the best that offered for thy advantage Some things being to likely to be proved, and by Some upon the Spott, that are of a very reprovable nature and Injustice to my own Character there & here, I could not any long[r] reject their request, to Change hands, & therefore I Petitioned the Queen in those Termes,[14] and that was all the reason I gave for praying her approbation of my Choice and Commission. Now know that I take thy care of my Int[rt] in Minerall matters very kindly, and Shall certainly hold my Self obliged if Mitchell[15] be made true, and that the vallue rises as I have heard by J. Logan &c who I perceive by thine Seems to Guess rather than know, this on that Subject was dated [this mo[th] a year or] near it,[16] Such an affair Judiciously and as honestly Performed will quickly end my misfortunes, and enable me to doe wonders for that poor Country after all the Ingratitude as well as Injustice of Some Perverse tempers in it whome God forgive I hope the Tenor of this Letter will not be able to provoke thee to either, but after w[t] has been Said, and reasons for it, rather quicken thee to recommend thy Self to the Services I and mine here away may be able to rend[r] thee in a future regard; and for the new Castle people, they may happen to find themselves mistaken at Last, I mean, the Lower Countys busy folks that have not used me wth Justice or gratitude or Common Civility, but I Committ my Cause to God ag[st] all my unworthy Enemys of whome R. Hallwell[17] I have heard is the Greatest, time fails me, the bearer is sent for to Leverpoole, where the Ship Lyes, he has taken passage in, and sets out to morrow early upon his Journey of w[ch] I had no notice till to day by himself, Lord Lovelace Sailes in a Month and I think by him to write w[t] I omitt now, and therefore Conclude, with the good wishes of me, mine and all thy best friends w[t] I am and desire to be

Thy assured friend to serve
thee when I may

29. 4[m] [June] 1708

I have yesterday thine of the 12 of the 11[m](Jan) 1707/8[18] and shall [improve] it the best I can w[th] [those] warmed ag[st thee]. But it comes 2 months to late, a pu[bl]ick war or a change of hands must be, & accordingly, Colonel Charles Gooking will Succeed thee, who will I hope give at least some content. He has commanded men, is about 48 years of age,[19] & intends to sow all he has in the Country & become a planter & will waite on Lord Lovelace that goes in 3 weeks they say. I hoped for a word about the oare thy last mention'd. Thy unckle Arter[20] brought thine yesterday, is well so thy Mother. Thy Frds wish the well, but nobody more than thy reall Friend

Wm Penn

T. Grey is wth me & gives thee his respects. Endeavours are for thy Service here by thy Frds.

LS. Weyerhauser Library, Macalester College. (*Micro.* 13:447.) Docketed: coppy to Colonel Evans | 27. 3m 1708. The closing section of the letter, dated 29 June, is in WP's hand. The editors have supplied, in brackets, words obliterated in the original, from a printed version in the *New England Historical and Genealogical Register,* 26:429.

1. Probably Thomas Evans; see doc. 63, n. 1.

2. See doc. 138.

3. Not found.

4. See doc. 133, text at nn. 9-11; *Micro.* 13:026, 135, 148, 200, 210.

5. Probably a mistake for "particularly." For the free right of entry to and exit from Pennsylvania specified in the 1681 charter, see *PWP,* 2:64.

6. Susanna Harwood, Jr. See doc. 147, n. 11.

7. Latter.

8. James Butler, second duke of Ormonde, had been replaced as lord lieutenant of Ireland in 1706 after a brief but stormy rule (*DNB*). Edward Hyde, Viscount Cornbury, after an equally controversial rule as captain general and governor-in-chief of New York, had just been recalled in Apr. 1708 (*CSPC, 1706-1708,* p. 720).

9. Charlwood Lawton.

10. Evan Evans, minister of Christ Church in Philadelphia.

11. Probably John Netterville, son of Robert Netterville, of Co. Meath, in Ireland, who was acting as an informant for Robert Harley. See *CTB, 1702-1707,* p. 384; HMC, *Report on the Manuscripts of . . . the Duke of Portland* (London, 1891-1931), 4:325-26; 8:278.

12. Arthur Evans. See below, n. 20.

13. George Whitehead, William Mead, and Thomas Lower. See doc. 147, n. 5.

14. See *Micro.* 13:464, where WP, "finding it convenient to Change Hands," petitions for approval of Charles Gookin as his new lieutenant governor.

15. François Luis Michel. See doc. 147, n. 38.

16. Not found.

17. Richard Halliwell.

18. Not found.

19. Yet see doc. 147, text at n. 15.

20. Arthur Evans was a London wine merchant. See Norris Papers, 7:104, HSP.

150

QUEEN ANNE'S APPROVAL OF GOVERNOR CHARLES GOOKIN

[18 July 1708]

At the Court at Windsor
the 18th of July 1708
Present
The Queens most Excellent Majesty

His Royal Highness[1]	Duke of Sommerset[5]
Lord Chancellor[2]	Earl of Sunderland[6]
Lord Treasurer[3]	Mr Secretary Boyle[7]
Lord President[4]	

Upon reading this Day at the Board a Representation from the Lords Commissioners of Trade and Plantations in the Words following Vizt

May it please your Majesty

In Obedience to your Maty's Order in Council of the 26th of last Month[8] relating to your Majesty's Royal Approbation of Captn Charles

Gookin to be Dept Govr of Pennsilvania and annexed Territories, We have required from Mr Penn the Performance of the Conditions therein expressed, and having accordingly received from him a Certificate of Security given in the Exchequer for Two Thousand Pounds[9] that the said Gookin shall duly observe the Acts of Trade, in the same Form as has been done for other Proprietary Governments, as likewise a Declaration and Promise under Mr Penns Hand that your Majesty's Approbation & Allowance of the said Gookin to be Dept Governour of the said Province & Territories shall not be construed in any Manner to diminish or set aside your Majesty's Claim of Right to the three lower Counties on Delaware River[10] whereupon we are humbly of Opinion that your Majesty do grant your Royal Approbation of the said Gookin to be Depty Governour of Pennsilvania without Limitation of Time and of the three Lower Counties during your Majesty's Pleasure only And we do further humbly lay before your Majesty a Draught of Instructions[11] for Mr Penn relating to the Acts of Trade to the like Effects as have been given to him and all other Proprietors of Plantations upon the like Occasion

Whitehall July the 8th 1708

All which is humbly submitted
Herbert J. Pulteny
Ph Meadows Cha Turner[12]

Her Majesty in Council is pleased to declare hereby her Royal Approbation of the said Gookin to be Depty Governour of Pennsilvania without Limitation of Time and of the three lower Counties on Delaware River during her Majesty's Pleasure only

William Blathwayt

Copy. Cadwalader Collection, HSP. (*Micro.* 13:502.)

1. Prince George of Denmark, Queen Anne's husband and lord high admiral.
2. Sir William Cowper.
3. Sidney Lord Godolphin.
4. Thomas Herbert (1656-1733), eighth earl of Pembroke and fifth earl of Montgomery.
5. Charles Seymour, sixth duke of Somerset.
6. Charles Spencer, third earl of Sunderland.
7. Henry Boyle.
8. See *CSPC, 1706-1708,* p. 771.
9. See *CSPC, 1708-1709,* p. 31.
10. This declaration (*Micro.* 13:494), dated 2 July 1708, follows exactly the same wording required by the Board of Trade in 1702 (see doc. 55C), except that Gookin's term as governor is unspecified, whereas in 1702 Gov. Hamilton had been approved for one year only.
11. Not found.
12. Three of these men were new members of the Board of Trade, appointed in 1707 and 1708: Henry Herbert (1654-1709), Lord Herbert of Cherbury; John Pulteney (d. 1726); and Sir Charles Turner (d. 1738). Sir Philip Meadows had served since 1696. *DNB;* Basil D. Henning, ed., *The House of Commons, 1660-1690* (London, 1983), 3:613; I. K. Steele, *Politics of Colonial Policy* (Oxford, 1968), pp. 20, 113, 175.

RENEWAL

September 1708–June 1709

By September 1708 the 63-year-old proprietor of Pennsylvania had been in debtor's prison for eight months, but his release was now in sight. The Fords had agreed to an out-of-court settlement of their Chancery suit, and WP reported that the lawyers were working out the final details (docs. 152–53). In October he paid the Fords £7600, all but £1000 of which was borrowed from a group of thirty-eight English and Irish Friends, including his father-in-law, Thomas Callowhill. Of these, nine became the trustees of Pennsylvania, with administrative power over the colony. WP told James Logan that he had recovered Pennsylvania "from the vilest of the earth" (doc. 158) and had granted the trustees "a fresh mortgage, without nameing that Base family therin" (doc. 155). In effect, the settlement of October 1708 gave WP some breathing room without resolving his financial problems. It transferred his debt from the hostile Fords to the friendly trustees, but it required him to pay back his new loan of £6600 in two years or lose possession of the colony to the trustees. He could raise little of this money from his English and Irish properties, which were heavily encumbered; the rents from his Irish estates were £2000 in arrears (doc. 156). In Pennsylvania, proprietary expenses continued to absorb much of WP's revenue. The trustees were empowered to collect all quitrents and taxes in the colony, but WP rather cavalierly disregarded this provision and instructed Logan to pay the new governor, Charles Gookin, his £200 salary out of proprietary funds.

After his release WP was able to visit his young children at school in Reading and to spend time with his wife, who was in poor health after the birth of their last child, who survived only a few months (docs. 152, 158). WP hinted broadly that he intended to move back to Pennsylvania with his family, provided the colonists assisted him financially (docs. 152–53, 159). He urged Logan to settle numerous land disputes in Pennsylvania and the Jerseys, to provide estates for his children, and to keep tabs on the mines being worked by former Governor Evans (docs. 154–55, 158–59). The resolution of the Ford case gave WP a marvelous sense of liberation and a renewed energy to address a wide range of problems that interested him. This can be seen in his two appeals to the English government on behalf of Pennsylvania merchants (docs. 151, 161); in his efforts to obtain naturalization for foreigners resident in Pennsylvania (docs. 154, 159); and in his proposals to the duke of Marlborough for a European parliament and for enlarged British territorial boundaries extending the North American empire west beyond the Mississippi (docs. 162, 163). Above all, he managed to quash the attempt Lord Baltimore had made while WP was in prison to gain legal title to the Lower Counties. On 23 June 1709 the Queen in Council affirmed the 1685 boundaries between Maryland, the Lower Counties, and Pennsylvania (doc. 166).

If WP was feeling renewed optimism about the years remaining to him, James Logan administered a strong antidote. There were bills to be paid, new commissioners of property to be named, complaints from Governor Gookin about his salary, anti-proprietary assemblies in Pennsylvania and the Lower Counties, difficulties in selling land because of the new mortgage, the necessity of repealing the Pennsylvania law for elections, and the knavery of David Lloyd and François Luis Michel (see docs. 157, 160). The Lower Counties posed a particularly serious problem. The Assembly at New Castle was contesting WP's right of proprietorship over them, and was preparing to petition Queen Anne. Logan believed that the New Castle representatives were hoping to establish their town as an independent trading center to rival Philadelphia. In May 1709 a French privateer plundered the town of Lewes, throwing into sharp relief the dilemma for the Quakers in power: how to defend the colony without sacrificing their peace testimony. They would not arm themselves; nor would they help to pay for military endeavors undertaken by non-Quakers, as shown in the Pennsylvania Assembly's refusal to support a proposed English expedition against the French in Canada (doc. 165). In June 1709 Logan told WP that he could no longer act effectively in Pennsylvania as his agent; he announced his intention to come to England to meet with his employer and discuss the future of the colony (doc. 165).

151
TO THE COMMISSIONERS OF THE CUSTOMS

[c. 11 September 1708][1]

Honrd Friends
The difficultys the Merchants of Pennsylvania lye under in their Trade are Soe many, that Should they not be removed commerce in that Colloney must drop wch may prove as fatall to the Islands as to my Goverm^{t} wch is known to be the Granary of the west Indies. It is the Interest of the Queen to Encourge Trade in all her Dominions, and

I'm sure we in our parts Shall not want it upon due application, but Gent the officers of the Customs being of yr appointment I shall without applying to any other Board lay Some of our Merchts grievances before yu, not doubting but yr Candor and prudence will redress them. in the first place the Merts Complain of the duty of 1d per £ for Tobacco is exacted in Cash upon entry before exportation wthout allowance for prompt payment, time given or allowance upon the Tob: being taken or lost, it cant be expected that in Pennsylvania where the greatest part of the Trade is Barter the Duty Should be paid in Cash,[2] therefore I hope yu will ordr it to be received in the Same Specie[3] unless yu Can think of Some other way to ease the Merts in this and the other part of their Complaint I have been allso Informed that the mistake of an officer in Clearings Coquets[4] Ignorance of mars [5] Inadvertences and very light mistakes wherein no wrong Could be done in the Queens Customs have been thought Sufficient reasons for a Seizure and Comdemnation,[6] in wch Cases it is not Just Merchts should Suffer for officers faults or Ignorance of a mar where no fraud is designed yet this would not be so hard could seizures be taken of Soe easyly and wth as Small Charge as in England, but there we must apply to the Admirallty, who when they find noe fraud Intended may discharge the Goods, yet not wthout rownd Charges Such are the fees of that Court.

Gent I offer not these things as Charges agst your officers who I hope performe their trust well but wt I aim at is to obtain from yu Such Certain Rules and directions for yr officers to walk by, that the Merts may be relieved in those matters. And once more be at Liberty to recover that part of their Trade, (I mean the Tob: Trade to the Islands) wch has been Some time at a stand and must Intirely fall Should the former methods Continue. I hope yu will excuse my recommending those matters once more to that Serious Consideration for they So nearly touch as well my owne Interest in particular as the Interest of the Merchts Collony in Generall that I am indispensibly oblieged in Justice to them and my Self to get wt relief I can in the Premises wch I am well assured will not be wanting to us from Gent of yr Character and reputaion[7] wthout puting our Selves to the Troube[8] of applying to any other place for redress and will be grate[fully received and] ever acknowledged by[9]

Your respectfull Friend
Wm Penn

P.S.
The Gentleman that brings this is my new Lieutnt Governour,[10] (well approved by the Queen who comes to wait upon you for your commands, wth a Gent lately arrived from that Province,[11] I am &c.

Copy. RG-21, Pennsylvania Historical and Museum Commission, Division of Archives and Manuscripts, Harrisburg. (*Micro.* 13:551.) Endorsed: A Letr to Comrs of | the Customs for | Trad. Docketed: Copy W Penn to Commrs of Cus[tom]s. The editors have identified, within brackets, obliterated words and sentences in the original from a printed version in *PA*, 1st ser., 1:149-50, erroneously dated Nov. 1703.

1. On 11 Sept. 1708 WP wrote to James Logan (*Micro.* 13:533) that he was enclosing a copy of the letter he had written to the commissioners of the customs.

2. On 9 Nov. 1705 Dep. Gov. Evans sent the Board of Trade an angry address "from all or most of the Traders of Note" in Pennsylvania, demanding that the tobacco customs collectors allow payment in kind. When WP in Feb. 1706 wrote to the Board of Trade about this matter, he was directed to the commissioners of the customs. See *Micro.* 12:377, 539, 645; *CSPC, 1704-1705*, pp. 682-84.

3. In kind.

4. A cocket is a document sealed by the customs officers and delivered to merchants as a certificate that their merchandise has been duly entered as having paid duty. *OED.*

5. Masters.

6. Here WP may be referring to the case of William Righton. See doc. 35, n. 16.

7. "Reputation."

8. "Trouble."

9. The remainder of the letter is taken from the printed version in *PA,* 1st ser., 1:150.

10. Charles Gookin.

11. Unidentified.

152
TO SAMUEL AND HANNAH CARPENTER

16. 7m [September] 1708

Deare samuell & Hannah Carpenter

I am truly sensible of, & thankfull for your love, & in that wch opened our hearts to the Lord & one an other, over all shortness, weakness, narrowness, Jealousy & the effects of the man's part, that has too much sway'd, & by it entangled, misguided, & frustrated us at one time or an other, to our wounding & exercise, I dearly salute you, & yours, and the worthy among you, as in the early day of our first & Innocent acquaintance, & wilderness Relation; desireing that the great & good God may renew us & preserve us to answear his many mercys & providences in our favour, before we lay down our heads, that it may be in peace & comfort wth his redeemed forever. amen. Dr. samll I leave outward things to J. Logan to informe thee of, & H. G. S. J. Gove, S. Wal.[1] &c: have also writt to thee[2] &c: in my affaire. 1o The agreemt is made wth the Fords & writeings neer adjusted by Counsill, & in two or three days will be engrost & Executed.[3] 2ly the sooner Frds there will quicken wt is due to me there, so as to pay off my assistants here, the sooner I shall, with my wife & children, be with you, the Lord enabling us as to our healths & Bodely ability. I hope wt my good Frds there will or can do, will be so Kinde in the manner of it (they justly being secured & repayd) as Frds here may see, they have no self ends in their helping of me. so soon as I am clear'd I goe to Reading school, for my childrens sake, & Board wth them.[4] hence in the Spring or 1st month, to Bristoll, for a month or two, & so to Haverford west[5] till 4th mo: Thence for Irland till the fall & so to you, if you are ready, & so I clear to come honorably to you. My heart has been ever almost with you, & no pretended necessitys (the mourning of my late years) shall call me over any more, as has been to my unspeakable griefe as well as prejudice every way. ~~I~~Well, I shall Say no more, but that I send you a new Gover^{r}.[6] I hope sober, & Friendly to us, & that will be Just to all & mercifull to Such as deserve it, & familier & humble as much as will Stand wth Goverm^{t}. I have refer'd him to thee, R: Hill, Is. N. Gr. O. Ca. P. T. S^{t} [7] & you to him, for hints & advice from time to time; and I hope neither I nor you will be {under} any disapointment in him.

The Ch. of Eng. Minister[8] comes, as ~~he assures me~~ I believe, wth an absolute disposition to be friendly & Neighbourly, & to meet us in Generall Dutys & virtues; pray be as easy, as truth will let you, towards him, for he professes to befriend ~~my~~ the Goverm^{t} & he has gott great Ground {here} of his enimys there, wch they will soon be Sensible of; thou mayst guess at them.[9] Now Know my Dr. wife has been safely delivered of a 2^{d} Hannah, the 5th instant, and our Stock is, 4 Boys, John, Thomas, Richard & Dennis, & 2 Girles, Margaret & Hannah, our first remarkable one, being at her Eternall rest.[10] she had the easiest time w^{n} it came, but the worst time since {of all of them} and yet so so, tho very weak. ~~our~~She Dear~~love~~y Salutes you all, as I do, & the inward family of Frds among you; and is no backfriend[11] to poor america. I desire thee give my love to Such as care for it; & communicate this to those to whom thou thinkest it may be serviceable. The Great and glorious God of Powr, of life of wisdom & Dominion, be with us & give us a blessed meeting in his own due time. amen.

I[12] Jonathan Dickeson & wife[13] be among you; pray let them have their share in our hearty remembrances.

now Dr. S~~h~~a~~s~~muell & Hannah fairwell {pray let none see that ab^{t} the Minister} I am

your affect Frd & Bro^{r} in the Truth
Wm Penn

we hope Is. N. & family are arrived[14] & poor Joan.[15] our love to them.

ALS. ACM. (*Micro.* 13:538.)

1. Henry Gouldney, Silvanus and Joseph Grove, and Samuel Waldenfield.
2. Not found.
3. See headnote to doc. 121.
4. WP was in Reading by February and stayed there for four or five months while eight-year-old John and six-year-old Thomas attended Joseph Nicholson's Quaker boarding school there. Nicholson (b. 1679), originally from Settle, Yorks., had married Mary Gome of Reading in 1705 and settled there. *Micro.* 14:010; Digests of Quaker Records, Berks. and Oxon., Yorks., GSP; docs. 158, 170, text at n. 27.
5. Haverfordwest is a seaport in Pembrokeshire, southwest Wales.
6. Charles Gookin.
7. Richard Hill, Isaac Norris, Griffith Owen, Caleb Pusey, and Thomas Story.
8. Evan Evans, minister of Christ Church in Philadelphia.
9. See doc. 148, n. 19.

10. Hannah Margarita Penn had died early in Feb. 1708. Digests of Quaker Records, Bristol and Som., GSP, does not provide the date of death but gives the burial date as 10 Feb.

11. False friend. *OED.*

12. Mistake for "If."

13. Jonathan and Mary Gale Dickinson had spent most of their time in Jamaica but were about to move permanently to Philadelphia. See doc. 132, n. 10.

14. Isaac Norris and his family had arrived in Philadelphia from England on 29 Aug. 1708. See Norris Papers, 7:191, HSP.

15. Apparently a former servant of the Penns. See doc. 159, text at n. 30.

153
TO SAMUEL CARPENTER AND OTHERS

Lond. 28. 7^{m} [September] 1708

Deare Friends & Bre^{r}

S. C. T. S. G. O. C: P. R. H. I. N. & R. E.[1]

My ancient Love, if you can beleive it, reaches to you as in times past & years that are gone, even in that divine root & Principle of love & life that made us neer to one an other, above all worldly considerations; where our life (I hope) is hid with X^{t}, even in God our Father, so that when he appeareth, we shall also appear wth him in Glory; & in the mean time through us, to those that love & waite for his appearance, as the desire of Nations; that we may Gloryfy God his & our ever lasting Father, in our bodys, soules & sprirts; In temporall & eternall affaires, being indeed none of our own, for so farr as we are, we are none of the Lords. A great mistery, but a great truth, & of absolute necessity to witness, & to be of the number of the chosen Nation, the Peculiar People, & Royal Priesthood of X^{t} & his glorious Kingdom. O my Friends! let all below this, keep on the left hand, & waite to feel these blessed things to inherit your right hand, & in faith & Courage Cry aloud to the Lord for his Renewings & refreshing powr, that may revive, & reenforce his work upon your hearts & mine, that our humility meekness, patience, self denial & charity, wth a Blameless walking may plainly appear & manifest the work of god upon our hearts to those that are without, wch is not only the way to bring up the Loyterers & gather in the careless ones to their Duty, but to fetch home & bring in the strainger & the very enimys of the blessed Truth to confess unto & to fall down before you & acknowledge that god is in you & for you of a Truth. If you please let thus far be read among Friends, & coppyed out.

Now my Dear Friends, as to outward things, thô I referr that off the Fords[2] &c: much to Frds, that writt before & now by this opertunity to you or some of you, yet I will hint particulars. 1. I have sent you a new Govern^{r} [3] of yeares & experience, of a quiet & easy Temper, that will give offence to none, nor too easily put up any, if offerd him, without hope of amendment. The Queen, very Graciously approv'd of him,[4] & at first offer, & gave him her hand to Kiss at last, being introduced by the Earle of Godolphin, Lord High Treasurer of Great Brittan, at windsor; & she added, *Sr I wish you a Good Journey & ~~am~~ Shall {be} ready to serve you.* He has promest me to avoide the Rock the former Govr split upon, as much as he can. He is sober, understands to command & obey; Moderate in his temper, & of ~~a~~ w^{t} they call a good family, his Grandfather Sr Vincent Gookin,[5] haveing been an early great Planter in Irland, in K. Jams the firsts time, & the First Charles's days, & intends if not ill treated, to Lay his bones as well as Substance among you; haveing taken leave of the War,[6] and both Irland & England, to live among you. And as he is not voluptuous, so he will be an examp{le} of thriftyness. In short, He has Instructions as much to the virtue, Justice & peace of the Country, as I can express my selfe, or you desire for your Comfortable liveing, I beleive. ~~p~~Pray therfore receive him Kindly, & express it by a modest subsistance, or rather Give it me to Give him, or how you please. He intends to board till a sister of his comes wth her family, ~~Comes~~ from Irland.

For the Fords business, Draughts are Engrosing, & doubt not but in 7 days they will be executed,[7] & if the Fleet is not sayled from Portsmouth, I may yet Send you word therof: tho Ld. Lovelace Govr of N. york (& a promessing on[e] indeed) presses, & the winde is faire, and the Admiralty Orders for sayling are gon down, & Govr Gookin leaves me to morrow.

I earnestly beseech you to assist J. Logan & who else the Trustees[8] for Repaym^{t} of the mony, here advanced, shall nominate, not only to get in, but turn into mony here, that best you are able, that I may come honorably to You, & Speedely, wch I purpose to do, as soon as you & these Frds here think fitt ~~& honorably~~ I should. Let me have this pledge of your love, and it shall be a lasting one, to advice & assist for the expedition of the matter; for be assured I long to be with you, & if the Lord bring me & mine well there, I hope not to returne, on almost any termes; at least not without y^{r} advice as well satisfaction For {Care of you, &} settling plantations for my poor Minors (for Planters {God wiling} they shall be in their Fathers {country &} (before great Merchants in their own native) land, and to visit Frds throughout the continent at least {will be ~~the~~ my chiefest business}. so my Deare Friends & Brethren, in first love, I leave you, commiting you & y^{rs} & all the Lords People among you, my own family & affaires to the mercifull Providences & orderings of our good Great & Gracious God, that welcom'd us in poor america wth his excellent love & presence, & will I hope once more, & remain

Your Faithfull & Loveing Friend & Brother
Wm Penn

Your School charter[9] goes with this Communicate this as[10]

ALS. Penn Papers, Tempsford Hall Papers, HSP. (*Micro.* 13:544.)

1. Samuel Carpenter, Thomas Story, Griffith Owen, Caleb Pusey, Richard Hill, Isaac Norris, and Rowland Ellis. WP regarded these Quakers as among his most trustworthy allies in Pennsylvania.

2. See headnote to doc. 108.

3. Charles Gookin.

4. See doc. 150.

5. Sir Vincent Gookin (1590?-1638), a Kentishman, settled in southern Ireland early in the seventeenth century and became one of the richest men in the region. In 1634 he published a bitter invective against the Irish people, which aroused a storm of protest and caused him to flee to England, where he remained until his death. *DNB*.

6. Gookin had served in the regiment of Lt. Gen. Thomas Erle during the War of the Spanish Succession. See *Micro.* 13:458.

7. The various documents ending the Ford affair were executed in the first week of Oct. 1708. See doc. 211.

8. In order to settle with the Fords, WP had borrowed £6600 from various English and Irish Quakers. As security for the loans, WP mortgaged Pennsylvania and the Lower Counties to a group of nine trustees who were given the right, until the debt was paid, to collect all rents, bonds, bills, and securities due to WP. See docs. 211F-H.

9. In Aug. 1706 Phila. Monthly Meeting had requested a new charter from WP for its free school (see doc. 131, n. 1). WP had delayed his response until this time because of objections raised by attorneys Robert West and Herbert Springett, and because of WP's preoccupation with the Ford case. See Norris Papers, 7:112-13, 119, HSP.

10. The letter ends at this point.

154
TO JAMES LOGAN

Lond. 29th 7m [September] 1708

James Logan
Lovg Friend
I have lately writt thee per I.N.[1] Thomas Potts,[2] & as I think, by Ephraim Jackson,[3] as also to Colonel evans:[4] at large, Since when, I have had a weak vindication from {him}[5] abt the Alarum[6] the N. Castle Act[7] &c: I am truly sorry at his over closeness from thee & other people honest & able to have advised him. However I have desired this Lieut Governr [8] to make his exit, as easy to him as possible. I perceive he intends to stay among you, & then it must be discoverys of Mines[9] there, or fear of meaner Circomstances here that detaines him. He owns to {me} he has not told thee of it, wch I took not so well of him, & fear there has not been that requisit good understanding, my affaires required. I impute it a good deale to thy dislike of his extreame craveing temper, wch in a young man is rare, & not so commendable. But for his Alarum, N. Castle act, his Beating the Conestable,[10] foulness wth young Harwood,[11] Reflexions upon his Conostogo journey;[12] & last, if not worst of all, his pardong of the Blackest crime in Gr. Jones's demure Son,[13] & that for mony, & as they say for so small a Summ as fifty pds that mony, wch is laying my reputation & that of the Govermt under me, & our character, in my

Judgemt very low indeed! I have shown my regard to him, & a faire mark I gave him to direct & excite his abilitys to, & his removall is made necessary to preserve the whole, as well as vindicate our Constitution & profession, to my great regrett. But I shall see, abt the new Discoverys, If he be a man of Cander & Gratitude or not. I have writt him, as plain, so very Kinde letters[14] yet to help & befriend wt I can, there or here; & expect his assistances. Now Know this is the Gentleman I send to Succeed him Colonel Gookin, read his character in mine to S.C. C.P. T.S Gr. O. &c:[15] He will entirely depend on thee for measures & Circumstances of Persons & things, In wch I will neither Doubt thy Sincerity nor ability; he has age, experience, virtue, moderation, good humour, a pretty nice Mathematician, & intends to begin a subscription for a Master of that & Macanickry in the Province, {(will not Ja: Tayler[16] be a fitt one)} Ingeneous Tollet[17] haveing been his Master 25 years agoe, who is now advanced to a commisr of the Navys place for his exceling abilitys in Mathematicall Knowledge by the Ministry. Give him the Knowledge of Partys, that he may direct his addresses & convers, as well as Politicks. E.E.[18] who gives the one from me, can say more, they are in a friendship; but the expression of it must be wth prudence. He has presented him {(E.E.)} for his Church 2 as Gawdy & Costly Common prayers Books, as the Queen has in her chapple, and intends as fine a Communion table {Cloth}, wch charms {the Baby in} the Bishop of Lond.[19] as well as Parson E. But is of a soldiers Religion; well dissended, & intends to lay his Bones as well as Lodge his substance among you, if well treated. *Make the best & the most of him.* I'le give him at the rate of two hundred pds per annum Eng. sterling till the assembly gives him a maintenance, wch will be 300l per annum upon the old calculation, & 250 as mony will be next Spring and no more pretentions of fines, forfietures and all other perquisits & Royaltys,[20] wch are to stand to me or my Revenue. Over wch pray super-intend with all care, that being all the Income I can call my own, till the Debt here, that redeems the Province &c: from the Fords, be answeared. & pray returne it as it comes, by the best opertunitys, and first.

Gett the Govr into a good Lodgeings, as a good substantiall Frds, or Robt Ashton or a churchmans, wel-affected to the Govermt and let them be reasonable; for he is a thrifty & Spareing man & easily satisfyed.

I Doubt not to send thee an exemplification of our end wth the Fords,[21] & It will not abate of thy Credit, that thy abilitys, industry & integrety are to come under the {Knowledge,} inspection & approbation of those ingeneous men, that will be their Trustes[22] who help me in this affaire. wherefore rouse up & be vigorous and executive, I desire thee, & beg Frds assistance once for all, that being delivered from this debt, I may come to you a free man, wch I purpose to do forthwith; But see that nothing be disposed of at under rates, for that is a dear help. I hope the Traders of all Perswasions, well affected to our Govermt or me in particular to accept of wt securitys & monys worth in thy hands, & make them Returnable hither the cheapest way to me. for more hast than good speed, may please the hasty to be reemburst, but make ~~me~~ {me} pay the whole claime of the Fords, by under rateing {Sales of} Lands &c: wch I refused to pay them. See {to} that, I desire thee. I know theyl choose no body that will not agree wth thee, I hope I. Norris will be the man they'le Joyn with thee, or that is to deal with thee for them. Fords assigne to me, and I give frds a fresh Mortgage, at two years Distance before possession,[23] only they have powr to make the best of my Debts owing me in the Country, & yearly income, of quitrents for their repaymt. Now, or Never. I have writt by Ch. Gookin to Frds,[24] I hope a moveing & effectuall letter, they will, I beleive, shew it thee, for their reall aid, without earnings by me, viz. S. Carpr. T. Story C. Pewsy, Gr. Owen, R. Hill, I. Norris, ~~E~~R. Ellis and to Communicate, as they Saw serviceable; especially the Genll part of it.

For the Naturalization of Straingers[25] I being now at liberty[26] & the Parliamt to sett, fear it not. yet send me per first a list of all in the Country: for the Speakers Proffit contests it,[27] no man endeavouring it more under a personall Confinemt than I did, but bid them be easy, do as formerly & not heed the empoysened breath of our Enimys, they are safe from me & mine, by my charter, and I shall get them either naturalised or endenisend by the Queen.

I have told thee I have gott the Comrs of the Customs to releive the Traders in reference to the Customs due on Tobacco,[28] a coppy of my letter {to them} goes now, & one I sent thee before, wch they answeared me ~~about~~ at their full bord, should be so no more.[29]

For the Laws,[30] they are delay'd by my Circumstances, as is the Runing of the line,[31] but the next ships shall bring you Directions, for Ld. Bal.[32] wilingly waved it as yet.

C. Q.[33] is the man I told thee, for because the man[34] thou so much recommended to[35] as an honest man, & writt by, had too much conscience to sacrefice wholy to his nett, he has writt as ill as he could agst him to the Bp.[36] & soci[e]ty for Prop. Evang.[37] & the worst of the Insinuation is that he too much countenances the Depty & Interest of me & my Hereticall Profession. verbum, sat.[38]

~~I have drawn upon thee~~ pray act accordingly, with great prudence, by advice of that black Gentleman,[39] & such other as you can trust, the Dept. Goverr [40] to be sure for one, who is naturally Silent. I shall not be unactive here &c.

I have an able & Smart man or two to refresh & give fresh motion to your Justice there, that will follow by the first ships after these of the present Fleet.

Samll Vause has, with acknowledgemt of his fault writt Large to thee[41] by way of the Barb. Packet. ship Dilligence alias Union & goods &

Freight is adjusted, at the best rates. but the mony will not be toucht except one hundred pds, in less than 3 months after Disposall. J. Ascew was for seling all to Coots,[42] as giveing the best price, agst S.V.s opinion who is a meek man. J. As. under vallues the tobacco for Virginia, & that loss will follow upon it. 40l per annum is all that the Gentlewoman[43] will be allowed, and the last Bill yet due. She is an Irish Knights[44] wife, & my Cousin[45] has nothing in his hand of hers. She must write & press, or thou must desist accommodation. a Small token comes now from Lady Bridges[46] per ~~Capt~~ Govr Gookin, I suppose Hood & scarfe.
Forget not my East & west Jerseys interest, not involved in this business; to Improve it the best thou canst. also to get ~~H~~W Hagues Mortgage If the Young Lad[47] be at N.Y. or N. Jersy 'twas offerd for ten pds to me long agoe {by his Mother,} all dead but he. pray look after the swiss Capts Plantation {(Charrier)}[48] for me, [illegible deletion] in N. Castle County, lately fallen; a good thing T. Grey says.
Hast thou done nothing yet wth w. Biddle abt Beumonts 300 acres upon Rancocas Creek[49] taken up at first by the w. Jersey Commisrs for poor Beumont, & if W. B. will not secure it to the man, to whom I am Assigne, at a dear purchass, let him Know I must seize the Island, ~~b~~fore Pensberry, of wch he has only permitt for 2 lives, as I remember it, & wt I would not Part with for 1000l this mony here, so much I vallue it. let not this be the meanest thing in thy thoughts, besides yt Island, tho the channel goes betwen it & Pennsberry, yet it alway belonged to the Indians of our Side that lived at Sepassin,[50] now Pennsberry. move in it as most prudent or advisable.
Give Capt. Cocks widdow[51] all reasonable satisfaction, her lettr [52] comes back. but I will pay none of Colonel Markhams Debts.[53] end wth Jacob Simcock, who threatens me to goe to Frds abt a story If not answeard {by me}. I aver I was to pay no Interest to his father. however hope to see you in a year and half at fathest, & may then end it. I am glad you have done wth Rabshaca Rakestraw,[54] one of wicked Loyds tools of clamour. I am pleasd to hear thy accusers are more so for thy zeal for me than reall faults of thy own,[55] & so I count upon.
I have had one hundred pds of Colonel Gookin, wch pay him so soon as Possible thou canst for his Supply and let Stephen Gould, my servt & now the Governors clark, Six pounds. He is an Ingenious Lad. a good Scholler, & somwt of a Lawyer, being abt 2 years in Counselor Poordons[56] service as clerk, a man of 8, or 900l per annum. his mother was a stony stratford Penn,[57] old Arthurs Daughter[58] that was housekeeper at Chelsea Colledge.[59] ~~sh~~ His fathers side, Gentleman of 3, or 400l per annum but left his Father ~~to be~~ [illegible deletion] {upon a religious acct}.
Here is a Complaint agst your Govermt that you suffer publick Mass, in a scandalous manner, pray send the matter of fact, for ill use is made of it agst us here.

watch the Queens officers that they Trade not, & wt thou canst detect of Indirect methods, or chargeing Traviling expences when they do not stir upon the Queens {acct,} Send me word of it.

Remember Byfields case, that I may have it, & trye to bring it to a reference there or here, or He will complain to Queen & Councill. Kings case.[60]

Stand by Pet. Bard agst that vile J. Moor.[61] I am extreamly Prest in poor An Harrisons case abt Calvert,[62] for she is reduced very Low, after her charitable disposition, & really wants it, fail not pray to give an act of it per first.

J. Hogg[63] of N. Castle is indebted to one here, who persecutes me for to urge him to return her the Improvemt of the Goods they entrusted him wth when he went over. ~~s~~He is a frd if alive, & the meeting was at his house at N. Castle when I was there.

Thou hast forgot, Birds, Blew & yellow, fine furs for {Muffs,} petticots {[illegible deletion]} {cloaks} or to Line mens Coats {or for Counterpans,[64] and Green wax, so easy to gett, & {would} excuse greater presents, wth a better acceptance also, among those that serve me. pray forget them not among thy more weighty affaires. ~~pray~~ also about the Naturalization, it will be necessary that the Partys send 10 shillings per head, over per first, wch will be an easy purchass ~~for~~ of their Freedom, & I will be responsable for its disposall.

Pray goe to the Bottom wth Colonel evans about the Mines & wt is become of Michel,[65] who are lett in the secreet where they are, & who have workt in them. & examin if they have not been workt & embezeld by & for {Persons of} other Colonys, if not much of the oare in Gross, or but once fined into some parts of Europe. It is a Test upon J. Evans's Honour & regard to me. I take his stay (if he stays) to be a proof he beleives it & Stays to benefit himselfe, by gain, & recommending his care, secrecy & justice {to me}.

Let not poor Pensberry be forgotten, or neglected, and employ Wm Watson (that comes from Bristoll, wth Innocent Tho: Potts (who brings a Packet for thee; if that honest man relishes him well, as to his sobriety & faithfulness. He gives thee a letter[66] to, as I remember) be employd, as first or 2d there, to keep up the Housen, the farme & Gardens, till we come. pray hast thou from Dr. Cox's son[67] a Bond of mine to John Etheridge[68] of two Hundred pds, to have his Interest in salem Tenth of upon Major Fenings Proprietys. & send me {an} acct per first returne. write per Packet boats as well as directly. I leave it open till I see Goverr Gookin come to me, for it may be he goes not till ~~2~~3 days hence, & then I can tell thee I have ended wth the Fords.

What ev Whatever thou doest, make up the acctt at 300l per annum your ~~Rate~~ rate & calculation, when I sent him over Governor John Evans I meane, & not one penny more, counting all over plus's, by fines, forfietures & all Royaltys, Proprietary or Governour benefits, to my credit & profitt, and If the honour I have done him {by such a station,} & Subsistance of 300^{l} per, to so young & unexperienced a man, obliges him not, but he must picke my bones in all my distresses (and truly, leaveing my prior Gifts of the People [illegible deletion] unreceiv'd, while those to him were carefully prest & gather'd that were 3 years after or more), I must chan[ge] my opinion of his justice as well as respect me. I have Given thee this direction let him have it Transcribd or read this to him. If he uses me as I hope, fairely ab^{t} the mines (if true, Gods peculier Providence to redeem & recruite me in a needfull time, I shall Show a gratefull resentm^{t}[69] & pray remember oare, if not oares to be sent per first, & once more w^{t} is become of Michell.

Colonel Gooking tonight & tomorrow Stays yet wth me the winde being at northwest, but the Fleet is ready at Spitt head for the first faire winde.

This the 4th day of the week, on 6th I hope to be at the Bull meeting,[70] & then to see t'other end of the town. the 12 of next month is appointed for Lord Baltemore & I to be wth the Lords of Trade & Plantations abt adjusting the Bound{s}[71] so that you will not long languish under that Complaint.

My poor wife had a quick & easy time for her last childe bearing, almost a month since, & has a Dafter of her own name in the room of an excellent childe that dyed last Spring[72] (the love, and I think the admiration of north, west, & south [tha]t Knew her). but it proves the weakest time Since she ever had, and is not forwarder at more than 3 weeks, than she used to be in half the time. she & her father,[73] salute thee, as does

Thy true Frd
Wm Penn

T. Grey has thy leter[74] inclosed to J. Jeffrys, imputes all the misfortune in latter business, to the Coldness between you two,[75] & that began his Coldness. that Gover^{r} being most Jealous of thy letters to me, & as if I was freer wth thee in his business than wth him; & on the Contrary I told T. Gr. thou often beggd me to avoide any such thing, to wch T.G. replyed he Knew it from thy mouth. T.G. confesses that they, the Go^{r} & he were greater [than] you two, but never to my prejudice. In the mine matters I beleive it. vale till more offers.

P.S.

I formerly writt to thee about Lotts in Severall Streets[76] I send thee the originall, wch it was some plain honest wellwisher that Informed me.

Pray take [all possible ca]re to preserve & [make the best use] of such vallua[ble discoveries. My] sons[77] family well [Deny m]y son aub^{s} attur[nys any] interest,[78] if the fault [be his he] has not {the} Principall, or Sale is not ratefyed by hi[m]. I thought to have sent thee w[ord] in this of the execution of the assignemt or Release of the Fords; but it is not done yet, cos. Springet[79] Standing candate for clark & atturny to Haberdashers hall,[80] 300l, & great Struggle, post[81]poning it till to morrow, or next 2d day, being now the 6th of the week. Yet hope to do it by this Fleet, not yet under sail, tho the winde be at north. My love to Frds and people at large. Allow an errata. vale.

Thy real Frd
Wm Penn.

ALS. Penn Papers, Letters of the Penn Family to James Logan, HSP. (*Micro.* 13:557.) Endorsed: Proprietor 29th 7 month 17098 | per Colonel Gookin | Copied. Missing letters and words have been supplied within brackets from Deborah Norris Logan's manuscript copy in Logan Papers, Selections from the Correspondence of the Honourable James Logan, HSP.

1. The letters sent by WP via Norris are probably docs. 147, 148. See *Micro.* 13:453.

2. Thomas Potts (d. 1719), a Quaker miller and traveling minister of Philadelphia, had been ministering in England and Ireland since the summer of 1707; Isaac Norris considered him "a Little Conceited and Whimsicall." The letter he carried to Logan may be doc. 144. Thomas M. Potts, *Historical Collections Relating to the Potts Family* (Canonsbury, Pa., 1901), pp. 201-11; Norris Papers, 7:146, HSP.

3. Ephraim Jackson (d. 1733), a Quaker yeoman and traveling minister of Chester Co., had worked briefly at Pennsbury; Isaac Norris described him as "Censorious & very Dogmaticall." *PMHB*, 9:231; 35:203; Chester Co. Will Bk. A, #394; Chester County Papers, 1684-1847, p. 93, HSP; Norris Papers, 7:161, HSP.

4. *Micro.* 13:530.

5. Not found, but see Evans's letter of 29 Sept. 1707 to the Board of Trade. *CSPC, 1706-1708*, pp. 554-55.

6. See doc. 129.

7. See doc. 138, n. 4.

8. Charles Gookin.

9. WP believed that Evans was secretly working mines in Pennsylvania in alliance with François Luis Michel; see *Micro.* 13:453.

10. Solomon Cresson. See doc. 138, text at n. 9.

11. Susanna Harwood. See docs. 147, text at n. 11; 149, text at n. 6.

12. See docs. 147, 149.

13. Joseph Jones. In June 1707 James Logan reported to WP: "Last first day in the morning meeting Jos: Jones . . . was by a paper publickly read disowned for Sodomy wch it seems he has long Practised" (*Micro.* 13:210). In Mar. 1708 Logan informed WP (*Micro.* 13:410), that Gov. Evans had pardoned Jones for £80 (not £50, as mentioned below). See also Phila. Monthly Meeting Records, Abstracts of Minutes, 1707-1730, pp. 10-11, GSP.

14. See *Micro.* 13:530.

15. Samuel Carpenter, Caleb Pusey, Thomas Story, and Griffith Owen. See doc. 153.

16. Jacob Taylor, the surveyor and mathematician.

17. George Tollett, father of the noted poet Elizabeth Tollett, was a commissioner of the navy in the reigns of William III and Anne. *DNB*.

18. Evan Evans.

19. Henry Compton.

20. Here WP is referring to former Gov. Evans's claims to perquisites as a supplement to his salary.

21. See doc. 211.

22. Henry Gouldney, Joshua Gee, Silvanus Grove, John Woods, Thomas Callowhill, Thomas Oade, Jeffrey Pinnell, John Field, and Thomas Cuppage. See doc. 211F-G.

23. That is, WP had two years in which to pay off his debt to Friends, at which time he could regain possession of his colony. See doc. 211G.

24. Doc. 153.

25. WP was lobbying for the naturalization of foreign-born residents of Pennsylvania. In 1709 Parliament passed an act for naturalizing foreign Protestants in Great

Britain and Ireland (7 Anne, c. 5, *Statutes at Large*), but this measure cannot have satisfied WP, since it made no mention of the colonies and required that foreigners take an oath of allegiance and receive the Anglican sacraments.

26. The exact date of WP's release from debtor's prison is not known. The wording of doc. 152 suggests that he was not yet "at liberty" on 16 Sept.

27. The speaker of the House of Commons, Sir Richard Onslow (1654-1717), M.P. for Surrey, presumably opposed the bill because it would deny him fees for allowing the introduction of private bills for naturalization.

28. See doc. 151.

29. The commissioners' response to WP has not been found.

30. Here WP is referring to the laws passed by the Pennsylvania Assembly in 1705, which he submitted to the Board of Trade for approval in June 1706. See *CSPC, 1706-1708*, p. 165.

31. The boundary line between Maryland, the Lower Counties, and Pennsylvania. See doc. 12, n. 5.

32. Charles Lord Baltimore. WP's optimism over Lord Baltimore's attitude was misplaced. See doc. 158, text at nn. 14-15.

33. Col. Robert Quary.

34. Evan Evans, minister of Christ Church, Philadelphia.

35. WP has omitted "me."

36. Quary's letter to Henry Compton, bishop of London, has not been found.

37. The Society for the Propagation of the Gospel in Foreign Parts. For Quary's letter, see Perry, *Historical Collections*, pp. 40-42.

38. Probably *verbum sat sapienti*—a word is sufficient to a wise man.

39. Evan Evans.

40. Charles Gookin.

41. Not found. Logan had written to Vaus on several occasions about insurance for the *Diligence*. See James Logan Letterbook, 2:97, 103, 110, HSP.

42. James Coutts.

43. Lady Mary Newcomen, alias Mary Phillips.

44. Sir Robert Newcomen.

45. Richard Rooth.

46. Probably the wife of Sir Matthew Bridges (d. 1714) and the daughter of Sir Richard Rooth, who was related to WP's father. Luttrell, 5:335; Rev. William Betham, *The Baronetage of England* (London, 1803), 3:192.

47. Either Obadiah or Francis Haige. See doc. 126, n. 25.

48. Jean Jacques Charrière (d. 1708), a Swiss nobleman and compatriot of François Louis Michel, had purchased land in New Castle, for which he paid James Logan £20 in July 1702 for quitrents. He was apparently killed in the War of the Spanish Succession; as a foreigner, his estate would revert to WP as proprietor of the Lower Counties. See *PWP*, 3:615; *Micro.* 9:870.

49. See doc. 76, nn. 20-21.

50. Sepassinck Is., later Biddle's Is., was in the middle of the Delaware River between Pennsbury and the Biddle manor of Mount Hope. *PWP*, 3:141.

51. Capt. Lasse Cock (1646-1699) had acted as Gov. Markham's interpreter and messenger to the Delaware Indians. After Cock's death, his widow, Martha, as executor of the estate, submitted a bill to WP for goods and services rendered to Markham. See *PWP*, 2:242; Phila. Will Bk. B, #14, GSP.

52. Not found.

53. Joanna Markham, William Markham's widow, claimed that WP owed her late husband for collecting proprietary quitrents. James Logan, on viewing the accounts, found them "So Confused, So unreasonable, and with an appearance of So much Disingenuity" that he could not look them over "without Amazement." James Logan Letterbook, 2:56, HSP. See also ibid., 2:66.

54. William Rakestraw. See doc. 144, n. 10.

55. At this time, Logan was under threat of impeachment by the Pennsylvania Assembly. See doc. 147, n. 23.

56. Possibly Ferdinando Poulton, of Desborough, Northants. *DNB*.

57. One branch of the Penn family lived in Stony Stratford, Bucks. See J. Henry Lea, *Genealogical Gleanings* (Boston, 1890-1900), p. 19.

58. Unidentified. Arthur Penn was the brother of Peter Penn and grandchild of Henry Penn, of Stony Stratford, Bucks. Ibid., pp. 19-20.

59. A seminary in London; the site of Chelsea Hospital, built in 1682. Peter Cunningham, *A Handbook for London, Past and Present* (London, 1849), 1:191-92.

60. For the suit of Thomas Byfield against the estate of John King, see doc. 44, n. 16.

61. John Moore had confiscated goods imported into Pennsylvania by Peter Bezaillion "because imported . . . by a foreignor." Logan had requested directions from WP on how to assist the Frenchman against such actions in the future. See *Micro.* 13:468.

62. For the case involving Judith Calvert and Ann Harrison, see doc. 38, n. 47.

63. Probably George Hogg (d. 1722), a Quaker cordwainer of New Castle, who was among the first Quakers to settle there, and who had held meetings in his house. See Scharf, *Delaware,* 2:711; Logan Papers, 2:76½; *A Calendar of New Castle County Wills, 1682-1800* (New York, 1911), p. 23.

64. Counterpanes, or bed covers. *OED.*

65. François Luis Michel.

66. Not found.

67. Col. Daniel Coxe.

68. John Edridge or Eldridge, a Middlesex Quaker tanner, had been involved in the 1670s and 1680s with Edmond Warner, another English Quaker, in West New Jersey, having mortgaged the bulk of the Salem "tenth" owned by John Fenwick. Warner bought out Edridge; WP, in turn, bought out Warner and Fenwick. See *PWP,* 2:300-302, 316-18; doc. 139, n. 22.

69. Appreciation. *OED.*

70. The Quaker meeting held at the sign of the Bull and Mouth, in Aldersgate St., London. See *PWP,* 1:296n.

71. The Board of Trade had set a deadline of 12 Oct. for WP and Lord Baltimore to reach an agreement on their boundary dispute; they met several times without resolution. In Jan. 1709 Baltimore was still trying to set aside the 1685 order in council that had ruled in favor of WP. On 23 June 1709 WP won another round in this endless contest when he obtained an order-in-council dismissing Baltimore's petition. See doc. 166; *Journal of the Commissioners for Trade and Plantations, 1704-1709,* pp. 538, 569-70, 575-77; *1709-1715,* p. 51.

72. Hannah Penn had given birth to a daughter, Hannah, on 5 Sept. 1708; her previous child of that name, Hannah Margarita Penn, had died in Feb. 1708.

73. Thomas Callowhill.

74. Not found.

75. John Evans and James Logan.

76. Not found.

77. William Penn, Jr.

78. William Aubrey's attorneys in Pennsylvania, Richard Hill and Reese Thomas, were attempting to force Logan to pay interest owed to their client. See docs. 100, 130.

79. Herbert Springett.

80. Haberdasher's Hall in Cheapside, London, occupied by the Haberdashers Company. Cunningham, *Handbook for London,* 1:366.

81. The remainder of this letter has been supplied by the editors from the Deborah Norris Logan transcript. See provenance note, above.

155
TO JAMES LOGAN

James Logan Kensington 29 x[br][December] 1708

Lov[g] Friend

The Ships being not gone from Spit-head I send this to lett thee know that a day or two after Colonel Gookin left me, the Fords were payd[1] & the Country Redeemed to & by me, & I graunted my assistants a fresh mortgage,[2] without nameing that Base family therin.

Secondly, I have sent you a new Lief[t] Gover[r3] and also a charter for a free school for Frds.[4] wch with orders to Colonel Quarry to accept the Customs upon Tobacco, in Kinde,[5] will, I hope, Strike all, even the worst of my enimys, with Fear, Respect, or Confusion. My poor wife is better that has been ill to a dangerous Circumstance. all mine by her, wch are 6 in number[6] are well, through mercy ~~well~~ & so is my son Penn[7] now (thou[gh] dubious a month agoe) & my Daugh[ter] Aubrey,[8] but my sons wife,[9] at present out of order. pray stop the occasion of more Interest to my son Aubrey for I will pay no more on acct of my Daughters 2000l.[10] my wife has had Jones letter[11] & glad she & the Frds[12] are gott well home. shee & John, Thomas & Margaret, (my Children) salute her & them wth my Selfe. ~~I~~We shall be also glad to hear the like of honest T. Potts company from Bristoll, & the other 2 ships, one from Bristoll, & {tother from} Leverpoole. And to be sure, it will be good news to hear yr Lieft Govr is safely arrived among you,[13] & my severall Packets. I add no more, but my Generall & Speciall love, as proper & suitable, & the best wishes for all your happiness, being their as well as

Thy reall Frd
Wm Penn

Salute me to the Governr &c:

ALS. Logan Papers, HSP. (*Micro.* 13:614.) Addressed: For James Logan | Secretary of Penn | sylvania at | Philadelphia | america. Docketed: Kensington 29th 7br 1708.

1. See headnote to doc. 108.
2. See doc. 211F-G.
3. Charles Gookin.
4. See docs. 131, n. 1; 153, n. 9.
5. See doc. 151.
6. John, Thomas, Margaret, Richard, Dennis, and Hannah.
7. William Penn, Jr.
8. Laetitia Penn Aubrey.
9. Mary Jones Penn.
10. See doc. 130, n. 32.
11. No letter from Joan, the Penns' former servant, has been found. See doc. 152, n. 15.
12. Isaac Norris and his family. See doc. 152, n. 14.
13. Charles Gookin arrived in Pennsylvania on 31 Jan. 1709. See doc. 157, text at n. 10.

156
TO AMOS STRETTLE

London 8th 11mo [January] 1708[/9]

Dear & Oblidgeing Frd

Thy Affecting, yet very kind letter,[1] gave that blow to my Spirit which for some time I have not been Able to Recover, My Self; for I have Lost a great Friend[2] and the Church a great Member, his parts tho' plain Were Masculine and strong his Integrity Incorruptable, his

Friendship firm & his Zeal {& love} for Truth Always Fresh & tender, a good plain pious & usefull Man. O My Dr Friend, May I wish to find So Able & so Compassionate A Friend In Eng: Irland or America Without Offence? I have Lost him too soon, & hope those My Sincere Friends that think With me so, Will please to still pitty & help Me, who have Neither been breád Nor Us'd to help My Self; but have My Dr Brethren In some Measure. this Suddain gráeat turn In my Affairs Must hasten My Journey for Ireland,[3] Unless my Able Corke Friends Will please to Make It useless & save Me so severe A Journey As the present season If It Continues Will Make Mine, & the More Difficult for the Weak Circumstances My poor Wife Is Under,[4] tho' I bless God she Rather Increases her strength, And Almost Longs to see that too much Dispised As well as hard used Country, I desire thee to bestow on Me A more Ample Account of thy Dr Brothers[5] Frame of Spirit, & Concerns If thou pleasest, & What his Dr & sweet Wife purposes to Do; Also I beg of thee to Lett the Friends of Corke Know, that the Money I drew Is to pay the Intrest of A morgage of 4 or 5 years Old, to My Son Aubrey[6] that if not pay'd, he May Enter upon the Western Estate of above 400l per Annum: which Must Not be;[7] And this thy Brother Knew as I writ to Tho Wight[8] When I drew the Bill of 1000l: & Indeed I had Never Drawn It, had Not the Arrears (which thy Brother tould me Would Amount to 2000l last November) been the Method proposed to Me by him for the payment of It. But If the Friends that Advanced that thousand pound Will Expect It out of present and growing Rents, I shall be post poned for my Bread, for I do Assure thee I now Borrow Money to be Able to put It Into My Childrens Mouths; & tho' I think to Write to Friends of Corke on this Subject, that they would Now & then Let me have fifty or an hundred pounds, whilst they Are Apaying off for My Subsistance (which I shall take for a great Kindness) yet I Intreat thee & My Dr Friends In & About Dublin to Write to them, Such as they Know, G: Rooke T Willson &c:[9] that they Would please to Receive their Money With some tenderness to My Circumstances; If they fear a Loss by My Death If I live Not till they be pay'd, My Son Penn[10] Will secure them. And Now Give thy Dr Sister Cuppage Mine & My Wifes Very Dr Love for We are Deeply Concern'd In her Affliction, & fear Least she Looks upon Me (by my Concerns he so heartily Espoused) as an accessary to her Unspeakable Loss,[11] tho I fear he Made a Little too much hast When he Return'd, for he Rode Above 40 Miles a day & often Complain'd of his Loyns to My Man that Waited on him to Chester, Dr Amos Let Me hear from thee & that freely & Largly and As soon As May be So With Dr Love to All Brethren & Friends (& hopeing thy Dr Child Is better) I close & End

Thy Affectionate & Faithful Friend
Wm Penn

Poor Edward Hastwell[12] was buried Last night.

LS. Huntington Library, San Marino, Calif. (*Micro.* 13:648.)

1. Not found.

2. Thomas Cuppage (d. c. Dec. 1708), an Irish Quaker gentleman of Lambstone, Co. Wexford, had been empowered by WP in 1704 to act as his attorney to sell or lease his Irish lands. Cuppage was also instrumental in forging the settlement between WP and the Ford family and became one of the trustees for Pennsylvania. See docs. 210A, 211F-G; Norris Papers, 7:86, 89, 114; 7½:15, 26, HSP.

3. WP did not, in fact, ever return to Ireland.

4. Hannah Penn had recently given birth to a daughter and was recovering very slowly.

5. Amos Strettle was married to Experience Cuppage, daughter of Robert Cuppage and sister of Thomas Cuppage. Myers, *Immigration*, p. 164.

6. See docs. 100, 130, n. 32.

7. Aubrey held a claim to WP's lands in the baronies of Ibaune and Barryroe, West Cork (see doc. 209G). In 1670 this "western estate" had totaled 4859 acres, with an annual rental value of about £364. *PWP*, 1:570-73.

8. Thomas Wight (c. 1640-1724), a Quaker clothier and minister of Cork, was the author of *A History of the Rise and Progress of the . . . Quakers in Ireland.* Wight, *Rise and Progress*, 4th rev. ed. by John Rutty (London, 1811), 279-81.

9. George Rooke (1652-1742) and Thomas Wilson (c. 1654-1725) were both Quaker traveling ministers originally from Cumberland. Rooke resided in Dublin and Wilson in Edenderry, King's Co., Ireland. Wight, *Rise and Progress*, pp. 281-88, 313-16.

10. William Penn, Jr.

11. Isaac Norris commented that Thomas Cuppage had worked very hard on behalf of WP in arranging a settlement with the Ford family: "Poor Thos I prceive Near Tyr'd with attendance upon that unhappy & Delatory buisiness." Norris Papers, 7:89.

12. Edward Haistwell died "of fever" in London on 4 Jan. 1709. Digests of Quaker Records, London and Middx., GSP.

157
FROM JAMES LOGAN

Philadelphia 3d of the 12th Month
[February] 1708/9

Honored Governour

/On the 22d of 9br [1] by way of Jamaica and the 17th of last Month[2] by Barbados I Sent two Letters intended by the Pacquet boat to hint Such Matters as I then thought more espetially Necessary, particularly that {all} thy Bills would be Answered that thou hadst been pleased to Advise me of: but that having Received none Concerning that to Jones[3] for 179l:4s that to Robt Raine[4] for 168l & that to Robt Frame[5] for 20l:7s their payment must be delay'd untill Advice is received According to the Tenour of the Drought. I mentioned also that Isaac Jennings Bill is drawn for 76l:13 but in thy Advice is but 60l:13 and that John Jeffery's is also drawn for 120l tho per Advice tis but 112l of all which some Speedy care ought to be taken that I may be Sufficiently Instructed.[6]

I Informed thee also that the Representatives of the Lower Counties by questioning thy Powers of Government in their Open Assembly had laid a Design to bring about a Re~~so~~volution there, but that means were found for that time to putt an end to it by breaking up the house, those that were for the design not making a Quorum tho' a Majority, but that it would Still be Indeavoured as opportunitys offered till Such time as that Affair Should be fully Settled at home[7] which for thy own Pea~~s~~ce & ease would be Indispensib~~e~~ly Necessary before thou leaves that Kingdom, otherwise we Shall Still be in the Same Confusion.

I told thee that Thomas Story was gone for the west Indies that Gr: Owen Intended for New England in the Spring, & therefore that our Commission[8] would be broke, for a time at least, if matters were to Continue on the Same foot as before, that if an Addition were to be made Samuel Carpenter Ri^{d} Hill & I: Norris or S: Preston (I now add)[9] would be very fitt men, if they would undertake it, In my last I again press'd that of the Lower Counties very close [as] a matter highly deserving thy Consideration which therefore I hope will be granted it.

I am now at length to give thee the good News of Coll^{o} Gookins Arrival ~~to~~ {at} this ~~twon~~ town from Virginia on the last day of last Month (which by the way was the last day ~~of~~ also of the term for which the Impost was Granted)[10] he was proclaimed the first of this Month & yesterday held a Councill, took the usuall oaths and issued a Proclamation for continueing of officers. The Gentleman as far as can be judged of him promises very fair (I mean not in words) to make good thy whole Character of him & therefore to make the people happy if they please to Consent to it themselves, wch I very much question. He has shew'd me a Receipt und^{r} thy hand for 100^{l} Ster: for wch thou promises to give him Bills on me at 25 per C^{t} Exchange but {he} never took any ~~Bill~~ for it, he says, nor has any thing besides to Shew, he adds, that he let thee have an other hundred pounds to furnish thy Son,[11] for wch thou gave him 2 bills for 50^{l} Ster each wch bills he was obliged to leave behind him upon the trouble that was unworthyly given him before his coming away. Now thou advises me only of one 100^{l} for wch I am to pay him at the rate of 60 per Cent {advance}, but Seeing he ownes he had bills for that Summ I cannot See how I can pay any untill the Bills appear this makes both him and me uneasy, and indeed upon the Small observations he has been able to make of the Country, he is apprehensive that he has changed for the worse being more particularly concerned at thy oblieging him at Portsmouth to Signe Articles that he Should receive no more than 200^{l} Ster: per annum including all perquisits after thou hadst at London he Sayes in express words given him an expectation of 400^{l} being paid him yearly by the Assembly. He seems to be a plain honest man and of a temper best Suiteing a Soldier; but of prudence enough to consider as well how he himself is to live in the world, as how he shall be helpfull to others in it, & therefore Seems Jealous, from the opportunitys he has had of considering matters in passing through virginia

& Maryland[12] that he shall be so far from being enabled by his new Post to make any provision for a Change if one should happen, that his whole allowance will scarce be a subsistance, and is the more anxious because he has he says but very litle now to shew of those 300^{l} wch by his care he had Saved in the Army or of the 350^{l} wch he had for his place,[13] he is also much troubled at that Story told thee in London of his having wronged his men of their pay, wch he affirms he could, if there, prove to be so far from true, that he could make it appear he had often wronged himself be advanceing his own money to them when they were in Straits to answer their necessitys but had never once acted what he was charged with, and that this report could never arise from any other grownds than his frugality in saving some part of his own pay when others squander'd more than their all. this is the substance of a discourse he had wth me yesterday, and I cannot but think it will prove a great unhappyness to us if his reflections upon the disappointm^{t} he may think he meets wth should discourage his zeal in the business he is engaged in for were he a Solomon, he will certainly meet wth enough to try his temper. but we shall doe our best. The alteration of the money[14] now Shortly coming on will lay us und[er] a necessity I Doubt of meeting the Assembly this Year wch otherwise would better be deferred till another Election, for the present is as bad as allmost it can be. D. Lloyd ought by all means to be prosecuted one way or other for that Remonstrance sent in 1704[15] but want the Originall papers under his hand wch we have long expected and are much disappointed they are not come now, but ought if possible to have them by Some Safe opportunity directed to York or Maryland before next yearly meeting[16] (at wch time friends generally convene) in 7^{br} and before the Same time if possible we ought to have a repeal! of that Law past 3 years agoe for Elections[17] wch while in force we shall scarce ever be able to gain a good ~~new~~ [?] one but then wth that repeall we should have the rest least it Should be represented to the disaffected as a particular designe agst the peoples privileges. It is now I assure thee the earnest desire of most of thy friends that that law may be repealed because instead of answering any good end our enemies are only strenthned by it.

I am extreamly troubled to find thee so angry wth Colonel Quary, I have been very intimate & free wth him ever since his last arrivall & have found good Service in it, once or twice (as tis prudence allways to watch an enemy newly reconsiled) I was somewhat Jealous of him, but the matter was Soon clear'd up if he writ Slightingly either of friends or thee when upon that head of parson Evans and the Church here,[18] perhaps it might be imputed to the remains of their old divisions wth that Gent. and common humour of the times or way of the world to consider only w^{t} will most directly Serve the present turn in hand without remembring who is a friend or who an Enemy, but in generall I can say that our intimacy has been sev^{ll} times of great

Service to me, for he has been my best oracle to find out the practices of our Enemies, in wch he has been often very communicative wth a great appearance of Sincerity upon the whole I am very sensible he is a variable man, & not easyly to be fixed so as to be intirely depended on, yet I am fully perswaded tis thy Interest to keep in wth him, & must therefore beg thy leave to act accordingly here. As for Jno Moore it will be a difficult matter ever to reclaim him, his Sowrness of temper is Scarce to be alter'd, and of this C.Q. has severall times complained to me & assured me wthall, that unless he would change his measures & forbear medling wth any thing relating to the Govermt he would endeavour to find an effectual way to make him Sensible of his Error, for he as to his own part was resolved never to concern himself in those points any more I request thee to considr this & let me have thy thought upon it, that I may know how to behave I perceive by thy last[19] that the Country is to be mortgaged de novo for the paymt of the money advanced to the Fords & is to remain in thy hands for a year or two, and then to come into possession of the Trustees.[20] but as the business now before us is to sell & raise money, I wish it had been remember'd that while the whole lyes undr Mortgage no Sufficient Title can afterward be made to any part of it, unless there be some other provision made than I can form any notion of, thou mayst be assured that while the people have this notion a full Stop will be put to all sales, nor untill we get an other law of Property[21] for the overplus shall we under any circumstances be able to perswade the people to buy, for the Lawyers wth help of Some of our late assembly members have generally spread it through the Country, that the former law of Property being repealed thou Canst come at no part of their Lands they certainly[22] in the wrong in this, but in the mean time it will give us great trouble, soe that a Law must be obtain'd if possible but till that method of our Elections be alterd I fear it will Scarce be practicable.

Pray if thou comes not speedily over thy self write a close leter to friends concerning D. Ll[23] fit to be communicated insisting chiefly on that Remonstrance & his directing leters to thy enemies,[24] for his indirect proceedings in that affair[25] and his making his privat Revenge wth a pretence of asserting only the Peoples right, I believe will prove the best Topick, but will require great care to guard it well, and yet at the Same time to make it close enough, with this should be sent the Originalls I have mentioned time enough to be here by Septr next.

There is nothing yet certainly discoverd about the mines,[26] Coll. Evans has been very free wth me upon that head, he designes to Stay no longer here, than to be ascertaind as far as he can be, and then will hasten over, there has been none opened, & I hartly wish I may ever be able to tell thee more of the mater hearafter, for I fear Mitchell[27] has tricked us all, he is gone over to England wth an intention we believe to put his Country men the Swiss upon purchasing a Tract of the Queen beyond Petomack[28] where he thinks they lie, and is as he accts a part of Virga It will therefore very nearly concern thee, to have an eye on all his motions there, and prevent him especially till Colonel Evans comes over, who I believe will be very free wth thee, for in all appearance he has been So wth me. I shall be extreamly puzzeld how to make up accts wth him, thou by thy last leter confines him to 300l per annum only & yet in a former allowed him 400l as long as the Assemblys grant continued besides that thou made mencion of some part of the fines to goe to him, How I shall be able to manage it is more than I at present can See.

thou hast severall times mencioned a designe some foreigners had of making a large purchase there,[29] I wish it were done 5000l Ster: paid in London would goe a great way to make thee easy, and I dare affirm would be beter to thee [than] 10000l of our present money, Returns are So extreamly difficult. In Maryland they have very lately past an act allowing only ten per Ct on protesting of a Bill of Exchange[30] wch will rendr all their Bills not worth the purchasing & indeed in generall for Some years past they have Studied all possible methods to discourage all kind of trade between us and them.[31] It were to be wished the merchts would oppose the confirmacion of that Law.

In the 3d article of thy Instructions to the Governor[32] thou art large in directing him to procure an union between the Province & lower Countys, but I am fully perswaded that it will be impossible ever to perswade the Province to it, they now know on wt foot they stand, and can plead the Kings Charter for their Laws, but to take in others within that who are locally Scituate wthout it is wt I believe they will never agree to, that mater having been soe largely canvased in the late Assemblys, that Scarce any body of years & Common Sense amongst us is {un}acquainted wth the whole notion. I have wrote Sevll times to this same purpose, and I believe it may be depended on, that wthout new powers or ordrs from the Crown it will be found Impracticable.

I have very earnestly pressed the Setlemt of the Lower Counties, as well the Govermt of them as their Boundaries wthout wch thou wilt never be as easy here as might be wished. Another Article of thy Instructions directs the Governor to dissolve the Assembly & Call another by writ, if untractable, but were that attempted, I Should be harder put to it to Justi{fie} my advising it then to answr ten times as much as all the 14 Articles agst me,[33] thy Character binds thee up from it & there must be noe breach of {that} wth this people. D. Ll. is noe longer in the Corporation, R Ashton being now Recordr[34] who I believe is really thy hearty friend but he has a great expensive family, & therefore is to be born with. T. Grey and I parted very good friends as we allways lived, and it was no small trouble to me that I missed him in Maryland, I must Say of him that after 7 years experience I allways found him to be both faithfull & able as well {as} of a Singular good temper but I must now conclude wth the paper

Thy most obedt sert

LBC. James Logan Letterbook, HSP. (*Micro.* 13:674.)

1. *Micro.* 13:605.
2. *Micro.* 13:661.
3. Charles Jones, Sr. (d. 1714), a prominent Bristol Quaker merchant, was the grandfather of WP's daughter-in-law, Mary Jones Penn. See Mortimer, 1:206.
4. Robert Raine (c. 1633-1714) was a Quaker of Southwark, London. Digests of Quaker Registers, London and Middx., GSP.
5. Robert Freame was a Quaker grocer in Aldersgate, London. Ibid.
6. Jennings's and Jeffreys's bills are listed in doc. 144.
7. Until the crown recognized WP's title to the government of the Lower Counties, or WP surrendered his governing powers to the crown.
8. The commissioners of property; with Story and Owen gone, Logan and Edward Shippen would be the only remaining members.
9. Logan had first suggested Samuel Preston as a commissioner of property on 17 Jan. 1709. *Micro.* 13:661.
10. In Jan. 1706 the Assembly had passed a three-year tax, part of which was to be used to pay the governor's salary. See doc. 129, n. 25.
11. William Penn, Jr.
12. The governors of these two colonies were much better paid than Pennsylvania's. WP preferred to compare Pennsylvania with Connecticut and Rhode Island, where the governors' salaries were small; see doc. 127, text at nn. 8, 9.
13. Gookin had evidently sold his officer's commission in the army for this price.
14. The need for a new revenue act; see n. 10, above.
15. See doc. 83.
16. The Quaker Phila. Yearly Meeting.
17. The Act to Ascertain the Number of Members of Assembly and to Regulate the Election, which was enacted in Jan. 1706. See *Statutes,* 2:212-21. It was not repealed.
18. For Quary's apparent efforts to have Evan Evans removed as minister of Christ Church, see doc. 148, n. 19.
19. Probably WP's letter of 11 Sept. 1708. See *Micro.* 13:533.
20. For WP's mortgage of Pennsylvania to nine Quaker trustees on 6-7 Oct. 1708, see doc. 211F-G. The settlement guaranteed secure title to all Pennsylvania landholders, thus allaying some of Logan's fears. But WP was obligated to pay his debt of £6600 within two years or lose possession of the colony.
21. See headnote to doc. 31.
22. "Are" is omitted.
23. No such general letter concerning David Lloyd has been found.
24. To George Whitehead, Thomas Lower, and William Mead. See doc. 127, n. 25.
25. That is, the Ford case. For example, see doc. 129, n. 6.
26. The possible discovery of copper or silver mines in Pennsylvania; see doc. 154, n. 9.
27. François Luis Michel.
28. In June 1709 George Ritter, of Berne, petitioned Queen Anne on behalf of 4-5000 Swiss Protestants for the right to settle a colony in Virginia near the settlement of François Luis Michel. This was granted in Sept. 1709. At the same time, Michel was granted 2500 acres of land in North Carolina. See *CSPC, 1708-1709,* pp. 398, 463, 465.
29. See doc. 126, text at nn. 21-22.
30. An Act Ascertaining What Damages Shall Be Allowed upon Protested Bills of Exchange, which allowed only 10 percent damages "over and above the Summe of money for which such bill shall be drawn." *Archives of Maryland,* 27:364.
31. See doc. 141, n. 2.
32. Not found.
33. The 14 articles of impeachment drawn up by the Assembly against Logan on 25 Feb. 1707. See *Minutes of the Provincial Council,* 2:344-47.
34. Robert Assheton was appointed recorder of Philadelphia on 3 Aug. 1708, replacing Lloyd who had served since 1702. Scharf, 3:1738.

158
TO JAMES LOGAN

Reding[1] 27 12m[February] 1708/9

James Logan
Lovg Friend
Tho I have writt many ways, & I think most amply, & especially by Colonel Gookin, & Tho: Potts,[2] yet haveing receiv'd thine of 7br last,[3] wch is the last, I thought fitt to lett thee Know, yt Michel has been wth me, is a little Clowdy, & would tell me wt is good out of our Province, & dubious of the vallue of wt is within it, as yet;[4] but promesses faire. T. Grey as yet cannot make him Selfe master of the papers thou hast twice writt about. comeing by N. Castle upon tine,[5] Sick, his chest in disorder Still, but is positive that one Sort of the papers thou hast every individuall of them. I'le mind him of it again. But Coll. evans & his company of Indians[6] both T.G. & Michell declare, can make 100l if {not} 2 or three, per diem neat. unhappy for me has that faling out been between you.[7] But end it the best that may be. He writes[8] of comeing over, but let him be Honorable there or he may repent it here. He is {a} Silliton[9] if he Stirr, & does not persue my last offer & advice by Colonel Gookin.[10] I hear Ld Lovelace is well arrived, I hope so is the Govr too. make the most of him to Frds & Service. He ~~hasd~~ hints enough to follow theirs & thine & was let in to every secreet of yr affaires that occur'd to me at his goeing. Give him measures of Persons & things. he writes well, is a good Mathimatician and I have desired him to keep a Diary for his security, or at least prudent discharge.

Now these five things thou hast to Ballance agst the Turbulent & ungratefull.

1. That I keep my Govermt
~~&~~2 I have sent a new Lieut or Dept
~~2~~3 That I have recovered the Province from the vilest of the earth;[11] & that Danger over.
~~3~~4 That I have Sent the School charter.[12]
~~4~~5 That Ld Baltr, laying hold of his Provinces address for settling our Boundarys,[13] [illegible deletion] Petitioned the Queen in order to it, to dismiss or repeale the order of Councill[14] in her Fathers time, & only run the line, & leave the Lower Countys to him as his by his graunt.

& he gott it referr'd to the Lords for Trade &c: I appeared to them, told them they could not be proper Judges, or Shake a definitive order or Sentence of King & Council. complain'd to Ld President Sommers[15] & Ld Sunderland se~~s~~cretr of state, they agreed with me excused the Inadvertency of the reference, and concurd wth me to Petit. the Queen, wch I have done,[16] setting forth the case & the long quiet possession upon that determination, & prayd to have so ill a President to American settlem[ts] {prevented & his Petition} dismist, & so it was, in high Council.[17] This may be an [illegible deletion] victory {(as Blaithwait[18] called it)} or advantage, If so base & sordid a people as my enimys[19] there are, can be obliged. But I really think, they will be sorry for my successes, that would have made my insuccesses a fault or mismanagemt. But almighty God forgive & change them or it will [illegible deletion] be a wofull day for them in close of time. I have lost my last Sweet nursery,[20] my wife a weekly woman, but hope the Spring will assist her, all else well. Oblige my fat[r] Callowhill w[t] may be.[21] pay as full as is possible; & a little while & I hope to see you all God permiting. in great hast farewell

Thy assured Friend
Wm Penn

Salute me to Colonel Gookin The Council, & frds of all Sorts.
more per vir. fleet Glad of I. Norris & familys so happy arrivall[22]
all our loves to them & relations, & poor Joan.[23]

ALS. This letter was found divided in two repositories: the first four pages (*Micro.* 13:691) are in ACM; the final two pages and cover (*Micro.* 13:697) are in Miscellaneous Manuscripts, Friends Historical Library, Swarthmore College, Swarthmore, Pa. Addressed in WP's hand: WPG[r] | For James | Logan Secret[r] of | Pennsylvania &c: | at Philadelphia | in America. Endorsed: p[r] the Union. Docketed: Prop[r] 27. 12 [mo] 1708/9 | per M Lisle.[24]

1. Reading, Berks. WP was perhaps visiting his children at school; see doc. 152, n. 4.

2. The letters sent via Gookin and Potts are docs. 154 and 144, respectively.

3. *Micro.* 13:515.

4. Here WP is referring to François Luis Michel's estimate of the potential value of mines in Pennsylvania.

5. Newcastle-upon-Tyne, a port in northeast England. The papers mentioned by WP relate to money paid by Thomas Grey to former Gov. Evans for licenses and regulating ships. See *Micro.* 13:410.

6. A group of Shawnee, having discovered a mine in Pennsylvania, were working it on behalf of former Gov. Evans. See doc. 159, text at n. 25.

7. For evidence of the estrangement between Evans and Logan, see docs. 129, 159; *Micro.* 12:721, 812; 13:026, 343, 410.

8. Not found.

9. Sillyton; that is, simpleton. *OED*.

10. Probably *Micro.* 13:530, much of which is missing. It appears that WP offered Evans the right to manage mines in Pennsylvania on his behalf. See also doc. 149.

11. The Ford family.

12. See doc. 153, n. 9.

13. In Apr. 1707 the Maryland House of Delegates petitioned the queen that the unsettled boundary with Pennsylvania had "already caused great Disputes Suits at Law and Uneasiness . . . to the great Loss and Impoverishmt of your Majestys People in each Province." They requested that royal directions be given to Penn and Baltimore "to settle and adjust their respective Bounds of the two Provinces." *Archives of Maryland*, 18:136.

14. On 13 Nov. 1685 the Privy Council effectively granted the Lower Counties to WP and defined their western and southern boundaries with Maryland (see *PWP*, 3:18-70). For Lord Baltimore's petition of 9 Jan. 1709, see *CSPC, 1708-1709*, p. 194.

15. John Lord Somers was lord president of the Privy Council from 1708 to 1710.

16. WP petitioned Queen Anne on 27 Jan. 1709. See *Micro.* 13:671.

17. On 27 Jan. 1709 Queen Anne in the Privy Council ordered that Lord Baltimore's petition (see n. 14, above) be dismissed (see *Micro.* 13:672). The matter, however, was soon reopened and a final order in WP's favor was issued on 23 June 1709 (doc. 166).

18. William Blathwayt.

19. Here begins *Micro.* 13:697.

20. Hannah Penn, who had been born in London on 5 Sept. 1708, died there on 24 Jan. 1709. Jenkins, p. 88.

21. James Logan was acting as Thomas Callowhill's agent in Pennsylvania. See doc. 139, n. 23.

22. See doc. 152, n. 14.

23. See doc. 152, n. 15.

24. Maurice Lisle was a factor in Jamaica. *PMHB*, 78:167.

159
*TO JAMES LOGAN**

Reding 3. 1m [March] 1709

James Logan
Lovg Friend
I writt to thee last week[1] by way of Bristoll, & will come by one short a shipright, that brings some letters from Fatr Callowhill, also Jeffery Pinnell, & Tho: Oads,[2] in wch I have been particular, & to wch I referr thee, wch pray take notice of & improve for my Just advantage. This goes by Marice Lisle, whom I suppose the Frds Concern'd wth me,[3] intends to recommend to thee so farr as he can be usefull to thee in their & my business; & if thou findest him capable & upright, I Shall like that he may be Encouraged by thee.

I inclose to thee the Queens Order in Council, to dismiss & discharge the Ld. Baltimores Petit:[4] wch inadvertantly was referr'd to the Lds of Trade & Plantations as thou wilt finde by sd order & the reason for that Lds proceeding to such a foolish as well as unfaire proceeding was, I presume, some privat encouragemt from not the most Judicious, to graft upon the Maryland Address for ascertaining our Common Boundarys, an abolition of the order of Councill 1685 for secureing {me} in the Possession of the Lower Countys,[5] & wch was indeed, a definitive sentence upon divers hearings for Queen or King & Council are reputed the last prerogative Jurisdiction, upon prerogative Graunts or Patents. one wo'd think such a quick & through turne of ill endeavours should convince our Enemys there, we are not left a prey to their designes. wch is an article to be insisted there more than here, while I am here.

I have thine of 7br [6] & one also from Colonel evans,[7] that tells me he is comeing hither to vindicate himselfe, wch In my opinion is a sleevless[8] errand; but let him do as he pleases. I hope a change it selfe is gratefull,[9] or they that desired it must be very Base to me as well as him, I mean evans.

T. Grey tells me he has not yet gone over his papers, & positively affirms thou hast the most profitable part of the acct of fines or perquisits, & he never had;[10] if I can see him or finde his note he gave me, Ile incert the terme of that par{t} of the getings he assures me he never medl'd with. By al means take care I have Justice from him;[11] for he cannot think I sent him to get an estate out of me; but to live, without State or the expence of it, & wch no body else would have done {for him}. And I hope he will be so reasonable as to think I am so in my expectation, under all my unspeakable Burdens. If he leaves you indeed, then try to secure for me his Plantation, for I think from abt Shackamaxon to the town, is ~~som~~ one of the pleasantest Scitituations upon the River, for a Goverr where one sees & hears wt one will & wn one will, & yet have a good deal of the sweetness & quiet of the Country.[12] and I do assure thee that If the Country would settle upon me 600l per annum as mony is now order'd, I would hasten over this following summer, God permiting me & mine, & leave my Frds here to pay them selves out of my European estate,[13] as well as wt that place in debts & Rents would afford to it. Cultivate this wth the best Frds.

Pray forget not Beaumonts purchass of wm Biddle,[14] that I have bought, to ~~Press~~ speak ~~Wm~~ of ~~with~~ it, the more to loosen his hold of the Island before Pensberry. I hope the lands of Jo. Blaklin, 1000 acres, John Nelson &c: I formerly writt about,[15] are layd out in valluable over plusses for my younger Brood; as also some lots in town as thou Canst not but remember in severall former letters.

Be sure to assist Colonel Gooken all that is possible, for he has promest to follow the measures my Frds & officers (truly in my honest Interest) shall give him from Time to time, or I had never sent him. and I have a bond of 2, or 3000l Security[16] for his just performances. All that can be preserve him out of all dangerous, or lessening measures that may expose him or me to mischiefe or contempt. and engage two or three able & sensible friends, and as many of others, to be of privat Frds & Council to him, in the nature of a Cabinet, for the better prevention of ill designing persons, & the popular performance of his duty in Govermt. advise him to Corrispond wth all Neighbouring Govrs especially Ld Lovelace & Seymer.[17] and also to Keep a Diary, or Journall, wch was one of my Instructions to him.[18]

Tho we have {here} a 2d Bill for Naturalizaton in the house,[19] & I think I never writt so Correctly as I did to some members of Parliamt (as well as discoursed them) upon that Subject, yet that point being a faire Flower in the Speakers Garland,[20] it moves but slowly; & least it should miscarry, faile not pray to send me over the names of all our Forriegners, not born in the Country; & I will put them into one act, or at least Patent for Denezation, to put them out of the trouble, that villan Lloyd put the Saxons & others into,[21] as the chiefest of them told me, & gave it me under his own hand wch I have to show. What is become of the mony for the Sadlers craiz'd sons Passage, that his unworthy Father refused m~~e~~y bill for, & the town promest to repay me.[22]

Peace is yet Dubious, yet I think it will be the last Campagne w[ch] is ready to open, and the mighty preparations on all hands & sides rather confirms me in my opinion, as well as our vehemences & faling out too much at home.[23] I think I have been pretty large, yet shall observe that Michell has been with me & by him & T.G. I learn the misunderstanding between the late Gov[r] & thy selfe,[24] if they Say true, has cost me deare. for they assure me, he & company may & they beleive do make 100[l] if not twice told weekly; the Indians chiefly discovered the mine, & work it on the Spot, & told me the way of it. It is the King of the Shanoe[25] Indians, & some few of his subjects that performs the business for him (viz) Coll. E.[26]—Pray Scruteny this matter well, & let me hear from thee wth all the Speed thou canst; for the assurance Michell gives me, makes me sollicitous to pry into that affaire, whence help & reward may arise to deliver me. A Duplicat of the Fords release[27] I desired might be sent thee, to putt the redemption of the Country (tho a meer Mock Title to them before, as forty instances show) out of all doubt.

We are through the Lords mercy pretty well, & send thee our remembrances. Give ours also to all our Frds, & Particularly, S.C. C.P. R.H. I.N. G.O. E.S. N.S. T.M. T.S. J.G. S.P. R.E.[28] with their familys, Ann P.[29] & Joan,[30] must not be forgotten our old Serv[t] to whom Johnne, Tomme, & Peggy[31] pray to be remembred. Salute me to the L[t] Gover[r] & his clark; to the Council & Magistrates. w[ch] closes this from

Thy assured Friend
Wm Penn

I hear nothing of Colonel Q.[32] complaints.

ALS. Letters of the Penn Family to James Logan, HSP. (*Micro.* 13:700.) Docketed: Propriet 3. 1 1709 | pr M. Lisle | Copied.

1. See doc. 158.
2. These letters have not been found.
3. The trustees for Pennsylvania; see doc. 153, n. 8.
4. See doc. 158, n. 17.
5. See ibid., nn. 13-14.
6. Probably Logan's letter of 1, 3 Sept. 1708, *Micro.* 13:515.
7. Not found.
8. Futile. *OED.*
9. The replacement of Dep. Gov. Evans with Charles Gookin.
10. See doc. 158, n. 5.
11. John Evans.
12. By June 1709 (*Micro.* 13:789) he was considering the purchase of land near Pegg's Run "or Such a remote place for me & famaly."
13. WP's English and Irish holdings.
14. See doc. 76, nn. 20-21.
15. For John Blaykling and John Elson's lands, see doc. 97, n. 51.
16. The amount was £2000; see *CSPC, 1708-1709,* p. 31.

17. Unfortunately for WP's strategy, both Gov. Lovelace of New York and Gov. Seymour of Maryland had died in office by the end of July 1709.

18. These instructions have not been found.

19. See doc. 154, n. 25.

20. See ibid., n. 27.

21. WP seems to be referring to Lloyd's role in the case of *John Henry Sproegel* v. *Frankford Land Co.*, in which Lloyd filed a fictitious writ in the Phila. Co. Court of Common Pleas, resulting on 12 Jan. 1709 in the ejection of the Frankford Co. from its Pennsylvania lands. It is unlikely, however, that WP would have learned of this action by 3 Mar. The Provincial Council, concerned over the impact such actions would have on future German immigration, denounced Lloyd on 1 Mar. 1709 as the "principal agent & Contriver of the whole." See Samuel W. Pennepacker, *Pennsylvania Colonial Cases* (Philadelphia, 1892), pp. 142-78; *Minutes of the Provincial Council,* 2:432.

22. On 12 Mar. 1709 (*Micro.* 13:732) WP asked Logan: "Has that unhappy German, that married our good Dorothy, payd thee w^{t} he borrowed of me here?" Possibly this is the sadler mentioned here by WP; his "craiz'd" son has not been identified.

23. By June 1709 peace talks at the Hague aimed at ending the War of the Spanish Succession had failed mainly because of allied intransigence. An allied army of 120,000 took the field at Lille, in Flanders, for the beginning of another campaign. Contrary to WP's expectations, further campaigns were necessary. See George M. Trevelyan, *The Peace and the Protestant Succession* (London, 1934), pp. 4-5, 222.

24. See doc. 158, n. 7.

25. Shawnee.

26. Colonel Evans.

27. See doc. 211C.

28. Samuel Carpenter, Caleb Pusey, Richard Hill, Isaac Norris, Griffith Owen, Edward Shippen, Nathan Stanbury, Thomas Masters, Thomas Story, Joseph Growden, Samuel Preston, and Rowland Ellis. In WP's view, these men were his staunchest allies in Pennsylvania.

29. Probably Ann Bax Parsons, a former servant at Pennsbury. See *PWP,* 3:434n.

30. Joan, a former servant of the Penns, had recently arrived in Pennsylvania with the Norris family. See doc. 152, nn. 14-15.

31. John, Thomas, and Margaret Penn.

32. Col. Robert Quary.

160
FROM JAMES LOGAN

Philadelphia 7th 2 month [April] 1709

Honored Governor

Hearing tis not improbable but the ships at Virginia may be yet overtaken by a vessel bound to their Capes. I send these few lines to inform thee That by the way of the West Indies in a Pacquet directed to Wm Popple & by a Letter[1] inclosed to T Loyd[2] by one of these Ships I sent thee a large Account of an Address sent home from 9 Members (being just one half of the Lower County Assembly) by Ja: Coutts who is to negotiate it, of wch in a shorter Letter[3] I have also sent thee advice by way of Boston & the Mast fleet.[4] This is now principally to inform thee that since J Coutt's departure, we have an Account that he resolves to be at the Charge of 2 or 300 Guineas to gett a Commission for the Goverment of those Counties to himself so much has his Ambition & most Arrogant Spirit blinded him. I cannot believe him capable of doing himself much good, tho the

Scotch are generally warm Canvassers & stick fast by one another, but I fear unless prevented he will give thee trouble

That ever he should obtain it is improbable, but if he should the Tyranny & haughtiness of that mans temper would soon be a means of thinning those Counties to a degree that the Propriety of them would scarce be worth asking & Philadelphia would be extreamly unhappy

By the next good Opportunity I design to write my thoughts of thy Affairs here at large in the mean time must again press thee to gett that most useful Law for collecting Quittrents (tho' it should cost 200 Guineas) confirm'd[5] & the Law for Elections repealed[6] & sent over with all speed for till 'tis done we shall have no Assembly to doe business the present will doe nothing and till matters are settled at home about the Lower Counties wch the Address will necessarily draw on, Affairs of Government will be much perplexed there.

I have by many Letters[7] requested that we may live at peace with Colonel Quary, the present Governor[8] seems not very well pleased with his Change, Meeting with so much fraud Self Interest & faction under sanctimonious outsides & from those whose consciences will not allow them even even to practice the Common forms of Civility Pray Inform me how much Money thou received of him that I am to repay, he sayes 200l sterling tho' he expects payment but of one hundred as yet. I desire full Orders how I shall make Returns of what I receive. Since the Repeal of the Property Act[9] the people refuse to purchase one Acre of their Overplus, claiming all within their Lines, but of this I design to be larger. J Sotcher is still at Pensbury R Assheton Recorder of Philadia I Norris S Preston & Captain Anth. Palmer are of the Council I cannot now add but that I am as ever

Thy most Obedient Servant
J L

Pray sell Lands there if to be done at a good price I mean those of Sasquehan.[10] & believe it necessary to watch Mitchel if he or the Swiss his Countreymen make proposals to the Cr.[11] for Land in these parts I wrote to the same effect with this Letter by the mast fleet[12]

LBC. James Logan Letterbook, HSP. (*Micro.* 13:744.) Docketed: per Jacob Leader Sloop Annap. Merchant to Virginia.

1. The "packet" mentioned by Logan included his letter of 5 Mar. 1709 (*Micro.* 13:707). The other letter via Thomas Lloyd was dated 6 Mar. 1709 (*Micro.* 13:703). See *Micro.* 13:735.

2. Thomas Lloyd (1675-1716), son of Thomas Lloyd, former deputy governor of Pennsylvania, was a Quaker merchant in London and brother-in-law of Isaac Norris, Samuel Preston, and Richard Hill. Thomas A. Glenn, ed., *Genealogical Notes Relating to the Families of Lloyd, Pemberton, Hutchinson, Hudson and Parke* (Philadelphia, 1898), pp. 11, 12-15.

3. Written 16 Mar. 1709. *Micro.* 13:735.

4. In Oct. 1708 the New Castle representatives in the Lower Counties' Assembly rejected WP's new governor and challenged his proprietary right over those counties. James Logan believed they were intent on establishing New Castle as a major port independent of Philadelphia. They offered outgoing Gov. Evans a commission to act as their governor if he would assist their anti-proprietary efforts with the crown; he refused. Their efforts were stymied when nine members of the Assembly refused to appear. Without a quorum, the remaining nine members, led by Speaker James Coutts, Jasper Yeates, Richard Halliwell, and Robert French, drew up a petition, ostensibly on behalf of the Assembly, to the Board of Trade outlining their grievances against WP. Logan urged that William Penn, Jr., a close friend of Coutts, should warn him of the consequences of his actions; alternatively, WP could show the Board of Trade relevant portions of Logan's correspondence on that issue. See *Micro.* 13:605, 703, 707, 735.

5. An Act for the More Easy and Effectual Collecting of the Proprietary's Quitrents, passed in Jan. 1706. The Queen in Council reviewed it in Oct. 1709 but did not act upon it, thereby allowing it to become law by lapse of time. *Statutes,* 2:224-31.

6. See doc. 157, n. 17.

7. See *Micro.* 12:812; 13:121, 135, 148, 233, 362.

8. Charles Gookin.

9. See doc. 139, n. 25.

10. The Susquehanna Valley. For WP's efforts to populate this area, see *PWP,* 3:671-78.

11. Crown. See doc. 157, n. 28.

12. On 16 Mar. 1709 Logan wrote by way of the Massachusetts fleet: "Pray guard ag[st] Mitchels projects for I doubt they may prove Injurious." *Micro.* 13:735.

161
TO THE EARL OF GODOLPHIN

[c. 2 May 1709]

A Memorial Humbly Offered to the Consideracion of Sidney Earle of Godolphin Lord High Treasurer of Great Brittain, by William Penn Proprittor and Governor of Pensilvania in behalfe of Several Merchants Viz[t] [1]

To furnish her Majes[ties] Ships of Warr in the West Indies Maryland and Virginia, wth Provissions from Pensilvania In America; at Cheaper Rates (more particularly at this juncture when the price of Corne is Considerably raised by the Scarcity therof in Europe) fresher and better then Usually is Sent from England; and Other parts of Europe; the badness of provissions in General from whence hass to Offten (it may be fear[d]) been one great Cause of the frequent distempers among our Seamen proceeding from the Length of time the same remains on Ship board from the first time of takeing in, till the delivery thereof

For Remidy of w[ch] it is proposed that the Queens Ships may be furnished by Us Espeicially wth Bread Flower Oatmeal and groats;[2] the few Impediments that Lye in Our way, (in Respect of the many on this side Europe,) Makeing the Voyages from Pensilvania to the Islands much more safe and Shorter, being generally Runn in fourteen or Eighteen day[s] at most; by Reason the Short Stay, Our Vessels make in Harbour; after their Ladeing is On board: the same being to be had from the Mill and Newly bolted and packt) which gives us always^{s} the Oppertunity to Supply the Islands wth Provissions Fresher and wholesomer then can come from Europe

Impr [3]: To Supply her Majes^{ties} Ships wth Provissions; Upon such terms as Shal be Agree^{d} on; her Majesty Runing the Resque[4] of Said good^{s} from Pensilvania to the Island^{s}; and Upon Shiping such goods at Pensilvania they be permited to draw bills for England On the proper Officers: at the price as then the Markett Rules; Allowing the Exchange[5] which will be in her Majesties favour

Otherwise the proposers are willing to Runn the Resque of said good^{s} and pay Freight to said Islands (her Majesty Allowing Convoy for Such Vessells) which may Alwayes be had, in Twenty four hours from New York & Virginia, where the Station is for her Majesties Ships of warr for the Securetty of Trade in those parts; delivering the quantities (Which they agree to perform) to her Majesties Officers: Appointed to Receive the Same; This Accepted: they will be willing to Settle & fix a price: and Upon delivery of Such good^{s} in the West Indies: be permitted to draw bills for England

The proposers will be ready On Agreement to give Sufficient Securetty to the Goverment to performe any Contract as Shall be Agree^{d} On here with her Majesties Officers According to this or any Reasonable Terms the Goverment Shall Approve of

It is Next desired that the Vessels Masters and Sailors belonging to Such Vessels; be protected from being prest[6] and all Other Mollestacions and hinderances dureing the time of their Imploy in her Majesties Service.

Whitehall Treasury Chambers 2^{d} May 1709

The Right Hono^{ble} the Lord High Treasurer is pleased to Referr this Memoriall to the Commissioners for Victualling Her Maj^{ts} Navy who are to Consider the same & hear the proposers thereupon and then to Report to his Lord^{p} what they thinke fit to be done for Her Ma^{ts} Service in relacion to the premises[7]

Wm Lowndes

DS. Treasury Papers, Anne, T 1/115/66-67, PRO. (*Micro.* 13:750.) Docketed by WP: Memorial | ab^{t} victualing | the Queens ships | in the west indias. Further docketed: 2 May 1709 | Ref. to Com^{rs} Vict^{g}.

1. These merchants have not been identified.
2. Hulled and crushed grain, chiefly oats. *OED.*
3. *Imprimis,* or in the first place. Ibid.
4. In effect, the crown would insure the cargoes.
5. The rate of exchange between English and Pennsylvania currency.
6. Impressed, or compelled to serve in the army or navy. *OED.*
7. On 23 July 1709 the commissioners for victualling the navy reported to the lord treasurer on WP's memorial. They had received tenders from the merchants in question but found the prices higher than those generally paid by their agent in Jamaica. The commissioners therefore recommended that the proposal be refused. *Calendar of Treasury Papers, 1708-1714,* p. 128.

162
TO THE DUKE OF MARLBOROUGH

6 3m (May) 1709

Noble Friend

Thy best Friends have been in some pain for thy quick & agreable passage,[1] which they now conclude because they have no news yet from thee.

It is by no means pleasing that the Duke chooses the Field before the Cabinet, Since the Enimys are so much abler there than in the field, & that the Duke, without a flattery, is equally able in both, & as he has no body of his Size in the field, so no body can be better furnisht for the Cabinet. and that so great a General should victoriously forward a peace, is certainly a great addition to his caracter, it being as wise as brave, and I think Christian too.

I have inclosed to the Duke my Novel, abt peace.[2] It is no more than Henry the 4th of france design'd[3] & the States of Holland have proved practicable, & therfore not chimericall.

For America, I hope, in a post o[4] two, under the Lady Dutches's[5] covert, to send a paper a few particulars, that may be worth our poor Country a million of mony yearly for ought I know.[6] Ld Treasurer[7] has not seen it, whose correct Judgement, I would be glad to have upon it. I add no more but that I am with great Sincerity & respect

Thy Faithfull Friend
Wm Penn

ALS. Additional Manuscripts 61,366, fols. 179-82, BL. (Not filmed.) Addressed: For my Noble | Friend the Duke | of Marleborough. Docketed: 3d May 1709, | From Mr Penn, | B.1.28. Endorsed, probably by Sarah, Duchess of Marlborough: I was desired by | mr penn to send | this which hee | sent me unseald.

1. On 4 May the duke of Marlborough had embarked from England for the peace conference at the Hague. Luttrell, 6:437.

2. This was WP's *An Essay Toward the Present and Future Peace of Europe,* first published in 1693 during the War of the League of Augsburg. It envisioned a European parliament with each nation proportionally represented in accordance with its economic power. See *PWP,* vol. 5, item 93.

3. Although WP attributes *The Grand Design* (1638) to King Henry IV (1589-1610) of France, it was more likely the work of Maximillian de Béthune (1560-1641), duc de Sully. This plan sought to create a balance of power among European states to reduce the power of the House of Hapsburg. See Mary Maples Dunn, *William Penn, Politics and Conscience* (Princeton, 1967), p. 165.

4. WP probably meant "or."

5. Sarah Churchill (1660-1744), duchess of Marlborough, wife of John Churchill, first duke of Marlborough, had been a confidant of Queen Anne but was gradually losing favor at court to Abigail Hill Masham, a close ally of Robert Harley. It had been rumored in Mar. 1708 that Sarah was prepared to assist WP in his legal struggle with the Ford family. See *DNB;* Norris Papers, 7:162, HSP.

6. This was WP's plan for an expanded and reorganized British North American Empire. See doc. 163.

7. Sidney Lord Godolphin.

163
TO THE DUKE OF MARLBOROUGH

Bristoll. 22 3^{m} (May) 1709

Noble Friend

I hope my last[1] came time enough for the Peace, especially Since all our news made us believe there would be none this year; But to days prints Speaking so very favourably of it,[2] I Send this in reference to our Northbounds in America.

The English Empire on the Contenent lyes upon the South Side, & we Claym to the North Sea of Hudsons Bay, but I should be glad if our North Bounds might be exprest & allowed to the South Side of St Lawrences River that Feeds Canaday eastward, & comes from the Lakes westward, w^{ch} {will} make a Glorious Country, & from those lakes due west to the ~~french~~ River of ~~Messippa~~ Messicippa,[3] & travers that River to the extream bounds of the Continent {westward}, whereby we may secure 1000 miles of that River down to the Bay of Mexico; and that the French demolish or at least quitt all their Settlem^{ts} within the bounds aforesayd.[4] The Duke may finde at any Noted Stationers in Holland or Flanders the Map of North America, & See how St L. River runs east & west through the length of the Continent, & that of Messicippa, wch lys 2000 miles cross the Continent, North & South; for without such a settlement of our American Bounds, we shall be in hazard of being dangerously Surpris'd at one time or other by the French & their Indians, especially if they send but 12 ships of war to attaque us by sea. I humbly referr it all to the Dukes English heart & Head, to secure to his Country so great an one & of that vallue on many acc^{ts} (and no more, I think, than we have a reall claime to) forgive the roughness of this, a Gen^{ll} assembly of our People[5] from the Countys ab^{t} this Citty so fill me wth Company & business, I cannot send it in a better Dress. God Speed the Plow; allow me thy Good Opinion & beleive me to be with great Respect

Thy obliged Faithfull Frend
Wm Penn

ALS. Additional Manuscripts 61,366, fol. 191, BL. (Not filmed.) Docketed: From Mr Penn.

1. Doc. 162.

2. In fact, the peace negotiations at The Hague had failed and the War of the Spanish Succession continued for four more years. Unfortunately for WP, the duke of Marlborough would soon fall from power and the Treaty of Utrecht in 1713 would be negotiated by his Tory opponents led by Viscount Bolingbroke. See John B. Wolf, *The Emergence of the Great Powers, 1685-1715* (New York, 1951), pp. 86-91.

3. Mississippi.

4. WP is here proposing boundary limits not achieved by the English settlers in America until the Louisiana Purchase. The Treaty of Utrecht failed to fulfil WP's

hopes. Britain did acquire Acadia (Nova Scotia) and forced the French to recognize the rights of the Hudson's Bay Company, but the residue of French North America was left intact.

5. The Bristol Yearly Meeting of Quakers.

164
FROM THE EARL OF PETERBOROUGH

[c. May-June 1709][1]

I heare you are att Bristoll, and would be glad to know how you dispose of your self, how long you stay there, and whether you come afterwards for any Time to the Bath.

your British physn^t Doctour Lane[2] advises my Drinking the watters there, I know my own distemper best, and the conversation of a True, & agreable Friend may give creditt to his prescriptions, if you stay any Time where you are, I will take The watters The sooner.

if your affaires require a quick return to London, let us meet however, I can send a Calash or very good Pads[3] if you will call at Dodington[4] & putt you into your Road, or let me know when you passe by the Bath.

I find your Great Generall will not disoblige his army with a peace[5] & it will be some time Longer ere we can reduce the world to your no fighting principle.

we heard the Whiggs were designing to make you a present of their Palatinat beggars,[6] I am so weary of this world, that I almost wished to be one of them, and Transported to your Territories.

Till we meet accept of the very sincere assurances I make you, that no man is with more affection

your humble servant & Friend
Peterborow

ALS. Penn-Forbes Collection, HSP. (*Micro.* 13:646.) Addressed: For Mr Pen | att Bristoll. Docketed: Lord Peterborough.

1. This undated letter was probably written in late May or early June 1709, when WP was in Bristol and when hopes for a truce in the war were failing. WP was in Bristol by 22 May and back in London by 9 June; he visited Bristol again from late July to late Sept. *Micro.* 13:763, 765, 767; 14:021, 031.

2. Unidentified. "British" here probably means "Welsh." *OED.*

3. Pad-nags, or easy-paced horses. *OED.*

4. Dodington, Glos., about 10 miles northeast of Bristol. Peterborough seems to have been staying at his estate in Dauntsey, Wilts., 15 miles further east. William Stebbing, *Peterborough* (London, 1890), p. 10.

5. At peace negotiations at the Hague in Apr.-May 1702, the duke of Marlborough had insisted on the Whig position of "no peace without Spain," whereby France would guarantee that the Bourbon Philip V of Spain would cede his throne to the Hapsburg candidate, Charles III. English hopes for peace rose as the negotiations continued but were dashed with the news of 2 June that Louis XIV, Philip's grandfather, had refused

to sign the treaty. Marlborough immediately began to prepare for battle and was accused of wanting to continue the war in order to bolster his own diminishing power. Peterborough, who had been the English commander in Spain until his dismissal in 1707, had often criticized Marlborough's strategy. David Chandler, *Marlborough as Military Commander* (New York, 1973), pp. 241-45.

6. Through the summer and fall of 1709 thousands of Palatine refugees poured into London and were temporarily housed in tents on the outskirts of the city until the government could arrange for their resettlement. Because the Whigs had pushed the naturalization bill through Parliament (see doc. 154, n. 25), they were generally blamed for the influx of refugees. WP's name is not mentioned in the records of the public debate over the refugees; the archbishop of Canterbury, however, believed that WP had been the one to invite them to England. Only a small group settled in Pennsylvania (see doc. 167, n. 9). The Board of Trade took special care to prevent the Palatines from being "decoy'd into Proprietary Governments," meaning Pennsylvania, and instead promoted their settlement in New York, Carolina, and the West Indies. *PMHB*, 2:117-23, 10:379-88; *CSPC,1708-1709*, pp. 290, 455-57, 560-61.*CSPC, 1708-1709*, pp. 455-57, 560; William L. Sachse, *Lord Somers* (Manchester, Eng., 1975), pp. 280-81; *The London Diaries of William Nicolson, Bishop of Carlisle, 1702-1718*, ed. Clyve Jones and Geoffrey Holmes (Oxford, 1985), p. 542.

165
FROM JAMES LOGAN

Philadelphia 14.4 month [June] 1709

Honored Governor

To my surprize I have been just now told that this Bearer Casp Hoodt is in a few Minutes to depart for Maryland in order to embarque for England, who should he leave this place without one line from me might not only take it unkind but it might perhaps be thought more strange there that I should omitt such an Opportunity therefore till I am called on shall goe on with a few Lines

By the Men of War from N York I have briefly hinted[1] to thee the heads of such affairs as have mostly employ'd our thoughts of late. the Town of Lewis having been plunder'd the 7th of last Month by a French Privateer[2] & divers others of the Enemy having been seen on the Coast wch has been much infested, has exceedingly Alarm'd the Countrey beyond what could be easily imagined from no more pressing a Danger, But so it has been, as the Bearer can much more particularly relate This threw those who are alwayes calling for a Defence under the greatest Uneasiness and has putt them upon forming an Address to the Queen or Lds wch I believe no Endeavours here will be sufficient to prevent[3] Friends are so tired out with the Clamours and Abuses of these men that the thoughts of Government become very uncomfortable to them And what heightens their Uneasiness is the Indignation of others at the Assemblies Refusal to doe any thing in Obedience to the Q's Commands towards the Expedition against Canada,[4] wch I have several times mentioned. Boston and Conecticot ha~~s~~ve far outdone what was desired of them Road Island the same, and York has at least come up to if not exceeded their proportion Jersey Voted 3000^{l}, they Voted the Bill for it twice Ord^{d} it to be engrossed but before the 3^{d} Reading their Minds it seems alter'd ('tis said upon some Advices from hence) & then they intirely rejected it, the Majority there are friends And at first they Voted it only to be given to the Queen Which all the friends of the Council & the Generality (I think all) the friends of the Ministry here not only thought but freely gave their Opinion to the Assembly that it might be safely done wthout breaking in upon their Principles. But all that could be obtained from ours was to vote 500^{l} to the Queen, but lest it should be employ'd in that Service, tho' the buying of Provisions to send to Boston was all the Governor at length proposed to doe wth it they deferr'd it till August to wch time they ~~deferr'd it~~ {adjourned themselves}[5] directly in Opposition to the Governors Commands. He must of necessity Answer the Qu's Letter to him[6] which is exceedingly positive in this business & for his Answer must Send a Copy of the Assemblies Proceedings, wch I am sure will be of no service to thee, this place or fr^{ds} of any other.

Baltimores Struggle for all the Lower Counties[7] their Address by Ja Coutts concerning their Government[8] & this coming all on the back of one another, will I doubt be too hard for thee to bear up against, but why thou shouldst contend for those who so litle regard thee, or consider any thing further than thy own just Interest & the Ease of such of thy friends here, who really deserve the title, as there are still a great many such, is what neither I nor they can easily understand. If friends after such a Profession of denying the World, Living out of it, & acting in opposition to its depraved wayes to which they have born a Testimony by the most distinguishing Characters from any other people, cannot be satisfied, but must involve themselves in Affairs of Government under another Power & Administration which Administration in many of its necessary parts is altogether inconsistent wth this Profession I say if this be the case, I cannot see why it should not be accounted singularly just in Providence to deal to their Portion Crosses Vexation & Disappointments to convince them of their Mistakes & own Inconsistency. I write freely as I think & as I have often of late been obliged to express my self, tho' thou well knows I am no very strict Pretender that way

The Settlement made upon the Advance of the Money paid the Fords[9] making a great Alteration in affairs of Property here, the Commissioners[10] cannot well proceed by any Powers they now have. I have received a Letter from Tho: Callowhill and others of Bristol[11] informing me that thou hast made over to them & others of London & Ireland not only the Province but all thy Debts of whatever kind here & therefore they desire me to gett in all I can to have it ready for their Orders. And this was done I perceive before any one of thy Bills was either paid or due, yet thou Assign'd all the Bonds that were to discharge those very Draughts & others since ~~made~~ drawn by thee to Coll Gookin &c Upon this I cannot but reflect upon the Dangers I exposed my self to before tho' unwittingly, from wch thrô the good Providence of God, I am now with thee & thine happily relieved, but must from thence take a Caution for the future. However I have adventured to pay the Bills at least the greatest part of them & hope I shall be able to justify it, but think it unsafe to proceed much further untill I have an opportunity of Seeing thee, wch because I fear the troubles I have already mentioned will not allow here I think this Fall to make a Trip over wthout waiting any further Advice.[12] I have many things to induce me to this besides what I have here hinted, and particularly that 'tis impossible for me to be easy, or any way enjoy my self under such a Load of Confusion as oppresses me in matters of Government. I resolved to be Patient & sitt quiet till the late threatning Storms blew over, but since I have no prospect of a Serenity under this Constitution as now modelled, I must endeavour to breath Liberty again & taste freedom once more. I hope my Voyage may prove of Service to thee as I fully design it as far as it may ~~reasonably~~ ly in my Power, for perhaps my presence there may not be amiss, if it should prove according to the Expectation of most here, that the Parliament who now so narrowly scan all publick Affairs should inquire next Winter into the Management of this Expedition & the reasons of our failures wch Inquiry 'tis feared will prove very litle to our Advantage when helped forward by the Remonstances & Complaints that in all probability will attend it, from Colonel Vetch[13] Colonel Nicholson[14] & many others. How great an Unhappiness doe I often think is this Complication of Misfortunes now in (what we {here} generally hope may prove the last or near) the ~~f~~last Year of the War![15] I wish thou may'st be able to secure thy self But if any surrender should be made[16] & a new Council thought of (wch is not very probable) before I arrive it may not be amiss to give thee a List of the Present, because I find Oldmixon in his Account of this place[17] has been very much misinformed

Divers things that I ought to take Notice of to thee, may I believe b[e] better omitted till I am personally there, Only I know not what to doe wth Colonel Evans, I have largely discoursed him not only by himself, but in Company of some of thy best friends chosen for that purpose, & he affirms that notwithstanding he has seldom spent a penny he could handsomly spare he shall scarce have enough to carry him off after his Debts here are pd and that he never either sent off or remitted directly nor indirectly since his Arrival 50l Sterling in all. That story of his getting by the mines I believe to be a very fiction.[18] Colonel Gookin thinks he has great Cause to be uneasy at his Change,

& fears unless some Provision be made for him, that he shall be a greater Loser than his fortunes now in his Advanced Years will by any means allow of or Bear Time will not allow me to add but that I am &c

Thy most Obed[t] Servant
J L

Pray take this as 'tis wrote w[th] a flying pen & w[th]out Copy
List of the Council ES. SC. JG. TS. GO. SF. CP. JY. WT. RH. GR. INor. SP. AP. JL[19]

LBC. James Logan Letterbook, HSP. (*Micro.* 13:772.) Docketed: per Caspar Hoodt.

1. Probably *Micro.* 13:757, dated 11, 12 May 1709.

2. On 7 May Capt. Cross, in a 20-gun captured English ship formerly called the *Queen Anne,* landed about 80 men in Lewes. They plundered the town thoroughly, ransomed four men for Indian corn and sheep, and shot a Maryland ship captain. See *Micro.* 13:757; Norris Papers, 7½:10-12, 15-16, HSP.

3. No address has been found. Isaac Norris claimed that the "Church Party" was so enraged against the Quakers that they were "Rudely & scandalously threatening they would as soon shoot us as a fr:man" (Norris Papers, 7½:16).

4. On 1 Mar. 1709 the Queen in Council approved a plan to invade Canada from New England (see n. 14, below). As their requirement for the expedition, Pennsylvania was to furnish 150 men. Dep. Gov. Gookin estimated the charge as £4000 which he expected the Assembly to raise. See *CSPC, 1708-1709,* pp. 230-32; *Votes and Proceedings,* 2:34.

5. The Assembly adjourned on 14 June. *Votes and Proceedings,* 2:42.

6. Dep. Gov. Gookin wrote to Cols. Vetch and Nicholson (see nn. 13-14, below) on 17 June 1709, explaining the Assembly's rejection of his demands, and asked them to justify his own behavior to the ministry in England. See *CSPC, 1708-1709,* p. 349.

7. See docs. 158, 159.

8. See doc. 160, n. 4.

9. See headnote to doc. 121.

10. Commissioners of Property.

11. Not found.

12. Logan sailed from New Castle aboard the *Hope Galley* on 3 Dec. 1709. See Frederick B. Tolles, *James Logan and the Culture of Provincial America* (Boston, 1957), p. 75.

13. Col. Samuel Vetch (1668-1732), a Scottish-born soldier, had fought in the army of William III. He came to America in 1700, acting as a negotiator for the English with the French and Indians. In 1708 his plan to conquer Canada and Acadia was approved by the British government, but after he had raised and trained colonial levies, his plan fell through when the British diverted promised forces to Portugal. G. M. Waller, *Samuel Vetch: Colonial Enterpriser* (Chapel Hill, 1960).

14. Col. Francis Nicholson, former governor of Virginia and Maryland, had been appointed by the British government as joint commander with Col. Samuel Vetch for the abortive invasion of Canada in 1709. *DNB.*

15. In fact, the War of the Spanish Succession continued until 1713.

16. WP did not resume active negotiations for the surrender of his government until July 1710; see doc. 179.

17. John Oldmixon (1673-1742), historian and pamphleteer, wrote a two-volume study of *The British Empire in America,* published in 1708. Since he had never visited America, he drew upon printed sources. He barely touched on Pennsylvania, noting that the colonists there had never fought the French or Indians and therefore very little of consequence had occurred. See *DNB;* Richard S. Dunn, "Seventeenth-Century English Historians of America," in James M. Smith, ed., *Seventeenth-Century America: Essays in Colonial History* (Chapel Hill, 1959), pp. 222-24.

18. See doc. 159, text at nn. 26-27.

19. Edward Shippen, Samuel Carpenter, Joseph Growden, Thomas Story, Griffith Owen, Samuel Finney, Caleb Pusey, Jasper Yeates, William Trent, Richard Hill, George Roche, Isaac Norris, Samuel Preston, Anthony Palmer, and James Logan.

166
ORDER IN PRIVY COUNCIL

At the Court at St James's,
the 23^d^ of June 1709

Present
The Queen's most Excellent Majesty

Lord Chancellor	Lord Dartmouth
Lord Treasurer	Mr Secretary Boyle
Lord President	Mr Comptroller
Duke of Queensbury	Mr Vice Chamberlain
Lord High Admiral	Mr Chancell^r^ of the Excheq^r^
Earl of Berkeley	Lord Chief Justice Holt
Earl of Radnor	Master of the Rolls
Earl of Loudoun	Lord Chief Justice Trevor[1]

Mr Vernon

Whereas upon the Humble Petition of Charles Lord Baltemore,[2] Proprietor under Her Majesty, of the Province of Maryland, Praying to be heard against an Order of Council of the 13th of November 1685,[3] Dividing an Isthmus or Tract of Land in America, lying between the Bay and River of Dellaware, and the Eastern Sea on the One Side, and Cheasaspeake Bay on the other; One Moiety to the Crown and another to the Petitioner, and that the Difference between the Petitioner and William Penn Esqr Proprietor of Pensylvania touching the Boundaries of their respective Province{s} may be adjusted; Which Order of the 13th of November 1685, the Petitioner Alledges to have been Obtained by the false Suggestions of Mr Penn, and without the Petitioner having been heard thereupon; Her Majesty was pleased by Order of the 19th of May last,[4] to appoint the Hearing of this Matter in Council, and Accordingly both parties this day attending and being fully heard with their Council Learned. And it appearing by Authentick Copies of Proceedings at this Board, that as well the Petitioner, as the said Mr Penn had been divers times heard before the Making of the said Order. Her Majesty with the Advice of Her Privy Council, is pleased to Order, That the Lord Baltimore's Petition be dismissed this Board; and that the abovementioned Order of Council of the 13th of November 1685, be ratifyed and Confirmed in all it's Points, And be put in Execution without any further delay. Whereof the Parties concerned are to take notice and Yeild Obedience Accordingly

John Povey[5]

DS. C.O. 5/1264/75, PRO. (*Micro.* 13:782.) Docketed: Pennsylvania | Copy of an Order of Council | of the 23[d] of June 1709, dismissing | the Lord Baltemore's Petition | against an Order of the 13th of Nov[r] | 1685 for Settling the Boundaries | between Pennsylvania and | Maryland | Received | Read | 5th July 1709.

1. Lord Chancellor Sir William Cowper; Lord Treasurer Sidney Lord Goldophin; Lord President John Lord Somers; James Douglas, second duke of Queensberry and duke of Dover, co-keeper of the Scottish privy seal; Lord High Admiral Thomas Herbert (1656-1733), eighth earl of Pembroke; William Berkeley, Baron Berkley of Stratton; Charles Bodvile Robartes (1660-1723), second earl of Radnor; Hugh Campbell (d. 1731), third earl of Loudoun, co-keeper of the Scottish privy seal; James Vernon; William Legge, earl of Dartmouth; Secretary of State (for the northern department) Henry Boyle; Comptroller of the Household Hugh Cholmondeley (d. 1724), first earl of Cholmondeley; Chancellor of the Exchequer John Smith (1655-1723); Lord Chief Justice Sir John Holt, of King's Bench; Master of the Rolls Sir John Trevor (1637-1717); and Lord Chief Justice Sir Thomas Trevor (1658-1730), of Common Pleas. The vice-chamberlain has not been identified. *DNB*.

2. See *CSPC, 1708-1709*, p. 194.

3. See *PWP*, 3:68-70.

4. See *CSPC, 1708-1709*, p. 304.

5. John Povey, the clerk of the Privy Council, was a cousin of William Blathwayt and, formerly, assistant auditor of colonial revenues and clerk of the old Lords of Trade. Steele, *Colonial Policy*, p. 24.

RECONCILIATIONS

June 1709–May 1711

The years 1709–11 marked the Indian summer of WP's career. After the humiliating experiences of 1705–8, in which his business incompetence had been publicly exposed by the Fords and his absentee management of Pennsylvania and the Lower Counties had been openly repudiated by the colonists, WP recovered his spirits and resumed his public activities—although on a more modest scale than before 1705. His surviving correspondence from the two years June 1709–May 1711 is notably genial in tone. Partly this is because James Logan, WP's most fulsome and pessimistic reporter from Pennsylvania, stopped writing as he prepared to visit his aging master in England; Logan left Pennsylvania in December 1709 and did not return until March 1712. In place of Logan's commentary on public affairs, we have an unusual group of fourteen private letters from WP to members of his family, written between 25 June 1709 and 7 February 1710; half of these are printed below. WP's letters to Hannah from this period (see docs. 167–69, 174, 175) are almost his only known letters to his second wife apart from his engagement letters written in 1695–96 (*PWP*, 3:413, 425–34). His letters to young John and Thomas Penn (see docs. 171, 173) are the only ones found from WP to his children by his second wife, and they are much more revealing than the formulaic letters of farewell written to Gulielma's three young children (*PWP*, 2:272–75, 280–81). These family letters supply details of WP's relationship with his family, showing his emotional dependence on Hannah and his affectionate concern for the children's health, education, and amusement, with his gifts of books, a new pony for "Johnne," a doll for "Pegge," and sweets for "poor Tomme."

Much of the family correspondence concerns WP's search for a house to rent. Since the sale of Warminghurst, the Penns had not had a satisfactory home of their own. They had stayed with the Callowhills or rented nearby in Bristol and had boarded with friends in Ealing, London, and Reading. While the rest of the family stayed in Bristol, WP combed the countryside surrounding London for the ideal house: large enough for a family with five children and several servants; near a good Quaker meeting and school; and close to the Bristol road for easier visits with Hannah's family and faster mail delivery. WP's household budget had shrunk radically in the three decades since he had purchased Warminghurst for £4450 (*PWP*, 1:649); now he was searching for a house at under £25 a year rent. By May 1710 the family had settled at Ruscombe near Twyford, Berks., and was attending Quaker meetings in Reading. John and Thomas probably went back to the small Quaker school they had attended in the early part of 1709.

In Pennsylvania and the Lower Counties, there was a significant movement toward a reconciliation between the proprietor and the colonists. When Logan left the colony in late 1709, the Pennsylvania Assembly under David Lloyd's leadership was stridently asserting its privileges and protesting WP's oppressive policies. In June 1710 WP wrote a strongly worded yet measured public letter (doc. 178), reproving the Assembly for its childish conduct. Fortunately for WP, in October 1710 the annual election produced a complete turnover in the Assembly. On learning that Lloyd and his allies were temporarily removed, WP wrote a letter of friendship and thanks (doc. 181) to his chief supporters in the Council and Assembly. In the Lower Counties, also, the assemblymen were far more conciliatory than in 1708–9. Still trying to foster Pennsylvania's economic growth, WP recruited new European immigrants (doc. 176) and contracted for the development of Pennsylvania's mines (doc. 177). At the same time—no doubt urged on by Logan after he reached England — WP resumed negotiations for the surrender of Pennsylvania's government to the crown (docs. 179, 180, 182). When WP's Quaker supporters in Pennsylvania heard about these renewed negotiations, they expressed their alarm (docs. 185, 186). The Anglicans in the colony were lobbying with the bishop of London to have all Quakers disqualified from officeholding because they refused to swear oaths. Queen Anne was no friend to dissenters, and should WP surrender his government to the queen, the Anglicans in Pennsylvania might well establish themselves as the new governing party. Almost too late the Pennsylvania Quakers were recognizing the value of WP's protective powers.

167
TO HANNAH PENN

Tish[es] [1] 25 4[m] [June] 1709

Myn Dearest H.

I bless the Lord I can tell thee I am pretty well, & much affected with thy very kinde letter of last post,[2] & humbly pray the almighty God to keep us to his eternal kingdom; & while here make us happy in our meetings together to our mutuall Comfort, again, & againe. I send thee by Arthur Thomas[3] 1 lb of chocolot, & ½ of coffee, & a Bottle of Hungary water,[4] & cos. Sprs Salve[5] for &c: I am just goeing for Colchester H. G. T. Brown, one Green, Christr Crow,[6] & son Penn,[7] with or after me. I have got out my order of Councill in my favour,[8] wch I think to send to America forthwith, by Jos. Guy, that Carrys the Palatinats over.[9] I purpose to return, if the Lord please, 5 night, & then, I shall look towards thee & thine, if something extreordinary dont hinder. our children & relations here are all pretty well, & often salute thee & ours &c: I dined at my good sisters[10] upon 6 {little} dishes yesterday, who Salutes, thee, & so pretty peggy,[11] & ours. It is neer 3 & by ½ after four I take chaise at honest T. Coxes[12] so myn own Dearest I embrace thee & my Dr. lambs, beyond words, & wth Dr. love to thy Far & Mor cosins & Frds & the family I close theirs & Thine own

WP.

ar. Th.[13] goes hence 2d day.

ALS. Penn Papers, Penn-Forbes Collection, HSP. (*Micro.* 13:787.) Addressed: For H. Penn | at T. Callowhills | Mert in | Bristoll.

1. Laetitia Aubrey lived at White Lyon Court off Cornhill St. in east London. Drinker, *Hannah Penn,* p. 32; Digests of Quaker Records, Sus. and Sur., GSP.

2. No letters from Hannah Penn to WP have been found for this period.

3. Arthur Thomas (d. 1720) was a Bristol pewterer and a frequent representative to London Yearly Meeting. Mortimer, 2:263.

4. Wine infused with rosemary leaves, used for medicinal purposes. *OED.*

5. Richard Springett (d. c. 1718), Gulielma Penn's cousin and Herbert Springett's younger brother, was a London apothecary. John Comber, ed., *Sussex Genealogies: Lewes Centre* (Cambridge, 1933), pp. 281-82; London Record Society, *London Inhabitants Within the Walls, 1695* (Chatham, Kent, 1966), p. 276.

6. WP, Henry Gouldney, and the others probably were going to attend a yearly meeting for worship in Colchester, Essex, an early center of Quaker activity. Christopher Crow may have been the Lombard St. barber surgeon or his father, who lived in Essex. Brown and Green have not been identified. Braithwaite, *Second Period,* pp. 276, 548; Digests of Quaker Records, London and Middx., GSP.

7. William Penn, Jr.

8. Doc. 166.

9. WP arranged for eight Palatine refugee families to settle in Pennsylvania, and London Yearly Meeting authorized £50 toward their expenses. WP was blamed for encouraging the flood of Palatine refugees to England in 1709 (see doc. 164, n. 6). *PMHB,* 2:122-23; London Yearly Meeting Minutes, 1709, p. 242, FLL; Walter A. Knittle, *Early Eighteenth-Century Palatine Emigration* (Philadelphia, 1937), p. 80.

10. Margaret Lowther must have been living in London, rather than Yorkshire, at this time.

11. Probably Margaret Penn, Hannah's only surviving daughter, then four years old.

12. Thomas Cox, a London Quaker vintner and grocer, was the son of Thomas Cox, Sr. (d. 1701), an early sufferer and investor in East New Jersey. Digests of Quaker Records, London and Middx., Sus. and Sur.; *PWP,* 2:102n.

13. Arthur Thomas.

168
TO HANNAH PENN

Buckingham court[1] 9 5m [July] 1709

This is to lett mine own Drst know that hers is, through the Lds mercy, pretty well, & rejoyces that her most acceptible letter tould me so of her & ours.[2] Tishe[3] r. Baker[4] & Dr. Phillips[5] are wth me, wth Counselor west,[6] & supt on some soles & smelts, & goeing home. I goe to morrow to Edgeworth,[7] wth many Frds, my ould way to Rickmansworth,[8] the first of this ~~ye~~ Earth. I have chid R. Bulls[9] people abt the coffee, & they desire it back to change. I cannot be with thee till this day week at soonest, because I would end with this wiked town & stay that away a month or two. I have got a Buck from the Dutchess[10] today, very generously; & the D. of Beufort[11] will give me a warrant for an other to treat our relations & Frds wn I come. Kiss & embrace my Dr. children for me, the lord keep you & give us a comfortable meeting if it be his blessed will. B. wall[12] will tell thee how I am, who calld upon me this morn in his way to Reding,[13] & so to Bristoll. tis past 11. tishe goeing, & so must break off writeing, but never loveing my dearest & hers, that are mine because I am, in the dearest love theirs & thine in the dearest tyes.

WP.

Love to relations & Frds. vale. all here salute.

ALS. Penn Papers, Penn-Forbes Papers, HSP. (*Micro.* 14:007.) Addressed: For H. Penn | Tho. Callowhills | Mert in | Bristoll.

1. Near Spring Gardens, then attached to the king's palace at Whitehall, between St. James's Park and Charing Cross. Peter Cunningham, *A Handbook for London, Past and Present* (London, 1849), 1:142, 2:767-68.
2. Hannah Penn's letter has not been found.
3. Laetitia Aubrey.
4. Perhaps Richard Baker (d. 1722) of Worplesdon, Sur., who was a member of Guildford Monthly Meeting. Digests of Quaker Records, Sus. and Sur., GSP.
5. Perhaps James Phillips, a Quaker physician of Turvill, Bucks. Digests of Quaker Records, London and Middx.
6. Robert West.
7. Edgware, a village now in north London.
8. Rickmansworth, Herts., 18 miles northwest of London, was the home of WP and his first wife, Gulielma, from 1672 to 1676. *PWP*, 1:241, 355.
9. Probably Robert Bullock, originally of Portishead, Som.; his son Daniel was helping WP find a house. See doc. 175, n. 20.
10. Sarah Churchill, the duchess of Marlborough, gave WP a warrant for a buck from the woods near Windsor Lodge, one of the Marlborough residences. *Micro.* 14:010; David Green, *Sarah, Duchess of Marlborough* (London, 1967).
11. Henry Somerset (1684-1714), the duke of Beaufort, was a Tory whose estate was in Badminton, Glos. *DNB*.
12. Benjamin Wall, a Quaker grocer, moved to London from Bristol in 1700. Mortimer, 2:264.
13. Reading, Berks., on the road from London to Bristol.

169
TO HANNAH PENN

Lond. 20. 5m July 1709
beg St Margarets day[1]
at Tishes.[2]

Myne own Dearest
I leave this behinde me to come by the post, that it may tell my beloved, I am following as swiftly as the 3 days Coach can carry me; wch considering wt blood I have lost, 20 z, &c:[3] It is as fast as is fitt.
I had this 3d night last, a good rest, & hope for the same ~~&~~ to morrow night at Reading as well as tonight at my Lodgeings.[4] I have so much to say that I omitt all till we meet; for a letter is too scanty a compass. Weigh my 3 last letters[5] & I shall not have much to say more, poor Lord Lovelace is dead & his sweat & beutifull wife, wth 2 of his Children are left behinde.[6] I purpose to ride to the Bath, upon my own Gelding; from Kings down[7] thither, if not part of the rest to Bristoll.

For my Dr. Boy, or Boys, send or keep them as thou pleasest, & as I am able, Ile ride on horse back or in Coach, or be with you next morning. Farewell to myn own Drst Hannah, & all her Dr offspring & mine, & the Lord send us well together, in his love & feare, in wch I am beyond all words, & Time & Distance, Theirs, & ~~beyond words~~ Likewise

Thine own from all woman kinde
Wm Penn

my deare love to Far & Mor & Relats & Frds as if named, & the family also. vale.
Newberry 22.[8]
I brought this with me to this place & her tell thee, I lay to night in our bed, & had good rest, tho it had been better if I had had my ould & beloved bedfellow. I fine my selfe the better for traveling. Manda[9] recovering. 11 borders there & 2 more comeing. W. Lamb[10] & family well & salutes thee as well as Josephs.[11] the Goverr of Carolina[12] & that Judge advocat goe to Bristoll wth me wth an old Cork[13] wth me

I think to come ~~to~~ by the Bath, & if the children will meet me there, or at the half way house please them in it. Tripe & {ox} muggets[14] wth some parcely guts,[15] I should not dislike for my supper tomorrow ~~&~~ tho nothing else were drest, wch I should desire rather. farewell to my own Drst. & my Dear lambs. I am yours in the deepest Love.

WP

We are got well to Marleborow.[16]

ALS. Penn Mutual Life Insurance Company, Philadelphia. (*Micro.* 14:014.) Addressed: For Tho: Callohill | Mert in | Bristoll.

1. The twentieth of July honors St. Margaret of Antioch, invoked especially by women in childbirth. *The Oxford Dictionary of the Christian Church*, ed. F. L. Cross (Oxford, 1978).

2. Laetitia Aubrey's house in London.

3. Twenty ounces; WP had evidently been bled.

4. WP's lodgings were probably at Buckingham Court. See doc. 168.

5. WP's previous three letters were probably those written 1, 9, and 14 July (*Micro.* 14:005, 007, 010).

6. Lovelace died in New York 6 May 1709. He and his wife, Charlotte, the daughter of Sir John Clayton of Richmond, had two sons, John and Nevil (d. 1736). *DNB;* Raimo, *Governors*, pp. 254-55.

7. Kingsdown Hill was on the London-Bath road, four miles east of Bath. Edward Mogg, ed., *Patterson's Roads . . . in England and Wales* (London, 1729), p. 99.

8. By 22 July WP had arrived at Newbury, Berks., on the road from London to Bristol.

9. Manda has not been identified; she was evidently a young relative or servant later living in the Penn household. The nickname appears often in later family correspondence of the period, as well as in Hannah Penn's Cashbook, HSP.

10. Probably William Lamboll (d. 1722) of Reading, with whom WP may have been staying. Thomas Story stayed at Lamboll's house on his later visits there. *A Journal of the Life of Thomas Story* (Newcastle upon Tyne, 1747), pp. 465, 607..

11. Perhaps Joseph and Elizabeth Coysgarne. Digests of Quaker Records, London and Middx., GSP.

12. Edmund Tynte (d. 1710), possibly of Somerset, was appointed governor of Carolina in Dec. 1708 but did not arrive in the colony until Nov. 1709. He died suddenly in June 1710. Raimo, *Governors*, p. 425.

13. Perhaps an old friend from Cork.

14. Intestines.

15. Probably sweetbreads. *OED.*

16. Marlborough, Wilts., about halfway between Reading and Bristol.

170
TO JAMES LOGAN

Pall-Mall 14 & my birth day of 8[br] [October] 1709

James Logan
Lov[g] Friend
This comes by David Brintnell,[1] to whom I would have thee justly kinde in reference to a small piece of land he has bought here for a childe of his not so fitt for town business. and now know that I have thine of the 12[m] 2[d] 3[d] & 4th two of each of the last months.[2] and for answear, I vallue not Coots[3] nor the disapointm[t] of Colonel Nicolson w[ch] Rainer Att. Gen[ll] of newyork has complained of,[4] but hope to weather them. Only the Assemblys not giveing Gov[r] Gookin any thing after the hundreds it has Cost me, to gett a Gover[r] of my own approved by the Queen & to prevent a Queens Governours outing of me, is so Barbarous, I can very uneasily put it up.[5] *Sampson killed more Philistians at his death than in his life,*[6] *let them have a care of provoaking me too farr. They are a pack of vile brutish spirits.* why will not the best of friends, & mine, stand and put by the *numskulls that D.L.*[7] *governs.* And I cannot think my selfe sincerely used, if this is not done & if they will not assist my affaires there. I must think my paines & charge ill

bestowed here for Frds administration & interest in Govermt for the story of Colonel Quarry, ask parson evans.[8] & know that I have writt to the Lt Goverr to desolve the present Councill (if not well without it) & make him first of a new one, & am not angry with him, only that Person,[9] thou so much recommended, tould me, he had made it an article agst him that he was too indulgent to my Frds & Govermt See the Goverrs letter[10] by way of Bristoll, a Pinck[11] goes thence directly Mitchell is a great undertaker, & has prevailed wth the Lds. of Carolina for land for 600 Palatines, by the help of the Swiss lords, who make him Agent.[12] also the Queen has graunted to the Swiss Lords a tract of land upon the Branches of Potomack, & is seekg ten or 20000 As of me.[13] Hele want for the Lds. a thousand Bushels of flowr not fine but midling,[14] & pay here for the Palatines in Carolina. They are Just now goeing, are on board, wch pray take notice of, since so plain & easy an opertunity of returnes hither. My son Aubrey is in so great a rage, saying thou hast not payd him anything, tho thou writt me word thou hadst payd in 1500l of the 2000l & the rest should not be long after,[15] & indeed he wants it extreamly, wherefore, pray minde that matter. he says thou telst his atturneys, I have orderd thee to pay them nothing, I tould him & her,[16] it was abt the interest of wt was payd to his atturneys, nor indeed will I. Pray ~~pu~~Let Capt Finny {be} in some Post,[17] tell Colonel Gook of it, & to show respect to Jos. Growden, for I hear they behave well,[18] & remember me to all that have deserved well from me, & the rest I wish better. wt would the fools be at? would they have me get law making here insteed of there by abuseing their authority? through whom had they it? how long would D. L. G. J. & Jos. Wil. &c: have lived in Eng. before they had been members of assembly & Justices of peace?[19] have they forgot their low Circumstances? I have not. In short If they will not maintaine a Goverr & settle a lasting Sallery on me or my Dept & to encourage a chief Justice & an atturny Generall, wth a decent allowance I will take care it shall be done by act of Parliamt here, & I will resigne upon that condition fore one.[20] Also know that a Good cheif Justice should so brow beat your quack lawyers that our primative law of every man teling his own Greivance, or by his frd, without Fees, should be renewed again. & without it we cannot hope it *for all wise men press that as the most Capitall thing to a quiet Govermt to Suffer no lawyers in it.* Forget not the Good & now poor widdow Harrison of Dublin,[21] Frds write me again & again. I admire thou hast never sent me Furs, creatures Birds, &c: I writt for that is as gratefull to the people I have obligations too, as greater things.[22] Thy head is too full of (thou thinkest) greater things. By Colonel G. letter I perceive thou intendest over to us,[23] wch I shall be glad to see, tho' it were but for 2 months time. but then I hope thou will putt my affaires in good hands. It Seems the quantity of flowr to be sent to the Palatines at Carolina, is 100 Barrels of ordinary Flowr, but let it be wheaten flowr. If we had 1000 quarters of Flowr here, it would be a noble cargoe, wheat being 10 & 11 shilings a bushell in this town, & then returns may be in our Growth, to an high advantage pray minde this. I hope Pennsberry is upon a good bottom & at least 150 if not more acres are cleared, if not 200, & some marsh for good Meddow. w. watson, makes heavy complaint of thee & J. Sacher:[24] you look upon all as your own & seem as if you were never to be called upon. but take little notice of it for I think to write a few lines perhaps. I fear I shall not be able to finde D. Llds Remonstrance,[25] but will endeavour it; for I am but just come from the west of England to town.[26] & my papers are partly in town, & partly at Reading where in our way to Bristoll we sojourned 4 or 5 months, for our Childrens Sake at School.[27] Tho I know not the use now to be made of it there. he being in such consideration wth some there. Pray give my love to I. N.[28] & family. He has sent several letters to Frds at Bristoll as well as here, but none to me,[29] wch I admire a little at. I admire thou hast not my orders abt Colonel Gs mony, pray faile not to do it, as before. I writt two letters to thee on that acct.[30] as also abt Ch. Jones & Robert—.[31] My poor wife collicall, but at times hearty, & so now. & my 5 pretty children[32] were two days agoe, hearty & well. so is my poor son P. & his,[33] also my son Daughter Aubrey. wch ends this at Present, (unless I have more time) from

Thy assured Friend
Wm Penn

ALS. Rare Book Section, State Library of Pennsylvania, Harrisburg. (*Micro.* 14:044.)

1. David Breintnall (d. 1732), a Quaker tailor of Derbyshire, immigrated in the 1680s to Philadelphia, where he acquired two city lots. In July 1709 he purchased a deed for 250 acres from a London First Purchaser who never emigrated, and in 1712 he was granted a city lot on the basis of that purchase. Breintnall had three sons, all of whom settled in Pennsylvania. *PWP,* 3:506n, 689; Phila. Will Bk. E, #282; Hinshaw, 2:339-40, 471; *PA,* 2d ser., 19:528, 544, 555, 576; *Micro.* 2:388; 8:119, 128; Breintnall Family Notes, B. Hoff Knight Collection, GSP; *PMHB,* 59:42-56; *Philological Quarterly,* 21:247-49.

2. Logan had written to WP on 3 Feb., 24 Feb., 7 Apr., 11 and 12 May, 9 June, and 14 June 1709. Docs. 157, 160, 165; *Micro.* 13:685, 757, 769.

3. James Coutts had left for England bearing complaints from the Lower Counties. Docs. 160, 165; *Micro.* 13:757.

4. John Rayner had been appointed attorney general of New York in July 1708 and had returned to England in July 1709 carrying complaints from Col. Nicholson, who was having difficulty raising money and men to support his planned expedition into Canada. Nicholson complained particularly of opposition from Quakers in Pennsylvania and New Jersey, and the expedition was eventually cancelled. *CSPC, 1708-1709,* pp. 33-34, 349, 405-7, 419-20, 502; *Minutes of the Provincial Council,* 2:449-67.

5. Since 1706 the governor's salary had come from revenues from an impost tax, which the Assembly failed to renew when it expired in 1709. By Sept. 1709 Gookin was refusing to take any action on other pending legislation until the Assembly had approved a bill to pay salaries for public officials. Doc. 157, n. 10.

6. Judges 16:28. WP is threatening to pull down Quaker officials in Pennsylvania with him if he is forced to surrender the government on unfavorable terms.

7. David Lloyd.

8. See docs. 148, n. 19; 157, text at n. 18.

9. Evan Evans; see doc. 154, text at n. 34.

10. WP's letter to Gookin has not been found.

11. A sailing ship. *OED*.

12. In September 1709 the Carolina proprietors granted François Luis Michel 2500 acres in North Carolina. *CSPC, 1708-1709*, p. 465.

13. Michel and his associates, George Ritter and Baron Graffenried, had petitioned in June for land on the southwest branch of the Potomac to settle 400 or 500 Swiss Protestants. Queen Anne granted the request on 10 Sept. (*CSPC, 1708-1709*, pp. 398, 425, 428-29, 463). No record has been found of the British government's negotiating with WP for land; in fact, the Board of Trade was determined to keep the Palatines out of Pennsylvania. See doc. 164, n. 6.

14. Coarsely ground wheat with bran.

15. For Logan's account of his payments to Aubrey as of 1706, see doc. 130.

16. Laetitia Aubrey. The Aubreys' attorneys in Pennsylvania were Richard Hill and Reese Thomas.

17. Capt. John Finney never received any post in Pennsylvania and returned to live in England in 1711. *Micro.* 14:289.

18. Joseph Growden, a provincial councilor and David Lloyd's former ally, was now defending Logan against Lloyd and the Assembly's attacks.

19. David Lloyd, Griffith Jones (a glover), and Joseph Willcox (a ropemaker) all had relatively humble origins in England and Wales. Roy N. Lokken, *David Lloyd, Colonial Lawmaker* (Seattle, 1959), p. 7; *PWP*, 2:646, 3:581n.

20. In fact, WP assured the Board of Trade in his surrender negotiations that Pennsylvanians were prepared to pay their governor a decent salary. *Minutes of the Provincial Council*, 2:493; doc. 180B.

21. See doc. 38, n. 47.

22. See doc. 154, text at n. 64.

23. Logan told WP in June 1709 that he was coming to England; he arrived in Mar. 1710. Gookin's letter to WP has not been found. Doc. 165, text at n. 12; Frederick B. Tolles, *James Logan and the Culture of Provincial America* (Boston, 1957), p. 81.

24. No letters have been found from William Watson, who was employed at Pennsbury.

25. Doc. 83.

26. WP had just come from Bristol.

27. See doc. 152, n. 4.

28. Isaac Norris.

29. Norris had written to Benjamin Coole of London on 24 May 1709 and to Henry Gouldney of London on 3 June. Deborah Logan and Edward Armstrong, eds., *Correspondence between William Penn and James Logan* (Philadelphia, 1872), 2:346-49. His first letter to WP after his return to Pennsylvania had never arrived: see doc. 172, text at n. 1.

30. See doc. 154, text at n. 20; doc. 160, text at n. 8.

31. WP had been slow in advising Logan to pay bills on Charles Jones and Robert Raine. Doc. 157, text at nn. 3, 4; *Micro.* 13:685, 732.

32. John, age nine; Thomas, seven; Margaret, four; Richard, three; and Dennis, two.

33. William Penn, Jr., had three children: Gulielma Maria, ten; Springett, eight; and William III, six.

171
TO THOMAS PENN

London 22. 8^{m} [October] 1709

My Dr. Boy

I was glad of thine yesterday,[1] but tell thy Dr. mother, that to get your letters at 4th hour, post days, is a great favour; for ~~it is~~ neerer 8 or 9 at night has severall times been the earliest {here,} as thine came last night. I salute you all, thy Dr & Beloved Mother, & you my Dr. children & so the family wth you; but especially your Grandf^{r} &

G Mother,[2] wth that family & our kinde Relations & Friends at Bristoll. Know that through the Lords mercy I am pretty well, & bless the Lord that you are so; I pray him to preserve you. And I charge thy Brother Johnne, & thee, to follow your ~~book~~ book 2 hours in the fore noon, & 2 hours in the after noon, & do readily wt you are bid, & you will comfort your Dr Mother, & your poor father to hear you do so. I sent thy Mother so full a letter last past,[3] that I shall write the less now, but let her know, that this week & next, I have thoughts of goeing both for Rochester, & for Reading; both on truths acct to one, & on our acct to the other;[4] & by that time, I may write more positively to thy Mother as to wt I have already writt to her about. The Great God & Lord of, & over us all, keep ~~us in his in~~ us in his fear & love, & then it shall be well wth us. I hear all our frds are well, but he Cos. Pool,[5] in this town. And tell Mother, I know not anyone here that can tell me the Lady Pools age, but I beleive she was abt 13 years oulder than I am. Married in 1654, & 20 when married.[6] I sent per Horse Carrier yesterday, that comes from the 3 Cups in Bred-Street,[7] his name Samll whippin,[8] a Box, directed for Brice Webb, Draper in ~~in~~ Wine Street;[9] tell mother also that I desire my love to Samll osborn;[10] & that I desire also to know how he does. Dont overdo the poor little Horse, & ask Mother leave wn you desire to ride him. so with my best love to her and next her, to you all, my Dr. Johnne, Tomme, Peggy, Richard, & Denis, I close hers & yrs.

W Penn

ALS. Penn Papers, Penn-Forbes Collection, HSP. (*Micro.* 14:052.) Addressed: These | to mr Thomas Callowhill | Merchant at | Bristoll | Frank[11] Cha: Cox.[12]

1. Not found.
2. Thomas and Hannah Callowhill, Sr.
3. Not found.
4. WP was house hunting in Reading, Berks., 39 miles west of London, and on a Quaker tour in Rochester, Kent, 28 miles east of London.
5. Benjamin Poole (1656-1714) was married to WP's niece, Margaret Lowther, Jr. He was the eldest son of Sir William Poole of Cheshire, and the grandson of Jonas Poole, who was WP's uncle; both William and Jonas Poole had served in the navy with Admiral Penn. ACM, vol. 49; R. B. Latham and W. Matthews, eds., *Diary of Samuel Pepys* (London, 1970-84), 8:403, 10:342.
6. Lady Margaret Hubbard Poole (b. c. 1634), actually about ten years older than WP, was assisted by WP and his father in the 1670s, when her husband was at sea. *PWP,* 1:584-85, 592, 597; ACM, vol. 49.
7. The tavern at the sign of the Three Crowns near Bread St. Bryant Lillywhite, *London Coffee Houses* (London, 1963), p. 746.
8. Samuel Whibben, or Whebbin, of Bristol was a carrier to and from London. Mortimer, 2:266.
9. Brice Webb, Hannah Penn's cousin, had a shop on Wine St. in Christchurch parish, Bristol, 1703-17, where John Penn served as apprentice. Mortimer, 2:265.
10. Samuel Osburne (d. 1711), a Bristol Quaker soapmaker. WP may have heard of the illness of another Samuel Osburne who died in 1709. Digests of Quaker Records, Bristol and Som.; Mortimer, 2:255; doc. 175, text at n. 4.
11. Mailed free of postage.
12. Probably Charles Cox (b. c. 1661), treasurer of Lincoln's Inn and an M.P. for Cirencester 1708-13 and Gloucester 1713-22. *Alumni Oxonienses.*

172
FROM ISAAC NORRIS

Philada: the 2d Xbr [December] 1709

Honod: Govr:

Upon my 1st Arrivall here I wrote to thee Vizt the 6: 7br 1708,[1] which I fear miscarried as severall did which I Sent to go by the Virga fleet then bound away.

I now salute thee with much duty & affection with thy good wife in which my wife[2] Joyns heartily Often Gratefully remembring the many Extraordinary civillities & favours received from You when there. as wel as thy Kind Son & Daughter Awbry's to whom also is our very kind Love

The hurry I have been put in by getting this Ship away for fear of the Ice makes me unfitt to adresse thee at this time. But considering who goes with it[3] I could not have chose a better opportunity to Say nothing of publick affairs.

Our Govr meets with great discouragments from the Assembly. his honesty and plainess as well as good Intentions, works too little on them. A strange unacountable humour (almost become a Custom now) of Straining & resenting Everything of Creating monsters & then Combating them, I think too much prevails. When Such a {collective} body wth whom buissness ought to be done (that should look at solids & substantials) sett up for witts and Criticks upon Everything that is said or done, and grow Voluminous, always remonstrating, and valluing the last word highly, I See no room to Expect much ~~done~~ effectuall buissness. The Air of Grandure & sacred care for the honour & Dignity of the house that runns thrô Everything is too Vissible & the secrett pride thereof ~~is~~ too ~~Vissible in~~ {plainly appears} Even in the {Great pretensions to & professions of} mean & Despicable thoughts of themselves.

The height things are come to between the Secretary & the house their manner of treating the Councill — The authority the Speaker has assum'd of Granting {a} Warrant[4] — will all come fully to thy knowledge — So that I Entreat Leave to conclude with True Love and Due Regards

Thy Much Oblidg'd frd &c
Isaac Norris

Please to remember us kindly to thy Son & Daughter Penn & to the rest of Your & their Children

My kind love If thou thinks of it To S W. J Fd H G. JG & S: G: {JF}[5] & all Other good frds that may think of mee

I would not send thus Interlin'd had I time to Coppy. they are Just going horseback.[6]

ALS. Society Collection, HSP. (*Micro.* 14:058.) Docketed: I. Norris 2d December | 1709. A copy, without postscripts, is in the Norris Letterbook, 1709-1716, p. 112, HSP.

1. Only the letterbook copy of Norris's letter of 6 Sept. 1708 has been found (*Micro.* 13:508).

2. Mary Lloyd Norris had arrived back in Pennsylvania with her husband on 29 Aug. 1708.

3. James Logan sailed on Isaac Norris's ship the *Hope Galley* on 3 Dec. 1709. Frederick B. Tolles, *James Logan and the Culture of Provincial America* (Boston, 1957), p. 75.

4. David Lloyd, speaker of the Assembly, had issued a warrant for Logan's arrest on charges of scandalous libel. Gov. Gookin ordered the sheriff to protect Logan rather than to arrest him, and the Assembly pronounced the governor's actions illegal. While the two sides continued to fight, Logan left for England. *Minutes of the Provincial Council,* 2:507-8; Tolles, *James Logan,* p. 75; Roy N. Lokken, *David Lloyd* (Seattle, 1959), pp. 183-86.

5. These men were all prominent London Quakers: Samuel Waldenfield, John Field, Henry Gouldney, Joshua Gee, Silvanus Grove, and John Freame.

6. Logan and his small party were riding to catch the ship at New Castle.

173
TO JOHN PENN

Buck-Court.[1] 15. Xbr [December] 1709

My Deare Childe

I was much pleased with thy letter,[2] & with thee for writeing of it; and I desire to be thankfull to the lord you are all so well as thine tells me you are: that thy Deare Mother is better, thy Gr:father so too, & can walk abroad so well; if they eat & sleep well, they will quickly be so. and that you my poor Dr. Children are so, tenders my heart to the Lord, our Common preserver, wth fear & praise. I am concerned Gr:Mother is but indifferent, & wish she may grow Stronger & better. Give My Dr. love to Mother, Gr.far & Gr:Mor, & kiss for me, thy Brors & pretty sister, also my Dr. love to cos Webbs,[3] & other relations, & Friends as If I named them; not forgeting Mary C. Sarah P. Bette L. & H. Cul. nor the Landlady.[4] Now know, I dined today at thy good Aunt Lowthers, who & cosen Margt [5] salute you all, so C. Lawton & thy Bror Penn[6] who dined there with me. also thy sist. Penn, where we called & poor Springet,[7] who has got a hoarsness, else is well, & looks very well as I ever saw him. also this family sends their respects.[8] I hope the things I sent per John Dyer,[9] as well as per carrier are come safe to hand, & please you & to heare therof from Mother tomorrows post. Let her know my Phisick workt six or 7 times, wch I took in the citty, where I lay 4 nights, & came to this end last night. Also tell her I ended with Michel, & the Swiss Barron today.[10] If shee or you my Dr children Love the Potatoes, I have sent already being excellent for Mothers Nourishment, & Gr. Fars & Gr Mors Thomas Tomkins[11] tell mother has sent me 4, or 5 lb more, for her. But O my

Dr. childe your life & health is more than all outward things, for which my soule is deeply engaged to the Lord, that we may live together & enjoy each others Company till I must leave you by age, see you in some condition to help yourselves, so should I lay down my head wth joy.

let M.[12] send me my calico drawrs, & dark gray & Colourd stockings per first opertunity of a frds comeing up. take care of thy little horse dayly & dont ride alone, nor in the Dirt without thy shosoons,[13] to fill the feet of the boot, to keep thee dry & warme, remember wt I say. & I desire both thou & bror Tomme may have as strong & thick shoes as frd Kippen[14] made for Arthur at his comeing away, & then you may goe in the wet & dirt more safely.

tell mother that Ed. Singleton has yet some Barbadoes Pepper for her, & is well & salutes her, & you all. also that J. Logan comes wth a 1000 quarters[15] of our wheat to Lisbon, & so hither.[16] Farewell my Dr Boy, be sober & dutifull, & God will bless thee, & thy relations will Dearly love thee (as they will all of you) and so farewell. Thy tender & afect Father

Wm Penn

I have sent thy Mos Lettr to Cos. Bl:[17]

ALS. Gratz Collection, Governors of Pennsylvania, HSP. (*Micro.* 14:062.)

1. Buckingham Court.
2. Not found.
3. Brice and Phoebe Webb.
4. Mary Clement (b. 1654) was Hannah Penn's aunt; Sarah North Pope Pike (b. 1668) was the sister-in-law of WP's business associate, Joseph Pike; Elizabeth Andrews Lloyd (d. 1731) was the wife of wine merchant Edward Lloyd; and Hannah Cullimore, the daughter of John Cullimore, married William Watson in 1711. The landlady has not been identified. Digests of Quaker Records, Bristol and Som., GSP.
5. Margaret Lowther Poole.
6. Charlwood Lawton and William Penn, Jr.
7. Mary Penn's eldest son, Springett, was a year younger than John Penn.
8. WP was staying with James and Elizabeth Taylor and their four children. *Micro.* 14:079, 094, 101. Digests of Quaker Records, London and Middx., GSP.
9. John Dyer (c. 1661-1741), a leading Bristol Quaker merchant. Mortimer, 2:241.
10. François Luis Michel and Baron Christoph von Graffenried (1661-1743) had agreed to operate mines for WP in Pennsylvania. Leo Schelbert and Hedwig Rappolt, *Alles ist ganz anders hier: Auswandererschicksale in Briefen aus zwei Jahrhunderten* (Freiburg, 1977), pp. 39-40; doc. 177.
11. Thomas Tompkins (d. 1715) was a Quaker wine broker of Seething Lane, London. Digests of Quaker Records, London and Middx., GSP.
12. Mother.
13. Sashoons, leather pads worn inside boots. *OED.*
14. Joseph Kippon (d. 1721) was a Quaker shoemaker of Wine St., Bristol. Mortimer, 1:207.
15. Eight thousand bushels (*OED.*). See doc. 170, text at nn. 23-24.
16. Delayed by storms and capture by a French privateer, Logan did not arrive in London until Mar. 1710. Frederick B. Tolles, *James Logan and the Culture of Provincial America* (Boston, 1957), pp. 79-81.
17. Rebecca Blackfan.

174
TO HANNAH PENN

Lodggs 20 Xbr [December] 1709

My most Dear Heart

I am not a little pleased nor Thankfull that thy dear letter[1] brings me an acct so very [a]greable to my hearty prayers to the Lord [i]n your behalf that you gett forward & that [t]hy father thinks himself well enough for the Orchard.[2] Yesterday I found out J. [F]reeman,[3] told him thy case, he sayd Hanna [Cu]ll[4] was in the same Condition, when she had her [co]ugh, her pains left her, & wn her Cough ceased [h]er pains renewed; & is of opinion that thy [tr]aveling will be helpfull to thee, & thou mayst remember it was so in thy goeing [d]own to Bristoll.[5] Commends strong port white wine & hot well water for thy Con[s]tant drink, & not to use malt liquers; & also that thou hast thy chocolat & tea made wth hot well water. And by the way, I hope thou doest not spoyle that precious Tea I sent the last wth milk, but drink it upon its own merrit, the flavour being much lost ~~by~~ thereby wch is its excellency. I shall send thee per carrier to morrow, or coach next day, ½ ll of good green at 16 & 18ss per ll, that you may use ~~Tea~~ milk wth. I shall also send some potatos of the same sort, that J. Fr. likes for thee, being made into pudings, like bred ones, or roasted, peeld & with Butter as excellent good & Nourishing. poor T. Tompkins sent them me for thee & thine. forgive me the Box I now send; because I know not but it may be the last, while thou art at Bristoll. There is raisons, & almonds, & Figs. 1 oz of every sort of comfitures, Maccaromes 1 lb ½ lb of Savoy Biskets[6] ½ lb of Barly sugar, 1 lb of oringo root,[7] very strengthening for thee, & the best of Ginger bred, good for all your Stomacks, wth wch regalia[8] all our Dr children not forgeting Far & Mor. also a little book for each childe, & M. Harris's Baby[9] for my Dr. little houskeeper[10] which I Know will please her. I salute & embrace ~~you~~ you all, in the arms of the best as well as the dearest love, & commit you to his holy keeping, that has shown himselfe so very gracious to us in man[y] respects, blessed be his holy name; & may a tr[ue] sence of his tender dealings live dayly wth [us] that he may Continue his favorable Providen[ce] over us.

And now for my Dears goeing down,[11] pleas[e] thy own minde; be sure all is aired, & smoa[ked] wth Pitch or Tarr, & some franckensence, & th[at] fires be made every day, & kept up, for 3 or [4] days runing before you remove, for it [is] a good preservative agst contagion, & the dam[p] & foggs that are very great here, by easterly windes blowing up the thick aires of the fla[ts] of Kent & hundreds of Essex upon us.

I will have Johnne & Tomme sett to their Books two hours every morning as if at schoo[l] & both read a chapter, & write an hour in the after noon. I will not have them ride the little horse, only to water, for a quarter of an hour, & where there is no danger, night & morning, or evening only. I think the house airy enough this weather, except dry & cleare while at Clifton,[12] & for the Orchard, let the back door of the best kitchen, be kept shutt continually, unless for a Coach, not to be opened; & the children not to goe but on the terras walk to the stable, or the like. This is my Charge, but stay a week {or 2} longer, after this comes to hand where you are; & stirr not ~~& last when~~ [illegible deletion] if any feaver be in your lane or neer it, nor {the children} goe to school if much by the way but if dry, let Humphry goe to school wth them & help them over wett places, & fetch them back. & charge them by my love to obey readily, & do as bid. and dont vex thy spt by their follys, I hope to make them good boys for all this. I admire the cloaths are not come, but I have writt to J. Wren abt it[13] They keptt the gowns till farther order, insteed of Manda,[14] tho I order'd other wise. I payd the widdow Hodges[15] (as she now is) 2l today for goods had of her. For my ~~coming~~ goeing down, I cannot yet see it, & to have you up before a place is fitt to receiv you, is improper, but besides raising mony, & the Govermt J. Logan, will perhaps [r]equire my stay the longer, & then I shall desire [y]ou up. next month the day[s] will be an hour long[er], & the month following the dawning of the Spring. [I] have writt to wm Smyth, both abt {2 or 3 months} bording, but if not, abt. Laycock house.[16] I have writt to Reding [ab]t Ruscomb house,[17] & w. Furniture. I write to [n]ight to Dr. Matthews[18] if they will bord us for 2 [or] 3 months, & every {other} day, a coach goes {through} from [N]ewberry to london as well as from Reading.

[O]ur distance growes very uncomfortable to me. [E]d. Sing.[19] has presented Tishe wth 2 pots & thee [w]th 3 of pickles, wch shall be kept for thee; [&] my sister has a Noble present for thee. 1 ll of [?]arepuff to make thee {a} silk Covering to lay upon thee on a bed; I beleive thou hast seen one at Cosin Pools,[20] & 2 pints of Cyprus wine, sould for 12ss or 15ss each. shall I send them to thee. The down is 3l the pound weight. I am tould by almost every body at Duke H.[21] ch. Lawson[22] & many more, that have known me long (& but to day, the Duke protested) they see no difference from 20 years ago, so that I am upon equall terms wth thee, it seems.[23] Well, I am pretty well, I praise the Lord, of all liveing for it; but I have not my Drst neerest Friend, & my Drly beloved Children with me. If thou likest my thoughts of a winter entertaimt let me heare per next pray. all ours are well, through the Lords mercy, & salute thee. To Tishe yesterday & to Daughter Penn[24] to day, where thy unckle clement[25] dined wth me [illegible deletion] today—tis time to close, & so my Drst farewell in the Lord, with all ourr Dr lambs, & relations, & Frds, and be assured I am

Thine own most Faithfll & affect
WP

I send a small penknife to thee or Johne.

ALS. Personal Miscellaneous Papers, New York Public Library. (*Micro.* 14:066.) Addressed: For Hannah | Penn at Thomas | Callowhills in | Bristol. This letter is torn at the fold, and the editors have supplied conjectural missing text within square brackets.

1. Not found.

2. Thomas Callowhill, who had been ill, was now well enough to attend meetings at Friars' Orchard, where the Quaker meetinghouse in Bristol stood.

3. James Freeman, a Bristol apothecary and leading Friend, moved to London in 1708. Mortimer, 1:200.

4. Hannah Cullimore.

5. Hannah Penn had returned to Bristol after a brief visit to London in Sept. 1709.

6. Savoy biscuits were spongy biscuits covered with sugar. *OED.*

7. Oringo, or orange, root is a North American plant similar to the buttercup, used medicinally. *OED.*

8. Regale, or entertain. *OED.*

9. Probably a doll made by Mary Harris, who did sewing for the Penns. Penn Papers, Hannah Penn Cashbook; Private Correspondence, 1:49, HSP.

10. Margaret Penn, then five years old.

11. To visit WP in London.

12. Thomas Callowhill owned property in Clifton, a suburb of Bristol known for its hot springs. *Micro.* 14:327.

13. Probably John Wren of London, who loaned WP £80 in 1712. He may have been the son of Admiral Penn's servant by the same name. *Micro.* 14:453; Penn-Forbes Manuscripts, 1:30, HSP; Digests of Quaker Records, London and Middx., GSP; *PWP,* 1:151n.

14. See doc. 169, n. 9.

15. The widow of John Hodges, a Quaker living on Drury Lane, who died 2 Nov. 1709 at the age of 36. Digests of Quaker Records, London and Middx.

16. Probably the manor house, a former convent, at Lacock, Wilts., south of Chippenham, where Quaker chapman William Smith lived. Samuel Lewis, *A Topographical Dictionary of England* (London, 1838), s.v. "Laycock"; Mortimer, 2:261.

17. Ruscombe, near Reading and Twyford, Berks., was to be WP's residence from 1710 until his death. The Penns seem to have paid an annual rent of £15 to John Foster of London. Penn Papers, Hannah Penn Cashbook, HSP.

18. James Matthews, a Quaker surgeon originally of Cheping Wiccomb, Bucks., moved to West Chalow, Berks., in 1684 and belonged to Reading and Warboro Monthly Meeting. Digests of Quaker Records, Berks. and Oxon.; Beatrice S. Snell, ed., *The Minute Book of the Monthly Meeting of the Society of Friends for the Upperside of Buckinghamshire, 1669-1690* (High Wycombe, Bucks., Eng., 1937), pp. 134-35.

19. Probably Edward Singleton.

20. Benjamin and Margaret Poole.

21. The duke of Hamilton.

22. Charlwood Lawton.

23. WP was then 65 years old, while Hannah was only 38.

24. Mary Penn.

25. Simon Clement.

175
TO HANNAH PENN

Lodgegs 19. 11m [January] 1709/10

I shall be very glad to hear my two last letters[1] have found their way to my Dearests hands, and that they are agreable to her, as hers of yesterday, came timely & most pleasingly {to} her most endeared &

affectionate & faithfull friends, that never longed, I think, more to see her & her,[2] and the blest fruits of their mutuall love, than now; & yet he begs her motions may be with the utmost precaution for her & Dr little Travellers Safety & Conveniency; & then they cannot well come too soon to him, he can assure her.[3] first, I am thankfull & desire to be so, more & more, for the Comfortable news of your Genll welfaire; and I bless the Lord I am not worse, wch I hope will be as agreable to thee to hear; for after all, nobody can love a creature better than I love her, & am so Just as to beleive she is not short of the same expression to him. I was truly glad to hear that poor S. Os.[4] was yet in the land of the liveing, & may he be a monumt of gods mercy if it be his heavenly will in being raised up again. I wait to hear wt Nick Says to 4 horses to Newberry or rather to Sandy lane;[5] for the plow[6] draws you up Bacon hill.[7] or at most to Marlborough, whither thy uncle clemt meets thee upon one of Ld Peterborows pads;[8] wch he lent him in my presence today to goe & meet thee; for he freely offer'd himselfe, wn I only askt him for Cos. D.[9] to do that part, & he is vigilent & handy. So soon as thou Sendest me word of the time, or day of thy Seting forth, I am to inform him, & he will at least meet thee at Marlborow, if thou hast not sufficient company to bring thee carefully forward. For poor Tomme I should be glad to see him, & hope the best of the poor Childe, & if he be not too provoaking, I should be glad he were under his Grandfathers eye; else at W. Jen.[10] if he must not come wth thee. If Nick drove, I should like it better, because so often used to the roade. pray let G. Rogers know, I had his lettr but have writt to T. wight to hear wt he has to say upon that head, & then intend to answear him; But I think that farm is {in} my sons settlemt & out of my possession.[11]

If Johnne Sees a horse a large handfull or two higher than his nag, & that pleases him as well, at 20ss, or 3ss [12] in the truck,[13] & it likes[14] his Grandfather & thee well (a good pacer) I shall be satisfyed, tho a better can hardly be found, & free of all faults but littleness. Thou canst not think how much peggy T. takes all in earnest, & calls me every where father. & therfore lett poor Johnne look to it.[15] my Dr. love to M. W.[16] & tell her hers were lately all well. I am glad the Sturgeon pleases, & that thou hast hopes of the Brawn Salt the liquer well.[17] I shall tomorrow Send for the wine, but keep it till thou comest, as my Sister[18] & I do other things. I sent per J. Newton,[19] a Basket of 6 civil & 4 china oranges & 6 lemons & a good many fine chesnuts, with a little gingerbread, some carraways & orange chips or peal (4 oz of both) for your Journy, costing me nothing to send, of wch let Tomme have some, tho' he should Stay. I have a Second lettr from D. Bul.[20] who has had J. Field & J. Kent[21] both like it, & the last sayd this will do. However I will not be hasty. But the goeing in is rather up than down into the house, has a good Pump & half as much Garden as t'other had,[22] & Brickwalled too, wth some fruit. more when

I have seen it. be sure to direct to D. B. for me per your 7th nights post. this is a good reserve, in case one neerer cant be had, but if one between Maidenhead & Colebrook, can as there was one lately by Stains (& ready furnisht) be had, I shall preferr it.[23] such an other as whiticars, at ham,[24] right agst secret. Jonstons,[25] was offerd me today, & new & well wainscoted, garden coach house & Stable & a bigger Garden than J. N.^{s} [26] for 25^{l} per annum. wert thou here, thou mightst chuse for thyselfe. I writ thee also that pretty house at Teding is now to be lett.[27] also Cos. Rooth[28] says a neat Brick one (as is that of 25^{l}) for 20^{l} per annum at Leather head, 3 miles from Darking,[29] a choise market, & good meeting[30] & the pleasure of Bansteed downs,[31] but Still wider from Bristoll roade, wch cools me to them. I think to Send thee J Jaggers[32] lett^{r} wth this wch I have answeard, bid him look out & meet me at Stow[33] 7th day. It is pitty we cannot compas[34] that; but I writt last night to Bro^{r} Wharly[35] ab^{t} it for Cos. Pool.[36] a lovely place. Ld Orkney[37] told me of it.

AL. Penn-Forbes Papers, HSP. (*Micro.* 14:094.) This letter is written on four sides of a single, folded sheet; the closing page or pages have not been found.

1. WP wrote to Hannah on 17 Jan. 1710 (*Micro.* 14:083); he apparently sent another letter a few days earlier, which has not been found. Hannah had already received his letter of 7 Jan. written to John (*Micro.* 14:079).

2. WP means "hers."

3. Hannah is thinking of bringing the children to London but is worried that the long winter would be bad for their health. Doc. 174, text at n. 12; *Micro.* 14:083, 101, 103.

4. For Samuel Osburne, see doc. 171, n. 10.

5. WP had advised Hannah to hire Nick, a Bristol ostler, to take her at least as far as Newbury, where she could take a stage coach to Reading, where he would meet her. Sandy Lane, Wilts., is en route between Bath and Reading. Nick has not been identified.

6. A team of horses harnessed to a wagon. *OED.*

7. Possibly Beacon Hill, Wilts.

8. Easy-paced horses. Hannah's uncle Simon Clement was employed by Peterborough. See doc. 53, n. 8; 164, n. 4.

9. Probably Simon Clement's son Dennis (b. 1688). Digests of Quaker Records, Bristol and Som., GSP.

10. William Jenkins (d. 1735) was the schoolmaster of Sidcot School near Bristol. Mortimer, 2:249.

11. George Rogers, a merchant and First Purchaser from Co. Cork, Ireland, was probably trying to acquire one of the Penn properties in Ireland that WP had already conveyed to William Penn, Jr. *PWP,* 1:604, 611; 2:360n, 652.

12. WP must mean "30 shillings."

13. Exchange. John wants to trade his small horse for a larger one. See doc. 173, text at n. 13.

14. Pleases.

15. Margaret Taylor (b. 1703), the seven-year-old daughter of James and Elizabeth Taylor, claimed that she was "engaged" to John Penn, then ten years old. WP mentions the engagement in letters to John: "Thy little wife stands by me, remembers dearly to thee, will call me father, . . . so remember to be just to thy engagemts." *Micro.* 14:079, 101.

16. Mary North Wall (d. 1723?), a leading Quaker in Bristol, had been a widow since 1684. Her daughter Mary had moved to London with her husband, apothecary James Freeman, in 1708. Her granddaughter Mary was married to WP's friend Nathaniel Marks. Mortimer, 1:200, 219; Digests of Quaker Records, Bristol and Som., London and Middx.

17. WP had sent his family "a barrel of cos. J L[s] [John Lowther's] Sturgion," and "a good peice of brawn [boar meat] in a box." The meat was probably pickled with salt to preserve it. *Micro.* 14:079.

18. Margaret Lowther.

19. WP had hoped to send "some of Colonell Gookins Liquer by little John Newton that keeps the faire." Newton has not been identified. *Micro.* 14:079.

20. Daniel Bullock (b. 1668), originally from Portishead, Som., had been looking for a house for the Penns near Reading, where he now lived. *Micro.* 14:074, 083.

21. Probably John Kent, a Quaker weaver of Stow, Glos., who now lived in Witney, Berks. Digests of Quaker Records, Berks. and Oxon., GSP.

22. WP had been considering renting another house near Twyford, which Bullock described as standing "on a noble large dry Gravelly green, & clean ways abt it." *Micro.* 14:074.

23. Maidenhead and Colnbrook, Berks., and Staines, Middx., now part of Greater London, were all on the Bristol Road and closer to London than Ruscombe, where WP finally decided to live. He was settled there by June 1710. *Micro.* 14:121.

24. Probably a house belonging to the Whitaker family in Ham, Sur. *VCH; Micro.* 14:083.

25. James Johnston (1643?-1737), formerly secretary for Scotland under William III, lived at Orleans House in Twickenham, Middx., adjacent to Ham. *DNB*.

26. Joseph Nicholson.

27. WP decided against the house at Teddington, Middx., 11 miles southwest of London, because it was not on the direct route to Bristol and the mail would have to come via London. *Micro.* 14:083.

28. Richard Rooth.

29. Leatherhead and Dorking, Sur.

30. WP had belonged to Dorking and Horsham Monthly Meeting while living at Warminghurst.

31. Banstead, or Epsom, Downs, popular for its spa waters, horse races, and other entertainments. Samuel Lewis, *A Topographical Dictionary of England* (London, 1838); John Ashton, *Social Life in the Reign of Queen Anne* (London, 1883), pp. 230, 333.

32. John Jagger, or Gigger (b. 1675), was the son of a servant to Gulielma Springett before her marriage to WP. The family had moved from Eton, Bucks., and had offered their house there to WP. Digests of Quaker Records, Bucks.; London and Middx.; *PWP*, 1:131n; L. V. Hodgkin, *Gulielma: Wife of William Penn* (London, 1947), pp. 99-101; *Micro.* 14:079; Pemberton Papers, 4:38, HSP.

33. Probably Stowe, Bucks., near Buckingham, about 50 miles from London and far from the London-Bristol road.

34. Obtain or contrive at.

35. WP's letter to Daniel Wharley has not been found.

36. Margaret Lowther Poole. WP had gone househunting with the Pooles in July 1709; he wrote Hannah on 14 July: "I have been to day with cos. Pools ab[t] the Houses by Croyden, w[ch] is by Scituation in its privacy as good as 30 miles of, & yet is but 11." *Micro.* 14:010.

37. George Hamilton, earl of Orkney (1666-1737), a distinguished Scottish soldier, served often in Parliament after the Union as one of the representative peers for Scotland. *DNB*.

176
TO VISCOUNT TOWNSHEND

4. 2[m] (Appr[ll]) 1710

My Noble Friend[1]
There being fifty or Sixty Swissers,[2] called Menonists,[3] comeing for Holland in order to goe for Pennsylvania, It is feard the States of

Holland will Stop them,[4] being well to pass {on}, & for as much as one Mitchell,[5] their Agent, has contracted wth m[6] for them, for lands &c: I humbly beg that If the States should stop them, It would please thee, as for the Queens Interest & service, It may be taken off or prevented, & thou wilt ~~please~~ much oblige

Thy very resectfll Friend
Wm Penn

Menonists or Menist are Annabaptists here.

ALS. Penn Papers, Tempsford Hall Collection, HSP. (*Micro.* 14:115.) Docketed: Mr William Peen | Aprill the 4 | Red Aprill 22 N S | 1710.

1. Charles Townshend (1674-1738), second viscount Townshend, had been privy councilor since 1707 and a supporter of religious liberty in the early years of Queen Anne's reign. In 1709 he became ambassador extraordinary and plenipotentiary to the States General, where he was involved in the peace negotiations in the spring of 1710. *DNB.*

2. This was probably a group of Mennonites expelled from the canton of Berne in 1710. The hundreds of exiled Bernese found refuge in the Palatinate, the Netherlands, and Prussia. Eventually many of them immigrated to Pennsylvania. Ernst H. Correll, *Das schweizerische Täufermennonitentum* (Tübingen, 1925), pp. 70-75.

3. The Mennonites were Anabaptists, named after Menno Simon (1496-1561) of Friesland, who gathered and led the Anabaptists scattered in the wake of the Münster revolt of 1536. The refugees described by WP were Swiss Anabaptists with beliefs similar to those of the Mennonites in the Netherlands.

4. After the mass exodus of 13,000 Palatines in 1709, Dutch officials were very cautious before granting emigrants permission to pass through their territories for fear that poor transients might become a burden to the Dutch taxpayers. Dutch West Indies Company Papers, Box 3, HSP.

5. François Louis Michel.

6. "Me."

177
TO CHARLES GOOKIN

London 14th 4mo [June] 1710

Hond Friend

Haveing made a Contract wth my friends Lewis Mitchel & Baron Graffenried[1] for the Discovering Opening & working certain Mines within the Bounds of that Province for wch I have Granted to the sd Mitchel my Commission wth Such full & ample Powers as may be Necessary to Carry on the sd Work: I Doe therefore desire thee to give the Sd L Mitchel & all persons Concearned for or under him all reasonable Encouragemt in the Sd Design, and particularly to take Care that the Indians at my Instance & Request be prevailed wth to be Assisting to him & his People in carrying on this Work & makeing Such settlements as may be Necessary for the Same: for the more ready obtaining of wch assistance he (I beleive) will be ready to make those of them that are principally Concearned Some suitable Presents: I also Desire that Martin Chartiere[2] who lives among the

Shawanois at Pedquean may be Particularly engaged in my behalf & that Peeter Bizaillon,[3] if he Still continue to Trade by the approbacion of the Governm[t] & remains faithfull as I hope he does, may be also made Assistant as far as the Undertakers Shall think Convenient or Safe, butt the Whole must be managed at first especially wth all Possible Privacy

Haveing mencioned the Baron Graffenried I must Particularly recommend him to thy favour and Notice, as a Gentleman of Worth that haveing made a very good figure, & born very Considerable Offices in his own Countrey, is now willing to retire, & Plant himself in a Land of more freedom & Ease;[4] I Desire also that my friends there of the Council & others may Shew him a particular respect, as one who I beleive will on ~~e~~ all Occasions Shew himself Deserveing of it for Such he has truly appeared here And I hope will prove of Service to our Colony

WP

Copy. Library Company Manuscripts, Read Family Papers, Autograph Letters, HSP. (*Micro.* 14:126.) Addressed: To Coll[o] Gookin. Docketed: Will: Pens brief | an Guverneur von Pensil:[5]

1. WP's contract with François Louis Michel and Christoph von Graffenried has not been found. See doc. 173, n. 10.
2. Martin Chartier, a French fur trader, had moved to the Conestoga Valley in 1700, where he lived among the Shawnees at Pequea Creek in present-day Lancaster Co. *PMHB,* 53:332.
3. Peter Bezaillion. See doc. 41, n. 6.
4. WP seems to have been unaware that Christoph von Graffenried embarked on this endeavor in the American colonies in an effort to recoup losses incurred during his tenure as Bernese governor of Iverdon and also as a result of unsuccessful speculation. Leo Schelbert and Hedwig Rappolt, eds., *Alles ist ganz anders hier* (Freiburg, 1977), pp. 39-40, 421n.
5. William Penn's letter to the governor of Pennsylvania.

178
TO FRIENDS IN PENNSYLVANIA

London 29th 4[mo] [June] 1710

My ould Friends
It is a mournfull consideration & the cause of deep Affliction to me that I am forc'd by the Oppressions and Disappointments w[ch] have faln to my share in this life to speak to the People of that Province in a language I once ~~more comfortably~~ hop'd I shou'd never have occasion to use. But the many troubles & Oppositions that I have mett with from thence oblige me in plainess & freedom to expostulate with you concerning the cause of them.

When it pleas'd ~~my~~ God to open a way for me to settle that Colony

I had reason to expect a solid comfort from the Services done to so many hundreds of People. And it is no small satisfaction to me that I have not been disappointed in seeing them prosper & grow up to a flourishing Countrey blest with Liberty Ease & Plenty beyond what many of themselves cou'd expect and wanting nothing to make themselves happy but what with a right temper of mind & prudent conduct they might give themselves.

But alas! as to my part instead of reaping the like Advantages some of the greatest of my troubles have rose from thence, the many Combats I have been engaged in, the great pains & incredible expences for your welfare & ease to the decay of my former Estate, of which (however some there would represent it) I too sensibly feel the effects, wth the undeserv'd oppositions I have mett with from thence, sink me into a Sorrow, that if not Supported by a Superiour hand, might have overwhelm'd me long agoe, And I cannot but think it hard measure, that while that has prov'd a Land of freedom & flourishing, it shou'd become to me by whose means it was principally made a Countrey the cause of Grief Trouble & Poverty.

For this reason I must desire you all even of all Professions and degrees, for though all have not been engag'd in the measures that have been taken,[1] yet every man who has an Interest there is or must be concern'd in them by their effects. I must therefore I say desire {you all} in a serious & true weightiness of Mind {to consider} what you are or have been doing why matters must be carry'd on wth those divisions and Contentions, & what real Causes have been given on my Side for that Opposition to me & my Interest wch I have mett with as if I were an Enemy & not a Friend after all I have done & spent both here & there, I am sure I know not {of any} cause whatsoever.

Were I sensible you {really} wanted any thing of me in the relation between us that would make you happier I should readily grant it, if any reasonable man could say it were fitt for you to demand provided you wou'd also take such measures as were fitt for me to joyn with.

Before any one family had transported themselves thither I earnestly endeavour'd to form such a Model of Goverm^t as might make all concern'd [in?] it easy which never the less was subject to be alterd as there should be occasion[.][2] Soon after we gott over that Model appear'd in some parts of it to be very inconvenient if not impracticable, the numbers of Members both in Council [&] Assembly were much too large some other matters also prov'd inconsistent with the Kings Charter to me So that according to the Power reserv'd for an Alteration, there was a necessity to make one in which if the Lower Counties we[re] brought in, it was well known at that time to be on a View of advantage to the Province it self, as well as the People of those Counties & to the general Satisfaction of those concern'd w^thout the least apprehension of any irregularity in the Method.

Upon this they had another Charter pass'd[3] Nemine Contradicente[4] wch I always desir'd might be continu'd, while you yourselves wou'd keep up to it, & putt it in practice, & many there know how much it was against my will that upon my last going over it was vacated.

But after this was laid aside[5] (wch indeed was begun by your selves in Colonel Fletchers time)[6] I according to my engagement left another[7] wth all the Priviledges that were found convenient for your good Govermt & if any part of it has been in any case infring'd it was never by my approbation I desir'd it might be enjoy'd fully.

But tho' Privileges ought to be tenderly preserv'd they shou'd not on the other hand be asserted under that name to a Licentiousness: The design of Govermt is to preserve good Order wch may be equally broke in upon by the turbulent Endeavours of the People, as well as by the overstraining of Power in a Govr.

I designd the People shou'd be secur'd of an Annual fix'd Election & Assembly & that they shou'd have the same Privileges in it that any other Assembly {has} in the Queens Dominions, among all which this is one constant rule, as in the Parlia[mt] here that {they} shou'd sitt on their own adjourments, but to strain this {expression} to a Power to meet at all times during the Year without the Govrs concurrence[8] wou'd be to distort Govermt to break the due proportion of ~~the~~ the parts of it, to establish {Confusion} in the place of Necessary Order & to make the Legislative the Executive part of the Gover[mt.]

Yet for obtaining this Power, I perceive much time & money has been spent {& great struggles have been made} not only for this but some other things that cannot at all be for the advantage of the People to be possess'd of; particularly the appointing of Judges[9] because the Administration might by such means {be} so clog'd that it would be difficult if possible under our Circumstances at some times to Support it.

As for my own part {as} I desire nothing more than the Tranquillity and Prosperity of the Province & Govermt in all its branches, cou'd I see that any of these things that have been contended for, wou'd certainly promote these ends it wou'd be a matter of indifference to me how they were settled. But seeing the frame of every Govermt ought to be regular in it self, well proportioned & subordinate in it's parts & every branch of it invested with Sufficient power to discharge it's respective duty for the Support of the whole I have cause to beleive that nothing wou'd be more destructive to it than to take so much of the Provision & Executive part of Govermt out of a Govrs hands and lodge it in an {un}certain collective body; And more especially since our Govermt is dependant, & I am answerable to the Crown if the Administration shou'd fail & a Stop be putt to the course of Justice. On these considerations I cannot think it prudent in the People to crave those Powers, because not only I but they themselves wou'd be in danger of suffering by it; Cou'd I beleive otherwise I shou'd not be against granting any thing of this kind that were asked of me wth any degree of common prudence & civility.

But instead of finding cause to beleive the Contentions that have been rais'd about these matters have proceeded only from mistakes in Judgemt with an earnest desire notwithstanding at the bottom to Serve the Publick (wch I hope has still been the Inducemt of several concern'd in them) I have had but too sorrowful a view & sight to complain of the manner in wch I have been treated

The Attacks on my Reputation the many Indignities putt upon me in papers sent over hither into the hands of those who cou'd not be expected to make the most discreet & charitable use of them;[10] The secret Insinuations against my Justice, besides the Attempt made on my Estate. Resolves past in Assemblies for turning my Quitrents never sold by me to the support of Govermt,[11] my lands enter'd upon without any regular Method, my Mannors invaded (under pretence I had not duly survey'd them) & both these by persons principally concern'd in these Attempts against me here; a right to my Overplus Lands unjustly claim'd, by the Professors of the Tracts in which they are ~~plainly~~ found ~~to be~~. My private Estate, continually exhausting for the support of that Govermt both here & there & no provision made for it by that Countrey. To all which I can not but, add the Violence that has been particularly shewn against my Secretary,[12] of wch (tho' I shall by no means protect him in any thing he can be justly charg'd with, but suffer him to stand or fall by his own Actions) I cannot but thus far take notice that from all these Charges I have seen or heard of agst him, I have cause to beleive that had he been as much ~~f~~in Opposition to me, as he has been understood to stand for me, he might have mett ~~h~~ wth a milder treatmt from his Prosecutors And to think that any man shou'd be the more expos'd there on my Account & instead of finding favour meet wth enmity for his being engaged in my Service is a melancholy Consideration. In short when I reflect on all those heads of wch I have so much cause to complain, & at the same time think of the hardships I & my Suffering Family have been reduced to in no small measure, owing to my endeavours for & Disappointments from that Province. I cannot but mourn the unhappiness of my Portion dealt to me from those of whom I had reason to expect much better & different things; Nor can I but lament the unhappiness that too many of them are bringing upon themselves, who instead of pursuing the amicable wayes of Peace Love & Unity wch I at first hop'd to find in that retirement are cherishing a Spirit of Contention & Opposition & blind to ~~your~~ {their} own Interest are oversetting that foundation on which your happiness might be built Friends The eyes of many are upon you. The People of many Nations in Europe look on that Countrey as a Land of ease & Quiet, wishing to themselves in vain the same blessings they conceive you may enjoy: But to See the use you make of them is no less the cause of Surprise to others while such bitter Complaints & Reflections are seen to come from you of wch it's difficult to conceive even the sense, ~~&~~ or meaning. Where are the Distresses Grievances & Oppressions that the Papers sent from thence so often say you languish under? while others have cause to beleive you have hitherto liv'd or might live ~~in~~ the happiest of any in the Queens Dominions. Is it such a grievous Oppression that the Courts are establish'd by my Power, founded on the Kings Charter, without a Law of your making when upon the same Plan you propose? If this disturb any, take but the advice of other able Lawyers on the Main without tying me up to the Opinion of principally one man, whom I can not think so very proper to ~~judge~~ direct in my Affairs (for I beleive the late Assembly have but had that one Lawyer amongst them)[13] & I am freely content you should have any Law that by proper Judges shall be found suitable. Is it your oppression that the Officers fees are not settled by an Act of Assembly?[14] No man can be a greater Enemy to extortion than my self: Doe therefore but allow such fees as may reasonably encourage fitt persons to undertake these Offices, & you shall soon have (& shou'd have alwayes chearfully had) mine & I hope my Lieutenants ready concurrence & approbation. Is it such an Oppression that Licenses for Publick Houses have not {been} settled ~~by an Act of Assembly?~~ as has been propos'd?[15] Tis a certain sign you are strangers to oppression, & know nothing but the name when you so lightly bestow it on matters so inconsiderable but that business I find is adjusted. Could I know any real Oppression you lie under that is not in your own Power to remedy (& what I wish you wou'd take proper measures to remedy if you truly feel any such) I wou'd be as ready on my part to remove them as you to desire it. But according to the best Judgement I can make of the Complaints I have seen (& you once thought I had a pretty good one) I must in a deep sense of sorrow say that I fear the kind hand of Providence that has so long favour'd & protected you, will by the Ingratitude of many there to the great Mercies of God hitherto shewn them, be at length provok'd to convince them of their Unworthiness, & by changing the blessing[s] that so litle care {has been taken by the Publick} to deserve, into calamities reduce those that have been so clamorous and causelesly discontented to a true but smarting Sense of their duty. I write not this with a design to include all. I doubt not but many of you have been burthen'd at, & can by no means joyn in the Measures that have been taken; but while such things appear under the name of an Assembly that ought to represent the whole, I can not but speak more generally than I wou'd desi~~gn~~re tho' I am not insensible what methods may be us'd to obtain the weight of such a Name.

I have already been tedious & shall {therefore} now briefly say that the opposition I have mett with from thence must at length force me to consider more closely of my own private & Sinking Circumstances in relation to that Province.[16] In the mean time I desire you all seriously to weigh wt I have wrote together wth your own duty to yourselves, to me, & to the World who have their Eyes upon you & are witnesses of my early & earnst care for you. I must think there is a regard due to me that has not of late been paid. Pray consider of it fully, & think soberly what you have to desire of me on the one hand, & ought to perform to me on the other, for from the next Assembly I shall expect to know what you resolve, & what I may depend on. If I must continue my regards to you, let me be engag'd to it by the like disposition in you towards me But if a plurality after this shall think they owe me none, or no more than for some years I have mett with let it upon a fair election be so declar'd & I shall then wthout further Suspence know what I have to rely on. God give you his wisdom & fear to direct you, that yet our poor Countrey may be blest wth peace love & Industry & we may once more meet good friends & live so to the end, our relation in truth having but the same true Interest.

I am wth great Truth & a most Sincere regard

Your reall frd
as well as Just Proprr
& Govr Wm Penn

LS. Gratz Collection, Governors of Pennsylvania, HSP. (*Micro.* 14:133.) Both the salutation and closing, beginning with "I am wth great Truth . . . ," are in WP's hand. Docketed in James Logan's hand: Proprietors Letter to friends &c | in Pensilvania | 1710. A copy of the letter, dated 27 June 1710, was printed in Philadelphia with the title *A Serious Expostulation with the Inhabitants of Pensilvania* (*PWP,* vol. 5, item 131).

1. A reference to the Pennsylvania colonists' strenuous recent efforts to expand the Assembly's privileges and reduce WP's political and economic powers. See docs. 157, text at n. 15; 160; 165, text at nn. 4-6; 172, text at nn. 3-4.

2. *The Frame of the Government of the Province of Pennsylvania in America: Together with certain Laws Agreed upon in England by the Governour and Divers Free-men of the aforesaid Province* (London, 1682). *PWP,* 2:211-27.

3. The Second Frame of Government (1683). Soderlund, *William Penn,* pp. 265-73.

4. Without opposition.

5. Replaced by the Frame of 1696. *PWP,* 3:456-64.

6. Under the governorship of Benjamin Fletcher, the Assembly gained the power to initiate legislation. *PWP,* 3:347.

7. The Charter of Privileges (1701). Doc. 28.

8. For the Assembly's fight with the governor about the right of the representatives to sit on the prorogation and dissolution of the house, see *Votes and Proceedings,* 1(pt. 2):12, 25.

9. For the Assembly's effort to control the judiciary see doc. 133, n. 3.

10. See docs. 83, 84.

11. See doc. 100, n. 8; *PWP,* 3:408, 682.

12. A reference to the impeachment proceedings against James Logan. See docs. 133; 147, n. 23.

13. David Lloyd.

14. A law of 1700 had set fees for some services by provincial officers, but it was considered inadequate; a far more extensive act was passed in 1711 but repealed by the Queen in Council in 1714. *Statutes,* 2:137-40, 331-48.

15. The governor had the power, upon recommendation from the county justices, to grant licenses for public houses. Doc. 28, text at n. 12; *Charter and Laws,* pp. 286-88; *Statutes,* 2:93-94.

16. A reference to WP's renewed negotiations for the surrender of the government of Pennsylvania to the crown. See docs. 179, 180, 182.

179
TO QUEEN ANNE

By July 1710 three years had elapsed since WP had last negotiated for the surrender of the government of Pennsylvania to the crown (doc. 140). His renewed application was subjected to the same administrative procedure as before. WP represented his case to the queen on 31 July 1710 (doc. 179); her minister, Lord Dartmouth, in turn submitted WP's memorial to the Board of Trade for its opinion (*Micro.* 14:163); the Board took the matter up three months later, only to require additional information from WP (doc. 180*a*). WP showed some impatience in his response to the Board's questions, since the queries very closely resembled those he had already answered (rather sketchily) in July 1707 (doc. 140B). Seeking a resolution of the matter, WP presented the Board with yet another elegantly and eloquently written memorial on 2 February 1711 (*Micro.* 14:209). The success of WP's lobbying is evident in the Board's recommendation to the queen, which adopts many of WP's arguments — often in his words — although it leaves the crucial question of the sale price for the surrender for the crown to determine (doc. 182). A few days later, on 17 February 1711, WP seems to have had an audience with the queen (cf. *Micro.* 14:232). Yet as he remarked in March 1711, the prospects for surrender remained "very uncertain" (doc. 184). The attorney general was asked for his opinion about WP's clauses for the surrender of Pennsylvania's government only in October 1711, and the queen did not announce her decision until September 1712 (doc. 198).

[c. 31 July 1710]

The Memorial of William Penn Proprietor and Governour of Pensilvania in relation to his Government in that Province.

The Settlement of Colonies having in all Ages been accounted a very great Advantage to the Governments from whence they were derived, this Kingdom has thought it her particular Interest to plant a large number of them in foreign parts, tho' with great Hazard and Charge, from whence they have received a vast Increase of Power and Wealth, by their Trade.

The Said William Penn, by his indefatigable Endeavours, and Interest in his Friends, with a great Expence to the Sensible Decay of his Patrimonial Estate, Undertook near 30 Years agoe, and has since compleated, the Settlement of a considerable Colony in that Tract of Land in America granted him by King Charles the Second,[1] and from an unhospitable Wilderness, has raised it to a flourishing Countrey, without the least Charge to the Crown of this Realm, from whence considerable Advantages have accrued to the Kingdom, as well by the constant Consumption of its Manufactures, and Improvement of Navigation, as by the Increase of Duties paid here on Goods from thence, which Duties have already amounted, in one Year, to above ten thousand pounds.

The Motives that induced the King to grant this Countrey to the Said Willm Penn, with all necessary Powers for the well Governing thereof, were not only from an Inclination to promote an Undertaking, So laudable in it Self, and Advantageous to the Publick, but also the Consideration of his Fathers Services, as is at large expressed in His Letters Patent, And further, that at that time, there was due to the Said William Penn from the Crown, for his fathers Disbursements in the Victualling Office, and Interest thereon, the Sum of Sixteen thousand Pounds, of which he never received one penny.[2]

And what principally engaged the Said William Penn in so difficult and hazardous an Enterprise, besides his Desire of promoting So great a Publick Good, was the hopes he conceived, that He, and his Posterity, might there enjoy a quiet Retirement, guarded with Such an Authority, as might render their Lives more comfortable and easy.

But instead of this, having twice transported himself thither, in hopes of this enjoyment, He had those Attacks made upon him, that obliged him as often to return, after a very short Stay there, to defend his Interest, And further, he has at other times, almost continually (notwithstanding his intire Complyance with the Laws of this Kingdom, relating to that Settlement) mett with such Disturbances, from the Uneasiness Some have been under, upon the Account of Proprietary Governments, that his Fatigues & Expence have become unsupportable to him, And it has been so fully received by many, that Such Governments are inconvenient to Trade, & inconsistent with the Dignity of the Crown, that he is no longer willing to contend, but will Surrender those Powers of Government with which he is invested, and deliver them intirely into the hands of the Queen, Provided he can receive such a reasonable Consideration, as may appear due to his Merits in settling the Said Colony, and be Secured in the enjoyment of what will be necessarily due to himself, and his friends who are now unmoveably fix'd there.

In consideration of this Surrender, he with humility conceives, that he ought to have Such a Sum, as may reimburse him of a reasonable part of his past Expences, and relieve him from the Necessities, that his Engagement in that Province has plunged him into,[3] which Sum may be raised out of any Such fund, as shall be found most convenient.

And whereas he was particularly at a very great Expence & Trouble in asserting the Right of the then Duke of York, to a Tract of Land on the lower parts of Delaware-Bay, against the Lord Baltimore, the principal part of which Tract the Said Duke had granted to W Penn, and afterwards, when upon the Throne, did actually give him the whole, but his Sudden *Removal* prevented the full execution of the Grant, intended for a more intire Confirmation thereof, with all necessary Powers of Government: the said W: Penn humbly craves that this Affair may be fully Settled and confirmed.[4]

He doubts not, but as that Colony was at first principally Settled and improved by Men, who being, for Conscience sake, unable in their Native Countrey, where in other respects they lived in Credit & Plenty, to comply with some things that the Laws required of them, did in hopes of greater Liberty and Ease, transport themselves thither, and upon that foundation are fixed with their families there: He doubts not therefore but it will be found necessary, as well as reasonable, to indulge these People, at all times, in such things, as they never could nor now can, either here or there comply with, while they are known in all other regards to be peaceable, Industrious and Obedient to Government, as any other Subjects whatsoever.

And as he proposes, his Posterity Shall fix themselves there, he hopes he may modestly crave some particular Mark of Respect to be continued to his Family, for distinguishing them above the Rank of those who have planted under him; as that the Proprietor for the time being may alwayes have a Place, and be the first in the Council there, or receive some other suitable Instance of the Regard due to them, in remembrance of Him that first made it a Colony.

These heads he humbly offers to the consideration of the Queen and Her Ministry, and for the more Speedy Dispatch of the Affair requests that persons may be appointed to adjust the whole matter, according as his Proposals shall be approved of.

D, in the hand of James Logan. CO 5/1264/102i, PRO. (*Micro.* 14:155.) Docketed: Mr Penn's memorial.

1. See *PWP,* 2:61-77; Soderlund, *William Penn,* pp. 38-50.
2. See *PWP,* 2:30-33.
3. For WP's comments on the cost of his colony, see docs. 13, text at nn. 10-11; 20, text at nn. 3-4; 62, text at nn. 2-4.
4. The insecurity of WP's title to the Lower Counties was a major reason for the separation of the Territories from Pennsylvania; it was also the basis on which representatives of New Castle Co. challenged WP's proprietary rights. *PWP,* 2:91n, 103-4, 281-84, 381-82; docs. 157, n. 7; 160, n. 4; 166.

180
QUERIES CONCERNING THE SURRENDER OF PENNSYLVANIA

A

From William Popple, Jr.

[4 November 1710]

Sr

The Lords Commissrs of Trade & Plantations, having under consideration, Your Proposal for a Surrender of Your Government of Pennsylvania,[1] and taking Notice that the Expence you have been at, in the setling of that Province, is among other things made a Ground of your Demand of a sum of Mony upon such surrender Wherefore In Order to their laying a full and Clear State of this matter before her Majesty, Their Lordships judge it Necessary, to have plain and distinct Answers to the Several following Queries. Viz[t]

First, What are the Profits you have made of that Province, computing the Yearly Value of Quitrents or other the property remaining in you.

2[d] How the said Profits have arisen, whether by Fines, Forfeitures, or otherwise.

3[d] What Benefit or Advantages will the Crown receive from that Colony by purchasing the Government, more than it now hath; and how the same may arise.

4th What is the Annual Charge of that Government.

5[ly] What Revenue is now subsisting for the support of that Government, the Yearly Value of such Revenue, and for what time Granted.

6[ly] Whether You have Granted any Priviledges and Immunities, by Charter, or otherwise, to the City of Philadelphia, or other Towns or Corporations in the Province of Pennsylvania, other than what are granted by the Charter to the City of Philadelphia; Dated the 25th October 1701,[2] and by the Charter of Priviledges to the People of Pennsylvania, Dated the 28th of October 1701.[3] Copies of which Charters are now lying before their Lordships.

So soon as you shal have Given in Your Answer to the Several abovemention'd Queries[4] (which you are desir'd to do as fully, and as far as may be without reference to any Papers formerly Deliver'd into this Office, or any former transactions thereon) Their Lordships will then proceed in the further consideration of this Affair, and confer with you, as occasion shal Require,[5] that the same receive all Possible dispatch. I am

S[r]

Whitehal. — Your most Humble Servant

Nov[r] 4th 1711[6] — W[m] Popple

Copy. CO 5/1292/231, PRO. (*Micro.* 14:167.) Docketed: Nov[r] 4th | Letter to M[r] | Penn with several Que- | ries, upon his propo- | sing to surrender the | Government of Penn- | sylvania.

B

To The Board of Trade

Whitehall 7 X[br] [December] 1710

Hon[rble] Frds

I have no other Accounts to Lay before You, of the Proffits and Charges of Pensilvania, but what You had from Me about two Years

agoe[7] So that I cannot So fully Answer Your 6 Queries as Perhaps You may Expect. If I could, Yet do I not conceive, how Your first and Second, have any Relation to the Surrender of my Governm[t]. For I do not Remember to have made an offer of Alienating any part of my Propriety, [(]strictly so called) but only the Governm[t] which will alone, I presume intitutle me upon a Surrender, to aske a considerable Sum of money, as well in consideration of the Expence I have been at, in makeing it a Country, as of the benefitt and Advantage, the Crown has already, and hereafter will receive thereby, in the increase of the Customs, as well as other parts of the Revenue. Which I am inform'd, have amounted for several Years, to between 10 and 12000[l] per Annum,[8] and sometimes, double that Sum. And Especially Surrendring it at a time: when in keeping it in my own hands, I may reasonably Expect, a great Profitt thereby. The Country being now come to that Maturity, to stand upon it's own leggs: that is able to raise Supplies, (Equall to most of the Neighbouring Collonies) more than Sufficient to defray all the Charges of Governm[t] which are less considerably in my Gov[rnmt], than in other places. I cannot Positively Say, what Revenue at present is Setled to Defray Such Charges: But the Same has been maintaind heretofore, partly out of my own private fortune, and partly by the People.[9]
Which I have been the more willing to Comply with: because it was my Opinion, Taxes in the Infancy of a Collony, would be a Cramping of the Industry of the People, and Experience has since shown, my Notion was not ill founded, by the Superiour Improvem[ts] and Trade, above many of their Neighbours. It having been during the Late Scarcity of Corn in Europe, not only the Granary of the W. Indies, (which it hath been many Years) but also of Some part of Europe, and what has been may be again. The Profitt The Crown will Gain by my Surrender, may ~~be~~ Easily be perceived to be very considerable. If it be considered, that Upwards of twenty five Years Since, the People made a free Gift of a {small} Duty, upon Goods Exported & Imported, which at that time of day, would have brought in by a Modest Calculation, 1200[l] per Annum. This I thought fitt to let fall in consideration of 600[l] and intended it should lye dormant for Sometime.[10] And Soon after coming for England, it was never revived. The Flourishing State of Pensilvania neither Requires nor Expects to put me to further Charge. But will, I am well assured upon my Going there Setle a handsom Revenue, (if the Same be not already done) to defray the Charges of Governm[t], and Enable their Governor honorably to Subsist. The Crown has formerly desired my Governm[t], when it was not Arrived at the Ability & Perfection it now is, And I am Sure it will appear, If I surrender my Government to the Crown that the Revenue will not fall Short of its Neighbours, and at the same time the Charge much less. So that Upon the whole, the Crown will be more a gainer by my Governm[t] than by Some others. I hope not only this, but the making a Wilderness, a fruitfull Country, without

any Expence to the Crown, who will reap the fruit of my Labour and Expence in the increase of the English Navigation and Customs: and the Maintaining, as well as making that Country, chiefly out of my own Estate, does intitule me to a good & Valuable consideration. And I doubt not but in Justice You will so Report it. that this affair may have a Speedy Issue.

Upon the Whole Matter, I expect 20000^{l} for my Governm^{t}, but am Content to allow seven Years, for the Compleating the full Paym^{t} thereof, receiving Yearly, Proporcionable Sums, till the whole be paid.[11] Which is so far from being a boon, that it has Sunk my Patrimony several hundred pounds per Annum to bring it to what it is. If You are not pleas'd with this Proposal, Then I only begg, that what was intended for a Satisfaction, as well as favour, (I mean the Grant of Pensilvania) may not be made the Ruin of my other Estate, and family to Support it, as it hath hitherto been, by the many interrupcions, and Avocacions, there, and here, for twenty eight Years past. I have been several times there, and as often called home, to my Great Expence, fatigue, and danger, to defend my Just Right, not to Say Merit, to the Crown. I am with respect

Your assured
& desire to be your
obliged Freind
Wm Penn

LS. CO 5/1264/106, PRO. (*Micro.* 14:184.) The dateline and closing, beginning with "I am with respect . . . ," are in WP's hand. Docketed: Pensilvania | Letter from Mr Penn of the 7th | Instant, relating to the Sur- | render of his Government of | Pensilvania for 20000^{l} to be | paid him in 7 Years. | Received: 8th December | 1710 | Read. 22th Do.

1. See doc. 179.
2. *Micro.* 9:682.
3. See doc. 28.
4. See doc. 180B, below.
5. WP attended the Board of Trade in conference about the surrender of his government on 22 Dec. 1710, 18 Jan., 2 and 12 Feb. 1711. *Journal of the Commissioners for Trade and Plantations from February 1708-9 to March 1714-5* (London, 1925), pp. 216, 228-29, 235, 237.
6. Copyist's mistake for 1710.
7. For WP's reply to essentially the same questions in 1707, see doc. 140B.
8. For WP's earlier figures of customs revenue from Pennsylvania, see doc. 88.
9. WP is being disingenuous here. He knows that Pennsylvania's revenue act of 1706 expired in 1709, and that Gov. Gookin has been unable to secure a new act from the Assembly. In 1710 Pennsylvania had no settled revenue. However, in 1711 the Assembly did pass a new supply bill. See doc. 185.
10. For WP's decision in 1684 to settle for a subscription of £500—not £600 as he claims here—instead of an annual income from duties, see *PWP*, 2:411-12, 558-59.
11. WP had asked for the same total sum in 1707 but with a different mode of payment. See doc. 140, text at n. 4.

181
TO FRIENDS IN PENNSYLVANIA

[10 February 1711]

Dear and worthy friends[1]
I herewith send you my hearty and affectionate Salutes & Remembrances & cannot but acknowledge your late eminent Zeal and Concurrence for the Publick Good & therein for my service,[2] & may they never be separated as I ever desired they never might. God be thanked I can say for the Blessing that has attended your ~~Endeavours~~ late noble Endeavours to rescue your poor Governour & Government out of the fallen selfish & ungrateful practices of some men, for whether I ever surrender or not, it will shew honest friends a discreet a wise & Just people & depend upon it nothing can ever carry me that length, but because I can not more be able to come to you without such a supply, than I can pay Debts without Money, but if such a thing which has been long in Agitation should come to pass, it shall not stop my coming among You, but rather the contrary, & I shall take care of your Property and Privileges both as Christians & Englishmen for as the News of those unruly spirits that have, I verily believe griev'd you is gott to the Ears of the Ministry here, so your Wisdom in recovering your spirits as you have done to doe just prudent & reasonable things begins to honour You as a People that have begun to doe your Duty to your own Benefit & preservation, For what with the Impracticable Designs of your Malignants & those not far from You a Resolution was taken here among both Merchants & the great Men of the Government of putting a period to your Assemblies & to leave your Legislation to the Parliament of England wch I hope now to prevent. The People of N York & of the Caribee Islands being wth You & the Jerseys represented unruly & impracticable to Governours, This Resolution as before, was thought necessary to prevent future Clamor, I am truly Joyful that it has been the good Providence of God among You and especially poor friends, that by all your last Accounts you cannot fall under the Displeasure of the great men at home, upon that great Objection. The wise Lord preserve you and renew your Courage to act the part of a Judicious People that will weigh your Duty to the Publick maugre[3] all the tricks of self designing men.

I doe dearly own & Accept {of} your Love in your kind & affectionate Letters[4] return[ing] You with the upright & honest hearts that Adhere to You My own & families Acknowledgements Assuring You that nothing but our Eternal felicity is more our prayer to the Lord than that we may live if not die among you & Yours & I truly hope that your & our Desires on that Account shall be acceptably heard

Wherefore Dear Brethern help me all you can & as soon as you can, for it shall ~~not~~ {never} be my fault that I am not yours as much as your honest hearts can desire Nay I can say that this comes not only from a Sense of Duty & Interest too but of long & deep Inclination ~~by~~ {&} choice Wherefore once more Lett me say goe on & prosper & the Lord bring us more & more near to each other & ours, that as God gave us that Copious & good Countrey so we may enjoy it & ours from Generation to Generation in fear & Love to the Lord & one to another Amen

Here have been some Changes in the Ministry[5] wch I hope will not turn to our prejudice, at le~~s~~{a}st I shall use all my Interest to turn to ~~m~~ our Advantage, but to be sure 'tis a time for you all there, as here too, to be wise & careful in our Conduct. I hope {after} what I mentioned in a former Letter to you[6] ~~&~~ {about Your} encouraging your present Governour to perform his Character & Duty among You, there will not now need any more to be said upon that Subject, nor what I hinted in my expostulatory Letter[7] concerning the Invasion of my poor Property, to wch, I cannot but Say I am sorry so many have shewn so slender a regard in detaining so much of my wanted Quittrents. Of wch I entreat your reminding those concern'd therein as well as in the Province. I beg you also to consider the Necessity of regulating the Courts of Justice there[8] that the unruly spirits that are too apt to disquiet them may not prevail as they did in the Notorious case of the Frankford Company, the Abhorrence here of all men of Law that have heard of it.[9] for the rest I shall refer You to what I shall send you by James Logan who intends over in a Month or 5 weeks.[10]

I bless God I am pretty well & so are mine saving my youngest son[11] that has 3 or 4 fits of a feaver, but {as} I heard to day from my little American[12] is better Pray give my Dr Love to yours & friends in General & believe that I am cordially Your faithful & Affectionate friend

WP

Whitehal~~l~~ 10. 12 month 1710/1

Copy (in James Logan's hand). Penn Papers, Private Correspondence, HSP. (*Micro.* 14:216.) Addressed: E Sh. S Carp. R H. T St. G Ow. I Nor. C Pus. S Pr. T Masters &c. Docketed: A Coppy of a | Letter to Frds in | Pennsilvania | 10: Fe~~y~~by 1710/11.

1. Edward Shippen, Samuel Carpenter, Richard Hill, Thomas Story, Griffith Owen, Isaac Norris, Caleb Pusey, Samuel Preston, Thomas Masters, and others. WP had written a collective letter to six of these nine men in 1708; see doc. 153.

2. A reference to the Oct. 1710 election, in which there was a complete turnover in the membership of the Pennsylvania Assembly. In the 1709 election, 17 of the 26 Assembly members had been reelected, including Speaker David Lloyd, but in the 1710 election none of the 1709 members was reelected. Richard Hill was the new speaker and a majority of the members were favorably inclined toward WP. *Votes and Proceedings*, 2:17, 61, 83.

3. In spite of.

4. See Isaac Norris's and Samuel Preston's letters of Nov. 1710 to WP. *Micro.* 14:172, 177.

5. A reference to the gradual replacement of Whig ministers under the leadership of Godolphin with Tories under Harley in Apr.—Aug. 1710. David Green, *Queen Anne* (New York, 1970), p. 232.

6. See doc. 153.

7. See doc. 178.

8. The Assembly passed a law regulating the courts in Feb. 1711. *Statutes,* 2:301-31.

9. A reference to the attempted recovery of land for the Frankford Land Company by writ of ejectment in 1708. David Lloyd had suggested this legal ploy that pitted members of the company against each other. In exchange for his counsel he received 1000 acres of land. Stephanie G. Wolf, *Urban Village* (Princeton, 1976), p. 176; doc. 159, n. 21.

10. Logan stayed nearly another year in England; he sailed for Pennsylvania in Jan. 1712.

11. Dennis Penn.

12. John Penn's letter has not been found.

182
THE BOARD OF TRADE TO QUEEN ANNE

[13 February 1711]

TO THE QUEEN'S MOST EXCELL^t MAJ^ty

MAY IT PLEASE YOUR MAJ^ty

IN obedience to your Maj^ty's commands Signifyed to us by the Ld Dartmouth, We have considered the Memoriall of William Penn Esq. Proprietor & Governour of Pensilvania in relation to his Governm^t of that Province,[1] & have severall times been attended by, & conferr'd with him on that occasion.[2] Whereupon We beg leave humbly to represent to your Maj^ty.

THAT by Lettres Patents bearing date the 4th day of March 1680 Your Maj^ty's Royall Uncle King Charles the 2^ed for the considerations therein mentioned Did Grant the Propriety & Governm^t of the s^d Province of Pensilvania to the s^d Willm Penn his Heirs & Assigns,[3] wherein are contain'd such large & ample powers Priviledges & Immunityes as in our humble opinion seem capable of being Extended to the diminution of the Prerogative of your Maj^ty's Crown from whence they were originally deriv'd.

THAT the s^d Willm Penn has since compleated the Settlem^t of a considerable Colony in that Tract of Land in America, & out of a desolate Wilderness has rais'd a flourishing Country from whence great benefit has accru'd to this Kingdom by a Consumption of British Manufactures from time to time Exported thither, by an improvm^t of Navigation, & by an Increase of Dutyes paid here on Goods imported from thence; wch Dutyes have yearly amounted to a considerable Sum as appears by the Custom house Accounts of Imports from that province.

That the s^{d} Settlem^{t} having been made by the great care & industry of the s^{d} Wm Penn (not without many difficultys & hardships) & an undertaking so chargeable, having been perform'd by him at his own expence, & thrö his Interest, 'tis reasonable to believe he has very much impair'd his Estate, as is set forth in his s^{d} memoriall.

That the s^{d} William Penn being very uneasy under the frequent attempts that have been made upon him in order to take that Governm^{t} out of his hands, & under such other disturbances & oppositions as he has met with on Account of its being a Proprietary Governm^{t}, he therefore declares that he is ready, & willing to Surrender all the Powers of Governm^{t} wherewith he is invested, & to deliver the same intirely into the hands of your Maj^{ty} upon such a consideration as may appear reasonable with regard to what he has meritted from the publick in having settled the s^{d} Colonys.

Whereupon We humbly offer our Opinion that the revesting the Governm^{t} of Pensilvania in your Maj^{ty} will be a benefit to the trade of this Kingdom, & particularly that it will tend.

To the Establishm^{t} of maintenance of your Maj$^{ty's}$ more immediate Authority in that Province.

To the more speedy & Impartiall Administration of Justice to all persons there.

To a more regular carrying on a legall trade in those parts conformable to the severall Acts of Parliam^{t} in that behalf.

To the better Security & defence of Your Maj$^{ty's}$ subjects in that Province, & the Strengthening the British Interest upon the Northern Continent of America.

In Consideration of wch Surrender the s^{d} Willm Penn by a Supplementall memoriall deliver'd to us,[4] does propose, that 20000^{l} be paid to him within the Term of Seven Years the same to be paid by equall Yearly paym^{ts}.

We presume Your Maj^{ty} will not expect that we should give an opinion as to the reasonableness of that sum, or that in this case We should propose a Sum with regard to the true Value of the Governm^{t} to be purchased, the nature of Governm^{t} not admitting of any Rule whereby it may be valued, as is done in other cases where the price to be paid & the profit to be purchas'd are to be equally consider'd. Therefore what ever sum your Maj^{ty} shall be graciously pleas'd to give to the said William Penn upon his Surrender of that Governm^{t} it is to {be} Estimated not only as a full & ample Consideration of that purchase, but as proceeding further from your Maj$^{ty's}$ wonted Goodness & Bounty on Account of his great Expence in the Settling that Colony to the Impairing his Estate, & of his good Services in having made that Settlem^{t} whereby the Trade & Navigation of this Kingdom, & Your Maj$^{ty's}$ Revenue has been increasd as before mention'd.

He Says he should think himself oblig'd on Surrendering his Governm^{t} to desire leave in all humility to recommend to Your Maj$^{ty's}$

Royall Protection & favour the people call'd Quakers (who under him first settled, cultivated & improv'd that Colony) were he not so sensible of Your Maj$^{ty's}$ great Justice & Goodness that he doubts not but they will be protected in a full enjoym^{t} of that Indulgence in Religious Matters, & of all those civill Rights & priviledges wch by Law they now Enjoy.

We Enquir'd of the s^{d} Willm Penn, what might be the Annual charges of that Governm^{t} & what Revenue there was subsisting for the support thereof, The Yearly value of such Revenue & for what time Granted

In answer whereunto he has inform'd us in generall that the charge of that Governm^{t} is less than in other Your Maj^{tys} Governm^{t} on that continent. That about 25 Years agoe the Assembly made a free Gift to him of a Duty on Goods exported & Imported, which he says at that time would have rais'd 1200^{l} per Annum; But in consideration of 600^{l} given to the s^{d} William Penn, and for that he was of opinion that Taxes in the Infancy of a Colony would cramp the Industry of the people, the s^{d} Duty of 1200^{l} was let fall, & it has not since been reviv'd.[5] However he does not doubt but the Assembly will readily Grant new Dutyes, and that as the Province is daily increasing in numbers of people & in Trade, such Dutyes, with the Fines of Courts, & forfeitures for illegall Trade, will, as he conceives, be more than sufficient for the expence of that Governm^{t}.

Having laid befor Your Maj^{ty} a State of Willm Penn's Case in relation to his Governm^{t} of Pensilvania as it has appear'd to us upon the best information we have been able to get, with our humble Opinion therein, We beg leave further to offer that if your Maj^{ty} shall think fit to acçept of a Surrender of that Governm^{t}, Such Surrender should be absolute, & that the s^{d} Wm Penn do thereby renounce all Right claim or pretension whatsoever as well to the s^{d} Governm^{t} of Pensilvania as to that of New Castle & the other two lower Countyes in such a manner & form as by your Maj$^{ty's}$ Councill learned in the Law shall be advis'd.

All which is most humbly
Submitted

Stamford
Phil: Meadows
J: Pulteney
Robt Monckton
Cha: Turner
Geo: Baillie
Arth: Moore[6]

Whitehall
February the 13th 1710/11

Whitehall February 26th 1710/11

HER Majty is graciously pleas'd to refer this Representation to the Rt Honble the Lords Commissioners of her Majty's Treasury to consider thereof & Report their opinion what may be fitly done therein Whereupon her Majty will declare her further pleasure

Dartmouth

Copy. Penn Papers, Miscellaneous Manuscripts of William Penn, HSP. (*Micro.* 14:224.) Docketed: 13th February 1710/11 | 26th February 1710 | Report from the Lord Commissioners | for trade upon Mr Penn's | Memoriall to Surrender his | Propriety of the Governmt of | Pensilvania. Referr'd to | the Treasury from the Queen | by Lord Dartmouth | 5th April 1711 | My Lords will take her | Majty's pleasure upon this | Report at their first | Attendance.

1. See doc. 179.
2. See doc. 180, n. 5.
3. See *PWP*, 2:61-77.
4. See doc. 180B.
5. This is taken directly from doc. 180B, text at n. 10.
6. Of the seven Board members who signed this document, three have been previously identified. Thomas Grey (1654-1720), second earl of Stamford, was a court Whig and president of the Board; Robert Monckton, a Yorkshire Lord Lieutenant from Newcastle, had joined the Board in 1707; George Baillie, a Scottish Whig, was appointed to the Board in 1710; and Arthur Moore (1666?-1730), a prominent Irish merchant and financier, became a member of the Board in 1710. Steele, *Colonial Policy*, pp. 113-14, 134-35.

183
FROM THOMAS CALLOWHILL

Bristoll the 1~~7~~6th of 12th month [February] 1710[/11]

Deare W P.

I have thine of the 13th Instant[1] and am sorry to perceive ~~thow have not payd~~ {that} Beringer[2] and Ja. St amand[3] ~~to cleare that affaire which thou~~ {is not payd & satisfied as thou} gave me Expectation thou would {doe} by the sale of the Kentish or Ireish Lands,[4] {~~that coming not about~~ {~~about time to their content~~} {~~Now~~} Since I am oblidged with thee to them ~~and I have assigned them the cheque order value~~ {& that not coming about in time to their content} why are they not payd off with the produce of the Exchequer {order &} annuity {which I assigned to Berringer for that purpose[5] ~~&~~ in case that failed} which at the vallue now Runing {as thou say} ~~is~~ at 5.0 per Cent is 777.15s besids about 23l due for halfe years Intrest makes above Eight hundred pounds — Sufficent to pay Moses Beringer 500l & Intrest ~~and Ja St amand 270 or there about~~ {~~I never thought it above 800l Vallew nor was fond of it and [thou] had my consent to dispose of it the Exheq-~~

~~uer annuity to that purpose and}~~ ~~& I would part with it rather then they should be longer unsatisfied, thou, might~~ {~~in Lew thereof~~} ~~have given me satisfaction when time might serve.~~
and Ja St Amand 270 or there about I never thought it above 800^{l} value nor was fond of it but consented to part with it to Serve thee & thou ~~might~~ {may} in Lew thereof ~~have given~~ {give} me satisfaction when time might serve {I pray thou let that be disposed & Ber & St Amands pd of without delay}

Df. Penn Papers, Private Correspondence, HSP. (*Micro.* 14:222.)

1. WP's letter of 13 Feb. 1711 has not been found.
2. Moses Beranger was a London merchant with whom Thomas Callowhill dealt in his efforts to help WP refinance his debts. *Micro.* 14:541, 543, 570, 577.
3. James St. Amand (1688-1727), who studied law at Oxford University and the Inner Temple, became a judge of the courts within the jurisdiction of the Tower of London. *Alumni Oxonienses,* 3:1300.
4. On 15 Dec. 1698 WP became indebted to St. Amand in the penal sum of £1000 for borrowing £500 (*Micro.* 7:771). On 10 Aug. 1699 he borrowed another £200, bringing the total, including interest, to £763.10.0 (*Micro.* 8:087). In an effort to settle this obligation, WP appointed trustees to manage lands in Ireland and England, with profits and rents going to repay the debt to St. Amand. As of July 1710 the debt was still outstanding and Thomas Callowhill agreed to repay £500, which he in turn borrowed from Beranger. *Micro.* 14:541, 543, 570, 577, 586, 775, 777; Penn Papers, Miscellaneous Manuscripts, Penn vs. Beranger, HSP.
5. As security for his loan from Beranger, Callowhill had used a government annuity assigned to him in 1706 by WP, who had held it since 1678. This annuity paid a yearly dividend of about £45 and had a cash value of about £800. In 1715, after a lawsuit brought by Hannah Penn, Beranger finally agreed to purchase the annuity outright, with the proceeds going to pay Beranger himself and to repay St. Amand's remaining debt, and the remainder going to the Penn family. See *Micro.* 13:090; 14:451, 543, 570, 775, 777.

184
TO CHARLES GOOKIN

London the 14 1mo (Mar:) 1711

Honoured Friend
About a Month agoe I wrote to thee[1] by the Pacquet Boat which I hope will come to Hand long before this
From my Letter by that oppertunity thou wilt find I am treating at Present, about the Surrender of my Goverm^{tt} [2] I am sensible that the Peoples late Endeavours to be more duely represented by such as will not make it their Bussiness to thwart me[3] and my Just (but suffering) Interest there, as has to long been done, may deservedly engage my Care over them, in a much different Manner, from what I have for several Years past been highly Provoked to, And accordingly they may assure them selves, no Regard of mine shall be wanting to

them; Butt from what I have already undergone, I have been soe far reduced to a Necessity of takeing these Measures which were entered on a considerable time agoe, that I still think it adviseable to Pursue them: The Circumstances of my Affairs & Family are such that I cannott butt think it expedient, as well for the People there as my Self, to wind up the matter, & make the best Terms, I can in my life time, for after my Decease, should I keep it till then, neither they nor I can be sure, that it would be an Advantage to them to have it continued as it is. I cannot however butt account it very providential should this Treaty goe on (as 'tis altogether ucertain, the Ministry haveing so many weighty Affaires on their hands) that the Country has so far considered their Interest as to send Representatives that will (I hope) be governed by reason and not think a merit to oppose me, & those concerned for me

I desire therefore that the Assembly may seriously & soberly consider what is fitt for them in modesty to ask (of the Crown as well as me) & have enacted under the Present Administration without shewing any fright at the Apprehensions of a Change. I desire they may propose only what is necessary & reasonable in itself, And to all such things as far as they shall be approved by the Council, I desire thee to concur, & I doubt not afterwards I shall get them pass'd here, for You see by the order of the Queen in Council wch I sent over, about the 11th Mo 1709[4] most of the last Laws are approved, the Assembly 1705 were pressing for an Act to Impower Religious Societies to buy & sell Lands,[5] to which Some of the Ch: of England (it seems) Shew'd themselves averse, butt soe far as it tended to enable them, only to purchase what might be necessary for accommodating any Community of People, with a Meeting-House, Burying-Ground, School-House & such like Conveniences & not to make Estates in Mortmain,[6] as far as I am able to Judge of Affairs here, I beleive there would be little or no Objection made to it, Yet if any there cannot think it safe; that their Wardens should be thus impowered to dispose of what has been appropriated to such Uses I see no reason, why they may not, if they please, have a Clause to guard againt it, Butt in short I am willing such an Act should pass, and if thou apprehends any blame in it, turn it upon the People & me, & I shall here be very ready to defend it.

The same also for any Act that they shall think necessary for a fitting & requisite Affirmation, to be taken in Evidence & for qualifying Officiers which I wish might be brought as neare as may be, to that passed in Coll Fletchers time and approved by the late King:[7] butt as tis absolutely necessary there should be some provision made in that Case, which is not to be done here, nor anywhere butt, among themselves, it will be Incumbent on thee to pass such a Bill for that Purpose as the House can agree to[8]

Butt while I propose to answer the Peoples Desires in what is for their Ease & Advantage, 'tis butt reasonable to expect they should also consider what is due to me. I have been greatly wronged in my Property. My Mannors have been invaded, my Lands entered on at pleasure without any regular Method, the Tax granted me not paid, and notwithstanding I have always been Ready to give the Inhabitants their full Allowance according to the Act of Property (so called) past at Newcle in the year 1700[9] yett divers have on their parts disputed my Rights, they have shewn themselves soe unjust as to covet what they never Purchased, that is, their Overpluss without paying for it. I will not enter into further particulars, Butt to settle both them, & me in our respective Rights I desire the Bill prepared 1705 Called an Act for preventing of Lawsuits[10] may be passed according to the Amendmts made to it, & sent to that House by the Goverr & Council takeing at the same time the further Advice of my Comms of Property there; This I am sensible will be for their own Advantage in maney Things they cannot soe directly claim as I can what is my due, butt I am desirious it should be now done, I hope they will Provide for my Security in other Respects

I would expect they will not need be put in mind of the Necessity of supporting the Govemt whether Surrendered or not (for I must again say that's very uncertain) nor of considering thee as well for thy past Services as the present & future: It will alsoe be their Interest I beleive to settle something Certain for the Time {to} come, even tho' I should resign

Upon what I have here said you will find it necessary that the Assembly shou'd sett to Bussiness 'till these Affairs be duly compleated

Pray fail not to recommend to them Unanimity & Dispatch & lett that Govemt for this Time be an Instance that the People in America are not everywhere Soe Contentious & full of themselves, but that some of them can at some time agree to see & Pursue their own Good as becomes reasonable & moderate Men

Acquaint those of the Lower Counties that I rec'd their kind Addresss for the Two Yeares Past,[11] & am heartily pleased to see them so well & peaceable Inclined. I am not forgetfull of what they Desire and would willingly labour it, both for their and in ~~your~~ {my} own Interest

I cannot at present see any other foundation for an Union but a Surrendr it must be done by the Crown, & the Ministry will not be forward to meddle in it till it's in their own Hands. I hope at the same time to gett the Division Line run between me and the Ld Baltimore;[12] that all Occasions of Difference may be effectually removed

Let this Letter be laid before the Council & so much of it as thou wth them, shall think convenient, be communicated to the Assembly[13] to all of whom (I mean the Council and both the Assemblies) I Desire to be kindly remmembr'd. I refer thee to Prints for the Publick News, and with my particular Regards to thy Self I close this from

thy Affectionte and Assured Friend
William Penn

Copy. Penn Papers, Additional Miscellaneous Letters, HSP. (*Micro.* 14:240.) Docketed: Copy of Wm Penn's | Letter in 1711.

1. Not found.

2. See doc. 182; *Micro.* 14:232.

3. A reference to the current Pennsylvania Assembly elected in Oct. 1710; see doc. 181, n. 2.

4. Not found. On 24 Oct. 1709 the Queen in Council had disallowed 6 of the 51 laws passed by the Assembly in Jan. 1706; the remaining laws were apparently approved. *Votes and Proceedings,* 1(pt. 2):80-81; *Acts of the Privy Council,* 2:851.

5. In Dec. 1705 the Pennsylvania Assembly had drawn up a bill enabling religious societies to buy and sell land, but in Jan. 1705 Lt. Gov. Evans deferred action on this measure until he had received further advice. The act was finally passed in 1712. *Votes and Proceedings,* 1(pt. 2):72, 76, 78, 80; *Statutes,* 2:424-25.

6. Alienation of land to an ecclesiastical corporation. *Black's Law Dictionary.*

7. In Nov. 1696, under Dep. Gov. Markham, the Pennsylvania Assembly passed a law allowing officials to affirm instead of taking oaths of office. The crown disallowed a similar law passed in 1700. WP may have been thinking of a 1694 law, passed under Gov. Fletcher, which permitted witnesses in all legal proceedings to testify "by Solemnly promising to speak the truth, the whole truth & nothing but the truth." The crown approved this law, but Anglicans later complained that it exceeded the 1696 English Affirmation Act, which permitted affirmations only in civil, not criminal, cases. *Charter and Laws,* pp. 228, 247-49; *PWP,* 3:399, 401, 444, 446, 449.

8. See *Micro.* 14:237.

9. An Act for the Effectual Establishment and Confirmation of the Freeholders of this Province and Territories, Their Heirs and Assigns, in Their Lands and Tenements. *Statutes,* 2:118-23.

10. WP probably means An Act for the Better Confirmation of the Owners of Lands and Inhabitants of this Province, in Their Just Rights and Possessions. *Statutes,* 2:191-94.

11. Not found.

12. See doc. 166.

13. On 9 Aug. 1711 the Council ordered an abstract of WP's letter for the Assembly. *Minutes of the Provincial Council,* 2:538.

185
FROM THE PROVINCIAL COUNCIL

[10 April 1711]

Honoured Propriry

Wee Salute thee with much duty and Love, and Crave Leave to acquaint thee that the Assembly hath made and the governour past fourteen Laws,[1] vizt An Act for Establishing Courts, 2d, Fees, 3d, Recording Deeds, 4th, The affirmation, 5th Publick Inns, 6th, Priviledges to a Freeman, 7th Riotous Sports, 8th Disputes about ~~deb~~ Dates of Conveyances, 1st-2d-3d months &c: 9, Priority of payments of Debts to Inhabitants of this province, 10, Improveing a good Correspondance With the Indians, 11th, Regulating party walls in Philada, 12th, Commissioners to Compell Collecting of All Arrearages of former Taxes, 13th, Supply of 2d per pound & 8/-per head, 14 Impost on Negros, Wine, Rum, & other Spirritts, Syder & Vessells,[2]

And in the Supply Act[3] have appropriated five hundred pounds

To the Governour towards his Support in the Lieutennancy and the Remainder to defray the Debts of the Country which because no mony hath been Raised Since 1705/6 are become very heavey and among those Debts The assembly has Reckoned the order of 200^{l} old Currancy to thy Selfe for Negotiating the laws made by that assembly, Accordingly have [illegible deletion] {Revivd} it to be now paid Since they find the mony Intended for that Use out of that tax 1705/6[4] to have been Drawn out & Expended under the name of Immediate Sevices

Some of us were appointed by the Assembly to Embrace the Same oppertunity which the Governour Shall take to transmitt the Laws, and write to thee Incloseing their Addresses to the Queen and thy Selfe[5] but are Obliged a little to anticipate that time, upon this Occation.

The affirmation act (of which Inclosed is a Coppy)[6] has Stir'd up great uneasiness & oposition In Some men of the Church and as we understand a vestry was Called under Couller of augmenting the Church and their a Collection made, and a letter writt to the Bishop of London[7] {&} as wee are {alsoe} Informed a Representation to the queen ag^{t} the Said Act, So that we Embrace this Conveyance to be as Earley as they, Entreating thy Interest and Care for a Confirmation if possible Otherwise our Condition here as friends will be very precarious and hard, as thou art fully sencible and this being a Law that was for the Ease of our Society and to the generall Satisfaction of friends here it was thought more just and hono^{ble} for fr^{ds} to Raise Some mony for that particular Charge of Negotiation, and accordingly Last Quarterly Meeting hath taken Some Care in it & in the meane time Desired Some {of us} ~~friends~~ to advance the Sum of 50^{l} Sterling and Remitt for that Service which is accordingly done herewith[8]

There was found great Occation for ~~wh~~ Such an Act upon the Tryall of Capt Pride[9] John Moor himselfe in barr to the Evidence declareing the Queen's order no Law and for want of a law in being here for an affirmation the Evidence was Rejected

The Governour has us'd his Endeavours to please and Oblige the Church men, has adapted his Commis^{rs} on our new Constitutions of Courts[10] Accordingly, putting in this County Seven of them to five Quakers,[11] and in the other Counties as Many as could be got or by any meane's thought fitt, Little or No Opposition was made till it past the Govr tho the assemblys ~~Minutes~~ Minnutes were weekly publisht,[12] but now it is So managed & wrought up that not one of the Church Magestrates Except Capt Finney (who now lyes Dengerously Ill) did or would act, ~~Soe that,~~ Soe that to Dissapoint the Suppos'd designe of bringing in oaths before friends on the bench there by to Strengthen their Complaint the Courts have been only Call^{d} & Adjournd & thus Matters now Stand.

We here Inclose Likewise Coppy of the 2 adresses;[13] and now with much Love to thee thy wife & Children Conclude and Remaine Thy True Friends

Philadelphia the 10th 2mo: 1711

Richd Hill	Edwd Shippen
Saml Preston	Tho Story
Jona Dickinson	Griff Owen
Isaac Norris	Saml Carpenter

P: S:

Since writeing this Letter we have got a Coppy of part of the vestrys Letter to the Bisp: & the heads or Substance as well as Could be Suddenly taken & privately had of the Remainder wch we Send thee herewith

The bills[14] are

Edward Shippen on John Crouch for	£12.10.0
Richd Hill on Thomas Loyd	12.10.0
Saml Preston on Ditto	12.10.0
Isaac Norris on Jon Askew	12.10.–
	£50. 0.0

Coppy

When the Interest of our holy Mother Church of England is attackt by her Restless Enemys the Quakers And her unworthy Members want admittance to Supplycate her most Sacred Majesty to Support and protect us. Wee the Minestr & vestery of this Church of Philadelphia Could Think of no other then your Lordship to doe Soe good an office, who have all along Stood So boldly in the gap for her Defence: And Your Lordships Constant adherance to her wise Conduct & Councill have now put her (we trust) beyond the Reach of her avowed Adersaryes the Sectaryes of all Sorts

We presume to Inclose to your Lord Ship an Humble address to her majesty in behalfe of this infant branch planted in the midst of a people Dangerouse to Church and State, to one Denying the benefit of the Laws to the other the use of armes, and altho we thought most proper to Address her majesty only Concerning this act, yet we begg leave to lay before you the Dangerous & pernicious Effects of severall other Laws made this Assembly wch when her majty please to Call for will appeare all of a peice, but above all our present Naked Circumstances—Thus farr is Coppy

Now follows Some of the heads or Substance of the Remaineing part of the Same Letter

The Naked Circumstances is the want of Defence Expressing how open we lye to the Enemy that the french have been Severall times up in the River & done Mischiefe in the out Skirts of the Country And that the Country is lyable to be destroyed by one Ship of force.

That Some thousands of pounds is Now Raised[15] & they know

not for what unless to Carry on their Designe of passing their Law or Act for affirmation or to that purpose & that the Laws of this kind have been Soe often Repealed or Disliked by the Queen yet nothing will obstruct them therefore We begg it may be put out of their power of doeing the Like hereafter, or to this purpose

the 3d 3mo [May] 1711

Hondd Frd

The foregoing is Coppy {the Orriginal} via Lisbon. Just now came up that hope Galley Jno Richmond[16] in 5 weeks from Lisbon by whom I had a Letter from James Logan of the 6 1mo [17] Giving a Large accot of the Progress toward a Surrender[18] it a Little damps us but as things are It may be for the better. May wee Submitt to the Great hand wch Is Over all: and I hope his direction will be with thee in it.

I am Sorry to hear of thy Indisposition, and Simpathiz in all thy Troubles. Our familys and frds Generally [are] well, and are full of Love to thee. I Desire thy Self and good wife will please to accept mine in a Perticular manner

Thy cordiall frd
Isaac Norris

Copy and ALS. Penn Papers, Official Correspondence, HSP. (*Micro.* 14:249.) Docketed: Isaac Norrys &c | 3d May 1711. Addressed: To William Penn Esqr | Proprietary & Governor | Pensilvania | in London. Docketed by WP: Isaac Norris.

1. Gov. Gookin and the Assembly passed these 14 laws on 28 Feb. 1711. *Votes and Proceedings,* 2:93.

2. For the texts of these 14 laws, see *Statutes,* 2:301-88.

3. The 13th law. Ibid., p. 381.

4. An Act for the Raising a Supply of Two Pence Halfpenny per Pound and Ten Shillings per Head. Ibid., p. 290.

5. *Micro.* 14:237.

6. Enclosure not found, but see *Statutes,* 2:355-57

7. See the copy of this letter to Bishop Compton, attached to the Provincial Council's letter.

8. The sum of £50 was sent to WP in four bills of exchange. *Micro.* 14:247; Quarterly Meeting Minutes of 5 Mar. 1711, Quaker Collection, Haverford College, Haverford, Pa.

9. Proceedings of this trial have not been found.

10. An Act for Establishing Courts of Judicature in this Province. *Statutes,* 2:301-31.

11. The names of the 12 Phila. Co. justices of the peace commissioned by Gookin are not known; in Mar. 1710 Gookin and the Council discussed what to do when the justices declined to serve. *Minutes of the Provincial Council,* 2:531.

12. See *Votes and Proceedings,* 2:76-92.

13. For a copy of the Anglican address to Bishop Compton, see this document, below. The Anglican address to Queen Anne has not been found.

14. See n. 8, above.

15. Actually £50. See n. 8, above.

16. The *Hope Galley* was built by Isaac Norris, who—together with WP and James Logan—invested in a cargo of Pennsylvania wheat destined for the Lisbon market in 1711. *PMHB,* 78:147n, 167, 169, 170, 172.

17. Not found.

18. See doc. 182.

186
FROM EDWARD SHIPPEN AND OTHERS

Philadelphia the 23^{d} 3^{d} moth [May] 1711

Hounred Friend
Prorietery & Govr

Thy kind and affectionate Letter per the pacquett Boat of the 10th 12 mo[1] came to hand the 12th Inst[2] and wee are truely glad that thou with thine were then In health and hope the Continuation of the Same. Wee Cann but take notice of thy kind Acceptance of our Late Endeavours which in Som measure has had the desired Successe & Effect Soe agreable to thee and us; after some Years prevalency of a Contrary party to that degre[e] that some of us could See but litle hopes of withstanding the Current, and with thee wee also ought to be thankefull to God for that Favour, And wee Earnestly desire that wee and all Friends concerned In our Severall Stations & places and upon all Occasions may make a Right Improvement and true use thereof by a prudent Conduct & management in the discharge of our duty to God to thee & the Country as becomes a people professing the holy peaceable truth, That those who watch for our halting, & Seeke occasions may be disapointed, and Such as have been prejudiced & misled by the artifices & Insinuations of designing men may come to a Sight & Sense {ther}of, Returne in true love & duty to thee & with us & wee with them may pursue those things which tend to mutuall Concord, the peace & welfare of the Province & therein thine & our owne true Interest.

Wee take notice of what thou hints about a Surrender which as wee have understood has been Long in Agitation & now Renewed; The matter seeming to us of Soe great moment to thee and the people If viewed on both Sides, we desire leave to take a Sutable Liberty & Freedome not by way of advice, For as wee Represent none but ourSelves wee are not Quallifyed for that, but only by way of Memoriall to thee and to put thee in mind of what thou well knowest & Soe Leave It to thee.

First therfore for thy Consideration on the one hand wee lay before thee that wheras It has pleased God in his wisdome and Providence and In favour to thee & the people to open the heart of our Late King Charles to grant this large and Fruitfull Countrey Soe Commodiously Scituated on a noble Capacious Navigable River and Bay, for trade as It were in the Center of the English Empire on the Maine; And {the} hearts of many Friends being as wee believe by the Good Will of God Inclined to come Into this Countrey [&] Severall other Conscienious people of other perswasions, with Expectacons no doubt that they & their Posterityes might Enjoy the Ease and Benefit of Thy Government dureing thy Life and ~~after~~ the Continuance therof under those that should Succed thee. Now as wee and the Generallity of the people are very {sensible} of the Ease Libertyes & privilidges wee have had & doe Enjoy under thy Mild and gentle Governm[t] for which wee are thankfull to God and under Just obligations of affections and duty to thee; And wee Should be heartily glad if the Same might be Continued to us & our Posterityes; And even some others who have taken the Liberty of shewing their dislike of thee in Some matters Seemes willing to Continue under thy Government by their writeing to thee[3] & Expressing themselves against a Surrender when at the Same time Some of the~~m~~se have made the Same not only difficult but uneasy for thee to hold. And as all men Generally love Ease & Liberty (though too often abuse it to their owne hurt,) And as wee Expect when a Chainge happens our taxes will Run much higher, and our Friends more perticulerly may be lyable to many Sufferings and Inconveniencyes on Severall accounts will not a volluntary Surrender give Occasion for Some people to Reflect upon thee for Soe doeing Especially thy Enemyes who will be ready to put the worst Constructions upon It?

2[dly] On the other hand ~~It~~ may be Considered, thy 28 years Tryall and Experience, the oppositions & difficultyes here and there, and the many groundlesse Complaints from time to time, and not only the unfair but false Colours turns & Suggestions of discontented partyes for above 20 years past upon Every thing done in the Government which did not please them, though never Soe well Intended & by men Impartiall might not be faulted but commended. (Thou knows the ground of these things and from whence they arise) and wee cannot Expect It will be better as long as the Governm[t] Is in the hands of Friends. Next thy Extraordinary Charges In makeing defences against these Complaints, the mean Supplyes raised here for the Support of the Government, thy great trouble and Exercises from Some assemblies and the uncertainty of being better upon a new Choice and the different Opinions among Friends in these matters, the great difficultyes which thou & Friends here Lye under in the Executive part of the Government for want of a Militia & defence & for not takeing and administring oathes, with out which some looke upon themselves unsafe, which growes worse & worse and is Come to that point by the refusall of the Church of England magestrates to Sit In Courts Ever since the Governour passed the Act for the affirmation[4] that a full Stop is {thereby} put to our Courts of Justice and thereupon Occasions are taken for Complaints to the Queen against Friends as being unfit to be Concerned in Government; The Constant Uneasinesse of the Church of England party under the Administracon of Friends and the frequent attempts to wrest the Government out of thy hands; and Endeavours to deprive us of the affirmation acts & other Lawes most suited to our Consciencious Circumstances, to bring us under Sufferings or render us obnoxious to our Superiors & to make thee & Friends dissenters under thy owne Governmt and these bold attempts being made against thee and us while thou sits at the helme, what may wee Expect when thou hast given up thy Charge when it will be out of thy Power to assit & defend us, and this Leads us to a third Consideration to lay before thee that if upon good advice thou should See Cause to Surrender, wee Intreat thee to make the best terms thou canst for us and other dissenters.

The Ease & Libertyes which wee Enjoy under Thy Government Seemes to us not to be of Long Continuation considering thy years for wee looke upon the Same as but dureing thy Life {~~considering thy years~~} (if soe long) therfore thou haveing been kindly pleased to Intimate to us that if thou Should Surrender thou wouldst take Care of the peoples propertyes & Privilidges both as Christians & Englishmen, thou knowing both better than wee can direct, wee wholly referre the matter & manner of Doeing It to thy Selfe, only wee put thee In mind of our Lawes & Charters In generall & perticulerly our Lawes for Liberty of Conscience {&} the affirmation act as Its now gone home, but If that cannot passe that then full Care may be taken for the generall Ease and ~~the~~ Service of Friends on that account, and that Friends and others who Conscientiously Scruple to take an oath~~e~~ may not only be Exempted from ~~taking~~ Oathes but that their not Swearing may not unquallyfy them to discharge their Dutyes as Englishmen, that Friends may be Exempted from bearing armes, and not be obliged to Support a ministry of other Societyes, which is what at present occurrs to our thoughts.

Wee take notice of thyne and thy wifes Earnest desires & Intentions to come {over} & to Live if not dye amongst us whether thou Surrender or not and desires Friends assistance; Wee heartily wish for thy sake that wee with ~~our~~ {other} Friends here were Capable to lay downe the money there to pay off the Friends who discharged thee from the Fords[5] & ~~wee~~ should Readily doe It in order to make thee and them Easy and to hasten thy Comeing.

It proved a very great Error or Neglect and a great damage to thee that the Trustees[6] did not wth the deeds of Mortgauge Send over a Sufficient power and orders to sell Lands & to discharge the Quitt Rents and debts, for want wherof the Advantageous oppertunityes of Lisbon Markett has been hetherto lost & Returnes Retarded, & how soone that may be quite over wee know not. For although James Logan should Speedily come over and be fully Impowred,[7] yet the last years Cropp being near gone litle more can be done till next Spring, and the Rents & debts as well as the Lands being secured to the trustees Severall have therby taken Occasion to detaine the Same as not being Safe In paying untill here be a Sufficient power to discharge them.

As to the opposition that is made against the affirmation Law & Endeavours by the Church of England party to vacate the same at home, wee Referre thee to former Letters[8] and doe Intreat thee if It be possible that wee may obtaine that Favour from the Crowne haveing therin Endeavoured to come up to thy owne directions to thy Lieft Govr [9] & to do the Satisfaction of Friends here, and without that Law or the Substance of It wee cannot See how Friends can be Capable of Serving in any Station, or be wittnesses or have Equall safety & ~~other~~ Privilidges wth other people.

Wee further Request In Case of a Surrender uppon the Annexing the Lower Countyes to the Province that It may be done upon an Equall and Just bottom, for their demands of Equal ~~eight~~ numbers of Representatives and In all Respects Equall Privilidges[10] seeme unreasonable they haveing but three Limitted Countyes which cannot be Enlarged, the province being farr Larger much more Improved, more populous and Capable of greater Growth & may It not be worth thy thoughts whether It would not be greatly the Intrest of the Crowne & thyne and the peoples that both Sides of the River & bay were under one Government, which being Joyned might very well Support a Govr without oppression, many arguments might be given for this, the Interest of the Crowne and Security of trade not the least

Considering the nature of the Case wee question not but thou wilt lay the whole state of the matter before Friends there and also before others Eminent for Integrity & abillity, whose opinion in the Case Concurring with thine may Justify thee agst the Clamours of thy Enimyes

Thy present neccessityes (which wee hope may be Remedyed by other wayes) doe not seeme to us to us to be the best arguments thou may use for a Surrender but the Uncertainty of the peoples Enjoying the Same Libertyes after thy time and that thou haveing Such an Intrest wth our Superiors art most Capable of obtaineing for us Such valluable privilidges on Such a juncture then wee can Expect hereafter will be better taken, which if obtained Seemes Somewhat to Compensate what the people must In that case part wth

Thou well knowes the hazards difficultyes & Charges In Setling this Remote Countrey & that Friends have been the most Early & Considerable therin and are the Majority In Number & Substance, and wee hope wee may without offence Say that they have Exceeded In Sobriety, Industry, & Readynesse to Improve the Country, promote trade & the publick good of the Province. And though wee would not vallue ourselves above others nor doe wee Request these privilidges as of Right or Merit but of Favour & bounty. Easily foreseing Considering the Oppositions made against us That if God be not pleased to Incline the heart of the Queen and her Ministers to Extend their Favours to Friends here by Granting Some Such Privilidges or at least the Law for the Affirmation, Frds will be laid by as uselesse Members In the Government and be Exposed to Sufferings, Though even our opposers themselves owne our usefullnesse and have nothing Justly against us as wee know of but their Insecurity as they alledge for want of Judiciall Oaths and Provisions for Defence. Wee shall Leave our Cause {to} God & the Queen & under thy Care for Us.

Wee are wth Sincere Affections
Thy Reall Friends.
Edwd Shippen
Sam Carpenter
Griffith Owen
Richard Hill
Jonathan Dickinson
Isaac Norris
Tho: Story
Samll Preston
Thomas Masters

Inclosed are Coppys of the 2 addresses[11] a Coppy of the Law for affirmation[12] the Coppy of our Last Letter of the 10th of the Second month, with an abstract ~~of the Coppy~~ or Substance of a Lre from our vestry to the Bishop of London.[13]

ALS. Cliveden Manuscripts, Chew Family Papers, HSP. (*Micro.* 14:279.) Addressed: For William Penn | Proprietary & Governour of | Pensilvania | In Bristoll or Elsewhere | In Great Brittain. | from | freinds of | Phillidel- | phia. Docketed: Friends in Pensilvania | 23d May 1711.

1. See doc. 181.
2. 12 May 1711.
3. For one of these letters of qualified support for WP's government in Pennsylvania, see Joseph Growdon to WP, 3 May 1711. *Micro.* 14:270.
4. An Act Directing an Affirmation to Such Who for Concience Sake Cannot Take an Oath, passed 28 Feb. 1711. *Statutes,* 2:355-57; see also doc. 185.
5. See docs. 153, n.8; 157, n. 20.
6. The nine trustees to whom WP had conveyed Pennsylvania in 1708 were Henry Gouldney, Joshua Gee, Silvanus Grove, John Woods, Thomas Callowhill, Thomas Oade, Jeffrey Pinnell, John Field, and Thomas Cuppage (who died in 1708).
7. In Nov. 1711 WP and his trustees gave full empowerment to the commissioners of property in Pennsylvania; see *PA,* 2d ser., 19:503-10.
8. See doc. 185.
9. See doc. 184, text at nn. 7-8.
10. The insistence of the Lower Counties on equality with the more populous Pennsylvania counties was the major reason for the separation of the two colonial governments.
11. For one of the Anglican addresses referred to here, see doc. 185.
12. See n. 4, above.
13. See doc. 185.

FINAL NEGOTIATIONS FOR SURRENDER

June 1711–December 1712

By mid-1711 WP was sixty-six years old and in obviously failing health. His few surviving letters from late 1711 to early 1712 are brief and disjointed. He seems to have spent most of his time in retirement at Ruscombe, but after James Logan sailed for Pennsylvania in December 1711, WP probably visited London where he lobbied for the resolution of his surrender of Pennsylvania to the crown, as well as for revision of the Affirmation Act (docs. 189, 190). As part of the latter effort, he reprinted his *Treatise of Oaths,* first printed in 1675 (*PWP,* vol. 5, item 38C–E). WP had published no major new work since *More Fruits of Solitude* in 1702; now he wrote his last brief essay, dated 23 February 1712, a preface to the *Journal of the Life* of John Banks (*PWP,* vol. 5, item 133). Although still active in the ministry, WP was by no means the dynamic Quaker leader and lobbyist he had once been. To his friend the earl of Oxford he could only write, "I am now Good for nothing"; WP had lost most of his influence among Friends and with members of Parliament.

He still had enough energy and presence, however, to push his surrender proposal through. Besides his informal meetings with Oxford, the leader of the queen's ministry, he met with treasury officials on at least two occasions, in March and July 1712, and garnered evidence to support his claim that Pennsylvania was valuable to the crown (doc. 191). By July he was able to write Logan that he hoped he had "made an end wth the Ld. Treasurer" (doc. 195), and in September he received an advance payment of £1000 from the treasury (doc. 198). WP had settled for £12,000 — much less than he had originally hoped for — to be paid by the crown within four years. As it turned out, no further payments were ever made. WP heard little news from Pennsylvania during this time. Logan, who arrived back in the colony in early March 1712, was virtually his only correspondent. Other colonists had little interest in dealing with their proprietor once they heard that he had sold his government.

WP was dangerously ill in February and April 1712. He drew up a new will (doc. 193) just before he experienced the first of several apoplectic strokes. Another blow was the death of his wife's parents, Hannah and Thomas Callowhill, in April and June 1712. Soon after he came to Bristol to help settle the Callowhill estate, WP suffered another stroke on October 4. Within a week he was sufficiently recovered to add a few lines to the letter he had begun to Logan (doc. 199), but this was the last letter he wrote. He managed to travel to London where he met with the Board of Trade. Soon after returning to Ruscombe, probably in late December 1712, he suffered his most crippling stroke. From then on WP would be unable to participate in public affairs of any sort. As Thomas Story later reflected, it was perhaps the only way this dynamic, restless man could retire; his illness gave him "a sort of Sequestration . . . from all the Concerns of this Life, which so much oppress'd him . . . that he might have rest, and not be oppress'd thereby to the End." *CTB*, vol. 26, pt. 2, pp. 17, 54; ACM, vol. 25; Drinker, *Hannah Penn*, p. 38.

187
TO THE EARL OF OXFORD

[22 June 1711][1]

My Noble & Worthy Friend[2]

The Inclosed is a letter to me[3] from a Person Perfectly verst in that Branch of the Revenue, relating to the wine License office & that of the Hawkers; and I dare assure thee a more able Person belongs not to the Revenue among the Subalterns. I earnestly begg thy perusall of it, & utmost expedition, for the nature of the thing, & Season calls for it; I will make good w[t] I also offerd,[4] for thy own accomodation & for [illegible deletion] a nest egg for {the Queen of} 100000[l] per annum (to the Crown) now so low in land Revenues. No man has a better Collection of Proposals for augmenting the Crowns Revenue than I had the 4 years of King Jamess raigne, as careless as I was of my Selfe, because I would not the world should think I used his favour that way, till I Saw him well establisht wth a Parliamentary Satisfaction.[5]

my Great Friend, please to remember & resolve

Thy most Faithfull as well as
affectionate Friend
Wm Penn

ALS. Loan Manuscripts 29/197/133-34, BL. (*Micro.* 14:280.)

1. This date does not appear on the document itself but is found in a printed version of the letter in HMC, *Harley Manuscripts* (London, 1899), 3:17-18.

2. In May 1711 Robert Harley was created a peer with the titles of Baron Harley, Earl of Oxford, and Earl of Mortimer. In the same month he was appointed lord high treasurer of England. *DNB*.

3. Enclosure not found.

4. The nature of WP's scheme for revenue raising is not known; in Apr. 1711 Harley set up a South Sea Company to fund the national debt. G. M. Trevelyan, *England Under Queen Anne: The Peace and the Protestant Succession* (London, 1934), pp. 123-24.

5. In 1687-88 WP had lobbied to pack a Parliament favorable to James II. *PWP*, 3:172-77.

188

THE TRUSTEES OF PENNSYLVANIA TO THE COMMISSIONERS OF PROPERTY

London the 30: 9mo [November] 1711

Esteemed Friends

Edw Shippey, Sam Carpenter, Richard Hill, Isaac Norris, James Logan[1]

This Accompanies our worthy friend James Logan, with whome we have sent You an ample power.[2] Signed by our Dear Friend Willm Penn in Conjunction with the Trustees[3] wherein we have invested You with full Authorities to sell and fully to Confirm unto Such purchasers that have or shall buy any Tracts of Land &c: belonging to the Province or Territories of Pensilvania, for want of which Instrument we percieve, no perso[ns] there deem themselves Sufficiently quallified to dispose off,[4] a counter part whereof is already sent by way of New York, by the Direction of James Logan, which we hope You will Recieve before his arivall.[5]

What we Earnestly Request of you is that You would heartily Ingauge in this affair, for therein You will greatly serve both the Interest and Reputation of Governor Penn, the Consid[er]ation Whereof we have as much at heart as our ow[n] perticuler Concern therein. Althô of late an Opertunity has presented in favour of Remittances from thence hither by way of Lisbon, Yet we have not Recieved so much as has paid of all the Interest that is due upon the principle,[6] but now You will be so fully Invested with power, we beseech You, make it Your Care Effectualy to Raise mony to set him free of this Incumbrance that we very well Remember Some of You Expresed a great Concern to have accomplishd, and Gave good assurances, that if he was assisted here, to Clear his Country out of the hands of Phillip Fords family, care would be taken there to Reimburse us Spedily, & Since it is of so much Importance, that this Debt is paid off, we Recommend to You, that good Incouragement be given to purchasers, Rather at an Easier Rate then Usuall, to Effect the Same we Understand it is Necessary to have these powers Enroll'd in the proper Rigester in Such Cases which we Request You will see done for the Security of the persons Consernd, we shall Conclude with Due Respects unto You from your Real Friends

Joshua Gee
Henry Gouldney
Silvan[s] Grove
John Woods
John Feild

LS. Pennsylvania Miscellaneous Papers, Penn & Baltimore, 1653-1724, HSP. (*Micro.* 14:334.) Addressed: For | Edw[d] Shippey | Sam[ll] Carpenter | Richard Hill | Isaac Norris | James Logan | In | Philadelphia | Pensilvania | America.

1. On 9 Nov. 1711 WP appointed Edward Shippen, Samuel Carpenter, Richard Hill, Isaac Norris, and James Logan as commissioners of property. *Micro.* 14:314, 316.

2. For this power of attorney to the commissioners, signed by WP and the trustees and dated 10 Nov. 1711, see *PA,* 2d ser., 19:505-11.

3. See doc. 186, n. 6.

4. See doc. 186, text at n. 6.

5. After James Logan arrived in Pennsylvania on 22 Mar. 1712, the power of attorney was entered into the minutes of the Board of Property on 9 Apr. 1712. *PA,* 2d ser., 19:503; *Micro.* 14:377.

6. In order to pay off the Fords, WP had mortgaged Pennsylvania and the Lower Counties in Oct. 1708 for the principal sum of £6600 at 6 percent interest. *Micro.* 14:322.

189
TO THE EARL OF OXFORD

December 6. 1711

I am heartily Sorry I am now Good for nothing. twas otherways in former days; & if I could think so to, I would not send this; but for thy sake as much as my own, I wish for a few moments, & for poor Englands also.[1] A man may be too close as well as too free; right timeing every thing is best. Thou art a great ~~J~~Genius & therfore a great Judge, & I am Thy Faithf[ll]

Friend
Wm Penn

ALS. Loan Manuscripts 29/198, BL. (*Micro.* 14:339.) Addressed: For the Earle | of oxford & Morti- | mer Ld High Treas[r] | of Great Britaine.

1. WP was writing the day before Parliament met to debate the peace treaty with France that Oxford had been negotiating. WP doubtless knew that Oxford was willing to accept the Bourbon Philip V as king of Spain, which the opposition Whigs were adamantly against. And he probably feared that Oxford supported the Occasional Conformity Bill—a pro-Anglican, anti-dissenter measure—which Parliament passed in this session. J. A. Downie, *Robert Harley and the Press* (Cambridge, 1979), pp. 134-48; Trevelyan, *England Under Queen Anne: The Peace and the Protestant Succession,* pp. 194-96.

190
TO THE EARL OF OXFORD

6 Curt [January or February][1] 1711/12

My Noble Friend

Pray permitt me to recommend the Petn of our Friends in Parlimt,[2] who are some of the most religious among us, & most Loyall to the Queens Govermt. We hope we have gain'd Some ground with severall worthy members, that wish thou wouldst please to like their endeavours for us, which constrains this Freedom, & we pray that Secretary St Johns[3] may have a kinde hint from thee, wch will Credit the good will of none of the meanest members of the house of Commons that will appear in our favour, & that (I will answear for them) shall deserve the priviledge desired by them; who am wth the greatest Sincerity & Respect

Thy Faithfull
& obliged Friend
to serve thee
Wm Penn

Transcript. ACM. (*Micro* 14:353.)

1. WP could have written this document in either Jan. or Feb. 1712. The Meeting for Sufferings Minutes referred to the Quaker lobbying effort on 14 Dec. 1711 and reported on the failure of their efforts on 15 Feb. 1712. See n. 2, below.

2. A group of Quakers was lobbying for a new affirmation bill modifying the act of 1696, due to expire in 1715. Many Friends — led by George Whitehead, Thomas Ellwood, Benjamin Coole, and Joseph Wyeth — were satisfied with the existing law, but they agreed that a "solicitation" could be presented to Parliament by the dissatisfied, who included WP, Robert Haydock, Joseph Pike, and Roderick Forbes. Braithwaite, *Second Period*, pp. 191-204; J. William Frost, "The Affirmation Controversy and Religious Liberty," in *The World of William Penn*, ed. Richard S. Dunn and Mary Maples Dunn (Philadelphia, 1986), pp. 314-15; Minutes of the Meeting for Sufferings, 1702-1715, 20:261, 280, FLL.

3. Henry St. John, later Viscount Bolingbroke, became secretary of state for the northern division in Sept. 1710. Since Harley's elevation to the peerage, St. John had become the government leader in the Commons; however, he sided increasingly with the High Tories against Oxford's moderates, and he would soon break completely with Oxford. For the outcome of the vote, see doc. 192, n. 8. *DNB; Sheila Biddle, Bolingbroke and Harley* (London, 1975), pp. 219-42.

191
FROM JOHN EVANS

[7 February 1712]

Sr

You was pleas'd to Enjoyn me,[1] to make Such an Estimate of the Revenue of the Govmt of Pensilvania as I was able from near Seven years Experience in the Province,[2] and found to be the Settled Income really & truly communibus Annis[3] which please to Accept as followeth,

Licenses for publick Houses and Permitts for Strong
Water Shops[4] £120.00.00
Registring Vessels & passes [?] & Bills of Health[5] 50.00.00
Fines and Forfeitures[6] 150.00.00
Seizures upon Unlawfull trade & the Crown's
Thirds[7] 250.00.00
Money Rais'd by Assembly in my time[8] 300.00.00
The Duty of 1 penny per pound upon Tobacco[9] 600.00.00

Besides which there appears by the Custom House Accounts to have been paid in England for Tobacco made in that province Several years above Ten Thousand pounds a year to the Crown,[10] to which may in all reason be added when you come upon a Valuable consideration for for your Surrend^r^ (wch you are pleas'd to inform me y^o^ are about) near 20000^l^ a Year that Pensilvania (planted and improv'd at yor Sole cost and care) takes off, of the English Manufacture,[11] and it may yett farther in justice be consider'd what it would have cost the crown of Great Brittain to have brought that Province to the perfection they will find it in. This {is} what at present occurr's to me in pursuance of yor Commands to

Yo^r^ most obedient humble Servt
John Evans

Lond^o^ Febry 7th 1711/12

ALS. TI/144, PRO. (*Micro.* 14:360.) Addressed: To | the Honble William Penn Esq Prop^r^ and | Govr of the Province of Pensilvania | near Whitehall | London. Docketed: From Mr Penn.

1. WP made this request while trying to assemble evidence to show the crown that a royal governor would be comfortably supported in Pennsylvania.

2. John Evans was deputy governor 1704-8; he was back in England by Sept. 1710. *Micro.* 14:165.

3. On annual average. *Black's Law Dictionary.*

4. On 12 Jan. 1706 the Assembly imposed a tavern licensing fee of 40s in Philadelphia and 20s elsewhere in the province, payable to the governor. The Assembly passed a new act on 7 Feb. 1711, requiring tavern keepers to be licensed by the governor, who collected fees of £3 in Philadelphia, and 30 or 40s elsewhere. *Statutes,* 2:291, 357-58.

5. In 1711 the Assembly granted the governor the following fees: 8s for registering and certifying any vessel; 6s for a let-pass or permit, if required, for a vessel of under 60 tons, and 8s for a vessel of over 60 tons; and 8s for a bill of health, required of all ships arriving from unhealthy ports. *Statutes,* 2:347.

6. The governor received a share of fines for selling adulterated liquor, or liquor without a license; he also received a share of forfeited estates belonging to convicted murderers and rapists. *Statutes,* 2:8, 14, 84, 107, 172, 288.

7. Under the Navigation Act of 1696, penalty receipts were shared equally by three parties: the crown, the proprietor or governor, and the informant. Ships and goods in violation of this act were subject to seizure and forfeiture. Merrill Jensen, ed., *English Historical Documents: American Colonial Documents to 1776* (London, 1955), pp. 359-64.

8. On 12 Jan. 1706 the Assembly levied £800 — not £300 — over a three-year period for Evans's salary and administrative expenses. See doc. 129, n. 25. Possibly Evans only received £300 of this money.

9. This was the plantation duty of 1d per pound levied by the British government on all tobacco exported from the American colonies. Gov. Evans had not, of course, received this duty, but if Pennsylvania became a crown colony, the money raised by taxing tobacco exported from the Lower Counties could be used to augment the local revenue.

10. For earlier statements on the growing size of English customs revenue from Pennsylvania imports, see doc. 62, n. 3; doc. 88, text at n. 4.

11. Imports.

192
TO JAMES LOGAN

Whitehall 7 1m [March] 1712

James Logan
Loveing Friend
pray be kinde as well as Just to this honest & kinde ould friend of mine, or his order, about the land he has in my Country, viz John Marlow,[1] also know that thru mercy we are all yet in the land of the liveing & so, so; the Report of the Att. Generall before the lord Treasr whence hope a quick Issue.[2] Genll Nicolson for the Crowns haveing all the Proprietarys Soyle rents &c: as well as Powrs, & likely to be consider'd this session[3]
Ric. Sneed of Bristoll & John Vaughton of this citty, are at rest.[4] A Peace, I beleive, will Issue the Congress at Utrickt in a month or 2 at the farthest.[5] a fearfull Trecaw[6] is upon the french Ks family his 2d Dolphin & wife & eldest son the Duke of Britain, Suddenly dead, not without Suspicion of Poysen, called the Spotted Measles:[7] The lords often at a stand, but the Commons entirely one with the Queen & her present Minstry. Our affirmation disapointed in the house of commons by 21 only, & many absent at puting the Question, wch we hope will be retreived next session if not this.[8] W. Lickfolds affaire is renewed, by bond for 12 days for an arbitration, & among the bundle {of} papers thou didst not think worth looking into, as he says, is found one note under cos. {Rebecca} Blackfans hand one hundred pds, which he says he pay'd to her, who tould me that W. Lickfold told my wife and her that William confest that we did not owe him above 56l & so she tould me; & get it from her under her hand & send it per first.[9] I am short but that will serve. No news of the New Castle business at the Councill of Trade,[10] nor of J. French wt is become of him.[11] Remember me to the Goverr & the councel &c: but especially my true & chosen Frds. I suppose J. Ascew has sent the papers in the hands of Counselor west by the virginia Fleet, but poor will has had a paraletick stroak,[12] but is better & recovering Doctor Heathcot our frd his Phisi[tian].[13]
Remember poor Pennsberry, the Island therby,[14] lands in both Jerseys

& all my poor Interests there as well as in Pennsylvania, of wch I waite thy good news. wch is wt now offers from

Thy reall Friend
Wm Penn

All our loves to thee & our true Frds.

ALS. Penn Papers, Letters of the Penn Family to James Logan, HSP. (*Micro.* 14:373.) Docketed: Proprietor London 7:1:1[2].[15]

1. John Marlow, a mariner from St. Katherine's, Middx., who had purchased 250 acres of Pennsylvania land in 1684, purchased another 250 acres of Gilbert Mace's First Purchase in 1711. In Mar. 1713 the Commissioners of Property gave him a patent for 250 acres on Pequea Creek in Chester County, as well as a city lot. *PWP,* 3:54n; *PA,* 2d ser., 19:548-51, 580.

2. The report of Attorney General Edward Northey on WP's surrender to the crown (*Micro.* 14:367) was received by the earl of Oxford on 25 Feb. 1712.

3. No record has been found of these lobbying efforts by Francis Nicholson in Parliament.

4. Richard Snead died on 2 Feb. 1712, and John Vaughton of London died 1 Mar. 1712. Digests of Quaker Records, Bristol and Som.; London and Middx., GSP.

5. The treaty of Utrecht was signed on 11 Apr. 1713.

6. Perhaps "tracas," French for "turmoil."

7. The French dauphin was Louis, duke of Burgundy (1682-1712), who was married to Marie-Adélaïde of Savoy (1685-1712). His eldest son, the duke of Brittany, was only five when all three died in a measles epidemic, leaving the infant duke of Anjou, the future Louis XV, as the heir to the throne. John B. Wolf, *Louis XIV* (New York, 1968), pp. xvii-xviii, 610-12.

8. For the Quakers' affirmation petition, see doc. 190, n. 2. Under pressure from the established church, the petition was "thrown out by the Commons" on 9 Feb. 1712 on a vote of 101 to 80. Friends did not bring the issue before Parliament again until 1715, when the Affirmation Act was due to expire. Clyve Jones and Geoffrey Holmes, eds., *The London Diaries of William Nicholson, Bishop of Carlisle, 1702-1718* (Oxford, 1985).

9. William Lickfold (c. 1644-1714), a Quaker from Ockham, Sur., had been WP's steward in England in 1704. The circumstances of WP's indebtedness to him are unclear. Apparently WP had borrowed £150 from Lickfold back in 1685; this debt with accumulated interest amounted to at least £550 by 1712 (see doc. 199). In 1707 WP had directed his Pennsylvania agents to pay Lickfold £608 within six months (see doc. 144); they sent payment in the form of tobacco, which was either lost or ruined when it reached England. Lickfold then went to court to collect; the final award may have been to satisfy the 1685 debt, finally settled in 1712. Digests of Quaker Records, Sus. and Sur., GSP; *Micro.* 11:221, 13:605; Isaac Norris Letterbook, 1:232.

10. James Coutts was supposedly bringing over complaints from the Lower Counties to the Board of Trade. See doc. 160, n. 4.

11. John French, the sheriff of New Castle, was on his way to England to vindicate himself in a controversy with admiralty officials in Delaware. French had accompanied the New Castle collector, Samuel Lowman, to inspect a ship said to be carrying an illegal cargo of sugar and indigo from the Spanish West Indies. Lowman went on board but declined to seize the ship, instead allowing French to do so. After French had the ship and cargo appraised (the value was £3730), Quary and Lowman complained and had a naval officer from New York come to New Castle, jail the local magistrates, and take both ships back to New York. Logan advised WP not to become personally involved in the matter, but WP helped French win his case and then arranged for the seizures to be part of the crown's payment to him for the surrender of Pennsylvania's government. *Micro.* 14:296, 381, 390; docs. 194, 195.

12. WP's lawyer, Robert West, was recovering from a stroke at the time he helped draft WP's will. See doc. 193; *Memoirs of the Historical Society of Pennsylvania,* 1:235.

13. The letter is torn here.

14. Sepassinck, or Biddle's Island.

15. Torn.

193
LAST WILL AND TESTAMENT

In April 1712, after he had suffered his first stroke, WP wrote a new will to replace that of 1705–7 (doc. 107). This was his final will, the one probated after his death, and its provisions differed markedly from his earlier wills. Writing in the midst of negotiations for the surrender of Pennsylvania's government, WP tried to insure the completion of the surrender by vesting his government in two prominent noblemen and longtime friends, the earl of Oxford and Earl Poulett, who were both members of the queen's cabinet. As for his lands, the most dramatic new provision was that the heir-at-law, William Penn, Jr., would receive only the English and Irish estates that descended to him through his mother and from his grandfather. All the Pennsylvania properties would go to Hannah Penn's children, with a double portion to her eldest son, John. This new arrangement reflected WP's final disillusionment with his thirty-one-year-old son, as well as his recognition of his obligations to his second wife's family. The new will made no charitable bequests such as those WP had made in earlier wills; he provided no money or land for poor Quakers and neither freed his slaves nor established charitable institutions.

The will was poorly drafted. When James Logan saw a copy of it after WP's death, he noted that the wording "gives me Some Uneasiness as being Drawn in hast I believe by himself only, when Such a Settlement Requir'd a hand better acquainted with affairs of that Nature." Simon Clement explained to Logan that WP had been assisted by attorney Robert West, who himself had been recovering from a stroke at the time. The main section of the will was not dated; the second and final codicil was not witnessed; the first name of Earl Poulett was mistakenly given as "William," not "John"; and the separation of Pennsylvania's government from its lands was of questionable legality. Lawyers puzzled over where the mortgagees, who had been empowered since 1708 to supervise WP's property in Pennsylvania, fit in; WP failed to mention them at all, except to specify that the trustees of his will should sell as much land as necessary to pay his debts. After WP's death, William Penn, Jr., challenged the will, claiming that his father had actually died intestate. The courts then distinguished separate groups of plaintiffs and defendants for the questions of land and government. In the end, the courts accepted the will, and in 1726 the title to Pennsylvania passed to the three surviving sons of WP and Hannah Penn: John, Thomas, and Richard (Dennis died in 1722, Hannah in 1726). Penn Papers, Private Correspondence, 1:55; *Memoirs of the Historical Society of Pennsylvania,* 1:235; Drinker, *Hannah Penn,* pp. 32, 185–86.

[c. 6 April 1712][1]

I William Penn, Esqr {so calld} Chief Proprietary ~~of~~ & Governour of the Province of Pensilvania & the Territories thereunto belonging being of sound mind & understanding for which I bless God doe make & declare this my last Will & testament

My Eldest son being well provided for by a settlement of his mothers & my Fathers Estate[2] I give & dispose of the rest of my Estate in manner following

The Government of my Province of Pensilvania & Territories thereunto belonging & all powers relating thereunto I give & devise to the most honourable the Earle of Oxford & Earle Mortimor & to Will Earle Poulet[3] so calld & their heires upon trust to dispose thereof to the Queen or any other Person to the best advantage & profit they can to be applied in such manner as I shall herin after direct

I give & devise to my dear wife Hannah Penn & her father Thomas Callowhill & to my good friends Margaret Lowther my Dear sister & to Gilbert Heathcote Physician samuel Waldenfield John Field Henry Goldney {all} living {in} England[4] & to my Frd samuel Carpenter Richd Hill Isaac Norris samuel Preston & James Logan living in or near Pensilvania[5] & their heirs all my Lands tenements & hereditaments whatever Rents & other profits scituate lying & being in Pensilvania & the Territories thereunto belonging or elsewhere in America upon trust that they shall sell & dispose of so much thereof as shall be sufficient to pay all my just debts & from & after payment thereof shall convey unto each of the {three} children of my son William Penn {Guli[el]ma maria Springet & william} respectively & to their respective heires ten thousand acres of Land in some proper & beneficiall places to be set out by my Trustees aforesaid[6] all the rest of my lands & hereditaments whatsoever scituate lying & being in America I will that my said Trustees shall convey to & amongst my children wc I have by my present wife in such proportions & for such Estates as my said wife shall think fitt[7]

but before such conveiance shall be made to my said children I will that my said Trustees shall convey to my ~~said~~ daughter Aubry whom I omitted to name before ten thousand Acres of my said Lands in such places as my Trustees shall think fit[8]

all my [illegible deletion] personall Estate in Pensilvania & ~~elswh~~ {elswhere} & arrears of rent due there I give ~~it~~ my said dear wife {(whom I make my sole executrix)} for the equall benefit of her & her children In Testimony whereof I have set my hand & seale to this my Will wc I declare to be my last {will} revoking all others formerly made by me[9]

Wm Penn

Signed sealed & Published by the Testator William Penn in the Presence of us who set our {names} as witnesses therof in the presence of the said Testator after the interlineation of the words above viz (whom I make my sole Executrix)

Sarah: West[10]   Robert West

Susanna reading[11]

Thos Pyle[12]

Robtt Lomax.[13]

This Will I made whn ill of a feaver at London,[14] with a clear understanding of what I did then, but because of some unworthy expressions belying gods goodness to me as if I knew not what I did I do now that I am recovered, through gods goodness hereby declare it is my last Will & Testament at Ruscomb in Berkshire this 27 of the 3m called may 1712.

Wm Penn

witnesses present

Elizabeth Penn[15]

Thos Pyle

Thomas Penn[16]

Elizabeth Anderson[17]

Mary Chandler[18]

Jonah Dee

mary dee[19]

Postscript in my own hand—

As a farther Testimony of my love to my Dr wife, I of my own minde give unto her out of the rents of america, viz, Pennsilvania &c three hundred pds a year for {her naturall life & for} her ~~care~~ {care & charge} over my children in their education of wch she knows my minde as also that I desire they may Settle at least in good part in america where I leave them so good an Interest to be for their Inheritance from Generation to Generation wch the lord Preserve & prosper[20] amen

Wm Penn

D. Prob. 1/10, PRO. (Not filmed.)

1. WP did not date this will, but Hannah Penn's lawyers later stated that he wrote it on or about 6 Apr. 1712. The codicil is dated 27 May 1712. Penn Papers, Granville Penn Book, p. 22, HSP.

2. William Penn, Jr.'s exact inheritance is unknown; he received much of Sir William Penn's property in Ireland and some of Gulielma Springett Penn's property in England. *PWP*, 1:570-73, 646-49. See also doc. 209.

3. In his sickness WP apparently confused two lords Poulett. Rather than William Baron Poulett, he meant John Poulett, or Powlett, created Earl Poulett in 1706, who was a staunch Harleyite and WP's friend since the 1690s. Earl Poulett was "a Somerset nobleman with a shrewd political brain, extensive estates, and useful electoral influence in the west country." In 1743, just before his death, Poulett conveyed his rights to Pennsylvania's government to John, Thomas, and Richard Penn; his son and heir, also named John, continued to be involved in the legal controversies over Pennsylvania's proprietorship. *DNB;* Geoffrey Holmes, *British Politics in the Age of Anne* (New York,

1967), pp. 85, 262, 326; Penn Papers, Official Correspondence, 4:235; Penn & Baltimore, 1740-1756, p. 81; Cadwalader Collection, Thomas Cadwalader Papers; Logan Papers, 10:111, HSP; *Micro.* 8:045; 9:427; 12:673, 793; 14:695.

4. As noted on a copy of this will (*Micro.* 14:354), two of the trustees named here had predeceased WP: Callowhill and Waldenfield. Margaret Lowther died a few months after her brother, before the will was probated. Gilbert Heathcote (c. 1664-1719), a London doctor, was a member of Westminster Monthly Meeting in his later years. He probably was the author of the anonymously published *Letter from a Satisfied to a Dissatisfyed Friend,* which quietly took a position opposite to WP's on the affirmation question (see doc. 190). *PWP,* 3:424n.; Smith, 1:50.

5. Of these five Pennsylvania trustees, only Samuel Carpenter predeceased WP.

6. In *Micro.* 14:354, a marginal note beside the grandchildren's names reads: "these were added by Testator after the execucion being intlined [interlined]." Whether William Penn, Jr.'s three children received 10,000 acres of Pennsylvania land apiece is unclear. When their father died in 1720, they inherited additional Pennsylvania properties from him. In the 1730s Hannah Penn's children paid off the Pennsylvania claims of William Penn III for £5500. Jenkins, pp. 127-31, 246-47.

7. After the will was probated 18 Nov. 1718, Hannah Penn assigned half the Pennsylvania and Delaware properties to John and divided the other half among Thomas, Richard, and Dennis. In 1726, after Dennis Penn's death, she executed a new deed of appointment; this time she assigned half the property to John, with the proviso that he give £2000 to his sister, Margaret, when she married or turned 21, and divided the other half between Thomas and Richard. When John Penn died unmarried, his share went to Thomas. Jenkins, pp. 130-31, 135-36.

8. Laetitia and William Aubrey sold their 10,000 acres to John Knight, who then sold them to John Page. Laetitia died childless and bequeathed her American estate to her nephew William Penn III for life, to pass to his daughter, Christiana Gulielma Penn, later Gaskell. Penn Photostats, HSP; Jenkins, pp. 65-66.

9. WP had made at least four earlier wills: the first, drawn up before his initial voyage to Pennsylvania, has not been found; the second, written before his return voyage to England in 1684, named his first wife, Gulielma, and her three children—Springett, William Jr., and Laetitia—as the chief beneficiaries (*PWP,* 2:585-86). The wills of 1701 and 1705-7 are printed above (docs. 30, 107).

10. Sarah West was the wife of WP's attorney Robert West. By Nov. 1718, when the will was probated, she was widowed and living in Cooke's Court, London. Penn Papers, Penn-Forbes Manuscripts, 1:27.

11. Susannah Reading (d. by 1718) was probably a servant. Ibid.

12. Thomas Pyle, probably a law clerk, witnessed another legal document in July 1712 (doc. 209L). In 1718 he was living in Parker's Court, Coleman St., London. Ibid.

13. Robert Lomax was Robert West's servant; after West's death in 1718 he went to work at Mitcham in Surrey. Ibid.; London Record Society, *London Inhabitants within the Walls* (London, 1966), p. 188.

14. WP had been ill in Feb. as well as in Apr.; he probably suffered his first stroke after making this will and before writing the codicil. See doc. 199.

15. Probably the Elizabeth Penn who married maltster Thomas Penn (d. 1693) of Adderbury, Oxon., at Peel Monthly Meeting in London in 1688. She may have been a distant relative; perhaps she was the "Cousen Betty" who stayed at Ruscombe while Hannah Penn was in London in Oct. 1716. The Elizabeth Penn who witnessed the will had died by 1718. Digests of Quaker Records, London and Middx.; Penn-Forbes Manuscripts, 1:27; Penn Papers, Hannah Penn Cashbook, HSP.

16. Probably Thomas Penn (b. 1690), the son of Elizabeth and Thomas Penn. By 1718 this witness to the will was reported to be living in the house of London Quaker linendraper James Larkes; he may have been the same Thomas Penn, a servant, named in the 1746 will of John Penn. Digests of Quaker Records, London and Middx.; Penn-Forbes Manuscripts, 1:27; Phila. Will Bk. H, #165.

17. Elizabeth Anderson, a servant of the Penns, was still living at Ruscombe in 1718. Penn-Forbes Manuscripts, 1:27.

18. Mary Chandler (1695-1718), the daughter of London Quakers Thomas and Mary Chandler, probably came to work in the Penn household at about this time. She died at Ruscombe of smallpox in September 1718, two months after WP's death. Digests

of Quaker Records, London and Middx., Berks. and Oxon.; John Penn to Thomas Penn, 25, 28, and 30 Sept. 1718, Gratz Collection, HSP; Mary Chandler to Thomas Penn, 30 Apr. 1715, Penn Papers, Provincial Council Records, HSP; Hannah Penn Cashbook.

19. Jonas (d. by 1718) and Mary Dee worked at Ruscombe; Mary continued there after his death. Penn-Forbes Manuscripts, 1:27; Hannah Penn Cashbook.

20. Of Hannah and WP's four children who reached adulthood, three visited Pennsylvania, but none of them settled there permanently. Thomas Penn was in the colony from 1732 to 1741 and took a close interest in the colony's affairs for the rest of his life, but as an absentee proprietor; after his marriage to Lady Juliana Fermor in 1751, he settled at Stoke Poges, Bucks. John Penn, accompanied by his sister and brother-in-law, Margaret and Thomas Freame, visited Pennsylvania in 1734-35. Jenkins, pp. 133-51.

194
FROM JAMES LOGAN

Phila^ia^ 12th 4mo [June] 1712

Hon^rd^ Governour

The Assembly have now finished their Session & passed several Laws (vizt a Dozen) wch will be sent all together by Jno Annis[1] who is to sail for England directly about the latter end of this Mo^th^. The Property Act called an Act for confirming Patents & Grants[2] has been laboured with all the Industry I could use & thô I would gladly have had some parts otherwise yet upon the whole I take it to be a very valuable Law between thee & the People & very well deserving thy care in regard to thy own Interest to gett it passed there.

The Repeal of the last Affirmation Act arriving while the Assembly sate they thought themselves Oblig'd not to suffer the Oppertunity to pass without making a further Provision and accordingly have done it[3] very much to the Dissatisfaction of the Church party, who Interpret this proceeding as a flying in the face of the Govm^t^ at home & will doubtless have it so represented, they have also gott the Bill impowering Religious Societies to buy & hold Lands Passed,[4] of both which coppies are Inclosed & I have procured 4 small Bills makeing up 50^l^ to come with them w^ch^ 'tis hoped may help the Negotiation if not too late Bills are so very Scarce that 'twas with much Intreaty even these could be obtain'd tho from the best fr^ds^ in the province the Drawers having little or no money in England Could more have been had they should have come upon Acc^t^ of the 200^l^ old Currency, granted by the Assembly for negotiating the Laws, wch was paid to Edwd Shippen & Isaac Norris & remitted by mistake to the Trustees via Lisbon, but shall be drawn out again from thy general Effects here to wch they have a Claim[5]

There is also an Act pass'd Confirming Skulkill Ferry to B. Chambers for 21 years,[6] for wch he pays thee 50^l^ of this Currency, the

Assembly were Earnest for it, believing he had Merit enough to deserve it, but we gott this summ from him for thy Consent provided it be passed by the Queen

We are told by the Post now come from N. York in the news Letter from that place[7] that thou hast Surrendred the Govmt wch alarms the people more then Could be expected after the fair warning they have repeatedly had from thy Lettrs last Year.

The Lt Governours unhappy Differences wth the Custom house Officers, will I fear prove very injurious to him, & I wish there may be no Inquiry made after his Security given in there[8] however unless some care be taken to provide for him he will be extreamly pittied, being regarded by the generality as one that meant honestly thô for want of skill & better advice he might miss his way.

By some hints from N. York 'tis a Current Report that Coll Evans Succeds & Comes wth the first Commission from the Queen[9] I wish it may be sufficiently thought of what Laws are in force with us since our Separation from the Lower Counties And how Consistent some of them may be wth the Queens ~~L~~ Commission espe~~s~~cially those for regulating Elections & Confirming the Provincial Charter as far as it relates to the Assembly Appointmt of Sheriffs &c all which have passed the Royal Approbation.[10]

I was often at a stand in my Self when there, whether I should enter on a Discourse of the persons fitt to be named for the Queens Council here,[11] but Chose rather to Leave it, knowing it would be Impossible so to order it, as not to give great disgust, if Coll Evans be Concern'd, he very well knows the Country & the Several Abilities of the People in it, as they have more lately shewn themselves

But since these last acts were past before any notice of a surrender it is hoped they will still be considered by the Queen[12]

I am concerned principally for the Property Act,[13] wch I take to be very valuable both to thee & the People & ought by no means to drop. I therefore beseech thee if it cannot pass there to have it well recommend to the first Assembly under the Queen in the words it now is or very near them, there being no Grant in it from thee but what was under thy own hand & Seal before but diverse from the People to thee that cannot easily b~~y~~e so effectually Settled any other way. I should except the the last of all wch notwithstanding all the Commissioners & Surveyors find to be so reasonable that without it the People have not Justice

Money is so extreamly Scarce that we cannot as yet get any in, but hope in a little time to have Considerable, at least the value of it, & shall send by all the ways that offer, I shall ship for thy own use a hogshead of the best Madeira wine the place at present affords on board John Annis who is to Sail shortly.

{19th 5mo}[14] We have been able to doe very little Yet for Wm Aubry the Witnesses to his power of Attorney being left behind[15] their ship at Madeira arrived not in this Country till this week & are not yet come to town, so that I should be sure of more blame there, & how to Remitt by Bills is what we cannot yet see.

Eliz Webb arriv'd here about 3 Weeks agoe[16] friends are generally well. I am with dutiful Regards to thy self & family

Thy faithfull & Obedient

J.L.

LBC. Logan Papers, Parchment Logan Letterbook, 1712-1715, HSP. (*Micro.* 14:406.)

1. John Annis (d. 1724), a London Quaker mariner, frequently carried letters between London and Philadelphia. At the time of his death he was captain of the *London Hope.* Digests of Quaker Records, London and Middx.; Phila. Will Bk. D, #279, 326; Edgar Heyl, comp., *Pennsylvania Vital Records* (Baltimore, 1983), p. 125; *PMHB,* 21:156, 62:479n.

2. This act was passed by the Assembly on 7 June 1712 and repealed by the Queen in Council on 20 Feb. 1714. *Statutes,* 2:400-409.

3. The law repealed was An Act Directing an Affirmation to Such Who for Conscience Sake Cannot Take an Oath, which was passed 28 Feb. 1711 and repealed by the Queen in Council on 19 Dec. 1711. The new law was called A Supplementary Act to a Law about the Manner of Giving Evidence, which was passed on 7 June 1712 and repealed on 20 Feb. 1714. *Statutes,* 2:355-57, 425-27.

4. Passed 7 June 1712 and repealed 20 Feb. 1714. *Statutes,* 2:424-25.

5. In Feb. 1706 the Assembly had voted £200 to WP to defray the charges of negotiating crown approval of the 51 laws just passed. This money was evidently diverted by accident to WP's trustees. *Votes and Proceedings,* 2(pt. 2):82.

6. *Statutes,* 2:427-29. Logan's draft of a license for Chambers is *Micro.* 14:477.

7. This newsletter has not been identified.

8. Logan feared that Gookin would have to forfeit his bond given to guarantee compliance with the Navigation Acts because of his role in the French-Lowman controversy. See doc. 192, n. 11.

9. WP had been trying since 1710 to have Evans appointed the first royal governor of Pennsylvania. *Micro.* 14:165.

10. For example, the Act to Ascertain the Number of Members of Assembly and to Regulate the Election, passed 12 Jan. 1706, which became law by lapse of time when the Privy Council took no action on it. This law concerned the three Pennsylvania counties only, and Logan was worried that a royal governor would not be able to persuade the Lower Counties to join in the new government unless his commission specifically ordered it. *Statutes,* 2:212-21.

11. The Provincial Council would have been reconstituted if Pennsylvania had become a royal colony.

12. The 12 acts passed on 7 June 1712 were all considered by the queen; 6 were repealed and 6 confirmed on 20 Feb. 1714. *Statutes,* 2:400-404.

13. See n. 2, above.

14. This date is written in the margin; it seems to mark the day when Aubrey's witnesses finally arrived in Philadelphia.

15. Josiah Rolfe (d. c. 1743), a Quaker merchant of Philadelphia and later of New Castle, and Thomas Norton, whom the editors have been unable to identify. Phila. Will Bk. G, #22; Digests of Quaker Records, London and Middx.; Parchment Logan Letterbook, 1712-1715, p. 10.

16. Elizabeth Webb (d. 1726), a Quaker minister, immigrated to Pennsylvania in about 1700 and settled in Birmingham Twp., Chester Co. She visited England in 1710 and returned to Pennsylvania in 1712. *JFHS,* 11:134; *PWP,* 3:558-60.

195
TO JAMES LOGAN

Ruscomb. 24 5^{m} [July] 1712

James Logan

I rejoyce I am yet alive to write to thee, & if ever thou lovest me or desirest my wellfaire, Show it now, I pray thee, in my poor Concerns; tho I hope I have made an end wth the Ld. Treasurer[1] ab^{t} my business. insteed of 7 years for 20000^{l} reduced to 16000^{l} ~~at 7 years pay~~, I hope {he will} at 12000^{l} in 4 years time ~~will~~ pay me if not sooner.[2] I have it on Stocks.[3] Never the less, know the Queens ⅓ of the sugars in Delaware is part,[4] & I hope mine to Colonel Hunter inclosed,[5] will prevaile wth him at his great Perrill, ~~wi~~ to restore the 2 ships in Statu quo, all wch I recommend to thy great care & dilligence; for since the Ld. has continued my life, I hope, by the same, to see an End of my encombrances. we long to hear *pathetically* from thee, thy last saying little more than that thou art landed safely.[6] we are all alive thou left so, save my wifes poor mother, that is gone to her long home, & dyed well.[7] my father is yet here he bringing home my wife from seeing her poor Mother before she dyed, which she did. If I can get away by the 7th month, I come, else must stay till next Spring. I hope by this occasion to write yet farther. French tryumphs over Lowman, & my takeing that as part of pay, has facilitated.[8] be kinde to french, but spare no body, neither he nor Colonel Gooking &c: ab^{t} the true vallue of the sugars & ships; and remitt to the trustees the rents, & to me the Queens ⅓ & mine by the very first. not forgetting w. aub. who is the great Bare[9] in Cornhill that troubles me. forget not poor Pennsberry, nor my purchass from Beaumont;[10] & let me know how althings are, & if frds will help me over as I desired of thee.[11] depend upon a peace, & trade accordingly. our love is to thee, desireing thy prosperity in a good way. & so I close wth love to frds, & all moderate minds, (not forgeting Jos. Growden)—

Thy reall Frd
Wm Penn

our love to John & Mary Sacher. let me know how things are there per first.[12]

ALS. Penn Papers, Letters of the Penn Family to James Logan, HSP. (*Micro.* 14:426.) Addressed: For Jame Lo | -gan Secret^{r} & | Receiver Generall | of Pennsylvania | & Territorys. Docketed: The Proprietor | Ruscomb 24th 5mo 1712.

1. Robert Harley, earl of Oxford.
2. The government at first settled on a payment of £16,000 to be paid over a seven-year period; WP agreed to reduce this to £12,000 in order to be paid within four years. He received only the initial payment of £1000; see doc. 198.
3. Planned and begun, but not completed. *OED*.
4. See doc. 192, n. 11.

5. WP's letter to Gov. Robert Hunter of New York has not been found. In his friendly but disappointing answer of 22 Dec. 1712 (*Micro.* 14:479), Hunter wrote that he could not restore the ships, since the Board of Trade was currently considering the case.

6. Logan left London in Dec. but did not arrive in Pennsylvania until 22 Mar. He wrote a brief note to WP on 31 Mar. 1712 (*Micro.* 14:377).

7. Hannah Callowhill, Sr., died 6 June 1712. Digests of Quaker Records, Bristol and Som., GSP.

8. See doc. 192, n. 11.

9. Bear.

10. See doc. 76, n. 20.

11. See doc. 200, text at nn. 23-24

12. Logan had told WP on 25 May that the Sotchers were still at Pennsbury but were "restless to be gone." *Micro.* 14:390.

196
TO FRIENDS IN PENNSYLVANIA

Ruscomb Berks, 24 5th mo. [July] 1712

DEARE AND WORTHY FRIENDS.

Haveing so faire an opertunity, and having heard from you by the Bearer, John French,[1] I chuse, by him to salute you and yours; and all unnamed friends, that you think worthy. for my heart loves such and heartily salutes them and theirs, and prays for your preservation in the Lord's everlasting truth to the end of time; and the way of it is, to take the Lord along with you in all your enterprises to give you right sight, true counsil, and a just temper or moderation in all things, you knowing right well the Lord our God is neer at hand. Now know, that tho I have not actually sold my Govermt. to our truly Good Queen, yet her able Ld treasurer[2] and I have agreed it, and that affaire of the Prizes, the Bearer came hither abt. is part of the Queen's payment, viz, her one third;[3] and the other comes very opertunely, that belongs to me, which I hope J. Logan will take care of, in the utmost farthing, and remit it to me first, to whom I suppose, orders will goe by this opertunity from the treasury to that effect.[4] But I have taken effectual care, that all the Laws and priviledges I have graunted to you, shall be observed by the Queen's Governors, &c: and that we who are friends shall be in a more particular manner regarded and treated by the Queen.[5] So that you will not, I hope and believe, have a less interest in the govermt. being humble and discreet in our conduct. and you will finde all the charters and Proprietary Governmts. annexed to the Crown by act of Parliament next winter;[6] and perhaps Col. Quarry, if not J. Moore, may happen to be otherwise employed, notwithstanding the politick opinion of one of my officers in that Governmt. that is still for gaining them which I almost think impossible. But be that as it will, I purpose to see you if God give me life this fall, but I grow ould and infirme, yet would Gladly see you once more before I dye, and my young sons and daughter also, settled upon good Tracts of Land, for them and theirs' after them, to clear and settle upon, as Jacob's sons did.[7] I close when I tell you that I desire fervent prayers to the Lord for continuing my life, that I may see pennsylvania once more, before I die, and that I am

your Faithful Loving
friend
Wm. Penn

Printed. *Memoirs of the Historical Society of Pennsylvania* (Philadelphia, 1826). (*Micro.* 14:430.) Addressed: For my De. Friends | S. Carpenter, Ed. Shippen, Ricd. Hill, J. | Norris, C. Peusy, S. Preston, T. Story, Gr. | Owen, &c.[8] at Philadelphia in Pennyslvania. | Pp. J. French.

1. French left Pennsylvania after Nov. 1711 and arrived in England before May 1712. The letter he brought from Pennsylvania Friends has not been found. See docs. 185, 186.

2. Robert Harley, earl of Oxford.

3. See doc. 192, n. 11.

4. No such orders from the treasury seem to have been sent.

5. When WP reopened negotiations with the crown in 1710 for surrendering his colony's government, he had asked the queen to "indulge" the Quaker colonists in their beliefs and practices (doc. 179). The Board of Trade agreed in 1711 that the Quakers should enjoy full religious liberty and civil rights (doc. 182), and in Feb. 1712 Attorney General Northey reported that WP was asking the queen to declare that she would take the Quakers "into her Maties Protection" (*Micro.* 14:367). However, WP never secured any explicit written guarantee of special treatment for Pennsylvania Quakers under a royal administration.

6. Parliament did not consider resumption in 1713, and the proprietary and chartered colonies continued in that status up until the time of the Revolution.

7. Jacob's 12 sons settled in Israel and became the progenitors of the 12 tribes of Israel. Gen. 48-50.

8. These men were all leading Quakers who had served WP's interests as members of the Provincial Council, the Assembly, and the Board of Property. "J. Norris" is Isaac Norris.

197
TO JAMES LOGAN

Bristoll 15. 6m [August] 1712

J. Logan
Log Friend

Being here on the most sorrowfull acct of the buriall of my Dr. wifes most humble & ingenious & able Father, who layd down his life at my house after he had brought home my poor wife from seeing her Dr Mother, that deceased about 8 weeks ~~af~~ before my father (wch often happens to ould people, as long married as they were, viz, 52 years)[1] & that layd me under the necessity of performing this duty of comeing wth her above 70 miles[2] to interr him a~~b~~mong his relations & Friends, where the ~~sore~~ severe illness of my poor Johnne detaines us, he being sorely aflicted with the present wonderfull epidemick,[3] half the people being taken in town & Country, tho but rarely mortall; thro' the Lords wonderfull mercy Here comes a ship of Frds, mostly; I think above 130 or therabouts. pray see that he answear his part to the poor people, & do them Justice, & urge the Gover[r] therin if need be. I have writt by Colonel French via London, & to my good Frds, & tould thee all I have done,[4] & above all, prest thee to double thy dilligence to redeem me & mine, wth w[t] the lord has given me there, from my entanglements here; tho I fear tis to late in the day for any advantage by way of lisbon. 3 years agoe, had been the time.[5] Never hardly Such an harvest known of grain as this; I committ all to thee, & pray faile not to let me heare from thee as often as may be; & pray to the purpose. wife Johnne, Tomme, & Pegge give their loves, as I & my wife do to thee, our best Frds, & all serv[ts] & sober Tennants. The Governm[t] & I have greed time & surrender but not formally executed on both Sides; but hope in a month or two to dispatch it wth Ld. Treasurer, under hand seale. of w[ch] more per first opertunity. These afflictions & the great business that attends me upon fathe[r] & mothers death, & the sale of my Goverm[t] & paym[t] of debts forbids my comeing this fall. w[ch] yet I hope to effect if I dye not suddenly. vale.

Thy reall Frd
Wm Penn

Ann Jones is gone & charles Stoops after her.[6] the Boat waits for this so cannot read it over. But a Peace, in Spight of [illegible][7]

ALS. Penn Papers, Letters of the Penn Family to James Logan, HSP. (*Micro.* 14:431.) Docketed: The Propriet. | Bristol 15th 6[mo] 1712 | death of his wifes Father.

1. Quaker records give 5 July 1712 as the date of Thomas Callowhill's burial; WP indicates that it was on 5 Aug. Thomas Callowhill and Hannah Hollister had been married on 27 or 29 Nov. 1660. Mortimer, 1:196.

2. The distance from Ruscombe to Bristol.

3. John Penn was particularly susceptible to illness, perhaps because he had had rheumatic fever as an infant. Drinker, *Hannah Penn*, pp. 124, 147.

4. Docs. 195, 196.

5. Wheat had sold at the highest price in Portugal in 1709; by 1712, the market there had collapsed. Logan Papers, Parchment Logan Letterbook, 1712-1715, pp. 24, 42, HSP.

6. Ann Jones, William Penn, Jr.'s mother-in-law, died on 1 Aug. 1712; her husband, Charles Jones, died in 1714. Digests of Quaker Records, Bristol and Som., GSP.

7. WP scribbled a name here and then changed it; both words are illegible.

198
QUEEN ANNE'S ORDER TO THE TREASURY

[9 September 1712]

WHEREAS Our trusty & Welbeloved William Penn Esq[r] hath made a proposall for surrendering & transferring unto us the several Powers of Governm[t] granted to him by Lrs Patents of our late Royall Unckle King Charles the second and by Deeds from our late Royall Father

King James the Second (when Duke of York) in Pennsilvania & other places in those parts And We having taken the same into our Royall Consideration as also the Reports of our Com^rs for Trade & Plantacions[1] & of our Attorney Generall[2] in Relacion to the s^d proposall & having thereupon resolved to Accept {of} the s^d Surrender & Conveyance & to allow him in Respect thereof a sum of 12000^l to be paid in four years time from the date of the s^d Surrender & Conveyance to which he the s^d Wm Penn hath Consented & agreed AND WHEREAS he hath humbly besought us to advance to him a summ of 1000^l in part of the s^d 12000^l so agreed for & intended to be p^d to him as afores^d untill such time as the s^d Deeds of Surrender & Conveyance can be drawn and perfected Our Will & pleasure is that by Vertue of our Generall Letters of Privy Seale bearing date the thirteenth day of March in the first year of our Reign[3] you issue & pay or cause to be issued & paid out of any our Treasure being and remaining in the receipt of our Exchequer applicable to the uses of our Civill Governm^t unto the s^d William Penn or his Assigns the afores^d sum of 1000^l by way of advance[4] to be taken & esteemed as part of the s^d summ of 12000^l agreed to be paid to him for the s^d Surrender & Conveyance within four years time from the date thereof as is above menconed And for so doing this shall be Your Warr^t given at our Court at Windsor Castle[5] the ninth day of September 1712 in the Eleventh year of our Reign

By her Majestys Comand
Signed Oxford

Copy. Penn Papers, Penn v. Baltimore, 1653-1724, HSP. (*Micro.* 14:437.) Addressed: To Robert Earle of Oxford &c | Our high Treasurer. Superscribed: Anne R. Docketed: 1712.

1. Doc. 182.
2. Attorney General Northey made his report to the lord treasurer on 25 Feb. 1712 (*Micro.* 14:367).
3. 1702. See *CSPD, 1702-1703*, p. 5.
4. The treasury issued WP the initial payment of £1000 on 28 Sept. 1712, but neither he nor his family ever received the remaining £11,000. *Micro.* 14:440; *CTP, 1708-1714*, p. 428.
5. Queen Anne had gone to Windsor for the summer and remained there until the end of Nov. David Green, *Queen Anne* (New York, 1970), pp. 272-77.

199
TO JAMES LOGAN

Bristoll 4: 8^m [October] 1712

James Logan
I have not mist any opertunity since thou left us; but upon Wm Lick—affaire, I have been a looser ~~thereby~~,[1] haveing been by that over easiness of that ingenious, &, I hope Ingennuous S.G.[2] & over ri-

gourousness of W. ~~P~~Wragg,[3] brought to pay 500l for the 150 l~~o~~eant 85, without allowing me one farthing for the fifty pds I repayd, as surely as I write now to thee; tho the many {subsequent} Revolutions of life, have not made me master of the Individuall memorandum abt it wch thy Stay, but as long as one week, or two at most, would have at least more reasonably ~~have~~ ended. I have found above 100l I payd him, for wch he has not given me any Credit, but being before T. Cps [4] conclusion, we were to desolve that by {Such a} retrospection. so that I am as much a looser by the fool as by the knave, such is that seeming milksop. In the mean time I desire thee move all Springs that may deliver me from my present thraldom, as thou will answear it to the great allseeing god, and all Just & good men; for it is my excessive expences upon Pennsylvania that sunck me so low, & nothing else, my expences yearly in England ever faling short of my yearly income in Irland & England.[5] And that wch urges me the more, is thy deep Silence, to my earnest expectation upon my presing order to thee, to dispose Frds there to come in wth frds here to Sinck the present Incumbrance on the Country.[6] It would be a kindness I should not have forgoten. But I see Such an hold fast disposition in the most of men, that I almost dispond of succeeding. yet the atturny Generall[7] assures me I might have made over by my Patent any number of my Frds, or a less number, as 48, 24 or 12, for the whole, as an Incorperated body to have ruled in my steed (Including my selfe, or family a double vote) & so frds had had a Country, wch Frds there & here may have time herafter to Consider of.[8] And truly so great is the number & Interest of Friends here, that they would always have had it in their powr to have preserved their interest in the Province to the end in all revolutions of Govermt here. But I am not {to} be heard either in Civils, or Spiritual{l}s, till I am dead.

I am now to tell thee that both my Daughter & son Aubrey, are under the greatest uneasiness for their mony, wch In the first place I desire as well as allow thee to returne wth the first. Tis an epedemick disease on that side the sea, & the worst of all the *Seasonings*[9] to be too oblivious of returnes, wch I beseech thee to contradict by the most speedy method possible. But as thou sayst the mony intended me was placed to the acct of my Mortgagees, but Still kept there, & so from me, so I have payd wm aubrey, wth a mad Bully & treatmt Into the Bargain but five hundred pds 500l, wch with severall hundred pds payd at severall times, makes neer 1000l besides what thou hast sould & put out upon interest there, wch is so deep a cutt to me here, & nothing but my sons tempestious & most rude treatmt of wife & me too should have ravisht (as I may say) from me. wherefore dont thou lessen thy care to return to pay me, or at least to secure my mony here, upon her Mannor of Mt Joy there, for a Plantation for me, or one of my Children. I writt to thee abt our great & unhappy loss & Revolution at Bristoll, by the Death of our neer & Dr Frds, Father & Mother

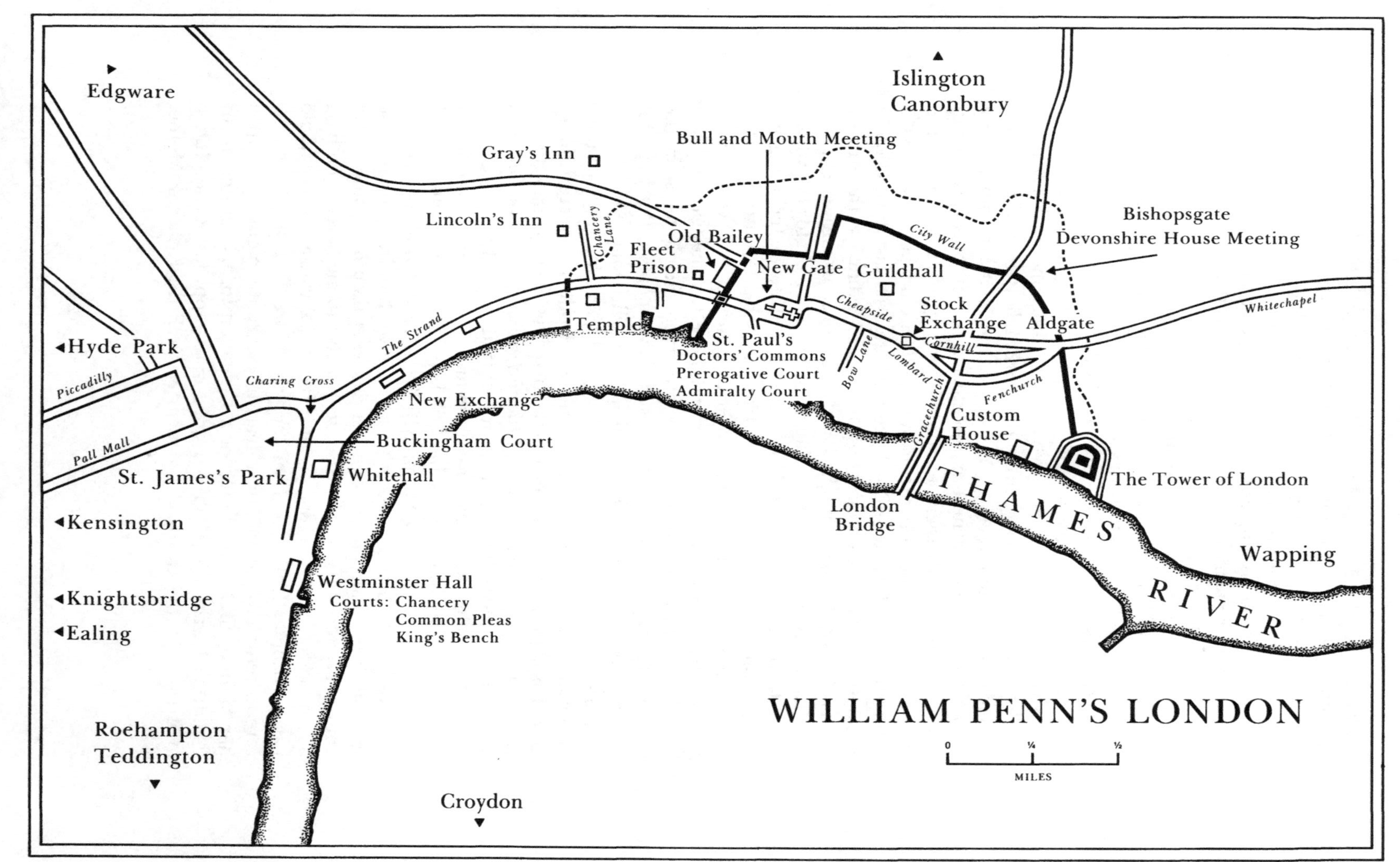

WILLIAM PENN'S LONDON
Edgware
Islington
Canonbury
Bull and Mouth Meeting
Gray's Inn
Lincoln's Inn
Chancery Lane
Old Bailey
Fleet
Prison
New Gate
Guildhall
City Wall
Bishopsgate
Devonshire House Meeting
Stock
Exchange
Aldgate
Whitechapel
Cheapside
Cornhill
Temple
St. Paul's
Doctors' Commons
Prerogative Court
Admiralty Court
Bow Lane
Lombard
Fenchurch
Gracechurch
Custom
House
The Tower of London
London
Bridge
THAMES
RIVER
Wapping
Hyde Park
Piccadilly
The Strand
Charing Cross
New Exchange
Buckingham Court
Pall Mall
St. James's Park
Whitehall
Kensington
Westminster Hall
Courts: Chancery
Common Pleas
King's Bench
Knightsbridge
Ealing
Roehampton
Teddington
Croydon
0
¼
½
MILES

Callowhill, so shall only say that he has left all his concerns in america to poor Johnne,[10] who has almost followed his Grandfather thru an excess of sorrow at his death, & Buriall also & Justifys my Speciall regards to him, as of an uncommon Genius & capacity {as also} by his behavour since, & thru the lords mercy is upon Recovery. & my Recovery is perfecting through the Lords goodness, that have been most dangerously Ill at london.[11]
a Peace certainly; whether the Dutch will or noe, & whom our folks threaten shall pay the Reconing of it too, wch will not be less then a million of mony;[12] & I advise you to be discreet in Those parts, & may the Simplicity, humility, & Serious Sincerity of the christian life & Doctrine be your aime & attainmt in the peace & Plenty you are blest withall. I am Glad to see Sib. Masters,[13] who is come down to this citty, & wth us, but sorry at Phillips comeing wthout a just hint of it.[14] She[15]

Bristoll the 13th 8br [October] 1712

Lo Frd
the Inclosed my poor husband wrot, but had not time to finish, before he was taken wth a second fitt of his Lethargick illness Like as about 6 months ago at London, which has been no small addition to my Late most severe Exercises;[16] But it has pleasd the Lord in the midst of Judgment, to shew us Mercy, in the ⱣComfortable Prospect of his recovery, tho as yett but weak, & I am orderd by the Docters to keep all buisness from him till he is stronger, and yett Loath to lett what he has wrot be Left behind, I therfore thought best to send it tho Unfinishd, for thee to make the best {use} of; there being severall things of Moment. And I pray thee Use thy Utmost dillegence to Setle things, & returns, for his Comfort & quiett of those that dwell near to the Lyon.[17] I ought to say more in answer to thine Intended for my poor dear (deceased) father[18] but time & trouble forbids my Inlarging, only pray show thy regards ~~to him~~ thou had to him, by thy ~~by and~~ dilligence for his poor helpless ~~of~~ Little ofspring. I am cald on in hast the Wind Coming fair, So conclude this hasty Scraule wth my well wishes to thee, & Love to my good, & kind, frds that ask after me

~~This~~ From Thy Reall Frd
H Penn

I had thine[19] by our [Frd] Sib. Masters, who is h[ere] & well.
My 3 Children {here} are [a]ll now, pretty well, as [ar]e my 2 little ones lately at Ruscom.[20]

I am through the the Lords mercy pretty well. I had I had begun an other sheet but not above {6 lines} more than the Inclosed. but being upon six, & I suppose the time, ready for the boat, send thee this & may yet more, if this goes not yet. so farewell, & persue former, earnest orders & thou wilt oblige thy reall Frd.[21]

Wm Penn

Dr. love to all my Dr Friends.

ALS. Penn Papers, Letters of the Penn Family to James Logan, HSP. (*Micro.* 14:441.) Addressed: For James Logan Secretary | of the Province | ~~Province~~ of Pensilvania | In | America. Endorsed: NY ll 10[d] | these | on the Harley. Docketed: M[rs] Ha: Penn Bristoll 13 8[br] 1712 | wth the Proprietors [torn] | Imperfe: | 4th Ditto | per the Harly 15. 12[mo].

1. For William Lickfold's lawsuit, see doc. 192, n. 9.

2. Possibly Stephen Gould.

3. Lickfold's lawyer may have been the William Wragg who was living in Blackfriars, London, in 1695. London Record Society, *London Inhabitants Within the Walls* (Chatham, Kent, 1966), p. 328.

4. Perhaps a reference to Thomas Cuppage, one of the trustees named to supervise WP's estate in 1708; he died in Dec. 1708. See doc. 156.

5. After WP's death his lawyers estimated his annual income in Ireland and England at £1500. Penn Papers, Granville Penn Book, p. 22.

6. WP felt that Pennsylvania Quakers should help to pay off some of the £6600 mortgage held by English Friends.

7. Edward Northey.

8. WP appears to be suggesting here—rather belatedly—that he could have sold the government of Pennsylvania to a corporate body of Quaker colonists rather than to the queen.

9. Diseases occuring during the time a person is becoming accustomed to a new climate; in this case, the American colonists' metaphorical "disease" is their failure to honor obligations in England. *OED.*

10. By lease and release dated 26 and 27 Nov. 1711, and in a will dated 28 Nov. 1711, Thomas Callowhill conveyed his property in England and Pennsylvania to Brice Webb, Charles Harford, and Richard Champion as trustees for his wife; his only child, Hannah Penn; and her children. Callowhill owned considerable property in Bristol and its suburbs and was part-owner of the Bristol Brass Company. He also held 6500 acres in Pennsylvania, plus 80 acres of liberty lands and a Philadelphia lot at Front and High Sts. that had been rented to Thomas Roberts. All the Pennsylvania property was to go to John Penn. *Micro.* 14:327; *PMHB,* 17:70-72; *PWP,* 2:639; *PA,* 2d ser., 19:66.

11. See n. 16, below.

12. British troops had been withdrawn from the war, and the Dutch agreed to take over and pay foreign units formerly under British command. David Chandler, *Marlborough as Military Commander* (New York, 1973), pp. 304-5.

13. Sybilla Masters had come to London to seek patents for her method of milling corn. See doc. 45, n. 24.

14. WP had not yet received Logan's letter of 29 June 1712, which mentioned that Lady Newcomen, alias Mary Phillips, was intending to go back to England "to gett her allowance more certainly Settled for the future." *Micro.* 14:414.

15. This is the bottom catchword on WP's fourth page. As he explains in his postscript, he started to write a fifth page but became ill before he could finish the letter. The next section of the letter is in Hannah Penn's hand.

16. WP had suffered a stroke in Mar. or Apr. 1712, shortly before the deaths of Hannah's parents in June and August.

17. William and Laetitia Aubrey.

18. Logan's letter to Thomas Callowhill, dated 2 July 1712, discussed rent collection on Callowhill's city lots, remittances to the Pennsylvania mortgagees in England, and an intractable Irish servant Logan had bought from the captain of the *Edgely,* a ship in which Callowhill was a part owner. Parchment Logan Letterbook, 1712-1715, pp. 22-24.

19. Probably Logan's letter of either 29 June or 4 July (*Micro.* 14:414, 418). This postscript by Hannah Penn is written on the verso of the last page of the letter; the text is worn away where the letter was folded.

20. The older children—John, Thomas, and Margaret—had accompanied their parents to Bristol for their grandfather's burial, while the younger ones—Richard and Dennis—stayed with the household staff at Ruscombe.

21. This postscript is in WP's hand. He repeats himself, and his language is confused, but his hand is still strong.

THE CLOSING YEARS

1713–1718

With WP's stroke of December 1712, at age sixty-eight, his participation in public life came to an end. For the next five-and-a-half years until his death, he was a helpless invalid, able to walk and speak, but without memory or the ability to communicate effectively. His wife, family, and friends tried to cover up the extent of his incapacity and to cope with the major problems he had left unresolved: repaying the mortgage on Pennsylvania; establishing the division line between Pennsylvania and Maryland; confirming the title to the Lower Counties; dealing with complaints about Governor Gookin; and completing the surrender of the colony's government to the crown. One of WP's lawyers wrote after his death, "had his health continued a Yeare longer the Governm[t] had been surrendered to the Queen" (John Page to Grimble Pauncefort, 6 Aug. 1719, Penn Papers, Official Correspondence, 1:73). If WP left many loose ends, he also left a network of loyal friends and patrons on whom his family could call for help. Among Quakers, Thomas Story and Henry Gouldney in England and James Logan and Isaac Norris in Pennsylvania supplied assistance. During the Ford case, WP had developed a team of lawyers, including Robert West, John Page, Grimble Pauncefort, and Herbert Springett, all of whom continued to advise the family during his final years and after his death.

During WP's years of invalidism, Hannah Penn became the effective head of the family. Although her five children were still young, she delegated considerable responsibility to them, as shown by her letter to thirteen-year-old Thomas (doc. 203). Forced to manage WP's business affairs, Hannah Penn proved herself extremely competent in utilizing WP's agents, friends, and patrons. She worked in close collaboration with Logan (doc. 201) to supervise affairs in Pennsylvania, including the appointment in 1716 of a new governor, William Keith, to replace Gookin. She turned to Springett (doc. 202) when an Irish landholder made a claim to some of WP's acreage in county Cork. She appealed to the earl of Sunderland (doc. 204) when another nobleman, the earl of Sutherland, tried to gain possession of the Lower Counties. In 1714 Hannah Penn and the trustees for Pennsylvania petitioned the queen to complete the surrender negotiated in 1712, and the Privy Council recommended that it be done by Act of Parliament. Anne died soon afterward, however, and the surrender was again put aside. By 1725, when the mortgage was almost totally paid off, the the Penn family quietly decided to drop the question of surrender altogether, and Pennsylvania remained a proprietorship down to the Revolution. Although none of WP's children settled permanently in the colony, and none of them as adults shared his Quaker beliefs, the colony proved a profitable legacy to them, enabling John, Thomas, and Richard Penn to live comfortable lives as absentee landlords in England.

From 1713 to 1715 WP's condition remained relatively stable. He still attended meetings in Reading, but he had lost his talent as a public speaker, which had been remarkable throughout his adult life, and (according to Joseph Besse) he could only speak "several sensible sentences." In 1715 Hannah Penn arranged a trip to Bath, where the waters provided a last hope (doc. 203); this trip provided a diversion from the family routine but no improvement in WP's condition. By 1716 he no longer went to meetings in Reading, and by July 1717 he had failed further; Besse wrote, "he could not well walk without leading; nor scarce express himself intelligibly." In the early morning hours of 30 July 1718, at the age of 73, WP died at Ruscombe. The death scene is movingly described in Hannah Penn's grief-stricken letter to Thomas Story (doc. 205). A large number of Quakers and non-Quakers attended his burial at Jordans, Bucks., on 5 August 1718. In memorial addresses from both sides of the Atlantic, WP was suitably eulogized. The governor of Pennsylvania spoke of "Mr. Penn's generous regard to Mankind, & his sublime Humanity that first fram'd the Scheme, & then laid the solid foundation of this flourishing Colony." And Berkshire Quakers (doc. 208), while acknowledging WP's "deficiencies" in managing his "Temporal Affairs," remembered him as a "Man of great Abilities" with "a Peculiar Sublimity of mind."

200
FROM JAMES LOGAN

Philadelphia, 26th 12 month [February], 1712/3

Honoured Governour

After a great Consternation we were putt into by repeated Accounts of thy Decease[1] We were at length revived by those the last Post gave us of thy Recovery, for not till then did we receive even these of October by the Harley from Bristol.[2]

By that Conveyance I was favoured with my Mistresses and thine of that Month which I opend with great Joy, but from thy late Sentiments of Me, I must prepare (I see) for a Mortification in all I am to Receive.

I am surprized at the Account thou gives me of the Award in W Lickfold's business viz that thou pays him 500l more. I know not what I might have done in Staying (as thou mentions) one Week longer, but believe if I could have mett you both together with the Arbitrators but one night, which for some Weeks before I left London I could not, it might have been ended somewhat differently.[3] I perceive also that Wm Aubry has received 500l of thee, and cannot but think that so dutiful a Child as his Wife deserves all the favours thou canst spare {that} way.

I know not what to doe as to thy Orders about her Lands, the whole business is long agoe Settled under hand and Seal, and therefore can be alter'd no other way. I am sorry that from the Resurveys, I have caused to be made of both her Mannors[4] Since my Return, upon the more ample Powers I brought over,[5] I can give thee no better account of them. They were both confirmed to her by Patents from thy Self before thy Departure,[6] and being done in a hurry, the Surveyors it seems had no other thought than to please thee by returning Land enough, without regarding whose it was, for in that on Skuylkill, above one third of the best of it belong'd to others, thou was fully apprized of the Swedes Claim (viz Rambo's Cocks &c:) to about 1750 Acres on the River, and left them thy Orders in writing that it Should be confirmed to them, but that proves not all, for the Survey took in other old purchased Settlements to all which I was {as} utterly a Stranger as she her Self was, being no other way concerned in it, than to expedite the Patent. And of her other Tract on Brandywine too much may be said to the Same purpose, besides the great Barrenness of a considerable quantity of this as well as the other.[7]

I am getting in and remitting her Money as fast as possibly as I can, but both that and Bills (to which alone we are confined in the Writings)[8] are exceedingly scarce with us, and the Countrey Produce is this Year as bad as either, Many families that used to sell, being likely before Harvest to want bread for their own Sustenance, thrô the shortness of the last Crop.

I hope, as thou charges me, that I shall alwayes remember I am to Answer to God for all my Conduct, and in some measure also to good Men more then which I shall not at present Say upon that head. I arrived here somewhat too late to doe much that Spring in the business of Quittrents: The times of Harvest wch are early here, will not admit of it in Summer, and I was unhappily confined almost all the Fall viz from the middle of the 6th to the 9th Month with a most afflicting Sciatica and Rheumatism, of wch last I am not yet wholly clear, but now as the Spring advances, am setting about it and shall proceed (the Lord willing) with the utmost Diligence and Application, but can never think it reasonable that I should be accountable for what is not in my Power. I have mentioned it in almost every Letter, and have divers times used the most Pathetick Language I could think of, to press thee to gett the Division Lines run between us and Maryland, for not only thousands of Pounds due for Lands already Sold and for Quittrents are detained,[9] but we cannot proceed to sell or Grant more Lands any where near the Bounds because of the Uncertainty, and yet there the greatest Demand is, because not far from Navigable Water.[10] In Maryland the Ld Baltimore Grants his Lands only for the Quittrent of 24 pounds of Tobacco per hundred Acres, but they bring it up in the high Fees which are paid to his Officers We on the other hand Sell thy Lands from 6 to 10 or 12^{l} per hundred to be paid at the first Purchase to thy Use. If after running the Lines any of his Grants fall without his Bounds, the Damage is small to him but while we receive the Purchasers Money, if he cannot hold it ~~if~~ by thy Grant that Money must be made good to him by Somebody. This is so dangerous a Point that the Commissioners think themselves obliged to hold their hands in all those Lands that may prove disputable, and in the mean time those of Maryland running no Risque by their Method, break in more & more upon us by their Surveys.

Now (I suppose) will be the time, if ever, to gett this matter fully Settled, and if it can be done by Lumping,[11] thou wilt have no cause, I believe, to repent it, I know not what may be made of the two different Capes Inlopen & Henlopen,[12] but am of Opinion if thou canst begin at the Mouth of the Indian River[13] as a Natural Boundary, it may be bore with, thô the more can be had the better, but if you begin at what the Sailors understand by Cape In- or Henlopen (& no body here has any notion of any other, thô the old Dutch Map[14] expresses it otherwise) 'twill leave out even the Town of Lewis.

As to the Division Line between the Province and Maryland, if any thing can be obtained by that Interpretation of the Beginning of the 40th Degree, viz that it must be where the 39th ends, thou wilt be a Gainer, but if taken according to the common acceptation, I have more reason than I care to mention to suspect that the Line will fall much more to the Northward than has generally been apprehended.[15]

This being of the greatest Importance to thee, not only to Settle thy Estate here in general, but also for getting in what is due, and raising more Money, I would willingly hope that, however long neglected, it will now at length obtain, as it highly merits, thy care and Application, for Shouldst thou be removed before 'tis effected, none afterwards will be so capable of managing it. I wrote a long Letter on this & some other heads to H Goldney on the first perplexing Report we had of thy Decease, in which I stated the matter as clearly as I was capable.[16]

In that Letter I mentioned a Replevin brought by one Berkly Codd in Sussex for Wheat distrained on by Tho: Fisher for Quittrents by my Order.[17] Codd was baffled at the Court by the Dexterity of our Lawyers Management without bringing the matter to Trial, for indeed I was altogether unwilling to bring in the Deeds of Feofment into Court because of the Reservation of one half of the Rents to the Duke & the Distress that is allow'd to be made in case of thy failing to pay them.[18] This however ~~is~~ {will (we hope) be} fully Settled by the Surrender but the People are so resolute in not paying till it be done that we know not how to manage them.

Besides what we shipt last Summer, We have Sent to Jamaica & Loaded on the Hope Gally[19] {to Carolina} about 250l and now send to Hen: Goldney a very good Bill for 200l sterling. As Effects can be gott in this Spring, We shall hasten all that's possible.

I know not what to say further than I have done in former Letters, about the Effects of Parks vessels,[20] I have not yet been able to gett any Satisfactory Account of them, but am well assured, that whoever claims them, no Great matter will be found, when compared with their first value. John French takes it to be his Right to dispose of ~~them~~ all that is left, which is only the ships Sails now almost rotten & Indigoe that the Governor could not come at, being in John's own, or his Cousin Robert's[21] Cellars, he expects to have the Charges of his voyage & Management in England bore out of them, and indeed upon the whole I am almost as much at a Loss to understand his way of thinking about them, as the Governours, 'tis certain unless he can gett some Compensation, he must be a great sufferer by his Negotiation, and if I may say so much of Colonel Gookin without Offence, I think his Conduct towards John Since his Return is Surprizing

I hope whoever comes with the Queen's Commission,[22] he will bring full Powers & Order about them, & that none will be putt upon touching with them, till they are sufficiently Warranted. I ~~he~~ would wish also that he might come fully Instructed & Impower'd in relation to what thou mayst have to say to Colonel Gookin, Some here affirm, that he is consulting how to keep those Effects of Parks to himself, but however that be, 'tis certain he is not unthoughtfull how to find his Account by coming over, he has lately taken some large fines that amounted to a hundred pounds at least, into his own hands, for he is Governor, (wch is more than ever Colonel Evans did) & yet he complains he shall be a Loser.

Thou seems to admire at my Silence about friends here lending Money to take off the Incumbrance on the Province. I know many would be willing to assist thee to their Power but I had been here but a very litle time, when the Publick News Letters gave an Account that thou hadst Surrendred the Government for wch thou was to have 14,000^{l} and common fame made it more, I could not venture to Say this was false, but knew it was much too late to think of Settling the Government, as thou mentions in thy last on a Number of friends here and when it was generally believ'd, being confirmed by many Letters from England, that thou was to receive Such a Sum, on account of this Government, 'twas in vain to propose any thing further, every body believing that that would absolutely clear the whole.

There was a necessity for M Philips or Newcomens going over, for unless her Affairs were better Settled, She could not be supplied for the future with Money. I thought there was some Risque in what I was obliged to at my Arrival for the preceeding time but Seeing I Sent thee what was sufficient to recover from her husband what was advanced, I hope there has been due care taken not to lett it be lost.[23]

I have since my Arrival follow'd but litle of my own business having putt the few Goods I had into the hands of others to sell, and thô some are of Opinion that I have made my self Master of great quantities of Land, I made but two Purchases of unsurvey'd Lands in this Province, the one from the Geerys of one thous^{d} Acres, the other for a larger quantity that was Hugh Lambs,[24] both these were in a manner forced upon me and {in} what I have taken or shall take up I have no other Privilege than what every man in the Province may according to our established Methods claim, without the least partiality. for in this particular I would not be tax'd on any consideration.

I design if it please God to Spare me Life & health, to spend the ensuing year with the utmost Application to thy business, in which time I hope to bring it into a pretty good Order, thô it has formerly been in the utmost Confusion, and to use my best Endeavours with I Norris to remit what we can receive, after which I doubt from the treatment I meet with, I shall find it necessary to look out for some calmer kind of Life in which I may be less accountable, I have now Spent near fourteen of the best of my Years in thy Service, in wch I can very safely say, I have generally had a much greater regard to thy Interest than my own, And yet it has pleased God in his Divine Providence to bless me beyond my own thoughts or Contrivances {thô far short of what some will Imagine}, I hope through his Assistance my Aim has been answered in this that I have not acquitted my self with any Disrepute to thy Affairs. And whatever happens, if there be any room left for it, I shall willingly give any reasonable Assistance for the future, provided it may be on terms not unbecoming a freeman, which I would willingly Still conceive my self to be.[25]

Having been prevented last fall by my Illness to goe to Salem, I have now appointed to take 3 or 4 Dayes, this next Month, to visit ~~the~~ & call upon the Tenants there,[26] but from what I have hitherto mett with, doubt the Success, as well as in the business of Quittrents at home here, thrô the hardness of the Year.

I design'd to have made up this Letter in it self to save Postage, Merchant-like, but must now putt it under a Cover. I am with true Respect

Thy faithful & Obedient Servant
J Logan

P.S. The trouble thy Unkindnesses gives me ha~~s~~ve forced me in this Letter upon expressing my Self in a manner that I doubt will scarce prove agreeable, but as I am far from intending any thing but what is handsome and honourable, I hope it will be construed in the softest Sense.

J.L.

ALS. Miscellaneous Manuscripts Collection, APS. (*Micro.* 14:484.) Docketed: (N°. 4). Further docketed: James Logan the 26th | of the 12th month 1712/3 | February. Endorsed: Jno Logan | 26th 12^{mon} 1712/3.

1. On 20 Jan. 1713 Logan wrote to Henry Gouldney that "A very Silly young Fellow" recently arrived in Pennsylvania reported seeing WP's funeral in London on 4 Nov. 1712. Parchment Logan Letterbook, 1712-1715, p. 81, HSP.

2. Doc. 199.

3. See doc. 192, n. 9.

4. Laetitia Aubrey's manors were Mount Joy on the Schuylkill in Chester Co. and Hening Manor on the Brandywine. Penn-Physick Papers, 6:22, HSP.

5. *Micro.* 14:341.

6. WP confirmed the patents to Laetitia on 23 Oct. 1701. Penn-Physick Papers, 6:22; Patents, Box 1a, HSP.

7. Thomas Holme and David Powell had laid out 500 acres to Peter Yocum in 1684; this and other smaller tracts fell within the Mount Joy tract laid out for Laetitia. In 1707, acting on WP's orders, Logan had confirmed the lands to Yocum and the other purchasers. *PA*, 2d ser., 19:266, 293, 432, 489.

8. William and Laetitia Aubrey specified in their power of attorney of 24 Dec. 1711 that Samuel Carpenter and James Logan should sell all their lands and remit the proceeds by bills of exchange or coin only. Penn-Physick Papers, 6:22.

9. According to Logan, the potential quitrent income from the Lower Counties was three times that of Pennsylvania. Parchment Logan Letterbook, 1712-1715, p. 81.

10. The head of Chesapeake Bay.

11. Treating everything (in this case, the disputed land claims) collectively, without regard for particulars. *OED*.

12. Cape Henlopen, by this time the accepted name for the southern cape at the mouth of Delaware Bay, had originally been the Dutch name for a section of the Atlantic coast 25 miles to the south. In a later, undated defense of the Penns' claim, Logan wrote, "The two main Capes which form the Bay of Delaware were by one Cornelius May a Dutchman call'd after his own Names: That on the Pensilvania Side Cape Cornelius, & that on the New Jersey side Cape May; but there is yet another Cape upon the Eastern Sea above twenty Miles to the Southward of that Cape Cornelius to wch he gave the name of Cape Hinlopen; and thus it appears in the old Dutch map which Mr Penn laid before the King In Council upon which the Devision Line was accordingly mark'd: But the later Maps have quite lost the name of Cape Cornelius, and transferr'd that of Hinlopen in its Place, setting no Name at all at the Place of the old Hinlopen, which now the Saylors call the false Cape." The present boundary was finally set at WP's "Cape Henlopen" in an agreement of 1732. *PWP*, 2:308n; *Micro.* 14:729; *PMHB*, 87:267-83.

13. The mouth of the Indian River is midway between present-day Cape Henlopen and the southern border of Delaware.

14. WP probably had a map by either Jan Jansson (1588-1664) or Nicolas Jansz Visscher I (1618-1679) or II (1649-1702). A copy of a Visscher map is found in the Cadwalader Collection, 3:90, HSP. See Tony Campbell, "The Jansson-Visscher Maps of New England," in R. V. Tooley, ed., *The Mapping of America* (London, 1980), pp. 279-94.

15. Logan is here citing Thomas Fairman's novel concept of degrees of latitude; see doc. 103. The Penns decided to employ a different strategy, arguing that the determining factor should not be the actual location of the 40th degree of latitude but instead its location in the old maps shown to the king when he made the grant to WP, "so that tho later observations should discover those imaginary Lines to have been wrong plac'd; the Grants however ought not to be extended or diminish'd according to any such corrected observations; but must be regulated by such other parts of the Discription as are visible, fix'd, certain, & subject to no variation." *Micro.* 14:729.

16. Logan had written Henry Gouldney on 20 Jan. 1713 and urged him to secure WP's title to the Lower Counties, "which was always intended to be a condition of the surrender." Parchment Logan Letterbook, 1712-1715, p. 81.

17. Berkeley Codd (d. 1724), an Anglican Supreme Court justice in the Lower Counties, was probably being sued for failure to pay quitrents. Thomas Fisher (d. 1713) had come to the Lower Counties in 1682 and later served as WP's secretary. Logan had retained Andrew Hamilton to act for WP in the case against Codd. *Governor's Register, State of Delaware* (Wilmington, 1926), 1:8; Leon de Valinger, Jr., comp., *Calendar of Sussex County, Delaware, Probate Records, 1680-1800* (Dover, Del., 1964), pp. 23, 25, 32; Scharf, *Delaware,* 2:1228; *PMHB,* 16:2, 42:170.

18. WP's deeds to the Lower Counties specified that he should pay a substantial portion of all rents and profits received to the duke of York, whose rights now belonged to the crown. *PWP,* 2:282-84.

19. The *Hope Galley,* in which WP owned a ⅛ share, was built by Isaac Norris and captained by John Richmond. *PMHB,* 78:147n, 167, 169, 170, 172; doc. 185.

20. Thomas Park was captain of the *St. John Baptist* and Robert Remer was captain of the *St. Joseph,* the two ships seized at Newcastle by John French. See doc. 192, n. 11; *Micro.* 14:296, 381.

21. Robert French, an Anglican, had once been anti-proprietary, but, according to Logan, by the time of his death he had become "a cordial Wellwisher" to WP. *PMHB,* 3:217-20, 22:104; *Micro.* 14:505.

22. The proposed royal governor of Pennsylvania.

23. Logan had advanced Lady Newcomen £95 of WP's own money, making a total of £425 given to her since her arrival in 1702, which Logan expected WP to collect from either her husband or her step-father, Richard Rooth. *Micro.* 14:414, 418.

24. Hugh Geary of Buckinghamshire and John Geary (d. 1696) of Hertfordshire were First Purchasers of 500 acres each; John had bequeathed his land to his cousin William Davy, who evidently then sold it to Logan. Hugh Lamb, a Middlesex hosier, was a First Purchaser of 2500 acres. By 1716 Logan had sold most of this land to Israel Pemberton. *PWP,* 2:643, 647; *PMHB,* 29:316-17.

25. Logan gave up this plan to retire from WP's service when he heard that the proprietor was a complete invalid.

26. For WP's landholdings in Salem, N.J., see *PWP,* 2:316-18.

201
HANNAH PENN TO JAMES LOGAN

Ruscomb the 17th 8br [October] 1713

Lo: Friend

I Recd lately thine of the 1st of the 4th mo past & have ~~It~~ a few days since, recd a duplicate therof,[1] as also an additionall Letter, wrot the 2d 5th month, by Henry Brook,[2] Who I have not yet seen, having not been In London for above 9 months past, for So Long it is, since my poor Dearest was taken wth his Last most fatall fitt,[3] And tho beyond our expectation, he is recovered to a degree of health & strength, Yet has never attaind his wonted strength in Expression, nor is he able to ~~Grable~~ {engage}[4] in buisness as formerly, wch throws a Great Load therof on me, & with respect to his American affairs I am scarce able to get through any part therof to advantage. it being so much beyond my Reach, However, was willing by this our dear friend Jno Salkield,[5] to lett thee know how tis with us, and that I have not only Considered the Contents of thy Letters my selfe, but have also Consulted wth our friend H Gouldney, Counselr West; Cous Rooth &c[6] about ~~w~~That part thou so much Insists on; Viz, about the division Line, and Setlemt of the Lower Countys; if they are so Unfixt as thou seems to suggest, I am heartily Consernd, it has been lett alone to this day, espesially since for some years past my husbands Life has Look'd so Precarious, and he is now unable to New Modell that Important affair of the surrender, which I am by all my frds advisd to get finishd, & Confirmed by an Act of Parliment before it is too late, but the blocks thou throws in my way are ready to stumble me, in it;[7] till I consider that what Steps my husband has taken, has been with great deliberation, & in the Soundness of his ~~Ju~~ Judgment, And therfore I cannot ~~now~~ see who can now mend it, However I purpose for my own, & frds, satisfaction, to Get a Coppy of the Surrender, and see if any thing Can be safely done in it. But as to the Line all Conclude it does not at all depend on the Goverment, & therfore as things are tis not best to stir in it: if thou Conclude the Contrary, & think thou could push it on to advantage by being here, & can Leave thy Charge there in good able hands, I should be Glad thou ~~was~~ Come {over} here, thô twere but for a few months.[8] But the distance, & precariousness of its success, forbids my pressing it, So I Leave it to thee to thee, to do as thou thinks will be most for our Reall Advantage.

The laws T: G[9] tells me are not yet, past, but we Intend next week, by a fee to make them Slip the easier through the Soliceters hands. tho I fear some of the most Meteriall for the people wont pass, at all, of which I presume Tho Grey Gives thee Accot, as also of the perticular Transactions of Parks's Owners, who Give things a Very different face to what Jno french did;[10] so that I see not room for us to say any thing, but Leave it to the Queen & Councell to determine, I am now Glad thou hast took so little of it, into thy possesion, but I fear twill Light hard somwhere; as to the Care thou Mentions of Inspecting &c I know not, as things are, Who can Impower, or be Impowerd to, Transact it throughly, nor can I as yet find writings sufficient to give Life to such an Onsett, but will search farther.

I have wrot & searchd all the Likly places for this deed thou Mentions relating to Haugs affair but cannot yet hear of it.[11]

I shall (since thou Insists so much on it,) send thee a Coppy of my dear Fathers will, when I can ~~also~~ get a letter of Atturney also, from the trustees wch I think is full as Nesessary.[12]

I am sorry to hear poor Peter Evans has met wth so unkind

treatment,[13] I wish I could help it, but cannot see how as things are, to move much in his, nor even {in} our own affairs, The bearer[14] can give thee a perticular act of our Circumstances & afflictions, to whom I referr &, if after weighing the matter, thou can by writing to H Gouldney, (in whom I Confide more than any one Man) my selfe ~~&~~ or any else, put us in away how to attack C G[15] to advantage, or how to get the other~~s~~ things setled, to a Generall satisfaction, and I doubt not but we should readyly Concur with it, but see not at presant how to make much alterations, I have not time to say much more the frds going sooner than ~~e~~I expected, My poor husband, if he was well enough, has scarce time to write to thee by this opertunity so sends by these his dear Love to all our Good frds as if Named, and with as great a fervency as ever, desires both theirs, & the Countrys welfare, In Which I Joyn, and with both our Loves to thy selfe, desiring thy Continued Care in all things that may Contribute to our, & the Countrys Benefitt, with which and desires for thy own Comfort also I conclude & remain Thy assured Frd

H Penn.

Pray let not my Cous R Blackfan Want Nessesarys[16]

ALS. Penn Papers, Letters of the Penn Family to James Logan, HSP. (Not filmed.) Docketed: Mises H Penn Ruscomb: 17. 8. 13 | per J Salkeld 11. 11 month 1713.

1. For Logan's letter of 1 June and 2 July 1713, see Parchment Logan Letterbook, 1712-1715, pp. 116-18, 122-23, HSP.

2. Henry Brooke, youngest son of an English baronet, emigrated to America in 1702 and became customs collector at Lewes, Del.; in 1721 he was on the Provincial Council. Brooke and Logan became good friends and Logan encouraged his efforts to write poetry. Edwin Wolf II, *The Library of James Logan of Philadelphia, 1674-1751* (Philadelphia, 1974), p. 552; *Micro.* 11:063, 312; 13:756; Logan Letterbooks, 2:164, 204; 3:195.

3. WP's third and most serious stroke evidently occurred in Dec. 1712.

4. Grapple with (*OED*). The word "Grable" has been struck through and replaced with "engage" by what appears to be a modern hand.

5. John Salkeld had come to England and was now returning to Pennsylvania.

6. Henry Gouldney, Robert West, and Richard Rooth.

7. See doc. 200. For Logan's insistence that the Penns' title to the Lower Counties had to be confirmed as part of the final surrender of the Pennsylvania government, see Parchment Logan Letterbook, 1712-1715, esp. pp. 94-95, 106-8, 116-18, 122-23.

8. Logan did not go to England at this time; he did make the trip in 1723-24 to negotiate an agreement with Lord Baltimore. Drinker, *Hannah Penn,* pp. 150-51; Frederick B. Tolles, *James Logan and the Culture of Provincial America* (Boston, 1957), pp. 128-31.

9. Thomas Grey was trying to obtain the queen's approbation for laws passed by the Assembly in June 1712; see doc. 194.

10. See doc. 200, text at n. 21.

11. In his letter of 14 May 1713 Logan asked Hannah Penn to search for William Haige's deed for New Jersey lands and his mortgage to Philip Ford on WP's account. Logan and WP had been looking for these documents since at least 1706; see doc. 126, n. 25.

12. Logan had assumed that he needed a power of attorney from WP and his wife as guardians for John Penn, the heir to Thomas Callowhill's Pennsylvania property. Actually Callowhill had named three prominent Bristol Friends — Brice Webb, Charles Harford, and Richard Champion — as trustees for his property. Parchment Logan Letterbook, 1712-1715, pp. 94-95, 116-18; doc. 199, n. 10.

13. Logan had reported that Peter Evans went twice to Col. Gookin to tell him that he had been commissioned register of wills, but Gookin called him "Rascal Villain &c" and refused to honor the commission. Parchment Logan Letterbook, 1712-1715, p. 118.

14. John Salkeld.

15. Col. Gookin, who, according to Logan, was now interested only in the "raking in of money" by any means for his personal use. Gookin was finally dismissed in 1717 and replaced by William Keith. Parchment Logan Letterbook, 1712-1715, p. 117; Drinker, *Hannah Penn,* pp. 99-101.

16. Rebecca Blackfan, recently widowed, was overseeing Pennsbury after the departure of John and Mary Sotcher. See doc. 70, n. 12.

202
CONTROVERSY WITH RALPH FREKE

A
From Ralph Freke

London July the 18th 1714

D^{r} S^{r}

tis with the Greates Concerne that may be that Obliges me to send my serv^{t} to you with ~~in~~ A supena butt I have soe long prest Mr Waite your Agent to A survey & A Devition of Bally Roe, & Bally Laurence,[1] that now I cant Avoyde itt he Constantly Putting that matter Allways off soe I hope now you'll Give your Directions in that matter {&} nott be Disobliged att this Comeing From D^{r} s^{r}

Your Affect^{t} Relation &
Hum^{bl} Servt
Ralph Freke[2]

B
Hannah Penn to Herbert Springett

Dear Cousen

I am forcd to be yet farther troublesom to thee, for the above letter & Incosed Coppy of a Supine came last night, ~~by~~ to my no small Surprise. I did not lett my husband see the Messenger, & ~~re~~ also refusd to take the paper my Selfe wch he left in the Window, & is here Inclosed, I told the Man it had been more kind if his Master would hav~~eing~~ given himselfe the trouble of writing me a letter, he sayd hiss Master had spoke to My husband son,[3] but to little porpose or it had never come to this.

I now request thy through Care in the affair to prevent farther trouble. for tho I have recd & thankfully {acknowledge} thy kind answer to my former letter, yet I now Conclude there must be more possitive orders Given. I therfore Intreet thou will Give thy selfe the trouble of Calling on this Sr Ralfe Freake, his man says he Lodges at one Mr Williamsons in Sheer Lane near the Temple.[4] he seems by his writing to be a Cousen but his action not much like a true friend. I pray thee discorrs & setle the Matter wth him, & what needfull Charge shall arise therefrom shall be allowed by

thy obliged Cous H.P.

pray as opertunity offers to [blotted] my son Pen know I take it unkindly of him that [blotted] had not stop'd, nor given me Notise of this, that I might have previnted it.

HP.

the Man had 2 things wch I supose was Originall & Coppy but he Left only the Inclosed.[5]

I have wrot this Sr Ralfe word that my husband is ill and that I will advise wth thee in the Matter. I have more to say but omitt it till Next, only if in the Mean time it should Lye in thy way to ~~b~~ hear of any reliefe, that may be gaind for my poor daughter Pen and Children I intret thee for their accomodation & my ease use thy best Endeavour[6]

ALS. Chester County Historical Society. (*Micro.* 14:522.) Addressed: For | Wm Pen Esqr att his | house att | Reading | these. Further addressed: To Harbert Springett | In George Yard | Lumbard Street[7] | London. Docketed in Robert West's hand: Sr Ra: Freke at | West Bilney[8] neare | Lynn Norffolk.

1. In the 1660s Sir William Penn had been granted more than 12,000 acres of Irish lands, including 64 acres in Ballyroe and Ballelowrace, part of the barony of Imokilly, East Cork. When this property was discovered to contain 112 acres, WP obtained a lease from the duke of York for the additional 48 acres, without setting out the boundaries of this leased land. After the Glorious Revolution, the 48 acres were granted by William III to his mistress, Elizabeth Villiers (later countess of Orkney), from whom WP obtained a new lease. Later the 48 acres were resumed by Parliament and sold to the Swordblade Company of London, which sold them to Ralph Freke. WP had admitted Freke's claim to the 48 acres but had argued about where to lay them out. WP insisted on his right to keep the house and cultivated land developed by his tenant; Freke had refused to accept any division that did not include the house. *PWP*, 1:570-73; *Micro.* 14:737; *DNB*.

2. Sir Ralph Freke (d. 1718), baronet of Castle Freke and Bilney, was the son of Percy and Elizabeth Freke, whose Irish lands had been seized by James II in the 1680s and restored by William III in 1690. His relationship to WP has not been determined, but he must have been related to William and John Freke, whom WP met in 1670 when they were tenants on his father's Irish lands. Another member of the family, John Freke—a friend of John Locke and Benjamin Furly—also was WP's cousin and had asked him for a grant of Pennsylvania land in 1687. William Playfair, *British Family Antiquity* (London, 1811), 6:788-89; Burke's *Landed Gentry*, 1:602-3; *PWP*, 1:124, 126, 128, 137n, 141n; E. S. De Beer, ed., *Correspondence of John Locke* (Oxford, 1978), 3:114, 135, 148, 159, 210, 265.

3. William Penn, Jr.

4. Probably Shire Lane, Temple Bar. Peter Cunningham *A Handbook for London, Past and Present* (London, 1849), 2:738. Mr. Williamson has not been identified.

5. Not found.

6. Mary Jones Penn was separated from her husband, William Penn, Jr. She and her three children were dependent on Hannah Penn, who may have been trying to find a way to force her stepson to support his wife and children. Penn Papers, Hannah Penn Cashbook, HSP; doc. 207, n. 3.

7. George Yard, Lombard St., is just south of Oxford St. above Grosvenor Sq. in the west end of London.

8. West Bilney is about five miles southeast of King's Lynn, Norf. Freke had inherited substantial property there through his mother. Playfair, *Family Antiquity*, 6:788-89.

203
HANNAH PENN TO THOMAS PENN

Bath the 11th of 3^{d} month [May] 1715

Dear Child

This brings Mine & thy fathers Dear Love to thee, & thy Brothers Richard, & Dennis, Who I hope mind your Books & do as Master orders.[1] At Neglect not to read in the Bible or in some Good {frds} book the Value of 2 Chapters every day, and hear thy brothers also, ~~and~~ A {a small} portiton,[2] out of the bible or J Frames book,[3] some of Which I would thee at thy Leacure hours ~~I would have thee~~ Learn them by heart, and be a good Example to them. I have the satisfaction to hear you were well first day from Hannahs Mother[4] Who also[5] the account of Honest Marg^{t} Chandler death,[6] at Which I have been much Consernd but wish to know of wh~~om~~att, & with whom she dyed. I shall lett thee know that, thy Poor father holds through the Lords mercy as well as at home he drinks about a q^{t} of the Bath Water, and has a good stomach after it. I am at presant also pretty well as {is} thy sister, & sister aubrey, Mary Chandler & M Wells Indiferent,[7] as is Hannah this day, But she has been very ill for the most part ever since she Came here, so as not able to attend thy father but rather wanted attendance her selfe having had a severe feavour & ague but Mist her fitt yesterday, and has been better to day than any day since she Came. I am at a Loss for severall things she should have remembred, and wch I would have sent by flying Coach[8] 6th day if this Comes time enough to hand. Viz thy fathers slippers 2 pair of New Gloves in the sheet Trunk. his old thin Wascoat of striped silk druggett.[9] Johnes thin surtoot[10] if not toren, if tis then send thy fathers {short one} to make one for him. We also want Pegges Blue shoes. Johnes new silk Hankercher & mine from Mary littleworths.[11] Send it by the man that meets H. Pratt for I fancy they will be most reasonable, but if Extortious than send by the Waggon, who will bring for 7s a hundred but I much Want thy fathers thin Wascoat & Johnes Coat, he & thy sisters gives their kind love to you all. Give mine to Thomas Kent[12] & to thy Master, if either of them desire any books out of thy fathes Closett thou may help them to the key & when done lett Rachell,[13] lock it up with the rest, in the draw as I left it. Give my Love to Rachell, to whom be the all kind & easy & if her Mother Inclines to Come as I oferd rachell, Lett her be kindly used. and tell her I would have Tho Kent accomodated to his satisfaction. I have not as yet heard from you since Thomas went hence, I desire sometimes to hear from thy Master, and sometimes from thee how you go on & are in health and how poor Manda does,[14] if thy Master has not made more Balsamack sirup[15] lett Thomas Get 2 or 3 ounces of it from Robt Deans,[16] & if {it} does her good lett her have more. or anything else that may turn to her advantage. for I am in Concern for her. but I must say no more now, but with my best desires for good and Comfort, and hearty salutes of dear Love to you all my dear Children I end and am thy Dear brothers &

Thy affectionate Mother
H Penn

My love to our frds at Reding. I would have Rachell bottle 6 or 8 bottles at least of Goosberry, when they are fitt. & Candy some J Angellca[17] if any is fitt. else make some {cake}, a reiceite of which is in my rciete Book which John[18] has and which I desire wth the Loose receits may be kept very Carefully.[19] I wish for a lattin book or 2 that Johne[20] might Imploy his time in here if John thinks any he has proper.

ALS. Dreer Collection, HSP. (*Micro.* 14:528.) Addressed: To Thomas Penn | At Ruscomb | Near Redding | Barks | postpayd. Docketed: Hannah Penn | 11 May 1715.

1. John Seward was employed as a tutor for the boys at Ruscombe; he left the Penn household in May 1716. Drinker, *Hannah Penn*, p. 67; Penn Papers, Hannah Penn Cashbook, HSP.
2. This word, written over the word "and," is probably meant to be "portion."
3. John Freame was the author of a popular Quaker schoolbook, *Scripture-Instruction* . . . (London, 1714). Smith, 1:706.
4. Probably Hannah Hoskins (b. 1693), the daughter of Reading Quakers Richard and Joan Hoskins, who were also occasionally employed by the Penns. Hannah was paid wages of £4 a year for the period from 25 Dec. 1712 to Dec. 1720; her primary responsibility seems to have been to care for the invalid WP. Digests of Quaker Records, Berks. and Oxon., GSP; Hannah Penn Cashbook.
5. Hannah Penn probably meant to write "brought" here.
6. Margaret Chandler was probably a relative of Mary Chandler.
7. Probably Mary Wells (b. 1688), the daughter of Nathaniel and Elizabeth Wells, members of Ratcliff and Barking Monthly Meeting in London. She may have been employed by Laetitia Aubrey. Digests of Quaker Records, London and Middx., GSP; Hannah Penn Cashbook.
8. A fast coach, especially coaches operating in relay to carry the mails. *OED*.
9. A thin woollen cloth, sometimes containing silk or linen. Ibid.
10. Overcoat. Ibid.
11. Mary May Littleworth, the daughter of Berkshire Friends Edward and Dorothy May, married clothworker John Littleworth in 1696. She operated a shop in Reading frequented by Hannah Penn. Digests of Quaker Records, Berks. and Oxon.; Hannah Penn Cashbook.
12. Thomas Kent (1690-1725), the son of Reading Quakers John and Ann Kent, had evidently just begun to work in the Penn household. Digests of Quaker Records, Berks. and Oxon.; Hannah Penn Cashbook.
13. Rachell Rose was the daughter of Berkshire Friends Richard and Susanna Rose, who died in Nov. 1715. Rachell married Michael Sargood of Reading in Mar. 1716 and probably left the Penn household then. Digests of Quaker Records, Berks. and Oxon.; Hannah Penn Cashbook.
14. See doc. 169, n. 9.
15. A soothing or healing ointment or medicine. *OED*.
16. Robert Dean has not been identified; his name appears several times in the Hannah Penn Cashbook.
17. Angelica, an herb cultivated for medicinal and culinary purposes, was used to make a confection known as candied angelica. *OED*.
18. John Seward.
19. Recipes for gooseberry jam and for angelica candy and cake are found in the Penn family recipe book. *Micro.* 10:558.
20. John Penn.

204
HANNAH PENN TO THE EARL OF SUNDERLAND

[27 March 1718]

I would be as Little troublesom to Lord Sunderland as possible, but as there is a Ne{ce}ssety for me to Make application to Secretary Craggs[1] to endeavour if possible to prevent the Earle of Southerlands getting from us, the Lower Countys of Pensylvania,[2] I Would hope from thy long friendship to my poor weak husband,[3] and in Compassion to {our} Younger Children,[4] who would be deprived of the Greatest part of the Provision made for them, if a Stranger should be permitted to reap the fruits of the Improvements, ~~of the~~ Which have been Made at the great expence of their Fathers Mony and Time; that thou woulds be pleasd favourably to Recomend our hard case to the Secretary, and Espesially that he will be pleasd to permitt my Uncle Clement,[5] or sometimes my Friend Lawton[6] to Wait upon him in my behalfe as Occasion may require. This is the Request I humbly make to thee and praying thy Excuse for this trouble I am

Thy most Obliged Friend
H Penn

27th of March 1718

ALS. Add. Ms. 61,647, fol. 211, BL. (Not filmed.) Docketed: H. Penn. 27 March 1718.

1. James Craggs (1686-1721) had been appointed secretary of state for the Southern Department on 16 Mar. 1718, after serving in the House of Commons since 1713 and as secretary of war since 1717. Both he and his father, Postmaster-General James Craggs, were clients of Sunderland and the duke of Marlborough. *DNB*.

2. John Gordon (1660?-1733), the 16th earl of Sutherland, had participated in the Glorious Revolution of 1688, served as a privy councilor under William III, and helped suppress the earl of Mar's rebellion in 1715. In 1716 he petitioned for a grant of the Lower Counties to repay the crown's debt to him of £20,000 incurred during the Revolution and the Scottish rebellion. By Dec. 1716 King George I was "inclined to favour his Lordship's request." The Board then solicited the opinion of the attorney and solicitor general, who determined that title to the Lower Counties did, in fact, belong to the crown and not to WP but that the title should be established in the court of Chancery. Sutherland and his son continued to press the issue into the 1730s, but the case was never heard in Chancery and the Penn family continued to hold the Lower Counties, although their title remained uncertain. *DNB; CSPC, 1716-1717*, pp. 233, 256, 271-72, 514; *1717-1718*, pp. 87-95; Shepherd, pp. 348-50; John A. Munroe, *Colonial Delaware: A History* (Millwood, N.Y., 1978), pp. 131-34.

3. Hannah Penn had requested Sunderland's help several times before. In 1715 she had asked him to facilitate the completion of WP's surrender to Pennsylvania's government, negotiated in 1712, and to counter malicious rumors that WP was "Disaffected" to the government of George I. In late 1716 or early 1717, when Sutherland was attempting to gain the Lower Counties, she had appealed to Sunderland again. On 12 Feb. 1717 she wrote Logan, "By the friendship of my good friend the Earl of Sunderland, I am assured it is quite put by and I believe he will stand by us against all such encroachments." Drinker, *Hannah Penn*, pp. 82-83, 101-2; *Micro*. 14:536.

4. Hannah Penn is referring here to Thomas, Margaret, Richard, and Dennis, since John Penn was due to receive a double portion of the Pennsylvania properties and had already inherited much of the Callowhill estate. See headnote to doc. 193.

5. Simon Clement.

6. Charlwood Lawton.

205
HANNAH PENN TO THOMAS STORY

Ruscomb the 28th of the 5th month [July] 1718

Dear Friend

I hope this will meet thee well, after thy Journey but am ready to wish thou had stayd a day longer with us,[1] ~~My~~ for tho I found my poor husband last night near as I left him, in the Morning; Yet this Morni{n}g {near noon,} he alterd Much, was taken with shivering & Lowness of Spiritt, and divers simptoms like a sudan Change, on which the Desolateness of my Circumstancs Looking me in the face, & no one frd with me that was Capable to advise in such a Juncture I then regreted the opertunity I lost, of ~~hav~~ Beging ~~taken~~ thy advice, and which Indeed I thought to have done in the Coach but was willing to put the evill day yet farther of. But fearing tis drawing Nigh I would Gladly have thy advice how to Act on such a surprise both with respect {to my own &} ~~of~~ my Childrens saftey, & for the quiett of Pensylvaina should it happen now Just On the ships going of. twould be sad if H G[2] should not Come to me On such an occasion. May I have strength & Wisdom to go through this trying day as I ought, and for which let me have thy Earnest supplycations, at the Throne of Grace, which will be kindly accepted by

Thy affte but afflicted Frd
H Penn

I hoped to have overtaken thee by flying Coach or otherwis, with this {but finding it to Late &} when our apothecary Coming in gave me hope it might terne to an Intermiting feavour, the heat Coming on as the Cold went of. I d~~a~~elayd till to late to recover thee till thou got Bath, & being also straitend least I should straiten thee in thy duty.[3] I uneasyly bear the burthen & Loss I sustain for Want of thy advice. for my poor husband is this day grown so Much Worse that I cant Expet his Continience till this time to morrow. on Which I speed this Messenger on purpose with my sons horse, & to let thee know how it is desiring thee to break the first Notice therof to him, & get leave of his Master[4] to {let him} come to me[5] but Which Enduce me yet more is to get thy {best} advice how to act, for should not H G. be able to come down, I should be most Desolate & fersaken. I must say no more but am ready to say wo is me, that I have Lived to ~~say~~ee this day of Striping this most Desolate day. My dear Love salutes thee & my Cousen Webbs.[6] I am your

aflicted frd H.P.

30th my poor Dearests last breath was fetcht this morning between 2 & 3 a Clock

{pray} give the Iclosed to Johne if thou think proper when thou hast broke the matter to him

ALS. This letter is one of several inserted in a copy of *A Journal of the Life of Thomas Story* (Newcastle upon Tyne, 1747), at FLL. (*Micro.* 14:601.) Addressed: To Thomas Story | these. Docketed: H. Penn 28. 5m 1718.

1. Thomas Story had stayed at Ruscombe 24-27 July 1718, en route from London to Bristol and Bath. This was his sixth visit to WP since his return to England in 1714. *Life of Thomas Story,* pp. 463-64, 525-26, 529-30, 578, 606-7.

2. Henry Gouldney.

3. Story received this letter in Bristol on 31 July. Being "much broken in my Spirit on reading the Letter," he wrote, "and a Concern taking hold of my Mind, to be at the Interment of his Corpse," he immediately set out from Bristol and reached Ruscombe on the evening of 1 Aug. Story stayed with the Penn family until 12 Aug. and was present for the burial at Jordans and the reading of WP's will. He then resumed his ministering travel. *Life of Thomas Story,* p. 607.

4. Brice Webb.

5. John Penn left Bristol with Story on 31 July 1718. *Life of Thomas Story,* p. 607.

6. Brice and Phoebe Webb, Hannah Penn's cousins, with whom Story usually stayed on his visits to Bristol. Ibid., p. 607 and passim.

206
WILLIAM KEITH TO THE TRUSTEES OF PENNSYLVANIA

[6 November 1718]

To Mr Joshua Gee, Henry Goldney and the rest of the rest of the Gentlemen Mortgagees claiming a right to the Governmt of Pensilvania &ca.[1]

Gentlemen

Upon certain Advice that the Honble Wm Penn late Proprietor of this Province died upon the 30th of July last, I summon'd the Council here who met immediately, & the Administration of the Governmt was continued in the Same maner as before and for the reasons given in that Day's Minute of Councill here inclosed.

I thought it a part of my Duty to acquaint you wth our proceedings on this occation & I am wth great respect

Gentlemen
Your most faithful and
obedient humble Servt
W: Keith[2]

Philadelphia
Novr 6th 1718

At Council held at Philadelphia the 3d Novr 1718

Present

The Honourable William Keith Esqr Lieutt Governour

Jasper Yeates	Samuel Preston
Richard Hill	James Logan
William Trent	Anthony Palmer
Isaak Norris	Robert Assheton
Jonathan Dickenson	John French[3]

The Governr having just received some Letters from Grt Brittain[4] spoke to the Council in these Words—

Gentlemen

The important occation of yr meeting at this time is that I may communicate unto you in the most decent & respectful manner the Accounts wch I have just recd of our late Lord Proprietor & Govr in chief the great Mr Penn's Death.

The exalted merit & Reputation whereby this Gentn has been Universaly known & distinguish'd for many Years most justly restrains me from presuming to touch so perfect a Piece as the genll Character of that greate Man.

But the dutiful regard to that Trust, in my present Station, wch I once receiv'd from him, as well as the respect wch is justly due to so many of his faithful Servants present, obliges me in the midst of Sorrow to put you in mind of the Duty which we in particular owe to the grateful Memory of a worthy & good Master.

In short, As it was Mr. Penn's generous regard to Mankind, & his sublime Humanity that first fram'd the Scheme, & then laid the solid foundation of this flourishing Colony,

So it is to his indefatigable Care & great Capacity in all manner of publick Business that we intirely owe those valuable Priveledges which we now enjoy, & wch the good People of this Province may justly expect to be regarded, especialy by those employed in the Administration of Government under the late Proprietor.

At this time therefore Gentlemen, I hope you will think I am in my Duty when I recommend it ~~so~~ to you so to proceed in every part of the publick Service as that our Soveraign Lord King George his supreme and Rightful Authority may in the first place be maintained over all his Maties Subjects within this Province

Secondly, That the Respect and Gratitude which is so justly due to the late worthy Proprietor's Family may on all occations be dutifully acknowledged & paid.

And lastly, That our behaviour towards each other may be such as in any event will clearly demonstrate that we are Loyal Subjects, faithful Servants, and Sincere Friends.

The Board Receiv'd the Govr's affectionate Condolence upon this melancholy occation wth Gratitude & Respect; and then the Act of Assembly pass'd in the Year 1712 and approved by the late Queen entituled, An Act for the further securing the Administration of the Government,[5] was called for and read; And a Motion being thereupon made that for the greater Satisfaction of the Inhabitants of this Province a Proclamation should be issued mentioning the Proprietor's Decease and reciting the last Clause in the said Act vizt:

"That in case the said Governour in chief shall happen to be removed by Death or otherwise Then it shall & may be Lawfull for his Deputy or Lieutenant for the time being to exercise all the Powers of Government as fully & amply as before until further order from Her Majesty her Heirs or Successors, or the Heirs of the said Proprietor & Governr in Chief wch shall first happen." And further That all Majistrates & Officers be required to discharge Their Duty with the same Vigour &c Application as formerly they were oblig'd to do: And the said Motion being unanimously approv'd & agreed unto by the Board, the Governour order'd such a Proclamation to be forthwith prepared and issued accordingly.[6]

DS. Penn Papers, Granville Penn Book, HSP. (*Micro.* 14:611.) Docketed: The Councill's | Proceedings on the | death of Wm Penn | 3d Novr 1718. | Publick Transactions | since 30th July 1718. The Council minute appears in *Minutes of the Provincial Council,* 3:58-59.

1. For the names of the other mortgagees, see doc. 211F-H.

2. William Keith (1680-1749) had been commissioned governor of Pennsylvania in Nov. 1716. The son of a Scottish baronet, he succeeded to the baronetcy in 1720. WP had probably met him in 1703, after Keith's return from France and before his implication in a Jacobite plot which resulted in his imprisonment in 1704. In 1714 he went to the colonies as surveyor general of customs, replacing Robert Quary. Keith was warmly received in Pennsylvania by the many provincial leaders disaffected with the government of Charles Gookin. Having obtained the governorship, he managed the colony from May 1717 until his dismissal in 1726, after which he served briefly in the Pennsylvania Assembly and then returned to England, where he published tracts on colonial affairs but was imprisoned for debt and died impoverished. *PMHB,* 12:1-33, 92:289-305; Raimo, *Governors,* pp. 329-30.

3. WP had personally known all these Council members, with the possible exception of Capt. Anthony Palmer, who moved from Barbados to Pennsylvania after WP's last visit to his colony. See docs. 129, n. 4; 160.

4. Hannah Penn had written Keith on 8 Aug. 1718 to inform him of WP's death. Penn Papers, Penn-Forbes Manuscripts, 1:80, HSP.

5. *Statutes,* pp. 436-38.

6. A copy of the proclamation is found in the Penn Papers, Granville Penn Book, p. 20, HSP.

207
HANNAH PENN TO WILLIAM PENN, JR.

Ruscomb. the 13th of 11th mo [January], 1718[/19]

Sonn Penn

When I last parted from thee twas in hope that thou would, as thou then sayd, be best pleasd, to have all our Matters Setled in a friendly, way, & to which I agreed as Choosing to have it so. But thy Mind soon alterd, & in thy first letter[1] I had threats insteed of friendship, and a stop to my Incombe,[2] before I had receaved even Enough to pay for thy poor Fathers funerall. a very aggravateing {Circumstance} after the Regards I had shown, in a Constant Expence on thy family,[3] & was a Sufficient Motive to make me Look out for my own safety in time to Come, & to seek reliefe from Chancery, if not Else to be had, but as I olnly flyed or desire to fly to it, ~~for~~ Only for my own & Childrens safty, So Left the Matter with John Page to treat with thee upon, Who wrot me word he had Left the writings in thy Lawyer's hands;[4] since which I have heard Little from him, but that the Matters goes on in Chancery, which as far as my safe'ty requires, I must asent to {& shall pursue} but have no desire of giving thee unnessessary trouble, nor, Increasing unnessesary Charge, and therefore if thou art of the same mind {as H G[5] gives me to Expect} I would have no~~t~~ longer time delayd, But on thy apoynting 2 proper persons, I will also Write to my Uncle Clement & Jno Page to meet ~~go~~ them; & there to setle all our differences that may be Ended without Chancery,[6] & to go {on} in that in a way of friendship, of which I desire thy answer ~~a~~by the next post, and am.

Thy Lo: Mother
H. Penn

ALS. Penn Papers, Granville Penn Book, HSP. (Not filmed.) Addressed: For | William Penn Esquire: These. Docketed: To Wm Penn | 13th Jan^ry^ 1718.

1. No letters have been found from William Penn, Jr., to Hannah Penn.

2. William Penn, Jr., challenged WP's will, which named Hannah Penn sole executrix, and especially the second codicil, which provided an annual income of £300 to the widow. The codicil had not been witnessed, but on 3 Nov. 1718 when it was probated, Simon Clement and John Page testified that it was written in WP's hand. Rawle-Cadwalader-Tate Collection, HSP; doc. 193.

3. Hannah Penn had provided money to Mary Penn and her children, who were evidently abandoned by William Penn, Jr., and without any means of support. Her cashbook records a total of almost £300 paid out from 1713 to 1718 for rent, clothing, food, and schooling for Mary's children. Hannah Penn Cashbook, HSP; see also doc. 202, n. 6.

4. Probably Grimble Pauncefort. See John Page's letter to him of 6 Aug. 1719, Penn Papers, Penn-Forbes Manuscripts, 1:73, HSP.

5. Henry Gouldney.

6. The case continued in Chancery and later in the Court of the Exchequer; it was concluded in favor of Hannah Penn and her children on 13 Dec. 1726. Drinker, *Hannah Penn,* p. 185.

208

READING QUARTERLY MEETING TO LONDON YEARLY MEETING

[c. 21 April 1719]

From the Quarterly Meeting held at Reading for the service of truth the 20th & 21st of the 2^d^ month 1719 to the yearely Meeting Ensuing

Dear Friends

After the Salutation of our Unfeigned love to you in the blessed & Unchangeable truth

These are to acquaint you that at this our meeting the Several meetings contain'd in this County were call'd over & Enquiry made into the state & Condition of friends therein Respecting their faithfulness to God & to the testimony of his truth: wch doth appear to us as followeth That Notwithstanding in some part of the County there are weights

& burdens to the exercise of the faithful, among them on whose spirits we find a travail in faith & patience for the Removal thereof to the releif of our spirits respecting the same Yet in other parts thereof Truth prospers & friends are generally in unity.

The Several Advices of the yearly meeting have been read & in good measure put in practice.

One Publick Friend deceas'd vizt: our worthy & honourable Elder William Penn of whom we have herewith sent our Testimony & in the remembrance of the precious Seasons that many of us have had wth him a supplication remains on our spirits to the great & merciful God that he would be pleas'd to fill up the rooms of such faithful Elders & Ministers to his own Glory & the Churches Edification

Our Friend William Penn departed this Life at his House at Ruscomb in the County of Berkshire the 30th of the 5th month 1718. & his Body was Convey'd thence the 7th of the 6th month following to Friends burying-ground at Jordans[1] in the County of Buckinghamshire where he was honourably interr'd being Accompanied by many friends; & others from divers parts & being a member from our monthly meeting at Reading at the time of his decease & some years before we can do no less but in giving the foregoing Acco^t say something respecting the Character of so worthy a man & not only refer to other Meetings where his residence was in former time who are Witnesses of the great Selfdenial he underwent in the Prime of his Youth & the patience wth wch he bore many a heavy Cross but Also think it our duty to cast in our mite to set forth in part his deserved Commendation.

He was a Man of great Abilities; of an Excellent sweetness of Disposition, quick of Thought, & ready utterance: full of the Quallification of true Discipleship, even Low without dissimulation as Extensive in Charity as Comprehensive in Knowledge & to whom Malice & Ingratitude were utter Strangers so ready to forgive Enemies that the Ungrateful were not excepted.

Had not the Management of his Temporal Affairs been Attended wth some deficiencies envy itself would be to seek for matter of Accusation & yet in Charity even that part of his Conduct may be Ascribed to a Peculiar Sublimity of mind.

Notwithstanding wch he may without straining his Character be ranked among the Learned good & great whose abilities are Sufficiently manifested throughout the Elaborate writings wch are so many lasting monuments of his admired Quallifications & are the Esteem of Learned & Judicious men Among all Perswasions.

And tho': in Old Age by reason of some shocks of a violent distemper his Intellects were much Impair'd yet his sweetness & loving disposition surmounted it's utmost efforts & remained when Reason almost fail'd.

In fine he was Learned without Vanity Apt without forwardness facetious in Conversation yet weighty & serious of an Extraordinary greatness of mind yet void of the Stain of Ambition as free from rigid gravity as he was Clear of unseemly levity.

A MAN, A SCHOLAR, A FRIEND; A MINISTER.

Surpassing in Superlative Endowments whose memorial will be val-ue'd by the wise & blessed wth the Just.

Signed on behalf & by the Appointment of the monthly meeting held at Reading aforsaid the 31st of the 1st month 1719

Wm Lamboll Junr [2]

The foregoing testimony being presented to us at our Quly Meeting held at Reading the 20th & 21st of the 2nd month 1719 was there Read & weightily Consider'd of & in respect of the Unfeigned Love we bore to so Eminent a Friend Could do no less then agree & Joyn wth our aforesaid friends therein.

Sign'd on behalf & by Appointment of the
Abovesaid Quly meeting by

John Buy[3]

Sent the aforesaid accots to the yearely Meeting 1719 by Wm Lamboll Junr One of our representatives Chosen to attend the same the other are Wm Millis Senr Edward May & Jno Fellers.[4]

Copy. Gratz Collection, Governors of Pennsylvania, HSP. (*Micro.* 14:631.)

1. WP's burial, which actually occurred on 5 Aug. 1718, was attended by "twenty or thirty publick Friends and a vast number of Friends and others," according to Rebekah Butterfield's journal. His first wife, Gulielma Maria, and their eldest son, Springett, as well as five of his other children who died as infants, had been buried at Jordans Burial Ground next to the meetinghouse in Jordans, Bucks. Hannah Penn and most of the rest of WP's immediate family were later interred there. *Journal of the Life of Thomas Story* (Newcastle upon Tyne, 1747), p. 607; *PMHB*, 74:100-112; 76:326-29; Jenkins, pp. 75, 85-86, 237, and illustration opposite p. 66. For one of Edward Hicks's paintings of the burial ground, see the frontispiece to this volume.

2. William Lamboll, Jr. (1686-1722), of Reading, Berks., was the third son of longtime Quaker and friend of WP, William Lamboll, Sr. Digests of Quaker Records, Berks. and Oxon., GSP.

3. John Buy, a Reading maltster originally from Tadley, Hants., married Ann Austell in 1674. Ibid.

4. William Millis, Sr., was from Reading; Edward May was from Thatcham, Berks.; and John Fellows was a maltster of Maidenhead, Berks., formerly of Wood-burn, Bucks. Digests of Quaker Records, Berks. and Oxon.; Bucks.

APPENDIX

209
CALENDAR OF MARRIAGE SETTLEMENTS, 1699–1712

Two of WP's priorities are illustrated in the following abstracted documents. First, he was anxious to provide a jointure for the support of his wife, Hannah, after his death, and marriage settlements for his two oldest children, William Penn, Jr., and Laetitia. Second, he needed to raise substantial sums of money to pay off the Ford family and other creditors. WP's primary asset was land in Ireland, England, and America. These lands he could divide among his family and use as security for loans. William Penn, Jr., married in January 1699, and Laetitia married in August 1702. Shortly before both marriages, WP concluded formal agreements (docs. 209A–B) that provided money or lands for the two children and their spouses, Mary Jones and William Aubrey. A preliminary agreement for the marriage of William, Jr., and Mary Jones also provided that WP would receive £2000 from Mary's father and grandfather, although this seems to have been used to pay off WP's debt to them for that amount (*Micro.* 8:078). WP then obtained a loan from William Aubrey of £2500 (doc. 209G), while William, Jr., borrowed £500 from the same source. The interest rate on the £3000 was 6 percent, which WP assumed for himself and his son. These arrangements caused manifold problems. William, Jr., was unhappy with his legacy, which prompted another agreement (doc. 209F), whereby Hannah Penn surrendered lands previously granted to her by WP as jointure in return for an equivalent in lands previously granted to William, Jr. WP felt forced to conciliate William, Jr., because he needed to use his son's lands in Ireland as security for the debt to Aubrey. WP had also agreed to the sale of Laetitia's lands in Pennsylvania, which he hoped would raise £2000 to be then used to purchase property for Laetitia and Aubrey in England, and was obliged until the Pennsylvania lands were sold to pay the Aubreys £120 per annum—an obligation that he had great difficulty in meeting. Perhaps because of WP's proclivity toward indebtedness, William, Jr., apparently demanded reassurance that the £2500 debt would be paid, and that his Irish lands which secured Aubrey's loan would be indemnified. WP therefore granted Pennsbury in trust to his son, along with over 40,000 other acres of land in Pennsylvania, and promised to pay Aubrey back. Unfortunately, the Aubrey loan and marriage agreement would prove to be a long-standing source of extreme annoyance to WP; his widow, Hannah; and their American agent, James Logan.

In the extracts printed below, proper names of witnesses are spelled as they are in the original documents.

A
Articles of Agreement

Source: Penn Manuscripts, FLL. (Not filmed.)
Date: 10 January 1699.
Parties: (1) WP and Laetitia Penn; (2) William Penn, Jr., and Mary Jones; (3) Charles Jones, the younger; (4) Nathaniel Wade, Charles Harford, Herbert Springett, Ambrose Galloway, and Joseph Pike.
Summary: I. Notes the forthcoming marriage of William Penn, Jr., and Mary Jones, and a tripartite agreement of 29 Oct. 1698 between (1) WP; (2) William Penn, Jr., and Mary Jones; (3) Charles Jones, the younger, whereby WP was to receive £1500 from Charles Jones, the younger, father of Mary Jones, and £500 from Charles Jones, the elder; and, whereby, if the marriage of William Penn, Jr., and Mary Jones were consummated within two months, William Penn, Jr., was to convey to four trustees lands valued at £300 to his use for life and then to Mary Jones and their children.

II. Now, however, because William Penn, Jr., is not yet 21, and because WP is concerned about a provision for Laetitia Penn, a new agreement provides that, if the marriage is consummated and when William Penn, Jr., reaches 21, WP is to convey:

A. The manor of Wicksham, parish of Ickelsham, Sus., with other enumerated lands in that parish (Thomas Reynolds, tenant), along with other lands situated there formerly belonging to Sir William Springett, deceased; one-half the manor of Kingston Dowry alias Kingston Bowsey, Sus., along with other enumerated lands in Kingston Bowsey, Southwick, and Shoreham, Sus.; all freehold lands in Shurlocks, Stocketts alias Stockard, and Leagues, Sus.; Rock Farm, in the parishes of Wicksham and Ratherford, Sus. (John Fraser, tenant).

B. The following lands in Imokilly, co. Cork: Killgillhen, Knocknegeiragh, and Knocknegappule (Francis Smith, Jr., tenant), Ballyhonick and Ballyline (Katherine Dawkins, tenant); Garrymore

(John Bredsford, tenant); Curroghticloghy, Ballycarrowny, Condon's acres, and Acredoan (Capt. John Wakeham, tenant).

C. The following lands in Ibaune and Barryroe, co. Cork: the south half ploughland of Carhow ([blank] Crook, tenant), Greaghbeg (David Jerman, tenant), Geiragh, Cnockelloage, and Dyrrinreene (Timothy Danavan, tenant).

III. All the English lands, except those of Thomas Reynolds and those in parish of Ickelsham; and all the Irish lands held by Francis Smith, John Bredsford, and John Wakeham, are to be held in trust by Nathaniel Wade and Charles Harford for the use of William Penn, Jr., for life, and then to pass to Mary Jones and her heirs by William, Jr., but if heirs are lacking, then the Sussex lands are for the heirs of the late Gulielma Penn, with the Irish lands going to WP.

IV. The residue of the above-mentioned lands are for WP and after his decease are to be put in trust to Herbert Springett, Ambrose Galloway, and Joseph Pike for 500 years to the uses as outlined in two agreements: 10 Jan. 1672 (see *PWP,* 1:646) between (1) Gulielma Maria Springett, (2) WP, (3) Richard Langhorne and Thomas Ellwood, (4) Henry Oxinden, James Masters, and Benjamin Worsden; and 10 Feb. 1672 between (1) WP, (2) Dame Margaret Penn and Richard Penn, (3) Gulielma Maria Springett, (4) William Holcroft, Daniel Whistler, Anthony Lower, and Sir Henry Oxindon; James Masters and Benjamin Worsley; (5) David Solome and John Reeves.

V. The rents next due are to be divided equally between WP and William Penn, Jr.

VI. On the death of WP, the trustees—Springett, Galloway, and Pike—are to raise £3000 to be paid to Laetitia Penn from the lands held by them in trust.

Witnesses: None given.

B
Articles of Agreement

Source: Wynne Papers, DD/WY/836, Bedfordshire Record Office, Bedford, England. (*Micro. 10:407.*)

Date: 6 August 1702.

Parties: (1) WP; (2) William Aubrey.

Summary: I. Notes that on 21–22 October 1681 WP granted 5000 acres in Pennsylvania, along with city lots and liberty lands, to Laetitia Penn.

II. WP now agrees with Laetitia's future husband, William Aubrey, to sell those lands and to post bond in a penal sum of £2000 to pay Aubrey £120 annually at the court house in Philadelphia until the lands are sold by trustees, but if the money raised from the sale is less than £2000 sterling, WP agrees to make up the difference. (On 19 August 1702 WP agreed that the £120 was to be paid in equal annual installments on 20 February and 20 August, and to make up the sale difference to £2000 within 20 days. See *Micro.* 10:455.)

III. Aubrey agrees to loan WP £3000 sterling for one year at 6 percent interest before marrying Laetitia, with WP agreeing, in return, to mortgage certain of his Irish lands (unnamed), valued at approximately £5000, as security. At the time of the marriage, Aubrey was then to assign the Irish mortgage and bond to trustees, along with sufficient securities, to raise an additional £3000. All of this income (£8000) was ultimately to be used to purchase unspecified English lands for Laetitia and William Aubrey.

IV. Aubrey agrees to convey the 5000 acres and associated lands to trustees for disposal. (On 18 August 1702 Aubrey agreed to post bond in a penal sum of £12,000 to convey the lands to Daniel Wharley, Samuel Waldenfield, and Henry Gouldney, and on that same date WP agreed with these future trustees that he would make up the difference between the sale price and £2000. These are mentioned in doc. 209E. On 3–4 May 1703 the Aubreys finally conveyed the lands in question to Wharley, Gouldney, and Waldenfield. See *Micro.* 10:913; doc. 209E.)

V. If the marriage, however, does not occur by 25 Dec. 1702, the agreement is void.

Witnesses: H. Springett, Wm. Martin.

C
Lease

Source: Dreer Collection, HSP. (*Micro.* 10:910.)
Date: 3 May 1703.
Parties: (1) WP; (2) Daniel Wharley and Henry Gouldney.
Summary: WP leases Pennsbury, with all its lands (4000 acres), rights, and profits for one year at 5s to Wharley and Gouldney.
Witnesses: John Meredith, Richd Jones, Peter Rive.

D
Release

Source: Mentioned in doc. 209I.
Date: 4 May 1703.
Parties: (1) WP; (2) William Penn, Jr.; (3) Daniel Wharley and Henry Gouldney.
Summary: WP now conveys Pennsbury for 99 years to Wharley and Gouldney to the use of WP for life, and after his death, to the use of William Penn, Jr.

E
Articles of Agreement

Source: Dreer Collection, HSP. (*Micro.* 10:918.)
Date: 4 May 1703.
Parties: (1) WP; (2) Samuel Waldenfield; Daniel Wharley; Henry Gouldney; (3) William and Laetitia Penn Aubrey.
Summary: I. All parties now agree that they have set up a trust to sell Laetitia Penn Aubrey's Pennsylvania lands (see doc. 209B) for the best possible price, with the proceeds to be used to purchase English land for the Aubreys for their use for life, and then to their heirs, but if they have no heirs, then to those of William Aubrey.

II. WP will pay for both the cost of transferring money from Pennsylvania to England and the differences in the exchange rate. All payments are to be made by bills of exchange to the trustees (Wharley, Waldenfield, and Gouldney) by the attorney or attorneys they appoint to sell the land. The proceeds are to be loaned at interest to either the Old or New East India companies (or another security of the Aubreys' choice) until the money is used for land purchases. The trustees are to be reimbursed for expenses out of rents and profits of the land and from the sale money.
Witnesses: Harb[t] Springett, John Page.

F
Indenture of Release

Source: Penn-Gaskell-Skillern Papers, HSP. (Not filmed.)
Date: 4 May 1703.
Parties: (1) William Penn, Jr., and Mary Jones Penn; (2) WP and Hannah Penn; (3) William Aubrey and Laetitia Penn Aubrey; (4) Herbert Springett; (5) Nathaniel Wade, esq., and Charles Harford the younger, mercer, both of Bristol; and Michael Jones and Samuel Vaus, London merchants; (6) Daniel Phillips, doctor, and Anthony Neate, haberdasher, both of London, and Margaret Lowther, widow of Anthony Lowther.
Summary: I. William Penn, Jr., unhappy over his marriage settlement (see doc. 209A) agrees with Hannah Penn, who has lands in Ibaune and Barryroe, co. Cork, to accept her lands in return for an equivalent amount of land from him.

II. Thus William Penn, Jr., for 5s from WP, and in order to settle jointures on Hannah Penn and Mary Jones Penn, grants to WP lands he has leased to him on 3 May 1703 (not found), in or near barony of Imokilly, co. Cork, Munster, Ire., as follows: Shannagarry, Kilmaghen, Killkeagh, Ballynamony, Ballygannybegg, Ballingogannigg, Ballingarrane, Ballylongan, Ballingarrane, Ruskemore, Ruskaghbegg, Ballylinnanee, and Ballymallobegg (Robert Foulke, tenant); Barries quarter, Ballelowrace, and Ballyroe (Samuel Rowle, tenant); Killgillhen, Knocknegeiragh, and Knocknegappule (Francis Smith, tenant); Inch, Doonepower, and Ballynatra (John Bowles, tenant, deceased); Lisshally, Ballinicoll, Ballyshane, Mucky, and Tullyplenebegg (Thomas Wallis, tenant); Lisally (Thomas Bent, tenant); Kilbrie, Sheanless, Carrigtoghir, Teadbegg, Ballyvillin, and Ballinevohir (John Bowles, tenant, deceased); Ballyronahane, Ballybraher, Coolenodigg, Garrigkilter, and Rathcully (Barry Frankland, tenant); Ballyhonick, and Ballyline (Katherine Dawkins, tenant); Garrymoore (John Bredsford, tenant); Old Meupre [Clonemane?] (Robert Fitzgerald, tenant); Kilderrig (James French, tenant); Curroghticloghy, Ballycarrowny, Condon's acres, and Acredoan (William Wakeham, tenant); Fenore and Knocknagihy (William Wakeham, tenant); Ballyvillin and Seskens Fowrie (William Wakeham, tenant); and lands in tenure of William Penn, Jr., or where he or any other persons in trust for him have any estate within Imokilly, along with houses, stables, mines, quarries, etc.

III. All the lands mentioned of John Bowles, Thomas Wallis, Barry Frankland, Catherine Dawkins, and James French are to be conveyed to Wade, Harford, Jones, and Vaus in trust for WP and after his death to Hannah Penn.

IV. All the lands of Francis Smith and John Bresford, along with some of William Wakeman's lands (Curroghticloghy, Ballycarrowny, Condon's acres, and Acredoan) are to be conveyed to Wade, Harford, Jones, and Vaus in trust for William Penn, Jr., and after his death to Mary Penn, which lands are for her jointure, along with certain lands in Sussex limited to her life by a seven-part indenture of 4 May 1703 (not found) between (1) William Penn, Jr., and Mary Penn; (2) WP and Hannah Penn; (3) William and Laetitia Aubrey; (4) John Page; (5) Nathaniel Wade, Charles Harford, Michael Jones, and Samuel Vaus; (6) Daniel Wharley, Samuel Waldenfield, and Henry Gouldney; (7) Daniel Phillips, Anthony Neate, and Sir Robert Fagg, bart., for the jointure of Mary Jones Penn.

V. The remainder of the above-listed lands are conveyed to Wade, Harford, Jones, and Vaus in trust for WP and after his death for William Penn, Jr., and after his death to Hannah Penn, and after her death to Mary Jones Penn, and after her death to the male heirs of her marriage to William Penn, Jr. If they have no male heirs, then the lands will revert to the use of WP's male heirs.

VI. The lands limited as jointure to Mary Jones Penn are to go after the deaths of her and William Penn, Jr., to their female heirs; if none, then to the heirs of William Penn, Jr.

VII. There are also provisoes for raising money from lands in Ibaune and Barryroe for the children of William Penn, Jr.

VIII. If Hannah Penn survives WP, the lands given her in jointure should not exceed yearly value of £300. If they do, the overplus is to go to the person or persons who have the right to the remainder of her lands at her death.

IX. The quitrents owed to the crown on the jointures of Mary and Hannah are to come from other lands.

X. William Penn, Jr., after Mary Jones Penn's death, can provide lands to the yearly value of £300 in trust to any future wife, out of lands given to Hannah Penn for her jointure.

XI. WP has paid William Aubrey £2000 as a marriage portion for Laetitia. (Actually WP has merely agreed that Laetitia's Pennsylvania lands be sold and he would make up the difference if the sale price did not reach £2000; see doc. 209B). This effectively replaces the proviso in doc. 209A whereby Herbert Springett, Ambrose Galloway, and Joseph Pike were to raise £3000 for Laetitia Penn as trustees for certain Irish lands. This indenture therefore witnesses that the Aubreys release Springett, Galloway, and Pike from having to raise the £3000.

Witnesses: Richard Jones, Peter Rice, John Page.

G
Indenture of Release

Source: Cadwalader Collection, HSP. (*Micro.* 10:925.)
Date: 4 May 1703.
Parties: (1) WP; (2) William Penn, Jr.
Summary: I. William Aubrey has loaned £2500 to WP and £500 to William Penn, Jr. In return, William Penn, Jr., who has an estate in tail after WP's death in lands in Ibaune and Barryroe, co. Cork, agrees that these lands be mortgaged to Aubrey for 400 years as security for the £3000 and 6 percent interest.

II. This previous proviso is voided, however, if WP and William Penn, Jr., pay Aubrey £3180 within one year (£2650 from WP, and £530 from William Penn, Jr.).

III. WP agrees to demise Pennsbury to William Penn, Jr., as security that he will pay his £2500 and interest debt to Aubrey.

IV. WP has previously conveyed Pennsbury for 99 years to Daniel Wharley and Henry Gouldney, to his use for life, and after his death, to the use of William Penn, Jr. (see docs. 209C-D).

V. This indenture now witnesses that, in return for his son's consent to use the Irish lands as security, thus enabling him to receive the £2500, and also to indemnify those Irish lands if he defaults, WP for 5s from his son grants Pennsbury to him for 99 years. WP also releases to him all quitrents, rents, services, and arrears due from Bucks, Chester, and Phila. Cos., but not the quitrents and rents from the Lower Counties.

VI. William Penn, Jr., will also receive for 1000 years 5000 acres in Rocklands Manor, preferably near Brandy Creek in New-castle Co., 5000 acres in Fryth Manor (Kent Co.), and 30,000 acres lying between the Delaware and Susquehanna rivers, as well as all city lots, town lots, and liberty lands.

VII. These terms between WP and his son are all invalidated if WP pays £2650 to William Aubrey at Lincoln's Inn (£75 on 5 November 1703 and £2575 on 5 May 1704) along with the costs incurred by William Penn, Jr., for setting out and surveying the said lands.

VIII. WP promises to pay Aubrey £2650 and to pay William Penn, Jr., the above-mentioned costs and charges, and he also claims full authority to make these grants (despite the Ford mortgages; see headnote to doc. 108).

IX. William Penn, Jr., can take full possession of the land if WP defaults, but until that time WP can occupy and possess the said premisses without interference from his son.
Witnesses: John Meredith, Rich[d] Jones, Peter Rice.

H
Lease

Source: Penn-Forbes Collection, HSP. (*Micro.* 10:1048.)
Date: 16 July 1703.
Parties: (1) WP and William Penn, Jr.; (2) Daniel Phillips, of London, doctor, and Anthony Neate, London, haberdasher.
Summary: I. For 5s WP and William Penn, Jr., lease Pennsbury to Philipps and Neate for 500 years in trust (along with the quitrents of Phila., Bucks, and Chester Cos. and other lands conveyed to William Penn, Jr., for 1000 years) as collateral security for payment of £2500 with interest to William Aubrey, for which William Penn, Jr., has mortgaged lands in Ibaune and Barryroe and for indemnifying the lands in Ireland against the sum of £2500 plus interest. (This presumably augments the previous trust of Daniel Wharley and Henry Gouldney, which remained in force; see doc. 209J).

II. After the £2500 is paid, the trustees can raise money on the estate to pay off WP's debts when he dies. After these debts have been paid, Phillips and Neate will hold the land in trust to wait upon reversion and inheritance. But WP and William Penn, Jr., reserve the right to make any different arrangement that suits them.
Witnesses: Harb[t] Springett, John Page.

I
Power of Attorney

Source: Logan Papers, Provincial Council, HSP. (*Micro.* 11:075.)
Date: 24 September 1703.
Parties: (1) Daniel Wharley, Samuel Waldenfield, and Henry Gouldney; (2) Samuel Carpenter and James Logan.
Summary: Wharley, Waldenfield, and Gouldney appoint James Logan and Samuel Carpenter as their attorneys to sell Laetitia Penn's land in Pennsylvania (see doc. 209B) and return money to England by bills of exchange.
Witnesses: Harb[t] Springett, John Page, and WP.
Endorsement: Enrolled at enrollment office in Phila. on 8 Jan. 1706 by Tho. Story, recorder.

J
Release

Source: Wynne Papers, WY 838, Bedfordshire Record Office, Bedford, England. (*Micro.* 13:314.)
Date: 21 October 1707.
Parties: (1) WP; (2) William Penn, Jr.
Summary: I. WP and William Penn, Jr., have this day settled accounts with each other (probably in connection to the sale of Warminghurst; see doc. 210). WP has secured £120 to William Aubrey for four years of interest payable on £500, which Aubrey had loaned to William Penn, Jr., at 6 percent interest, and which was due on 4 May 1707.

II. WP releases all claims or disputes with William Penn, Jr., except those remaining from the 1000-year lease to William Penn, Jr., of 4 May 1703 (see doc. 209G), the lease of 3–4 May 1703 between himself, William Penn, Jr., Daniel Wharley, and Henry Gouldney for Pennsbury (see docs. 209C-D), and the 500-year lease of 16 July 1703 to Daniel Phillips and Anthony Neate (doc. 209H).
Witnesses: Robt West, H. Springett, John Page, Joseph Davis.

K
Release

Source: Endorsement to doc. 209G.
Date: 3 August 1711.
Parties: (1) William Penn, Jr.; (2) WP.
Summary: I. William Penn, Jr., notes that the £2500 debt to William Aubrey, secured by estates in Ibaune and Barryroe, has been paid and cleared off by sale of those estates by himself and WP.

II. William Penn, Jr., desires therefore that the said security and all other securities from WP touching that debt be discharged.
Witness: John Page.

L
Release

Source: Endorsement to doc. 209G.
Date: 14 July 1712.
Parties: (1) William Penn, Jr.; (2) WP.
Summary: William Penn, Jr., citing the payment of £2500, has by the consent and direction of WP, released all lands securing that sum and also releases to WP the terms of 99 and 1000 years relating to Pennsbury and specified lands in Pennsylvania and the Lower Counties (see doc. 209G).
Witnesses: Jo[n] Page, Tho Pyle, Alpsley Newton.

M
Release

Source: Endorsement to doc. 209G.
Date: 14 July 1712.
Parties: (1) William Penn, Jr.; (2) WP; (3) Richard Rooth.
Summary: I. Cites the payment of £2500 to William Aubrey.
II. William Penn, Jr., now directs Rooth to release to WP the 1000-year term relating to the province of Pennsylvania, New Castle, and the Lower Counties (see doc. 211I).
III. Rooth, by virtue of executing this document, has executed the said release.
Witnesses: John Page, Apsley Newton.

210
THE SALE OF WARMINGHURST, 1707

In June 1676 WP and Gulielma Penn purchased Warminghurst Place, in Sussex, about three hundred acres, with a large three-story building, for £4500 (see *PWP,* 1:366, 646). It was WP's primary residence from September 1676 until his second voyage to Pennsylvania in 1699. Thereafter, his eldest son, William, Jr., and his wife, Mary Jones Penn, became the resident tenants. WP had described the house as "ugly," but with "room enough for 12 or twenty People more than our . . . family" (see *PWP,* 3:432). Aesthetics aside, Warminghurst had proved to be a costly venture. WP had negotiated a loan of £4700 from Sir James Rushout and William Jarrett to help pay for this house; by 1692 WP's debt to Rushout had increased to £6231, leading to a new mortgage which seriously tied up WP's Sussex lands (see *PWP,* 1:647). As the following document abstracts indicate, in 1707 the debt involving the Warminghurst property still totalled at least £5962. On 10 June 1707 WP wrote James Logan (doc. 139) that William, Jr., had "at last resignd for sale" Warminghurst, apparently overcoming stubborn opposition from his wife who, WP added, "could have no pretence, either by family or portion." The purchaser, Sir James Butler, a member of Parliament, agreed to pay £6053 for the land and £334 for livestock, equipment, and hay (see doc. 145). Although virtually all of the money received went to pay off some of WP's debt, he was happy with the sale. "I gave 4500^l for it," he wrote to James Logan, "& sould it for 6050^l after I had cutt down 2000^l of Timber" (doc. 148). The following documents, in conjunction with doc. 145, represent the only agreements found concerning the sale. It is not known if the draft agreement between WP and his son (210A) was ever completed. In any event, the sale of Warminghurst was a significant step by WP toward retirement of his burdensome debts.

A
Draft of Agreement to Sell Warminghurst

Source: Miscellaneous Manuscripts of William Penn, HSP. (Not filmed.)
Date: c. 22 November 1707.
Parties: (1) WP; (2) William Penn, Jr.
Summary: I. WP and William Penn, Jr., will sell Warminghurst, with all money from the sale to be applied to payment of the debt now owing thereupon and upon Fryth, in Kent, and Bridges, in Sussex.

II. For better securing Fryth and Bridges against the Ford family (see headnote to doc. 108), they are now made a collateral security for WP's debt of £2500 owed to William Penn, Jr. (actually to William Aubrey; see docs. 209G-H).

III. Lands now in possession of Daniel Sevell (probably Coolcoors, co. Meath, Ire., which had been leased in 1704 for 21 years by George Sevell, of Dublin, from Thomas Cuppage, WP's agent in Ireland; see *Micro.* 11:428) shall be sold, and in order thereto WP is to convey his estate for life to his son. It is then to be valued by Thomas Cuppage, and William Penn, Jr., is to allow that value out of the £2500 taken up on the lands in Ireland (see doc. 209G).

IV. The settlement made on William Penn, Jr., and his wife should have been £170 per annum over and above the quitrents, but in actuality, it fell short by about £60 per annum. The difference is to be made good out of the Irish estate mortgaged to William Aubrey for his loan of £2500 to WP and £500 to William Penn, Jr. (see doc. 209G).

V. WP will also order his steward to pay £200 out of the rents of the land mortgaged to Aubrey to Thomas Cuppage for paying the interest on the £3000 owed to William Aubrey.
Witnesses: None given.

B
Indenture of Release

Source: Penn Papers, HSP. (*Micro.* 13:321.)
Date: 22 November 1707.
Parties: (1) WP; (2) Thomas Bedford, of Middle Temple, and his wife, Abigail; William Calderott, of London, gentleman, and his wife, Mary; Anne Cullen, of Horton, Bucks., spinster; (3) Edmund Poley, of Lincoln's Inn, esq., brother and heir of Henry Poley, late of Lincoln's Inn, esq., deceased, and sole executor of Henry Poley's will; (4) Elizabeth Dickson, of St. Andrew Holborn, Middx., spinster; (5) James Butler, of Michaelgrove, Sus., esq., and Henry Penrice of Doctor's Commons, London.
Summary: I. James Butler has contracted with WP for purchase of Warminghurst for £6053 15s.

II. Thomas and Abigail Bedford (£1000), William and Mary Calderott (£1200), Anne Cullen (£1200), Edmund Poley (£1200), and Elizabeth Dickson (£1200) all had claims on Warminghurst. Those claims had now been satisfied by James Butler, including an additional £162 for interest, out of the sale price of the property. In consideration of these payments, and that of the residue of £91 15s to WP, all parties acquit James Butler from any further claim on the property.

III. The sum of £6053 15s is the same as in the indentures of sale of 22 November 1707 between WP and James Butler.

IV. Also in consideration of 10s to the parties by Henry Penrice, they confirm, at WP's request, James Butler and Charles Penrice in possession by force of an indenture of 21 November 1707 for one year commencing on 20 November 1707.

V. This includes the advowson of the parish church of Warminghurst.

VI. In all 166 acres are to go to James Butler and Charles Penrice in trust for Butler, along with certain enumerated meadows from Thomas and Abigail Bedford, William and Mary Calderott, Anne Cullen, Edmund Poley, Elizabeth Dickson, and WP with the appurtenances formerly in lands and hereditaments of Henry Bigland, of Gray's Inn.
Witnesses: Robt Sherard, Peniston Lamb, John Page, William Hall.

C

Covenant of Indemnity

Source: Penn Papers, Leases/Mortgages, HSP. (*Micro.* 13:324.)
Date: 22 November 1707.
Parties: (1) WP and Herbert Springett; (2) James Butler and Henry Penrice.
Summary: I. Recites lease and release of 21–22 November 1707 and release of WP and others to Warminghurst.

II. Now WP and Herbert Springett agree to indemnify James Butler and Charles Penrice for one year against any suits relating to Warminghurst.
Witnesses: Robt West, Peniston Lamb.

D

Covenant of Indemnity

Source: Penn-Forbes Manuscripts, HSP. (*Micro.* 13:328.)
Date: 22 November 1707.
Parties: (1) WP; (2) Herbert Springett.
Summary: I. Recites covenant of 22 November 1707 with James Butler and Charles Penrice (see doc. 210C).

II. Now WP agrees to indemnify Herbert Springett for one year against any suits relating to Warminghurst.
Witnesses: Robert West, Peniston Lamb.

211
THE SETTLEMENT OF THE FORD CASE, 1708

The following documents represent both a victory and defeat for WP in his embarrassing lawsuit with the Ford family (see headnote to doc. 108). Although the Fords did not gain Pennsylvania, they did receive £7600, a substantial sum of money, which added to WP's legacy of indebtedness. The new landlords of Pennsylvania were nine trustees on behalf of themselves and twenty-nine others, who had loaned WP £6600. In effect, WP had merely substituted new creditors, and his right of proprietorship was still in jeopardy. Nonetheless, the trustees would now be Friends in good standing, including his father-in-law, Thomas Callowhill.

A

Release of Claims on Money Paid to Free Society of Traders

Source: Wynne Papers, DD/WY/778, Bedfordshire Record Office, Bedford, England. (*Micro.* 13:580.)
Date: 2 October 1708.

Parties: (1) WP, William Penn, Jr., and Thomas Callowhill (2) Bridget Ford, John Hall, Thomas Moss, Philip Ford, Jr., James and Bridget Ayrey, Anne Ford, and Susanna Ford.
Summary: I. Recites 1682 establishment of the Free Society of Traders and subscriptions paid by WP, William Penn, Jr., Thomas Callowhill, and others, and that officers were appointed, with Philip Ford to take subscriptions.

II. Now WP, William Penn, Jr., and Thomas Callowhill agree to release the Fords from any claim they would have made against them (to recover money from Ford for subscriptions made to the Free Society of Traders) in return for 5s each, although this is not to pertain to their rights in lands, tenements, or hereditaments of the Free Society in Pennsylvania or elsewhere.
Witnesses: Harb[t] Springett, John Page, J. Davis, John Round.

B
Lease of Pennsylvania by the Fords

Source: Cadwalader Collection, Thomas Cadwalader, HSP. (*Micro.* 13:583.)
Date: 4 October 1708.
Parties: (1) Bridget Ford, Thomas Moss, John Hall, and Philip Ford, Jr.; (2) WP.
Summary: WP will pay 10s to John Hall, Thomas Moss, and Philip Ford, Jr., in return for a one-year lease of 5000 acres in Philadelphia, with city lots and liberty lands, devised by Philip Ford to his son Philip Ford, Jr., and the rest of Pennsylvania, New Castle, and the Lower Counties to Cape Henlopen.
Witnesses: Harb[t] Springett, John Round, John Page, Joseph Davis.

C
Release of Pennsylvania by the Fords

Source: Cadwalader Collection, Thomas Cadwalader, HSP. (*Micro.* 13:585.)
Date: 5 October 1708.
Parties: (1) Bridget Ford, John Hall, Thomas Moss, Philip Ford, Jr., James and Bridget Ayrey, Ann Ford, Susannah Ford; (2) WP.
Summary: I. WP will pay Philip Ford, Jr., £1500, John Hall and Thomas Moss (for James and Bridget Ayrey) £1500, Anne Ford £1000, Susannah Ford £1000, and Bridget Ford £2600, a total of £7600, in return for Pennsylvania and an agreement to drop any pending suits.

II. WP to pay 10s for the release.

III. Endorsements acknowledge receipt of the above-mentioned sums.
Witnesses: John Round, Harb[t] Springett, John Page, Joseph Davis.

D

Release by John Hall and Thomas Moss

Source: Penn Papers, Ford vs. Penn, HSP. (*Micro.* 13:589.)
Date: 5 October 1708.
Parties: (1) John Hall and Thomas Moss; (2) WP.
Summary: I. Recites Philip Ford's will and legacies.

II. Acknowledges that the lands in question have been reconveyed to WP for £7600.

III. Because James Ayrey is bankrupt, John Hall and Thomas Moss (who received £1500 in the settlement for the Ayreys) agree to indemnify WP against further claims on their behalf.
Witnesses: John Round, Harb[t] Springett, John Page, Joseph Davis.

E

Release of Pennsylvania by Thomas Ellwood and Philip Ford

Source: Wynne Papers, DD/WY/779, Bedfordshire Record Office, Bedford, England. (*Micro.* 13:590.)
Date: 6 October 1708.
Parties: (1) Thomas Ellwood (2) Bridget Ford, Thomas Moss, John Hall, Philip Ford, Jr., James and Bridget Ayrey, Anne Ford, and Susannah Ford; (3) WP.
Summary: I. Recites the demise of 11 April 1687 where WP conveyed Pennsylvania to Philip Ford for 5000 years.

II. Notes that Ford then conveyed the land to Thomas Ellwood in 1690 in trust for Philip Ford for the rest of the term of 5000 years.

III. Recites Philip Ford's last will, in which he left Pennsylvania to his wife and, in trust, to John Hall and Thomas Moss for them to sell and pay specified legacies.

IV. Recites lease and release of 4–5 October 1708.

V. Now Thomas Ellwood reconveys Pennsylvania to WP for 10s.
Witnesses: Harb[t] Springett, John Page, Joseph Davis.

F

Lease of Pennsylvania to Silvanus Grove and Others

Source: Penn Papers, HSP. (*Micro.* 13:593.)
Date: 6 October 1708.
Parties: (1) WP and William Penn, Jr.; (2) Henry Gouldney, Joshua Gee, Silvanus Grove, John Woods, Thomas Callowhill, Thomas Oade, Jeffrey Pinnell, John Field, Thomas Cuppage.
Summary: I. Silvanus Grove and the others lease Pennsylvania, New Castle, and the Lower Counties for one year for 10s each to WP and William Penn, Jr.

II. The following lands are excluded from the agreement:
A. Pennsbury and 5000 acres, conveyed to WP by lease and release of 21 and 22 October 1681.
B. Lands conveyed on 11–12 August 1699 to Tobias Collett, William Russell, Daniel Quary, and Henry Gouldney (the London Company).
C. 5000 acres conveyed by William Penn, Jr., to Isaac Norris and William Trent.
D. Any other lands previously granted by WP for which quitrents, rents, etc. have been reserved.
Witnesses: James Thomas, Harb[t] Springett, John Page, Joseph Davis.

G
Release of Pennsylvania

Source: Cadwalader Collection, Thomas Cadwalader, HSP. (*Micro.* 13:598.)
Date: 7 October 1708.
Parties: (1) WP and William Penn, Jr.; (2) Henry Gouldney, Joshua Gee, Silvanus Grove, John Woods, Thomas Callowhill, Thomas Oade, Jeffrey Pinnell, John Field, Thomas Cuppage.
Summary: I. £6600 has been paid to WP for lands in Pennsylvania, New Castle, and the Lower Counties (actually has been loaned to WP to pay off the Fords), except the exclusions cited in doc. 210F.

II. The £6600 was paid as follows: £3100 from Henry Gouldney, Joshua Gee, Silvanus Grove, and John Woods; £1000 from Thomas Callowhill; £1500 from Thomas Callowhill, Thomas Oade, and Jeffrey Pinnell, and £1000 from John Field and Thomas Cuppage.

III. William Penn, Jr., will be given 10s.

IV. However, if WP pays £6600 and 6 percent annual interest on or before 8 October 1710, then the mortgage is voided.

V. If WP defaults, then the land will pass to the abovementioned trustees with the right to sell.

VI. Until that time, the trustees have power of attorney to keep all rents and bonds, bills, and securities for any money due to WP within the province, and to compound for any rent or debt.
Witnesses: James Thomas, Harb[t] Springett, John Page, Joseph Davis.

H
Declaration of Trust

Source: Wynne Papers, DD/WY/785, Bedfordshire Record Office, Bedford, England. (*Micro. 13:594.*)
Date: 7 October 1708.
Parties: (1) Henry Gouldney, Silvanus Grove, Joshua Gee, and John Woods on behalf of: Samuel Waldenfield, linendraper; John Freame, goldsmith; Thomas Cox, vintner; Joseph Grove, merchant; Nathan-

iel Markes, glover; Richard Baker, woollendraper; Simon and John Warner, merchants; John Padley and Richard Partridge, merchants; John Kent, merchant; John Sandow, merchant; Beatrice Fisher, widow; Thomas Barber, merchant; John Harman, haberdasher; Gilbert Moleson, silkman; Thomas Bond, merchant; Edward Doyly, linendraper; Edward Haistwell, merchant; Mary Russell, widow; Jonathan Scarth, merchant; James Taylor, linendraper; John Tanner, merchant; James Larkes, cornfactor; William Beech, vintner; John Hitchcock, merchant; Mary Mason, widow; Elizabeth Kay, widow; John Partridge, goldsmith; Henry Gouldney; Joshua Gee, Silvanus Grove, and John Woods, all of London.

Summary: I. Recites the lease and release of 6–7 October 1708 (docs. 211F-G).

II. Recites that each of the contributors (or pairs of contributors) gave £100 for a total of £3100.

III. Henry Gouldney, Silvanus Grove, Joshua Gee, and John Woods are to act as their trustees.

Witnesses: Harb[t] Springett, John Page, Joseph Davis.

I
Tripartite Indenture

Source: Wynne Papers, DD/WY/839, Bedfordshire Record Office, Bedford, England. (*Micro.* 13:601.)

Date: 8 October 1708.

Parties: (1) WP; (2) William Penn, Jr.; (3) Richard Rooth, of Epsom, Sur.

Summary: I. Recites the indenture of 4 May 1703 between WP and William Penn, Jr. (see doc. 209G).

II. Some of the Irish lands securing William Aubrey's loan of £2500 to WP, will now be demised to Rooth for a term of 1000 years subject to redemption on payment of the £2500 plus interest.

III. William Penn, Jr., has agreed to provide these Irish lands now conveyed to Richard Rooth on trust as security for the £6600 loaned to WP (the money he borrowed to redeem Pennsylvania; see doc. 211G), subject to equity of redemption after payment of £6600.

IV. Recites the lease and release of 6–7 October 1708 (docs. 211F-G).

V. WP, as security to William Penn, Jr., that he will pay £2500 for discharging the indemnity on the Irish estate mortgaged to William Aubrey, will for 5s from Richard Rooth convey Pennsylvania, New Castle, and the Lower Counties, with the exceptions already noted, in trust for William Penn, Jr., for 1000 years.

VI. If WP pays £2500 by 9 October 1711, the lease is void.

Witnesses: James Thomas, Harb[t] Springett, John Page, Joseph Davis.

CALENDAR OF MICROFILMED WP DOCUMENTS, 1701–1718

In the following list, figures in the first column give the reel and frame numbers of documents in the microfilm edition of The Papers of William Penn. Numbers in bold type identify documents printed in this volume.

9:005 To William and Claus Rittinghousen, [c. 1701]
9:007 To William Penn, Jr., 2 January 1701, **1**
9:015 From Edward Hunloke, [c. 1701]
9:017 *The Case of William Penn, Esq, as to the Proprietary Government of Pensilvania,* [1701]
9:019 To the Justices of New Castle, 8 January 1701
9:024 From William III, 19 January 1701
9:030 To Nathaniel Blakiston, 20 January 1701
9:034 From Andrew Hamilton, 23 January 1701
9:039 Petition from Philadelphia Citizens, February 1701, **2**
9:043 Warrant to Edward Penington to Resurvey the Welsh Tract, 4 February 1701
9:044 To John Nanfan, 12 February 1701
9:045 From Inhabitants of Chichester, [14 February 1701]
9:052 From Francis Daniel Pastorius, 17 February 1701, **3**
9:058 Marriage Certificate of Samuel Powell and Abigail Willcox, 19 February 1701
9:061 From Andrew Hamilton, 19 February 1701
9:064 From Francis Daniel Pastorius, 19 February 1701
9:068 Patent to Richard Pearce and Others, 24 February 1701
9:074 Abstract of Instructions to Thomas Fairman, 25 February 1701
9:078 From William Clark, 27 February 1701
9:082 From James Vernon, 4 March 1701
9:083 From Samuel Carpenter, 5 March 1701
9:086 To Nathaniel Blakiston, 6 March 1701
9:088 From Andrew Hamilton, 6 March 1701
9:091 To the Commissioners of the Customs, 6 March 1701, **4**
9:096 To the Board of Trade, 6 March 1701
9:105 Proclamation to Prorogue the Assembly, 6 March 1701
9:108 Warrant to Edward Penington to Survey Springtown Manor, 6 March 1701
9:110 Hannah Penn to Elizabeth Taylor, 6 March 1701, **5**

9:117 From Andrew Hamilton, 8 March 1701
9:119 Commission to Samuel Carpenter as Treasurer, 8 March 1701
9:121 Commission to Naval Officer at Dover River, 10 March 1701
9:126 To the New York Council, 17 March 1701
9:132 Warrant to Thomas Fairman to Survey Road in Dublin Township, 21 March 1701
9:135 To Nathaniel Blakiston, 26 March 1701
9:137 From the Commissioners of the Treasury, 27 March 1701, **7**
9:141 From Griffith Jones, 28 March 1701
9:147 To the New York Council, 29 March 1701
9:151 To Christopher Codrington, Jr., 31 March 1701
9:153 To Robert Harley, [c. April 1701], **9**
9:179 To the Countess of Bellomont, [c. 17 March 1701], **6**
9:181 From Richard Roberts, 2 April 1701
9:184 To Andrew Hamilton, 3 April 1701, **10**
9:189 To the Proprietors of East New Jersey, [c. March 1701], **8**
9:194 To John Hans Steelman, 12 April 1701
9:197 From John Richardson, Robert Dale, and Henry Fuller, 14 April 1701
9:201 From the Board of Trade, 15 April 1701
9:206 To Ralph Grey, 23 April 1701
9:209 To the New York Council, 23 April 1701
9:211 Articles of Agreement with the Susquehanna Indians, 23 April 1701
9:220 To [the New York Council?], 26 April 1701
9:223 To [the New York Council?], 27 April 1701
9:226 To [William Popple?], 29 April 1701
9:228 To Jonathan Bayly, 3 May 1701
9:230 To Francis Jenkins and William Whittington, 6 May 1701
9:234 To the New York Council, 17 May 1701
9:237 From John Holt, 23 May 1701
9:241 To Nathaniel Blakiston, 23 May 1701, **12**
9:243 Commission to James Logan to Settle Land Titles, 26 May 1701
9:248 To Nathaniel Blakiston, 26 May 1701
9:250 To James Logan, 28 May 1701
9:254 Commission to John Moore as Attorney General, 31 May 1701
9:257 Warrant to Edward Penington to Resurvey for Elizabeth Beakes, 31 May 1701
9:259 To Francis Cook and Others, 2 June 1701
9:263 To John Nanfan, 4 June 1701
9:266 To James Logan, 11 June 1701
9:268 To James Logan, 15 June 1701
9:272 Minutes of the Meeting for Sufferings, 20 June 1701
9:274 Extracts from Minutes of Meeting for Sufferings, 27 June 1701
9:284 Petition from Francis Daniel Pastorius, 28 June 1701
9:285 To James Logan, 30 June 1701
9:288 To the Commissioners of the Customs, [Summer 1701]
9:294 To the Board of Trade, 2 July 1701
9:306 To John Nanfan, 2 July 1701
9:309 To Charlwood Lawton, 2 July 1701, **13**
9:314 To James Logan, 13–14 July 1701, **14**
9:321 Instructions to William Rodney, 14 July 1701

9:324 Writ to the Pennsylvania Assembly, [c. 14 July 1701]

9:326 To James Logan, 17 July 1701

9:329 To James Logan, 23 July 1701

9:333 Naturalization of Caspar Hoodt, 25 July 1701

9:335a To the Meeting for Sufferings, [late 1701?]

9:336 To the Pennsylvania Assembly, 29 September 1701

9:339 To James Logan, 30 July 1701

9:344 From Joseph Willcox, 16 August 1701

9:349 Speech to the Pennsylvania Assembly, 2 August 1701

9:351 Speech to the Pennsylvania Assembly, 2 August 1701

9:352 Speech to the Pennsylvania Assembly, 4 August 1701

9:353 Speech to the Pennsylvania Assembly, 5 August 1701

9:354 John Jones to Edward Penington, 6 August 1701

9:356 From the Pennsylvania Assembly, 6 August 1701, **15**

9:361 Address of Representatives from the Lower Counties, 6 August 1701

9:365 To James Logan, [12] August 1701, **16**

9:370 From Abraham Depeyster, 12 August 1701, 16 September 1701

9:376 To James Logan, 13 August 1701

9:381 To Sir John Lowther, 16 August 1701, **17**

9:385 To Charlwood Lawton, 18, 27 August 1701, **18**

9:404 Writ to Samuel Beakes, 23 August 1701

9:409 Writ to John Hoskins, 23 August 1701

9:414 To Jonathan Bayly, 23 August 1701

9:418 To the Duke of Devonshire, 25 August 1701

9:420 To John How, 26 August 1701

9:424 To the Marquis of Normanby, 26 August 1701

9:427 To Earl Poulett, 26 August 1701

9:431 To the Duke of Somerset, 26 August 1701

9:434 To John Jefferys, 26 August 1701

9:437 To the Board of Trade, 26 August 1701, **19**

9:448 To the Earl of Dorset, 27 August 1701

9:452 To Robert Harley, 27 August 1701

9:468 To Robert Harley, 27 August 1701

9:477 To Heneage Finch, 27 August 1701

9:484 Commission to John Guest, 2 September 1701

9:488 From Darby Inhabitants, 3 September 1701

9:492 To James Logan, 6 September 1701

9:497 To the Earl of Romney, 6 September 1701, **20**

9:513 To the Earl of Romney, 6 September 1701

9:521 To James Logan, 8 September 1701, **21**

9:525 Charter for Marcus Hook, 12 September 1701

9:527 Speech to the Pennsylvania Assembly and the Assembly's Reply, 15, 16 September 1701

9:533 Address from the Pennsylvania Assembly, 16 September 1701

9:536 Inhabitants of Philadelphia to the Pennsylvania Assembly, 17 September 1701

9:547 From the Pennsylvania Assembly, 20 September 1701, **22**

9:553 To Abraham Depeyster, 20 September 1701

9:555 Order of the Provincial Council, 23 September 1701

9:558 Warrant to Survey a Tract for Servants, 27 September 1701, **23**

9:560 To the Pennsylvania Assembly, 29 September 1701, **24**
9:569 From the Pennsylvania Assembly, 30 September 1701
9:576 From William Rodney, [c. October 1701]
9:579 To the Commissioners of Property, [c. October 1701]
9:580 Certificate of Removal from Falls Meeting, [c. 8 October 1701], **26**
9:586 To James Logan, 5 October 1701
9:587 From the Susquehannock and Shawnee Indians, [c. 7 October 1701], **25**
9:591 To Phineas Pemberton, 7 October 1701
9:595 Petition from William Clark, 8 October 1701
9:596 Grant to William Davies, David Evans and William Willis, 9 October 1701
9:602 From the Assemblymen of the Lower Counties, 10 October 1701
9:606 Agreement with John Fitch, 14 October 1701
9:608 From Assemblymen of the Lower Counties, 14 October 1701, **27**
9:613 Proposed Act of Assembly, 14 October 1701
9:616 Petition from Dennis Konder, with response, [15] October 1701
9:617 To the Pennsylvania Assembly, [15 October 1701]
9:619 To John Nanfan, 18 October 1701
9:622 Address of the Lower Counties Assembly, [c. 6 August 1701]
9:627 From Benjamin Israel, 20 October 1701
9:634 From Charles Jones [Jr.], 21 October 1701
9:639 From Juan Corso, [c. 22] October 1701
9:643 Warrant to Thomas Fairman, 23 October 1701
9:645 Patent to Samuel and Joshua Carpenter, 24 October 1701
9:652 Deed to Richard Stockton, 25 October 1701
9:663a Opinion re William Clayton's Claim, 25 October 1701
9:664 To the Commissioners of Property, 25 October 1701
9:665 To the Pennsylvania Assembly, 25 October 1701
9:668 To James Logan, 25 October 1701
9:669 Lower Counties Assemblymen to the Board of Trade, 25 October 1701
9:672 Concessions to Susquehanna Purchasers, 25 October 1701
9:682 Charter of the City of Philadelphia, 25 October 1701
9:703 Charter of Friends Public School, 25 October 1701
9:715 To the Commissioners of Property, 26 October 1701
9:716 Commission to Andrew Hamilton, 27 October 1701
9:721 Commission to James Logan, 27 October 1701
9:724 To James Logan, 27 October 1701
9:727 The Charter of Privileges, 28 October 1701
9:741 The Charter of Privileges, 28 October 1701, **28**
9:742 Warrant to Survey the Boundary Between Chester and New Castle Counties, 28 October 1701
9:744 From the Pennsylvania Assembly, 28 October 1701
9:747 Commission to the Provincial Council, 28 October 1701, **29**
9:751 Commission to the Commissioners of Property, 28 October 1701
9:754 Draft of the Charter of Property, [c. 28 October 1701]
9:770 The Charter of Property, 28 October 1701
9:786 The Charter of Property [incomplete], [c. 28 October 1701]
9:793 Reduction in Quitrent for Andrew Rudman, 29 October 1701

10:379 To John Winthrop, 27 July 1702
10:382 To James Logan, 28 July 1702, **48**
10:385 To Samuel Carpenter or James Logan, 27 June 1702
10:400 From James Logan, 29 July 1702
10:407 Articles of Agreement between WP and William Aubrey, 6 August 1702, abstracted in **209B**
10:412 Benjamin Furly's Letter of Attorney, 6 August 1702
10:416 Epistle to Friends Meetings in Pennsylvania, 9 August 1702
10:427 Petition from Gabriel Thomas to Queen Anne, 10 August 1702
10:431 To the Board of Trade, [c. 12 August 1702]
10:444 From Nicholas Bayard, 12 August 1702
10:449 From James Logan, 13 August 1702
10:455 Bond to William Aubrey, 19 August 1702
10:460 From the Earl of Nottingham, 19 August 1702
10:463 To James Logan, 19 August 1702, **49**
10:467 To the Earl of Nottingham, 22 August 1702, **50**
10:470 To William Popple, Jr., 27 August 1702
10:475 To James Logan, 6 September 1702
10:485 To John Sotcher, 8 September 1702
10:488 To the Board of Trade, 9 September 1702
10:491 From William Popple, Jr., 9 September 1702
10:493 From James Logan, 11 September 1702
10:496 From Prince de Mario Plati, 11 September 1702
10:502 From Andrew Hamilton, 19 September 1702, **51**
10:506 To James Logan, 23 September 1702
10:510 Petition to Queen Anne, [c. 2 October 1702]
10:514 From James Logan, 2 October 1702, **52**
10:530 Charles Hedges to the Board of Trade, 2 October 1702
10:532 From the Earl of Peterborough, 3 October 1702, **53**
10:536 From the Earl of Peterborough, 6 October 1702
10:538 From James Logan, 18 October 1702
10:544 From Andrew Hamilton, 21 October 1702
10:558 Recipes for Cooking, Preserving, and Surgery, 25 October 1702
10:617 Gabriel Thomas to the Board of Trade, [c. 24 November 1702]
10:627 To the Board of Trade, [c. 30 November 1702], **54**
10:632 From [William Popple?], 1 December 1702
10:634 From James Logan, 1 December 1702
10:678 Declaration on the Crown's Claim of Right to the Lower Counties [First Draft], 2 December 1702, **55A**
10:681 To the Board of Trade, 4 December 1702
10:683 Declaration on the Crown's Claim of Right to the Lower Counties [Second Draft], 4 December 1702, **55B**
10:685 To the Board of Trade, 7 December 1702
10:688 Declaration Required by the Board of Trade, 8 December 1702, **55C**
10:691 To William Popple, 10 December 1702
10:694 Declaration on the Crown's Claim of Right to the Lower Counties, 10 December 1702
10:697 From Andrew Hamilton, 11 December 1702
10:704 To the Board of Trade, 15 December 1702
10:707 From William Popple, Jr., 8 January 1703
10:709 To Edward Shippen, Thomas Story and others, 10 January 1703

10:1024 To the Board of Trade, 6 July 1703
10:1026 From William Popple, 7 July 1703
10:1028 To the Board of Trade, 8 July 1703, **63**
10:1031 From James Logan, 9 July 1703
10:1038 From Daniel Defoe, 12 July 1703, **64**
10:1045 Declaration on the Crown's Claim of Right to the Lower Counties, 13 July 1703
10:1048 Lease of Pennsbury Manor to Daniel Phillips and Anthony Neate, 16 July 1703, abstracted in **209H**
10:1056 To [the Earl of Nottingham?], 18 July 1703
10:1058 From John Pennyman, 19 July [1703]
10:1059 From William Popple, 23 July 1703
10:1061 To the Board of Trade, 28 July 1703
10:1063 From the Queen in Council, 30 July 1703
10:1066 From the Queen in Council, 30 July 1703
10:1069 Commission to John Evans, 2 August 1703
10:1073 From William Popple, 3 August 1703
10:1075 From William Popple, 6 August 1703
10:1077 To John Evans, 9 August 1703
10:1087 From the Provincial Council, 26 August 1703, **66**
11:005 To James Logan, 27 August 1703, **67**
11:018 From [William Clark?], 6 September 1703
11:022 From James Logan, 8 September 1703
11:026 From James Logan, 11 September 1703
11:031 To James Logan, 13 September 1703
11:034 From James Logan, 2, 7 September 1703
11:063 From James Logan, 20, 29 September 1703
11:075 Power of Attorney from Daniel Wharley and Others to Samuel Carpenter and James Logan, 24 September 1703, abstracted in **209I**
11:079 To [the Earl of Sunderland?], 24 September 1703
11:083 To James Logan, 24 September 1703
11:085 From Hannah Penn, 13 October 1703, **68**
11:085 To Hannah Penn, [c. 1705?]
11:089 To James Logan, 4, 7 December 1703
11:105 From James Logan, 5 December 1703, **69**
11:114 To John Evans and the Provincial Council, 15 December 1703
11:118 From Lady Mary Culpeper and Lady Catherine Fairfax, 16 December 1703
11:121 To the Board of Trade, 22 December 1703
11:126 From Hannah Penn, 27 December 1703, **70**
11:131 To the Provincial Council, 31 December 1703, **71**
11:136 To James Logan, 31 December 1703, 8 April 1704
11:143 From William Popple, Jr., 12 January 1704
11:145 To Robert Harley, 9 February 1704, **72**
11:153 From William Penn, Jr., 15 February 1704, **73**
11:156 From James Logan, 15, 18 February 1704, **74**
11:167 To Ambrose Galloway, 19 February 1704, **75**
11:169 To Robert Harley, 3 March 1704
11:172 To John Evans, 5 March 1704
11:174 To John Evans, 5 March 1704
11:178 To James Logan, 10 March–10 July 1704, **76**

11:466 From William Popple, Jr. and the Board of Trade, 11 January 1705
11:468 To the Board of Trade, 11 January 1705, **90**
11:474 To James Logan, 16 January 1705, **91**
11:495 To Edward Southwell, 20 January 1705
11:499 From James Logan, 11 February 1705, **92**
11:504 From Isaac Norris, 13 February 1705
11:512 To Roger Mompesson, 17 February 1705, **93**
11:520 To Edward Southwell, 20 February 1705
11:524 To Friends in Pennsylvania, 26 February 1705, **94**
11:531 To John Evans, 26 February 1705, **95**
11:539 To the Board of Trade, 9 March 1705
11:542 From William Popple, Jr., 9 March 1705
11:545 To John Penn, 1 April 1705
11:546 Proposal for Surrender of the Government of Pennsylvania, April 1705, **96**
12:005 From James Logan, 5 April 1705
12:029 To James Logan, 30 April, 10 May, 1705, **97**
12:045 To Robert Harley, 1 May 1705
12:049 To the Earl of Seafield, 12 May 1705
12:053 From James Logan, 17 May 1705
12:061 From James Logan, 28 May 1705
12:063 To the Board of Trade, 3 June 1705
12:066 To the Board of Trade, 6 June 1705, **99**
12:074 To the Board of Trade, 20 June 1705
12:076 From John Toland, 26 June 1705
12:085 From William Popple, Jr., 27 June 1705
12:087 From James Logan, 4 July 1705, **100**
12:103 From James Logan, 13, 18 July 1705, **101**
12:109 From David Lloyd, 19 July 1705, **102**
12:140 The Board of Trade's Objections to the Laws of Pennsylvania, 26 July 1705, **104A**
12:156 From James Logan, 22, 24 August 1705
12:198 To Robert Harley, 24 August 1705
12:201 From Thomas Fairman, 27 August 1705, **103**
12:207 [?] to Robert Harley, 28 August 1705
12:211 The Proprietor's Answer on the Laws of Pennsylvania, [c. 31 August 1705], **104B**
12:217 Abstract of Proposed Terms of Surrender of the Government of Pennsylvania, [c. 1 September 1705]
12:221 Requests to Queen Anne, 1 September 1705, **105**
12:223 To James Logan, 7 September 1705
12:227 To Robert Harley, 8 September 1705
12:229 To James Logan, 14, 21 September 1705
12:245 To John Evans, 22 September 1705, **106**
12:251 To John Evans, 30 September 1705
12:253 To James Logan, 3 October 1705
12:255 To John and Mary Sotcher, 12 October 1705
12:256 Attorney General Northey to the Board of Trade, 19 October 1705
12:263 Last Will and Testament, 20 October 1705, 21 August 1707, **107**
12:270 From William Popple, Jr., 23 October 1705
12:272 From James Logan, 24 October 1705

12:275 The Fords' Bill of Complaint, 31 October 1705
12:362 Draft Defense to the Fords' Bill of Complaint, [c. 1–19 November 1705], **109**
12:368 From James Logan, 8 November 1705
12:377 John Evans to the Board of Trade, 9 November 1705
12:391 From Griffith Owen, 9 November 1705, **122**
12:397 To Samuel Carpenter and Others, 18 November 1705–3 February 1706, **123**
12:416 From James Logan, 18 November 1705
12:420 From William Popple, Jr., 20 November 1705
12:422 To the Board of Trade, 21 November 1705
12:424 From William Popple, Jr., 21 November 1705
12:426 From the Earl of Peterborough, 29 November 1705
12:431 To Sir William Cowper, 30 November 1705, **124**
12:434 Samuel Browning to Herbert Springett, 1 December 1705
12:436 Assignment to Thomas Callowhill, 7 December 1705
12:442 From James Logan, 12, 13 December 1705
12:451 Plea for Delay in Answering the Fords' Bill of Complaint, [c. 4–15 December 1705]
12:459 Grant of Extension of Time to Answer the Fords' Bill of Complaint, 15 December 1705
12:463 To James Logan, 28 December 1705, **125**
12:470 Statement of the Case Against Bridget Ford and Others, [c. summer 1707], **116**
12:482 Draft of WP's Affirmation, [1706]
12:484 Brief of the Plea and Demurrer by Bridget Ford and Others, [c. July 1706], **113**
12:487 Draft of Tripartite Indenture, *Ford* v. *Penn*, [c. 1705]
12:494 From the Pennsylvania Assembly, 12 January 1706
12:495 From James Logan, 29 January 1706
12:502 Answer of John Hall and Thomas Moss [incomplete], 1706
12:505 To John Evans, 7 February 1706
12:512 To James Logan, 7 February 1706, **126**
12:520 To James Logan, 9 February 1706, **127**
12:531 To John Evans, 16 February 1706
12:535 To James Logan, 16 February 1706
12:539 To the Board of Trade, 22 February 1706
12:544 Draft of Cross Bill of Complaint against the Fords and Others, 23 February 1706
12:602 Cross Bill of Complaint Against the Fords and Others, 23 February 1706, **110**
12:645 From William Popple, Jr., 1 March 1706
12:647 To James Logan, 2 March 1706
12:656 Attestation of Articles of Agreement Between Thomas Callowhill and Philip Russell, 2 March 1706
12:659 To Jonathan and Caleb Dickinson, 6 March 1706
12:663 Order to Bridget Ford, defendant, 30 March 1706
12:664 Alleged Overcharges in the Ford Accounts, [c. April 1706], **121A**
12:667 Plea for Injunction to Stay the Fords' Proceedings, 10 April 1706
12:668 The Fords' Petition to Sir John Trevor for Extension of Time, 13 April 1706
12:671 To Sir William Trumbull, 17 April 1706, **128**

12:673 From Earl Poulett, 27 May 1706
12:676 From James Logan, 28 May 1706, **129**
12:688 To Jonathan and Caleb Dickinson, 30 May 1706
12:691 Statement of Accounts with Philip Ford, [c. June 1706], **111**
12:698 Draft of Bridget Ford Defendant vs. WP, 5 June 1706
12:719 J. Kelley to Herbert Springett, 8 June 1706
12:721 From James Logan, 12 June 1706
12:732 To Jonathan and Caleb Dickinson, 20 June 1706
12:734 From William Popple, Jr., 28 June 1706
12:735 Draft of Plea to Stay Injunction, [c. June 1706]
12:791 Affidavits of John Page in re *Ford* v. *Penn,* 6 July 1706
12:792 To Robert Harley, 14 July 1706
12:793 From Earl Poulett, 15 July [1706?]
12:795 Order for the Fords and WP to Join in Commission to Examine Witnesses in Pennsylvania, 16 July 1706
12:796 From James Logan, 25 July 1706, **130**
12:802 From James Logan, 27 July 1706
12:804 Commission for WP to Examine Witnesses in Pennsylvania, [July 1706?]
12:806 From Philadelphia Monthly Meeting, 7 August 1706
12:811 From Benjamin Furly, 10 August 1706
12:812 From James Logan, 10, 14 August 1706
12:823 From Samuel Carpenter, 15, 18 August 1706, **131**
12:828 Bond and Receipts to John Wright, 23 August 1706
12:829 From Charlwood Lawton, 6 September 1706
12:831 To Grimbole Paunceforte, 7 September 1706
12:835 To Robert Harley, 8 September 1706
12:837 From James Logan, 15 September 1706
12:838 From James Logan, 15, 18 September, 6 October 1706
12:850 From Jonathan Dickinson, 17 September 1706, **132**
13:005 From James Logan, 12 October 1706
13:007 John Page's Affidavit to Bridget Ford, 22 October 1706
13:008 Lord Keeper Cowper's Report on the Defendants' Plea and Demurrer, 8 November 1706, **114**
13:012 William Cowper's Order that Ford's Plea Stand for an Answer, 8–12 November 1706
13:013 To [Thomas Curtis?], 14 November 1706
13:015 From James Logan, 26, 30 November 1706, **133**
13:021 From James Logan, 5 December 1706
13:022 From the Earl of Sunderland, 8 December 1706
13:023 Order Dismissing WP's Suit, 14 December 1706
13:025 From Benjamin Furly, 18 December 1706
13:026 From James Logan, 20 December 1706
13:036 Bill of Complaint Against Philip Ford, 23 December 1706
13:058 Interrogatories, [1706?]
13:060 Alleged Overcharges in the Ford Accounts, [late 1706?], **121B**
13:063 Estimated Cost and Charges of Pennsylvania, [c. 1706?], **135**
13:065 To Dr. Edward Baynard, [c. 1706], **134**
13:067 From William Popple, Jr., 4 January 1707
13:069 Notice to Hear *Penn* v. *Ford,* 17 January 1707
13:070 The Fords' Bill of Costs with Exceptions, 20 January 1707
13:083 From Francis Robartes, 21 January 1707

13:084 Notice to Hear *Penn* v. *Ford,* 23 January 1707
13:085 Notice re Hearing of *Penn* v. *Ford,* 27 January 1707
13:086 To the Board of Trade, 29 January 1707
13:090 Assignment of Government Annuities to Thomas Callowhill, 29 January 1707
13:095 Receipt of WP's Payment of Bill of Costs, *Ford* v. *Penn,* 1, 5 February 1707
13:097 The Board of Trade to the Earl of Sunderland, 5 February 1707, **136**
13:104 To the Duke of Ormonde, 8 February 1707
13:108 Writ to Trevor Sheffield in re *Ford* v. *Penn,* 11 February 1707
13:110 To Jonathan and Caleb Dickinson, 14 February 1707, **137**
13:116 To Edward Smith, 18 February 1707
13:121 From James Logan, 2,3 March 1707
13:128 From the Earl of Shrewsbury, 2 April 1707
13:130 From Isaac Norris, 3 April 1707
13:133 From the Earl of Shrewsbury, 7 April 1707
13:135 From James Logan, 12 April 1707
13:147 Bridget Ford's Plea and Demurrer, 21 April 1707
13:148 From James Logan, 5 May 1707
13:156 From Jonathan and Caleb Dickinson, 10 May 1707
13:162 From William Popple, Jr., 12 May 1707, **140A**
13:165 Replication to the Fords' Plea & Demurrer, 14 May 1707
13:177 To John Evans, 15 May 1707, **138**
13:185 Brief on Action on Parol Lease in *Ford* v. *Penn,* [before 20 May 1707]
13:187 Action in Debt upon Parol Lease in *Ford* v. *Penn,* [before 20 May 1707]
13:190 Draft of Bridget Ford vs. WP, [before 20 May 1707]
13:194 Brief on Action of Parol Lease in *Ford* v. *Penn,* [before 20 May 1707]
13:196 Action of Debt in Bridget Ford vs. WP, [before 20 May 1707]
13:199 Action of Covenant in Bridget Ford vs. WP, [before 20 May 1707]
13:200 From James Logan, 20 May 1707
13:207 To Jonathan and Caleb Dickinson, [May 1707?]
13:210 From James Logan, 6 June 1707
13:214 To James Logan, 10 June, 8 July 1707, **139**
13:223 Remonstrance from the Pennsylvania Assembly, 10 June 1707
13:226 The Earl of Fairfax, Richard Rooth, and others to Edward Smith, 16 June 1707
13:230 To Jonathan and Caleb Dickinson and Captain Gomerson, 17 June 1707
13:232 John Round to Herbert Springett re. *Ford* v. *Penn,* 19 June 1707
13:233 From James Logan, 28 June 1707
13:237 Brief for the Defense in Suit for Arrears in Rent, [c. 28 June 1707], **117**
13:238 To William Popple, Jr., 2 July 1707, **140B**
13:243 To James Logan, 8 July 1707
13:244 From William Popple, Jr., 19 July 1707
13:246 To Richard Hill, 22 July 1707, **141**
13:250 From Isaac Norris, 30 July 1707
13:255 To "Loveing Friend," 2 August 1707
13:257 From Isaac Norris, 4 August 1707
13:260 To the Board of Trade, 14 August 1707, **142B**

13:269 Case of Ford v. Penn, [c. 16 August 1707]
13:270 To th Earl of Seafield, 2 September 1707
13:273 The Case of *Ford* v. *Penn,* [c. September 1707]
13:274 From James Logan, [c. September 1707]
13:288 To Samuel Carpenter and Others, 7 October 1707, **143**
13:291 Brief with Special Verdict in *Ford* v. *Penn,* 11 October 1707
13:307 Order to hear Council in *Ford* v. *Penn,* 11 October 1707
13:309 Order to Hear Council in *Ford* v. *Penn,* 16 October 1707
13:311 To James Logan, 16 October 1707, **144**
13:314 Release to William Penn, Jr., 21 October 1707, abstracted in **209J**
13:317 Bill of Exchange to James Logan, 31 October 1707
13:319 Herbert Springett's Affidavit Notice, 6 November 1707
13:321 Indenture of Release Concerning Sale of Warminghurst, 22 November 1707, abstracted in **210B**
13:324 Covenant of Indemnity Concerning Sale of Warminghurst, 22 November 1707, abstracted in **210C**
13:328 Covenant of Indemnity Concerning Sale of Warminghurst, 22 November 1707, abstracted in **210D**
13:331 Covenant of Indemnity to James Butler and Henry Penrice, 22 November 1707
13:335 Covenant of Indemnity to James Butler and Henry Penrice, 22 November 1707
13:338 The Sale of Livestock and Equipment at Warminghurst, 27 November 1707, **145**
13:343 From James Logan, [late 1707]
13:349 Brief for an Answer to the Defendants' Second Plea and Demurrer, [c. April, 1707], **115**
13:357 From Robert West, [c. late January, 1708]
13:359 Francis Hill's Map of Warminghurst Parish, 1707 [see pp. 598–99]
13:360 To Noble Friend, 27 Curr[t] [1707?]
13:362 From James Logan, 5 January 1708
13:367 Petition of Bridget Ford Against WP, [after 10 January 1708]
13:371 Petition to Queen Anne by Bridget Ford and Others, [c. 22 January 1708], **118**
13:374 Order to Hear the Fords' Petition to Queen Anne, 2 February 1708
13:375 Interrogatories, 4 February 1708
13:382 Interrogatories, [incomplete draft], 4 February 1708
13:386 Brief in Response to Bridget Ford's Petition, [c. 9 February 1708], **119**
13:392 From James Logan, 17 February 1708
13:394 Bridget Ford's Petition to Set New Date for Hearing Petition to Queen Anne, 19 February 1708
13:395 William Cowper's Order to Hear Petition of Bridget Ford on WP's Title to Pennsylvania, 19 February 1708
13:397 From William Popple, Jr., 20 February 1708
13:399 To Henry Cane, 28 February 1708, **146**
13:401 From William Popple, Jr., 3 March 1708
13:403 To William Popple, 3 March 1708
13:406 Lord Chancellor Cowper's Report on Petition by Bridget Ford and Others, 9 March 1708, **120**
13:410 From James Logan, 12 March 1708
13:416 From William Popple, 23 March 1708

13:593 Lease of Pennsylvania to WP's Trustees, 6 October 1708, abstracted in **211F**
13:594 Declaration of Trust by WP's Trustees, 7 October 1708, abstracted in **211H**
13:598 Release of Pennsylvania to WP's Trustees, 7 October 1708, abstracted in **211G**
13:601 Indenture Tripartite Between WP, William Penn, Jr., and Richard Rooth, 8 October 1708, abstracted in **211I**
13:605 From James Logan, 22 November 1708
13:612 From William Popple, Jr., 18 December 1708
13:614 To James Logan, 29 December 1708, **155**
13:618 John Jeffery's Calculations of Philip Ford's Overcharge, [c. 1708]
13:622 The Case of *Penn* v. *Ford,* [c. 1708]
13:626 Alleged Overcharges in the Ford Accounts, [c. July 1708], **121C**
13:629 Exceptions to Ford's Account, [c. 1708]
13:632 Complaint Against Philip Ford's Charges, [c. 1708]
13:635 Complaint Against Ford's Charges, [c. 1708]
13:643 To the Earl of Sunderland, [c. 18 January 1709]
13:646 From the Earl of Peterborough, [c. May–June 1709], **164**
13:648 To Amos Strettle, 8 January 1709, **156**
13:652 Case against Lord Baltimore, [c. 12 January 1709]
13:659 From William Popple, 13 January 1709
13:661 From James Logan, 17 January 1709
13:666 From the Earl of Limerick, 25 January 1709
13:671 Petition to Queen Anne, 27 January 1709
13:672 Order of Queen in Council, 27 January 1709
13:674 From James Logan, 3 February 1709, **157**
13:685 From James Logan, 24 February 1709
13:691 To James Logan, 27 February 1709, **158** [opening]
13:697 To James Logan, 27 February 1709, **158** [closing]
13:700 To James Logan, 3 March 1709, **159**
13:703 From James Logan, 6 March 1709
13:707 From James Logan, 5 March 1709
13:729 James Logan to William Penn, Jr., 10 March 1709
13:732 To James Logan, 12 March 1709
13:735 From James Logan, 16 March 1709
13:738 To Baron Somers, 31 March 1709
13:741 To the Board of Trade, 6 April 1709
13:744 From James Logan, 7 April 1709, **160**
13:747 To Queen Anne, 16 April 1709
13:748 To Charles Gookin, 28 April 1709
13:750 To the Earl of Godolphin, [c. 2 May 1709], **161**
13:755 To the Duke of Marlborough, 6 May 1709
13:756 James Logan to Charles Gookin, 11 May 1709
13:757 From James Logan, 11, 12 May 1709
13:763 To the Duke of Marlborough, 22 May 1709
13:765 To Baron Somers, 1 June 1709
13:767 To William Popple, 9 June 1709
13:769 From James Logan, 9 June 1709
13:772 From James Logan, 14 June 1709, **165**
13:779 To the Board of Trade, 17 June 1709
13:782 Order in Privy Council, 23 June 1709, **166**

13:787 To Hannah Penn, 25 June 1709, **167**
13:789 To James Logan, 26 June 1709
13:793 The Case of WP Against Lord Baltimore, [after 23 June 1709]
14:005 To Hannah Penn, 1 July 1709
14:007 To Hannah Penn, 9 July 1709, **168**
14:010 To Hannah Penn, 14 July 1709
14:014 To Hannah Penn, 20 July 1709, **169**
14:019 Report of Commissioners for Victualling the Navy, 23 July 1709
14:021 From Henry Gouldney, 26 July 1709
14:023 From James Logan, 29 August 1709
14:027 From William Popple, 8 September 1709
14:029 To William Popple, 12 September 1709
14:031 From William Popple, 15 September 1709
14:033 From James Logan, 17 September 1709
14:035 From Samuel Carpenter, 1 October 1709
14:044 To James Logan, 14 October 1709, **170**
14:052 To Thomas Penn, 22 October 1709, **171**
14:056 From William Popple, 28 October 1709
14:058 From Isaac Norris, 2 December 1709, **172**
14:062 To John Penn, 15 December 1709, **173**
14:066 To Hannah Penn, 20 December 1709, **174**
14:074 To Hannah Penn, 24 December 1709
14:079 To John Penn, 7 January 1710
14:083 To Hannah Penn, 17 January 1710
14:091 From the Board of Trade, 19 January 1710
14:094 To Hannah Penn, 19 January 1710, **175**
14:101 To Hannah Penn, 4 February 1710
14:103 To Hannah Penn, 7 February 1710
14:106 From William Popple, 20 February 1710
14:109 From John Beeke, 4 March 1710
14:111 Draft of Memorial to the Earl of Sunderland, [27 March 1710?]
14:115 To Viscount Townshend, 4 April 1710, **176**
14:118 From the Earl of Galway, 28 April 1710
14:121 Thomas Grey's Release to James Logan, 3 June 1710
14:122 Bond to Charles Dunster, 7 June 1710
14:126 To Charles Gookin, 14 June 1710, **177**
14:129 From Samuel Carpenter, 14 June 1710
14:133 To the Pennsylvania Assembly, 29 June 1710, **178**
14:145 Receipt Book, 5 July 1710–24 October 1717
14:148 Assignment to Thomas Callowhill, 19 July 1710
14:155 To Queen Anne, [c. 31 July 1710], **179**
14:163 The Earl of Dartmouth to the Board of Trade, 31 July 1710
14:165 To the Earl of Dartmouth, 30 September 1710
14:167 From William Popple, 4 November 1710, **180A**
14:172 From Isaac Norris, 23, 29 November 1710
14:177 From Samuel Preston, 28 November 1710
14:184 To the Board of Trade, 7 December 1710, **180B**
14:190 Henry Gouldney's Account Book, 1710–1725
14:206 To the Earl of Dartmouth, 20 Cur[t] 1711
14:209 Memorial to the Board of Trade, [c. 2 February 1711]
14:216 To Friends in Pennsylvania, 10 February 1711, **181**
14:222 From Thomas Callowhill, 16 February 1711, **183**

14:224 The Board of Trade to Queen Anne, 13 February 1711, **182**
14:232 From the Earl of Dartmouth, 15 February 1711
14:234 From the Pennsylvania Assembly, 28 February 1711
14:237 The Pennsylvania Assembly to Queen Anne, 28 February 1711
14:240 To Charles Gookin, 14 March 1711, **184**
14:247 Bill of Exchange from Isaac Norris, 10 April 1711
14:249 From the Provincial Council, 10 April, 3 May 1711, **185**
14:258 From John French, 21 April 1711
14:268 To the Bristol Yearly Meeting, 28 April 1711
14:270 From Joseph Growdon, 3 May 1711
14:279 From Edward Shippen and Others, 23 May 1711, **186**
14:280 To the Earl of Oxford, 22 June 1711, **187**
14:284 From Griffith Owen, 24 June 1711
14:289 From John Finney, 28 June 1711
14:292 Petition to the Duke of Ormond, [c. 14 August 1711]
14:293 Thomas Harley to Attorney General Edward Northey, Enclosing Clauses of Surrender, 6 October 1711
14:296 From John French, 6 November 1711
14:314 Commission to Commissioners of Property [Draft], 9 November 1711
14:316 Commission to the Commissioners of Property, 9 November 1711
14:318 Letter of Attorney to Commissioners of Property, 10 November 1711
14:322 Letter of Attorney to Commissioners of Property, 10 November 1711
14:324 Letter of Attorney from from the Trustees of Pennsylvania to the Commissioners of Property, 10 November 1711
14:327 Thomas Callowhill's Release in Trust to Brice Webb, Charles Harford, and Richard Champion, 27 November 1711
14:331 Charter for the Public School in Philadelphia, 29 November 1711
14:334 The Trustees of Pennsylvania to the Commissioners of Property, 30 November 1711, **188**
14:337 To the Commissioners of Property, 5 December 1711
14:339 To the Earl of Oxford, 6 December 1711, **189**
14:341 To the Commissioners of Property, 8 December 1711
14:344 From Robert Assheton, 15 December 1711
14:348 To Sir John Pakington, 16 January 1712
14:353 To the Earl of Oxford, 6 [January or February] 1712, **190**
14:354 Last Will and Testament, [c. 6 April], 27 May 1712
14:358 From John Evans, 7 February 1712
14:360 From John Evans, 7 February 1712, **191**
14:363 Benefits to the Crown on WP's Surrender, [c. February 1712]
14:366 Preface to John Banks, *Journal of the Life,* 23 February 1712
14:367 Edward Northey's Report on WP's Proposed Surrender, 25 February 1712
14:371 To the Earl of Oxford, 28 February 1712
14:373 To James Logan, 7 March 1712, **192**
14:377 From James Logan, 31 March 1712
14:379 From [Richard?] Gibson, March 1712
14:381 Petition to the Earl of Oxford, [c. 11 April 1712]
14:384 Jacob Taylor to Josiah Burchett, 14 April 1712
14:386 From John French, 13 May 1712
14:388 To Widow Thornton, 15 May 1712
14:390 From James Logan, 25 May 1712
14:395 To the Earl of Oxford, 12 May 1712

14:398 From Thomas Grey, 31 May 1712
14:401 From Richard Hill, 7 June 1712
14:403 From the Pennsylvania Assembly, 7 June 1712
14:406 From James Logan, 12 June 1712, **194**
14:411 From Peter Evans, 23 June 1712
14:414 From James Logan, 29 June 1712
14:418 From James Logan, 4 July 1712
14:423 Treasury Minute Recommending Acceptance of Surrender, 17 July 1712
14:425 Clauses of Government to be Surrendered, [c. 24 July 1712]
14:426 To James Logan, 24 July 1712, **195**
14:430 To Friends in Pennsylvania, 24 July 1712, **196**
14:431 To James Logan, 15 August 1712, **197**
14:437 Queen Anne's Order to the Treasury, 9 September 1712, **198**
14:440 The Treasury's Entry of Payment to WP, 28 September 1712
14:441 To James Logan, 4, 13 October 1712, **199**
14:451 William Penn, Jr., to James Logan, 4 November 1712
14:453 Promissory Note to John Wren, 8 November 1712
14:454 From Matthias Bagger, 17 November 1712
14:456 From John French, 18 November 1712
14:460 From James Logan, 24 November 1712
14:468 From James Logan, 11 December 1712
14:471 From William Bradford, 15 December 1712
14:474 From William Bradford, 15 December 1712
14:477 Draft of Ferry License to Benjamin Chambers, 20 December 1712
14:479 From Robert Hunter, 22 December 1712
14:482 From James Logan, 6 January 1713
14:484 From James Logan, 26 February 1713, **200**
14:496 Bond to George Dakeyne, Collector of Quitrents, 28 February 1713
14:497 From Samuel Trafford, 27 March 1713
14:500 Power of Attorney to James Logan, 9 May 1713
14:501 From John Brooks, 12 June 1713
14:504 Release from Francis Daniel Pastorius, 22 July 1713
14:505 From James Logan, 8 September 1713
14:514 James Logan to Charles Gookin, 15 October 1713
14:516 Release from Thomas Fairman, 10 December 1713
14:518 Petition to Queen Anne, [c. 1713]
14:519 From James Steel, 24 June 1714
14:522 Controversy with Ralph Freke, 18 July 1714, **202**
14:524 From Edward Bathurst, 24 December 1714
14:525 Hannah Penn to Thomas Story, 27 February 1715
14:527 Account of Trunk of Goods from Pennsbury sent to James Logan, 27 April 1715
14:528 Hannah Penn to Thomas Penn, 11 May 1715, **203**
14:532 From the Provincial Council, 12 August 1715
14:536 Hannah Penn to the Earl of Sunderland, 1 September 1715
14:538 From the Assemblymen of the Lower Counties, 14 October 1715
14:541 Attorney General Edward Northey's Opinion on Procedure in re *Penn et al.* v. *Beranger*, 23 March 1716
14:543 Bill of Complaint Against Moses Beranger, 5 July 1716
14:570 Decretal Order in re *Penn* v. *Beranger*, 27 July 1716
14:577 Release to Moses Beranger, 18 August 1716

14:578 Petition to George, Prince of Wales, for Approval of Governor William Keith, [c. 13 September 1716]
14:580 From the Assemblymen of the Lower Counties, 15 October 1716
14:581 Declaration on George I's Claim of Right to the Lower Counties, 25 October 1716
14:583 William Keith to Hannah Penn, 17 November 1716
14:586 Account of Transactions with Thomas Callowhill, James St. Amand, and Moses Beranger, [c. 1710]
14:588 From Thomas Fairman, Jr., 20 August 1717
14:599 Receipt from Thomas Callowhill's Trustees to WP and William Penn, Jr., 28 December 1717
14:600 Memorial from the Amish in Pennsylvania, 20 May 1718
14:601 Hannah Penn to Thomas Story, 28, 30 July 1718, **205**
14:605 Hannah Penn to Thomas Story, 4 September 1718
14:608 Will and Probate, 3 November 1718
14:611 William Keith to the Trustees of Pennsylvania, 6 November 1718, **206**
14:615 "An Elegy upon William Penn," 21 November 1718
14:618 Friends' Memorial in Behalf of Pennsylvania, [before 9 December 1718]
14:631 Reading Quarterly Meeting to London Yearly Meeting, c. 21 April 1719, **208**
14:644 Recipes for Ointments and Sauces, [c. 1702]
14:654 Remedies for Sore Eyes, Ears, and Other Ailments, [c. 1670?]
14:676 Security Bond from Jonas Potts
14:687 To Baron Fairfax, [c. 1705]
14:688 To Henry Boyle, 28 Curr[t] [c. 1709–10]
14:689 To the Pennsylvania Assembly, [c. 15 September 1701]
14:693 Estimate of Charges of Pennsylvania, [c. 1704]
14:694 To Robert Harley,, 21 September [1702?]
14:695 From Earl Poulett, 28 August [1709?]
14:699 From Sir Heneage Finch, [c. 1702?]
14:717 Robert Quary to the Commissioners of the Customs, [c. 1702]
14:723 Abstract of the Case for the Surrender of Pennsylvania, [c. 1711]
14:726 To the Earl of Oxford, [c. 1711–12]
14:728 Abstract of the Case for the Surrender of Pennsylvania, [c. 1715]
14:729 The State of the Dispute over the Boundaries of Pennsylvania and Maryland, [after 1714]
14:737 Robert West to Hannah Penn, [c. April 1715]
14:741 From Samuel Morris, 26 May [after 1710]
14:749 Memorial to the Board of Trade, [c. 1717–18]
14:762 Petition from Hannah Penn to George I, [c. 12 May 1715]
14:775 Summary of the Case Against Moses Beranger, [c. July 1716]
14:777 Brief of the Defendants' Answer in re *Penn et al.* v. *Beranger,* [c. July 1716]
14:780 To "My Ould Friend," [c. 1702?]

CALENDAR OF DOCUMENTS NOT FILMED, 1701–18

In the following list of documents accessioned since the publication of the microfilm edition of The Papers of William Penn, numbers in bold type identify documents printed in this volume.

1. Articles of Agreement Concerning Marriage Settlement of William Penn, Jr., 10 January 1699, abstracted in **209A**
2. Will of Philip Ford, 20 January 1700 (Prob. 11/484, PRO)
3. Map and Description of Pennsbury by D. Powell, 13 March 1700 (Bureau of Land Records, Harrisburg)
4. Warrant to Henry Hollingsworth to Survey Land for John Simcock, 22 March 1701 (ACM, 39:141)
5. Agreement with the Susquehanna Indians, 23 April 1701, **11**
6. To Ralph Grey, 23 April 1701 (ACM, 39:220)
7. Warrant to Survey Land for Jonathan Wynne and Edward Jones, 9 October 1701 (Bureau of Land Records, Harrisburg)
8. Warrant to Edward Penington to Survey Land for the German Company, 14 October 1701 (William J. Buck, *William Penn in America*)
9. Instructions to James Logan to Issue Warrant to George Brown, 20 October 1701 (*PA*, 2d ser., 19:358)
10. Warrant to Survey Land for Andrew Rudman and Swedish Inhabitants, 21 October 1701 (Buck, *Penn in America*)
11. Warrant to Confirm Lands in Laetitia Penn's Manor to Gunnar Rambo, John Rambo, and Peter Cock, 28 October 1701 (*PA*, 2d ser., 19:296)
12. Proposal to Reunite Proprietary Colonies to the Crown, [c. 17 February 1702], **40**
13. Abstract of Robert Quary's Complaint, [c. 16 April 1702], **44A**
14. Reply to Robert Quary's Complaint, [c. 28 April 1702] (CO 5/1261/85, PRO)
15. Robert Quary's Rejoinder, 12 May 1702 (CO 5/1261/94, PRO)
16. Proposal to Address the Queen, 30 May 1702 **46A**
17. Address to Queen Anne, [c. 3 June 1702], **46B**
18. Recipes for Medicines and Waters, [c. October 1702] (Miscellaneous Manuscripts of William Penn, HSP)
19. To the Commissioners of Property, 13 February 1703 (privately owned)
20. Indenture of Release Between WP and Hannah Penn, and William Penn, Jr., 4 May 1703, abstracted in **209F**
21. To John Evans, 9 August 1703, **65**
22. Indenture of Release from Sir John Fagg, 1 March 1704 (Wynne DDWY/792, 793, Bedfordshire Record Office, Bedford, England)
23. To James Logan, 10 March–10 July 1704, **76**
24. Epistle from Bristol Yearly Meeting, 17 May 1704 (Port. 42, FLL)

25. From James Logan, 22 November 1704 (Deborah Norris Logan Notebooks, HSP)
26. From William Popple, Jr., and the Board of Trade, 11 January 1705, **89**
27. To James Logan, 30 April–10 May 1705, **97** [opening]
28. Draft of a New Patent for Pennsylvania, 23 May 1705, **98**
29. The Fords' Bill of Complaint, 31 October 1705, **108**
30. Order in Council Repealing Pennsylvania Laws, 7 February 1706 (Chew Manuscripts, HSP)
31. Writ to Bridget Ford to Reply to WP's Cross Bill of Complaint, 10 April 1706 (Penn Manuscripts, Ford vs. Penn, HSP)
32. Writ to Produce Deeds in re *Ford* v. *Penn,* 27 April 1706 (Penn Manuscripts, Penn vs. Baltimore, HSP)
33. Answer of John Hall and Thomas Moss, 14 June 1706, **112**
34. Herbert Springett's Notice in re *Penn* v. *Ford,* 4 July 1706 (Penn Manuscripts, Ford vs. Penn, HSP)
35. Order to Allow Plaintiffs to Amend Bill, 25 September 1706 (Penn Manuscripts, Ford vs. Penn, HSP)
36. Lord Keeper's Order for Extension of Time in re *Ford* v. *Penn* 11 October 1706 (Penn Manuscripts, Ford vs. Penn, HSP)
37. Lord Keeper's Order to Continue Injunction Against Proceedings, 18 October 1706 (Penn Manuscripts, Ford vs. Penn, HSP)
38. Notice from John Round to Samuel Browning in re *Penn* v. *Ford,* 12 November 1706 (Penn Manuscripts, Ford vs. Penn, HSP)
39. Writ to Bridget Ford, 8 February 1707 (Wynne DDWY/777, Bedfordshire Record Office)
40. George Wilcox's Memorial to the Board of Trade, 6 November 1706, **142A**
41. Draft of Agreement to Sell Warminghurst, [c. 22 November 1707], abstracted in **210A**
42. To the Duke of Marlborough, 6 May 1709, **162**
43. To the Duke of Marlborough, 22 May 1709, **163**
44. The Board of Trade to John Evans, 15 April 1708 (*CSPC, 1706–8,* p. 718)
45. From Simon Clement, 15 April 1711 (Penn Papers, Photostats, HSP)
46. Thomas Callowhill's Lease in Trust to Brice Webb, et al., 26 November 1711 (Wynne DDWY/614, Bedfordshire Record Office)
47. To the Earl of Oxford, 24 December 1711 (Loan Manuscripts 29/198, BL)
48. Last Will and Testament, [c. 6 April], 27 May 1712, **193**
49. Last Will and Testament, [c. 6 April], 27 May 1712 (Penn-Forbes Manuscripts, HSP)
50. James Logan to William Penn, Jr., 9 July 1713 (Parchment Logan Letterbook, 1712–1715, HSP)
51. Hannah Penn to James Logan, 17 October 1713, **201**
52. Petition of Hannah Penn and Others to George I, [after August 1714] (Egerton Manuscripts, 2168/5, BL)
53. Hannah Penn to Thomas Penn, 25 February 1716 (Granville Penn Book, HSP)
54. Draft Bill of Complaint Against Moses Beranger, 5 July 1716 (Penn Manuscripts, Penn vs. Beranger, HSP)
55. Hannah Penn to the Earl of Sunderland, 27 March 1718, **204**
56. Hannah Penn to William Penn, Jr., 13 January 1719, **207**
57. The Case of Earl Poulett as Trustee for Pennsylvania, c. 1719 (Penn Manuscripts, Penn vs. Baltimore, 1653–1724, HSP)

INDEX

Page references to identifications are set in **bold face type.**

My Dr. Boy London 22. 8th. 1709

I was glad of thine yesterday, but let thy Dr. mother yt I get yr letters all four post days, is a great favour, for never 8 or 9 at night has severall times been ye earliest here as there came last night. I Salute you all, thy Dr & beloved Mother, & you my Dr. children & so ye family with you; but especially yr Grandfr. & Mother, wth yt family & our Kin & Relations & friends at Bristoll. Know yt through ye Lords mercy I am pretty well, & bless God yt you are so; I pray him to preserve you. And I charge thy Brother Johnne, & thee, to follow yr book 2 hours in ye fore noon, & 2 hours in ye afternoon, & do readily wt you are bid, & you will comfort your Dr Mother, & your poor Father to hear you do so. I sent thy Mother so full a lett.r last post, yt I shall write the less now,

CPSIA information can be obtained
at www.ICGtesting.com
Printed in the USA
BVHW010811100620
581173BV00017B/108